Post Office Box 1005
Mount Sterling, KY 40353

Jacks GALLER

Established in 1966

Email - bestrelics@aol.com
or alex@jacksongalleries.com

Visit our website at
www.jacksongalleries.com

QUALITY ANCIENT ARTIFACTS

CATALOG SALES / INTERNET SALES / CONSIGNMENTS
ARTIFACT BROKERAGE AND ESCROW SERVICE

Our specialty is North American flint and stone artifacts. We also offer a large selection of unique antiquities and artifacts from Meso-America, Europe, Egypt, Asia and elsewhere. Our reputation has been built by consistently offering the very finest *Authentic* artifacts available anywhere in the world. Simply stated, Jackson Galleries is your *#1 choice* for buying *or* selling prehistoric relics.

Collectors - Our Artifact Brokerage service allows you to get the proper exposure for your artifacts without the high cost of marketing the relics yourself. Let our years of experience in marketing artifacts help you get your pieces sold!

NOW ACCEPTING QUALITY CONSIGNMENTS!

Please call us for a *FREE* Catalog or visit our website for more information or subscribe for $15./year

AUTHENTICATION AND GRADING SERVICES

The '*Standard*' For the Collecting Community

Jackson Galleries is the preferred choice of collectors the world over for authentication of prehistoric artifacts. Our evaluations aid in preserving the integrity of ancient artifacts and in safeguarding the investments of the serious collector. We welcome individual pieces or entire collections. Our scientific authentication method is '*second to none*'. Call for details...

1-800-466-3836

Our Extended Services Include
Authentication - Artifact Grading - Appraisals
Pre-Auction Inspections - Evaluation Training

We also offer a wide selection of Collector's supplies
Microscopes - Black Lights
Reference Books - Display Cases
And MORE!!!

Alex Przygoda
Authenticator

Bill Jackson
Authenticator

http://www.jacksongalleries.com

Post Office Box 1005 - Mount Sterling, Kentucky 40353

Arrowheads.com

#1 Artifact Related Web Site
8 Years Running

Your banner here

IN SITU
PROS
CATALOG
AUCTIONS

Artifacts	Magazines
Auctions	Journals
Dealers	T-Shirts
Collectors	Display Cases
Authenticators	Advertising
Resources	Paleo
Links	Archaic
Discussions	Woodland
Associations	Mississippian
Supplies	Potery
Books	Bannerstones
Microscopes	Axes

ArrowheadAuctions.com

Memberships Available

Arrowheads.com Members enjoy
free unlimited access to listing on
the auction site which has been
steadily growing since 1/10/2004.
All sellers guarantee there artifacts,
so authenticity is the norm and the
risks of purchasing at online auction
are greatly reduced. By January, 2006
only members will be able to sell.

It all happens here, so Join the Fun Today!!

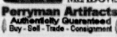

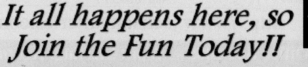

BACK TO EARTH ®

Rocks and Relics

Larry Garvin
Dept. 10
17 North LaSalle Drive
South Zanesville, OH 43701

Subscription

Relic List

Published quarterly - Feb., May, Aug., & Nov.
Artifact photos w/descriptions. - Usually 40 pages.
All prices shown - No "price on request"

In 1992 Back to Earth began publishing this very popular listing, which pictures a well-rounded variety of Indian artifacts (flint, stone tools, pottery, beads, ornaments, mini-collections, etc.), Civil War items, old world antiquities, fossils, a large selection of Indian related books (specializing in autographed copies), trade pipes, Pre-Columbian artifacts, collector frames, and unusual gift ideas. Authenticity guaranteed with a reasonable return policy. Visa, Mastercard, Amex, and Discover/Novus accepted for your ordering convenience.

$6⁰⁰/year (1st class)

Sample copy $2⁰⁰
Canada $3⁰⁰ - Foreign $5⁰⁰

2 years - $11⁰⁰
1 year priority mail - $16⁰⁰
1 year - Canada (air) - $8⁰⁰
1 year - Foreign (air) - $12⁰⁰

WWW.RIVERSOFTIME.COM
WE BUY AND CONSIGN 1-800-851-0924

RIVERS OF TIME

Quality Artifacts and Fossils from the Southeast

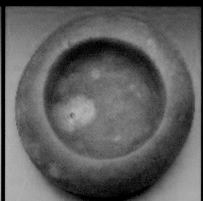
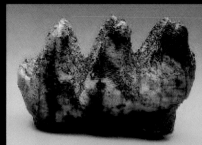

OFFICIAL OVERSTREET INDIAN ARROWHEADS IDENTIFICATION AND PRICE GUIDE

10th Edition

by Robert M. Overstreet

SPECIAL CONTRIBUTORS TO THIS EDITION:
Richard Michael Gramly, PhD • Duncan Caldwell

SPECIAL ADVISORS TO THIS EDITION:

David Abbott • Mark Berreth • Pete Bostrom
Tommy Beutell • John Byrd
Joel Castanza • Dave Church • Jerry Chubbuck
Vernon Crites • Gary Davis • Tom Davis
Winston Ellison • Gary Fogelman • Jacky Fuller
Richard Michael Gramly, PhD
Ron L. Harris • Jim Hogue • Bill Jackson
Sam Johnson • Glenn Leesman • Randy McNeice
Bob McWilliams • Donald Meador
Roy Motley • Lyle Nickel • John T. Pafford
Rodney Peck • Alan L. Phelps • Floyd Ritter
Dwain Rogers • Mike Speer • Art Tatum
Carlos Tatum • Jim Tatum, PhD
Pete Timoch • Larry Troman • Michael Troman
Greg Truesdell • Eric C. Wagner
Sam Williams • Warner Williams
Jack Willhoit • Brian Wrage

HOUSE OF COLLECTIBLES **NEW YORK**
GEMSTONE PUBLISHING, INC.

Gemstone Publishing, Inc. supplies books directly to the relic market. This book is available at special quantity discounts for bulk purchases or single copy orders. For ordering information please call or write:

GEMSTONE PUBLISHING, INC.
1966 GREENSPRING DR.
TIMONIUM, MD 21093
Call Toll Free (888) 375-9800

ABOUT THE FRONT COVER: The cover features a selection of Paleo Period Cumberland points all from central Tennessee. Most Cumberland points are found in an area from Northern Alabama through central Tennessee into Kentucky which is the heart of the Cumberland focus. Recently Dr. Richard Michael Gramly, PhD has (arguably) dated Cumberland to 13,000-14,000 calendar years old. (see his article "The Cumberland Tradition And Earliest Americans" in this book). Cumberland fluted points have always been prized possessions of collectors and hobbyists since the earliest times of hunting occurring over the past two centuries.

Important Notice: All of the information, including valuations, in this book has been compiled from reliable sources, and efforts have been made to eliminate errors and questionable data. Nevertheless, the possibility of error always exists in a work of such immense scope. The publisher and the author will not be held responsible for losses which may occur in the purchase, sale, or other transaction of items because of information contained herein. Readers who feel they have discovered errors are invited to *write* and inform us so that the errors may be corrected in subsequent editions. All advertising is accepted in good faith. If any item advertised is not as represented, and enough unsolved complaints are received, Gemstone will discontinue advertising space with that vendor. Gemstone also reserves the right to reject any advertisement without explanation.

THE OFFICIAL OVERSTREET INDIAN ARROWHEADS IDENTIFICATION AND PRICE GUIDE. Copyright © 2007 by Gemstone Publishing, Inc. All rights reserved. No part of this book may be reproduced in any form or by any means, electronic or mechanical, including photocopying, recording, or by any information storage and retrieval system, without permission in writing from the publisher.

THE OFFICIAL OVERSTREET INDIAN ARROWHEADS IDENTIFICATION AND PRICE GUIDE is an original publication of Gemstone Publishing Inc. and House of Collectibles. Distributed by The Random House Information Group, a division of Random House, Inc., New York, and simultaneously in Canada by Random House of Canada Limited, Toronto. This edition has never before appeared in book form.

HOUSE OF COLLECTIBLES
Random House Information Group
1745 Broadway
New York, NY 10019

www.houseofcollectibles.com

Overstreet is a registered trademark of Gemstone Publishing, Inc.

House of Collectibles is a registered trademark and the colophon is a trademark of Random House, Inc.
Published by arrangement with Gemstone Publishing, Inc.

Printed in the United States of America

ISSN: 1073-8622

ISBN: 9780375722462

10 9 8 7 6 5 4 3 2 1

Tenth Edition-July 2007

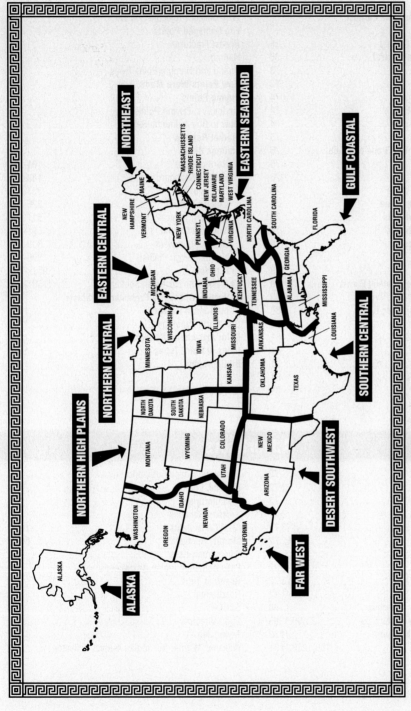

THE TEN REGIONS MAP KEY

This book is divided into ten regions and is set up starting with the Northeast and ending with the Alaska (east to west, right to left on this map). The Great Basin Westward region from the previous editions has been renamed the Far West region. This is your key to the contents of this book, and versions of the map highlighting each individual section appear at the beginning of each regional section.

Table of Contents

Advertisers

PALEO
ENTERPRISES

YOUR PREMIER SOURCE FOR QUALITY AUTHENTIC FLORIDA ARTIFACTS

We pride ourselves in providing you with the largest inventory of fine Florida artifacts and fossils available today.

AUTHENTICATION SERVICES

Authentication certificate with color photo: $25 each
Regional lithic authentications for Florida and Southern Georgia.

WE BUY ARTIFACTS AND FOSSILS COLLECTIONS OR SINGLE ITEMS

ALL ARTIFACTS GUARANTEED 100%

Jim Tatum Ph.D., Owner
(386) 454-1916
P.O. Box 2035
High Springs, Florida 32643

Carlos Tatum, Authenticator
(813) 765-6099
P.O. Box 82098
Tampa, Florida 33682

www.paleoenterprises.com

Authentication
of Stone Artifacts

➤ Roy Motley ➤

▼ Specializing in Midwestern
  Flint and Axes
▼ Appraisal Service
▼ Over 25 Years of Experience

Regional Consultant
Dave Church
Buyer of old flint and stone artifacts.
One piece or whole collection.

KRM CONSULTANTS
Karen and Roy Motley
29802 SE Moreland Sch Rd.
Blue Springs, MO 64014
(816)229-6025
E-Mail-Krmconsultants@aol.com

Jeb Taylor Artifacts
High Plains Artifact Sales and Evaluation

PO Box 882, Buffalo, WY. 82834 ~ 307-737-2347 ~ jeb@rangeweb.net

SALES:

Artifacts sold by Jeb Taylor Artifacts

- Always have been and always will be unconditionally guaranteed to be authentic and free of modern enhancements
- Are issued with COA's

EVALUATIONS:

COA's are on bonded watermarked paper, numbered, and permanent copies are kept on file. When submitting artifacts for evaluation, please include:

- Where they were found (county and state at least)
- When they were found
- Who found them
- $30 for each artifact + return shipping and insurance

BOOK SALES:

Projectile Points of the High Plains

- 477 Pages, cloth bound
- Includes life size quality color images of the most diagnostic points from virtually all of the type and important representational sites on the High Plains.
- An extremely comprehensive chapter specifically on tool stone
- Organized chronologically including information regarding climate and fauna.
- $145 + $10 for Priority Mail shipping

BLUEGRASS
Case Company

www.bluegrasscase.com
Box 982,
272 Airport Road
Stanton, KY 40380
1-800-668-9871
(606) 663-9871 or (606) 663- 6897
Fax-(606) 663-6369
support@bluegrasscase.com

Buy directly from the manufacturer and safely display your collectibles. We produce all of the standard sized cases or can custom make any size you need. We use only select oak, walnut, cherry, and cedar woods. We also make an economy case from poplar. All cases have double strength glass and dowelled corners. Black display cases also available in sizes from 3x4 to 14X20. Call, write, or go online to get our free catalog. Wholesale also available.

CADDO TRADING CO., INC.
P.O. Box 669
Murfreesboro, Arkansas 71958

Sam Johnson
President
Office: (870) 285-3736

* Prehistoric Indian Art
* Fine Art • Folk Art
* Historic Indian Art
* Pre-Columbian Art
* Jewelry • Tribal Art

* Books on Art and
  Artifacts
* Artifact Appraisals and
  Liquidations
* Authentication Service

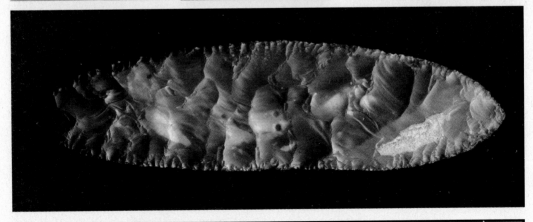

FINE ARTIFACTS FOR SALE
WEB SITE: *http://www.caddotc.com* **E-Mail:** *caddotc@alltel.net*

13

Acknowledgements

A very special thanks to Richard Michael Gramly, PhD for his ground breaking article specifically for this edition and for his contribution of photographs. Special gratitude is also given to my good friend Duncan Caldwell for his excellent article on "Collecting Old World Prehistoric Artifacts" and his contribution of many photographs as well.

Many thanks to Joel Castanza who previously photographed and researched Alaska point types included again in this edition.

My gratitude is also due the following people that so generously provided important data and or photographs used in this reference work: Peter Allen, Jeremy Anderson, Bret Bile, Dave Bowling, Gaylon Brickley, Hayden Bybee, John Byrd, Chris Carneal, Norman Carte, Louis Chavez, Dana Andrea Chepey, Eugene Colpitts, Lee Colpitts, Mathew Cox, Vern Crites, William Dean, Al Downs, Ryan Fain, Mark Fisher, Gary Fogelman, Steven Fox, Kim Fultz, Mike Gant, Rick Giesse, Slade Griffiths, Karl Hagler, Justin Hazuga, Henry H. Helene, Gary Henson, Charles W. Hinkle, Dave Imler, Wynn Isom, Chase Jennings, Brian Johnson, Oliver Johnson, Sam Johnson, Jason L. Kendrick, Leroy Kohl, Jimmy Lambert, Richard A. Laughlin, Anthony Martinez, Greg Mellinger, Phil Mize, Adam Morris, Dave Moulton, Lyle Nickel, Doug Nortier, Joshua Orick, John Pafford, David Pendleton, Monty R. Pennington, Nicholas Pray, Ruben Rankin, David Reed, Steven Rich, George Roberts, Dr. David Rozier, Cecil E. Scholl, Don Seamans, J.E. Smith, John Smith, William Jason Sockwell, Jim Stone, Dean Thompson, Tim Thompson, Pete Timoch, Robert Walter, William C. Weathers, Kent C. Westbrook, M.D., Mike Wilber, Robert Woodruff, James Wright.

I am also in debt to Pete Bostrom and Dr. Michael Gramly for their valuable advice in keeping me up to date with changes in the archaeological arena.

This book also contains photos from the collections of Ray Acra, Tom Addis, Dick Agin, Ralph Allen, Chuck Andrew, Robert Beasley, Jerry Beaver, Jim Bergstrom, Tommy Beutell, Ken Bovat (photographer, N.Y.), John Byrd, Roland Callicutt, Phillip H. Cain, Jerry Chubbuck, John Cockrell (deceased), Jim & Janice Cunningham, Leo Paul Davis, Kevin L. Dowdy, Tom Evans, Ted Filli, Gary Fogelman, Tom Fouts, Steven Fox, Jeff Galgoci, William German, Kenneth Hamilton, Scott Hanning, Jim Hill, Frank & Kathy Hindes, Bill Jackson, Mark L. Jewell, Glen Kizzia, Glenn Leesman, Mike Long, Skip Mabe, Edward Mason, Charles D. Meyer (deceased), Ron Miller, Sherri A. Monfee, Buzzy Parker, Floyd Ritter, George Roberts, Bob Roth, Arlene & Lori Rye, Richard Savidge (deceased), Charles Shewey (deceased), Mike Speer, Larry Allan Stanley, Scott Tickner, Brian K. Tilley, Kirk Trivalpiece, P.K. Veazey, R.S. Walker, Blake Warren, Warner Williams, Lyons D. Woody and John W. Young. We want to sincerely thank these people for making their collections available to us.

Gratitude is also due Vern Crites, Tom Davis, Gary Fogelman, Jacky Fuller, Don Meador, Roy Motley, Dwain Rogers, George E. Rodieck, Jr. and Jack Willhoit who spent so much of their valuable time submitting photographs; to Art Tatum and Alan Phelps for their many hours of expert help, photographs and points sent in for photographing.

Thanks is also given to Jim Hogue who spent countless hours photographing collections in his area and writing descriptions of new types for this edition as well as for his excellent research into previously published reports on types.

Very special credit is due my wife Caroline, who not only advises cover and layout designs, but is of tremendous help to me at the artifact shows visiting and talking with collectors and dealers.

Thanks also to the staff of Gemstone Publishing--J. C. Vaughn (Executive Editor & Associate Publisher), Brenda Busick (Creative Director), Mark Huesman (Production Coordinator), Brandon DeStefano (Editor), Tom Gordon III (Managing Editor), Jamie David (Director of Marketing), Stacia Brown (Editorial Coordinator), and Heather Winter (Office Manager)--for their invaluable assistance in the production of this edition.

Our gratitude is given to all of our special advisors for their dedicated advice and input as well as help in typing, grading, and pricing; and to those who wish their names not to be listed and to all of our advertisers in this edition.

THE CUMBERLAND TRADITION AND EARLIEST AMERICANS

By Richard Michael Gramly, PhD
American Society for Amateur Archaeology
North Andover, Massachusetts

The European philosopher and natural historian, Montaigne, is the reputed author of the statement: "Nothing is so firmly believed as that which is least known" (cited in Crichton 2004: 144). His admonition applies well to our search for the Earliest Americans. Since the 1920s and 1930s, when studies of early hunters came of age at the Clovis and Folsom type sites in New Mexico, there has been much speculation. The factual basis for theories is often slight. Repeated often enough, ideas (even poorly founded ones) tend to be accepted unquestioningly; therefore, there is a need for archaeological science to re-examine concepts, including ones constituting its foundation. Expressing doubt is not a sign of weakness, but rather a testament of vigor and strength. The current controversies: Who were the Earliest Americans?, from what continents did they come (Asia, Western Europe, Africa)?, and when did they arrive? ask us to think fresh thoughts and to re-examine cherished notions.

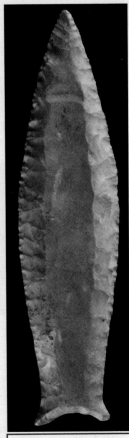

One concept of North American archaeology that stands to benefit from rethinking is the Cumberland archaeological tradition. The fact that ancient Clovis and Cumberland people both made fluted points has disposed researchers to believe that they and their cultures were akin and that Cumberland must be derived from the better-known, more widespread Clovis. At an earlier time even the writer held such views (Gramly and Funk 1991: 21). Fifteen years and thousands of hours of archaeological fieldwork later, I find this position untenable. Cumberland, it appears to me, is not younger than Clovis and derived from it; rather it may be antecedent. For awhile, too, these cultures even may have existed side-by-side within the same landscapes – much as we observe today among Amish and non-Amish people. Such a reversal of thinking has not been easy as it flies in the face of conventional wisdom. Nor do I feel that the thesis is proved.

Yet, in order to progress in archaeological science, like a horseman preparing to undertake a long journey, you had better know what is the "head end" of your horse before saddling up. To understand the evolution of New World palaeolithic cultures, their temporal succession must be made clear at the outset.

What, indeed, is the direction that our "horse" faces? Was Clovis or Cumberland the first on the scene?

Figure 1: Cumberland point from Montgomery Co., Tennessee. Fluted to the tip on both faces. Length 4-1/4 inches. Made from Fort Payne chert and is one of the finest examples for this state. Photo by Bob Overstreet

Conventional Wisdom

Most writers assign Cumberland fluted points to a nebulous "Middle Paleoindian period" dating between 10,500 and 11,000 radio-carbon years before present (Anderson, O'Steen and Sassaman 1996: Figure 1.2). They are thought to follow upon the several varieties of

Clovis points, which are presumed to belong to a more ancient "Early Paleoindian period". In actual fact, NO stratified archaeological site has evidence in support of such a temporal relationship aLthough both Cumberland and Clovis points have been discovered together at several places across the Mid-South (Barker and Broster 1996; Norton and Broster 1992). Remarkably, both Cumberland and Clovis workshops have been observed at the same archaeological site (Carson/Conn/Short – Broster *et al.* 1996); however, none of these separate cultural remains overlapped in a stratigraphic relationship with one another. Since there is at present NO stratigraphic evidence proving that Clovis precedes Cumberland, on what grounds do prehistorians assert that Cumberland is of lesser antiquity?

The belief that Cumberland points are younger than Clovis is based upon an hypothesized technological superiority, that is to say, the "quality" of the fluting shown on Cumberland points. Indeed, the length of flutes or channel flakes on both faces of a Cumberland point usually exceeds anything observed on a Clovis point. A long flute is obtained by setting up a medial ridge on a Cumberland point preform – the ridge serving to direct the force of a knapper's billet blow. Clovis point preforms seldom exhibit a medial ridge, and in modern replications the force of the strike is dissipated over a broader area, making the fluting scar relatively wider and shorter.

Figure 2: Cumberland point from Ross Co. /Highland Co. line, Ohio. Fluted to the tip on both faces. Length 3-1/2 inches. Cumberland points are rare north of the Ohio River, and this is one of the finest examples for this state. Photo courtesy Robert Converse.

But is Cumberland fluting really an "advance" over Clovis fluting and, thus, a later development as analysts would have us believe? (See Jolly 1972 for a clear presentation of the common view that Cumberland fluting is superior.) Any channel flake traveling beyond the hafting area of a point was to no purpose and served only to weaken it. Setting up a medial ridge on both faces of a Cumberland point preform dictates that the striking platform (and thus the haft) will be thick and the cutting blade will be narrow. While thick, narrow penetrating instruments are useful against some game (such as the tapir with its thick hide – see Squier 1855 for a description of a hunt), a thinner and wider instrument with a more rounded tip might have been better for causing bleeding. In this regard, Clovis points are perhaps superior to Cumberland points. Further, in contrast to Cumberland, the hafting area of most Clovis points is relatively thin, and channel flakes may not extend very far past the haft. A sleek cutting instrument capable of deep penetration was created, and since channel flakes were not allowed to travel too far, the tip of a Clovis point remained strong. It could also be resharpened easily and more often, perhaps, than a Cumberland point could. In sum, despite their long channel flakes, which so impress fanciers of flaked stone tools, Cumberland fluting is less functional or practical than Clovis fluting. The Cumberland weapon tip may also have been less effective against a variety of quarry. It strikes me that Cumberland fluted points are more rudimentary than Clovis points and, therefore, possibly older – not younger.

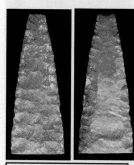

Figure 3: Tip fragment from a Cumberland point showing collateral flaking to a median ridge with reverse face fully fluted to the tip from the Nuckolls site in Humphreys Co., Tenn. Length =1-3/4 inches

Another argument used to support a lesser antiquity for Cumberland is the confined distribution of Cumberland points, centering upon northern Alabama, Tennessee, Kentucky, and northeastern Mississippi (Anderson 2004). It is felt that

Figure 4: An example of a Cumberland point variant with fluting on only one face, from Tennessee. The channel flake is uncharacteristically short. Length = 3-5/8 inches.

Cumberland cannot represent an ancient, colonizing population as its vestiges are not as widely distributed as those of Clovis – suggesting that makers of Cumberland points were specialized or adapted to quarry found within specific regions or environments (Anderson and Faught 2000). Such a belief is faulty for two reasons. First, while Cumberland point distribution, strictly defined, is delimited and has few outliers, the Cumberland Tradition is not. Descendant forms – the Barnes and Folsom types – occur over a broad area. Second, there is nothing illogical about earliest populations colonizing and then multiplying within favored environments, from which they radiated to all corners of northern North America. The unglaciated lands bordered by the Appalachian Mountains on the east and the Ohio, Tennessee, and Mississippi Rivers may have been one of these favored regions and could have supported a large and diverse animal population.

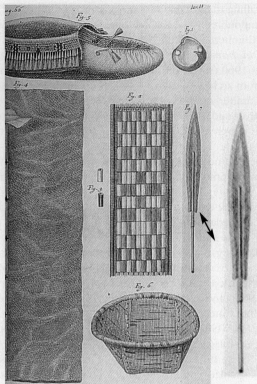

Figure 5: Earliest known illustration of a fluted point of the Cumberland Tradition. Likely collected in Massachusetts in 1785. From Luigi Castiglione's *Viaggio* (1790). Image courtesy of William Reese Company (New Haven, Connecticut).

What Is a Cumberland Point?

The earliest detailed illustration of a North American flaked stone point is a Cumberland (Barnes) point shown in Figure 7, Plate IV of Luigi Castiglione's *Viaggio*, which documents his travels in the United States during 1785-1787. Although the collection locality is not given, it is likely that the point was presented to Castiglione by fellow naturalist, Rev, Manasseh Cutler, a resident of Ipswich, Massachusetts (Pace 1983: 26). A late expression of the Cumberland Tradition exists in New England (Carty and Spiess 1992); fluted points, as large as the one figured by Castiglione appears to be, are on record (see Spiess and Hedden 2000: 72 for an example). The present whereabouts of Castiglione's Cumberland specimen are unknown; perhaps it lies forgotten in some desk drawer of a home in his native Milan, Italy?

During the nineteenth century Cumberland points found places in public and private collections. Although their particular character was sometimes recognized, at that time they were not given special designations. In his monumental *The Antiquities of Tennessee*, Gates Thurston illustrated a Cumberland fluted point from Maury County, Tennessee, which he describes as a "specialty" of that county (1890: 232, Figure 139). Also, some time before 1898 a Cumberland/Barnes point was collected at Big Bone Lick, Boone County, Kentucky – an important Pleistocene fossil locality long known to natural historians. Not until 60 years after Herbert Schiefer had secured it from its original finder, was the specimen finally illustrated by Prufer (1960) in his *Survey of Ohio Fluted Points*.

Among the earliest illustrations of Cumberland points in archaeological publications we note Plate V in Figgins' 1935 report about "Folsom and Yuma artifacts" for the Colorado Museum of Natural History. Two indubitable Cumberland points from Ohio are shown, which Figgins classed as Folsom. A colleague of his, Edgar B. Howard, as Figgins himself acknowledged, preferred the designation "Folsom-like". In 1939 these same Cumberland points illustrated by Figgins were termed "generalized Folsom points" by Wormington (1939: 10). By 1957 in a later edition of her classic *Ancient Man in North America* Wormington had dropped this designation in favor of calling them "Ohio or Cumberland Fluted points" (Figure 29, page 82). Working in the West, undoubtedly she had become familiar with Thomas M. N. Lewis' newly-coined name, "Cumberland point," which was presented within a 1954 volume of the *Bulletin of the Oklahoma Anthropological Society.* Although usage of the term "Ohio Fluted" persisted as late as 1960 (see Hyde 1960 for an example of its application), within a few years it had disappeared from archaeologists' vocabulary. Analysts had come to understand that the distribution of Cumberland points was far wider than just the Ohio River region — or even the Cumberland River and its tributaries. Since so many examples of Cumberland points had been collected within the greater Cumberland River valley, however, this name stuck (Perino 1985: 94).

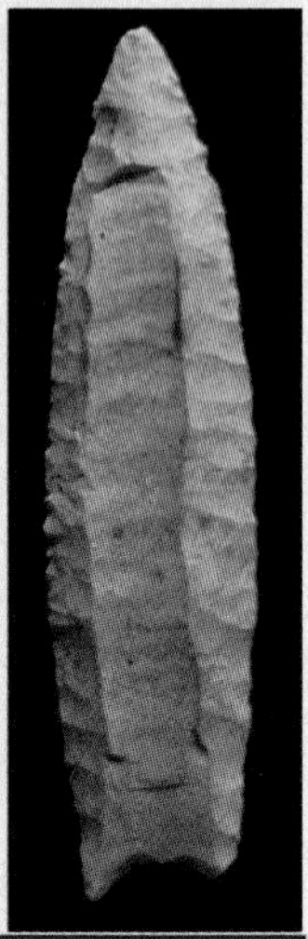

We note at this juncture that by 1957 Marie Wormington had become aware of Folsom points with fluting on one side only and of others without fluting (1957: 41). Likely her published commentaries did not pass unnoticed; analysts working east of the Mississippi found the distinction to be equally pertinent to Cumberland points.

The shift away from designating Cumberland points as "Folsom" or "Folsom-like" began only a few years after the appearance of Webb's 1951 report about the Parrish Village site, Hopkins County, Kentucky. This multi-component site, which contained both Clovis and Cumberland types, had been known since the 1930s, and at least one Cumberland point collected upon its surface was sent to John Cotter (excavator of the Clovis type locality at Blackwater Draw, NM) in 1938. Webb's fieldwork at Parrish during 1939 added more specimens to the assemblage.

By 1964, use of the term, Cumberland, to designate thick, flaring-based (auriculate) points showing long flutes on one, but more often both, faces was well entrenched. Martha Ann Rolingson published a detailed trait-list for the Cumberland type (1964: 37), and (inspired by Marie Wormington?) she presented evidence of several sub-types. Building upon her research or in step with it, studies of fluted point distribution were generated for Indiana (Dorwin 1966), Ohio (Prufer and Baby 1963; Seeman and Prufer 1982), and Tennessee (see various issues of the *Tennessee Archaeologist* from 1964 onward). In all these works Cumberland points were illustrated.

Figure 6: Large, unresharpened Barnes point belonging to late phase of the Cumberland Tradition. Unearthed at the Thedford II site, Ontario Province. Length approx. 4-1/4 inches. Note absence of fish-tailing. The point is thin in comparison to Cumberland type points; also, secondary flaking ("Barnes finishing") is present on its base.

Also in the 1960s, archaeologists in Michigan and Ontario Province began to document actual habitation sites and isolated finds of a Cumberland point variant – a form now recognized as the Barnes type. These highly distinctive fluted points were named after a site in Michigan, which was first described in 1962-3. It was not until several years later that a fuller treatment of the entire flaked tool-kit was published (Wright and Roosa 1966) and photographs more widely disseminated (Fitting 1970: 43). Since then, several sites with Barnes points have been investigated, including the Parkhill site, for which a "Parkhill Phase" was named (Ellis and Deller 2000). Barnes points undoubtedly fall at the end of the Cumberland Tradition. Although they have never been dated absolutely and directly, Barnes points may be the northeastern North American equivalent of Folsom points, as revealed by the remarkable similarity of their preforms.

Although Folsom and Barnes points were crafted from preforms having painstakingly made medial

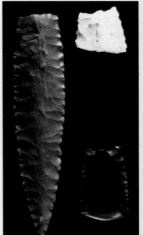

Figure 7: Unfluted preform for a Cumberland point (note medial ridge), found in Alabama, length = 5-1/2 inches. *Upper right,* Folsom point preform base showing nippled striking platform and medial ridge, Lake Ilo site, North Dakota; *lower right,* fluted Folsom point preform fragment with traces of a nippled platform, Lake Ilo site.

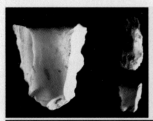

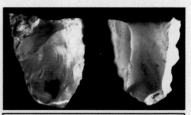

ridges — just like Cumberland point preforms – there were, in addition, nippled striking platforms set up for fluting both faces. In the manufacture of Cumberland points nippled platforms were seldom required for fluting the first, and even second, face. Folsom and Barnes points, because of their delicacy, are more surely fluted using pressure or perhaps indirect per-

Figure 8: *Left,* basal fragment of Cumberland point preform that failed during fluting. The fragment is the proximal end of a very large prismatic blade (estimated 8-9 inches long); *right,* matching fragments of a Cumberland point preform (of ordinary size) that failed during fluting.

Figure 9: Depending upon the quality and size of the raw material available to them, Cumberland knappers at the Phil Stratton site made fluted points either by "center-ing" chert nodules (*left*) or reducing massive prismatic blades (*right*). Had they not failed, both preforms would have yielded very large Cumberland points. Width of both fragments = 3 inches.

cussion. Cumberland points, on the other hand, had channel flakes removed either by carefully controlled direct percussion or by resorting to a jig. These less delicate methods had the advantage, however, of yielding very large points. Genuine ancient Cumberland points as long as 8-9 inches are known; lengths of 6-7 inches were routinely achieved (see Irons 2002 for an intact preform of this size). Few Folsom and Barnes points ever attained such a length.

Our answer to the question, "What is a Cumberland point?" must necessarily exclude Folsom and Barnes points with their delicate nippled preforms and reliance upon pressure-flaking (and perhaps some indirect percussion) for fluting. Although Folsom and Barnes are omitted from our definition of type, we are aware that both forms have their place within a greater Cumberland Tradition.

Before presenting a definition, we must consider the possibility that Cumberland points themselves may have undergone changes through time? Among the group of more than 100 authentic Cumberland points from Tennessee, Kentucky and Ohio studied by me in preparation for writing this paper, three classes of finished specimens were obvious. A) Most common are specimens corresponding to Rolingson's "subtype 1," that is to say, thick, auriculate points, fluted on both sides, with fish-tailed or flaring bases. B) Much

Figure 10: *Left,* Folsom point and mid-section of another; *right,* failed fluted point preforms, perhaps intended as Barnes or Folsom points. Specimens from Fox Farm Road site, near Warsaw, Kosciusko County, north-central Indiana – a productive, surficial, Palaeo-American encampment.

less common are thinner, shorter points with fluting on one face only (or no fluting at all). The tendency for Cumberland points rather than Clovis points to have an unfluted side was noted by McNutt (1972: 11) for a group of specimens originating primarily within Logan County,

Figure 11: Rare example of very thick, early variant of a Cumberland point showing only slight "fish-tailing" of its base, from Tennessee. Lithic Casting Lab photo.

Kentucky. C) Rare are very thick points, fluted on both faces, that exhibit hardly any flaring of their bases. The latter "style" is almost straight-sided and were it not fluted, it would be best described as a lanceolate point with slight indenting of its lower edges to facilitate hafting.

Are Cumberland Variants B and C of the same age as Variant A or were they predominant forms during some earlier or later sub-phase of the Cumberland Tradition? For reasons that I will make clear later in this paper, I believe that Variants A and B were contemporary; while, the thick, almost straight-sided Variant C may be the most ancient Cumberland form.

Finally, it should not go unsaid that fake or modernlymade "Cumberland points" abound, and caution is advised for students of the subject. Even fragmentary, recently-knapped specimens are offered in the marketplace. As testimony to the degree modern replicas are confounded with authentic, ancient specimens, readers should turn the pages G. E. Van Buren's typology book, *Arrowheads and Projectile Points* (1974) – especially pages 196-215. Such a deplorable situation reinforces the need for more scientific investigations of Cumberland sites and the witnessed recovery of data.

Figure 12: Modernly made "Cumberland point" by Dan Theus. This elegant form, 11 inches long, was knapped of Ste. Genevieve chert from a nodule collected in Logan County, Kentucky by Phil Stratton. Photo by Lithic Casting Lab.

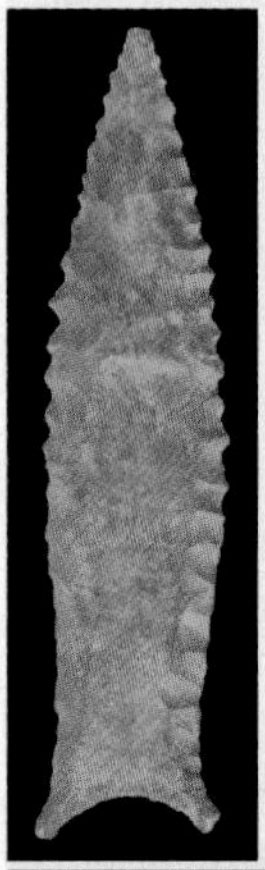

Definition of a Cumberland point:

A Cumberland point belongs to the initial phase of the Cumberland Tradition. A later phase of this tradition is characterized by Barnes and Folsom points. It is most commonly a relatively thick point with pronounced medial ridges on both faces and a flattened, diamond-shaped cross-section (where fluting has not obliterated these features). A single channel flake scar, sometimes running all the way to a sharply pointed tip, is present on each face.

Figure 13: Serrated Cumberland point from Humphreys Co., Tennessee made of Dover chert. Length = 3-1/4 inches.

Rare, pristine examples, purported to be authentic, show fine serration near the tip. The base of a typical point is thick and constricted along its lower edges where it is ground for hafting. The angle of the ears with the point's long axis is variable but often centers around 45 degrees. The edge of the basal concavity may exhibit short, fine trimming flakes and grinding.

A rare variant of a Cumberland point conforms in all respects to the common type but is thicker than average specimens and also less auriculate with ears at a lower angle (30 degrees) to the main axis.

A variant of a Cumberland point that is more often seen is plano-convex in cross-section with a channel flake scar (if any at all) only on the convex face. Points of this sort tend to be short and will have a vestigial medial ridge if it has not been removed during fluting. Most Beaver Lake and Quad point types, which are frequently confused with this Cumberland variant, lack a medial ridge (Barker and Broster 1996: 116). They also date to the Very Early Archaic era and are not part of the Cumberland Tradition.

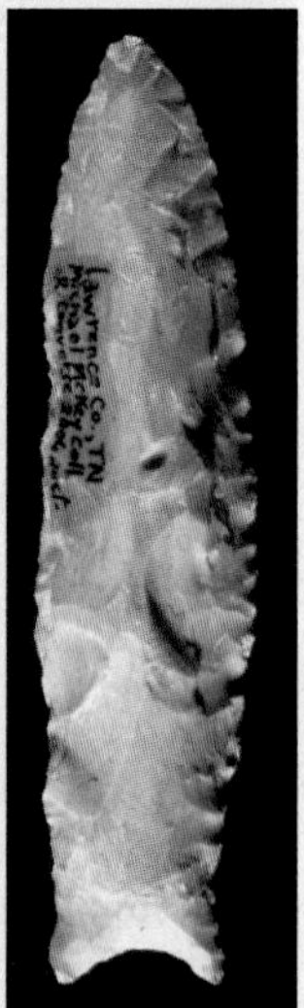

Figure 14: A Beaver Lake point (length 3-5/8 inches), from Lawrence Co., Tennessee. This type, which dates to the Very Early Archaic, is often mistaken for a much rarer, more ancient, unfluted Cumberland point.

The Cumberland Tool-kit

With few exceptions the earlier phase of the Cumberland Tradition, the Cumberland archaeological culture *per se*, is known only from bifaces that have been collected upon the surface, at deflated sites, or within eroded and redeposited sediments. As these discoveries are often mixed with cultural materials of lesser antiquity, or in some cases with Clovis and other Palaeo-American artifacts, what constitutes the full Cumberland tool-kit has been difficult to understand.

Figure 15: Classic fish-tailed Beaver Lake point with medial ridge and collateral flaking from Smith Co., Tennessee. Heavily ground ears and stem sides. Length = 3-3/8 inches

I am aware of just five archaeological sites with isolatable Cumberland artifacts that lay (or still lie) within excavatable contexts,

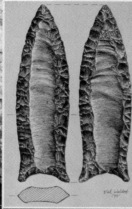

Figure 17: Illustration of the only Cumberland point from the Trinity site, northern Kentucky, to have escaped damage by farming machinery. Length = 3-1/2 inches. Artist Val Waldorf.

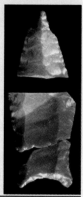

Figure 18: Damaged Cumberland point with missing mid-section from the Trinity site, northern Kentucky. Cumberland points retouched as drills are exceedingly rare.

Figure I6: Entrance to Dutchess Quarry Cave No. 8, southeastern New York state. This small cave yielded five Cumberland points, bones of extinct giant beaver and flat-headed peccary as well as caribou. Dates on these bones were 11,530-14,200 radiocarbon years BP.

which have been witnessed by trained observers. Four of these five have been visited by me. The **first** to be discovered was Dutchess Quarry Caves (Funk 1969 *et al.*; Funk and Steadman 1994), which is located in unglaciated southeastern New York State. Although strata within Dutchess Quarry Caves 1 and 8 yielded some fossil animal bones and surprisingly old radiocarbon dates, only fragmentary and intact fluted points were recovered. The **second** site to be made known to science was the Cumberland component of the Carson/Conn/Short site along the Tennessee River, Benton County, Tennessee (Broster and Norton 1996 and elsewhere). This component, thought to cover an area 15 meters in diameter, appears to be a lithic workshop. Artifacts recovered during preliminary testing have not been published. Two years later a **third** Cumberland site was announced – the Trinity site, which is situated upon a fossil terrace of the Ohio River in northern Kentucky (Gramly, Vesper, and McCall 1999; Gramly and Vesper 2005). Like Dutchess Quarry Caves, Trinity yielded only Cumberland points to excavators. Unfortunately it had been severely disturbed by farming activities. In 1999 I was made aware of the archaeological potential of a **fourth** Cumberland site, which we have named the Phil Stratton site after its owner and discoverer (Gramly and Stratton 2005). This Cumberland encampment overlooks a ford of the Red River in Logan County, western Tennessee and would have been strategically situated for the interception of game. The large and growing assemblage of stone tools from the Phil Stratton site will be treated here. Finally, the writer was guided to a **fifth** site on a terrace bordering Knob Creek, Lawrence County, south-central Tennessee, by a local resident and ASAA Member — Roy McKey. Our 2005 test excavations there confirmed that Cumberland artifacts lie well beneath the reach of the plow within fluvial sediments. Like the Carson/Conn/Short Cumberland locality elsewhere in Tennessee, the Houser site (for so it has been named after property abutters) appears to be a lithic workshop. Cobbles of superior Ft. Payne chert, likely picked up in the bed of Knob Creek, were transformed into preforms and finished Cumberland points as well as various unifacial tools. Some of the fluted points achieved impressive sizes,

Figure 20: Badly damaged Cumberland point assembled from four fragments discovered separately at the Trinity site, northern Kentucky. Length = 4-3/8 inches, fluted on both faces. The Trinity "cache" of 11 points is one of only two known for the Cumberland Tradition.

Figure 19: Damaged Cumberland point, fluted on both faces — one of 11 discovered at Trinity, Lewis County, northern Kentucky. Length = 3-7/8 inches.

Figure 21 Canoeing on the Red River below the Phil Stratton Cumberland site, Logan County, Kentucky. The ancient encampment is located above these sheer cliffs and overlooks a ford, which presumably was used by ancient quarry of Cumberland hunters.

to judge by fragments discovered at the site. The archaeological potential of the Houser site is high although it has suffered disturbance by artifact collectors. Since Houser is culturally zoned, future excavators will have to pay close attention to the depths of artifacts and stratigraphy.

Of these several stations of the Cumberland archaeological tradition, the Phil Stratton encampment is most useful for understanding the full tool-kit. Of course, one would expect Cumberland flaked tool assemblages to differ from each other according to the activities that took place at the several sites. The ancient inhabitants of the Houser and Carson/Conn/Short sites may have focused upon lithic procurement and reduction; while, residents of the Phil Stratton encampment performed a wider range of tasks connected with food-getting, crafts, and tool maintenance.

Table 1 (at the end of this article) is a breakdown of the 11,912 flaked and rough stone objects and 13 manuports recovered from the Cumberland zone at the Phil Stratton site. Not included are nine Neo-Indian artifacts (primarily whole projectile points), spanning the Early Archaic through Mississippian periods, that were left anciently upon its surface during hunts.

Several facts about the assemblage are immediately obvious. **First**, the flaked tool-kit is diverse with no fewer than 22 types of finished tools. It is an impressive inventory for such a small sample (N = 410), making it unique among Palaeo-American vestiges that have come to my attention. **Second**, utilized flakes and utilized prismatic blades dominate the industry with 45% of the tally. This figure is certainly very high; for example, it is over twice the percentage of utilized pieces (19%) that was observed at the Vail Clovis site in northwestern highland Maine (Gramly 1995: 51, Table 2). **Third**, prismatic blades were being produced by direct percussion from conical blade cores of nodular Ste.

Figure 22: Prismatic blade core of Ste. Genevieve chert, five inches tall, discovered at the Phil Stratton Cumberland site, Logan County, Kentucky. Blades struck from conical cores were used as knives and retouched as scrapers. Also, blades were transformed into Cumberland points with fluting on only one face.

Genevieve chert at the Phil Stratton site. Prismatic blades with one and two arises are among the assemblage along with core "tablets" (core rejuvenation flakes). Obviously, prismatic blades and cores yielding them can no longer be seen as exclusive to Clovis or the Llano Complex (Green 1963; Collins 1999). Although most prismatic blades of the Phil Stratton assemblage were used in an unmodified state or "fresh off the core" for cutting and slicing, some blades were transformed into small Cumberland points. **Fourth**, the ancient inhabitants of this site were discarding twice the number of sidescrapers as endscrapers. This statistic is the reverse of what one would expect to observe at a Clovis encampment. The flaked stone assemblage from the Vail Clovis site, it is worth noting, had four times as

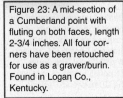

Figure 23: A mid-section of a Cumberland point with fluting on both faces, length 2-3/4 inches. All four corners have been retouched for use as a graver/burin. Found in Logan Co., Kentucky.

Figure 24: Utilized prismatic blades and flake-blades from the Phil Stratton Cumberland encampment, Logan County, Kentucky. Length of longest blade = 3 inches.

many endscrapers as it did sidescrapers. This disparity has been observed at Clovis encampments across North America. The ratio of sidescrapers to endscrapers at Phil Stratton is noteworthy; the difference hints at possibly different origins for Cumberland and Clovis industries. Analyses of more Cumberland tool-kits, however, will be required to substantiate this notion.

Fifth, and finally, judging by the flaked stone waste, both bifaces and unifaces were being manufactured and maintained at Phil Stratton's. Too, usage of unmodified flakes and prismatic blades produced at the site from nodular chert is assumed by the heavy amount of damage their edges had sustained.

Another curious fact about the tool assemblage at the Phil Stratton site is the absence of *pièces esquillées*. This toolform, which I believe served as a wedge or chisel, is abundant at Clovis Tradition encampments east of the Mississippi (see Lothrop and Gramly 1982 for a discussion). It is, however, rare or lacking altogether at Cumberland Tradition sites featuring Barnes points (Deller and Ellis 1992: 127). The dearth of *pièces esquillées* during early and late phases of the Cumberland Tradition, as well as an emphasis upon sidescrapers at the expense of endscrapers, which we observe at Phil Stratton's, give an unique flavor to Cumberland industry. These qualities set it apart from Clovis.

Figure 25: Small utilized prismatic blades from the Phil Stratton Cumberland encampment. The blade balanced on the finger has silica phytolith sheen on an edge and was used to cut plants. Length = 1-1/4 inches.

For what purposes unmodified flakes and prismatic blades and the many shapes of unfacial and bifacial tools were used may become known when these objects are examined for traces of wear left upon them. Interestingly, there are a few tools and flakes with silica phytolith sheen upon them. The sheen appears identical to that accumulated upon tools used to sever grasses and other plants having colloidal silica within their tissues. Perhaps these plants were foodstuffs, or perhaps they were intended for making cordage, baskets, or other artifacts?

Finally, a word should be said about Cumberland points in the Phil Stratton site assemblage. A full point, which was restored from four fragments found separately, and a large tip fragment represent the most common variety, that is to say, a thick point with a channel flake on both faces and well-developed medial ridges. Two basal fragments, on the other hand, are examples of a rarer variant with a channel flake on only one face or none at all. Interesting to note, a failed Cumberland

Figure 26: Classic fish-tailed Cumberland point with fluting on both faces, restored from four fragments excavated separately at the Phil Stratton site, Logan County, Kentucky. Ste. Genevieve chert. Length = 4-5/8 inches.

Figure 27: Both sides of a Cumberland point preform on a prismatic blade of Ste. Genevieve chert that failed during fluting. Phil Stratton site. Had the point been completed, it would have been short and plano-convex in cross-section with a channel flake on one face only. Length = 3 inches.

other hand, are examples of a rarer variant with a channel flake on only one face or none at all. Interesting to note, a failed Cumberland point abandoned during fluting shows that it was being transformed from a prismatic blade. Only the ridged dorsal face would have been fluted.

Locally occurring Ste. Genevieve chert was the favored raw material at Phil Stratton. A small amount of Ft. Payne chert is also present in the form of finished unifaces and bifaces. The nearest extensive outcrops of Ft. Payne chert lie 50-55 miles to the southwest along bluffs above the Tennessee River in Stewart County, Tennessee (Marcher 1962: 11-16). Its presence and the apparent lack of any raw materials from the north indicate that the ancient inhabitants of the Phil Stratton site arrived from the south.

From Whence Came Cumberland?

The origin of Cumberland is inextricably linked to the appearance of fluted points. Until now no industry has been suggested as a credible progenitor. It is true that the Nenana Complex of Alaska seems to be older than fluted point manifestations farther south in North America, and it shares many well known, non-bifacial tool types with Clovis and Cumberland. Yet, the thin, tear drop-shaped Chindadn points characteristic of Nenana have no counterparts elsewhere on the continent. Likewise, the short, almost triangular, lanceolate points known for the Cactus Hill (Virginia) and Meadowcroft (Pennsylvania) sites, which have been advanced as products of a "pre-Clovis" industry, seem too specialized to be in the line of direct innovation of fluted points. With these facts in mind, some thinkers have abandoned models of *in situ* development – looking, instead, outside North America for the origin of Clovis (and Cumberland).

These days the most articulate spokesmen for an European origin of fluted point industries are Dennis Stanford and Bruce Bradley, who believe that the Solutrean archaeological culture (tradition) of southwest Europe furnishes a likely candidate (Stanford and Bradley 2002). Although their idea is hardly new – the remarkable similarity of some Solutrean bifaces to New World specimens having long been recognized (Obermaier 1925: 206)

— only they have built a credible model for trans-Atlantic spread of Upper Palaeolithic culture. A detailed presentation of their arguments will settle the issue.

Another candidate for an extra-continental origin of fluted point industries, perhaps one even stronger than a Solutrean connection, is the El Jobo Industry (Joboid Series) of Venezuela (Rouse and Cruxent 1963). Known primarily from Pleistocene mega-fauna kill sites such as Taima-Taima at *circa*. 13,000 radiocarbon years before present (Ochsenius and Guhn 1979), the age of El Jobo appears to be considerably older than Clovis in North

Figure 28: Mid-Solutrean laurel leaf point. Pressure flaked projectile point with steeply retouched back. Black Vèzére flint with soil sheen. Laugerie Haute, Dordogne, France, excavated in 1862. ca. 21,000 B.P. Size = 5 1/8 inches. Courtesy Duncan Caldwell.

America. El Jobo points, which are medially ridged lanceolates, are scattered far and wide in South America and have even been identified as far south as Monte Verde, Chile. The inventory of toolforms accompanying El Jobo points is, however, quite unlike anything known for Clovis (Oliver 2006 – website). Although some critics have dismissed the association of El Jobo lanceolate points and dated mastodont remains (Roosevelt *et al.* 2002), others see merit in the

Figure 29: Double-edged sidescraper with graver spur, Ste. Genevieve chert. Unearthed at the Phil Stratton Cumberland encampment, Logan County, Kentucky. Lithic Casting Lab photograph.

argument (Lavallee 1995).

Published drawings and photographs of El Jobo points (Rouse and Cruxent, *ibid.*, Bryan 1983: Figure 10.1; etc.), specimens on exhibit in North American museums, and a photograph of other examples provided by to me by Alan Bryan show them to be medium to large (as long as nine inches), narrow bifaces with a pronounced medial ridge on each face. Their bases may be excurvate or flat – seldom incurvate – and show no edge-grinding. The cross-section of an El Jobo point is a flattened diamond, as is the common form of Cumberland point. In my opinion an El Jobo point could be fluted easily to its tip by setting up a striking platform, which any experienced flintknapper could accomplish in a minute or two.

El Jobo, points because of their size and overall shape, are the best candidates on any conti-nent for a Cumberland point precursor. Ancient Cumberland point preforms bear a startling resemblance to an El Jobo point, and would be identical if both medial ridges were present on preforms. In practice, however, medial ridges for fluting were set up sequentially – as the writer's study of actual Cumberland points broken during fluting reveals.

Figure 30: Examples of sidescrapers of Ste. Genevieve and Ft. Payne cherts, Phil Stratton Cumberland site, Kentucky. Sidescrapers are more common than endscrapers at this site – a relationship seldom noted for Clovis assemblages.

Since no excavation report of a well-preserved, single-com-ponent El Jobo encampment with a large tool assemblage has been published, analysts must content themselves with qualita-tive "trait-lists" (of tools) compiled from various sources. Oliver (*ibid.*) gives the following:

1) Lanceolate points (El Jobo points)
2) Awls
3) Sidescrapers
4) Wide bifaces – presumed to be knives
5) Hand-axes

Significantly, no mention is made of endscrapers and *pièces esquillées*; and because analyses of flaked stone waste have not been published, existence of a core and prismatic blade industry is uncertain.

Figure 31: Bifacially flaked celt *in situ* with-in loess at 35 cm below surface, Phil Stratton Cumberland site, Logan County, Kentucky. Length = 2-3/4 inches.

On the face of it, the tool industry purportedly associat-ed with El Jobo points vaguely resembles the assemblage from the Phil Stratton site. A noteworthy difference is the possible absence of prismatic blades for El Jobo. Manufacture of prismatic blades, however, may have been rooted in the practice of strik-ing blade-like channel flakes from point pre-forms. For the Cumberland Tradition, at least, making and using prismatic blades may have been authigenic, that is to say, the practice was an outcome of learning to flute ridged lanceolate (El Jobo) points.

A serious flaw in our argument that Cumberland developed from El Jobo is the belief that evolution occurred in South America or some other locality far-removed from lands between the Ohio and Tennessee Rivers where Cumberland points are concentrated. But are El Jobo points really confined to South America? Are there none in the American Southeast, which offered rich opportunities to early hunter-gatherers during the terminal Pleistocene? Do we really expect colo-nizing populations armed with El Jobo points to have eschewed such bounty in favor of food-getting in more southern regions?

Ovoid to lanceolate bifacial points of medium size, known as "Lerma," have long been known in south

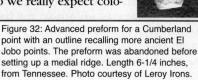

Figure 32: Advanced preform for a Cumberland point with an outline recalling more ancient El Jobo points. The preform was abandoned before setting up a medial ridge. Length 6-1/4 inches, from Tennessee. Photo courtesy of Leroy Irons.

Figure 33: Heavily resharpened El Jobo point, collected in south-central Tennessee/northern Alabama. Length approx. 3 inches. In Venezuela similar points have been found with Pleistocene mega-fauna dating to 13,000 years (radiocarbon age). Photo courtesy of Lithic Casting Lab.

tered them, as well. While most Lerma points may be Archaic in age, the general form may be much older, to judge by discoveries in association with Pleistocene mega-fauna in Mexico (see, for example, the biface from Tlapacoya 1, Valley of Mexico; Mirambell 1978: 227). Illustrated examples show a variable basal configuration, and some points are even medially ridged like El Jobo points. During 2005 the writer procured an El Jobo point from the private Ollenhausen Collection that had been assembled in Lawrence County, Tennessee and adjacent northern Alabama. Although some collectors might class this specimen together with Lerma points, in my opinion it conforms closely to the El Jobo "type," as it is thick, narrow, medially ridged and unground along its edges. It is also heavily resharpened and might have been long when freshly made.

If true El Jobo points and accompanying toolforms exist within the Cumberland "heartland" of Kentucky, Tennessee, northern Alabama and northeastern Mississippi, as suggested by the above specimen, it is reasonable to expect that the Cumberland Tradition arose here and perhaps nowhere else. In searching for hypothesized cultural "roots" of Cumberland within the immediate region, amateur and professional archaeologists will have to pay close attention to lanceolate points in the hope of distinguishing among varieties. The search for closed components featuring El Jobo or early Lerma points will not be easy, but the rewards will be great.

Environments and Antiquity of the Cumberland Tradition

Dating the Cumberland Tradition has proved challenging. Only one of its late phases, Folsom, has been dated securely by absolute means at *circa* 10,500 radiocarbon years or roughly 12,000 calendar years (Meltzer 2006: 147). Although Barnes (or the Parkhill Phase as it is sometimes termed), has yet to furnish a credible series of radiocarbon dates, an association of sites with fossil Lake Algonquin strandlines suggests that it dates to the interval 10,400-11,000 radiocarbon years (Ellis and Deller 2000: 27).

Despite the fact that Folsom and Barnes are of the same general antiquity, their bearers had different hunting proclivities. Folsom hunters were adept at ambushing and slaying now-extinct, giant *Bison* (Frison 2004); while a dietary mainstay of Barnes is thought to have been caribou (*Rangifer tarandus*).

Cumberland hunters have shown long-standing interest in caribou. This species was a quarry of Cumberland point-using hunters who inhabited the Dutchess Quarry Caves west of the Hudson River in southern New York State. Also present (within Dutchess Quarry Cave No. 8) were bones of giant beaver (*Castoroides ohioensis*) and flat-headed peccary (*Platygonus compressus*) – representing a North American genus that was widespread during the Pleistocene (Harris 1985: 34-35).

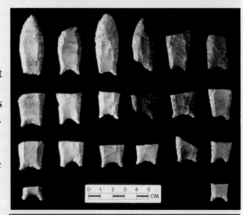

Figure 34: Series of Barnes points from the Parkhill site, Ontario. Hunters at the end of the Cumberland Tradition living around the Great Lakes, it is thought, depended upon caribou. Barnes points are thinner than older Cumberland points and may have been used to tip hand-held lances. Photo courtesy of C. Ellis.

The hunters who sought refuge within the Dutchess Quarry Caves belonged to the early phase of the Cumberland Tradition and used the common form of Cumberland fluted point. It is worth noting that the single intact point from Dutchess Quarry Caves is almost identical in shape and style to specimens from the Trinity Cumberland site, northern Kentucky (Gramly, Vesper and McCall *ibid.*). Because of this remarkable similarity, the sites are undoubtedly close in age despite the 450 miles separating them.

The first radiocarbon date to be reported from the Dutchess Quarry Caves was obtained on collagen from caribou bone that had been anciently cracked for extracting marrow (Funk *et al.* 1969). An uncalibrated age of 12,530+/-370 years initially was viewed with skepticism (Gramly and Stratton 2005); however, doubts began to subside after a series of additional dates (on amino acids extracted from collagen) evidenced comparable antiquity (Funk and Steadman 1994: 74). The new radiocarbon dates (at two standard deviations) gave a range of 11,530-14,200 years before present. When calibrated and at two standard deviations, the gross bracketing ages of Dutchess Quarry Caves animal bones proved to be 13,430-17,030 years before present (Gramly and Stratton *ibid.*). This impressively old series was based upon samples taken from bones of caribou, flat-headed peccary, and giant beaver.

Ending roughly 12,000 calendar years ago but with beginnings 1,500-5,000 years earlier, the Cumberland Tradition belonged to the terminal Pleistocene era. In that era a wasting Laurentide ice sheet generated abundant silt, which was carried seaward by the Mississippi River. Much of it was also picked up by winds and deposited as fine, yellow-brown loess across the upper Mid-West and upon a narrow strip of land bordering the Mississippi to the east (Buckman and Brady 1969: 291). These massive deposits date from 12,000 to 29,000 years ago (Porter 1988: 6), with a few researchers advocating 10,000 years as an end-point.

A claim for an association of ancient flaked tools with Peorian loess (10/12,000-25,000 years before present) has been made for the Shriver site, Missouri (Rowlett 1981). No projectile points were discovered with this assemblage, although a purported Palaeo-American fluted point (likely a fluted Dalton point) was recovered in a separate cultural zone nearer the surface. The marked slope of the Shriver's surface suggests that washing and redepositing of loess may be a compli-cating factor. Artifacts deep within the loess, and therefore possibly coeval with the end of a Peorian episode, included endscrapers (some with spurs), a backed knife, burins, various other scrapers and utilized flakes, fragmentary early stage bifaces, and a core (not conical). Although no fluted points were found, the assemblage deep within the loess would be at home on most Clovis sites.

The Palaeo-American manifesta-tion at Shriver is unlike the Cumberland assemblage we have garnered at the Phil Stratton site since 1999. The sites do have one thing in common, however — both are deeply buried by loess. The prob-lem of slopewash and colluvial depo-sition does not appear to be so acute at Phil Stratton's – at least in the sector of the site where our principal discoveries have been made. Here erosion has not been a major factor, and we observe that large Cumberland artifacts are con-centrated at 30-35 cm below surface. Forty centime-ters beneath the Cumberland zone, at 75 cm below surface the age of the loess has been found to be 16,720+/-1300 years; while, at 90 cm below surface

Figure 35: Phil Stratton at the Phil Stratton Cumberland encampment, Logan County, southwest-ern Kentucky. The Cumberland zone, perhaps dating to 13,000-14,000 years ago, is embedded within this section of windblown silt (loess) of the glacial era.

– the **bottom** of the loess blanket – a date of 29,980+/-2320 years was obtained. Other age deter-minations are pending.

These dates indicate that the loess at the Phil Stratton site is the Peoria Loess with bracket-ing ages of 10,000-25,000 years (Forman and Pierson 2002: 26). Corroborating an age for the **top** of loess at Phil Stratton's, is a Kirk Serrated projectile point. This 10,000 year-old artifact was found just beneath the surface. Its position suggests that loess had ceased accumulating by that time if not even earlier.

If the rate of build-up of the Peoria loess at the Phil Stratton encampment can be established (it may have varied through time), it should be possible to estimate the age of the Cumberland occupation with a fair degree of precision. At this stage of our investigation a "best guess" is 13,000-14,000 calendar years before present. Such an estimate exceeds or equals the oldest absolute dates for Clovis (Fiedel 2004).

We envision that from time to time while the Phil Stratton site was inhabited the western sky was clouded with glacial dust. There may have been memorable colorful sunsets especially during dry, cold periods. Kentucky's Red River region may have been covered by a boreal forest with predominating jackpines and spruce (Rolingson 1964: 16-17); while, just to the south in Tennessee oaks, hickory and other pines prevailed (Anderson *et al.* 1996: 5). The Tennessee forests may have been similar to those in southwestern Kentucky today. Here and there in south-central Tennessee, northern Alabama and in "burns" among the pines farther north in Kentucky prairies may have held sway (Hulse and Wright 1989: 122-123). Upon them special suites of plants would have provided fodder for an animal population quite unlike that to be seen in the region today. Extensive flat plains, like the one stretching west of Lawrenceburg, Tennessee, for 30 miles, might have been covered at certain seasons with herds of animals. Some of this game may have been migratory causing the hunting societies who depended upon it to become sea-sonally transhumant.

Prior to Cumberland, when hypothesized pioneering "El Jobo" groups inhabited the virgin land, animals also may have crossed vegetational ecotones in step with changing seasons. Throughout the period when El Jobo was being replaced by Cumberland, caribou and *Bison*, we may expect, were two of the desirable species who moved to and fro. There must have been oth-ers who either migrated or resided within territories the year round. Faunal records from caves in the immediate vicinity of the Phil Stratton site include tapir (Hilltop Cave, Trigg County; see Schubert *et al.* 2003) and peccary (Savage Cave, Logan County; see Schenian 1988: 71); while, a mastodon skeleton with marks of butchering is known from north-central Kentucky, about 200 miles away (Harrison County; see Walters 1988).

The number of animal species exploited by El Jobo and Cumberland hunters may have been great, unusually so, for it may have included animals who, given the chance, would have pre-ferred to live far apart. The push to the south by Wisconsin glaciers caused many habitats to be lost and for awhile engendered crowded conditions for animals living north of the Gulf of Mexico. Such an hypothesized "compressed fauna" (Rolingson 1964: 12-17) would have afforded rich opportunities to technologically adept hunters.

On the face of it, we should not be surprised that lands west of the Appalachians and bor-dered by the Ohio, Tennessee, and Mississippi Rivers with their bounty of game witnessed the blossoming of early Palaeo-American culture. From this "forcing area" bearers of the Cumberland Tradition followed migrating caribou and other favorite prey ever northward towards the Great Lakes and eastward into New England. Separately, perhaps, another group who bore the Cumberland Tradition moved north and afterward crossed the Mississippi, branching out upon the Great Plains. Their toolkit evolved into Folsom industry. In some cases Cumberland Tradition hunters were the first on the scene; elsewhere, they may have competed with resident Clovis groups. As we infer from the distribution of Cumberland points (see Appendix), some regions were never settled by bearers of the Cumberland Tradition, as for example, land east of the Appalachians and south of Pennsylvania's Ridge and Valley province. In this region representa-tives of the Clovis archaeological culture had staked a claim, which they neither shared nor ever relinquished.

The story of interacting Palaeo-American cultures, we are beginning to perceive, was perhaps no less complex than the mosaic of linguistic groups and cultures existing across eastern North America on the eve of European colonization. Played out against a backdrop of (now) extinct or extirpated animal species in lands freed of glaciers' grip, these interactions have their own special fascination for students of the past.

R.M.G., 12/27/06

Acknowledgements

I wish to thank ASAA Members Dennis Vesper and Pete Bostrom for suggestions about content and providing illustrations and textual references. The cheerful labor of over 100 other ASAA Members at the Phil Stratton, Trinity and Houser sites has forever indebted me. Walter Philip and Ann Stratton, together with their family and friends, made us feel welcome in Logan County, Kentucky, becoming strong advocates for the discipline of archaeology in their beautiful homeland.

Funding for optically stimulated luminescence determinations (OSL dates) at the Phil Stratton site was provided by ASAA Members, T. Beutell, L. Pfeiffer, and D. Walley.

The support and encouragement of Bob Overstreet was most welcome.

APPENDIX: A NOTE ABOUT THE DISTRIBUTION OF FLUTED POINTS OF THE CUMBERLAND TRADITION

Because of their distinctive appearance and aura of antiquity, Cumberland points have been a lightning rod for controversies and ruses since the 1930s. Modernly made pieces have been misrepresented as ancient; as a result, every newly discovered Cumberland point must be assessed critically. Even artifacts from controlled excavations should be witnessed by trained observers as a safeguard against hoaxes.

In 1939 Marie Wormington reported a heavily reworked Cumberland fluted point from Angus, Nebraska (1939: 11-13). This find (made in 1931) was noteworthy as it lay among the bones of a large, early mammoth (*Archidiskodon meridionalis*). By 1957, however, this association of a "mid-Pleistocene" mammoth and Cumberland point had been dismissed as the handiwork of an unknown "forger" (Wormington 1957: 43). The reputations of gullible scientists who promulgated the bogus (?) discovery had been compromised.

Twenty-two years later and 1,500 miles away, another find of Cumberland artifacts aroused interest. Known as the Moosehorn Fluted Point Discovery, it was named after its purported findspot under a rock overhang on the Moosehorn National Wildlife Refuge, near Calais, on the border of Maine and New Brunswick Province. It consisted of four complete fluted Cumberland points, a large "flake knife," and a fragmentary biface (perhaps a knife). Although the find was clouded by certain "ambiguities," the discovery was deemed possibly genuine (Bonnichsen *et al.* 1983). To this day, however, the pinkish raw material of two surviving Cumberland points, remains unidentified. In my opinion it may be heat-treated Burlington chert, which is a favored toolstone of modern flintknappers – now and during the 1970s when the Moosehorn artifacts came to light. Were they authentic, the Moosehorn Cumberland points would be the easternmost occurrence of the type. Elsewhere in New England, only the Barnes type, representing the later phase of the Cumberland Tradition, is on record. The Moosehorn discovery remains anomalous. More verification is needed.

Another favorite target of charlatans and frauds is the Folsom type, which like Barnes, belongs at the end of the Cumberland Tradition. Since the 1940s Folsom points have been successfully and painstakingly reproduced by commercial knappers and hobbiests. The very high prices that authentic Folsom command are added inducement for producing copies. *Caveat emptor!*

Although Cumberland has suffered from the attentions of deceitful persons, it has been spared the severe blows received by Clovis. The number of whole, shapely Clovis points in museums and private collections is wholly out of proportion to the low number observed within archaeological contexts. At the Vail Clovis site in northwestern highland Maine (Gramly 1982), for example, fewer than 25 whole fluted projectile points have been recorded. Of these 25 only one had not undergone resharpening of the tip. Likely, that particular specimen was lost by an ancient hunter. An additional 80 fluted points from the Vail encampment are represented merely by basal and tip fragments; also, it is highly likely that most of the 60-65 fluted drills excavated by archaeologists from Vail site habitations were converted from fragmentary fluted projectile points. Whole points then, constitute less than 20% of the entire sample of fluted points; while, shapely pristine Clovis points are once-in-a-lifetime finds (less than 1% of the sample)!

Clovis, because it is commonly perceived as the most ancient Palaeo-American point type, has been a preferred target of replicators. At a relic show I have observed an entire table heaped with modernly made specimens that were "sold out" at the conclusion of the event! All these unsigned, spurious specimens find their way into public and private collections, ultimately confounding archaeologists who are systematically investigating the distribution of Palaeo-American points (Moeller 1983).

With these problems in mind, I prefer to work with fragmentary or uncompleted Cumberland points when seeking to understand ancient technology and the distribution of projectile point variants. The identity of raw materials used for making Cumberland points may prove important in deciding whether or not the claim of a discovery is real. In the Mid-West Cumberland hunters seem not to have ranged as widely as Clovis and relied more heavily upon lithic raw materials of the immediate region (Tankersley 1990: Figures 10 and 11). Their trading networks may also have been more poorly developed. When I observe Cumberland points made of some foreign or extra-regional raw material, as is possibly the case for two fluted points of Maine's Moosehorn discovery, naturally suspicions arise.

In this brief overview of the distribution of points belonging to the Cumberland Tradition, the following types and variants are addressed:

I. Early Phase

Variant C, Cumberland point – presumed to be oldest

Variant B, Cumberland point – fluted on one face and unfluted

Variant A, Cumberland point – most common form

II. Late Phase

Barnes point – belongs to Parkhill Complex

Folsom points

I (A). Cumberland Point, Variant C

Specimens are known from south-central Tennessee. Examples represent the thickest and narrowest Cumberland points.

I (B). Cumberland Point, Variant B

Known at present only from northern Tennessee and Kentucky. Points of this variant with fluting on one face were being manufactured from prismatic blades at the Phil Stratton site, Logan County, Kentucky.

The range in size of Variant B has not been established although small points seem to be the rule.

I (C). Cumberland Point, Variant A

This common variant is known from northern Alabama, northeastern Mississippi (McGahey 2000: 11-14), Tennessee, northern Georgia, Kentucky, Indiana (Dorwin 1966: 157-159), Ohio (Converse 1994: 12-13), northern West Virginia (Hyde 1960: 36-37), Pennsylvania (Fogelman and Lantz 2006: 26-27 and elsewhere), southeastern New York (Funk and Steadman 1994), and perhaps New Jersey's coastal plain (Mounier et al. 1993). An outstanding specimen made of local felsite is also on record from western North Carolina (Williams as told to Mitchell 2004). It may represent a "sortie" through the Appalachian Mountains by Cumberland folk coming from the west (Tennessee).

The longest, authentic points of this variant approach nine inches; rumors of even lengthier specimens are the stuff of legend.

Points with finely serrated tips have been reported from Kentucky, Tennessee, Mississippi and Alabama with the greatest number perhaps coming from the Tennessee River and its tributaries.

II (A). Barnes Point

Barnes points are present in the Ohio River region (at Big Bone Lick, Kentucky; see Prufer 1960), north-central Ohio (Prufer 1961: 12), northern Indiana (Gramly 2005), at many localities in Pennsylvania (Fogelman and Lantz 2006), across New York State (Ritchie 1957: Plate 4A; Gramly and Lothrop 1984: 149; Tankersley 1994), Michigan (the Barnes type site), Ontario Province (numerous sites), New Jersey (Staats 1993), Massachusetts (Carty and Spiess 1992; Finneran 2003), New Hampshire (Boisvert 1998), and as far "down-east" as Maine (see Spiess and Wilson 1987 for examples).

A summary statement about the distribution of this point type may be found in a website based upon a publication entitled "Barnes fluted point," *KEWA* 84-6 and authored by B. Deller and C. Ellis.

II (B). Folsom Point

East of the Mississippi River Folsom points are on record for Wisconsin, Illinois, and northern Indiana. I have firsthand knowledge of an authentic specimen that was discovered in western Tennessee, 50-100 miles inland from the Mississippi River. The Indiana occurrence – two typical Folsom points, complete in every detail and made of local raw materials – is a large, open site along the Tippecanoe River in the northern and central part of the state (see Gramly 2005: 98 for illustrations of one of the two complete points together with a mid-section of a third Folsom). It may constitute the most easterly occurrence of Folsom points known to science. The same site, as well, yielded Barnes points and other Palaeo-American point types – all of equivalent antiquity.

Ultimately makers of Folsom points would spread westward to the Rockies and northward and southward along this mountain chain. Their movements were rapid, in step with the ranging habits of their preferred quarry (bison). Interactions with descendants of Clovis folk undoubtedly occurred; however, there was room enough for both cultural groups to co-exist.

Table 1. Flaked and Rough Stone Artifacts of the Cumberland Phase,
Phil Stratton Site, Logan County, Kentucky, 1999-2006

ARTIFACT TYPE AND CLASS   NUMBER/PERCENTAGE
Flaked Tools..(410)
   A. Utilized flakes (unbacked & backed)   116/28%
   B. Utilized prismatic blades (backed & unbacked)   71/17%
   C. Tool fragments (many are prismatic blades)   92/22%
   D. Early stage bifaces and bifacial preforms   34/8%
   E. Gravers (3 are on prismatic blades)   32/8%
   F. Sidescrapers   18/4%
      Simple (one is on a prismatic blade) 10
      Also with "utilization" 2
      Also with graver 3
      Also with beak 1
      Also with denticulate 1
      Shows "alternating" scraper edges ...1
   G. Irregular scrapers (opportunistically placed working   14/4%
      Edges; one is combined with a denticulate)
   H. Endscrapers   7/2%
      Typical endscrapers 2
      Atypical endscrapers 3
      Denticulate endscrapers 2

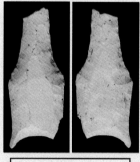

Figure 36: Cumberland drill from Leighton, Alabama. Missing tip and one ear. 2-1/8 inches.

I. Cumberland points (whole count; one point is in four Fragments)	6/2%
J. Burins (one is a technical burin)	5/1%
K. Denticulates (one also has a burin, another a denticulate)	5/1%
L. Celts/Adzes (whole count)	4/1%
M. Awls	2/.5%
N. Bifacial knives	1/.25%
O. Drills	1/.25%
P. Choppers	1/.25%
Q. Nosed scrapers	1/.25%
TOTAL	**410/99.5%**

Cores (one has three chunks refitted to it) . . . . .(10)
Manuports (cobbles from river) . . . .(13)
Rough Stone Tools . . . .(12)

A. Hammerstones	9/75%
B. Abraders/abradingstones	3/25%
TOTAL	**12/100%**

Debitage . . . .(11,480)
A. Uncatalogued and unsorted   11,091
B. Catalogued and sorted   389
    Prismatic blade fragments 197
    Cortex removal flakes 124
    Unidentified flakes 19
    Channel flakes 16
    Angular waste flakes 10
    Biface reduction flakes 8
    Uniface resharpening flakes 3
    Flakes with phytolith sheen 2
    Rolled flakes 2
    Flake blades 2
    Proofed chert cobbles from river 3
    Burin spalls 1
    Chunks 1
    Flake fragments 1

References Cited

Anderson, David G.
    2004 Paleoindian occupations in the southeastern United States. Pp. 119-128 in Bradley T. Lepper and Robson Bonnichsen (eds.) *New Perspectives on the First Americans.* Center for the Study of the First Americans. Texas A&M University.

Anderson, David G. and Michael K. Faught
    2000 Paleoindian artefact distributions: evidence and implications. *Antiquity* 74: 507-513.

Anderson, David G., Lisa D. O'Steen and Kenneth E. Sassaman
    1996 Environmental and chronological considerations. Pp. 3-15 in David G. Anderson and Kenneth E. Sassaman (eds.) *The Paleoindian and Early Archaic Southeast.* The University of Alabama Press. Tuscaloosa.

Barker, Gary and John B. Broster
    1996 The Johnson site (400Dv400): A dated Paleoindian and Early Archaic occupation in Tennessee's Central Basin. *Journal of Alabama Archaeology* 42(2): 97-152.

Boisvert, Richard A.
    1998 The Intervale fluted point. Reprinted from the *New Hampshire Archaeological Society Newsletter* (Volume 1, new series).

Bonnichsen, Robson, Bruce Bourque, and David E. Young
    1983 The Moosehorn Fluted Point Discovery, northern Maine. *Archaeology of Eastern North America* 11: 36-48.

Broster, John B. and Mark R. Norton
    1996 Recent Paleoindian research in Tennessee. Pp. 288-297 in David G. Anderson and Kenneth E. Sassaman (eds.) *The Paleoindian and Early Archaic Southeast.* The University of Alabama Press. Tuscaloosa.

Broster, John B., Mark B. Norton, Dennis J. Stanford, C. Vance Haynes, Jr., and Margaret A. Jodry
    1996 Stratified fluted point deposits in the Western Valley of the Tennessee. Pp. 1-11 in *Proceedings of the 14th Annual Mid-South Archaeological Conference.* Pan-American Consultants, Inc.

Bryan, Alan
    1983   South America. Pp. 137-146 in Richard Shutler, Jr. (ed.) *Early Man in the New World*. Sage Publications. Beverly Hills.

Buckman, Harry O. and Nyle C. Brady
    1969   *The Nature and Properties of Soils*. The Macmillan Company. New York.

Carty, Frederick M. and Arthur E. Spiess
    1992   Neponset Paleoindian site in Massachusetts. *Archaeology of Eastern North America* 20: 19-38.

Collins, Michael B.
    1999   *Clovis Blade Technology*. University of Texas Press. Austin.

Converse, Robert N.
    1994   *Ohio Flint Types*. The Archaeological Society of Ohio. Columbus.

Crichton, Michael
    2004   *State of Fear*. Avon Books. New York.

Deller, D. Brian and Christopher J. Ellis
    1992   Thedford II: A Paleo-Indian Site in the Ausable River Watershed of Southern Ontario. *Memoirs, Museum of Anthropology, University of Michigan* 24. Ann Arbor.

Dorwin, John T.
    1966   Fluted Points and Late-Pleistocene Geochronology in Indiana. *Indiana Historical Society, Prehistory Research Series* IV(3): 141-188. Indianapolis.

Ellis, Christopher and D. Brian Deller
    2000   An Early Paleo-Indian Site Near Parkhill, Ontario. *Mercury Series, Archaeological Survey of Canada* 159. Canadian Museum of Civilization. Hull, Quebec.

Fiedel, Stuart
    2004   Clovis age in calendar years: 13,500 – 13,000 CALYBP. Pp. 73-78 in Bradley T. Lepper and Robson Bonnichsen (eds.) *New Perspectives on the First Americans*. Center for the Study of the First Americans. Texas A & M University. College Station, Texas.

Figgins, J. D.
    1935   Folsom and Yuma artifacts (Part II). *Proceedings of the Colorado Museum of Natural History* XIV(2): 1-7 plus plates.

Finneran, Joseph
    2003   Following the toolstone to "Wamsutta." *The Amateur Archaeologist* 9(2): 45-68.

Fitting, James E.
    1970   *The Archaeology of Michigan*. The Natural History Press. New York.

Fogelman, Gary L. and Stanley W. Lantz
    2005   *The Pennsylvania Fluted point Survey*. Fogelman Publishing. Turbotville, Pennsylvania.

Forman, Steven L. and James Pierson
    2001   Pleistocene luminescence chronology of loess deposition in the Missouri and Mississippi River valleys, United States. *Palaeogeography, Palaeoclimatology, & Palaeoecology* 186: 25-46. Elsevier Science B.V.

Frison, George C.
    2004   *Survival by Hunting*: Prehistoric Human Predators and Animal Prey. University of California Press.

Funk R. E. and D. W. Steadman
    1994   *Archaeological and Paleoenvironmental Investigations in the Dutchess Quarry Caves, Orange County, New York*. Persimmon Press. Buffalo, New York.

Funk, Robert E., George R. Walters, and William F. Ehlers, Jr.
    1969   The archeology of Dutchess Quarry Cave, Orange County, New York. *Pennsylvania Archaeologist* XXXIX (1-4): 7-22.

Gramly, Richard Michael
    1982   The Vail Site: A Palaeo-Indian Encampment in Maine. *Bulletin of the Buffalo Society of Natural Sciences* 30. Buffalo, New York.
    1995   The Vail Palaeo-Indian site: Fifteen years after the excavation. *The Amateur Archaeologist* 1(2): 46-64.
    2005   A multi-component, Palaeo-American site near Warsaw, Indiana. *The Amateur Archaeologist* 11(1): 91-101.

Gramly, Richard Michael and Robert E. Funk
    1991   What is known and not known about the human occupation of the Northeastern United States until 10,000 B.P. *Archaeology of Eastern North America* 18: 5-32.

Gramly, Richard Michael and Jonathan Lothrop
    1984   Archaeological investigations of the Potts site, Oswego County, New York, 1982 and 1983. *Archaeology of Eastern North America* 12: 122-158.

Gramly, Richard M. and Walter Phillip Stratton
    2005   Archaeological investigations of the Phil Stratton site, 1999-2004: A component of the Cumberland/Barnes Tradition. *The Amateur Archaeologist* 11(2): 39-47.

Gramly, Richard Michael and Dennis Vesper
    2006   Additional discoveries at the Trinity Cumberland site: A tribute to Dave McCall. *The Amateur Archaeologist* 11(1): 103-110.

Gramly, Richard Michael, Dennis Vesper and Dave McCall
  1999   A Cumberland site near Trinity, Lewis County, northern Kentucky. *The Amateur Archaeologist* 6(1): 63-80.

Green, F. E.
  1963   The Clovis blades: An important addition to the Llano Complex. *American Antiquity* 29(2): 145-165.

Harris, John M.
  1985   Treasures of the Tar Pits. *Science Series, Natural History Museum of Los Angeles County* 31. Los Angeles, California.

Hulse, David C. and Joe L. Wright
  1989   The Pine Tree-Quad-Old Slough Complex. *Tennessee Anthropologist* XIV(2): 102-125.

Hyde, E. W.
  1960   Mid-Ohio Valley Paleo-Indian and Suggested Sequence of the Fluted point Cultures. *West Virginia Archeological Society, Publication Series* 5. Blennerhassett Chapter, Parkersburg, West Virginia.

Irons, Leroy
  2002   A Cumberland preform: Fluting 101. *Central States Archaeological Journal* 49(1): 38

Jolly, Fletcher III
  1972   Unfinished fluted points and fluted point manufacture in the Tennessee Valley. *Tennessee Archaeologist* XXVIII(2): 60-97.

Lavallee, Daniele (transated by Paul G Bahn)
  1996   *The First South Americans.* The University of Utah Press. Salt Lake City.

Lothrop, Jonathan C, and Richard Michael Gramly
  1982   *Pieces esquillees* from the Vail site. *Archaeology of Eastern North America* 10: 1-22.

Marcher, Melvin V.
  1962   Geology of the Dover Area, Stewart County, Tennessee. *Report of Investigations* 16. State of Tennessee, Department of Conservation and Commerce, Division of Geology. Nashville.

McGahey, Samuel O.
  2000   Mississippi Projectile Point Guide. *Mississippi Department of Archives and History, Archaeological Report* 31. Jackson.

McNutt, Charles H.
  1972   Pre-fluted "Paleo" points from the Southeast: A preliminary note. Unpublished ms., 11 pp. With the author and on file at the American Society for Amateur Archaeology. North Andover.

Meltzer, David J.
  2000   *Folsom: New Archaeological Investigations of a Classic Paleoindian Bison Kill.* University of California Press. Berkeley.

Mirambell, Lorena
  1978   Tlapacoya: A Late Pleistocene site in central Mexico. Pp. 221-230 in Alan Lyle Bryan (ed.) Early Man in America. *Occasional Papers, Department of Anthropology, University of Alberta* 1. Edmonton.

Mitchell, Jessie Tucker
  2004   Point guard. (A youthful fascination with American Indian arrowheads has evolved into a lifelong love and a priceless collection of artifacts for Asheboro's Warner B. Williams). *Our State* (September issue): 28-32.

Moeller, Roger W.
  1983   There is a fluted baby in the bath water. *Archaeology of Eastern North America* 11: 27-28.

Mounier, R. Alan, Jack Cresson, and John W. Martin
  1992   New evidence of Paleoindian biface fluting from the Outer Coastal Plain of New Jersey at 28-OC-100. *Archaeology of Eastern North America* 21: 1-23.

Norton, Mark R. and John B. Broster
  1992   40HS200: The Nuckolls Extension site. *Tennessee Anthropologist* XVII(1): 13-32.

Obermaier, Hugo
  1925   *Fossil man in Spain.* Yale University Press. New Haven.

Ochsenius, Claudio and Ruth Gruhn
  1979   *Taima-Taima. A Late Pleistocene Paleo-Indian Kill Site in Northernmost South America.* South American Quaternary Documentation Program. Distributed by Texas A&M University Press.

Oliver, Jose
  2007   Untitled website devoted to Venezuela Palaeo-Americans. www.bradshawfoundation.com/journey/taima-taima-text3.html, 7 pp. including illustrations.

Pace, Antonio (editor and translator)
  1983   *Viaggio* (by Luigi Castiglione). Syracuse University Press.

Perino, Gregory
  1985   *Selected Preforms, Points and Knives of the North American Indians* (Volume 1). Idabel, Oklahoma.

Porter, Stephen C.
  1988   Landscapes of the last Ice Age in North America. Pp. 1-24 in Ronald C. Carlisle (ed.) Americans Before Columbus: Ice-Age Origins. *Ethnology Monographs, Department of Anthropology, University of Pittsburgh* 12. Pittsburgh, Pennsylvania.

Prufer, Olaf H.
    1960 *Survey of Ohio Fluted Points* (No. 1). Cleveland Museum of Natural History.
    1961 *Survey of Ohio Fluted Points* (No. 4). Cleveland Museum of Natural History.

Prufer, O. H. and R. S. Baby
    1962 *Palaeo-Indians of Ohio.* Ohio Historical Society. Columbus.

Ritchie, William A.
    1957 Traces of Early Man in the Northeast. *New York State Museum and Science Service Bulletin* 358. Albany.

Rolingson, Martha Ann
    1964 Paleo-Indian Culture in Kentucky. *University of Kentucky, Studies in Anthropology* 2. Lexington.

Rouse, Irving and Jose M. Cruxent
    1963 *Venezuelan Archaeology.* Yale University Press. New Haven.

Roosevelt, A. C., John Douglas, and Linda Brown
    2002 The migrations and adaptations of the First Americans: Clovis and Pre-Clovis viewed from South America. Pp. 159-236
          in Nina G. Jablonski (ed.) The First Americans. *Memoirs of the California Academy of Sciences* 27. San Francisco.

Rowlett, Ralph M.
    1980 A lithic assemblage stratified beneath a fluted point horizon in Northwest Missouri. *The Missouri Archaeologist* 42: 7-16.

Schenian, Pamela A.
    1988 An overview of the Paleoindian and Archaic period occupations of the Savage Cave site. Pp. 67-84 in
          Charles D. Hockensmith, David Pollack and Thomas N. Sanders (eds.) *Paleoindian and Archaic Research in Kentucky.*
          Kentucky Heritage Council. Frankfort.

Schubert, Blaine, Jim Mead and Russell Graham (eds.)
    2003 *Ice Age Cave Faunas of North America.* Indiana University Press. Bloomington.

Seeman, Mark F. and Olaf H. Prufer
    1982 An updated distribution of Ohio fluted points. *Midcontinental Journal of Archaeology* 7(2): 155-169.

Spiess, Arthur and Mark Hedden
    2000 Avon: A small Paleoindian site in the western Maine foothills. *Archaeology of Eastern North America* 28: 63-80.

Spiess, Arthur R. and Deborah Brush Wilson
    1986 Michaud: A Paleoindian Site in the New England Maritimes Region. *Occasional Publications in Maine Archaeology* 6.
          Maine Historic Preservation Commission. Augusta.

Squier, Ephraim G. (writing as Samuel A. Bard)
    1855 *Waikna: Adventures on the Mosquito Shore.* Harper and Brothers. New York.

Stanford, Dennis and Bruce Bradley
    2001 Ocean trails and prairie paths? Thoughts about Clovis origins. Pp. 255-272 in Nina G. Jablonski (ed.)
          The First Americans: The Pleistocene Colonization of the New World. *Memoirs of the California Academy
          of Sciences* 27. San Francisco.

Staats, F. Dayton
    1993 An update on a fluted point from northwestern New Jersey. *Bulletin of the Archaeological Society of New Jersey* 48: 64.

Tankersley, Kenneth B.
    1989 Late Pleistocene lithic exploitation in the Midwest and Midsouth. *Research in Economic Anthropology*
          (Supplement 8): 259-299. JAI Press, Inc.
    1994 Devil's Nose: A Parkhill Complex site in western New York. *Current Research in the Pleistocene* 11: 51-53.

Thruston, Gates
    1890 *The Antiquities of Tennessee.* Robert Clarke and Co. Cincinnati.

Turner, Ellen Sue and Thomas R. Hester
    1995 *A Field Guide to Stone Artifacts of Texas Indians* (second edition). Gulf Publishing. Houston, Texas.

Van Buren, G. E.
    1973 *Arrowheads and Projectile Points.* Arrowhead Publishing Company. Garden Grove, California.

Walters, Matthew M.
    1988 The Adams Mastodon site, Harrison County, Kentucky. Pp. 43-46 in Charles D. Hockensmith, David Pollack, and
          Thomas N. Sanders (eds.) *Paleoindian and Archaic Research in Kentucky.* Kentucky Heritage Council. Frankfort.

Webb, Wm. S.
    1951 The Parrish Village Site (Site 45, Hopkins County, Kentucky). *The University of Kentucky Reports in
          Anthropology* VII(6): 407-461. Lexington.

Wormington, H. M.
    1939 *Ancient Man in North America* (first edition). Colorado Museum of Natural History. Denver.
    1957 *Ancient Man in North America* (sixth edition). Colorado Museum of Natural History. Denver.

Wright, Henry T. and William B. Roosa
    1965 The Barnes site: A fluted point assemblage from the Great Lakes region. *American Antiquity* 31(6): 850-860.

WHY CONSIGN *with* MORPHY AUCTIONS ?

- All items are on display at Morphy Auctions two months prior to the sale.

- Your collection is securely housed and insured to guarantee ultimate protection and safekeeping.

- All items are available to view online at www.morphyauctions.com and www.liveauctioneers.com one month prior to the sale.

- Over 85,000 full-color brochures and 10,000 hardbound catalogs are printed.

- Morphy Auctions promotes its sales at the top antique shows in the country.

- A well-planned marketing and advertising campaign is launched to maximize exposure.

- Consignors paid within 30 days.

SOLD $77,000

SOLD $8,800

SOLD $6,600

SOLD $8,960

SOLD $5,750

SOLD $7,500

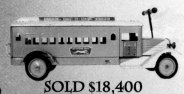

SOLD $18,400

SOLD $5,600

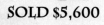

SOLD $10,450

SOLD $8,800

SOLD $2,500

SOLD $14,950

SOLD $14,300

SOLD $14,300

SOLD $29,120

SOLD $5,040

SOLD $25,300

ACCEPTING QUALITY
CONSIGNMENTS
Single Pieces & Collections

SOLD $14,375

SOLD $14,300

SOLD $12,000

SOLD $8,250

SOLD $3,300

SOLD $4,760

SOLD $8,250

SOLD $30,800

FOR THE UTMOST CARE IN
YOUR COLLECTION...

MORPHY
AUCTIONS

2000 N. READING RD
DENVER, PA 17517
717-335-3435
MORPHYAUCTIONS.COM

LAKE MOHAVE
13,200 B.P., Steens Mountain,
OR, ground stem, obsidian

LAKE MOHAVE
13,200 B.P., Navajo Co., AZ,
ground stem

LAKE MOHAVE
13,200 B.P., S.W.
CO, conglomerate

HASKETT
12,000 B.P., Harney Co., OR,
obsidian, ground stem

LAKE MOHAVE
13,200 B.P., Carson Sink,
NV, ground stem

LAKE MOHAVE
13,200 B.P.,
Humboldt Co., NV,
basalt

HASKETT
12,000 B.P.,
Humboldt Co.,
NV, mahagony
obsidian;
ground stem

CLOVIS
11,500 B.P., Logan
Co., CO, agate

CLOVIS
11,500 B.P., WY, petrified wood

CLOVIS
11,500 B.P., Lake Co., OR,
Malheur chert. Clovis is rare
in the Northwest

CLOVIS
11,500 B.P., Benton Co., TX

CLOVIS
11,500 B.P., Greene Co., IN,
hornstone

CLOVIS
11,500 B.P., Dekalb Co., IL,
Kaolin chert

CLOVIS
11,500 B.P., IL, Hixton sandstone

CLOVIS
11,500 B.P. Blount Co., AL,
petrified wood

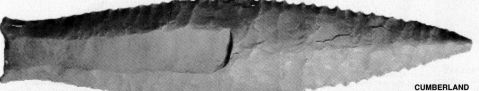

CUMBERLAND
11,250 B.P., Coffee Slough, AL, Fort Payne
chert. Cumberlands are rarely serrated

CUMBERLAND-BARNES
11,250 B.P., Chester Co., PA, Jasper

BEAVER LAKE
11,250 B.P., W. TN, Fort Payne chert

CUMBERLAND
11,250 B.P., Humphreys Co., TN, Buffalo River chert

CUMBERLAND
11,250 B.P., Mid, TN, Fort Payne chert

CUMBERLAND
11,250 B.P., Weakley Co., TN, Fort Payne chert

CUMBERLAND
11,250 B.P., Nashville, TN Nicknamed "Big Red"

BEAVER LAKE
11,250 B.P., Dayton, TN, gray flint

BEAVER LAKE
11,250 B.P., N. FL

PLAINVIEW
11,250 B.P., WY, jasper

BEAVER LAKE
11,250 B.P., Johnson Co., TN

CUMBERLAND
11,250 B.P., Christian Co., KY, Fort Payne chert

PLAINVIEW
11,250 B.P., Wilson Co., TX

PLAINVIEW
11,250 B.P., N.W. Chihuahua, MX

BLACK ROCK CONCAVE
11,000 B.P., N.W. NV, agate

BLACK ROCK CONCAVE
11,000 B.P., N.W. NV, jasper

BLACK ROCK CONCAVE
11,000 B.P., N.W. NV, agate

BLACK ROCK CONCAVE
11,000 B.P., Klamath Co., OR, obsidian; side cut used for water hydration age test

COUGAR MOUNTAIN
11,000 B.P., Harney Co., OR, agate

COUGAR MOUNTAIN
11,000 B.P., Lake Co., OR, ground stem

CRESCENT
11,000 B.P.,
Columbia Riv., OR

CRESCENT
11,000 B.P., N. NV, jasper

CRESCENT
11,000 B.P., S. OR

COUGAR MOUNTAIN
11,000 B.P., Lake Co., OR,
obsidian, ground stem

CRESCENT
11,000 B.P., N. NV

CRESCENT
11,000 B.P., Lake
Co., OR

CRESCENT
11,000 B.P., Black
Rock Desert, OR

FOLSOM BASE
11,000 B.P., San
Luis Valley, CO,
chert

CROWFIELD
11,000 B.P., Chautauqua Co.,
NY, black flint

EARLY OVOID KNIFE
11,000 B.P., Fulton Co., IL,
Burlington chert

FOLSOM
11,000 B.P., Culbertson
Co., TX, chalcedony

FOLSOM
11,000 B.P., OK, agate

FOLSOM
11,000 B.P., Hooker
Co., NE, agate

FOLSOM
11,000 B.P., Burnet Co., TX

HAW RIVER
11,000 B.P., Grayson Co., KY

LIND COULEE
11,000 B.P., Burns, OR,
chisel tip, obsidian

LIND COULEE
11,000 B.P., Lake Co.,
OR, jasper

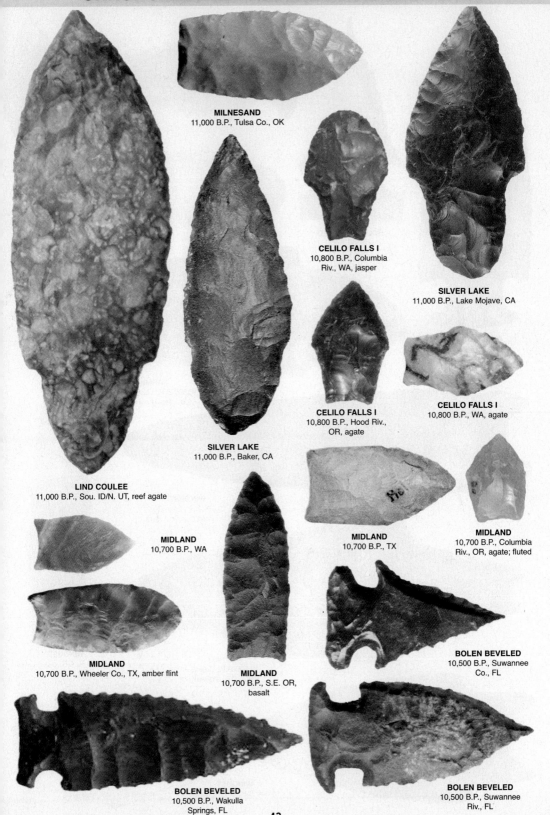

MILNESAND
11,000 B.P., Tulsa Co., OK

CELILO FALLS I
10,800 B.P., Columbia
Riv., WA, jasper

SILVER LAKE
11,000 B.P., Lake Mojave, CA

CELILO FALLS I
10,800 B.P., Hood Riv.,
OR, agate

CELILO FALLS I
10,800 B.P., WA, agate

SILVER LAKE
11,000 B.P., Baker, CA

LIND COULEE
11,000 B.P., Sou. ID/N. UT, reef agate

MIDLAND
10,700 B.P., WA

MIDLAND
10,700 B.P., TX

MIDLAND
10,700 B.P., Columbia
Riv., OR, agate; fluted

MIDLAND
10,700 B.P., Wheeler Co., TX, amber flint

MIDLAND
10,700 B.P., S.E. OR,
basalt

BOLEN BEVELED
10,500 B.P., Suwannee
Co., FL

BOLEN BEVELED
10,500 B.P., Wakulla
Springs, FL

BOLEN BEVELED
10,500 B.P., Suwannee
Riv., FL

43

BOLEN BEVELED
10,500 B.P., N. FL

PARMAN
10,500 B.P.,
OR, chisel tip,
obsidian

BOLEN BEVELED
10,500 B.P.,
Leon Co., FL

PARMAN
10,500 B.P., OR, agate

BOLEN PLAIN
10,500 B.P.,
Suwannee Riv., FL

PARMAN
10,500 B.P., Lake Co., OR,
obsidian, ground stem

WINDUST
10,500 B.P., Lake Co.,
OR, basalt, ground stem

WINDUST
10,500 B.P., Crump
Lake, OR, obsidian

WINDUST
10,500 B.P., OR, ground stem

WINDUST
10,500 B.P., S. OR, basalt

WINDUST
10,500 B.P., WA, yellow
jasper

WINDUST
10,500 B.P., Lake
Co., OR, jasper

HELL GAP
10,300 B.P., Osage
Co., OK, Foraker flint

HELL GAP
10,300 B.P.,
Mountrail Co., ND,
Knife River flint

AGATE BASIN
10,200 B.P.,
Tulsa Co., OK

HELL GAP
10,300 B.P., ND,
Knife River flint

AGATE BASIN
10,200 B.P.,
Logan Co., CO,
petrified wood

AGATE BASIN
10,200 B.P., Garden
Co., ND, moss agate

AGATE BASIN
10,200 B.P.,
Sinclair Co., IL

AGATE BASIN
10,200 B.P.,
Hooker Co.,
NE, chalc.

AGATE BASIN
10,200 B.P.,
Madison Co., IL

BIG SANDY
10,000 B.P., Meigs Co., TN

BIG SANDY
10,000 B.P.,
Cullman Co., AL

BIG SANDY
10,000 B.P., Jackson
Co., AL

ALBERTA
10,000 B.P., Massacre Lake, NV, chalc.

BIG SANDY
10,000 B.P., N.W. AL,
jasper

ALBERTA
10,000 B.P., WY, petrified wood

DALTON
10,000 B.P.,
Stoddard Co., MO

CACHE RIVER
10,000 B.P.,
Greene Co., AR

DALTON
10,000 B.P.,
Boone Co., IA

CODY KNIFE
10,000 B.P.,
Sask., CAN,
Knife River flint

DALTON
10,000 B.P., Jackson Co., MO, Mozarkite chert

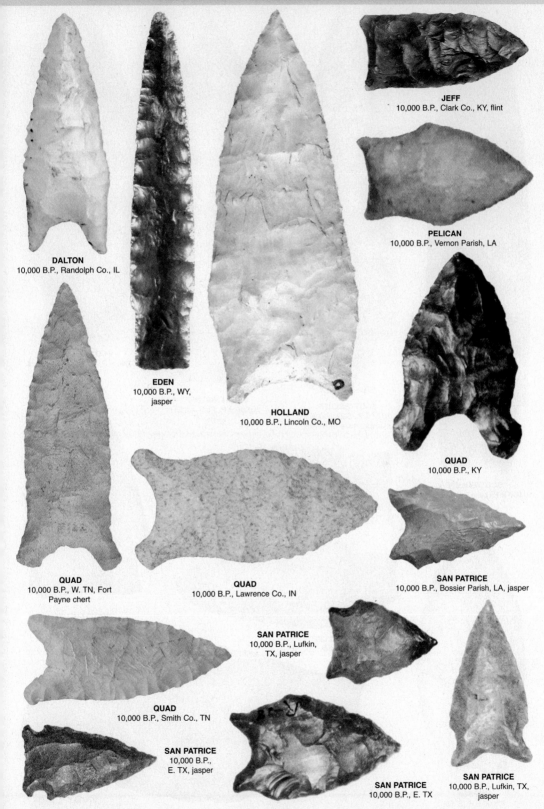

DALTON
10,000 B.P., Randolph Co., IL

EDEN
10,000 B.P., WY, jasper

HOLLAND
10,000 B.P., Lincoln Co., MO

JEFF
10,000 B.P., Clark Co., KY, flint

PELICAN
10,000 B.P., Vernon Parish, LA

QUAD
10,000 B.P., KY

QUAD
10,000 B.P., W. TN, Fort Payne chert

QUAD
10,000 B.P., Lawrence Co., IN

SAN PATRICE
10,000 B.P., Bossier Parish, LA, jasper

QUAD
10,000 B.P., Smith Co., TN

SAN PATRICE
10,000 B.P., Lufkin, TX, jasper

SAN PATRICE
10,000 B.P., E. TX, jasper

SAN PATRICE
10,000 B.P., E. TX

SAN PATRICE
10,000 B.P., Lufkin, TX, jasper

SCOTTSBLUFF
10,000 B.P., WY, Knife River flint

SCOTTSBLUFF
10,000 B.P., Saskatchewan,
Canada, Knife River flint

SCOTTSBLUFF
10,000 B.P., Portland, OR,
jasper

SCOTTSBLUFF
10,000 B.P., Lake Co., OR, basalt

SCOTTSBLUFF
10,000 B.P., WA

SCOTTSBLUFF
10,000 B.P., TX

SCOTTSBLUFF
10,000 B.P., Nuckolls Co., NE

SIMPSON
10,000 B.P., S. GA

SIMPSON
10,000 B.P., S. GA

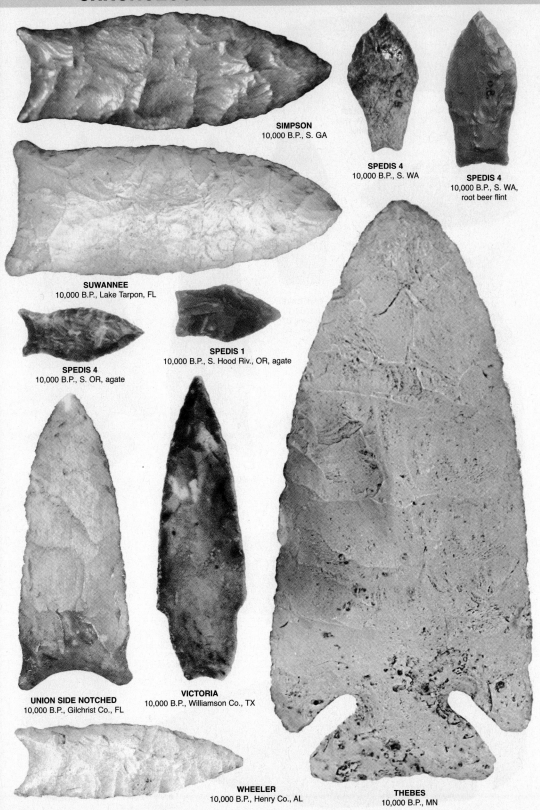

SIMPSON
10,000 B.P., S. GA

SPEDIS 4
10,000 B.P., S. WA

SPEDIS 4
10,000 B.P., S. WA,
root beer flint

SUWANNEE
10,000 B.P., Lake Tarpon, FL

SPEDIS 1
10,000 B.P., S. Hood Riv., OR, agate

SPEDIS 4
10,000 B.P., S. OR, agate

UNION SIDE NOTCHED
10,000 B.P., Gilchrist Co., FL

VICTORIA
10,000 B.P., Williamson Co., TX

WHEELER
10,000 B.P., Henry Co., AL

THEBES
10,000 B.P., MN

WHEELER
10,000 B.P., Trigg
Co., KY

WHEELER
10,00 B.P. TN/AL
border

ST. CHARLES
9,500 B.P., KY,
Carter Cave chert

OWL CAVE
9,500 B.P., N. Cent.
UT, obsidian

OWL CAVE
9,500 B.P.
N. Cent. UT

HARDAWAY
9,500 B.P., Nuckolls
site, TN

MESERVE
9,500 B.P., Mitchell, SD,
Knife River, flint

ST. CHARLES
9,500 B.P., Clark
Co., KY, flint

ST. CHARLES
9,500 B.P., Decatur Co.,
TN, Buffalo River flint

ST. CHARLES
9,500 B.P., Warren Co.,
TN, red/blue/white
Del Rio flint

ST. CHARLES
9,500 B.P., Davidson
Co., TN, flint

ST. CHARLES
9,500 B.P.,
Madison Co., IL

EARLY TRI-ANGULAR
9,000 B.P.,
Webb Co., TX

DECATUR
9,000 B.P., TN,
hornstone,
fractured base

ST. CHARLES
9,500 B.P., Fulton Co.,
Il, LaSalle chert

HARDIN
9,000 B.P., IN

FREDERICK
9,000 B.P., Walworth Co.,
SD, agatized wood

KIRK STEMMED
9,000 B.P., Summit
Co., OH, Upper
Mercer flint

HARPETH RIVER
9,000 B.P., Humphreys
Co., TN, Dover chert

KIRK STEMMED
9,000 B.P., Marion
Co., FL

KIRK CORNER NOTCHED
9,000 B.P., Jefferson Co., MS

SAN JOSE
9,000 B.P., S.W.
CO

LOST LAKE
9,000 B.P., Hardin Co.,
KY, Sonora flint

LOST LAKE
9,000 B.P., Saltillo, TN,
Dover chert

SAN JOSE
9,000 B.P., San Juan
Co., UT

LERMA
9,000 B.P., Wilson Co., TX,
root beer flint

SAN JOSE
9,000 B.P., S.W. CO,
jasper

WILDCAT CANYON
9,000 B.P., WA,
petrified wood

LOST LAKE
9,000 B.P.,
Turner Co., GA

ZEPHYR
9,000 B.P., S.W.
CO, jasper

WAHMUZA
9,000 B.P., Columbia
Riv., OR, jasper

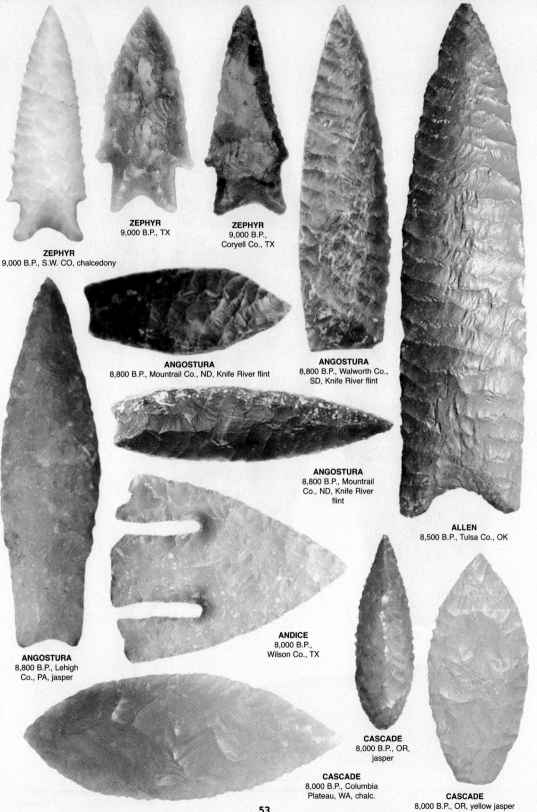

ZEPHYR
9,000 B.P., S.W. CO, chalcedony

ZEPHYR
9,000 B.P., TX

ZEPHYR
9,000 B.P.,
Coryell Co., TX

ANGOSTURA
8,800 B.P., Mountrail Co., ND, Knife River flint

ANGOSTURA
8,800 B.P., Walworth Co.,
SD, Knife River flint

ANGOSTURA
8,800 B.P., Mountrail
Co., ND, Knife River
flint

ALLEN
8,500 B.P., Tulsa Co., OK

ANGOSTURA
8,800 B.P., Lehigh
Co., PA, jasper

ANDICE
8,000 B.P.,
Wilson Co., TX

CASCADE
8,000 B.P., OR,
jasper

CASCADE
8,000 B.P., Columbia
Plateau, WA, chalc.

CASCADE
8,000 B.P., OR, yellow jasper

CASCADE
8,000 B.P.,
Columbia
Plateau, WA,
petrified wood

CASCADE
8,000 B.P., Warner Valley, OR, agate

CASCADE
8,000 B.P., OR, ground stem, obsidian

CASCADE
8,000 B.P., Lake Co., OR, obsidian

CASCADE
8,000 B.P., Harney Co., OR, chalcedony

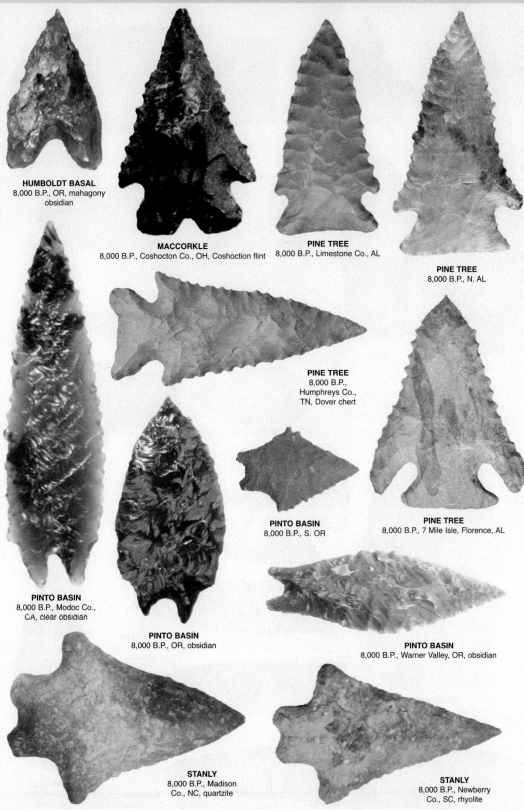

HUMBOLDT BASAL
8,000 B.P., OR, mahagony obsidian

MACCORKLE
8,000 B.P., Coshocton Co., OH, Coshoction flint

PINE TREE
8,000 B.P., Limestone Co., AL

PINE TREE
8,000 B.P., N. AL

PINE TREE
8,000 B.P., Humphreys Co., TN, Dover chert

PINE TREE
8,000 B.P., 7 Mile Isle, Florence, AL

PINTO BASIN
8,000 B.P., S. OR

PINTO BASIN
8,000 B.P., Modoc Co., CA, clear obsidian

PINTO BASIN
8,000 B.P., OR, obsidian

PINTO BASIN
8,000 B.P., Warner Valley, OR, obsidian

STANLY
8,000 B.P., Madison Co., NC, quartzite

STANLY
8,000 B.P., Newberry Co., SC, rhyolite

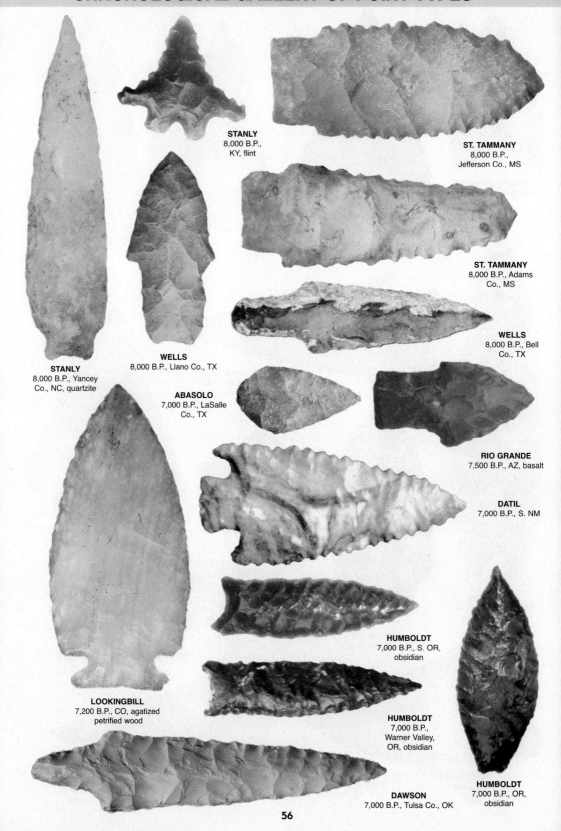

STANLY
8,000 B.P.,
KY, flint

ST. TAMMANY
8,000 B.P.,
Jefferson Co., MS

ST. TAMMANY
8,000 B.P., Adams
Co., MS

WELLS
8,000 B.P., Bell
Co., TX

STANLY
8,000 B.P., Yancey
Co., NC, quartzite

WELLS
8,000 B.P., Llano Co., TX

ABASOLO
7,000 B.P., LaSalle
Co., TX

RIO GRANDE
7,500 B.P., AZ, basalt

DATIL
7,000 B.P., S. NM

HUMBOLDT
7,000 B.P., S. OR,
obsidian

LOOKINGBILL
7,200 B.P., CO, agatized
petrified wood

HUMBOLDT
7,000 B.P.,
Warner Valley,
OR, obsidian

HUMBOLDT
7,000 B.P., OR,
obsidian

DAWSON
7,000 B.P., Tulsa Co., OK

HUMBOLDT
7,000 B.P., Lake Co., OR

HUMBOLDT
7,000 B.P., Warner Valley, OR

HUMBOLDT
7,000 B.P., S. OR, obsidian

MORROW MOUNTAIN
7,000 B.P., Madison Co., NC, red quartzite

HUMBOLDT
7,000 B.P., Humboldt Co., NV

NEWNAN
7,000 B.P., Pasco Co., FL. Coastal Plain chert

NEWNAN
7,000 B.P., Alachua Co., FL; restored base

NEWNAN
7,000 B.P., Alachua Co., FL, coastal plain chert

MARION
7,000 B.P., Dixie Co. FL

NIGHTFIRE
7,000 B.P., OR, obsidian

NIGHTFIRE
7,000 B.P., Klamath
Co., OR, obsidian

NORTHERN
7,000 B.P., Warner Valley,
OR, obsidian

NORTHERN
7,000 B.P., Warner Valley,
OR, obsidian

NORTHERN
7,000 B.P., Warner Valley,
OR, obsidian

NIGHTFIRE
7,000 B.P., Warner Valley,
OR, obsidian

NORTHERN
7,000 B.P., Warner Valley, OR

NORTHERN
7,000 B.P., Warner Valley,
OR, mahagony obsidian

NORTHERN
7,000 B.P., Warner Valley,
OR, obsidian

NORTHERN
7,000 B.P., OR, obsidian

NORTHERN
7,000 B.P., Warner
Valley, OR, obsidian

NORTHERN
7,000 B.P., Warner
Valley, OR, obsidian

NORTHERN
7,000 B.P., OR, petrified
wood agate

SIMONSEN
6,800 B.P., Mountrail Co., ND, agate

ESCOBAS
6,500 B.P., S.W. CO

GUILFORD
6,500 B.P., NC,
quartzite

WENDOVER
7,000 B.P., Harney
Co., OR, basalt

WENDOVER
7,000 B.P., Lake Co., OR

SUDDEN
6,300 B.P., Cent.
UT, chert

BAJADA
6,000 B.P.,
S.W. CO,
jasper

BENTON
6,000 B.P.,
Florence, AL

BENTON
6,000 B.P., Sumner
Co., TN, red, blue,
white Del Rio flint

BENTON
6,000 B.P.,
W. TN,
Dover chert

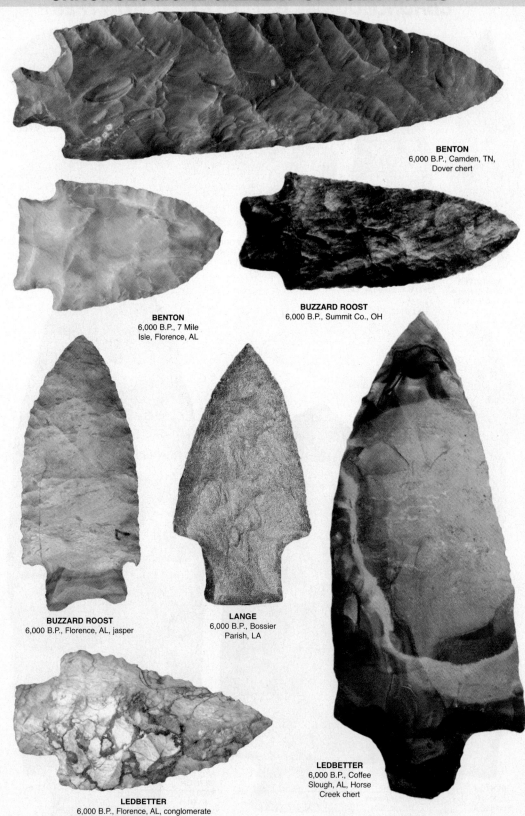

BENTON
6,000 B.P., Camden, TN,
Dover chert

BENTON
6,000 B.P., 7 Mile
Isle, Florence, AL

BUZZARD ROOST
6,000 B.P., Summit Co., OH

BUZZARD ROOST
6,000 B.P., Florence, AL, jasper

LANGE
6,000 B.P., Bossier
Parish, LA

LEDBETTER
6,000 B.P., Coffee
Slough, AL, Horse
Creek chert

LEDBETTER
6,000 B.P., Florence, AL, conglomerate

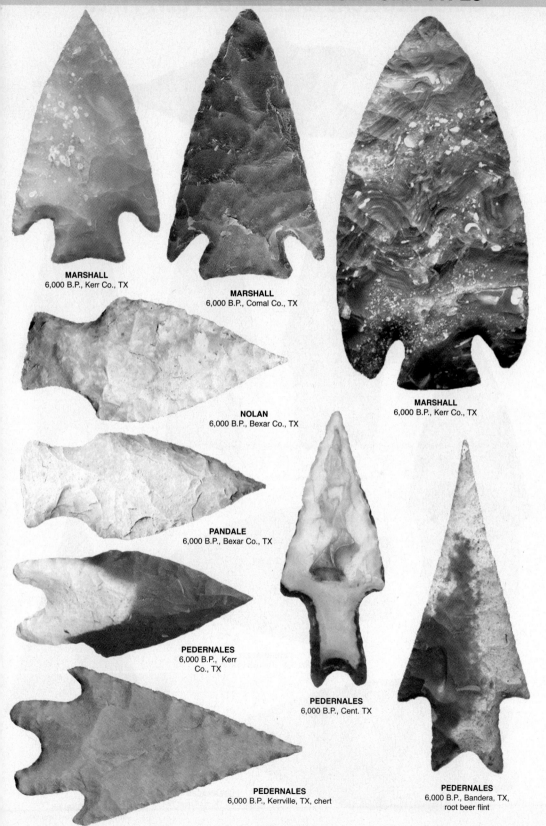

MARSHALL
6,000 B.P., Kerr Co., TX

MARSHALL
6,000 B.P., Comal Co., TX

MARSHALL
6,000 B.P., Kerr Co., TX

NOLAN
6,000 B.P., Bexar Co., TX

PANDALE
6,000 B.P., Bexar Co., TX

PEDERNALES
6,000 B.P., Kerr
Co., TX

PEDERNALES
6,000 B.P., Cent. TX

PEDERNALES
6,000 B.P., Kerrville, TX, chert

PEDERNALES
6,000 B.P., Bandera, TX,
root beer flint

PEDERNALES
6,000 B.P., TX,
root beer flint

PEDERNALES
6,000 B.P., TX, root beer flint

PEDERNALES
6,000 B.P., TX, root beer flint

PEDERNALES
6,000 B.P., TX, root beer flint

PEDERNALES
6,000 B.P., TX, root beer flint

PEDERNALES
6,000 B.P., TX, root beer flint

PEDERNALES
6,000 B.P., TX, root beer flint

PEDERNALES
6,000 B.P., TX, root beer flint

PEDERNALES
6,000 B.P., TX, root beer flint

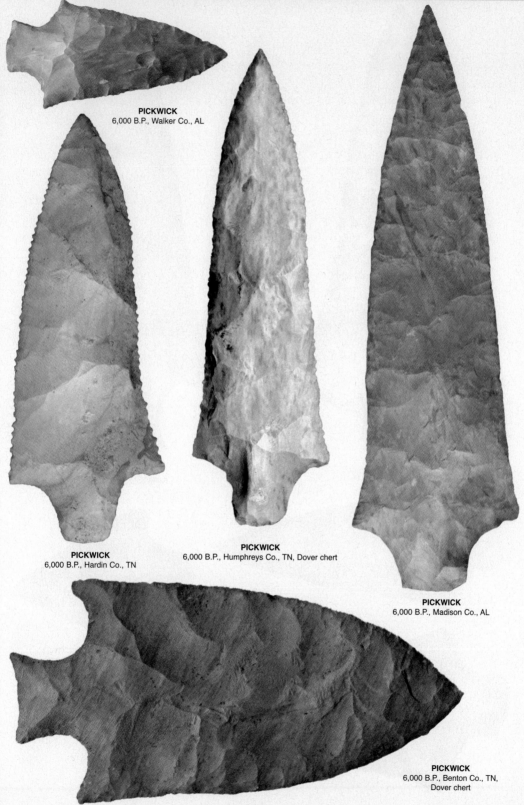

PICKWICK
6,000 B.P., Walker Co., AL

PICKWICK
6,000 B.P., Hardin Co., TN

PICKWICK
6,000 B.P., Humphreys Co., TN, Dover chert

PICKWICK
6,000 B.P., Madison Co., AL

PICKWICK
6,000 B.P., Benton Co., TN,
Dover chert

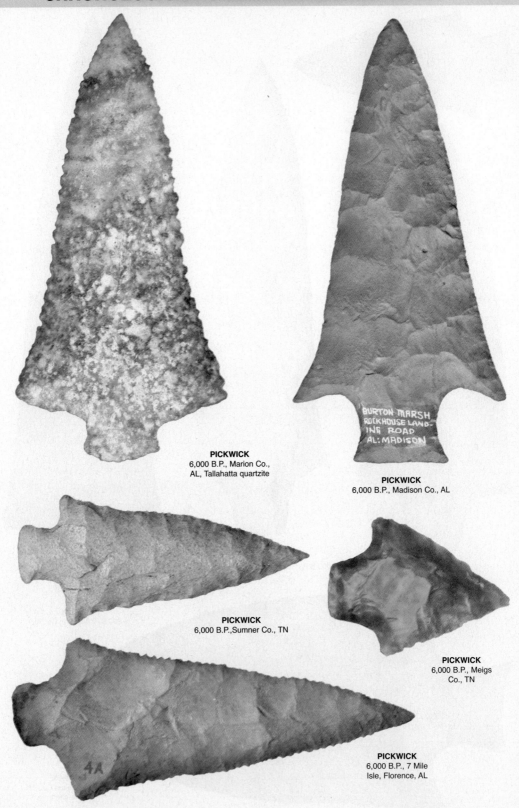

PICKWICK
6,000 B.P., Marion Co.,
AL, Tallahatta quartzite

PICKWICK
6,000 B.P., Madison Co., AL

PICKWICK
6,000 B.P.,Sumner Co., TN

PICKWICK
6,000 B.P., Meigs
Co., TN

PICKWICK
6,000 B.P., 7 Mile
Isle, Florence, AL

SAN JACINTO
6,000 B.P., S.E. TX

SIERRA CONTRACTING STEM
6,000 B.P., S. OR, obsidian

TORTUGAS
6,000 B.P., S. TX

WILLIAMS
6,000 B.P., Bossier
Parish, LA, jasper

BUFFALO GAP
6,000 B.P., Walworth Co., SD,
chalcedony

HIGH DESERT KNIFE
5,500 B.P., OR

**HIGH DESERT
KNIFE**
5,500 B.P., Harney
Co., OR, obsidian

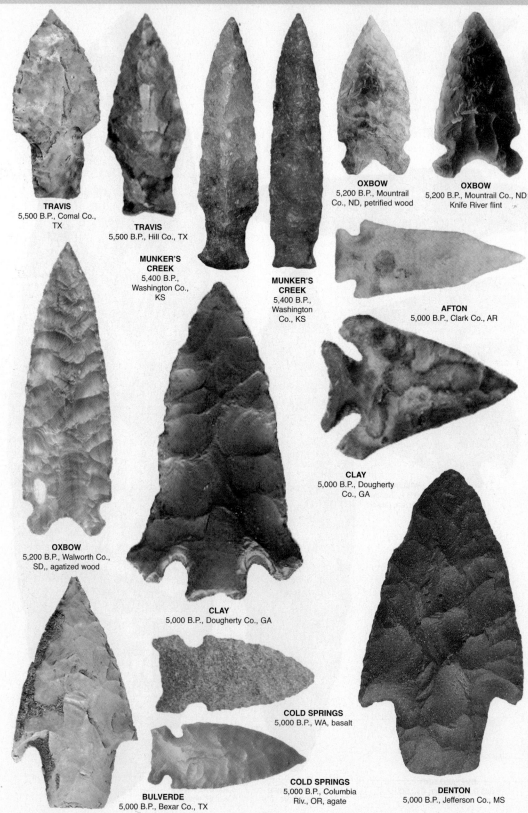

TRAVIS
5,500 B.P., Comal Co.,
TX

TRAVIS
5,500 B.P., Hill Co., TX

**MUNKER'S
CREEK**
5,400 B.P.,
Washington Co.,
KS

**MUNKER'S
CREEK**
5,400 B.P.,
Washington
Co., KS

OXBOW
5,200 B.P., Mountrail
Co., ND, petrified wood

OXBOW
5,200 B.P., Mountrail Co., ND
Knife River flint

AFTON
5,000 B.P., Clark Co., AR

CLAY
5,000 B.P., Dougherty
Co., GA

OXBOW
5,200 B.P., Walworth Co.,
SD,, agatized wood

CLAY
5,000 B.P., Dougherty Co., GA

COLD SPRINGS
5,000 B.P., WA, basalt

BULVERDE
5,000 B.P., Bexar Co., TX

COLD SPRINGS
5,000 B.P., Columbia
Riv., OR, agate

DENTON
5,000 B.P., Jefferson Co., MS

GATECLIFF
5,000 B.P., Harney Co., OR

GATECLIFF
5,000 B.P., Harney
Co., OR, obsidian

GATECLIFF
5,000 B.P., OR, agate

GATECLIFF
5,000 B.P., Harney
Co., OR, obsidian

KAYS
5,000 B.P., Meigs Co., TN

KINNEY
5,000 B.P., Webb Co., TX

KINNEY
5,000 B.P., Bexar Co., TX

GATECLIFF
5,000 B.P., Twin Falls, ID,
orange agate

LANGTRY
5,000 B.P., Webb
Co., TX

LANGTRY
5,000 B.P., Bexar Co., TX

MENDOCINO CONCAVE
5,000 B.P., Santa Barbara Co., CA, agate

MONTELL
5,000 B.P., Boerne, TX

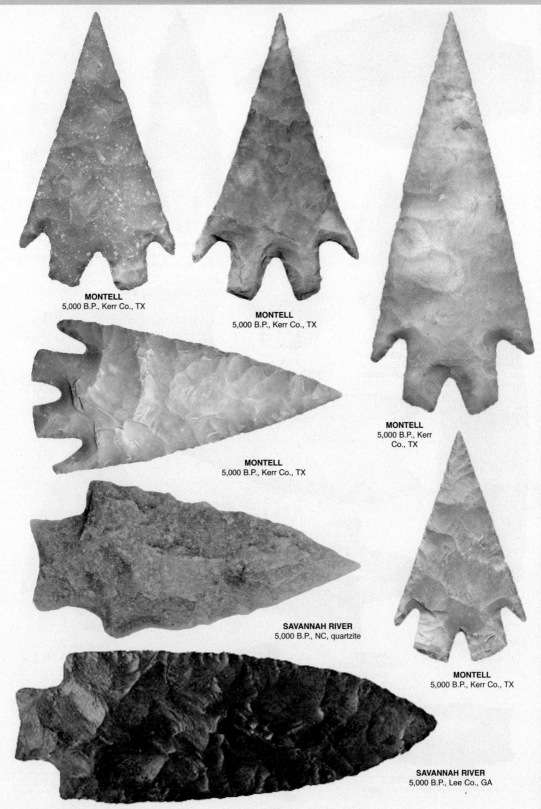

MONTELL
5,000 B.P., Kerr Co., TX

MONTELL
5,000 B.P., Kerr Co., TX

MONTELL
5,000 B.P., Kerr Co., TX

MONTELL
5,000 B.P., Kerr Co., TX

SAVANNAH RIVER
5,000 B.P., NC, quartzite

MONTELL
5,000 B.P., Kerr Co., TX

SAVANNAH RIVER
5,000 B.P., Lee Co., GA

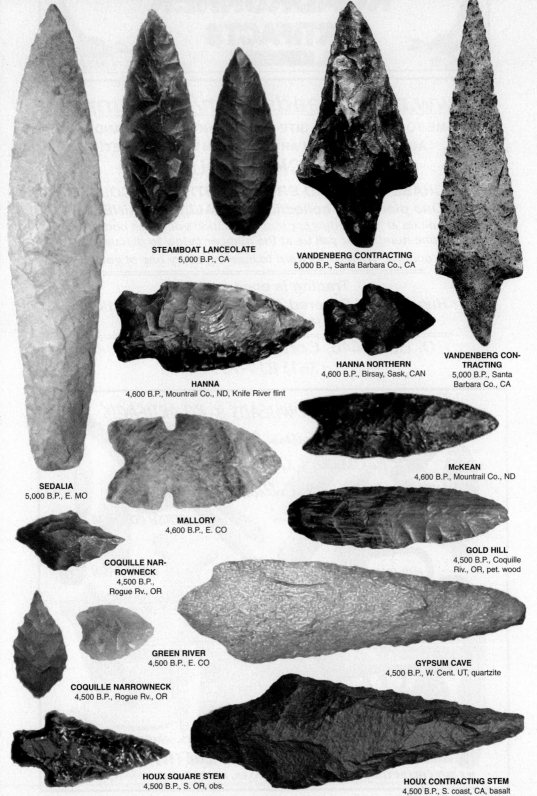

STEAMBOAT LANCEOLATE
5,000 B.P., CA

VANDENBERG CONTRACTING
5,000 B.P., Santa Barbara Co., CA

HANNA NORTHERN
4,600 B.P., Birsay, Sask, CAN

**VANDENBERG CON-
TRACTING**
5,000 B.P., Santa
Barbara Co., CA

HANNA
4,600 B.P., Mountrail Co., ND, Knife River flint

McKEAN
4,600 B.P., Mountrail Co., ND

SEDALIA
5,000 B.P., E. MO

MALLORY
4,600 B.P., E. CO

GOLD HILL
4,500 B.P., Coquille
Riv., OR, pet. wood

**COQUILLE NAR-
ROWNECK**
4,500 B.P.,
Rogue Rv., OR

GREEN RIVER
4,500 B.P., E. CO

GYPSUM CAVE
4,500 B.P., W. Cent. UT, quartzite

COQUILLE NARROWNECK
4,500 B.P., Rogue Rv., OR

HOUX SQUARE STEM
4,500 B.P., S. OR, obs.

HOUX CONTRACTING STEM
4,500 B.P., S. coast, CA, basalt

ROADRUNNER
ARTIFACTS
AL KENNEDY

www.arrowheads.com/roadrunner/

WELCOME TO THE PREMIER SITE FOR BUYING, SELLING, AND TRADING AUTHENTIC INDIAN ARTIFACTS ON THE INTERNET!

CHECK US OUT!

WE PURCHASE, SELL AND BROKER AUTHENTIC COLLECTIONS,
One piece or a collection (LEGALLY OBTAINED).
Email us at akennedy@stx.rr.com (include your area code and phone number) or call us at the number below to discuss the options. We look forward to meeting every one of you!

Trading is encouraged!
Hundreds of Papered Artifacts for your Selection!
Happy Hunting!

P.O. Box 8646, Corpus Christi, Texas 78468
(361) 814-1314

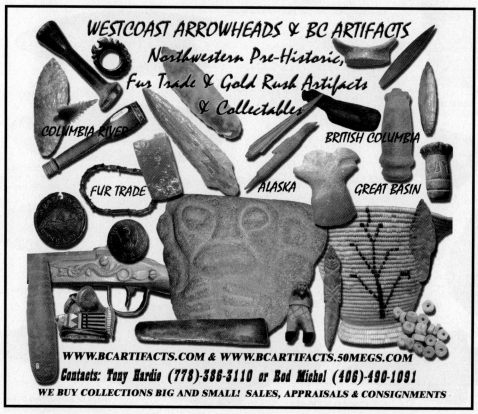

WESTCOAST ARROWHEADS & BC ARTIFACTS
Northwestern Pre-Historic, Fur Trade & Gold Rush Artifacts & Collectables

COLUMBIA RIVER

BRITISH COLUMBIA

FUR TRADE

ALASKA

GREAT BASIN

WWW.BCARTIFACTS.COM & WWW.BCARTIFACTS.50MEGS.COM
Contacts: Tony Hardie (778)-386-3110 or Rod Michel (406)-490-1091
WE BUY COLLECTIONS BIG AND SMALL! SALES, APPRAISALS & CONSIGNMENTS

Pat's Authentic Indian Arrowheads

Quality Points at Fair Prices

Over 100 Close-up Photos Online

Best Prices Available on Artifact Reference Books

Visit our Website at

www.Arrowheads-Relics.com

or call toll-free at

1-888-841-9386

teddun @ itexas.net

P.O. Box 156, Gustine, TX 76455

HD Enterprises, Inc.

➢ Indian Artifacts & Pottery
➢ Pre-Colombian Gold & Artifacts
➢ Antiquities
➢ Ancient Coins
➢ Antique Bottles
➢ Old West & Indian War Relics
➢ Ancient Egyptian
➢ And Much More

ALL FULLY GUARANTEED

HANK & MARY ANN JOHNSON
P.O. BOX 22082VS
DENVER, CO 80222

(303) 695-1301 • FAX: (303) 751-3281

WEBSITE: WWW.HDE-INC.COM
E-MAIL: maj@ix.netcom.com
EBAY SELLER NAME: hd_enterprises

BUY - SELL - TRADE

DO YOU HAVE A COLLECTION WORTHY OF APPEARING IN THIS BOOK? SHOULD IT BE RECORDED FOR POSTERITY & SHARED WITH YOUR FELLOW ENTHUSIASTS? IF SO, GIVE US A CALL ON OUR TOLL FREE LINE!

CALL:
(888) 375-9800
ext. 466

OR E-MAIL:
roverstreet1@mac.com

ROBERT M. OVERSTREET
AUTHOR & PUBLISHER

WE WANT YOUR HELP!

www.AmazingCo.com

info@amazingco.com
(631) 567-8069

Visit our website for authentic, reasonably priced artifacts and other fine collectibles.

Bob Nastasi
Amazing Comics
12 Gillette Ave. Sayville NY 11782

LONNIE HARTLINE

Route 4, Box 10020
Eufaula, OK 74432
(918) 689-1552
email: hartz@cwis.net

Collector of Indian Relics
Buy, Sell or Trade

ArrowheadsOnline

All Artifacts Guaranteed Authentic for life

www.arrowheadsonline.com

Chris Merriam   P.O. Box 6268
(405) 366-1960   Norman, OK. 73070

25 years   Charter Member
Experience   A.A.C.A.

DO YOU HAVE A COLLECTION WORTHY OF APPEARING IN THIS BOOK? IF SO, GIVE US A CALL ON OUR TOLL FREE LINE!

1-888-375-9800 ext. 466
roverstreet1@mac.com

ROBERT M. OVERSTREET
AUTHOR & PUBLISHER

Directory Listings

ARKANSAS

Caddo Trading Co., Inc.
P.O Box 669
Murfreeboro, AK 71958
Ph: (870) 285-3736
Email: caddotc@alltel.net
Web: www.caddotc.com

FLORIDA

Paleo Enterprises
P.O Box 82098
Tampa, FL 33682
Ph: (813) 632-8579
Web:
www.paleoenterprises.com

KENTUCKY

Bluegrass Case Company
P.O. Box 982
272 Airport Rd.
Stanton, KY 40380
Ph: (800) 668-9871
Fax: (606) 663-6369
Email: support
@bluegrasscase.com
Web:
www.bluegrasscase.com

Davis Artifacts Inc.
P.O. Box 676
449 Oak Ridge Drive
Stanton, KY 40380-0676
Fax: (606) 663-4370
PH: (606) 663-2741
Email: tomdavis@mis.net
Web:
www.tomdavisartifacts.com

Jackson Galleries
P.O. Box 1005
Mt. Sterling, KY 40353
Ph: (800) 466-3836
Web:
www.jacksongalleries.com

MISSOURI

KRM Consultants
29802 SE Moreland Sch. Rd.
Blue Springs, MO 64014
Ph: (816) 229-6025
Email: krmconsultants
@aol.com

OHIO

Back to Earth
17 North LaSalle Drive
South Zanesville, OH 43701

OKLAHOMA

Merriam Station Books
8716 Old Brompton Rd
Oklahoma City, OK. 73132
PH: (405) 721-0484
Web:
www.merriamstationbooks
.com

RHODE ISLAND

Arrowheads.com Karl Kilguss & Associates
535 Centerville Rd.
Warwick, RI 02886
Ph: (401) 737-0500
Email: kkilguss@aol.com
Web: www.arrowheads.com

WYOMING

Jeb Taylor Artifact Evaluation
P.O. Box 882
Buffalo, WY 82834
Ph: (307) 737-2347
Email: jeb@rangeweb.net

CANADA

BC Artifacts
P.O. Box 71088
7921 120 Street
Delta, BC V4C 8E7
Ph: (604) 501-1768
Cell: (778) 386-3110
Web: www.bcartifacts.com

Introduction

Hunting arrowheads has been a popular pastime for many Americans over the past one hundred years. Even the Indians themselves cherished and collected rock crystals, gem stones, and points. In the past, large collections were put together with very little effort, since few people hunted and the supply of good artifacts was plentiful. Plowed fields along creeks and rivers, as well as river banks and dry lake beds, are the most popular places for hunting relics, as the early Indians built their villages and hunted game in such locations. The Indians' food supply, such as fish, game, mussels, etc. lived in or along rivers, creeks, springs, ponds, swamps and lakes. Early man preyed on this abundant food supply, migrating along these water routes, moving from place to place in search of better hunting grounds, as the game became depleted.

Fields are plowed in the Fall or Spring of each year. The most likely sites for hunting, of course, would be the large flat areas close to the original river or creek banks. Hunting in areas that may be large enough to support a small village and are on high ground, protected from a flooding river, are especially productive places. Village sites were usually built where a creek converged with a large river. Field hunting should be attempted after a hard rain. Heavy rains will create deep gullies and washed-out areas exposing the relics.

Here is where you can get lucky, especially if you are the first person in the field. All a collector has to do is walk along and pick up pieces of history. Be sure to ask permission before entering private property. Most farmers will give permission to enter their land if approached in a friendly manner.

Plowed fields next to springs and cave openings have also produced relics. Such a place is Castillian Springs, just above Nashville, Tennessee. Here, next to the spring, there are salt licks for animals. The Indians occupied and lived in this area for thousands of years from the Paleo to Woodland periods and later. The herd animals would always migrate here for salt and watering, providing the Indians with plentiful meat and nourishment right in their own backyard. Erosion around the spring has in the past produced many excellent artifacts. From fluted points to Doves, to Lost Lakes, to stemmed types, this area has been rich with many types of points.

Another similar site is Nickajack Cave and its surrounding fields, just below Chattanooga, Tennessee. Overhangs and rock shelters along rivers and creeks where early man lived, as well as river lands, have produced fine artifacts as well.

In the 1930s, the blow-outs, or dust storms, in the plains states produced many fine projectile points. The top layer of soil blew away, exposing relics left centuries ago by the Indians.

Sand bar hunting along the Tennessee River became possible after the Tennessee Valley Authority built their dams and began controlling the river level in the 1930's. During the development of the TVA system, hunting was excellent. Lake levels were dropped during the winter months, exposing the sand bars which were originally high areas in the now inundated fields along the river channel, where the early Indians built their villages and camp sites. As winter storms raged through the Tennessee Valley, the lake levels would rise and fall and the racing river would cut into the sand bars, exposing relics for anyone to merely come along and pick up.

Today most of the sand bars and plowed fields in many states have been "hunted out." But the energetic hunter can still find new relic-producing sites if he gathers his facts, follows all leads, studies maps of likely areas and hunts whenever he can. Sooner or later he will get lucky.

However, most collectors are neither energetic nor imaginative, and build their collections by systematically purchasing specimens one at a time. **Genuine** points can be found for sale at relic shows, and sometimes in local collections that come up for sale. **Warning:** fake relics (all recently made and aged) are being offered to the public everywhere as genuine prehistoric artifacts. Knowing the history or pedigree of a point is very important in the process of determining whether or not it is a genuine pre-Columbian piece. Before purchasing a relic from anyone, be sure the dealer will guarantee it to be a genuine, pre-Columbian artifact, and will give you your money back should you later discover otherwise. Many reputable dealers will give you a money back guarantee. Whenever possible, you should have an expert examine any and every piece for its authenticity before you buy.

Most points illustrated in this book are shown actual size and are believed to be genuine prehistoric artifacts. We have gone to great lengths to insure that only authentic points are included. Any errors discovered will be deleted in future editions. This is not a "For Sale" list of points. The illustrated examples are for identification and value purposes only.

HOW TO USE THIS BOOK

This book is set up by regions of the country to make it easy for you to classify your collection. All points in each region are arranged in alphabetical order. First turn to the region that applies to you. The book is set up beginning with the Northeast section, continuing westward to the Alaska section. The ten regions are: Northeastern, Eastern Seaboard, Gulf Coastal, Eastern Central, Southern Central, Northern Central, Desert Southwest, Northern High Plains, Far West and Alaska.

CLASSIFICATION: Projectile points come in many shapes, colors and sizes. Their quality varies from thick, crude forms to very thin, beautifully flaked, symmetrical specimens. Over the past fifty years, hundreds of points have been classified and given names. The names of people, rivers, creeks, lakes, mountains, towns, etc. have been used in naming point types. Many of the types come from sites that were excavated from undisturbed stratigraphic layers where carbon dating was made. These forms of data are important in placing each type in time and showing the relationship of one type to another. You will soon see that most of the early types evolved into the later forms.

This book includes as many point types as possible with the idea of expanding to more types in future updated editions as the information becomes available to us. The point types are arranged in alphabetical order by section of the country. The archeological period and approximate dates of popular use are given for each point type. A general distribution area is given, along with a brief description of each type. There are several factors that determine a given type: 1-Shape or form. 2-Size. 3-Style or flaking. 4-Thickness or thinness. 5-Kind of material.

NEW ARROWHEADS LISTED

The field of Archaeology is an on-going science where sites are constantly being found and excavated. Occasionally, new types are discovered, named and reported in their published literature. As a result, the interrelationship of types, their age, as well as geographical dispersion is always changing. Due to this, the region boundaries may change in future editions. We are constantly on the outlook for photographs as well as the documentation of these types so they can be added to future volumes of this book. The author would appreciate receiving any photos and reports of this nature.

ARROWHEAD VALUES LISTED

Values listed in this book are for your information only. None of the points shown are for sale. Under each type, we have attempted to show a photographic spread of size, quality and variation of form (where available), from low to high grade, with corresponding prices. All values listed in this book are in U.S. currency and are wholesale/retail prices based on (but not limited to) reports from our extensive network of experienced advisors which include convention sales, mail order, auctions and unpublished personal sales. Overstreet, with several decades of market experience, has developed a unique and comprehensive system for gathering, documenting, averaging and pricing data on arrowheads. The end result is a true fair market value for your use. We have earned the reputation for our cautious, conservative approach to pricing arrowheads. You, the collector, can be assured that the prices listed in this volume are the most accurate and useful in print.

The low price is the wholesale price (the price dealers may pay for that point). The high price is the retail price (the price a collector may pay for that point). Each illustration also gives a brief description pointing out special features when applicable. The prices listed have been averaged from the highest and lowest prices we have seen, just prior to publication. We feel that this will give you a fair, realistic price value for each piece illustrated. If your point matches the illustrated example in both size, color, and quality, the listed value would then apply. Warning: The slightest dings or nicks can dramatically drop the grade and value of a point. Please see Grade vs. Value following this section.

HIGH PRICE- RETAIL PRICE, LOW PRICE - WHOLESALE PRICE

IMPORTANT NOTE: This book is not a dealer's price list, although some dealers may base their prices on the values listed. The true value of any arrowhead is what you are willing to pay. The top price listed is an indication of what collectors would pay while the lower price is what dealers would possibly pay. For one reason or another, these collectors might want a certain piece badly and will pay over the list price for comparable quality. This commonly occurs on many high grade, rare points.

DEALER'S POSITION

Dealers are not in a position to pay the full prices listed, but work on a percentage depending largely on the amount of investment required and the quality of material offered. What a dealer will pay depends on how long it will take him to sell the individual piece or collection after making the investment; the higher the demand and better the grade, the more the percentage. Most dealers are faced with expenses such as advertising, travel, telephone and mailing, rent, employee salaries, plus convention costs. These costs all go in before the relics are sold.

The high demand relics usually sell right away but the lower grades are difficult to sell due to their commonality and low demand. Sometimes a dealer will have cost tied up for several years before finally selling everything. Remember, his position is that of handling, demand, and overhead. Most dealers are victims of these economics.

How to Grade Points

Before a point's true value can be assessed, its condition or state of preservation as well as quality must be determined. The better the quality and condition, and the larger the size, the more valuable the point. Perfect points that are classic for the type, thin, made of high quality materials with perfect symmetry and flaking are worth several times the price of common, but complete, low grade field points.

FACTORS THAT INFLUENCE THE GRADE AND VALUE OF POINTS:

Condition: Perfection is the rule. Nicks, chips, and breakage reduce value.

Size: Everything else being equal, a larger point will grade higher than a smaller point and larger points are worth more.

Form: The closer a point comes to being a classic for the type, the higher the grade and value.

Symmetry: Points with good balance and design are higher grade and worth more.

Flaking: Points with precision percussion and secondary flaking, a minimum of hinge fractures and problem areas are higher grade and worth more. Points with unusual flaking patterns, such as collateral or oblique transverse, enhance grade and value.

Thinness: The thinner the better.

After all the above steps have been considered, then the reader can begin to assign a grade to his point. Points are graded on a scale of 1 to 10+, where a 10+ is the best and a 1 is the lowest grade for a complete point.

GRADING DEFINITIONS

Grade 10+: The exceptional perfect point. One of the few half dozen best known to exist. Perfect in every way, including thinness, flaking, material, symmetry and form. The best example you would ever expect to see of any given type. This grade is extremely rare, and applies to medium to large size points that normally occur in a given type.

Grade 10: A perfect point, including thinness, flaking, symmetry and form. This grade is extremely rare, and applies to <u>all sizes</u> of points that normally occur in a given type. A point does not have to be the largest known to qualify for this grade.

Grade 8 or 9: Near perfect but lacking just a little in size or material or thinness. It may have a small defect to keep it out of a 10 category. Still very rare, most high grade points would fall into this category.

Grade 6 or 7: Better than the average grade but not quite nice enough to get a high ranking. Flaking, size, and symmetry are just a little above the average. Points in this grade are still very hard to find in most states. A very collectible grade.

Grade 4 or 5: The average quality that is found. The flaking, thickness, and symmetry is average. 2 or 3 very minute nicks may be seen but none that would be considered serious.

Grade 1-3: Field grade points that have below average overall quality. Better points with more serious faults or dings would fall into this grade. The most common grade found and correspondingly, the least valuable.

Broken points: Usually little to no value. However, good high grade broken backs of popular type points have fetched good prices. Examples would be Paleo points and many of the rare Archaic beveled and notched types.

PRICING POINTS

After a point has been graded and assigned a grade number, it should be compared with similar points in the alphabetical listings. The prices listed will give the reader a guide as to the probable value of his point, but be careful, compare grade with grade. If your point has a little ear or tip broken, the value is affected drastically. Of course, state of perfection, thinness, rarity of type, quality of material and flaking, and size all enter into determining a value. Usually with everything being equal, the larger the size the higher the price.

Many factors affect value and should be considered when determining a price for your point. Besides those listed under Grading Points, the following should be considered:

FACTORS THAT INFLUENCE VALUE:

Provenance: When a point has been properly documented as to where and when it was found and by whom, the value increases. Points from key sites such as the Clovis site in New Mexico, the Quad site in Alabama, the Nuckolls site in Tennessee, the Hardaway site in North Carolina, etc. increases value. Well documented points from famous collections show increased value. Points that have been published show an increase in demand and makes them easier to sell (the wise investor should have all points checked before purchase, whether published or not, because many fakes have been published as genuine). Local points usually bring higher prices than imports from other states.

Material & Color: Most points are made of common local gray to brown cherts, but the type of material can enhance value. Points made from colorful or high quality material such as agate, petrified wood, agatized coral, quartz, crystal, flint, jasper, Horse Creek chert, Buffalo River chert, Flint Ridge chert, Carter Cave chert, Dover chert, etc. will increase value. Some materials became glassier and more colorful when heat treated by the Indians and would enhance the appearance. Certain local materials are more collectible in various states, such as rhyolite in North and South Carolina, Dover in Tennessee, Carter Cave chert or Kentucky hornstone in Kentucky, Flint Ridge chert in Ohio, Knife River flint in North and South Dakota, jasper in Pennsylvania, agatized coral in Florida or petrified wood in Arizona and New Mexico. Usually, points that are transparent or have pretty colors alone will sell for higher prices.

Symmetry: The left and right sides of points must be balanced to receive the highest grades. Value decreases as symmetry is lost.

Rarity: Obviously, some point types are scarcer and much harder to find than others. For instance, Clovis, which is found in most of North America, is more common than Folsom, which is rarely found in just a few western states. Paleo points are much more rare out west than in the east.

Popularity of Type: Market demand for certain point types can greatly influence the supply and value. The value of these points can vary with changing market demands and available supplies. Points with slight damage, such as a nick off the tip or wing, suffer a cut in value of about 60 percent. Medium damage, such as a missing wing, will cut the value about 90 percent. Field grade pieces and halves are usually sold at five dollars per gallon. The very best points have no top retail price and are always in very high demand. Local points are usually worth more in the area where they are found.

Grade and Its Effect on Value

Presented below are examples of the same point type in grades 10 through 3 and the effect on value. All are equal size and quality, except for the defects. These examples illustrate how value drops with grade. True number 10s are rare and the slightest dings or nicks can easily cause the value to drop dramatically.

When the novice grades points to determine value, it is a common mistake to grade his #5s and #6s as #9s and 10s. True 9s and 10s must be superb. They have to be perfect for 10s and near perfect for 9s, thin, symmetrical, and of high quality to reach this grade. Color, translucency and high quality material enhance value.

When dealers look at a collection to buy, they are faced with the economics of having to buy the whole collection to get the few points that they really want. For example, a virgin collection of 1000 complete points, all found by the owner, that is still intact and not picked over, would break down as follows: 92% (920 points) would be low grade, worth below $20 each with the remaining 8% worth $20 or more each. As you can see, most collections are loaded with low grade points making it very difficult for anyone to pay a large price just to get the few choice pieces.

Material increases value

"Bullseye" in hornstone

Perfect corners

Dovetail, grade 10
Value $1500

Dovetail, grade 10
Value $1000

Slight edge nick

Small tang nick

Dovetail, grade 9
Value $600

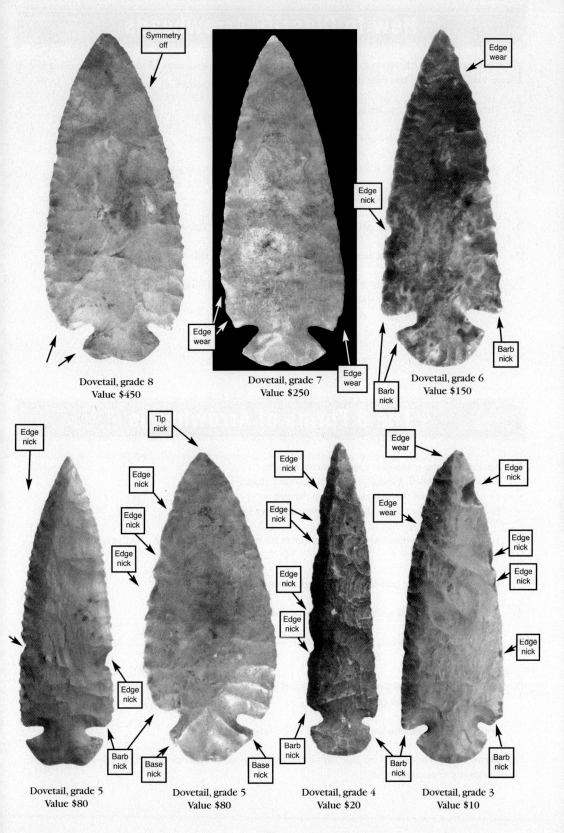

Dovetail, grade 8
Value $450

Dovetail, grade 7
Value $250

Dovetail, grade 6
Value $150

Dovetail, grade 5
Value $80

Dovetail, grade 5
Value $80

Dovetail, grade 4
Value $20

Dovetail, grade 3
Value $10

How to Classify Arrowheads

It's as easy as **one, two, three** (well, seven actually) if you take the following steps. All arrowheads, according to their shape, have been divided into eight different forms listed below.

1. The country is divided into ten sections.

2. Decide which of the categories #1-8 listed below that your point belongs.

3. Go to the Thumbnail Guide at the beginning of the section that applies to your locale.

4. Match your arrowhead to one of the photos in that section.

5. Look up the name under the photo that matches your point in the alphabetical section.

6. Look at the numerous examples, actual size, and make a more detailed comparison.

7. If your point still does not match exactly, go back to the **Thumbnail Guide Section** and look for another match and start over with step four.

The 8 Forms of Arrowheads

1. **Auriculate.** These points have <u>ears</u> and a concave base.
   A. Auriculate Fluted. A fluted point is one that has a <u>**channel flake**</u> struck off one or both faces from the base.
   B. Auriculate Unfluted. All other eared forms are shown here.

2. **Lanceolate.** Points without **notches** or **shoulders** fall into this group. Bases are round, straight, concave or convex.

3. **Corner Notched.** The base-end has corner notches for **hafting**.

4. **Side Notched.** The base-end has side notches for **hafting**.

5. **Stemmed.** These points have a **stem** that is short or long, expanding or contracting. All stemmed points have **shoulders**.

6. **Stemmed-Bifurcated.** Since a number of stemmed points occur that have the base split into two **lobes**, they have been grouped together.

7. **Basal Notched.** This form has notches applied at the **base**.

8. **Arrow Points.** These points are generally small, thin triangle and other forms grouped for easy identification.
   *See glossary for underlined words.

Identification/Classification

The following drawings illustrate point nomenclature used by collectors and professionals everywhere for point shapes and features.

Auriculate Forms

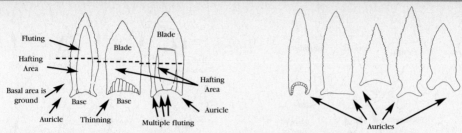

This is the basic form of the Paleo Period. Flaking tends to be parallel and the entire hafting area is usually ground.

Lanceolate Forms

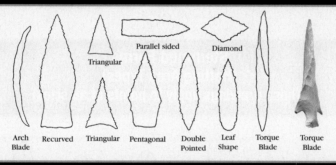

Basal, Corner & Side Notched Forms

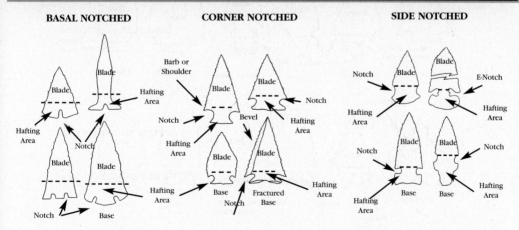

BASAL NOTCHED

CORNER NOTCHED

SIDE NOTCHED

Basal notched forms appeared in the early Archaic Period and reappeared in the Woodland Period. Not a popular form of hafting since only a few types are known.

Corner notched forms appeared in the early Archaic Period and reappeared again in the Woodland Period and lasted to Historic times.

Side notched forms began in Transitional Paleo times and persisted through the Archaic Period, reappearing in Woodland times lasting into the Historic Period.

Stemmed Forms
(These drawings apply to points of all sizes)

Basal edge types

Shoulder types

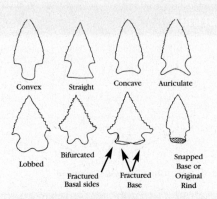

Note: The **Basal Edge** begins the hafting area of a point.

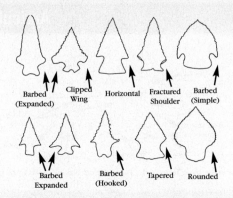

Note: The **shoulder** divides the blade from the hafting area.

Stemmed Forms
(Hafting Area Types)
(These drawings apply to points of all sizes)

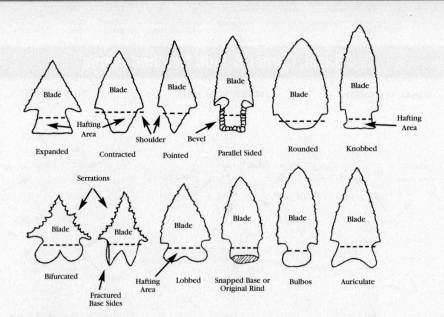

Note: Stemmed types began as early as the Paleo Period, but didn't really become popular until the Woodland Period. Consequently, this form has the most types and is the most difficult to classify.

Blade Beveling Types

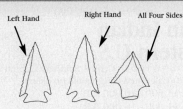

Left Hand   Right Hand   All Four Sides

Blade Edge Types

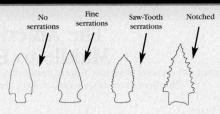

No serrations   Fine serrations   Saw-Tooth serrations   Notched

Note: Alternate blade beveling began in the early Archaic Period and continued into the Woodland Period. Beveled points are very popular among collectors.

Distal Ends

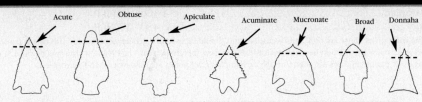

Acute   Obtuse   Apiculate   Acuminate   Mucronate   Broad   Donnaha

Note: The distal end of a point is located at the very tip and describes the shape of the penetrating part of the knife or projectile point.

Point Cross-Sections
(These drawings apply to points of all sizes)

Elliptical   Round   Uniface or Plano-convex   Median Ridged   Rhomboid   Flattened   Fluted

Note: The cross-section of a point represents its form if broken at mid-section.

Flaking Types
(These drawings apply to points of all sizes)

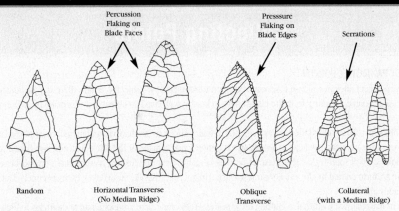

Percussion Flaking on Blade Faces   Presssure Flaking on Blade Edges   Serrations

Random   Horizontal Transverse (No Median Ridge)   Oblique Transverse   Collateral (with a Median Ridge)

Note: Points are rough shaped with an elk antler billet or hammer stone. Then fine pressure flaking is applied to the blade and stem edges with a sharp pointed antler. Billet and deer antler are alternated until the point is finally finished. During the flaking process, edges are lightly ground to prevent hinge fracturing on the blade edges.

The American Indian
Middle to Eastern U.S.

(Includes sections: Northeast, Eastern Seaboard, Gulf Coastal, Eastern Central, Southern Central and Northern Central)(Only carbon dates are used)(Calculated dates would be older)

Paleo ....c. 11,500 - 10,000 B.P.
Late Paleo...c. 11,000 - 10,000 B.P.
Transitional Paleo..c. 10,500 - 9,000 B.P.
Early Archaic ....c. 10,000 - 7,000 B.P.
Middle Archaic ....c. 7,500 - 4,000 B.P.
Late Archaic ....c. 5,000 - 3,000 B.P.
Woodland..c. 3,000 - 1,300 B.P.
Mississippian...c. 1,300 - 400 B.P.
Historic ....c. 450 - 170 B.P.

Note: The dates given above are only approximations and should be used in a general context only. This data is constantly being revised as new information becomes available. **B.P. means "before present."** In 1998 new data was released to correct previously published dates acquired through carbon dating. All points are now older than first realized.

The American Indian West

(Includes sections: Desert Southwest, Northern High Plains and Great Basin-Westward)

Paleo ....c. 13,200 - 8,000 B.P.
Early Archaic ....c. 8,000 - 5,000 B.P.
Middle Archaic ....c. 5,100 - 3,300 B.P.
Late Archaic ....c. 3,400 - 2,300 B.P.

Desert Traditions:

Transitional ....c. 2,300 - 1,600 B.P.
Developmental ....c. 1,600 - 700 B.P.
Classic ....700 - 400 B.P.
Historic ....c. 400 - 170 B.P.

Note: The dates given above are only approximations and should be used in a general context only. This data is constantly being revised as new information becomes available. **B.P. means "before present."**

Collecting Points

WHY COLLECT PROJECTILE POINTS?

Whether you collect ancient Chinese cloisonné, Egyptian tomb pieces, or projectile points, there is a particular satisfaction in possessing a piece of history from the distant past–to hold in your hand an object that was made by someone thousands of years ago.

Projectile points may very well be the earliest evidence of man's ability to create, style, and manufacture objects of symmetry and beauty. If you ever have the privilege of seeing an exceptional piece, made of the finest material, and flaked to perfection, take a close look. You will soon realize that these early tools of man were made for two reasons: function and beauty. They represent a unique art form crafted by the world's earliest artists. Unique, because, like snowflakes, each specimen is an original and no two are exactly alike.

Many different materials were utilized in crafting these points. From crude slate, conglomerate or quartzite, to high quality flint, agate, jasper, chalcedony, petrified wood or volcanic obsidian, the list is endless. The Indians went to great lengths to obtain high quality material from the popular flint and chert quarries known to them, such as Dover in Northwest Tennessee, Flint Ridge in Ohio, and the many obsidian sources of the west. It is believed that extensive trade networks for flint and other objects were established in the earliest times and extended over vast areas from coast to coast.

The variations in shape and flaking style are clues to dating and identifying point types. The novice should study points from the different periods illustrated in this book and become familiar with the various styles produced. Generally speaking, the older Paleo and Archaic types are better made, exhibiting the finest flaking, thinness, edge work, and symmetry ever produced by man. The earliest points are mostly auriculate or eared. Some are grooved in the center or fluted. Later, these forms basically became side-notched, corner-notched, basal-notched or stemmed. With the introduction of the bow, most points became smaller and lighter with stemmed bases. However, during the Woodland period, Paleo auriculate and Archaic notched forms reappeared for a short period of time.

Some collectors specialize in a particular type, while others try to assemble a collection of many shapes and types. Most collectors are only interested in points from their immediate locale, and only if found by them. However, this author has learned after many years of hunting, that the only way to put together a quality collection is through intelligent buying. It's a rare occurrence today to find an outstanding piece for your collection by hunting in the field.

FIRE DAMAGED POINTS

Points made of flint, chert, chalcedony, and other materials are susceptible to damage when in close contact with fire and heat. This can occur when points shot at an animal are left in the butchered meat that is cooked over a fire. Fire damaged flint reflects a rather unique appearance, usually a circular pitted, or pock-marked look not unlike miniature moon craters.

There have been theories that the intense heat of fire actually brings about a molecular change or rearrangement of molecules. This undue stress or tension causes a change in the material which induces the pock-marks to form. This has been questioned and criticized by some geologists who flatly state that no such action takes place.

(Examples of fire damaged points) Note typical pitting damage to the surfaces.

The acceptable and more logical explanation is that the change is purely physical. That is, the heat from the fire is applied and transferred in such a random and uneven manner that the coefficients of contraction and expansion cause the damage or pitting.

The resultant conflict of expansion and non-expansion coefficients flake off the flint material due to tensions within itself. The resultant flake is quite different from a pressure or percussion flake in that it is circular and, of course, non-controllable. The examples illustrated show points with the typical pitting associated with fire damage.

Example of a repaired impact fracture. The point was retipped.

Impact fracture located at the tip

Left: Example of a long impact fracture that runs almost to the base.

IMPACT FRACTURES

When spear and arrow points are thrown or shot, they sometimes collide with hard objects such as bone in animals or rock or wood when the target is missed. If the angle at the point of impact is just right, the resulting blow will fracture the point, forming a flute or channel that runs from the tip toward the base. In other examples the fracturing will run up the side, or the tip of the point will simply snap off. Occasionally, these broken points with impact fluting are remade into new points with the flute channel still visible (see illustration). These should not be confused with real fluted Paleo points that were found by later Indians and rechipped into a more recent point, also with the fluting still present. Points with well defined impact fractures are interesting additions to any collection and should not be overlooked when going through the junk boxes.

HAFTING

All finished arrow points and most knives were made to be inserted or tied onto a shaft or handle. To prevent movement, sinew, gut, and rawhide were used to tie the stone blades onto the shafts or handles. Fibers from hair and plants (grasses, tree bark, yucca, vines, etc.) were also employed for lashing.

Pitch, asphalt and resin were used as adhesives (when available) to glue the lashings to the stone and shaft. In some of the western states where climates are very dry, complete specimens of arrows and knives have been found preserved in caves. On rare occasions complete arrows and knives have been found with hafting completely intact. Of course, during the Indian wars

Above: A very rare example of an 9,000 year old Kirk Corner Notched point with original hafting petrified to the base. Reverse side shows a brown stain where hafting was.

Above: A complete knife with bone handle and flint blade recovered in eastern Colorado. Note drilled hole in handle

Above: Rare examples of hafted arrow-points on wooden shafts. All were found in New Mexico or Nevada. The binding is fashioned of fibres from a local plant.

Above: A complete knife with bone handle and flint blade recovered 4 feet below the floor of a dry cave in Fort Rock desert in south central Oregon. Note the tally marks at the rear of the handle and the gut hafting and gum or asphaltum adhesive cementing the blade to the handle.

out west in the 1800s, perfect hafted specimens were collected and saved from the battlefields as well. Cane and many types of wood were employed for arrow shaft usage while bone, ivory and wooden handles were crafted for holding the knives.

DATING AND NAMING POINT TYPES

For decades, professional archaeologists and collectors have been interested in the age and classification of projectile points. Of course the best information has come from archaeologically controlled scientific excavations where exact locations, cultural association, and carbon dating of associated matter with point types was made.

The carbon deposits from animal and vegetable remains are taken from these stratigraphic layers and dated through the carbon-14 process and other techniques. This gives an age for each layer and its associated artifacts. In 1997, it was reported that all previously published carbon-14 dates are now slightly older than realized. Adjustments should be made on a logarithmic scale with age. **Clovis** is now believed to be about 2,000 years earlier.

Many of these sites were occupied for thousands of years by various peoples who left projectile points around their campfires, buried for future discovery with thousands more lost through usage and breakage. The face of the land next to rivers where many of these sites are, is always changing due to flooding. Indian villages and campsites were either being eroded away or buried under silt deposited by the flooding river. Later, the sites that were destroyed would become occupied again, waiting for the next inundation. Over a period of thousands of years, these sites accumulated many stratified layers of silt, some of which contain evidence of human occupation. The most recent culture would be near the top with the oldest at the deepest levels.

Some of these excavated areas produce important point types which were named after the site from which they were found. Sometimes popular "type styles" such as **Clovis** are found all across the country while others are very localized and found only in a few counties. Some of the more famous type sites are **Cahokia** at St. Clair and Madison counties in Illinois, **Eva** and **Nuckolls** in northwest Tennessee, **Quad** and **Pine Tree** in northwest Alabama, **Black Rock Concave** in Black Rock Desert, Nevada, **Clovis** near Clovis, New Mexico, **Folsom** near Folsom, New Mexico, **Golondrina** in Val Verde Co., Texas, **Graham Cave** in Montgomery Co., Missouri, **Hardaway** in Stanly Co., North Carolina, **Hell Gap** from Hell Gap Valley in Wyoming, **LeCroy** in Hamilton Co., Tennessee, **Midland** near Midland, Texas, **Milnesand** in Milnesand, New Mexico, **Motley** in northeast Louisiana, **Plainview** near Plainview, Texas, **San Patrice** in DeSoto Co., Louisiana and **Sandia** from the Sandia Cave near Albuquerque, New Mexico. There are many more sites too numerous to list here.

These excavations have provided valuable information about point types and their cultural relationships. Papers published (by the archaeologists who worked the sites) about these excavations were the first attempt at typing or classifying projectile points. These papers and books are still important reference sources today and belong in every reference library.

How Points Were Made

Decades ago this author was spending his weekends hunting rivers, fields and streams for the elusive #9s and 10s but usually coming home with the average 3s and 4s. His hunting territory covered several states including dozens of private farms, rivers, creeks and lakes. The usual procedure when hunting on private land was always to ask permission. This required a short visit with the owner who would be sizing you up before allowing access to his land. Some of the farmers were very suspicious of strangers because of their hidden whiskey stills.

During these interesting visits, I would hear stories of how the farmers thought the Indians made arrowheads. A common tale was that the Indians would heat up a container of water. After getting it as hot as they could, they would take an eagle feather, dipping it in the scoulding water, then carefully releasing drops onto the flint causing an immediate fracturing to occur. Eventually they would end up with a finished arrowhead. Although this story was pretty common, I don't think any of the farmers ever tried it to see if it would really work.

Actually flint tools are made by the art of knapping flint. Hundreds of thousands of years ago, far away from this country, early homo erectines learned how to knap flint. The earliest forms from Africa have been dated to 2.2 million years ago. Secrets of the knappers art came with the first peoples to inhabit the Americas. Beginning with Paleo Man the best sources for quarrying flint and chert were soon found. The technique of exposing flint to heat to change its molecular structure making it more "glassy" and easier to flake was learned prior to Paleo times. Heat treating changes the color as well, sometimes making it difficult to match the altered stone with local sources.

Examples of a group of spent cores made from spalls.

Although small points were crafted from local materials such as small nodules that can be found along rivers and streams, the larger points were made from a large nodule. The flintknapper takes the nodule and knocks off a chunk forming a spall. He then strikes off long slivers that can be crafted into points. As the slivers are struck off, a circular core is formed. Eventually the core is discarded and the process starts over. Flint flakes can be removed easily in the direction of the force applied. Indians used hammer stones, elk billits, and other tools in rough shaping the stone through percussion blows. After a suitable form was achieved with the proper thickness, the final shaping was accomplished using tools such as the fine tips of antlers. This procedure is called "pressure flaking" and was carefully applied to all edges and was used to create the notches on side and corner notched points.

Buying Points

FINDING VERSUS BUYING POINTS

Why would a collector want to buy points instead of just finding his own? The answer to this question is very simple. Many people who collect just don't have the time to spend hunting in the field. In most cases, you can buy points cheaper than you can find them, when you consider travel, lodging, food, and the money you could be earning if you were at home. But the best reason for buying is to acquire quality pieces that are not available or found in your immediate area of hunting. Not all collectors are fortunate enough to live in an area that produces high quality material. Many collectors hunt in plowed fields that do sometimes produce high quality points, but unfortunately most are broken or chipped by the plow and cutting harrow.

One collector lived and hunted in central Alabama and Mississippi for ten years, keeping every piece that was found. Later, when he took a realistic look at his collection, it was only worth about $1,000.00 and the points in the collection looked very common. He began selling everything but the most perfect pieces. He used the money to finance hunting trips to other areas that were strong with quality points, and also began to buy nice pieces as they became available. His previous collection was basically all the same color. He soon found that points from other areas were more colorful, and within three years he had built a large collection that anyone would be proud to own. He kept up this style of collecting for several years and has owned many super quality pieces worth a substantial amount of money. If he had not ventured out into other hunting areas his collection today would still be worth little and of low quality. Try acquiring a quality item, whether it be stone, bone, pottery, or flint. After all, isn't this what collecting is all about?

HOW TO BUY AUTHENTIC RELICS

The best way to recognize an old point is by knowing how both river and field patination affect the type of flint from which the point is made. Each point type also has its own style of chipping that you should study and understand. A Paleo point never has random flaking, while Archaic and Woodland points do. You should understand that changes in patination along the edges or near the tip of an arrowhead are signs of rechipping. Hinge fractures are good indicators to the authenticity of a point. An old point will patinate underneath the hinge fractures while recently applied patina will only be on the surface. Hold the point up to a light source and look along the edges for restoration. You can also lightly tap the surface of a point with a steel knife blade to find a restored area. The restored spot will have a dull sound. Restored areas will also look different under a black light.

If you go to a show, flea market, or someone's house to buy relics, you should first size up the collection or inventory that is for sale. Look for any questionable pieces. If the relics past the test, then you must assess the seller. If he looks untrustworthy, you should probably not take the risk.

But if you are convinced the person is of good character and the piece you want really looks good and authentic, you could use the following guidelines to protect yourself. First, ask for a money back guarantee in writing. Some dealers will comply but may put a time limit on it. Also ask if the point has been restored or rechipped. Second, you could ask for a satisfaction guarantee. This means that if you do get a piece that becomes questionable later, you would be able to trade it for another item of equal value that you feel is a good authentic piece. This arrangement would help you feel more secure about what you are buying. Third, especially if a lot of money is at risk, you should tell the person that you want to send the relic to someone for authentication before the sale is final. If a lot of money is at risk, you may want to get more than one opinion. Ask around to find out who the best authenticators are for your area.

There is a lot of competition in the Indian relic market. Some people will condemn a competitor's piece to persuade you to buy from them. They will also try to buy a good item from you at a cheap price. Others may say a relic is bad just to convince you that they are experts. To be truly knowledgeable in Indian relics, this book will help, but you need to learn as much as you can. Study the flint types of your collecting area and how they look with natural patination. Learn to match flaking styles with types. Simply look at as many good authentic points as you can. Remember, the people who think they know more than everyone else are usually the ones who get burned.

Market Reports

Photographs of needed types have been pouring in from collectors over the past two years. It has been impressive how many individuals now have scanners and/or digital cameras and have been able to email pictures to me for inclusion in future editions of this book. If you have points worthy of inclusion, shoot or scan at 300 pixels/inch with a ruler along side and email to: (roverstreet1@mac.com). Be sure to send location, type, material, etc. with each picture.

The arrowhead market has continued to show growth in many areas with points from the Paleo period leading the way. Fluted points of all types continue to sell for record prices everywhere. Early Archaic beveled types have shown increased demand as have the smaller, true arrowpoints. Points made of exotic or colorful materials are in the most demand as are all higher grade examples of most types. Low, field grade points continue to languish with slow sales.

Certification has become more and more widely used. It is important before spending a large sum of money for a point that you have the benefit of an expert opinion, and it should be someone of your choice. There are quite a number of people papering points across the country. Be sure to check their reputation before choosing the right certifier to certify your points. On expensive points, it might be wise to have at least a couple of experts see the point before spending your money.

The following market reports were prepared by some of our advisors from around the country and are included here for your information.

Mark Berreth - (Relics From the Past)
Far West Section

Arrowhead sales of Western points and blades has continued to remain strong and steady. Everything from field grade to museum quality G-10 relics has had strong demand the last 2 years and with the dwindling availability of new collections coming up for sale, this trend should continue.

Great Basin relic prices seem to have caught up to Columbia River pricing in many areas. There has been a very strong demand for Great Basin relics over the last few years and pricing increases have accompanied the demand. Some examples are a G-10 Blackrock selling for $5000, a 5 inch G-10 Eden made of butterscotch and maroon jasper selling for $6000, and large Bi-point blades selling for $1000 to $2000 on a regular basis. Cody Complex and Paleo material continue to be in high demand and prices have continued to soar for them.

Finding new supplies of Columbia River material has become virtually impossible. It seems that nobody is willing to part with their collections. I foresee a larger rise in the prices of Columbia River relics over the next few years due to the extremely limited supply of relics available. If you collect Columbia River material and are given the opportunity to buy it, then you better act fast because it will probably be quite some time before you get another chance.

G-10 Columbia River relics have continued to explode due to the non-existent availability. When G-10 material is available it goes for a significant premium over high book in many instance. I have seen G-10 Klickitat daggers go for $1000 to $1300, G-10 Columbia Plateaus go for $1000-$1500 and G-10 Quillomene/Hells Canyon points go for $800-$1500 on a regular basis. The most prominant Columbia River Gem sale the last 2 years was a 8 1/8" golden agate Blade with a slight concave base sold for $10,000. This was one of the finest Gem blades ever to come off the Columbia River. Anything G-10 from the Columbia River is very valuable now and should continue to increase due to the virtual non-existence of new material becoming available.

Western relics are some of the prettiest and most intricately flaked relics in the world and will always have a high demand because of these factors. As with any collecting hobby you should only collect what you like and can afford.

Obtaining the provenance of the relics you obtain is another thing you should do and keep that provenance with the relics you buy. Good provenance will help your points retain their value and be more desireable than relics that do not have any provenance. Obtaining and keeping provenance is pretty standard in all collectible fields.

The last thing I will touch upon in my report this year is who to buy from. Buying relics can be very frustrating and also very fun and profitable! The most fun way to collect in my opinion is direct from the finder or family members who have inherited collections, unless that is, you have access to private property to hunt them yourself.

You will have to do some advertising and also spread the word to everyone you come in contact with that you collect artifacts and are interested in buying collections. You must know what you doing when you buy this way because this is also the easiest way to lose alot of money if the relics have been rechipped or modernly made to look like ancient artifacts. Everyone I know including myself has been taken at one or more times buying this way. You usually learn the hard way at first if you have not properly educated yourself on knowing how to determine what is good and what is bad. You will also want to make sure you get a note from the seller stating when and where they were found so can guarantee they were legally obtained. DO NOT buy if they were not obtained legally. Buying direct like this usually gives you a better investment return if you ever sell your artifacts. It takes alot of time and money to buy this way because entire collections usually run from a few thousand dollars to hundreds of thousands of dollars.

A second way to build a collection is by going to auctions either online or in person. I cannot stress enough that you absolutely must know good from bad relics when doing this. It will be impossible to tell if the relics are good if you are bidding online or from a catalogue, so you must make sure the seller has a good return policy and good references or feedback in order to guarantee you will get your money back if you do not like the relics once you receive them. I follow the guideline that the seller in an internet auction should have a 30 day or longer return period and guarantee they take the relic back for any reason within that 30 days if I do not like it. I also look to see that the seller has a 99% or better feedback rating if buying on eBay. Buying at auctions in person just plain requires you know what you are doing because once the hammer goes down–it's yours!

The final way to buy relics is direct from a dealer. If you buy from a dealer you will pay a retail price for their knowledge and guarantee that the relics you are buying are authentic and legally collected. You are also paying a retail price because the dealer has what you want. You must realize the dealer has usually done extensive traveling, research and has invested alot of money into the inventory they have and it may take years to sell what they have. Any dealer advertising in this publication must adhere to high standards and know what they are doing. I require a dealer be a member of AACA, have a 30 day return period at minimum and if I need more time than that to get a second opinion I require them to let me talk to them personally and agree to whatever longer time period I need to make my decision. I have not had a problem with any reputable dealer getting this guarantee and you should not settle for anything less!

Good luck with your collection and happy collecting. This is a very interesting hobby and a very enjoyable one if done responsibly and only with funds you can afford to collect with. Only buy what you like and you will never be disappointed.

John Byrd - Piedmont, SC
High Plains Section

Because the artifact market is so complex and continually changing, knowledge of current trends is the greatest tool any collector or dealer can possess. If you read all of the different market reports being presented in this edition, and compare them to find what trends they have in common, you will better understand the overall artifact market and where it is headed over the next couple of years. Armed with this knowledge you will be better prepared to have an actual collecting strategy instead of a shotgun approach. As you refine your area of interest there are several recommendations we would make to develop a collection with the most potential for providing a reasonable return on your investment.

Obviously, authentic prehistoric artifacts will have more value and be easier to sell than those that are questionable. It doesn't matter if you are buying at an artifact show or over the internet, the number of reproduction or very questionable items outnumber the authentic specimens offered for sale. As a result, authentication of high end artifacts has become a necessity as well as a booming business. But, this legitimate need is often times abused. First of all, not everybody offering authentication services has the knowledge and experience to do so with a reasonable amount of accuracy, so you need to choose your authenticator carefully. I come into possession of "papered" artifacts all the time that are fakes and the authentications are totally worthless. Most authenticators might be very good within a certain geographical region or with a particular artifact type, but I honestly know of none whose expertise I would depend upon across the board. The majority of the major authenticators will be quick to tell you what they feel qualified to appraise and what they do not. As valuable as these authenticators may be, there is nothing to compare with you investing the time to learn the basics yourself. Once you do, and become fairly comfortable within your area of interest, then follow this advice; "If you have any question on an item, it is best to pass on it."

You also need to consider spending your authentication money wisely. Most COA's (Certificate of Authenticity) cost from $20 to $25 each plus the shipping fees. I am amazed that collectors will spend that kind of money to get a certificate on artifacts in the $10 to $30 value range. If you do that you will probably never break even on your investment when you resell an item. If your funds are limited you may want to consider only having the higher value or key items in your collection evaluated.

The second recommendation we would make, if you are hoping for the best possible increase in the value of your collection, would be to purchase the best quality items you can afford. These are the pieces that will always be easiest to sell and will most likely experience the greatest increase in value. Personally, I would rather have one nice frame of high quality artifacts than ten frames of lower quality.

As we look at the trends and changes that have occurred in this market over the past two years we will be able to better judge where the next two are headed. In the last edition I mentioned the falling value for the average High Plains paleo point and the dynamic that caused this to happen. This situation has now leveled off and though nice paleo material from the region is selling for as much as 25% less than it was five years ago, it is now in a more realistic alignment with other artifact values from the same area. This actually creates a more healthy overall artifact market than existed when these select items were skyrocketing.

Though overall artifact prices are steadily increasing, one particular area has seen surprising gains in the past two years. This is for the high quality arrow points of the Late Prehistoric period. These are what would generally be described as the small side-notched arrowheads between 300 and 1200 years old. Though these have always been one of my favorites, most collectors tended to prefer paleo and early archaic types. In my opinion this advance in recognition was long overdue. That being said, I expect this increase to now slow as it has caught up with the rest of the market.

In the last edition several dealers, including myself, made note of the fact that obsidian was finally coming into its own (after many years of being undervalued) and beginning to be appreciated more by collectors far removed from the source areas. That has definitely come into being these past two years and aided tremendously by the fact that there are now a couple of very competent authenticators who are from the west and have handled enough obsidian to know what they are looking at. In the past two years I have sold around 12,000 obsidian artifacts and at least half of those have gone to collectors east of the Mississippi. That would have been unimaginable ten years ago.

Another prediction I made in the last edition that has proven to be right on the mark was the increase in value for the high quality African material, usually referred to as Saharan Neolithic. This was aided greatly by the long overdue publication of a book covering the various items one will encounter in this collecting arena. The supply is definitely decreasing, especially in quality. In the last two years I have sold about 150,000 of these nice gemmy little arrowheads and they are becoming much harder to get in decent condition. As predicted, the finer ones have doubled in price and I expect this to happen again over the next several years. There is still time to get in on this collecting nitch and put together a great collection for a minimal investment, but within five years I expect the supply to disappear.

I have talked to lots of people in the past couple of years who are gun-shy of the internet and especially Ebay because they have been burned so many times by unscrupulous dealers selling bogus material. Unfortunately, I have to tell them the fault is their own. It only makes sense, buy from and bid on those auctions where people are willing to offer you a money back guarantee of authencity with a reasonable inspection period. Most of the reputable dealers are now members of the AACA (Authentic Artifact Collector's Association) and as such follow strict guidelines that were created to make your buying experience a positive one. Many of those dealers will display the AACA logo, so look for it or ask if they are a member. I am a member myself but I have also offered a lifetime money back guarantee for over 35 years and it has paid off many times over.

In closing I have state the obvious, this is supposed to be a hobby. It's not about who has the most valuable or the best, it's about enjoying what you are doing. Nearly all of you have had the experience of finding arrowheads yourself. The ones you personally found may not be as fine or valuable as some you have purchased, but there is nothing to compare with the thrill of picking one out of the dirt that has been there for thousands of years. Take this same appreciation of the individual artifact into your collecting. These things are many hundreds or thousands of years old. Every time I hold even the most mundane projectile point in my hand I marvel at the person who's very life depended on that little piece of stone or bone I have been entrusted with.

Vern Crites
Desert Southwest Section

My personal experience with points is primarily with the four corners area, New Mexico, Arizona, Utah & Colorado. I have other types in my collection, but have decided to market them so I can concentrate on Southwest types only. My experience has been that good points, drills, blades etc. continue to appreciate. I have seen an increase in both interest and pricing in the last year or two for good southwest material. I also hear constant complaints about how difficult it is to find good pieces in the field anymore, in fact I tell people that it is easier and less expensive to purchase them than to find them, but of course not as much fun.

I never cease to be amazed at the price increase in the past few years for good material. Points that were priced at ten to twenty dollars a few years ago are now commanding several times that much.

I am not sure about other regions, but I have seen a new interest and enthusiasm for southwest points, even the so called "bird points". Although I have been collecting prehistoric pottery for over forty five years, I find myself evolving more toward stone as my first love in collecting.

I personally know of several people who are spending a substantial amount of time and money beating the bushes looking for quality southwest material. I personally believe that they are setting a precedent for higher prices and greater demand. which is understandable.

My philosophy is that a person should always buy the best that they can afford and it will appreciate faster, in other words quality over quantity, and of course always beware of fakes and reproductions. Only buy from reputable people and of course when possible get certificates of authenticity signed by reputable authenticators.

Best luck collecting.

Winston H. Ellison - Fair Oaks Ranch, TX
Southern Central Section

The artifact market in Texas has been very healthy these past several years, finally reaching and surpassing the pre 9-11-2001 paces. Demand has been equally strong for late pre-historic, archaic, and paleo pieces of high quality. Points made from Texas root beer flint, alibates and Tecovas jasper continue to demand premium prices.

This past year saw Texas shows achieve record levels of attendance. Many new collectors are joining our hobby, a large number of these being young people. This speaks well for the future.

Modern made and altered relics continue to be a problem, one that will probably only increase as we move into the future. I constantly suggest to collectors that they learn all they can about their hobby. The use of a respected and well-known authenticator is almost essential. This can and will help the collector build a collection he will be very satisfied with today and in the future. We have a great hobby, one I have been priviledged to be a part of for the last 54 of my 60 years of life. I wish you all the best for your collecting future.

Gary L. Fogelman
Pennsylvania and the Northeast Section

Another year has rolled by and throughout the year there were a number of auctions, sales and shows attended which allow for some observations on the health of the artifact market place in Pennsylvania and the greater Northeast. All of the auctions, shows and sales were well attended if the merchandise being offered was worth it. Shows continue to draw reasonable crowds and would probably do better with efforts in the advertising area.

As before, the statement can be made that artifacts are holding their own, or increasing in value. This has been the case each year. There is still a great demand for artifacts of all types and quality. The better quality items have no trouble finding homes, and these usually experience the highest gains in value as well.

Paleo items, fluted points in particular, continue to be a collector favorite. Even the smaller specimens, that used to be in the $200-400 range, bring on average a couple of hundred more than that. Consider two items, both of the Clovis type. One was a small (1.5") jasper point from Lancaster Co., PA. The other was a 2-

3/4" long point of mottled gray flint, purportedly Butler Co., PA. There were questions on the Butler County origins of that point and it held the value down. Each sold for $700, whereas the one should have been almost double that. A Barnes type point, 2-3/4" long of red Munsungun Chert purportedly from Lancaster Co., PA., sold for $1400. A 2" Crowfield of Onondaga chert sold for $800. A really nice Northumberland type from Westmoreland County, PA., 3-5/8" long and made of Upper Mercer chert went through one of the big dealers and was being offered for $3500. Whether it actually brought that much I don't know.

Provenience does count for something in value consideration, and the stronger the history of any piece the greater its value.

Paleo-form tools such as endscrapers, side scrapers, gravers, etc., can sell between $25-$400, depending on size, material, and provenience. A piece from a known site or assemblage will go 3-4 times what an unprovenienced piece will bring. A 4" jasper uniface knife/side scraper tool sold for $400.

Late Paleo, in the form of Agate Basin and Ohio Lanceolates, etc., are rarer than fluted points. Western Pennsylvania has a good share of the lanceolates, usually well made of Upper Mercer and Nellie cherts. The average for most is $35-$250; the extra-fine example will bring more. Agate Basin points turn up scattered across the Northeast. A couple of jasper appeared this past year and the 3-4" specimens sold for $250-$400.

All point types have people who like or specialize in them, and values are only held back by the limitations of the points themselves. A G10 Lamoka point, if one exists, will only be in the $10-$15 range. A G10 bifurcate or LeCroy type will be in the $50-$100 range, a rare one may bring more, but most average LeCroys will be in the $5-$15 area. A frame of 16 average bifurcates from Lancaster Co., PA. sold for $225. A larger MacCorkle type, of jasper, 2" long can get a couple of hundred dollars. Material, size, workmanship and eye appeal all play a role.

Perkiomen Broadpoints, and the other broadpoints as well, Susquehanna and Lehigh, continue to be collector favorites, as do their relatives the Atlantic Phase Blades and Boats Blades. Average size Perkiomens, 1-1/2" to 2-1/2", usually of brown jasper, will be in the $75-$400 range, depending on finesse or uniqueness of the point or material. Larger points will be double or triple that, at least.

Points of the Piedmont Tradition, long and slender fishtails to stemmed types like the Poplar Island and Bare Islands, to the larger, broader Morrow Mtn., and Savannah River types (Long, Swatara) have their attractions, especially if long, slender, perfect, etc., It's hard to find really good examples as the materials themselves don't lend to fine or pretty end products. These people purposely chose the harder, less cryp-

tocrystalline materials for their points. Often crude to begin with, the years are not kind to argillite, rhyolite or indurated shales for the most part. Quartzite specimens can be pretty nice and sometimes beautifully flaked. Average 2-3" Piedmont points go for $5-$25, while points in the 4" range will begin fetching $200-$300 and more.

Archaic point types are the most common types around. The Archaic period stretched for many thousands of years. It seems some point styles were on the scene for almost as long. Points of the Laurentian Tradition, namely Brewerton, Otter Creek, Vosburg, etc., are everywhere and made of all kinds of materials with subtle variations in styles around the Northeast. Examples 1/2" to 2" are $.50 - $4 each. Good examples are in the $5-$15 range. Early Archaic types like Kirk, Stanley, Amos, etc., are usually eye-catchers as they're well made and often of pretty flints. Here are a few more examples of prices realized:

Genesee point, 4" long brought $90.
Perkiomen point, 1.8" long, jasper, x-D. Staats coll., $350.
Amos point, jasper, 1.6" long, $240.
Adena point, Butler Co., PA., 4.7" long, $325.
Lehigh Broadpoint, 3.1" long, jasper, $1000.
Frame, 15 points, Lanc. Co., PA., $80.
Six points, Transitional types, $50.
Frame, 19 white quartz points, $85.
Orient Fishtail point, jasper, 3.5" long, $500.

Stone tools have not really come into their own, perhaps they never will in the Northeast. They don't have the eye appeal of flint points; perhaps they don't capture the imagination as much. Too, when they're used up and worn out they really look it, whereas flint can retain some shape and beauty.

The average ax will be in the $75-$300 range. Beater axes can be had for $10-$20 and/or are often thrown into box lots. At a couple of auctions over the past summer the best any stone could do was in the $400-$500 range, for a couple of axes, and one of those was from Indiana! It's the same for celts, adzes and pestles. Not a lot of variation in materials, not a lot of pretty materials, and lots of them. So prices are $5-$20 for the common, $30-$75 for better grade. Rare ones get into the hundreds.

Gouges are an exception, but then they have a little more character perhaps, and they're rarer. An average gouge will be $50-$125, a great one $750 and up. Ground slate points and ulus, Northeast types, are again rare and good ones hard to find. An average 2" slate point starts at $250. A 4" piece would be $750 or more. Ulus do even better.

The Slate Categories - gorgets, pendants, bannerstones, birdstones: There are some good and fine slate pieces in the Northeast, especially in New York, and the New England states have produced some exquisite examples of all the above, but still it's not like Ohio, Indiana or Michigan for example. Thus, these are highly collectible and represent some unique, interesting, even art-form items.

Common slate pendants and gorgets, often gray slate, or green banded slate, average quality with no or minor damage, $65-$150. A solid average piece goes $200-$400. Fine quality with pretty material - $500-$1500.

Bannerstones will out-value pendants and gorgets. Forms can be more interesting, unique or rare and materials are more varied. It's always been that a complete banner of any condition is pretty hard to find. Small, simple examples or damaged ones will be $75-$150, maybe even up to $250. When size, shape and material kick in values of $500-$1500 are more common and the rare, fine specimen may bring $3000-$5000.

Birdstones trump bannerstones, as far fewer are found in the Northeast, and fewer get to auction. One that did, with a re-worked head, 4" fantail type, brought $800. Pipes are fun to watch. A plain pipe, complete, of any type is worth several hundred dollars to start. A bit of restoration is quite acceptable, and clay pipes, mostly Iroquois styles, of 4-8" length will go from $300-$1000. Put effigies on the pies and prices jump considerable, often double at least. Even plain specimens, if they're fine, will jump in price. A rare effigy Adena tubular pipe adorned with the head of a duck sold for $4000. A plain hatchet-shaped Micmac sold for $400. Several clay Iroquois elbow pipes sold for $350-$900. Catlinite pipes of the late 19th century, elbow type, are $150-$300. Older ones, with wooden stems, are in the thousands.

Clay vessels continue their upward climb. A small (4.5" dia.) Susquehannock pot brought $1000. They should be worth this much, as there aren't that many of them. This one was about perfect, though some restoration is acceptable on clay pots.

Not a lot of the reservation type material, like beaded moccasins, beaded pipe bags, and etc., came up this year in the Northeast, but some did. These things almost always top the list of top-selling items at auctions. Some nice beaded Apache moccasins, late 19th century, sold for $400 and $700. A beaded pipe bag brought $1400. A fully painted parfiech was worth $2300.

Other trade items, such as brass points and glass beads, mainly of Susquehannock and Iroquois origins, re-surface from older collections. Brass points bring $10-$35, as do brass jangles. Glass beads, loops of common types go for $75-$150. Loops with some rare types can fetch $300-500. Some individual beads will bring $25-$50 apiece, maybe $75-$150 if a really scarce type.

Bone and antler items are likewise scarce items and I don't feel they've reached their potential yet. Bone awls will bring $20-$35. Antler harpoons go for $100-$250. Bone fishhooks go for $50-$300. Most, if not all, of these things are also originating in older collections. Not a whole lot more of them will be coming out of the ground. They're a perishable item and they should be worth a good value.

The value of artifacts continues to keep apace, with most items of any quality, trending upward. Low grade or field grade items will likely never rise above the $.50-$1.00 level, there's just too many of them. Fine quality or art quality artifacts also continue upwards, with higher and higher prices being ever realized and, so long as one doesn't drastically over-pay for things, they should end up being a good investment. Besides, they're so much more interesting and fun to play with and learn about than, you know, dollar bills or stock certificates.

Jacky Fuller
Gulf Coastal Section

The ancient cultures that are unique to the deep southeastern U.S. created an amazing array of aesthetically pleasing point styles made from some of the most beautiful high quality lithic materials in the country. This has made for some of the most fascinating and beautiful collections in the world. Collectors are now, through web based sites and Ebay being introduced to these gems, and interest is growing as is their confidence in the material. Fraudulent relics are not as pervasive in the extreme southeast as in other areas of the country due to the close knit collector organizations and the difficulty in replicating the patinas present on ancient relics here. Artifact Shows in south Georgia, southeast Alabama and Florida are numerous and well attended. There are new people beginning to collect along with a large group of seasoned veterans whose focus is collecting the choice material. A wonderful trend to see is the growing interest in documenting these collectables and the demand for good provenience particularly with choice pieces. This will ensure that the story these relics tell will not be lost.

The market continues to be strong with good prices being paid for high quality material.

Colorful Newnans, Hillsboroughs made of high grade coral or translucent chalcedony are fetching top dollar especially if they have a little size.

Paleos remain strong, especially Clovis and Simpson points. Chipolas and Gilchrist points from the late Paleo era are also gaining in popularity.

Bolens, Lost Lakes, Kirk Corner-Notch and Hardins of exceptional quality are moving well. Especially ones over 3 inches.

Hernandos are among the most popular and are bringing high prices for the finest examples.

Large high quality Uniface Tools with fine edgework are quite sought after.

Cobbs Blades, Waller Knives, Savannah Rivers, Levys, Pickwicks, Clays, Tallahassees are all popular point and blade types to collect. Just about any point type with nice colors, workmanship and larger than average in size seems to be in high demand. Even points with dings are bringing high prices if the point quality is exceptional. Minor restoration of fine points seems to be gaining more and more acceptance.

Ron L. Harris - Hickory, NC
Eastern Seaboard Section

Arrowheads are the most common of objects left by the ancient Native Americans. Although once plentiful in many parts of the country we now come to the stark realization that authentic ancient points are a non-renewable resource and finding or acquiring a quality intact point today is indeed a rarity. Yes, average grade and/or broken points may still be found in some locales but their demand obviously is not as great as that of high-grade G-8 to G-10 points, which in today's market are eagerly sought by seasoned collectors, buyers, sellers or traders. Arrowheads are in effect "Shadows of the past" or "Pieces of the puzzle" to avocational and professional archaeologists. They serve as cultural time markers when cross-referenced with similar point types recovered in controlled excavations at stratified sites. They also represent a small sampling of the diverse ways that early man created tools used in their everyday lives and today are considered extraordinary expressions of beauty and art to many. Collecting arrowheads is a hobby or passion for many and an obsession for others. There are many reasons to collect including but not limited to; education, acquiring ancient "art", preserving prehistory, and investment or business purposes when it comes to buying, selling or trading for profit or gain. Points of flint and chert are found in all parts of North America. They vary in size, shape, lithic material and typology. Decades ago they were found in abundant quantities by farmers, acquired by collectors of antiquities, studied by scholars, displayed in museums all over the country and sold and traded by dealers. The same holds true today with one exception. No longer are arrowheads found in abundance as they once were. This has contributed to increased demand and value bringing us to today's market status.

Here in the Piedmont and rolling Foothills regions of the Carolinas and Virginia the interest in Indian arrowhead collecting has jumped by leaps and bounds during the past decade. Never has the interest or enthusiasm been greater. Prices steadily increase even for average grade arrowheads but especially for high-grade specimens and this reflects in the continu-ing upward market trend. Newcomers are fast entering the collecting arena every year. Some have the financial means and enthusiasm for building highly respectable collections. Others settle for more-or-less average grade assemblages. The increasing interest in the hobby is evidenced by attendance and support of archaeological society shows such as those sponsored by the Piedmont Archaeological Society of N.C. & S.C. and the Genuine Indian Relic Society (GIRS). Displays of fine regional artifacts at these shows have been phenomenal and have peaked the interest and desire of the young and old alike. In this the age of electronic purchases many novice and serious collectors as well resort to the Internet for building or supplementing their collections by online purchases such as thru Ebay auctions. However, a word to the wise, as the old saying goes, is "buyer beware." It is evident that over 75% of Indian artifacts or what appears to be "above average" artifacts sold on Ebay are actually reproductions or fakes that are misrepresented as "authentic" and frequently "documented" by various homespun scenarios and stories in an attempt to validate their so called "antiquity". Today the discriminating collector, dealer or hobbyist relies heavily on updated versions of *The Overstreet Indian Arrowhead Identification & Price Guide* books as a valuable resource in researching the type, grade and value range of points they intend to purchase, sell or have personally found. In the Piedmont Market Area, recent trend and range of sales recognized are as follows:

Paleo type points are now and always will be of prime interest to the collecting community due to their value that is driven by antiquity, scarcity, publicity and demand. Paleo type points in this Market Report area include: Eastern Fluted or Clovis, Alamance, Redstone and some forms of the Hardaway tradition that some scholars now place in the late Paleo period. Procurement prices observed for these Paleo types in the Market Report area range from $250 to $6000 depending on the size, shape, thinness, color, material and overall quality.

Early Archaic points such as certain Hardaway tradition types, Palmer, Kirk, Decatur, Lecroy and the like are very desirable and depending on the size, quality and material command prices anywhere from $25 to $2500.

Mid Archaic points such as Stanly, Guilford, Morrow Mountain, etc., have a mediocre demand unless they are exceptionally large, undamaged and of classic form. The price range for these type points generally runs from $50 to $1200 on the average.

Late Archaic points such as large Savannah River and Appalachian blades has seen some high-dollar purchases in recent years. Some of these points in the 5" to 7" plus range have brought prices from $600 to $2000.

Early Woodland points such as Yadkin and Yadkin-Eared Points are highly desirable and collectible in the Market area and command prices from $15 to $400, again depending on size and quality of workmanship.

Late Woodland triangle type points are small, simple and generally plentiful. The types are: Uwharrie, Pee Dee, Caraway and Randolph. Points of this type usually bring from $5 to $200 depending on the size, specific type and quality of workmanship.

In closing please remember that accurate detailed provenance contributes greatly to the value of points, especially the high grade ones. One should always strive to ascertain who found it, when it was found, and exactly where it was found (town, county, state) because this is very important in preserving the history and integrity of the artifact and in many cases it also increases the value as well.

Paul V. Hilton - Silver Springs, FL
Gulf Coastal Section

Paleo points in grades 9 and 10 seem to have stabilized in price over the last year. At the Gainesville Artifact Show a very fine land-find 5 inch Simpson sold for $10,000 - a fabulous point! Large, well made archaic points are still bringing top dollar from collectors and dealers alike.

Bolens have jumped up in price considerably along with Hernandos and nicely made Greenbriers.

Mid and low grade points have not changed much in price at all during the past year.

As you have probably heard by now, it is illegal to collect artifacts in Florida's rivers which will no doubt drive the prices of these particular artifacts through the roof. My advice to collectors - if you have got river pieces, hang onto them! Good Hunting!

Randy McNeice - Spokane, WA
Far West Section

Over the last two years, I have seen a significant change in the marketing process for Indian arrowheads. From 1999 through 2004, the popularity of the internet auction process stimulated the sales of artifacts. This forum tremendously increased the number of collectors and contributed significantly to the market value. However over the past two years, high quality pieces have not been showing up for sale on the various online auction sites. The reason is simple. Those auction sites did not take the necessary steps to insure the authenticity of the item being sold and refused to police their own sites. As a result, the buyers assumed a certain level of skepticism about authenticity and placed their buying bids at prices that reflected that concern. Prices declined on well known auction sites. In a reaction to the declining prices, sellers of high end authentic pieces refuse to sell on popular online auction sites. The end result has been high end pieces selling privately at much increased prices and the lower end pieces continuing to sell online at reduced prices. My assessment and experience over the past two years has been that the higher end material is selling at higher prices and lower end pieces are either flat to lower.

Supply and demand continue to weigh in on the pricing structure for Indian arrowheads from the western region. Most of the material that has been available over the past ten years has come from old time well known collections that were assembled prior to 1979. Those collections are now mostly sold to serious collectors who do not resell the high end pieces. The supply of grade 8, 9 and 10 Columbia River and Great Basin lithics is greatly reduced from the levels of five years ago. Prices are high and will likely continue to rise as more collectors appreciate the beauty and worksmanship of western artifacts. More collectors with more money to spend and a reduction in supply can only result in a continuation of escalating prices.

Some examples of sales from the western area for high end material in private sales are as follows. A grade 10 three inch northern side notch point made of banded translucent obsidian recently sold for $2500. Honest, accurately graded G10 Columbia Plateau points now sell from $1500 and up depending on material type. Quilomene Bar points of grade 9 and 10 command from $500 to $1500 each depending on size and material. The late paleo pieces from the Great Basin are exceptionally hard to find for sale. Grade 9 and 10 examples of Haskett points are currently selling in excess of $3000 each and up. Great Basin blades over 6 inches long will sell for $750 and up depending on flaking and material quality. Grade 9 and 10 Rogue River points command at least $500 per point. Mule Ear knives from the Columbia River have been in demand. Grade 9 and 10 examples sell for $200 and up depending on toolstone quality. Nightfire points are in demand with high end pieces selling for $600 and up.

With more and more collectors with more money recognizing the high quality artifacts available for the Western region and the supply decreasing quickly, prices should continue to be stable to substantially higher.

Donald E. Meador - Dallas, TX
Southern Central Section

The Texas market is good, and I am seeing a lot of new collectors. The number of Artifact shows has dwindled down to about half of what it used to be.

However, there are better crowds at these shows.

Most collectors are looking for specific pieces to add to their collections. Paleo points have led the way and prices seem to be going up depending on the quality.

Some prices:

Grade 9-10 Allens, 4"-5" long - $3,000-$10,000
Barber, 4" to 5" - $5,000-$15,000
Clovis, 4" to 5" - $5,000-$20,000
Eden, 4" to 5" - $4,000-$20,000
First View, 4" - $5,000-$15,000
Folsom, 2-1/2" - $5,000-$20,000
Midland, 3" to 4-1/2" - $3,000-$10,000
Milnesand, 3" to 4-1/2" - $2,000-$10,000
Pelican, 2" to 4", $1,000-$3,000
Plainview, 4" to 6", $3,000-$10,000
Scottbluff, 4" to 6", $3,000-$15,000
Alberta, 4" to 6", $2,500-$10,000

Top quality archaic are still a very good investment. Bird points have held steady and top Woodland pieces seem to have held steady. Most sought after materials are root beer, Georgetown alibates, jasper, petrified wood, and good quality agate.

Collecting is a very healthy activity and a good investment tool. I suggest going to shows and finding yourself a good mentor to help find the pieces you need. For the inexperienced, always ask for an authentication paper with the top pieces. Find out as much provenance on a piece as possible. Always ask for a 15 to 30 day return privilege on pieces that you buy.

Good luck in your collecting future.

Roy Motley and Dave Church
Northern Central Section

The Indian artifact-collecting hobby has continued to grow in the Mid-West. The market for middle grade artifacts remains steady with large numbers of new collectors entering the market. Artifacts in the $50 to $250 range appeal to the newer collectors, with the large numbers of new collectors, the "online auctions" on the Internet help this price range remain very strong.

The demand for "High End" high quality artifacts has been increasing faster than most had imagined. More and more people are seeing this hobby as a fun way to invest some of their hard earned money. Paleo and Archaic points still remain highly sought after and have set some record prices.

"Old Time" collections are still entering the market and there is an increasing desire by both collectors and dealers to have their artifacts authenticated by qualified individuals.

In closing, the market for ancient points is stronger than ever, prices continue to climb, business is good, ancient points are still being found, old collections are being sold, and there are a lot of points to be collected.

John T. Pafford - Eva, Tennessee
Eastern Central Section

Over the past two years, the artifact collecting market has experienced continuing growth and interest. While numerous high quality artifacts from old collections are being offered on the market, the increase in supply has not outpaced the growing demand from an ever increasing collecting community. The result of this demand has pushed prices higher and forced budget conscious collectors to seek diversification in their collecting interests. Consequently, artifact types that have experienced little or no growth over recent years have demonstrated surprising price increases. At the same time, high quality modern reproductions with fraudulent provenances and convincing patination have become an insidious problem for active collectors.

However, in the face of growing demand and ever increasing attempts at fraud, well-documented, classic high quality Paleo and Archaic flint artifacts have dramatically increased in price. Clovis, Cumberland, Lost Lake and Dovetail remain the most coveted point types and prime examples continue to bring record prices. For example, a 3-3/4" colorful Clovis sold at $7500, a 4" Lost Lake at $5500 and an offer of $12,500 was refused for a 5-1/2" Dovetail. Woodland point types such as Adena and Buck Creek have also demonstrated an increase in demand, as well as the best Mississippian triangular points, which have sold for as much as $300 each. Overall, the market bodes well for collectors in general with increasing interest, available quality pieces and an increasing awareness of the importance of documentation.

Jim C. Tatum, Ph.D. & Carlos P. Tatum
Gulf Coastal Section

First the bad news: in the southeast, especially Florida, more and more sites are being closed down due mainly to housing developments, urban sprawl and huge tracts of land falling under control of the state (either bought outright by preservation or water management groups or leased for state control), small political groups yell loudly about historic preservation and the destruction of our heritage by artifact collectors who buy and sell artifacts, choosing to ignore the fact that responsible collectors have revealed many sites and significant artifacts to the professional archaeologists.

We also lament the demise of the Isolated Finds Policy, successfully killed by a few people in power who passionately oppose the collecting and preservation of artifacts by anyone other than themselves. Ironically, several archaeologists (among them Florida's best known and most productive) and professional groups supported the policy and we are trying to reinstate this or a similar policy. As an example of the importance of the collector, a recent Ph.D. dissertation in Florida revealed that of the 1,088 Paleo points studied in the work, the author estimated that professional archaeologists found 20, the rest were found by amateur collectors. The same author stated that he did not know of a single Paleo site in Florida that had been discovered by professionals, all had been found by amateurs.

The good news: I would venture to say that the hobby has never been stronger nor interest higher in artifact collecting. In spite of the negative aspects described above, there are more and more active collectors out looking for artifacts. Some of these people spend the majority of their time in the field: some go every weekend, some go two or three times a week and some go daily. New material appears at every show. As old sites become off-limits or are destroyed, new ones are discovered. Fortunately the southeast is blessed with an abundance of sites from Paleo to Historic times, as well as a great variety of high grade, colorful stone which, in part, explains the popularity of the artifacts, which extends well beyond the geographical area of the southeast.

In the past two years, several large collections in the southeast have been sold, some outright to an individual, some dispersed piece by piece. Although medium and lower grade artifacts are moving slowly, as always, there is no suppressed market for good pieces. If the artifact is choice, the buyer is there and he is paying record prices, at times, far beyond previously established guidelines. The point types accruing most in value continue to be outstanding Hillsboroughs and Newnans of good color, often of coral. Running a close second in appreciation are fluted Paleos and Bull Tongue Simpsons, followed by other high quality Paleos. Hardins and Lost Lakes have jumped in popularity, and good quality Edgefields and Wallers disappear quickly at shows, for much higher prices than formerly. Unless of outstanding quality, Bolens, basal notched and later period points have not increased in value as much as others. Recently I have seen outstanding tools sell for several hundred dollars. Some advanced collectors seem to be pursuing high grade but less common artifacts, such as those of bone and wood. It seems that more and more advanced collectors are drastically thinning their collections, concentrating only on extremely high quality artifacts. A reliable source reported to me that there is one southeast collector dispersing his collection, but buying and retaining only points in the five-figure range.

Shows are strong in the southeast. A new one has successfully begun near Columbia SC, in January and another new one is in Ocala, FL around the beginning of April. A fourth edition of Dowdy's extremely popular Best of the Best is due out soon. If the quality of the third edition is maintained, it should be a winner, as the photographs in the last edition were of unsurpassed quality. This book is truly a credit to southern artifact collecting and Dowdy, Reed and Sowell are to be commended. A revised edition of Lloyd Schroder's excellent The Anthropology of Florida Points and Blades appeared in 2006. Important revisions are the inclusion of Florida pottery types and also photographs as well as line drawings. This work has probably the best bibliography on Florida archaeology that exists anywhere. Likewise, Schroder is to be commended and we are looking forward to a new work by him on the Bolen complex, currently in progress.

Pete Timoch
Eastern Central Section

Artifact sales for shows are good, and individual trading is always high. The artifact auctions for this region have been very strong, and high prices for quality artifacts reached new record sales over and over. The overall prices of artifacts of all kinds have increased steadily. The fantastic Rienhart Dovetail made from fine Flint Ridge material is 7.31" long, and is reportedly the largest Dovetail ever to be auctioned. It reached the highest price ever paid for a single piece of flint. Its final bidding reached a lofty $110,000! (Note: All auction results reported require an additional 10% buyer's premium added to the final bid.) An 8" leaf-shaped Adena Cache Blade made of chalcedony and a fine 18" celt both reached $12,000. Great results like these have an upward effect on artifacts in all classes. These results reflect not only the value of high quality artifacts, but conditions of the market and confidence of collectors as well. All indications are upward. With a $110,000 bid on a single piece, who could argue otherwise?

Clovis points and other Paleo artifacts are always high interest items for collectors, and current conditions are no different. According to numerous dealers, any perceived easing of Clovis prices or the market in general is over. Depending on how and what you sell, you may have never felt it. Prices have moved upward, and auction sales are hot. Each time fine Paleo materials are auctioned, they reach a new high mark. Recent auction results: a 3.5" B.W. Stevens Clovis sold for $700, a 2.75" average fluted point for $1700, and an ex-Vietzen collection 3.5" Clovis for $2000. A 3.5" pictured Clovis sold for $5800, a 4" black Clovis for $6500, and a 4" Paleo Square Knife for $2000. Also sold was an ex-Vietzen collection 7" Paleo Uniface Knife for $1000, and a 4.25" black Agate Basin for $2000. A frame of broken Paleo backs and tools went for $400. A frame of Transitional Paleo blades with a pre-auction estimate of $200 finished at $2000. A 4.5" Stringtown eared lance for $2100, and a 3" fine black stemmed lance for $800.

Archaic Dovetails, Lostlakes, and Thebes are also collector favorites. Archaic notched forms are popular not only with Ohio collectors, but with collectors everywhere. Prices for early Archaic notched points are always moving upward, and this year is no different. Several old collections were brought to the auction block. More Dovetails in the 3"- 5" size were brought to market this year than in many recent years. 3"- 4" early Archaic forms were among the fastest risers in the last 2 years. If a favorite Archaic point is made of an attractive material, it has easily changed from its previous benchmark of $200 to its new winning bid of $800 or more. Results at auction are as follows: Dovetails: almost 7": $6000, 5": $5000, 4.9": $5000, 3.25": $900, 3.2": $825, and 3": $500. Results of Thebes points at auction are as follows: 2.5" black: $700, 3" black: $1700. Two 3.25" black examples both went for $2900, and a 4.25" piece sold for $10,250. The Thebes points listed all sold for much higher than book prices. Daltons have enjoyed the same trend, with a 4.5" Dalton classic being bid up to $1600.

Frames of well-documented caches or original type site material such as Glover's Cave, Lost City, or the Reeve Site are always prized by collectors. Winning bids at auction can reach $5000 for a large frame of points, slate pendants and bone tools. A fabulous large double frame of Northern Ohio antler and bone harpoons and tools was given away for $5000. High dollar values for these elite items represent a cumulative effect of the individual artifacts, history and documentation. It is part of our hobby to archive and curate these prized groups for the next generation. Frames like these are rare, so when they are available, they command a premium.

Neolithic points are a fantastic buy if you can get in on the good ones. Neolithic points are still in large supply in the lower grades. However, traders report: the higher-grade points are no longer coming in. This may be the beginning of the drying up of this supply. The last of the Neolithic ground floor. Get in on it. Steep appreciation of investor grade relics will follow.

Saharan Paleolithic Choppers and Bifaces are in the same boat as the Neolithic points. For 6 years, collectors of Paleolithic material have been enjoying low prices due to increased availability. Paleolithic Bifaces are fantastic Early Man tools. From our earliest ancestors, a "hand-axe" is the granddaddy of all artifacts. Currently, many average to fine examples are out there to collect at auctions or artifact shows, at a fraction of their value. A new collector could easily acquire an awesome collection at a modest cost. Certainly, every artifact cabinet should have some. They are fabulous and are going to move up steeply as supply decreases. Label it; display it. This is an underdeveloped part of collections everywhere.

On a related topic, since the last issue, a large collection of fossilized Giant Cave Bear teeth from the Ural Mountains in Romania / Russia is being dispersed. These fossil teeth are unbelievable in preservation and size (up to 5.5" long). Many have retained nearly 100% of their original enamel. Initial auction results for average specimens have been up to $300 a tooth. With supply up, prices are moving down a little. Now is a good time to get fine examples at good prices. Prices are certain to move higher later. Ten years ago a 3" Cave Bear tooth, with nearly all its enamel, was advertised for $250 - $300. In today's market, a 5.5" tooth should be double that price. Remember, the fossils in this collection were graded out and sold in reverse order. There are still fine examples out there. The best is yet to come.

What will happen next? The future market is very strong. The next several years will enjoy good appreciation, like the last 2 years. Sources will dry up for legally acquired artifacts. Investment prices and appreciation will be even steeper than what we have seen in the last 5 to 10 years. Same as the past – better than the past. The big hoards are gone. What will collecting be like when the Neolithic points are no longer easily acquired? When the collectors buying them spend their investment dollars on American artifacts, driving them up even further? Protect your investment; become involved in new collector recruitment and education.

Help keep a great hobby great.

Eric C. Wagner - AACA Vice President
Eastern Central Section

It's an honor to write a market report for another Overstreet Price Guide.

I'll start off with discussing the Internet. The net has made it a small world for artifact collectors, and information travels fast. In the past ten years the number of collectors has increased greatly, and this is largely due (in my opinion) to the number of people accessing the internet.

There are many dealer websites with thousands of relics listed for sale, many with multiple pictures of each relic, with some websites going as far as including microscopic pictures. There are several relic forums that discuss the latest artifact news, including recent finds, legislation, and reproductions. There are also several online organizations for artifact collectors, with the most popular being the AACA (Authentic Artifact Collectors Association). The AACA is free to join and holds its members to a professional standard of ethics in artifact dealing. The AACA has also standardized a minimum return period for its member dealers. The AACA fights artifact fraud by education, communication and mediation. Artifact auctions also are popular on the net. There are several with Ebay being the largest. On Ebay, there are hundreds of relics that are up for auction 24 hours a day. There are so many collectors using Ebay now that a "steal" is about impossible to find. Relics bring fair market value in most cases.

My observations over the past two years on relic sales are as follows: On hard stone, fine celts and axes sell fast and for a premium. When watching Flint sell, the most highly sought out relics are anything Paleo, Dovetails, Lostlakes and Thebes. I've also noticed an increased trend in Woodland relics. Any G-7 and up Adena , Hopewell, or Snyders point are highly collectable and in demand, and their respective prices are up. Bone and pottery prices have remained unchanged. Slate is still very popular among collectors with moderate increases in price.

In my opinion slate and pottery are still undervalued as well as drills and Intrusive mound points. These flint artifact types are fragile and it is rare to find/buy one in undamaged condition.

Artifact collecting is not only a great hobby, but also a growing hobby. With careful buying you can build a collection that will give you a lifetime of enjoyment. Happy collecting!

Warner B. Williams
Eastern Seaboard Section

The market in our region continues to increase for the top quality points. Points in the 9 and 10 category usually bring what a collector is willing to pay while the lower grade points in the 1 to 5 category have become less desirable. The 6 through 8 category points have had a nominal increase since the publication of the 9th edition of the *Overstreet Identification and Price Guide*.

Collectiors are still cautious more than ever due to the impact of modern day points. The risk is high when the collector is purchasing an arrowhead made of stone for which they are totally unfamiliar. Knowing the patina, type, flaking, appearance and feel of the stone is very important.

I have collected Indian arrowheads for 60 years and 95% of the collection is from the central North Carolina region. My policy is: buy only stone that you are familiar with and from your area. If you have doubt, walk away.

Each year, I display my entire collection the first weekend in March at our local library. In the past 10 years, over 8,000 have signed the register to see the collection. We must do all we can to create interest among the youth in our hobby.

HARDSTONE HOUSE AUTHENTICATION
SERVICE AND SALES
Maury Meadows
33232 East US Highway 146
Bethany, MO 64424
660-425-8348

THE MOST RESPECTED CERTIFICATE OF AUTHENTICITY
IN THE HOBBY TODAY

SPECIALIZING IN AXES, BANNERSTONES AND
MIDWESTERN FLINT

visit our web site at
www.hardstonehouseauthentication.com

Advertise!

is your ticket to the relic and arrowhead market!

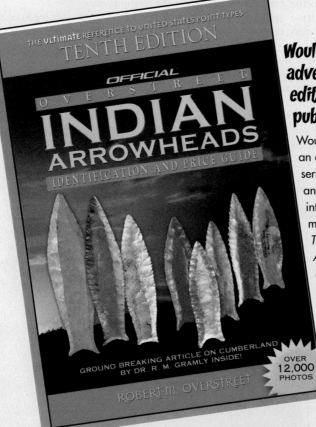

Would you like to advertise in a future edition of one of our publications?

Wouldn't you like to reach an audience made up of serious collectors, dealers and historians who are interested in the same material you are?

The Overstreet Indian Arrowhead Identification and Price Guide is your golden ticket! Call today for advertising rates for our next edition!

**Just call toll free (888)375-9800 ext. 466
or e-mail ads@gemstonepub.com for details!**

Visit us on the web at www.gemstonepub.com

IS YOUR COLLECTION WORTHY?

Should your collection be recorded for posterity and shared with your fellow enthusiasts? If you'd like to submit photos or be an advisor, please contact Bob Overstreet by email at
roverstreet1@mac.com
or contact Gemstone Publishing on our toll free line at (888) 375-9800 ext. 466

When photographing your collection for submission, photos should be 300 dpi in full color with a ruler showing in the picture for reference size.

We want your help!

HAKE'S
IS THE PLACE!

SOLD Peanuts Art $41,264

SO

All Winners Comics $95,2...

Consign your high quality collectibles today!

Our worldwide clientel is always looking to add to their collections

CONTACT!
Deak Stagemyer
sdeak@hakes.com
toll free 866-404-9800 ext. 448
Hake's Americana & Collectibles
1966 Greenspring Drive,
Timonium, Maryland 21093

SOLD Mickey $4,643

WORLD'S GREATEST SUPER-HEROES!
ROBIN THE BOY WONDER

SO

Robin Mego Figure $12,19...

AMERICANA & COLLECTIBLES
A Division Diamond International Galleries

1915 Cracker Jack Christy Mathewson Card $1,910

SOLD John W. Davis Button $13,622

Dr. Frankenstein Toy $5,019

SO

SOLD

www.hakes.com

NORTHEASTERN SECTION:

This section includes point types from the following states:
Connecticut, Delaware, Maine, Maryland, Massachusetts, New Hampshire,
New Jersey, New York, Pennsylvania, Vermont.

The points in this section are arranged in alphabetical order and are shown **actual size**. All types are listed that were available for photographing. Any missing types will be added to future editions as photographs become available. We are always interested in receiving sharp, black and white or color glossy photos, color slides or high resolution (300 pixels/inch) digital pictures of your collection. Be sure and include a ruler in the photograph so that proper scale can be determined.

Lithics: Materials employed in the manufacture of projectile points from this region are: argillite, Coshocton chert, Coxsackie chert, crystal quartz, dolomite, felsite, Helderberg cherts, jasper, Ledge Ridge chert, milky quartz, Onondaga chert, quartzite, rhyolite, shale, siltstone, slate, vein quartz.

Important sites: Bull Brook (Paleo, Ipswich, Mass.), Burwell-Karako (Conn.), John's Bridge (Early Archaic, Conn.), Neville (Early Archaic, Manchester, NH), Plenge (Paleo, NJ), Shoop (Paleo, Dauphin Co., PA), Vail (Paleo, Maine), Titicut (Early Archaic, Bridgewater, MA), Wapanucket (Middleboro, MA).

Regional Consultant:
Gary Fogelman

Special Advisors:
Dr. Richard Michael Gramly

In memory of Richard Savidge

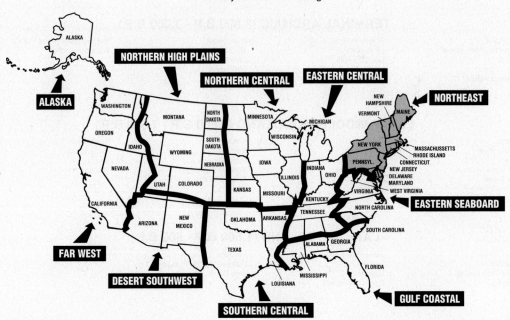

NORTHEASTERN POINT TYPES
(Archaeological Periods)

PALEO (11,500 B.P - 8,000 B.P.)

Agate Basin	Crowfield	Holcomb	Scraper
Amos	Debert	Northumberland	
Barnes(Cumberland)	Graver	Ohio Lanceolate	
Clovis	Haw River	Redstone	

EARLY ARCHAIC (10,000 B.P - 6,500 B.P.)

Angostura	Kessel	Neville	Strike-A-Lite I
Arden	Kirk Corner Notched	Palmer	Stringtown
Brodhead Side-Notched	Kirk Stemmed	Parallel Lanceolate	Susquehanna Bifurcate
Charleston Pine Tree	Kline	Penn's Creek Series	Taunton River Bifurcate
Dalton Classic	Lake Erie	Penn's Creek Bifurcate	Thebes
Dalton Nuckolls	LeCroy	St. Albans	Varney
Decatur	Lost Lake	St. Charles	
Hardaway	MacCorkle	Stanly	
Kanawha	Muncy Bifurcate	Stark	

MID-LATE ARCHAIC (6,000 B.P - 4,000 B.P.)

Atlantic Phase Blade	Drill	Lycoming County	Squibnocket Stemmed
Bare Island	Duncan's Island	Merrimack Stemmed	Squibnocket Triangular
Beekman Triangular	Eshback	Morrow Mountain	Swatara-Long
Boats Blade	Exotic	Newmanstown	Taconic Stemmed
Bone/Antler	Genesee	Otter Creek	Vestal Notched
Brewerton Corner Notched	Ground Slate	Patuxent	Virginsville
Brewerton Eared Triangular	Guilford	Pentagonal Knife	Vosburg
Brewerton Side Notched	Hoover's Island	Piedmont, Northern	Wading River
Burwell	Jim Thorpe	Piney Island	Wapanucket
Chillesquaque	Kittatiny	Poplar Island	
Crooked Creek	Lacawaxan	Savannah River	
Dewart Stemmed	Lamoka	Snook Kill	

TERMINAL ARCHAIC (3,800 B.P - 3,000 B.P.)

Ashtabula	Forest Notched	Meadowood	Susquehanna Broad Point
Conodoquinet/Canfield	Frost Island	Normanskill	Wayland Notched
Cresap	Koens Crispin	Orient Fishtail	
Drill	Lehigh Broadpoint	Perkiomen	
Drybrook Fishtail	Mansion Inn Blade	Schuylkill	

EARLY-MIDDLE WOODLAND (2,800 B.P - 1,500 B.P.)

Adena	Greene	Piscataway	Strike-A-Lite II
Adena Blade	Hellgramite	Port Maitland	Tocks Island
Adena (Robbins)	Hopewell	Randolph	Vernon
Erb Basal Notched	Kiski Notched	Sandhill Stemmed	Waratan
Fox Creek	Oley	Shark's Tooth	
Garver's Ferry	Ovates	Snyders	

LATE WOODLAND (1,500 B.P - 500 B.P.)

Erie Triangle	Jacks Reef Pentagonal	Rossville
Goddard	Levanna	Susquehannock Triangle
Jacks Reef Corner Notched	Madison	Web Blade
	Raccoon Notched	

HISTORIC (350 B.P - 200 B.P.)

Trade Points

NORTHEASTERN UNITED STATES
THUMBNAIL GUIDE SECTION

The following references are provided to aid the collector in easier and quicker identification of point types. All photos are exactly 30% of actual size and are proportional to each other. Each point pictured in this section represents a classic form for the type. When a match is found, go to the alphabetical location of that type for more examples in true actual size.

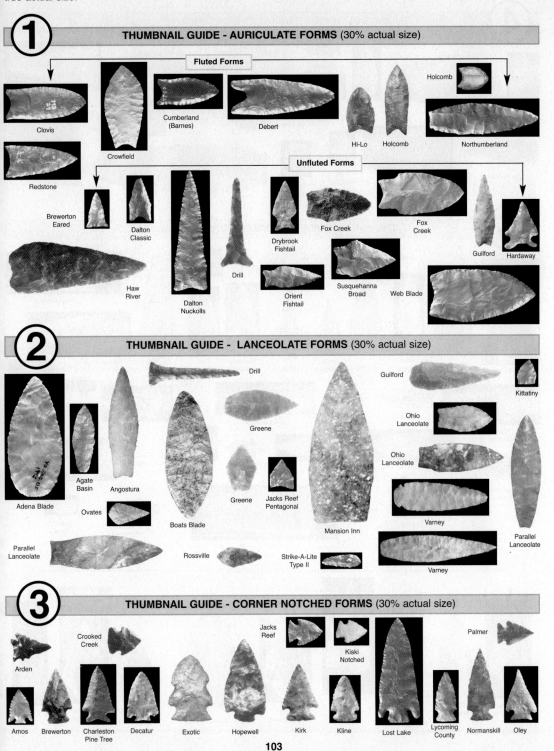

① THUMBNAIL GUIDE - AURICULATE FORMS (30% actual size)

Fluted Forms

Clovis — Crowfield — Cumberland (Barnes) — Debert — Hi-Lo — Holcomb — Holcomb — Northumberland

Redstone — Brewerton Eared — Dalton Classic

Unfluted Forms

Drybrook Fishtail — Fox Creek — Fox Creek — Guilford — Hardaway

Haw River — Dalton Nuckolls — Drill — Orient Fishtail — Susquehanna Broad — Web Blade

② THUMBNAIL GUIDE - LANCEOLATE FORMS (30% actual size)

Drill — Guilford — Kittatiny

Adena Blade — Agate Basin — Angostura — Greene — Ohio Lanceolate

Ovates — Greene — Jacks Reef Pentagonal — Ohio Lanceolate

Boats Blade — Varney

Parallel Lanceolate — Rossville — Strike-A-Lite Type II — Mansion Inn — Varney — Parallel Lanceolate

③ THUMBNAIL GUIDE - CORNER NOTCHED FORMS (30% actual size)

Arden — Crooked Creek — Jacks Reef — Kiski Notched — Palmer

Amos — Brewerton — Charleston Pine Tree — Decatur — Exotic — Hopewell — Kirk — Kline — Lost Lake — Lycoming County — Normanskill — Oley

THUMBNAIL GUIDE - Corner Notched Forms (continued)

Perkiomen   St. Charles   Snyders   Susquehanna Broad   Thebes   Vestal Notched   Vosburg   Wayland Notched

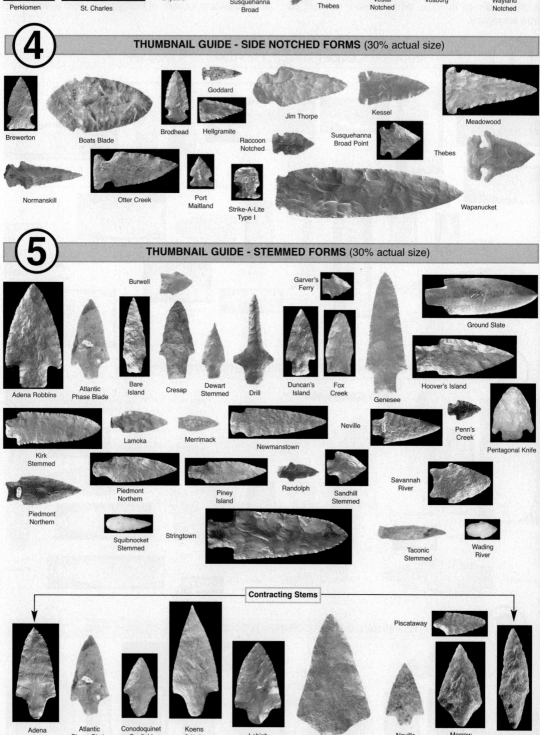

(4) THUMBNAIL GUIDE - SIDE NOTCHED FORMS (30% actual size)

Brewerton   Boats Blade   Brodhead   Hellgramite   Goddard   Jim Thorpe   Kessel   Meadowood

Raccoon Notched   Susquehanna Broad Point   Thebes

Normanskill   Otter Creek   Port Maitland   Strike-A-Lite Type I   Wapanucket

(5) THUMBNAIL GUIDE - STEMMED FORMS (30% actual size)

Burwell   Garver's Ferry   Ground Slate

Adena Robbins   Atlantic Phase Blade   Bare Island   Cresap   Dewart Stemmed   Drill   Duncan's Island   Fox Creek   Genesee   Hoover's Island

Kirk Stemmed   Lamoka   Merrimack   Newmanstown   Neville   Penn's Creek   Pentagonal Knife

Piedmont Northern   Piney Island   Randolph   Sandhill Stemmed   Savannah River

Piedmont Northern   Squibnocket Stemmed   Stringtown   Taconic Stemmed   Wading River

Contracting Stems

Piscataway

Adena   Atlantic Phase Blade   Conodoquinet Canfield   Koens Crispin   Lehigh Broadpoint   Mansion Inn   Neville   Morrow Mountain   Poplar Island

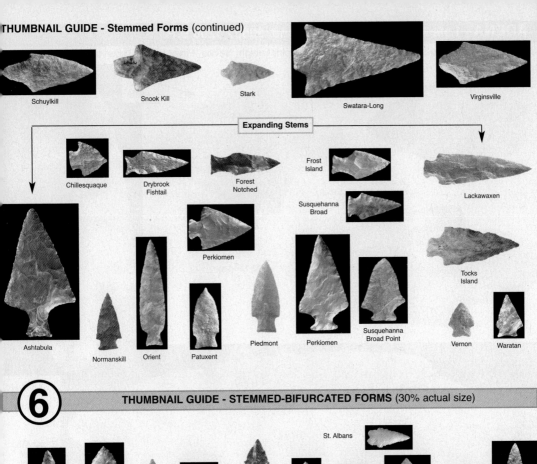

Schuylkill

Snook Kill

Stark

Swatara-Long

Virginsville

Expanding Stems

Chillesquaque

Drybrook
Fishtail

Forest
Notched

Frost
Island

Susquehanna
Broad

Lackawaxen

Perkiomen

Tocks
Island

Ashtabula

Normanskill

Orient

Patuxent

Piedmont

Perkiomen

Susquehanna
Broad Point

Vernon

Waratan

(6) THUMBNAIL GUIDE - STEMMED-BIFURCATED FORMS (30% actual size)

St. Albans

Kanawha

Kirk
Stemmed

Lake Erie

LeCroy

MacCorkle

Muncy
Bifurcated

Penn's
Creek

Stanly

Susquehanna
Bifurcate

Taunton
River
Bifurcate

(7) THUMBNAIL GUIDE - BASAL NOTCHED FORMS

Erb Basal

Eshback

(8) THUMBNAIL GUIDE - TRIANGLES

Beekman
Triangular

Erie
Triangle

Levanna

Madison

Squibnocket
Triangle

Susquehannock
Triangle

ADENA - Late Archaic to late Woodland, 3000 - 1200 B.P.

(Also see Adena Blade, Koens Crispin, Lehigh, Neville, Piney Island, Turkeytail)

Felsite

Narrow stem Adena

G6, $8-$15
Bridgewater, MA

G6, $12-$20
W. PA

G7, $35-$50
W. PA

G7, $40-$70
Columbia
Co., PA

G8, $150-
$250
NJ

LOCATION: Northeastern to South- eastern states. **DESCRIPTION:** A medium to large, thin, narrow, triangular blade with a medium to long, narrow to broad rounded "beaver tail" stem. Most examples are from average to excellent quality. Bases can be ground. Has been found with *Nolichucky, Camp Creek, Candy Creek, Ebenezer* and *Greenville* points (Rankin site, Cocke Co., TN). **I.D. KEY:** Rounded base, woodland flaking.

ADENA BLADE - Late Archaic to Woodland, 3000 - 1200 B.P.

(Also see Adena, Turkeytail)

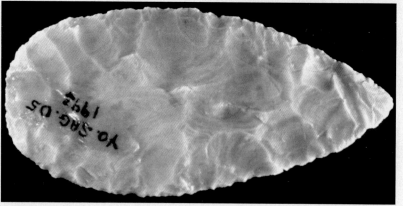

LOCATION: Southeastern to Northeastern states. **DESCRIPTION:** A large size, thin, broad, ovate blade with a rounded base and is usually found in caches. **I.D. KEY:** Woodland flaking, large direct strikes.

G8, $80-$150
York Co., PA

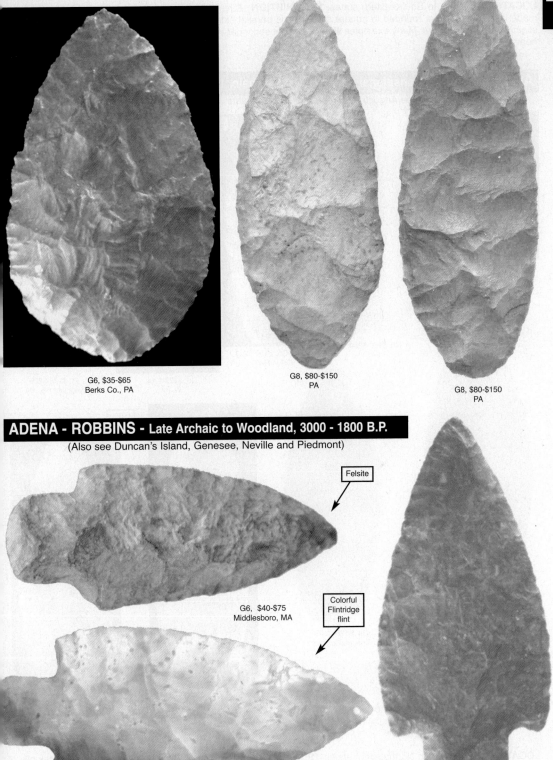

G6, $35-$65
Berks Co., PA

G8, $80-$150
PA

G8, $80-$150
PA

ADENA - ROBBINS - Late Archaic to Woodland, 3000 - 1800 B.P.

(Also see Duncan's Island, Genesee, Neville and Piedmont)

Felsite

G6, $40-$75
Middlesboro, MA

Colorful
Flintridge
flint

G9, $300-$500
Beaver Co., PA

G8, $100-$175
W. NY

107

ADENA-ROBBINS (continued)

LOCATION: Eastern to Southeastern states. **DESCRIPTION:** A large, broad, triangular point that is thin and well made with a long, wide, rounded to square stem that is parallel sided. The blade has convex sides and square to slightly barbed shoulders. Many examples show excellent secondary flaking on blade edges. **I.D. KEY:** Square base, heavy secondary flaking.

AGATE BASIN - Transitional Paleo to early Archaic, 10,500 - 8000 B.P.

(Also see Angostura, Greene, Ohio Lanceolate, Parallel Lancelote, Varney)

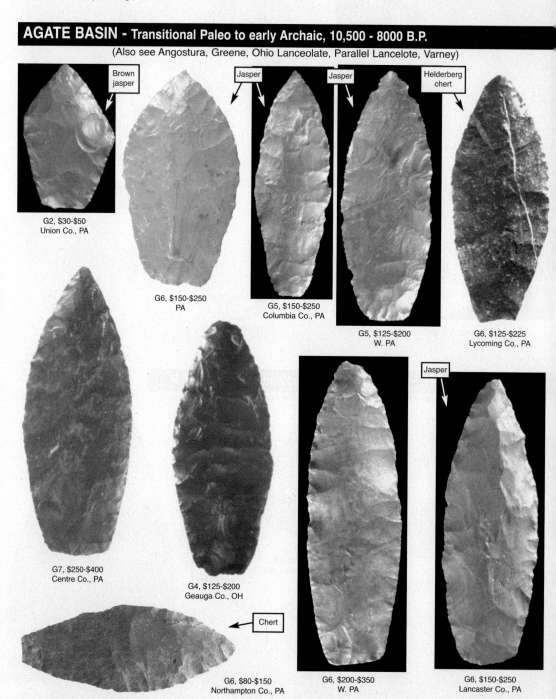

Brown jasper

G2, $30-$50
Union Co., PA

G6, $150-$250
PA

Jasper

G5, $150-$250
Columbia Co., PA

Jasper

G5, $125-$200
W. PA

Helderberg chert

G6, $125-$225
Lycoming Co., PA

G7, $250-$400
Centre Co., PA

G4, $125-$200
Geauga Co., OH

Jasper

Chert

G6, $80-$150
Northampton Co., PA

G6, $200-$350
W. PA

G6, $150-$250
Lancaster Co., PA

LOCATION: Midwestern to Northeastern states. **DESCRIPTION:** A medium to large size lanceolate blade, usually of high quality. Bases are either convex, concave or straight, and are usually ground. Some examples are median ridged and have random to parallel flaking. **I.D. KEY:** Basal form and flaking style.

108

Worn tip

Ground stems

G8, $300-$500
Mercer Co., PA

G9, $350-$650
Union Co., PA

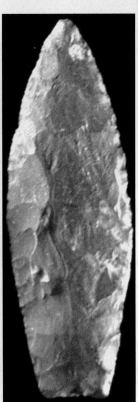

G7, $250-$450
Warren Co., PA

G7, $300-$550
OH

AMOS - Early Archaic, 10,000 - 9000 B.P.

(Also see Charleston Pine Tree, Kirk Corner Notched, Palmer)

Restored

Black chert

Serrated edge

G2, $5-$10
Snyder Co., PA

G4, $25-$45
Lycoming Co., PA

G7, $20-$35
Lycoming Co., PA

G7, $35-$65
Montgomery Co., PA

G6, $25-$40
Lycoming Co., PA

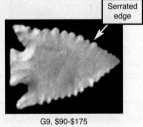

G9, $90-$175
MD

Red/yellow jasper

G8, $40-$75
Lycoming Co., PA

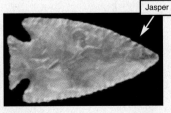

Jasper

LOCATION: Northeastern states.
DESCRIPTION: A small to medium size corner notched point with serrated edges and barbed shoulders. The base is straight to convex. **I.D. KEY:** Edgework.

G9, $80-$150
Luzerne Co., PA

ANGOSTURA - Early Archaic, 10,000 - 8000 B.P.

(Also see Agate Basin, Clovis-unfluted, Greene, Guilford, Ohio Lanceolate, Parallel Lanceolate,)

ANGOSTURA (continued)

LOCATION: Eastern states. **DESCRIPTION:** A medium to large size lanceolate blade with a contracting, concave base. Both broad and narrow forms occur. Flaking can be parallel oblique to random. Bases are not usually ground but are thinned. **I.D. KEY:** Basal form, early flaking on blade. Very rare for the NE.

Yellow jasper

G9, $250-$500
Lehigh Co., PA

G8, $250-$400
Barry, MA

Black/brown chert

Note parallel diagonal flaking

ARDEN - Early Archaic, 9000 - 8000 B.P.

(Also see Charleston Pine Tree)

LOCATION: Northeastern states, especially New York. **DESCRIPTION:** A small to medium size, serrated, corner notched point with barbed shoulders and an expanded stem. **I.D. KEY:** Basal form, one barb round and the other stronger.

G2, $2-$4
NY

ASHTABULA - Late Archaic to Woodland, 4000 - 2500 B.P.

(Also see Koens Crispin, Lehigh, Perkiomen and Susquehanna Broad)

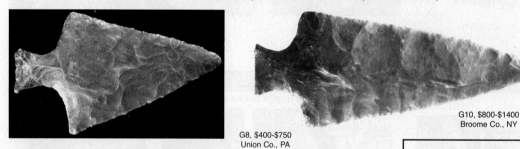

G10, $800-$1400
Broome Co., NY

G8, $400-$750
Union Co., PA

IMPORTANT:
These Ashtabulas are shown half size

LOCATION: Northeastern states, especially Northeastern Ohio and Western Penn. **DESCRIPTION:** A medium to large size, broad, thick, expanded stem point with tapered shoulders. **I.D. KEY:** Basal form, one barb round and the other stronger.

ATLANTIC PHASE BLADE - Late-Terminal Archaic, 4300 - 3700 B.P.

(Also see Boats Blade, Koens Crispin, Savannah River, Schuylkill and Snook Kill)

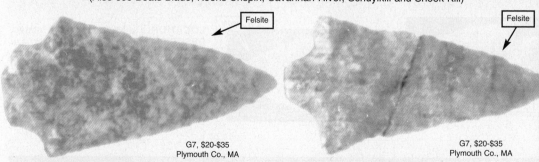

Felsite

Felsite

G7, $20-$35
Plymouth Co., MA

G7, $20-$35
Plymouth Co., MA

LOCATION: Massachusetts and surrounding states. **DESCRIPTION:** A medium to large size point with squared to tapered shoulders and a short, parallel sided to tapered stem. The base is generally straight. **I.D. KEY:** Base form.

Felsite

Felsite

G7, $12-$20
Bristol Co., MA

G7, $12-$20
Bristol Co., MA

G7, $15-$30
Bristol Co., MA

G7, $20-$35
Bristol Co., MA

G9, $300-$550
Bridgewater, MA

BARE ISLAND - Late Archaic, 4500 - 1500 B.P.

(Also see Duncan's Island, Lackawaxen, Lamoka, Neville, Newmanstown, Piedmont, Piney Island, Poplar Island, Snook Kill)

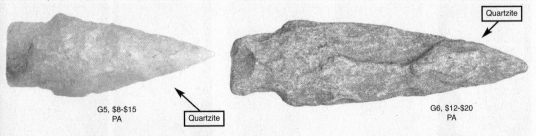

Quartzite

G5, $8-$15
PA

Quartzite

G6, $12-$20
PA

LOCATION: Northeastern states. **DESCRIPTION:** A medium to large size, narrow, thick stemmed point with tapered shoulders. One shoulder is higher than the other and the blade is convex to straight. The stem is parallel to expanding. Similar to *Little Bear Creek* in the Southeast. **I.D. KEY:** Narrow stemmed point.

111

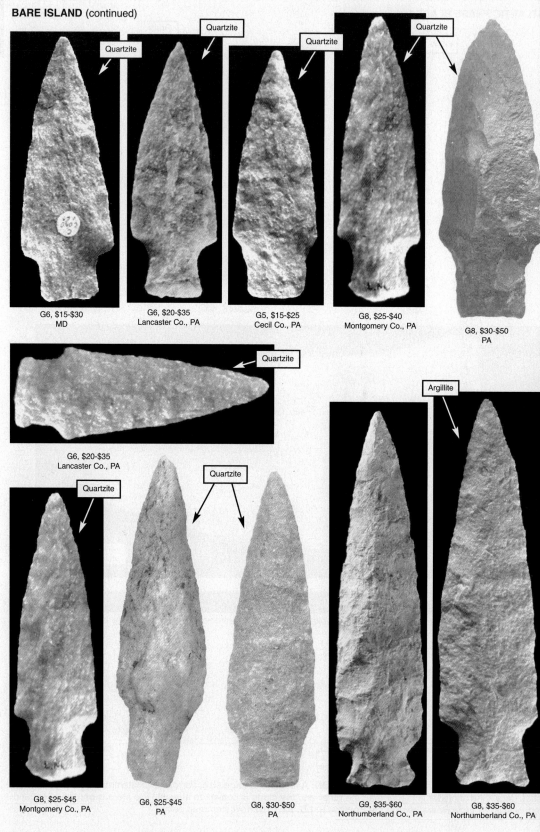

Quartzite

Quartzite

Quartzite

Quartzite

Quartzite

G6, $15-$30
MD

G6, $20-$35
Lancaster Co., PA

G5, $15-$25
Cecil Co., PA

G8, $25-$40
Montgomery Co., PA

G8, $30-$50
PA

Quartzite

G6, $20-$35
Lancaster Co., PA

Argillite

Quartzite

Quartzite

G8, $25-$45
Montgomery Co., PA

G6, $25-$45
PA

G8, $30-$50
PA

G9, $35-$60
Northumberland Co., PA

G8, $35-$60
Northumberland Co., PA

BARE ISLAND (continued)

Argillite

G8, $35-$65
Northumberland
Co., PA

BEEKMAN TRIANGULAR - Mid-late Archaic, 4800 - 4500 B.P.

(Also see Madison, Squibnocket Triangle and Susquehannock Triangle)

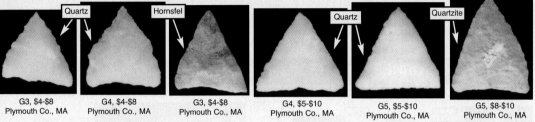

| Quartz | | Hornsfel | | Quartz | | Quartzite |

| G3, $4-$8 | G4, $4-$8 | G3, $4-$8 | G4, $5-$10 | G5, $5-$10 | G5, $8-$10 |
| Plymouth Co., MA | Plymouth Co., MA | Plymouth Co., MA | Plymouth Co., MA | Plymouth Co., MA | Plymouth Co., MA |

LOCATION: Northern Pennsylvania into New York, New Jersey and Massachusetts. **DESCRIPTION:** A small size, short, triangular point with a broad, straight to concave base. Bases are ground. **I.D. KEY:** Equilateral triangle with ground base.

BOATS BLADE - Late to Terminal Archaic, 4300 - 3700 B.P.

(Also see Adena Blade, Atlantic Phase Blade, Mansion Inn, Web Blade)

Glued

G3, $30-$50
Bridgewater, MA

Rare
notched
form

Half
restored

G6, $25-$40
Middleboro, MA

$12-$20
Bridgewater, MA

LOCATION: Southern New England states. Type site is in Dighton, MA. **DESCRIPTION:** A large size, broad, bi-pointed blade of good quality. Rarely, examples exist with side notches.

BONE/ANTLER - Mid-Archaic to Historic, 4500 - 100 B.P.

(Also see Trade Points)

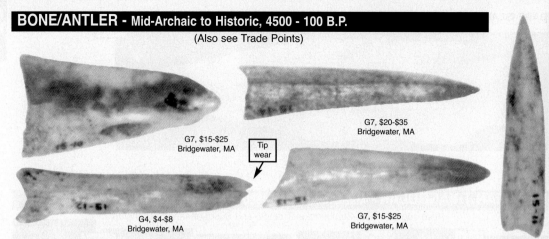

G7, $15-$25
Bridgewater, MA

Tip
wear

G7, $20-$35
Bridgewater, MA

G4, $4-$8
Bridgewater, MA

G7, $15-$25
Bridgewater, MA

G6, $12-$20
Bridgewater, MA

LOCATION: Northeastern states. **DESCRIPTION:** A medium to large size lanceolate point carved from deer or Elk antler or from bone.

BREWERTON CORNER NOTCHED - Middle to late Archaic, 6000 - 4000 B.P.

(Also see Crooked Creek, Jacks Reef, Kirk, Kiski, Lycoming County, Normanskill, Palmer & Snyders)

Jasper

Gray
chert

Onondaga
chert

G5, $6-$12
Luzurne Co., PA

G5, $6-$12
Luzurne Co., PA

G5, $6-$12
Montgomery Co., PA

Black
flint

Black
chert

G5, $6-$12
Lycoming Co., PA

G5, $6-$12
Columbia Co.,
NY

G4, $6-$12
Columbia Co., NY

G5, $8-$15
Lycoming
Co., PA

G5, $6-$12
Monroe Co., PA

Onondaga
chert

G6, $6-$12
Lycoming Co., PA

G10, $25-$40
Columbia Co., NY

G7, $15-$30
Columbia Co., NY

G7, $35-$60
Columbia Co., NY

LOCATION: Eastern to midwestern states. **DESCRIPTION:** A small to medium size, thick, triangular point with faint corner notches and a concave, straight or convex base. Called *Freeheley* in Michigan. **I.D. KEY:** Width, thickness.

BREWERTON EARED-TRIANGULAR - Middle to late Archaic, 6000 - 4000 B.P.

(Also see Fox Creek, Kittatiny, Steubenville & Yadkin)

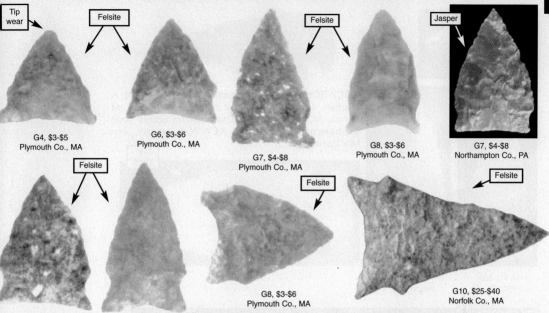

Tip wear

Felsite

Felsite

Jasper

G4, $3-$5
Plymouth Co., MA

G6, $3-$6
Plymouth Co., MA

G7, $4-$8
Plymouth Co., MA

G8, $3-$6
Plymouth Co., MA

G7, $4-$8
Northampton Co., PA

Felsite

Felsite

Felsite

G8, $3-$6
Plymouth Co., MA

G10, $25-$40
Norfolk Co., MA

G7, $5-$10
Plymouth Co., MA

G8, $8-$15
Plymouth Co., MA

LOCATION: Eastern to midwestern states. **DESCRIPTION:** A small size, triangular, eared point with a concave base. **I.D. KEY:** Small basal ears.

BREWERTON SIDE-NOTCHED - Late Archaic, 6000 - 4000 B.P.

(Also see Meadowood, Otter Creek, Perkiomen, Susquehanna Broad)

Rhyolite

Black flint

Black chert

Restored

G5, $4-$8
Lycoming Co., PA

G5, $4-$8
Northum. Co., PA

G5, $4-$8
Union Co., PA

G5, $4-$8
Monroe Co., PA

G5, $4-$8
Lycoming Co., PA

G2, $2-$5
Brewerton Co., PA

G8, $8-$15
Luzerne Co., PA

G8, $20-$35
Lycoming Co., PA

G8, $15-$25
Luzerne Co., PA

G4, $4-$8
CT

LOCATION: Eastern to midwestern states. **DESCRIPTION:** A small size, thick, triangular point with shallow side notches and a concave to straight base. **I.D. KEY**. Small side notched point.

115

BRODHEAD SIDE-NOTCHED - Early Archaic , 9000 - 7000 B.P.

(Also see Bennington Quail Tail, Brewerton, Crooked Creek, Kiski, Lycoming Co. & St. Charles)

G5, $5-$10
Lycoming Co., PA

G6, $8-$15
Lycoming Co., PA

Gray chert

LOCATION: Northeastern states. **DESCRIPTION:** A medium size, side to corner notched point with an expanded, convex base. The notching occurs near the base and are wide. **I.D. KEY:** Wide notches, convex base.

Gray chert

G7, $12-$20
Lycoming Co., PA

G7, $12-$20
Lancaster Co., PA

G7, $15-$25
Lycoming Co., PA

G7, $15-$25
PA

BURWELL - Late Archaic, 5000 - 4000 B.P.

LOCATION: Northeastern states. **DESCRIPTION:** A small size, parallel stemmed point with weak, tapered shoulders and a short blade. The base is concave. **I.D. KEY:** Broad, parallel stem, tapered shoulders.

G6, $4-$8
Washingtonboro, PA

CHARLESTON PINE TREE - Early Archaic, 8000 - 7000 B.P.

(Also see Arden, Kirk Corner Notched, Lycoming Co., Oley, Palmer, Vestal Notched, Vosburg)

G3, $5-$10
Lycoming Co., PA

G6, $25-$40
Lycoming Co., PA

Oblique flaking & median ridge

Gray chert

G6, $35-$65
Mifflin Co., PA

G9, $35-$65
NY

Restored ear

G5, $25-$50
Lycoming Co., PA

LOCATION: Eastern to Southeastern states. The St. Albans site is in West Virginia. Points here were dated to 9,900 B.P. **DESCRIPTION:** A medium to large size, corner notched, usually serrated point with parallel flaking to the center of the blade forming a median ridge. The bases are ground and can be concave, convex, straight, bifurcated or auriculate. Called *Pine Tree* in the Southeast. **I.D. KEY:** Archaic flaking with long flakes to the center of the blade.

CHILLESQUAQUE SERIES - Mid Archaic, 6,000 - 5,000 B.P.

(Also see Crooked Creek, Lycoming County Series and Penn's Creek Series)

LOCATION: Northeastern states. **DESCRIPTION:** A series of points that are Laurentian in nature like Brewerton, with slight an subtile variations in material and shape from drainage to drainage.

G5, $5-$10
Lancaster Co., PA

CLOVIS - Early Paleo, 11,500 - 10,600 B.P.

(Also see Crowfield, Cumberland, Debert, Holcomb & Redstone)

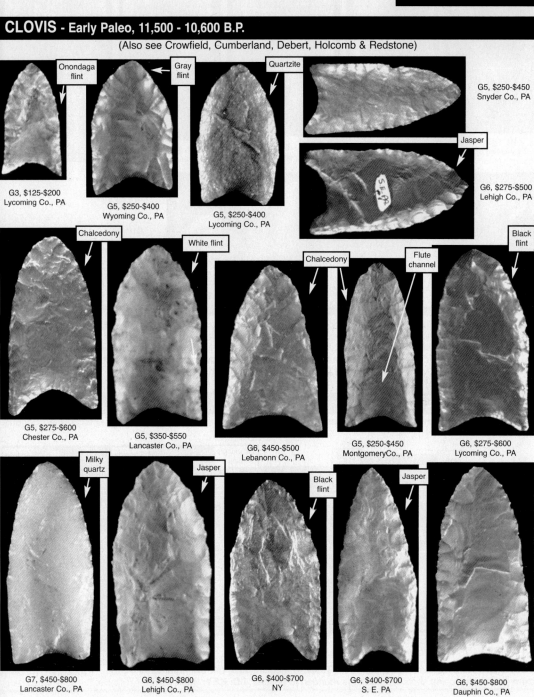

Onondaga flint

Gray flint

Quartzite

G5, $250-$450
Snyder Co., PA

Jasper

G6, $275-$500
Lehigh Co., PA

G3, $125-$200
Lycoming Co., PA

G5, $250-$400
Wyoming Co., PA

G5, $250-$400
Lycoming Co., PA

Chalcedony

White flint

Chalcedony

Flute channel

Black flint

G5, $275-$600
Chester Co., PA

G5, $350-$550
Lancaster Co., PA

G6, $450-$500
Lebanonn Co., PA

G5, $250-$450
MontgomeryCo., PA

G6, $275-$600
Lycoming Co., PA

Milky quartz

Jasper

Black flint

Jasper

G7, $450-$800
Lancaster Co., PA

G6, $450-$800
Lehigh Co., PA

G6, $400-$700
NY

G6, $400-$700
S. E. PA

G6, $450-$800
Dauphin Co., PA

CLOVIS (continued)

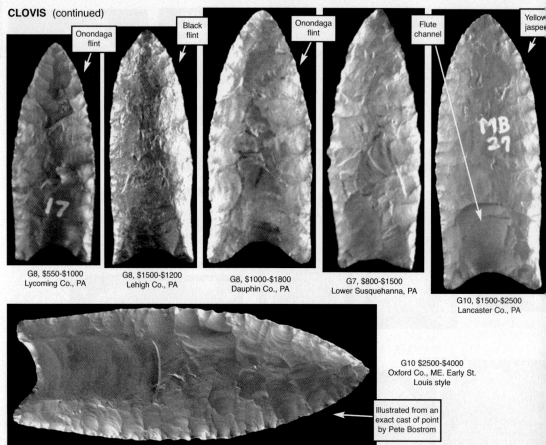

Onondaga flint

Black flint

Onondaga flint

Flute channel

Yellow jasper

G8, $550-$1000
Lycoming Co., PA

G8, $1500-$1200
Lehigh Co., PA

G8, $1000-$1800
Dauphin Co., PA

G7, $800-$1500
Lower Susquehanna, PA

G10, $1500-$2500
Lancaster Co., PA

G10 $2500-$4000
Oxford Co., ME. Early St.
Louis style

Illustrated from an exact cast of point by Pete Bostrom

LOCATION: All of North America. **DESCRIPTION:** A medium to large size, auriculate, fluted, lanceolate point with convex sides and a concave base that is ground. Most examples are fluted on both sides about 1/3 the way up from the base. The flaking can be random to parallel. The oldest point type in the hemisphere. Materials used in this area are: Argillite, black flint, chalcedony, conglomerate, coshocton, coxsackie, jasper, Onondaga, quartz crystal, quartzite, rhyolite, shale & upper Mercer black chert. **I.D. KEY:** Auricles and fluting.

CONODOQUINET/CANFIELD - Late Archaic, 4000 - 3500 B.P.

(Also see Dewart Stemmed, Duncan's Island, Lehigh, Lamoka, Morrow Mountain, Neville, Piscataway, Sandhill Stemmed)

Gray chert

Chert

Onondaga flint

Siltstone

Argillite

G4, $4-$8
Union Co., PA

G4, $4-$8
Lycoming Co., PA

G5, $4-$8
Lycoming Co., PA

G5, $4-$8
Lycoming Co., PA

G4, $4-$8
Lycoming Co., PA

LOCATION: Northeastern states. **DESCRIPTION:** A medium size, narrow, contracted stem point with sloping shoulders. Base is rounded to pointed. **I.D. KEY:** Base form.

CRESAP - Late Archaic to Woodland, 3000 - 2500 B.P.

(Also see Adena, Adena Robbins)

Felsite

G6, $35-$60
Bridgewater, MA

LOCATION: West Virginia, Kentucky, into Massachusetts. **DESCRIPTION:** A medium to large size point that has a medium-long contracting stem and slight shoulders. The base is usually straight. Stems can be ground. Associated with the early Adena culture. **I.D. KEY:** Long "squarish" tapered stem.

CROOKED CREEK SERIES - Archaic, 6000 - 4000 B.P.

(Also see Brewerton, Chillesquaque Series, Decatur, Dovetail, Kiski, Lycoming County, Palmer & Penn's Creek Series)

LOCATION: Northeastern states. **DESCRIPTION:** A series of points that are Laurentian in nature like Brewerton, with slight an subtile variations in material and shape from drainage to drainage.

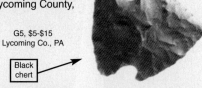

G5, $5-$15
Lycoming Co., PA

Black chert

CROWFIELD - Late Paleo, 11,000 - 10,000 B.P.

(Also see Clovis, Cumberland, Debert, Holcomb, Parallel Lanceolate, Plainview)

Jasper

Onondaga chert

Delaware chert

Hand held to show quality and size

G8, $400-$750
NY

G8, $600-$1000
Chilhowie, VA

G8, $800-$1500
Lancaster/York Co., PA

Multiple fluting

G10, $1400-$2500
Cuyahoga Co., NY

Not fluted

Restored tip

Flute channel

$700-$1200
Chautauqua Co., NY

G10, $1000-$1800
NY

White chert

LOCATION: Northeastern states. **DESCRIPTION:** A medium size, very thin, auriculate, fluted point with a concave base. Commonly multiple fluted and the basal area is ground. This point is widest near the tip. Believed to be later than *Clovis*. Cross section is as thin as *Folsoms*. **I.D. KEY:** Multiple flutes, blade form.

CROWFIELD (continued)

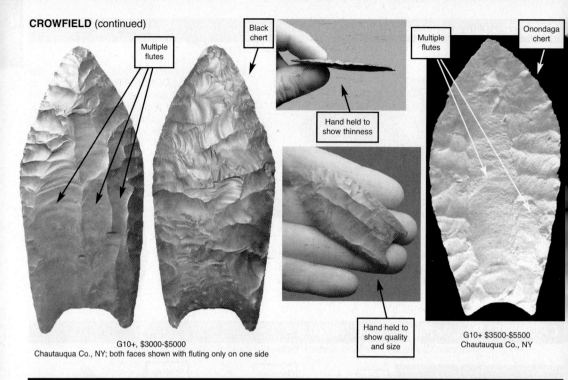

Multiple flutes

Black chert

Hand held to show thinness

Multiple flutes

Onondaga chert

Hand held to show quality and size

G10+, $3000-$5000
Chautauqua Co., NY; both faces shown with fluting only on one side

G10+ $3500-$5500
Chautauqua Co., NY

CUMBERLAND (Barnes) - Paleo, 11,250 - 10,000 B.P.

(Also see Beaver Lake, Clovis, Crowfield, Debert, Holcomb)

Flute channel

Yellow jasper

Black chert

Yellow jasper

Yellow jasper

G5, $450-$800
Chester Co., PA

G7, $300-$500
PA

G9, $800-$1500
Lycoming Co., PA

G5, $500-$800
PA

Broken ears

Yellow jasper

Restored tip

G7, $600-$1000
Lancaster Co., PA

G9, $1600-$3000
NY

120

CUMBERLAND (Barnes) (continued)

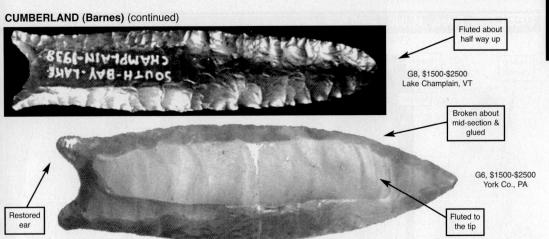

Fluted about half way up

G8, $1500-$2500
Lake Champlain, VT

Broken about mid-section & glued

G6, $1500-$2500
York Co., PA

Restored ear

Fluted to the tip

LOCATION: Southeastern states to Canada **DESCRIPTION:** A medium to large size, lanceolate form that is usually fluted on both faces. The fluting and flaking technique is an advanced form as in *Folsom*, with the flutes usually extending the entire length of the blade. Bases are ground on all examples. **I.D. KEY:** Paleo flaking, indirect pressure fluted.

DALTON CLASSIC - Early Archaic, 10,000 - 9200 B.P.

(Also see Clovis, Crowfield, Debert, Hardaway, Holcomb, Plainview)

Tip wear

Quartzite

Red jasper

Milky quartz

White flint

White flint

G3, $25-$40
Lycoming Co., PA

G4, $40-$75
Jefferson Co., PA

G7, $30-$50
Plymouth Co., MA

G3, $25-$40
Berks Co., PA

G6, $80-$150
Lebanon Co., PA

LOCATION: Midwestern to Eastern states. **DESCRIPTION:** A medium to large size, thin, auriculate, fishtailed point. Usually finely serrated and sometimes fluted. Beveling may occur on one side of each face but is usually on the right side. All bases are ground. **I.D. KEY:** Basal form and flaking style. **Rare** for area.

DALTON-NUCKOLLS - Early Archaic, 10,000 - 9200 B.P.

(Also see Angostura, Dalton Classic, Plainview)

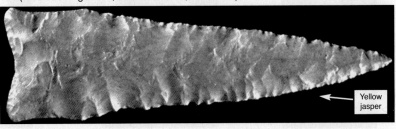

G10, $1200-$2000
Chester Co., PA

LOCATION: Midwestern to Northeastern states. Type site is in Humphreys Co., TN. **DESCRIPTION:** A medium to large size variant form, probably occuring from resharpening the

Yellow jasper

Greenbrier Dalton. Bases are squared to lobbed to eared, and have a shallow concavity. Bases are ground and some examples are fluted. **I.D. KEY:** Broad base and shoulders, flaking on blade. **Very Rare** for area.

DEBERT - Paleo, 11,000 - 9500 B. P.

(Also see Clovis, Crowfield, Cumberland, Dalton, Holcomb)

Fluting channel

Tip wear

Jasper

Broken & glued

Both pieces found at diff. times separated from kill and camp site. Note patination variation.

Classic form

Note deeply indented bases

G5, $350-$600
Vail site, ME. Photo by Dr. Gramly

G5, $350-$600
Lycoming Co., PA

G6, $600-$1000
Vail Debert site, ME, Photo courtesy Dr. R.M. Gramly.

Conjoined point

G2, $125-$200
Vail Devert site. ME.
Photo courtesy
Dr. R. M. Gramly

G9, $2500-$4000
Snyder Co., PA. Yellow Jasper.

LOCATION: Northeastern states. Type site is the Vail site in Maine. **DESCRIPTION:** A medium to large size, thin, auriculate point that evolved from *Clovis*. Most examples are fluted twice on each face resulting in a deep basal concavity. The second flute usually removed traces of the first fluting. A very rare form of late *Clovis*. **I.D. KEY:** Deep basal notch.

DECATUR - Early Archaic, 9000 - 3000 B.P.

(Also see Charleston Pine Tree, Dovetail, Kirk, Kiski, Lost Lake, Palmer)

Gray flint

Tip damage

Gray flint

Fractured base

Gray flint

Fractured base

G2, $3-$5
Lancaster Co., PA

G5, $25-$40
Northumberland Co., PA

G6, $25-$45
Northumberland Co., PA

DECATUR (continued)

LOCATION: Eastern states.
DESCRIPTION: A small to medium size, thin, serrated, corner notched point that is usually beveled on one side of each face. The base is usually broken off (fractured) by a blow inward from each corner of the stem. Sometimes the sides of the stem and backs of the tangs are also fractured, and rarely the tip may be fractured by a blow on each side directed towards the base. Bases are usually ground and flaking is of high quality. **I.D. KEY:** Squared base, one barb shoulder.

Fractured base

Base wear

G7, $125-$200
Union Co., PA

G6, $80-$150
Indiana Co., PA

DEWART STEMMED - Late Archaic, 5000 - 2500 B.P.

(Also see Bare Island, Duncan's Island, Garver's Ferry, Lamoka, Merrimack, Neville, Piney Island)

Vein quartz

G4, $3-$5
Divers Isle, PA

G4, $4-$8
Peach Bottom, PA

G4, $4-$8
Northumberland Co., PA

G6, $5-$10
Northumberland Co., PA

G6, $5-$10
Lycoming Co., PA

LOCATION: Northeastern states. **DESCRIPTION:** A medium size, narrow, stemmed point with strong shoulders. Tips are sharp and the stem is parallel to contracting. The base is normally unfinished. **I.D. KEY:** Unfinished base.

DOVETAIL (See St. Charles)

DRILL - Paleo to Historic, 11,500 - 200 B.P.

(Also see Graver, Randolph and Scraper)

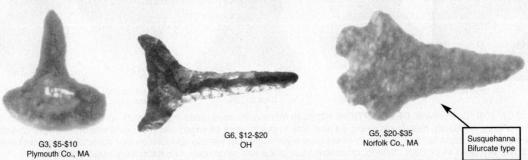

G3, $5-$10
Plymouth Co., MA

G6, $12-$20
OH

G5, $20-$35
Norfolk Co., MA

Susquehanna Bifurcate type

123

DRILL (continued)

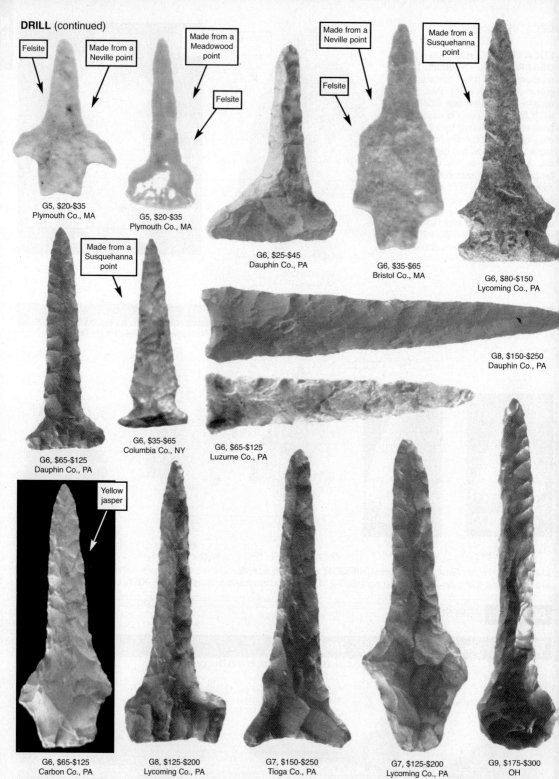

Felsite

Made from a
Neville point

Made from a
Meadowood
point

Felsite

Made from a
Neville point

Felsite

Made from a
Susquehanna
point

G5, $20-$35
Plymouth Co., MA

G5, $20-$35
Plymouth Co., MA

G6, $25-$45
Dauphin Co., PA

G6, $35-$65
Bristol Co., MA

G6, $80-$150
Lycoming Co., PA

Made from a
Susquehanna
point

G8, $150-$250
Dauphin Co., PA

G6, $65-$125
Dauphin Co., PA

G6, $35-$65
Columbia Co., NY

G6, $65-$125
Luzurne Co., PA

Yellow
jasper

G6, $65-$125
Carbon Co., PA

G8, $125-$200
Lycoming Co., PA

G7, $150-$250
Tioga Co., PA

G7, $125-$200
Lycoming Co., PA

G9, $175-$300
OH

LOCATION: Everywhere. **DESCRIPTION:** Although many drills were made from scratch, all point types ended up in the drill form. Usually, heavily resharpened and broken points were salvaged and rechipped into drills. These objects were certainly used as drills (evidence of extreme edge wear), but there is speculation that some of these forms may have been used as pins for clothing, ornaments, ear plugs and other uses. **I.D. KEY:** Very narrow blade form.

DRYBROOK FISHTAIL - Late Archaic to Woodland, 3500 - 2500 B.P.

(Also see Forest Notched, Frost Island, Orient, Patuxent, Perkiomen, Susquehanna Broad)

G4, $8-$15
Luzurne Co., PA

G3, $5-$10
Washingtonboro, PA

G6, $20-$35
Luzurrne Co., PA

G6, $15-$30
Lycoming Co., PA

Rhyolite

G8, $35-$60
Luzurne Co., PA

G7, $30-$50
Luzurne Co., PA

G7, $35-$60
Luzurne Co., PA

G2, $12-$20
Monroe Co., PA

Restored ear

G8, $45-$80
Lancaster Co., PA

LOCATION: Northeastern states. **DESCRIPTION**: A medium size, narrow, triangular point that expands towards the base. Shoulders are rounded and taper into an expanded base. The base is straight to concave. Some examples have basal ears that are rounded to pointed. **I.D. KEY:** Basal form, rounded shoulders.

DUNCAN'S ISLAND - Mid to late Archaic, 6000 - 4000 B. P.

(Also see Bare Island, Dewart Stemmed, Neville, Newmanstown, Piedmont, Piney Island)

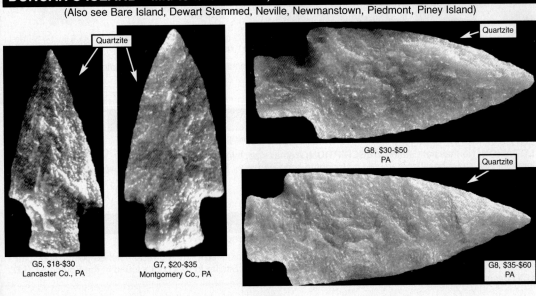

Quartzite

Quartzite

Quartzite

G8, $30-$50
PA

Quartzite

G8, $35-$60
PA

G5, $18-$30
Lancaster Co., PA

G7, $20-$35
Montgomery Co., PA

DUNCAN'S ISLAND
(continued)

LOCATION: Northeastern states. **DESCRIPTION:** A medium to large size stemmed point with convex sides and a medium length square stem. The base is usually straight to slightly convex. Shoulders are straight to tapered. **I.D. KEY:** Square stem.

Argillite

G6, $45-$80
PA

ERB BASAL NOTCHED - Mid-Woodland, 2000 - 1200 B.P.

(Also see Eshback, Oley)

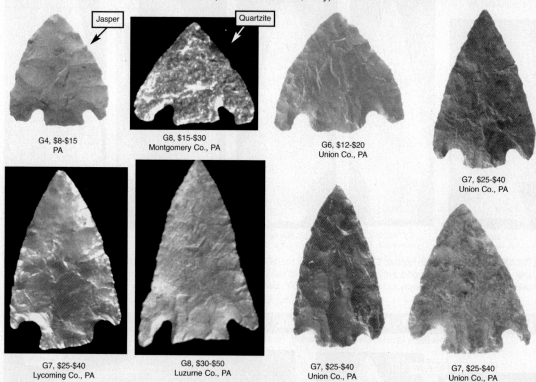

Jasper

Quartzite

G4, $8-$15
PA

G8, $15-$30
Montgomery Co., PA

G6, $12-$20
Union Co., PA

G7, $25-$40
Union Co., PA

G7, $25-$40
Lycoming Co., PA

G8, $30-$50
Luzurne Co., PA

G7, $25-$40
Union Co., PA

G7, $25-$40
Union Co., PA

LOCATION: Northeastern states. **DESCRIPTION:** A small to medium size, broad, basal notched point. Tangs can drop even with or below the base. **I.D. KEY:** Basal form.

ERIE TRIANGLE - Late Woodland, 1500 - 200 B.P.

(Also see Levanna, Madison, Susquehannock Triangle, Yadkin)

LOCATION: Northeastern states. **DESCRIPTION:** A small size, thin, triangular point with sharp basal corners and a straight to concave base. **I.D. KEY:** Triangular form.

G5, $3-$8
Lycoming Co., PA

ESHBACK - Late Archaic, 5500 - 3500 B.P.

(Also see Erb Basal Notched, Oley)

LOCATION: Northeastern states. **DESCRIPTION:** A small to medium size, broad, basal notched point. Tangs can extend beyond the base. Bases are straight, concave or convex. Similar to *Eva* points found in the Southeast. **I.D. KEY:** Basal form.

126

ESHBACK(continued)

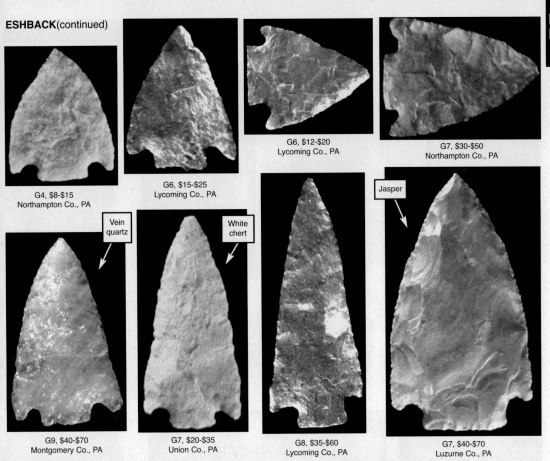

G4, $8-$15
Northampton Co., PA

G6, $15-$25
Lycoming Co., PA

G6, $12-$20
Lycoming Co., PA

G7, $30-$50
Northampton Co., PA

Vein quartz

White chert

Jasper

G9, $40-$70
Montgomery Co., PA

G7, $20-$35
Union Co., PA

G8, $35-$60
Lycoming Co., PA

G7, $40-$70
Luzurne Co., PA

EXOTIC - Mid-Archaic to Mississippian, 5000 - 1000 B.P.

Double notching

LOCATION: Throughout North America. **DESCRIPTION:** Many of these forms are altered, known point types. Others resemble animal effigy forms while others may be no more than unfinished and unintentional doodles.

G9, $40-$70
PA

FOREST NOTCHED - Early Woodland, 3000 - 2000 B.P.

(Also see Drybrook, Frost Island, Orient, Patuxent, Perkiomen and Susquehanna Broad, Table Rock)

LOCATION: Northeastern. **DESCRIPTION:** A medium size, narrow point with very wide side notches. The basal area is relatively long and expands. The base is straight. Shoulders are rounded. **I.D. KEY:** Base form and rounded shoulders.

G7, $15-$25
Clinton Co., PA

(Also see Steubenville)

Shale

Black flint

Yellow Jasper

Rhyolite

G5, $12-$20
Lycoming Co., PA

G7, $30-$50
Lycoming Co., PA

G7, $35-$60
Luzurne Co., PA

G6, $33-$50
NJ

Yellow Jasper

Purple argilite

G3, $12-$20
Lycoming Co., PA

Argilite

G3, $15-$25
Lycoming Co., PA

G9, $100-$175
Dauphin Co., PA

G8, $90-$160
Paramus Woods, NJ

Slate

G8, $70-$130
PA

LOCATION: Northeastern states. **DESCRIPTION:** A medium size blade with a squared to tapered hafting area and a straight to concave base. Shoulders, when present are very weak and tapered. **I.D. KEY:** Basal form.

G9, $125-$200
Big Flats, NY

FROST ISLAND - Late Archaic - Early Woodland, 3200 - 2500 B.P.

(Also see Drybrook, Forest Notched, Orient, Patuxent, Perkiomen, Susquehanna Broad)

Black chert

G6, $15-$25
Lycoming Co., PA

Yellow Jasper

G6, $15-$25
Lycoming Co., PA

Yellow Jasper

G6, $15-$25
Centre Co., PA

Black chert

G6, $15-$30
Lycoming Co., PA

G7, $30-$50
Clinton Co., PA

Yellow Jasper

LOCATION: Northeastern states. **DESCRIPTION:** A medium to large size expanded stem point with rounded shoulders. Side notches are broader than the *Forest Notched* type. **I.D. KEY:** Long expanded base, rounded shoulders.

G9, $275-$500
Lycoming Co., PA

GARVER'S FERRY - Late Woodland, 1800 - 1300 B.P.

(Also see Crooked Creek, Dewart Stemmed, Lamoka, Merrimack, Neville, Wading River)

LOCATION: Northeastern states. **DESCRIPTION:** A small size dart point with a short stem that is slightly expanding. The base is straight. Some examples are corner notched. **I.D. KEY:** Basal form, early flaking. **I.D. KEY:** Expanded stem, small size.

Yellow Jasper

G6, $5-$10
Lycoming Co., PA.
Red Jasper.

GENESEE - Late Archaic, 5000 - 4000 B.P.

(Also see Bare Island, Neville, Newmanstown, and Piedmont)

Slate

G4, $15-$25
NY

G7, $25-$40
NY

G9, $250-$375
NY

G10, $275-$500
NY

G10, $350-$600
NY

Onondaga chert

G10, $275-$500
Lancaster Co., PA

LOCATION: Northeastern states. Named for the Genesee Valley located in New York state. **DESCRIPTION:** A medium to large size point with prominent shoulders, a thick cross section and a squarish base. Shoulders can be straight to tapered to slightly barbed. Basal area can be ground. **I.D. KEY:** Squarish stem, strong shoulders.

GODDARD - Mississippian, 1000 - 800 B.P.

(Also see Jacks Reef & Raccoon Notched)

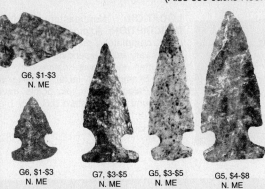

G6, $1-$3
N. ME

G6, $1-$3
N. ME

G7, $3-$5
N. ME

G5, $3-$5
N. ME

G5, $4-$8
N. ME

G7, $5-$10
N. ME

LOCATION: Northeastern states. Type site is located at Penobscot Bay, Maine. **DESCRIPTION:** A small to medium side, thin, narrow, side to corner notched point with a straight to convex base. Similar in style to *Jacks Reef Corner Notched* and *Raccoon Creek* points. Also similar to *Knight Island* points of the Southeast. A late Ceramic Period point. Some examples in the type area are made of high grade, colorful material that would be worth more. **I.D. KEY:** Thin, side notched point.

GRAVER - Paleo to Archaic, 11,500 - 4000 B.P.

(Also see Drill & Scraper)

LOCATION: Paleo and Archaic sites everywhere **DESCRIPTION:** An irregular shaped uniface tool with sharp, pointed projections used for puncturing, incising, tattooing, etc. Some examples served a dual purpose for scraping as well. In later times, *Perforators* took the place of *Gravers*.

Graver tips

All from the Shoop site, Dauphin Co., PA. Onondaga chert.

Graver tips

Graver tips

G7, $15-$30

G8, $20-$40

G8, $20-$40

GREENE - Middle to late Woodland, 1700 - 1200 B.P.

(Also see Agate Basin, Angostura, Mansion Inn, Ohio Lanceolate, Parallel Lanceolate & Varney)

Flint

Felsite

Flint

G6, $8-$15
Plymouth Co., MA

G6, $8-$15
Plymouth Co., MA

G6, $8-$15
Plymouth Co., MA

Felsite

Flint

G7, $15-$25
Plymouth Co., MA

G7, $20-$35
Plymouth Co., MA

Felsite

G7, $20-$35
Plymouth Co., MA

LOCATION: New York into Massachusetts and Connecticut. **DESCRIPTION:** A medium size, fairly broad lanceolate point with a tapering basal area and a straight base. Some examples form a pentagonal shape. **I.D. KEY:** Ovate to pentagonal form.

131

GROUND SLATE - Archaic, 6000 - 4500 B.P.

(Also see Bare Island)

LOCATION: Northeastern states. **DESCRIPTION:** A large size stemmed point completely ground from slate. Bases vary from expanding to contracting. Often found with notches in the stem. Examples of facial grinding of flaked Paleo and Archaic points have been found in the Eastern U.S.

G6, $125-$200
E. PA

GUILFORD - Middle Archaic, 6500 - 5000 B.P.

(Also see Agate Basin)

G6, $15-$25
MD

Guilford Yuma form

G8, $40-$75
NY

Round base form

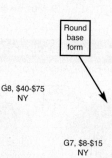

G7, $8-$15
NY

LOCATION: Eastern seaboard to Northeastern states. **DESCRIPTION:** A medium to large size, thick, narrow lanceolate point. The base varies from round to straight to eared. Another variation has weak shoulders defining a stemmed area. **I.D. KEY:** Thickness, early parallel flaking.

HARDAWAY - Early Archaic 9500 - 8000 B.P.

(Also see Dalton-Greenbrier and Palmer)

G7, $55-$100
Taunton, MA

Felsite

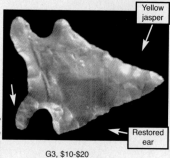

Yellow jasper

Restored ear

G3, $10-$20
Lycoming Co., PA

LOCATION: Eastern states. Type site is in Stanly Co., NC, Yadkin River. Very rare in Northeast. **DESCRIPTION:** A small to medium size point with shallow side notches and expanded auricles forming a wide, deeply concave base. Ears and base are usually ground. This type evolved from the *Dalton* point. **I.D. KEY:** Eared form, heavy grinding in shoulders, paleo parallel flaking.

132

HAW RIVER - Transitional Paleo, 11,000 - 8000 B.P.

LOCATION: Eastern seaboard to Northeastern states. **DESCRIPTION:** A medium to large size, broad, elliptical blade with a basal notch and usually rounded barbs that turn inward. **I.D. KEY:** Notched base.

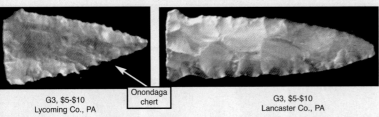

G8, $150-$250
NY

HELLGRAMITE - Early Woodland, 3000 - 2500 B.P.

(Also see Brewerton, Kessel, Kirk, Meadowood)

LOCATION: Northeastern states. **DESCRIPTION:** A small to medium size triangular point with very weak side notches. The blade edges are finely serrated and the base is straight to convex. **I.D. KEY:** Weak notches, serrated edges.

G3, $5-$10
Lycoming Co., PA

Onondaga chert

G3, $5-$10
Lancaster Co., PA

HI-LO - Late Paleo, 10,000 - 8,000 B.P.

(Also see Clovis, Crowfield, Cumberland, Dalton, Debert)

LOCATION: Western Pennsylvania into Michigan & N. Ohio. **DESCRIPTION:** A small to medium size, thin, auriculate point with a concave base. Basal area is ground. Most examples have basal thinning and are not fluted. Three forms known: convex sides, parallel sides and weak shoulders. **I.D. KEY:** Small fluted point.

Black/tan chert

Jasper

G6, $150-$250
Northumberland Co., PA

G7, $150-$250
Lancaster Co., PA

HOLCOMB - Paleo, 11,000 - 10,000 B.P.

(Also see Clovis, Crowfield, Cumberland, Dalton, Debert)

LOCATION: Northeastern states. **DESCRIPTION:** A small to medium size, thin, fluted point with a concave base. Basal area is ground. More than one fluting strike is common. **I.D. KEY:** Small fluted point.

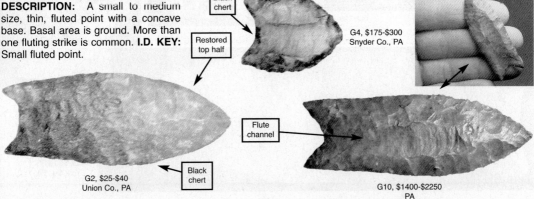

Black chert

Restored top half

G4, $175-$300
Snyder Co., PA

Flute channel

G2, $25-$40
Union Co., PA

Black chert

G10, $1400-$2250
PA

HOLCOMB (continued)

Jasper

Restored tip

Jasper

Jasper

Restored top half

Jasper

Not fluted

G2, $25-$40
Chester Co., PA

G2, $15-$30
Snyder Co., PA

G2, $25-$40
Lycoming Co., PA

Clovis/Holcomb cross type

G9, $2000-$3000
Gibson Co., IN

HOOVER'S ISLAND - Archaic, 6000 - 4000 B.P.

(Also see Bare Island, Duncan's Island, Genesee, Lackawaxen, Newmanstown, Patuxent, Piedmont, Piney Island)

Classic form

Yellow jasper

G6, $15-$25
Northumberland Co., PA

G6, $25-$40
Northumberland Co., PA

G8, $35-$65
Northumberland Co., PA

G9, $90-$175
York Co., PA

G9, $90-$175
York Co., PA

HOOVER'S ISLAND (continued)

LOCATION: Pennsylvania to northern Maryland. **DESCRIPTION:** A medium to large size, broad, expanded to parallel stemmed point. Bases are straight to concave. Basal corners are sharp. Shoulders are tapered to rounded. **I.D. KEY:** Sharp basal corners, tapered shoulders. Belongs to the Piedmont series and is also known as *Southern Piedmont.*

HOPEWELL - Woodland, 2500 - 1500 B.P.

(Also see Brewerton, Normanskill)

Preform

G6, $15-$30
PA

G5, $25-$40
PA

LOCATION: Midwestern to eastern states. **DESCRIPTION:** A large size, broad, corner notched point that is similar to *Snyders.* Made by the Hopewell culture.

JACKS REEF CORNER NOTCHED - Late Woodland to Mississippian, 1500 - 1000 B.P.

(Also see Kiski, Lycoming Co., Oley, Palmer, Raccoon Notched, Vosburg)

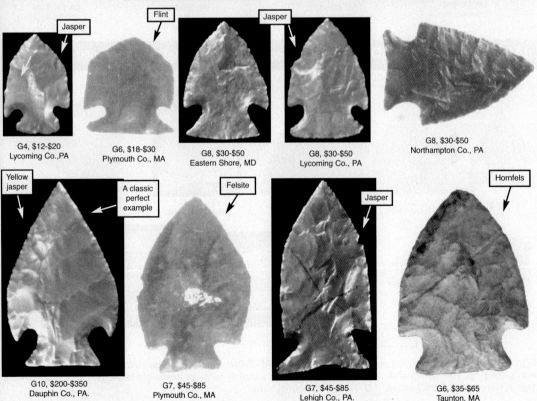

Jasper

Flint

Jasper

G4, $12-$20
Lycoming Co.,PA

G6, $18-$30
Plymouth Co., MA

G8, $30-$50
Eastern Shore, MD

G8, $30-$50
Lycoming Co., PA

G8, $30-$50
Northampton Co., PA

Yellow jasper

A classic perfect example

Felsite

Jasper

Hornfels

G10, $200-$350
Dauphin Co., PA.

G7, $45-$85
Plymouth Co., MA

G7, $45-$85
Lehigh Co., PA.

G6, $35-$65
Taunton, MA

LOCATION: Southeastern to Northeastern states. **DESCRIPTION:** A small to medium size, very thin, corner notched point that is well made. The blade is convex to pentagonal. Some examples are widely corner notched and appear to be expanded stem points with barbed shoulders. **I.D. KEY:** Thinness, sharp corners.

JACKS REEF CORNER NOTCHED (continued)

G6, $25-$45
Lycoming Co., PA

G5, $20-$35
Union Co., Pa

G6, $25-$45
Lycoming Co., PA

Pentagonal form

Jasper

G6, $30-$50
Union Co.,PA

G9, $125-$225
Ripley, NY

G7, $65-$125
NJ

G8, $80-$150
Lycoming Co.,PA

JACKS REEF PENTAGONAL - Late Woodland to Mississippian, 1500 - 1000 B.P.

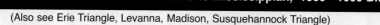

(Also see Erie Triangle, Levanna, Madison, Susquehannock Triangle)

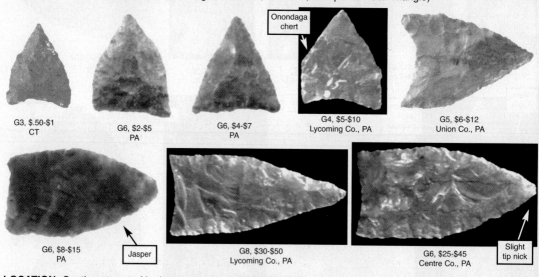

G3, $.50-$1
CT

G6, $2-$5
PA

G6, $4-$7
PA

Onondaga chert

G4, $5-$10
Lycoming Co., PA

G5, $6-$12
Union Co., PA

G6, $8-$15
PA

Jasper

G8, $30-$50
Lycoming Co., PA

G6, $25-$45
Centre Co., PA

Slight tip nick

LOCATION: Southeastern to Northeastern states. **DESCRIPTION:** A small to large size, very thin, five sided point with a sharp tip. The hafting area is usually contracted with a slightly concave to straight base. This type is called *Pee Dee* in North and South Carolina. **I.D. KEY:** Pentagonal form.

JIM THORPE - Archaic, 6000 - 4000 B.P.

(Also see Brodhead and Piedmont)

LOCATION: Pennsylvania. **DESCRIPTION:** A medium size, side notched point with tapered to square shoulders and a bulbous stem. The base is convex and the side notches are broad. Random flaking was employed. **I.D. KEY:** Bulbous stem.

G6, $25-$40
PA

KANAWHA - Early Archaic, 9000 - 5000 B.P.

(Also see Kirk Serrated, Lake Erie, LeCroy, MacCorkle, St. Albans, Stanly, Susquehanna Birfurcate)

LOCATION: Southeastern to Northeastern states. Type site is in Kanawha Co., WVA. **DESCRIPTION:** A small to medium size, fairly thick, shallowly bifurcated stemmed point. The basal lobes are usually rounded and the shoulders are tapered. Believed to be the ancestor to the *Stanly* type. Very similar to the *Fox Valley* point found in Illinois. Shoulders can be clipped wing, turning towards the tip. **I.D. KEY:** Archaic flaking, weak basal lobes.

G5, $12-$20
Union Co., PA

G6, $18-$30
Chester Co., PA

KESSEL - Early Archaic, 10,000 - 8000 B.P.

(Also see Cache River, Goddard, Hellgramite, Meadowood, Raccoon Notched)

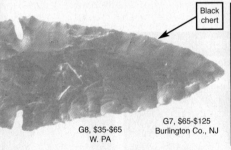

Black chert

G8, $35-$65
W. PA

G7, $65-$125
Burlington Co., NJ

LOCATION: Northeastern states. **DESCRIPTION:** A medium to large size, thin, triangular side notched point. Notches are close to the base, are very narrow and angle in from the sides. The base is concave. Almost identical in form and age to the *Cache River* type from Arkansas. **I.D. KEY:** Basal notches, thinness.

KIRK CORNER NOTCHED - Early to mid-Archaic, 9000 - 6000 B.P.

(Also see Amos, Brewerton, Charleston Pine Tree, Crooked Creek, Kline & Palmer)

Barb nick

Onondaga chert

G2, $3-$5
Montgomery Co., PA

G2, $3-$5
Lycoming Co., PA

G2, $3-$5
Lycoming Co., PA

KIRK CORNER NOTCHED (continued)

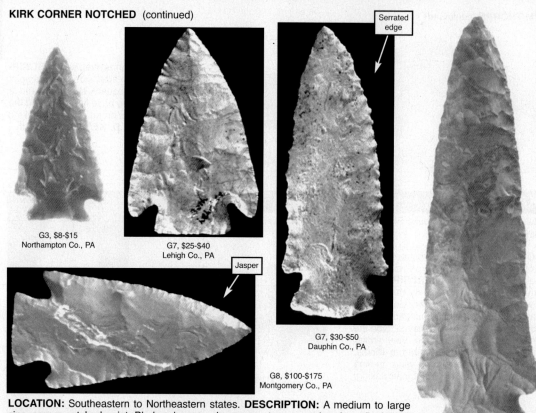

G3, $8-$15
Northampton Co., PA

G7, $25-$40
Lehigh Co., PA

Jasper

G8, $100-$175
Montgomery Co., PA

Serrated edge

G7, $30-$50
Dauphin Co., PA

G6, $65-$125
Northumberland Co., PA

LOCATION: Southeastern to Northeastern states. **DESCRIPTION:** A medium to large size, corner notched point. Blade edges can be convex to recurved and are finely serrated on many examples. The base can be convex, concave, straight, bifurcated or auriculate. Points that are beveled on one side of each face would fall under the *Lost Lake* or *Hardin* type. **I.D. KEY:** Secondary edgework.

KIRK STEMMED - Early to mid-Archaic, 9000 - 6000 B.P.

(Also see Bare Island, Duncan's Island, Fountain Creek, Genesee, Heavy Duty, Lackawaxen, Neville, Newmanstown)

G3, $2-$5
Lycoming Co., PA

Vein quartz

Jasper

Onandaga chert

Restored

Slate

G3, $2-$5
Lycoming Co., PA

G3, $2-$5
Luzurne Co., PA

G5, $8-$15
MD

G6, $8-$15
Lycoming Co., PA

G6, $5-$10
Northumberland Co., PA

LOCATION: Eastern states. **DESCRIPTION:** A medium to large size, barbed, stemmed point with deep notches or fine serrations along the blade edges. The stem is parallel, contracting or expanding. The base can be concave, convex or straight, and can be very short. The shoulders are usually strongly barbed. This form is believed to have evolved into *Stanly* and other types. **I.D. KEY:** Serrations.

KIRK STEMMED (continued)

G9, $150-$250
Northumberland Co., PA

KISKI NOTCHED - Late Woodland, 2000 - 1400 B.P.

(Also see Brewerton, Crooked Creek, Jacks Reef, Lycoming Co., Palmer)

Gray chert

White Flint Ridge flint

G6, $5-$10
Crawford Co., PA

LOCATION: Northeastern states. **DESCRIPTION:** A small size side or corner notched point. **I.D. KEY:** Notching and size.

G6, $5-$10
Crawford Co., PA

KITTATINY - Middle Archaic, 6000 - 5000 B.P.

(Also see Brewerton Eared, Jacks Reef Pentagonal, Levanna)

LOCATION: Northeastern states. **DESCRIPTION:** A small size lanceolate blade with recurved side edges. The base is straight, with the corners forming tiny ears. The stem is square to expanding. The *Nolichucky* type found in the Southeast is similar in outline. **I.D. KEY:** Triangular and basal form.

Yellow jasper

G5, $5-$10
Lycoming Co., PA

KLINE - Early Archaic, 9000 - 7000 B.P.

(Also see Brodhead Side Notched, Kirk, Lycoming Co., St. Charles, Susquehanna Broad)

Restored tip

Note early archaic parallel flaking

LOCATION: Northeastern states. **DESCRIPTION:** A medium to large size corner notched point with a convex base that is ground. Shoulders are strong and are horizontal to slightly barbed. Basal corners are rounded. **I.D. KEY:** Corner notching, early flaking.

G3, $8-$15
Lycoming Co., PA

G2, $15-$25
Lycoming Co., PA

KOENS CRISPIN - Late Archaic, 4000 - 3000 B.P.

(Also see Adena, Atlantic Phase Blade, Lehigh, Morrow Mountain, Poplar Island, Schuylkill, Virginsville)

Quartzite

LOCATION: Northeastern states. **DESCRIPTION:** A medium to large size, broad, contracted stem point with a rounded base. Shoulders are tapered to straight. Generally poorer quality than the *Lehigh* type. **I.D. KEY:** Contracted stem, strong shoulders.

G9, $300-$550
Carbon Co., PA

Jasper

G7, $200-$350
Lancaster Co., PA

G7, $65-$125
Lancaster Co., PA

G10, $350-$650
Lehigh Co., PA

LACKAWAXEN - Archaic, 6000 - 4000 B.P.

(Also see Bare Island, Duncan's Island, Neville, Piedmont, Tocks Island)

LOCATION: Northeastern states. **DESCRIPTION:** A medium to large size, narrow, expanded to contracting to parallel stemmed point with strong, tapered shoulders. **I.D. KEY:** Long, narrow stemmed point.

G6, $65-$125
Northampton Co., PA

G5, $15-$25
Northampton Co., PA

Minor
tip damage

LAKE ERIE - Early to mid-Archaic, 9000 - 5000 B.P.

(Also see Erie Triangle, Fox Valley, Kirk-Bifurcated, LeCroy, MacCorkle, Penn's Creek, St. Albans, Stanly, Susquehanna Bifurcate)

LOCATION: Northeastern states. **DESCRIPTION:** A small to medium size, thin, deeply notched or bifurcated stemmed point. The basal lobes are parallel with a tendency to turn inward and are pointed. The outward sides of the basal lobes are usually fractured from the base towards the tip and can be ground. **I.D. KEY:** Pointed basal lobes.

LAKE ERIE (continued)

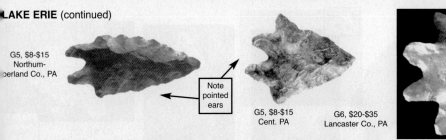

G5, $8-$15
Northum-
berland Co., PA

Note
pointed
ears

G5, $8-$15
Cent. PA

G6, $20-$35
Lancaster Co., PA

LAMOKA - Middle Archaic, 5500 - 4500 B.P.

(Also see Dewart Stemmed, Duncan's Island, Garver's Ferry, Merrimack, Neville, Piney Island, Randolph, Sandhill Stemmed, Wading River)

G4, $2-$4
Lycoming Co. PA

G5, $2-$5
Lycoming Co. PA

G5, $3-$6
Lycoming Co. PA

G8, $8-$15
Monroe Co. PA

Black
chert

G6, $6-$12
Lycoming Co. PA

G6, $6-$12
PA

G8, $12-$20
Columbia Co., NY

G8, $12-$20
Columbia Co., NY

G8, $12-$20
Columbia Co., NY

G6, $15-$25
Columbia Co., NY

G8, $15-$25
Lycoming Co. PA

G6, $15-$25
Lycoming Co., PA

G8, $20-$35
Lycoming Co., PA

G8, $20-$35
Monore Co., PA

LOCATION: Northeastern states. **DESCRIPTION:** A small to medium size, narrow, thick, spike point. The shoulders are tapered and the stem is square to contracting to expanding. The base on some examples shows the natural rind of the native material used. Called *Bradley Spike* in the Southeast. **I.D. KEY:** Thin, spike point.

LECROY - Early to mid-Archaic, 9000 - 5000 B.P.

(Also see Decatur, Kanawha, Kirk Serrated, Lake Erie, MacCorkle, Charleston Pine Tree, St. Albans, Stanly, Susquehanna Bifurcate & Taunton River Bifurcate)

Resharpened
many times

G9, $12-$20
Union Co., PA

G6, $8-$15
Centre Co., PA

G6, $12-$20
Lycoming Co., PA

G6, $12-$20
Northumb. Co., PA

G6, $12-$20
Lycoming Co., PA

G6, $12-$20
Union Co., PA

LECROY (continued)

G3, $4-$8
Union Co., PA

G5, $8-$15
Northumberland Co., PA

Serrated edge

G7, $15-$25
Union Co., PA

G6, $5-$15
Lycoming Co., PA

G9, $15-$25
Lancaster Co., PA

Serrated edge

Milky quartz

Serrated edge

Yellow jasper

Vein quartz

G6, $15-$25
Berks Co., PA

G8, $15-$30
Union Co., PA

G9, $20-$35
MD

G8, $15-$25
Lancaster Co., PA

G9, $20-$35
Union Co., PA

LOCATION: Eastern states. Type site is in Hamilton Co., Tennessee. **DESCRIPTION:** A small to medium size, thin, bifurcated point with deeply notched or serrated blade edges. Basal ears can either droop or expand out. The base is usually large in comparison to the blade size. Bases can be ground. **I.D. KEY:** Basal form, thinness.

LEHIGH BROADPOINT - Late Archaic, 4000 - 3000 B.P.

(Also see Adena, Koens Crispin, Morrow Mountain, Poplar Island, Schuylkill, Virginsville)

G5, $15-$25
Northampton Co., PA

Yellow jasper

G5, $25-$40
Northampton Co., PA

Yellow jasper

Yellow jasper

Yellow jasper

Made into a scraper

G65, $40-$70
Northampton Co., PA

G7, $80-$150
Luzurne Co., PA

G5, $12-$20
Northampton Co., PA

LOCATION: Northeastern states. **DESCRIPTION:** A medium to large size, broad, contracted to square stemmed point. Shoulders are horizontal to contracting. The base is straight to rounded. **I.D. KEY:** Broad, contracting stem.

142

Speckled
rhyolite

G9, $125-$225
Burlington Co., NJ

G9, $175-$300
Lancaster Co., PA

LEVANNA - Late Woodland to Mississippian, 1300 - 600 B.P.

(Also see Madison, Susquehannock Triangle)

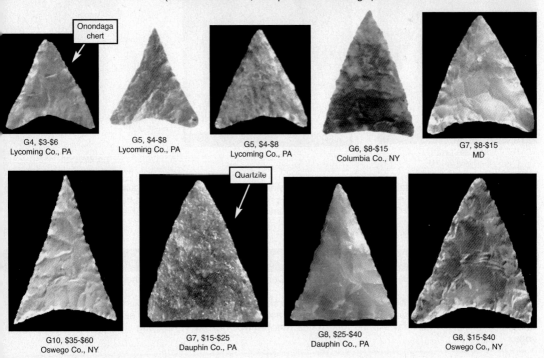

Onondaga
chert

G4, $3-$6
Lycoming Co., PA

G5, $4-$8
Lycoming Co., PA

G5, $4-$8
Lycoming Co., PA

G6, $8-$15
Columbia Co., NY

G7, $8-$15
MD

G10, $35-$60
Oswego Co., NY

Quartzite

G7, $15-$25
Dauphin Co., PA

G8, $25-$40
Dauphin Co., PA

G8, $15-$40
Oswego Co., NY

LEVANNA (continued)

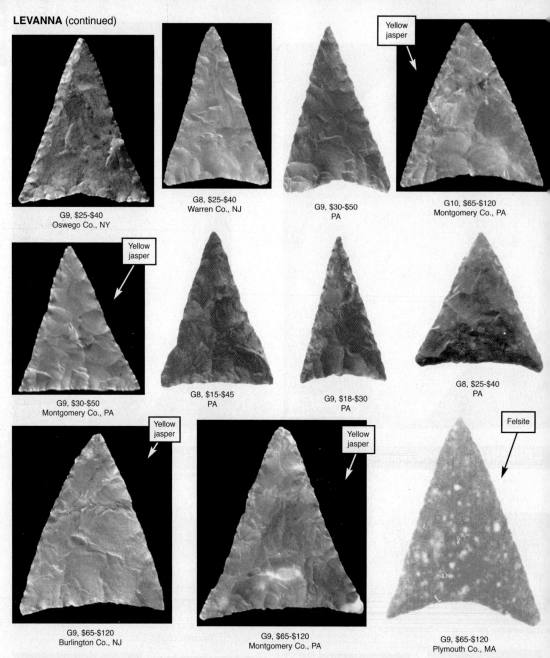

G9, $25-$40
Oswego Co., NY

G8, $25-$40
Warren Co., NJ

G9, $30-$50
PA

Yellow jasper

G10, $65-$120
Montgomery Co., PA

Yellow jasper

G9, $30-$50
Montgomery Co., PA

G8, $15-$45
PA

G9, $18-$30
PA

G8, $25-$40
PA

Yellow jasper

G9, $65-$120
Burlington Co., NJ

Yellow jasper

G9, $65-$120
Montgomery Co., PA

Felsite

G9, $65-$120
Plymouth Co., MA

LOCATION: Northeastern states. **DESCRIPTION:** A small to medium size, thin, triangular point with a concave to straight base. Believed to be replaced by *Madison* points in later times. Some examples have the basal corners fractured. Called *Yadkin* in North Carolina. **I.D. KEY:** Medium thick cross section triangle.

LOST LAKE - Early Archaic, 9000 - 6000 B.P.

(Also see Charleston Pine Tree, Decatur, Kirk, St. Charles and Thebes)

LOCATION: Southeastern, Midwestern to Northeastern states. **DESCRIPTION:** A medium to large size, broad, corner notched point that is beveled on one side of each face. Some examples are finely serrated. Bases are ground. Unbeveled examples would fall into the *Kirk Corner Notched* type. **I.D. KEY:** Notching and opposite beveled blade edge.

LOST LAKE(continued)

G8, $350-$650
NJ

LYCOMING COUNTY SERIES - Middle Archaic, 6000 - 4000 B.P.

(Also see Brewerton, Chillesquaque Series, Crooked Creek, Garver's Ferry, Otter Creek, Penn's Creek)

LOCATION: Pennsylvania. **DESCRIPTION:** Local variations of the Laurentian Archaic. Includes side notched, corner notched, basal notched & stemmed varieties.

Tip nick

G3, $4-$8
Lycoming Co., PA

Jasper

MacCORKLE - Early Archaic, 8000 - 6000 B.P.

(Also see Kanawha, Kirk Serrated, Lake Erie, LeCroy, St. Albans, Stanly, Susquehanna Bifurcate)

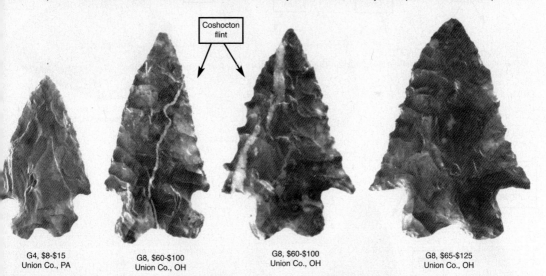

Coshocton
flint

G4, $8-$15
Union Co., PA

G8, $60-$100
Union Co., OH

G8, $60-$100
Union Co., OH

G8, $65-$125
Union Co., OH

LOCATION: Midwestern to Eastern states. **DESCRIPTION:** A medium to large size, thin, usually serrated, widely corner notched point with large round ears and a deep notch in the center of the base. Bases are usually ground. Called *Nottoway River Bifurcate* in Virginia. **I.D. KEY:** Basal notching, early Archaic flaking.

MADISON - Mississippian, 1100 - 200 B.P.

(Also see Jacks Reef, Levanna, Squibnocket Triangle, Susquehannock triangle)

LOCATION: Midwestern to Eastern states. Type site is in Madison Co., IL. Found at Cahokia Mounds (un-notched Cahokias). Used by the Kaskaskia tribe into the 1700s. **DESCRIPTION:** A small to medium size, thin, triangular point with usually straight sides and base. Some examples are notched on two to three sides. Many are of high quality and some are finely serrated. **I.D. KEY:** Thin triangle.

MADISON (continued)

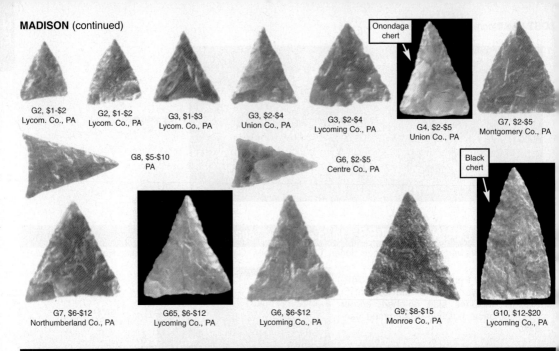

G2, $1-$2
Lycom. Co., PA

G2, $1-$2
Lycom. Co., PA

G3, $1-$3
Lycom. Co., PA

G3, $2-$4
Union Co., PA

G3, $2-$4
Lycoming Co., PA

Onondaga chert

G4, $2-$5
Union Co., PA

G7, $2-$5
Montgomery Co., PA

G8, $5-$10
PA

G6, $2-$5
Centre Co., PA

Black chert

G7, $6-$12
Northumberland Co., PA

G65, $6-$12
Lycoming Co., PA

G6, $6-$12
Lycoming Co., PA

G9, $8-$15
Monroe Co., PA

G10, $12-$20
Lycoming Co., PA

MANSION INN BLADE - Early Woodland, 3700 - 2700 B.P.

(Also see Koens Crispin, Greene, Lehigh, Morrow Mountain, Schuylkill, Virginsville, Wayland Notched & Web Blade)

Felsite

Dudley form

Dudley form

Felsite

Purple felsite

G6, $25-$40
Brodgewater Co., MA

G5, $15-$25
Plymouth Co., MA

G5, $15-$25
Plymouth Co., MA

G6, $25-$40
Plymouth Co., MA

G6, $25-$40
Plymouth Co., MA

IMPORTANT:
All Mansion Inn's shown half size

Watertown form

Argillite

Felsite

Watertown form

Classic form

G9, $250-$450
MA

G8, $175-$300
Burlington Co., NJ

G8, $250-$400
Plymouth Co., MA

G9, $275-$500
Plymouth Co., MA

146

MANSION INN BLADE (continued)

IMPORTANT: All Mansion Inn's shown half size

Watertown form

Watertown form

Coburn form

Felsite

G8, $200-$350
Easter Showe, MD

G9, $250-$500
Eastern NY

G8, $250-$450
Plymouth Co., MA

G9, $300-$550
Bridgewater, MA

LOCATION: Maine southward into New Jersey. Type site is in Massachusetts. **DESCRIPTION:** A medium to large size, broad, blade with a short, contracting stem. Believed to be preforms related to the *Perkiomen* and *Susquehanna* types. Three forms have been identified: Coburn, Dudley and Watertown. **I.D. KEY:** Size and base form.

MEADOWOOD - Late Archaic to early Woodland, 4000 - 2500 B.P.

(Also see Kessel, Otter Creek, Wapanucket)

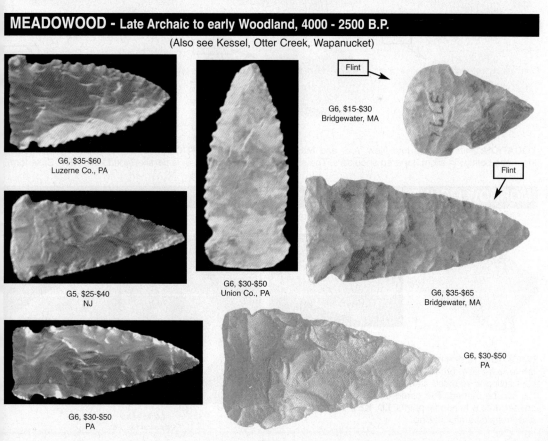

Flint

G6, $15-$30
Bridgewater, MA

Flint

G6, $35-$60
Luzerne Co., PA

G5, $25-$40
NJ

G6, $30-$50
Union Co., PA

G6, $35-$65
Bridgewater, MA

G6, $30-$50
PA

G6, $30-$50
PA

147

MEADOWOOD (continued)

LOCATION: Northeastern states. **DESCRIPTION:** A medium to large size point with shallow side notches near the base. The base can be straight to slightly convex. Blade edges can be straight to slightly convex to recurved. Some specimens show a lot of reworking and may be used up and asymmetrical.

G5, $65-$125
NY

G8, $80-$150
NY

MERRIMACK STEMMED - Mid-Archaic, 6000 - 5000 B.P.

(Also see Dewart Stemmed, Lamoka, Taconic Stemmed, Wading River)

Felsite

G4, $3-$5
Plymouth Co., MA

Felsite

G6, $5-$10
Plymouth Co., MA

Felsite

Felsite

G6, $5-$10
Plymouth Co., MA

Felsite

G4, $3-$5
Plymouth Co., MA

Quartzite

G6, $8-$15
Plymouth Co., MA

G6, $8-$15
Plymouth Co., MA

LOCATION: Pennsylvania into New York and Massachusetts. **DESCRIPTION:** A small to medium size, narrow, stemmed point with slight, tapered shoulders. The stem expands, contracts or is parallel sided. **I.D. KEY:** Base form.

MORROW MOUNTAIN - Mid-Archaic, 7000 - 5000 B.P.

(Also see Koens Crispin, Lehigh, Piscataway, Poplar Island, Stark, Swatara/Long, Virginsville)

Jasper

Quartzite

G4, $8-$15
PA

G4, $8-$15
PA

LOCATION: Northeastern states. **DESCRIPTION:** A medium to large size, broad, triangular point with a very short, contracting to rounded stem. Shoulders are usually weak but can be barbed. The blade edges on some examples are serrated with needle points. **I.D. KEY:** Contracted base and Archaic parallel flaking.

G6, $25-$40
Lancaster Co., PA

MORROW MOUNTAIN (continued)

G5, $15-$30
PA

Quartzite

G5, $15-$30
Lancaster Co., PA

G7, $80-$150
Northampton Co., PA

MUNCY BIFURCATE - Archaic, 8500 - 7000 B.P.

(Also see Fox Valley, Kanawha, Neville and Stanly)

Rhyolite

LOCATION: North eastern states. **DESCRIPTION:** A small to medium point with prominent shoulders and a contracting to parallel sided stem. The Base has a shallow notch. Possibly related to *Neville.* **I.D. KEY:** Base form.

G6, $5-$10
Lycoming Co., PA

G4, $3-$6
Lycoming Co., PA

G5, $4-$8
Union Co., PA

NEVILLE - Archaic, 7000 - 6000 B.P.

(Also see Adena Robbins, Bare Island, Duncan's Island, Genesee, Merrimack, Muncy Bifurcate, Newmanstown, Snook Kill, Stark)

Jasper

Felsite

G7, $15-$25
Chester Co., PA

G7, $15-$25
Plymouth Co., MA

G6, $15-$25
PA

LOCATION: Northeastern states. **DESCRIPTION:** A medium size, triangular point with barbed to horizontal shoulders and a short, square to contracting stem. **I.D. KEY:** Stem form.

149

NEVILLE (continued)

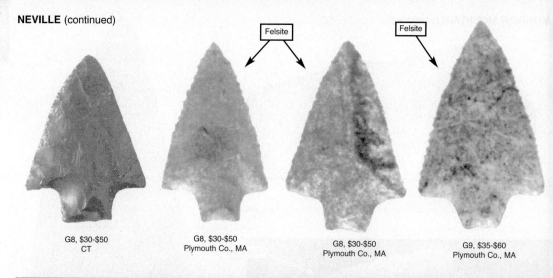

G8, $30-$50
CT

G8, $30-$50
Plymouth Co., MA

G8, $30-$50
Plymouth Co., MA

G9, $35-$60
Plymouth Co., MA

NEWMANSTOWN - Archaic, 7000 - 5000 B.P.

(Also see Bare Island, Duncan's Island, Lackawaxen, Neville, Piedmont, Taconic Stemmed, Tocks Island)

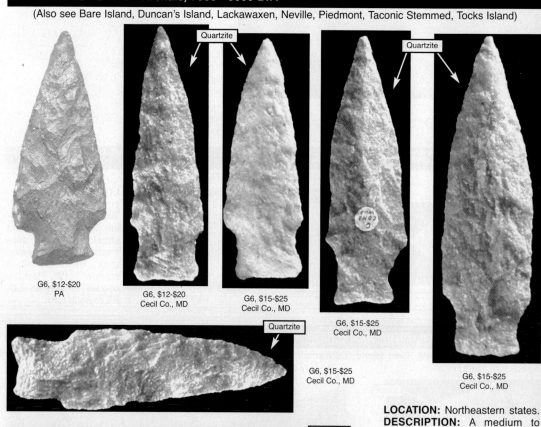

G6, $12-$20
PA

G6, $12-$20
Cecil Co., MD

G6, $15-$25
Cecil Co., MD

G6, $15-$25
Cecil Co., MD

G6, $15-$25
Cecil Co., MD

G6, $15-$25
Cecil Co., MD

G7, $25-$40
Luzurne Co., PA

LOCATION: Northeastern states.
DESCRIPTION: A medium to large size, narrow, stemmed point with a sharp tip and a short, expanding base.

150

NORMANSKILL - Late Archaic to early Woodland, 4000 - 2500 B.P.

(Also see Brewerton Corner Notched, Drybrook, Meadowood, Orient, Susquehanna Broad, Tocks Island)

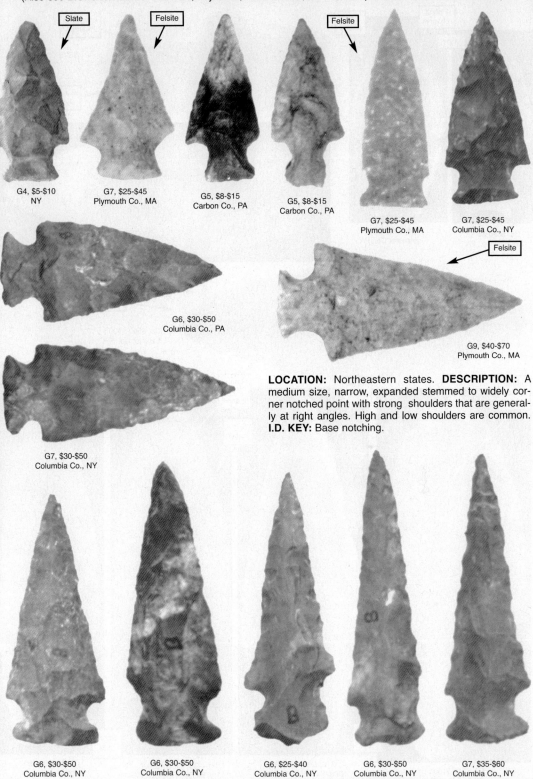

Slate

Felsite

Felsite

Felsite

G4, $5-$10
NY

G7, $25-$45
Plymouth Co., MA

G5, $8-$15
Carbon Co., PA

G5, $8-$15
Carbon Co., PA

G7, $25-$45
Plymouth Co., MA

G7, $25-$45
Columbia Co., NY

G6, $30-$50
Columbia Co., PA

G9, $40-$70
Plymouth Co., MA

G7, $30-$50
Columbia Co., NY

LOCATION: Northeastern states. **DESCRIPTION:** A medium size, narrow, expanded stemmed to widely corner notched point with strong shoulders that are generally at right angles. High and low shoulders are common. **I.D. KEY:** Base notching.

G6, $30-$50
Columbia Co., NY

G6, $30-$50
Columbia Co., NY

G6, $25-$40
Columbia Co., NY

G6, $30-$50
Columbia Co., NY

G7, $35-$60
Columbia Co., NY

NORTHUMBERLAND - Paleo, 11,250 - 10,000 B. P.

(Also see Clovis, Crowfield, Cumberland, Debert, Holcomb)

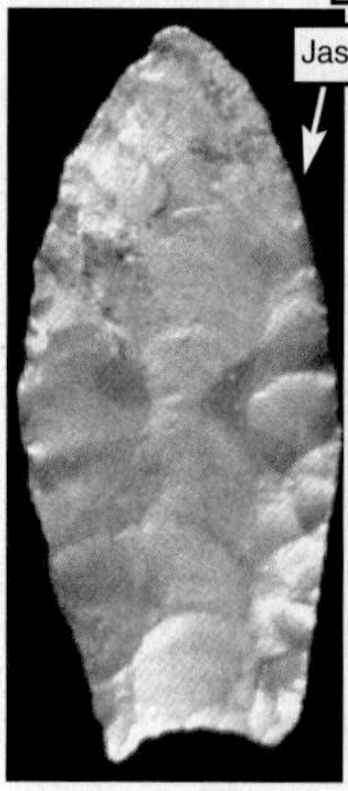

Jasper

G6, $350-$600
Dauphin Co., PA

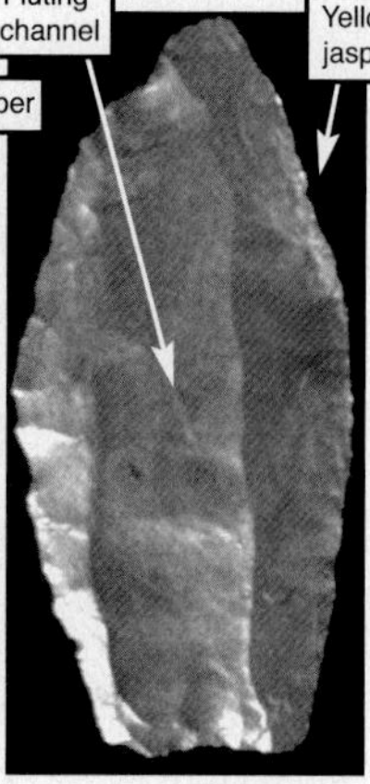

Fluting channel
Yellow jasper

G4, $300-$500
Lancaster Co., PA

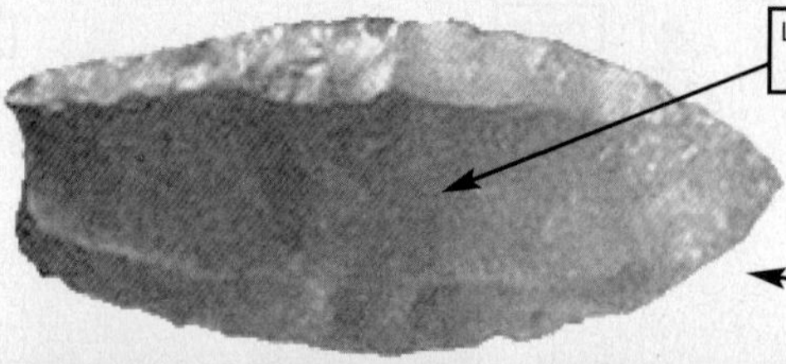

Long flute channel
Black chert

G5, $800-$1500
PA

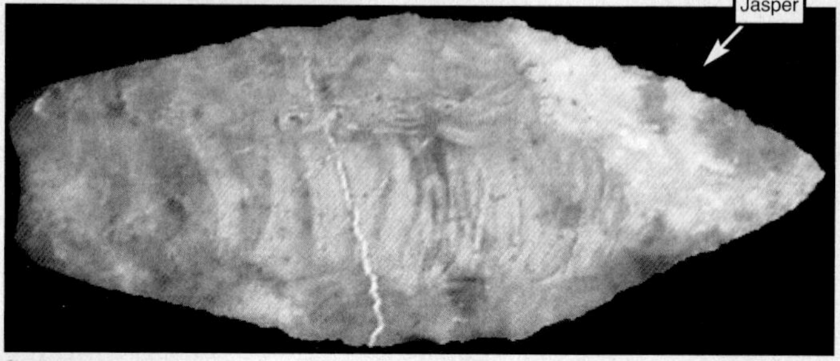

Jasper

G5, $1500-$2500
Indiana Co., PA

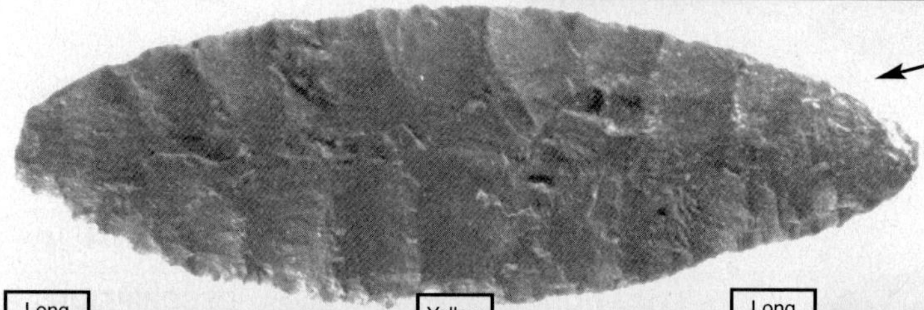

Collateral flaking
Not fluted

G8, $500-$900
Lancaster Co., PA

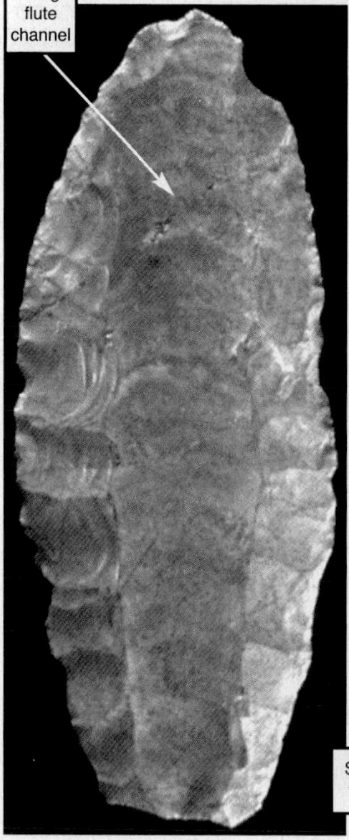

Long flute channel

G6, $800-$1500
Bedford Co., PA

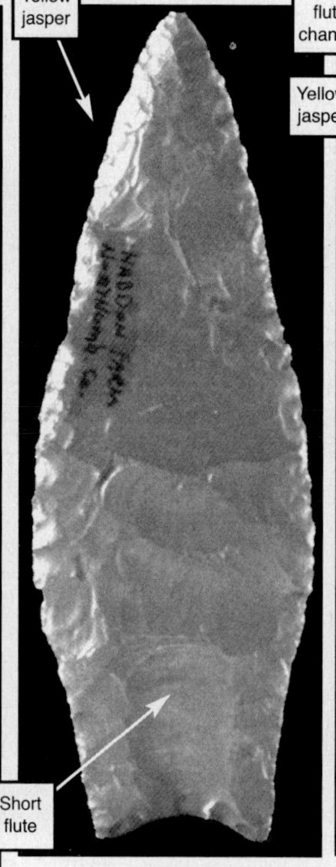

Yellow jasper
Short flute

G10, $2500-$4500
Northumberland Co., PA

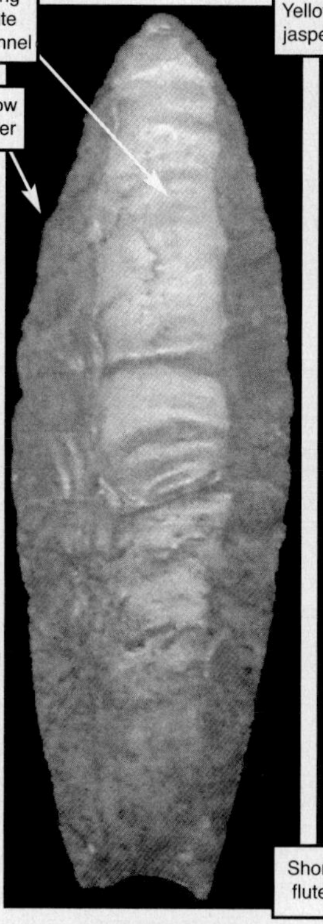

Long flute channel
Yellow jasper

G9, $2000-$3800
Montgomery Co., PA

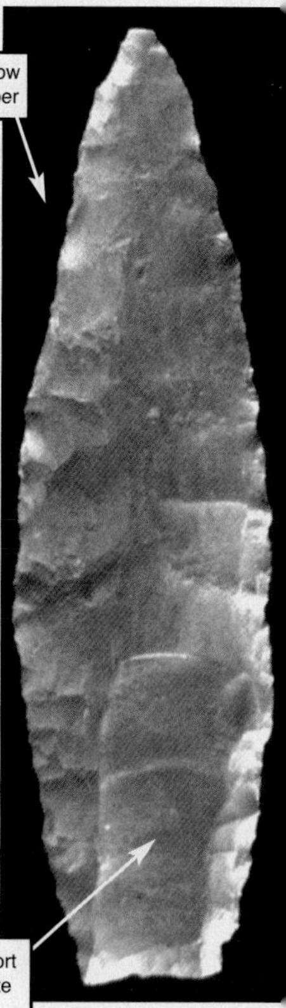

Yellow jasper
Short flute

G5, $1000-$1800
Schuylkill Co., PA

NORTHUMBERLAND (continued)

LOCATION: Northeastern states. **DESCRIPTION:** A medium to large size, lanceolate form that is usually fluted on one side only. Fluting usually extends to the tip. **I.D. KEY:** Paleo flaking, indirect pressure fluted.

Jasper

Not fluted

G6, $250-$450
Montgomery Co., PA

Fluting channel

G6, $800-$1500
Northumberland Co., PA

OHIO LANCEOLATE - Late Paleo, 10,500 - 7000 B.P.

(Also see Angostura, Clovis, Dalton, Cumberland, Parallel Lanceolate & Varney)

Flint Ridge flint

Blue/white Upper Mercer chert

Blue/black Upper Mercer chert

G9, $25-$45
PA

LOCATION: Ohio into W. Pennsylvania. **DESCRIPTION:** A medium to large size lanceolate point with parallel to convex sides and a concave base that is ground. Flaking is early collateral to oblique transverse. Base has light grinding, not fluted or basally thinned. Thinner than *Clovis* or *Agate Basin*. **I.D. KEY:** Base form and parallel flaking.

Waisted

Light Gray/brown Coshocton chert

Waisted

G6, $30-$55
PA

G10 $35-$65
PA

Stemmed/ shouldered

G5, $25-$45
PA

Narrowing stem

G7, $25-$45
PA

G6, $20-$35
PA

Upper Mercer chert

153

OLEY - Woodland, 2200 - 1500 B. P.

(Also see Charleston Pine Tree, Erb Basal Notched, Eshbach, Vestal Notched)

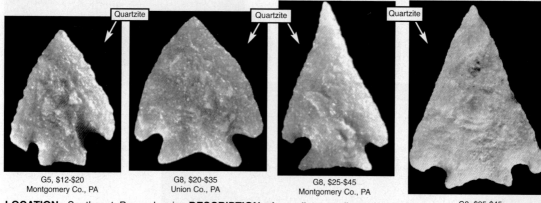

G5, $12-$20
Montgomery Co., PA

G8, $20-$35
Union Co., PA

G8, $25-$45
Montgomery Co., PA

G8, $25-$45
Lancaster Co., PA

LOCATION: Southeast Pennsylvania. **DESCRIPTION:** A small to medium size corner notched barbed point with an expanding base. Blade edges are concave to recurved. Base is concave. **I.D. KEY:** Base form and barbs.

ORIENT FISHTAIL - Late Archaic to Woodland, 4000 - 2500 B. P.

(Also see Drybrook, Forest Notched, Frost Island, Susquehanna Broad, Perkiomen & Taconic Stemmed)

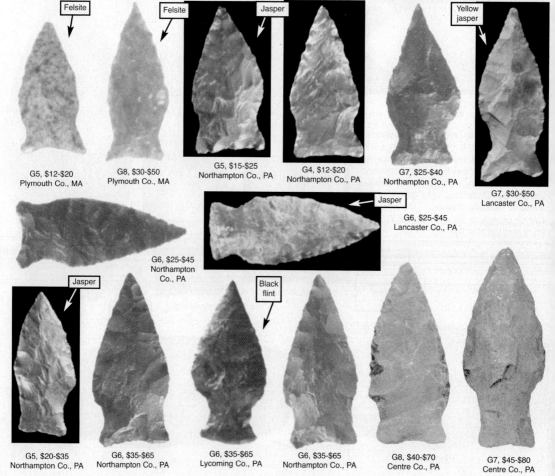

G5, $12-$20
Plymouth Co., MA

G8, $30-$50
Plymouth Co., MA

G5, $15-$25
Northampton Co., PA

G4, $12-$20
Northampton Co., PA

G7, $25-$40
Northampton Co., PA

G7, $30-$50
Lancaster Co., PA

G6, $25-$45
Northampton Co., PA

G6, $25-$45
Lancaster Co., PA

G5, $20-$35
Northampton Co., PA

G6, $35-$65
Northampton Co., PA

G6, $35-$65
Lycoming Co., PA

G6, $35-$65
Northampton Co., PA

G8, $40-$70
Centre Co., PA

G7, $45-$80
Centre Co., PA

154

ORIENT FISHTAIL(continued)

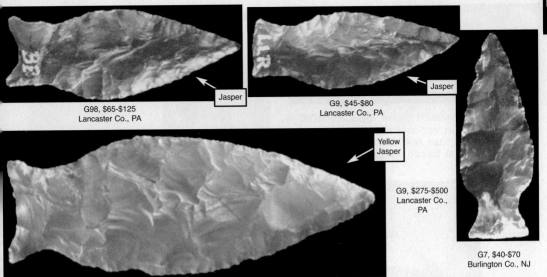

G98, $65-$125
Lancaster Co., PA

Jasper

G9, $45-$80
Lancaster Co., PA

Jasper

Yellow
Jasper

G9, $275-$500
Lancaster Co.,
PA

G7, $40-$70
Burlington Co., NJ

LOCATION: Northeastern states. **DESCRIPTION:** A small to medium size point with broad side notches, rounded shoulders and an expanding base. The base on some examples form auricles. **I.D. KEY:** Base form and rounded shoulders.

OTTER CREEK - Mid to late Archaic, 5000 - 3500 B.P.

(Also see Brewerton Side Notched, Goddard, Perkiomen, Raccoon Notched, Susquehanna Broad)

Onondaga
chert

G5, $8-$15
Lycoming Co., PA

G5, $12-$20
Lycoming Co., PA

G5, $12-$20
Washingtonboro Co., PA

G5, $20-$35
Columbia Co., NY

G5, $20-$35
PA

Gray
chert

G8, $20-$35
Milton, VT

G7, $30-$50
Lycoming Co., PA

G5, $15-$30
Washingtonboro, PA

G5, $15-$25
NY

G7, $30-$50
Union Co., PA

Black
chert

155

OTTER CREEK (continued)

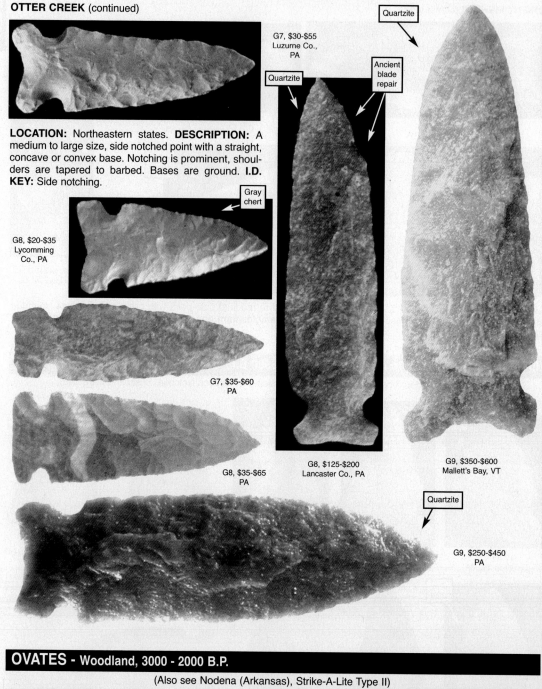

G7, $30-$55
Luzurne Co.,
PA

Quartzite

Quartzite

Ancient blade repair

LOCATION: Northeastern states. **DESCRIPTION:** A medium to large size, side notched point with a straight, concave or convex base. Notching is prominent, shoulders are tapered to barbed. Bases are ground. **I.D. KEY:** Side notching.

Gray chert

G8, $20-$35
Lycomming
Co., PA

G7, $35-$60
PA

G8, $35-$65
PA

G8, $125-$200
Lancaster Co., PA

G9, $350-$600
Mallett's Bay, VT

Quartzite

G9, $250-$450
PA

OVATES - Woodland, 3000 - 2000 B.P.

(Also see Nodena (Arkansas), Strike-A-Lite Type II)

G4, $5-$10
Berks Co., PA

G4, $5-$10
Berks Co., PA

G4, $5-$10
Montgomery Co., PA

G5, $8-$15
Chester Co., PA

LOCATION: Northeastern states. **DESCRIPTION:** A small size tear-drop shaped point with rounded shoulders and base. **I.D. KEY:** Ovoid form.

OVATES (continued)

G5, $8-$15
Chester Co., PA

G6, $15-$25
Berks Co., PA

G6, $15-$25
Montgomery Co., PA

PALMER - Early Archaic, 9000 - 8000 B.P.

(Also see Amos, Brewerton, Charleston Pine Tree, Kirk Corner Notched, Kiski, Kline)

Jasper

G5, $15-$25
Union Co., PA

G6, $20-$35
Monroe Co., PA

G5, $15-$25
Luzurne Co., PA

G5, $15-$25
Lycoming Co., PA

G6, $20-$35
Union Co., PA

G6, $25-$40
Luzurne Co., PA

LOCATION: Eastern states. **DESCRIPTION:** A small to medium size, corner-notched point with a ground concave, convex, or straight base. Shoulders are barbed to contracting. Many are serrated and large examples would fall under the *Charleston Pine Tree* or *Kirk* Type. **I.D. KEY:** Basal form and notching.

PARALLEL LANCEOLATE- Early Archaic, 9500 - 8500 B.P.

(Also see Agate Basin, Angostura, Ohio Lanceolate, Varney)

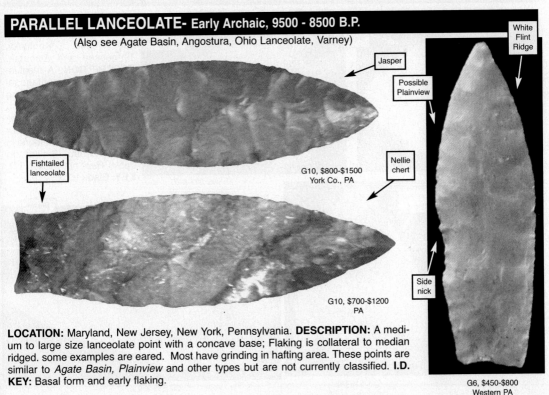

White
Flint
Ridge

Jasper

Possible
Plainview

Nellie
chert

Fishtailed
lanceolate

G10, $800-$1500
York Co., PA

G10, $700-$1200
PA

Side
nick

LOCATION: Maryland, New Jersey, New York, Pennsylvania. **DESCRIPTION:** A medium to large size lanceolate point with a concave base; Flaking is collateral to median ridged. some examples are eared. Most have grinding in hafting area. These points are similar to *Agate Basin, Plainview* and other types but are not currently classified. **I.D. KEY:** Basal form and early flaking.

G6, $450-$800
Western PA

157

PATUXENT - Late Archaic, 4000 - 3000 B.P.

(Also see Bare Island, Duncan's Island, Frost Island, Orient, Piedmont)

LOCATION: Southeastern PA., MD., VA. **DESCRIPTION:** A small to medium size point with weak, tapered shoulders and an expanding base. The base is concave forming ears. **I.D. KEY:** Basal form and weak shoulders.

G6, $15-$30
Montgomery
Co., PA

Quartzite

PENN'S CREEK BIFURCATE - Early Archaic, 9000 - 7000 B.P.

(Also see Kirk Stemmed, LeCroy, MacCorkle, St. Albans, Susquehanna Bifurcate)

LOCATION: Northeastern states. **DESCRIPTION:** A small size bifurcated point with Archaic flaking. Shoulders are weakly barbed and the base expands to ears. **I.D. KEY:** Basal form and early flaking.

G4, $12-$20
Northumberton
Co., PA

PENN'S CREEK SERIES - Early Archaic, 9000 - 7000 B.P.

(Also see Chillesquaque Series, Crooked Creek Series, Lycoming County Series)

LOCATION: Central Pennsylvania. **DESCRIPTION:** A series of points that are Laurentian in nature like Brewerton, with slight an subtle variations in material and shape from drainage to drainage.

G4, $4-$8
Peach Bottom, PA

PENTAGONAL KNIFE - Mid-Archaic, 6500 - 4000 B.P.

(Also see Jacks Reef Corner Notched)

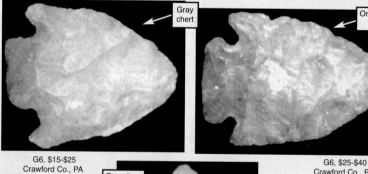

Gray chert

Onondaga chert

LOCATION: Pennsylvania into Ohio, Kentucky, Tennessee and Alabama. **DESCRIPTION:** A medium to large size pentagonal shaped point with a flaring or corner notched stem. Some examples are base notched. Similar to but older than the *Afton* point found in the Midwest. Similar to *Jacks Reef* but thicker. **I.D. KEY:** Blade form.

G6, $15-$25
Crawford Co., PA

G6, $25-$40
Crawford Co., PA

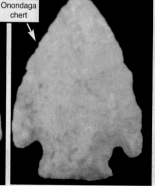

Onondaga chert

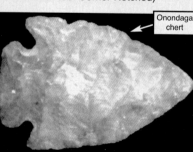

Brown chert

G6, $8-$15
Crawford Co., PA

G6, $15-$25
Crawford Co., PA

G6, $35-$50
Crawford Co., PA

PERKIOMEN - Late Archaic to early Woodland, 4000 - 2500 B.P.

(Also see Ashtabula, Frost Island, Manson Inn, Susquehanna Broad, Waratan)

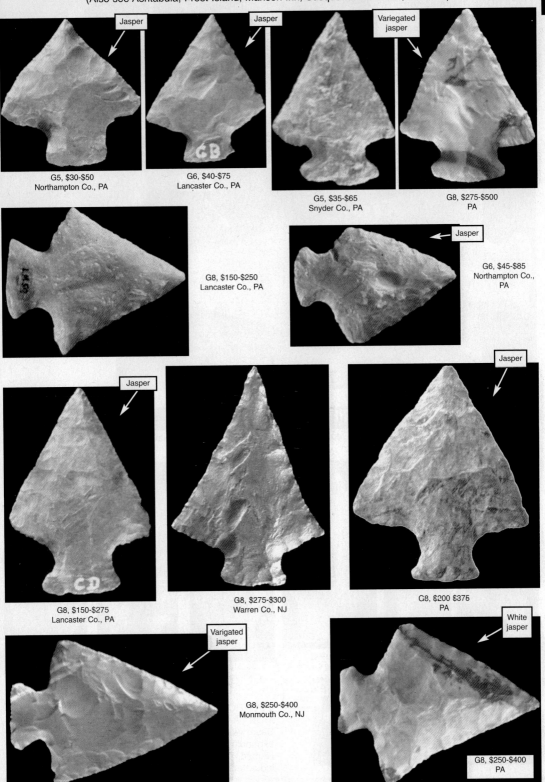

Jasper

G5, $30-$50
Northampton Co., PA

Jasper

G6, $40-$75
Lancaster Co., PA

Variegated jasper

G5, $35-$65
Snyder Co., PA

G8, $275-$500
PA

G8, $150-$250
Lancaster Co., PA

Jasper

G6, $45-$85
Northampton Co.,
PA

Jasper

Jasper

G8, $150-$275
Lancaster Co., PA

G8, $275-$300
Warren Co., NJ

G8, $200 $375
PA

White jasper

Varigated jasper

G8, $250-$400
Monmouth Co., NJ

G8, $250-$400
PA

PERKIOMEN (continued)

LOCATION: Northeastern states. **DESCRIPTION:** A medium to large size broad point with strong shoulders and a small, expanding base that is usually bulbous. Shoulders usually slope upwards. Blades can be asymmetrical. **I.D. KEY:** Broad shoulders and small base.

G7, $150-$275
Montgomery Co., PA

Jasper

Jasper

G8, $175-$300
Berks Co., PA

G10, $3000-$5000
Dauphin Co., PA

PIEDMONT-NORTHERN VARIETY - Archaic, 6000 - 4000 B.P.

(Also see Bare Island, Duncan's Island, Genesee, Hoover's Island, Neville, Lackawaxen, Newmanstown, Patuxent, Piney Island, Tocks Island)

Indurated shale

Indurated shale

Indurated shale

G3, $5-$10
Lycoming Co., PA

G4, $8-$15
Lycoming Co., PA

G6, $12-$20
Lycoming Co., PA

G6, $12-$20
Lycoming Co., PA

G5, $12-$20
Lycoming Co., PA

G8, $15-$25
Lycoming Co., PA

Indurated shale

G6, $15-$25
Lycoming Co., PA

LOCATION: Central Pennsylvania northward. **DESCRIPTION:** A medium to large size, narrow stemmed point. Base varies from straight to convex, from square to expanding or contracting. Shoulders are usually tapered. Named by Fogelman. Usually made of siltstone and indurated shale. **I.D. KEY:** Base form and narrow width.

160

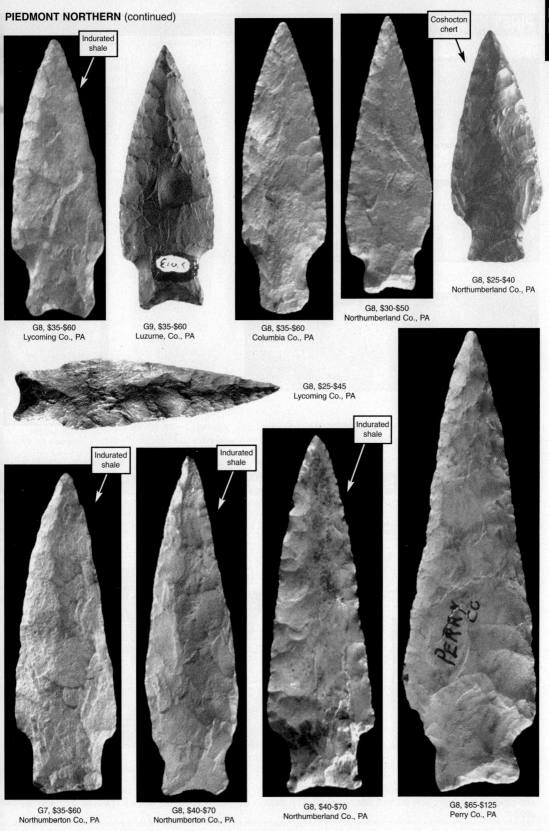

Indurated shale

Coshocton chert

G8, $35-$60
Lycoming Co., PA

G9, $35-$60
Luzurne, Co., PA

G8, $35-$60
Columbia Co., PA

G8, $30-$50
Northumberland Co., PA

G8, $25-$40
Northumberland Co., PA

G8, $25-$45
Lycoming Co., PA

Indurated shale

Indurated shale

Indurated shale

G7, $35-$60
Northumberton Co., PA

G8, $40-$70
Northumberton Co., PA

G8, $40-$70
Northumberland Co., PA

G8, $65-$125
Perry Co., PA

PINEY ISLAND - Late Archaic, 6000 - 2000 B.P.

(Also see Bare Island, Duncan's Island, Lamoka, Patuxent, Piedmont, Squibnocket Stemmed)

G6, $20-$35
Northampton Co., PA

G6, $20-$35
Columbia Co., PA

G8, $25-$40
Columbia Co., PA

Black chert

G8, $35-$60
Carbon Co., PA

G8, $40-$70
Lycoming Co., PA

LOCATION: Northeastern states. **DESCRIPTION:** A medium size, narrow, long stemmed point with tapered shoulders. **I.D. KEY:** Basal form and narrow width.

PISCATAWAY - Mid to late Woodland, 2500 - 500 B.P.

(Also see Morrow Mountain, Poplar Island, Schuylkill, Stark, Virginsville)

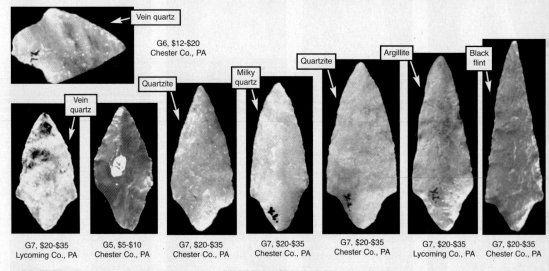

Vein quartz

G6, $12-$20
Chester Co., PA

Quartzite

Milky quartz

Quartzite

Argillite

Black flint

Vein quartz

G7, $20-$35
Lycoming Co., PA

G5, $5-$10
Chester Co., PA

G7, $20-$35
Chester Co., PA

G7, $20-$35
Chester Co., PA

G7, $20-$35
Chester Co., PA

G7, $20-$35
Lycoming Co., PA

G7, $20-$35
Chester Co., PA

LOCATION: Eastern to Northeastern states. **DESCRIPTION:** A small to medium size, very narrow triangular point with tapered shoulders and a short tapered stem. The base is pointed to rounded. **I.D. KEY:** Basal form and narrow width.

(Also see Koens Crispin, Morrow Mountain, Piscataway, Schuylkill, Stark, Virginsville)

Quartzite

G6, $30-$50
PA

G8, $30-$50
Northampton Co., PA

G4, $15-$30
Northampton Co., PA

G6, $30-$50
Carbon Co., PA

G6 $12-$20
NJ

Argillite

Quartzite

G8, $125-$200
NJ

G7, $125-$200
Lancaster Co., PA

G9, $125-$225
Montgomery Co., PA

G9, $150-$275
Carbon Co., PA

LOCATION: Northeastern states. **DESCRIPTION:** A medium to large size, narrow, triangular point with tapered shoulders and a long contracting base. The base can be pointed to rounded. **I.D. KEY:** Basal form and narrow width.

163

PORT MAITLAND - Mid-Woodland, 2500 - 1400 B.P.

(Also see Brewerton, Goddard, Raccoon Notched)

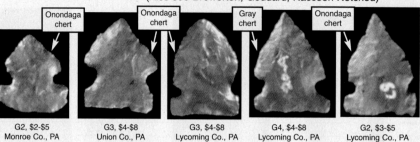

Onondaga chert

Onondaga chert

Gray chert

Onondaga chert

G2, $2-$5
Monroe Co., PA

G3, $4-$8
Union Co., PA

G3, $4-$8
Lycoming Co., PA

G4, $4-$8
Lycoming Co., PA

G2, $3-$5
Lycoming Co., PA

LOCATION: North eastern states. **DESCRIPTION:** A small size side notched point with a straight to slightly concave base. Side notches form square corners at the base. **I.D. KEY:** Notching form and small size.

RACCOON NOTCHED - Late Woodland, 1500 - 1000 B.P.

(Also see Brewerton, Goddard, Jacks Reef, Port Maitland)

LOCATION: Northeastern states. **DESCRIPTION:** A small to medium size, thin, side notched point. Blade edges are convex to pentagonal shape. Known as *Knight Island* in Southeast. **I.D. KEY:** Side notching and thinness.

Onondaga flint

Red jasper

G4, $12-$20
NY

G5, $25-$40
Union Co., PA

RANDOLPH - Woodland to Historic, 2000 - 200 B.P.

(Also see Dewart Stemmed, Lamoka, Merrimack, Wading River)

G7, $5-$10
Union Co., PA

G5, $3-$7
Union Co., PA

LOCATION: Eastern to Northeastern states. **DESCRIPTION:** A medium size, narrow, thick, spike point with tapered shoulders and a short to medium, contracted, rounded stem. Many examples have exaggerated spikes along the blade edges. **I.D. KEY:** Blade form and spikes.

REDSTONE - Paleo, 13,000 - 9000 B.P.

(Also see Clovis, Crowfield, Cumberland, Debert, and Holcomb)

LOCATION: Southeastern to Northeastern states. **DESCRIPTION:** A small to large size, thin, auriculate, fluted point with convex sides expanding to a wide, deeply concave base. Fluting can extend most of the way down each face. Multiple flutes are usual. A very rare type. **I.D. KEY:** Baton fluted, edgework on the hafting area.

Restored tip

Fluting channel

G7, $350-$600
Lycoming Co., PA. Coshocton chert.

ROSSVILLE - Late Woodland, 1500 - 1100 B.P.

(Also see Ovates, Morrow Mountain, Piscataway and Stark)

G3, $2-$5
Middleboro, MA

G4, $3-$6
Middleboro, MA

G5, $5-$10
Middleboro, MA

ROSSVILLE (continued)

G3, $5-$10
Middleboro, MA

G7, $15-$25
Middleboro, MA

G6, $12-$20
Middleboro, MA

LOCATION: Southern New England into New Jersey, E. Pennsylvania, Maryland and Virginia. **DESCRIPTION:** A small diamond shaped, lanceolate point with a pointed, to rounded, tapered stem. Tips are sharp and blade edges are straight to convex. **I.D. KEY:** Long tapered stem.

ST. ALBANS - Early to mid-Archaic, 9000 - 5000 B.P.

(Also see Charleston Pine Tree, Decatur, Kanawha, Kirk Serrated, Lake Erie, LeCroy, MacCorkle, Stanly & Susquehanna Bifurcate)

Milky quartz

Serrated edges

Classic form

G4, $8-$15
Lycoming Co., PA

G5, $15-$25
Lycoming Co., PA

G5, $15-$25
MD

G8, $25-$40
Lycoming Co., PA

G8, $30-$50
Lycoming Co., PA.

Chert

G9, $40-$75
Union Co., PA

G9, $35-$65
Union Co., PA

G6, $15-$30
Montour Co., PA

LOCATION: Eastern to Northeastern states. Type site is in Kanawha Co., WVA. **DESCRIPTION:** A small to medium size, usually serrated, bifurcated point. Basal lobes usually flare outward, and are weakly bifurcated. **I.D. KEY:** Weak bifurcation, base more narrow than shoulders.

ST. ANNE   (see Varney)

ST. CHARLES - Early Archaic, 9500 - 8000 B.P.

(Also see Brodhead Side Notched, Decatur, Kirk, Kline, Lost Lake & Thebes)

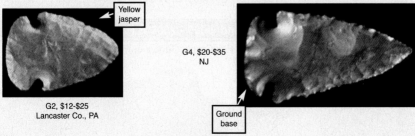

Yellow jasper

G4, $20-$35
NJ

G2, $12-$25
Lancaster Co., PA

Ground base

LOCATION: Midwest to Eastern states. **DESCRIPTION:** Also known as *Dovetail*. A medium to large size, corner notched, dovetailed base point. The blade is beveled on one side of each face when resharpened. Bases are straight, convex or bifurcated and are ground and can be fractured from both corners of the base. **I.D. KEY:** Dovetailed base.

ST. CHARLES (continued)

G4, $25-$40
PA

G6, $65-$125
MD

G8, $275-$500
Monmouth Co., NJ

G6, $135-$250
Lancaster Co., PA

SANDHILL STEMMED - Mid-Woodland, 2200 - 1700 B.P.

(Also see Dewart Stemmed, Garver's Ferry, Lamoka, Merrimack, Wading River)

G7, $6-$12
Lycoming Co., PA

G5, $6-$12
Lycoming Co., PA

G5, $4-$8
Lycoming Co., PA

G8, $8-$15
Lycoming Co., PA

G7, $8-$15
Monroe Co., PA

LOCATION: Northeastern states. **DESCRIPTION:** A small point with a straight to contracting base. Shoulders are tapered to slightly barbed.

SAVANNAH RIVER - Mid Archaic to Woodland, 5000 - 2000 B.P.

(Also see Atlantic Phase Blades, Fox Creek, Genesee, Piedmont)

G6, $15-$25
PA

G4, $5-$10
PA

SAVANNAH RIVER (continued)

LOCATION: Southeastern to Eastern states. **DESCRIPTION:** A medium to large size, straight to contracting stemmed point with a concave, straight or bifurcated base. The shoulders are tapered to square. The stems are narrow to broad. Believed to be related to the earlier *Stanly* point.

Quartzite

Tip nick

G4, $8-$15
Northumberland Co., PA

G7, $30-$50
PA

G5 $12-$20
PA

SCHUYLKILL - Late Archaic, 4000 - 2000 B.P.

(Also see Adena, Atlantic Phase Blades, Condoquinet Canfield, Koens Crispin, Lehigh, Morrow Mountain, Piscataway, Poplar Island, Stark, Virginsville)

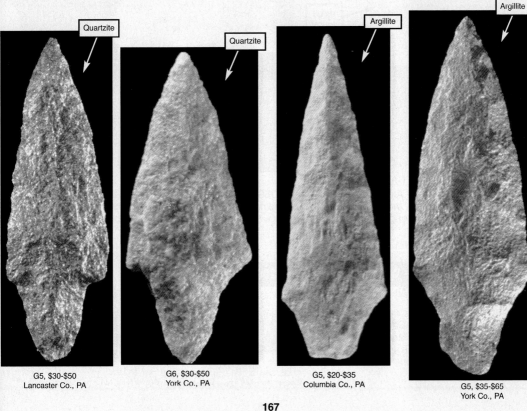

Quartzite

Quartzite

Argillite

Argillite

G5, $30-$50
Lancaster Co., PA

G6, $30-$50
York Co., PA

G5, $20-$35
Columbia Co., PA

G5, $35-$65
York Co., PA

SCHUYLKILL (continued)

LOCATION: Northeastern states. **DESCRIPTION:** A medium to large size, narrow point with a long, tapered, rounded stem. Shoulders are usually at a sharper angle than Poplar Island. **I.D. KEY:** Sharp corners, narrow blade, long tapering stem.

G7, $40-$75
PA

SCRAPER - Paleo to Archaic, 14,000 - 5000 B.P.

(Also see Drill, Graver, Strike-A-Lite)

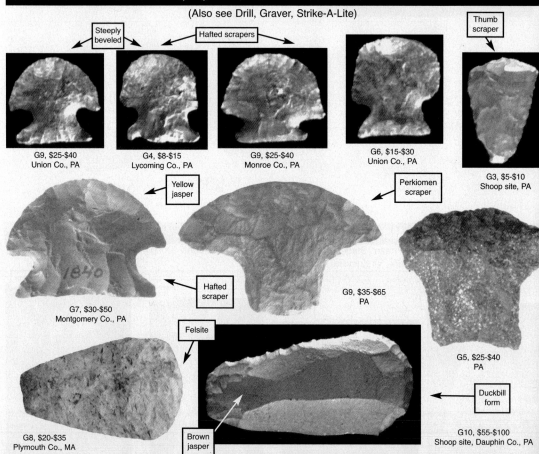

Steeply beveled

Hafted scrapers

Thumb scraper

G9, $25-$40
Union Co., PA

G4, $8-$15
Lycoming Co., PA

G9, $25-$40
Monroe Co., PA

G6, $15-$30
Union Co., PA

G3, $5-$10
Shoop site, PA

Yellow jasper

Perkiomen scraper

Hafted scraper

G7, $30-$50
Montgomery Co., PA

G9, $35-$65
PA

G5, $25-$40
PA

Felsite

Duckbill form

G8, $20-$35
Plymouth Co., MA

Brown jasper

G10, $55-$100
Shoop site, Dauphin Co., PA

LOCATION: Paleo to early Archaic sites everywhere. **DESCRIPTION:** Thumb, Duckbill, and Turtleback forms are small to medium size, thick, ovoid shaped, uniface, scraping tools that are steeply beveled, especially at the broadest end. Side scrapers are long hand-held uniface flakes with beveling on all blade edges of one face. Broken points are also utilized as scrapers.

SHARK'S TOOTH - Woodland to Historic, 2000 - 100 B.P.

(Also see Bone/Antler)

LOCATION: Coastal states from Maine to Florida. **DESCRIPTION:** Salvaged from Shark remains and as fossilized teeth found along the shoreline. Used as arrowpoints by Woodland Indians into historic times.

G5, $6-$12
Seaver farm, MA

G6, $6-$15
Seaver farm, MA

G7, $12-$20
Seaver farm, MA

G7, $15-$25
Seaver farm, MA

SNOOK KILL - Late Archaic, 4000 - 2000 B.P.

(Also see Atlantic Phase Blades, Dewart Stemmed, Koens Crispin, Lehigh, Merrimack, Sandhill Stemmed, Stark & Taconic Stemmed)

Flint

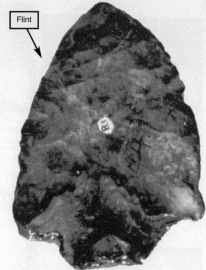

Flint

G9, $30-$50
Middlesboro, MA

LOCATION: New York and adjoining states. **DESCRIPTION:** A medium size point with tapered shoulders and a short, contracting to parallel sided stem. Base can be straight to convex. Believed to be related to *Koens Crispin* and *Lehigh*. **I.D. KEY:** Short stem, tapered tangs.

G5, $15-$30
Middlesboro, MA

SNYDERS - Woodland, 2500 - 1500 B.P.

(Also see Brewerton and Lycoming County)

LOCATION: West. New York eastward into Ohio. **DESCRIPTION:** A medium to large size, broad, thin, wide corner notched point. Made by the Hopewell culture. **I.D. KEY:** Size and broad corner notches.

IMPORTANT:
Snyders point shown
half size

G7, $80-$150
Western NY

SQUIBNOCKET STEMMED - Mid-late Archaic, 4200 - 4000 B.P.

(Also see Lamoka, Merrimack, Piney Island, Snook Kill, Taconic Stemmed)

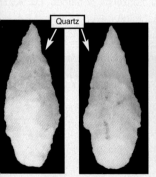

Quartz

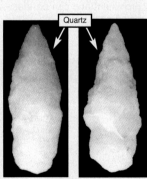

Quartz

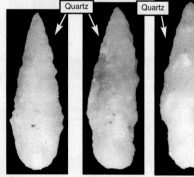

Quartz

Quartz

Quartz

G6, $6-$12	G7, $8-$15	G5, $5-$10	G7, $8-$15	G8, $12-$20	G5, $5-$10	G5, $5-$10
Bridgewater, MA	Bridgewater, MA	Bridgewater, MA	Bridgewater, MA	Bridgewater, MA	Bridgewater, MA	Bridgewater, MA

LOCATION: Conn., Massachusetts into New York. **DESCRIPTION:** A medium size, narrow, stemmed point with very weak shoulders and a rounded stem. **I.D. KEY:** Narrowness and weak shoulders.

SQUIBNOCKET TRIANGLE - Mid-late Archaic, 4500 - 4000 B.P.

(Also see Levanna, Madison and Susquehannock Triangle)

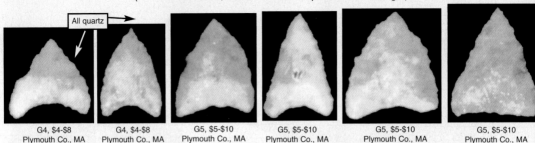

All quartz

| G4, $4-$8 | G4, $4-$8 | G5, $5-$10 | G5, $5-$10 | G5, $5-$10 | G5, $5-$10 |
| Plymouth Co., MA | Plymouth Co., MA | Plymouth Co., MA | Plymouth Co., MA | Plymouth Co., MA | Plymouth Co., MA |

LOCATION: Conn., Massachusetts into New York. **DESCRIPTION:** A small size, broad, triangular point with excurvate sides and an incurvate base. Basal corners turn inward. **I.D. KEY:** Narrowness and weak shoulders.

STANLY - Early Archaic, 8000 - 5000 B.P.

(Also see Kanawha, Kirk-Bifurcated, LeCroy, Muncy, Savannah River)

Black flint

G5, $20-$35
Lycoming Co., PA

G6, $20-$35
Union Co., PA

G9, $25-$40
NJ

Jasper

G5, $20-$35
Lycoming Co., PA

Classic form

Called Stanly Narrow Blade in North Carolina

G6, $15-$25
MD

LOCATION: Southeastern to Northeastern states. **DESCRIPTION:** A small to medium size, broad shoulder point with a small birfurcated stem. Some examples are serrated and show high quality flaking. The shoulders are very prominent and can be tapered, horizontal or barbed. **I.D. KEY:** Tiny bifurcated base.

G8, $35-$60
Lancaster Co., PA

STARK - Early Archaic, 7000 - 6500 B.P.

(Also see Adena, Koens Crispin, Lehigh, Morrow Mountain, Neville, Piscatawa, Poplar Island, Schuylkill & Stark)

Felsite

Felsite

| G6, $12-$20 | G5, $12-$20 | G5, $12-$20 |
| Middleboro, MA | Plymouth Co., MA | Plymouth Co., MA |

STARK (Continued)

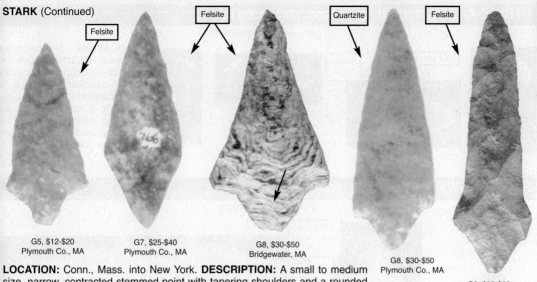

Felsite

Felsite

Quartzite

Felsite

Felsite

G5, $12-$20
Plymouth Co., MA

G7, $25-$40
Plymouth Co., MA

G8, $30-$50
Bridgewater, MA

G8, $30-$50
Plymouth Co., MA

G8, $35-$60
Middleboro, MA

LOCATION: Conn., Mass. into New York. **DESCRIPTION:** A small to medium size, narrow, contracted stemmed point with tapering shoulders and a rounded to pointed stem. Similar to **Piscataway** and **Rossville** points found further south.

STRIKE-A-LITE, type I - Early to late Archaic, 9000 - 4000 B.P.

(Also see Drill, Scraper)

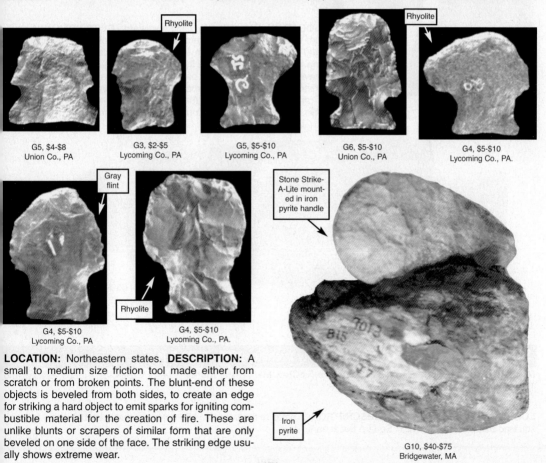

Rhyolite

Rhyolite

G5, $4-$8
Union Co., PA

G3, $2-$5
Lycoming Co., PA

G5, $5-$10
Lycoming Co., PA

G6, $5-$10
Union Co., PA

G4, $5-$10
Lycoming Co., PA.

Gray flint

Stone Strike-A-Lite mounted in iron pyrite handle

Rhyolite

G4, $5-$10
Lycoming Co., PA

G4, $5-$10
Lycoming Co., PA.

Iron pyrite

G10, $40-$75
Bridgewater, MA

LOCATION: Northeastern states. **DESCRIPTION:** A small to medium size friction tool made either from scratch or from broken points. The blunt-end of these objects is beveled from both sides, to create an edge for striking a hard object to emit sparks for igniting combustible material for the creation of fire. These are unlike blunts or scrapers of similar form that are only beveled on one side of the face. The striking edge usually shows extreme wear.

STRIKE-A-LITE, type II - Woodland, 3000 - 1000 B.P.

(Also see Drill, Ovates)

All Helderberg chert

Striking area

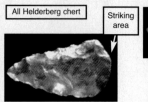

G1-5, $1-$2 ea.
All Lycoming Co., PA

LOCATION: Northeastern states. **DESCRIPTION:** A small size, narrow, tear drop form created for striking a hard object to emit sparks for igniting combustible material for the creation of fire. The striking edge usually shows extreme wear.

STRINGTOWN - Early Archaic, 9500 - 7000 B.P.

(Also see Scottsbluff)

White/blue Upper Mercer chert

Onondage chert

G7, $25-$45
PA

LOCATION: Pennsylvania, Ohio westward.. **DESCRIPTION:** A medium to large size, broad stemmed point with convex to parallel sides and square shoulders. The stem is parallel sided to slightly expanding. The base is eared and the hafting area is ground. Most examples have horizontal to oblique parallel flaking and are of high quality and thinness. The Eastern form of the *Scottsbluff* type made by the Cody Complex people. The *Eastern Stemmed Lanceolate* is a variation of this form. **I.D. KEY:** Base form and ground stem.

G8, $30-$50
Geauga, OH

G4, $12-$20
PA

Note knobbed base

G8, $175-$300
NY

SUSQUEHANNA BIFURCATE - Early Archaic, 9000 - 6000 B.P.

(Also see Kanawha, Kirk Stemmed, Lake Erie, LeCroy, MacCorkle, Muncy, Penn's Creek, St. Albans, Stanly, and Taunton River Bifurcate)

LOCATION: Northeastern states. **DESCRIPTION:** A small to medium size bifurcated point with barbed shoulders and squared basal ears. **I.D. KEY:** Square basal ears.

SUSQUEHANNA BIFURCATE (Continued)

Serrated edge

Yellow jasper

G4, $8-$15
MD

G8, $15-$25
Union Co., PA

G7, $15-$25
Lycoming Co., PA

G8, $15-$25
Lycoming Co., PA

G8, $25-$40
Lycoming Co., PA

Yellow jasper

Tip wear

G7, $25-$40
Dauphin Co., PA

G6, $15-$30
Lycoming Co., PA

G7, $25-$40
Lycoming Co., PA

G7, $25-$40
Berks Co., PA

Chert

Yellow jasper

G9, $70-$135
Luzurne Co.,
PA

G8, $45-$85
Union Co., PA

SUSQUEHANNA BROAD POINT - Early Woodland, 3700 - 2700 B.P.

(Also see Ashtabula, Drybrook, Frost Island, Orient, Patuxent, Perkiomen and Waratan)

Felsite

Yellow jasper

Rhyolite

G4, $8-$15
Plymouth Co., MA

G5, $12-$20
Plymouth Co., MA

G5, $12-$20
Centre Co., PA

G6, $30-$50
Lancaster Co., PA

G5, $15-$25
Lycoming Co., PA

G6, $15-$25
Northampton Co., PA

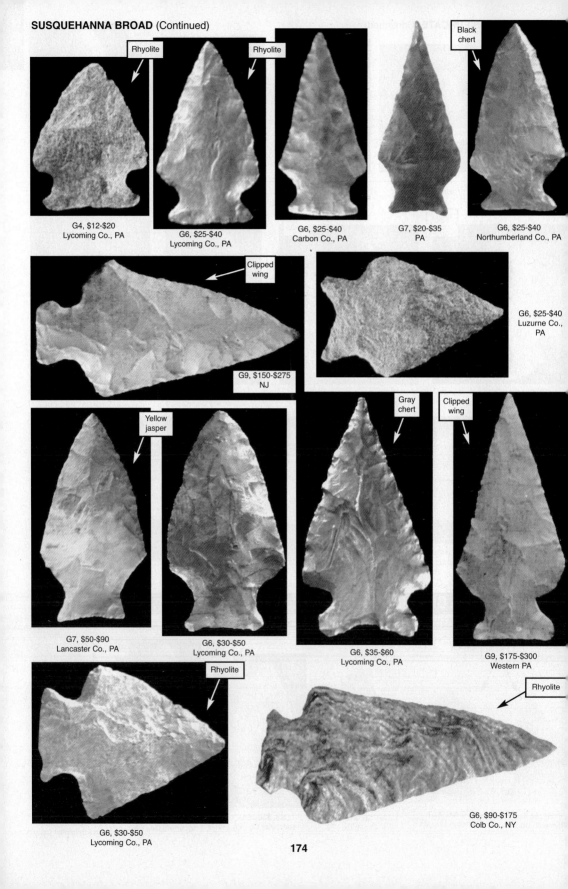

SUSQUEHANNA BROAD (Continued)

Rhyolite

Rhyolite

Black chert

G4, $12-$20
Lycoming Co., PA

G6, $25-$40
Lycoming Co., PA

G6, $25-$40
Carbon Co., PA

G7, $20-$35
PA

G6, $25-$40
Northumberland Co., PA

Clipped wing

G6, $25-$40
Luzurne Co., PA

G9, $150-$275
NJ

Yellow jasper

Gray chert

Clipped wing

G7, $50-$90
Lancaster Co., PA

G6, $30-$50
Lycoming Co., PA

G6, $35-$60
Lycoming Co., PA

G9, $175-$300
Western PA

Rhyolite

Rhyolite

G6, $30-$50
Lycoming Co., PA

G6, $90-$175
Colb Co., NY

SUSQUEHANNA BROAD (Continued)

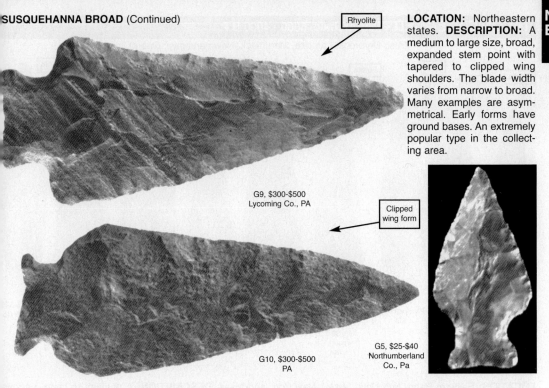

Rhyolite

LOCATION: Northeastern states. **DESCRIPTION:** A medium to large size, broad, expanded stem point with tapered to clipped wing shoulders. The blade width varies from narrow to broad. Many examples are asymmetrical. Early forms have ground bases. An extremely popular type in the collecting area.

G9, $300-$500
Lycoming Co., PA

Clipped wing form

G5, $25-$40
Northumberland Co., Pa

G10, $300-$500
PA

SUSQUEHANNOCK TRIANGLE - Late Woodland, 1500 - 400 B.P.

(Also see Erie Triangle, Levanna, Madison, Squibnocket Triangle, Yadkin)

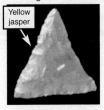

Yellow jasper

LOCATION: Pennsylvania. **DESCRIPTION:** A small to medium size triangle. Some examples can be serrated. **I.D. KEY:** Triangle.

G6, $15-$25
Lycoming Co., PA

Serrated edge

Yellow jasper

G7, $25-$40
NJ

SWATARA-LONG - Archaic, 5000 - 4000 B.P.

(Also see Koens Crispin, Lehigh, Morrow Mountain, Poplar Island & Virginsville)

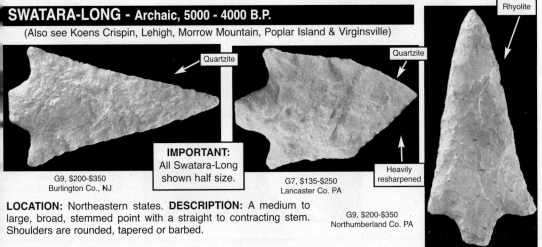

Quartzite

Quartzite

Rhyolite

IMPORTANT:
All Swatara-Long shown half size.

G9, $200-$350
Burlington Co., NJ

G7, $135-$250
Lancaster Co. PA

Heavily resharpened

G9, $200-$350
Northumberland Co. PA

LOCATION: Northeastern states. **DESCRIPTION:** A medium to large, broad, stemmed point with a straight to contracting stem. Shoulders are rounded, tapered or barbed.

TACONIC STEMMED - Mid-Archaic, 5000 - 4000 B.P.

(Also Drybrook, Lamoka, Merrimack, Newmanstown, Orient)

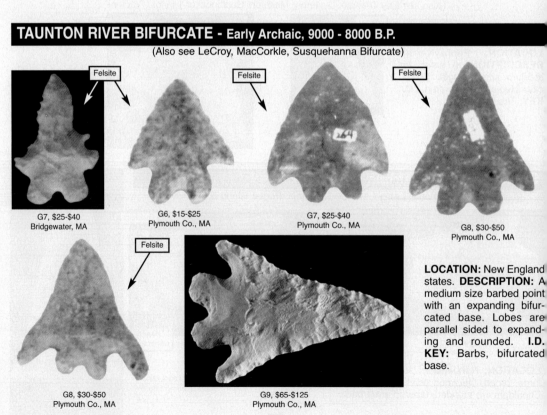

Felsite

Argillite

Flint

Felsite

Felsite

Felsite

Argillite

G4, $5-$10
Plymouth Co.,
MA

G4, $5-$10
Plymouth Co.,
MA

G4, $5-$10
Plymouth Co.,
MA

G5, $8-$15
Plymouth Co.,
MA

G7, $15-$25
Plymouth Co.,
MA

G6, $12-$20
Plymouth Co.,
MA

G7, $15-$25
Plymouth Co.,
MA

G7, $15-$25
Plymouth Co.,
MA

G7, $15-$25
Plymouth Co
MA

LOCATION: Easterm Penn. into New Jersey, New York and Mass. **DESCRIPTION:** A medium to large, narrow, stemmed point with a straight, or contracting or expanding stem. Shoulders are weak and are tapered.

TAUNTON RIVER BIFURCATE - Early Archaic, 9000 - 8000 B.P.

(Also see LeCroy, MacCorkle, Susquehanna Bifurcate)

Felsite

Felsite

Felsite

Felsite

G7, $25-$40
Bridgewater, MA

G6, $15-$25
Plymouth Co., MA

G7, $25-$40
Plymouth Co., MA

G8, $30-$50
Plymouth Co., MA

Felsite

G8, $30-$50
Plymouth Co., MA

G9, $65-$125
Plymouth Co., MA

LOCATION: New England states. **DESCRIPTION:** A medium size barbed point with an expanding bifurcated base. Lobes are parallel sided to expanding and rounded. **I.D. KEY:** Barbs, bifurcated base.

176

THEBES - Early Archaic, 10,000 - 8000 B.P.

(Also see Lost Lake and St. Charles)

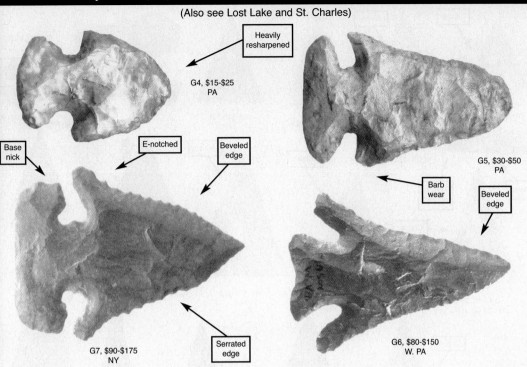

Heavily resharpened

G4, $15-$25
PA

Base nick

E-notched

Beveled edge

G5, $30-$50
PA

Barb wear

Beveled edge

Serrated edge

G7, $90-$175
NY

G6, $80-$150
W. PA

LOCATION: New York eastward into Ohio. **DESCRIPTION:** A medium to large size, wide blade with deep, angled side notches that are parallel sided and squared. Resharpened examples have beveling on one side of each face. The bases have broad proportions and are concave, straight or convex and are ground. Some examples have unusual side notches called *Key notch*. This type of notch is angled into the blade to produce a high point in the center, forming the letter E.

TOCKS ISLAND - Early to mid-Woodland, 1700 - 1500 B.P.

(Also see Bare Island, Duncan's Island, Lackawaxen, Merrimack, Susquehanna Broad)

G3, $12-$20
Carbon Co., PA

G5, $45-$80
Monmouth Co., NJ

White quartz

LOCATION: Lower Hudson river area. **DESCRIPTION:** A small to medium size stem- med point with a small, expanding base. Shoulders are barbed. **I.D. KEY:** Short expanding stem.

TRADE POINTS - Historic, 400 - 170 B.P.

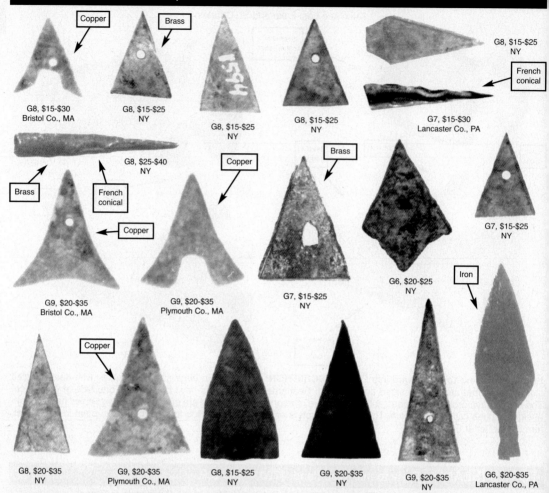

Copper
G8, $15-$30
Bristol Co., MA

Brass
G8, $15-$25
NY

G8, $15-$25
NY

G8, $15-$25
NY

G8, $15-$25
NY

French conical
G7, $15-$30
Lancaster Co., PA

G8, $25-$40
NY

Copper

Brass

Copper

French conical

Copper

G9, $20-$35
Bristol Co., MA

G9, $20-$35
Plymouth Co., MA

Brass
G7, $15-$25
NY

G6, $20-$25
NY

G7, $15-$25
NY

Iron

Copper

G8, $20-$35
NY

G9, $20-$35
Plymouth Co., MA

G8, $15-$25
NY

G9, $20-$35
NY

G9, $20-$35
NY

G6, $20-$35
Lancaster Co., PA

LOCATION: All States. These points were made of copper, iron and steel and were traded to the Indians by the French, British and others from the 1600s to the 1800s. Examples have been found all over the United States. Similar points were used against Custer at the battle of the Little Big Horn.

VARNEY - Early Archaic, 9000 - 8000 B.P.

(Also see Agate Basin, Angostura, Ohio Lanceolate, Parallel Lanceolate)

Classic parallel flaked, Notched variety

G3, $40-$75
Upper Deleware Valley, PA

Restored base

Dark green chert

Gray Onondaga? chert

G6, $150-$250
NY

Tip wear

LOCATION: Northeastern states into eastern Canada. **DESCRIPTION:** A small to medium size, narrow, lanceolate point with very weak shoulders. The base is rectangular shaped and is ground. Similar to *Eden* points found further west. **I.D. KEY:** Weak shoulders, narrow blade.

178

VERNON - Early Woodland, 2800 - 2500 B.P.

(Also see Brewerton, Kiski, Kline, Lycoming Co.)

G4, $3-$6
Long Level, PA

LOCATION: Northeastern states. **DESCRIPTION:** A small to medium size triangular point with a short, expanding stem. The base has rounded corners and the shoulders are usually barbed. **I.D. KEY:** Expanded base, barbed shoulders.

VESTAL NOTCHED - Late Archaic, 4500 - 4000 B.P.

(Also see Brewerton, Kiski, Kline, Lycoming Co.)

LOCATION: Northeastern states. **DESCRIPTION:** A small to medium size triangular point with a short, expanding stem. The base has rounded corners and the shoulders are usually barbed. **I.D. KEY:** Expanded base, barbed shoulders.

G6, $5-$15
Luzurne Co., PA

G6, $5-$15
Luzurne Co., PA

VIRGINSVILLE - Mid-Archaic, 5000 - 3000 B.P.

(Also see Adena, Conodoquinet Canfield, Lehigh, Koens-Crispin, Morrow Mountain, Piscataway, Poplar Island, Schuylkill)

G4, $8-$15
PA

Quartzite

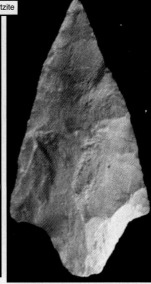

Quartzito

G4, $12-$20
Montgomery Co., PA

G6, $15-$25
PA

G6, $15-$25
Lancaster Co., PA

VIRGINSVILLE (Continued)

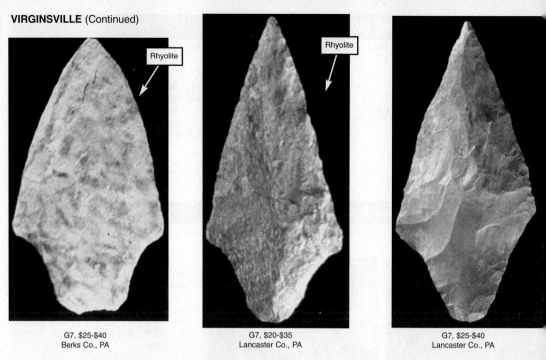

G7, $25-$40
Berks Co., PA

G7, $20-$35
Lancaster Co., PA

G7, $25-$40
Lancaster Co., PA

LOCATION: Northeastern states. **DESCRIPTION:** A medium to large size triangular point with contracting shoulders and base that is usually rounded. **I.D. KEY:** Diamond shape.

VOSBURG - Archaic, 5000 - 4000 B.P.

(Also see Brewerton, Crooked Creek, Goddard, Jacks Reef, Kiski)

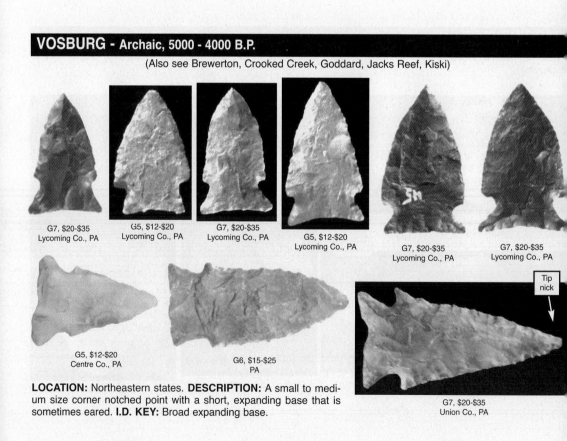

G7, $20-$35
Lycoming Co., PA

G5, $12-$20
Lycoming Co., PA

G7, $20-$35
Lycoming Co., PA

G5, $12-$20
Lycoming Co., PA

G7, $20-$35
Lycoming Co., PA

G7, $20-$35
Lycoming Co., PA

G5, $12-$20
Centre Co., PA

G6, $15-$25
PA

G7, $20-$35
Union Co., PA

LOCATION: Northeastern states. **DESCRIPTION:** A small to medium size corner notched point with a short, expanding base that is sometimes eared. **I.D. KEY:** Broad expanding base.

VOSBURG (Continued)

G7, $20-$35
Centre Co., PA

G10, $150-$250
Columbia Co., NY

WADING RIVER - Archaic, 4200 - 4000 B.P.

(Also see Dewart Stemmed, Garver's Ferry, Lamoka, Merrimack, Sandhill Stemmed,)

Flint | Felsite | Quartz | Quartz | Felsite | Quartz

G2, $1-$3
Plymouth Co.,
MA

G3, $2-$4
Plymouth Co.,
MA

G6, $5-$10
Plymouth Co.,
MA

G6, $5-$10
Plymouth Co.,
MA

G6, $4-$8
Plymouth Co., MA

G5, $4-$8
Plymouth Co., MA

G6, $4-$8
Plymouth Co.,
MA

LOCATION: Massachusetts and surrounding states. **DESCRIPTION:** A small size, thick, stemmed point. Stem can be contracting, expanding or parallel sided. Base is straight to rounded. **I.D. KEY:** Small size and thick cross section.

WAPANUCKET - Mid-Archaic, 6000 - 4000 B.P.

(Also see Bare Island, Benton (Central East), Genesee, Lackawaxen, Meadowood, New- manstown, Piedmont, Tocks Island)

IMPORTANT:
All
Wapanuckets
shown half size

Jasper

G8, $200-$350
Monmouth Co., NJ

G7, $125-$200
Burlington Co., NJ

G10, $350-$600
MA

LOCATION: Northeastern states. **DESCRIPTION:** A medium to very large size short stemmed point. Bases can be corner or side notched, knobbed, bifurcated or expanded. Found in caches and closely resembles the *Benton* point found further south. **I.D. KEY:** Large size, notched blade.

WARATAN - Woodland, 3000 - 1000 B.P.

(Also see Drybrook, Perkiomen, Susquehanna Broad)

LOCATION: Eastern states. **DESCRIPTION:** A small to medium size point with usually broad, tapered shoulders, weak corner notches and a very short, broad, concave base. The base expands on some examples giving the appearance of ears or auricles. **I.D. KEY:** Short, broad, eared base.

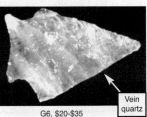

Vein
quartz

G6, $20-$35
Montgomery Co., PA

181

WAYLAND NOTCHED - Late Archaic, 3700 - 2700 B.P.

(Also see Ashtabula, Frost Island, Mansion Inn, Orient, Perkiomen, Susquehanna Broad)

Felsite

Pink quartzite

Felsite

G7, $30-$50
Plymouth Co., MA

G8, $60-$100
Plymouth Co., MA

G9, $80-$150
Plymouth Co., MA

G9, $150-$250
Norfolk Co., MA

LOCATION: Maine southward into New Jersey. **DESCRIPTION:** A large size, broad, expanding stem point with tapered shoulders. Similar in form to the *Susquehanna Broad* point in which it is related. See *Mansion Inn* points which represent the preform for this type. **I.D. KEY:** Large size, broad, tapered shoulders.

WEB BLADE - Woodland, 1500 - 500 B.P.

(Also see Adena Blade)

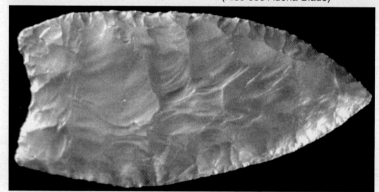

G8, $350-$500
NJ

LOCATION: Northeastern states. **DESCRIPTION:** A large size, lanceolate blade with a thin cross section. Bases can be concave to straight. Believed to be related to the Adena culture. **I.D. KEY:** Large, thin blade.

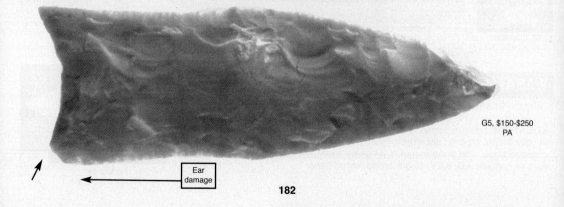

G5, $150-$250
PA

Ear damage

EASTERN SEABOARD SECTION:

This section includes point types from the following states:
North Carolina, South Carolina, Virginia and West Virginia

The points in this section are arranged in alphabetical order and are shown **actual size**. All types are listed that were available for photographing. Any missing types will be added to future editions as photographs become available. We are always interested in receiving sharp, black and white or color glossy photos, color slides or high resolution (300 pixels/inch) digital pictures of your collection. Be sure to include a ruler in the photograph so that proper scale can be determined.

Lithics: Argillite, crystal, chalcedony, chert, Coastal Plain Chert, flint, jasper, limestone, quartz, quartzite, rhyolite, shale, siltstone, slate, vein quartz.

Important sites: Baucom site, Union Co., N.C., Hardaway site in Stanly Co., NC., St. Albans site, Kanawha Co., WVA., Williamson site, Dinwiddie Co., VA.

Regional Consultants:
David Abbott, Ron L. Harris
Rodney Peck, Jack Willhoit
Warner Williams

Special Advisors:
Tommy Beutell
Tom Davis

EASTERN SEABOARD POINT TYPES
(Archaeological Periods)

PALEO (11,500 B. P. - 10,500 B. P.)

Clovis	Drill
Clovis Unfluted	Redstone

LATE PALEO (10,500 B. P. - 10,000 B. P.)

Alamance	Quad	Simpson

EARLY ARCHAIC (10,000 B. P. - 7,000 B. P.)

Amos	Fishspear	Kirk Corner Notched	Stanly
Big Sandy	Fountain Creek	Kirk Stemmed	Stanly Narrow Stem
Bolen Bevel	Garth Slough	Kirk Stemmed-Bifurcated	Taylor
Bolen Plain	Guilford Yuma	Lecroy	Thebes
Charleston Pine Tree	Hardaway	Lost Lake	Van Lott
Culpepper Bifurcate	Hardaway Blade	Palmer	Waller Knife
Dalton	Hardaway-Dalton	Patrick Henry	
Dalton Greenbrier	Hardaway-Palmer	Rowan	
Decatur	Hardin	St. Albans	
Ecusta	Jude	St. Charles	
Edgefield Scraper	Kanawha Stemmed	Southampton	

MIDDLE ARCHAIC (7,500 B. P. - 5,000 B. P.)

Appalachian	Chesapeake Diamond	Halifax	Pentagonal Knife
Benton	Conerly	Heavy Duty	Pickwick
Brewerton Eared	Guilford Round Base	Morrow Mountain	
Brewerton Side Notched	Guilford Stemmed	Morrow Mountain Straight Base	
Buffalo Stemmed	Guilford Staright Base	Otter Creek	

LATE ARCHAIC (5,000 B. P. - 3,000 B. P.)

Dismal Swamp	Meadowood
Exotic Forms	Savannah River
Holmes	

EARLY WOODLAND (3,000 B. P. - 2,100 B. P.)

Adena	Fox Creek	Piscataway	Wateree
Adena Robbins	Greeneville	Potts	Will's Cove
Armstrong	Gypsy	Snyders	Yadkin
Dickson	Ovates	Waratan	Yadkin Eared

MIDDLE WOODLAND (2,100 B. P. - 1,500 B. P.)

Randolph

LATE WOODLAND (1,600 B. P. - 1,000 B. P.)

Badin	Pee Dee
Jack's Reef Corner Notched	Uwharrie

LATE PREHISTORIC (1,000 B. P. - 500 B. P.)

Caraway	Occaneechee
Clarksville	

HISTORIC (450 B. P. - 170 B. P.)

Hillsboro	Trade Points

EASTERN SEABOARD
THUMBNAIL GUIDE SECTION

The following references are provided to aid the collector in easier and quicker identification of point types. All photos are exactly 30% of actual size and are proportional to each other. Each point pictured in this section represents a classic form for the type. When a match is found, go to the alphabetical location of that type for more examples in actual size.

ES

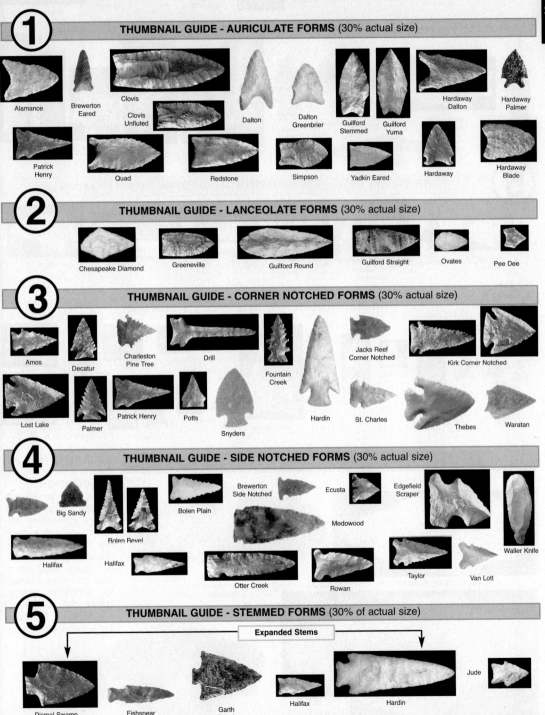

① THUMBNAIL GUIDE - AURICULATE FORMS (30% actual size)

Alamance | Brewerton Eared | Clovis | Clovis Unfluted | Dalton | Dalton Greenbrier | Guilford Stemmed | Guilford Yuma | Hardaway Dalton | Hardaway Palmer

Patrick Henry | Quad | Redstone | Simpson | Yadkin Eared | Hardaway | Hardaway Blade

② THUMBNAIL GUIDE - LANCEOLATE FORMS (30% actual size)

Chesapeake Diamond | Greeneville | Guilford Round | Guilford Straight | Ovates | Pee Dee

③ THUMBNAIL GUIDE - CORNER NOTCHED FORMS (30% actual size)

Amos | Decatur | Charleston Pine Tree | Drill | Fountain Creek | Jacks Reef Corner Notched | Kirk Corner Notched

Lost Lake | Palmer | Patrick Henry | Potts | Snyders | Hardin | St. Charles | Thebes | Waratan

④ THUMBNAIL GUIDE - SIDE NOTCHED FORMS (30% actual size)

Big Sandy | Bolen Bevel | Bolen Plain | Brewerton Side Notched | Ecusta | Medowood | Edgefield Scraper | Waller Knife

Halifax | Halifax | Otter Creek | Rowan | Taylor | Van Lott

⑤ THUMBNAIL GUIDE - STEMMED FORMS (30% of actual size)

Expanded Stems

Dismal Swamp | Fishspear | Garth Slough | Halifax | Hardin | Jude

185

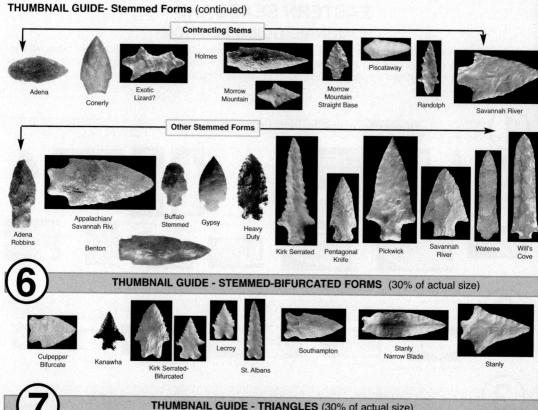

Contracting Stems

Adena · Conerly · Exotic Lizard? · Holmes · Morrow Mountain · Morrow Mountain Straight Base · Piscataway · Randolph · Savannah River

Other Stemmed Forms

Adena Robbins · Appalachian/ Savannah Riv. · Benton · Buffalo Stemmed · Gypsy · Heavy Duty · Kirk Serrated · Pentagonal Knife · Pickwick · Savannah River · Wateree · Will's Cove

⑥ THUMBNAIL GUIDE - STEMMED-BIFURCATED FORMS (30% of actual size)

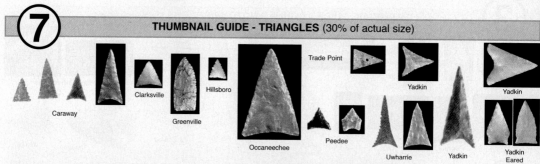

Culpepper Bifurcate · Kanawha · Kirk Serrated-Bifurcated · Lecroy · St. Albans · Southampton · Stanly Narrow Blade · Stanly

⑦ THUMBNAIL GUIDE - TRIANGLES (30% of actual size)

Caraway · Clarksville · Greenville · Hillsboro · Occaneechee · Trade Point · Peedee · Yadkin · Uwharrie · Yadkin · Yadkin · Yadkin Eared

ADENA - Late Archaic to early Woodland, 3000 - 1200 B. P.

(Also see Dickson)

Vein quartz

G3, $1-$3, Dinwiddie Co., VA

G4, $2-$4 Kanawha Co., WVA

G5, $5-$10 Dinwiddie Co., VA

G4, $2-$4 Kanawha Co., WVA

LOCATION: Tenn. into Ohio and West Virginia. **DESCRIPTION:** A medium to large, thin, narrow, triangular blade that is sometimes serrated, and with a medium to long, narrow to broad rounded "beaver tail" stem. Most examples are from average to excellent quality. Bases can be ground. **I.D. KEY:** Rounded base, woodland flaking.

ADENA ROBBINS - Late Archaic to early Woodland, 3000 - 1200 B. P.

(Also see Savannah River)

E S

G4, $3-$5
Putnam Co., WVA

Tip damage

G3, $2-$4
Putnam Co., WVA

LOCATION: Tenn. into Ohio and West Virginia. **DESCRIPTION:** A medium to large, thin, narrow, triangular blade that is sometimes serrated, and with a medium to long, narrow to broad stem that is parallel sided. Base can be straight to rounded. Most examples are from average to excellent quality. Bases can be ground. **I.D. KEY:** Rounded base, woodland flaking.

ALAMANCE - Late Paleo, 10,000 - 8000 B. P.

(Also see Hardaway & Hardaway Dalton)

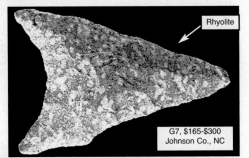

Rhyolite

G7, $165-$300
Johnson Co., NC

Rhyolite

G6, $200-$350
Johnson Co., NC

G6, $125-$225
Granville Co., NC

G6, $150-$250
Randolph Co., NC

LOCATION: Coastal states from Virginia to Florida. **DESCRIPTION:** A broad, short, auriculate point with a deeply concave base. The broad basal area is usually ground and can be expanding to parallel sided. A variant form of the *Dalton-Greenbrier* evolving later into the *Hardaway* type. **I.D. KEY:** Width of base and strong shoulder form.

AMOS - Early Archaic, 9900 - 8900 B. P.

(Also see Decatur, Kirk Corner Notched and Palmer)

All-black
Kanawha chert

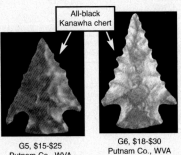

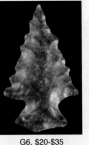

G5, $15-$25
Putnam Co., WVA

G6, $18-$30
Putnam Co., WVA

G6, $18-$30
Putnam Co., WVA

G6, $20-$35
Putnam Co., WVA

G8, $40-$75
Putnam Co., WVA

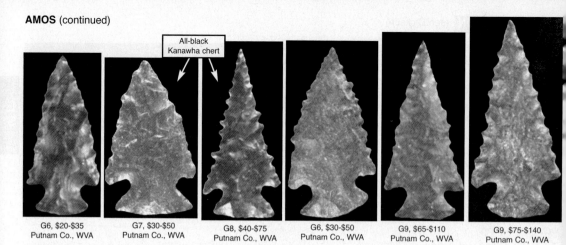

All-black
Kanawha chert

G6, $20-$35
Putnam Co., WVA

G7, $30-$50
Putnam Co., WVA

G8, $40-$75
Putnam Co., WVA

G6, $30-$50
Putnam Co., WVA

G9, $65-$110
Putnam Co., WVA

G9, $75-$140
Putnam Co., WVA

LOCATION: West Virginia into Pennsylvania and New York. Type site is in Kanawha Co., WVA. **DESCRIPTION:** A medium size, serrated, corner notched point with an expanding stem. Bases are straight, concave or convex and are ground. Basal corners are sharp to rounded. **I.D. KEY:** Deep serrations and expanding stem.

ANGELICO CORNER-NOTCHED (See Decatur)

APPALACHIAN - Middle Archaic, 6000 - 3000 B. P.

(Also see Savannah River and Southampton)

Quartzite

Gray/red
Quartzite

G8, $55-$100
Yancey Co., NC

G8, $70-$125
Yancey Co., NC

G7, $55-$100
Madison Co., NC

Yellow
Quartzite

G9, $150-$250
Haywood Co., NC

LOCATION: East Tennessee and Georgia into the Carolinas. **DESCRIPTION:** A medium to large size, rather crudely made stemmed point with a concave, straight or convex base. Most examples are made of quartzite. Shoulders are tapered and the base is usually ground. This point was named by Lewis & Kneberg for examples found in East Tenn. and Western North Carolina which were made of quartzite. However, this is the same type as *Savannah River*. **I.D. KEY:** Material Quartzite used.

Quartzite

G8, $70-$125
Haywood Co., NC

Quartzite

G8, $90-$175
McDowell Co., NC

Red quartzite

G7, $80-$150
Randolph Co., NC

G8, $125-$200
Yancey Co., NC

G9, $275-$500
Cent. NC

189

ARMSTRONG - Woodland, 2450 - 1600 B. P.

(Also see Brewerton, Ecusta, Palmer, Patrick Henry and Potts)

LOCATION: West Virginia and neighboring states. **DESCRIPTION:** A small, short, corner notched point with barbed shoulders. Base is straight to convex and expands. **I.D. KEY:** Tangs and broad notches.

G4, $4-$8
Kanawha Co., WVA

BADIN - Woodland, 2000 - 1200 B. P.

(Also see Fox Creek)

LOCATION: Carolinas to Virginia. **DESCRIPTION:** A medium size triangular point that is larger and thicker than Hillsboro. Sides are convex with straight to slightly convex or concave bases. **I.D. KEY:** Thickness and crudeness.

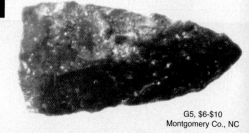

G5, $6-$10
Montgomery Co., NC

BENTON - Middle Archaic, 6000 - 4000 B. P.

(Also see Savannah River, Stanly)

LOCATION: Eastern to midwestern states. **DESCRIPTION:** A medium to very large size, broad, stemmed point with straight to convex sides. Bases can be corner or side notched, double notched, knobbed, bifurcated or expanded. **I.D. KEY:** Wide squared, eared or notched base.

G6, $15-$30
Beaufort Co., SC

BIG SANDY - Early to Late Archaic, 10,000 - 3000 B. P.

(Also see Bolen, Pine Tree, Rowan and Taylor)

Milky quartz

G2, $3-$6
Mason Co., WVA

G5, $4-$8
Moore Co., NC

G6, $8-$15
Dinwiddie Co., VA

G8, $35-$60
Randolph Co., NC

G8, $25-$45
Randolph Co., NC

Restored

G6, $8-$15
Putnam Co., WVA

LOCATION: Southeastern states. **DESCRIPTION:** A small to medium size, side notched point with early forms showing heavy basal grinding, serrations, and horizontal flaking. **I.D. KEY:** Basal form and blade flaking.

190

BOLEN BEVEL - Early Archaic, 10,000 - 7000 B. P.

(Also see Big Sandy, Patrick Henry, Taylor & Van Lott)

Beveled edge

Beveled edge

| G4, $8-$15 Spartanburg Co.,SC | G7, $25-$40 Colquittl Co., GA | G5, $25-$40 Randolph Co., NC | G5, $20-$35 Edgefield Co.,SC | G7, $50-$90 Lexington Co., SC |

LOCATION: Coastal states into South Carolina. **DESCRIPTION:** A small to medium size, side-notched point with early forms showing basal grinding, beveling on one side of each face, and serrations. Bases can be straight, concave or convex. The side notch is usually broader than in *Big Sandy* points. E-notched or expanded notching also occurs on early forms. **I.D. KEY:** Basal form and notching.

BREWERTON EARED - Middle Archaic, 6000 - 4000 B. P.

(Also see Hardaway, Yadkin Eared)

G3, $3-$5
Kanawha Co., WVA

LOCATION: Eastern to midwestern states. **DESCRIPTION:** A small size, triangular, eared point with a concave base. Shoulders are weak and tapered. Ears are the widest part of the point. **I.D. KEY:** Small ears, weak shoulders.

BREWERTON SIDE NOTCHED - Middle Archaic, 6000 - 4000 B. P.

(Also see Big Sandy, Hardaway and Palmer)

LOCATION: Eastern to midwestern states. **DESCRIPTION:** A small to medium size triangular point with broad side notches. Bases are straight to convex to concave. **I.D. KEY:** Thickness and width.

G4, $5-$9
Mason Co., WVA

G5, $8-$15
Mason Co., WVA

Quartzite

G4, $5-$9
VA

BUFFALO STEMMED - Middle Archaic, 6000 - 4000 B. P.

(Also see Holmes and Savannah River)

Altered to a scraper

G3, $2-$5
Putnam Co., WVA

LOCATION: West Virginia. **DESCRIPTION:** A medium size, broad, parallel stemmed point with tapered shoulders. **I.D. KEY:** Width, squared stem.

CARAWAY - Late Prehistoric, 1000 - 200 B. P.

(Also see Clarksville, Hillsboro, Uwharrie and Yadkin)

CARAWAY (continued)

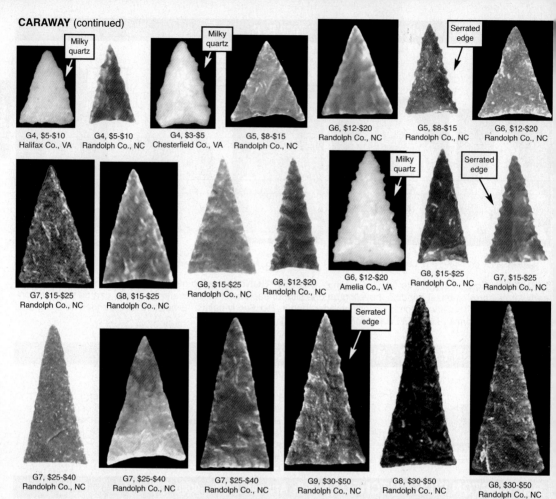

Milky quartz

G4, $5-$10
Halifax Co., VA

G4, $5-$10
Randolph Co., NC

Milky quartz

G4, $3-$5
Chesterfield Co., VA

G5, $8-$15
Randolph Co., NC

G6, $12-$20
Randolph Co., NC

Serrated edge

G5, $8-$15
Randolph Co., NC

G6, $12-$20
Randolph Co., NC

G7, $15-$25
Randolph Co., NC

G8, $15-$25
Randolph Co., NC

G8, $15-$25
Randolph Co., NC

G8, $12-$20
Randolph Co., NC

Milky quartz

G6, $12-$20
Amelia Co., VA

Serrated edge

G8, $15-$25
Randolph Co., NC

G7, $15-$25
Randolph Co., NC

G7, $25-$40
Randolph Co., NC

G7, $25-$40
Randolph Co., NC

G7, $25-$40
Randolph Co., NC

Serrated edge

G9, $30-$50
Randolph Co., NC

G8, $30-$50
Randolph Co., NC

G8, $30-$50
Randolph Co., NC

LOCATION: Coincides with the Mississippian culture in the Eastern states. **DESCRIPTION:** A small to medium size, thin, triangular point with usually straight sides and base, although concave bases are common. Some examples are notched on two to three sides. Many are of high quality and some are finely serrated. Similar to *Madison* found elsewhere.

CACTUS HILL (This small triangular point was dated approx. 15,000 B.P. in Virginia but verification is needed from other sites.)

CHARLESTON PINE TREE - Early Archaic, 8000 - 5000 B. P.

(Also see Kirk and Palmer)

LOCATION: Southeastern states. **DESCRIPTION:** A medium to large size, side notched, sometimes corner notched, usually serrated point with parallel flaking to the center of the blade forming a median ridge. The bases are ground and can be concave, convex, straight, or auriculate. Small examples would fall into the Palmer type. **I.D. KEY:** Archaic flaking with long flakes to the center of the blade.

Serrated edge

Serrated edge

G8, $35-$65
Tug Fork, WVA

G8, $40-$75
Tug Fork, WVA

CHESAPEAKE DIAMOND - Mid-Archaic, 6000 - 5000 B. P.

(Also see Morrow Mountain, Ovates)

LOCATION: Maryland into Virginia and North Carolina. **DESCRIPTION:** A medium to large size double tipped point with broad shoulders. Many are made of quartzite. After many resharpenings, the blade is reduced to the size of the stem.

G6, $12-$20
Halifax Co., VA

E
S

CLARKSVILLE - Late Prehistoric, 1000 - 500 A. D.

(Also see Caraway, Hillsboro, Uwharrie and Yadkin)

LOCATION: Far Eastern states. **DESCRIPTION:** A small size triangular point with all three sides approximately the same width. The base is straight to slightly concave. Examples made from quartzite and quartz tend to be thick in cross section.

G5, $5-$10
Randolph Co., NC

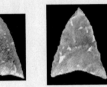

G4, $4-$8
Randolph Co., NC

G4, $3-$6
Randolph Co., NC

G3, $2-$5
Newberry Co., SC

G3, $3-$6
Randolph Co., NC

CLOVIS - Early Paleo, 11,500 - 10,600 B. P.

(Also see Redstone, Quad and Simpson)

G4, $125-$225
Laurens Co., SC

G4, $150-$250
NC

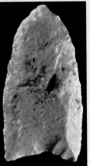

G5, $150-$275
Greensville Co., VA

G6, $300-$550
Mecklenburg Co., VA

G5, $200-$350
Brunswick Co., VA

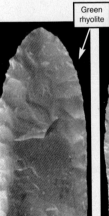

Green rhyolite

G8, $450-$800
Randolph Co., NC

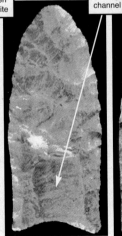

Fluting channel

G7, $500-$900
Greensville Co., VA

Fluting channel

G8, $550-$1000
Smith Co., VA

G6, $350-$650
Randolph Co., NC

G5, $300-$550
Randolph Co., NC

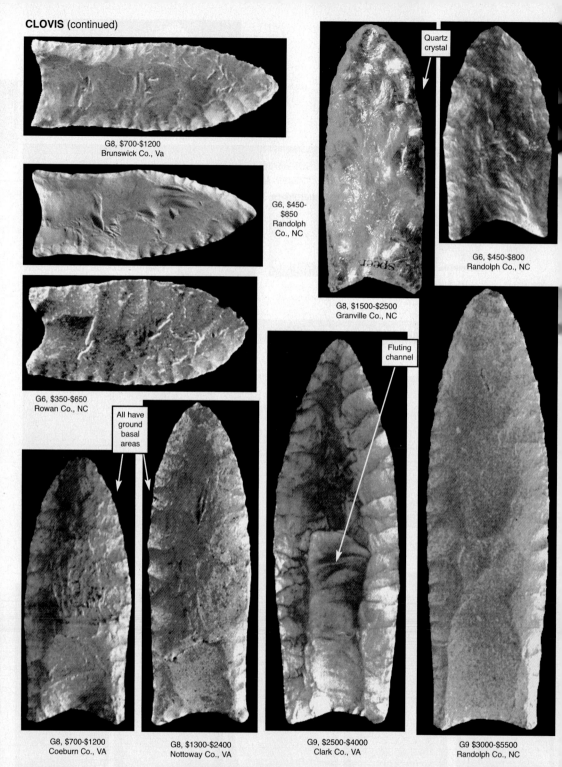

G8, $700-$1200
Brunswick Co., Va

G6, $450-$850
Randolph Co., NC

Quartz crystal

G6, $450-$800
Randolph Co., NC

G8, $1500-$2500
Granville Co., NC

G6, $350-$650
Rowan Co., NC

All have ground basal areas

Fluting channel

G8, $700-$1200
Coeburn Co., VA

G8, $1300-$2400
Nottoway Co., VA

G9, $2500-$4000
Clark Co., VA

G9 $3000-$5500
Randolph Co., NC

LOCATION: All of North America. **DESCRIPTION:** A medium to large size, auriculate, fluted, lanceolate point with convex sides and a concave base that is ground. Most examples are fluted on both sides about 1/3 the way up from the base. The flaking can be random to parallel. *Clovis* is the earliest point type in the hemisphere. *Clovis* technology more closely matches European *Solutrean* forms than anything else. There is no pre-*Clovis* evidence here (crude forms that would pre-date *Clovis*). **I.D. KEY:** Paleo flaking, shoulders, baton or billet fluting instead of indirect style.

CLOVIS-UNFLUTED - Paleo, 11,500 - 10,600 B. P.

(Also see Dalton, Fox Creek and Simpson)

G5, $150-$250
Sussex Co., VA.
Basal thinning.

LOCATION: All of North America.
DESCRIPTION: A medium to large size, auriculate point identical to fluted *Clovis,* but not fluted. A very rare type.

CONERLY - Middle Archaic, 7500 - 4500 B. P.

(Also see Guilford)

Coastal Plain chert

G7, $70-$125
Edgefield Co., SC

LOCATION: Southern southeastern states including South Carolina. **DESCRIPTION:** A medium to large size, auriculate point with a contracting, concave base which can be ground. On some examples, the hafting area can be seen with the presence of very weak shoulders. The base is usually thinned. Believed to be related to the *Guilford* type. **I.D. KEY:** Base concave, thickness, flaking.

CULPEPPER BIFURCATE - Early Archaic, 7500 - 6500 B. P.

(Also see Kanawha, Kirk Serrated Bifurcate, Lecroy, Southampton)

G5, $8-$15
VA

Rhyolite

LOCATION: North Carolina and Virginia. **DESCRIPTION:** A medium size point with barbed shoulders and an expanded stem that is bifurcated. Common with only one barbed shoulder. **I.D. KEY:** Bifurcated base.

G6, $12-$20
Chesterfield Co., VA

DALTON - Early Archaic, 10,000 - 9200 B. P.

(Also see Hardaway)

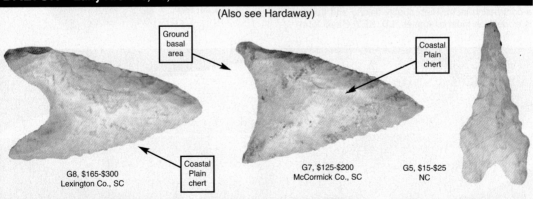

Ground basal area

Coastal Plain chert

G8, $165-$300
Lexington Co., SC

Coastal Plain chert

G7, $125-$200
McCormick Co., SC

G5, $15-$25
NC

LOCATION: Southeastern states including South & North Carolina. **DESCRIPTION:** A medium to large size, auriculate fishtailed point. Many examples are finely serrated and exhibit excellent flaking. Beveling may occur on one side of each face but is usually on the right side. All have basal grinding. This early type spread over most of the Eastern and Midwestern U.S. and strongly influenced many other types to follow. **I.D. KEY:** Concave base with auricles.

G4, $15-$25
NC

195

DALTON-GREENBRIER - Early Archaic, 10,000 - 9200 B. P.

(Also see Hardaway)

LOCATION: Southeastern states including South & North Carolina. **DESCRIPTION:** A medium size, auriculate form with a concave base and drooping to expanding auricles. Many examples are serrated, some are fluted on both sides, and all have basal grinding. **I.D. KEY:** Expanded auricles.

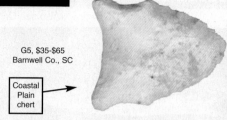

G5, $35-$65
Barnwell Co., SC

Coastal Plain chert

DECATUR - Early Archaic, 9000 - 3000 B. P.

(Also see Amos, Charleston Pine Tree, Dalton, Ecusta, Palmer and St. Charles)

Serrated edge

Fractured base

Edge nick

G5, $15-$25
VA

G8, $80-$150
Randolph Co., NC

G6, $40-$70
Pocahantas Co., WVA

LOCATION: Eastern states. **DESCRIPTION:** A small to medium size, serrated, corner notched point that is usually beveled on one side of each face. The base is usually broken off (fractured) by a blow inward from each corner of the stem. Sometimes the side of the stem and backs of the tangs are also fractured, and rarely the tip may be fractured by a blow on each side directed towards the base. Bases are usually ground and flaking is high quality. Basal and shoulder fracturing also occurs in *Abbey, Dovetail, Eva, Kirk, Motley* and *Snyders*. Unfractured forms are called *Angelico Corner-Notched* in Virginia.

DICKSON - Woodland, 2500 - 1600 B. P.

(Also see Adena)

LOCATION: W. Virginia to Missouri. **DESCRIPTION:** A small to large size point with tapered shoulders and a contracting stem. High quality flaking and thinness is evident on most examples. **I.D. KEY:** Basal form.

G4, $4-$8
Putnam Co., WVA

Resharpened many times

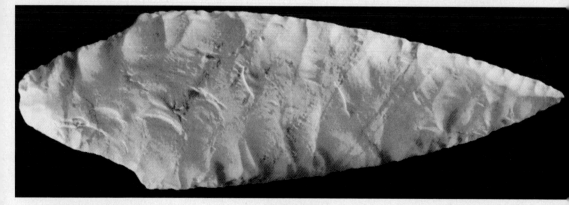

G10, $350-$600
Smyth Co., VA

DISMAL SWAMP - Late Archaic to early Woodland, 3500 - 2000 B. P.

(Also see Garth Slough, Savannah River and Waratan)

LOCATION: North Carolina to Virginia. Similar to *Perkiomen* found in Pennsylvania. **DESCRIPTION:** A medium to large size, broad point with strong shoulders and a small, expanding base that is usually bulbous, blades can be asymmetrical. **I.D. KEY:** Broad shoulders and small base.

G6, $25-$45
Bethany, WVA

DOVETAIL (See St. Charles)

DRILL - Paleo to Historic, 11,500 - 200 B. P.

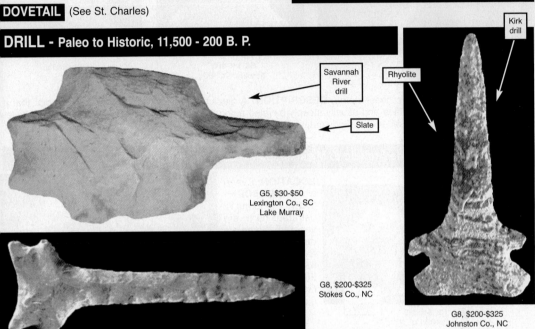

Savannah River drill

Slate

Rhyolite

Kirk drill

G5, $30-$50
Lexington Co., SC
Lake Murray

G8, $200-$325
Stokes Co., NC

G8, $200-$325
Johnston Co., NC

LOCATION: All of North America. **DESCRIPTION:** Although many drills were made from scratch, all point types were made into the drill form. Usually, heavily resharpened and broken points were salvaged and rechipped into drills. These objects were certainly used as drills (evidence of extreme edge wear), but there is speculation that some of these forms may have been used as pins for clothing, ornaments, ear plugs and other uses.

ECUSTA - Early Archaic, 8000 - 5000 B. P.

(Also see Bolen Plain, Palmer and Potts)

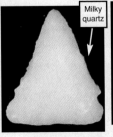

Milky quartz

G4, $4-$8
Prince Edward Co., VA

G5, $6-$12
Bethany, WVA

G6, $10-$18
Bethany, WVA

LOCATION: Southeastern states. **DESCRIPTION:** A small size, serrated, side-notched point with usually one side of each face steeply beveled, although examples exist with all four sides beveled and flaked to a median ridge. The base and notches are ground. Very similar to *Autauga*, with the latter being corner-notched.

197

EDGEFIELD SCRAPER - Early Archaic, 9000 - 6000 B. P.

Beveled edge.
Back side is flat

Beveled edge.
Back side is flat

G8, $45-$80
Edgefield Co., SC

G8, $45-$80
Edgefield Co., SC

G8, $55-$100
Edgefield Co., SC

LOCATION: Southern Atlantic coast states. **DESCRIPTION:** A medium to large size corner notched point that is asymmetrical. Many are uniface and usually steeply beveled along the diagonal side. The blade on all examples leans heavily to one side. Used as a hafted scraper.

EXOTIC FORMS - Late Archaic to Mississippian, 5000 - 1000 B. P.

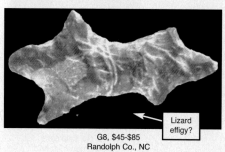

LOCATION: Everywhere. **DESCRIPTION:** The forms illustrated here are very rare. Some are definitely effigy forms while others may be no more than unfinished and unintentional doodles.

Lizard effigy?

G8, $45-$85
Randolph Co., NC

G8, $45-$85
Granville Co., NC

FISHSPEAR - Early to Mid-Archaic, 9000 - 6000 B.P.

(Also see Randolph)

FISH SPEAR (continued)

LOCATION: Northeastern states. **DESCRIPTION:** A medium to large size, narrow, thick, stemmed point with broad side notches to an expanding stem. Bases are usually ground and blade edges can be serrated. Named due to its appearance that resembles a fish. **I.D. KEY:** Narrowness, thickness and long stem.

G3, $8-$15
Kanawha Co., WVA

FOUNTAIN CREEK - Early Archaic, 9000 - 7000 B. P.

(Also see Kirk Stemmed)

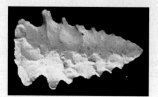

G6, $15-$25
Wayne Co., NC

G7, $30-$50
Nash Co., NC

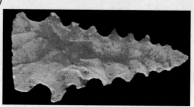

FOUNTAIN CREEK
(continued)

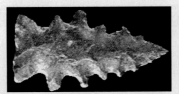

G7, $20-$35
Chatham Co., NC

Note strong barbs

E
S

G9, $70-$125
Randolph Co., NC

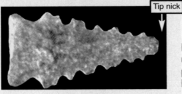

Tip nick

G4, $6-$12
Amelia Co., VA

G4, $10-$18
Randolph Co., NC

LOCATION: Eastern states. **DESCRIPTION:** A medium size, narrow corner notched to expanded stemmed point with notched blade edges and a short, rounded base which is ground. **I.D. KEY:** Exaggerated barbs.

FOX CREEK - Woodland, 2500 - 1200 B. P.

(Also see Badin, Clovis Unfluted and Guilford Stemmed)

G6, $12-$20
Bethany, WVA

LOCATION: Northeastern states. **DESCRIPTION:** A medium size blade with a squared to tapered hafting area and a straight to slightly concave base. Shoulders, when present are very weak and tapered.

FOX VALLEY (See Kanawha Stemmed; See N. Central section for Fox Valley points)

GARTH SLOUGH - Early Archaic, 9000 - 4000 B. P.

(Also see Kanawha Stemmed and Stanly)

LOCATION: Southeastern states. **DESCRIPTION:** A small size point with wide, expanded barbs and a small squared base. Rare examples have the tangs clipped (called clipped wing). The blade edges are convex with fine serrations. A similar type of a later time period, called *Catahoula*, is found in the Midwestern states. A bifurcated base would place it into the *Kanawha Stemmed* type. **I.D. KEY:** Expanded barbs, early flaking.

G6, $30-$50
Pearson Co., NC

GREENEVILLE - Woodland, 3000 - 1500 B.P.

(Also see Caraway, Clarksville, Madison)

G8, $15-$25
Davidson Co., NC

LOCATION: Southeast to eastern states. **DESCRIPTION:** A small to medium size lanceolate point with convex sides becoming contracting to parallel at the base. The basal edge is slightly concave, convex or straight. This point is usually wider and thicker than *Guntersville*, and is believed to be related to *Camp Creek*, *Ebenezer* and *Nolichucky* points.

199

GUILFORD-ROUND BASE - Middle Archaic, 6500 - 5000 B. P.

(Also see Cobbs and Lerma in other sections)

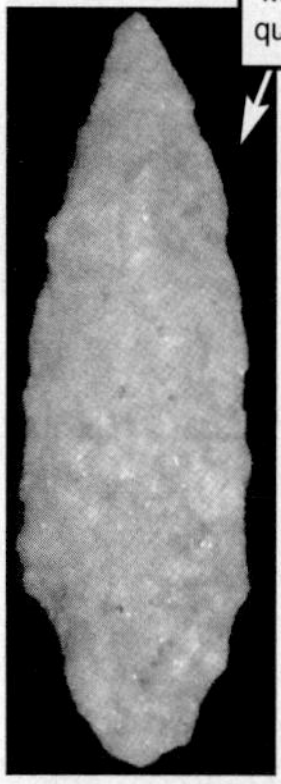

Milky quartz

Clear quartz

Milky quartz

Clear vein quartz

G5, $6-$12
Sussex Co., VA

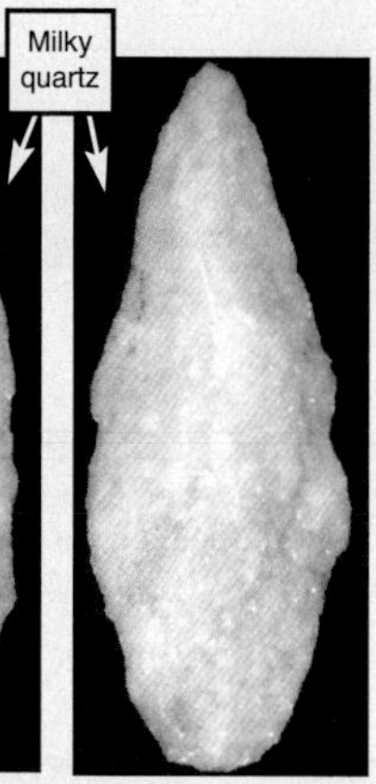

G5, $6-$12
Sussex Co., VA

G6, $6-$12
NC

G7, $8-$15
Fairfield Co., SC

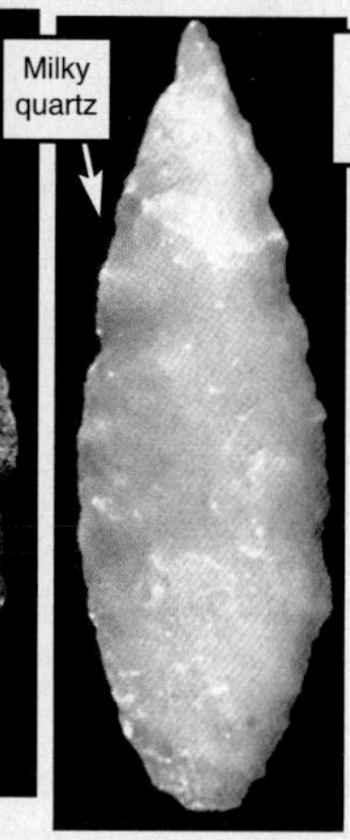

G6, $8-$15
Randolph Co., NC

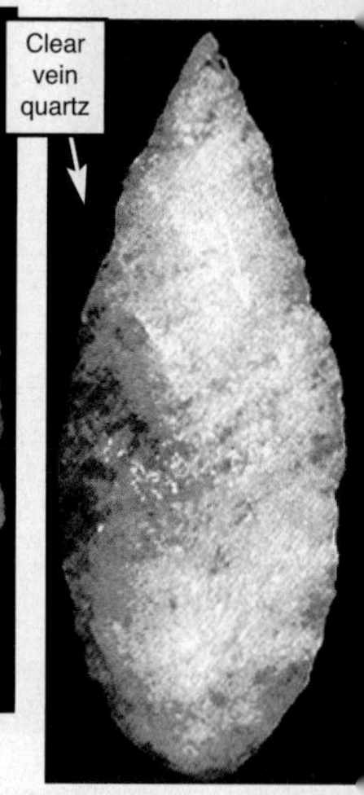

G6, $12-$20
Fairfield Co., SC

Vein quartz

Quartzite

Red/yellow quartzite

G7, $15-$25
Rancolph Co., NC

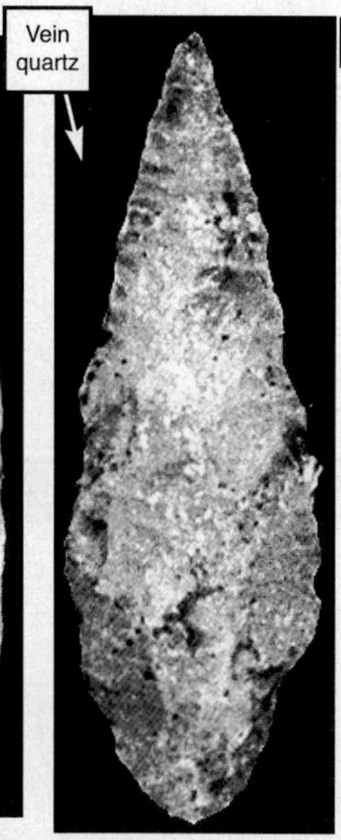

G6, $12-$20
Fairfield Co., SC

G8, $30-$50
NC

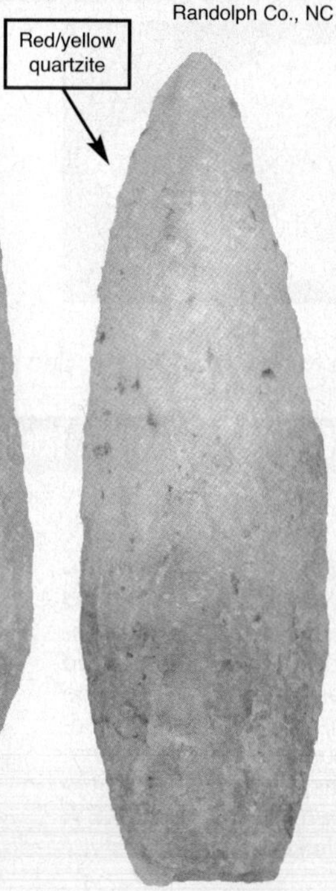

G8, $35-$65
NC

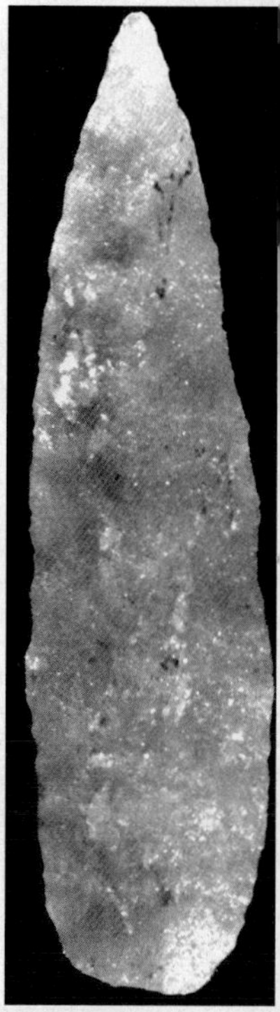

G6, $15-$25
NC

G8, $35-$65
Anderson Co., SC

North Carolina and surrounding areas. **DESCRIPTION:** A medium to large size, thick, narrow, lanceolate point with a convex, contracting base. This type is usually made of Quartzite or other poor quality flaking material which - al which results in a more crudely chipped form than *Lerma* (its ancestor). **I.D. KEY:** Thickness, archaic blade flaking.

GUILFORD-STEMMED - Middle Archaic, 6500 - 5000 B. P.

(Also see Stanly Narrow Stem, Waratan and Yadkin Eared)

E S

G5, $6-$12
Sussex Co., VA

G7, $8-$15
Guilford Co., NC

G5, $5-$10
Prince Edward Co., VA

G8, $8-$15
Dinwiddie Co., VA

G7, $15-$25
Wayne Co., NC

G9, $35-$65
Rockingham Co., NC

G7, $15-$25
Daw Island, SC

G5, $8-$15
Dinwiddie Co., VA

LOCATION: Far Eastern states. **DESCRIPTION:** A medium size, thick, narrow, lanceolate point with a straight to concave, contracting base. All examples have weak, tapered shoulders. Some bases are ground. Called *Brier Creek* in Georgia.

GUILFORD-STRAIGHT BASE - Middle Archaic, 6500 - 5000 B. P.

(Also see Fox Creek)

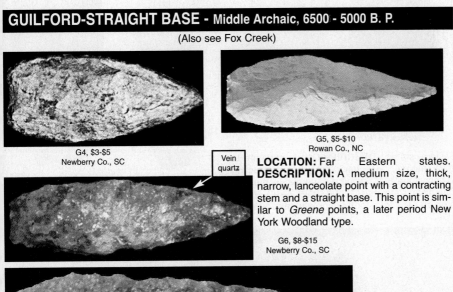

G5, $5-$10
Rowan Co., NC

G4, $3-$5
Newberry Co., SC

Vein quartz

LOCATION: Far Eastern states. **DESCRIPTION:** A medium size, thick, narrow, lanceolate point with a contracting stem and a straight base. This point is similar to *Greene* points, a later period New York Woodland type.

G6, $8-$15
Newberry Co., SC

G9, $45-$80
Pearson Co., NC

G7, $20-$35
NC

(Also see Clovis Unfluted and Yadkin Eared)

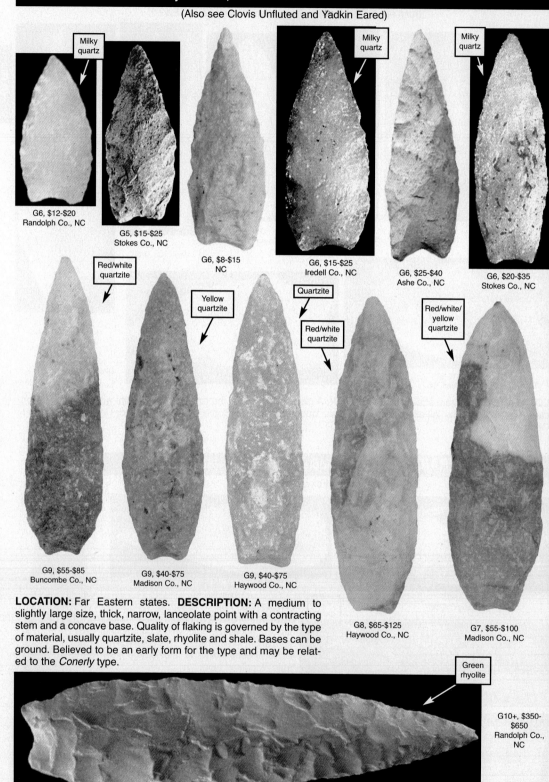

Milky quartz

G6, $12-$20
Randolph Co., NC

G5, $15-$25
Stokes Co., NC

G6, $8-$15
NC

Milky quartz

G6, $15-$25
Iredell Co., NC

G6, $25-$40
Ashe Co., NC

Milky quartz

G6, $20-$35
Stokes Co., NC

Red/white quartzite

Yellow quartzite

Quartzite

Red/white quartzite

Red/white/yellow quartzite

G9, $55-$85
Buncombe Co., NC

G9, $40-$75
Madison Co., NC

G9, $40-$75
Haywood Co., NC

G8, $65-$125
Haywood Co., NC

G7, $55-$100
Madison Co., NC

LOCATION: Far Eastern states. **DESCRIPTION:** A medium to slightly large size, thick, narrow, lanceolate point with a contracting stem and a concave base. Quality of flaking is governed by the type of material, usually quartzite, slate, rhyolite and shale. Bases can be ground. Believed to be an early form for the type and may be related to the *Conerly* type.

Green rhyolite

G10+, $350-$650
Randolph Co., NC

202

GYPSY - Woodland, 2500 - 1500 B. P.

(Also see St. Charles)

G8, $20-$35
Surry Co., NC

G7, $15-$25
Randolph Co., NC

LOCATION: North Carolina. **DESCRIPTION:** A small to medium size triangular point with a bulbous stem. Shoulders are usually well defined and can be barbed. **I.D. KEY:** Bulbous base.

HALIFAX - Middle to Late Archaic, 6000 - 3000 B. P.

(Also see Holmes, Rowan and Southampton)

G3, $1-$3
Pearson Co., NC

G3, $1-$3
Bethany, WVA

G4, $2-$5
Southampton
Co., VA

Milky quartz

G4, $2-$5
Southampton Co.,
VA

Milky quartz

G4, $3-$6
Randolph Co., NC

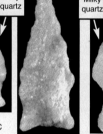

Milky quartz

G6, $4-$8
Dinwiddie Co., VA

Milky quartz

G6, $4-$8
Halifax Co., VA

Vein quartz

G7, $5-$10
Amelia, VA

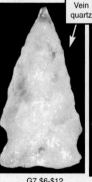

Vein quartz

G7 $6-$12
Caroline Co., VA

G6, $5-$10
Southampton Co.,
VA

Milky quartz

G6, $6-$12
Sussex Co., VA

G8, $12-$20
Randolph Co., NC

G8, $10-$18
Sussex Co., VA

LOCATION: Southeastern states. **DESCRIPTION:** A small to medium size, narrow, side notched to expanded stemmed point. Shoulders can be weak to strongly tapered. Typically one shoulder is higher than the other. North Carolina examples are made of quartz, rhyolite and shale.

HARDAWAY - Early Archaic, 9500 - 8000 B. P.

(Also see Alamance, Hardaway-Dalton, Patrick Henry and Taylor)

LOCATION: Southeastern states, especially North Carolina. Type site is Stanly Co. NC, Yadkin River. **DESCRIPTION:** A small to medium size point with shallow side notches and expanded auricles forming a wide, deeply concave base. Wide specimens are called *Cow Head Hardaways* in North Carolina by some collectors. Ears and base are usually heavily ground. This type evolved from the *Dalton* point. **I.D. KEY:** Heavy grinding in shoulders, paleo flaking.

Tip wear

Milky quartz

Milky quartz

G6, $55-$100
Montgomery Co., NC

G7, $80-$150
Moore Co., NC

G8, $90-$175
Southampton Co., VA

G6, $75-$140
Sussex Co., VA

G8, $125-$225
Mecklinburg Co., NC

Cowhead form

Tip wear

G8, $125-$225
Randolph Co., NC

G9, $125-$225
Moore Co., NC

G7, $150-$250
Alamance Co., NC

G6, $150-$250
Randolph Co., NC

Cowhead form

Cowhead form

G8, $150-$250
Moore Co., NC

G10, $175-$300
NC

G10, $275-$500
Cent. NC

G7, $150-$275
Moore Co., NC

Rhyolite

Indurated shale

Tip wear

G9, $175-$300
Rowan Co., NC

G6, $175-$325
Cent. NC

G7, $250-$450
Montgomery Co., NC

HARDAWAY BLADE - Early Archaic, 9500 - 9000 B. P.

(Also see Alamance)

LOCATION: North Carolina. **DESCRIPTION:** A small to medium size, thin, broad, blade with a concave base. The base usually is ground and has thinning strikes. A preform for the *Hardaway* point.

G4, $20-$35
Cent. NC

E
S

HARDAWAY-DALTON - Early Archaic, 9500 - 8000 B. P.

(Also see Alamance and Hardaway)

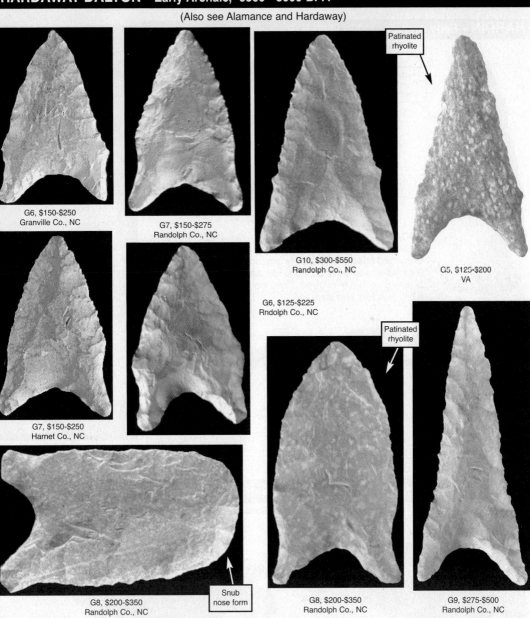

G6, $150-$250
Granville Co., NC

G7, $150-$275
Randolph Co., NC

G10, $300-$550
Randolph Co., NC

Patinated rhyolite

G5, $125-$200
VA

G7, $150-$250
Harnet Co., NC

G6, $125-$225
Rndolph Co., NC

Patinated rhyolite

Snub nose form

G8, $200-$350
Randolph Co., NC

G8, $200-$350
Randolph Co., NC

G9, $275-$500
Randolph Co., NC

LOCATION: Southeastern states. **DESCRIPTION:** A small to medium size, serrated, auriculate point with a concave base. Basal fluting or thinning is common. Bases are ground. Ears turn outward or have parallel sides. A cross between *Hardaway* and *Dalton*. **I.D. KEY:** Width of base, location found.

HARDAWAY-PALMER - Early Archaic, 9500 - 8000 B. P.

(Also see Hardaway and Palmer)

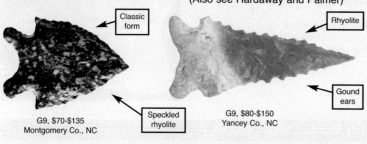

Classic form

Rhyolite

Gound ears

Speckled rhyolite

G9, $70-$135
Montgomery Co., NC

G9, $80-$150
Yancey Co., NC

LOCATION: Southeastern states. **DESCRIPTION:** A cross between *Hardaway* and *Palmer* with expanded auricles and a concave base that is ground.

HARDIN - Early Archaic, 9000 - 6000 B. P.

(Also see Kirk and Lost Lake)

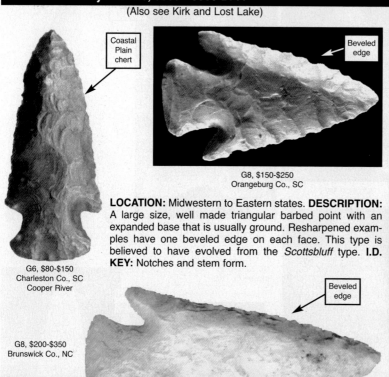

Coastal Plain chert

Beveled edge

G8, $150-$250
Orangeburg Co., SC

LOCATION: Midwestern to Eastern states. **DESCRIPTION:** A large size, well made triangular barbed point with an expanded base that is usually ground. Resharpened examples have one beveled edge on each face. This type is believed to have evolved from the *Scottsbluff* type. **I.D. KEY:** Notches and stem form.

G6, $80-$150
Charleston Co., SC
Cooper River

Beveled edge

G8, $200-$350
Brunswick Co., NC

Coastal Plain chert

G7, $165-$300
Tyler Co., WVA

HEAVY DUTY - Middle Archaic, 7000 - 5000 B. P.

(Also see Appalachian, Kirk Stemmed and Southampton)

G4, $8-$15
Putnam
Co., WVA

G4, $12-$20
Bethany, WVA

206

HEAVY DUTY (continued)

LOCATION: Ohio into West Virginia. **DESCRIPTION:** A medium to large size, thick, serrated point with a parallel stem and straight to slightly concave base. A variant of *Kirk Stemmed* found in the Southeast. **I.D. KEY:** Base, thickness, flaking.

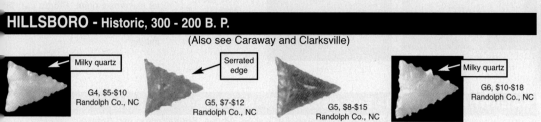

HILLSBORO - Historic, 300 - 200 B. P.

(Also see Caraway and Clarksville)

Milky quartz

G4, $5-$10
Randolph Co., NC

Serrated edge

G5, $7-$12
Randolph Co., NC

G5, $8-$15
Randolph Co., NC

Milky quartz

G6, $10-$18
Randolph Co., NC

LOCATION: North Carolina. **DESCRIPTION:** A small size, thin, triangular, arrow point with a straight to concave base. Blade edges can be serrated. Smaller than Badin to very small size.

HOLMES - Late Archaic, 4000 - 3000 B. P.

(Also see Savannah River, Southampton and Stanly Narrow Blade)

LOCATION: Far Eastern states. **DESCRIPTION:** A medium size, narrow point with weak, tapered shoulders and a slight concave base.

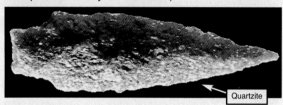

G4, $8-$15
Sussex Co., VA

Quartzite

JACKS REEF CORNER NOTCHED - Late Woodland to Mississippian, 1500 - 1000 B. P.

(Also see Kirk Corner Notched and Peedee)

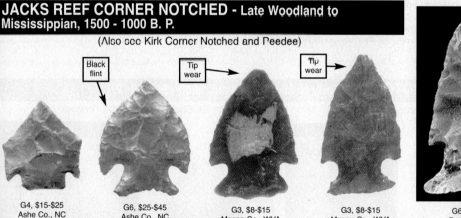

Black flint

Tip wear

Tip wear

G4, $15-$25
Ashe Co., NC

G6, $25-$45
Ashe Co., NC

G3, $8-$15
Mason Co., WVA

G3, $8-$15
Mason Co., WVA

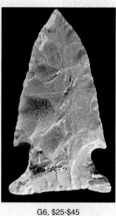

G6, $25-$45
Bethany, WVA

LOCATION: Southeastern states. **DESCRIPTION:** A small to medium size, very thin, corner notched point that is well made. The blade is convex to pentagonal. Some examples are widely corner notched and appear to be expanded stem points with barbed shoulders. Rarely, they are basal notched. **I.D. KEY:** Thinness, made by the birdpoint people.

Barb nick

G6, $20-$35
Mason Co., WVA

JACKS REEF PENTAGONAL (See Peedee)

JUDE - Early Archaic, 9000 - 6000 B. P.

(Also see Garth Slough and Halifax)

JUDE (continued)

G5, $8-$15
Montgomery Co., NC

G4, $5-$10
Amelia Co., VA

LOCATION: Southeastern states. **DESCRIPTION**: A small size, short, barbed, expanded to parallel stemmed point. Stems can be as large as the blade. Rare in this area. **I.D. KEY**: Basal form and flaking.

KANAWHA STEMMED - Early Archaic, 8200 - 5000 B. P.

(Also see Kirk Stemmed-Bifurcated, LeCroy, St. Albans, Southampton and Stanly)

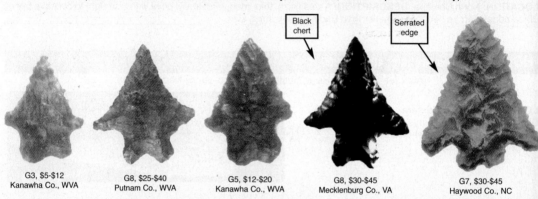

Black chert

Serrated edge

G3, $5-$12
Kanawha Co., WVA

G8, $25-$40
Putnam Co., WVA

G5, $12-$20
Kanawha Co., WVA

G8, $30-$45
Mecklenburg Co., VA

G7, $30-$45
Haywood Co., NC

LOCATION: Eastern to Southeastern states. Type site is in Kanawha Co., WVA. **DESCRIPTION:** A small to medium size, fairly thick, shallowly bifurcated stemmed point. The basal lobes are usually rounded and the shoulders tapered or clipped wing turning towards the tip. Believed to be the ancestor to the *Stanly* type. The St. Albans site dated *Kanawha* to 8,200 B.P. Similar to *Fox Valley* found in Illinois.

KIRK CORNER NOTCHED - Early to Middle Archaic, 9000 - 6000 B. P.

(Also see Amos, Bolen, Hardin, Jacks Reef, Lost Lake, St. Charles, Taylor and Thebes)

Serrated edge

Serrated edge

G2, $6-$12
VA

G6, $15-$25
Randolph Co., NC

G9, $55-$100
Ashe Co., NC

G7, $25-$45
Catawba Co., NC

G7, $35-$50
Ashe Co., NC

LOCATION: Eastern states. **DESCRIPTION:** A medium to large size, corner notched point. Blade edges can be convex to recurved and are finely serrated on many examples. The base can be convex, concave, straight or auriculate. Points that are beveled on one side of each face would fall under the *Lost Lake* type. **I.D. KEY:** Secondary edgework.

ES

Flint

Rhyolite

Green rhyolite

G8, $40-$75
Alleghany Co., NC

G6, $30-$50
Haywood Co., NC

G8, $70-$125
Randolph Co., NC

G9, $90-$175
Randolph Co., NC

Rhyolite

G8, $40-$75
Randolph Co., NC

Serrated edge

G8, $125-$225
Montgomery Co., NC

G7, $125-$200
Randolph Co., NC

Edge wear

Rhyolite

G5, $30-$50
Randolph Co., NC

G8, $125-$225
Johnston Co., NC

G9, $550-$1000
Surry Co., NC

KIRK STEMMED - Early to Middle Archaic, 9000 - 6000 B. P.

(Also see Bolen, Fountain Creek, Heavy Duty, and Stanly)

G3, $4-$8
Cent. NC

Banded
Rhyolite

G7, $12-$20
NC

Serrated
edges

G6, $15-$30
Cent. NC

G5, $20-$35
Wilson Co., NC

G6, $12-$20
NC

G6, $25-$45
NC

Serrated
edges

Banded
slate

G6, $25-$45
Randolph Co., NC

G8, $125-$225
Randolph Co., NC

G9, $125-$225
Randolph Co., NC

G6, $65-$125
Randolph Co., NC

LOCATION: Southeastern to Eastern states. **DESCRIPTION:** A medium to large size, barbed, stemmed point with deep notches or fine serrations along the blade edges. The stem is parallel to expanding. The stem sides may be steeply beveled on opposite faces. Some examples also have a distinct bevel on the right side of each blade edge. The base can be concave, convex or straight, and can be very short. The shoulders are usually strongly barbed. Believed to have evolved into *Stanly* and other types. The St. Albans site dated this type from 8,850 to 8,980 B.P. **I.D. KEY:** Serrations.

KIRK STEMMED-BIFURCATED - Early Archaic, 9000 - 7000 B. P.

(Also see Cave Spring, Fox Valley, LeCroy, St. Albans, Southhampton and Stanly)

Serrated edges

Slate

Serrated edges

G6, $20-$35
Randolph Co., NC

G7, $20-$35
Randolph Co., NC

G4, $12-$20
Saluda Co., SC

G6, $25-$45
Randolph Co., NC

Serrated edges

G8, $35-$65
Randolph Co., NC

G5, $15-$30
Randolph Co., NC

G5, $15-$30
Randolph Co., NC

LOCATION: Southeastern to Eastern states. **DESCRIPTION:** A medium to large point with deep notches or fine serrations along the blade edges. The stem is parallel sided to expanded and is bifurcated. Believed to be an early form for the type which later developed into *Stanly* and others. Tennessee examples have a steep bevel on the right side of each blade edge.

LECROY - Early to Middle Archaic, 9000 - 5000 B. P.

(Also see Decatur, Kanawha Stemmed, Kirk Stemmed-Bifurcated, St. Albans, Southampton and Stanly)

Milky quartz

Milky quartz

Milky quartz

G4, $10-$20
Emporia Co., VA

G4, $10-$20
Stokes Co., NC

G6, $12-$20
NC

G8, $25-$40
Wayne Co., NC

G4, $10-$20
Surry Co., NC

G8, $25-$45
Alleghany Co., NC

Milky quartz

Milky quartz

Milky quartz

G7, $20-$35
Randolph Co., NC

G8, $20-$35
Randolph Co., NC

G5, $15-$25
Ashe Co., NC

G5, $15-$25
Sussex Co., VA

G8, $25-$40
Randolph Co., NC

G7, $20-$35
Stokes Co., NC

211

LECROY (continued)

G6, $15-$25
Randolph Co., NC

Milky quartz

G9, $15-$25
Randolph Co., NC

Slate

G5, $15-$25
Fairfield Co., SC

G5, $15-$25
Randolph Co., NC

G6, $25-$40
Randolph Co., NC

G7, $25-$45
Randolph Co., NC

G7, $25-$40
Iredell Co., NC

G7, $20-$35
Randolph Co., NC

G8, $30-$50
Cent. NC

G8, $30-$50
Alleghany Co., NC

LOCATION: Southeastern into northeastern states. Type site-Hamilton Co., TN. **DESCRIPTION:** A small to medium size, thin, usually broad point with deeply notched or serrated blade edges and a deeply bifurcated base. Basal ears can either droop or expand out. The stem is usually large in comparison to the blade size. Some stem sides are fractured in Northern examples *(Lake Erie)*. Bases are usually ground. St. Albans site dated *LeCroy* to 8,300 B.P. **I.D. KEY:** Basal form.

LOST LAKE - Early Archaic, 9000 - 6000 B. P.

(Also see Bolen, Decatur, Hardin, Kirk, Palmer, St. Charles, Taylor and Thebes)

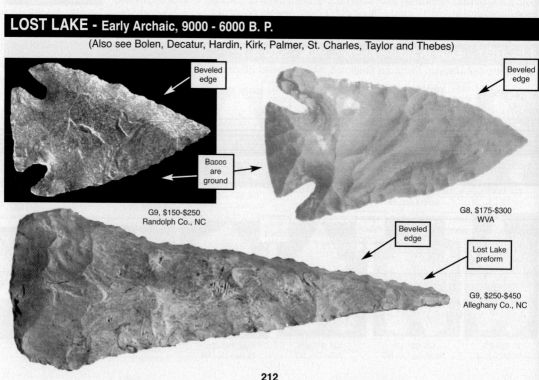

Beveled edge

Bases are ground

G9, $150-$250
Randolph Co., NC

Beveled edge

G8, $175-$300
WVA

Beveled edge

Lost Lake preform

G9, $250-$450
Alleghany Co., NC

LOST LAKE (continued)

LOCATION: Southeastern states. **DESCRIPTION:** A medium to large size, broad, corner notched point that is beveled on one side of each face. The beveling continues when resharpened and creates a flat rhomboid cross section. Most examples are finely serrated and exhibit high quality flaking and symmetry. Also known as *Deep Notch.* **I.D. KEY:** Notching, secondary edgework is always opposite creating at least slight beveling.

Beveled edge

E
S

G9, $350-$650
Pitt Co., NC

MEADOWOOD - Late Archaic to early Woodland, 4000 - 2500 B. P.

(Also see Otter Creek and Rowan)

G7, $25-$45
VA

LOCATION: Northeastern states into Virginia. **DESCRIPTION:** A medium to large size point with shallow side notches near the base. The base can be straight to slightly convex. Blade edges can be straight to slightly convex to recurved. Some specimens show a lot of reworking and my be used up and asymmetrical. **I.D. KEY:** Notches close to base

MORROW MOUNTAIN - Middle Archaic, 7000 - 5000 B. P.

(Also see Adena, Chesapeake Diamond, Ovates, Piscataway and Randolph)

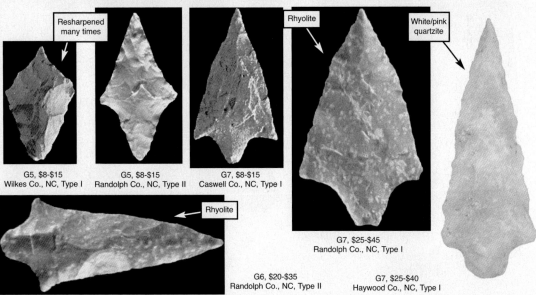

Resharpened many times

Rhyolite

White/pink quartzite

G5, $8-$15
Wilkes Co., NC, Type I

G5, $8-$15
Randolph Co., NC, Type II

G7, $8-$15
Caswell Co., NC, Type I

Rhyolite

G6, $20-$35
Randolph Co., NC, Type II

G7, $25-$45
Randolph Co., NC, Type I

G7, $25-$40
Haywood Co., NC, Type I

LOCATION: Midwestern to Southeastern states. **DESCRIPTION:** A medium to large size, triangular point with a very short contracting to rounded stem. Shoulders are usually weak but can be barbed. The blade edges on some examples are serrated with needle points. **I.D. KEY:** Contracted base and Archaic parallel flaking.

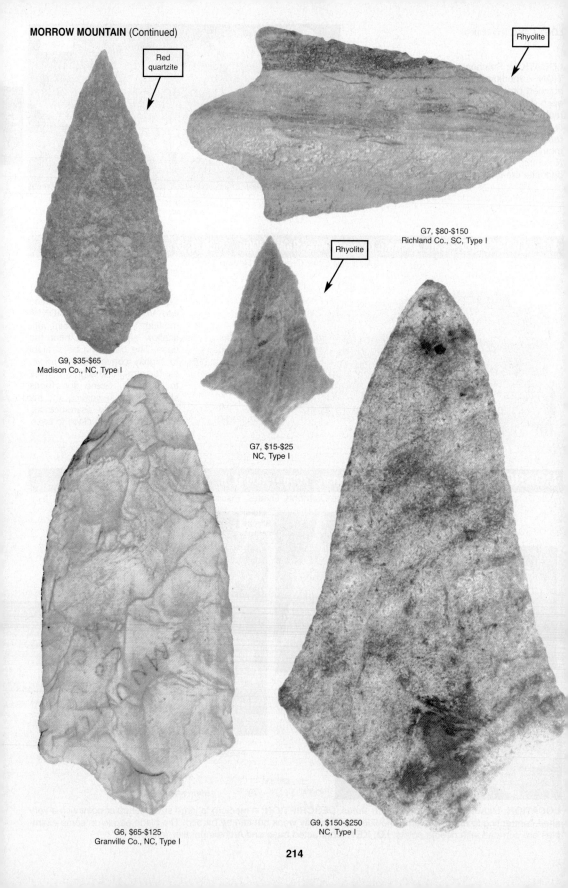

MORROW MOUNTAIN (Continued)

Red quartzite

Rhyolite

Rhyolite

G7, $80-$150
Richland Co., SC, Type I

G9, $35-$65
Madison Co., NC, Type I

G7, $15-$25
NC, Type I

G6, $65-$125
Granville Co., NC, Type I

G9, $150-$250
NC, Type I

MORROW MOUNTAIN STRAIGHT BASE - Middle Archaic, 7000 - 5000 B. P.

(Also see Adena and Savannah River)

G7, $8-$15
Bristol, VA

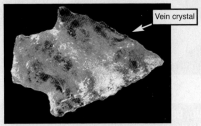

Vein crystal

G9, $35-$60
Johnson Co., NC

LOCATION: Southeastern states. **DESCRIPTION:** A medium size, thin, strongly barbed point with a contracting stem and a straight base. Some examples are serrated and have a needle tip. Look for Archaic parallel flaking.

E S

OCCANEECHEE - Mississippian to Historic, 600 - 400 B. P.

(Also see Yadkin)

LOCATION: North Carolina. **DESCRIPTION:** A large size triangular point with a concave base. Base corners can be sharp to rounded.

G8, $200-$350
Randolph Co.,
NC

OTTER CREEK - Middle to Late Archaic, 6000 - 3500 B. P.

(Also see Big Sandy, Meadowood and Rowan)

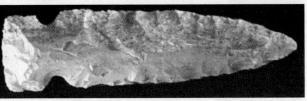

G6, $25-$40
Bethany, WVA

G6, $40-$70
WVA

G5, $15-$25
WVA

LOCATION: Northeastern states. **DESCRIPTION:** A medium to large size, narrow side-notched point with a straight, concave or convex base. Notching is prominent, shoulders are tapered to barbed. Bases are ground. **I.D. KEY:** Side notching.

OVATES - Woodland, 3000 - 2000 B. P.

(Also see Amos, Chesapeake Diamond, Ecusta, Hardaway-Palmer, Kirk Corner Notched and Taylor)

G3, $3-$6
Sussex Co., VA

G5, $5-$10
Chesterfield Co., VA

LOCATION: Northeastern statesinto Virginia. **DESCRIPTION:** A small size, tear-drop shaped point with rounded shoulders and base.. **I.D. KEY:** Ovoid form.

PALMER - Early Archaic, 9000 - 6000 B. P.

(Also see Amos, Ecusta, Hardaway-Palmer, Kirk Corner Notched and Taylor)

G6, $8-$15
Bethany, WVA

Milky quartz

G6, $12-$20
Randolph Co., NC

G6, $12-$20
Wayne Co., NC

G6, $12-$20
Bethany, WVA

G8, $30-$45
Davidson Co., NC

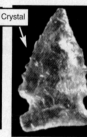

Crystal

G6, $20-$35
Randolph Co., NC

G5, $20-$35
Ashe Co., NC

G5, $15-$25
Lexington Co., SC

G9, $65-$125
Rockingham Co., NC

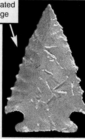

Serrated edge

G9, $55-$100
Stanly Co., NC

G9, $40-$75
Randolph Co., NC

G10, $40-$75
Surry Co., NC

Serrated edges

G9, $65-$125
Yadkin Co., NC

G7, $30-$50
Ashe Co., NC

Serrated edge

G8, $30-$50
Randolph Co., NC

G6, $25-$40
Ashe Co., NC

G9, $55-$75
Surry Co., NC

G10+ $175-$300
Randolph Co., NC

G8, $40-$75
Randolph Co., NC

LOCATION: Southeastern to Eastern states. **DESCRIPTION:** A small size, corner notched, triangular point with a ground concave, convex or straight base. Many are serrated and large examples would fall under the *Pine Tree* or *Kirk* type. This type developed from *Hardaway* in North Carolina where cross types are found.

216

PATRICK HENRY - Early Archaic, 9500 - 8500 B. P.

(Also see Bolen, Decatur, Palmer and Taylor)

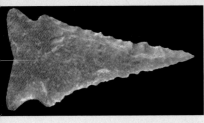

G8, $60-$100
Randolph Co., NC

G8, $65-$125
NC

E
S

LOCATION: Eastern seaboard states. **DESCRIPTION:** A medium size corner notched point with a fish-tailed base. Blade edges can be serrated and the basal area is ground.

PEE DEE - Late Woodland to Mississippian, 1500 - 1000 B. P.

(Also see Caraway and Jacks Reef)

G3, $5-$10
Smyth Co., VA

G3, $5-$10
Yadkin Co., NC

G5, $15-$30
Randolph Co., NC

G5, $15-$25
Yadkin Co., NC

G6, $15-$25
Wilkes Co., NC

G8, $15-$30
Randolph Co., NC

Pentagonal
form

G6, $15-$30
Randolph Co., NC

G5, $15-$30
Wilkes Co., NC

G6, $25-$40
Randolph Co., NC

G8, $30-$50
SC

G5, $15-$25
VA

LOCATION: Eastern seaboard states. **DESCRIPTION:** A small to large size, very thin, five sided point with a sharp tip. The hafting area is usually contracted with a slightly concave to straight base. Called *Jacks Reef* elsewhere.

PENTAGONAL KNIFE - Mid-Archaic, 6500 - 4000 B. P.

(Also see Kirk)

G8, $35-$65
Surry Co., VA

LOCATION: Ohio into Kentucky, Tennessee, North Carolina & Alabama. **DESCRIPTION:** A medium to large size pentagonal shaped point with a flaring or corner notched stem. Some examples are base notched. Similar to but older than the *Afton* point found in the Midwest. Similar to *Jacks Reef* but thicker. **I.D. KEY:** Blade form.

G8, $125-$200
Rockingham Co., NC

PICKWICK - Middle to Late Archaic, 6000 - 3500 B. P.

(Also see Savannah River and Stanly)

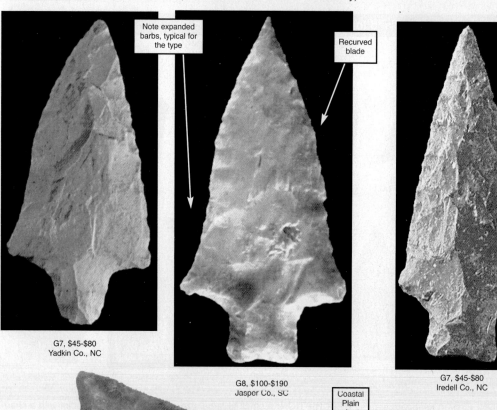

Note expanded barbs, typical for the type

Recurved blade

G7, $45-$80
Yadkin Co., NC

G8, $100-$190
Jasper Co., SC

G7, $45-$80
Iredell Co., NC

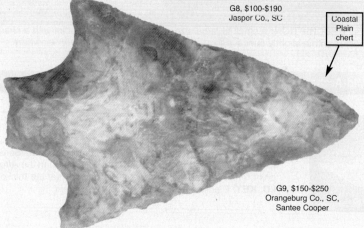

Coastal Plain chert

G9, $150-$250
Orangeburg Co., SC,
Santee Cooper

LOCATION: Southeastern states into North and South Carolina. **DESCRIPTION:** A medium to large size, expanded shoulder, contracted to expanded stem point. Blade edges are recurved, and many examples show fine secondary flaking with serrations. Some are beveled on one side of each face. The bevel is steep and shallow. Shoulders are horizontal, tapered or barbed and form sharp angles. Some stems are snapped off or may show original rind. **I.D. KEY:** Barbs and blade form.

PISCATAWAY - Mid to late Woodland, 2500 - 500 B. P.

(Also see Morrow Mountain and Randolph)

G5, $8-$15
Amelia Co., VA

LOCATION: Far Eastern states. **DESCRIPTION:** A medium size triangular point with a short, straight base that has shallow corner notches.

E
S

POTTS - Woodland, 3000 - 1000 B. P.

(Also see Ecusta and Waratan)

LOCATION: Far Eastern states. **DESCRIPTION:** A medium size triangular point with a short, straight base that has shallow corner notches.

G5, $8-$15
Rockingham Co., NC

QUAD - Late Paleo, 10,000 - 6000 B. P.

(Also see Simpson and Waratan)

G5, $125-$200
Myrtle Beach, SC

G7, $200-$375
Orangeburg Co., SC

LOCATION: Southeastern states. **DESCRIPTION:** A medium to large size lanceolate point with flaring "squared" auricles and a concave base which is ground. Most examples show basal thinning and some are fluted. **I.D. KEY:** Paleo flaking, squarish auricles.

RANDOLPH - Historic, 550 - 170 B. P.

(Also see Morrow Mountain)

G3, $3-$6
Randolph Co., NC

G4, $5-$10
Randolph Co., NC

G6, $5-$10
Guilford Co., NC

G6, $8-$15
Randolph Co., NC

G6, $8-$15
Randolph Co., NC

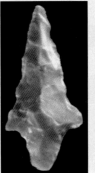

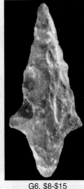

G6, $8-$15
Randolph Co., NC

G6, $8-$15
Randolph Co., NC

G6, $5-$10
Guilford Co., NC

LOCATION: Far Eastern states. Type site is Randolph Co., NC. **DESCRIPTION:** A medium size, narrow, thick, spike point with tapered shoulders and a short to medium contracted, rounded stem. Many examples from North Carolina have exaggerated spikes along the blade edges.

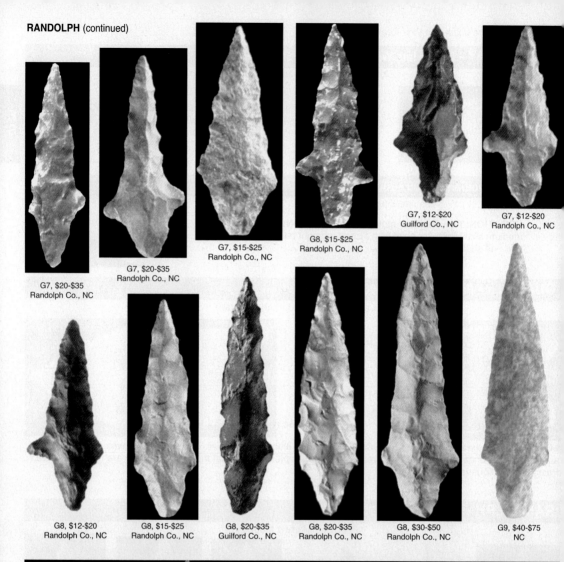

G7, $20-$35
Randolph Co., NC

G7, $20-$35
Randolph Co., NC

G7, $15-$25
Randolph Co., NC

G8, $15-$25
Randolph Co., NC

G7, $12-$20
Guilford Co., NC

G7, $12-$20
Randolph Co., NC

G8, $12-$20
Randolph Co., NC

G8, $15-$25
Randolph Co., NC

G8, $20-$35
Guilford Co., NC

G8, $20-$35
Randolph Co., NC

G8, $30-$50
Randolph Co., NC

G9, $40-$75
NC

REDSTONE - Paleo, 11,500 - 10,600 B. P.

(Also see Clovis)

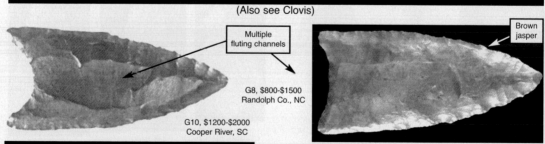

Multiple
fluting channels

Brown
jasper

G8, $800-$1500
Randolph Co., NC

G10, $1200-$2000
Cooper River, SC

G7, $650-$1200
Edgefield Co., SC

LOCATION: Southeastern states. **DESCRIPTION:** A medium to large size, thin, auriculate, fluted point with convex sides expanding to a wide, deeply concave base. The hafting area is ground. This point is widest at the base. Fluting can extend most of the way down each face. Multiple flutes are usual. (**Warning:** The more common resharpened *Clovis* point is often sold as this type. *Redstones* are extrememly rare and are almost never offered for sale.) **I.D. KEY:** Baton fluted, edgework on the hafting area.

(Also see Big Sandy and Bolen)

E S

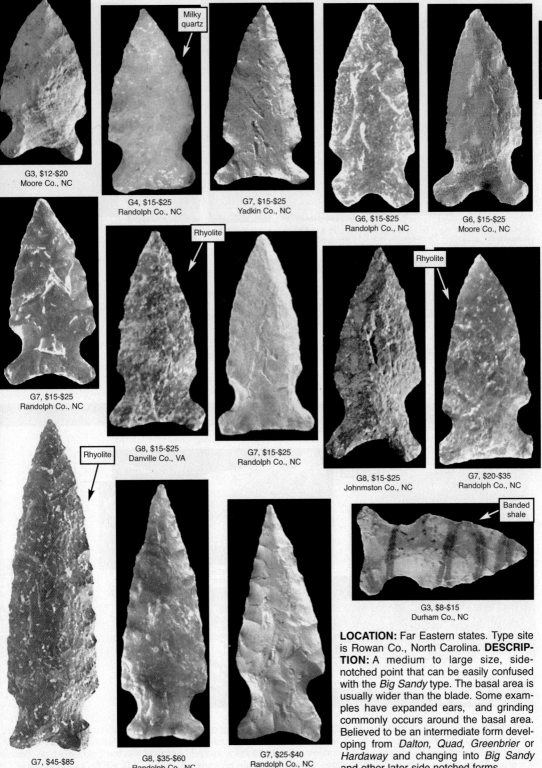

G3, $12-$20
Moore Co., NC

Milky quartz

G4, $15-$25
Randolph Co., NC

G7, $15-$25
Yadkin Co., NC

G6, $15-$25
Randolph Co., NC

G6, $15-$25
Moore Co., NC

G7, $15-$25
Randolph Co., NC

Rhyolite

G8, $15-$25
Danville Co., VA

G7, $15-$25
Randolph Co., NC

Rhyolite

G8, $15-$25
Johnmston Co., NC

G7, $20-$35
Randolph Co., NC

Rhyolite

Banded shale

G3, $8-$15
Durham Co., NC

G7, $45-$85
Iredell Co., NC

G8, $35-$60
Randolph Co., NC

G7, $25-$40
Randolph Co., NC

LOCATION: Far Eastern states. Type site is Rowan Co., North Carolina. **DESCRIPTION:** A medium to large size, side-notched point that can be easily confused with the *Big Sandy* type. The basal area is usually wider than the blade. Some examples have expanded ears, and grinding commonly occurs around the basal area. Believed to be an intermediate form developing from *Dalton, Quad, Greenbrier* or *Hardaway* and changing into *Big Sandy* and other later side notched forms.

221

ST. ALBANS - Early to Middle Archaic, 9000 - 5000 B. P.

(Also see Decatur, Kanawha, Kirk Stemmed-Bifurcated, LeCroy, Southampton and Stanly)

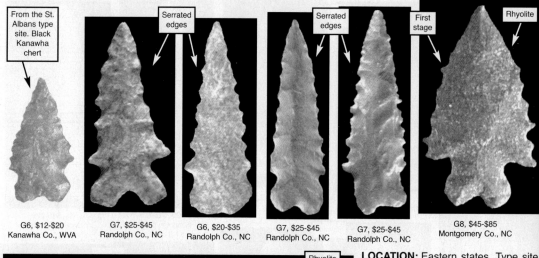

From the St. Albans type site. Black Kanawha chert

Serrated edges

Serrated edges

First stage

Rhyolite

G6, $12-$20
Kanawha Co., WVA

G7, $25-$45
Randolph Co., NC

G6, $20-$35
Randolph Co., NC

G7, $25-$45
Randolph Co., NC

G7, $25-$45
Randolph Co., NC

G8, $45-$85
Montgomery Co., NC

Rhyolite

G8, $65-$115
Randolph Co., NC

LOCATION: Eastern states. Type site is in Kanawha Co., WVA. **DESCRIPTION:** A small to medium size, narrow, usually serrated, bifurcated point. Basal lobes usually flare outward and most examples are sharply barbed. The basal lobes are more shallow than in the *LeCroy* type, otherwise they are easily confused. St. Albans site dated this type to 8,850 B.P. **I.D. KEY:** Shallow basal lobes and narrowness.

ST. CHARLES - Early Archaic, 9500 - 8000 B. P.

(Also see Bolen Beveled, Decatur, Lost Lake and Thebes)

Beveled edge

Beveled edge

G6, $35-$60
Mason Co., WVA

G4, $20-$35
Ashe Co., NC

Beveled edge

Beveled edge

Tip wear

G8, $200-$350
Stokes Co., NC

G5, $25-$40
Ashe Co., NC

LOCATION: Midwest into the southeast. **DESCRIPTION:** Also known as *Dovetail* and *Plevna*. A medium to large size, corner notched, dovetailed base point. The blade is beveled on one side of each face (usually the left side) on resharpened examples. Bases are always convex. Straight bases would place a point into the *Lost Lake* type. Bases are ground and can be fractured on both sides or center notched on some examples. **I.D. KEY:** Dovetailed base.

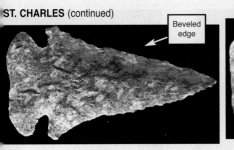

Beveled edge

Beveled edge

ES

G8, $65-$125
Central NC

G8, $175-$300
Randolph Co., NC

SAVANNAH RIVER - Late Archaic to Woodland, 5000 - 2000 B. P.

(Also see Appalachian, Kirk and Stanly)

Quartz

Milky quartz

G4, $8-$15
Newberry Co., SC

G4, $8-$15
Southampton Co., VA

G3, $8-$15
Amelia Co., VA

G6, $12-$20
Randolph Co., NC

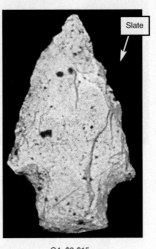

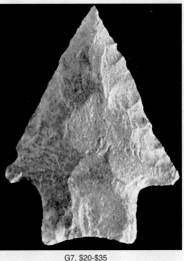

Slate

G5, $15-$25
Cent. NC

G4, $8-$15
Newberry Co., SC

G7, $20-$35
Yadkin Co., NC

LOCATION: Southeastern to Eastern states. **DESCRIPTION:** A medium to large size, straight to contracting stemmed point with a straight or concave to bifurcated base. The shoulders are tapered to square. The stems are narrow to broad. Believed to be related to the earlier *Stanly* point. Aka *Appalachian* points in East Tenn. & Western North Carolina.

223

Quartzite

G6, $20-$35
Randolph Co., NC

G8, $45-$80
Randolph Co., NC

G6, $30-$55
Randolph Co., NC

Rhyolite

Red
quartzite

G9, $55-$100
Sussex Co., VA

G9, $70-$125
Davidson Co., NC

G8, $125-$200
Randolph Co., NC

Rhyolite

G7, $30-$55
Randolph Co., NC

224

Quartzite

Rhyolite

E
S

G6, $50-$90
NC

G8, $125-$200
Randolph Co., NC

G8, $125-$200
Randolph Co., NC

Shale

Banded
slate

G7, $65-$125
Randolph Co., NC

G6, $55-$100
Montgomery Co., NC

G9, $150-$250
Randolph Co., NC

SCRAPER - Paleo to Archaic, 11,500 - 5000 B. P.

(Also see Drill)

G8, $12-$20
Chesterfield Co., VA

G8, $12-$20
Amelia Co., VA

LOCATION: Paleo to Archaic sites throughout North America. **DESCRIPTION:** Thumb, duck-bill and turtleback forms are small to medium size, thick, ovoid shaped, uniface, scraping tools that are steeply beveled, especially at the broadest end. Side scrapers are long hand-held uniface flakes with beveling on all blade edges of one face. Scraping was done primarily from the sides of these blades. Broken points were also rechipped into scrapers.

SIMPSON - Late Paleo, 10,000 - 9000 B. P.

(Also see Clovis-unfluted and Quad)

LOCATION: Southern Southeastern states. **DESCRIPTION:** A medium to large size lanceolate, auriculate blade with recurved sides, outward flaring ears and a concave base. The hafting area constriction is more narrow than in the *Suwannee* type. Fluting is absent.

G8, $150-$250
Edgefield Co.,
SC

SNYDERS (Hopewell) - Woodland, 2500 - 1500 B. P.

(Also see Jack's Reef)

LOCATION: Midwestern to eastern states. **DESCRIPTION:** A medium to large size, broad, thin, wide corner notched point of high quality. Blade edges and base are convex. This point has been reproduced in recent years. I.D. KEY: Size and broad corner notches.

G8, $40-$75
VA

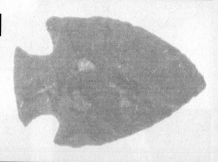

SOUTHAMPTON - Early Archaic, 8000 - 6000 B. P.

(Also see Kanawha, St. Albans and Stanly)

G4, $4-$8
Dinwiddie Co., VA

G4, $5-$10
Amelia Co., VA

G3, $5-$10
Amelia Co., VA

G3, $4-$8
Chesterfield Co., VA

G3, $5-$10
Amelia Co., VA

G5, $5-$12
Amelia Co., VA

G4, $4-$8
Sussex Co., VA

G6, $6-$12
Disputanta Co., VA

LOCATION: Far Eastern states. **DESCRIPTION:** A medium to large size, narrow, thick, bifurcated stemmed point. The basal lobes can expand and the center notch is shallow. Bases are usually ground.

SOUTHAMPTON (continued)

Quartzite

G5, $5-$10
Sussex Co., VA

Milky quartz

G5, $4-$8
Sussex Co., VA

Quartzite

G8, $6-$12
Southampton Co., VA

Quartzite

G6, $6-$12
Dinwiddie Co., VA

Quartzite

G6, $6-$12
Dinwiddie Co., VA

ES

STANLY - Early Archaic, 8000 - 5000 B. P.

(Also see Garth Slough, Kanawha Stemmed, Kirk Stemmed-Bifurcated, Savannah River and Southampton)

G8, $35-$65
Randolph Co., NC

Quartzite

G7, $15-$30
Amelia Co., VA

Milky quartz

G6, $15-$30
Amelia Co., VA

Milky quartz

G6, $30-$50
Chesterfield Co., VA

Milky quartz

G3, $15-$25
Dinwiddie Co., VA

G9, $40-$75
Randolph Co., NC

G8, $35-$65
Randolph Co., NC

LOCATION: Southeastern to Eastern states. Type site is Stanly Co., NC.
DESCRIPTION: A small to medium size, broad shoulder point with a small bifurcated stem. Some examples are serrated and show high quality flaking. The shoulders are very prominent and can be tapered, horizontal or barbed.
I.D. KEY: Small bifurcated base.

227

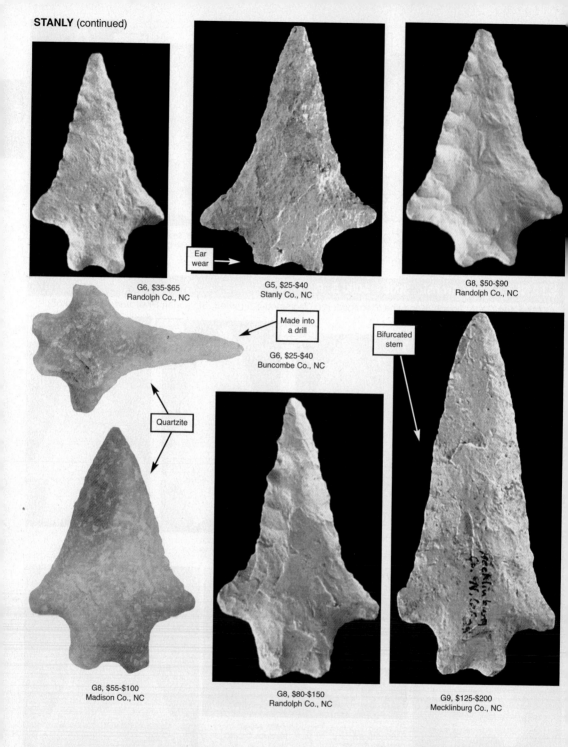

G6, $35-$65
Randolph Co., NC

Ear wear

G5, $25-$40
Stanly Co., NC

G8, $50-$90
Randolph Co., NC

Made into a drill

G6, $25-$40
Buncombe Co., NC

Bifurcated stem

Quartzite

G8, $55-$100
Madison Co., NC

G8, $80-$150
Randolph Co., NC

G9, $125-$200
Mecklinburg Co., NC

STANLY NARROW STEM - Early Archaic, 8000 - 5000 B. P.

(Also see Kirk Stemmed-Bifurcated, St. Albans, Savannah River & Southampton)

LOCATION: Far Eastern states. **DESCRIPTION:** A medium size, narrow shoulder point with a parallel sided stem and a concave base. Believed to have evolved from *Kirk* points and later evolved into *Savannah River* points. Similar to *Northern Piedmont* in Penn.

Bifurcated stem

Quartzite

Bifurcated stem

Quartzite

E S

Bifurcated stem

Quartzite

Quartzite

Quartzite

Bifurcated stem

G6, $15-$25
Stokes Co., NC

G5, $15-$25
Southampton Co., VA

G5, $15-$30
Randolph Co., NC

G4, $15-$30
Stokes Co., NC

G8, $20-$35
Sussex Co., VA

G6, $15-$30
Randolph Co., NC

G6, $20-$35
Catawba Co., NC

G8, $25-$40
Randolph Co., NC

G8, $15-$25
Sussex Co., VA

G8, $15-$30
Montgomery Co., NC

G8, $15-$30
Randolph Co., NC

G8, $30-$45
Randolph Co., NC

G7, $15-$30
Randolph Co., NC

G8, $20-$35
Randolph Co., NC

G7, $15-$25
Moore Co., NC

229

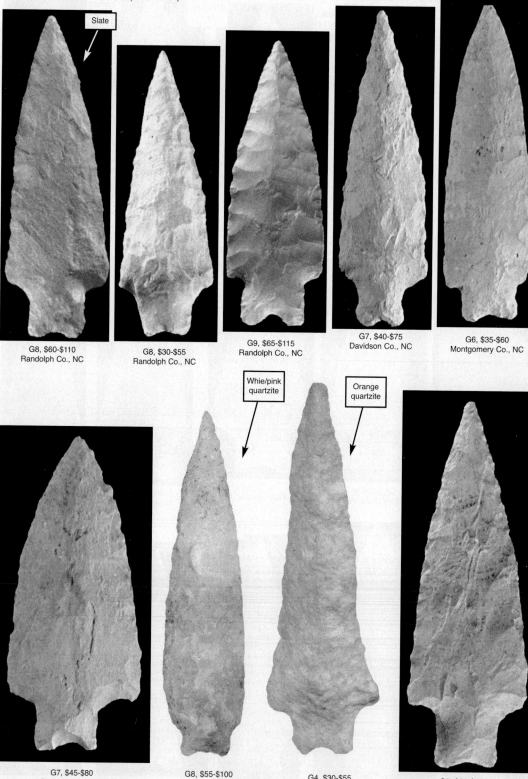

Slate

G8, $60-$110
Randolph Co., NC

G8, $30-$55
Randolph Co., NC

G9, $65-$115
Randolph Co., NC

G7, $40-$75
Davidson Co., NC

G6, $35-$60
Montgomery Co., NC

Whie/pink quartzite

Orange quartzite

G7, $45-$80
Randolph Co., NC

G8, $55-$100
Yancey Co., NC

G4, $30-$55
Swain Co., NC

G8, $80-$165
Moore Co., NC

TAYLOR - Early Archaic, 9000 - 6000 B. P.

(Also see Big Sandy, Bolen, Ecusta, Hardaway, Kirk and Palmer)

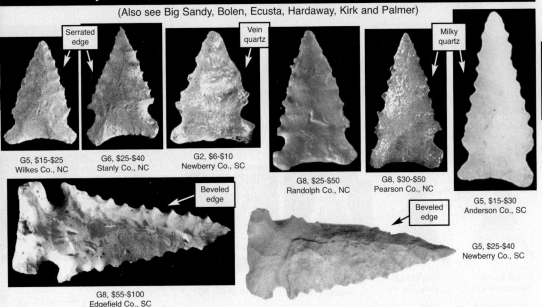

Serrated edge

Vein quartz

Milky quartz

Beveled edge

Beveled edge

G5, $15-$25
Wilkes Co., NC

G6, $25-$40
Stanly Co., NC

G2, $6-$10
Newberry Co., SC

G8, $25-$50
Randolph Co., NC

G8, $30-$50
Pearson Co., NC

G5, $15-$30
Anderson Co., SC

G5, $25-$40
Newberry Co., SC

G8, $55-$100
Edgefield Co., SC

LOCATION: Far Eastern states. **DESCRIPTION:** A medium to large size, side notched to auriculate point with a concave base. Basal areas are ground. Blade edges can be serrated. A cross between *Hardaway* and *Palmer*. Called *Van Lott* in South Carolina.

THEBES - Early Archaic, 10,000 - 8000 B. P.

(Also see Big Sandy, Bolen, Kirk Corner Notched, Lost Lake and St. Charles)

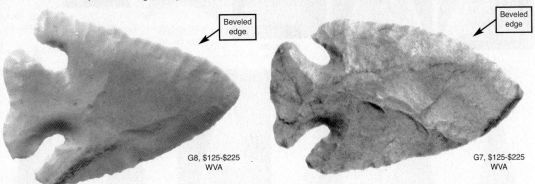

Beveled edge

Beveled edge

G8, $125-$225
WVA

G7, $125-$225
WVA

LOCATION: Midwestern to Eastern states. **DESCRIPTION:** A medium to large size, wide, blade with deep, angled side notches that are parallel sided and squared. Resharpened examples have beveling on one side of each face. The bases of this type have broad proportions and are concave, straight or convex and are ground. Some examples have unusual side notches called Key Notches. This type of notch is angled into the blade to produce a high point in the center, forming the letter E.

TRADE POINTS - Historic, 400 - 170 B. P.

$12-$20
NC, Copper,
circa 1800.

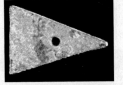

$15-$30
NC, Copper,
circa 1800.

These points were made of copper, iron, and steel and were traded to the Indians by the French, British and others from the 1600s through the 1800s. Examples have been found all over the United States.

(Also see Caraway, Clarksville, Hillsboro, Pee Dee and Yadkin)

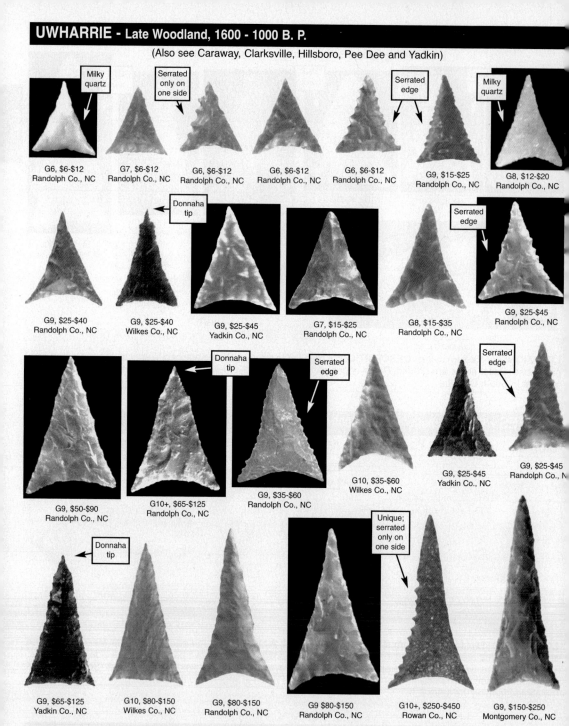

Milky quartz

G6, $6-$12
Randolph Co., NC

Serrated only on one side

G7, $6-$12
Randolph Co., NC

G6, $6-$12
Randolph Co., NC

G6, $6-$12
Randolph Co., NC

G6, $6-$12
Randolph Co., NC

Serrated edge

G9, $15-$25
Randolph Co., NC

Milky quartz

G8, $12-$20
Randolph Co., NC

G9, $25-$40
Randolph Co., NC

Donnaha tip

G9, $25-$40
Wilkes Co., NC

G9, $25-$45
Yadkin Co., NC

G7, $15-$25
Randolph Co., NC

G8, $15-$35
Randolph Co., NC

Serrated edge

G9, $25-$45
Randolph Co., NC

G9, $50-$90
Randolph Co., NC

Donnaha tip

G10+, $65-$125
Randolph Co., NC

Serrated edge

G9, $35-$60
Randolph Co., NC

G10, $35-$60
Wilkes Co., NC

G9, $25-$45
Yadkin Co., NC

Serrated edge

G9, $25-$45
Randolph Co., N

Donnaha tip

G9, $65-$125
Yadkin Co., NC

G10, $80-$150
Wilkes Co., NC

G9, $80-$150
Randolph Co., NC

G9 $80-$150
Randolph Co., NC

Unique; serrated only on one side

G10+, $250-$450
Rowan Co., NC

G9, $150-$250
Montgomery Co., NC

LOCATION: North and South Carolina. **DESCRIPTION:** A small to medium size, thin, triangular arrow point with concave sides and base. Tips and corners can be very sharp. Side edges are straight to concave. Called *Hamilton* in Tennessee. Some examples have special constricted tips called *Donnaha Tips*. Smaller than *Yadkin*.

VAN LOTT - Early Archaic, 9000 - 8000 B. P.

(Also Palmer & Taylor Side Notched)

Serrated edge

Beveled edge

Coastal Plain chert

Milky quartz

Serrated edges

Vein quartz

ES

G6, $25-$45
Moore Co., NC

G10, $90-$175
Lexington Co., SC, Van Lott type site

G6, $15-$30
Abbeville, SC

G6, $25-$40
Anderson Co., SC

G6, $25-$45
Randolph Co., NC

G5, $15-$30
Elberton Co., GA

Beveled edge

Beveled edge

Beveled edge

Beveled edge

G9, $90-$165
Richmond Co., NC

Slate

Serrated edge

G9, $100-$190
Kershaw Co., SC

Rhyolite

G6, $25-$40
Lexington Co., SC

G7, $30-$50
Lexington Co., SC

G8, $70-$135
Lexington Co., SC

LOCATION: Eastern Seaboard states. **DESCRIPTION:** A small to medium size, side notched point with drooping basal ears and a deeply concave base. Some examples are beveled on opposite faces when resharpened and are serrated. Bases and ears are ground. **I.D. KEY:** Expanded auricles.

WALLER KNIFE - Early Archaic, 9000 - 5000 B. P.
(Also see Edgefield Scraper)

LOCATION: Southern Southeastern states.
DESCRIPTION: A medium size double uniface knife with a short, notched base, made from a flake. Only the cutting edges have been pressure flaked.

G7, $40-$75
SC

WARATAN - Woodland, 3000 - 1000 B. P.
(Also see Potts and Yadkin)

Quartzite

Vein quartz

Tip wear

Quartzite

G4, $8-$15
Southampton Co., VA

G5, $12-$20
Sussex Co., VA

G6, $20-$35
Davidson Co., NC

G5, $6-$12
Sussex Co., VA

LOCATION: Far Eastern states. **DESCRIPTION:** A medium to large size point with usually broad, tapered shoulders, weak corner notches and a very short, broad, concave base. The base expands on some examples giving the appearance of ears or auricles.

WATEREE - Woodland, 3000 - 1500 B. P.

(Also see Will's Cove)

LOCATION: Far Eastern states.
DESCRIPTION: A medium size, narrow point with a recurvate blade, horizontal shoulders and a very short stem. Similar to North Carolina's *Will's Cove*.

G5, $20-$35
Fairfield Co., SC

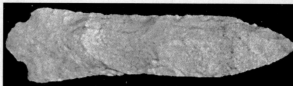

WILL'S COVE - Woodland, 3000 - 1000 B. P.

(Also see Wateree)

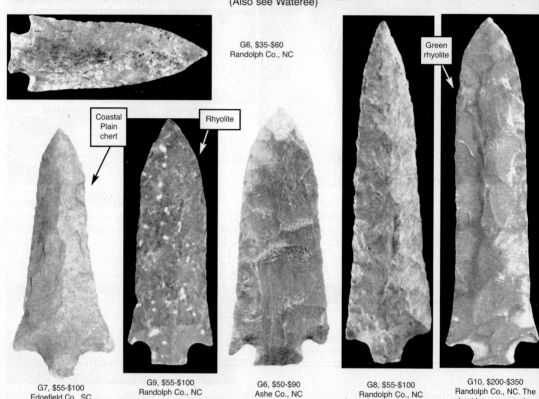

G6, $35-$60
Randolph Co., NC

Green rhyolite

Coastal Plain chert

Rhyolite

G7, $55-$100
Edgefield Co., SC

G9, $55-$100
Randolph Co., NC

G6, $50-$90
Ashe Co., NC

G8, $55-$100
Randolph Co., NC

G10, $200-$350
Randolph Co., NC. The best known example.

LOCATION: Far Eastern states. **DESCRIPTION:** A medium size, very narrow point with horizontal shoulders and a short, narrow stem with parallel sides and a straight base.

YADKIN - Woodland to Mississippian, 2500 - 500 B. P.

(Also see Caraway, Clarksville, Hillsboro, Occaneechee, Peedee, Uwharrie and Yadkin)

Jasper

LOCATION: Southeastern and Eastern states. Type site is Yadkin River in central North Carolina. **DESCRIPTION:** A small to medium size, broad based, fairly thick, triangular point with a broad, concave base and straight to convex to recurved side edges. Called *Levanna* in New York.

G6, $12-$20
Wilkes Co., NC

G6, $12-$20
Randolph Co., NC

G8, $25-$45
Randolph Co., NC

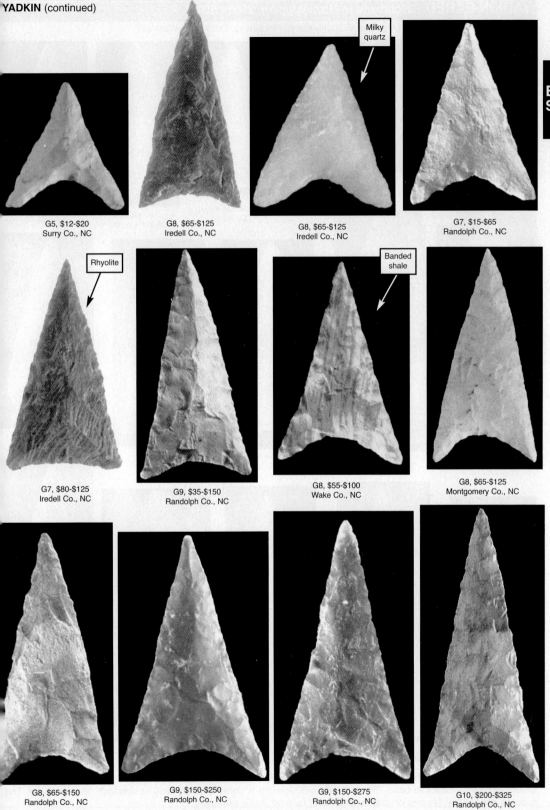

ES

G5, $12-$20
Surry Co., NC

G8, $65-$125
Iredell Co., NC

Milky quartz

G8, $65-$125
Iredell Co., NC

G7, $15-$65
Randolph Co., NC

Rhyolite

G7, $80-$125
Iredell Co., NC

G9, $35-$150
Randolph Co., NC

Banded shale

G8, $55-$100
Wake Co., NC

G8, $65-$125
Montgomery Co., NC

G8, $65-$150
Randolph Co., NC

G9, $150-$250
Randolph Co., NC

G9, $150-$275
Randolph Co., NC

G10, $200-$325
Randolph Co., NC

YADKIN-EARED - Woodland to Mississippian, 2500 - 500 B. P.

(Also see Guilford-Yuma, Hardaway, Potts, and Waratan)

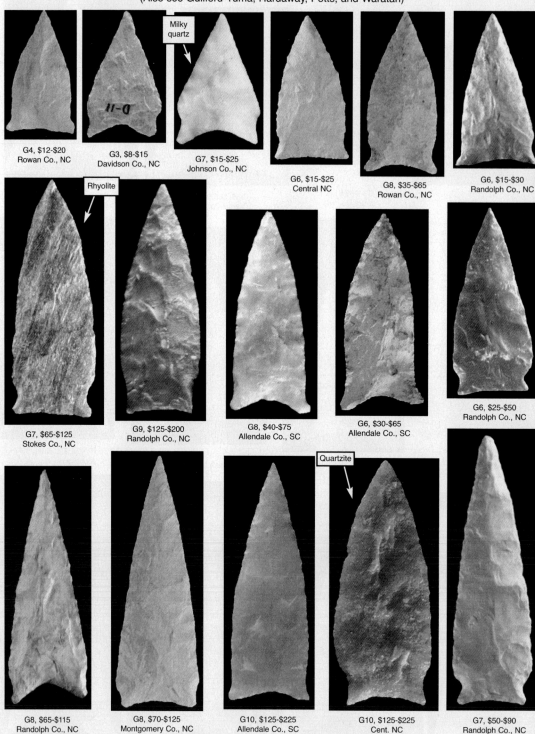

Milky quartz

Rhyolite

Quartzite

G4, $12-$20
Rowan Co., NC

G3, $8-$15
Davidson Co., NC

G7, $15-$25
Johnson Co., NC

G6, $15-$25
Central NC

G8, $35-$65
Rowan Co., NC

G6, $15-$30
Randolph Co., NC

G7, $65-$125
Stokes Co., NC

G9, $125-$200
Randolph Co., NC

G8, $40-$75
Allendale Co., SC

G6, $30-$65
Allendale Co., SC

G6, $25-$50
Randolph Co., NC

G8, $65-$115
Randolph Co., NC

G8, $70-$125
Montgomery Co., NC

G10, $125-$225
Allendale Co., SC

G10, $125-$225
Cent. NC

G7, $50-$90
Randolph Co., NC

LOCATION: Eastern Seaboard states, esp. North Carolina. **DESCRIPTION:** A small to medium size triangular, auriculate point with a concave base. The ears are produced by a shallow constriction or notching near the base. The notches are steeply beveled on one edge of each face on some examples.

GULF COASTAL SECTION:

This section includes point types from the following states:
Florida, S. Alabama, S. Georgia, S. Mississippi, S. South Carolina and
S.E. Louisiana.

The points in this section are arranged in alphabetical order and are shown **actual size**. All types are listed that were available for photographing. Any missing types will be added to future editions as photographs become available. We are always interested in receiving sharp, black and white, color glossy photos, color slides or high resolution (300 pixels/inch) digital pictures of your collection. Be sure to include a ruler in the photograph so that proper scale can be determined.

Lithics: Agate, agatized coral, agate, chalcedony, chert, Coastal Plain chert, conglomerate, crystal quartz, flint, hematite, petrified palmwood, quartzite, Tallahatta quartzite and vein quartz.

Special note: Points that are clear, colorful, made of coral, fossilized palmwood or other exotic material will bring a premium price when offered for sale. Exotic materials are pointed out where known.

Regional Consultants:
Tommy Beutell, Gary Davis
Jacky Fuller, Carlos Tatum
Jim Tatum, Jack Willhoit

GULF COASTAL
(Archaeological Periods)

PALEO - LATE PALEO (11,500 B. P. - 10,000 B. P.)

Beaver Lake	Drill	Scraper	Suwannee
Bone Pin	Paleo Knife	Simpson	Withlacoochee
Clovis	Redstone	Simpson-Mustache	

TRANSITIONAL PALEO (10,500 B. P. - 9,000 B. P.)

Cowhouse Slough	Stanfield	Wheeler
Marianna	Union Side Notched	

EARLY ARCHAIC (10,500 B. P. - 7,000 B. P.)

Agate Basin	Conerly	Hardin	Thonotosassa
Boggy Branch	Dalton	Kirk Corner Notched	Wacissa
Bolen Beveled	Edgefield Scraper	Kirk Stemmed	Waller Knife
Bolen Plain	Gilchrist	Lost Lake	
Chipola	Hamilton	Osceola Greenbrier	
Cobbs	Hardaway	Taylor Side Notched	

MIDDLE ARCHAIC (7,500 B. P. - 4,000 B. P.)

Abbey	Cottonbridge	Marion	Sumter
Alachua	Cypress Creek	Morrow Mountain	Westo
Arredondo	Elora	Newnan	
Bascom	Hardee Beveled	Pickwick	
Benton	Hillsborough	Putnam	
Buzzard Roost	Ledbetter	Savannah River	
Clay	Maples	Six Mile Creek	

LATE ARCHAIC (5,000 B. P. - 3,000 B. P.)

Citrus	Lafayette	South Prong Creek
Culbreath	Levy	Tallahassee
Evans	Santa Fe	
Hernando	Seminole	

WOODLAND (3,000 B. P. - 1,300 B. P.)

Adena	Copena	Leon	Sting Ray Barb
Bradford	Durant's Bend	Manasota	Taylor
Broad River	Duval	Ocala	Weeden Island
Broward	Gadsden	O'leno	Yadkin
Columbia	Jackson	Sarasota	

MISSISSIPPIAN (1300 B. P. - 400 B. P.)

Harahey	Pinellas	Tampa
Ichetucknee	Safety Harbor	Trade

GULF COASTAL
THUMBNAIL GUIDE SECTION

The following references are provided to aid the collector in easier and quicker identification of point types. All photos are exactly 30% of actual size and are proportional to each other. Each point pictured in this section represents a classic form for the type. When a match is found, go to the alphabetical location of that type for more examples in actual size.

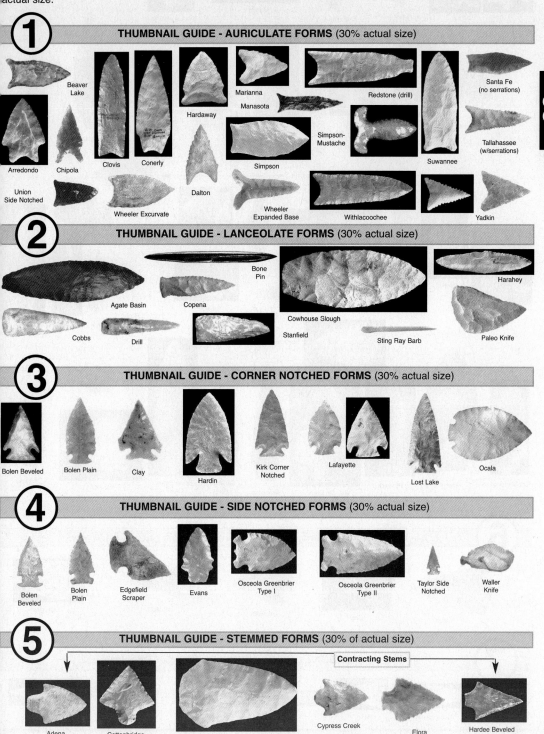

① THUMBNAIL GUIDE - AURICULATE FORMS (30% actual size)

Beaver Lake · Marianna · Manasota · Redstone (drill) · Santa Fe (no serrations) · Hardaway · Arredondo · Chipola · Clovis · Conerly · Simpson-Mustache · Simpson · Suwannee · Tallahassee (w/serrations) · Union Side Notched · Dalton · Wheeler Excurvate · Wheeler Expanded Base · Withlacoochee · Yadkin

② THUMBNAIL GUIDE - LANCEOLATE FORMS (30% actual size)

Bone Pin · Harahey · Agate Basin · Copena · Cobbs · Drill · Stanfield · Cowhouse Slough · Sting Ray Barb · Paleo Knife

③ THUMBNAIL GUIDE - CORNER NOTCHED FORMS (30% actual size)

Bolen Beveled · Bolen Plain · Clay · Hardin · Kirk Corner Notched · Lafayette · Lost Lake · Ocala

④ THUMBNAIL GUIDE - SIDE NOTCHED FORMS (30% actual size)

Bolen Beveled · Bolen Plain · Edgefield Scraper · Evans · Osceola Greenbrier Type I · Osceola Greenbrier Type II · Taylor Side Notched · Waller Knife

⑤ THUMBNAIL GUIDE - STEMMED FORMS (30% of actual size)

Contracting Stems

Adena · Cottonbridge · Bascom · Cypress Creek · Elora · Hardee Beveled

THUMBNAIL GUIDE - Stemmed Forms (continued)

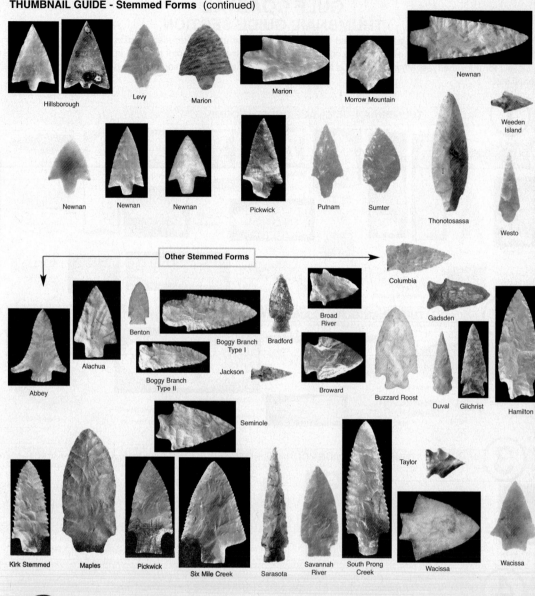

Hillsborough

Levy

Marion

Marion

Morrow Mountain

Newnan

Weeden Island

Newnan

Newnan

Newnan

Pickwick

Putnam

Sumter

Thonotosassa

Westo

Other Stemmed Forms

Columbia

Benton

Boggy Branch Type I

Bradford

Broad River

Gadsden

Abbey

Alachua

Boggy Branch Type II

Jackson

Broward

Buzzard Roost

Duval

Gilchrist

Hamilton

Seminole

Taylor

Kirk Stemmed

Maples

Pickwick

Six Mile Creek

Sarasota

Savannah River

South Prong Creek

Wacissa

Wacissa

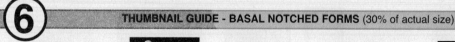

6 **THUMBNAIL GUIDE - BASAL NOTCHED FORMS** (30% of actual size)

Citrus

Clay

Culbreath

Hernando

Lafayette

7 **THUMBNAIL GUIDE - ARROW POINTS** (30% of actual size)

Durant's Bend

Ichetucknee

O'leno

Pinellas

Safety Harbor

Tampa

ABBEY - Middle Archaic, 6000 - 4000 B. P.

(Also see Alachua, Cottonbridge, Elora, Levy, Notchaway, Pickwick, Savannah River, Six Mile Creek, South Prong Creek and Wacissa)

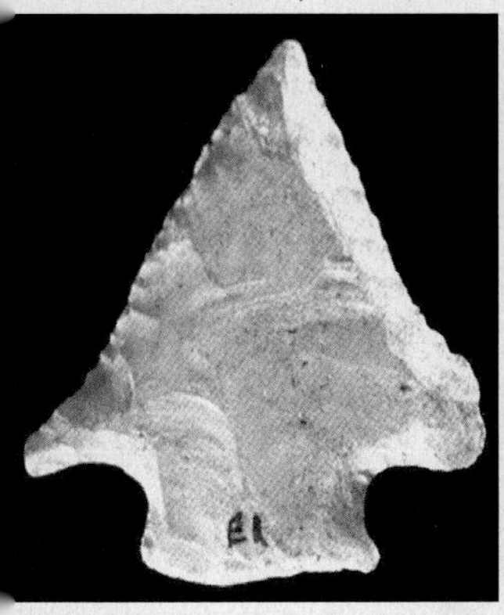

G3, $8-$15
Decatur Co., GA

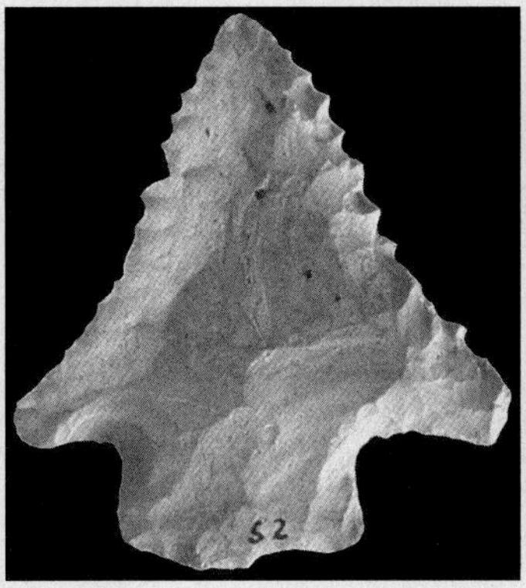

G4, $20-$35
Decatur Co., GA

Classic form

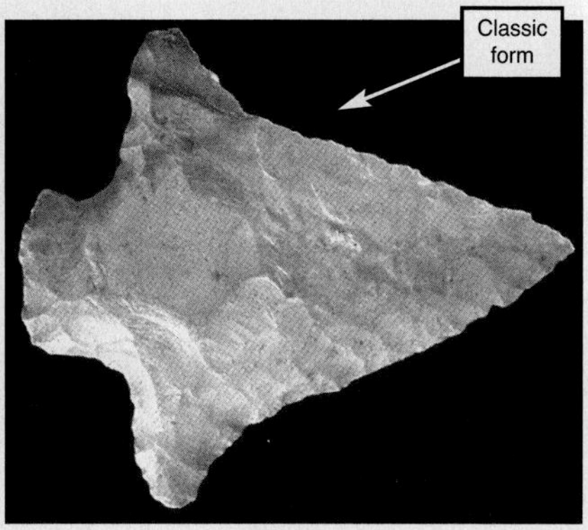

G7, $35-$65
Decatur Co., GA

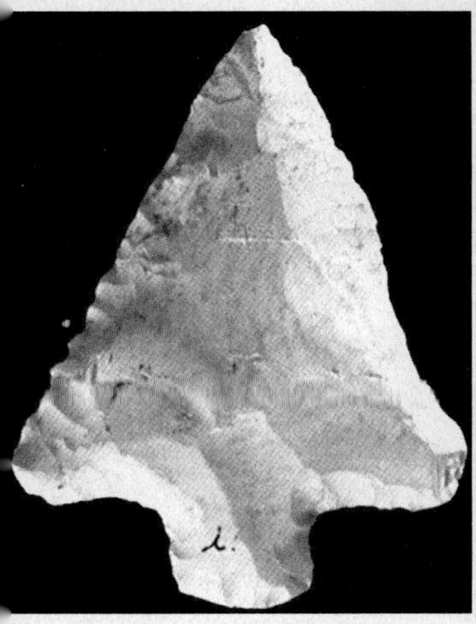

G6, $30-$50
Decatur Co., GA

Serrated edge

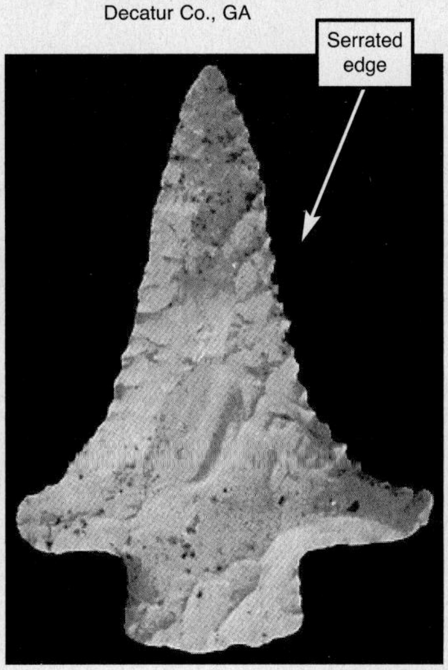

G8, $80-$150
S.W. GA

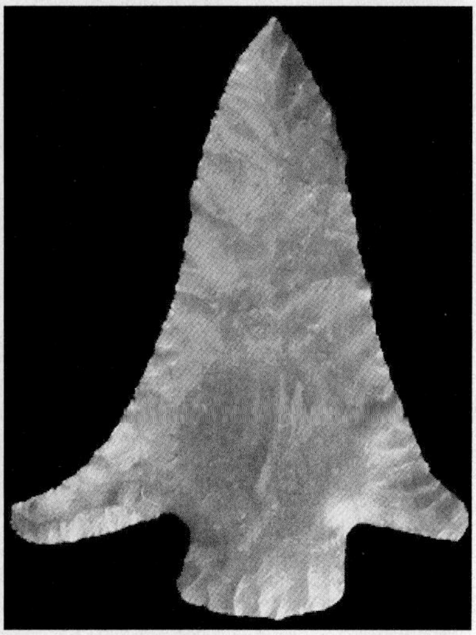

G9, $250-$450
Chipola Riv., FL

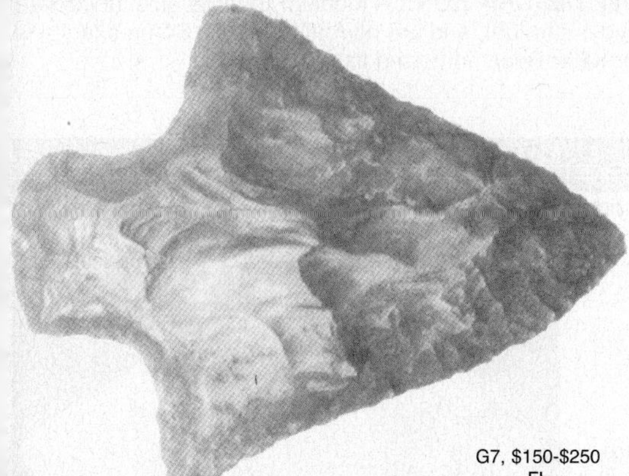

G7, $150-$250
FL

Serrated edge

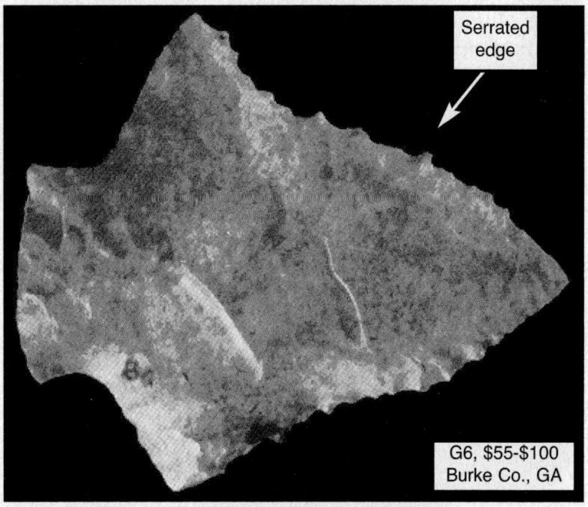

G6, $55-$100
Burke Co., GA

LOCATION: GA, AL, FL. **DESCRIPTION:** A medium sized, broad, stemmed point that is fairly thick and is steeply beveled on all four sides of each face. Blade edges are concave to straight. Shoulders are broad and tapered. A relationship to *Elora, Maples* and *Pickwick* has been suggested. **I.D. KEY:** Expanded barbs & fine edgework.

ADENA - Late Archaic to late Woodland, 3000 - 1200 B. P.

(Also see Cypress Creek, Elora, Levy, Pickwick, Putnam, Sumter & Thonotosassa)

Coral

G6, $15-$25
Pasco Co., FL

G5, $25-$40
Suwannee Co., FL

G9, $125-$225
Jackson Co., FL

LOCATION: Eastern to Southeastern states. **DESCRIPTION:** A medium to large, thin, narrow, triangular blade that is sometimes serrated, and with a medium to long, narrow to broad rounded "beaver tail" stem. Most examples are from average to excellent quality. **I.D. KEY:** Rounded base, woodland flaking.

AGATE BASIN - Transitional Paleo to Early Archaic, 10,200 - 8500 B. P.

Chert

G9, $400-$750
Aucilla River, FL

LOCATION: Florida to Pennsylvania & westward to Montana. **DESCRIPTION:** A medium to large size lanceolate blade of usually high quality. Bases are either convex, concave or straight, and are normally ground. Some examples are median ridged and have a random to parallel flaking. **I.D. KEY:** Basal form and flaking style.

ALACHUA - Middle Archaic, 5500 - 4000 B. P.

(Also see Abbey, Cypress Creek, Hardee Beveled, Levy, Marion, Morrow Mountain, Newnan, Putnam, Six Mile Creek)

G8, $60-$100
Alachua Co., FL

G6, $35-$65
Jefferson Co., FL

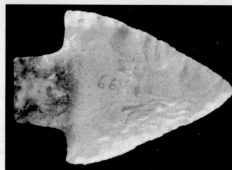

ALACHUA (continued)

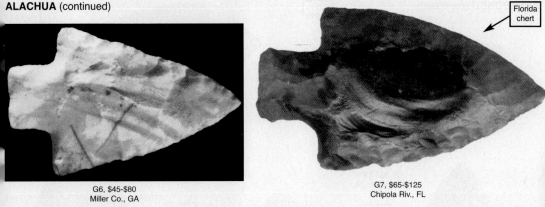

G6, $45-$80
Miller Co., GA

G7, $65-$125
Chipola Riv., FL

Florida chert

LOCATION: Gulf Coastal states. **DESCRIPTION:** A rare type with straight horizontal shoulders and straight stems that don't contract as much. **I.D. KEY:** Squared base, one barb shoulder.

ARREDONDO - Middle to Late Archaic, 6000 - 3500 B. P.

(Also see Buzzard Roost Creek, Hamilton, Kirk Stemmed, Savannah River, Seminole and Wacissa)

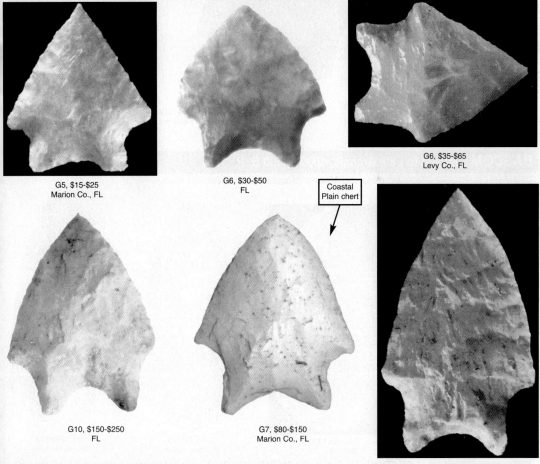

G5, $15-$25
Marion Co., FL

G6, $30-$50
FL

G6, $35-$65
Levy Co., FL

Coastal Plain chert

G10, $150-$250
FL

G7, $80-$150
Marion Co., FL

G9, $150-$250
Marion Co., FL

LOCATION: AL, GA, FL. **DESCRIPTION:** A thick, medium to large size point with a short, broad blade and a wide, concave to bifurcated base which can be thinned. Basal ears are rounded to pointed. Could be related to *Hamilton* points. **I.D. KEY:** Basal form and thickness.

ARREDONDO (continued)

Chert

Agate

G6, $55-$100
Marion Co., FL

G9, $125-$200
Alachua Co., FL

Chert

Chert

G8 $200-$325
Marion Co., FL

G6, $35-$65
FL

G7, $125-$200
Marion Co., FL

BASCOM - Middle to Late Archaic, 4500 - 3500 B. P.

(Also see Morrow Mountain and Savannah River)

G6, $35-$65
Jefferson Co., FL

G7, $55-$100
Burke Co., GA

G9, $65-$125
SC coast cache.

G10, $90-$150
SC coast cache.

IMPORTANT:
All Bascoms shown
half size.

LOCATION: AL, GA. & SC. **DESCRIPTION:** A large size, broad point with weak shoulders tapering to the base which is usually straight but can be convex. A preform for the *Savannah River* point. A cache of *Bascom* and *Savannah River* were found together. **I.D. KEY:** Basal form.

BEAVER LAKE - Paleo to Early Archaic, 11,250 - 8000 B. P.

(Also see Dalton, Manasota, Santa Fe, Simpson, Suwannee and Tallahassee)

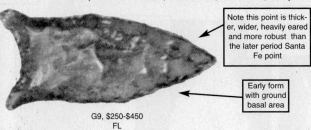

Note this point is thicker, wider, heavily eared and more robust than the later period Santa Fe point

Early form with ground basal area

G9, $250-$450
FL

LOCATION: Central Gulf coast to Northern Florida into Alabama. **DESCRIPTION:** Florida examples are very rare and are smaller than their northern counterparts. Narrow, thin examples of this form have been found in caches associated with *Hernandos* and *Santa Fes* and are confused as this type. **I.D. KEY:** Wide, heavier form with heavy basal grinding.

BENTON - Middle Archaic, 6000 - 4000 B. P.

(Also see Buzzard Roost Creek, Hamilton, Savannah River)

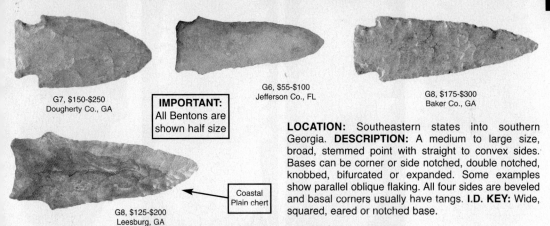

G7, $150-$250
Dougherty Co., GA

G6, $55-$100
Jefferson Co., FL

G8, $175-$300
Baker Co., GA

IMPORTANT: All Bentons are shown half size

G8, $125-$200
Leesburg, GA

Coastal Plain chert

LOCATION: Southeastern states into southern Georgia. **DESCRIPTION:** A medium to large size, broad, stemmed point with straight to convex sides. Bases can be corner or side notched, double notched, knobbed, bifurcated or expanded. Some examples show parallel oblique flaking. All four sides are beveled and basal corners usually have tangs. **I.D. KEY:** Wide, squared, eared or notched base.

BOGGY BRANCH-TYPE I - Early to Middle Archaic, 9000 - 6000 B. P.

(Also see Kirk Stemmed and South Prong Creek)

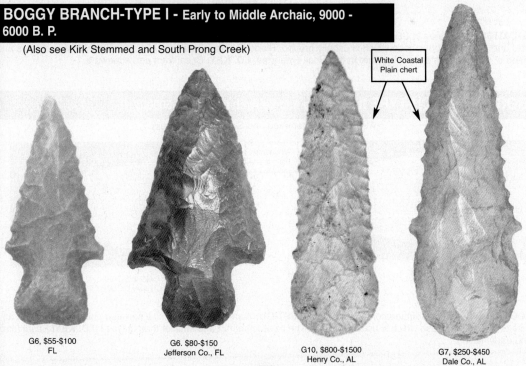

White Coastal Plain chert

G6, $55-$100
FL

G6. $80-$150
Jefferson Co., FL

G10, $800-$1500
Henry Co., AL

G7, $250-$450
Dale Co., AL

245

BOGGY BRANCH, TYPE 1 (continued)

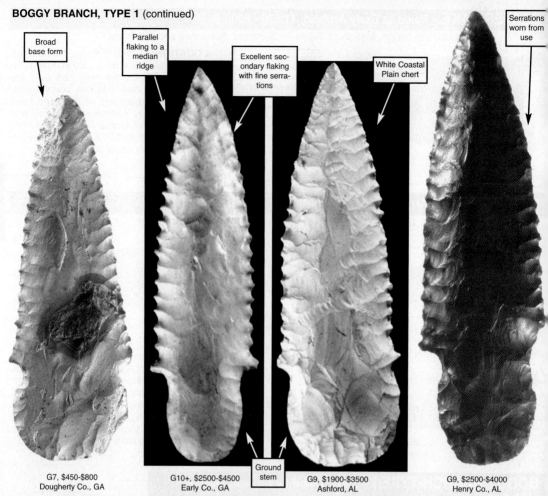

Broad base form

Parallel flaking to a median ridge

Excellent secondary flaking with fine serrations

White Coastal Plain chert

Serrations worn from use

Ground stem

G7, $450-$800
Dougherty Co., GA

G10+, $2500-$4500
Early Co., GA

G9, $1900-$3500
Ashford, AL

G9, $2500-$4000
Henry Co., AL

LOCATION: Small area in SE AL & SW GA. **DESCRIPTION:** A medium to large size serrated point with weak shoulders and a large bulbous base which is usually ground. Blade flaking is similar to *Kirk Stemmed.* Most examples are made of coastal plain chert. Very rare in the small type area. **I.D. KEY:** Basal form and edgework.

BOGGY BRANCH-TYPE II - Early to Middle Archaic, 9000 - 6000 B. P.

(Also see Kirk Stemmed and South Prong Creek)

All Coastal Plain chert

Ground base

G4, $30-$50
S.W. GA

G6, $55-$100
Henry Co., AL

LOCATION: Southern Southeastern states. **DESCRIPTION:** A small to medium size serrated point with weak shoulders and a bulbous base which is usually ground. The base is shorter and smaller than in type I. **I.D. KEY:** Basal form and early flaking.

246

BOGGY BRANCH, TYPE II (continued)

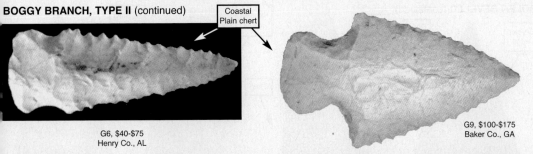

Coastal Plain chert

G6, $40-$75
Henry Co., AL

G9, $100-$175
Baker Co., GA

BOLEN BEVELED - Early Archaic, 10,500 - 8000 B. P.

(Also Clay, Lafayette, Lost Lake and Osceola Greenbriar)

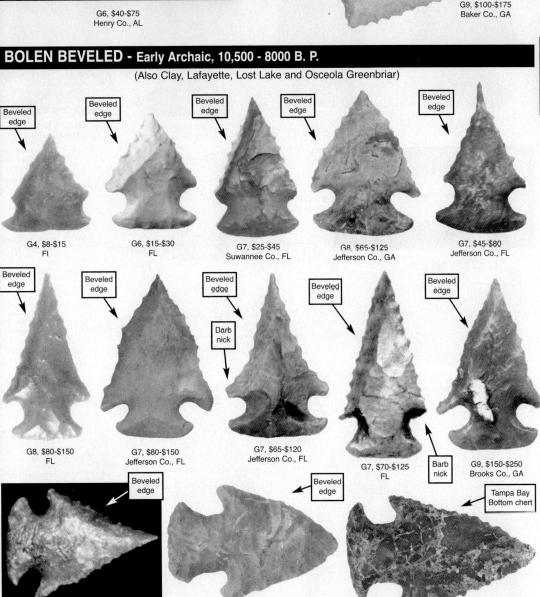

Beveled edge

G4, $8-$15
FI

Beveled edge

G6, $15-$30
FL

Beveled edge

G7, $25-$45
Suwannee Co., FL

Beveled edge

G8, $65-$125
Jefferson Co., GA

Beveled edge

G7, $45-$80
Jefferson Co., FL

Beveled edge

G8, $80-$150
FL

Beveled edge

G7, $80-$150
Jefferson Co., FL

Beveled edge

Darb nick

G7, $65-$120
Jefferson Co., FL

Beveled edge

G7, $70-$125
FL

Beveled edge

Barb nick

G9, $150-$250
Brooks Co., GA

Beveled edge

G7, $55-$100
Alachua Co., FL

Beveled edge

G6, $30-$50
Jefferson Co., MS

Tampa Bay Bottom chert

G9, $200-$350
Alachua Co., FL

LOCATION: Southeastern states including Florida. **DESCRIPTION:** A small to medium size, side to corner notched point with early forms showing basal grinding, beveling on one side of each face, and serrations. Bases can be straight, concave or convex. The side notch is usually broader than in *Big Sandy* points. E-notched or expanded notching also occurs on early forms. **Note:** *Bolens* have been found with horse remains in Florida indicating use in killing the horse which was probably hunted into extinction in the U.S. about 7,000 years ago. **I.D. KEY:** Basal form and notching.

BOLEN BEVELED (continued)

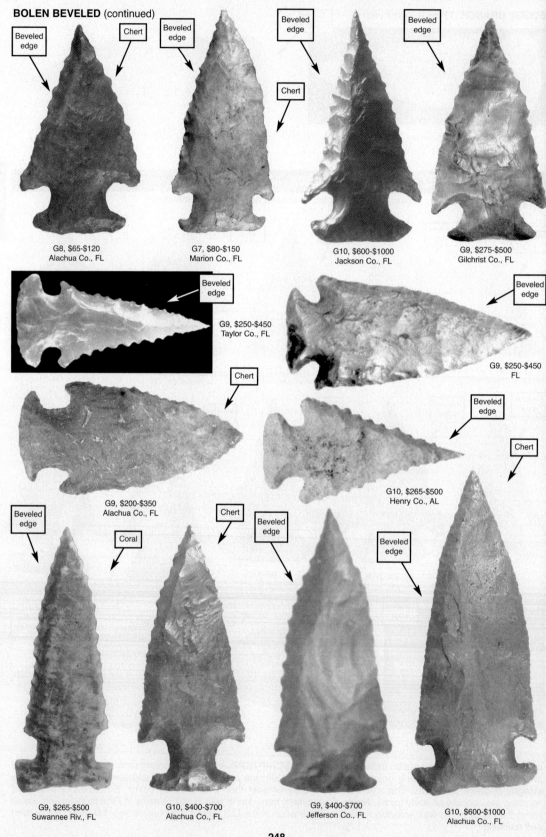

Beveled edge
Chert
Beveled edge
Beveled edge
Beveled edge
Chert

G8, $65-$120
Alachua Co., FL

G7, $80-$150
Marion Co., FL

G10, $600-$1000
Jackson Co., FL

G9, $275-$500
Gilchrist Co., FL

Beveled edge

G9, $250-$450
Taylor Co., FL

Beveled edge

G9, $250-$450
FL

Chert

Beveled edge

Chert

G9, $200-$350
Alachua Co., FL

G10, $265-$500
Henry Co., AL

Beveled edge

Coral

Chert

Beveled edge

Beveled edge

G9, $265-$500
Suwannee Riv., FL

G10, $400-$700
Alachua Co., FL

G9, $400-$700
Jefferson Co., FL

G10, $600-$1000
Alachua Co., FL

248

BOLEN PLAIN - Early Archaic, 9000 - 7000 B. P.

(Also see Kirk Corner Notched, Lafayette, Osceola Greenbriar and Taylor)

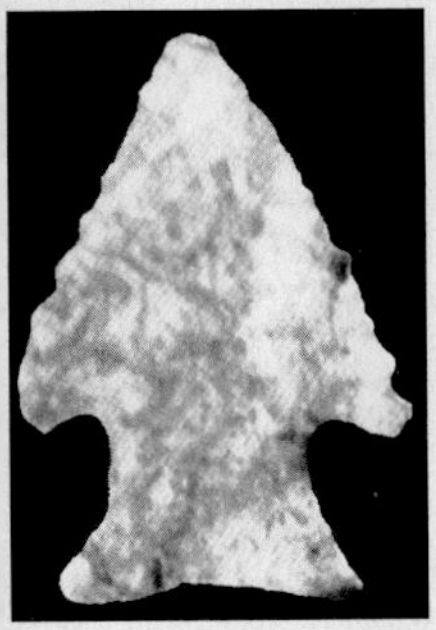

G5, $15-$30
FL

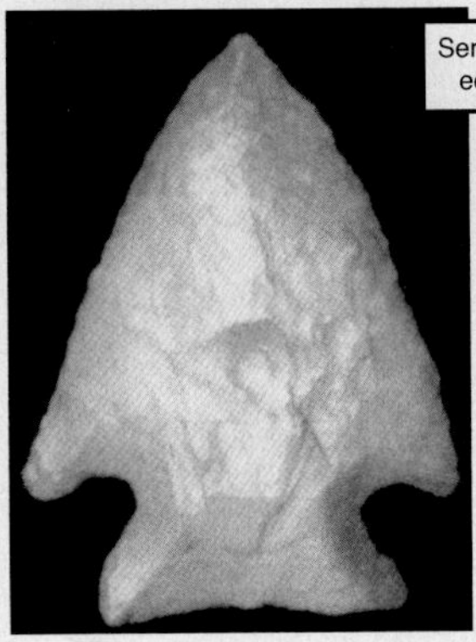

G6, $45-$80
FL

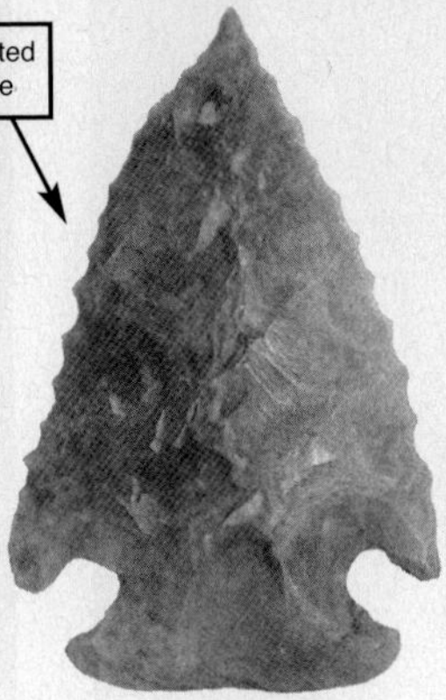
Serrated edge

G8, $125-$200
Jefferson Co., FL

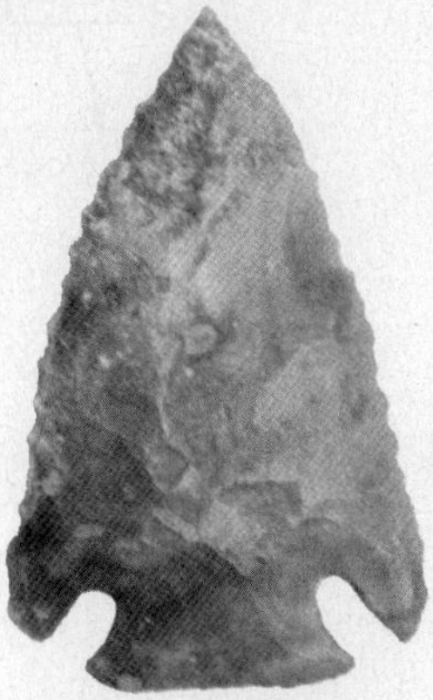

G7, $80-$150
Jefferson Co., FL

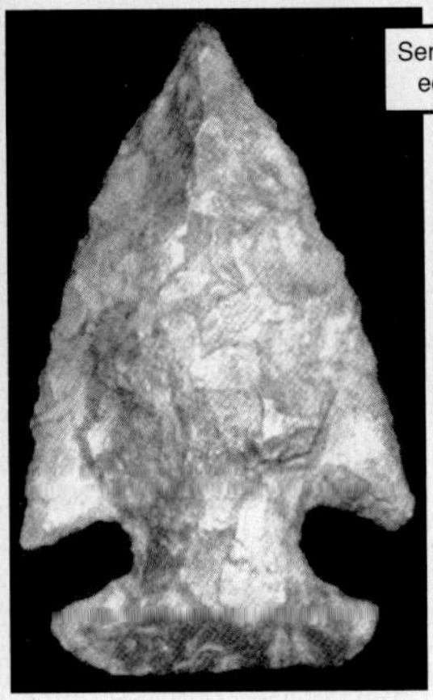

G8, $150-$250
FL

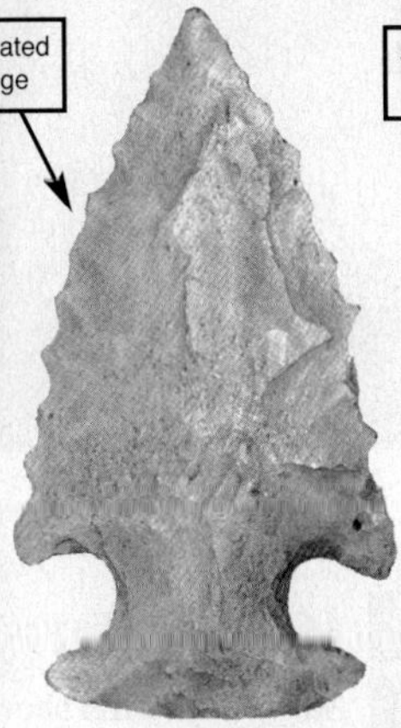
Serrated edge

G9, $200-$350
Jefferson Co., FL

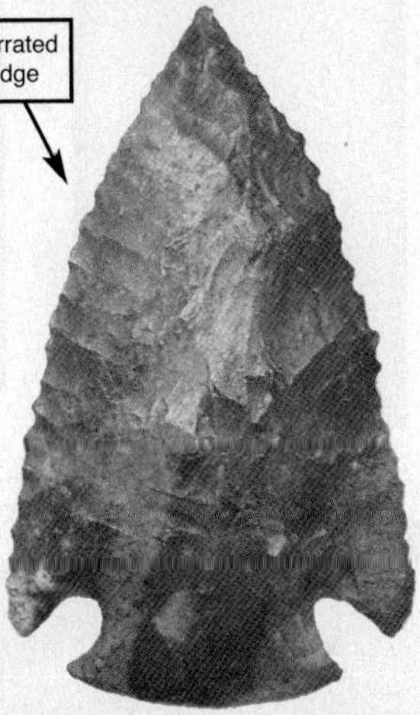
Serrated edge

G10, $250-$450
Jefferson Co., FL

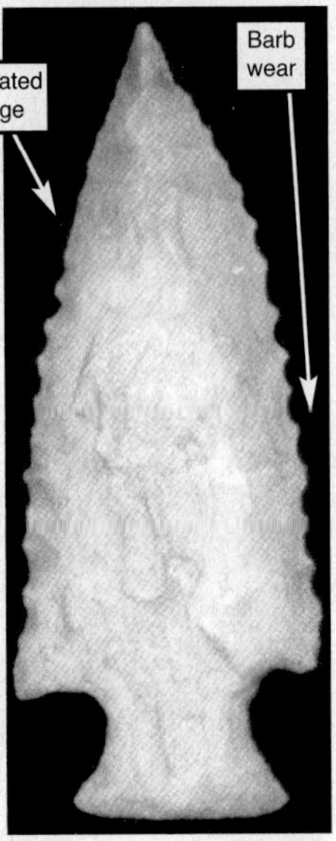
Serrated edge
Barb wear

G6, $125-$225
FL

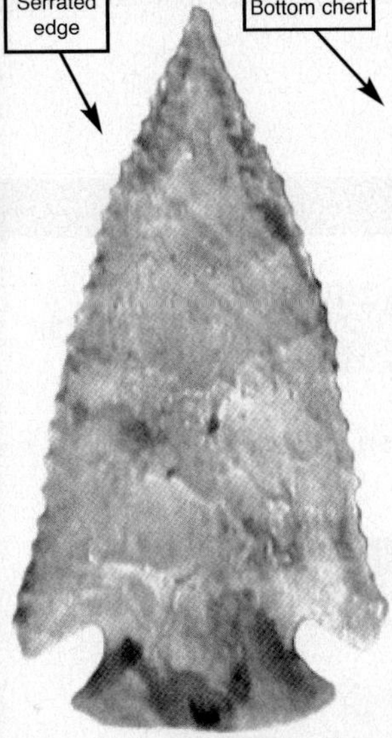
Serrated edge

G8, $250-$450
Jefferson Co., FL

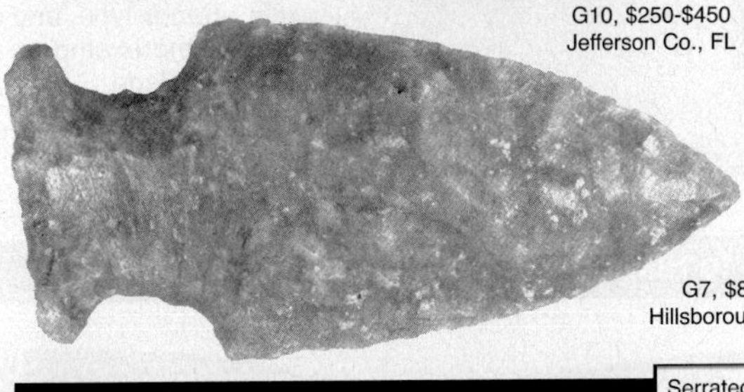
Tampa Bay Bottom chert

G7, $80-$150
Hillsborough Co., FL

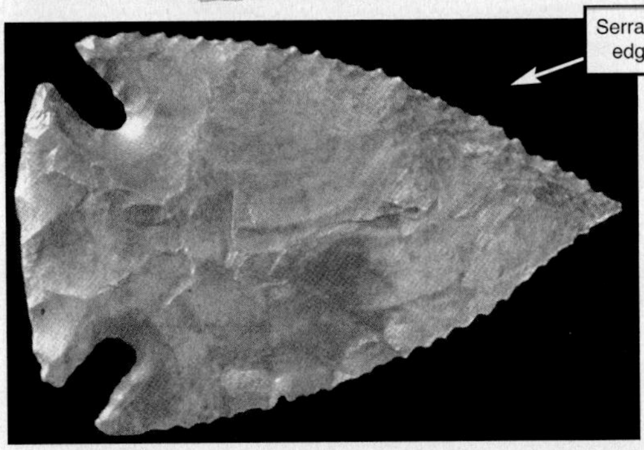
Serrated edge

G10, $800-$1500
Aucilla Riv., FL

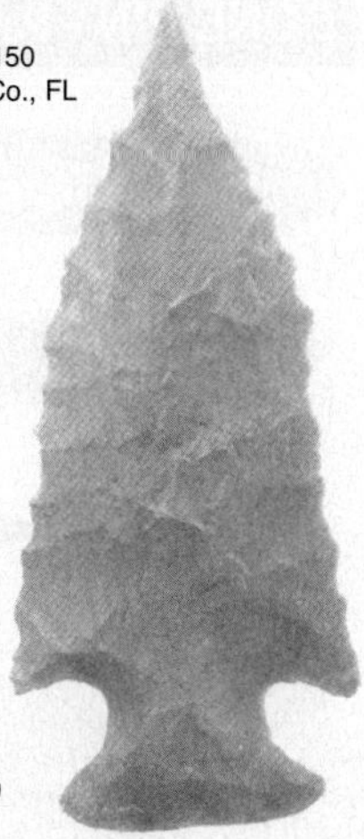

G10, $200-$350
FL

BOLEN PLAIN (continued)

Minor restoration

$150-$250
FL

G7, $250-$450
Jefferson Co., FL

G10, $600-$1000
Pasco Co., FL

G9, $400-$700
Jackson Co., FL

Serrated edge

LOCATION: Eastern states. **DESCRIPTION:** A small to medium size, side to corner notched point with early forms showing basal grinding and serrations. Bases are straight, concave or convex. The side notches are usually broader than in the *Big Sandy* type, and can be expanded to E-notched on some examples. **I.D. KEY:** Basal form and flaking on blade.

G10, $350-$650
Columbia Co., FL

BONE PIN - Paleo to Historic, 11,500 - 200 B. P.

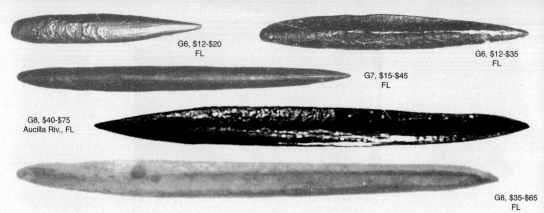

G6, $12-$20
FL

G6, $12-$35
FL

G7, $15-$45
FL

G8, $40-$75
Aucilla Riv., FL

G8, $35-$65
FL

BONE PIN (continued)

LOCATION: Florida. **DESCRIPTION:** Medium to large size, slender, double pointed spear pins made from deer leg bone, some camel and rarely mammoth. Less than 1% are mammoth ivory. The bone is usually blackened with age if found under water.

BRADFORD - Woodland to Mississippian, 2000 - 800 B. P.

(Also see Broward, Columbia and Sarasota)

G8, $35-$60
Suwannee Co., FL

G3, $3-$6
Hillsborough Co., FL

LOCATION: Southern Southeastern states. **DESCRIPTION:** A medium size, narrow, expanded stem point with tapered to rounded shoulders. Basal corners can also be rounded. Bases are straight to slightly convex.

BROAD RIVER - Woodland, 3000 - 1500 B. P.

(Also see Broward, Columbia, Sarasota, Savannah River and Wacissa)

LOCATION: Southern Southeastern states. **DESCRIPTION:** A small size, thick point with small shoulder barbs, a parallel sided stem and a straight to concave base.

G5, $8-$12
Beaufort Co., SC

G6, $10-$15
Henry Co., AL

BROWARD - Woodland to Mississippian, 2000 - 800 B. P.

(Also see Bradford, Broad River, Columbia, Gadsden and Sarasota)

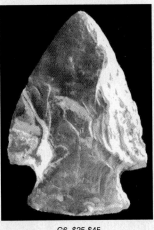

G8, $20-$35
FL

G6, $25-$45
Choctaw Co., AL

G5, $15-$25
FL

251

BROWARD (continued)

G8, $25-$45
FL

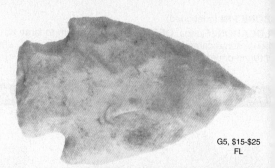

G5, $15-$25
FL

LOCATION: Southern Southeastern states. **DESCRIPTION:** A medium to large size triangular point with tapered to square shoulders and a short expanding stem. The base can be straight, concave or convex. Basal corners are usually rounded. An uncommon type. **I.D. KEY:** High and low barbs.

BUZZARD ROOST - Middle Archaic, 6000 - 4000 B. P.

(Also see Benton)

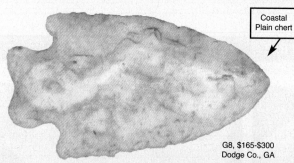

Coastal
Plain chert

G8, $165-$300
Dodge Co., GA

LOCATION: Southeastern states. **DESCRIPTION:** A medium to large size, stemmed point with a bifurcated base. Believed to be related to the *Benton* point. **I.D. KEY:** Bifurcated base and basal width. Found with *Benton* points. A notched base *Benton*.

CHIPOLA - Early Archaic, 10,000 - 8000 B. P.

(Also see Dalton, Gilchrist and Hardaway)

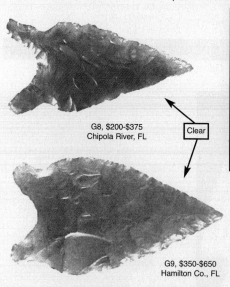

G8, $200-$375
Chipola River, FL

Clear

G9, $350-$650
Hamilton Co., FL

G10, $550-$950
Pasco Co., FL

Rare Chipola
variant

LOCATION: Southern southeastern states. **DESCRIPTION:** A small to medium size triangular point with long, expanding auricles and a tapered shoulder. Bases are deeply concave and are thinned. A *Dalton* variant form. Similar to *San Patrice* points found in Louisiana and Texas. May be related to *Gilchrist*. Rare in type area.

CITRUS - Late Archaic to Woodland, 3500 - 2000 B. P.

(Also see Culbreath and Hernando)

252

G8, $125-$200
FL

G9, $200-$375
Citrus Co., FL

Chert

G6, $80-$150
Marion Co., FL

G
C

Tip
wear

Chert

Tampa Bay
Bottom chert

G6, $55-$100
Lake Apopka, FL

G9, $125-$200
FL

G6, $55-$100
Marion Co., FL

Chert

G10, $450-$850
N.W. Cent. FL

G9, $250-$450
FL

G10, $400-$700
Alachua Co., FL

LOCATION: Southern Southeastern states including Florida. **DESCRIPTION:** A medium to large size basal-notched point. The stem is wider than *Hernando*. The base and tangs usually forms an arc on most examples. **I.D. KEY:** Notches and random flaking on blade.

(Also see Kirk Corner Notched and Lafayette)

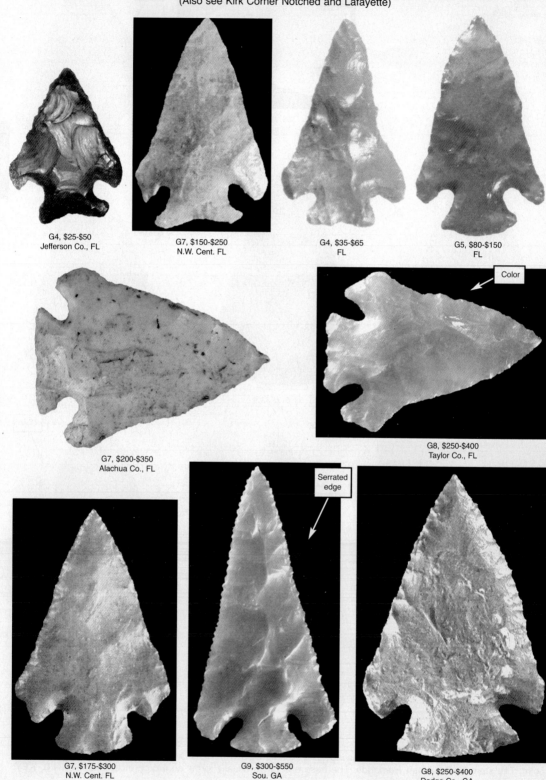

G4, $25-$50
Jefferson Co., FL

G7, $150-$250
N.W. Cent. FL

G4, $35-$65
FL

G5, $80-$150
FL

G7, $200-$350
Alachua Co., FL

Color

G8, $250-$400
Taylor Co., FL

Serrated edge

G7, $175-$300
N.W. Cent. FL

G9, $300-$550
Sou. GA

G8, $250-$400
Dodge Co., GA

CLAY (continued)

LOCATION: Southern Southeastern states including Florida.
DESCRIPTION: A medium to large size basal-notched point with outward-flaring, squared shoulders (clipped wing). Blades are recurvate. Related to *Lafayette* points.
I.D. KEY: Deep notches and squared barbs. Asymmetrical examples with one squared and one pointed or rounded barb also occur.

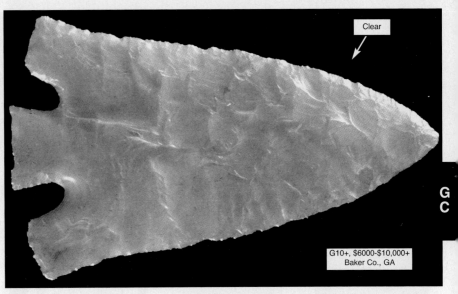

Clear

G C

G10+, $6000-$10,000+
Baker Co., GA

CLOVIS - Early Paleo, 11,500 - 10,600 B. P.

(Also see Chipola, Redstone, Simpson, Suwannee and Withlacoochee)

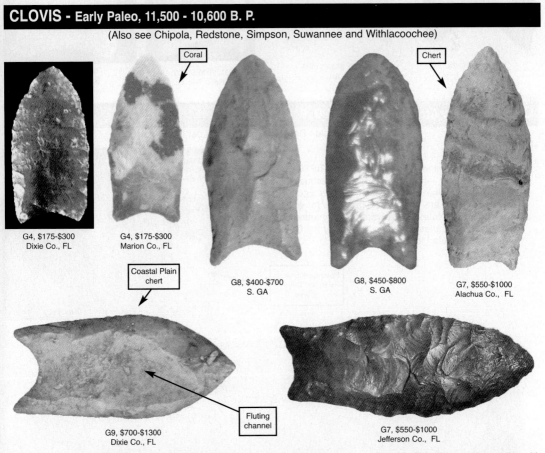

Coral

Chert

G4, $175-$300
Dixie Co., FL

G4, $175-$300
Marion Co., FL

Coastal Plain chert

G8, $400-$700
S. GA

G8, $450-$800
S. GA

G7, $550-$1000
Alachua Co., FL

Fluting channel

G9, $700-$1300
Dixie Co., FL

G7, $550-$1000
Jefferson Co., FL

LOCATION: All of North America. **DESCRIPTION:** A medium to large size, auriculate, fluted, lanceolate point with convex sides and a concave base that is ground. Most examples are fluted on both sides about 1/3 the way up from the base. The flaking can be random to parallel. *Clovis* is the earliest point type in the hemisphere. The origin of *Clovis* is unknown. *Clovis* technology more closely matches European *Solutrean* forms than anything else. **I.D. KEY:** Paleo flaking, shoulders, batan fluting instead of indirect style.

255

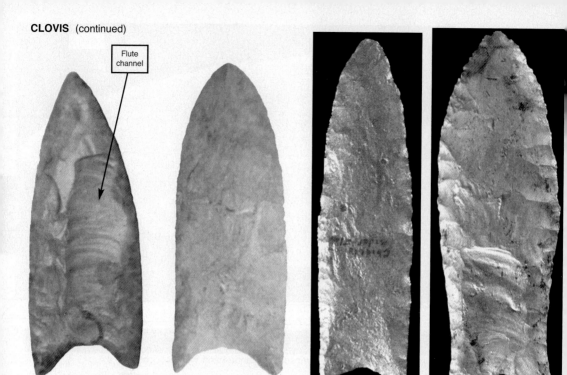

Flute channel

G8, $1500-$2500
S. GA

G9, $800-$1500
S. GA

G7, $900-$1600
Chipola Riv., FL

G8, $2500-$4000
Randolph Co., GA

COBBS - Early Archaic, 9000 - 5000 B. P.

(Also see Bolen Beveled, Hardin and Lost Lake)

LOCATION: Southeastern states. **DESCRIPTION:** A medium to large size, lanceolate blade with a broad, rounded to square base. One side of each face is usually steeply beveled. These are un-notched preforms for early Archaic beveled types. Note: *Cobbs* were recently found with dovetail base (St. Charles) points in a cache at the Olive Branch site in Illinois dated to 9300-9400 B.P.

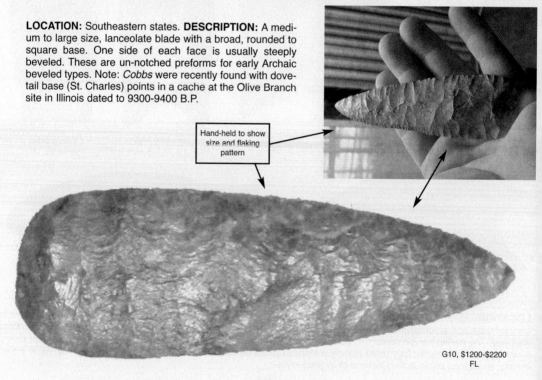

Hand-held to show size and flaking pattern

G10, $1200-$2200
FL

256

COBBS (continued)

G8, $1500-$2500
Jefferson Co., FL

COLUMBIA - Woodland, 2000 - 1000 B. P.

(Also see Bradford, Hamilton, Ledbetter, Sarasota and Thonotosassa)

Translucent

Chert

Clear

G7, $30-$50
Marion Co., FL

G7, $25-$45
FL

G4, $12-$20
Brooks Co., GA

Chert

G5, $35-$60
FL

G9, $200-$350
FL

G9, $160-$260
Levy Co., FL

G7, $80-$150
Dixie Co., FL

G8, $90-$175
Jefferson Co., FL

LOCATION: Southern Southeastern states. **DESCRIPTION:** A medium to large size stemmed point. Shoulders are tapered to horizontal and are weak. Stem is short and slightly expanding. Base is straight.

G8, $65-$120
Jefferson Co., FL

CONERLY - Middle Archaic, 7500 - 4500 B. P.

(Also see Beaver Lake, Simpson and Suwannee)

G5, $25-$40
Burke Co., GA

G10, $250-$450
Burke Co., GA

G10, $250-$450
Savannah River, GA
Brier Creek

G6, $40-$75
Burke Co., GA

G8, $80-$150
Burke Co., GA, Brier Creek

LOCATION: Southern Southeastern states, especially Tennessee and Georgia. **DESCRIPTION:** A medium to large auriculate point with a contracting, concave base which can be ground. On some examples, the hafting area can be seen with the presence of very weak shoulders. The base is usually thinned. Believed to be related to the *Guilford* type. **I.D. KEY:** Base concave, thickness, flaking.

G7, $175-$300
Burke Co., GA, Brier Creek

COPENA - Woodland, 2500 - 1500 B. P.

(Also see Duval and Safety Harborl)

Serrated edge

G7, $65-$125
Brooks Co., GA

LOCATION: Southern Gulf states. **DESCRIPTION:** A medium size lanceolate point with recurved blade edges and a straight to slightly convex base. Florida Copenas are usually smaller than those found further north. **I.D. KEY:** Recurved blade edges.

COTTONBRIDGE - Middle Archaic, 6000 - 4000 B. P.

(Also see Abbey and Elora)

LOCATION: Southern Gulf states. **DESCRIPTION:** A medium size, broad, stemmed point that is fairly thick and beveled on all four sides. Shoulders are tapered and blade edges are straight. Base is small and rounded with contracting sides. **I.D. KEY:** Small, round base, broad shoulders.

COTTONBRIDGE (continued)

G7, $35-$60
Henry Co., AL

G7, $25-$45
FL

COWHOUSE SLOUGH - Transitional Paleo, 10,000 - 6000 B. P.

(Also see Stanfield)

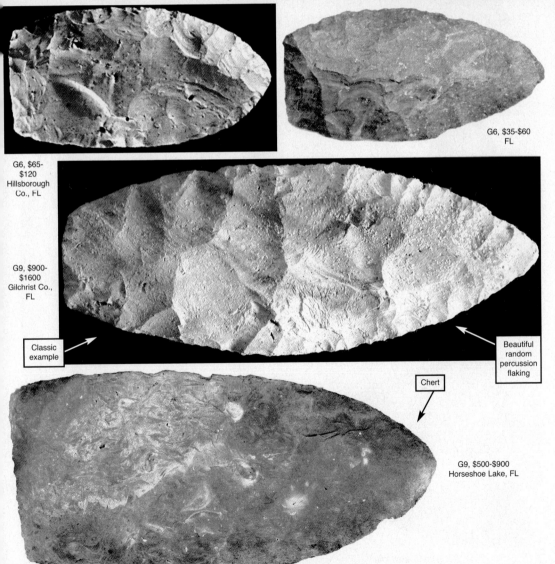

G6, $35-$60
FL

G6, $65-$120
Hillsborough Co., FL

G9, $900-$1600
Gilchrist Co., FL

Classic example

Beautiful random percussion flaking

Chert

G9, $500-$900
Horseshoe Lake, FL

COWHOUSE SLOUGH (continued)

LOCATION: Gulf Coastal states. **DESCRIPTION:** A medium to large size, broad, lanceolate blade with a contracting, straight to slightly convex base which may be ground as well as fluted or thinned. This type may possibly be a preform. **I.D. KEY:** Paleo flaking.

CULBREATH - Late Archaic to Woodland, 5000 - 3000 B. P.

(Also see Citrus, Clay, Hernando, Kirk Corner Notched and Lafayette)

Chert

G6, $40-$75
FL

Chert

G7, $125-$200
Marion Co., FL

Coral

Side
wear

G9, $200-$375
FL

G7, $125-$200
Marion Co., FL

G6, $150-$250
St. Pete, FL

G10, $400-$700
FL

G9, $200-$375
FL

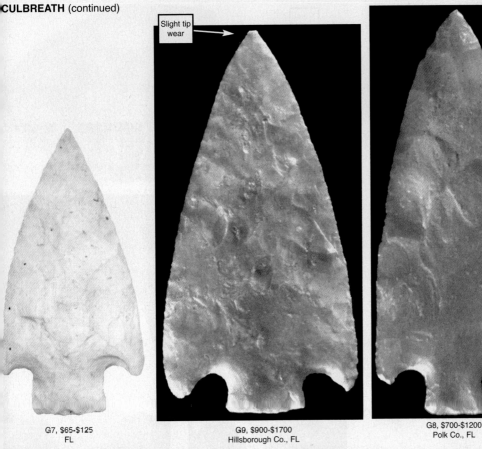

Slight tip wear

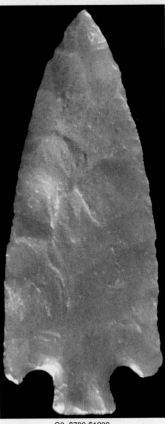

G7, $65-$125
FL

G9, $900-$1700
Hillsborough Co., FL

G8, $700-$1200
Polk Co., FL

G C

LOCATION: Southern Gulf states. **DESCRIPTION:** A medium to large size, broad, basal notched point, barbs are rounded and blade edges are convex. On some examples, the barbs do not reach the base. The earlier *Eva* point found in Kentucky and Tennessee could be a Northern cousin. **I.D. KEY:** Notching. Barb is always straight or contracting, never expanding.

CYPRESS CREEK - Middle Archaic, 5500 - 3000 B. P.

(Also see Alachua, Hillsborough, Levy, Morrow Mountain, Putnam and Sumter)

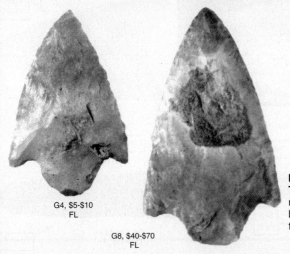

G4, $5-$10
FL

G8, $40-$70
FL

G8, $35-$60
FL

LOCATION: Lower southeastern states. **DESCRIPTION:** A medium size point with a short, pointed to rounded contracting base. Shoulders have short barbs and can be asymmetrical with one barbed and the other tapered.

261

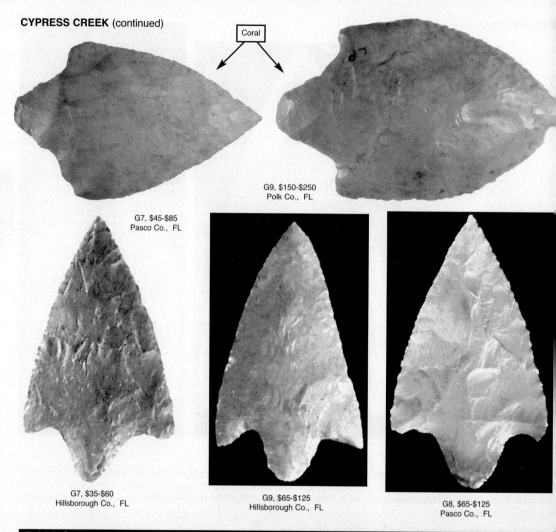

Coral

G9, $150-$250
Polk Co., FL

G7, $45-$85
Pasco Co., FL

G7, $35-$60
Hillsborough Co., FL

G9, $65-$125
Hillsborough Co., FL

G8, $65-$125
Pasco Co., FL

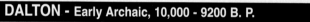

DALTON - Early Archaic, 10,000 - 9200 B. P.

(Also see Beaver Lake, Chipola, Hardaway, Safety Harbor, Santa Fe, Tallahassee & Withlacoochee)

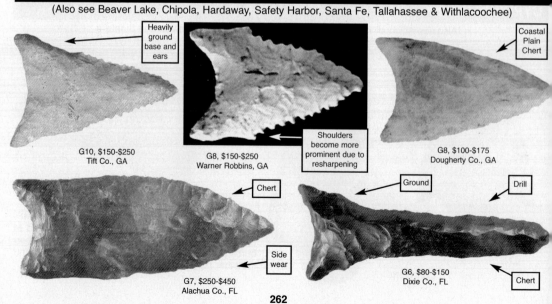

Heavily
ground
base and
ears

Coastal
Plain
Chert

G10, $150-$250
Tift Co., GA

Shoulders
become more
prominent due to
resharpening

G8, $150-$250
Warner Robbins, GA

G8, $100-$175
Dougherty Co., GA

Chert

Ground

Drill

Side
wear

G7, $250-$450
Alachua Co., FL

G6, $80-$150
Dixie Co., FL

Chert

Coastal Plain Chert

Florida chert

Basal area grinding

Beveled edge

G
C

G9, $200-$350
Screven Co., GA

G9, $150-$250
Seminole Co., GA

G9, $350-$600
Alachua Co., FL

G10, $550-$1000
S. GA

First stage, unsharpened form

G10, $700-$1200
Blakely, GA

LOCATION: North Florida into Georgia and Alabama. **DESCRIPTION:** A medium to large size, auriculate, fishtailed point. Resharpened examples are serrated and exhibit excellent flaking. Beveling does not usually occur on Florida examples. All have heavier basal grinding and most are thicker and wider than the look-alike *Santa Fe* and *Tallahassee* points. **I.D. KEY:** Thicker cross section, broader, heavier grinding than *Santa Fe* and *Tallahassees*.

DRILL - Paleo to Historic, 11,500 - 200 B. P.

(Also see Edgefield Scraper)

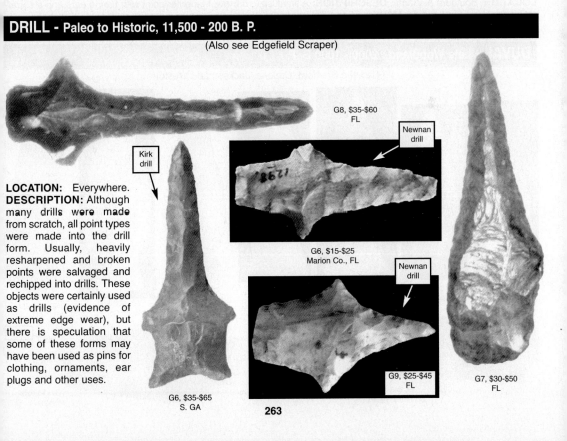

G8, $35-$60
FL

Newnan drill

Kirk drill

LOCATION: Everywhere. **DESCRIPTION:** Although many drills were made from scratch, all point types were made into the drill form. Usually, heavily resharpened and broken points were salvaged and rechipped into drills. These objects were certainly used as drills (evidence of extreme edge wear), but there is speculation that some of these forms may have been used as pins for clothing, ornaments, ear plugs and other uses.

G6, $15-$25
Marion Co., FL

Newnan drill

G6, $35-$65
S. GA

G9, $25-$45
FL

G7, $30-$50
FL

DRILL (continued)

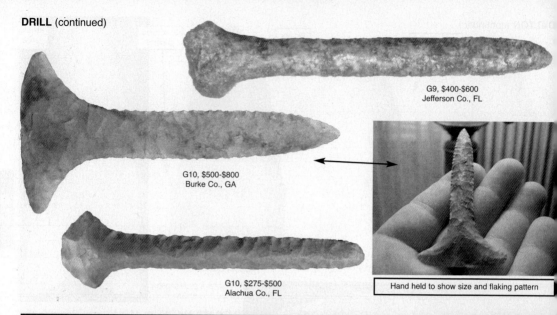

G9, $400-$600
Jefferson Co., FL

G10, $500-$800
Burke Co., GA

G10, $275-$500
Alachua Co., FL

Hand held to show size and flaking pattern

DURANT'S BEND - Woodland-Mississippian, 1600 - 1000 B. P.

(Also see Pinellas)

G8, $12-$20
Dallas Co., AL

G8, $12-$20
Dallas Co., AL

G8, $12-$20
Dallas Co., AL

G10, $35-$65
Sou. AL

G10, $55-$100
Dallas Co., AL

LOCATION: Southern Alabama. **DESCRIPTION:** A small size, narrow, triangular point with flaring ears and a serrated blade. Made from nodular black chert or milky quartz.

DUVAL - Late Woodland, 2000 - 1000 B. P.

(Also see Bradford, Copena, Jackson and Westo)

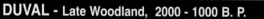

G6, $15-$25
Marion Co., FL

G5, $12-$20
Marion Co., FL

G8, $25-$40
Marion Co., FL

G7, $15-$30
Marion Co., FL

G7, $15-$30
Marion Co., FL

G7, $30-$50
Marion Co., FL

G9, $35-$65
FL

Chert

G9, $45-$85
St. Johns Rv., FL

Chert

G7, $30-$50
Marion Co., FL

264

LOCATION: Gulf states. **DESCRIPTION:** A small to medium size, narrow, spike point with shallow side notches, an expanding stem and a straight to convex base. The stem can be slight to moderate. Similar to *Bradley Spike* points from Tennessee.

EDGEFIELD SCRAPER - Early Archaic, 10,500 - 8000 B. P.

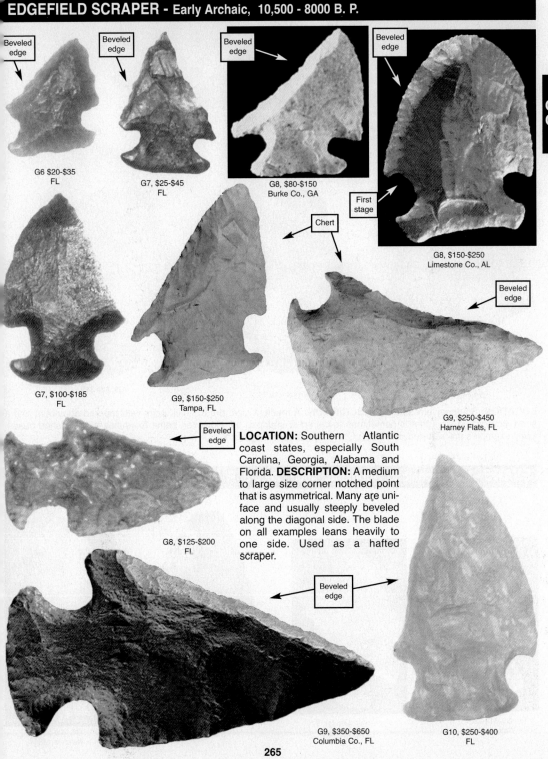

Beveled edge

G6 $20-$35
FL

Beveled edge

G7, $25-$45
FL

Beveled edge

G8, $80-$150
Burke Co., GA

Beveled edge

First stage

G8, $150-$250
Limestone Co., AL

Chert

Beveled edge

G7, $100-$185
FL

G9, $150-$250
Tampa, FL

G9, $250-$450
Harney Flats, FL

Beveled edge

G8, $125-$200
FL

LOCATION: Southern Atlantic coast states, especially South Carolina, Georgia, Alabama and Florida. **DESCRIPTION:** A medium to large size corner notched point that is asymmetrical. Many are uniface and usually steeply beveled along the diagonal side. The blade on all examples leans heavily to one side. Used as a hafted scraper.

Beveled edge

G9, $350-$650
Columbia Co., FL

G10, $250-$400
FL

GC

ELORA - Middle to Late Archaic, 6000 - 3000 B. P.

(Also see Abbey, Alachua, Cottonbridge, Kirk Stemmed, Levy, Newnan, Notchaway, Pickwick, Putnam, Savannah River, Six Mile Creek and South Prong Creek)

Base snapped off

Serrated edge

Serrated edge

G8, $20-$35
FL

G3, $8-$15
Decatur Co., GA

G7, $15-$30
Jefferson Co., FL

G5, $15-$25
Jefferson Co., FL

G8, $25-$45
FL

LOCATION: Southeastern states. **DESCRIPTION:** A medium size, broad, thick point with tapered shoulders and a short, contracting stem that is sometimes fractured or snapped off. However, some examples have finished bases. Early examples are serrated. **I.D. KEY:** One barb sharper, edgework.

EVANS - Late Archaic to Woodland, 4000 - 2000 B. P.

(Also see Merkle)

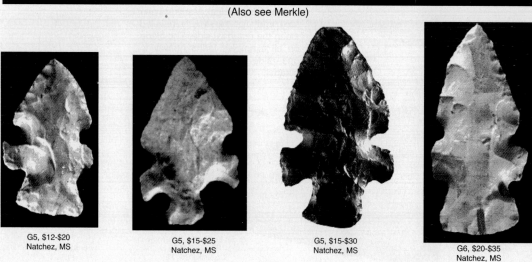

G5, $12-$20
Natchez, MS

G5, $15-$25
Natchez, MS

G5, $15-$30
Natchez, MS

G6, $20-$35
Natchez, MS

EVANS (continued)

LOCATION: Southeastern states into southern Alabama and Mississippi. **DESCRIPTION:** A medium to large size stemmed point that is notched on each side somewhere between the point and shoulder. **I.D. KEY:** Side notches with stem.

GADSDEN - Woodland to Mississippian, 2000 - 800 B. P.

(Also see Broward)

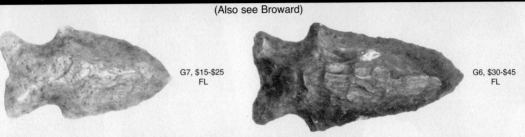

G7, $15-$25
FL

G6, $30-$45
FL

LOCATION: Easter to northwest Florida southward. **DESCRIPTION:** A small to medium size point with an expanding stem that forms ears. Bases are deeply concave. Shoulders are obtuse to rounded. This is a subtype of the **Broward** point. Named by Ripley Bullen. **I.D. KEY:** Bifurcated base.

GILCHRIST - Early Archaic, 10,000? - 7000 B. P.

(Also see Chipola, Beaver Lake and Taylor)

Coral

Chert

Coral

G7, $15-$30
Aiken, SC

G8, $125-$200
Marion Co., FL

G9, $150-$250
Marion Co., FL

G9, $165-$300
Alachua Co., FL

G10, $250-$400
Hernando Co., FL

Clear

G8, $275-$500
FL

LOCATION: Southern Southeastern states. **DESCRIPTION:** A small to medium size, broad point with a short stem that is square, bifurcated or auriculate. Shoulders are weak and can be tapered, horizontal or slightly barbed. The blade can be straight or concave and could be ground. Early forms may be related to *Suwannee.*

GREENBRIAR   (See Osceola Greenbriar)

HAMILTON - Early Archaic, 8000 - 5000 B. P.

(Also see Columbia, Kirk, Savannah River, Seminole and Thonotosassa)

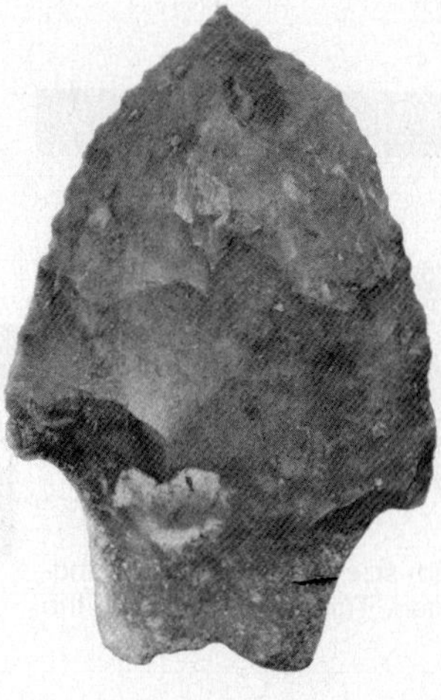

G5, $15-$30
Jefferson Co., FL

G6, $25-$40
FL

G8, $65-$125
Jefferson Co., FL

Chert

G5, $30-$50
Jefferson Co., FL

G9, $80-$150
Fellowship, FL

G8, $200-$350
FL

Chert

G8, $350-$600
Hernando Co., FL

HAMILTON (continued)

LOCATION: Southern Southeastern states. **DESCRIPTION:** A large size, thick, broad stemmed point with a concave base. Shoulders are horizontal to slightly tapered to barbed and are weaker than *Savannah River* points. Basal corners are slightly rounded **I.D. KEY:** Broad shoulders, basal form; i.e. short, wide barbs with a concave base. Confused with *Savannah Rivers* which have straight to concave bases, stronger shoulders and are not as old. Related to *Arredondo* points.

G8, $150-$250
FL

HARAHEY - Mississippian, 700 - 350 B. P.

Beveled edge on opposite corners

G8, $175-$350
Early Co., GA

IMPORTANT: ALL HARAHEYS SHOWN HALF SIZE

G8, $50-$90
SC

G7, $80-$150
SC

LOCATION: Midwestern to Eastern states. **DESCRIPTION:** A large, double pointed knife that is usually beveled on one or all four sides of each face. The cross section is rhomboid. The true buffalo skinning knife. **I.D. KEY:** Two and four beveled double pointed form.

HARDAWAY - Early Archaic, 9500 - 8000 B. P.

(Also see Chipola, Dalton, Santa Fe, Tallahassee and Union Side Notched)

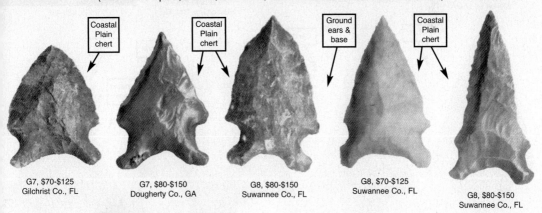

Coastal Plain chert

Coastal Plain chert

Ground ears & base

Coastal Plain chert

G7, $70-$125
Gilchrist Co., FL

G7, $80-$150
Dougherty Co., GA

G8, $80-$150
Suwannee Co., FL

G8, $70-$125
Suwannee Co., FL

G8, $80-$150
Suwannee Co., FL

Ground hafting area

G6, $80-$150
FL

LOCATION: The Carolinas into Florida. **DESCRIPTION:** A small to medium size point with shallow side notches and expanding auricles forming a wide, deeply concave base. Ears and base are usually heavily ground. This type evolved from the *Dalton* point. **I.D. KEY:** Heavy grinding in shoulders, paleo flaking.

Ground hafting area

Chert

Chert

Ground hafting area

G5, $40-$75
Columbia Co., FL

G7, $65-$125
Marion Co., FL

G6, $75-$140
Marion Co., FL

G9, $90-$175
Silver Springs, FL

HARDEE BEVELED - Middle Archaic, 5500 - 3000 B. P.

(Also see Alachua, Levy, Marion and Putnam)

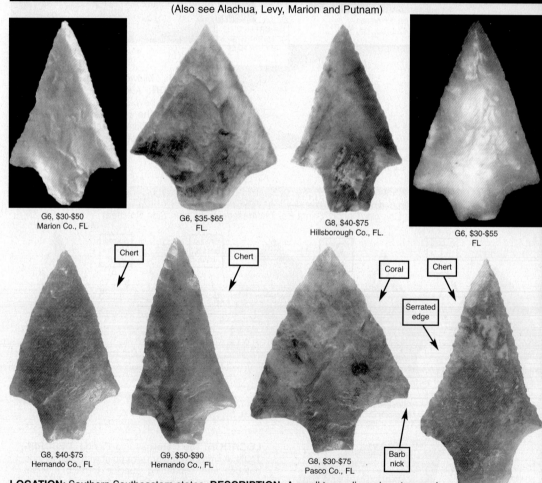

G6, $30-$50
Marion Co., FL

G6, $35-$65
FL.

G8, $40-$75
Hillsborough Co., FL.

G6, $30-$55
FL

Chert

Chert

Coral

Chert

Serrated edge

G8, $40-$75
Hernando Co., FL

G9, $50-$90
Hernando Co., FL

G8, $30-$75
Pasco Co., FL

Barb nick

G8, $125-$200
Hernando Co., FL

LOCATION: Southern Southeastern states. **DESCRIPTION:** A small to medium size stemmed point that occurs in two forms. One has a distinct bevel on the right side of each face. The other has the typical bifacial beveling. Shoulders are tapered to horizontal and are sharp. This type resembles the other Florida Archaic stemmed points (see above) except for the bevel and may be their ancestor. Found mostly in Tampa Bay vicinity. **I.D. KEY:** Beveling on right side of each face and sharp shoulders.

HARDEE BEVELED (continued)

Coral

G9, $200-$350
Hernando Co., FL

Barb
nick

Beveled
edge

G8, $150-$250
Hillsborough Co., FL.

Chert

G
C

G9, $175-$300
Citrus Co., FL

PASCO CO.
FL.

G8, $175-$300
Pasco Co., FL

G8, $125-$200
Orange Lake, FL

Classic
example

Fine
serrations

Fine
serrations

Fine
serrations

G7, $90-$175
FL

G10, $350-$600
Citrus Co., FL

G5, $45-$85
Marion Co., FL.

HARDIN - Early Archaic, 9000 - 6000 B. P.

(Also see Cypress Creek, Kirk Corner Notched, Lafayette and Ocala)

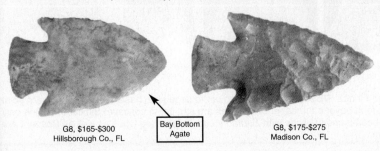

LOCATION: Midwestern to Eastern states. **DESCRIPTION:** A large, well made triangular barbed point with an expanded base that is usually ground. Re-sharpened examples have one beveled edge on each face. This type is believed to have evolved from the *Scottsbluff* type. **I.D. KEY:** Notches and stem form.

G8, $165-$300
Hillsborough Co., FL

Bay Bottom
Agate

G8, $175-$275
Madison Co., FL

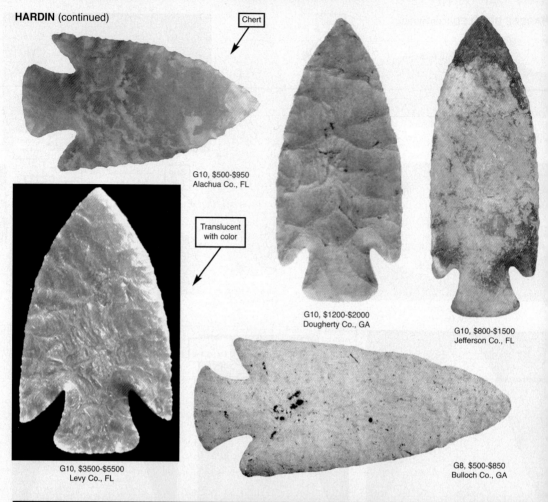

Chert

G10, $500-$950
Alachua Co., FL

Translucent
with color

G10, $1200-$2000
Dougherty Co., GA

G10, $800-$1500
Jefferson Co., FL

G10, $3500-$5500
Levy Co., FL

G8, $500-$850
Bulloch Co., GA

HERNANDO - Late Archaic, 4000 - 2500 B. P.

(Also see Citrus and Culbreath)

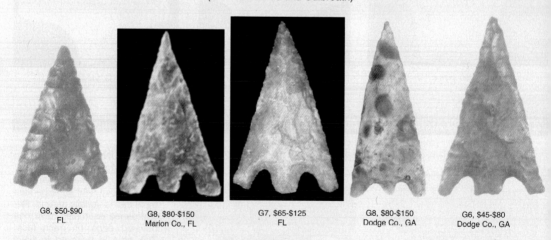

G8, $50-$90
FL

G8, $80-$150
Marion Co., FL

G7, $65-$125
FL

G8, $80-$150
Dodge Co., GA

G6, $45-$80
Dodge Co., GA

LOCATION: Georgia, Alabama and Florida. **DESCRIPTION:** A medium to large size, basal notched, triangular point with wide flaring tangs that may extend beyond the base. Side edges are straight to concave. Similar in outline only to the much earlier *Eva* type. Has been found in cache with *Santa Fe* and *Tallahassee* types as well as *Beaver Lake* style points. **I.D. KEY:** Narrow stem.

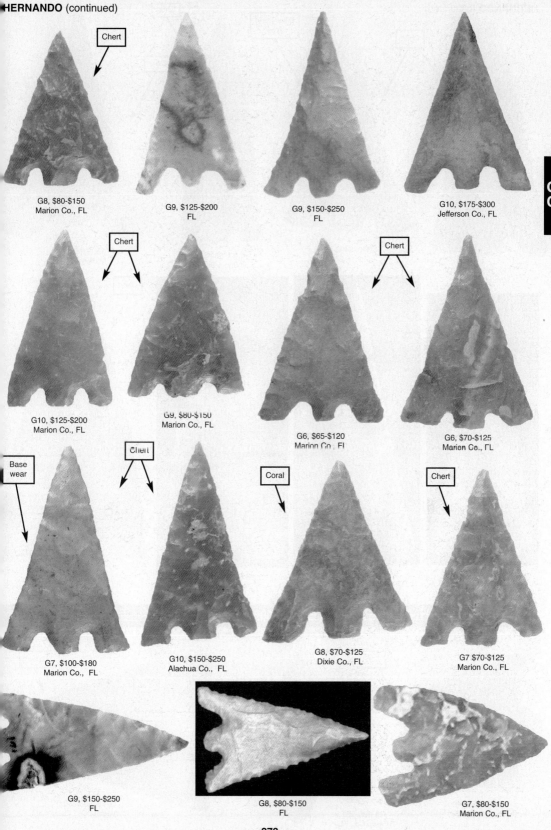

Chert

G8, $80-$150
Marion Co., FL

G9, $125-$200
FL

G9, $150-$250
FL

G10, $175-$300
Jefferson Co., FL

GC

Chert

G10, $125-$200
Marion Co., FL

G9, $80-$150
Marion Co., FL

Chert

G6, $65-$120
Marion Co., FL

G6, $70-$125
Marion Co., FL

Base wear

Chert

G7, $100-$180
Marion Co., FL

G10, $150-$250
Alachua Co., FL

Coral

G8, $70-$125
Dixie Co., FL

Chert

G7 $70-$125
Marion Co., FL

G9, $150-$250
FL

G8, $80-$150
FL

G7, $80-$150
Marion Co., FL

273

HERNANDO (continued)

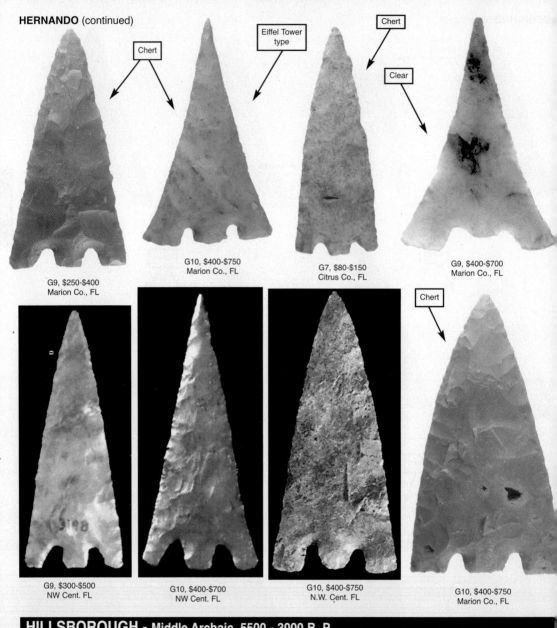

Chert

Eiffel Tower type

Chert

Clear

Chert

G9, $250-$400
Marion Co., FL

G10, $400-$750
Marion Co., FL

G7, $80-$150
Citrus Co., FL

G9, $400-$700
Marion Co., FL

G9, $300-$500
NW Cent. FL

G10, $400-$700
NW Cent. FL

G10, $400-$750
N.W. Cent. FL

G10, $400-$750
Marion Co., FL

HILLSBOROUGH - Middle Archaic, 5500 - 3000 B. P.

(Also see Marion and Newnan)

Coral

Chert

G8, $125-$200
Pasco Co., FL

G6, $30-$50
Pasco Co., FL

G7, $150-$250
Alachua Co., FL

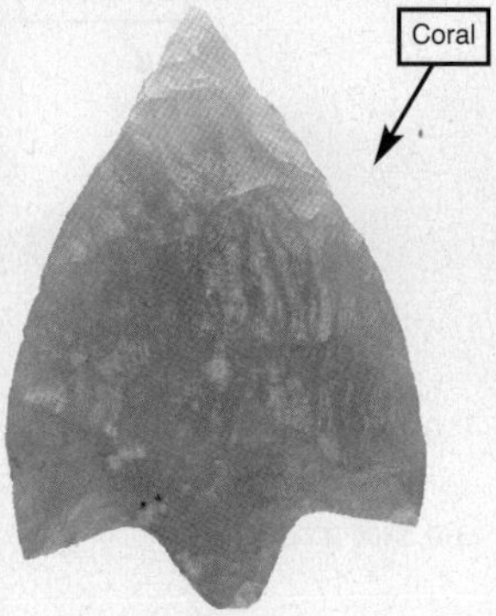

Coral

Clear
with color

G
C

G9, $275-$500
Pasco Co., FL

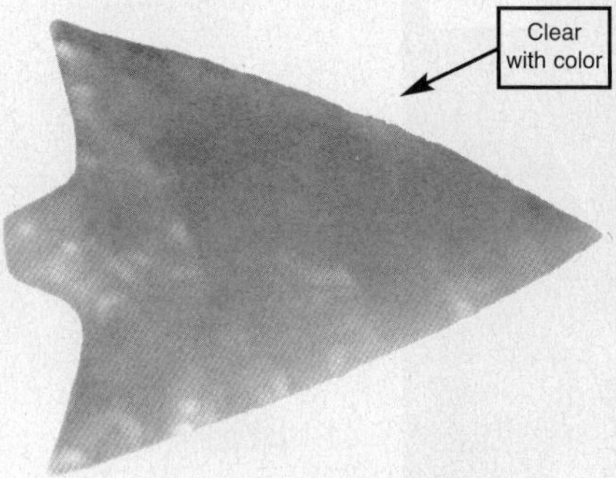

G9, $600-$1000
FL

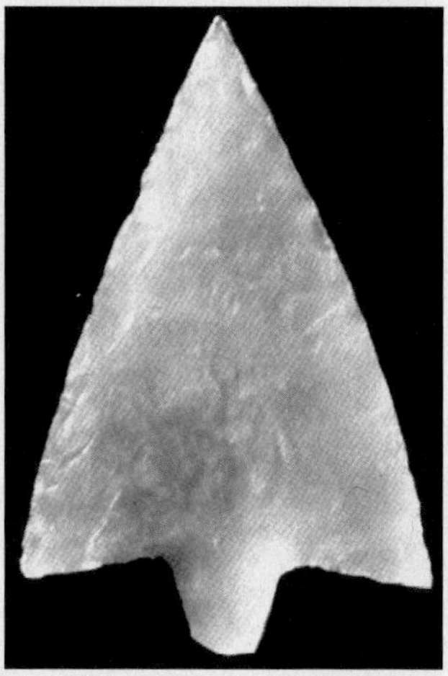

G9, $500-$900
Pasco Co., FL

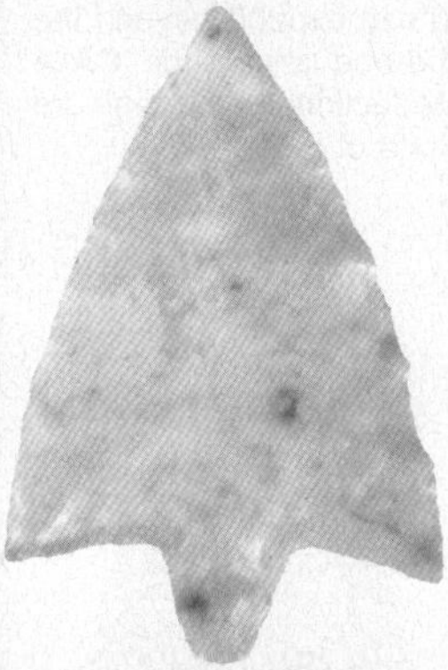

Color

G9, $350-$600
FL

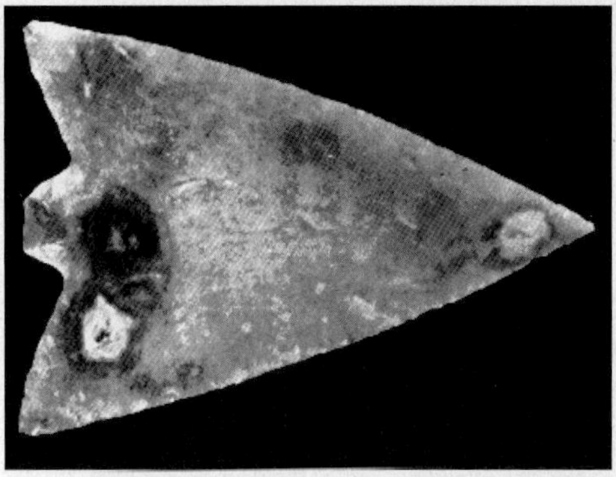

G9, $275-$500
N.W. Cent. FL

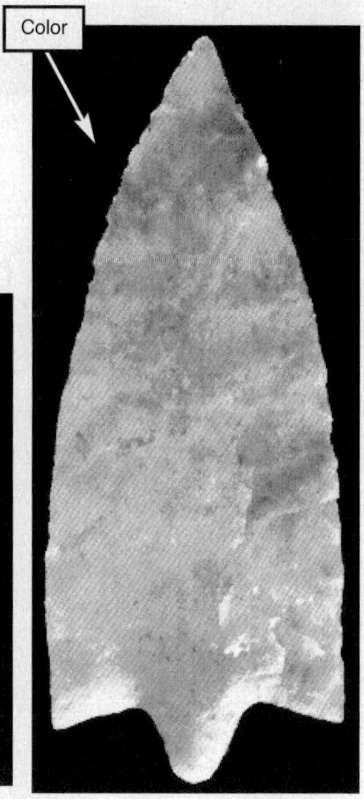

G7, $150-$250
Hillsborough Co., FL

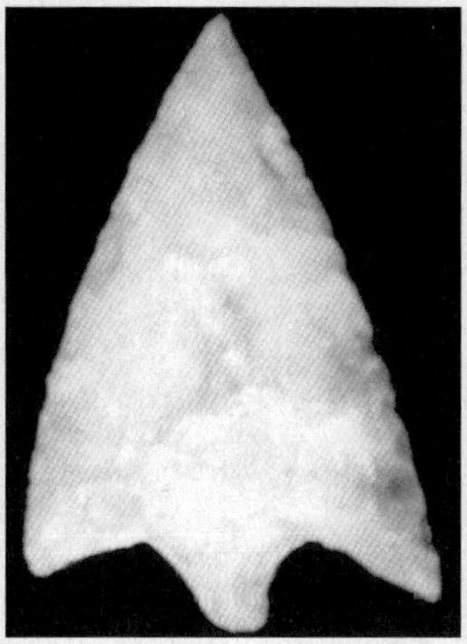

G6, $125-$200
Marion Co., FL

G9, $550-$1000
Hillsborough Co., FL

Coral

G7, $250-$400
Marion Co., FL

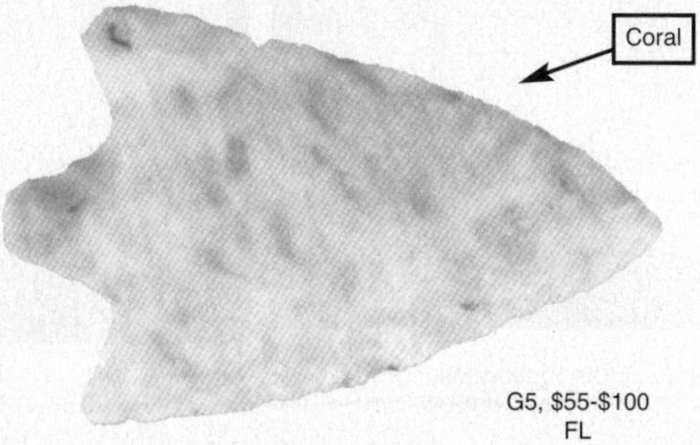

G5, $55-$100
FL

275

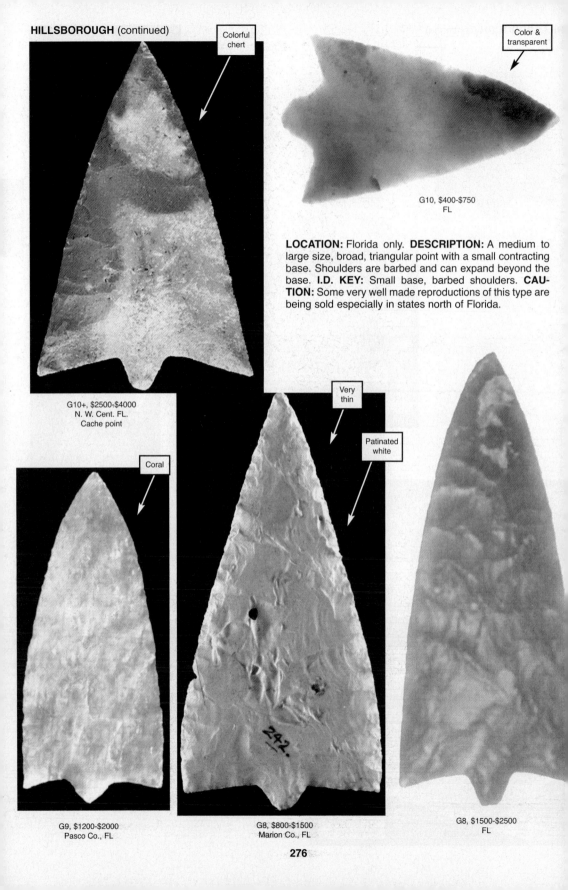

Colorful chert

Color & transparent

G10, $400-$750
FL

LOCATION: Florida only. **DESCRIPTION:** A medium to large size, broad, triangular point with a small contracting base. Shoulders are barbed and can expand beyond the base. **I.D. KEY:** Small base, barbed shoulders. **CAUTION:** Some very well made reproductions of this type are being sold especially in states north of Florida.

G10+, $2500-$4000
N. W. Cent. FL.
Cache point

Coral

Very thin

Patinated white

G9, $1200-$2000
Pasco Co., FL

G8, $800-$1500
Marion Co., FL

G8, $1500-$2500
FL

ICHETUCKNEE - Mississippian to Historic, 700 - 200 B. P.

(Also see Pinellas)

G7, $50-$75
Marion Co., FL

G8, $30-$50
Marion Co., FL

G8, $15-$25
Marion Co., FL

G8, $8-$15
Marion Co., FL

LOCATION: Southeastern states. **DES-CRIPTION:** A small to medium size, thin, narrow, lanceolate point with usually a straight base. Flaking quality is excellent. This point is called *Guntersville* to the north. **I.D. KEY:** Narrowness and blade expansion; blade edges curve inward at base.

JACKSON - Late Woodland to Mississippian, 2000 - 700 B. P.

(Also see Duval)

G6, $8-$15
Marion Co., FL

G10, $20-$35
FL

G8, $25-$45
FL

LOCATION: Coastal states. **DESCRIPTION:** A small size, thick, narrow, triangular point with wide, shallow side notches. Some examples have an unfinished rind or base. Called *Swan Lake* in upper Southeastern states

KASKASKIA POINT   (See Trade Points)

KIRK CORNER NOTCHED - Early to Middle Archaic, 9000 - 6000 B. P.

(Also see Bolen, Hardin, Lafayette and Ocala)

G8, $250-$450
Dixie Co., FL

G8, $100-$175
FL

LOCATION: Southeastern states. **DESCRIPTION:** A medium to large size, corner notched point. Blade edges can be convex to recurved and are finely serrated on many examples. The base can be concave, convex, straight or auriculate. **I.D. KEY**: Secondary edgework.

KIRK STEMMED - Early to Middle Archaic, 9000 - 6000 B. P.

(Also see Abbey, Arredondo, Boggy Branch, Bolen, Elora, Hamilton and Six Mile Creek)

G
C

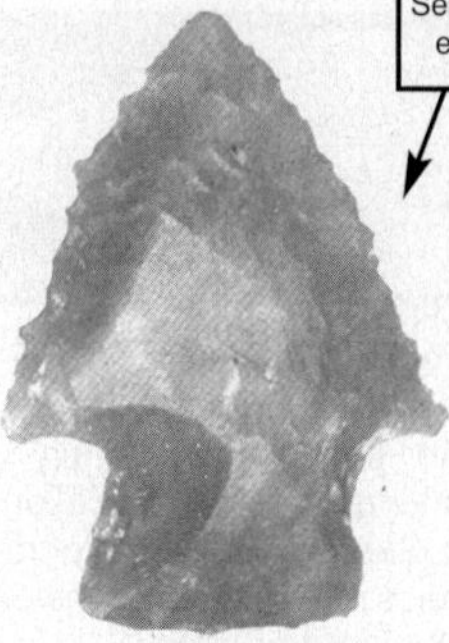

Serrated
edge

Coastal
Plain
chert

G3, $8-$15
FL

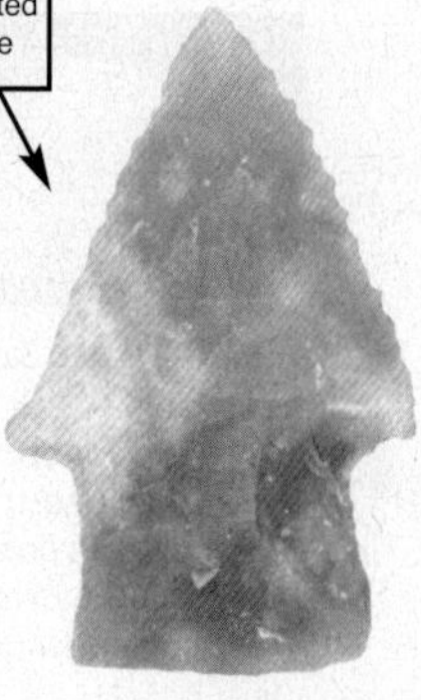

G5, $12-$20
FL

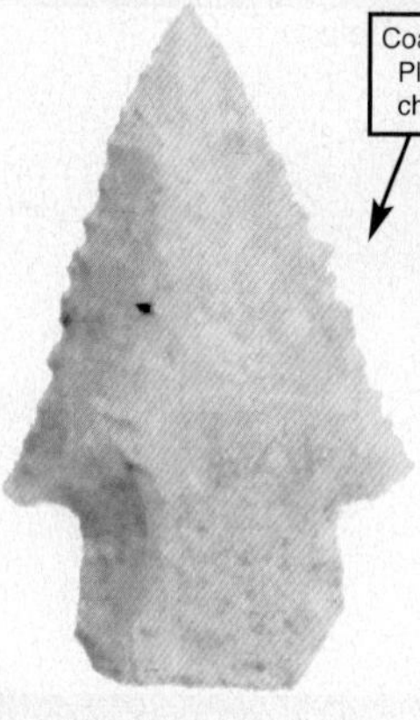

G5, $18-$30
FL

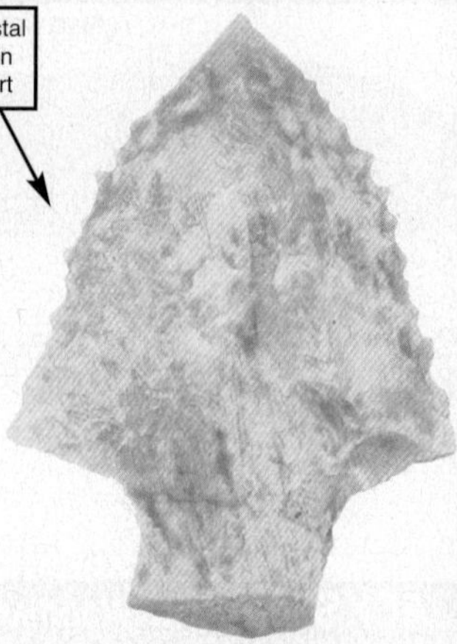

G8, $25-$45
Jefferson Co., FL

G6, $35-$60
FL

G9, $65-$125
FL

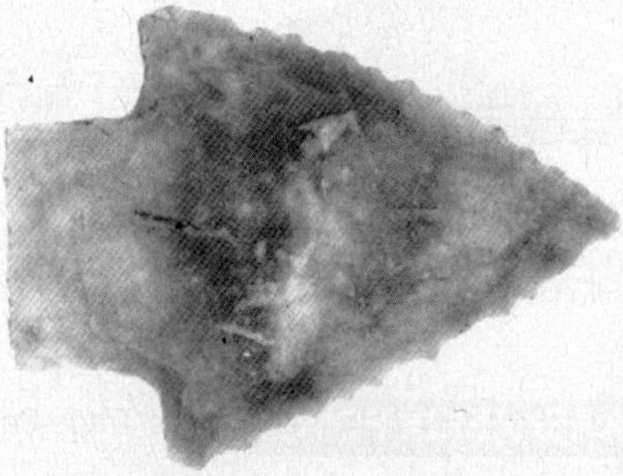

G6, $20-$35
FL

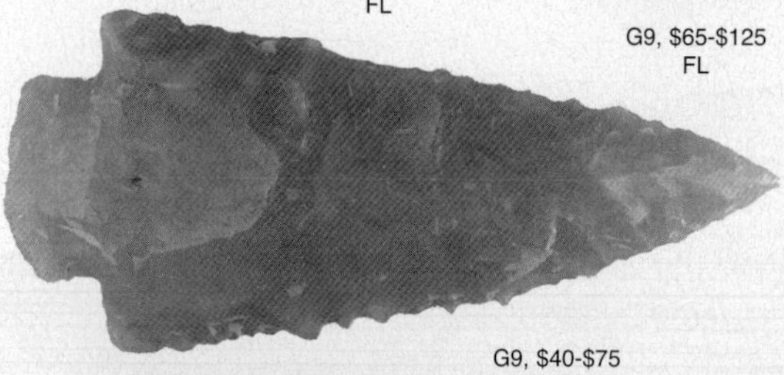

Chert

G9, $40-$75
Alachua Co., FL

Chert

Chert

G8, $35-$60
Alachua Co., FL

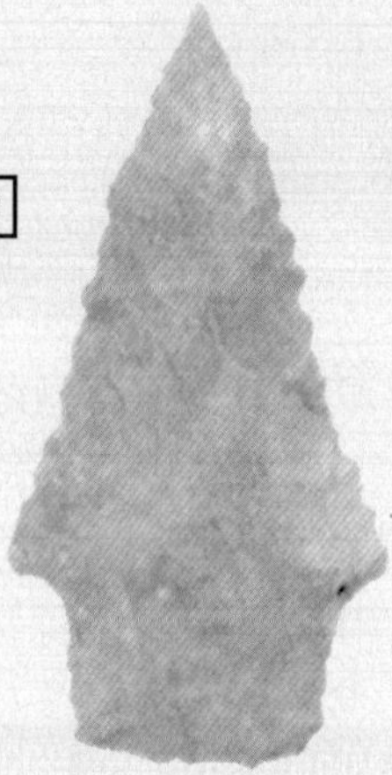

G6, $25-$45
FL

G9, $200-$350
Marion Co., FL

LOCATION: Eastern to Gulf Coastal states.
DESCRIPTION: A medium to large size, barbed, stemmed point with deep notches or fine serrations along the blade edges. The stem is parallel, contracting or expanding. The base can be concave, convex or straight, and can be very short. The shoulders are usually strongly barbed. **I.D. KEY:** Serrations.

KIRK STEMMED (continued)

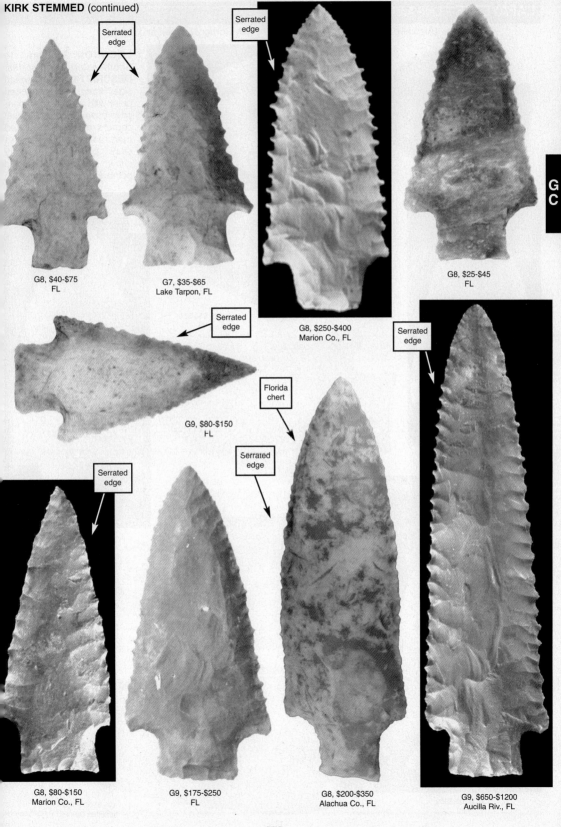

Serrated edge

Serrated edge

G8, $40-$75
FL

G7, $35-$65
Lake Tarpon, FL

Serrated edge

G8, $250-$400
Marion Co., FL

G8, $25-$45
FL

G C

Serrated edge

G9, $80-$150
FL

Serrated edge

Florida chert

Serrated edge

Serrated edge

G8, $80-$150
Marion Co., FL

G9, $175-$250
FL

G8, $200-$350
Alachua Co., FL

G9, $650-$1200
Aucilla Riv., FL

279

LAFAYETTE - Late Archaic, 4000 - 3000 B. P.

(Also see Bolen Plain, Clay, Culbreath, Kirk Corner Notched and Ocala)

LOCATION: Southern to Southeastern states.
DESCRIPTION: A medium size, broad, corner-notched point with a straight to concave base. Barbs and basal corners are more rounded than pointed. Related to *Clay* points. Previously shown (in error) as *Ocala* points. Barbs expand.

G5, $35-$60
Jefferson Co., FL

G8, $85-$165
Marion Co., FL

Classic example

G5, $30-$50
FL

G9, $150-$250
Pinellas Co., FL

G5 $25-$45
Jefferson Co., FL

G10, $400-$700
Gilchrist Co., FL

Chert

G9, $150-$275
Marion Co., FL

G7, $200-$350
FL

G9, $250-$475
Jefferson Co., FL

LEDBETTER - Mid to late Archaic, 6,000 - 3500 B. P.

(Also see Pickwick and Levy)

Note asymmetrical blade

G8, $90-$175
Jefferson Co., FL

G8, $90-$175
Dougherty Co., GA

G7, $80-$150
Marion Co., FL

LOCATION: Southeastern into the Gulf states. **DESCRIPTION:** A medium to large size *Pickwick* point that is asymmetrical with one side of the blade curving to the tip more than the other. Bases are contracting to expanding. Blade edges can be serrated. **I.D. KEY:** Asymmetrical blade.

LEON - Woodland - Mississippian, 1500 - 1000 B. P.

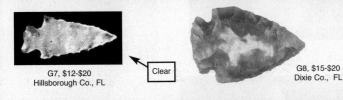

LOCATION: Southern to Southeastern states. **DESCRIPTION:** A small size corner notched point. Blade edges are straight to convex. Bases expand with sharp to rounded basal corners. **I.D. KEY:** Size and corner notching.

G7, $12-$20
Hillsborough Co., FL

Clear

G8, $15-$20
Dixie Co., FL

LEVY - Late Archaic, 5000 - 3000 B. P.

(Also see Abbey, Alachua, Cypress Creek, Elora, Hardee Beveled, Ledbetter, Marion, Newnan, Putnam, Savannah River and Sumter)

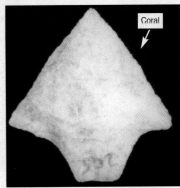

Coral

G6, $20-$35
FL

G6, $40-$75
FL

G7, $30-$50
FL

Colorful purple coral

G6, $150-$265
Hillsborough Co., FL

G6, $85-$125
Jefferson Co., FL

G5, $25-$40
Hillsborough Co., FL

G7, $35-$65
FL

G6, $80-$150
N.W. Cent. FL

G7, $55-$100
FL

G8, $40-$75
FL

G8, $85-$165
FL

LOCATION: Southern to Southeastern states. **DESCRIPTION:** A medium size, broad, contracted stemmed point with wide, tapered to slightly barbed shoulders. May have evolved from the earlier *Newnan* form. **I.D. KEY:** Edgework and one ear is stronger. *Levy* shoulders have concave edges connecting base and shoulder corners.

(Also see Bolen Beveled, Kirk Corner Notched)

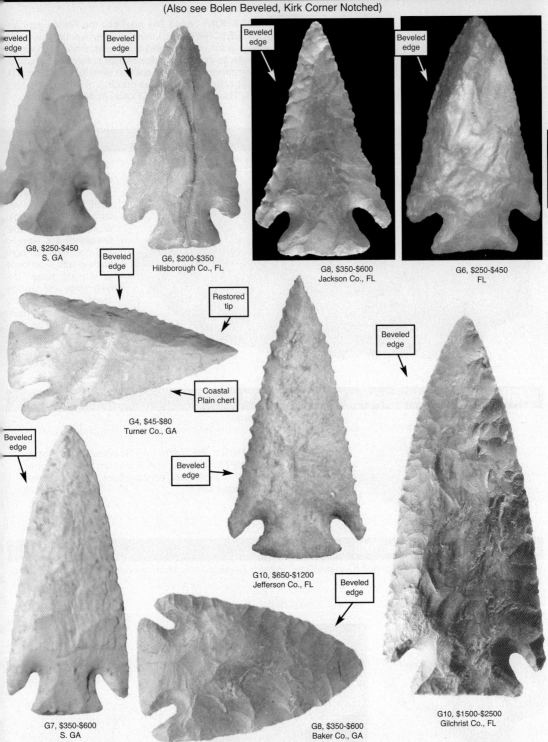

Beveled edge

Beveled edge

Beveled edge

Beveled edge

G8, $250-$450
S. GA

Beveled edge

G6, $200-$350
Hillsborough Co., FL

G8, $350-$600
Jackson Co., FL

G6, $250-$450
FL

G
C

Beveled edge

Restored tip

Coastal Plain chert

G4, $45-$80
Turner Co., GA

Beveled edge

Beveled edge

Beveled edge

Beveled edge

G10, $650-$1200
Jefferson Co., FL

G7, $350-$600
S. GA

G8, $350-$600
Baker Co., GA

G10, $1500-$2500
Gilchrist Co., FL

LOCATION: Southeastern states. **DESCRIPTION:** A medium to large size, broad, corner notched point that is beveled on one side of each face. The beveling continues when resharpened which created a flat rhomboid cross section. Also known as Deep Notch. **I.D. KEY:** Notching, secondary edgework is always opposite creating at least slight beveling.

283

MANASOTA - Woodland 3,000 - 1500 B. P.

(Also see Beaver Lake and Safety Harbor)

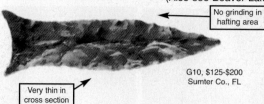

No grinding in hafting area

Very thin in cross section

G10, $125-$200
Sumter Co., FL

LOCATION: Tampa Bay area into the Florida panhandle. **DESCRIPTION:** A medium size, thin, narrow, auriculate point with recurved blade edges and a sharp tip. Similar to the much earlier *Beaver Lake* point but usually smaller and narrower and the stem is not ground. **I.D. KEY:** Narrowness and no grinding. See Schroder, pg. 194, The Anthropology of Florida Points and Blades.

MAPLES - Middle Archaic, 4500 - 3500 B. P.

(Also see Elora, Morrow Mountain and Savannah River)

Jasper

G7, $150-$250
Dodge Co., GA

LOCATION: N. Florida into Georgia. **DESCRIPTION:** A very large, broad, thick, short stemmed blade. Shoulders are tapered and the stem is contracting with a concave to straight base. Usually thick and crudely made, but fine quality examples have been found. Not to be confused with Morrow Mountain which has Archaic parallel flaking.

MARIANNA - Transitional Paleo, 10,000 - 8500 B. P.

(Also see Conerly)

G5, $8-$15
FL

LOCATION: Southern to Southeastern states. **DESCRIPTION:** A rare type. A medium size lanceolate point with a constricted, concave base. Look for parallel to oblique flaking.

MARION - Middle Archaic, 7000 - 3000 B. P.

(Also see Adena, Alachua, Cottonbridge, Cypress Creek, Hardee Beveled, Levy, Morrow Mountain, Newnan, Pickwick and Putnam)

G4, $12-$20
FL

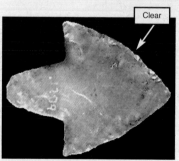

Clear

G9, $150-$250
Lake Mattie, FL

G5, $12-$20
FL

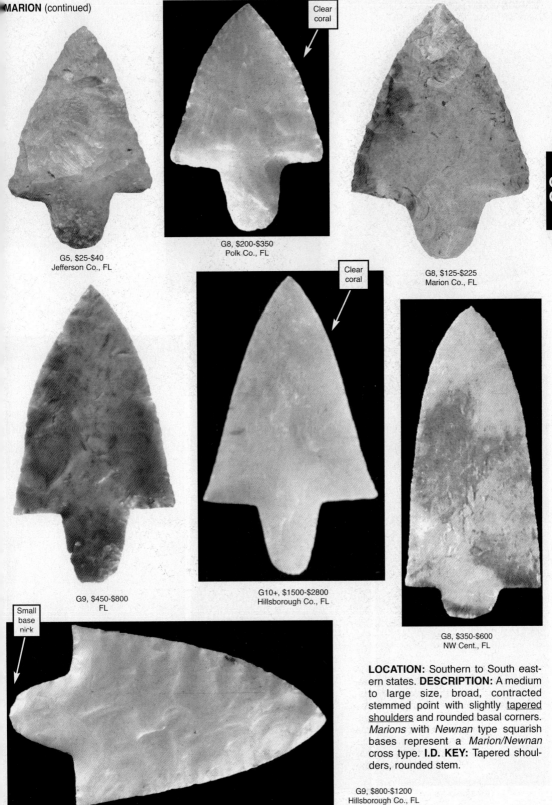

Clear coral

G5, $25-$40
Jefferson Co., FL

G8, $200-$350
Polk Co., FL

G C

G8, $125-$225
Marion Co., FL

Clear coral

G9, $450-$800
FL

G10+, $1500-$2800
Hillsborough Co., FL

G8, $350-$600
NW Cent., FL

Small base nick

LOCATION: Southern to South eastern states. **DESCRIPTION:** A medium to large size, broad, contracted stemmed point with slightly <u>tapered shoulders</u> and rounded basal corners. *Marions* with *Newnan* type squarish bases represent a *Marion/Newnan* cross type. **I.D. KEY:** Tapered shoulders, rounded stem.

G9, $800-$1200
Hillsborough Co., FL

G7, $125-$225
Hillsborough Co., FL

G8, $175-$300
Marion Co., FL

G6, $65-$125
Jefferson Co., FL

Colorful
chert

G8, $700-$1200
FL

G10, $2500-$4500
Hillsborough Co., FL

G10, $2500-$4000
Hillsborough Co., FL

(Also see Bascom, Cypress Creek, Eva, Maples, Marion, Putnam and Thonotosassa)

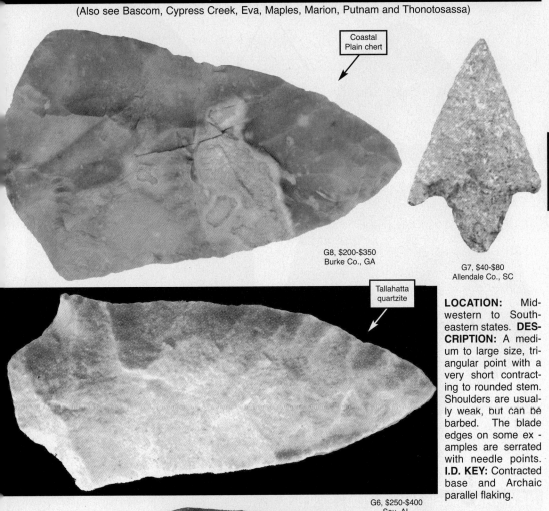

Coastal Plain chert

G8, $200-$350
Burke Co., GA

G7, $40-$80
Allendale Co., SC

G C

Tallahatta quartzite

LOCATION: Midwestern to Southeastern states. **DESCRIPTION:** A medium to large size, triangular point with a very short contracting to rounded stem. Shoulders are usually weak, but can be barbed. The blade edges on some examples are serrated with needle points. **I.D. KEY:** Contracted base and Archaic parallel flaking.

G6, $250-$400
Sou. AL

Chert

G9, $250-$400
Pasco Co., FL

287

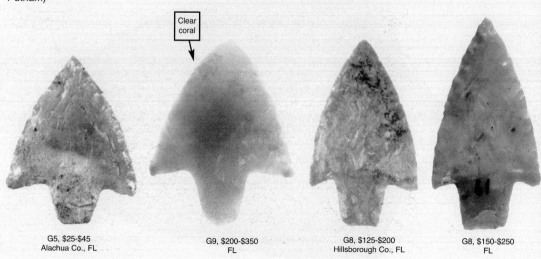

Chert

G9, $250-$400
Pasco Co., FL

G9, $250-$450
Pasco Co., FL

NEWNAN - Middle Archaic, 7000 - 3000 B. P.

(Also see Adena, Alachua, Cypress Creek, Hardee Beveled, Hillsborough, Levy, Marion, Morrow Mountain, and Putnam)

Clear coral

G5, $25-$45
Alachua Co., FL

G9, $200-$350
FL

G8, $125-$200
Hillsborough Co., FL

G8, $150-$250
FL

Coral

Tampa Bay Bottom chert

Chert

Base nick

G6, $45-$80
Hillsborough Rv., FL

G8, $125-$200
Pasco Co., FL

G9, $150-$250
Hillsborough Co., FL

G9, $150-$250
Orange Lake, FL

G C

Coral

Chert

G9, $80-$150
Alachua Co., FL

Coral

G8, $250-$400
Pasco Co., FL

G9, $250-$400
Lake, Apopka, FL

G9, $175-$300
Marion Co., FL

Coral

Chert

G9, $350-$600
Pasco Co., FL

G10, $200-$350
Withlachochee Rv., FL

G10, $250-$450
Marion Co., FL

NEWNAN (continued)

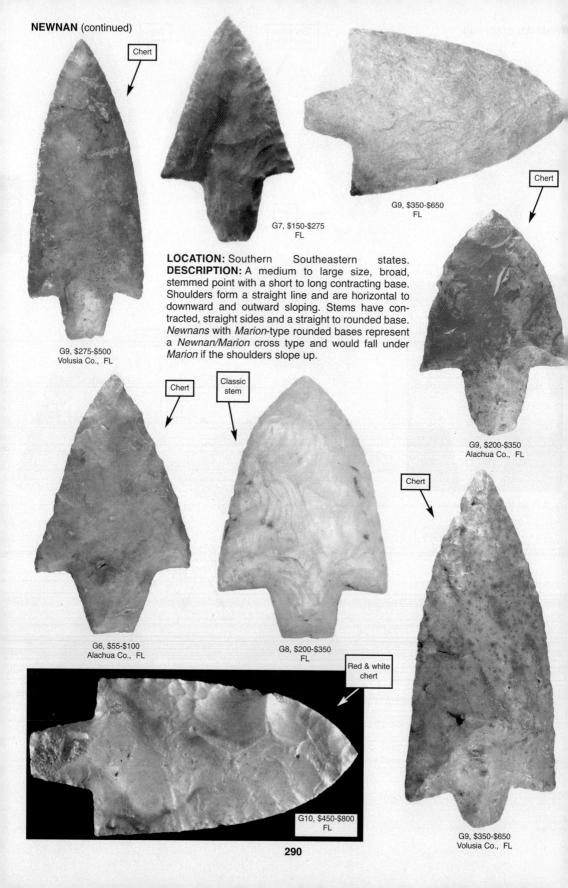

Chert

Chert

G9, $350-$650
FL

G7, $150-$275
FL

Chert

LOCATION: Southern Southeastern states. **DESCRIPTION:** A medium to large size, broad, stemmed point with a short to long contracting base. Shoulders form a straight line and are horizontal to downward and outward sloping. Stems have contracted, straight sides and a straight to rounded base. *Newnans* with *Marion*-type rounded bases represent a *Newnan/Marion* cross type and would fall under *Marion* if the shoulders slope up.

G9, $275-$500
Volusia Co., FL

Chert

Classic
stem

G9, $200-$350
Alachua Co., FL

Chert

G6, $55-$100
Alachua Co., FL

G8, $200-$350
FL

Red & white
chert

G10, $450-$800
FL

G9, $350-$650
Volusia Co., FL

290

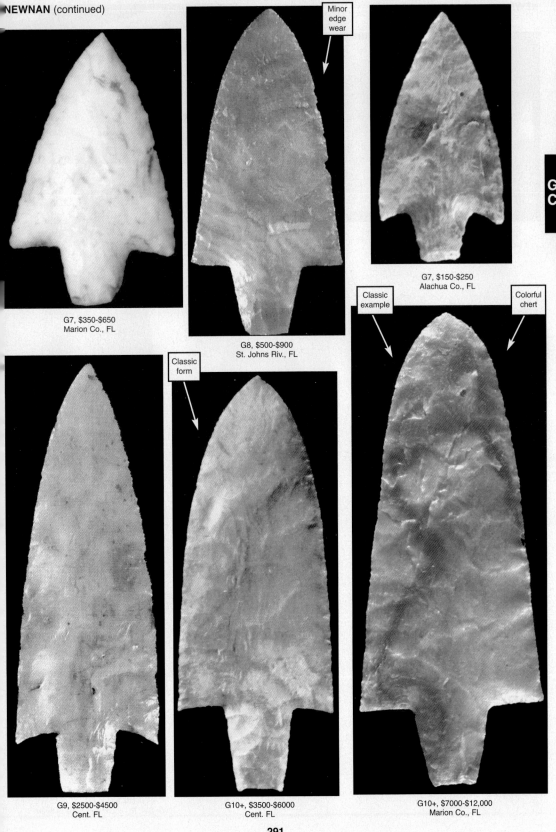

G C

G7, $350-$650
Marion Co., FL

Minor edge wear

G8, $500-$900
St. Johns Riv., FL

G7, $150-$250
Alachua Co., FL

Classic example

Colorful chert

Classic form

G9, $2500-$4500
Cent. FL

G10+, $3500-$6000
Cent. FL

G10+, $7000-$12,000
Marion Co., FL

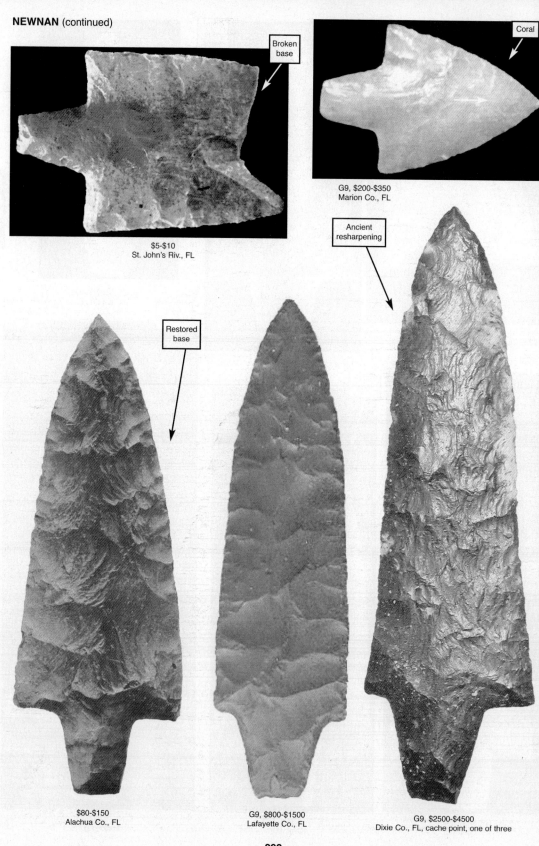

Broken base

$5-$10
St. John's Riv., FL

Coral

G9, $200-$350
Marion Co., FL

Ancient resharpening

Restored base

$80-$150
Alachua Co., FL

G9, $800-$1500
Lafayette Co., FL

G9, $2500-$4500
Dixie Co., FL, cache point, one of three

OCALA - Woodland, 2500 - 1500 B. P.

(Also see Bolen, Clay, Culbreath, Kirk Corner Notched & Lafayette)

Chert

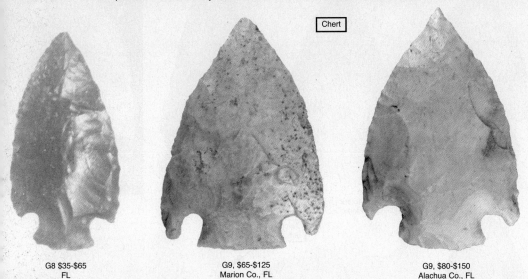

G8 $35-$65
FL

G9, $65-$125
Marion Co., FL

G9, $80-$150
Alachua Co., FL

LOCATION: Gulf Coastal states. **DESCRIPTION:** A medium to large size broad corner-notched point with a straight to convex base. Some examples have a base similar to *Dovetails*. Barbs and basal corners are sharp to rounded. Barbs curve inward. Rare in Florida. According to Bullen this type is larger and better crafted than *Bolens* or *Lafayettes* and dates to 2500 B.P. **I.D. KEY:** Size and corner notching.

O'LENO - Woodland, 2000 - 800 B. P.

(Also see Pinellas, Tampa and Yadkin)

G7, $20-$35
Henry Co., AL

G6, $15-$25
Marion Co., FL

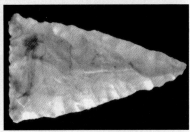

G6, $15-$25
N.W. FL

LOCATION: Southern Southeastern states. **DESCRIPTION:** A medium size, broad, triangle point with a straight to slightly concave base.

OSCEOLA-GREENBRIAR - Early Archaic, 9500 - 6000 B. P.

(Also see Bolen)

G2, $12-$20, type II
FL

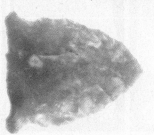

G6, $25-$40, type I
FL

G7, $80-$150, type I
FL

"Buttonbase" form

G6, $40-$75, type I
Jefferson Co., FL

G9, $45-$85, type II
Hernando Co., FL

G8, $150-$250, type I
Gilchrist Co., FL

G7, $175-$300, type I
Taylor Co., FL

Tampa Bay Bottom chert

G9, $40-$75, type II
Hernando Co., FL

G8, $175-$300, type II
Hillsborough Co., FL

LOCATION: Gulf Coastal states. **DESCRIPTION:** A medium to large size, broad, side-notched point with two base variations. The base is either concave or has two shallow notches creating a high point in the center. Bases and notches are usually heavily ground. This type is found in the same layer with *Bolen* points in Florida.

G8, $200-$350, type I
Jefferson Co., FL

G8, $150-$250, type II
Jefferson Co., FL

G8 $300-$550, type II
N.W. Cent. FL

G8, $350-$650, type II
Gilchrist Co., FL

G10, $600-$1100, type II
Suwannee Co., FL

PALEO KNIFE - Paleo, 10,000 B. P.

(Also see Scraper)

Dorsal side shown

G C

G8, $15-$25
Suwannee Co., FL

G6, $20-$35
Suwannee Co., FL

G10, $75-$135
Suwannee Co., FL

Florida. **DESCRIPTION:** A medium to large size, uniface blade found with bison, mammoth and mastodon mastodon remains. Flat on one face and steeply beveled on the opposing face. **I.D. KEY:** Uniface and steep beveling.

PICKWICK - Middle to Late Archaic, 6000 - 3500 B. P.

(Also see Elora, Ledbetter and Savannah River)

G5, $5-$10
Jefferson Co., FL

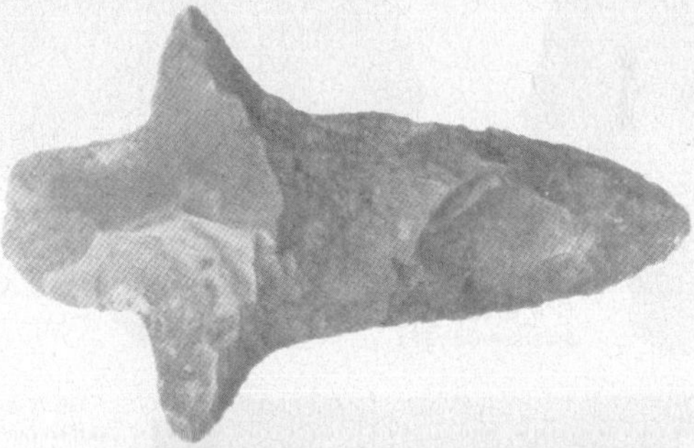

G8, $35-$60
FL

Tallahatta quartzite

LOCATION: Found North of the Suwannee River into Georgia and Alabama. **DESCRIPTION:** A medium to large size, expanded shoulder, contracted to expanded stem point. Blade edges are recurved, and many examples show fine secondary flaking with serrations. Alabama and Tennessee examples are beveled on one side of each face. The bevel is steep and shallow. Shoulders are horizontal, tapered or barbed and form sharp angles. Some stems are snapped off or may show original rind.

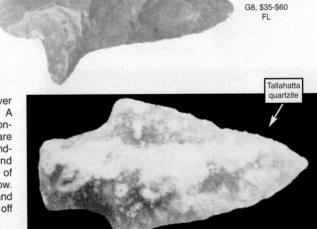

G7, $95-$175
Sou. AL

295

PICKWICK (continued)

G5, $15-$25
Jefferson Co., FL

G7, $35-$65
FL

G5, $30-$50
Jefferson Co., FL

G6, $40-$75
Jefferson Co., FL

Needle
tip

Serrated
edge

G10, $125-$200
Jefferson Co., FL

G9, $80-$150
Jefferson Co., FL

G9, $150-$250
Jefferson Co., FL

Tallahatta
quartzite

G9, $250-$450
FL

G6, $80-$150
Marion Co., FL

Tallahatta
quartzite

G6, $40-$75
Union Co., FL

Shoulder
wear

Minor
tip
nick

G
C

G9, $275-$500
Sou. AL

G6, $80-$150
Jackson Co., FL

G6, $125-$200
Jefferson Co., FL

G9, $200-$350
Jackson Co., FL

G9, $250-$400
Jefferson Co., FL

PINELLAS - Mississippian, 800 - 400 B. P.

(Also see O'Leno, Safety Harbor, Tallahassee and Yadkin)

G6, $5-$8
FL

G6, $6-$12
FL

G6, $4-$6
FL

G6, $8-$15
FL

G8, $25-$45
FL

G8, $25-$45
Marion Co., FL

G8, $25-$45
FL

Chert

G7, $25-$45
Dixie Co., FL

Serrated edge

Chert

G9, $25-$45
Madison Co., FL

G8, $45-$85
Marion Co., FL

G9, $25-$45
Suwannee Co., FL

G8, $30-$55
FL

G9, $30-$55
Burke Co., GA

Chert

G8, $30-$55
FL

G7, $25-$45
Alachua Co., F

Chert

G7, $45-$85
Marion Co., FL

G7, $45-$50
FL

Translucent steel blue flint

Clear

G10 $45-$85
Jefferson Co., FL

G9, $35-$65
Marion Co., FL

G9, $70-$135
FL

G8, $25-$40
FL

G9, $45-$80
FL

G9, $40-$75
Jefferson Co., FL

LOCATION: Gulf Coastal states. **DESCRIPTION:** A small, narrow, thick to thin, triangular point with a straight to slightly concave base. Blade edges can be serrated.

PUTNAM - Middle Archaic, 6500 - 3000 B. P.

(Also see Cypress Creek, Hardee Beveled, Levy, Marion, Morrow Mountain, Newnan, Sumter and Thonotosassa)

LOCATION: Southern Southeastern states. **DESCRIPTION:** A medium to large size, broad, contracted stemmed point with rounded to sharp shoulders. The stem is short to long with a convex base. The shoulders are tapered and can be rounded. Believed to have evolved from the *Marion* type. **I.D. KEY:** Weak shoulders, rounded barbs formed by continuous recurved edges.

G6, $15-$25
FL

Coral

G8, $25-$45
FL

G6, $20-$35
FL

G7, $15-$30
Jefferson Co., FL

Classic
example

G
C

G7, $25-$40
FL

Chert

G6, $30-$50
Jefferson Co., FL

Chert

G9, $200-$350
Polk Co., FL

G9, $150-$250
Marion Co., FL

Semi-clear

G9, $800-$1500
Aucilla Riv., FL

Minor
edge
nick

REDSTONE - Paleo, 11,500 - 10,500 B. P.

(Also see Clovis, Simpson, Suwannee & Withlachoochee)

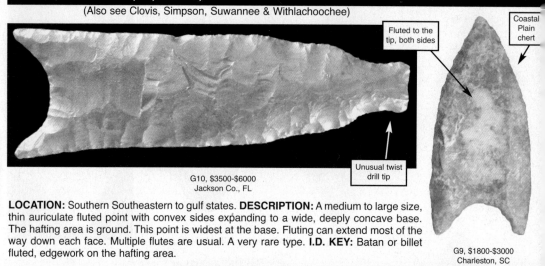

Fluted to the tip, both sides

Coastal Plain chert

G10, $3500-$6000
Jackson Co., FL

Unusual twist drill tip

LOCATION: Southern Southeastern to gulf states. **DESCRIPTION:** A medium to large size, thin auriculate fluted point with convex sides expanding to a wide, deeply concave base. The hafting area is ground. This point is widest at the base. Fluting can extend most of the way down each face. Multiple flutes are usual. A very rare type. **I.D. KEY:** Batan or billet fluted, edgework on the hafting area.

G9, $1800-$3000
Charleston, SC

SAFETY HARBOR - Mississippian to Historic, 1100 - 300 B. P.

(Also see Manasota, O'Leno, Pinellas, Santa Fe, Tallahassee and Yadkin)

Serrated edge

G5, $15-$25
Sumter Co., FL

Classic angular base

G9, $80-$150
Sou. AL

G9, $95-$185
Sumter Co., FL

Chert

G10, $165-$300
Sumter Co., FL

G8, $125-$200
Marion Co., FL

LOCATION: The Tampa Bay area of Florida. Named in the 1960s by Jarl Malwin. **DESCRIPTION:** A medium size, narrow, thin, triangular point with a concave to angular base. Basal corners are sharp. Blade edges can be serrated. These are similar points to *Santa Fe* and *Tallahassee* found in other areas but are not as old. Basal edges of *Safety Harbor* points are not ground.

SANTA FE - Late Archaic to Woodland 4000 - 1500 B.P

(Also see Beaver Lake, Dalton, Hardaway, Safety Harbor and Tallahassee)

Chert

Coral

G6, $12-$20
FL

G6, $15-$30
FL

G7, $30-$50
FL

G7, $30-$50
FL

G7, $35-$60
Marion Co., FL

G8, $40-$75
Tift Co., GA

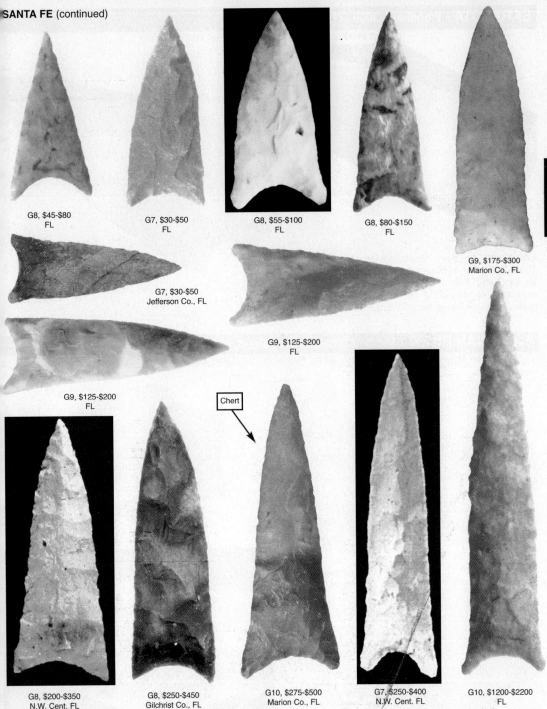

G C

G8, $45-$80
FL

G7, $30-$50
FL

G8, $55-$100
FL

G8, $80-$150
FL

G9, $175-$300
Marion Co., FL

G7, $30-$50
Jefferson Co., FL

G9, $125-$200
FL

G9, $125-$200
FL

Chert

G8, $200-$350
N.W. Cent. FL

G8, $250-$450
Gilchrist Co., FL

G10, $275-$500
Marion Co., FL

G7, $250-$400
N.W. Cent. FL

G10, $1200-$2200
FL

LOCATION: From the Tampa Bay area of Florida northward into southern Alabama, Georgia and South Carolina.
DESCRIPTION: A medium size, thin, narrow, auriculate point with expanding auricules and a concave base. Hafting area is not well defined and can be lightly ground although many examples are not ground. Blade edges are not serrated as in *Tallahassee* which is the serrated form of the two types. **Note:** This type along with the *Tallahassee* point have been confused with a much earlier *Dalton* type found in Northern Florida into Southern Alabama, Georgia and South Carolina. Compared to the *Dalton* type, the *Santa Fe* and the *Tallahassee* points are narrower and much thinner and have less patination. The *Dalton* is a heavier point being thicker and wider with heavy grinding around the entire basal area. the blade edge serrations are also formed differently on *Dalton* points. **I.D. KEY:** Thinness, narrowness, light grinding around base.

301

SARASOTA - Woodland, 3000 - 1500 B. P.

(Also see Bradford, Columbia, Ledbetter and Pickwick)

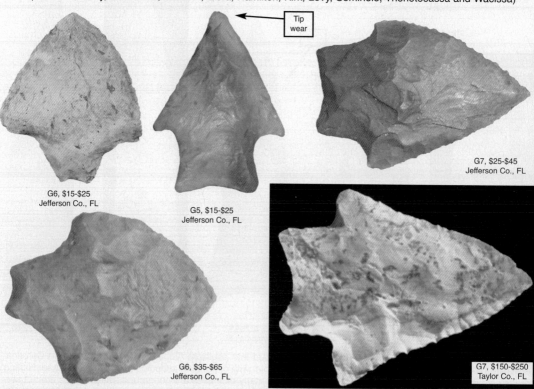

G5, $12-$20
FL

G7, $55-$100
Hernando Co., FL

LOCATION: Southern Southeastern states. **DESCRIPTION:** A medium to large size stemmed point with horizontal shoulders. The stem can be parallel sided to slightly expanding or contracting. Blade edges are slightly convex to recurved. Similar to the northern *Pickwick* type.

SAVANNAH RIVER - Middle Archaic to Woodland, 5000 - 2000 B. P.

(Also see Abbey, Arredondo, Bascom, Elora, Hamilton, Kirk, Levy, Seminole, Thonotosassa and Wacissa)

Tip
wear

G7, $25-$45
Jefferson Co., FL

G6, $15-$25
Jefferson Co., FL

G5, $15-$25
Jefferson Co., FL

G6, $35-$65
Jefferson Co., FL

G7, $150-$250
Taylor Co., FL

LOCATION: Southeastern to Eastern states. **DESCRIPTION:** A medium to large size, straight to contracting stemmed point with a straight to concave base. The shoulders are tapered to square and are strong. The stems are narrow to broad. Believed to be related to the earlier *Stanly* point. The preform is called *Bascom*. A large cache of *Bascom* and *Savannah River* points were found together in South Carolina. **KEY:** Stems have straight to concave bases, shoulders are strong, *Savannah River* points are usually large. Similar to *Hamilton* points which are much older and have concave bases and weaker shoulders.

G7, $25-$45
Jefferson Co., FL

G7, $25-$45
FL

G8, $30-$50
Jefferson Co., FL

G
C

Coral

G8, $150-$250
Dixie Co., FL

Tallahatta
Quartzite

G8, $150-$250
So. AL

G8, $150-$300
Clay Co., GA

Serrated
edge

G10, $250-$400
Lee Co., GA

G8, $150-$500
Daugherty Co., GA

G6, $275-$500
Jefferson Co., FL

G6, $250-$400
Jefferson Co., FL

G7, $200-$350
Jefferson Co., FL

G9, $275-$500
Madison Co., FL

G9, $400-$750
Jefferson Co., FL

G8, $400-$700
FL

Chert

G8, $275-$500
Jefferson Co., FL

G9, $80-$150
Marion Co., FL

G
C

G9, $450-$850
FL

G10, $1200-$2000
FL

SCRAPER - Paleo to Historic, 11,500 - 200 B. P.

(Also see Abbey, Elora, Hamilton, Levy, Paleo Knife, Savannah River and Wacissa)

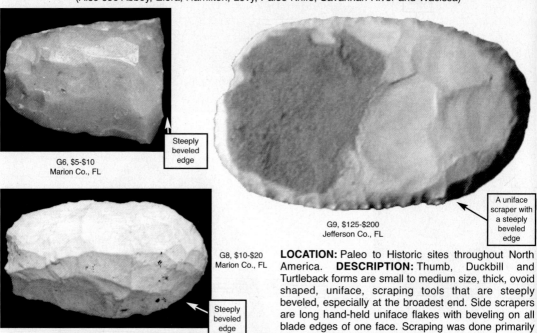

G6, $5-$10
Marion Co., FL

Steeply beveled edge

A uniface scraper with a steeply beveled edge

G9, $125-$200
Jefferson Co., FL

G8, $10-$20
Marion Co., FL

Steeply beveled edge

LOCATION: Paleo to Historic sites throughout North America. **DESCRIPTION:** Thumb, Duckbill and Turtleback forms are small to medium size, thick, ovoid shaped, uniface, scraping tools that are steeply beveled, especially at the broadest end. Side scrapers are long hand-held uniface flakes with beveling on all blade edges of one face. Scraping was done primarily from the sides of these blades.

SEMINOLE - Late Archaic, 5000 - 3500 B. P.

(Also see Abbey, Elora, Hamilton, Levy, Savannah River and Wacissa)

G9, $40-$75
Decatur Co., GA

G8, $80-$150
Burke Co., GA

G8, $125-$200
Gadsden Co., FL

LOCATION: Gulf Coastal states. **DESCRIPTION:** A medium to large size, broad point with barbed shoulders and a concave base. A variation of the Savannah River point.

306

(Also see Beaver Lake, Clovis, Conerly, Simpson-Mustache, Suwannee & Withlacoochee)

Chert

Crystal quartz

G C

G9, $2000-$3500
Gilchrist Co., FL

G5, $150-$275
Southern AL

G9, $500-$900
Alachua Co., FL

G8, $450-$800
FL

G8, $400-$700
FL

G8, $350-
$600
N. FL

LOCATION: Gulf Coastal states.
DESCRIPTION: A medium to large size lanceolate, auriculate blade with recurved sides, outward flaring ears and a concave base. The hafting area constriction is usually more narrow than in the *Suwannee* type. Fluting is absent or weak. Basal areas are ground.

G8, $550-$1000
S. GA

G9, $900-$1600
S. GA

G9, $700-$1200
Jefferson Co., FL

G7, $1500-$2500
S. GA

307

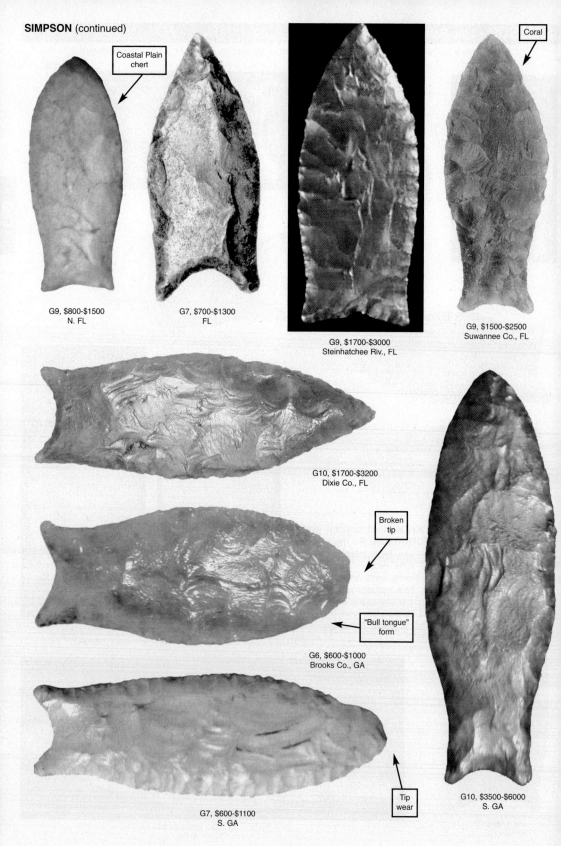

Coastal Plain chert

G9, $800-$1500
N. FL

G7, $700-$1300
FL

G9, $1700-$3000
Steinhatchee Riv., FL

Coral

G9, $1500-$2500
Suwannee Co., FL

G10, $1700-$3200
Dixie Co., FL

Broken tip

"Bull tongue" form

G6, $600-$1000
Brooks Co., GA

Tip wear

G7, $600-$1100
S. GA

G10, $3500-$6000
S. GA

Basal thinning

"Bull tongue" form

Semi-clear

G C

G8, $800-$1500
NW Cent. FL

G8, $1500-$2800
S. GA

G10, $1700 $3000
S. GA

G10, $2500-$4000
FL

G6, $800-$1500
S. GA

G10, $2500-$4500
Jefferson Co., GA

G10+, $2700-$5000
Jefferson Co., FL

G9, $3000-$5500
Jackson Co., FL

SIMPSON-MUSTACHE - Late Paleo, 12,000 - 8000 B. P.

(Also see Beaver Lake, Conerly, Suwannee and Wheeler Expanded Base)

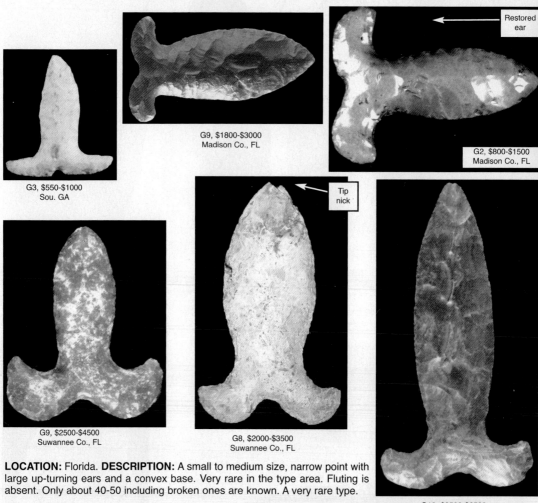

G3, $550-$1000
Sou. GA

G9, $1800-$3000
Madison Co., FL

Restored ear

G2, $800-$1500
Madison Co., FL

Tip nick

G9, $2500-$4500
Suwannee Co., FL

G8, $2000-$3500
Suwannee Co., FL

G10, $3500-$6500
Suwannee Co., FL

LOCATION: Florida. **DESCRIPTION:** A small to medium size, narrow point with large up-turning ears and a convex base. Very rare in the type area. Fluting is absent. Only about 40-50 including broken ones are known. A very rare type.

SIX MILE CREEK - Middle Archaic, 7500 - 5000 B. P.

(Also see Cottonbridge, Elora, Kirk Serrated and South Prong Creek)

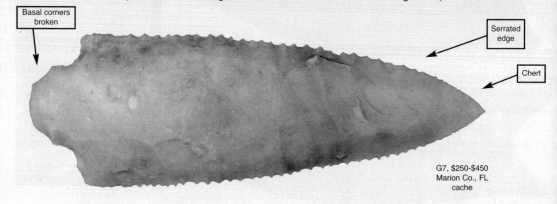

Basal corners broken

Serrated edge

Chert

G7, $250-$450
Marion Co., FL
cache

Note fine edgework was only pressure flaked on this one face.

High quality, excellent example. Classic form.

Chert

Serrated edge

G C

G10+, $900-$1600
Taylor Co., FL

Serrated edge

Ground stem

G10, $275-$500
Marion Co., FL, cache

Ground stem

G9, $150-$250
Marion Co., FL, cache

Chert

Serrated edge

Serrated edge

Chert

Ground stem

G10, $250-$450
Marion Co., FL, cache

Serrated edge

Ground stem

G8, $150-$250
Marion Co., FL, cache

G8, $150-$250
Marion Co., FL, cache

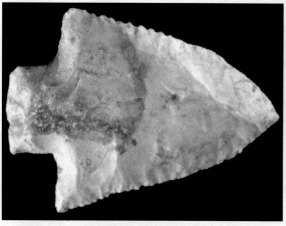

G7, $80-$150
Burke Co., GA

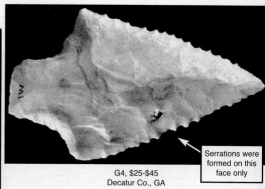

G4, $25-$45
Decatur Co., GA

Serrations were
formed on this
face only

LOCATION: Gulf Coastal states. **DESCRIPTION:** A medium to large size, broad, stemmed, serrated point. The serrations are uniquely formed by careful pressure flaking applied from the side of only one face. Normal *Kirk* serrations are pressure flaked alternately from both faces. Believed to be a later *Kirk* variant.

SOUTH PRONG CREEK - Late Archaic, 5000 - 3000 B. P.

(Also see Abbey, Cottonbridge, Elora, Savannah River and Six Mile Creek)

G5, $20-$35
Decatur Co., GA

Broad serrations
on this type

G8, $150-$250
Burke Co., GA

G7, $65-$125
Seminole Co., GA

G7, $40-$75
Henry Co., AL

G8, $125-$200
FL

312

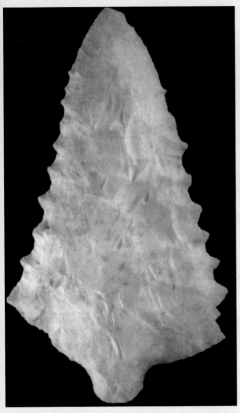

G6, $275-$500
Alexander City, AL

G10, $1200-$2200
Jackson Co., FL

G
C

Note how serrations end here

G9, $1100-$2000
Early Co., GA

Clear

LOCATION: Southern Southeastern states. **DESCRIPTION:** A large size, broad shouldered point with a small rectangular stem. Blade edges are usually bifacially serrated beginning at each shoulder and terminating about 1/3 the way from the tip.

STANFIELD - Transitional Paleo, 10,000 - 8000 B. P.

(Also see Cottonbridge, Elora, Kirk Serrated and South Prong Creek)

G10, $150-$250
FL

IMPORTANT: Stanfields shown half size

G9, $250-$400
Madison Co., FL

STANFIELD (continued)

G9, $200-$350
Brooks Co., GA

> **IMPORTANT:**
> Stanfields
> shown half size

G9, $250-$450
Henry Co., AL

LOCATION: Southeastern states. **DESCRIPTION:** A medium to large size, narrow, lanceolate point with parallel sides and a straight base. Some rare examples are fluted. Bases are ground.

STING RAY BARB - Woodland-Historic, 2500 - 400 B. P.

LOCATION: Florida. **DESCRIPTION:** Not only bone and wood were utilized as arrow points. These barbs taken from rays were hafted to shafts as well. Found on coastal occupation sites.

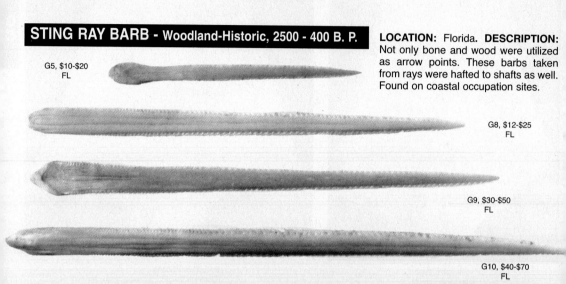

G5, $10-$20
FL

G8, $12-$25
FL

G9, $30-$50
FL

G10, $40-$70
FL

SUMTER - Middle Archaic, 7000 - 5000 B. P.

(Also see Adena, Elora, Kirk, Levy, Putnam, Thonotosassa & Westo)

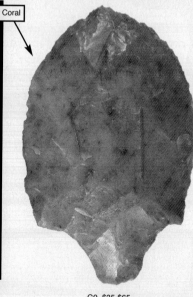

Coral

Coral

G8, $25-$40
Polk Co., FL

G8, $30-$50
Hillsborough Co., FL

G9, $35-$65
Polk Co., FL

314

LOCATION: Southern Southeastern states. **DESCRIPTION:** A medium to large size, broad, thick point with weak, tapered shoulders and a contracting stem. These may be small versions of the *Thonotosassa* type and are believed to be related.

SUWANNEE - Late Paleo, 10,000 - 9000 B. P.

(Also see Beaver Lake, Clovis, Conerly, Simpson, Union Side Notched & Withlacoochee)

G | C

G7, $350-$600
FL

G6, $275-$500
FL

G4, $55-$100
Taylor Co., FL

G7, $200-$350
Allendale Co., SC

Clear

G10, $1700-$3000
FL

LOCATION: Southern Southeastern states. **DESCRIPTION:** A medium to large size, fairly thick, broad, auriculate point. The basal constriction is not as narrow as in *Simpson* points. Most examples have ground bases and are usually unfluted. **I.D. KEY:** Thickness and broad hafting area, expanding ears, less waisted than *Simpsons*.

Agatized
coral

G7, $250-$450
FL

G9, $1500-$2500
N.W. Cent. FL

G9, $1700-$3000
N.W. Cent. FL

G8, $800-$1200
FL

G7, $700-$1200
Harris Co., GA

G7, $800-$1500
Columbia Co., GA

G9, $1200-$2000
FL

Chert

G9, $2500-$4000
Hernando Co., FL

G10, $2500-$4000
FL

Flute channel

G6, $650-$1200
Dixie Co., FL

Ground basal area

G10, $3500-$6500
Gilchrist Co., FL

(Also see Beaver Lake, Dalton, Hardaway, Safety Harbor, Pinellas, Santa Fe and Yadkin)

G
C

Serrated edge

G9, $100-$175
Tift Co., GA

G9, $125-$200
Jefferson Co., FL

G8, $125-$200
N.W. Cent. FL

G8, $150-$250
FL

G9, $150-$250
Jefferson Co., FL

G9, $175-$300
Jefferson Co., FL

Serrated edge

G9, $175-$300
Jefferson Co., FL

G9, $175-$300
Jefferson Co., FL

Slight serrations

Serrated edge

G10, $185-$350
FL

G9, $185-$350
N.W. Cent. FL

G9, $200-$350
Jefferson Co., FL

G9, $390-$700
Taylor Co., FL

G10, $400-$750
N.W. Cent. FL

LOCATION: Tampa Bay Area northward into Alabama, Georgia and South Carolina. **DESCRIPTION:** A medium size, thin, narrow, auriculate, serrated, triangular point with expanding auricules and a concave base. Hafting area is not well defined and can be lightly ground. Blade edges are serrated (see *Santa Fe*) and are resharpened on each face rather than the usual *Dalton* procedure of beveling on opposite faces. **Note:** This type along with the *Santa Fe* point have been confused with a much earlier *Dalton* type found in Northern Florida into southern Alabama, Georgia and South Carolina. Compared to the *Dalton* type, the *Tallahassee* is narrower and much thinner and has less patination. The Dalton is a heavier point being thicker and wider with heavy grinding around the entire basal area. The blade edge serrations are formed differently than on *Dalton* points. **I.D. KEY:** Thinness, narrowness and light grinding.

TAMPA - Mississippian, 800 - 400 B. P.

(Also see O'Leno and Pinellas)

G6, $8-$15
Jefferson Co., FL

G7, $15-$25
FL

G7, $35-$65
Hillsborough Co., FL

G9, $35-$65
FL

G9, $35-$65
FL

G9, $35-$65
FL

G9, $35-$150
FL

G10, $175-$350
FL

G10, $90-$175
FL

G10, $150-$225
Hernando Co., FL

LOCATION: Gulf Coastal states. **DESCRIPTION:** A small size, narrow to broad, tear drop shaped point with a rounded base. Similar to the *Nodena* type found further north and west. A rare point.

TAYLOR - Woodland, 2500 - 2200 B. P.

(Also see Bolen Plain and Kirk)

G5, $8-$15
FL

G7, $15-$25
FL

LOCATION: Gulf Coastal states. **DESCRIPTION:** A small to medium size, corner notched point with a straight to incurvate base. Basal areas are not ground. Blade edges are straight to excurvate and shoulders are weak.

TAYLOR SIDE-NOTCHED - Early Archaic, 9000 - 8000 B. P.

(Also see Bolen Beveled Plain and Osceola Greenbrier)

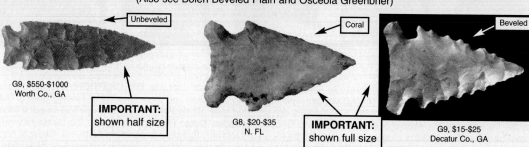

Unbeveled

Coral

Beveled

G9, $550-$1000
Worth Co., GA

IMPORTANT:
shown half size

G8, $20-$35
N. FL

IMPORTANT:
shown full size

G9, $15-$25
Decatur Co., GA

LOCATION: South Carolina into southern Georgia. **DESCRIPTION:** A medium size, side-notched point with a slightly concave base. Some examples are beveled and serrated. Base and notches are ground. Shoulders are pointed. Blade edges are straight to slightly concave or convex.

G8, $65-$125
FL

G8, $80-$150
FL

G8, $150-$250
Hillsborough Co., FL

G8, $125-$200
Hillsborough Co., FL

G10, $400-$750
Six Mile Creek, FL

LOCATION: Florida only. **DESCRIPTION:** A large size, narrow, usually heavy, crudely made blade with weak shoulders and a stem that can be parallel sided to contracting. The base can be straight to rounded. Believed to be related to the smaller *Sumter* type. Also believed to be the first Florida point with heated stone. Found almost exclusively in Central Florida.

G9, $350-$600
Hillsborough Co., FL

TRADE POINTS - Historic, 400 - 170 B. P.

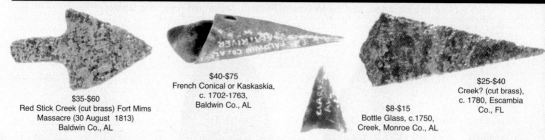

$35-$60
Red Stick Creek (cut brass) Fort Mims
Massacre (30 August 1813)
Baldwin Co., AL

$40-$75
French Conical or Kaskaskia,
c. 1702-1763,
Baldwin Co., AL

$8-$15
Bottle Glass, c.1750,
Creek, Monroe Co., AL

$25-$40
Creek? (cut brass),
c. 1780, Escambia
Co., FL

LOCATION: All of United States and Canada. **DESCRIPTION:** Trade points were made of copper, iron and steel and were traded to the Indians by the French, British and others from the 1600s to the 1800s. The French Conical point (above) is known as Kaskaskia in the midwest.

UNION SIDE NOTCHED - Trans. Paleo, 10,000 - 9000 B. P.

(Also see Beaver Lake, Hardaway, Osceola Greenbrier and Suwannee)

Chert

G6, $55-$100
FL

G8, $150-$250
Alachua Co., FL

5729

G7, $200-$350
FL

G8, $250-$450
Jefferson Co., FL

G9, $350-$600
Alachua Co., FL

G9, $400-$700
Gilchrist Co., FL

G8, $150-$250
FL

LOCATION: Gulf Coastal states. **DESCRIPTION:** A medium to large size, broad blade with weak side notches expanding into auricles. Base can be straight to slightly concave or convex and is usually heavily ground all around the basal area.

WACISSA - Early Archaic, 9000 - 6000 B. P.

(Also see Abbey, Arredondo, Bolen, Elora, Hamilton, Kirk Stemmed, Savannah River and Seminole)

LOCATION: Gulf Coastal states. **DESCRIPTION:** A small to medium size, thick, short, broad stemmed point that is beveled on all four sides. Shoulders are moderate to weak and horizontal to slightly barbed. Some examples are serrated.

Chert

G8, $30-$50
Marion Co., FL

G9, $55-$100
Colquitt Co., GA

Chert

G9, $80-$150
Marion Co., FL

G C

Clear

Needle tip

Serrated edge

Chert

G9, $200-$350
FL

G10, $200-$350
Jefferson Co., FL

G9, $275-$300
Dixie Co., FL

Serrated edge

G10+ $700-$1200
Jackson Co., FL

G9, $45-$85
S. GA

321

(Also see Edgefield Scraper)

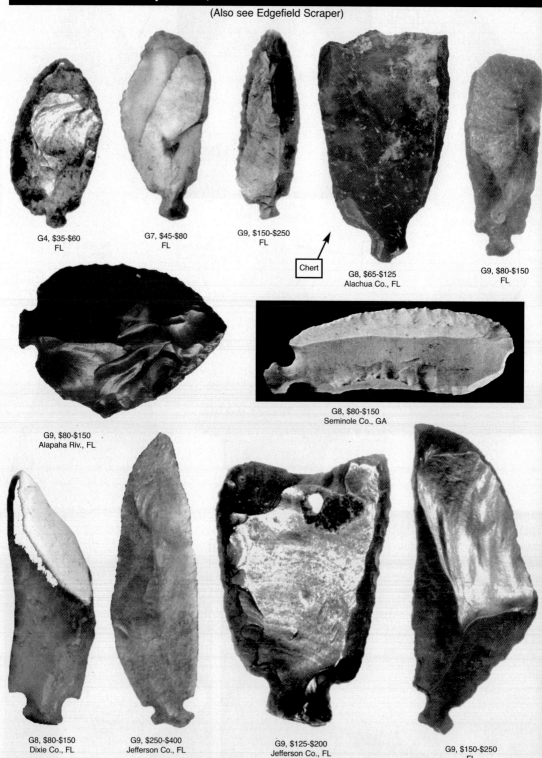

G4, $35-$60
FL

G7, $45-$80
FL

G9, $150-$250
FL

Chert

G8, $65-$125
Alachua Co., FL

G9, $80-$150
FL

G9, $80-$150
Alapaha Riv., FL

G8, $80-$150
Seminole Co., GA

G8, $80-$150
Dixie Co., FL

G9, $250-$400
Jefferson Co., FL

G9, $125-$200
Jefferson Co., FL

G9, $150-$250
FL

LOCATION: Gulf Coastal states. **DESCRIPTION:** A medium size double uniface knife with a short, notched base, made from a flake. Only the cutting edges have been pressure flaked. The classical Waller exhibits a dorsal ridge.

WEEDEN ISLAND - Woodland, 2500 - 1000 B. P.

(Also see Jackson)

Chert

Chert

G6, $5-$10
FL

G6, $8-$15
Marion Co., FL

G8, $8-$15
FL

G7, $15-$25
Marion Co., FL

G6, $8-$15
Marion Co., FL

G7, $15-$25
Marion Co., FL

G8, $20-$35
FL

G8, $20-$35
Marion Co., FL

LOCATION: Gulf Coastal states. **DESCRIPTION:** A small size triangular point with a contracting stem. Shoulders can be tapered to barbed. Bases are straight to rounded.

WESTO - Middle Archaic, 5000 - 4000 B. P.

(Also see Duval, Sumter)

G7, $30-$50
FL

LOCATION: Northern Florida into Georgia. **DESCRIPTION:** A small to medium size, narrow to broad point with a straight to convex blade edge and a short, rounded stem. Shoulders are tapered and many examples are made of quartz and are relatively thick in cross section. **I.D. KEY:** Thickness & short, rounded stem.

WHEELER - Transitional Paleo, 10,000 - 8000 B. P.

(Also see Beaver Lake and Simpson-Mustache)

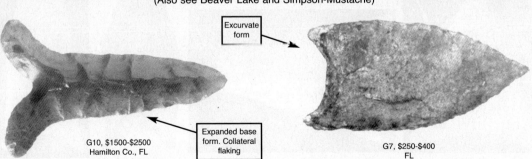

Excurvate form

Expanded base form. Collateral flaking

G10, $1500-$2500
Hamilton Co., FL

G7, $250-$400
FL

LOCATION: Southeastern states to Florida. **DESCRIPTION:** A small to medium size triangular, auriculate point with a concave base. The ears are produced by a shallow constriction or notching near the base. This form occurs in three forms: Excurvate, recurvate and expanded base. Excurvate and expanded base forms are shown. A very rare type in Florida.

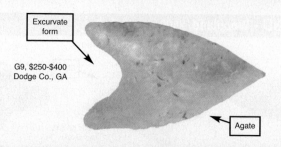

Excurvate form

G9, $250-$400
Dodge Co., GA

Agate

WITHLACOOCHEE - Late Paleo, 10,500 - 10,000 B. P.

(Also see Clovis, Dalton, Simpson and Suwannee)

LOCATION: Withlacoochie Riv. area of Northern Florida, sou. Alabama and Georgia. **DESCRIPTION:** A small to medium size triangular, auriculate point with a concave base. Believed to be a cross between *Clovis* and *Dalton*. Thinner and much better made than Suwannee and not waisted like Simpson. Entire hafting area is ground. Blade edges can have fine serrations. See Perino, Vol. 3.

Translucent

G10+ $1800-$3400
Wakulla Co., FL

YADKIN - Woodland to Mississippian, 2500 - 500 B. P.

(Also see Pinellas, Safety Harbor, Santa Fe and Tallahassee)

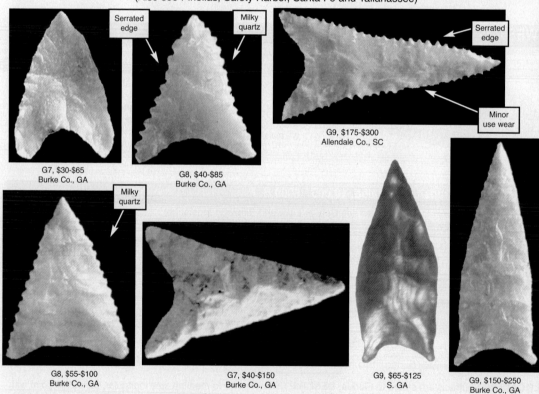

Serrated edge

Milky quartz

Serrated edge

Minor use wear

G9, $175-$300
Allendale Co., SC

G7, $30-$65
Burke Co., GA

G8, $40-$85
Burke Co., GA

Milky quartz

G8, $55-$100
Burke Co., GA

G7, $40-$150
Burke Co., GA

G9, $65-$125
S. GA

G9, $150-$250
Burke Co., GA

LOCATION: Florida into the Carolinas & southern Georgia. **DESCRIPTION:** A small to medium size, broad based, sometimes serrated, triangular point with a broad, concave base and straight to convex to recurved side edges. Bases are not ground. **I.D. KEY:** Broadness of base tangs, lack of grinding.

EASTERN CENTRAL SECTION:

This section includes point types from the following states:
Alabama, Georgia, Indiana, Kentucky, Michigan, Mississippi, Ohio and Tennessee.

The points in this section are arranged in alphabetical order and are shown **actual size**. All types are listed that were available for photographing. Any missing types will be added to future editions as photographs become available. We are always interested in receiving sharp, black and white or color glossy photos, color slides or high resolution (300 pixels/inch) digital pictures of your collection. Be sure to include a ruler in the photograph so that proper scale can be determined.

Lithics: Materials employed in the manufacture of projectile points from this region include: agate, chalcedony, chert, coshocton, crystal, flint, jasper, limestone, quartz, quartzite, silicified sandstone and upper mercer.

Important Sites: Nuckolls, Humphreys Co., TN.; Cotaco, Cotaco Creek, Morgan Co., AL.; Cumberland, Cumberland River Valley, TN.; Damron, Lincoln Co., TN.; Elk River, Limestone Co., AL.; Eva, Benton Co., TN.; Quad, Limestone Co., AL.; Pine Tree, Limestone Co., AL.; Dover Flint, Humphreys Co., TN.; Redstone, Madison Co., AL.; Plevna (Dovetail), Madison Co., AL.; Stone Pipe, Wheeler Reservoir, Limestone Co., AL. for Wheeler and Decatur points.

Regional Consultants:
Tom Davis,
John T. Pafford and Eric C. Wagner

E
C

EASTERN CENTRAL
(Archaeological Periods)

PALEO (11,500 B. P. - 10,000 B. P.)

Anzick	Clovis-Hazel	Debert	Redstone
Beaver Lake	Clovis Unfluted	Graver	Scraper
Clovis	Cumberland	Lancet	

TRANSITIONAL PALEO (10,500 B. P. - 9,000 B. P.)

Agate Basin	Hinds	Paint Rock Valley	Square Knife	Wheeler Recurvate
Early Ovoid Knife	Jeff	Pelican	Stanfield	Wheeler Triangular
Haw River	Marianna	Plainview	Wheeler Excurvate	
Hi-Lo	Ohio Lanceolate	Quad	Wheeler Expanded	

EARLY ARCHAIC (10,000 B. P. - 7,000 B. P.)

Alamance	Dalton Hemphill	Hardin	Lost Lake	Stanly
Alberta	Dalton Nuckolls	Harpeth River	MacCorkle	Steubenville
Angostura	Damron	Heavy Duty	Meserve	Stilwell
Autauga	Decatur	Hidden Valley	Neuberger	Stringtown
Big Sandy	Decatur Blade	Holland	Newton Falls	Tennessee River
Big Sandy Broad Base	Eastern Stemmed Lanceolate	Johnson	Palmer	Tennessee Saw
Big Sandt Contracted Base	Ecusta	Jude	Perforator	Thebes
Big Sandy E-Notched	Elk River	Kanawha Stemmed	Pine Tree	Warrick
Big Sandy Leighton Base	Eva	Kirk Corner Notched	Pine Tree Corner	Watts Cave
Cave Spring	Fishspear	Kirk Snapped Base	Notched	White Springs
Cobbs Triangular	Fountain Creek	Kirk Stemmed	Rice Lobbed	
Coldwater	Frederick	Kirk Stemmed-Bifur.	Russel Cave	
Conerly	Garth Slough	Lake Erie	San Patrice-Hope	
Crawford Creek	Graham Cave	Lecroy	St. Albans	
Dalton Classic	Greenbrier	Leighton	St. Charles	
Dalton Colbert	Hardaway	Lerma	St. Helena	
Dalton Greenbrier	Hardaway Dalton	Limeton Bifurcate	St. Tammany	

MIDDLE ARCHAIC (7,500 B. P. - 4,000 B. P.)

Appalachian	Buck Creek	Kays	Mountain Fork	Tortugas
Benton	Buggs Island	Ledbetter	Mulberry Creek	Turkeytail Tupelo
Benton Blade	Buzzard Roost Creek	Limestone	Patrick	Wade
Benton Bottle Neck	Copena Auriculate	Maples	Pentagonal Knife	Warito
Benton Double Notched	Cypress Creek	Matanzas	Pickwick	
Benton Narrow Blade	Elora	McIntire	Ramey Knife	
Big Slough	Epps	McWhinney Heavy Stemmed	Savage Cave	
Brewerton Corner Notched	Exotic Forms	Morrow Mountain	Savannah River	
Brewerton Eared Triangular	Frazier	Morrow Mountain Round Base	Searcy	
Brewerton Side Notched	Guilford Round Base	Morrow Mountain Straight Base	Smith	
Brunswick	Halifax	Motley	Sykes	

LATE ARCHAIC (5,000 B. P. - 3,000 B. P.)

Ashtabula	Dagger	Merom	Smithsonia	Turkeytail-Harrison
Bakers Creek	Etley	Mud Creek	Snake Creek	Turkeytail-Hebron
Beacon Island	Evans	Orient	Square-end Knife	
Bradley Spike	Flint Creek	Pontchartrain Type I & II	Sublet Ferry	
Copena Classic	Little Bear Creek	Rankin	Swan Lake	
Copena Round Base	Meadowood	Rheems Creek	Table Rock	
Copena Triangular	Merkle	Shoals Creek	Turkeytail-Fulton	

WOODLAND (3,000 B. P. - 1,300 B. P.)

Addison Micro-Drill	Chesser	Gibson	Morse Knife	Spokeshave
Adena	Collins	Greeneville	Mouse Creek	Tear Drop
Adena Blade	Coosa	Hamilton	New Market	Vallina
Adena-Narrow Stem	Cotaco Creek	Hamilton Stemmed	Nolichucky	Washington
Adena-Notched Base	Cotaco Creek Blade	Hopewell	North	Waubesa
Adena Robbins	Cotaco-Wright	Intrusive Mound	Nova	Yadkin
Adena Vanishing Stem	Cresap	Jacks Reef Corner Notched	Ohio Double Notched	
Alba	Dickson	Jacks Reef Pentagonal	Red Ochre	
Benjamin	Duval	Knight Island	Ross	
Camp Creek	Ebenezer	Lowe	Sand Mountain	
Candy Creek	Fairland	Montgomery	Snyders	

MISSISSIPPIAN (1300 B. P. - 400 B. P.)

Duck River Sword	Harahey	Mace	Sun Disc
Fort Ancient	Keota	Madison	Washita
Fort Ancient Blade	Levanna	Nodena	
Guntersville	Lozenge	Pipe Creek	

HISTORIC (450 B. P. - 170 B. P.)

Trade Points

326

EASTERN CENTRAL
THUMBNAIL GUIDE SECTION

The following references are provided to aid the collector in easier and quicker identification of point types. All photos are exactly 30% of actual size and are proportional to each other. Each point pictured in this section represents a classic form for the type. When a match is found, go to the alphabetical location of that type for more examples in actual size.

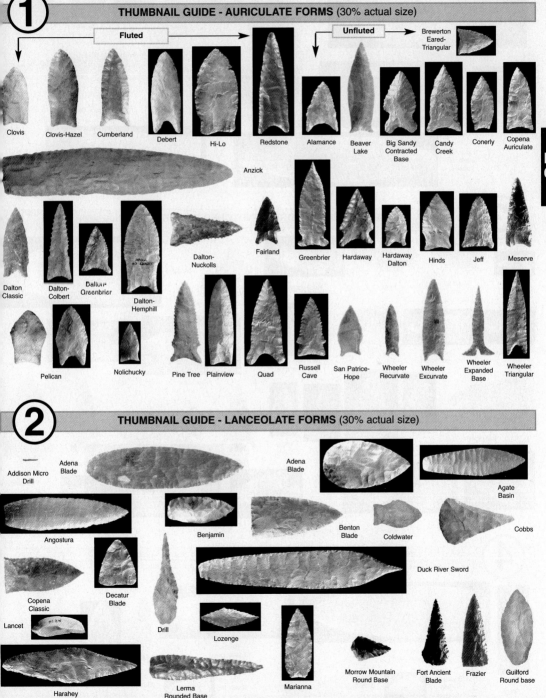

① THUMBNAIL GUIDE - AURICULATE FORMS (30% actual size)

Fluted → Unfluted → Brewerton Eared-Triangular

Clovis · Clovis-Hazel · Cumberland · Debert · Hi-Lo · Redstone · Alamance · Beaver Lake · Big Sandy Contracted Base · Candy Creek · Conerly · Copena Auriculate

Anzick

Dalton-Nuckolls · Fairland · Greenbrier · Hardaway · Hardaway Dalton · Hinds · Jeff · Meserve

Dalton Classic · Dalton-Colbert · Dalton-Greenbrier · Dalton-Hemphill

Pelican · Nolichucky · Pine Tree · Plainview · Quad · Russell Cave · San Patrice-Hope · Wheeler Recurvate · Wheeler Excurvate · Wheeler Expanded Base · Wheeler Triangular

② THUMBNAIL GUIDE - LANCEOLATE FORMS (30% actual size)

Addison Micro Drill · Adena Blade · Adena Blade · Agate Basin

Angostura · Benjamin · Benton Blade · Coldwater · Cobbs

Copena Classic · Decatur Blade · Duck River Sword

Lancet · Drill · Lozenge · Morrow Mountain Round Base · Fort Ancient Blade · Frazier · Guilford Round base

Harahey · Lerma Rounded Base · Marianna

EC

327

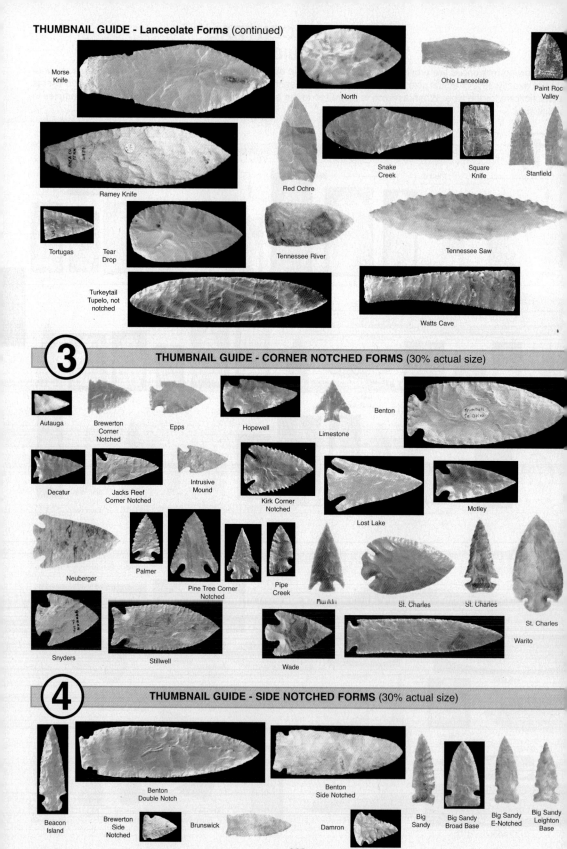

THUMBNAIL GUIDE - Lanceolate Forms (continued)

Morse Knife

North

Ohio Lanceolate

Paint Roc Valley

Ramey Knife

Red Ochre

Snake Creek

Square Knife

Stanfield

Tortugas

Tear Drop

Tennessee River

Tennessee Saw

Turkeytail Tupelo, not notched

Watts Cave

③ THUMBNAIL GUIDE - CORNER NOTCHED FORMS (30% actual size)

Autauga

Brewerton Corner Notched

Epps

Hopewell

Limestone

Benton

Decatur

Jacks Reef Corner Notched

Intrusive Mound

Kirk Corner Notched

Lost Lake

Motley

Neuberger

Palmer

Pine Tree Corner Notched

Pipe Creek

Franklin

St. Charles

St. Charles

St. Charles

Warito

Snyders

Stillwell

Wade

④ THUMBNAIL GUIDE - SIDE NOTCHED FORMS (30% actual size)

Beacon Island

Benton Double Notch

Benton Side Notched

Brewerton Side Notched

Brunswick

Damron

Big Sandy

Big Sandy Broad Base

Big Sandy E-Notched

Big Sandy Leighton Base

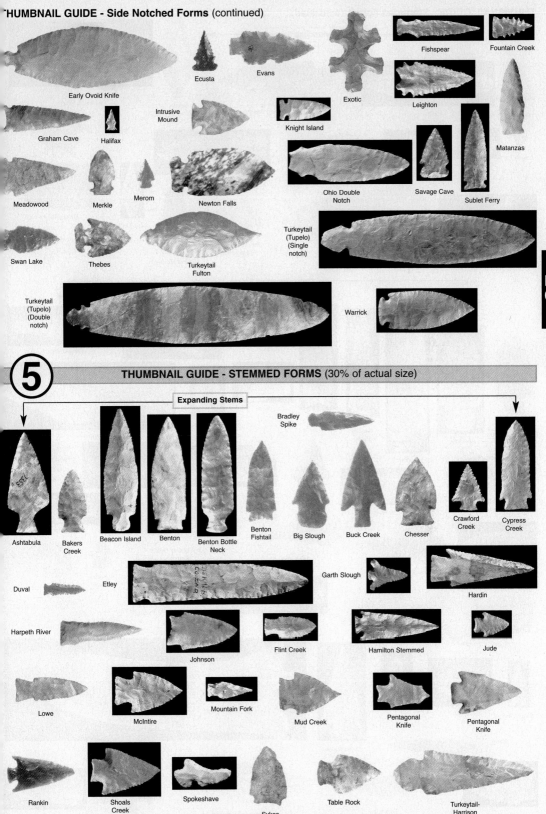

Early Ovoid Knife

Ecusta

Evans

Exotic

Fishspear

Fountain Creek

Leighton

Graham Cave

Halifax

Intrusive Mound

Knight Island

Matanzas

Meadowood

Merkle

Merom

Newton Falls

Ohio Double Notch

Savage Cave

Sublet Ferry

Swan Lake

Thebes

Turkeytail Fulton

Turkeytail (Tupelo) (Single notch)

Turkeytail (Tupelo) (Double notch)

Warrick

E
C

5 THUMBNAIL GUIDE - STEMMED FORMS (30% of actual size)

Expanding Stems

Bradley Spike

Ashtabula

Bakers Creek

Beacon Island

Benton

Benton Bottle Neck

Benton Fishtail

Big Slough

Buck Creek

Chesser

Crawford Creek

Cypress Creek

Duval

Etley

Garth Slough

Hardin

Harpeth River

Johnson

Flint Creek

Hamilton Stemmed

Jude

Lowe

McIntire

Mountain Fork

Mud Creek

Pentagonal Knife

Pentagonal Knife

Rankin

Shoals Creek

Spokeshave

Sykes

Table Rock

Turkeytail-Harrison

329

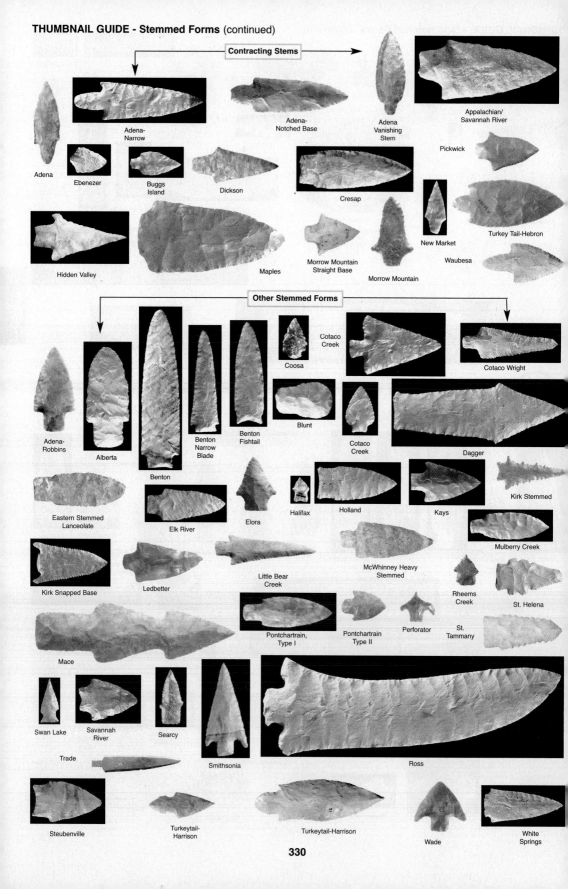

Contracting Stems

Adena-Narrow

Adena-Notched Base

Adena Vanishing Stem

Appalachian/ Savannah River

Adena

Ebenezer

Buggs Island

Dickson

Cresap

Pickwick

Turkey Tail-Hebron

New Market

Hidden Valley

Maples

Morrow Mountain Straight Base

Morrow Mountain

Waubesa

Other Stemmed Forms

Adena-Robbins

Alberta

Benton

Benton Narrow Blade

Benton Fishtail

Coosa

Blunt

Cotaco Creek

Cotaco Creek

Cotaco Wright

Dagger

Eastern Stemmed Lanceolate

Elk River

Elora

Halifax

Holland

Kays

Kirk Stemmed

Mulberry Creek

Kirk Snapped Base

Ledbetter

Little Bear Creek

McWhinney Heavy Stemmed

Rheems Creek

St. Helena

Mace

Pontchartrain, Type I

Pontchartrain Type II

Perforator

St. Tammany

Swan Lake

Savannah River

Searcy

Trade

Smithsonia

Ross

Steubenville

Turkeytail-Harrison

Turkeytail-Harrison

Wade

White Springs

330

6 THUMBNAIL GUIDE - STEMMED-BIFURCATED FORMS (30% of actual size)

Buzzard Roost Creek

Cave Spring

Fox Valley

Frederick

Haw River

Heavy Duty

Patrick

Kirk Stemmed-Bifurcated

Kanawha

Lake Erie

LeCroy

Limeton

MacCorkle

Neuberger

Pine Tree

Rice Lobbed

St. Albans

Stanly

7 THUMBNAIL GUIDE - BASAL NOTCHED FORMS (30% of actual size)

E
C

Eva

Buck Creek

Garth Slough

Hamilton Stemmed

Rankin

Smith

Wade

8 THUMBNAIL GUIDE - ARROW POINTS (30% of actual size)

Collins

Alba

Camp Creek

Fort Ancient

Greeneville

Guntersville

Hamilton

Jacks Reef Corner Notched

Jacks Reef Pentagonal

Knight Island

Keota

Levanna

Madison

Montgomery

Mouse Creek

Nodena

Nova

Sand Mountain

Valina

Washington

Washita

Yadkin

ADDISON MICRO-DRILL - Late Woodland to Mississippian, 2000 - 1000 B. P.

(Also see Drill, Flint River Spike and Schild Spike)

LOCATION: Examples have been found in Alabama, Kentucky, Illinois, North Carolina, North Georgia and Tennessee. Named after the late Steve Addison who collected hundreds of examples. **DESCRIPTION:** Very small to medium size, narrow, slivers, flattened to rectangular in cross section. Theory is that this is the final form of a drilling process. The original form was flint slivers with sharp edges that were used as drills. As the sliver was turned in the drilling process, the opposite edges in the direction of movement began to flake off. As the drilling operation proceeded, the edges became steeper as more and more of each side was flaked. Eventually a thin, steeply flaked, rectangular drill form was left and discarded. Unique in that these micro artifacts are not made and then used, but are created by use, and discarded as the edges became eroded away by extremely fine flaking, thus reducing their effectiveness as a cutting edge.

$4-$8 each
Shown actual size. All found
in Bradley & Hamilton Co.,
TN.

ADENA - Late Archaic to Late Woodland, 3000 - 1200 B. P.

(Also see Adena Blade, Bakers Creek, Dickson, Kays, Little Bear Creek, Turkeytail and Waubesa)

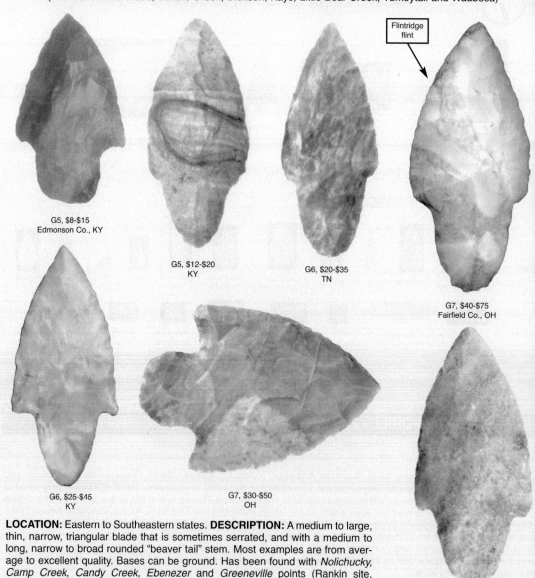

Flintridge flint

G5, $8-$15
Edmonson Co., KY

G5, $12-$20
KY

G6, $20-$35
TN

G7, $40-$75
Fairfield Co., OH

G6, $25-$45
KY

G7, $30-$50
OH

G8, $30-$50
AL

LOCATION: Eastern to Southeastern states. **DESCRIPTION:** A medium to large, thin, narrow, triangular blade that is sometimes serrated, and with a medium to long, narrow to broad rounded "beaver tail" stem. Most examples are from average to excellent quality. Bases can be ground. Has been found with *Nolichucky, Camp Creek, Candy Creek, Ebenezer* and *Greeneville* points (Rankin site, Cocke Co., TN). **I.D. KEY:** Rounded base, woodland flaking.

E
C

G7, $35-$65
KY

G10, $150-$250
Jefferson Co., KY

G7, $40-$70
IN

G6, $30-$50
AL

G9, $175-$300
McCracken Co., KY

Heat Treated

Hornstone

G6, $25-$40
Colbert Co., AL

G9, $400-$700
Livingston Co., KY

G8, $165-$300
Louisville, KY

333

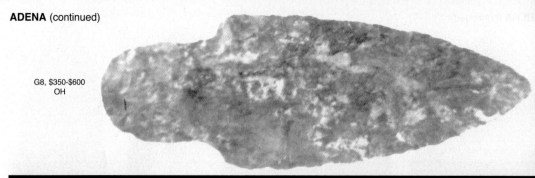

G8, $350-$600
OH

G9, $600-$1000
Crawford Co., IN

ADENA BLADE - Late Archaic to Woodland, 3000-1200 B. P.
(Also see Copena, North, Tear Drop and Tennessee River)

IMPORTANT
Adena Blades
Shown half
size

Dover
chert

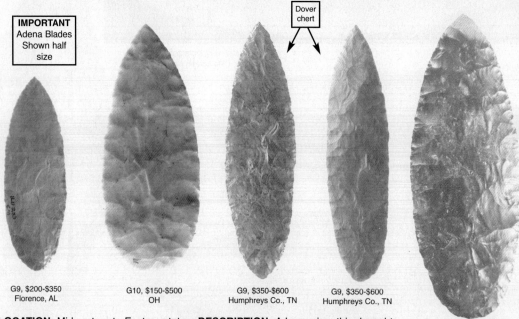

G9, $200-$350
Florence, AL

G10, $150-$500
OH

G9, $350-$600
Humphreys Co., TN

G9, $350-$600
Humphreys Co., TN

G10, $550-$1000
OH

LOCATION: Midwestern to Eastern states. **DESCRIPTION:** A large size, thin, broad to narrow, ovate blade with a rounded to pointed base. Blade edgework can be very fine. Usually found in caches. **I.D. KEY:** Woodland flaking, large direct primary strikes.

ADENA BLADE (continued)

IMPORTANT
Adena Blades
Shown half size

G7, $55-$100
TN

G9, $350-$600
OH

ADENA-DICKSON (see Dickson)

ADENA-NARROW STEM - Late Archaic-Woodland, 3000 - 1200 B. P.

(Also see Little Bear Creek and Waubesa)

Serrated edge

G6, $12-$20
N. W. AL

G7, $20-$35
OH

G5, $12-$20
KY

G6, $25-$40
TN

G8, $90-$175
Florence, AL

G7, $25-$45
AL

G9 $250-$400
Humphreys Co., TN

G9, $350-$650
Clifton, TN

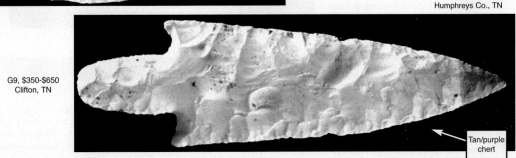

Tan/purple chert

ADENA NARROW STEM (continued)

LOCATION: Eastern to Southeastern states. **DESCRIPTION:** A medium to large, thin, narrow triangular blade that is sometimes serrated, with a medium to long, narrow, rounded stem. Most examples are well made. **I.D. KEY:** Narrow rounded base with more secondary work than ordinary *Adena*.

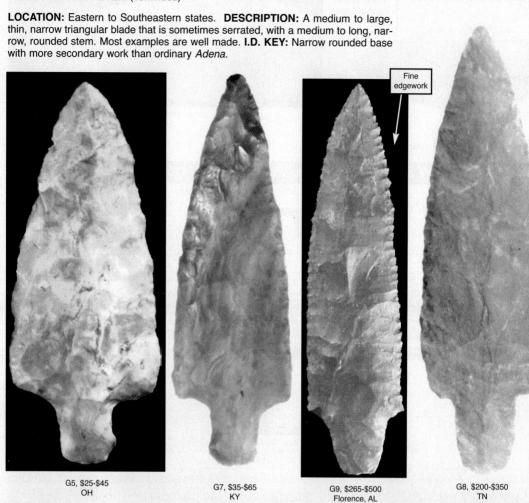

Fine edgework

G5, $25-$45
OH

G7, $35-$65
KY

G9, $265-$500
Florence, AL

G8, $200-$350
TN

ADENA-NOTCHED BASE - Late Archaic-Woodland, 3000 - 1200 B. P.

(Also see Adena and Little Bear Creek)

LOCATION: Southeastern states. **DESCRIPTION:** Identical to *Adena*, but with a notched or snapped-off concave base. **I.D. KEY:** Basal form different.

G8, $35-$60
Coffee Lake, AL

ADENA-ROBBINS - Late Archaic to Woodland, 3000 - 1800 B. P.

(See Alberta, Cresap, Dickson, Kays, Little Bear Creek, Mulberry Creek and Pontchartrain)

LOCATION: Eastern to Southeastern states. **DESCRIPTION:** A medium to large, broad, triangular point that is thin and well made with a long, wide, rounded stem that is parallel sided. The blade has convex sides and square shoulders. Many examples show excellent secondary flaking on blade edges. **I.D. KEY:** Squared base, heavy secondary flaking.

336

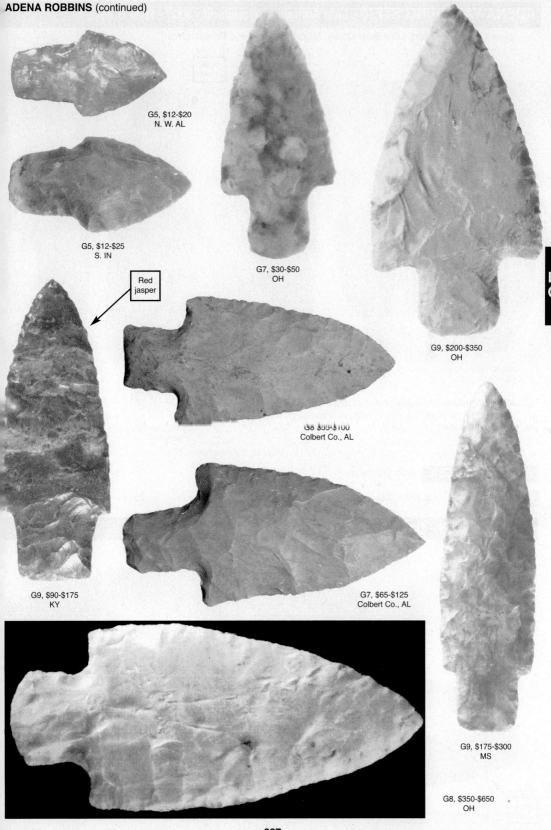

G5, $12-$20
N. W. AL

G5, $12-$25
S. IN

G7, $30-$50
OH

G9, $200-$350
OH

E
C

Red
jasper

G8, $55-$100
Colbert Co., AL

G9, $90-$175
KY

G7, $65-$125
Colbert Co., AL

G9, $175-$300
MS

G8, $350-$650
OH

ADENA-VANISHING STEM - Late Archaic to Woodland, 3000 - 1800 B. P.

(See Cresap, Dickson, Little Bear Creek, Mulberry Creek and Pontchartrain)

Boyle chert

G8, $35-$65
Jessamine Co., KY

G6, $20-$35
KY

G5, $20-$35
KY

G8, $65-$125
Madison Co., KY

G6, $35-$65
TN

LOCATION: Eastern to Southeastern states. **DESCRIPTION:** A medium to large size point with a small, narrow, short stem that is rounded. **I.D. KEY:** Small stem.

ADENA-WAUBESA   (see Waubesa)

AFTON   (see Pentagonal Knife)

AGATE BASIN - Transitional Paleo to Early Archaic, 10,500 - 8000 B. P.

(Also see Angostura, Lerma, Ohio Lanceolate and Sedalia)

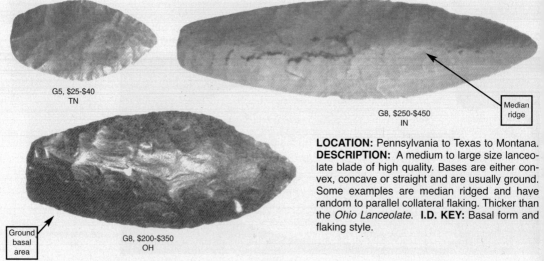

G5, $25-$40
TN

G8, $250-$450
IN

Median ridge

Ground basal area

G8, $200-$350
OH

LOCATION: Pennsylvania to Texas to Montana. **DESCRIPTION:** A medium to large size lanceolate blade of high quality. Bases are either convex, concave or straight and are usually ground. Some examples are median ridged and have random to parallel collateral flaking. Thicker than the *Ohio Lanceolate*. **I.D. KEY:** Basal form and flaking style.

338

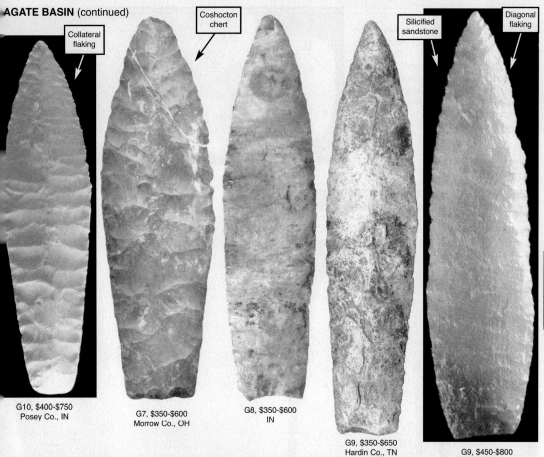

Collateral flaking

Coshocton chert

Silicified sandstone

Diagonal flaking

G10, $400-$750
Posey Co., IN

G7, $350-$600
Morrow Co., OH

G8, $350-$600
IN

G9, $350-$650
Hardin Co., TN

G9, $450-$800
Errien Springs, MI

E
C

ALAMANCE - Early Archaic, 10,000 - 8000 B. P.

(Also see Dalton, Hardaway and Haw River)

LOCATION: Coastal states from Virginia to Florida. **DESCRIPTION:** A broad, short, auriculate point with a deeply concave base. The broad basal area is usually ground and can be expanding to parallel sided. A variant form of the *Dalton-Greenbrier* evolving later into the *Hardaway* type. **ID. KEY:** Width of base and strong shoulder form.

Minor blade nick

G6, $55-$100
Autauga Co.,
AL

ALBA - Woodland to Mississippian, 2000 - 400 B. P.

(Also see Agee, Bonham, Colbert, Cuney, Hayes, Homan, Keota, Perdiz, Scallorn and Sequoyah in SC section)

LOCATION: Eastern Texas, Arkansas and Louisiana. **DESCRIPTION:** A small to medium size, narrow, well made point with prominent tangs, a recurved blade and a bulbous stem. Some examples are serrated. **I.D. KEY:** Rounded base and expanded barbs.

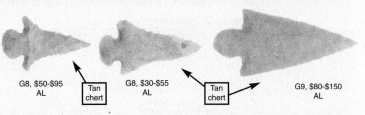

G8, $50-$95
AL

Tan chert

G8, $30-$55
AL

Tan chert

G9, $80-$150
AL

ALBERTA - Early Archaic, 9500 - 8000 B. P.

(Also see Eastern Stemmed Lanceolate, Holland, Scottsbluff and Stringtown)

ALBERTA (continued)

LOCATION: Northern states and Canada from Pennsylvania, Michigan to Montana. **DESCRIPTION:** A medium to large size point with a broad, long, parallel stem and weak shoulders. Believed to belong to the *Cody Complex* and is related to the *Scottsbluff* type. **I.D. KEY:** Long stem, short blade.

Very rare in the Eastern U.S.

G6, $350-$650
MI

ANGOSTURA - Early Archaic, 9000 - 8000 B. P.

(Also see Browns Valley, Clovis-Unfluted, Paint Rock Valley, Plainview and Wheeler)

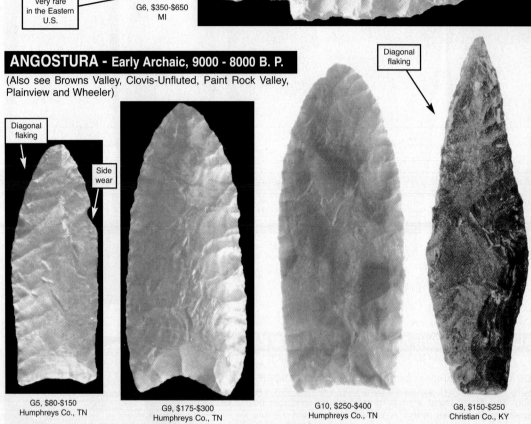

Diagonal flaking

Diagonal flaking

Side wear

G5, $80-$150
Humphreys Co., TN

G9, $175-$300
Humphreys Co., TN

G10, $250-$400
Humphreys Co., TN

G8, $150-$250
Christian Co., KY

LOCATION: South Dakota southward to Texas and W. Tenn. **DESCRIPTION**: A medium to large size lanceolate blade with a contracting, concave base. Both broad and narrow forms occur. Flaking can be parallel oblique to random. Bases are not usually ground but are thinned. **I.D. KEY:** Basal form, early flaking on blade.

ANZICK - Early Paleo, 11,500 - 10,600 B. P.

(Also see Clovis,Cumberland, Dalton and Redstone)

**IMPORTANT:
This point is
shown half size**

G10, Unique, $20,000+
Greenup Co., KY
Actual size is 8-1/4" long

Fluting channel

LOCATION: Kentucky, Illinois into Montana. **DESCRIPTION:** A large fluted point with generally parallel sides and a straight base. Tips are usually rounded and fluting is short in relation to the length of the blade. Perino believes this point was used as a knife. This type is extremely rare with only a few examples known. **I.D. KEY:** Size, form and short fluting.

APPALACHIAN - Mid-Archaic, 6000 - 3000 B. P.

(Also see Ashtabula, Hamilton and Savannah River)

LOCATION: Southeastern states. **DESCRIPTION:** A medium to large size, rather crudely made stemmed point with a concave base. Most examples are made of quartzite. Shoulders are tapered and the base is usually ground. This form was named by Lewis & Kneberg for examples found in East Tenn. and Western North Carolina which were made of quartzite. However, this is the same type as *Savannah River*. **I.D. KEY:** Basal form.

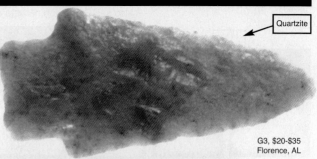

Quartzite

G3, $20-$35
Florence, AL

Quartzite

G8, $125-$225
Norris Lake, TN

E
C

ASHTABULA - Late Archaic, 4000 - 1500 B. P.

(Also see Appalachian and Table Rock)

G8, $250-$450
Shelby, OH

G8, $250-$450
Cleveland, OH

G8, $350-$600
Monroe Co., OH

G8, $400-$700
OH

G8, $500-$900
OH

G8, $400-$750
OH

G9, $90-$175
OH

IMPORTANT:
All Ashtabulas shown half size

LOCATION: Northeastern states, especially Northeastern Ohio and Western Penn. **DESCRIPTION:** A medium to large size, broad, thick, expanded stem point with tapered shoulders. **I.D. KEY:** Basal form, one barb round and the other stronger.

AUTAUGA - Early Archaic, 9000 - 7000 B. P.

(Also see Brewerton, Ecusta and Palmer)

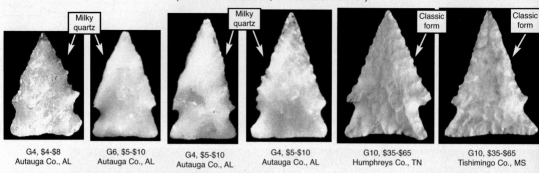

Milky quartz

Milky quartz

Classic form

Classic form

G4, $4-$8
Autauga Co., AL

G6, $5-$10
Autauga Co., AL

G4, $5-$10
Autauga Co., AL

G4, $5-$10
Autauga Co., AL

G10, $35-$65
Humphreys Co., TN

G10, $35-$65
Tishimingo Co., MS

LOCATION: Southeastern states. **DESCRIPTION:** A small, weakly corner notched point with a straight base, that is usually ground, and straight blade edges that are serrated. Blades can be beveled on one side of each face. **I.D. KEY:** Archaic flaking on blade.

BAKERS CREEK - Late Archaic to Woodland, 4000 - 1300 B. P.

(Also see Chesser, Copena, Harpeth River, Lowe, Mud Creek, Swan Lake & Table Rock)

Tip wear

G4, $3-$6
W. TN

G6, $8-$15
W. TN

G5, $8-$15
W. TN

G8, $15-$25
S. E. TN

G6, $25-$45
Parsons, TN

Breathitt chert

Dover chert

G6, $12-$20
S. IN

G8, $35-$60
Coffee Slough, AL

G8, $70-$135
Cent. KY

G8, $55-$100
Humphreys Co., TN

G9, $90-$175
Coffee Slough, AL

342

E
C

Needle tip →

Needle tip →

Chert ↘

G10, $170-$325
TN

G10+, $250-$450
Lauderdale Co., AL

G10, $275-$500
Humphreys Co., TN

G10, $275-$500
Hardin Co., TN

LOCATION: Southeastern states. **DESCRIPTION:** A small to large size expanded stem point with tapered or barbed shoulders. Bases are concave to convex to straight. Related to *Copena* (found with them in caches) and are called Stemmed *Copenas* by some collectors. Called *Lowe* and *Steuben* in Illinois. **I.D. KEY:** Expanded base, usually thin.

BEACON ISLAND - Late Archaic, 4000 - 3000 B. P.

(Also see Big Slough and Flint Creek)

G4, $6-$12
Lauderdale Co., AL

G4, $12-$20
Lauderdale Co., AL

G3, $4-$8
Meigs Co., TN

G4, $12-$20
Jessamine Co., KY

G6, $20-$35
Bolivar Co., MS

G8, $25-$45
Decatur, AL

343

BEACON ISLAND (continued)

Colorful Boyle chert

G7, $35-$65
TN

G8, $45-$85
TN

G8, $125-$200
Humphreys Co., TN

G10, $450-$800
Montgomery Co., KY

G8, $150-$250
Colbert Co., AL

LOCATION: Southeastern states. **DESCRIPTION:** A small to large size triangular point with a bulbous stem. Shoulders are usually well defined and can be barbed. Similar to *Palmillas* in Texas. **I.D. KEY:** Bulbous base.

BEAVER LAKE - Paleo, 11,250 - 8000 B. P.

(Also see Candy Creek, Cumberland, Dalton, Golondrina and Quad)

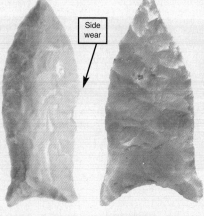

Side wear

G5, $40-$75
Maury Co., TN

G8, $175-$325
Hardin Co., TN

G8, $175-$325
Humphreys Co., TN

G5, $45-$80
KY

G6, $125-$200
KY

LOCATION: Southeastern states. **DESCRIPTION:** A medium to large size lanceolate blade with flaring ears and a concave base. Contemporaneous and associated with *Cumberland*, but thinner than unfluted *Cumberlands*. Bases are ground and blade edges are recurved. Has been found in deeper layers than *Dalton*. **I.D. KEY:** Paleo flaking, shoulder area.

344

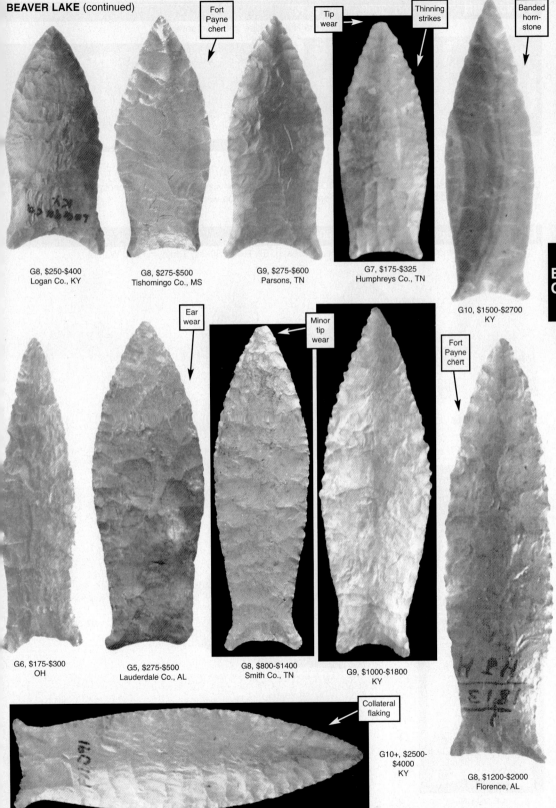

Fort Payne chert

Tip wear

Thinning strikes

Banded hornstone

G8, $250-$400
Logan Co., KY

G8, $275-$500
Tishomingo Co., MS

G9, $275-$600
Parsons, TN

G7, $175-$325
Humphreys Co., TN

G10, $1500-$2700
KY

E
C

Ear wear

Minor tip wear

Fort Payne chert

G6, $175-$300
OH

G5, $275-$500
Lauderdale Co., AL

G8, $800-$1400
Smith Co., TN

G9, $1000-$1800
KY

Collateral flaking

G10+, $2500-$4000
KY

G8, $1200-$2000
Florence, AL

BENJAMIN - Woodland, 3000 - 1600 B. P.

(Also see Copena Round Base and Montgomery)

G5, $6-$10
Limestone Co., AL

G5, $8-$15
Limestone Co., AL

LOCATION: Southeastern states. **DESCRIPTION:** A medium to large size, thin, narrow, lanceolate point with random flaking and a rounded base. This point has been found in association with *Copena*.

BENTON - Middle Archaic, 6000 - 4000 B. P.

(Also see Buzzard Roost Creek, Cresap, Elk River, Sykes, Turkeytail and Warito)

G4, $5-$10
N.W. AL

G6, $12-$20
AL

G8, $30-$55
Florence, AL

G7, $45-$80
TN

G6, $25-$45
N.W. AL

G8, $80-$150
Lee Co., MS

G8, $80-$150
TN

346

BENTON (continued)

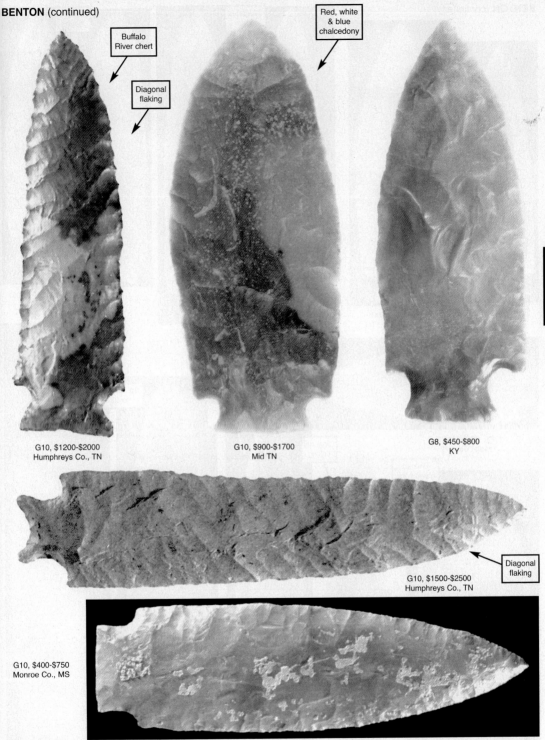

Buffalo
River chert

Diagonal
flaking

Red, white
& blue
chalcedony

E
C

G10, $1200-$2000
Humphreys Co., TN

G10, $900-$1700
Mid TN

G8, $450-$800
KY

Diagonal
flaking

G10, $1500-$2500
Humphreys Co., TN

G10, $400-$750
Monroe Co., MS

LOCATION: Southeastern to Midwestern states. **DESCRIPTION:** A medium to very large size, broad, stemmed point with straight to convex sides. Bases can be corner or side notched, double notched, knobbed, bifurcated or expanded. Some examples show parallel oblique flaking. All four sides are beveled and basal corners usually have tangs. Examples have been found in Arkansas with a steeply beveled edge on one side of each face (Transition form?). Found in caches with *Turkeytail* points in Mississippi on *Benton* sites. *Bentons* and *Turkeytails* as long as 16-3/4 inches were found together on this site and dated to about 4750 B.P. **I.D. KEY:** Wide squared, eared or notched base.

347

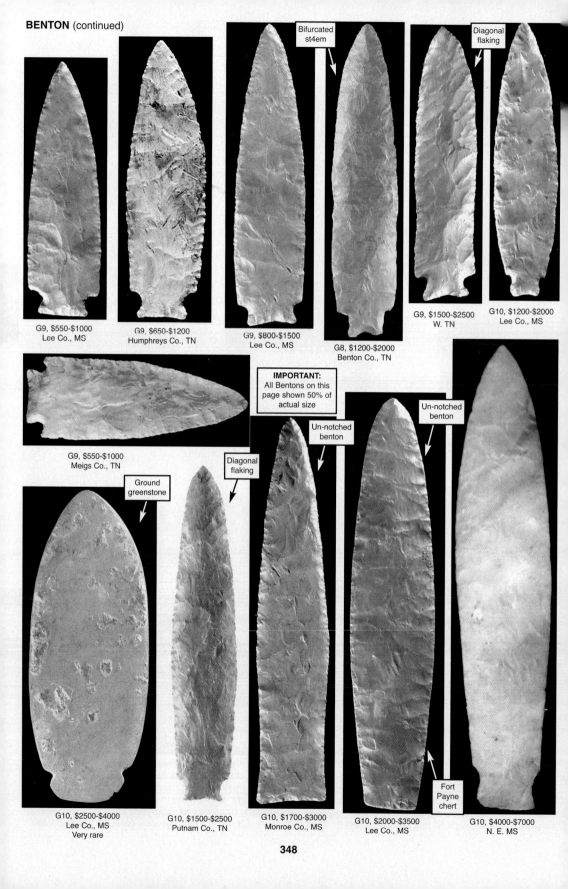

BENTON (continued)

G9, $550-$1000
Lee Co., MS

G9, $650-$1200
Humphreys Co., TN

Bifurcated st4em

G9, $800-$1500
Lee Co., MS

G8, $1200-$2000
Benton Co., TN

Diagonal flaking

G9, $1500-$2500
W. TN

G10, $1200-$2000
Lee Co., MS

G9, $550-$1000
Meigs Co., TN

IMPORTANT:
All Bentons on this page shown 50% of actual size

Ground greenstone

Diagonal flaking

Un-notched benton

Un-notched benton

G10, $2500-$4000
Lee Co., MS
Very rare

G10, $1500-$2500
Putnam Co., TN

G10, $1700-$3000
Monroe Co., MS

Fort Payne chert

G10, $2000-$3500
Lee Co., MS

G10, $4000-$7000
N. E. MS

348

BENTON BLADE - Middle Archaic, 6000 - 4000 B. P.

(Also see Benton and Copena)

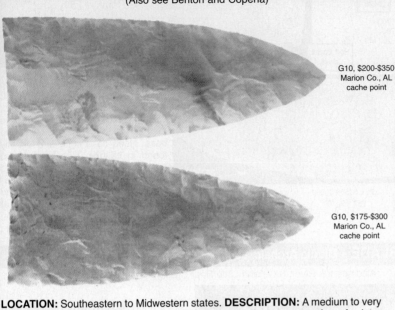

G10, $200-$350
Marion Co., AL
cache point

G10, $175-$300
Marion Co., AL
cache point

LOCATION: Southeastern to Midwestern states. **DESCRIPTION:** A medium to very large size, broad, finished blade used either as a knife or as a preform for later knapping into a *Benton* point. Usually found in caches. **I.D. KEY:** Archaic flaking similar to the *Benton* type.

G9, $250-$400
Marion Co., AL
cache point

E
C

BENTON-BOTTLE NECK - Middle Archaic, 6000 - 4000 B. P.

(Also see Benton and Table Rock)

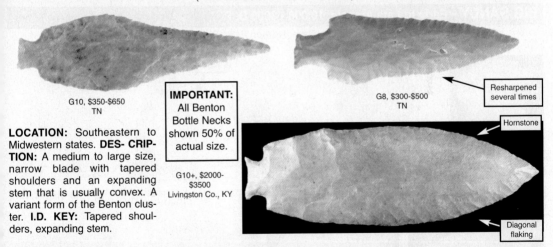

G10, $350-$650
TN

G8, $300-$500
TN

Resharpened several times

IMPORTANT: All Benton Bottle Necks shown 50% of actual size.

LOCATION: Southeastern to Midwestern states. **DES- CRIP-TION:** A medium to large size, narrow blade with tapered shoulders and an expanding stem that is usually convex. A variant form of the Benton cluster. **I.D. KEY:** Tapered shoulders, expanding stem.

G10+, $2000-$3500
Livingston Co., KY

Hornstone

Diagonal flaking

BENTON DOUBLE-NOTCHED - Middle Archaic, 6000 - 4000 B. P.

(Also see Benton and Turkeytail)

IMPORTANT: All double notched Bentons shown 50% of actual size

G6, $1200-$2000
Egypt, MS

Broken & glued

BENTON DOUBLE-NOTCHED (continued)

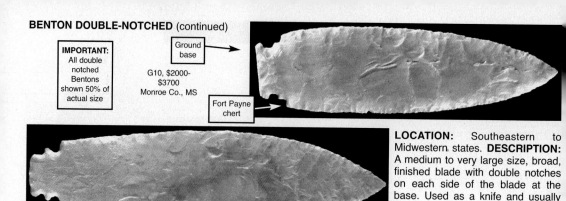

IMPORTANT: All double notched Bentons shown 50% of actual size

Ground base

G10, $2000-$3700
Monroe Co., MS

Fort Payne chert

G10, $3500-$6000
Lee Co., MS

Fort Payne chert

LOCATION: Southeastern to Midwestern states. **DESCRIPTION:** A medium to very large size, broad, finished blade with double notches on each side of the blade at the base. Used as a knife and usually found in caches. Has been found associated with un-notched and double to triple-notched *Turkeytail* blades in Mississippi. Unique and rare. **I.D. KEY:** Multiple notching at base.

BENTON-NARROW BLADE - Middle Archaic, 6000 - 4000 B. P.

(Also see Elk River, Kays and Little Bear Creek)

G8, $250-$450
Morgan Co., AL

LOCATION: Southeastern to Midwestern states. **DESCRIPTION:** A medium to large size, narrow, stemmed variant of the *Benton* form.

BIG SANDY - Early to Late Archaic, 10,000 - 3000 B. P.

(Also see Cache River, Graham Cave, Newton Falls, Pine Tree and Savage Cave)

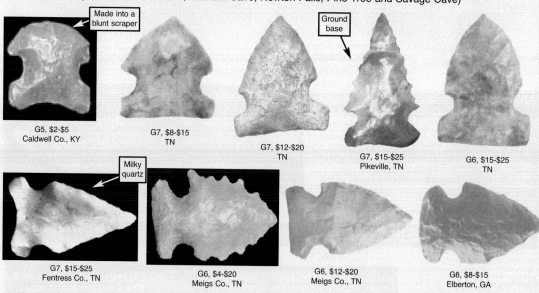

Made into a blunt scraper

Ground base

G5, $2-$5
Caldwell Co., KY

G7, $8-$15
TN

G7, $12-$20
TN

G7, $15-$25
Pikeville, TN

G6, $15-$25
TN

Milky quartz

G7, $15-$25
Fentress Co., TN

G6, $4-$20
Meigs Co., TN

G6, $12-$20
Meigs Co., TN

G6, $8-$15
Elberton, GA

LOCATION: Southeastern states. **DESCRIPTION:** A small to medium size, side-notched point with early forms showing heavy basal grinding, serrations, and horizontal flaking. This type may be associated with the *Frazier* point, being an unnotched form. Some examples have been carbon dated to 10,000 B.P., but most are associated with Mid-Archaic times. **I.D. KEY:** Basal form and blade flaking.

G8, $12-$20
KY

G6, $15-$25
Jackson Co., AL

G7, $15-$30
N. E. AL

G7, $15-$30
Jackson Co., AL

G7, $8-$15
KY

G6, $15-$25
N. W. AL

Blunt
tip

E
C

G8, $30-$50
Davidson Co., TN

G8, $40-$75
Jessamine Co., KY

G9, $35-$65
KY

G7, $25-$40
Humphreys Co., TN

G8, $40-$75
N. W. AL

G7, $40-$75
Humphreys Co., TN

G6, $40-$75
N. W. AL

G9, $200-$375
TN

G10, $800-$1500
Jefferson Co., KY

351

BIG SANDY-BROAD BASE - Early Archaic, 10,000 - 7000 B. P.

(Also see Cache River, Newton Falls and Savage Cave)

Black chert

G6, $20-$35
TN/KY

G8, $20-$35
TN

LOCATION: Southeastern states. **DESCRIPTION:** A small to medium size, side notched point with a broad base that is usually ground. The base is wider than the blade.

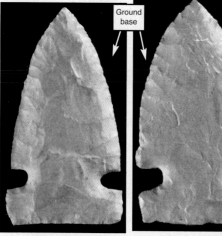

Ground base

G9, $125-$200
Humphreys Co., TN

G6, $35-$60
Humphreys Co., TN

G9, $175-$300
Humphreys Co., TN

G10, $400-$750
Meade Co., KY

BIG SANDY-CONTRACTED BASE - Early Archaic, 10,000 - 7000 B. P.

(Also see MacCorkle, Pine Tree and Quad)

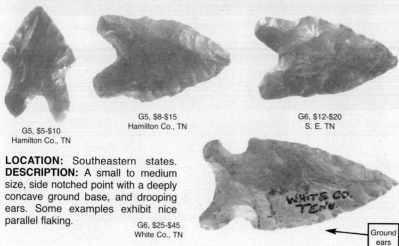

Flaki
a me
rid

G5, $5-$10
Hamilton Co., TN

G5, $8-$15
Hamilton Co., TN

G6, $12-$20
S. E. TN

LOCATION: Southeastern states. **DESCRIPTION:** A small to medium size, side notched point with a deeply concave ground base, and drooping ears. Some examples exhibit nice parallel flaking.

G6, $25-$45
White Co., TN

WHITE CO. TENN.

Ground ears

G6, $25-$45
Castalian Springs, TN

BIG SANDY E-NOTCHED - Early Archaic, 10,000 - 7000 B. P.

(Also see Leighton & Thebes)

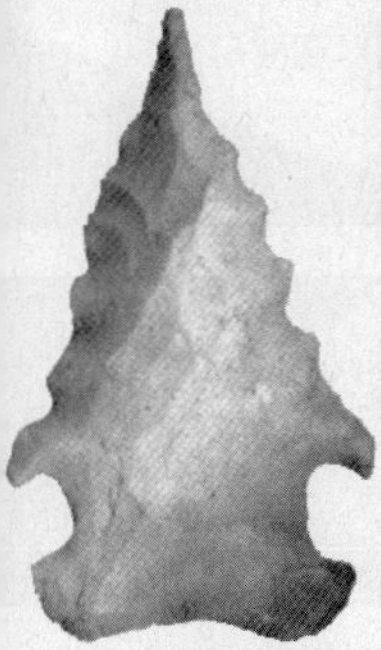

G6, $25-$40
Houston Co., AL

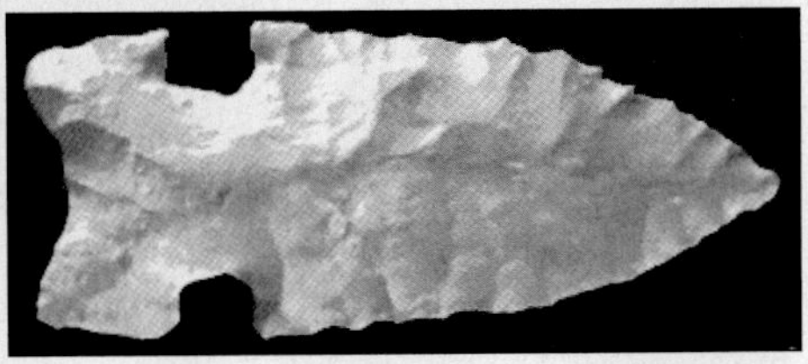

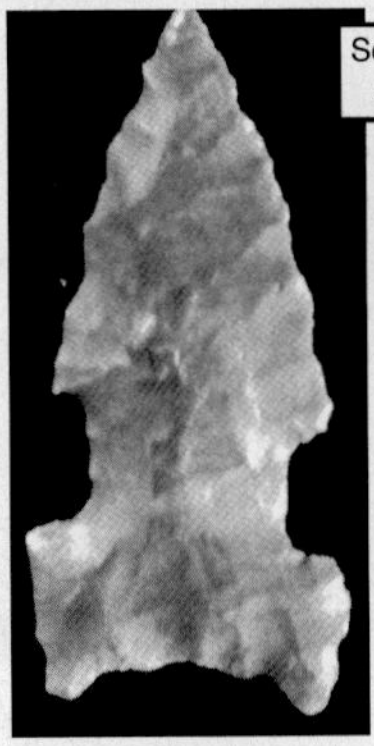

G5, $20-$35
Humphreys Co., TN

Serrated
edge

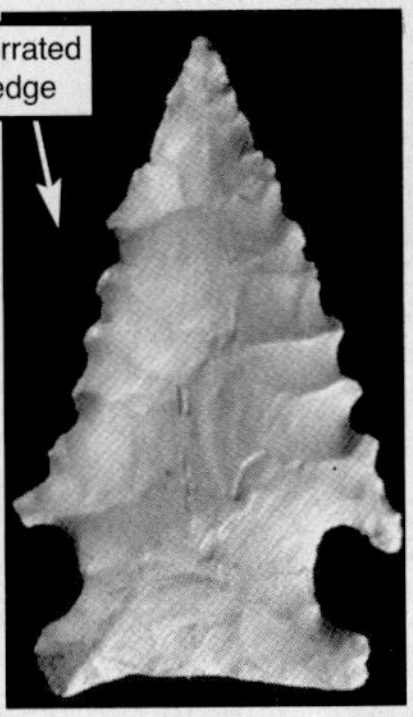

G8, $30-$55
Jackson Co., AL

G8, $70-$135
Coffee Lake, AL

Patinated
white

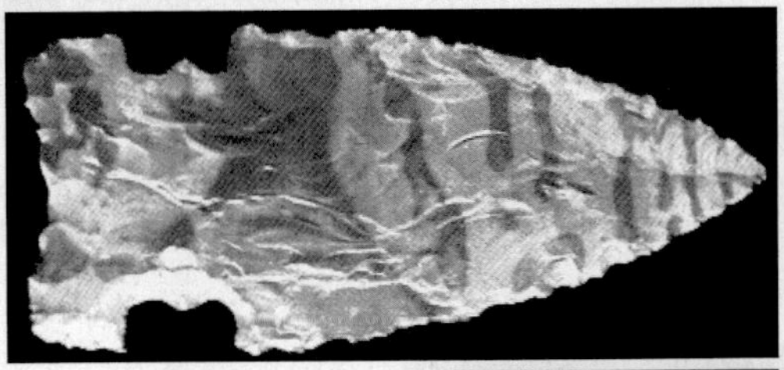

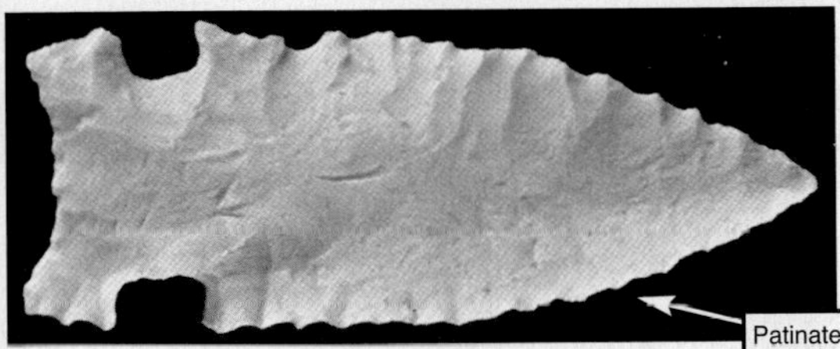

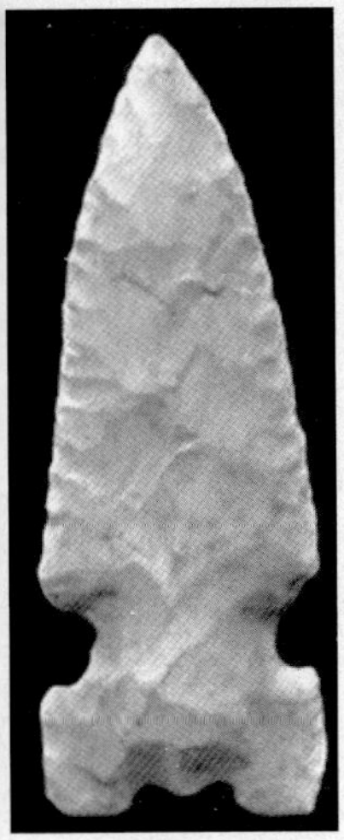

G10, $250-$425
Humphreys Co., TN

Prominent
E-notches
Purple
& beige
Buffalo
River
chert

G10, $400-$750
Humphreys Co., TN

G8, $90-$175
TN

G9, $150-$250
Humphreys Co., TN

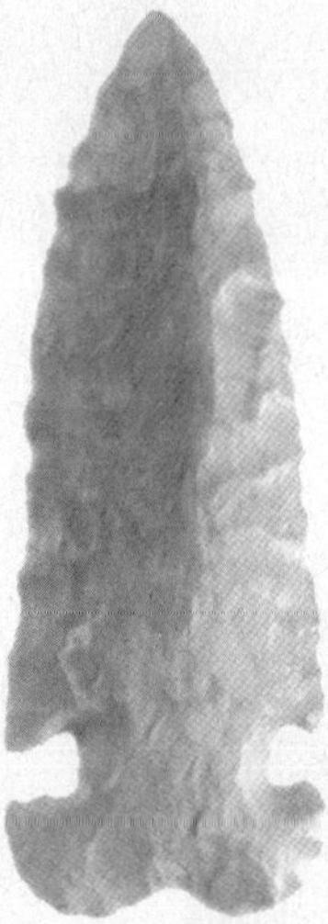

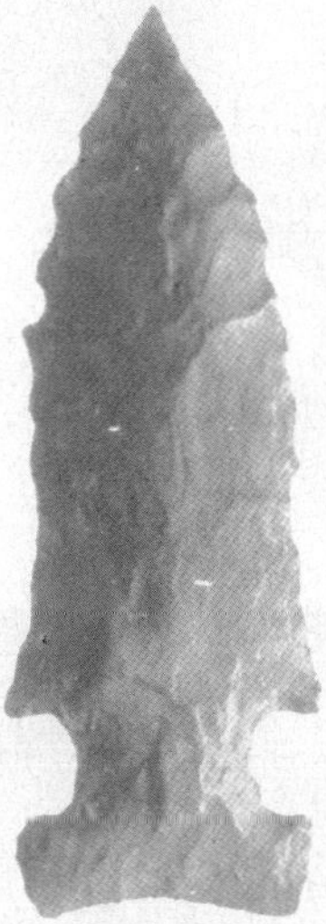

G10, $200-$375
Humphreys Co., TN

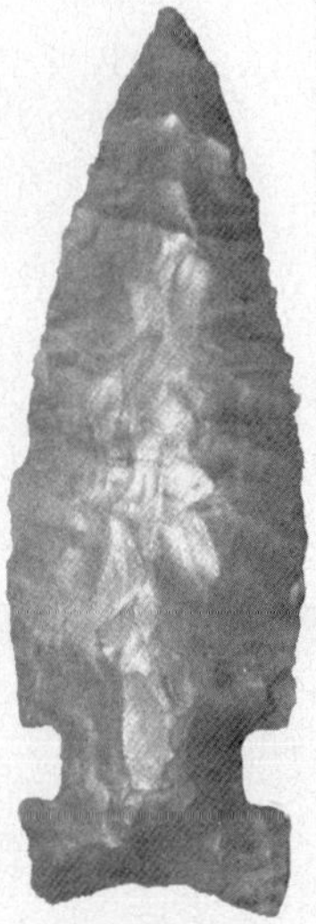

G9, $150-$250
N.W. AL

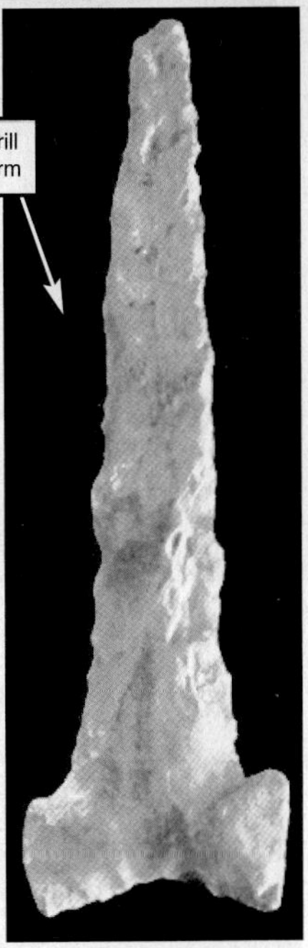

Drill
form

G9, $150-$250
Humphreys Co., TN

LOCATION: Southeastern states. **DESCRIPTION:** A small to medium size expanded side-notched point. The notching is unique and quite rare for the type. This type of notch is angled into the blade to produce a high point or nipple in the center, forming the letter E. Also called key-notched. Rarely, the base is also E-notched. The same notching occurs in the *Bolen* and *Thebes* types. **I.D. KEY:** Two flake notching system.

BIG SANDY-LEIGHTON BASE - Early Archaic, 10,000 - 7000 B. P.

(Also see Leighton and Thebes)

BIG SANDY-LEIGHTON (continued)

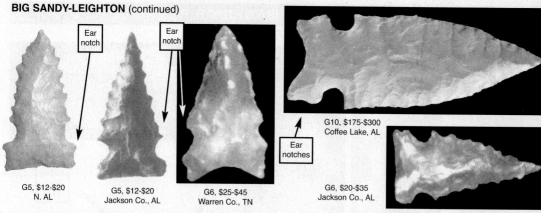

Ear notch

Ear notch

Ear notches

G10, $175-$300
Coffee Lake, AL

G5, $12-$20
N. AL

G5, $12-$20
Jackson Co., AL

G6, $25-$45
Warren Co., TN

G6, $20-$35
Jackson Co., AL

LOCATION: Southeastern states. **DESCRIPTION:** A small to medium size side notched point with a small notch in one or both sides of the base (see *Leighton* points). The notch or notches were used to facilitate hafting. **I.D. KEY:** Basal side notching.

BIG SLOUGH - Middle Archaic, 7000 - 4000 B. P.

(Also see Beacon Island and Elk River)

G8, $65-$125
Parsons, TN

G5, $15-$25
Bradley Co., TN

G6, $35-$70
Florence, AL

G10, $250-$450
Humphreys Co., TN

G7, $90-$175
KY

LOCATION: Southeastern states. **DESCRIPTION:** A medium to large size, broad, stemmed point with a bulbous base. The blade is convex to recurved. The shoulders may show a weak to medium tang. **I.D. KEY:** Basal form and barbs.

G8, $40-$75
TN

G9, $175-$300
Humphreys Co., TN

BLUNT - Paleo to Woodland, 11,500 - 1000 B. P.

(Also see Drill, Perforator and Scraper)

E
C

$.50-$1
IN

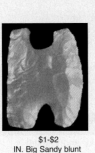

$1-$2
IN. Big Sandy blunt

$2-$4
IN. Big Sandy blunt

Adena
blunt

G6, $20-$35
IN

LOCATION: Throughout North America. **DESCRIPTION:** Blunts are usually made from broken points that are rechipped into this form, but can be made from scratch. All point types can occur as blunts. Some collectors call this form Stunners believing they were made to stun animals, not to kill. However, most archaeologists think they were used as knives and for scraping hides. Many blunts show excessive wear on the blunt edge proving their use as scrapers.

BRADLEY SPIKE - Late Archaic to Woodland, 4000 - 1800 B. P.

(Also see Buggs Island, Collins, Mountain Fork, New Market and Schild Spike)

Black
chert

Black
chert

G4, $4-$8
S.E. TN

G5, $4-$8
Dunlap, TN

G6, $5-$10
S. E. TN

G6, $8-$12
Jackson Co., AL

G6, $6-$12
Meigs Co., TN

G7, $8-$15
Pikeville, TN

G9, $15-$25
Hiwassee Isle, TN

G10, $20-$35
Limestone Co., AL

LOCATION: Southeastern states. **DESCRIPTION:** A small to medium size, narrow, thick, spike point. The shoulders are tapered and the stem contracts. The base on some examples shows the natural rind of the native material used.

BREWERTON CORNER NOTCHED - Middle to Late Archaic, 6000 - 4000 B. P.

(Also see Autauga)

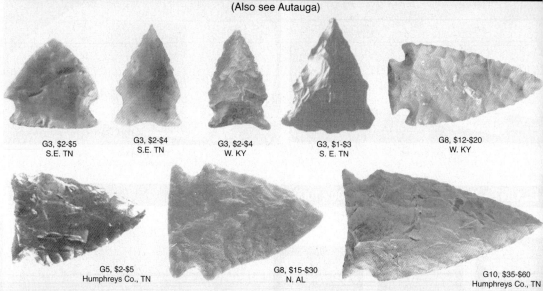

G3, $2-$5
S.E. TN

G3, $2-$4
S.E. TN

G3, $2-$4
W. KY

G3, $1-$3
S. E. TN

G8, $12-$20
W. KY

G5, $2-$5
Humphreys Co., TN

G8, $15-$30
N. AL

G10, $35-$60
Humphreys Co., TN

LOCATION: Eastern to Midwestern states. **DESCRIPTION:** A small size, triangular point with faint corner notches and a straight to concave base. Called *Freeheley* in Michigan. **I.D. KEY:** Width, thickness.

BREWERTON EARED-TRIANGULAR - Mid-Archaic, 6000 - 4000 B. P.

(Also see Autauga, Camp Creek, Candy Creek, Nolichucky and Yadkin)

G3, $1-$3
Polk Co., TN

G6, $3-$6
Autauga Co., AL

G3, $2-$4
Jessamine Co., KY

G3, $2-$5
Walker Co., AL

G3, $2-$5
Walker Co., AL

LOCATION: Eastern to Midwestern states. **DESCRIPTION:** A small size, triangular, eared point with a concave base. Shoulders are weak and tapered. Ears are widest part of point.

G3, $2-$5
Trimble Co., KY

BREWERTON SIDE NOTCHED - Mid-Archaic, 6000 - 4000 B. P.

(Also see Big Sandy, Brunswick, Hardaway and Matanzas)

G3, $1-$2
Trimble Co., KY

G4, $1-$3
Walker Co., GA

G3, $1-$2
Dallas Isle, TN

G4, $1-$3
Jessamine Co., KY

LOCATION: Eastern to Midwestern states. **DESCRIPTION:** A small to medium size, triangular point with shallow side notches and a concave to straight base.

356

G4, $1-$3
Harrison Co., IN

G5, $2-$5
Harrison Co., IN

G5, $2-$5
Harrison Co., IN

G4, $1-$3
Jessamine Co., KY

G8, $8-$15
Jessamine Co., KY

G7, $8-$15
Jessamine Co., KY

BRUNSWICK - Middle Archaic, 5000 - 4500 B. P.

(Also see Brewerton, Greenbrier and Matanzas)

G7, $40-$75
KY

G6, $35-$65
KY

LOCATION: Kentucky, Indiana. **DESCRIPTION:** A medium sized point with weak side notches. The base can be slightly concave to straight. **I.D. KEY:** Weak notching.

BUCK CREEK - Middle to Late Archaic, 6000 - 3500 B. P.

(Also see Hamilton, Motley, Rankin, Smithsonia, Table Rock and Wade)

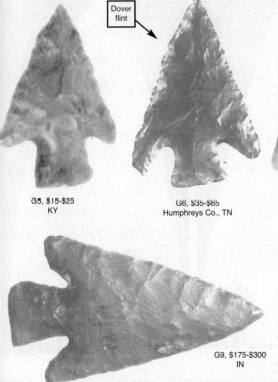

Dover flint

Needle tip

G5, $15-$25
KY

G6, $35-$65
Humphreys Co., TN

G7, $25-$45
TN

G10+, $2000-$3000
Pulaski Co., KY

G9, $175-$300
IN

LOCATION: Kentucky and surrounding states. **DESCRIPTION:** A large, thin, broad, stemmed point with strong barbs and high quality flaking. Some have needle tips, blade edges are convex to recurved. Blade width can be narrow to broad. **I.D. KEY:** Barb expansion and notching.

357

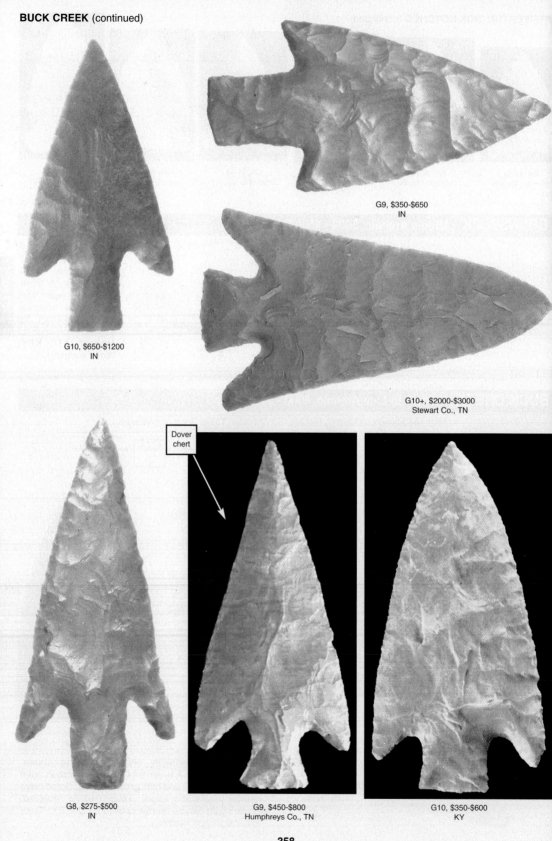

G9, $350-$650
IN

G10, $650-$1200
IN

G10+, $2000-$3000
Stewart Co., TN

Dover chert

G8, $275-$500
IN

G9, $450-$800
Humphreys Co., TN

G10, $350-$600
KY

BUGGS ISLAND - Mid to Late Archaic, 5500 - 3500 B. P.

(Also see Bradley Spike, Coosa, Ebenezer and New Market)

G3, $2-$4
S.E. TN

G4, $2-$4
Whitwell, TN

G5, $3-$6
Dunlap, TN

G6, $6-$12
Meigs Co., TN

G6, $6-$12
S.E. TN

Milky quartz

G5, $4-$8
S.E. TN

E
C

LOCATION: Eastern states. **DESCRIPTION:** A small to medium size point with a contracting stem and tapered shoulders. The base is usually straight.

BUZZARD ROOST CREEK - Middle Archaic, 6000 - 4000 B. P.

(Also see Benton and Kirk Stemmed)

Red jasper

G6, $8-$15
Meigs Co., TN

G8, $35-$65
TN

G7, $35-$65
Lawrence Co., TN

G8, $40-$75
Coffee Lake, AL

G9, $35-$65
TN

G5, $20-$35
OH

LOCATION: Southeastern states. **DESCRIPTION:** A medium to large size, stemmed point with a bifurcated base. Believed to be related to the *Benton* point. Found in Arkansas with the blade steeply beveled on one side of each face (transition form?). **I.D. KEY:** Bifurcated base and basal width. Found with *Benton* points. A notched base *Benton*.

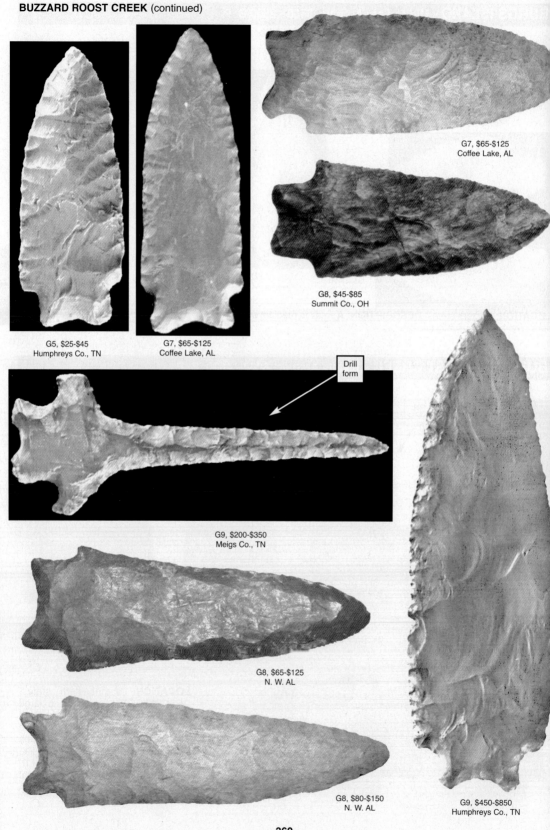

G7, $65-$125
Coffee Lake, AL

G8, $45-$85
Summit Co., OH

G5, $25-$45
Humphreys Co., TN

G7, $65-$125
Coffee Lake, AL

Drill
form

G9, $200-$350
Meigs Co., TN

G8, $65-$125
N. W. AL

G8, $80-$150
N. W. AL

G9, $450-$850
Humphreys Co., TN

CAMP CREEK - Woodland, 3000 - 1500 B. P.

(Also see Copena, Greeneville, Hamilton, Madison, Nolichucky and Yadkin)

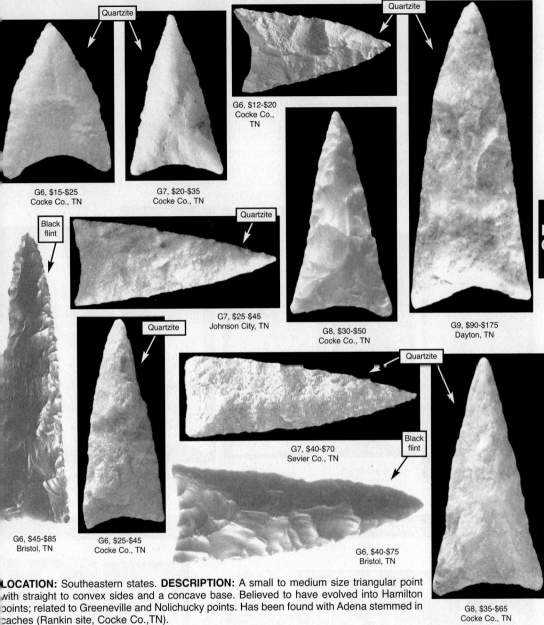

Quartzite

Quartzite

Quartzite

Quartzite

Quartzite

Black flint

Black flint

E C

G6, $12-$20
Cocke Co.,
TN

G6, $15-$25
Cocke Co., TN

G7, $20-$35
Cocke Co., TN

G7, $25-$45
Johnson City, TN

G8, $30-$50
Cocke Co., TN

G9, $90-$175
Dayton, TN

G7, $40-$70
Sevier Co., TN

G6, $45-$85
Bristol, TN

G6, $25-$45
Cocke Co., TN

G6, $40-$75
Bristol, TN

G8, $35-$65
Cocke Co., TN

LOCATION: Southeastern states. **DESCRIPTION:** A small to medium size triangular point with straight to convex sides and a concave base. Believed to have evolved into Hamilton points; related to Greeneville and Nolichucky points. Has been found with Adena stemmed in caches (Rankin site, Cocke Co.,TN).

CANDY CREEK - Early Woodland, 3000 - 1500 B. P.

(Also see Beaver Lake, Brewerton, Camp Creek, Copena, Dalton, Nolichucky and Quad)

LOCATION: Southeastern states. **DESCRIPTION:** A medium size, lanceolate, eared point with a concave base and recurved blade edges. Bases may be thinned or fluted and lightly ground. Flaking is of the random Woodland type and should not be confused with the earlier auriculate forms that have the parallel flaking. These points are similar to *Cumberland, Beaver Lake, Dalton* and *Quad*, but are shorter and of poorer quality. It is believed that Paleo people survived in East Tennessee to 3,000 B.P., and influenced the style of the *Candy Creek* point. Believed to be related to *Copena, Camp Creek, Ebenezer, Greenville* and *Nolichucky* points. **I.D. KEY:** Ears, thickness and Woodland flaking.

CANDY CREEK (continued)

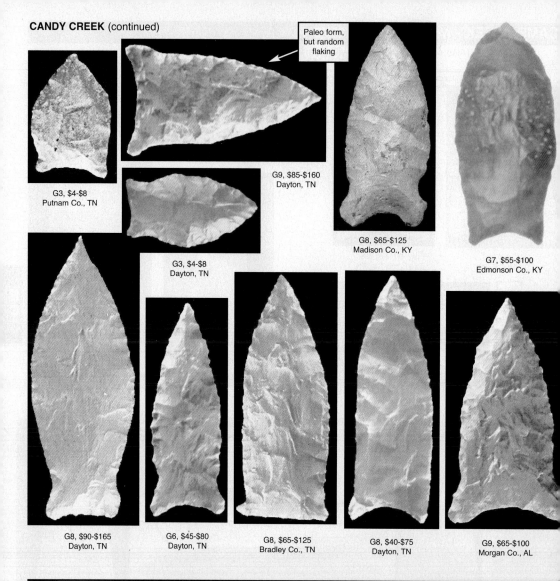

Paleo form, but random flaking

G3, $4-$8
Putnam Co., TN

G9, $85-$160
Dayton, TN

G3, $4-$8
Dayton, TN

G8, $65-$125
Madison Co., KY

G7, $55-$100
Edmonson Co., KY

G8, $90-$165
Dayton, TN

G6, $45-$80
Dayton, TN

G8, $65-$125
Bradley Co., TN

G8, $40-$75
Dayton, TN

G9, $65-$100
Morgan Co., AL

CAVE SPRING - Early Archaic, 9000 - 8000 B. P.

(Also see Frederick, Jude, LeCroy and Patrick)

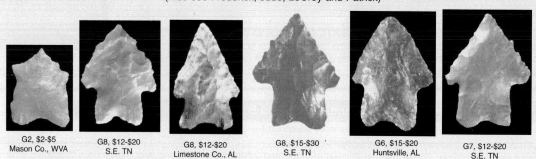

G2, $2-$5
Mason Co., WVA

G8, $12-$20
S.E. TN

G8, $12-$20
Limestone Co., AL

G8, $15-$30
S.E. TN

G6, $15-$20
Huntsville, AL

G7, $12-$20
S.E. TN

LOCATION: Southeastern states. **DESCRIPTION**: A *Jude* with a bifurcated base. A small to medium size, stemmed point with a shallow bifurcated base. Blade edges are usually straight; shoulders are either tapered or barbed, and the stem usually expands with a tendency to turn inward at the base which is usually ground. **ID. KEY:** Early Archaic flaking.

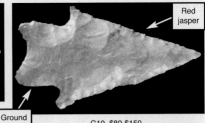

G8, $20-$35
Colbert Co., AL

G7, $25-$45
Humphreys Co., TN

Red jasper

Ground base

G10, $80-$150
Marion Co., AL

CHESSER - Late Woodland-Miss., 1600 - 1200 B. P.

(Also see Bakers Creek, Lowe, McIntire, Mud Creek)

LOCATION: Ohio into Pennsylvania.
DESCRIPTION: A medium size, broad point with a short, expanding stem. Bases are generally straight. Blade edges are convex to recurved and the shoulders are slightly barbed to tapered. **ID. KEY:** Broad, expanding stem.

G9, $80-$150
Hocking Co., OH

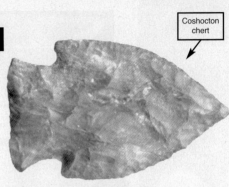

Coshocton chert

E C

CLOVIS - Early Paleo, 11,500 - 10,600 B. P.

(Also see Angostura, Browns Valley, Cumberland, Dalton, Folsom and Redstone)

Broken base

Hornstone

Quartzite

G7, $175-$300
KY

$25-$45
TN

G7, $350-$600
Greene Co., IN

G8, $400-$700
IN

G9, $650-$1200
Pickett Co., TN

Dover chert

Fluting channel

G6, $350-$600
TN

G8, $450-800
Lee Co., MS

LOCATION: All of North America. **DESCRIPTION:** A medium to large size, auriculate, fluted, lanceolate point with convex sides and a concave base that is ground. Most examples are fluted on both sides about 1/3 the way up from the base. The flaking can be random to parallel. *Clovis* is the earliest point type in the hemisphere. *Clovis* technology more closely matches European Solutrean forms than anywhere else. There is no pre-*Clovis* evidence here (crude forms that would pre-date *Clovis*). The first *Clovis* find associated with Mastodons was in 1979 at Mastodon State Park, Jefferson Co., MO. in the Kimmswick bone bed dated to 12,000 B.P. carbon years. **I.D. KEY:** Paleo flaking, shoulders, baton or billet fluting instead of indirect style.

CLOVIS (continued)

Edge wear

Paoli flint

Tip was taken with flute

$450-$800
N.W. AL

G8, $650-$1200
Perry Co., TN

Fluting channel

G7, $800-$1500
TN

G9, $1200-$2000
OH

G10+, $10,000-$20,000+
Estill Co., KY

Fluting channel

Ear damage

G10, $4000-$7500
OH

G9, $1800-$3500
KY

G8, $1700-$3200
IN

G6, $1000-$1800
KY

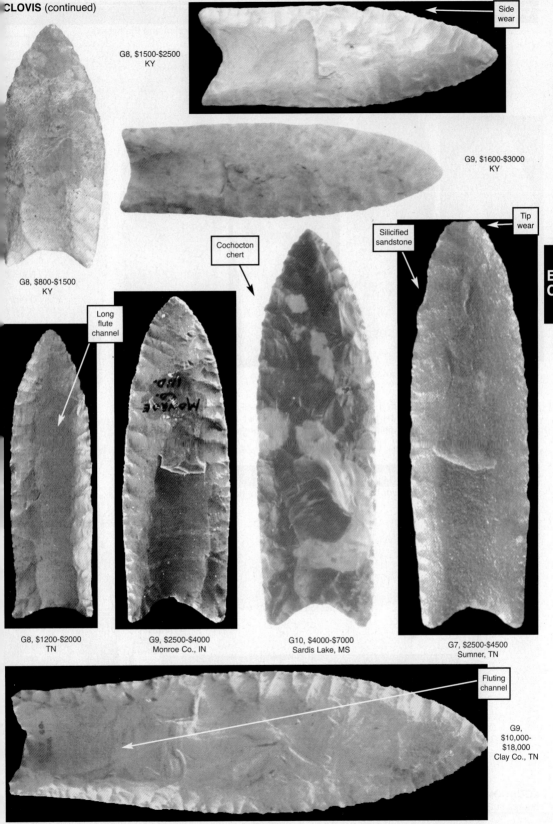

CLOVIS (continued)

Side wear

G8, $1500-$2500
KY

G9, $1600-$3000
KY

G8, $800-$1500
KY

Cochocton chert

Silicified sandstone

Tip wear

E
C

Long flute channel

G8, $1200-$2000
TN

G9, $2500-$4000
Monroe Co., IN

G10, $4000-$7000
Sardis Lake, MS

G7, $2500-$4500
Sumner, TN

Fluting channel

G9,
$10,000-
$18,000
Clay Co., TN

CLOVIS-HAZEL - Paleo, 11,500 - 10,600 B. P.

(Also see Angostura, Beaver Lake, Candy Creek, Golondrina and Plainview)

G9, $700-$1200
Lewis Co., KY

G10, $1200-$2000
KY

G10, $1500-$2500
KY

G8, $800-$1500
KY

G7, $700-$1200
KY

Flute channel

Tip wear

LOCATION: Eastern U.S. from Florida, Alabama, Tennessee, Kentucky, Ohio westward. **DESCRIPTION:** A medium to large size, auriculate point that has similarities to the Ross County variety, but with a more fishtailed appearance and a longer hafting area.

CLOVIS-UNFLUTED - Paleo, 11,500 - 10,600 B. P.

(Also see Angostura, Beaver Lake, Candy Creek, Golondrina and Plainview)

Knox chert

Ear nick

Basal thinning

G7, $550-$900
W. TN

Ross County type

Dover chert

G8, $300-$550
Clark Co., KY

G6, $550-$1000
Hickman, KY

G8, $1500-$2700
Humphreys Co., TN

LOCATION: All of North America. **DESCRIPTION:** A medium to large size, auriculate point identical to fluted *Clovis*, but not fluted. A very rare type as most *Clovis* points are fluted in their finished form.

COBBS TRIANGULAR - Early Archaic, 9000 - 5000 B. P.

(Also see Abasolo, Decatur, Lerma, Lost Lake and St. Charles)

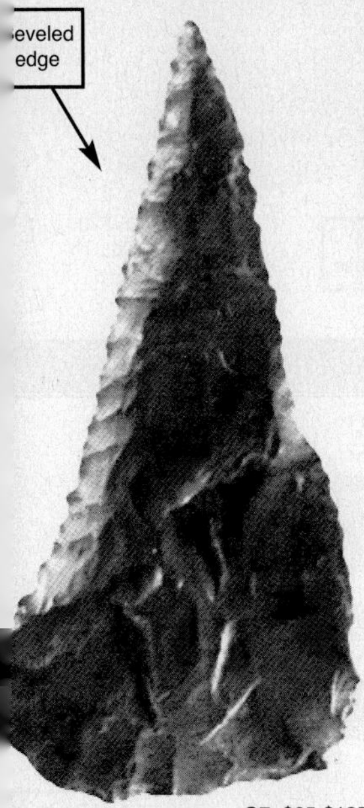

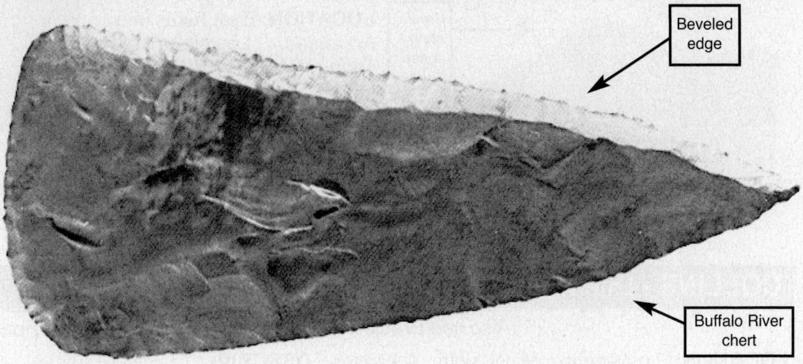

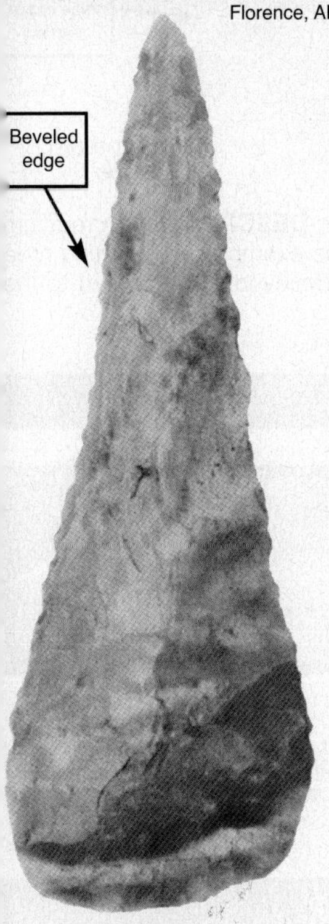

Beveled
edge

G7, $65-$125
Florence, AL

Beveled
edge
Buffalo River
chert

G10, $250-$450
Florence, AL

Beveled
edge

G8 $150-$250
KY

Beveled
edge

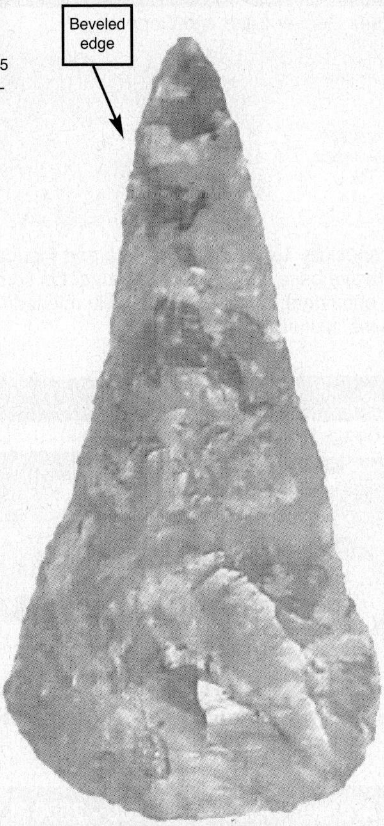

G9, $200-$350
Sequatchie Valley, TN

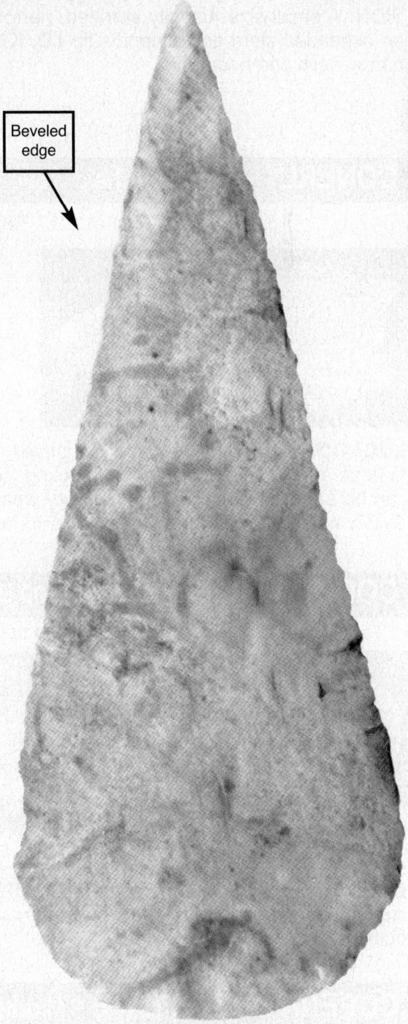

Beveled
edge

G10, $350-$650
TN

LOCATION: Southeastern states. **DESCRIPTION:** A medium to large size, thin, lanceolate blade with a broad, rounded to square base. One side of each face is usually steeply beveled. These are un-notched preforms for early Archaic beveled types such as *Decatur, Dovetail, Lost Lake,* etc. Has been found with St. Charles points in a cache at the Olive Branch site and dated to 9300-9400 carbon years before present.

COLDWATER - Trans. Paleo, 10,000 - 8000 B. P.

(Also see Hinds and Pelican)

G6, $80-$150
AL

Jasper

Ground stem & base

LOCATION: East Texas into Arkansas, Louisiana & Tenn. **DESCRIPTION:** A medium size, Lanceolate point with a longer waist than *Pelican* and a straight to concave base which is ground. The blade expands up from the base.

Ground stem & base

G8, $125-$200
Hardin Co., TN

COLLINS - Late Woodland, 1500 - 1200 B. P.

(Also see Bradley Spike, Clifton, Duval & Mountain Fork)

LOCATION: Louisianna, Mississippi, Arkansas. **DESCRIPTION:** A small size, usually serrated, narrow arrow point with an expanded stem and a needle tip **I.D. KEY:** Serrated blade narrowness and needle tip.

G10, $40-$75
Jefferson Co., MS

CONERLY - Middle Archaic, 7500 - 4500 B. P.

(Also see Beaver Lake and Copena)

G7, $25-$45
Nickajack Lake, TN

Fairly thick cross section

G10, $65-$125
Bradley Co., TN

LOCATION: Southern Southeastern states, especially Tennessee, Georgia and Florida. **DESCRIPTION:** A medium to large auriculate point with a contracting, concave base which can be ground. On some examples, the hafting area can be seen with the presence of very weak shoulders. The base is usually thinned. Believed to be related to the *Guilford* type. **I.D. KEY:** Base concave, thickness, flaking.

COOSA - Woodland, 2000 - 1500 B. P.

(Also see Buggs Island and Crawford Creek)

G5, $1-$2
Nickajack Lake, TN

G5, $1-$3
Jackson Co., AL

G5, $1-$3
Jackson Co., AL

LOCATION: Southeastern states. **DESCRIPTION:** A medium size, usually serrated medium grade point with a short stem. Some examples are shallowly side-notched. Shoulders are roughly horizontal. **I.D. KEY:** Serrated blade edges, bulbous stem.

COPENA-AURICULATE - Middle Archaic-Woodland, 5000 - 2500 B. P.

(Also see Beaver Lake, Camp Creek, Candy Creek, Clovis, Quad and Yadkin)

LOCATION: Southeastern states. **DESCRIPTION:** A medium to large size, lanceolate point with convex, straight to recurved blade edges and a concave, auriculate base. Could be confused with *Beaver Lake, Candy Creek, Clovis, Cumberland* or other auriculate forms. Look for the random Woodland flaking on this type. Stems are not ground. **I.D. KEY:** Concave base.

COPENA AURICULATE (continued)

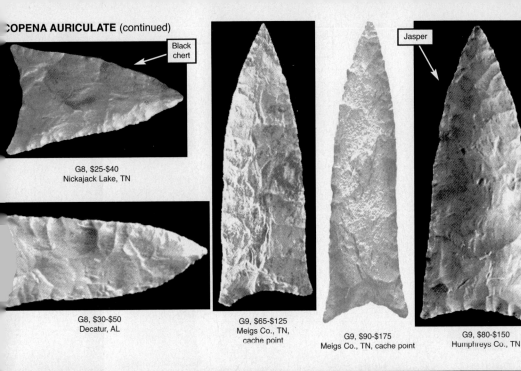

Black chert

G8, $25-$40
Nickajack Lake, TN

G8, $30-$50
Decatur, AL

G9, $65-$125
Meigs Co., TN,
cache point

Jasper

G9, $90-$175
Meigs Co., TN, cache point

G9, $80-$150
Humphreys Co., TN

E
C

COPENA-CLASSIC (Shield form) - Late Archaic to Woodland, 4000 - 1200 B. P.

(Also see Bakers Creek & Nolichucky)

Dover chert

Dover chert

G7, $65-$125
Humphreys Co., TN

G7, $45-$80
TN

G8, $80-$150
Hardin Co., KY

G9, $280-$450
TN

G7, $55-$100
TN

Buffalo River chert

G9, $150-$250
TN

LOCATION: Southeastern states. **DESCRIPTION:** A medium to large size, lanceolate point with recurved blade edges and a straight to slightly convex base. This point usually occurs in Woodland burial mounds, but is also found in late Archaic sites in Tennessee. The Alabama and Tennessee forms are usually very thin with high quality primary and secondary flaking.

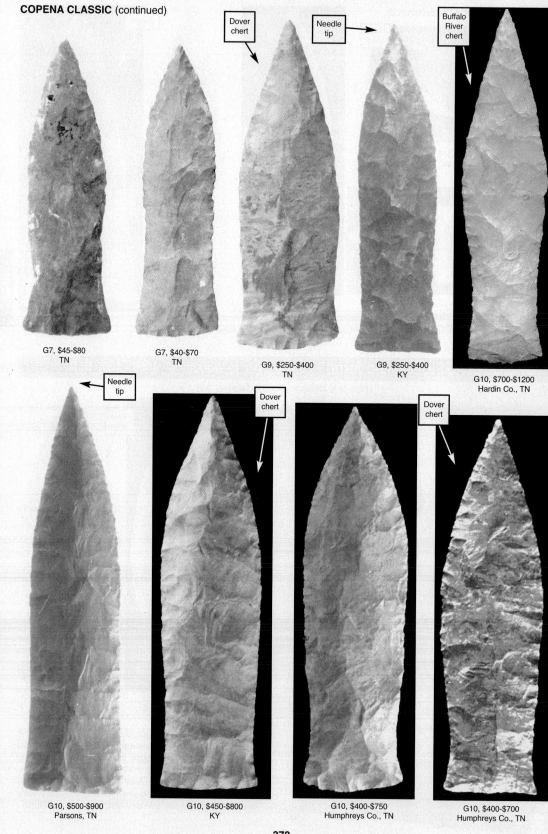

Dover chert

Needle tip

Buffalo River chert

G7, $45-$80
TN

G7, $40-$70
TN

G9, $250-$400
TN

G9, $250-$400
KY

G10, $700-$1200
Hardin Co., TN

Needle tip

Dover chert

Dover chert

G10, $500-$900
Parsons, TN

G10, $450-$800
KY

G10, $400-$750
Humphreys Co., TN

G10, $400-$700
Humphreys Co., TN

COPENA-ROUND BASE - Late Archaic to Woodland, 4000 - 1200 B. P.

(Also see Frazier & Tennessee River)

LOCATION: Southeastern states. **DESCRIPTION:** A medium to large size lanceolate blade with a rounded base. Blade edges become parallel towards the base on some examples.

Pink jasper

G9, $95-$185
Savannah, TN,
Snake Creek

G6, $12-$20
Florence, AL

G5, $20-$35
W. TN

E
C

COPENA-TRIANGULAR - Late Archaic to Woodland, 4000 - 1800 B. P.

(See Benton Blade, Frazier and Stanfield)

Sharp basal corners

G6, $20-$35
Parsons, TN

G5, $20-$35
TN

G7, $30-$50
W. KY

G8, $30-$50
Hardin Co., TN

G10, $125-$200
Florence, AL

G9, $125-$225
Decatur Co., TN

LOCATION: Southeastern states. **DESCRIPTION:** A medium to large size lanceolate blade with a straight base. Blade edges become parallel towards the base. Some examples show a distinct hafting area near the base where the blade edges form a very weak shoulder and become slightly concave.

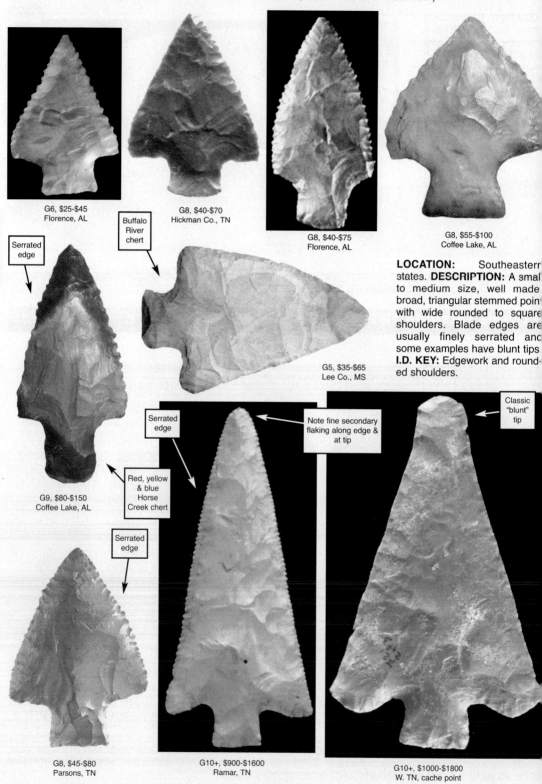

(Also see Flint Creek, Little Bear Creek, Smithsonia and Table Rock)

G6, $25-$45
Florence, AL

Buffalo River chert

G8, $40-$70
Hickman Co., TN

G8, $40-$75
Florence, AL

G8, $55-$100
Coffee Lake, AL

Serrated edge

LOCATION: Southeastern states. **DESCRIPTION:** A small to medium size, well made broad, triangular stemmed point with wide rounded to square shoulders. Blade edges are usually finely serrated and some examples have blunt tips. **I.D. KEY:** Edgework and rounded shoulders.

G5, $35-$65
Lee Co., MS

G9, $80-$150
Coffee Lake, AL

Red, yellow & blue Horse Creek chert

Serrated edge

Note fine secondary flaking along edge & at tip

Classic "blunt" tip

Serrated edge

G8, $45-$80
Parsons, TN

G10+, $900-$1600
Ramar, TN

G10+, $1000-$1800
W. TN, cache point

COTACO CREEK BLADE - Woodland, 2500 - 2000 B. P.

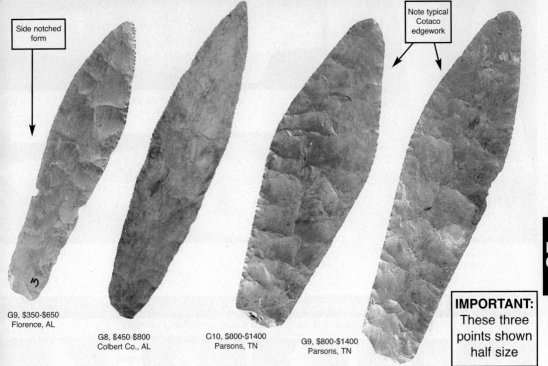

Side notched form

Note typical Cotaco edgework

G9, $350-$650
Florence, AL

G8, $450 $800
Colbert Co., AL

G10, $800-$1400
Parsons, TN

G9, $800-$1400
Parsons, TN

IMPORTANT: These three points shown half size

LOCATION: Southeastern states. **DESCRIPTION:** A medium to large size lanceolate blade with a rounded base. Blade edges expand past mid-section. Some examples are side notched for hafting.

COTACO-WRIGHT - Woodland, 2500 - 1800 B. P.

(Also see Flint Creek and Little Bear Creek)

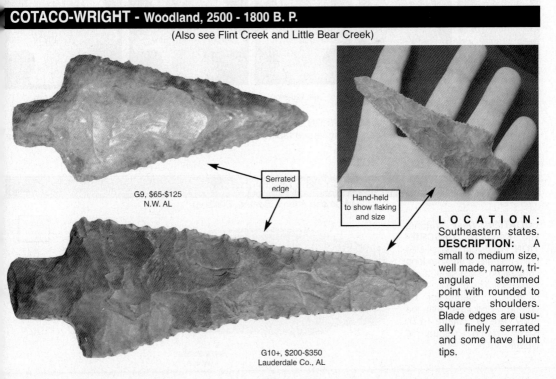

G9, $65-$125
N.W. AL

Serrated edge

Hand-held to show flaking and size

G10+, $200-$350
Lauderdale Co., AL

LOCATION: Southeastern states. **DESCRIPTION:** A small to medium size, well made, narrow, triangular stemmed point with rounded to square shoulders. Blade edges are usually finely serrated and some have blunt tips.

E
C

COTACO-WRIGHT (continued)

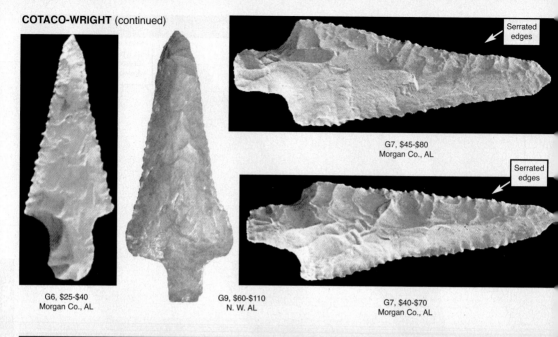

Serrated edges

G7, $45-$80
Morgan Co., AL

Serrated edges

G6, $25-$40
Morgan Co., AL

G9, $60-$110
N. W. AL

G7, $40-$70
Morgan Co., AL

CRAWFORD CREEK - Early Archaic, 8000 - 5000 B. P.

(Also see Coosa, Kirk Corner, Mud Creek and White Springs)

Serrated edges

G9, $25-$40
Meigs Co., TN

G7, $12-$20
Nickajack Lake, TN

G9, $25-$40
Morgan Co., AL

G10, $30-$50
Limestone Co., AL

G10, $30-$50
Limestone Co., AL

LOCATION: Southeastern states. **DESCRIPTION:** A small to medium size point that is usually serrated with a short, straight to expanding stem. Shoulders are square to tapered. Blade edges are straight to recurved. **I.D. KEY:** Early edgework.

CRESAP - Late Archaic to Woodland, 3000 - 2500 B. P.

(Also see Adena, Benton, Dickson)

LOCATION: West Virginia into Kentucky. **DESCRIPTION:** A medium to large size point that has a medium-long contracting stem and slight shoulders. The base is usually straight. Stems can be ground. Associated with the early Adena culture. **I.D. KEY:** Long "squarish" tapered stem.

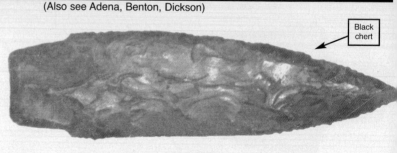

Black chert

G9, $175-$300
W. KY

374

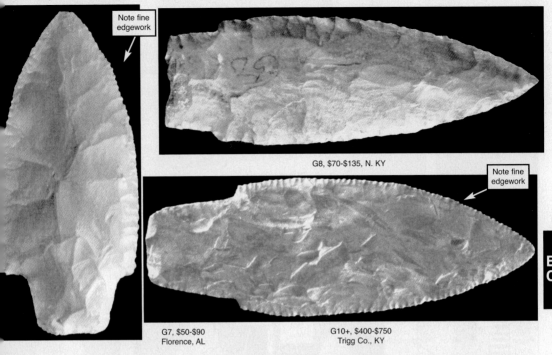

Note fine edgework

G8, $70-$135, N. KY

Note fine edgework

G7, $50-$90
Florence, AL

G10+, $400-$750
Trigg Co., KY

E
C

CUMBERLAND - Paleo, 11,250 - 10,000 B. P.

(Also see Beaver Lake, Clovis, Copena Auriculate and Quad)

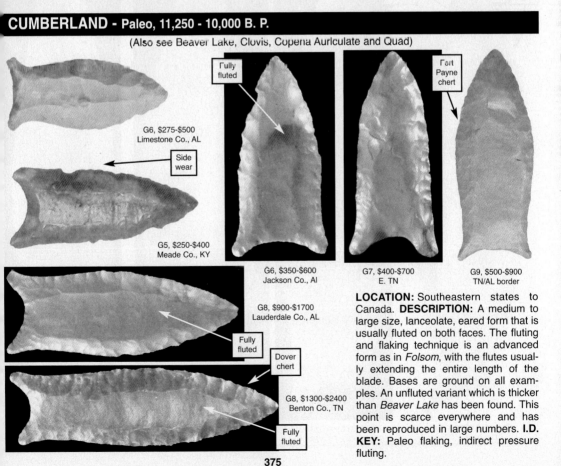

G6, $275-$500
Limestone Co., AL

Side wear

G5, $250-$400
Meade Co., KY

Fully fluted

G6, $350-$600
Jackson Co., Al

Fort Payne chert

G7, $400-$700
E. TN

G9, $500-$900
TN/AL border

G8, $900-$1700
Lauderdale Co., AL

Fully fluted

Dover chert

G8, $1300-$2400
Benton Co., TN

Fully fluted

LOCATION: Southeastern states to Canada. **DESCRIPTION:** A medium to large size, lanceolate, eared form that is usually fluted on both faces. The fluting and flaking technique is an advanced form as in *Folsom*, with the flutes usually extending the entire length of the blade. Bases are ground on all examples. An unfluted variant which is thicker than *Beaver Lake* has been found. This point is scarce everywhere and has been reproduced in large numbers. **I.D. KEY:** Paleo flaking, indirect pressure fluting.

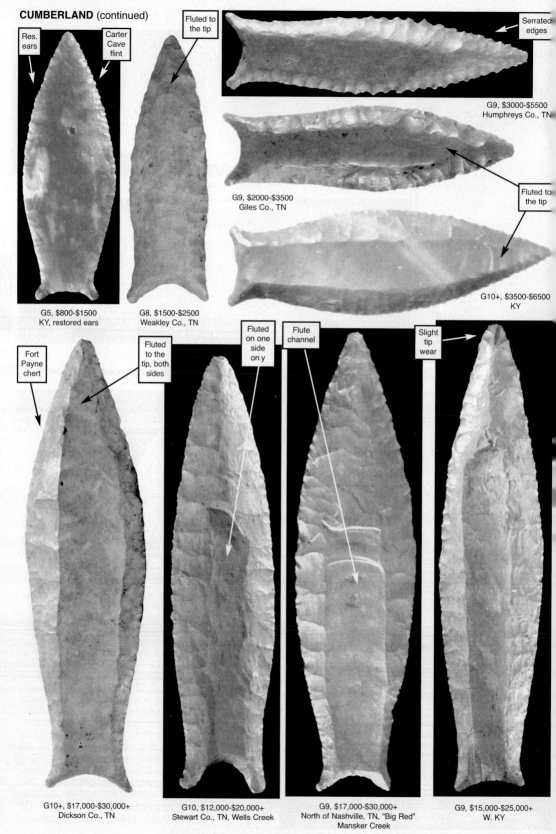

CUMBERLAND (continued)

Res. ears

Carter Cave flint

Fluted to the tip

Serrated edges

G9, $3000-$5500
Humphreys Co., TN

G9, $2000-$3500
Giles Co., TN

Fluted to the tip

G10+, $3500-$6500
KY

G5, $800-$1500
KY, restored ears

G8, $1500-$2500
Weakley Co., TN

Fort Payne chert

Fluted to the tip, both sides

Fluted on one side only

Flute channel

Slight tip wear

G10+, $17,000-$30,000+
Dickson Co., TN

G10, $12,000-$20,000+
Stewart Co., TN, Wells Creek

G9, $17,000-$30,000+
North of Nashville, TN, "Big Red"
Mansker Creek

G9, $15,000-$25,000+
W. KY

CYPRESS CREEK - Middle to Late Archaic, 5000 - 3000 B. P.

Also see Benton, Hardin, Kirk Corner Notched, Harpeth River, Lost Lake & McIntire)

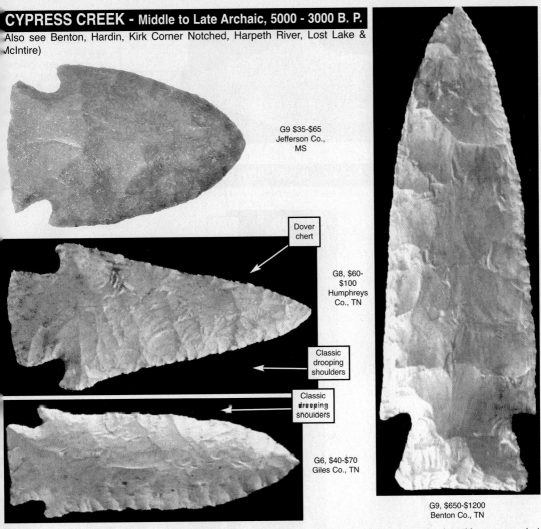

G9 $35-$65
Jefferson Co.,
MS

Dover chert

G8, $60-$100
Humphreys Co., TN

Classic drooping shoulders

Classic drooping shoulders

G6, $40-$70
Giles Co., TN

G9, $650-$1200
Benton Co., TN

E C

LOCATION: Southeastern states. **DESCRIPTION:** A medium to large size, broad stemmed point with an expanded base and drooping "umbrella" shoulder tangs. A cross between Lost Lake and Kirk Corner Notched. The blade is beveled on all four sides. **I.D. KEY:** Archaic flaking, shoulders droop.

DAGGER - Late Archaic to Woodland, 4000 - 1500 B. P.

(Also see Duck River Sword and Mace)

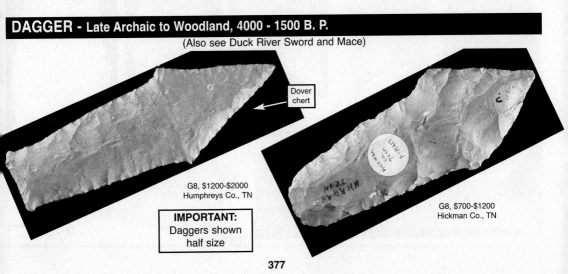

Dover chert

G8, $1200-$2000
Humphreys Co., TN

IMPORTANT:
Daggers shown
half size

G8, $700-$1200
Hickman Co., TN

DAGGER (continued)

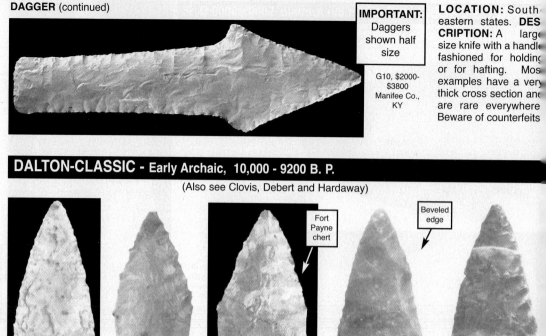

IMPORTANT: Daggers shown half size

G10, $2000-$3800 Manifee Co., KY

LOCATION: South-eastern states. **DESCRIPTION:** A large size knife with a handle fashioned for holding or for hafting. Most examples have a very thick cross section and are rare everywhere. Beware of counterfeits.

DALTON-CLASSIC - Early Archaic, 10,000 - 9200 B. P.

(Also see Clovis, Debert and Hardaway)

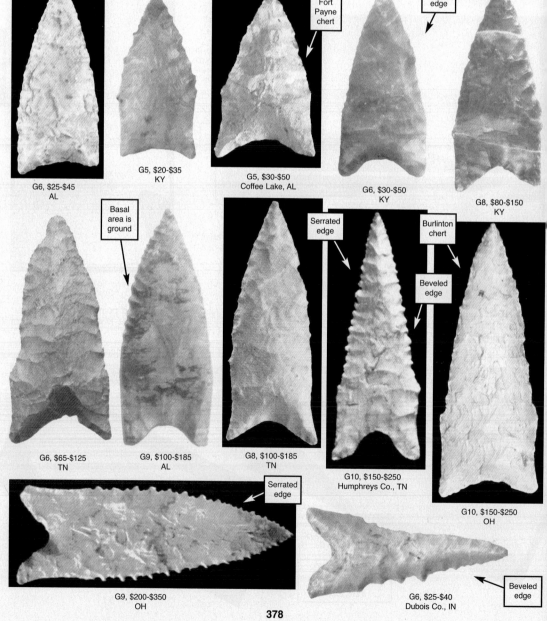

G6, $25-$45
AL

G5, $20-$35
KY

Fort Payne chert

G5, $30-$50
Coffee Lake, AL

Beveled edge

G6, $30-$50
KY

G8, $80-$150
KY

Basal area is ground

G6, $65-$125
TN

G9, $100-$185
AL

G8, $100-$185
TN

Serrated edge

Beveled edge

G10, $150-$250
Humphreys Co., TN

Burlinton chert

G10, $150-$250
OH

Serrated edge

G9, $200-$350
OH

G6, $25-$40
Dubois Co., IN

Beveled edge

DALTON CLASSIC (continued)

Serrated edge

G10, $200-$350
TN

LOCATION: Midwestern to Southeastern states. **DESCRIPTION:** A medium to large size, thin, auriculate, fishtailed point. Many examples are finely serrated and exhibit excellent flaking. Beveling may occur on one side of each face but is usually on the right side. All have basal grinding. This early type spread over most of the Eastern and Midwestern U.S. and strongly influenced many other types to follow.

DALTON-COLBERT - Early Archaic, 10,000 - 9200 B. P.

(Also see Beaver Lake, Dalton-Nuckolls, Plainview and Searcy)

E C

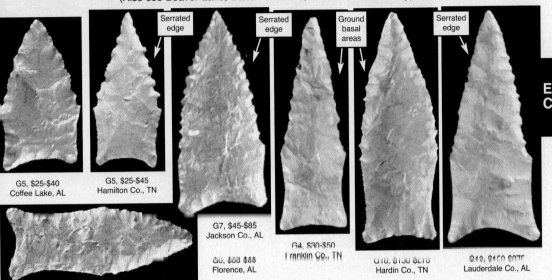

Serrated edge

Serrated edge

Ground basal areas

Serrated edge

G5, $25-$40
Coffee Lake, AL

G5, $25-$45
Hamilton Co., TN

G7, $45-$85
Jackson Co., AL

G4, $30-$50
Franklin Co., TN

G0, $00-$00
Florence, AL

G10, $150-$270
Hardin Co., TN

G10, $150-$275
Lauderdale Co., AL

LOCATION: Midwestern to Southeastern states. **DESCRIPTION:** A medium size, auriculate form with a squared stem and a weakly defined hafting area which is ground. Some examples are serrated and exhibit parallel flaking of the highest quality. **I.D. KEY:** Squarish basal area.

DALTON-GREENBRIER - Early Archaic, 10,000 - 9200 B. P.

(Also see Beaver Lake, Greenbrier, Hardaway and Haw River)

Serrated edge

G6, $12-$20
TN

G6, $20-$35
Meigs Co., TN

G6, $25-$40
Adams Co., MS

G6, $30-$50
Jackson Co., AL

G6, $25-$40
Jackson Co., AL

LOCATION: Midwestern to Eastern states and Florida. **DESCRIPTION:** A medium to large size, auriculate form with a concave base and drooping to expanding auricles. Many examples are serrated, some are fluted on both sides, and all have basal grinding. Resharpened examples are usually beveled on the right side of each face although left side beveling does occur. Thinness and high quality flaking is evident on many examples. This early type spread over most the U.S. and strongly influenced many other types to follow. **I.D. KEY:** Expanded auricles.

DALTON GREENBRIER (continued)

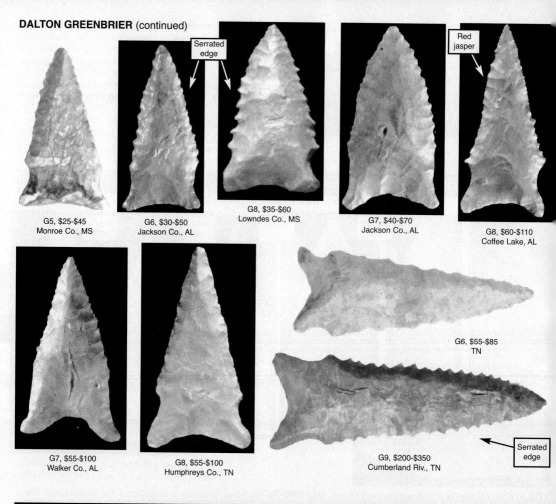

Serrated edge

G5, $25-$45
Monroe Co., MS

G6, $30-$50
Jackson Co., AL

G8, $35-$60
Lowndes Co., MS

G7, $40-$70
Jackson Co., AL

Red jasper

G8, $60-$110
Coffee Lake, AL

G7, $55-$100
Walker Co., AL

G8, $55-$100
Humphreys Co., TN

G6, $55-$85
TN

G9, $200-$350
Cumberland Riv., TN

Serrated edge

DALTON-HEMPHILL - Early Archaic, 10,000 - 9200 B. P.

(Also see Cave Spring, Hardaway and Holland)

Tip nick

Serrated edge

G5, $30-$50
Humphreys Co., TN

G8, $150-$260
KY

G8, $350-$650
Obion Co., TN

Basal thinning strikes

G8, $250-$475
Henry Co., TN

Dover chert

Serrated edge

380

LOCATION: Midwestern to Eastern states. **DESCRIPTION:** A medium to large size point with expanded auricles and horizontal, tapered to weak shoulders. Blade edges are usually serrated and bases are ground. In later times, this variant developed into the *Hemphill* point. **I.D. KEY:** Straightened extended shoulders.

G7, $250-$450
S. W. KY

DALTON-NUCKOLLS - Early Archaic, 10,000 - 9200 B. P.

(Also see Dalton-Colbert and Hardaway)

E
C

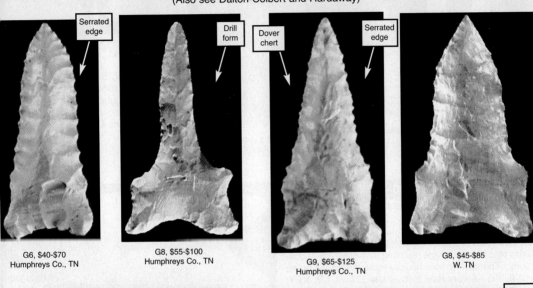

G6, $40-$70
Humphreys Co., TN

G8, $55-$100
Humphreys Co., TN

G9, $65-$125
Humphreys Co., TN

G8, $45-$85
W. TN

G8, $55-$100
Humphreys Co., TN

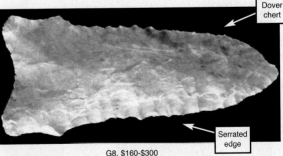

G8, $160-$300
Humphreys Co., TN

G8, $275-$500
Barkley Lake, KY

LOCATION: Midwestern to Southeastern states. Type site is in Humphreys Co., TN. **DESCRIPTION:** A medium to large size variant form, probably occuring from resharpening the Greenbrier Dalton. Bases are squared to lobbed to eared, and have a shallow concavity. **I.D. KEY:** Broad base and shoulders, flaking on blade.

DAMRON - Early to Middle Archaic, 8000 - 4000 B. P.

(Also see Autauga, Ecusta, Gibson, Palmer and St. Charles)

G6, $8-$15
S.E. TN

G7, $15-$25
Limestone Co., AL

G7, $15-$30
Humphreys Co., TN

G5, $15-$25
Limestone Co., AL

G4, $3-$6
Fayette Co., AL

G6, $12-$20
Sou. AL

G6, $12-$20
Dunlap, TN

LOCATION: Southeastern states. **DESCRIPTION:** A small to medium size, triangular, side-notched point with a wide, prominent, convex to straight base. **I.D. KEY:** Basal form.

DEBERT- Paleo, 11,000 - 9500 B. P.

(Also see Clovis and Dalton)

LOCATION: Northeastern to Eastern states. **DESCRIPTION:** A medium to large size, thin, auriculate point that evolved from *Clovis*. Most examples are fluted twice on each face resulting in a deep basal concavity. The second flute usually removed traces of the first fluting. A very rare form of late *Clovis*. **I.D. KEY:** Deep basal notch.

G8, $1000-$1800
KY

Fluting channel

DECATUR - Early Archaic, 9000 - 3000 B. P.

(Also see Cobbs Triangular, Ecusta, Hardin, Kirk, Lost Lake, Palmer and St. Charles)

Beveled edge

Burinated tip

Fracture shoulder and base sides

G8, $55-$100
Hamilton Co., TN

All Decaturs have ground basal areas

Fractured base

Beveled edge

Beveled edge

Actual size photos of an excellent example found in Hamilton Co., TN. These oblique photos illustrate the fractured tangs, stem sides and base that occur on this type. In rare cases the tip is also fractured on both sides. Shoulder and base fracturing also occurs in Abbey, Dovetail, Kirk and other Archaic forms.

G3, $12-$20
Sullivan Co., TN

G6, $35-$60
KY

G5, $20-$35
Walker Co., AL

G6, $35-$60
Florence, AL

382

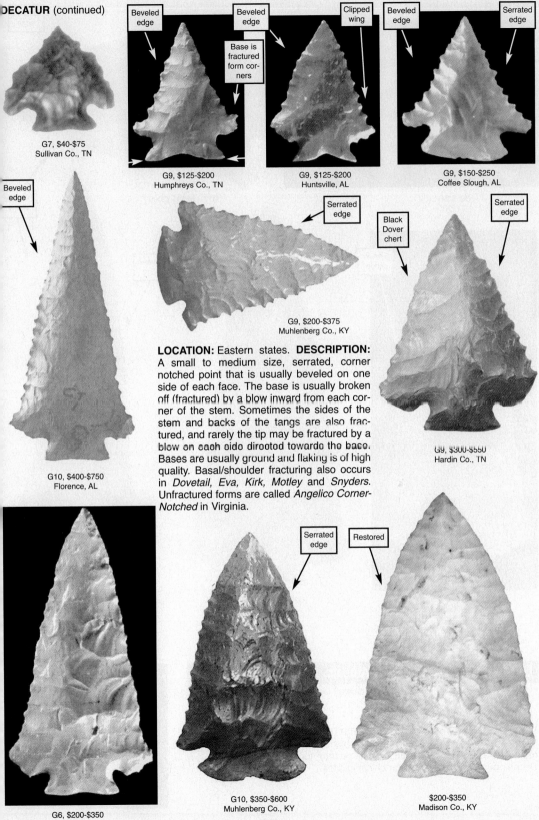

DECATUR (continued)

G7, $40-$75
Sullivan Co., TN

Beveled edge

Beveled edge

Base is fractured form corners

Clipped wing

Beveled edge

Serrated edge

G9, $125-$200
Humphreys Co., TN

G9, $125-$200
Huntsville, AL

G9, $150-$250
Coffee Slough, AL

Beveled edge

Serrated edge

Black Dover chert

Serrated edge

G9, $200-$375
Muhlenberg Co., KY

G9, $300-$550
Hardin Co., TN

G10, $400-$750
Florence, AL

E C

LOCATION: Eastern states. **DESCRIPTION:** A small to medium size, serrated, corner notched point that is usually beveled on one side of each face. The base is usually broken off (fractured) by a blow inward from each corner of the stem. Sometimes the sides of the stem and backs of the tangs are also fractured, and rarely the tip may be fractured by a blow on each side directed towards the base. Bases are usually ground and flaking is of high quality. Basal/shoulder fracturing also occurs in *Dovetail, Eva, Kirk, Motley* and *Snyders*. Unfractured forms are called *Angelico Corner-Notched* in Virginia.

Serrated edge

Restored

G6, $200-$350
OH

G10, $350-$600
Muhlenberg Co., KY

$200-$350
Madison Co., KY

DECATUR (continued)

Beveled edge

Serrated edge

Serrated edge

Serrated edge

Beveled edge

G9, $350-$650
KY

G10+, $1200-$2000
KY

G9, $1000-$1800
KY

G10+, $2000-$3500
KY

G9, $1200-$2200
Lauderdale Co., AL

DECATUR BLADE - Early Archaic, 9000 - 3000 B. P.

(Also see Hardaway Blade)

LOCATION: Eastern states. **DESCRIPTION:** A medium to large size, broad triangular blade with rounded corners and a straight base. A preform for *Decatur* points found on Decatur chipping sites.

G7, $5-$10
Morgan Co., AL. Found on a Decatur chipping site along with dozens of Decatur points.

DENTON - Woodland, 2500 - 1500 B. P.

(Also see Adena, Cresap, Gary, Morrow Mountain and Waubesa)

G6, $30-$50
Jefferson Co, MS

G6, $30-$50
Jefferson Co, MS

G4, $15-$25
Adams Co, MS

LOCATION: Southwestern Mississippi into southwestern Tennessee. **DESCRIPTION:** A medium to large size crudely flaked, thick point with barbed to tapered shoulders and a medium sized tapered to parallel sided to slightly expanding stem with rounded corners. **I.D. KEY:** Basal form.

DICKSON - Woodland, 2500 - 1500 B. P.

(Also see Adena, Cresap, Gary, Morrow Mountain and Waubesa)

G6 $5-$10
Meigs Co., TN

G7, $30-$50
KY

G6 $25-$40
KY

G8, $45-$80
AL

DICKSON (continued)

G9, $80-$150
KY

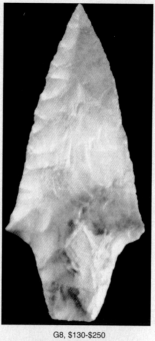

G8, $130-$250
OH

G9, $160-$300
OH

G9, $150-$275
OH

LOCATION: Midwestern states. Type site: Fulton Co., MO., Dickson mounds, Don F. Dickson, 1927. **DESCRIPTION:** A medium to large size point with tapered shoulders and a contracting stem. High quality flaking and thinness is evident on most examples. **I.D. KEY:** Basal form.

DOVETAIL (See St. Charles)

DRILL - Paleo to Historic, 14,000 - 200 B. P.

(Also see Addison Micro-Drill and Scraper)

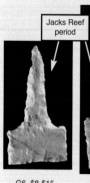

Jacks Reef period

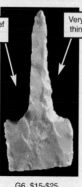

Very thin

G6, $8-$15
Humphreys Co., TN

G6, $15-$25
Humphreys Co., TN

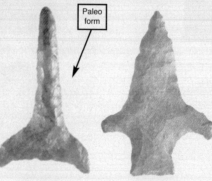

Paleo form

G6, $25-$40
OH

G6, $12-$20
KY

LOCATION: Everywhere. **DESCRIPTION:** Although many drills were made from scratch, all point types were made into the drill form. Usually, heavily resharpened and broken points were salvaged and rechipped into drills. These objects were certainly used as drills (evidence of extreme edge wear), but there is speculation that some of these forms may have been used as pins for clothing, ornaments, ear plugs and other uses.

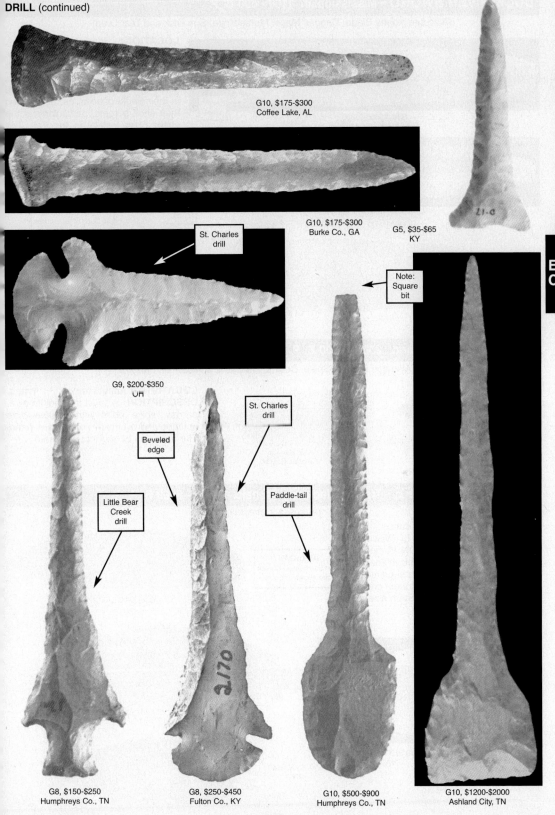

G10, $175-$300
Coffee Lake, AL

G10, $175-$300
Burke Co., GA

G5, $35-$65
KY

St. Charles
drill

Note:
Square
bit

E
C

G9, $200-$350
OH

Beveled
edge

St. Charles
drill

Little Bear
Creek
drill

Paddle-tail
drill

G8, $150-$250
Humphreys Co., TN

G8, $250-$450
Fulton Co., KY

G10, $500-$900
Humphreys Co., TN

G10, $1200-$2000
Ashland City, TN

DUCK RIVER SWORD - Mississippian, 1100 - 600 B. P.

(Also see Adena Blade, Dagger, Mace, Morse Knife, Sun Disk and Tear Drop)

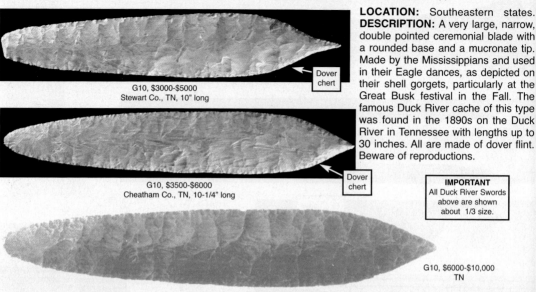

G10, $3000-$5000
Stewart Co., TN, 10" long

Dover chert

G10, $3500-$6000
Cheatham Co., TN, 10-1/4" long

Dover chert

LOCATION: Southeastern states. **DESCRIPTION:** A very large, narrow, double pointed ceremonial blade with a rounded base and a mucronate tip. Made by the Mississippians and used in their Eagle dances, as depicted on their shell gorgets, particularly at the Great Busk festival in the Fall. The famous Duck River cache of this type was found in the 1890s on the Duck River in Tennessee with lengths up to 30 inches. All are made of dover flint. Beware of reproductions.

IMPORTANT
All Duck River Swords above are shown about 1/3 size.

G10, $6000-$10,000
TN

DUVAL - Late Woodland, 2000 - 1000 B. P.

(Also see Bradley Spike, Collins, Fishspear & Mountain Fork)

G6, $20-$35
Bristol, TN

G6, $20-$35
Catoosa Co.,GA

LOCATION: Southeastern states. **DESCRIPTION:** A small to medium size, narrow, spike point with shallow side notches and a straight to concave base. The base can be slight to moderate.

EARLY OVOID KNIFE - Trans. Paleo-early Archaic, 11,000 - 8000 B. P.

(Also see Turkeytail)

LOCATION: Midwestern states from Kentucky, Arkansas north to Wisconsin and Michigan. **DESCRIPTION:** A medium to very large size, broad, thin blade that comes in two forms. It can be bi-pointed or it can have a small, rounded stem created by side notches. **I.D. KEY:** Stem size and blade form.

IMPORTANT
All Early Ovoid Knives are shown 1/2 size.

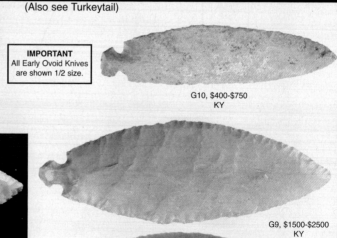

G10, $400-$750
KY

G9, $1500-$2500
KY

IMPORTANT
All Early Ovoid Knives are shown 1/2 size.

G10 $1200-$2000
KY

G10, $350-$650
KY

388

EASTERN STEMMED LANCEOLATE - Early Archaic, 9500 - 7000 B. P.

(Also see Alberta and Stringtown)

Upper Mercer chert

Impact fracture

Ground stem

G6, $50-$100
Washington Co., OH

Coshocton chert

G7, $150-$250
OH

G7, $125-$200
Delaware Co., OH

E C

LOCATION: Pennsylvania, Ohio westward. **DESCRIPTION:** A medium to large size, broad stemmed point with convex to parallel sides and square shoulders. The stem is parallel sided to slightly expanding. The hafting area is ground. Most examples have horizontal to oblique parallel flaking and are of high quality and thinness. The Eastern form of the *Scottsbluff* type made by the Cody Complex people. The *Stringtown* is an eared version of this type. **I.D. KEY:** Base form and parallel flaking.

EBENEZER - Woodland, 2000 - 1500 B. P.

(Also see Buggs Island, Gary, Montgomery and Morrow Mountain)

G5, $2-$4
Morgan Co., AL

G4, $2-$4
Dallas Co., AL

Milky quartz

G4, $2-$4
Dallas Co., AL

Milky quartz

G4, $2-$4
Dallas Co., AL

LOCATION: Southeastern states. **DESCRIPTION:** A small size, broad, triangular point with a short, rounded stem. Some are round base triangles with no stem. Shoulders are tapered to square. Very similar to the earlier *Morrow Mountain Round Base* but with random Woodland chipping. Related to *Candy Creek, Camp Creek* and *Nolichucky*.

ECUSTA - Early Archaic, 8000 - 5000 B. P.

(Also see Autauga, Brewerton, Damron, Decatur and Palmer)

Vein quartz

G7, $5-$10
Dalton, GA

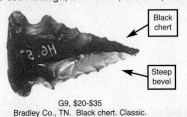

Black chert

Steep bevel

G9, $20-$35
Bradley Co., TN. Black chert. Classic.

LOCATION: Southeastern states. **DESCRIPTION:** A small size, serrated, side-notched point with usually one side of each face steeply beveled. Although examples exist with all four sides beveled and flaked to a median ridge. The base and notches are ground. Very similar to *Autauga*, with the latter being corner-notched and not beveled.

ECUSTA (continued)

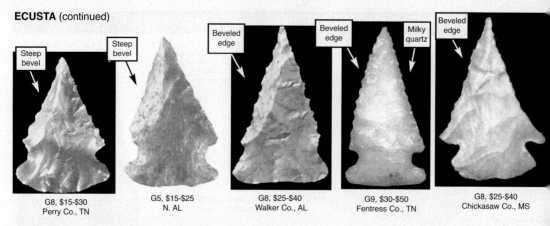

Steep bevel

Steep bevel

Beveled edge

Beveled edge

Milky quartz

Beveled edge

G8, $15-$30
Perry Co., TN

G5, $15-$25
N. AL

G8, $25-$40
Walker Co., AL

G9, $30-$50
Fentress Co., TN

G8, $25-$40
Chickasaw Co., MS

ELK RIVER - Early Archaic, 8000 - 5000 B. P.

(Also see Benton and Buzzard Roost Creek)

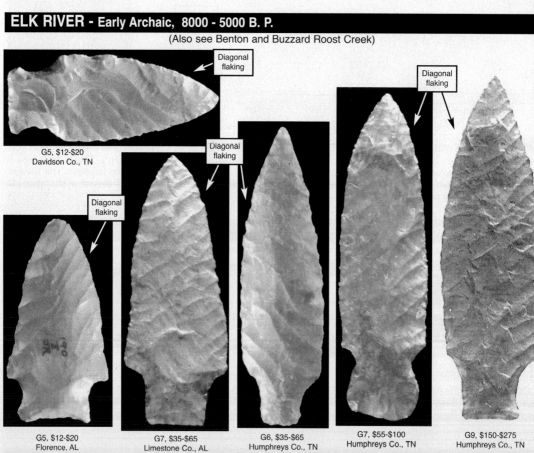

Diagonal flaking

Diagonal flaking

Diagonal flaking

Diagonal flaking

Diagonal flaking

G5, $12-$20
Davidson Co., TN

G5, $12-$20
Florence, AL

G7, $35-$65
Limestone Co., AL

G6, $35-$65
Humphreys Co., TN

G7, $55-$100
Humphreys Co., TN

G9, $150-$275
Humphreys Co., TN

G7, $200-$350
Parsons, TN

ELK RIVER (continued)

LOCATION: Southeastern states. **DESCRIPTION:** A medium to large size, narrow, stemmed blade with oblique parallel flaking. Shoulders are tapered, straight or barbed. Stems are parallel, contracting, expanding, bulbous or bifurcated. Believed to be related to *Benton* points. **I.D. KEY:** Squared base, diagonal parallel flaking.

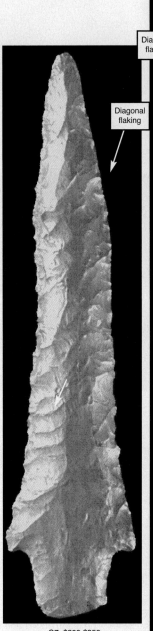

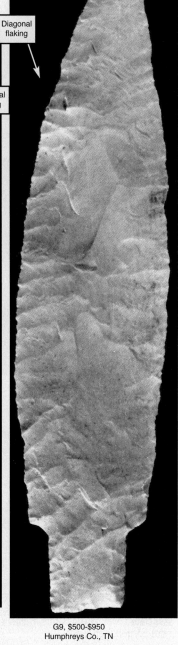

Diagonal flaking

Diagonal flaking

Diagonal flaking

Diagonal flaking

G7, $80-$150
Humphreys Co., TN

G7, $125-$200
Humphreys Co., TN

G7, $200-$350
Humphreys Co., TN

G9, $500-$950
Humphreys Co., TN

ELORA - Middle to Late Archaic, 6000 - 3000 B. P.

(Also see Maples, Morrow Mountain, Pickwick, Savannah River and Shoals Creek)

LOCATION: Southeastern states. **DESCRIPTION:** A medium size, broad, thick point with tapered shoulders and a short, contracting stem that is sometimes fractured or snapped off. However, some examples have finished bases. Early examples are serrated. **I.D. KEY:** One barb sharper, edgework.

G4, $2-$5
Polk Co., TN

ELORA (continued)

G4, $2-$5
W. TN

G4, $2-$5
Bartow Co., GA

Milky
quartz

G5, $4-$8
GA

Classic
rind
base

Note fine
serrations

G6, $25-$40
GA

G7, $15-$30
GA

G9, $30-$50
GA

EPPS - Late Archaic to Woodland, 4500 - 2500 B. P.

(Also see Buck Creek, Smithsonia, Motley, Snyders)

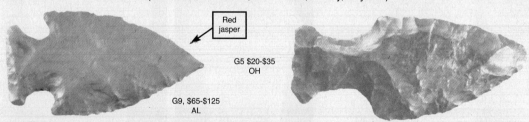

Red
jasper

G5 $20-$35
OH

G9, $65-$125
AL

LOCATION: Southeastern states. **DESCRIPTION:** A Motley variant. A medium to large size, expanded stemmed to widely corner notched point with strong barbs. The blade edges and the base are convex to straight. Has been found associated with *Wade* points in caches. Similar to *Epps* found in Louisiana which has a straight base; *Motley*s are more barbed than *Epps*.

ETLEY - Late Archaic, 4000 - 2500 B. P.

(Also see Hardin, Mehlville, Pickwick and Stilwell)

**IMPOR-
TANT:**
Etley shown
half size

G8, $200-$350
Dekalb Co., IN

LOCATION: Midwestern states. **DESCRIPTION:** A large size, narrow point with barbed shoulders, recurved blade edges and an expanding stem. **I.D. KEY:** One barb sharper edgework.

(Also see Hamilton Stemmed and Wade)

G4, $12-$20
TN

G6, $20-$35
Humphreys Co., TN

Black Dover chert

G6, $20-$35
KY

G8, $30-$50
W. TN

E
C

G6, $40-$75
TN

Early col-lateral flak-ing

G8, $65-$125
TN

G8, $65-$125
KY

G9, $150-$250
TN

G8, $125-$200
TN

G9, $90-$175
Giles Co., TN

LOCATION: West Tennessee to SW Kentucky. Type site, Eva island in Humphreys Co., TN. **DESCRIPTION:** A medium to large size, triangular point with shallow basal notches, recurved sides and sometimes flaring barbs. Early examples show parallel flaking. A large Eva cache was found that included a Pickwick point. **I.D. KEY:** Basal notches, Archaic flaking.

G8, $800-$1500
Humphreys Co., TN, Eva site

EVANS - Late Archaic to Woodland, 4000 - 2000 B. P.

(Also see Benton, Leighton, Merkle, Ohio Double-Notched, St. Helena, St. Tammany & Turkeytail)

G5, $15-$25
Florence, AL

G5, $12-$20
Natchez, MS

G5, $15-$25
MS

G6, $25-$45
Natchez, MS

G6, $20-$35
MS

G9, $65-$125
Choctaw Co., AL

G10, $50-$90
Adams Co., MS

LOCATION: Midwestern to Southeastern states. **DESCRIPTION:** A medium to large size stemmed point that is notched on each side somewhere between the point and shoulders. A similar form is found in Ohio and called *Ohio Double-Notched.*

EXOTIC FORMS - Mid-Archaic to Mississippian, 5000 - 1000 B. P.

LOCATION: Throughout North America. **DESCRIPTION:** The forms illustrated on this and the following pages are very rare. Some are definitely effigy forms while others may be no more than unfinished and unintentional doodles.

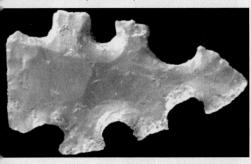

G9, $125-$225
N. TN

G7, $65-$125
Lauderdale Co., AL

FAIRLAND - Woodland, 3000 - 1500 B. P.

(Also see Bakers Creek, Hardaway, Johnson, Limestone and Steubenville)

LOCATION: Texas, Arkansas, and Mississippi. **DESCRIPTION:** A small to medium size, thin, expanded stem point with a concave base that is usually thinned. Shoulders can be weak and tapered to sightly barbed. **I.D. KEY:** Basal form, systematic form of flaking.

E
C

G6, $12-$20
MS

G6, $15-$25
Linden, TN

FISHSPEAR - Early to Middle Archaic, 9000 - 4000 B. P.

(Also see Duval and Table Rock)

G5, $12-$20
S.E. TN

G5, $12-$20
TN

G7, $30-$50
W. TN

G8, $35-$60
OH

LOCATION: Eastern states. **DESCRIPTION:** A medium to large size, narrow, thick, point with wide side notches. Bases are usually ground and blade edges can be serrated. Named due to its appearance that resembles a fish.

G9, $80-$150
Tallahatchie Co., MS

G9, $90-$165
Parsons, TN

G9, $125-$225
West TN

FLINT CREEK - Late Archaic to Woodland, 3500 - 1000 B. P.

(Also see Cotaco Creek, Elora, Kirk Stemmed, Mud Creek and Pontchartrain)

LOCATION: Southeastern and Gulf states. **DESCRIPTION:** A medium to large size, narrow, thick, serrated, expanded stem point. Shoulders can be horizontal, tapered or barbed. Base can be expanded, parallel sided or rounded. **I.D. KEY:** Thickness and flaking near point.

FLINT CREEK (continued)

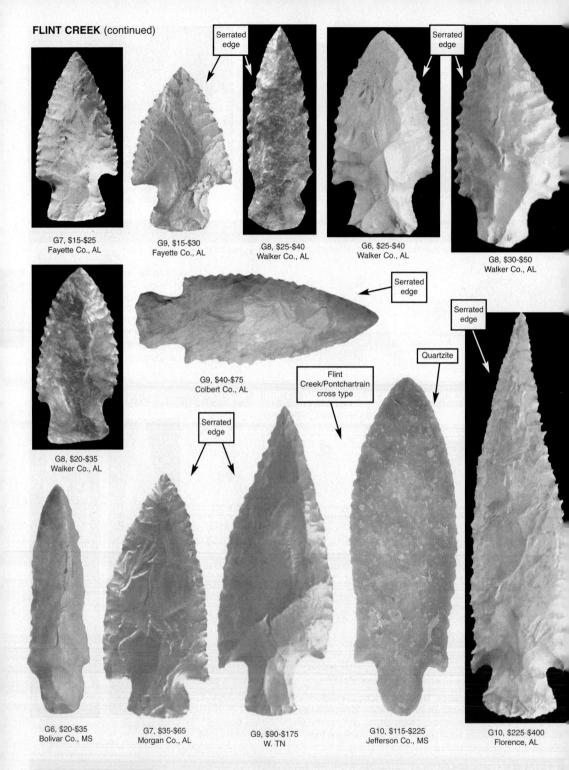

Serrated edge

G7, $15-$25
Fayette Co., AL

G9, $15-$30
Fayette Co., AL

G8, $25-$40
Walker Co., AL

Serrated edge

G6, $25-$40
Walker Co., AL

Serrated edge

G8, $30-$50
Walker Co., AL

Serrated edge

G8, $20-$35
Walker Co., AL

G9, $40-$75
Colbert Co., AL

Serrated edge

Flint Creek/Pontchartrain cross type

Quartzite

Serrated edge

G6, $20-$35
Bolivar Co., MS

G7, $35-$65
Morgan Co., AL

G9, $90-$175
W. TN

G10, $115-$225
Jefferson Co., MS

G10, $225-$400
Florence, AL

FLINT RIVER SPIKE   (see McWhinney Heavy Stemmed)

FORT ANCIENT - Mississippian to Historic, 800 - 400 B. P.

(Also see Hamilton, Madison and Sand Mountain)

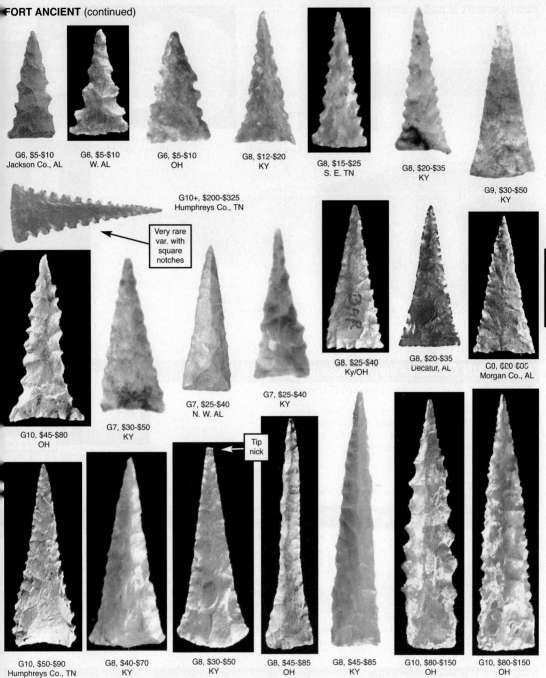

G6, $5-$10
Jackson Co., AL

G6, $5-$10
W. AL

G6, $5-$10
OH

G8, $12-$20
KY

G8, $15-$25
S. E. TN

G8, $20-$35
KY

G9, $30-$50
KY

G10+, $200-$325
Humphreys Co., TN

Very rare
var. with
square
notches

E
C

G8, $25-$40
Ky/OH

G8, $20-$35
Decatur, AL

G0, $20 $05
Morgan Co., AL

G10, $45-$80
OH

G7, $30-$50
KY

G7, $25-$40
N. W. AL

G7, $25-$40
KY

Tip
nick

G10, $50-$90
Humphreys Co., TN

G8, $40-$70
KY

G8, $30-$50
KY

G8, $45-$85
OH

G8, $45-$85
KY

G10, $80-$150
OH

G10, $80-$150
OH

LOCATION: Southeastern states into Ohio. **DESCRIPTION:** A small to medium size, thin, narrow, long, triangular point with concave sides and a straight to slightly convex or concave base. Some examples are strongly serrated or notched. **I.D. KEY:** Edgework.

FORT ANCIENT BLADE - Mississippian to Historic, 800 - 400 B. P.

(Also see Copena)

LOCATION: Eastern to Southeastern states. **DESCRIPTION:** A medium size triangular blade with a squared base. Blade edges expand to meet the base **I.D. KEY:** Basal form.

FORT ANCIENT BLADE (continued)

G8, $45-$85
Mason Co., KY

Red, yellow & blue Horse Creek chert

Thin cross section

G8, $50-$90
Whitwell, TN

G6, $65-$125
Coffee Lake, AL

G5 $15-$30
N.E. AL

FOUNTAIN CREEK - Early Archaic, 9000 - 7000 B. P.

(Also see Kirk Stemmed)

LOCATION: North Carolina into east Tennessee.
DESCRIPTION: A medium size, narrow point with notched blade edges and a short, rounded base which is ground. **I.D. KEY:** Edgework.

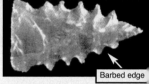

G10, $20-$35
Dayton, TN

Barbed edge

FOX VALLEY   (See Kanawha for a similar type found in Ky, TN, AL to WVA)

FRAZIER - Middle to Late Archaic, 7000 - 3000 B. P.

(Also see Big Sandy, Copena and Stanfield)

Black flint

G9, $25-$40
W. TN

LOCATION: Southeastern states. **DESCRIPTION:** A generally narrow, medium to large size lanceolate blade with a slightly concave to straight base. Flaking technique and shape is identical to that of *Big Sandy* points (minus the notches) and is found on *Big Sandy* sites. Could this type be unnotched *Big Sandy's*? **I.D. KEY:** Archaic flaking.

FREDERICK - Early to Middle Archaic, 9000 - 4000 B. P.

(Also see Cave Spring, Fox Valley, Garth Slough, Jude, Kanawha, Kirk, LeCroy, Rice Lobbed and Stanly)

Shoulder nick

G4, $8-$15
TN

G5, $12-$20
Walker Co., GA

G6, $20-$35
Cookeville, TN. Classic form.

398

FREDERICK (continued)

LOCATION: Southeastern states. **DESCRIP-TION:** A small to medium size point with flaring, up-lifting shou- lders and an extended narrow bifurcated base. A variation of the *Fox Valley* type. In the classic form, shoulders are almost bulbous and exaggerated.

G7, $40-$75
S.E. TN. Classic form.

GARTH SLOUGH - Early Archaic, 9000 - 4000 B. P.

(Also see Frederick, Jude, Kanawha and Stanly)

G7, $25-$40
AL

G8, $25-$40
W. TN

G9, $30-$55
Morgan Co., AL

Drooping shoulders

G9, $75-$140
Humphreys Co., TN

Knobbed shoulders

G8, $25-$45
Morgan Co., AL

G7, $35-$60
Morgan Co., AL

G10, $85-$160
Morgan Co., AL. Classic.

G9, $85-$160
Walker Co., AL

E C

GIBSON - Woodland, 2000 - 1500 B. P.

(Also see Hopewell, St. Charles and Snyders)

G6, $35-$65
Trimble Co., KY

G7, $35-$65
KY

LOCATION: Midwestern to Eastern states. Type site is in Calhoun Co., Illinois. **DESCRIPTION:** A medium to large size side to corner notched point with a large, convex base. The base is typically broader than the blade. Made by the *Snyders* people. **I.D. KEY:** Short, broad base.

GIBSON (continued)

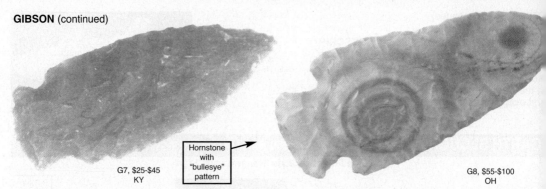

G7, $25-$45
KY

Hornstone with "bullesye" pattern

G8, $55-$100
OH

LOCATION: Southeastern states. **DESCRIPTION:** A small size point with wide, expanded barbs and a small square base. Rare examples have the tangs clipped (called clipped wing). The blade edges are concave with fine serrations. A similar type of a later time period, called *Catahoula,* is found in Louisiana. A bifurcated base would place it into the *Kanawha* type. **I.D. KEY:** Expanded barbs, early flaking.

GRAHAM CAVE - Early to Mid-Archaic, 9000 - 5000 B. P.

(Also see Big Sandy, Newton Falls)

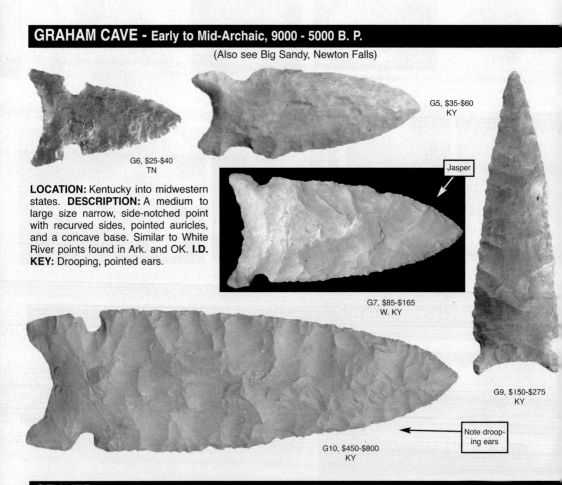

G5, $35-$60
KY

G6, $25-$40
TN

Jasper

LOCATION: Kentucky into midwestern states. **DESCRIPTION:** A medium to large size narrow, side-notched point with recurved sides, pointed auricles, and a concave base. Similar to White River points found in Ark. and OK. **I.D. KEY:** Drooping, pointed ears.

G7, $85-$165
W. KY

G9, $150-$275
KY

G10, $450-$800
KY

Note drooping ears

GRAVER - Paleo to Archaic, 11,500 - 4000 B. P.

(Also see Perforator and Scraper)

LOCATION: Found on Paleo and Archaic sites throughout North America. **DESCRIPTION:** An irregular shaped uni face tool with sharp, pointed projections used for puncturing, incising, tattooing, etc. Some examples served a dual purpose for scraping as well. In later times, *Perforators* took the place of *Gravers*.

GRAVER (continued)

Graver points

G5, $8-$15
Humphreys Co., TN

G6, $20-$40
Humphreys Co., TN

GREENBRIER - Early Archaic, 9500 - 6000 B. P.

(Also see Brunswick, Dalton-Greenbrier, Hardaway and Pine Tree)

E C

Serrated edge

Dover chert

Thinning strikes

Needle tip

Dover chert

G9, $90-$175
TN

G8, $125-$200
Humphreys Co., TN

G9, $150-$250
Hardin Co., KY

G9, $90-$175
Humphreys Co., TN

G10, $150-$275
Parsons, TN

Thinning strikes

Serrated edge

Serrated edge

G9, $150-$275
KY

G10, $150-$275
Coffee Lake, AL

Serrated edge

Fort Payne Chert

Flute channel

G10, $300-$550
KY

Black Dover chert

G9, $250-$400
W. TN

LOCATION: Southeastern states. **DESCRIPTION:** A medium to large size, auriculate point with tapered shoulders and broad, weak side notches. Blade edges are usually finely serrated. The base can be concave, lobbed, eared, straight or bifurcated and is ground. Early examples can be fluted. This type developed from the *Dalton* point and later evolved into other types such as the *Pine Tree* point. **I.D. KEY:** Heavy grinding in shoulders, good secondary edge-work.

401

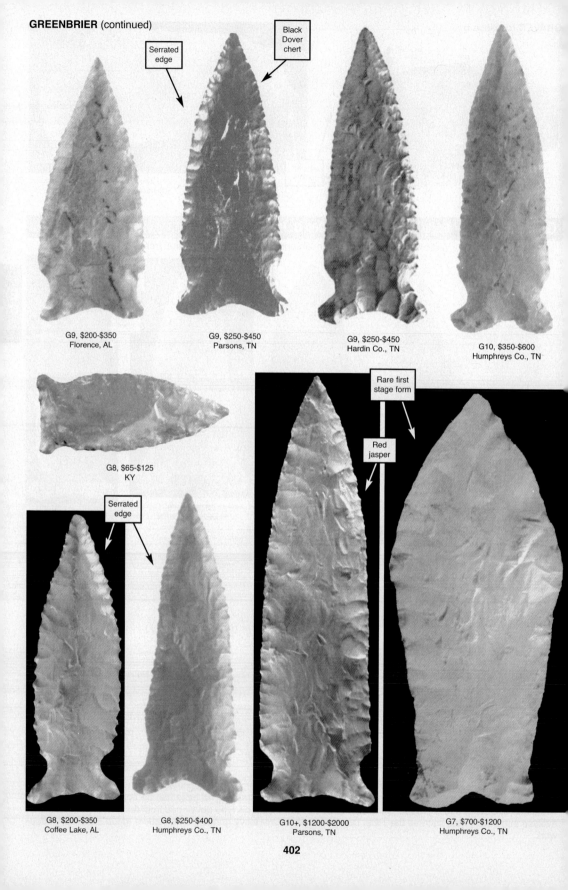

Serrated edge

Black Dover chert

G9, $200-$350
Florence, AL

G9, $250-$450
Parsons, TN

G9, $250-$450
Hardin Co., TN

G10, $350-$600
Humphreys Co., TN

G8, $65-$125
KY

Serrated edge

Rare first stage form

Red jasper

G8, $200-$350
Coffee Lake, AL

G8, $250-$400
Humphreys Co., TN

G10+, $1200-$2000
Parsons, TN

G7, $700-$1200
Humphreys Co., TN

GREENEVILLE - Woodland, 3000 - 1500 B. P.

(Also see Camp Creek, Guntersville, Madison and Nolichucky)

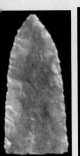

G6, $12-$20
E. KY

G6, $12-$20
Hamilton Co., TN

G8, $20-$35
Humphreys Co., TN

G8, $20-$35
E. TN

G8, $25-$40
Dayton, TN

G9, $45-$85
Humphreys Co., TN

LOCATION: Southeastern states. **DESCRIPTION:** A small to medium size lanceolate point with convex sides becoming contracting to parallel at the base. The basal edge is slightly concave, convex, or straight. This point is usually wider and thicker than *Guntersville*, and is believed to be related to *Camp Creek, Ebenezer* and *Nolichucky* points.

GUILFORD-ROUND BASE - Middle Archaic, 6500 - 5000 B. P.

(Also see Cobbs, Copena Round, Lerma & Morrow Mountain Round)

G6, $20-$35
Jessamine Co., KY

G6, $20-$35
Polk Co., TN

LOCATION: North Carolina and surrounding areas into East Tennessee and Georgia. **DESCRIPTION:** A medium to large size, thick, narrow, lanceolate point with a convex, contracting base. This type is usually made of Quartzite or other poor quality flaking material which results in a more crudely chipped form than *Lerma* (its ancestor). **I.D. KEY:** Thickness, archaic blade flaking.

GUNTERSVILLE - Mississippian to Historic, 700 - 200 B. P.

(Also see Camp Creek, Greeneville, Madison and Nodena)

G6, $8-$15
Meigs Co., TN

G5, $5-$10
Adams Co., MS

G5, $5-$10
Meigs Co., TN

G6, $15-$25
Dayton, TN

G6, $15-$25
Coffee Lk., AL

G6, $20-$35
Cherokee Co., AL

G9, $20-$35
IN

G9, $25-$45
TN

G10, $40-$70
Hardin Co., TN

E C

GUNTERSVILLE (continued)

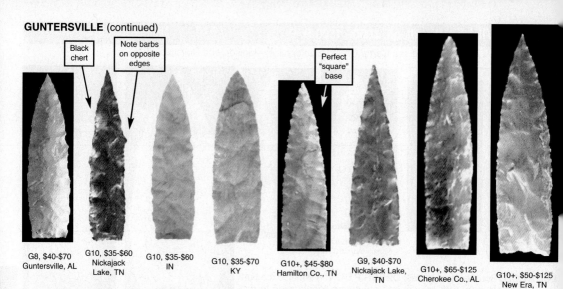

Black chert

Note barbs on opposite edges

Perfect "square" base

G8, $40-$70
Guntersville, AL

G10, $35-$60
Nickajack Lake, TN

G10, $35-$60
IN

G10, $35-$70
KY

G10+, $45-$80
Hamilton Co., TN

G9, $40-$70
Nickajack Lake, TN

G10+, $65-$125
Cherokee Co., AL

G10+, $50-$125
New Era, TN

LOCATION: Southeastern states. **DESCRIPTION:** A small to medium size, thin, narrow, lanceolate point with usually a straight base. Flaking quality is excellent. Formerly called *Dallas* points. **I.D. KEY:** Narrowness & blade expansion.

HALIFAX - Middle to Late Archaic, 6000 - 3000 B. P.

(Also see Bakers Creek, Jude, Rheems Creek and Swan Lake)

G5, $2-$3
Jassamine Co., KY

G5, $2-$3
Hinds Co., MS

G4, $2-$3
Hinds Co., MS

G5, $2-$3
Leflore Co., MS

G6, $2-$5
Jassamine Co., KY

G5, $4-$8
Jassamine Co., KY

G6, $4-$8
Jassamine Co., KY

G6, $5-$10
Walker Co., AL

G6, $5-$10
S. E. TN

G6, $5-$10
Jassamine Co., KY

G6, $5-$10
Hamilton Co., TN

LOCATION: Southeastern states. **DESCRIPTION:** A small to medium size, narrow, side notched to expanded stemmed point. Shoulders can be weak to strongly tapered. Typically one shoulder is higher than the other. North Carolina examples are made of quartz, rhyolite and shale.

HAMILTON - Woodland to Mississippian, 1600 - 1000 B. P.

(Also see Camp Creek, Fort Ancient, Madison and Sand Mountain)

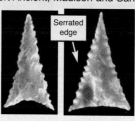
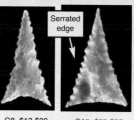
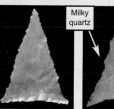

Serrated on one side

Serrated edge

Milky quartz

G8, $12-$20
Bradley Co., TN

G5, $5-$10
Hamilton Co., TN

G5, $8-$15
Bradley Co., TN

G8, $12-$20
Hamilton Co., TN

G10, $30-$50
Morgan Co., AL

G8, $15-$30
Limestone Co., AL

G9, $20-$35
Burke Co., GA

404

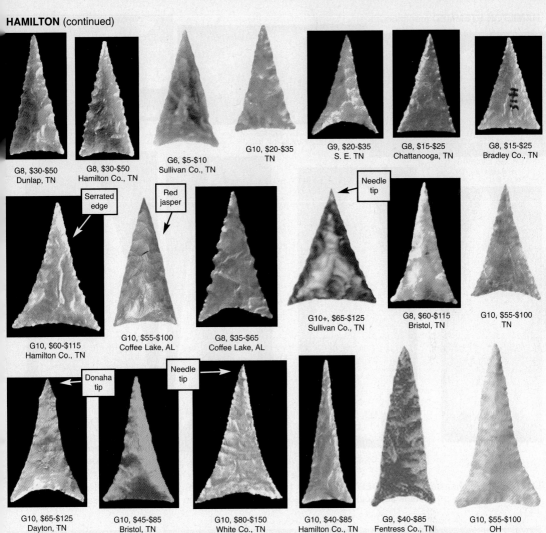

G8, $30-$50
Dunlap, TN

G8, $30-$50
Hamilton Co., TN

G6, $5-$10
Sullivan Co., TN

G10, $20-$35
TN

G9, $20-$35
S. E. TN

G8, $15-$25
Chattanooga, TN

G8, $15-$25
Bradley Co., TN

Serrated
edge

Red
jasper

Needle
tip

G10, $60-$115
Hamilton Co., TN

G10, $55-$100
Coffee Lake, AL

G8, $35-$65
Coffee Lake, AL

G10+, $65-$125
Sullivan Co., TN

G8, $60-$115
Bristol, TN

G10, $55-$100
TN

Donaha
tip

Needle
tip

G10, $65-$125
Dayton, TN

G10, $45-$85
Bristol, TN

G10, $80-$150
White Co., TN

G10, $40-$85
Hamilton Co., TN

G9, $40-$85
Fentress Co., TN

G10, $55-$100
OH

LOCATION: Southeastern states. **DESCRIPTION:** A small to medium size triangular point with concave sides and base. Many examples are very thin, of the highest quality, and with serrated edges. Side edges can also be straight. This type is believed to have evolved from *Camp Creek* points. Called *Uwharrie* in North Carolina. Some North Carolina and Tennessee examples have special constricted tips called *Donnaha Tips.*

HAMILTON-STEMMED - Late Woodland to Mississippian, 3000 - 1000 B. P.

(Also see Buck Creek, Motley, Rankin, Smithsonia and Wade)

Chalcedony

G4, $8-$15
Fentress Co., TN

G5, $20-$35
Putnam Co., TN

G9, $55-$100
Pulaski Co., KY

HAMILTON STEMMED (continued)

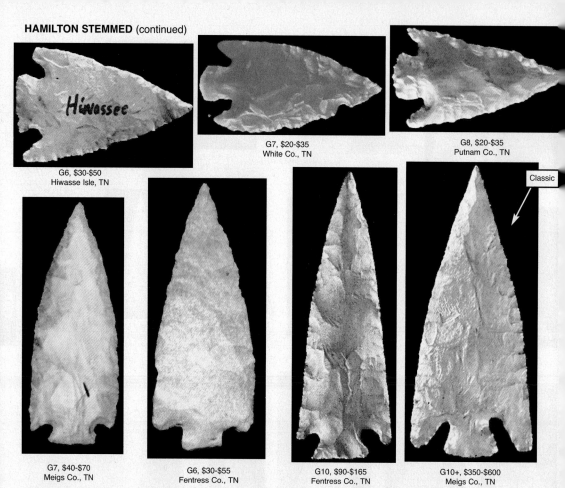

G6, $30-$50
Hiwasse Isle, TN

G7, $20-$35
White Co., TN

G8, $20-$35
Putnam Co., TN

Classic

G7, $40-$70
Meigs Co., TN

G6, $30-$55
Fentress Co., TN

G10, $90-$165
Fentress Co., TN

G10+, $350-$600
Meigs Co., TN

LOCATION: Southeastern states. **DESCRIPTION:** A medium to large size, barbed, expanded stem point. Most examples have a sharp needle like point, and the blade edges are convex to recurved. Called *Rankin* in Northeast Tenn.

HARAHEY - Mississippian, 700 - 350 B. P.

(Also see Lerma, Ramey Knife and Snake Creek)

G7, $80-$150
KY

LOCATION: Kentucky to Texas, Arkansas and Missouri. **DESCRIPTION:** A large size, double pointed knife that is usually beveled on one side of each face. The cross section is rhomboid.

HARDAWAY - Early Archaic, 9500 - 8000 B. P.

(Also see Alamance, Dalton-Greenbrier, Haw River, Russel Cave, San Patrice and Wheeler)

HARDAWAY (continued)

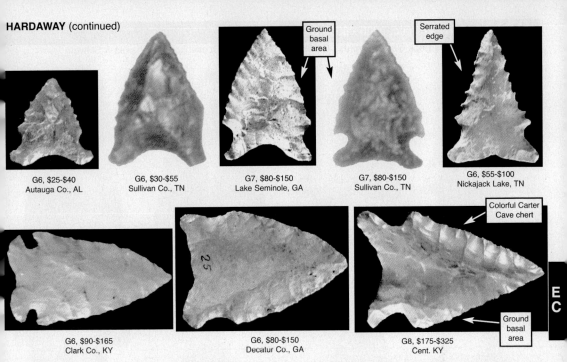

Ground basal area

Serrated edge

G6, $25-$40
Autauga Co., AL

G6, $30-$55
Sullivan Co., TN

G7, $80-$150
Lake Seminole, GA

G7, $80-$150
Sullivan Co., TN

G6, $55-$100
Nickajack Lake, TN

Colorful Carter Cave chert

Ground basal area

G6, $90-$165
Clark Co., KY

G6, $80-$150
Decatur Co., GA

G8, $175-$325
Cent. KY

LOCATION: Southeastern states. **DESCRIPTION:** A small to medium size point with shallow side notches and expanded auricles forming a wide, deeply concave base. Wide specimens are called *Cow Head Hardaways* by some collectors in North Carolina. Ears and base are usually heavily ground. This type evolved from the *Dalton* point. **I.D. KEY:** Heavy grinding in shoulders, paleo flaking.

HARDAWAY-DALTON - Early Archaic, 9500 - 8000 B. P.

(Also see Alamance and Dalton)

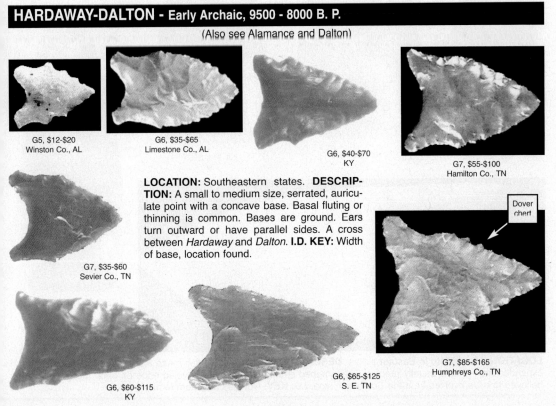

G5, $12-$20
Winston Co., AL

G6, $35-$65
Limestone Co., AL

G6, $40-$70
KY

G7, $55-$100
Hamilton Co., TN

G7, $35-$60
Sevier Co., TN

LOCATION: Southeastern states. **DESCRIPTION:** A small to medium size, serrated, auriculate point with a concave base. Basal fluting or thinning is common. Bases are ground. Ears turn outward or have parallel sides. A cross between *Hardaway* and *Dalton*. **I.D. KEY:** Width of base, location found.

Dover chert

G6, $60-$115
KY

G6, $65-$125
S. E. TN

G7, $85-$165
Humphreys Co., TN

(Also see Buck Creek, Cypress Creek, Kirk, Lost Lake, Scottsbluff, St. Charles & Stilwell)

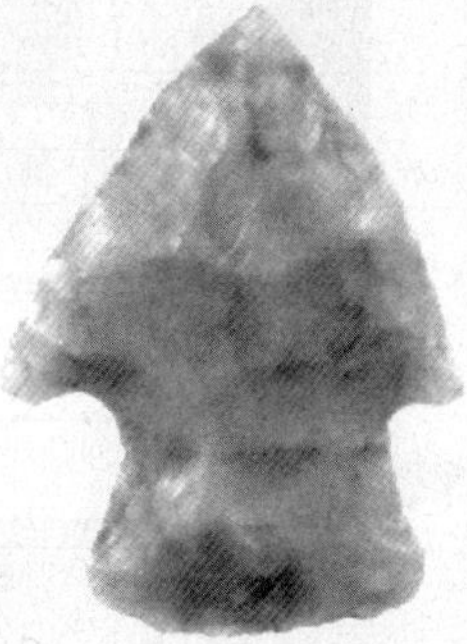

G6, $15-$25
OH

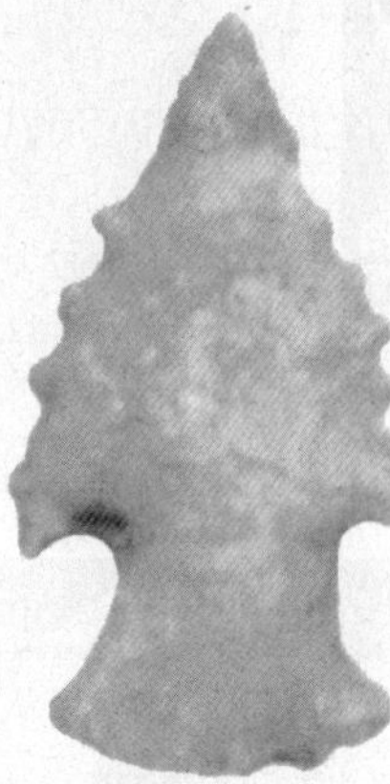

G7, $25-$45
OH

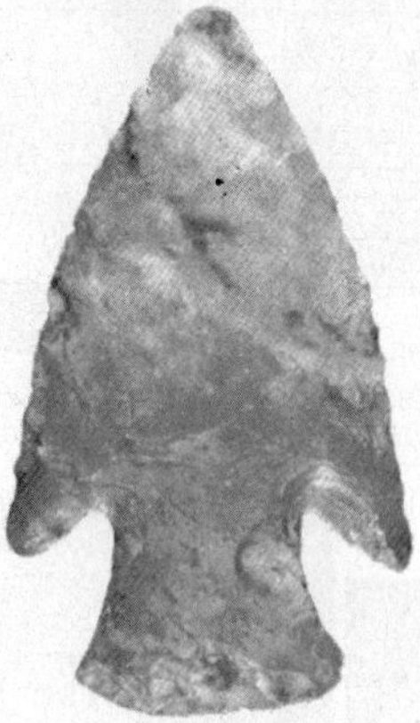

G8, $50-$90
Tishomingo Co., MS

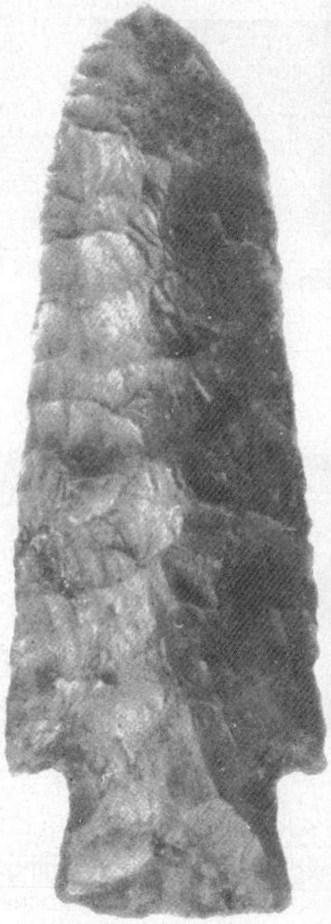

G8, $150-$250
IN

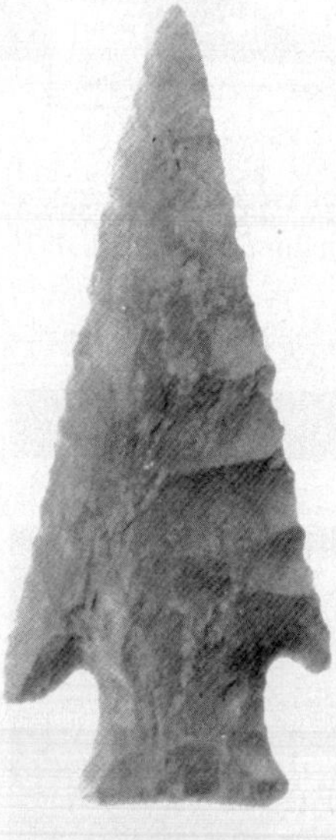

G9, $65-$125
KY

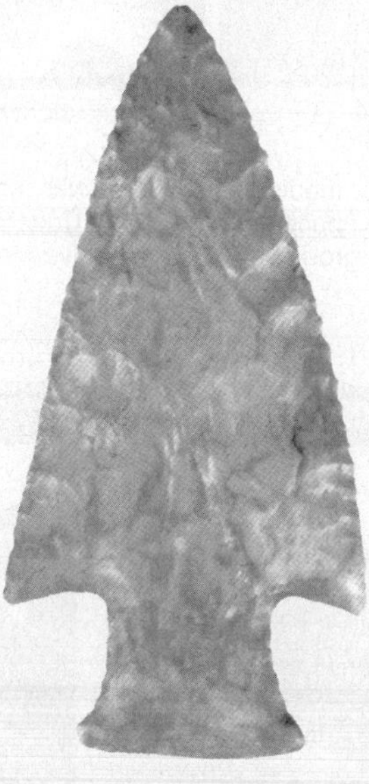

G10, $350-$650
MS

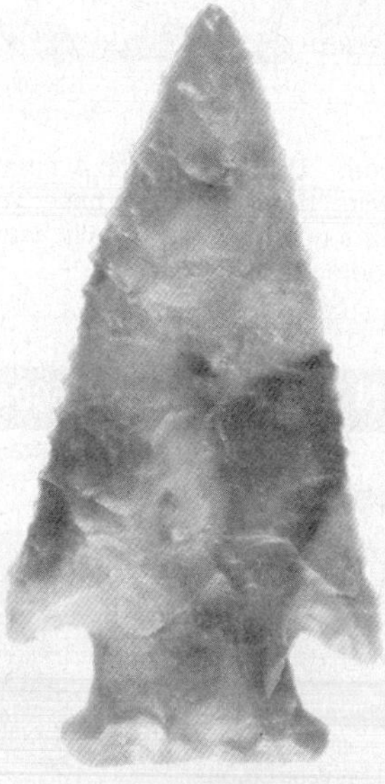

G9, $100-$250
IN

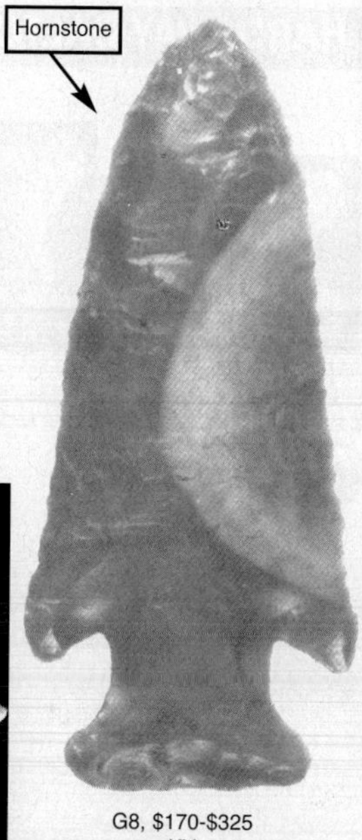

Hornstone

G8, $170-$325
KY

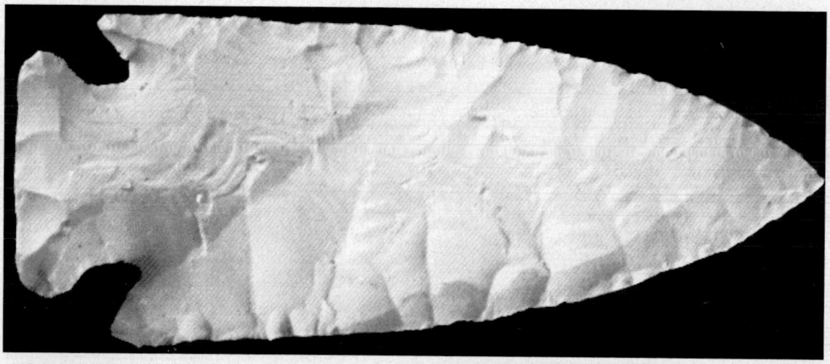

G9, $1700-$3000
OH

LOCATION: Midwestern to Eastern states. **DESCRIPTION:** A large size, well made triangular barbed point with an expanded base that is usually ground. Resharpened examples have one beveled edge on each face. This type is believed to have evolved from the *Scottsbluff* type. **I.D. KEY:** Notches and stem form.

HARDIN (continued)

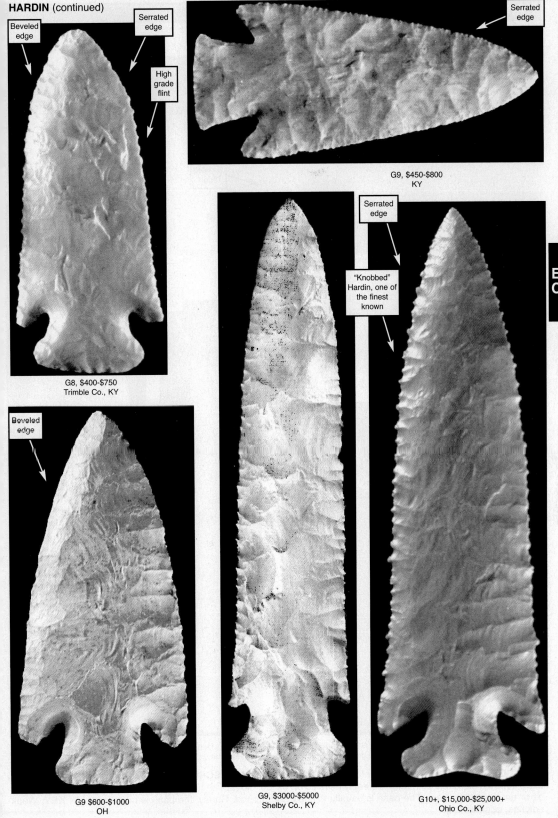

Beveled edge

Serrated edge

High grade flint

Serrated edge

Serrated edge

"Knobbed" Hardin, one of the finest known

Beveled edge

G9, $450-$800
KY

G8, $400-$750
Trimble Co., KY

G9 $600-$1000
OH

G9, $3000-$5000
Shelby Co., KY

G10+, $15,000-$25,000+
Ohio Co., KY

EC

409

HARPETH RIVER - Early Archaic, 9000 - 8000 B. P.

(Also see Bakers Cr., Cypress Cr., Dalton-Nuckolls, Mud Creek, Russell Cave and Searcy)

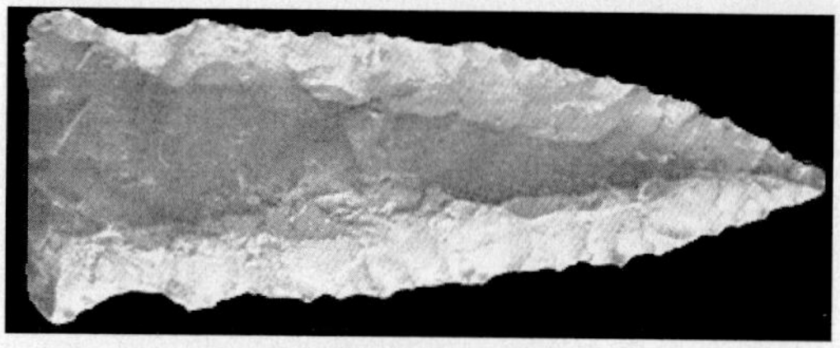

G6, $35-$65
Davidson Co., TN

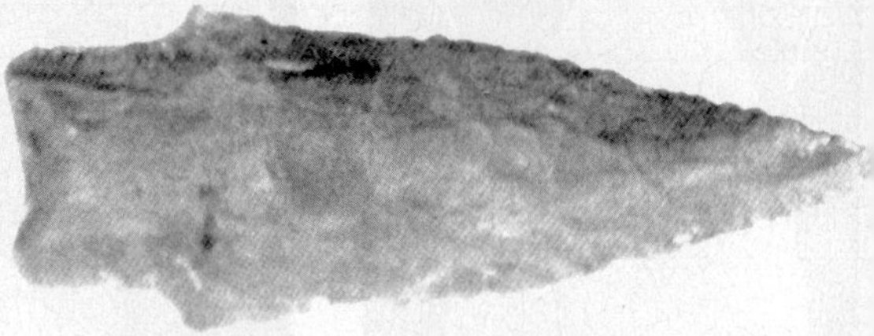

G8, $40-$75
TN

Serrated
edge

G10, $300-$550
TN

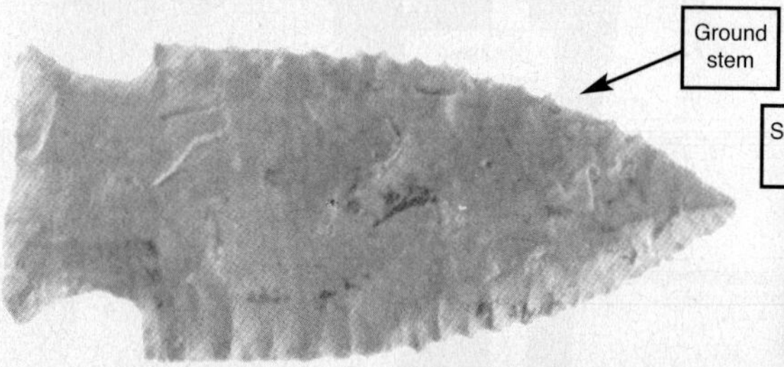

Ground
stem

G8, $150-$250
Davidson Co., TN

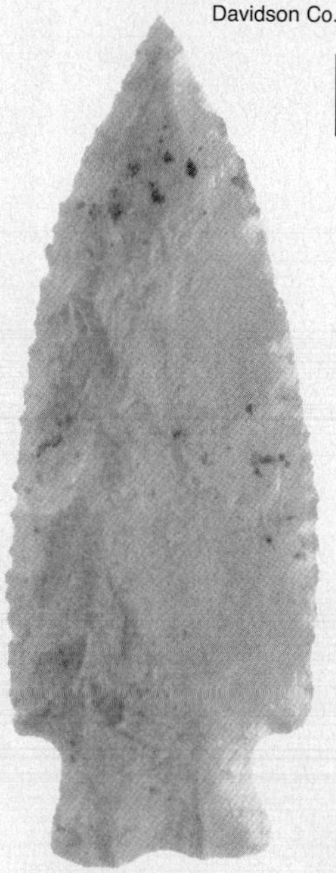

G10, $250-$450
Davidson Co., TN

Serrated
edge
Dover
chert

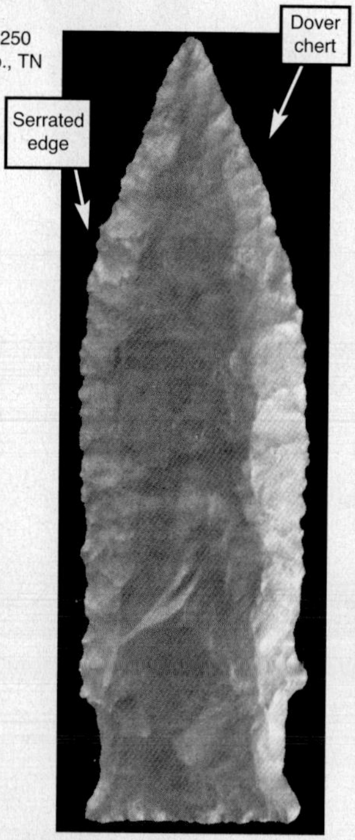

G10, $300-$550
Humphreys Co., TN

Serrated
edge
Dover
chert

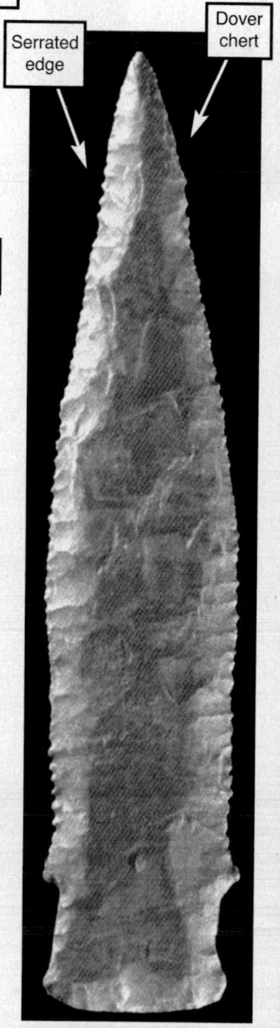

G10+, $1200-$2000
Humphreys Co., TN

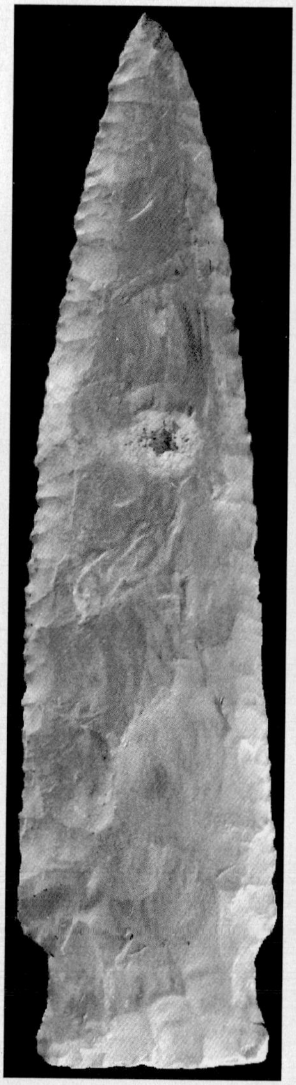

G9, $500-$900
Davidson Co., TN

LOCATION: Southwestern Kentucky into the Southeastern states. **DESCRIPTION:** A medium to large size, narrow, thick, serrated stemmed point that is steeply beveled on all four sides. The hafting area either has shallow side notches or an expanding stem. The base is usually thinned and ground. Rarely, the base is bifurcated. **I.D. KEY:** Weak notches, edgework.

HAW RIVER - Transitional Paleo, 11,000 - 8000 B. P.

(Also see Golondrina and Hardaway)

G10, $2500-$4000
Grayson Co., KY

G8, $800-$1500
Coffee Lake, AL

LOCATION: AL, KY, NC, PA & VA. **DESCRIPTION:** A medium to large size, thin, broad, elliptical blade with a basal notch and usually, rounded barbs that turn inward. Believed to be ancestral to the *Alamance* point. **I.D. KEY:** Notched base.

E C

HEAVY DUTY - Early to Middle Archaic, 7000 - 5000 B. P.

(Also see Harpeth River and Kirk Stemmed, McWhinney and Russell Cave)

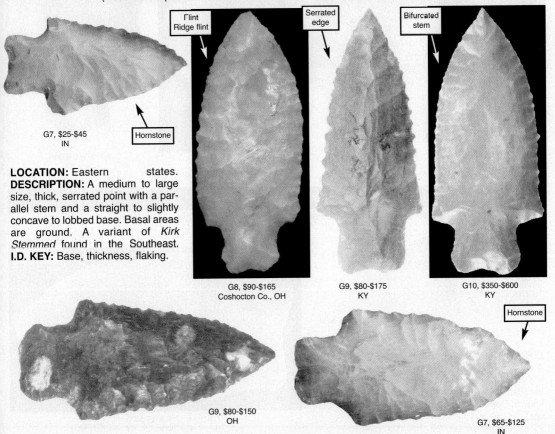

Flint Ridge flint

Serrated edge

Bifurcated stem

G7, $25-$45
IN

Hornstone

LOCATION: Eastern states. **DESCRIPTION:** A medium to large size, thick, serrated point with a parallel stem and a straight to slightly concave to lobbed base. Basal areas are ground. A variant of *Kirk Stemmed* found in the Southeast. **I.D. KEY:** Base, thickness, flaking.

G8, $90-$165
Coshocton Co., OH

G9, $80-$175
KY

G10, $350-$600
KY

Hornstone

G9, $80-$150
OH

G7, $65-$125
IN

411

HEAVY DUTY (continued)

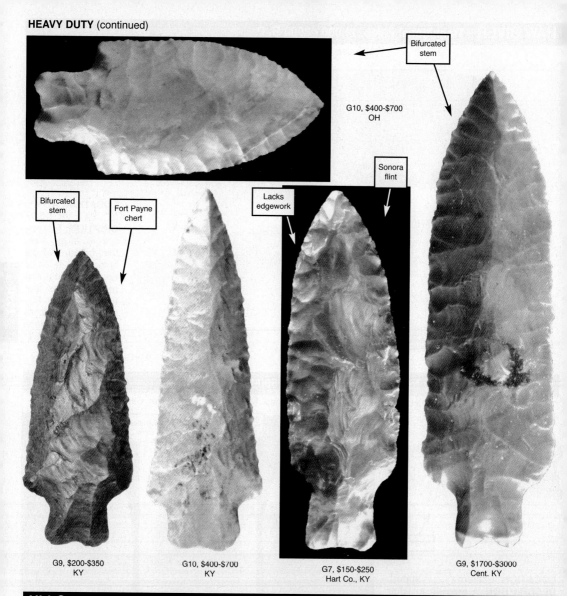

G10, $400-$700
OH

Bifurcated stem

Bifurcated stem

Sonora flint

Lacks edgework

Bifurcated stem

Fort Payne chert

G9, $200-$350
KY

G10, $400-$700
KY

G7, $150-$250
Hart Co., KY

G9, $1700-$3000
Cent. KY

HI-LO - Transitional Paleo, 10,000 - 8000 B. P.

(Also see Angostura, Golondrina, Jeff, Johnson and Paint Rock Valley)

G8, $125-$225
IN

LOCATION: Midwestern states. **DESCRIPTION:** A small to medium size, broad, eared, lanceolate point with a concave base. Believed to be related to *Plainview* and *Dalton* points. Three forms known: Convex sides, parallel sides & weak shoulders.

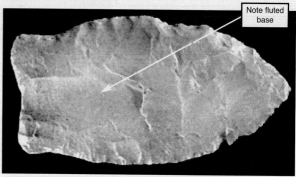

Note fluted base

G6, $150-$275
Barren Co., KY

HIDDEN VALLEY - Early to Middle Archaic, 8000 - 6000 B. P.

(also see Dickson and Morrow Mountain)

LOCATION: Arkansas, West Tennessee to Wisconsin. **DESCRIPTION:** A medium size point with square to tapered shoulders and a contracting base that can be pointed to straight. Flaking is earlier and more parallel than on *Gary* points. Called *Rice Contracted Stemmed* in Missouri.

G10, $150-$250
TN

HINDS - Transitional Paleo, 10,000 - 6000 B. P.

(Also see Pelican and Quad)

LOCATION: Tennessee, N. Alabama, Mississippi, Louisiana and Arkansas. **DESCRIPTION:** A short, broad, auriculate point with basal grinding. Shoulders taper into a short expanding stem. Some examples are basally thinned or fluted. Related to *Pelican* and *Coldwater* points found in Texas.

Classic form

Fine serrations

Serrated edge

G6, $65-$125
Dyersburg, TN

G9, $125-$200
Lee Co., MS

E C

HOLLAND - Early Archaic, 9500 - 7500 B. P.

(Also see Dalton, Hardin and Scottsbluff)

Knobbed base

Note early diagonal flaking

G7, $65-$125
KY.

G8, $125-$225
West Memphis, TN

LOCATION: Midwestern states. **DESCRIPTION:** A medium to large size lanceolate blade that is very well made. Shoulders are weak to nonexistent. Bases can be knobbed to auriculate and are usually ground. Some examples have horizontal to oblique transverse flaking. **I.D. KEY:** Weak shoulders, early flaking.

Ground basal area

G8, $500-$900
Harrison Co., IN

HOPEWELL - Woodland, 2500 - 1500 B. P.

(Also see Dickson, Gibson, North, St. Charles and Snyders)

Flintridge flint

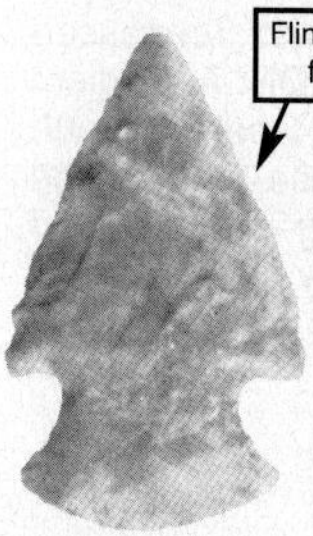

G6, $20-$35
OH

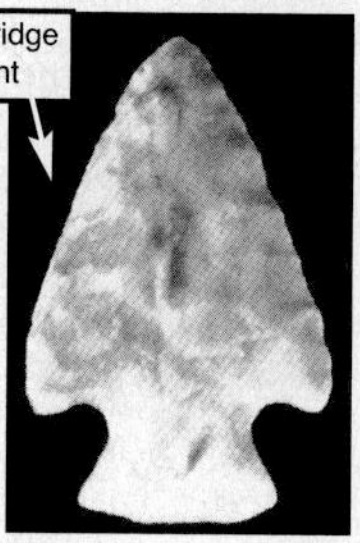

G6, $20-$35
OH

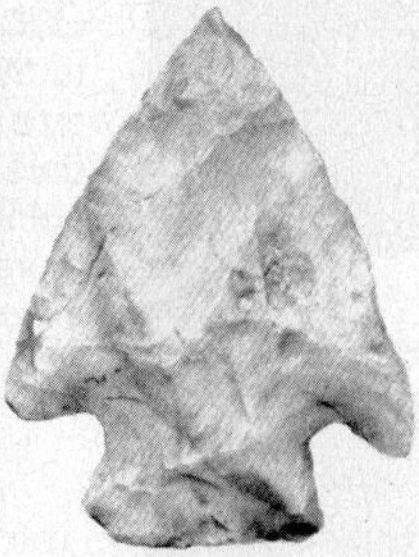

G6, $15-$25
Fentress Co., TN

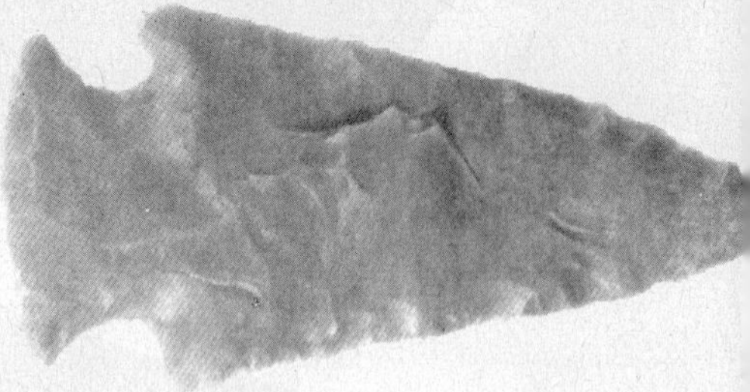

G6, $30-$50
OH

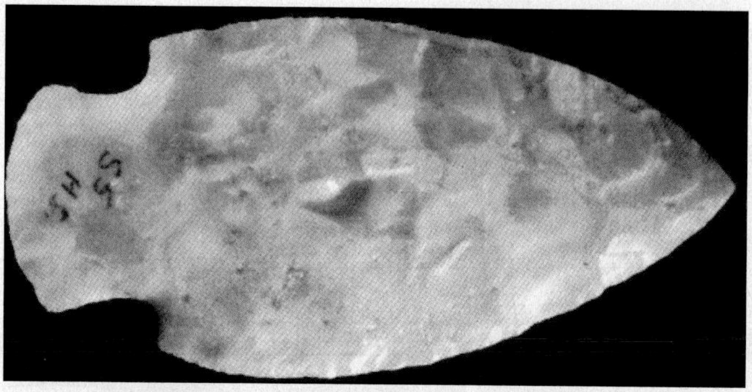

G9, $90-$175
OH

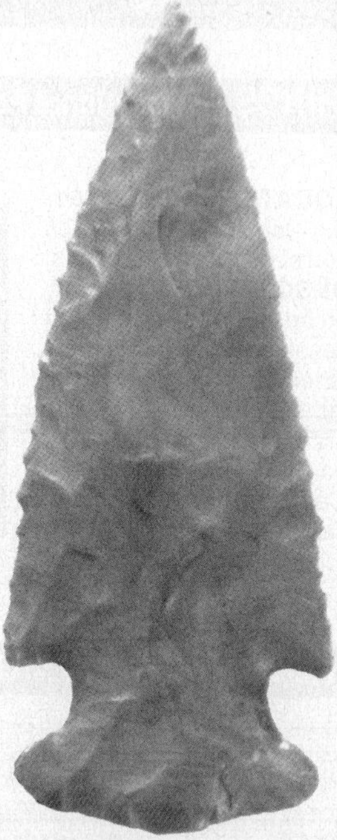

G9, $85-$165
KY

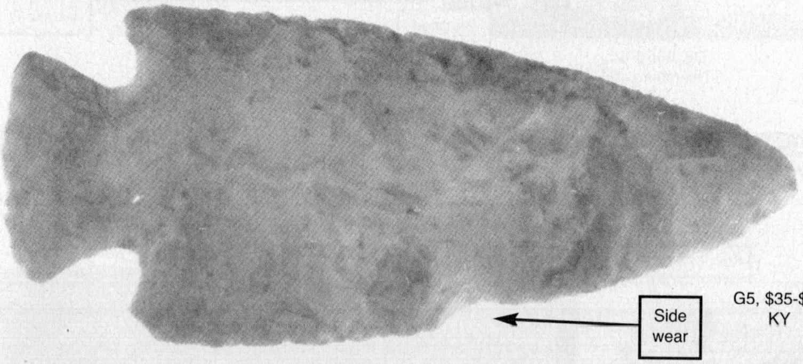

Side wear

G5, $35-$65
KY

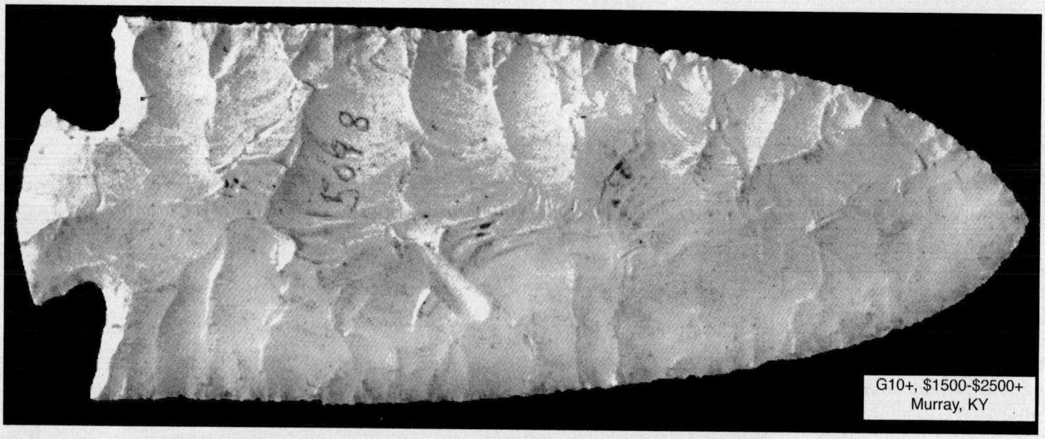

G10+, $1500-$2500+
Murray, KY

LOCATION: Midwestern to Eastern states. **DESCRIPTION:** A large size, broad, corner notched point that is similar to *Snyders.* Made by the Hopewell culture.

HOWARD COUNTY - Early Archaic., 7500 - 6500 B. P.

(also see Big Sandy, Gibson & St. Charles)

G6, $150-$250
Boyd Co., KY

LOCATION: Missouri, Illinois into Kentucky. **DESCRIPTION:** A small to medium size, thin, well-made point, The blade is long and triangular with slightly convex edges. Notches are narrow and fairly low on the sides, entering at a slight diagonally upward angle. The basal edge may range from straight to slightly convex or concave. Basal edge has light grinding to none.

INTRUSIVE MOUND - Late Woodland-Miss., 1500 - 1000 B. P.

(also see Jacks Reef, Knight Island)

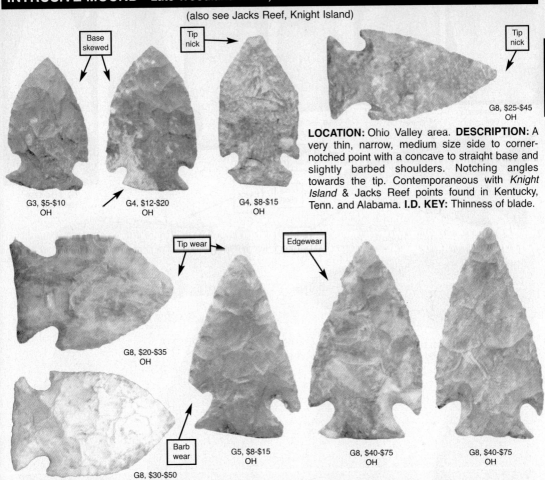

E
C

Base skewed

Tip nick

Tip nick

G8, $25-$45
OH

G3, $5-$10
OH

G4, $12-$20
OH

G4, $8-$15
OH

LOCATION: Ohio Valley area. **DESCRIPTION:** A very thin, narrow, medium size side to corner-notched point with a concave to straight base and slightly barbed shoulders. Notching angles towards the tip. Contemporaneous with *Knight Island* & Jacks Reef points found in Kentucky, Tenn. and Alabama. **I.D. KEY:** Thinness of blade.

Tip wear

Edgewear

G8, $20-$35
OH

Barb wear

G8, $30-$50
OH

G5, $8-$15
OH

G8, $40-$75
OH

G8, $40-$75
OH

JACKS REEF CORNER NOTCHED - Late Woodland to Mississippian, 1500 - 1000 B. P.

(Also see Intrusive Mound, Knight Island & Pentagonal Knife)

Southeastern states. **DESCRIPTION:** A small to medium size, very thin, corner notched point that is well made. The blade is convex to pentagonal. Some examples are widely corner notched and appear to be expanded stem poin stem points with barbed shoulders. Rarely, they are basal notched. **I.D. KEY:** Thinness, made by the birdpoint people.

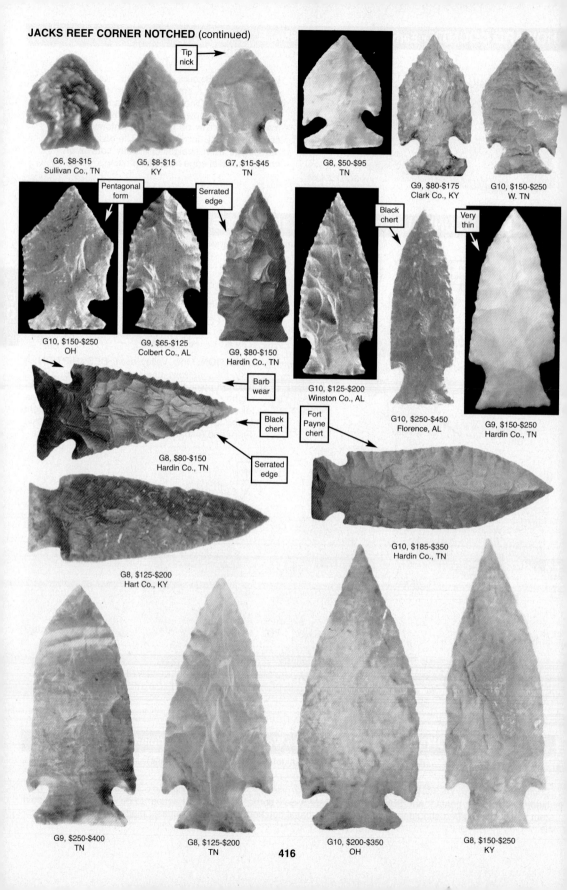

JACKS REEF CORNER NOTCHED (continued)

Tip nick

G6, $8-$15
Sullivan Co., TN

G5, $8-$15
KY

G7, $15-$45
TN

G8, $50-$95
TN

G9, $80-$175
Clark Co., KY

G10, $150-$250
W. TN

Pentagonal form

Serrated edge

G10, $150-$250
OH

G9, $65-$125
Colbert Co., AL

G9, $80-$150
Hardin Co., TN

Black chert

Very thin

G10, $125-$200
Winston Co., AL

Barb wear

Black chert

Serrated edge

Fort Payne chert

G10, $250-$450
Florence, AL

G9, $150-$250
Hardin Co., TN

G8, $80-$150
Hardin Co., TN

G10, $185-$350
Hardin Co., TN

G8, $125-$200
Hart Co., KY

G9, $250-$400
TN

G8, $125-$200
TN

G10, $200-$350
OH

G8, $150-$250
KY

416

(Also see Madison and Mouse Creek)

G6, $5-$10
Dallas Co., AL

G6, $6-$12
Morgan Co., AL

G6, $5-$10
KY

G6, $5-$10
Florence, AL

G5, $5-$10
N. E. AL

G5, $6-$12
W. TN

G9, $35-$65
Dayton, TN

LOCATION: Southeastern states.
DESCRIPTION: A small to large size, very thin, five sided point with a sharp tip. The hafting area is usually contracted with a slightly concave to straight base. This type is called *Pee Dee* in North and South Carolina.

E
C

G9, $25-$45
Morgan Co., AL

G9, $40-$75
Morgan Co., AL

G9, $55-$100
OH

G9, $25-$45
Morgan Co., AL

Knife
form

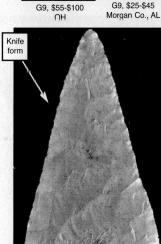

G8, $125-$200
Coffee Lake, AL

G9, $80-$150
TN

G9, $150-$250
Florence, AL

G9, $55-$100
TN

G10+, $225-$400
Warren Co., TN

G10+, $200-$350
TN

G9, $200-$350
Humphreys Co., TN

G10+, $150-$600
AL

G10, $350-$600
Humphreys Co., TN

417

JEFF - Late Paleo, 10,000 - 8000 B. P.

(Also see Angostura, Browns Valley, Golondrina, Hi-Lo, Paint Rock Valley and Quad)

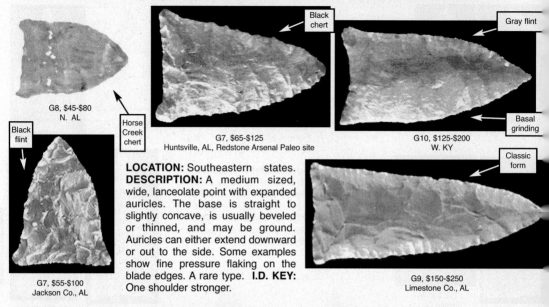

G8, $45-$80
N. AL

Black
chert

Gray flint

Horse
Creek
chert

Black
flint

G7, $65-$125
Huntsville, AL, Redstone Arsenal Paleo site

G10, $125-$200
W. KY

Basal
grinding

Classic
form

LOCATION: Southeastern states. **DESCRIPTION:** A medium sized, wide, lanceolate point with expanded auricles. The base is straight to slightly concave, is usually beveled or thinned, and may be ground. Auricles can either extend downward or out to the side. Some examples show fine pressure flaking on the blade edges. A rare type. **I.D. KEY:** One shoulder stronger.

G7, $55-$100
Jackson Co., AL

G9, $150-$250
Limestone Co., AL

JOHNSON - Early to Middle Archaic, 9000 - 5000 B. P.

(Also see Fairland, Hi-Lo, Limestone, McIntire, Savannah River and Steubenville)

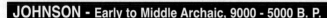

G5, $15-$30
Natchez, MS

G5, $15-$30
W. TN

G5, $15-$30
N.E. AL

G7, $35-$60
Coffee Lake, AL

G70, $15-$30
TN

LOCATION: Midwestern to Southeastern states. **DESCRIPTION:** A medium size, thick, well made, expanded stem point with a broad, concave base. Shoulders can be slightly barbed, straight or tapered. Basal corners are rounded to pointed to auriculate. Bases are thinned and ground. **I.D. KEY:** Pointed ears and thickness.

JUDE - Early Archaic, 9000 - 6000 B. P.

(Also see Cave Spring, Garth Slough, Halifax, Kanawha Stemmed, LeCroy, McIntire and Rheems Creek)

Red jasper

Diagonal flaking

Carter Cave flint

G5, $8-$15
Walker Co., AL

G5, $12-$20
Christian Co., KY

G6, $12-$20
Henegar, AL

G9, $35-$65
Colbert Co., AL

G6, $15-$30
Dickson, TN

G8, $25-$45
Marion Co., KY

Milky quartz

Classic form

G6, $8-$15
Walker Co., AL

G9, $35-$65
N. AL

G6, $15-$25
Humphreys Co., TN

LOCATION: Southeastern states. **DESCRIPTION:** A small size, short, barbed, expanded to parallel stemmed point with straight to convex blade edges. Stems are usually as large or larger than the blade. Bases are straight, concave, convex or bifurcated. Shoulders are either square, tapered or barbed. This is one of the earliest stemmed points along with *Pelican*. Some examples have serrated blade edges that may be beveled on one side of each face. **I.D. KEY:** Basal form and flaking.

E
C

KANAWHA STEMMED - Early Archaic, 0200 - 5000 B. P.

(Also see Frederick, Jude, Kirk Stemmed-Bifurcated, LeCroy, St. Albans and Stanly)

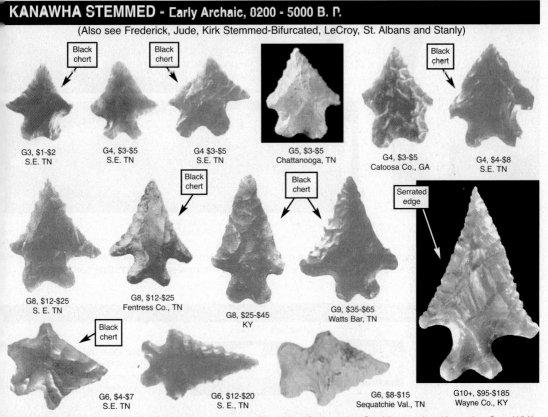

Black chert

Black chert

Black chert

G3, $1-$2
S.E. TN

G4, $3-$5
S.E. TN

G4 $3-$5
S.E. TN

G5, $3-$5
Chattanooga, TN

G4, $3-$5
Catoosa Co., GA

G4, $4-$8
S.E. TN

Black chert

Black chert

Serrated edge

G8, $12-$25
S. E. TN

G8, $12-$25
Fentress Co., TN

G8, $25-$45
KY

G9, $35-$65
Watts Bar, TN

Black chert

G6, $4-$7
S.E. TN

G6, $12-$20
S. E., TN

G6, $8-$15
Sequatchie Val., TN

G10+, $95-$185
Wayne Co., KY

LOCATION: West Virginia into Southeastern states. First identified at the St. Albans site, Kanwaha Co., WVA. **DESCRIPTION:** A small to medium size, fairly thick, shallowly-bifurcated stem- med point. The basal lobes are usually rounded, expanding and the shoulders tapered to horizontal and can turn towards the tip. Believed to be the ancestor to the *Stanly* type.

419

KAYS - Middle Archaic to Woodland, 5000 - 2000 B. P.

(Also see Adena Robbins, Cresap, Little Bear Creek, McIntire and Pontchartrain)

G5, $8-$15
Meigs Co., TN

G6, $12-$20
Florence, AL

G5, $8-$15
Morgan Co., AL

G6, $15-$25
Limestone Co., AL

G8, $65-$125
Decatur, AL

G6, $35-$60
Walker Co., AL

G9, $80-$150
Parsons, TN

LOCATION: Southeastern states. **DESCRIPTION:** A medium to large size, narrow, parallel sided stemmed point with a straight base. Shoulders are tapered to square. The blade is straight to convex. **I.D. KEY:** One barb is higher.

KEOTA - Mississippian, 800 - 600 B. P.

(Also see Merom)

G4, $1-$2
Meigs Co., TN

G4, $1-$2
Meigs Co., TN

G5, $5-$10
Wash. Co., AL

LOCATION: Okla, Ark, S.E. TN. & N. AL. **DESCRIPTION:** A small size, thin, triangular, side to corner-notched point with a rounded base.

KIRK CORNER NOTCHED - Early to Middle Archaic, 9000 - 6000 B. P.

(Also see Crawford Creek, Cypress Creek, Lost Lake, Neuberger, Pine Tree and St. Charles)

Serrated edge

G6, $3-$15
Dayton, TN

G5, $5-$10
KY

G8, $35-$60
W. TN

Serrated edge

G9, $65-$125
E. TN

Serrated edge

G8, $40-$75
KY

G8, $30-$50
KY

G8, $65-$125
KY

G10, $150-$250
Coffee Lake, AL

Coshocton chert

Serrated edge

G8, $65-$125
OH

G8, $65-$125
Spencer Co., OH

Serrated edge

Serrated edge

G8, $150-$250
W. KY

G9, $130-$250
Jefferson Co., MS

G9, $55-$100
Meade Co., KY

LOCATION: Southeastern states. **DES- CRIPTION:** A medium to large size, corner notched point. Blade edges can be convex to recurved and are finely serrated on many examples. The base can be convex, concave, straight or auriculate. Points that are beveled on one side of each face would fall under the *Lost Lake* type. **I.D. KEY:** Secondary edgework.

G8, $125-$200
KY

Ground basal area

Serrated edge

G9, $200-$350
Humphreys Co., TN

Serrated edge

G6, $80-$150
Davidson Co., TN

Serrated edge

G8, $150-$250
Humphreys Co., TN

G10, $275-$500
Coffee Lake, AL

Serrated edge

G10, $800-$1500
KY

G8, $250-$450
KY

G10+, $1000-$1800
Humphreys Co., TN

KIRK SNAPPED BASE - Early to Middle Archaic, 9000 - 6000 B. P.

G9, $80-$150
Humphreys Co., TN

G7, $40-$75
Coffee Lake, AL

Base snapped off

Base snapped off

High grade example

Base snapped off

Dover chert

G7, $15-$30
Humphreys Co., TN

G10, $165-$300
Hardin Co., TN

E
C

LOCATION: Southeastern to Eastern states. **DESCRIPTION:** A medium to large size, usually serrated, blade with long tangs and a base that has been snapped or fractured off. The shoulders are also fractured on some examples. This proves that the fracturing was intentional as in *Decatur* and other types.

KIRK STEMMED - Early to Middle Archaic, 9000 - 6000 B. P.

(Also see Elora, Flint Creek, Hamilton, Heavy Duty, St. Tammany and Stanly)

G2, $1-$3
Polk Co., TN

G7, $2-$5
AL

G6, $6-$12
Jackson Co., AL

G5, $6-$20
KY

G6, $12-$20
TN

Serrated edge

G5, $12-$20
KY

LOCATION: Southeastern to Eastern states. **DESCRIPTION:** A medium to large size, barbed, stemmed point with deep notches or fine serrations along the blade edges. The stem is parallel to expanding. The stem sides may be steeply beveled on opposite faces. Some examples also have a distinct bevel on the right side of each blade edge. The base can be concave, convex or straight, and can be very short. The shoulders are usually strongly barbed. Believed to have evolved into *Stanly* and other types. **I.D. KEY:** Serrations.

423

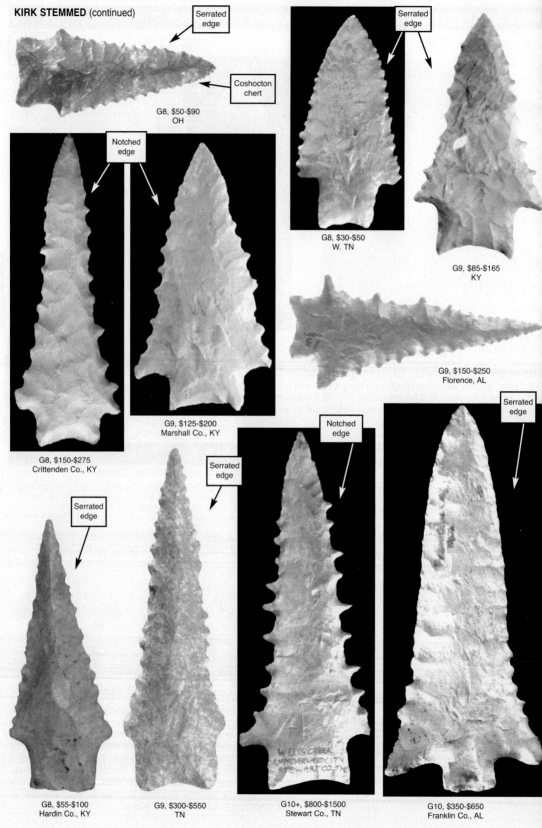

KIRK STEMMED (continued)

Serrated edge

Coshocton chert

G8, $50-$90
OH

Serrated edge

G8, $30-$50
W. TN

Serrated edge

G9, $85-$165
KY

Notched edge

G8, $150-$275
Crittenden Co., KY

G9, $125-$200
Marshall Co., KY

Serrated edge

G9, $150-$250
Florence, AL

Serrated edge

G8, $55-$100
Hardin Co., KY

Serrated edge

G9, $300-$550
TN

Notched edge

G10+, $800-$1500
Stewart Co., TN

Serrated edge

G10, $350-$650
Franklin Co., AL

424

KIRK STEMMED-BIFURCATED - Early Archaic, 9000 - 7000 B. P.

(Also see Cave Spring, Fox Valley, Heavy Duty, LeCroy, St. Albans and Stanly)

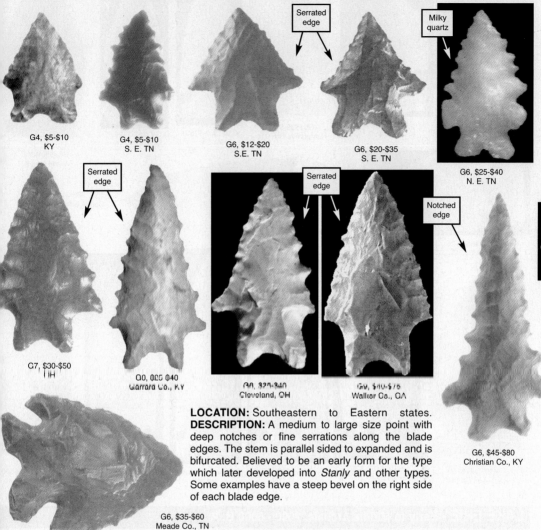

Serrated edge

Milky quartz

Serrated edge

Serrated edge

Notched edge

G4, $5-$10
KY

G4, $5-$10
S. E. TN

G6, $12-$20
S.E. TN

G6, $20-$35
S. E. TN

G6, $25-$40
N. E. TN

G7, $30-$50
TN

G0, $25-$40
Garrard Co., KY

G8, $25-$40
Cleveland, OH

G8, $40-$75
Walker Co., GA

G6, $45-$80
Christian Co., KY

G6, $35-$60
Meade Co., TN

E
C

LOCATION: Southeastern to Eastern states. **DESCRIPTION:** A medium to large size point with deep notches or fine serrations along the blade edges. The stem is parallel sided to expanded and is bifurcated. Believed to be an early form for the type which later developed into *Stanly* and other types. Some examples have a steep bevel on the right side of each blade edge.

KNIGHT ISLAND - Late Woodland, 1500 - 1000 B. P.

(Also see Cache River, Intrusive Mound and Jacks Reef)

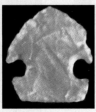

G8, $20-$35
Humphreys Co., TN

G8, $20-$35
Humphreys Co., TN

G5, $20-$35
Humphreys Co., TN

G6, $20-$35
S. E. TN

G5, $12-$20
TN

G8, $25-$45
Jessamine Co., KY

LOCATION: Southeastern states. **DESCRIPTION:** A small to medium size, very thin, narrow, side-notched point with a straight base. Longer examples can have a pentagonal apperarance. Called *Raccoon Creek* in Ohio. A side-notched Jacks Reef. **I.D. KEY:** Thinness, basal form. Made by the bird point people.

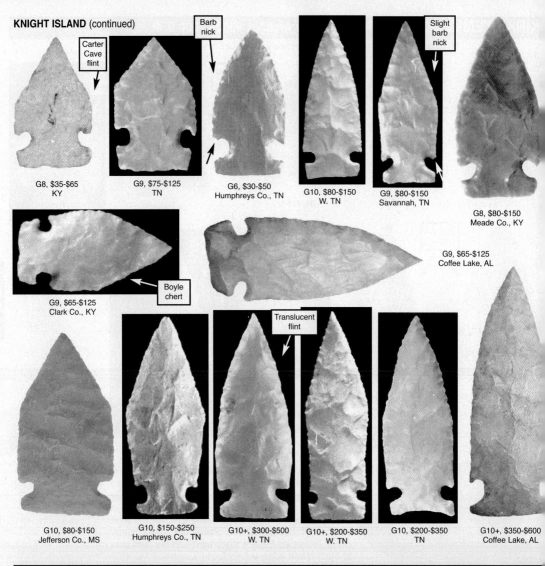

Barb
nick

Carter
Cave
flint

Slight
barb
nick

G8, $35-$65
KY

G9, $75-$125
TN

G6, $30-$50
Humphreys Co., TN

G10, $80-$150
W. TN

G9, $80-$150
Savannah, TN

G8, $80-$150
Meade Co., KY

G9, $65-$125
Coffee Lake, AL

Boyle
chert

G9, $65-$125
Clark Co., KY

Translucent
flint

G10, $80-$150
Jefferson Co., MS

G10, $150-$250
Humphreys Co., TN

G10+, $300-$500
W. TN

G10+, $200-$350
W. TN

G10, $200-$350
TN

G10+, $350-$600
Coffee Lake, AL

LAKE ERIE - Early to Middle Archaic, 9000 - 5000 B. P.

(Also see Jude, Kanawha, Kirk Stemmed-Bifurcated, LeCroy, MacCorkle, St. Albans and   Stanly)

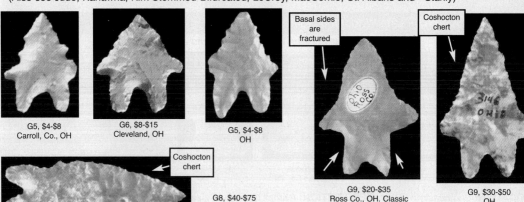

G5, $4-$8
Carroll, Co., OH

G6, $8-$15
Cleveland, OH

G5, $4-$8
OH

Basal sides
are
fractured

Coshocton
chert

Coshocton
chert

G8, $40-$75
Carroll Co., OH

G9, $20-$35
Ross Co., OH. Classic

G9, $30-$50
OH

426

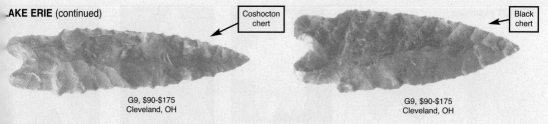

Coshocton chert

Black chert

G9, $90-$175
Cleveland, OH

G9, $90-$175
Cleveland, OH

LOCATION: Northeastern states. **DESCRIPTION:** A small to medium size, thin, deeply notched or serrated, bifurcated stemmed point. The basal lobes are parallel with a tendency to turn inward and are pointed. The outward sides of the basal lobes are usually fractured from the base towards the tip and can be ground.

LANCET - Paleo to Archaic, 11,500 - 5000 B. P.

(Also see Drill and Scraper)

All are Flint Ridge flint

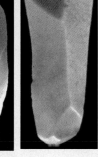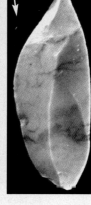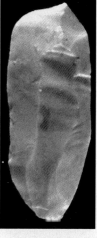

$3-$5 ea.
All from Flint Ridge, OH

LOCATION: Found on all early man sites. **DESCRIPTION:** A medium to large size sliver used as a knife for cutting. Recent experiments proved that these knives were sharper than a surgeon's scalpel. Similar to *Burins* which are fractured at one end to produce a sharp point.

LECROY - Early to Middle Archaic, 9000 - 5000 B. P.

(Also see Decatur, Jude, Kanawha Stemmed, Kirk Stemmed-Bifurcated, Lake Erie, MacCorkle, Pine Tree, Rice Lobbed, St. Albans and Stanly)

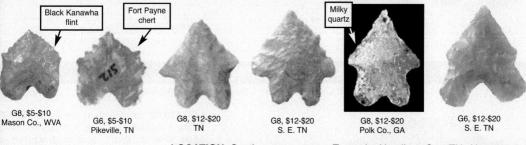

Black Kanawha flint

Fort Payne chert

Milky quartz

G8, $5-$10
Mason Co., WVA

G6, $5-$10
Pikeville, TN

G8, $12-$20
TN

G8, $12-$20
S. E. TN

G8, $12-$20
Polk Co., GA

G6, $12-$20
S. E. TN

G7, $8-$15
OH

LOCATION: Southeastern states. Type site-Hamilton Co., TN. Named after Archie LeCroy. **DESCRIPTION:** A small to medium size, thin, usually broad point with deeply notched or serrated blade edges and a deeply bifurcated base. Basal ears can either droop or expand out. The stem is usually large in comparison to the blade size. Some stem sides are fractured in Northern examples *(Lake Erie)*. Bases are usually ground. **I.D. KEY:** Basal form.

LECROY (continued)

Serrated edge

G7, $12-$25
KY

G7, $15-$25
Citico, TN

Serrated edge

G9, $20-$35
Hamilton Co., TN

G8, $25-$40
Lauderdale Co., AL

G10+, $40-$75
Dayton, TN

Double uniface

G9, $30-$50
Hamilton Co., TN

G8, $30-$50
Lauderdale Co., AL

G8, $30-$50
Jackson Co., AL

Serrated edge

G10, $40-$75
S. E. TN

G8, $35-$65
KY

Serrated edge

G9, $40-$75
TN

Serrated edge

Serrated edge

G9, $65-$125
Florence, AL

G8, $35-$65
KY

G10, $55-$100
Coffee Lake, AL

G6, $40-$70
KY

LEDBETTER - Middle to Late Archaic, 6000 - 3500 B. P.

(Also see Little Bear Creek, Mulberry Creek, Pickwick and Shoals Creek)

G5, $12-$20
N.W. AL

LOCATION: Southeastern states. **DESCRIP-TION:** A medium to large size asymmetric point with a short, usually fractured o snapped base. One blade edge is curve more than the other. Shoulders are tapered squared or slightly barbed. Some example show fine pressure flaking along the blad edges. Believed to be *Pickwick* knives. **I.D KEY:** Blade form.

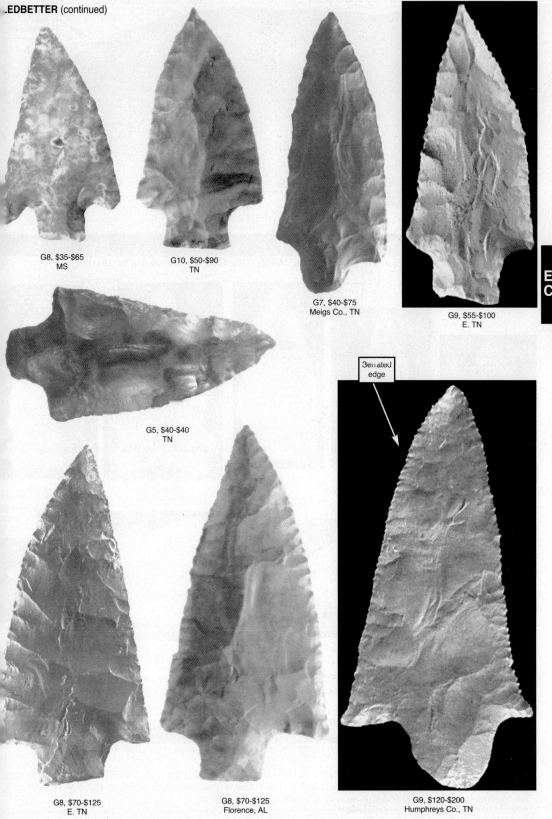

G8, $35-$65
MS

G10, $50-$90
TN

G7, $40-$75
Meigs Co., TN

E
C

G9, $55-$100
E. TN

G5, $40-$40
TN

Serrated
edge

G8, $70-$125
E. TN

G8, $70-$125
Florence, AL

G9, $120-$200
Humphreys Co., TN

429

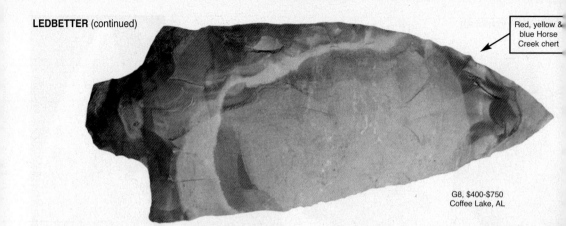

Red, yellow & blue Horse Creek chert

G8, $400-$750
Coffee Lake, AL

LEIGHTON - Early Archaic, 8000 - 5000 B. P.

(Also see Benton, Big Sandy, Evans, Merkle, Ohio Double Notched and St. Helena)

Serrated edge

Serrated edge

G6, $15-$25
Dayton, TN

G7, $30-$50
Florence, AL

G7, $35-$65
W. TN

G9, $125-$225
Lauderdale Co., AL

G6, $35-$50
Humphreys Co., TN

Dover chert

Serrated edge

Serrated edge

Note double notched base

G8, $150-$250
Humphreys Co., TN

G10, $350-$600
Colbert Co., AL

LOCATION: Southeastern states. **DESCRIPTION:** A medium to large size, double side-notched point that is usually serrated and has a concave base that is ground. **I.D. KEY:** Basal notching, archaic flaking.

LERMA - Early to Mid-Archaic, 10,000 - 5000 B. P.

(Also see Adena Blade, Harahey, North, Paleo Knife, Snake Creek, Tear Drop & Tenn. Saw)

LOCATION: Siberia to Alaska, Canada, Mexico, South America, and across the U.S. **DESCRIPTION:** A large size, narrow, thick, lanceolate blade with a rounded base. Some Western examples are beveled on one side of each face. Flaking tends to be collateral and finer examples are thin in cross section.

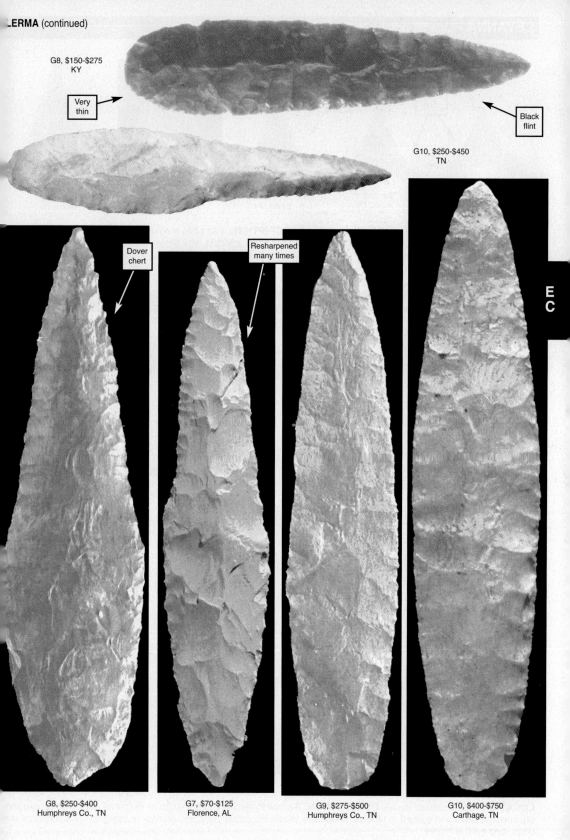

G8, $150-$275
KY

Very
thin

Black
flint

G10, $250-$450
TN

Dover
chert

Resharpened
many times

E
C

G8, $250-$400
Humphreys Co., TN

G7, $70-$125
Florence, AL

G9, $275-$500
Humphreys Co., TN

G10, $400-$750
Carthage, TN

431

LEVANNA - Late Woodland to Mississippian, 1300 - 600 B. P.

(Also see Hamilton, Madison, Tortugas and Yadkin)

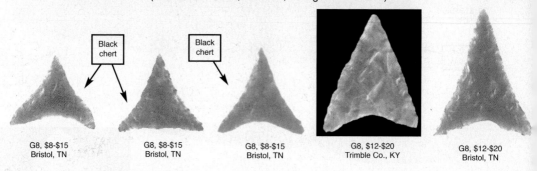

Black chert

Black chert

G8, $8-$15
Bristol, TN

G8, $8-$15
Bristol, TN

G8, $8-$15
Bristol, TN

G8, $12-$20
Trimble Co., KY

G8, $12-$20
Bristol, TN

LOCATION: Southeastern to Northeastern states. **DESCRIPTION:** A small to medium size, thin, triangular point with a concave to straight base. Believed to be replaced by Madison points in later times. Called *Yadkin* in North Carolina. **I.D. KEY:** Medium thick cross section.

LIMESTONE - Late Archaic to Early Woodland, 5000 - 2000 B. P.

(Also see Fairland, Johnson, McIntire)

G4, $6-$10
Walker Co., AL

G5, $8-$15
KY

G4, $8-$15
Limestone Co., AL

G4, $8-$15
Fayette Co., AL

G5, $12-$20
Fayette Co., AL

G7, $30-$55
Limestone Co., AL

G9, $40-$75
Limestone Co., AL

G8, $50-$90
Morgan Co., AL

G10, $55-$100
Morgan Co., AL

LOCATION: Southeastern states. **DESCRIPTION:** A small to medium size, triangular stemmed point with an expanded, concave base and barbed to tapered shoulders. Blade edges are concave, convex or straight. **I.D. KEY:** Concave base, one barb is higher.

LIMETON BIFURCATE - Early Archaic, 9000 - 6000 B. P.

(Also see Haw River)

LOCATION: Eastern states. **DESCRIPTION:** A medium size, crudely made, broad, lanceolate blade with a central notch in the base.

G6, $5-$10
Southeast, TN

LITTLE BEAR CREEK - Late Archaic to late Woodland, 4000 - 1500 B. P.

(Also see Adena, Kays, McWhinney, Mulberry Creek, Pickwick and Ponchartrain)

E
C

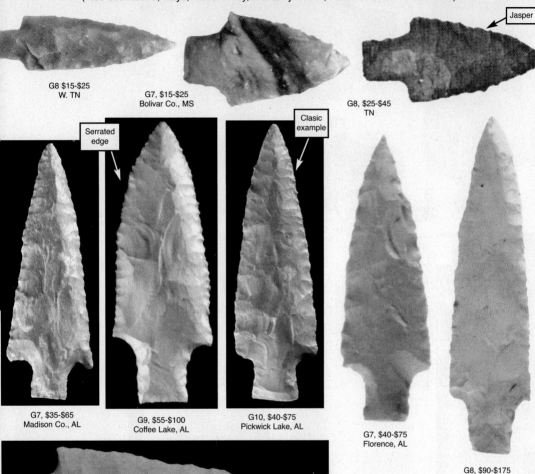

G8 $15-$25
W. TN

G7, $15-$25
Bolivar Co., MS

G8, $25-$45
TN

Jasper

Serrated edge

Clasic example

G7, $35-$65
Madison Co., AL

G9, $55-$100
Coffee Lake, AL

G10, $40-$75
Pickwick Lake, AL

G7, $40-$75
Florence, AL

G8, $90-$175
Florence, AL

G7, $45-$85
Lauderdale Co., AL

G9, $55-$100
TN

LOCATION: Southeastern states. **DESCRIPTION:** A medium to large size, narrow point with a long parallel stem that may contract or expand slightly. Blade edges are slightly convex. Shoulders are usually squared, tapered or slightly barbed. The base can be fractured or snapped off. Blade edges can be beveled on one side of each face and finely serrated. Called *Sarasota* in Florida. **I.D. KEY:** Straight base, woodland flaking.

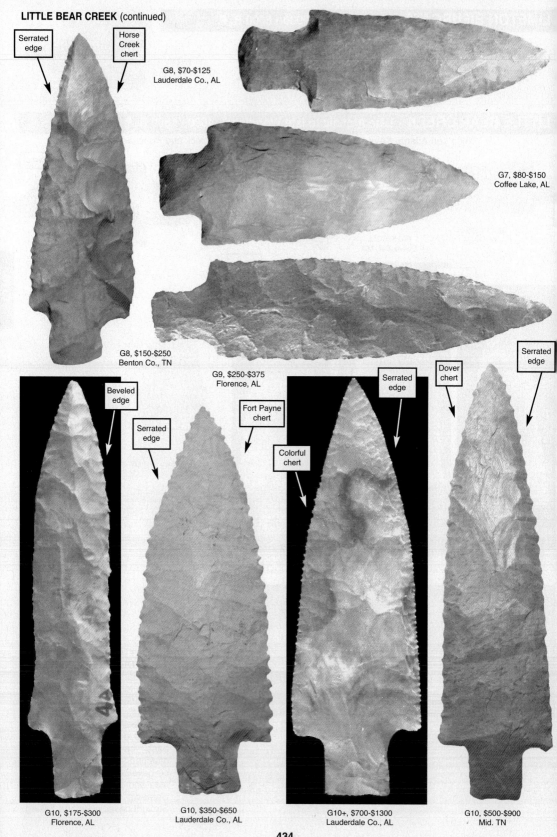

Serrated edge

Horse Creek chert

G8, $70-$125
Lauderdale Co., AL

G7, $80-$150
Coffee Lake, AL

G8, $150-$250
Benton Co., TN

G9, $250-$375
Florence, AL

Beveled edge

Serrated edge

Fort Payne chert

Colorful chert

Serrated edge

Dover chert

Serrated edge

G10, $175-$300
Florence, AL

G10, $350-$650
Lauderdale Co., AL

G10+, $700-$1300
Lauderdale Co., AL

G10, $500-$900
Mid. TN

LOST LAKE - Early Archaic, 9000 - 6000 B. P.

(Also see Cobbs, Cypress Creek, Hardin, Kirk Corner Notched, St. Charles and Thebes)

Beveled edge

Beveled edge

Beveled edge

Sunfish style

G3, $25-$40
Jackson Co., AL

Beveled edge

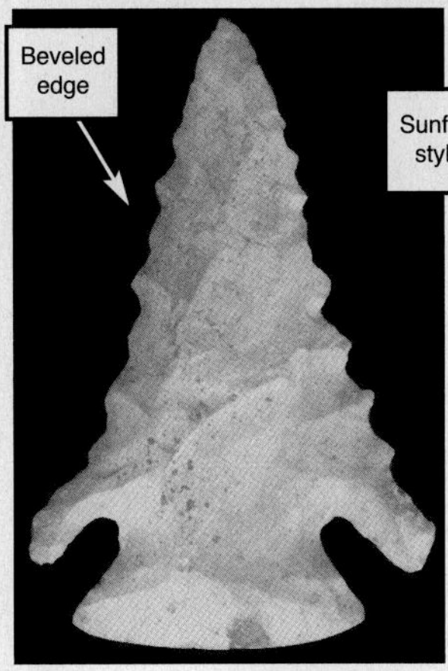

G7, $65-$125
Shelby Co., IN

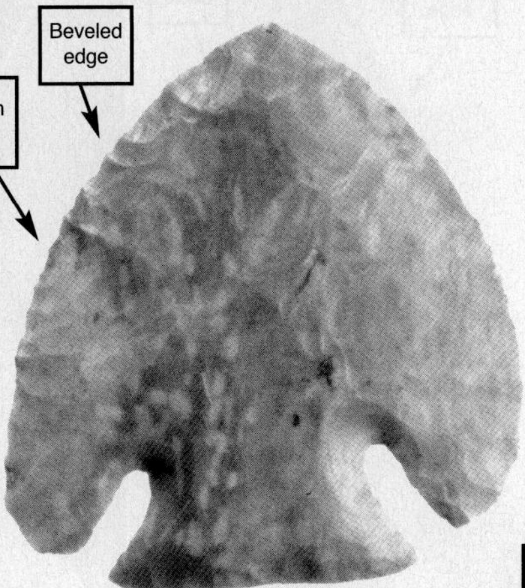

G9, $275-$500
KY

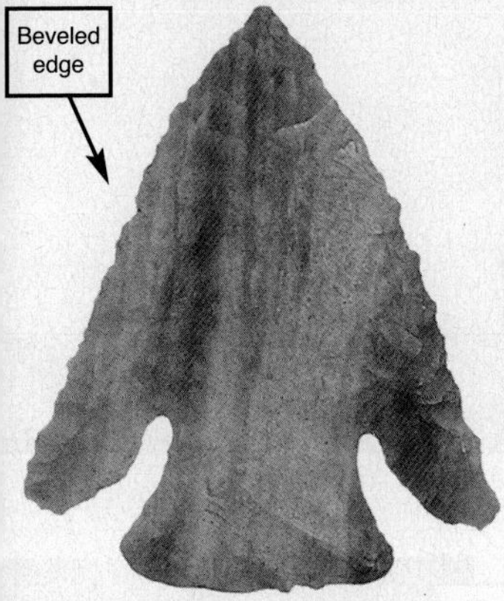

E
C

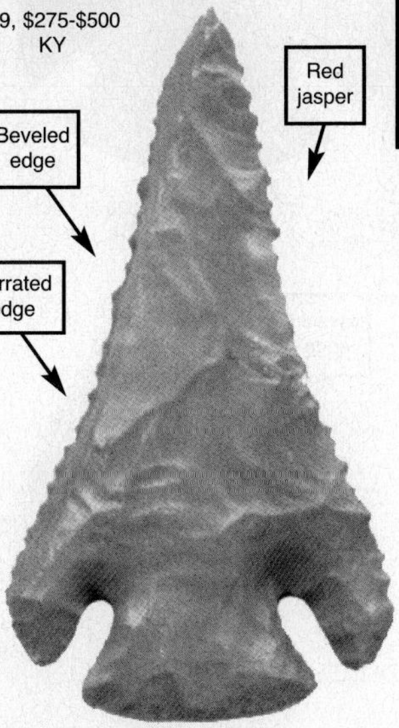

Red jasper

Beveled edge

Beveled edge

Serrated edge

Sonora flint

G10, $650-$1200
Clay Co., KY

Beveled edge

Serrated edge

G10+, $2500-$4000
Hardin Co., KY

G9, $350-$600
Perry Co., TN

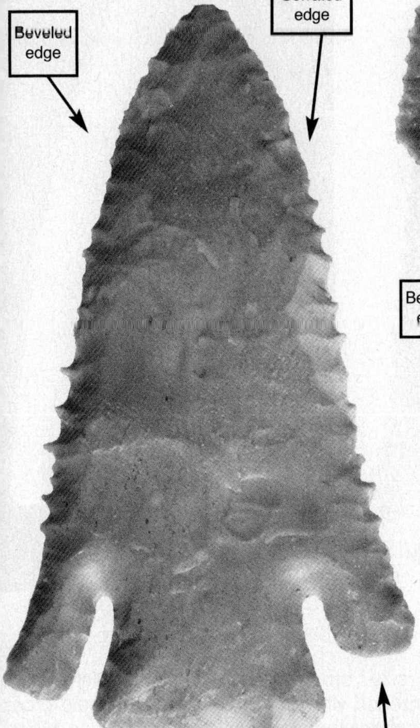

Beveled edge

Beveled edge

G8, $550-$1000
Meade Co., KY

Ancient repaired barb

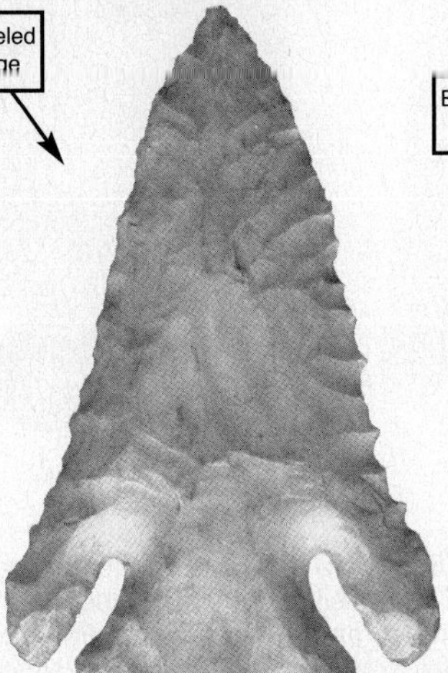

G9, $300-$500
IN

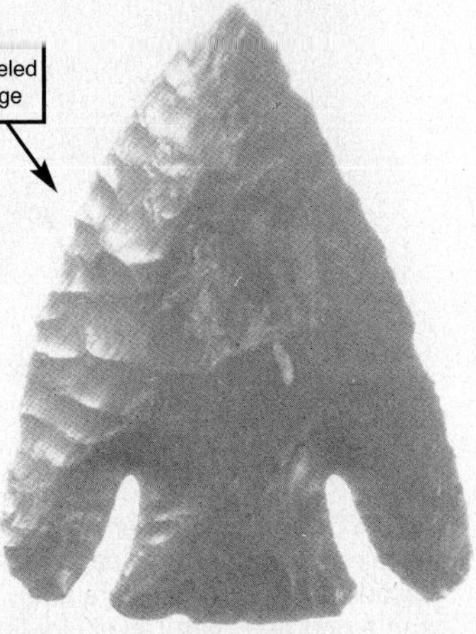

G8, $150-$275
KY

435

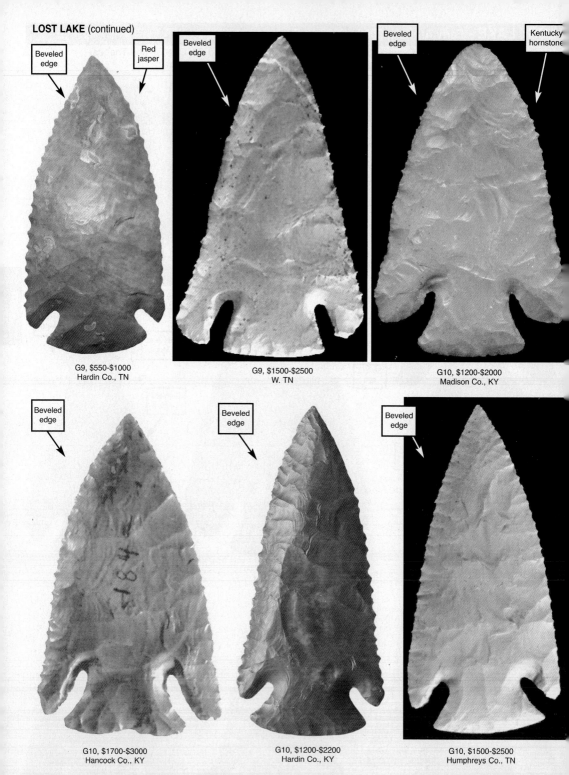

Beveled edge — Red jasper

G9, $550-$1000
Hardin Co., TN

Beveled edge

G9, $1500-$2500
W. TN

Beveled edge — Kentucky hornstone

G10, $1200-$2000
Madison Co., KY

Beveled edge

G10, $1700-$3000
Hancock Co., KY

Beveled edge

G10, $1200-$2200
Hardin Co., KY

Beveled edge

G10, $1500-$2500
Humphreys Co., TN

LOCATION: Southeastern states. **DESCRIPTION:** A medium to large size, broad, corner notched point that is beveled on one side of each face. The beveling continues when resharpened which created a flat rhomboid cross section. Most examples are finely serrated and exhibit high quality flaking and symmetry. Also known as *Deep Notch*, and typed as *Bolen Bevel Corner Notched* in Florida. **I.D. KEY:** Notching, secondary edgework is always opposite creating at least slight beveling.

LOWE - Mississippian, 1650 - 1450 B. P.

(Also see Bakers Creek, Chesser, McIntire, Mud Creek and Table Rock)

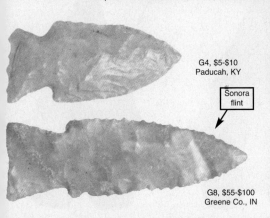

G4, $5-$10
Paducah, KY

Sonora flint

Hornstone

G8, $80-$150
Greene Co., IN

G8, $55-$100
Greene Co., IN

LOCATION: Indiana into Kentucky and Eastern Illinois. **DESCRIPTION:** A medium to large size, narrow point with a long expanding stem. Bases are straight. Shoulders are horizontal to slightly tapered. Related to *Bakers Creek, Chesser* and *Rice Side Notched.* **I.D. KEY:** Long expanding stem.

LOZENGE - Mississippian, 1000 - 400 B. P.

(Also see Nodena)

LOCATION: Midwestern to Southeastern states. **DESCRIPTION:** A small size, narrow, thin, double pointed arrow point.

G8, $12-$20
KY

MACCORKLE - Early Archaic, 8000 - 6000 B. P.

(Also see Kanawha Stemmed, Kirk Stemmed-Bifurcated, LeCroy, Rice Lobbed and St. Albans)

G5, $20-$35
Dayton, TN

G6, $15-$25
S. E. TN

Tip wear

Coshocton flint

G8, $30-$55
Trimble Co., KY

G5, $35-$65
OH

Upper Mercer flint

G8, $30-$50
Polk Co., TN

G5, $15-$30
OH

LOCATION: Midwestern to Southeastern states. **DESCRIPTION:** A medium to large size, thin, usually serrated, widely corner notched point with large round ears and a deep notch in the center of the base. Bases are usually ground. The smaller examples can be easily confused with the *LeCroy* point. Shoulders and blade expand more towards the base than *LeCroy*, but only in some cases. Called *Nottoway River Bifurcate* in Virginia. **I.D. KEY:** Basal notching, early Archaic flaking.

Serrated edge

Coshocton chert

G8, $55-$100
Union Co., OH

G10, $70-$125
KY

G9, $70-$125
Coshocton Co., OH

Coshocton flint

Serrated edge

Serrated edge

G7, $55-$100
Coshocton Co., OH

G9, $80-$150
OH

G9, $150-$275
KY

MACE - Mississippian, 1100 - 600 B. P.

(Also see Dagger and Sun Disc)

All Maces shown half size

G9, $2000-$3500
Stewart Co., TN

MACE (continued)

Dover chert

All Maces shown half size

G10, $2000-$3800
Henry Co., TN

G8, $1500-$2800
Stewart Co., TN

Dover chert

G8, $1200-$2200
Montgomery Co., TN

E C

LOCATION: Southeastern states. **DESCRIPTION:** A very large, thick, hand-held barbed dagger used in the Sun dance ceremony along with the Duck River Swords, Sun Discs and shell gorgets by the Mississippian culture. Such dances are depicted on the shell gorgets themselves. These objects are made from high grade flint and are flaked to perfection. **Warning:** Absolute provinence is needed to prove authenticity. Very rare, existing mostly in museum collections. **I.D. KEY:** Thickness, notching, flaking.

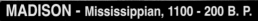

MADISON - Mississippian, 1100 - 200 B. P.

(Also see Camp Creek, Fort Ancient, Guntersville, Hamilton, Levanna, Sand Mountain and Valina)

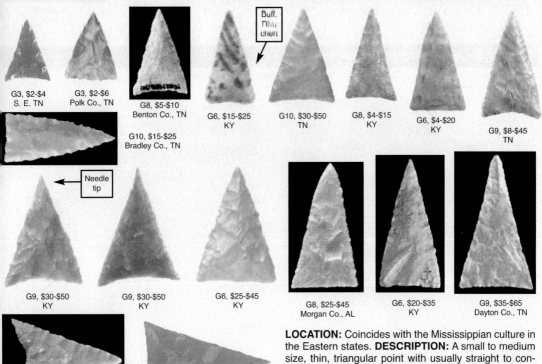

G3, $2-$4
S. E. TN

G3, $2-$6
Polk Co., TN

G8, $5-$10
Benton Co., TN

G10, $15-$25
Bradley Co., TN

Buff. flint chert

G6, $15-$25
KY

G10, $30-$50
TN

G8, $4-$15
KY

G6, $4-$20
KY

G9, $8-$45
TN

Needle tip

G9, $30-$50
KY

G9, $30-$50
KY

G6, $25-$45
KY

G8, $25-$45
Morgan Co., AL

G6, $20-$35
KY

G9, $35-$65
Dayton Co., TN

G8, $12-$35
E. KY

G9, $35-$65
Parsons, TN

LOCATION: Coincides with the Mississippian culture in the Eastern states. **DESCRIPTION:** A small to medium size, thin, triangular point with usually straight to convex sides. Bases are straight to concave. Some examples are notched on one to two sides. Many are of high quality and some are finely serrated.

439

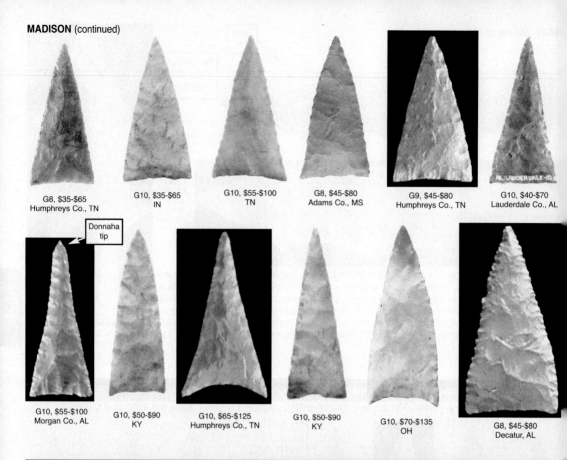

G8, $35-$65
Humphreys Co., TN

G10, $35-$65
IN

G10, $55-$100
TN

G8, $45-$80
Adams Co., MS

G9, $45-$80
Humphreys Co., TN

G10, $40-$70
Lauderdale Co., AL

Donnaha tip

G10, $55-$100
Morgan Co., AL

G10, $50-$90
KY

G10, $65-$125
Humphreys Co., TN

G10, $50-$90
KY

G10, $70-$135
OH

G8, $45-$80
Decatur, AL

MAPLES - Middle Archaic, 4500 - 3500 B. P.

(Also see Elora, Morrow Mountain and Savannah River)

Quartzite

G9, $200-$350
N. E. GA

LOCATION: Southeastern states. **DESCRIPTION:** A very large, broad, thick, short stemmed blade. Shoulders are tapered and the stem is contracting with a convex to straight base. Usually thick and crudely made, but fine quality examples have been found. Flaking is random and this type should not be confused with *Morrow Mountain* which has Archaic parallel flaking. **I.D. KEY:** Thickness, notching, flaking.

G9, $150-$250
Hardin Co., KY

G7, $125-$200
Taylor Co., KY

E
C

G9, $185-$350
Coffee Lake, AL
from a cache of 6

MARIANNA - Transitional Paleo, 10,000 - 8500 B. P.

(Also see Angostura, Browns Valley and Conerly)

LOCATION: Southern to Southeastern states. **DESCRIPTION:** A medium size lanceolate point with a constricted, concave base. Look for parallel to oblique flaking.

G7, $15-$25
Dayton, TN. Note
diagonal flaking

MATANZAS - Mid-Archaic to Woodland, 4500 - 2500 B. P.

(Also see Brewerton Side Notched, Brunswick and Swan Lake)

LOCATION: Ohio westward to Iowa. **DESCRIPTION:** A narrow, medium size point with broad side notches to an expanding stem.

MATANZAS (continued)

G6, $15-$25
KY

Base
nick

G4, $4-$8
TN

MCINTIRE - Middle to Late Archaic, 6000 - 4000 B. P.

(Also see Bakers Creek, Chesser, Kays, Limestone, Lowe, Mud Creek and Smithsonia)

G5, $12-$20
N. W. AL

G6, $20-$35
Morgan Co., AL

G8, $35-$65
Decatur, AL

G8, $30-$50
Meigs Co., TN

G7, $30-$50
N. W. AL

LOCATION: Southeastern states. **DESCRIPTION:** A medium to large point with straight to convex blade edges and a broad parallel to expanding stem. Shoulders are square to slightly barbed and the base is usually straight.

G6, $15-$25
Morgan Co., AL

G9, $35-$65
Humphreys Co., TN

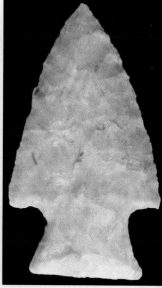

G9, $45-$85
TN

MCWHINNEY HEAVY STEMMED - Mid-Late Archaic, 6000 - 3000 B. P.

(Also see Heavy Duty, Little Bear Creek, Mud Creek, Mulberry Creek and Pickwick)

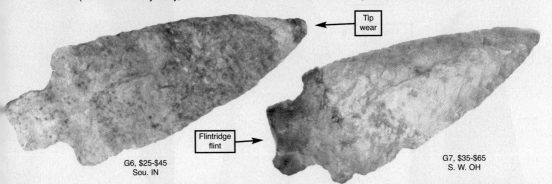

Tip wear

Flintridge flint

G6, $25-$45
Sou. IN

G7, $35-$65
S. W. OH

LOCATION: Illinois, Ohio into Kentucky. **DESCRIPTION:** A medium size, fairly thick point with a short stem and squared shoulders. Stems can be bulbous, straight to expanding. On some examples side notches occur where the stem and shoulders intersect. Previously known as the *Flint River Spike* point.

MEADOWOOD - Late Archaic to Woodland, 4000 - 2000 B. P.

(Also see Big Sandy and Newton Falls)

Foraker chert

G6, $25-$45
OH

G7, $35-$65
OH

G7, $40-$75
KY

G10, $150-$265
Boyle Co., KY

G8, $165-$300
OH

443

MEADOWOOD (continued)

Coshocton chert

Upper Mercer flint

G8, $90-$175
Fairfield Co., OH

G8, $150-$285
Dearborne Co., IN

G8, $150-$285
Shelby Co., IN

LOCATION: Northeastern to Eastern states. **DESCRIPTION:** Medium to large size, thick, broad side notched point. Notches occur close to the base. This point is found from Indiana to New York.

MERKLE - Late Archaic to Woodland, 4000 - 2000 B. P.
(Also see Evans, Leighton and Tangipahoa)

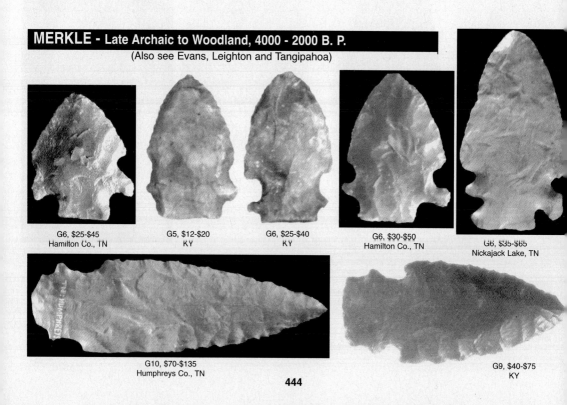

G6, $25-$45
Hamilton Co., TN

G5, $12-$20
KY

G6, $25-$40
KY

G6, $30-$50
Hamilton Co., TN

G6, $35-$65
Nickajack Lake, TN

G10, $70-$135
Humphreys Co., TN

G9, $40-$75
KY

444

MERKLE (continued)

LOCATION: Midwestern states into Tennessee. **DESCRIPTION:** A medium size point with a short stem and broad side notches and corner notches at the base. Bases are usually straight to convex. **I.D. KEY:** Double notching.

MEROM - Late Archaic, 4000 - 3000 B. P.

(Also see Keota)

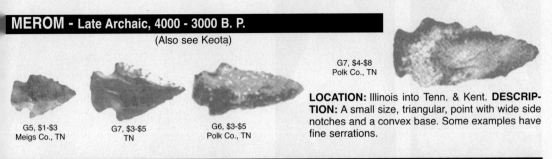

G7, $4-$8
Polk Co., TN

G5, $1-$3
Meigs Co., TN

G7, $3-$5
TN

G6, $3-$5
Polk Co., TN

LOCATION: Illinois into Tenn. & Kent. **DESCRIPTION:** A small size, triangular, point with wide side notches and a convex base. Some examples have fine serrations.

MESERVE - Early to Middle Archaic, 9500 - 4000 B. P.

(Also see Dalton)

G8, $60-$110
OH

G9, $70-$135
TN

E
C

LOCATION: Midwestern states, rarely into Ohio & Tennessee. **DESCRIPTION:** A medium size, auriculate form with a blade that is beveled on one side of each face. Beveling extends into the basal area. This type is related to *Dalton* points.

MONTGOMERY - Woodland, 2500 - 1000 B. P.

(Also see Benjamin, Ebenezer and Morrow Mountain)

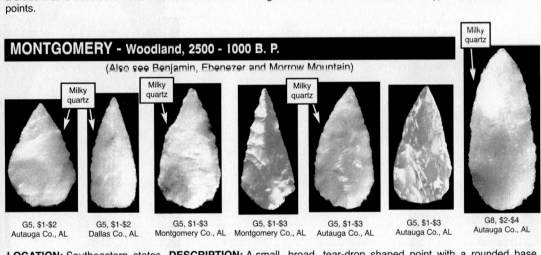

Milky quartz

Milky quartz

Milky quartz

Milky quartz

G5, $1-$2
Autauga Co., AL

G5, $1-$2
Dallas Co., AL

G5, $1-$3
Montgomery Co., AL

G5, $1-$3
Montgomery Co., AL

G5, $1-$3
Autauga Co., AL

G5, $1-$3
Autauga Co., AL

G8, $2-$4
Autauga Co., AL

LOCATION: Southeastern states. **DESCRIPTION:** A small, broad, tear-drop shaped point with a rounded base. Flaking is random. This type is similar to *Catan* found in Texas.

MORROW MOUNTAIN - Middle Archaic, 7000 - 5000 B. P.

(Also see Buggs Island, Cypress Creek, Ebenezer, Elora, Eva and Maples)

Milky quartz

G2, $1-$2
Burke Co., GA

G6, $8-$15
Polk Co., TN

G6, $8-$15
Bristol, TN

445

Needle tip

G8, $30-$50
Benton Co., TN

G6, $12-$25
OH

G8, $20-$35
Lauderdale Co., AL

G9, $45-$80
TN

G6, $5-$20
TN

G7, $15-$20
Limestone Co., AL

High grade flint

G9, $55-$100
Lauderdale Co., AL

G10, $90-$175
AL

G10+, $175-$325
Hamilton Co., TN

LOCATION: Midwestern to Southeastern states. **DESCRIPTION:** A medium to large size, triangular point with a very short contracting to rounded stem. Shoulders are usually weak but can be barbed. The blade edges on some examples are serrated with needle points. **I.D. KEY:** Contracted base and Archaic parallel flaking.

MORROW MOUNTAIN ROUNDED BASE - Middle Archaic, 7000 - 5000 B. P.

(Also see Ebenezer, Guilford Round Base and Montgomery)

G3, $1-$2
Polk Co., TN

G3, $1-$2
S. E. TN

Crystal

G4, $12-$20
Burke Co., GA

G5, $2-$4
Jessamine Co., KY

G5, $2-$4
Dunlap, TN

Chalcedony

G8 $25-$40
Nickajack
Lake, TN

G10, $40-$75
N. W. AL

E
C

LOCATION: Midwestern to Southeastern states. **DESCRIPTION:** A small to medium size tear-drop point with a pronounced, short, rounded base and no shoulders. Some examples have a straight to slightly convex base. This type has similarities to Gypsum Cave points found in the western states.

MORROW MOUNTAIN STRAIGHT BASE - Middle Archaic, 7000 - 5000 B. P.

(Also see Hidden Valley, Mud Creek)

G6, $8-$15
Jessamine Co., KY

G6, $12-$20
Hamilton Co., TN

Transparent
quartz

Serrated
edge

G6, $15-$25
Decatur Co., AL

G6, $12-$20
Jessamine Co., KY

G9, $25-$45
S.E. TN

LOCATION: Southeastern states. **DESCRIPTION:** A medium size, thin, strongly barbed point with a contracting stem and a straight base. Some examples are serrated and have a needle tip. Look for Archaic parallel flaking.

447

MORSE KNIFE - Woodland, 3000 - 1500 B. P.

(Also see Cotaco Creek, Duck River Sword, Ramey Knife and Snake Creek)

IMPORTANT:
Morse Knives are shown half size

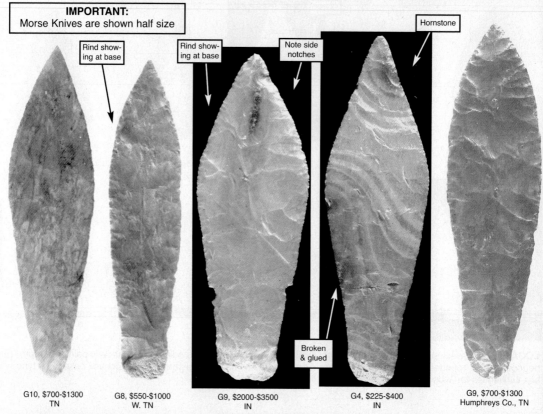

Rind showing at base

Rind showing at base

Note side notches

Hornstone

Broken & glued

G10, $700-$1300
TN

G8, $550-$1000
W. TN

G9, $2000-$3500
IN

G4, $225-$400
IN

G9, $700-$1300
Humphreys Co., TN

LOCATION: Midwestern to Southeastern states. **DESCRIPTION:** A large lanceolate blade with a long contracting stem and a rounded base. The widest part of the blade is towards the tip.

MOTLEY - Late Archaic to Woodland, 4500 - 2500 B. P.

(Also see Buck Creek, Epps, Hamilton, Smithsonia, Snyders and Wade)

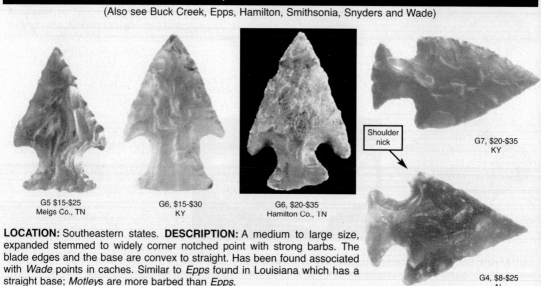

Shoulder nick

G7, $20-$35
KY

G5 $15-$25
Meigs Co., TN

G6, $15-$30
KY

G6, $20-$35
Hamilton Co., TN

G4, $8-$25
AL

LOCATION: Southeastern states. **DESCRIPTION:** A medium to large size, expanded stemmed to widely corner notched point with strong barbs. The blade edges and the base are convex to straight. Has been found associated with *Wade* points in caches. Similar to *Epps* found in Louisiana which has a straight base; *Motley*s are more barbed than *Epps*.

448

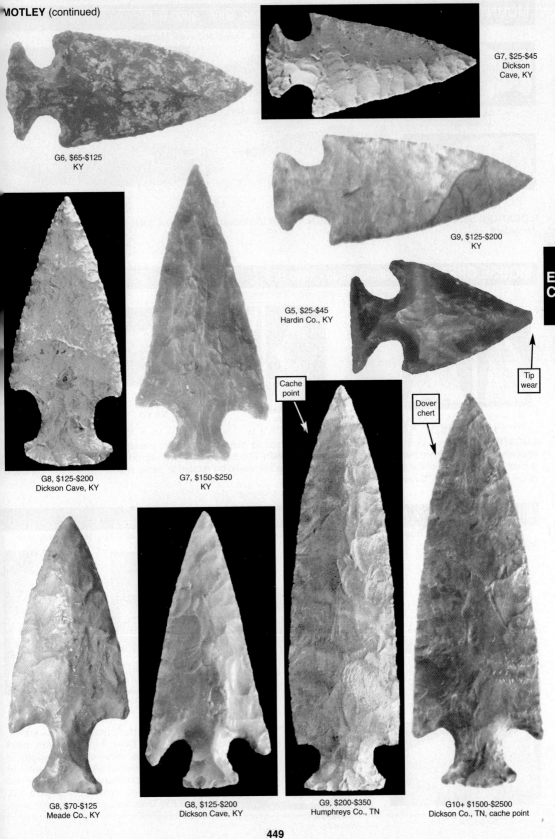

G6, $65-$125
KY

G7, $25-$45
Dickson
Cave, KY

G9, $125-$200
KY

G5, $25-$45
Hardin Co., KY

Tip
wear

G8, $125-$200
Dickson Cave, KY

G7, $150-$250
KY

Cache
point

Dover
chert

G8, $70-$125
Meade Co., KY

G8, $125-$200
Dickson Cave, KY

G9, $200-$350
Humphreys Co., TN

G10+ $1500-$2500
Dickson Co., TN, cache point

EC

449

MOUNTAIN FORK - Middle Archaic to Woodland, 6000 - 2000 B. P.

(Also see Bradley Spike, Collins, Duval and New Market)

G4, $8-$15
Decatur, AL

G6, $15-$25
S.E. TN

G4, $8-$15
Ft. Payne, AL

G4, $8-$15
Decatur, AL

G6, $20-$35
Limestone Co., AL

G6, $12-$20
W. TN

LOCATION: Southeastern states. **DESCRIPTION:** A small to medium size, narrow, thick, stemmed point with tapered shoulders.

MOUSE CREEK - Woodland, 1500 - 1000 B. P.

(Also see Jacks Reef Pentagonal)

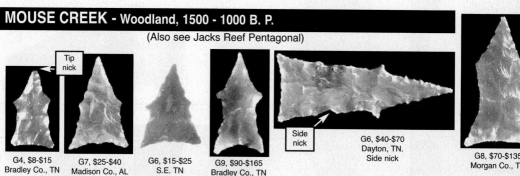

Tip nick

Side nick

G4, $8-$15
Bradley Co., TN

G7, $25-$40
Madison Co., AL

G6, $15-$25
S.E. TN

G9, $90-$165
Bradley Co., TN

G6, $40-$70
Dayton, TN.
Side nick

G8, $70-$135
Morgan Co., TN

LOCATION: Southeastern states. **DESCRIPTION:** A small to medium size, thin, pentagonal point with prominent shoulders, a short pointed blade and a long, expanding stem. The base is concave with pointed ears. The hafting area is over half the length of the point. This type is **very rare** and could be related to Jacks Reef. A similar form is found in OK, TX, & LA called "Snow Lake."

MUD CREEK - Late Archaic to Woodland, 4000 - 2000 B. P.

(Also see Bakers Creek, Beacon Island, Chesser, Flint Creek, Little Bear Creek, Lowe, McIntire, McWhinney and Mulberry Creek)

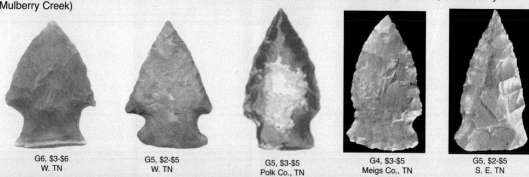

G6, $3-$6
W. TN

G5, $2-$5
W. TN

G5, $3-$5
Polk Co., TN

G4, $3-$5
Meigs Co., TN

G5, $2-$5
S. E. TN

G6,$5-$10
Dunlap, TN

G6, $5-$10
Walker Co., AL

LOCATION: Southeastern states. **DESCRIPTION:** A medium size point with slightly recurved blade edges, a narrow, needle like tip, square to tapered shoulders and an expanded stem. Called *Patuxent* in Virginia. **I.D. KEY:** Thickness, point form, high barb.

450

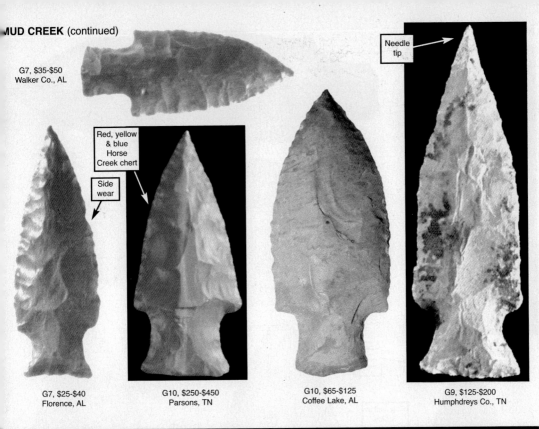

G7, $35-$50
Walker Co., AL

Red, yellow & blue Horse Creek chert

Side wear

Needle tip

G7, $25-$40
Florence, AL

G10, $250-$450
Parsons, TN

G10, $65-$125
Coffee Lake, AL

G9, $125-$200
Humphdreys Co., TN

E C

MULBERRY CREEK - Mid-Archaic to Woodland, 5000 - 3000 B. P.
(Also see Little Bear Creek, McWhinney and Pickwick)

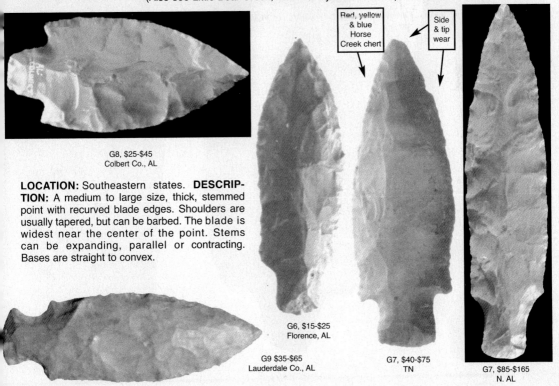

G8, $25-$45
Colbert Co., AL

LOCATION: Southeastern states. **DESCRIPTION:** A medium to large size, thick, stemmed point with recurved blade edges. Shoulders are usually tapered, but can be barbed. The blade is widest near the center of the point. Stems can be expanding, parallel or contracting. Bases are straight to convex.

Red, yellow & blue Horse Creek chert

Side & tip wear

G6, $15-$25
Florence, AL

G9 $35-$65
Lauderdale Co., AL

G7, $40-$75
TN

G7, $85-$165
N. AL

451

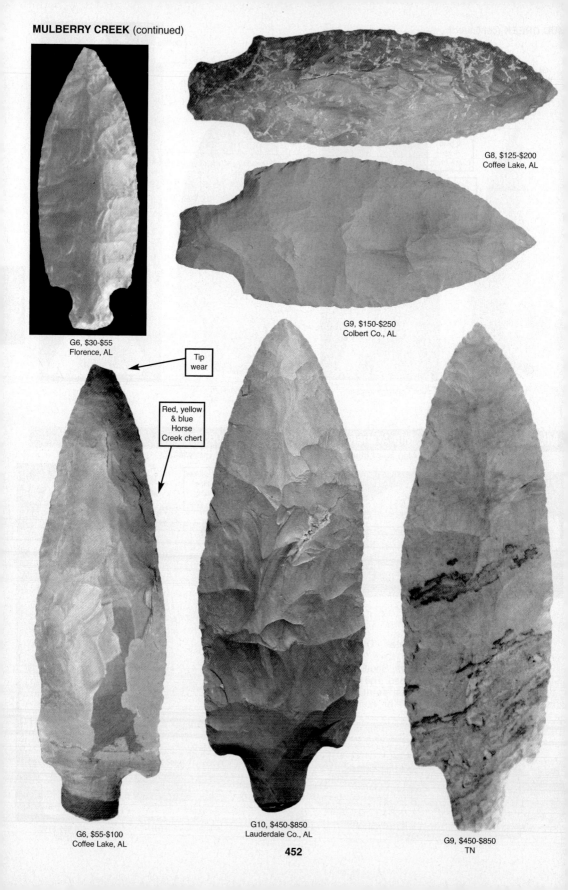

MULBERRY CREEK (continued)

G8, $125-$200
Coffee Lake, AL

G6, $30-$55
Florence, AL

G9, $150-$250
Colbert Co., AL

Tip wear

Red, yellow & blue Horse Creek chert

G6, $55-$100
Coffee Lake, AL

G10, $450-$850
Lauderdale Co., AL

G9, $450-$850
TN

452

NEUBERGER - Early-Mid Archaic, 9000 - 6000 B. P.

(Also see Kirk Corner Notched and Pine Tree)

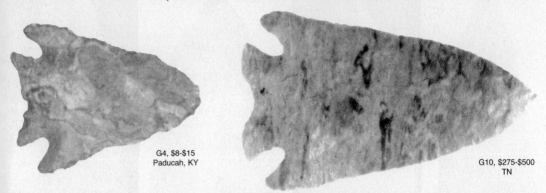

G4, $8-$15
Paducah, KY

G10, $275-$500
TN

LOCATION: Tennessee, Kentucky, Ohio to Illinois. **DESCRIPTION:** A medium to large size, broad, corner notched point with a short, auriculated base. Blade edges are recurved and the base is indented. Shoulders curve in towards the base.

E
C

NEW MARKET - Woodland, 3000 - 1000 B. P.

(Also see Bradley Spike, Buggs Island, Duval and Flint River)

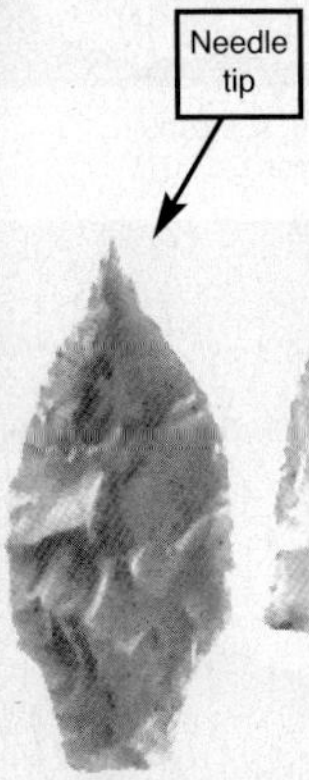

Needle tip

Needle tip

G5, $6-$12
Limestone Co.,
AL

G6, $8-$15
Humphreys Co., TN

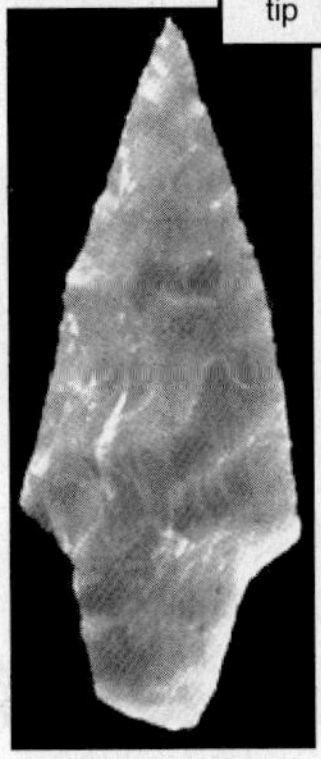

G7, $20-$35
Morgan Co., AL

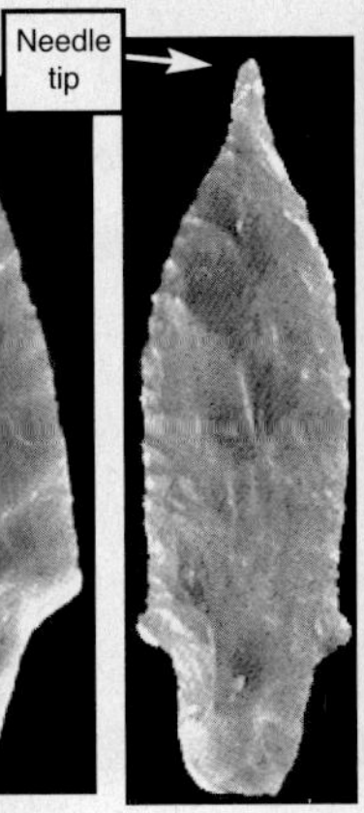

G10+, $65-$125
New Market, AL

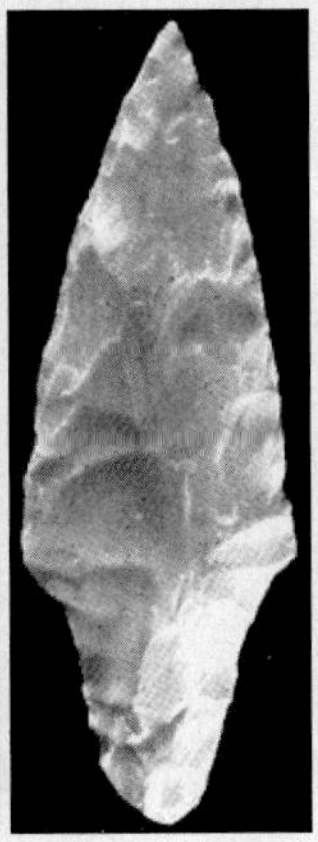

G8, $25-$40
Decatur, AL

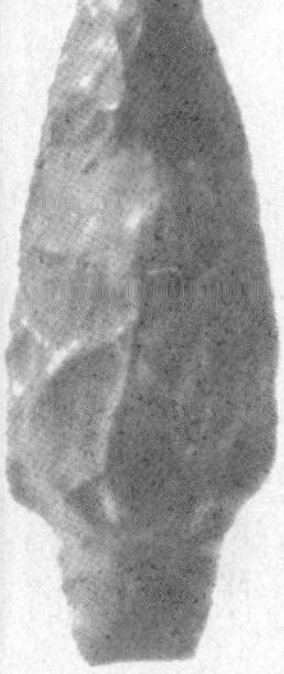

G8, $20-$35
Walker Co., AL

G8, $25-$40
TN

LOCATION: Southeastern states. **DESCRIPTION:** A small to medium size point with tapered shoulders and an extended, rounded base. Shoulders are usually asymmetrical with one higher than the other.

NEWTON FALLS - Early to Mid-Archaic, 7000 - 5000 B. P.

(Also see Benton, Big Sandy, Cache River, Graham Cave and Meadowood)

G8, $30-$50
OH

G8, $90-$165
OH

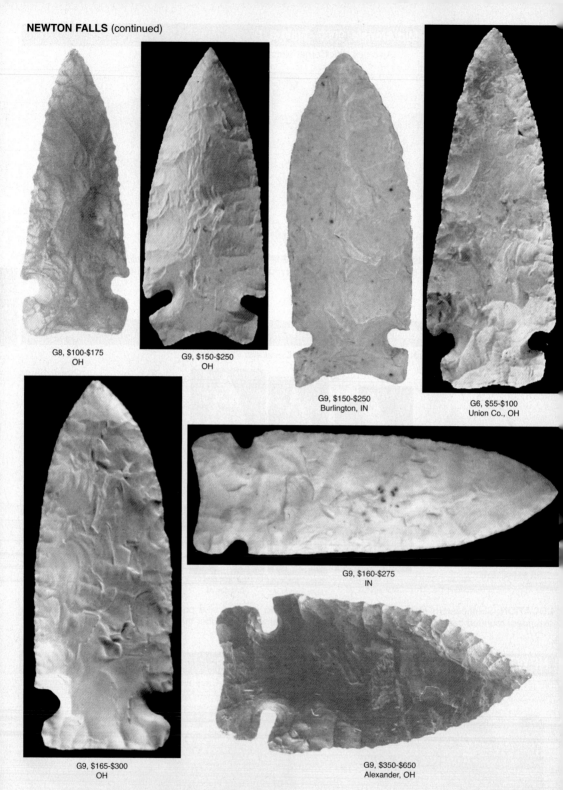

G8, $100-$175
OH

G9, $150-$250
OH

G9, $150-$250
Burlington, IN

G6, $55-$100
Union Co., OH

G9, $160-$275
IN

G9, $165-$300
OH

G9, $350-$650
Alexander, OH

LOCATION: Ohio and surrounding states. **DESCRIPTION:** A medium to large size, narrow, side notched point with paralled sides on longer examples and a straight to concave base which could be ground. Similar to *Big Sandy*, *Godar*, *Hemphill* and *Osceola* found in other areas. **I.D. KEY:** Size and narrowness.

454

NODENA - Mississippian to Historic, 600 - 400 B. P.

(Also see Guntersville and Lozenge)

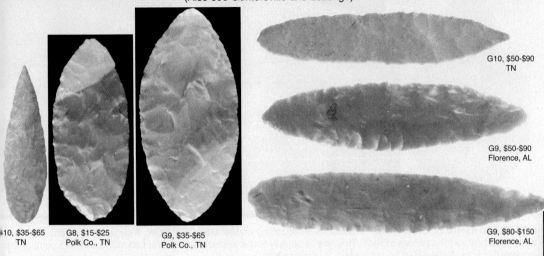

G10, $50-$90
TN

G9, $50-$90
Florence, AL

G9, $80-$150
Florence, AL

10, $35-$65
TN

G8, $15-$25
Polk Co., TN

G9, $35-$65
Polk Co., TN

LOCATION: Midwestern to Southeastern states. **DESCRIPTION:** A small to medium size, narrow, thin elliptical shaped arrow point with a pointed to rounded base. Some examples have oblique, parallel flaking. Called *Tampa* in Florida. Used by the Quapaw Indians.

NOLICHUCKY - Woodland, 3000 - 1500 B. P.

(Also see Camp Creek, Candy Creek, Copena Auriculate, Greeneville and Yadkin)

Chalce-dony

Needle tip

G5, $2-$5
Newport, TN

G6, $5-$10
Bristol, TN

G6, $12-$20
Bristol, TN

G5, $4-$8
Bristol, TN

G6, $12-$20
Meigs Co., TN

G9, $30-$50
Bradley Co., TN

G6, $12-$20
Meigs Co., TN

G9, $35-$60
Dayton, TN

G9, $30-$50
Dayton, TN

LOCATION: Southeastern states. **DESCRIPTION:** A small to medium size, triangular point with recurved blade edges and a straight to concave base. Most examples have small pointed ears at the basal corners. Bases could be ground. Believed to have evolved from *Candy Creek* points and later developed into *Camp Creek*, *Greeneville* and *Guntersville* points. Found with *Ebenezer*, *Camp Creek*, *Candy Creek* and *Greeneville* in caches (Rankin site, Cocke Co. TN.) **I.D. KEY:** Thickness and hafting area.

NORTH - Woodland, 2200 - 1600 B. P.

(Also see Adena Blade, Hopewell, Snyders and Tear Drop)

OHIO LANCEOLATE (continued)

Flint Ridge flint

G6, $40-$75
OH

G8, $200-$350
Sidney, OH

LOCATION: Kentucky, Ohio, Illinois, Missouri & surrounding states. **DESCRIPTION:** A large, thin, elliptical, broad, well made blade with a concave blade. This type is usually found in caches and is related to the *Snyders* point of the Hopewell culture. Believed to be unnotched *Snyders* points.

NOVA - Woodland to Mississippian, 1600 - 1000 B. P.

(Also see Durant's Bend and Washington)

LOCATION: Southeastern states. **DESCRIPTION:** A small point shaped like a five pointed star.

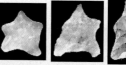

| G8, $3-$5 | G5, $1-$2 | G6, $1-$3 | G2, $1-$2 |
| Dallas Co., AL | Dallas Co., AL | Dallas Co., AL | Dallas Co., AL |

OHIO DOUBLE NOTCHED - Woodland, 3000 - 2000 B. P.

(Also see Benton, Evans, Leighton and St. Helena)

G5, $40-$75
OH

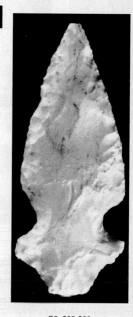

G8, $150-$250
Trimble Co., KY

G5, $35-$60
OH

LOCATION: Ohio and surrounding states. **DESCRIPTION:** A medium to large size, narrow, rather crude, point with side notches on both sides and a short base that is usually notched.

OHIO LANCEOLATE - Trans. Paleo-Early Archaic, 10,500 - 8000 B. P.

(Also see Agate Basin, Angostura, Browns Valley, Sedalia)

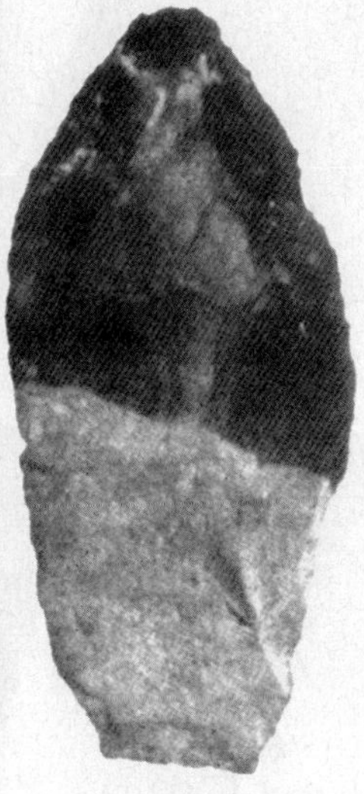

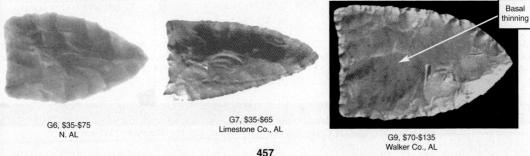

G5, $20-$35
Coshocton, OH

Black flint

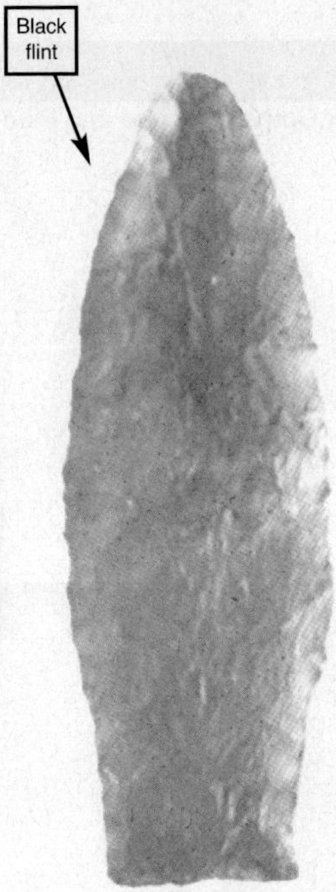

G7, $80-$150
Geauga Co., OH

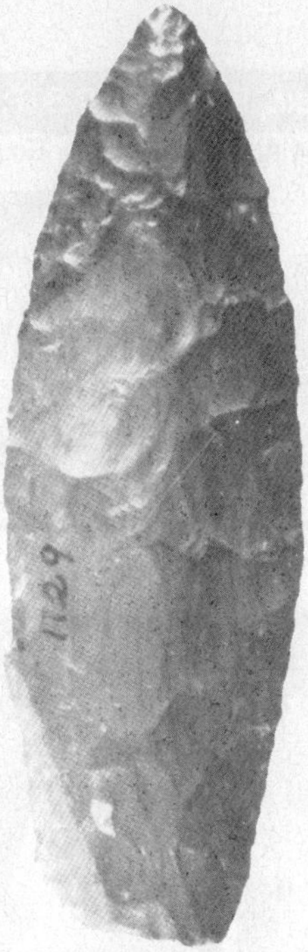

G8, $175-$325
OH

G10, $275-$525
Richland Co., OH

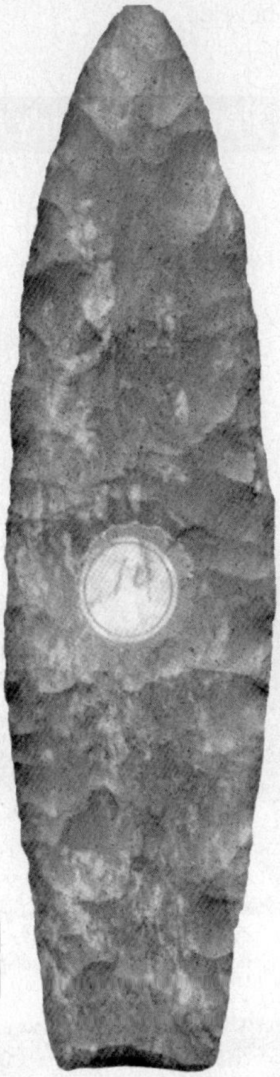

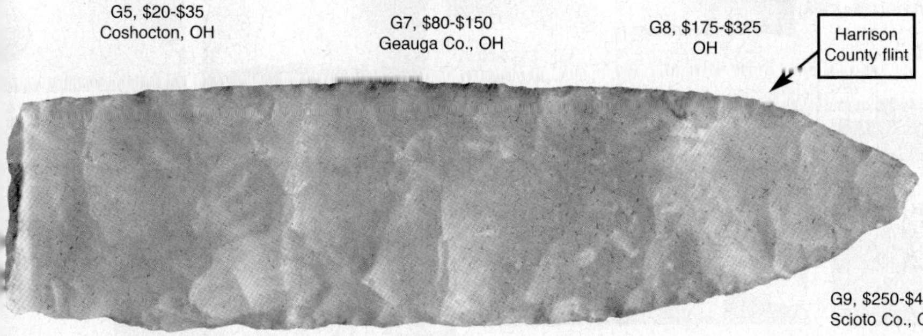

Harrison County flint

G9, $250-$475
Scioto Co., OH

LOCATION: Ohio and surrounding states. **DESCRIPTION:** A medium to large size lanceolate point with a straight base. Blade edges are slightly recurved becoming constricted at the basal hafting area. Thinner than *Clovis* or *Agate Basin.* Not fluted or basally thinned. Has light grinding at the stem.

PAINT ROCK VALLEY - Transitional Paleo, 10,000 - 6000 B. P.

(Also see Angostura, Browns Valley, Frazier, Hardaway Blade, Jeff and Tortugas)

G6, $35-$75
N. AL

G7, $35-$65
Limestone Co., AL

Basal thinning

G9, $70-$135
Walker Co., AL

PAINT ROCK VALLEY (continued)

LOCATION: Southeastern states. **DESCRIPTION:** A medium size, wide, lanceolate point with a concave base. Flaking is usually parallel with fine secondary work on the blade edges. The bases may be multiple fluted, thinned or beveled.

PALMER - Early Archaic, 9000 - 6000 B. P.

(Also see Autauga, Decatur, Ecusta, Kirk Corner Notched and Pine Tree)

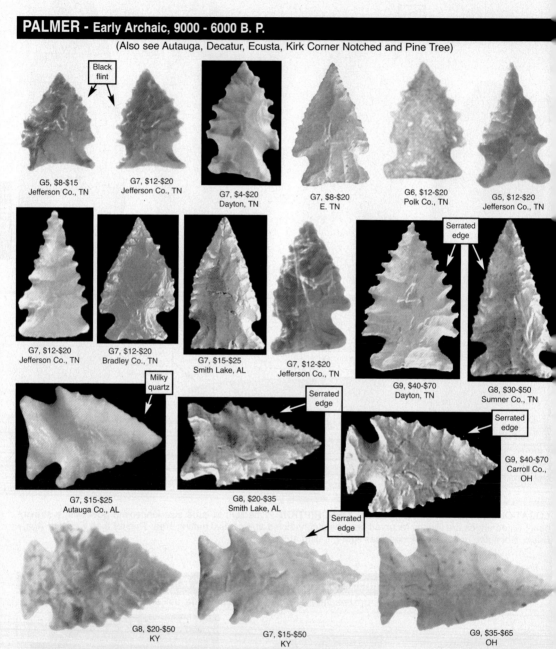

Black flint

G5, $8-$15
Jefferson Co., TN

G7, $12-$20
Jefferson Co., TN

G7, $4-$20
Dayton, TN

G7, $8-$20
E. TN

G6, $12-$20
Polk Co., TN

G5, $12-$20
Jefferson Co., TN

G7, $12-$20
Jefferson Co., TN

G7, $12-$20
Bradley Co., TN

G7, $15-$25
Smith Lake, AL

G7, $12-$20
Jefferson Co., TN

Serrated edge

G9, $40-$70
Dayton, TN

G8, $30-$50
Sumner Co., TN

Milky quartz

Serrated edge

Serrated edge

G9, $40-$70
Carroll Co., OH

G7, $15-$25
Autauga Co., AL

G8, $20-$35
Smith Lake, AL

Serrated edge

G8, $20-$50
KY

G7, $15-$50
KY

G9, $35-$65
OH

LOCATION: Southeastern to Eastern states. **DESCRIPTION:** A small size, corner notched, triangular point with a ground concave, convex or straight base. Many are serrated and large examples would fall under the *Pine Tree* or *Kirk* type. This type developed from *Hardaway* in North Carolina where cross types are found.

PATRICK - Mid-Archaic, 5000 - 3000 B. P.

(Also see Cave Spring, Fox Valley, Kanawha Stemmed, LeCroy, Stanly and Wheeler)

PATRICK (continued)

G5, $3-$6
Sequatchie Valley, TN

G5, $5-$10
KY

G7, $8-$15
Dunlap., TN

LOCATION: Eastern states. **DESCRIPTION:** A small to medium size, narrow point with very weak shoulders and a long, parallel sided, bifurcated stem.

PELICAN - Transitional Paleo, 10,000 - 6000 B. P.

(Also see Hinds and Arkabutla and Coldwater in SW Section)

Ground basal area

G9, $225-$400
Sou. MS

E
C

G9, $200-$350
Sou. MS

G9, $250-$450
Sou. MS

LOCATION: Mississippi, Tennessee westward intro Texas and Arkansas. **DESCRIPTION:** A short, broad, usually auriculate point with basal grinding. Shoulders taper into a long contracting stem. Some examples are basally thinned or fluted. **I.D. KEY:** Basal contraction, small size.

PENTAGONAL KNIFE - Mid-Archaic, 6500 - 4000 B. P.

(Also see Intrusive Mound, Jacks Reef Corner Notched)

Flintridge flint

Upper Mercer flint

G6, $30-$50
OH

G9, $80-$150
Lorain Co., OH

G8, $70-$135
OH

G8 $70-$135
Ashland, KY

PENTAGONAL KNIFE (continued)

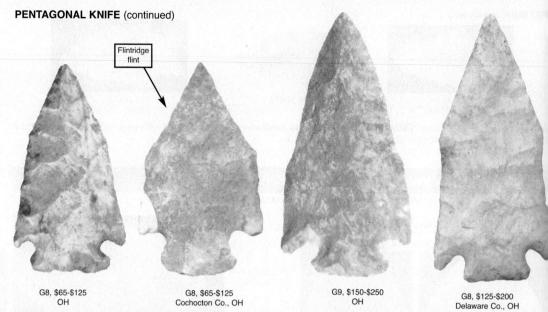

Flintridge flint

G8, $65-$125
OH

G8, $65-$125
Cochocton Co., OH

G9, $150-$250
OH

G8, $125-$200
Delaware Co., OH

LOCATION: Ohio into Kentucky, Tennessee and Alabama. **DESCRIPTION:** A medium to large size pentagonal shaped point with a flaring or corner notched stem. Some examples are base notched. Similar too but older than the *Afton* point found in the Midwest. Similar to *Jacks Reef* but thicker. **I.D. KEY:** Blade form.

PERFORATOR - Archaic to Mississippian, 9000 - 400 B. P.

(Also see Drill, Graver and Lancet)

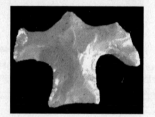

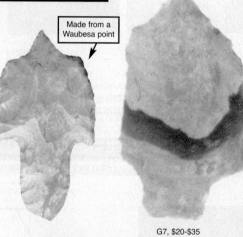

Made from a Waubesa point

G3, $1-$2
Meigs Co., TN

G3, $3-$6
Walker Co., GA

G10, $40-$75
TN

G7, $20-$35
TN

LOCATION: Archaic and Woodland sites everywhere. **DESCRIPTION:** A jabbing projection at the tip would qualify for the type. It is believed that *perforators* were used for tattooing, incising or to punch holes in leather or other materials or objects. Paleo peoples used *Gravers* for the same purpose. All Archaic and Woodland cultures converted their points into this type. Therefore, most point types could occur in this form.

PICKWICK - Middle to Late Archaic, 6000 - 3500 B. P.

(Also see Elora, Ledbetter, Little Bear Creek, McWhinney, Mulberry Creek and Shoals Creek)

LOCATION: Southeastern states. **DESCRIPTION:** A medium to large size, expanded shoulder, contracted to expanded stem point. Blade edges are recurved, and many examples show fine secondary flaking with serrations. Some are beveled on one side of each face. The bevel is steep and shallow. Shoulders are horizontal, tapered or barbed and form sharp angles. Some stems are snapped off or may show original rind.

G5, $8-$15
Meigs Co., TN

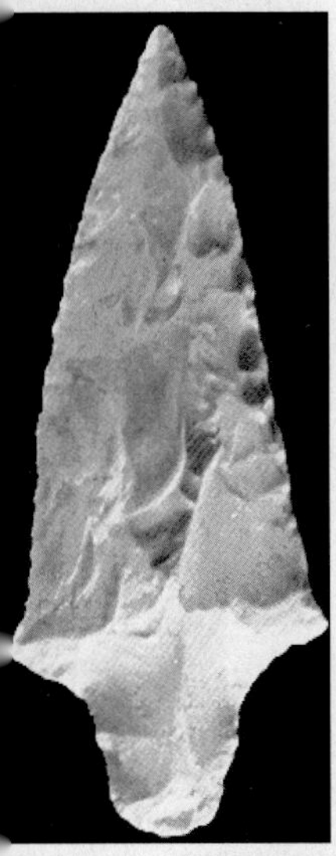

Snap base

E
C

G7, $25-$45
Meigs Co., TN

G6, $35-$65
Florence, AL

G6, $30-$45
KY

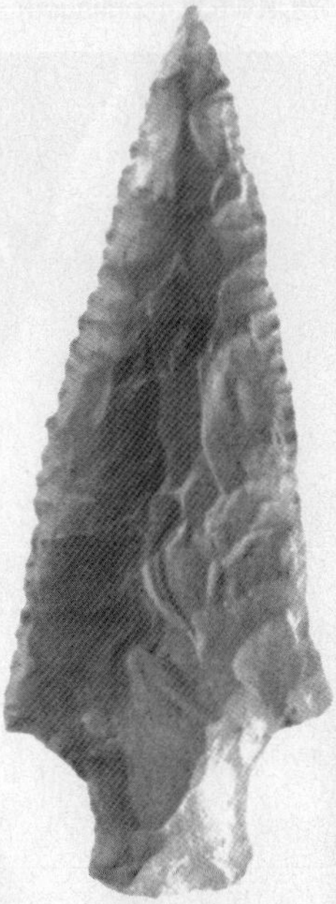

G9, $65-$125
Florence, AL

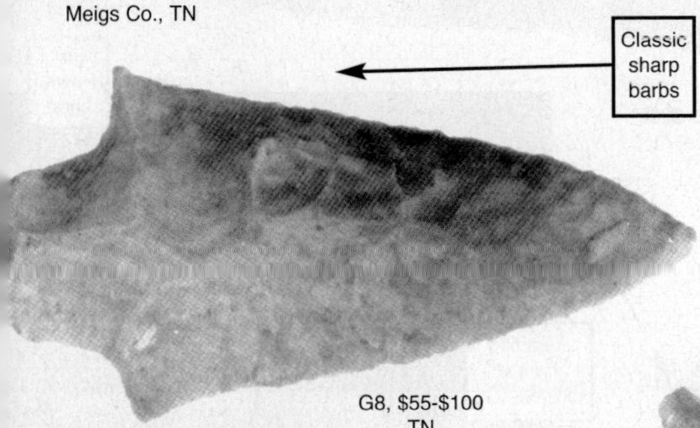

Classic sharp barbs

G8, $55-$100
TN

G7, $35-$65
TN

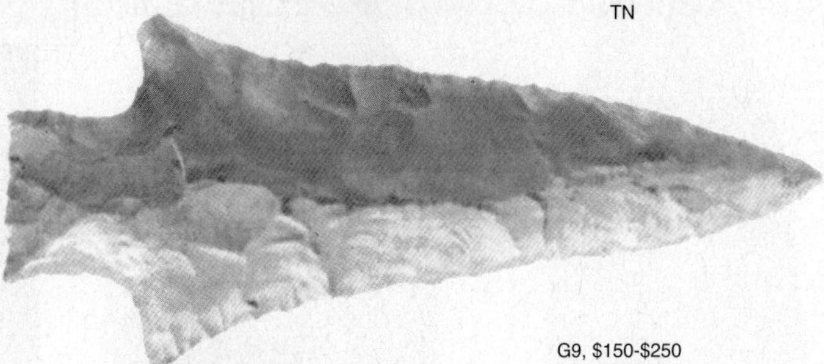

Red jasper

Serrated edge

G9, $150-$250
Florence, AL

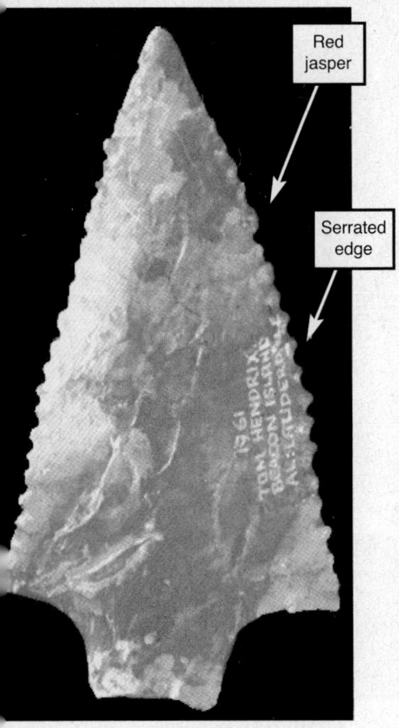

G10, $150-$250
Lauderdale Co., AL

G10, $170-$325
Colbert Co., AL,
Buffalo Riv., cache point

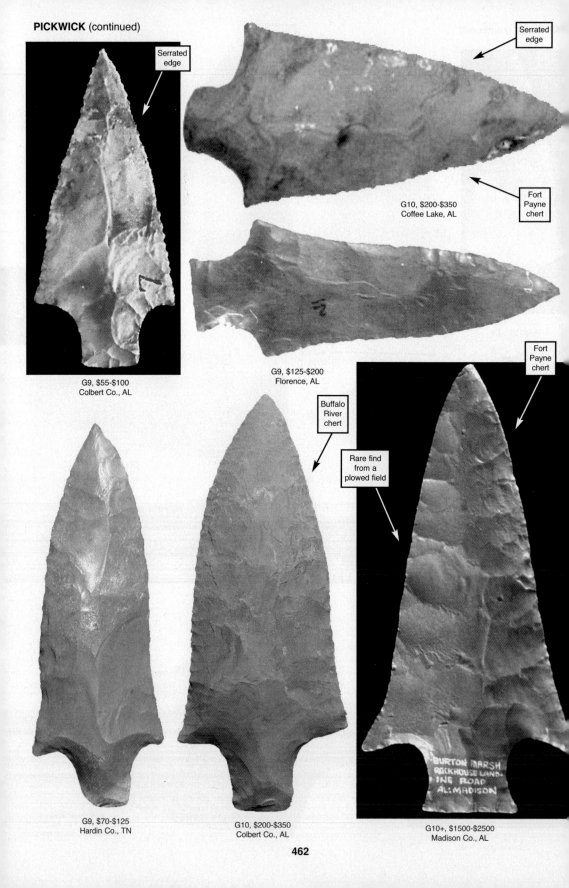

Serrated edge

Serrated edge

Fort Payne chert

G10, $200-$350
Coffee Lake, AL

G9, $55-$100
Colbert Co., AL

G9, $125-$200
Florence, AL

Fort Payne chert

Buffalo River chert

Rare find from a plowed field

G9, $70-$125
Hardin Co., TN

G10, $200-$350
Colbert Co., AL

BURTON MARSH
ROCKHOUSE LAND
ING ROAD
AL:MADISON

G10+, $1500-$2500
Madison Co., AL

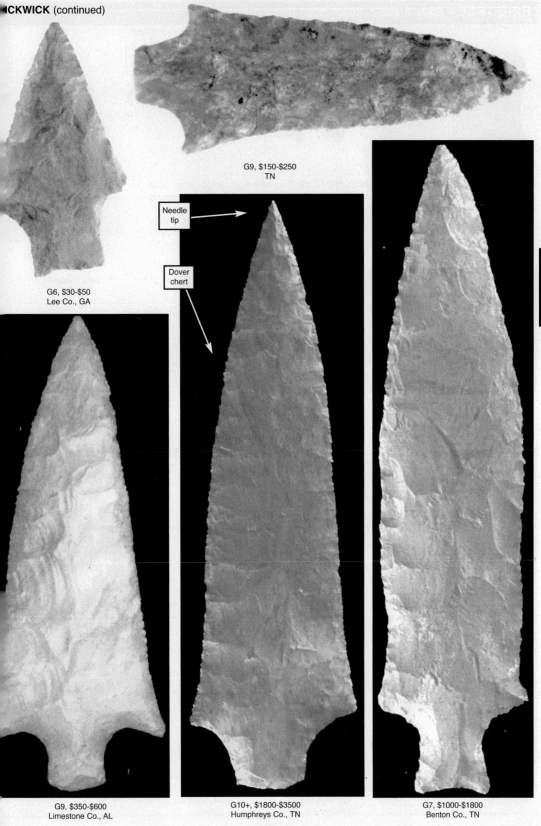

G9, $150-$250
TN

Needle
tip

Dover
chert

G6, $30-$50
Lee Co., GA

E
C

G9, $350-$600
Limestone Co., AL

G10+, $1800-$3500
Humphreys Co., TN

G7, $1000-$1800
Benton Co., TN

PINE TREE - Early Archaic, 8000 - 5000 B. P.

(Also see Big Sandy, Decatur, Greenbrier, Kirk and Palmer)

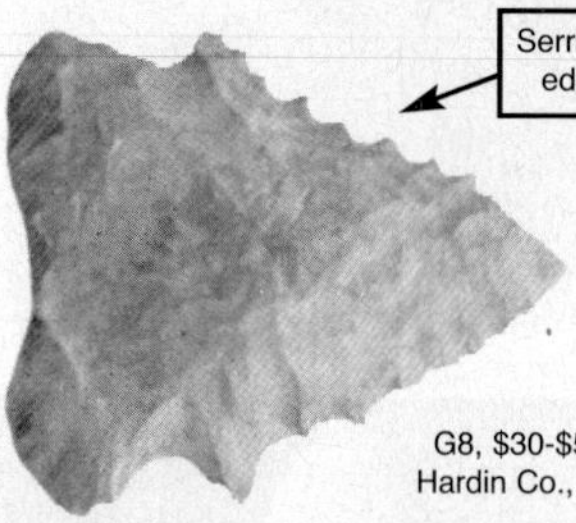

Serrated
edge

G8, $30-$55
Hardin Co., TN

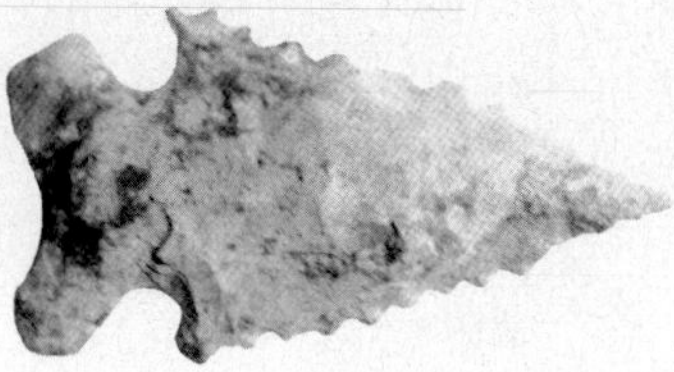

G7, $20-$35
S. IN

Bifurcated
base

G9, $125-$250
KY

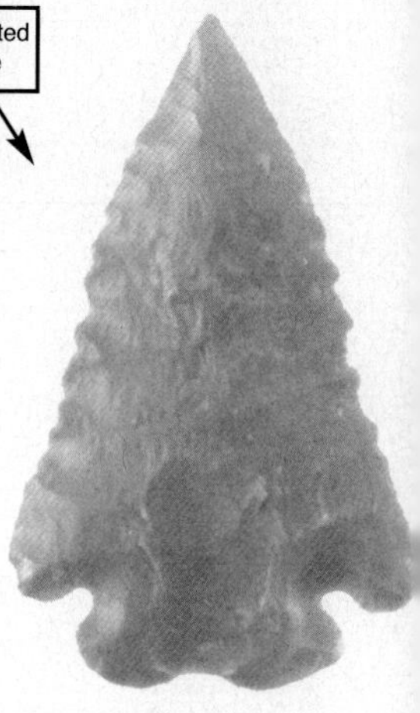

LOCATION: Southeastern states. **DESCRIPTION:** A medium to large size, side notched, usually serrated point with parallel flaking to the center of the blade forming a median ridge. The bases are ground and can be concave, convex, straight, or auriculate. This type developed from the earlier *Greenbrier* point. Small examples would fall into the *Palmer* type. **I.D. KEY:** Archaic flaking with long flakes to the center of the blade.

Serrated
edge

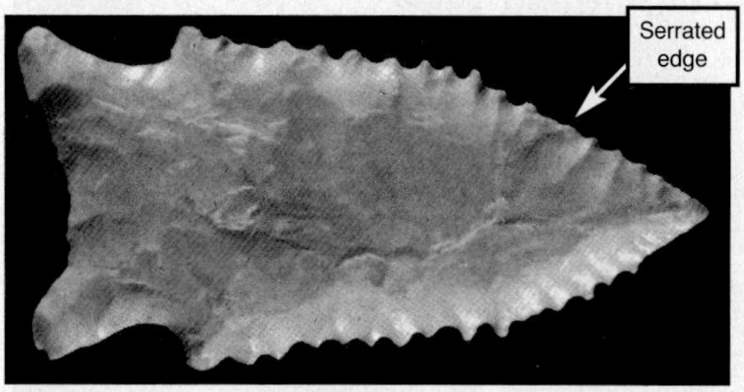

G10, $250-$375
Coffee Lake, AL

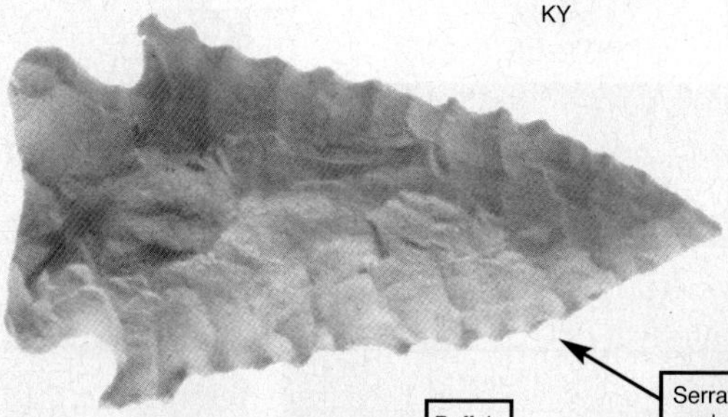

Serrated
edge

G9, $125-$200
Coffee Lake, AL

G7, $250-$400
W. KY

Dover
chert
Serrated
edge

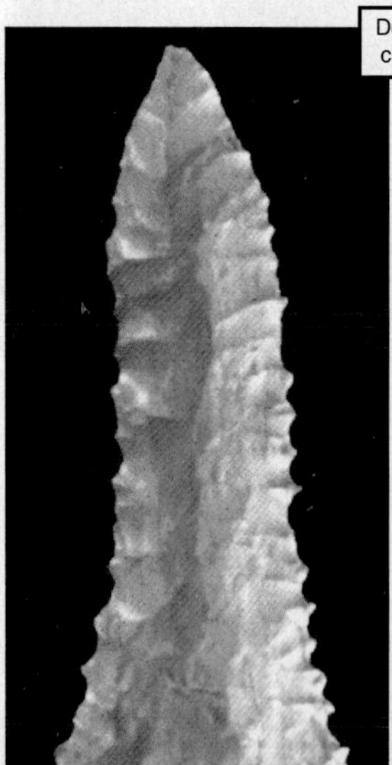

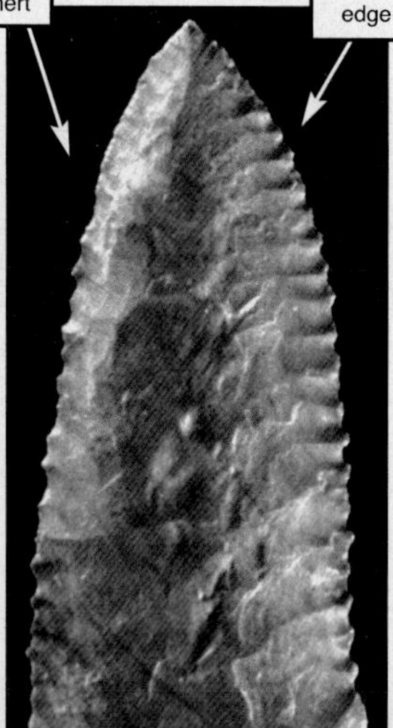

G8, $250-$450
Humphreys Co., TN

Found in
a plowed
field
Fort
Payne
chert

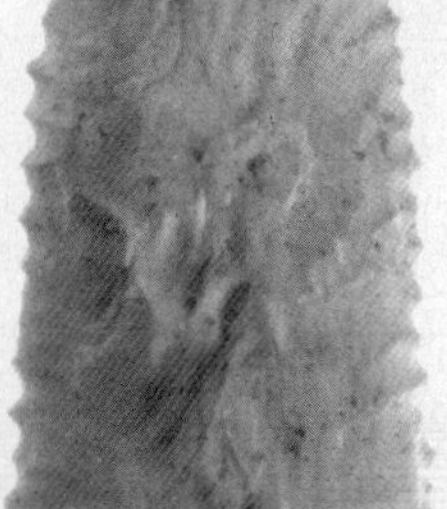

G10+, $750-$1400
Giles Co., TN

Buffalo
River
chert

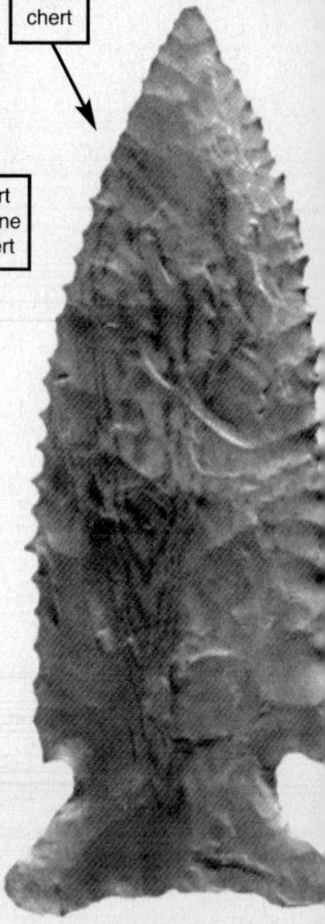

G10, $350-$600
Humphreys Co., TN

(Also see Kirk, Neuberger and Palmer)

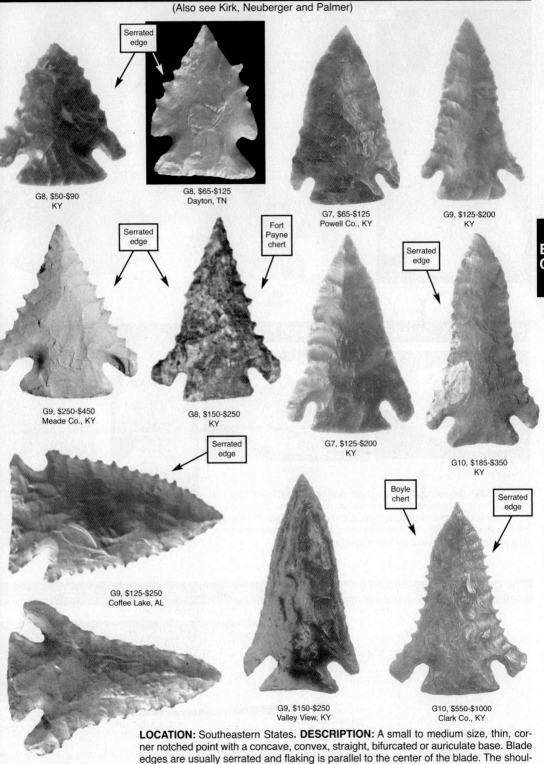

Serrated edge

G8, $50-$90
KY

G8, $65-$125
Dayton, TN

G7, $65-$125
Powell Co., KY

G9, $125-$200
KY

E
C

Serrated edge

Fort Payne chert

Serrated edge

G9, $250-$450
Meade Co., KY

G8, $150-$250
KY

G7, $125-$200
KY

G10, $185-$350
KY

Serrated edge

Boyle chert

Serrated edge

G9, $125-$250
Coffee Lake, AL

G9, $150-$250
Valley View, KY

G10, $550-$1000
Clark Co., KY

G10, $300-$350
Humphreys Co., TN

LOCATION: Southeastern States. **DESCRIPTION:** A small to medium size, thin, corner notched point with a concave, convex, straight, bifurcated or auriculate base. Blade edges are usually serrated and flaking is parallel to the center of the blade. The shoulders expand and are barbed. The base is ground. Small examples would fall under the *Palmer* type. **I.D. KEY:** Archaic flaking to the center of each blade.

PINE TREE CRONER NOTCHED (continued)

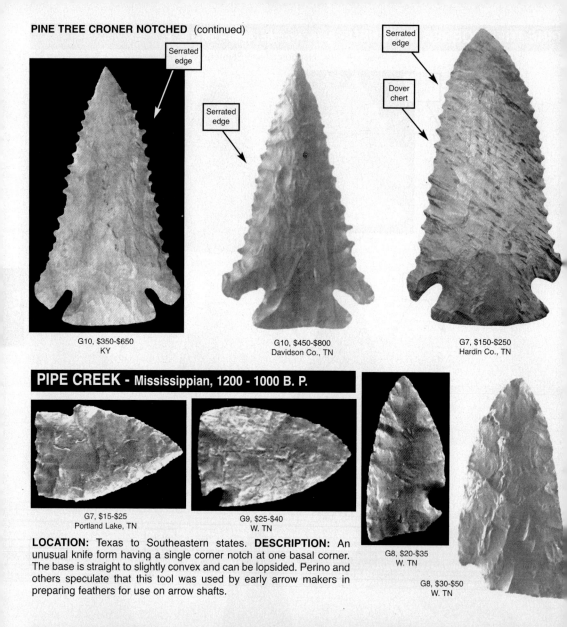

Serrated edge

Serrated edge

Serrated edge

Dover chert

G10, $350-$650
KY

G10, $450-$800
Davidson Co., TN

G7, $150-$250
Hardin Co., TN

PIPE CREEK - Mississippian, 1200 - 1000 B. P.

G7, $15-$25
Portland Lake, TN

G9, $25-$40
W. TN

G8, $20-$35
W. TN

G8, $30-$50
W. TN

LOCATION: Texas to Southeastern states. **DESCRIPTION:** An unusual knife form having a single corner notch at one basal corner. The base is straight to slightly convex and can be lopsided. Perino and others speculate that this tool was used by early arrow makers in preparing feathers for use on arrow shafts.

PLAINVIEW- Late Paleo, 10,000 - 7000 B. P.

(Also see Angostura, Browns Valley, Clovis and Dalton)

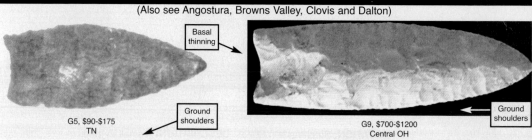

Basal thinning

Ground shoulders

G5, $90-$175
TN

Ground shoulders

G9, $700-$1200
Central OH

LOCATION: DESCRIPTION: A medium size, thin, lanceolate point with usually parallel sides and a concave base that is ground. Some examples are thinned or fluted and are believed to be related to the earlier *Clovis* and contemporary *Dalton* type. Flaking is of high quality and can be collateral to oblique transverse.

PONTCHARTRAIN (Type I) - Late Archaic-Woodland, 4000 - 2000 B. P.

(Also see Kays, Little Bear Creek and Mulberry Creek)

G6, $25-$45
Clarksville, TN

G6, $20-$40
S. E. TN

G6, $20-$40
W. TN

Good symmetry

G10, $250-$475
Parsons, TN. Classic.

G8, $35-$65
W. TN

E
C

LOCATION: Mid-southeastern states. **DESCRIPTION:** A medium to large size, thick, narrow, stemmed point with weak, tapered or barbed shoulders. The stem is parallel sided with a convex base. Some examples are finely serrated and are related and similar to the *Flint Creek* type.

G8, $90-$175
TN. Classic.

PONTCHARTRAIN (Type II) - Woodland, 3400 - 2000 B. P.

(Also see Buck Creek, Hardin and Hamilton Stemmed)

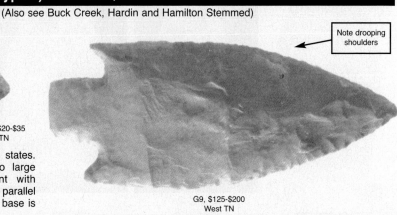

Note drooping shoulders

G7, $20-$35
TN

LOCATION: Mid-southeastern states. **DESCRIPTION:** A medium to large size, broad, stemmed point with barbed shoulders. The stem is parallel to slightly contracting and the base is straight to convex.

G9, $125-$200
West TN

467

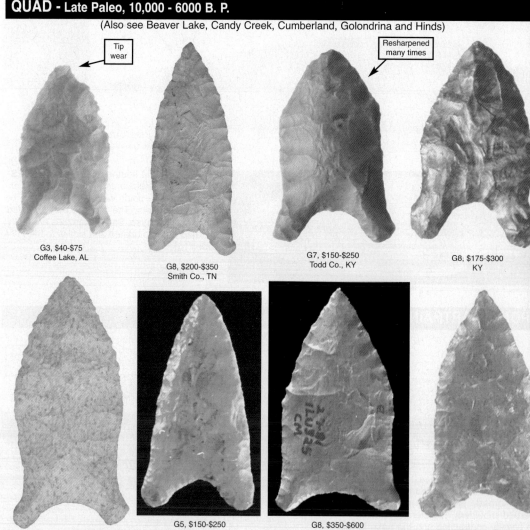

G9, $200-$375
West TN

G8, $35-$60
Noxubee Co., MS

QUAD - Late Paleo, 10,000 - 6000 B. P.

(Also see Beaver Lake, Candy Creek, Cumberland, Golondrina and Hinds)

Tip wear

Resharpened many times

G3, $40-$75
Coffee Lake, AL

G8, $200-$350
Smith Co., TN

G7, $150-$250
Todd Co., KY

G8, $175-$300
KY

G6, $400-$750
Lawrence Co., IN

G5, $150-$250
Lauderdale Co., AL

G8, $350-$600
Lauderdale Co., AL

G8, $350-$650
Wayne Co., KY

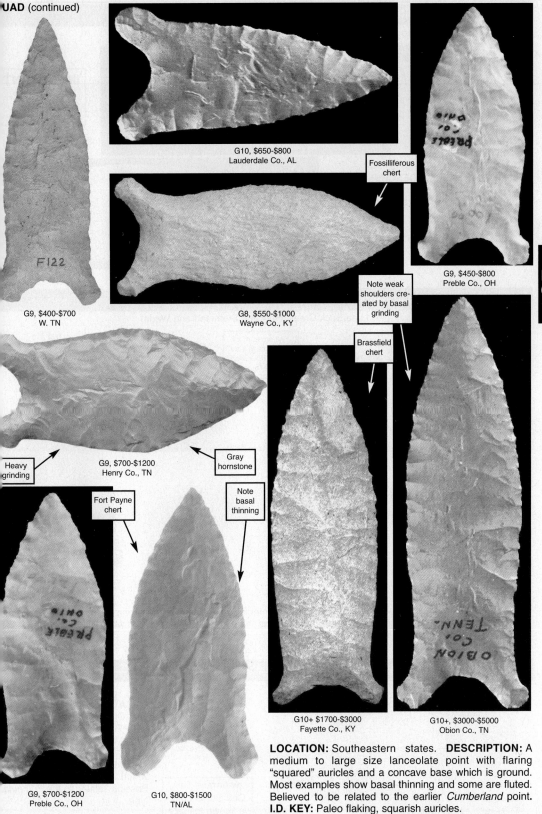

G10, $650-$800
Lauderdale Co., AL

G9, $400-$700
W. TN

F122

G8, $550-$1000
Wayne Co., KY

Fossilliferous chert

G9, $450-$800
Preble Co., OH

E
C

Note weak shoulders cre-ated by basal grinding

Brassfield chert

Heavy grinding

G9, $700-$1200
Henry Co., TN

Gray hornstone

Fort Payne chert

Note basal thinning

G9, $700-$1200
Preble Co., OH

G10, $800-$1500
TN/AL

G10+ $1700-$3000
Fayette Co., KY

G10+, $3000-$5000
Obion Co., TN

LOCATION: Southeastern states. **DESCRIPTION:** A medium to large size lanceolate point with flaring "squared" auricles and a concave base which is ground. Most examples show basal thinning and some are fluted. Believed to be related to the earlier *Cumberland* point. **I.D. KEY:** Paleo flaking, squarish auricles.

469

RAMEY KNIFE - Middle Archaic, 5000 - 4000 B. P.

(Also see Cotaco Creek, Morse Knife and Snake Creek)

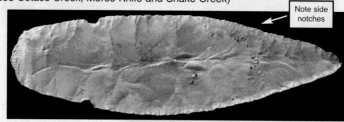

Note side notches

G8, $450-$800
KY

IMPORTANT:
Shown 50% actual size.

LOCATION: Type site is at the Cahokia Mounds in IL. **DESCRIPTION:** A large size broad, lanceolate blade with a rounded base and high quality flaking. The Tenn. form is similar to the Illinois form.

G8, $450-$800
Rhea Co., TN

RANKIN - Late Archaic-Woodland, 4000 - 2500 B. P.

(Also see Buck Creek, Hamilton Stemmed and Wade)

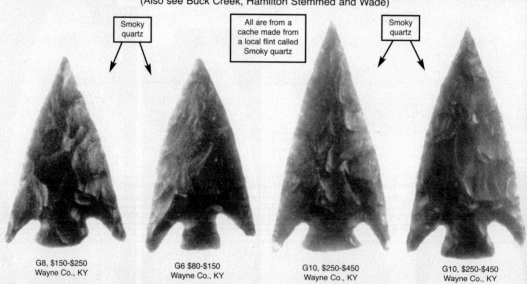

Smoky quartz

All are from a cache made from a local flint called Smoky quartz

Smoky quartz

G8, $150-$250
Wayne Co., KY

G6 $80-$150
Wayne Co., KY

G10, $250-$450
Wayne Co., KY

G10, $250-$450
Wayne Co., KY

LOCATION: Tennessee into Kentucky. **DESCRIPTION:** A medium size, thin, well made barbed dart point with a short, expanding stem. Barbs are pointed and can extend beyond the base. Blade is recurved with a needle tip. **I.D. KEY:** Drooping barbs, short base.

RED OCHRE - Woodland, 3000 - 1500 B. P.

G8, $125-$200
KY

IMPORTANT: This Red Ochre point is shown full size

LOCATION: Mid-western states into Ohio and Kentucky. **DESCRIPTION:** A large, thin, broad blade with a contracting basal area. The base is convex to straight. Very similar to *Wadlow* which has parallel sides. Possibly related to the *Turkeytail* type.

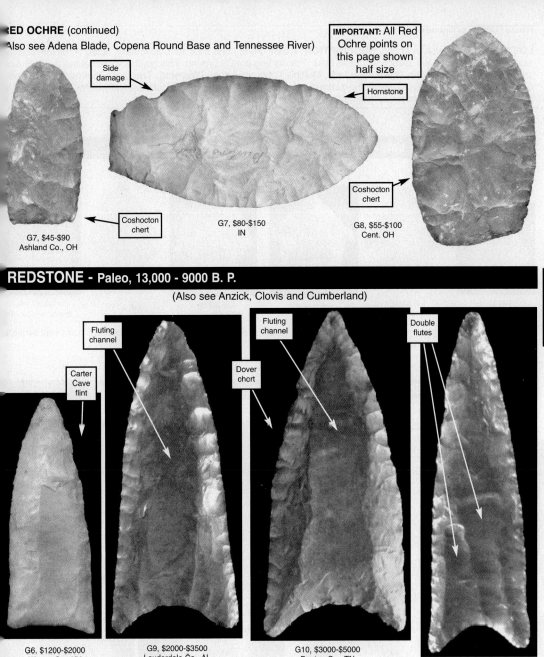

(Also see Adena Blade, Copena Round Base and Tennessee River)

IMPORTANT: All Red Ochre points on this page shown half size

Side damage

Hornstone

Coshocton chert

Coshocton chert

G7, $80-$150
IN

G8, $55-$100
Cent. OH

Coshocton chert

G7, $45-$90
Ashland Co., OH

REDSTONE - Paleo, 13,000 - 9000 B. P.

(Also see Anzick, Clovis and Cumberland)

E
C

Fluting channel

Fluting channel

Double flutes

Carter Cave flint

Dover chert

G6, $1200-$2000
Wayne Co., KY

G9, $2000-$3500
Lauderdale Co., AL

G10, $3000-$5000
Benton Co., TN

G10, $2000-$3500
N. AL

Dover chert

G9, $4000-$7500
Humphreys Co., TN

Minor tip wear

From a cache of three

Fluting channel

471

REDSTONE (continued)

LOCATION: Southeastern states. **DESCRIPTION:** A medium to large size, thin, auriculate, fluted point with conve. sides expanding to a wide, deeply concave base. The hafting area is ground. This point is widest at the base. Flutin can extend most of the way down each face. Multiple flutes are usual. (**Warning:** The more common resharpene Clovis point is often sold as this type. *Redstones* are extremely rare and are almost never offered for sale.) **I.D. KEY** Baton or billet fluted, edgework on the hafting area.

RHEEMS CREEK - Late Archaic to Woodland, 4000 - 2000 B. P.

(Also see Halifax and Jude)

G2, $1-$2
Meigs Co., TN

G2, $1-$2
N. AL

G3, $2-$4
Huntsville, AL

G5, $3-$6
Meigs Co., TN

G5, $3-$6
N. AL

G3, $2-$4
Jessamine Co., KY

LOCATION: Southeastern states. **DESCRIPTION:** A small size, stubby, parallel sided, stemmed point with straigh shoulders. Similar to *Halifax* which expands at the base.

RICE LOBBED - Early Archaic, 9000 - 5000 B. P.

(Also see Kanawha, LeCroy, MacCorkle and Pine Tree)

Basal lobes
are ground

Serrated
edge

G8, $65-$125
OH

G8, $65-$125
Salt Lick, KY

G8, $90-$175
Salt Lick, KY

G8, $90-$175
Salt Lick, KY

LOCATION: Midwestern to Northeastern states. **DESCRIPTION:** A medium to large size bifurcated to lobbed base point with serrated blade edges. The base has a shallow indentation compared to the other bifurcated types. Shoulders are sharp and prominent. Called *Culpepper Bifurcate* in Virginia.

ROSS - Woodland, 2500 - 1500 B. P.

(Also see Hopewell, North & Snyders)

LOCATION: Midwestern to Eastern states. **DESCRIPTION:** A very large size blade with an expanded, rounded base. Some examples have a contracting "V" shaped base. **I.D. KEY:** Size, base form.

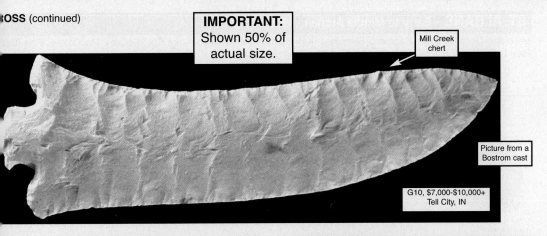

IMPORTANT:
Shown 50% of
actual size.

Mill Creek
chert

Picture from a
Bostrom cast

G10, $7,000-$10,000+
Tell City, IN

RUSSELL CAVE - Early Archaic, 9000 - 7000 B. P.

(Also see Hardaway, Harpeth River, Heavy Duty, Pine Tree and Searcy)

E
C

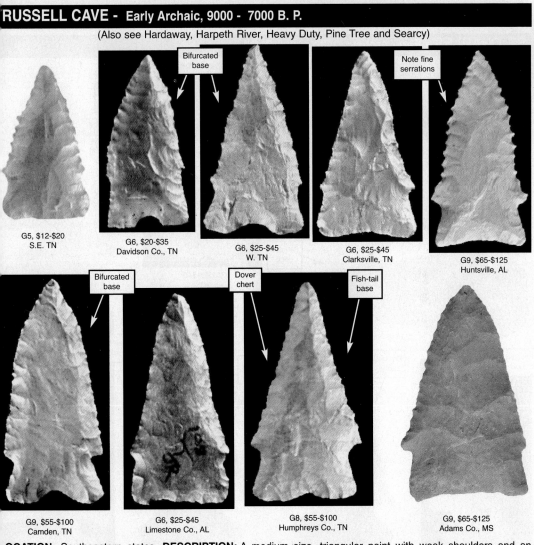

Bifurcated
base

Note fine
serrations

G5, $12-$20
S.E. TN

G6, $20-$35
Davidson Co., TN

G6, $25-$45
W. TN

G6, $25-$45
Clarksville, TN

G9, $65-$125
Huntsville, AL

Bifurcated
base

Dover
chert

Fish-tail
base

G9, $55-$100
Camden, TN

G6, $25-$45
Limestone Co., AL

G8, $55-$100
Humphreys Co., TN

G9, $65-$125
Adams Co., MS

LOCATION: Southeastern states. **DESCRIPTION:** A medium size, triangular point with weak shoulders and an expanding to auriculate base. The stem appears to be an extension of the blade edges, expanding to the base. Most examples are serrated and beveled on one side of each face, although some examples are beveled on all four sides. The base is straight, concave, bifurcated or auriculate. **I.D. KEY:** Notched base and edgework.

ST. ALBANS - Early to Middle Archaic, 8900 - 8000 B. P.

(Also see Decatur, Jude, Kanawha Stemmed, Kirk Stemmed-Bifurcated, Lake Erie, LeCroy, MacCorkle, Pine Tree Rice Lobbed and Stanly)

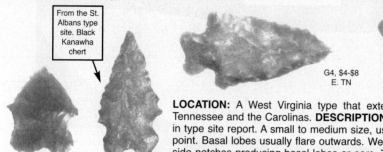

From the St. Albans type site. Black Kanawha chert

G4, $4-$8
E. TN

G5, $5-$10
GA

G5, $3-$6
Hamilton Co., TN

G6, $12-$20
Kanawha Co., WVA

LOCATION: A West Virginia type that extends into Pennsylvania, Virginia, Tennessee and the Carolinas. **DESCRIPTION:** Called *St. Albans Side Notched* in type site report. A small to medium size, usually serrated, narrow, bifurcated point. Basal lobes usually flare outwards. Weak shoulders are formed by slight side notches producing basal lobes or ears. The basal lobes are more shallow than in the *LeCroy* type, otherwise they are easily confused. **I.D. KEY:** Shallow basal lobes.

ST. CHARLES - Early Archaic, 9500 - 8000 B. P.

(Also see Decatur, Gibson, Kirk Corner Notched, Thebes and Warrick)

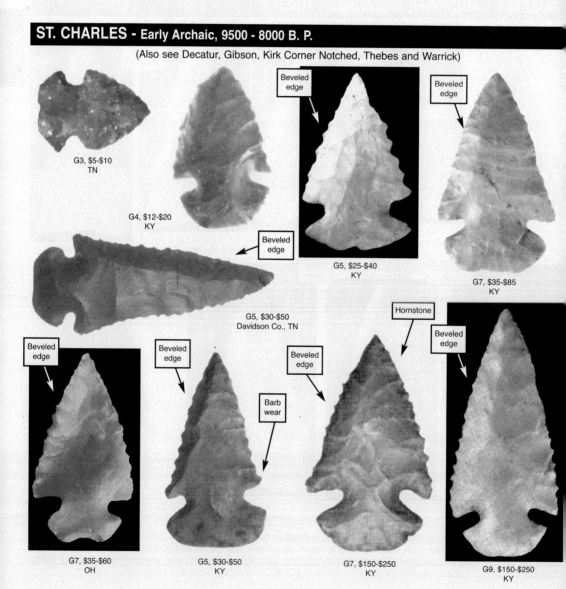

G3, $5-$10
TN

G4, $12-$20
KY

Beveled edge

Beveled edge

Beveled edge

G5, $25-$40
KY

G7, $35-$85
KY

G5, $30-$50
Davidson Co., TN

Hornstone

Beveled edge

Beveled edge

Beveled edge

Barb wear

Beveled edge

G7, $35-$60
OH

G5, $30-$50
KY

G7, $150-$250
KY

G9, $150-$250
KY

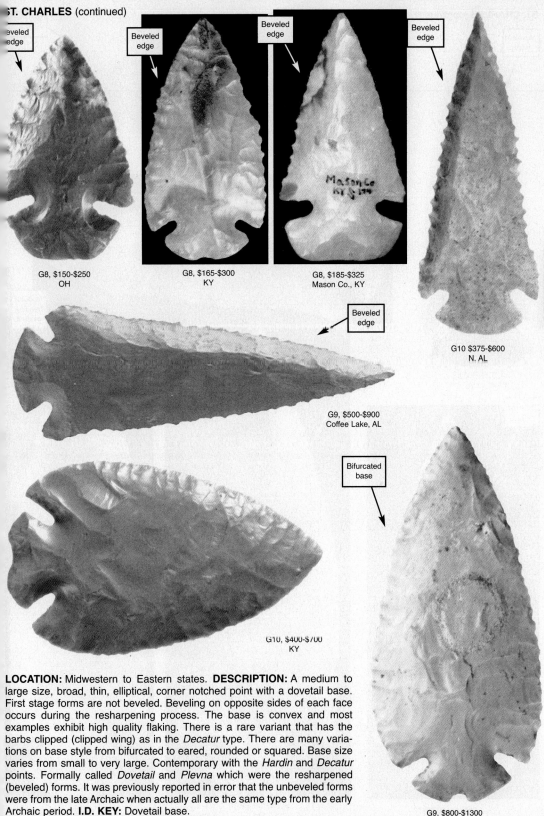

Beveled edge

Beveled edge

Beveled edge

Beveled edge

G8, $150-$250
OH

G8, $165-$300
KY

G8, $185-$325
Mason Co., KY

G10 $375-$600
N, AL

Beveled edge

G9, $500-$900
Coffee Lake, AL

Bifurcated base

G10, $400-$700
KY

G9, $800-$1300
IN

E
C

LOCATION: Midwestern to Eastern states. **DESCRIPTION:** A medium to large size, broad, thin, elliptical, corner notched point with a dovetail base. First stage forms are not beveled. Beveling on opposite sides of each face occurs during the resharpening process. The base is convex and most examples exhibit high quality flaking. There is a rare variant that has the barbs clipped (clipped wing) as in the *Decatur* type. There are many variations on base style from bifurcated to eared, rounded or squared. Base size varies from small to very large. Contemporary with the *Hardin* and *Decatur* points. Formally called *Dovetail* and *Plevna* which were the resharpened (beveled) forms. It was previously reported in error that the unbeveled forms were from the late Archaic when actually all are the same type from the early Archaic period. **I.D. KEY:** Dovetail base.

475

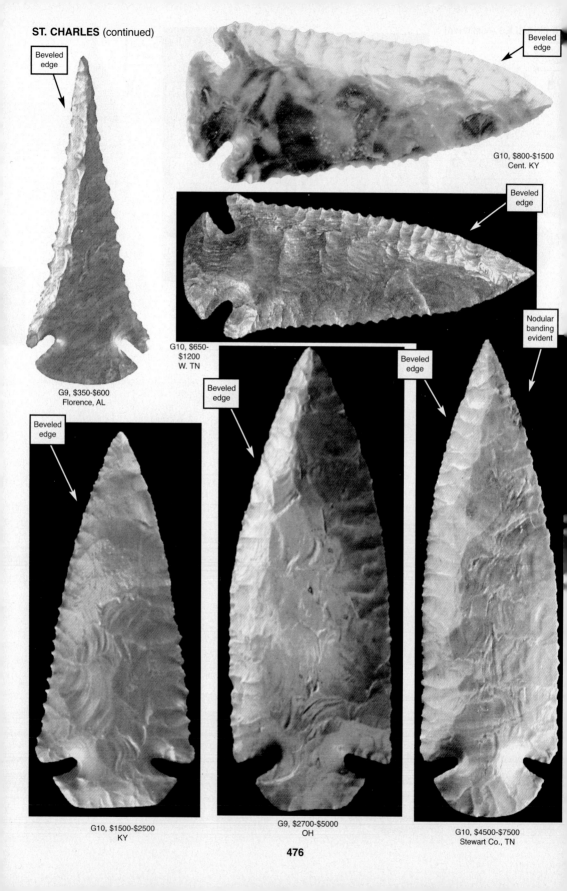

ST. CHARLES (continued)

Beveled edge

Beveled edge

G10, $800-$1500
Cent. KY

Beveled edge

G10, $650-$1200
W. TN

G9, $350-$600
Florence, AL

Beveled edge

Beveled edge

Beveled edge

Nodular banding evident

G10, $1500-$2500
KY

G9, $2700-$5000
OH

G10, $4500-$7500
Stewart Co., TN

ST. HELENA - Early to Mid-Archaic, 8000 - 5000 B. P.

(Also see Benton, Evans, Leighton and Ohio Double Notched)

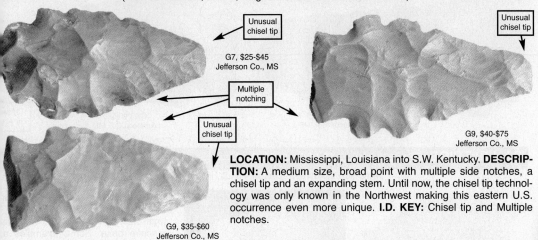

Unusual chisel tip

G7, $25-$45
Jefferson Co., MS

Unusual chisel tip

Multiple notching

Unusual chisel tip

G9, $40-$75
Jefferson Co., MS

G9, $35-$60
Jefferson Co., MS

LOCATION: Mississippi, Louisiana into S.W. Kentucky. **DESCRIPTION:** A medium size, broad point with multiple side notches, a chisel tip and an expanding stem. Until now, the chisel tip technology was only known in the Northwest making this eastern U.S. occurrence even more unique. **I.D. KEY:** Chisel tip and Multiple notches.

E
C

ST. TAMMANY - Early to Mid-Archaic, 8000 - 5000 B. P.

(Also see Evans, Kirk Stemmed and St. Helena)

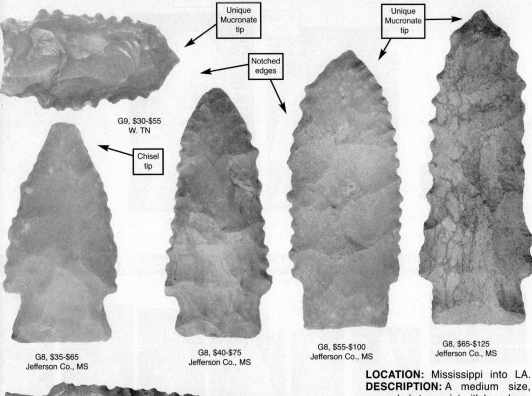

Unique Mucronate tip

Unique Mucronate tip

Notched edges

G9, $30-$55
W. TN

Chisel tip

G8, $35-$65
Jefferson Co., MS

G8, $40-$75
Jefferson Co., MS

G8, $55-$100
Jefferson Co., MS

G8, $65-$125
Jefferson Co., MS

LOCATION: Mississippi into LA. **DESCRIPTION:** A medium size, expanded stem point with broad serrations on the blade edges. Base is straight to convex and an apiculate distal end. Some examples have a chisel tip. **I.D. KEY:** Apiculate distal end, blade notching.

G10, $80-$150
Adams Co., MS

G8, $55-$100
Jefferson Co., MS

G8, $40-$80
Jefferson Co., MS

Unique
chisel t

SAN PATRICE - Early Archaic, 10,000 - 8000 B. P.

(Also see Coldwater, Dalton, Hinds, Palmer, Pelican)

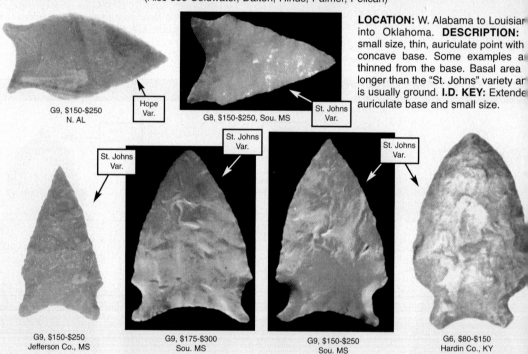

LOCATION: W. Alabama to Louisian into Oklahoma. **DESCRIPTION:** small size, thin, auriculate point with concave base. Some examples a thinned from the base. Basal area longer than the "St. Johns" variety an is usually ground. **I.D. KEY:** Extende auriculate base and small size.

G9, $150-$250
N. AL

Hope
Var.

G8, $150-$250, Sou. MS

St. Johns
Var.

St. Johns
Var.

St. Johns
Var.

St. Johns
Var.

G9, $150-$250
Jefferson Co., MS

G9, $175-$300
Sou. MS

G9, $150-$250
Sou. MS

G6, $80-$150
Hardin Co., KY

SAND MOUNTAIN - Late Woodland to Mississippian, 1500 - 400 B. P.

(Also see Durant's Bend, Fort Ancient and Madison)

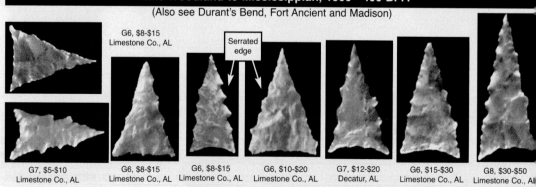

G6, $8-$15
Limestone Co., AL

Serrated
edge

G7, $5-$10
Limestone Co., AL

G6, $8-$15
Limestone Co., AL

G6, $8-$15
Limestone Co., AL

G6, $10-$20
Limestone Co., AL

G7, $12-$20
Decatur, AL

G6, $15-$30
Limestone Co., AL

G8, $30-$50
Limestone Co., Al

LOCATION: Southeastern states. **DESCRIPTION:** A small size, triangular point with serrated blade edges and a con cave base. A straight base would place it in the *Fort Ancient* type. **I.D. KEY:** Basal corners are not symmetrical.

SAVAGE CAVE - Early to Middle Archaic, 7000 - 4000 B. P.

(Also see Big Sandy and Newton Falls)

LOCATION: Kentucky and surrounding states. **DESCRIPTION:** A medium to large size, broad, side notched point that is usually serrated. Bases are generally straight but can be slightly concave or convex.

G5, $8-$15
Meigs Co., TN

G6, $10-$20
Henry Co., AL

SAVANNAH RIVER - Middle Archaic to Woodland, 5000 - 2000 B. P.

(Also see Appalachian, Elora, Hamilton, Johnson, Kirk, Maples and Stanly)

EC

G6, $6-$12
Polk Co., TN

G5, $5-$10
Dayton, TN

G6, $15-$25
Dayton, TN

G7, $35-$60
Andersonville, GA

G6, $30-$50
GA

G7, $40-$75
GA

479

SAVANNAH RIVER (continued)

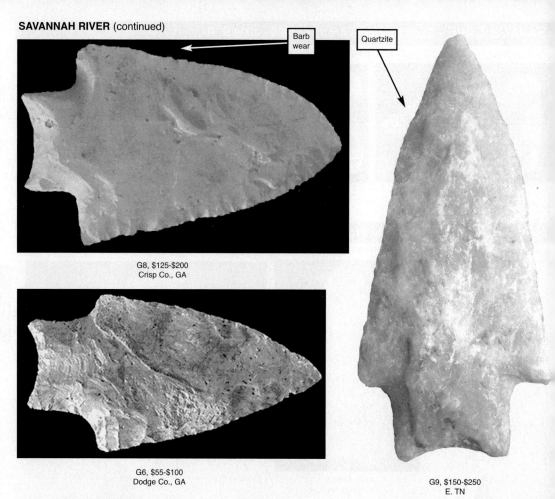

Barb wear

Quartzite

G8, $125-$200
Crisp Co., GA

G6, $55-$100
Dodge Co., GA

G9, $150-$250
E. TN

LOCATION: Southeastern to Eastern states. **DESCRIPTION:** A medium to large size, straight to contracting stemmed point with a straight, concave or bifurcated base. The shoulders are tapered to square. The stems are narrow to broad. Believed to be related to the earlier *Stanly* point.

SCRAPER - Paleo to Archaic, 14,000 - 5000 B. P.

(Also see Drill, Graver, Lancet and Spokeshave)

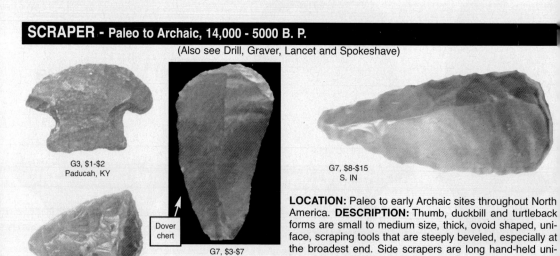

G3, $1-$2
Paducah, KY

Dover chert

G7, $8-$15
S. IN

G7, $3-$7
Humphreys Co., TN

Thumb scraper

G6, $2-$5
Carter Cave, KY

LOCATION: Paleo to early Archaic sites throughout North America. **DESCRIPTION:** Thumb, duckbill and turtleback forms are small to medium size, thick, ovoid shaped, uniface, scraping tools that are steeply beveled, especially at the broadest end. Side scrapers are long hand-held uniface flakes with beveling on all blade edges of one face. Scraping was done primarily from the sides of these blades.

480

SCRAPER (continued)

Circular scraper

G7, $12-$20
Lawrence Co., TN

Dover chert

G7, $4-$8
Humphreys Co., TN

G5, $8-$15
Humphreys Co., TN

Duckbill form

Dover chert

Duckbill form

Dover chert

G8, $15-$25
Humphreys Co., TN

G10+ $55-$100
Humphreys Co., TN

E C

SEARCY - Early to Middle Archaic, 7000 - 5000 B. P.

(Also see Dalton-Colbert, Harpeth River, Kirk Stemmed and Russell Cave)

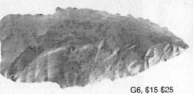

G6, $15 $25
W. TN

G7, $35 $65
New Market, AL

G5, $15-$25
Meigs Co., TN

LOCATION: Midwestern states. **DESCRIPTION:** A small to medium size, thin, lanceolate point with a squared hafting area that (usually) has concave sides and base which is ground. Many examples are serrated.

SHOALS CREEK - Late Archaic to Woodland, 4000 - 2000 B. P.

(Also see Elora, Kirk Stemmed, Ledbetter, Little Bear Creek, Pickwick and Smithsonia)

LOCATION: Southeastern states. **DESCRIPTION:** A medium to large size point with serrated edges, an expanded base and sharp barbs.

SHOALS CREEK (continued)

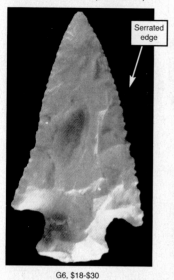

Serrated edge

G6, $18-$30
Lawrence Co., AL

Serrated edge

G7, $20-$35
Lawrence Co., AL

Serrated edge

G6, $20-$35
Lawrence Co., AL

SMITH - Middle Archaic, 7000 - 4000 B. P.

(Also see Eva, Hamilton, Rankin and Wade)

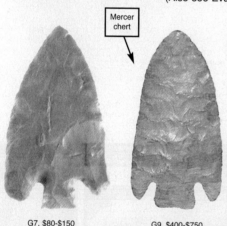

Mercer chert

G7, $80-$150
Florence, AL

G9, $400-$750
IN

G7, $175-$300
OH

G9, $800-$1500
OH

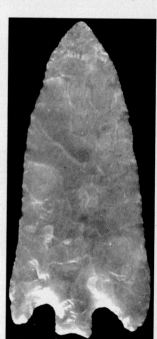

G9, $650-$1200
IN

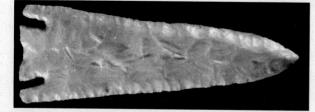

LOCATION: Midwestern states into Ohio. **DESCRIPTION:** A very large size, broad, point with long parallel shoulders and a squared to slightly expanding base. Some examples may appear to be basally notched due to the long barbs.

IMPORTANT: Smith points shown 50% actual size.

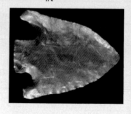

G7, $80-$150
N. AL

482

(See Buck Creek, Cotaco Cr., Hamilton, Motley, Shoals Creek, Table Rock and Wade)

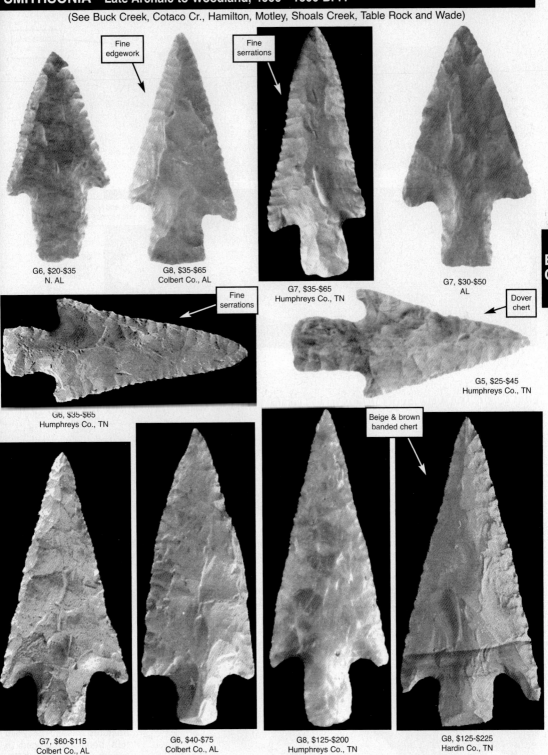

Fine edgework

Fine serrations

Fine serrations

Dover chert

Beige & brown banded chert

E
C

G6, $20-$35
N. AL

G8, $35-$65
Colbert Co., AL

G7, $35-$65
Humphreys Co., TN

G7, $30-$50
AL

G6, $35-$65
Humphreys Co., TN

G5, $25-$45
Humphreys Co., TN

G7, $60-$115
Colbert Co., AL

G6, $40-$75
Colbert Co., AL

G8, $125-$200
Humphreys Co., TN

G8, $125-$225
Hardin Co., TN

LOCATION: Southeastern states. **DESCRIPTION:** A medium size, triangular point with tapered to barbed shoulders and a parallel sided stem with a straight base. Many examples have finely serrated blade edges which are usually straight. **I.D. KEY:** High barb on one side and fine edgework.

483

SNAKE CREEK - Late Archaic, 4000 - 3000 B. P.

(Also see Harahey, Lerma, Morse, Ramey Knife and Tear Drop)

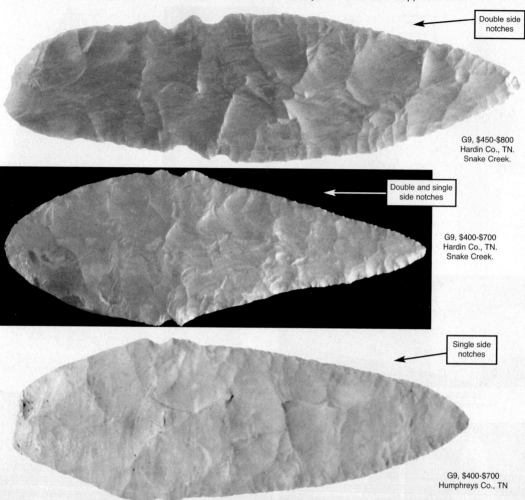

Double side notches

G9, $450-$800
Hardin Co., TN.
Snake Creek.

Double and single side notches

G9, $400-$700
Hardin Co., TN.
Snake Creek.

Single side notches

G9, $400-$700
Humphreys Co., TN

LOCATION: Tennessee and Kentucky **DESCRIPTION:** A large size, broad, ovoid blade with shallow side notches about 30 to 40% of the way between the base and tip. Double side notches are common. The stem contracts to a rounded base.

SNYDERS (Hopewell) - Woodland, 2500 - 1500 B. P.

(Also see Buck Creek, Hopewell, Motley and North)

G7, $55-$100
IN

G6, $25-$45
KY

LOCATION: Midwestern to Eastern states. **DESCRIPTION:** A medium to large size, broad, thin, wide corner notched point of high quality. Blade edges and base are convex. Many examples have intentional fractured bases. This point has been reproduced in recent years. **I.D. KEY:** Size and broad corner notches.

484

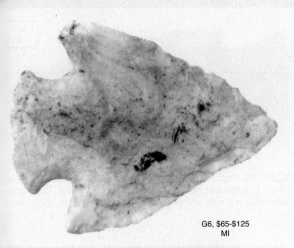

G6, $65-$125
MI

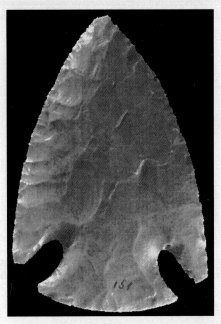

G8, $265-$500
IN

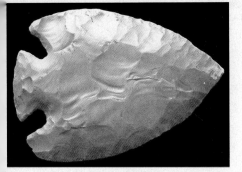

G9, $150-$250
Franklin Co., IN

Blue
flint

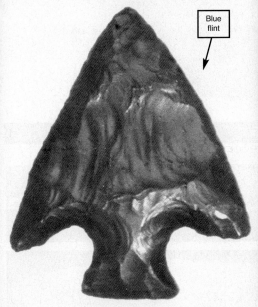

G10, $250-$350
KY

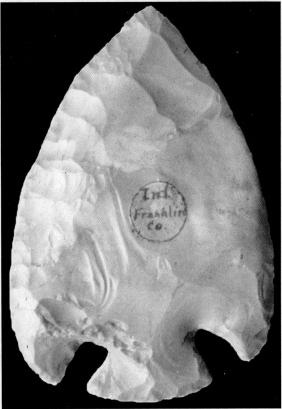

G8, $200-$350
Franklin Co., IN

EC

SPOKESHAVE - Woodland, 3000 -1500 B. P.

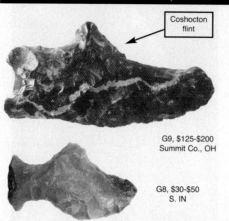

Coshocton flint

Hardin point

G9, $125-$200
Summit Co., OH

G8, $30-$50
S. IN

G8, $125-$200
Mercer Co., OH

LOCATION: Kentucky, Ohio into Indiana. **DESCRIPTION:** A medium to large size stemmed tool used for scraping. The blade is asymmetrical with one edge convex and the other concave.

SQUARE-END KNIFE - Late Archaic to Historic, 3500 - 400 B. P.

(Also see Angostura, Fort Ancient Blade, Frazier and Watts Cave Knife)

LOCATION: Midwestern states. **DESCRIPTION:** A medium to large size rectangular blade. Edges are generally straight to slightly convex.

G7, $45-$75
Humphreys Co., TN

Dover chert

G8, $80-$150
TN

G7, $80-$150
TN

STANFIELD - Transitional Paleo, 10,000 - 8000 B. P.

(Also see Angostura, Copena, Fort Ancient Blade, Frazier and Tennessee River)

G6, $25-$40
Colbert Co., AL

G8, $25-$45
Colbert Co., AL

Basal grinding

G6, $30-$50
Colbert Co., AL.

G8, $25-$45
Colbert Co., AL

STANFIELD (continued)

LOCATION: Southeastern states. Type site is in Colbert Co., AL. **DESCRIPTION:** A medium size, narrow, lanceolate point with parallel sides and a straight base. Some rare examples are fluted. Bases are usually ground and flattened. Flaking is to the center of the blade. This point has been confused with the *Tennessee River* point which is simply a preform for early non-beveled Archaic types. This type is smaller, narrowerer and is flaked to the center of the blade and is much rarer than the type with which it is often confused.

STANLY - Early Archaic, 8000 - 5000 B. P.

(Also see Frederick, Garth Slough, Kanawha Stemmed, Kirk Stemmed -Bifurcated and Savannah River)

G5, $3-$5
KY

G5, $3-$5
S.E. TN

G7, $12-$20
KY

G7, $15-$30
Bakewell, TN

G7, $12-$20
KY

E
C

G6, $12-$20
KY

G6, $12-$20
S.E. TN

G6, $12-$20
S.E. TN

G6, $12-$20
S.E. TN

Grey
flint

G10, $50-$90
KY

Tip
nick

G5, $8-$15
Bradley Co., TN

G10, $35-$60
S.E. TN

G6, $12-$20
N. E. AL

G8, $35-$60
OH

G6, $12-$20
KY

LOCATION: Southeastern to Eastern states. Type site is Stanly Co., N.C. **DESCRIPTION:** A small to medium size, broad shoulder point with a small bifurcated stem. Some examples are serrated and show high quality flaking. The shoulders are very prominent and can be tapered, horizontal or barbed. **I.D. KEY:** Tiny bifurcated base.

STEUBENVILLE - Early Archaic, 9000 - 6000 B. P.

(Also see Holland and Johnson)

STEUBENVILLE (continued)

G6, $40-$75
W. TN

G7, $65-$125
W. TN

LOCATION: Ohio into the Northeast. **DESCRIPTION:** A medium to large size, broad, triangular point with weak tapered shoulders, a wide parallel sided stem and a concave base. The basal area is ground. Believed to be developed from the *Scottsbluff* type.

STILWELL - Early Archaic, 9000 - 7000 B. P.

(Also see Kirk Corner Notched, Neuberger and Pine Tree)

G8, $50-$90
OH

G6, $55-$100
IN

Serrated edge

G9, $80-$150
Shelby Co., IN

G8, $80-$150
IN

G9, $350-$600
KY

G10, $400-$700
W. TN

Serrated edge

488

Serrated edge

Diagonal flaking

E C

G10, $1200-$2200
Limestone Co., AL

G9, $500-$900
KY

G9, $850-$1500
OH

LOCATION: Midwestern to Eastern states. **DESCRIPTION:** A medium to large size, corner notched point with usually serrated blade edges. The shoulders are barbed. The base is concave and ground. The blade edges are convex, parallel or recurved. This type may be related to *Kirk*.

STRINGTOWN - Early Archaic, 9500 - 7000 B. P.

(Also see Alberta and Eastern Stemmed Lanceolate)

Jasper

Note eared base

Coshocton chert

G6, $30-$50
OH

G5, $30-$50
OH

LOCATION: Pennsylvania, Ohio westward. **DESCRIPTION:** A medium to large size, broad stemmed point with convex to parallel sides and square shoulders. The stem is parallel sided to slightly expanding. The base is eared and the hafting area is ground. Most examples have horizontal to oblique parallel flaking and are of high quality and thinness. The Eastern form of the *Scottsbluff* type made by the Cody Complex people. The Eastern Stemmed Lanceolate is a variation of this form. **I.D.KEY:** Base form and parallel flaking.

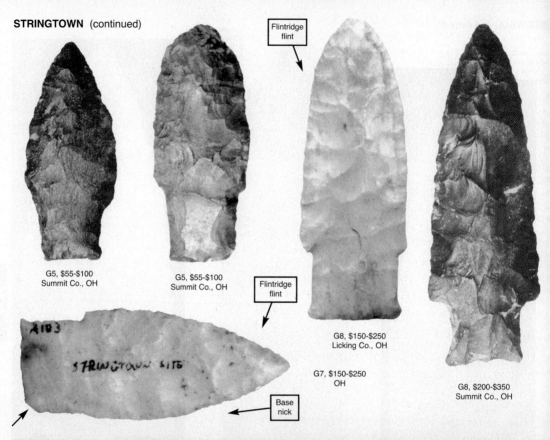

Flintridge
flint

G5, $55-$100
Summit Co., OH

G5, $55-$100
Summit Co., OH

Flintridge
flint

Base
nick

G8, $150-$250
Licking Co., OH

G7, $150-$250
OH

G8, $200-$350
Summit Co., OH

SUBLET FERRY - Late Archaic to Woodland, 4000 - 2000 B. P.

(Also see Big Sandy, Brewerton Side Notched, Coosa and Meadowood)

G6, $8-$15
Trimble Co., KY

G9, $45-$80
TN

G8, $20-$35
Humphreys Co., TN

Dover
chert

G9, $55-$100
Humphreys Co., TN

G6, $15-$25
Putnam Co., TN

LOCATION: Southeastern states. **DES- CRIP-TION:** A small to medium size point with side notches that are very close to the base. The base is straight to slightly convex. Blade edges are straight to convex and may be serrated.

SUN DISC - Mississippian, 1100 - 600 B. P.

(Also see Duck River Sword and Mace)

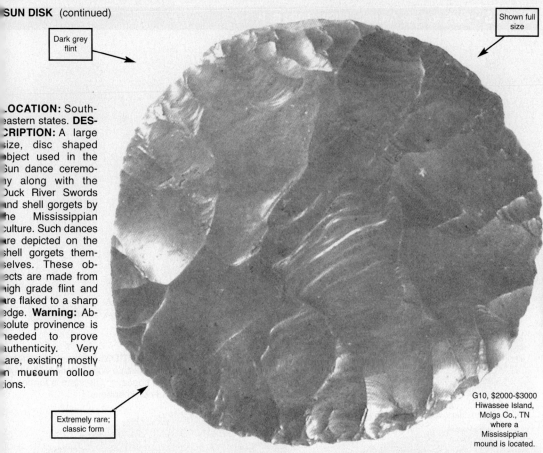

Dark grey flint

Shown full size

LOCATION: Southeastern states. **DESCRIPTION:** A large size, disc shaped object used in the Sun dance ceremony along with the Duck River Swords and shell gorgets by the Mississippian culture. Such dances are depicted on the shell gorgets themselves. These objects are made from high grade flint and are flaked to a sharp edge. **Warning:** Absolute provinence is needed to prove authenticity. Very rare, existing mostly in museum colloctions.

Extremely rare; classic form

G10, $2000-$3000 Hiwassee Island, Mcigs Co., TN where a Mississippian mound is located.

E C

SWAN LAKE - Late Archaic to Woodland, 3500 - 2000 B. P.

(Also see Bakers Creek, Brewerton, Durst, Halifax and Matanzas)

LOCATION: Southeastern to Eastern states. **DESCRIPTION:** A small size, thick, triangular point with wide, shallow side notches. Some examples have an unfinished rind or base. Similar to the side-notched *Lamoka* in New York. Called *Jackson* in Florida.

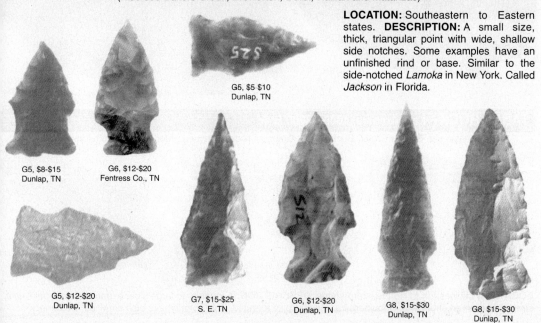

G5, $5 $10
Dunlap, TN

G5, $8-$15
Dunlap, TN

G6, $12-$20
Fentress Co., TN

G5, $12-$20
Dunlap, TN

G7, $15-$25
S. E. TN

G6, $12-$20
Dunlap, TN

G8, $15-$30
Dunlap, TN

G8, $15-$30
Dunlap, TN

SYKES - Early to Late Archaic, 6000 - 5000 B. P.

(Also see Benton)

G6, $15-$25
KY

G7, $20-$35
TN

G9, $40-$75
Adams Co., MS

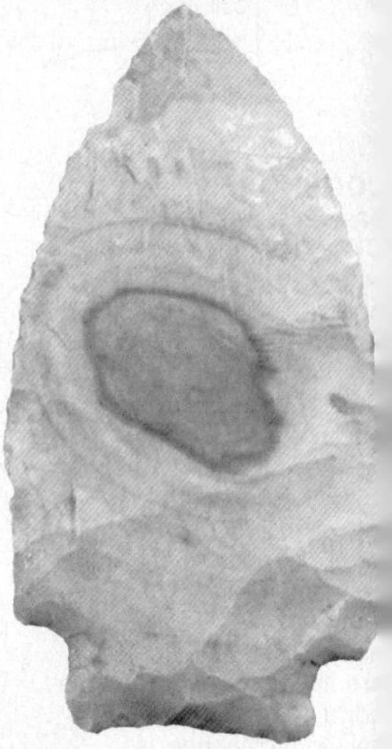

G7, $35-$60
TN

Ground
basal
area

G8, $25-$40
Adams Co., MS

LOCATION: Southeastern states. **DESCRIPTION:** Believed to be related to *Benton* points. A medium size, point with a broad blade and a very short, broad stem. Bases are straight to concave. The stem is formed by corner notches. **I.D. KEY:** Short stem and broadness.

G9, $30-$50
Adams Co., MS

G10, $80-$150
Adams Co., MS

TABLE ROCK - Late Archaic, 4000 - 3000 B. P.

(Also see Bakers Creek, Buck Creek, Cotaco Creek, Fishspear, Motley and Smithsonia)

G5, $15-$30
KY

G8, $25-$45
Meigs Co., TN

G7, $25-$45
OH

LOCATION: Midwestern to Northeastern states. **DESCRIPTION:** A medium to large size, expanded stem point with straight to tapered shoulders. Shoulders can be sharp or rounded. This point type is also know as "Bottleneck".

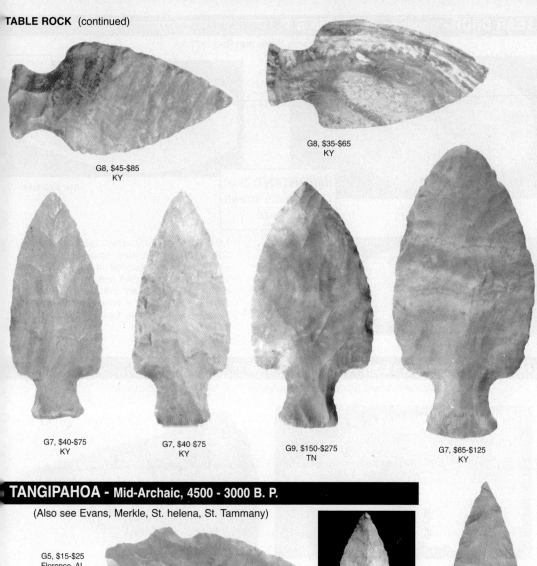

G8, $35-$65
KY

G8, $45-$85
KY

E
C

G7, $40-$75
KY

G7, $40 $75
KY

G9, $150-$275
TN

G7, $65-$125
KY

TANGIPAHOA - Mid-Archaic, 4500 - 3000 B. P.

(Also see Evans, Merkle, St. helena, St. Tammany)

G5, $15-$25
Florence, AL

G8, $25-$45
Wilkinson Co., MS

G7, $30-$55
Natchez, MS

G7, $30-$50
Natchez, MS

G10+, $150-$250
Adams Co., Ms

LOCATION: Louisiana into central Mississippi. **DESCRIPTION:** A medium size, fairly thick point with one to four notches on each side. Stems are straight to contracting. Basal corners are sharp to rounded. Shoulders are horizontal, tapered or barbed like angel wings. Mostly percussion flaked and believed to be related to the earlier *St. Helena* and *St. Tammany* points from the same region. Similar to the *Evans* point that only has single notches and an expanding stem. **I.D. KEY:** Angel wings barbs.

493

TEAR DROP - Woodland, 2000 - 1000 B. P.

(Also see Adena Blade and Red Ochre)

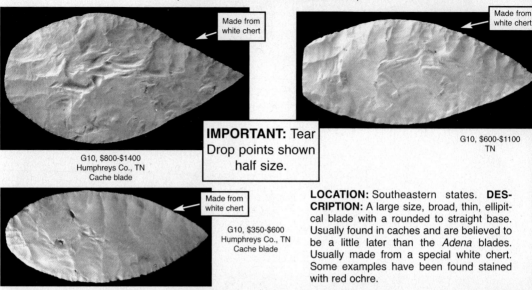

Made from white chert

Made from white chert

G10, $800-$1400
Humphreys Co., TN
Cache blade

G10, $600-$1100
TN

IMPORTANT: Tear Drop points shown half size.

Made from white chert

G10, $350-$600
Humphreys Co., TN
Cache blade

LOCATION: Southeastern states. **DESCRIPTION:** A large size, broad, thin, elliptical blade with a rounded to straight base. Usually found in caches and are believed to be a little later than the *Adena* blades. Usually made from a special white chert. Some examples have been found stained with red ochre.

TENNESSEE RIVER - Early Archaic, 9000 - 6000 B. P.

(Also see Adena Blade, Cobbs Triangular, Kirk, Red Ochre and Stanfield)

G7, $25-$45
Lauderdale Co., AL

G5, $25-$45
Summit Co., OH

G6, $30-$55
Florence, AL

G7, $40-$75
KY

LOCATION: Southeastern states. **DESCRIPTION:** These are unnotched preforms for early Archaic types such as *Kirk, Eva*, etc. and would have the same description as that type without the notches. Bases can be straight, concave or convex. **I.D. KEY:** Archaic style edgework. **NOTE:** This type has been confused with the *Stanfield* point which is a medium size, narrow, thicker point. A beveled edge would place your point under the *Cobbs Triangular* type

Kirk preform

G8, $200-$350
Dickson Co., TN

TENNESSEE SAW - Early Archaic, 8000 - 6000 B. P.

(Also see Lerma)

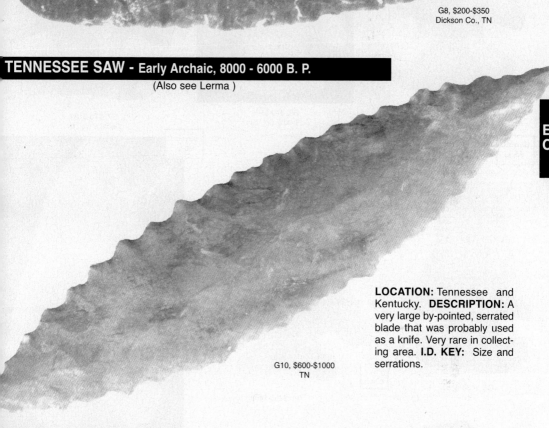

E
C

LOCATION: Tennessee and Kentucky. **DESCRIPTION:** A very large by-pointed, serrated blade that was probably used as a knife. Very rare in collecting area. **I.D. KEY:** Size and serrations.

G10, $600-$1000
TN

TENNESSEE SWORD (See Duck River Sword)

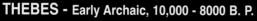

THEBES - Early Archaic, 10,000 - 8000 B. P.

(Also see Big Sandy E-Notched, Lost Lake and St. Charles)

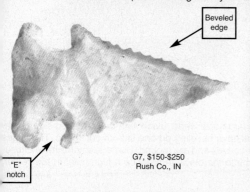

Beveled edge

"E" notch

G7, $150-$250
Rush Co., IN

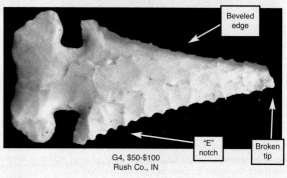

Beveled edge

"E" notch

Broken tip

G4, $50-$100
Rush Co., IN

Beveled edge

Tip nick

Beveled edge

Beveled edge

Beveled edge

Beveled edge

"E" notch

Beveled edge

G5, $55-$100
Decatur Co., IN

G8, $70-$125
Shelby Co., IN

G7, $70-$125
Decatur Co., IN

G8, $150-$250
IN

G8, $250-$400
IN

G10, $350-$600
OH

G6, $165-$300
IN

G7, $65-$125
OH

LOCATION: Midwestern states. **DESCRIPTION:** A medium to large size, wide, blade with deep, angled side notch-es that are parallel sided and squared. Resharpened examples have beveling on one side of each face. The bases of this type have broad proportions and are concave, straight or convex and are ground. Some examples have unusu-al side notches called Key notch. This type of notch is angled into the blade to produce a high point in the center, forming the letter E. See *Big Sandy E-Notched.*

Coshocton chert

Beveled edge

"Eared" base

Coshocton chert

G6, $300-$550
OH

G8, $300-$700
IN

G8, $350-$650
IN

E
C

Bifurcated base

Beveled edge

Beveled edge

G8, $250-$450
Meade Co., KY

G8, $285-$550
Scott Co., IN

G8, $400-$700
Shelby Co., IN

TORTUGAS - Middle Archaic to Woodland, 6000 - 1000 B. P.

(Also see Frazier, Levanna and Paint Rock Valley)

Dover chert

G5, $4-$8
Tishomingo Co., MS

G5, $4-$8
Decatur, AL

G7, $12-$20
Florence, AL

G7, $12-$20
W. TN

G9, $25-$45
Camden, TN

G8, $20-$35
Limestone Co., AL

G8, $20-$35
Parsons, TN

LOCATION: Typically found in northern Mexico into southern Texas. Similar points (shown here) are also found in Mississippi, Alabama and western Tenn. **DESCRIPTION:** A medium size, fairly thick, triangular point with straight to convex sides and base. Some examples are beveled on one side of each face. Bases are usually thinned. This type is much thicker than *Madison* points and are more triangular than *Frazier* points.

TRADE POINTS - Historic, 400 - 170 B. P.

$10-$20
Tellico Plains, TN
Cherokee

$15-$25, TN, Cherokee
c. 1810-1830 (cut sheet iron)

$65-$125, TN, Cherokee
c. 1810-1830 (cut sheet iron)

$20-$40, French conical (Kaskaskia)
Elmore Co., AL. Circa 1700-1763

$75-$150
Eastern U.S.

These points were made of copper, iron, and steel and were traded to the Indians by the French, British and others from the 1600s to the 1800s. Examples have been found all over the United States.

TURKEYTAIL-FULTON - Late Archaic to Woodland, 4000 - 2500 B. P.

(Also see Adena, Early Ovoid Knife and Turkeytail-Tupelo)

LOCATION: Midwestern to Eastern states. **DESCRIPTION:** A medium to large size, wide, thin, elliptical blade with shallow notches very close to the base. This type is usually found in caches and has been reproduced in recent years. Made by the Adena culture. A similar form, but much earlier, is found in late *Benton* caches in Mississippi. **I.D. KEY:** Smaller base than the Harrison Var.

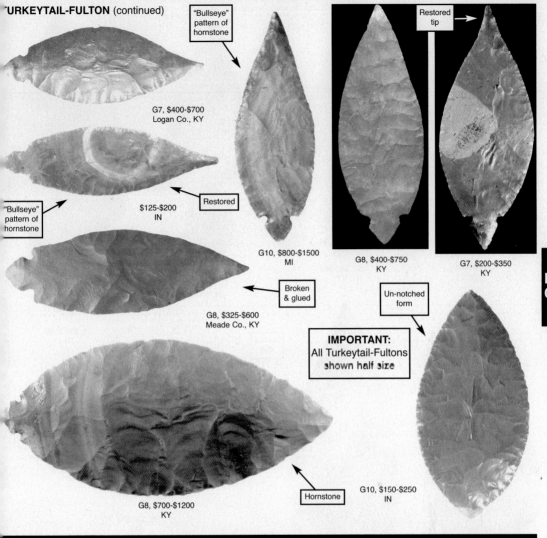

"Bullseye" pattern of hornstone

G7, $400-$700
Logan Co., KY

Restored tip

"Bullseye" pattern of hornstone

Restored

$125-$200
IN

G10, $800-$1500
MI

G8, $400-$750
KY

G7, $200-$350
KY

E C

Broken & glued

G8, $325-$600
Meade Co., KY

Un-notched form

IMPORTANT:
All Turkeytail-Fultons shown half size

Hornstone

G8, $700-$1200
KY

G10, $150-$250
IN

TURKEYTAIL-HARRISON - Late Archaic to Woodland, 4000 - 2500 B. P.

(Also see Adena and Beacon Island)

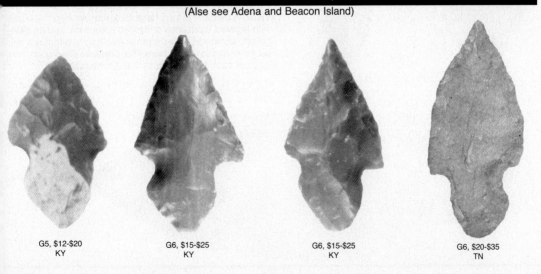

G5, $12-$20
KY

G6, $15-$25
KY

G6, $15-$25
KY

G6, $20-$35
TN

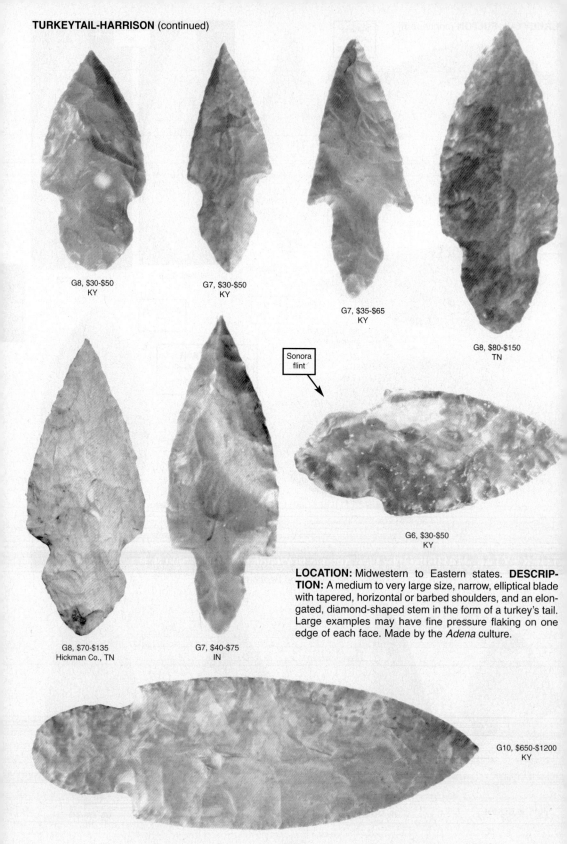

G8, $30-$50
KY

G7, $30-$50
KY

G7, $35-$65
KY

G8, $80-$150
TN

Sonora flint

G8, $70-$135
Hickman Co., TN

G7, $40-$75
IN

G6, $30-$50
KY

LOCATION: Midwestern to Eastern states. **DESCRIPTION:** A medium to very large size, narrow, elliptical blade with tapered, horizontal or barbed shoulders, and an elongated, diamond-shaped stem in the form of a turkey's tail. Large examples may have fine pressure flaking on one edge of each face. Made by the *Adena* culture.

G10, $650-$1200
KY

TURKEYTAIL-HEBRON - Late Archaic to Woodland, 3500 - 2500 B. P.

(Also see Waubesa)

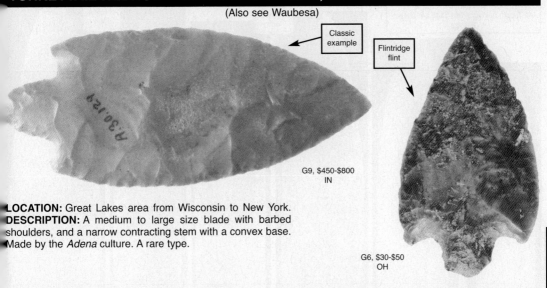

Classic example

Flintridge flint

G9, $450-$800
IN

G6, $30-$50
OH

E
C

LOCATION: Great Lakes area from Wisconsin to New York.
DESCRIPTION: A medium to large size blade with barbed shoulders, and a narrow contracting stem with a convex base. Made by the *Adena* culture. A rare type.

TURKEYTAIL-TUPELO - Late Archaic, 4750 - 3900 B. P.

(Also see Benton and Warito)

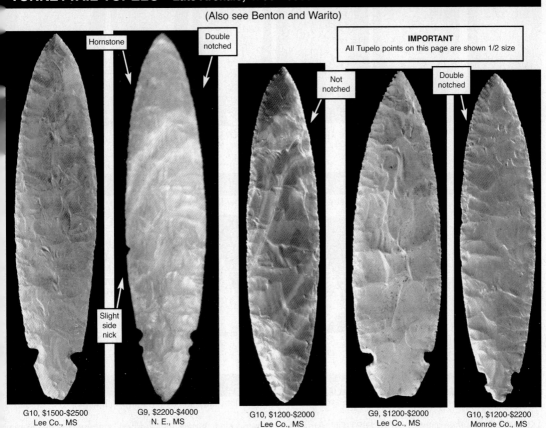

Hornstone

Double notched

IMPORTANT
All Tupelo points on this page are shown 1/2 size

Not notched

Double notched

Slight side nick

G10, $1500-$2500
Lee Co., MS

G9, $2200-$4000
N. E., MS

G10, $1200-$2000
Lee Co., MS

G9, $1200-$2000
Lee Co., MS

G10, $1200-$2200
Monroe Co., MS

LOCATION: Mississippi, Alabama and Tennessee. **DESCRIPTION:** A large size, thin, well-made blade that is found in caches with large *Benton* and *Warito* points. Some are not notched, but most have single, double or triple notches. Polishing occurs on the edges and surfaces of a few examples, possibly used as dance blades. These are unique and 1000 years older than the northern type.

TURKEYTAIL-TUPELO (continued)

IMPORTANT
All Tupelo points on this page are shown 1/2 size

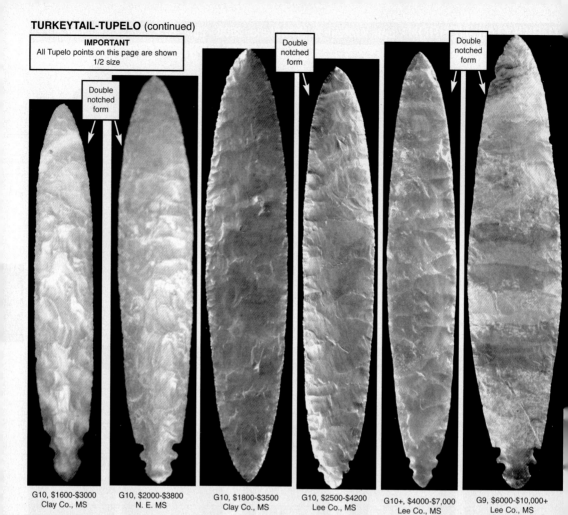

Double notched form

Double notched form

Double notched form

Double notched form

G10, $1600-$3000
Clay Co., MS

G10, $2000-$3800
N. E. MS

G10, $1800-$3500
Clay Co., MS

G10, $2500-$4200
Lee Co., MS

G10+, $4000-$7,000
Lee Co., MS

G9, $6000-$10,000+
Lee Co., MS

VALINA - Woodland, 2500 - 1000 B. P.

(Also see Madison and Morrow Mountain)

LOCATION: Eastern states. **DESCRIPTION:** A small size, broad triangle with rounded basal corners and a convex base.

G5, $1-$2
Sequatchie Valley, TN

G5, $1-$2
Meigs Co., TN

G7, $1-$3
Meigs Co., TN

G7, $1-$3
S. E. TN

WADE - Late Archaic to Woodland, 4500 - 2500 B. P.

(Also see Buck Creek, Eva, Hamilton Stemmed, Motley, Rankin, Smith and Smithsonia)

LOCATION: Southern states. **DESCRIPTION:** A medium to large size, broad, well barbed, stemmed point. Some examples appear to be basal notched. The blade is straight to convex. The stem is straight to expanding or contracting. On some examples, the barbs almost reach the base and are rounded to pointed. Has been found with *Motley* points in caches.

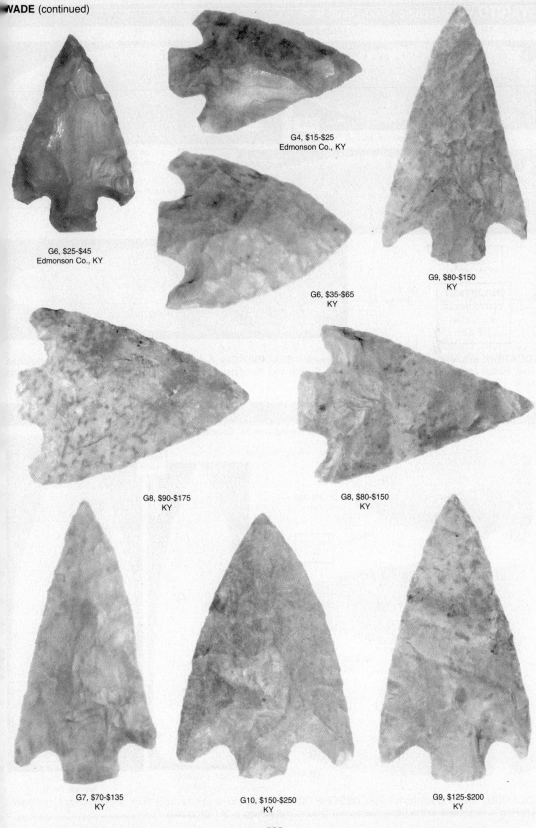

G4, $15-$25
Edmonson Co., KY

G6, $25-$45
Edmonson Co., KY

G6, $35-$65
KY

G9, $80-$150
KY

E
C

G8, $90-$175
KY

G8, $80-$150
KY

G7, $70-$135
KY

G10, $150-$250
KY

G9, $125-$200
KY

WARITO - Mid-Archaic, 5500 - 4500 B. P.

(Also see Benton and Turkeytail)

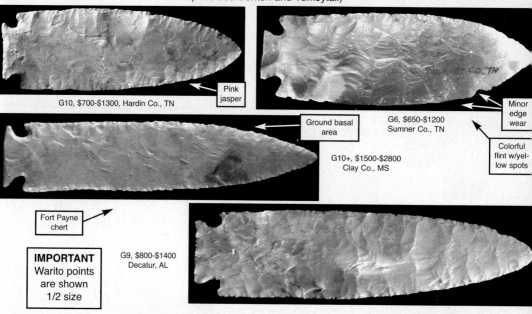

G10, $700-$1300, Hardin Co., TN

Pink jasper

Ground basal area

G6, $650-$1200
Sumner Co., TN

Minor edge wear

Colorful flint w/yellow spots

G10+, $1500-$2800
Clay Co., MS

Fort Payne chert

IMPORTANT
Warito points are shown 1/2 size

G9, $800-$1400
Decatur, AL

LOCATION: Mississippi, Alabama and Tennessee. **DESCRIPTION:** A medium to very large size corner notched point. Bases are ground. Found in caches with *Benton* and *Turkeytail Tupelo* points. **I.D. KEY:** Large corner notched point.

WARRICK - Early Archaic, 9000 - 5000 B. P.

(Also see Hardin and St. Charles)

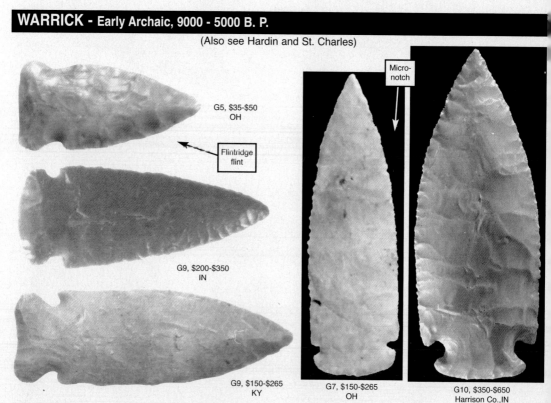

G5, $35-$50
OH

Flintridge flint

Micro-notch

G9, $200-$350
IN

G9, $150-$265
KY

G7, $150-$265
OH

G10, $350-$650
Harrison Co.,IN

LOCATION: Ohio and adjacent states. **DESCRIPTION:** A medium to large size, fairly thick, sturdy side notched point. Notching is very close to the base. Bases are ground and flaking is of high quality.

WASHINGTON - Woodland, 3000 - 1500 B. P.

(Also see Durant's Bend and Nova)

LOCATION: Southeastern states. **DESCRIPTION:** A small size, serrated, corner to side notched point with a concave, expanded base.

G5, $8-$15
Dallas Co., AL. Classic.

WASHITA - Mississippian, 800 - 400 B. P.

(Also see Keota)

G2, $.50-$1
S.E. TN

G2, $.50-$1
Hiwassee Isle, TN

G6, $5-$10
Meigs Co., TN

G8, $8-$15
Lauderdale Co., AL

LOCATION: Midwestern states into Tenn. and Ala **DESCRIPTION:** A small size, thin, triangular side notched arrow point with a concave base. Basal area is usually large in proportion to the blade size. A Mississippian point probably transported between the Mississippian sites.

WATTS CAVE - Trans. Paleo to Early Archaic, 10,000 - 8000 B. P.

(Also see Square End Knife)

E
C

Finely serrated
edge

IMPORTANT
This knife
shown
1/2 size

G10, $450-$800
Dickson Cave, KY

LOCATION: Tennessee into Kentucky and Ohio. **DESCRIPTION:** A large size, serrated, knife form with squared corners and the blade expanding towards both ends. First recognized as a type from Watts Cave in Kentucky. Some examples are fluted.

WAUBESA - Woodland, 2500 - 1500 B. P.

(Also see Adena, Dickson and Turkeytail-Hebron)

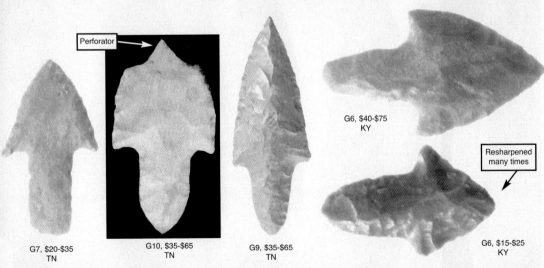

Perforator

G6, $40-$75
KY

Resharpened
many times

G7, $20-$35
TN

G10, $35-$65
TN

G9, $35-$65
TN

G6, $15-$25
KY

LOCATION: Eastern to Southeastern states. **DESCRIPTION:** A medium to large, narrow, thin, well made point with a contracting stem that is rounded or pointed. Some examples exhibit unusually high quality flaking and saw-tooth serrations. Blades are convex to recurved. Shoulders are squared to barbed. **I.D. KEY:** Basal form pointed or near pointed, good secondary flaking and thin. **NOTE:** Believed to be associated with the Hopewell culture.

G10, $70-$125
TN

G6, $35-$65
KY

G7, $35-$65
KY

Dover
chert

G8, $40-$75
Stewart Co., TN

G9, $25-$45
TN

Red
jasper

G9, $70-$125
KY

G7, $35-$75
TN

Red & Black
Horse
Creek chert

G7, $65-$125
KY

G9, $80-$150
KY

G9, $125-$200
KY

G8, $175-$300
KY

G10+, $700-$1200
Hardin Co., TN

G6, $35-$65
KY

Dover chert

Serrated edge

E C

G10, $350-$600
Humphreys Co., TN

G8, $185-$350
Hardin Co., KY

G9, $300-$550
Hamilton Co., OH

G10+, $700-$1200
Parsons, TN

WHEELER EXCURVATE - Transitional Paleo, 10,000 - 8000 B. P.

(Also see Angostura)

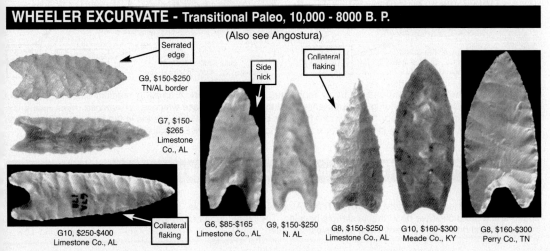

Serrated edge

Side nick

Collateral flaking

G9, $150-$250
TN/AL border

G7, $150-$265
Limestone Co., AL

Collateral flaking

G10, $250-$400
Limestone Co., AL

G6, $85-$165
Limestone Co., AL

G9, $150-$250
N. AL

G8, $150-$250
Limestone Co., AL

G10, $160-$300
Meade Co., KY

G8, $160-$300
Perry Co., TN

WHEELER EXCURVATE (continued)

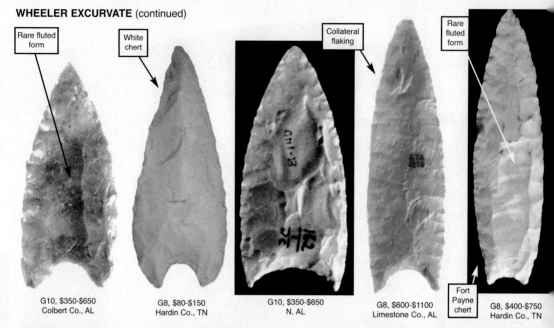

Rare fluted form

White chert

Collateral flaking

Rare fluted form

Fort Payne chert

G10, $350-$650
Colbert Co., AL

G8, $80-$150
Hardin Co., TN

G10, $350-$650
N. AL

G8, $600-$1100
Limestone Co., AL

G8, $400-$750
Hardin Co., TN

LOCATION: Southeastern states. **DESCRIPTION:** A small to medium size, lanceolate point with a deep concave base that is steeply beveled. Some examples are fluted, others are finely serrated and show excellent quality collateral flaking. Most bases are deeply notched but some examples have a more shallow concavity. Basal grinding does occur but is usually absent. The ears on some examples turn inward. Blade edges are excurvate. **I.D. KEY:** Base form and flaking style.

WHEELER EXPANDED BASE - Transitional Paleo, 10,000 - 8000 B. P.

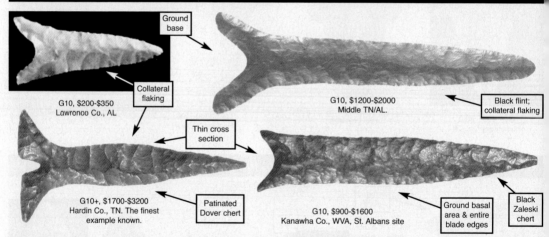

Ground base

Collateral flaking

Black flint; collateral flaking

G10, $200-$350
Lawrence Co., AL

G10, $1200-$2000
Middle TN/AL.

Thin cross section

Patinated Dover chert

G10+, $1700-$3200
Hardin Co., TN. The finest example known.

G10, $900-$1600
Kanawha Co., WVA, St. Albans site

Ground basal area & entire blade edges

Black Zaleski chert

LOCATION: Northwest Alabama and southern Tennessee. **DESCRIPTION:** A small to medium size, very narrow, thin, lanceolate point with expanding, squared ears forming a "Y" at the base which is "V" notched. Most examples have high quality collateral flaking. This very rare type has been found on *Wheeler* sites in the type area. Scarcity of this type suggests that it was not in use but for a short period of time. **I.D. KEY:** Notch and ears.

WHEELER RECURVATE - Transitional Paleo 10,000 - 8000 B. P.

(Also see Patrick)

LOCATION: Southeastern states. **DESCRIPTION:** A small to medium size, lanceolate point with recurved blade edges and a deep concave base that is steeply beveled. The blade edges taper towards the base, forming the hafting area. Basal grinding is absent. Rare examples are fluted.

G8, $350-$650
Smith Co., TN

G8, $65-$125
Hamilton Co., TN

G8, $65-$125
Hamilton Co., TN

G8, $150-$250
W. TN

G7, $450-$800
Trigg Co., KY

Hornstone

Very rare
fluted form

G9, $600-$1000
Trigg Co., KY

Classic
form

G9, $1500-$2500
Colbert Co., AL (Found on a Wheeler site)

E C

WHEELER TRIANGULAR - Transitional Paleo 10,000 - 8000 B. P.

(Also see Camp Creek, Copena, Madison and Sand Mountain)

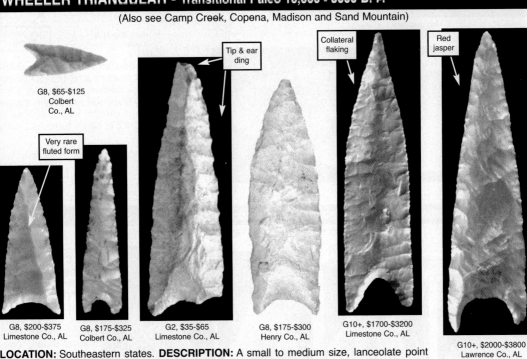

G8, $65-$125
Colbert
Co., AL

Tip & ear
ding

Collateral
flaking

Red
jasper

Very rare
fluted form

G8, $200-$375
Limestone Co., AL

G8, $175-$325
Colbert Co., AL

G2, $35-$65
Limestone Co., AL

G8, $175-$300
Henry Co., AL

G10+, $1700-$3200
Limestone Co., AL

G10+, $2000-$3800
Lawrence Co., AL

LOCATION: Southeastern states. **DESCRIPTION:** A small to medium size, lanceolate point with straight sides and a deep concave base that is steeply beveled. On some examples, the ears point inward toward the base. This is a rare form and few examples exist. **I.D. KEY:** Beveled base and Paleo flaking.

WHITE SPRINGS - Early to Middle Archaic, 8000 - 6000 B. P.

(Also see Benton)

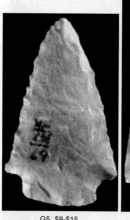

G5, $8-$15
Limestone Co., AL

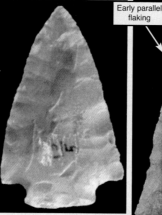

Early parallel flaking

G6, $15-$30
Limestone Co., AL

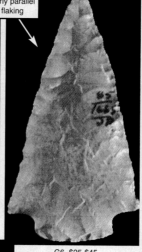

G6, $25-$45
Limestone Co., AL

G7, $35-$65
Madison Co., AL

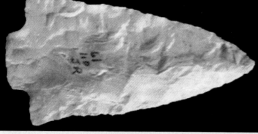

G7, $25-$40
Limestone Co., AL

G10, $60-$110
Colbert Co., AL

Early parallel flaking

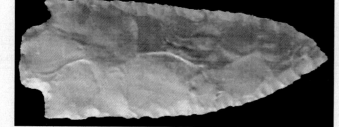

G9, $60-$110
Limestone Co., AL

LOCATION: Southeastern states. **DESCRIPTION:** A medium size, broad, triangular point with a medium to wide very short straight stem. Shoulders are usually square and the base is straight, slightly convex or concave. **I.D. KEY:** Short base and early flaking.

YADKIN - Woodland to Mississippian, 2500 - 500 B. P.

(Also see Camp Creek, Hamilton, Levanna and Nolichucky)

Black flint

G6, $15-$25
Bristol, TN

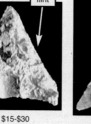

Black flint

G6, $15-$30
Bristol, TN

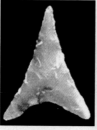

G8, $25-$45
Bristol, TN

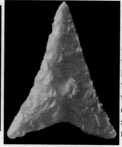

G8, $25-$45
Bristol, TN

LOCATION: Southeastern and Eastern states. **DESCRIPTION:** A small to medium size, broad based, fairly thick, triangular point with a broad, concave base and straight to convex to recurved side edges.

510

SOUTHERN CENTRAL SECTION:

This section includes point types from the following states:
Arkansas, Louisiana, Oklahoma, Texas

The points in this section are arranged in alphabetical order and are shown **actual size**. All types are listed that were available for photographing. Any missing types will be added to future editions as photographs become available. We are always interested in receiving sharp, black and white or color glossy photos, color slides or high resolution (300 pixels/inch) digital pictures of your collection. Be sure and include a ruler in the photograph so that proper scale can be determined.

Lithics: Materials employed in the manufacture of projectile points from this region are: basalt, chalcedony, chert, conglomerate, crystal, flint, novaculite, obsidian, quartz, quartzite with lesser amounts of agate, jasper, and petrified wood.

Regional Consultant:
Dwain Rogers

Special Advisors:
Tom Davis, Glen Kizzia, Bob McWilliams, Donald Meador,
Lyle Nickel, Michael Speer, Art Tatum, Sam Williams

S
C

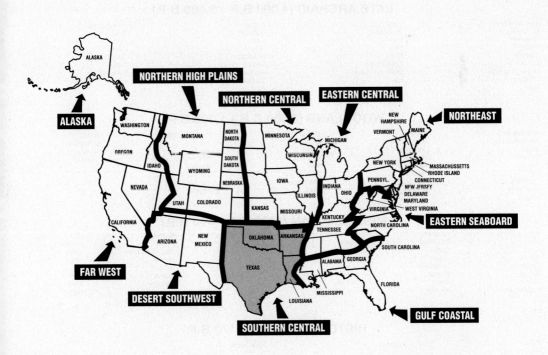

SOUTHERN CENTRAL
(Archaeological Periods)

PALEO (11,500 B.P. - 10,600 B.P.)

Chopper	Clovis	Drill	Graver	Scraper

LATE PALEO (11,250 B.P. - 9,000 B.P.)

Folsom	Frederick	Goshen	Midland	Milnesand	Plainview

TRANSITIONAL PALEO (10,700 B.P. - 8,000 B.P.)

Agate Basin	Arkabutla	Coldwater	Hell Gap	Pelican
Allen	Barber	Crescent Knife	Mahaffey	Plainview
Archaic Knife	Browns Valley	Golondrina	Paleo Knife	

EARLY ARCHAIC (10,000 B.P. - 7,000 B.P.)

Albany Knife	Dalton Classic	Frederick	Lerma Rounded	San Patrice-Geneill
Alberta	Dalton Colbert	Gower	Martindale	San Patrice-Hope Var.
Andice	Dalton Greenbrier	Graham Cave	Meserve	San Patrice-Keithville Var.
Angostura	Dalton Hemphill	Hardin	Ocala	San Patrice-St. Johns Var.
Baker	Dalton Hempstead	Hidden Valley	Perforator	Scottsbluff I & II
Bandy	Darl Stemmed	Holland	Pike County	Victoria
Big Sandy	Early Stemmed	Hoxie	Red River Knife	Wells
Cache River	Early Stemmed Lanceolate	Jakie Stemmed	Rice Lobbed	Zella
Calf Creek	Early Triangular	Jetta	Rio Grande	Zephyr
Cosotat River	Eden	Johnson	Rodgers Side Hollowed	
Dalton Breckenridge	Firstview	Lerma Pointed	St. Charles	

MIDDLE ARCHAIC (7,000 B.P. - 4,000 B.P.)

Abasolo	Carrolton	La Jita	Motley	Searcy
Afton	Coryell	Lange	Nolan	Tortugas
Almagre	Dawson	Langtry	Ouachita	Travis
Axtel	Exotic	Langtry-Arenosa	Paisano	Uvalde
Bell	Frio	Little River	Palmillas	Val Verde
Brewerton Eared	Hemphill	Marshall	Pandale	White River
Brewerton Side Notched	Hickory Ridge	Matanzas	Pedernales	Williams
Bulverde	Kerrville Knife	McKean	San Jacinto	Zorra
Calcasieu	Kings	Merkle	Savage Cave	
Carrizo	Kinney	Montell	Savannah River	

LATE ARCHAIC (4,000 B.P. - 3,000 B.P.)

Base Tang Knife	Delhi	Friday	Pontchartrain I, II
Big Creek	Desmuke	Gahagan	Refugio
Castroville	Elam	Gary	Sabine
Catan	Ellis	Hale	Smith
Coahuila	Ensor	Marshall	Table Rock
Conejo	Ensor Blade	Marcos	Trinity
Corner Tang Knife	Ensor Split-Base	Mid-Back Tang	Turkeytail
Covington	Epps	Morhiss	
Dallas	Evans	Pandora	

WOODLAND (3,000 B.P. - 1,300 B.P.)

Adena Blade	Dickson	Gibson	Peisker Diamond	Sinner
Adena-Robbins	Duran	Godley	Pogo	Spokeshave
Burkett	Edgewood	Grand	Reed	Steuben
Charcos	Edwards	Hare Biface	Rice Shallow Side Notched	Yarbrough
Cupp	Fairland	Kent	Rockwall	
Darl	Figueroa	Knight Island	San Gabriel	
Darl Blade	Friley	Matamoros	San Saba	
Deadman's	Gar Scale	Morill	Shumla	

MISSISSIPPIAN (1300 B.P. - 400 B.P.)

Agee	Caracara	Harrell	Keota	Nodena	Starr
Alba	Catahoula	Haskell	LeFlore Blade	Perdiz	Steiner
Antler	Cliffton	Hayes	Livermore	Round-End Knife	Talco
Bassett	Colbert	Homan	Lott	Sabinal	Toyah
Bayogoula	Dardanelle	Howard	Maud	Sallisaw	Turner
Blevins	Fresno	Huffaker	Mineral Springs	Scallorn	Washita
Bonham	Garza	Hughes	Moran	Schustorm	Washita-Peno
Caddoan Blade	Harahey	Kay Blade	Morris	Sequoyah	Young

HISTORIC (450 B.P. - 170 B.P.)

Cuney	Guerrero	Trade Points

SOUTHERN CENTRAL
THUMBNAIL GUIDE SECTION

The following references are provided to aid the collector in easier and quicker identification of point types. All photos are exactly 30% of actual size and are proportional to each other. Each point pictured in this section represents a classic form for the type. When a match is found, go to the alphabetical location of that type for more examples in true actual size.

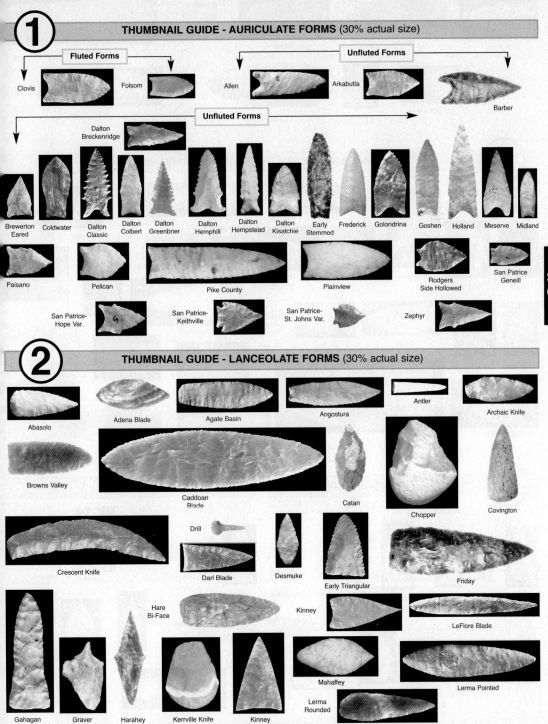

① THUMBNAIL GUIDE - AURICULATE FORMS (30% actual size)

Fluted Forms: Clovis, Folsom

Unfluted Forms: Allen, Arkabutla, Barber

Unfluted Forms: Dalton Breckenridge, Brewerton Eared, Coldwater, Dalton Classic, Dalton Colbert, Dalton Greenbrier, Dalton Hemphill, Dalton Hempstead, Dalton Kisatchie, Early Stemmed, Frederick, Golondrina, Goshen, Holland, Meserve, Midland

Paisano, Pelican, Pike County, Plainview, Rodgers Side Hollowed, San Patrice Geneill

San Patrice-Hope Var., San Patrice-Keithville, San Patrice-St. Johns Var., Zephyr

S C

② THUMBNAIL GUIDE - LANCEOLATE FORMS (30% actual size)

Abasolo, Adena Blade, Agate Basin, Angostura, Antler, Archaic Knife

Browns Valley, Caddoan Blade, Catan, Chopper, Covington

Crescent Knife, Drill, Darl Blade, Desmuke, Early Triangular, Friday

Hare Bi-Face, Kinney, LeFlore Blade

Gahagan, Graver, Harahey, Kerrville Knife, Kinney, Mahaffey, Lerma Rounded, Lerma Pointed

513

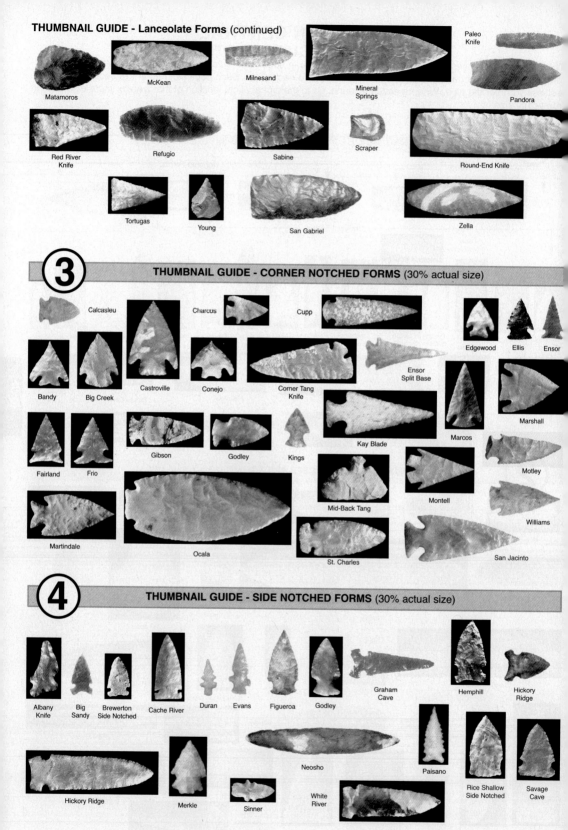

THUMBNAIL GUIDE - Lanceolate Forms (continued)

Matamoros

McKean

Milnesand

Mineral Springs

Paleo Knife

Pandora

Red River Knife

Refugio

Sabine

Scraper

Round-End Knife

Tortugas

Young

San Gabriel

Zella

③ THUMBNAIL GUIDE - CORNER NOTCHED FORMS (30% actual size)

Calcasleu

Charcos

Cupp

Edgewood

Ellis

Ensor

Bandy

Big Creek

Castroville

Conejo

Corner Tang Knife

Ensor Split Base

Marshall

Fairland

Frio

Gibson

Godley

Kings

Kay Blade

Marcos

Motley

Martindale

Ocala

Mid-Back Tang

Montell

Williams

St. Charles

San Jacinto

④ THUMBNAIL GUIDE - SIDE NOTCHED FORMS (30% actual size)

Albany Knife

Big Sandy

Brewerton Side Notched

Cache River

Duran

Evans

Figueroa

Godley

Graham Cave

Hemphill

Hickory Ridge

Hickory Ridge

Merkle

Sinner

Neosho

White River

Paisano

Rice Shallow Side Notched

Savage Cave

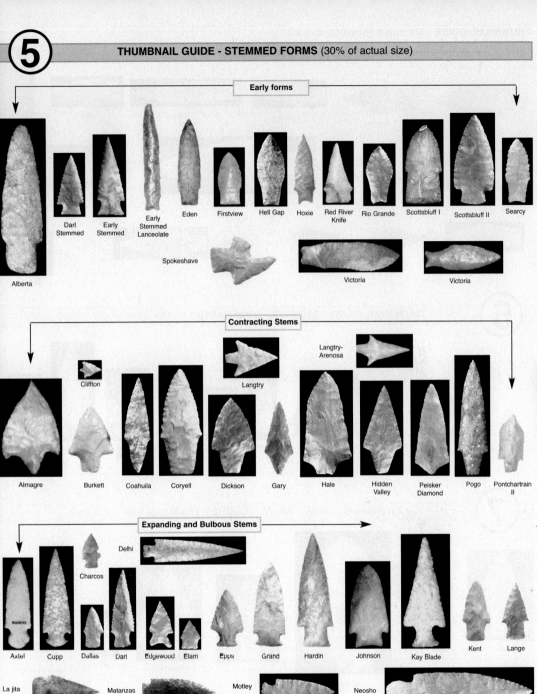

Early forms

Alberta · Darl Stemmed · Early Stemmed · Early Stemmed Lanceolate · Eden · Firstview · Hell Gap · Hoxie · Red River Knife · Rio Grande · Scottsbluff I · Scottsbluff II · Searcy

Spokeshave · Victoria · Victoria

Contracting Stems

Cliffton · Langtry · Langtry-Arenosa

Almagre · Burkett · Coahuila · Coryell · Dickson · Gary · Hale · Hidden Valley · Peisker Diamond · Pogo · Pontchartrain II

S C

Expanding and Bulbous Stems

Axtel · Cupp · Charcos · Delhi · Dallas · Darl · Edgewood · Elam · Epps · Grand · Hardin · Johnson · Kay Blade · Kent · Lange

La jita · Matanzas · Motley · Neosho

Palmillas · Pandale · Ponchartrain I · Rice Lobbed · Steuben · Table Rock · Trinity

Uvalde · Val Verde · Williams · Yarbrough

THUMBNAIL GUIDE - Stemmed Forms (continued)

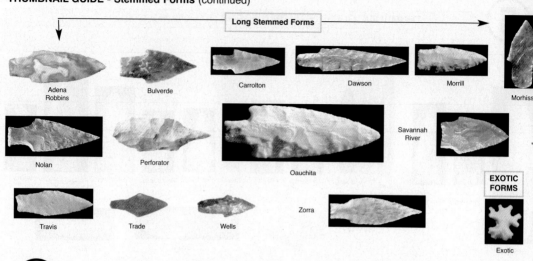

Long Stemmed Forms

Adena
Robbins

Bulverde

Carrolton

Dawson

Morrill

Morhiss

Nolan

Perforator

Oauchita

Savannah
River

Travis

Trade

Wells

Zorra

EXOTIC
FORMS

Exotic

⑥ THUMBNAIL GUIDE - STEMMED-BIFURCATED FORMS (30% of actual size)

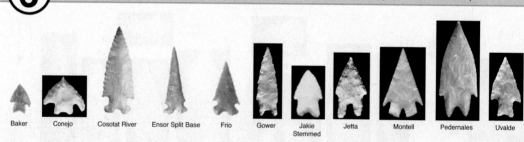

Baker | Conejo | Cosotat River | Ensor Split Base | Frio | Gower | Jakie Stemmed | Jetta | Montell | Pedernales | Uvalde

⑦ THUMBNAIL GUIDE - BASAL NOTCHED FORMS (30% of actual size)

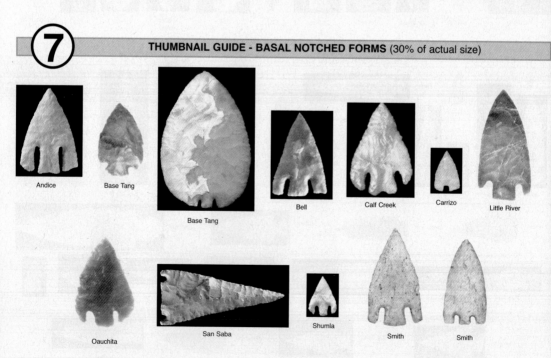

Andice

Base Tang

Base Tang

Bell

Calf Creek

Carrizo

Little River

Oauchita

San Saba

Shumla

Smith

Smith

Bayogoula Colbert Deadman's

Homan

Toyah

Agee Alba Basset Blevins Bonham Caracara Catahoula Cuney Dardanelle Edwards Fresno Friley

Garza Guerrero Harrell Haskell Hayes Howard Huffaker Hughes Keota Knight Island Livermore Lott Maud Moran Morris Nodena

Perdiz Reed Rockwall Sabinal Sallisaw Scallorn Schustorm Sequoyah Starr Steiner Talco Turner Washita Washita-Peno

S C

ABASOLO - Early to Middle Archaic, 7000 - 5000 B. P.

(Also see Catan and Matamoros)

G7, $1-$2
S. TX

G7, $2-$4
S. TX

G6, $2-$5
Zapata Co., TX

G7, $3-$6
Zapata Co., TX

G7, $3-$6
S. TX

G7, $4-$9
Travis Co., TX

G6, $5-$10
Starr Co., TX

LOCATION: Southern Midwestern states and Mexico. **DESCRIPTION:** A medium to large size, broad, lanceolate point with a rounded base. The blade can be beveled on one side of each face and the base can be thinned. **I.D. KEY:** Early form of flaking on blade with good secondary edgework and rounded base.

ADENA - Late Archaic to Late Woodland, 3000 - 1200 B. P.

(Also see Adena Blade, Adena Robbins, Dickson & Gary)

LOCATION: Southeast into Arkansas, W. Texas, Sou, New Mexico, Chihuahua, Mex. **DESCRIPTION:** A medium to large, thin, triangular blade that is sometimes serrated, and with a medium to long, narrow to broad rounded "beaver tail" stem. Bases can be ground. **I.D. KEY:** Rounded stem

G6, $8-$15
Bell Co., TX

ADENA (continued)

G7, $15-$25
AR

G7, $12-$20
Titus Co., TX

ADENA BLADE - Late Archaic to Late Woodland, 3000 - 1200 B. P.

(Also see Harahey, Lerma, Pandora)

G9, $150-$250
Zapata Co., TX

LOCATION: Arkansas eastward. **DESCRIPTION:** A large size, thin, broad, ovate blade with a rounded to pointed base and is usually found in caches. **I.D. KEY:** Woodland flaking, large direct strikes.

ADENA-DICKSON   (See Dickson)

ADENA-ROBBINS - Late Archaic to Woodland, 3000 - 1800 B. P.

(Also see Bulverde, Carrolton, Dickson, Kent and Wells)

G5, $35-$65
AR

LOCATION: Arkansas eastward. **DESCRIPTION:** A large, broad, triangular point that is thin and well made with a long, wide, rounded to rectangular stem that is parallel sided. The blade has convex sides and square shoulders. Many examples show excellent secondary flaking on blade edges. **I.D. KEY:** Squared base, heavy secondary flaking.

G5, $12-$20
AR

G5, $15-$25
AR

(Also see Apple Creek, Ferry and Helton)

G6, $40-$75
Clark Co., AR

G5, $30-$50
W. TX

G7, $90-$175
N.E. OK

G5, $30-$50
N.E. OK

G10+, $1200-$2000
OK

LOCATION: Midwestern states and is rarely found in some Eastern and Southeastern states. **DESCRIPTION:** A medium to large size pentagonal shaped point with a flaring or corner notched stem. Some examples are base notched and some are stemmed. **I.D. KEY:** Blade form.

AGATE BASIN - Transitional Paleo to Early Archaic, 10,200 - 8500 B. P.

(Also see Allen, Angostura, Hell Gap, Lerma, Mahaffey and Sedalia)

Heavily
resharpened

G8, $200-$350
Wagoner Co., OK

G4, $35-$65
N.E. OK

LOCATION: New Mexico to Montana eastward to Pennsylvania. **DESCRIPTION:** A medium to large size lanceolate blade of usually high quality. Bases are either convex, concave or straight, and are normally ground. Some examples are median ridged and have random to parallel flaking. **I.D. KEY:** Basal form and flaking style.

AGATE BASIN
(continued)

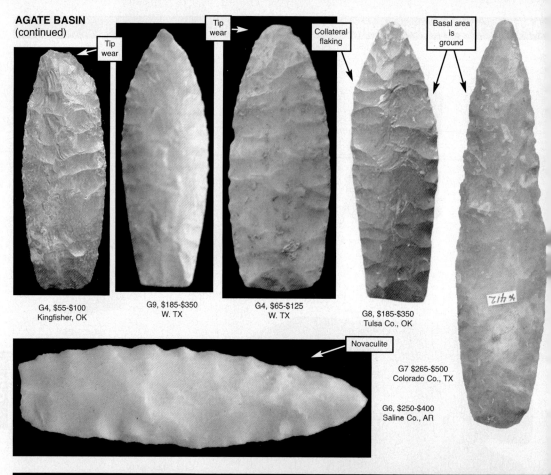

Tip wear

Tip wear

Collateral flaking

Basal area is ground

G4, $55-$100
Kingfisher, OK

G9, $185-$350
W. TX

G4, $65-$125
W. TX

G8, $185-$350
Tulsa Co., OK

Novaculite

G7 $265-$500
Colorado Co., TX

G6, $250-$400
Saline Co., AR

AGEE - Mississippian, 1200 - 700 B. P.

(Also see Alba, Dardanelle, Hayes, Homan and Keota)

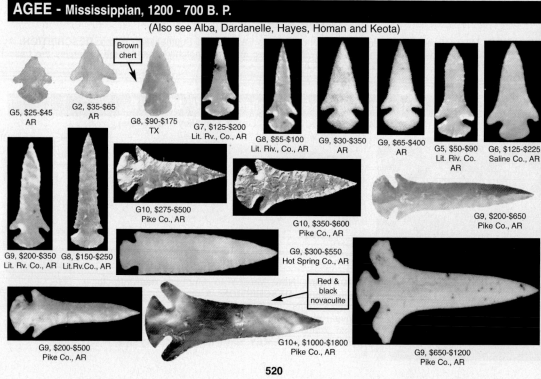

Brown chert

G5, $25-$45
AR

G2, $35-$65
AR

G8, $90-$175
TX

G7, $125-$200
Lit. Rv., Co., AR

G8, $55-$100
Lit. Riv., Co., AR

G9, $30-$350
AR

G9, $65-$400
AR

G5, $50-$90
Lit. Riv. Co.
AR

G6, $125-$225
Saline Co., AR

G10, $275-$500
Pike Co., AR

G10, $350-$600
Pike Co., AR

G9, $200-$650
Pike Co., AR

G9, $200-$350
Lit. Rv. Co., AR

G8, $150-$250
Lit.Rv.Co., AR

G9, $300-$550
Hot Spring Co., AR

Red & black novaculite

G9, $200-$500
Pike Co., AR

G10+, $1000-$1800
Pike Co., AR

G9, $650-$1200
Pike Co., AR

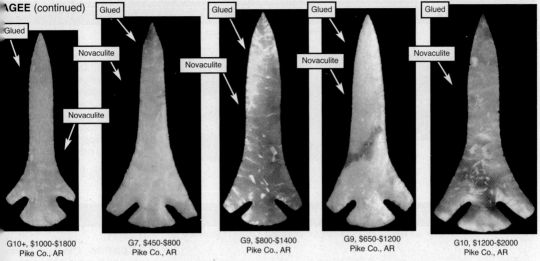

G10+, $1000-$1800
Pike Co., AR

G7, $450-$800
Pike Co., AR

G9, $800-$1400
Pike Co., AR

G9, $650-$1200
Pike Co., AR

G10, $1200-$2000
Pike Co., AR

LOCATION: Arkansas Caddo sites. **DESCRIPTION:** The finest, most exquisite arrow point made in the United States. A small to medium size, narrow, very thin, expanded barbed, corner notched point. Tips are needle sharp. Some examples are double notched at the base. A rare type that has only been found on a few sites. Total estimated known examples are 1100 to 1200. **I.D. KEY:** Basal form and barb expansion.

ALBA - Woodland to Mississippian, 1100 - 800 B. P.

(Also see Agee, Bonham, Colbert, Cuney, Hayes, Homan, Keota, Perdiz, Scallorn, Sequoyah and Turner)

S C

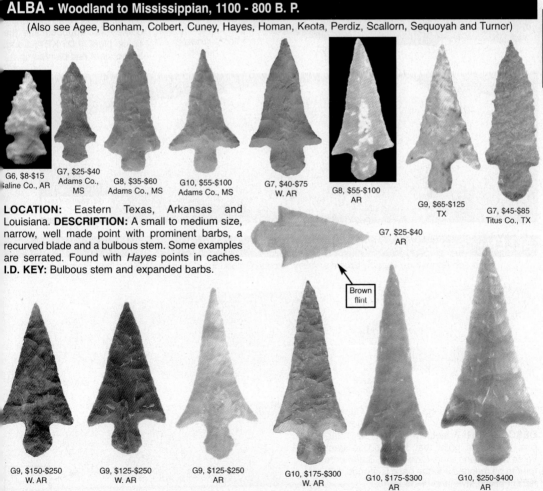

G6, $8-$15
Saline Co., AR

G7, $25-$40
Adams Co., MS

G8, $35-$60
Adams Co., MS

G10, $55-$100
Adams Co., MS

G7, $40-$75
W. AR

G8, $55-$100
AR

G9, $65-$125
TX

G7, $45-$85
Titus Co., TX

G7, $25-$40
AR

Brown flint

LOCATION: Eastern Texas, Arkansas and Louisiana. **DESCRIPTION:** A small to medium size, narrow, well made point with prominent barbs, a recurved blade and a bulbous stem. Some examples are serrated. Found with *Hayes* points in caches. **I.D. KEY:** Bulbous stem and expanded barbs.

G9, $150-$250
W. AR

G9, $125-$250
W. AR

G9, $125-$250
AR

G10, $175-$300
W. AR

G10, $175-$300
AR

G10, $250-$400
AR

ALBANY KNIFE - Early Archaic 10,000 - 8000 B. P.

(Also see Red River Knife and San Patrice)

G6, $15-$30
Angelina Co., TX

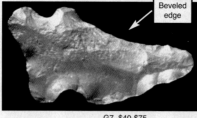

G7, $40-$75
Angelina Co., TX

LOCATION: Louisiana, E. Texas and Arkansas. **DESCRIPTION:** A small to medium size knife form of the *San Patrice* point. Form is asymmetrical with a steeply beveled edge on the diagonal side. Bases are ground. Similar to the Edgefield Scraper found in Florida. **I.D. KEY:** Symmetry & beveling.

ALBERTA - Early Archaic, 10,000 - 8500 B. P.

(Also see Angostura, Brown's Valley, Clovis, Plainview and Scottsbluff)

G9, $1200-$2000
N.E. OK

LOCATION: Oklahoma northward to Canada and eastward to Michigan. **DESCRIPTION:** A medium to large size, broad stemmed point with weak, horizontal to tapered shoulders. Made by the Cody Complex people who made *Scottsbluff* points. A very rare type. Basal corners are rounded and the tip is blunt. **I.D. KEY:** Long, broad stem and blunted tip.

G6, $600-$1000
Kay Co., OK

ALLEN - Transitional Paleo to Early Archaic, 8500 - 7500 B. P.

(Also see Angostura, Barber, Brown's Valley, Clovis, Golondrina, Goshen, McKean and Plainview)

G5, $125-$200
Comanche Co., TX

G10, $1000-$1800
N. OK

G10, $800-$1500
N. OK

Translucent Alibates dolomite

LOCATION: Midwestern states to Canada. Named after Jimmy Allen of Wyoming. **DESCRIPTION:** A medium to large size, narrow, lanceolate point that has oblique transverse flaking and a concave base. Basal ears tend to be rounded and the base is ground. **I.D. KEY:** Flaking style and blade form.

522

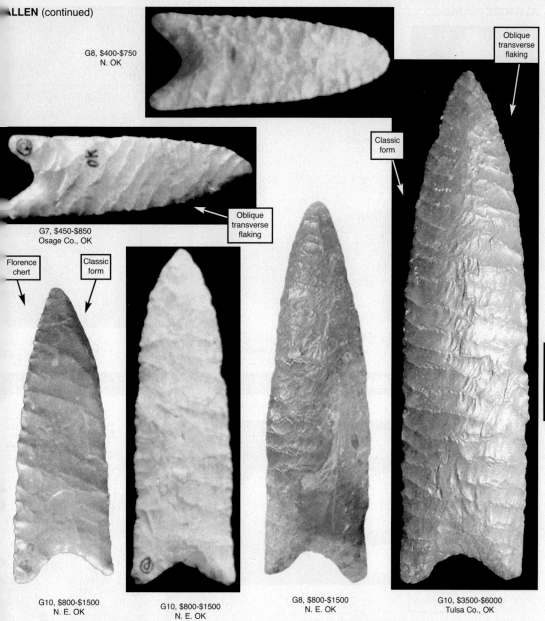

G8, $400-$750
N. OK

Oblique transverse flaking

Classic form

Oblique transverse flaking

G7, $450-$850
Osage Co., OK

Florence chert

Classic form

S C

G10, $800-$1500
N. E. OK

G10, $800-$1500
N. E. OK

G8, $800-$1500
N. E. OK

G10, $3500-$6000
Tulsa Co., OK

ALMAGRE - Early Archaic, 6000 - 4500 B. P.

(Also see Gary, Hidden Valley, Langtry-Arenosa and Morrow Mountain)

G6, $5-$10
E. TX

G4, $12-$20
Val Verde Co., TX

G8, $55-$100
W. TX

ALMAGRE (continued)

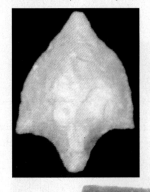

LOCATION: Midwestern states. **DESCRIPTION:** A broad, triangular point with pointed barbs and a long contracted pointed to rounded base. This point could be a preform for the *Langtry-Arenosa* type.

G6, $25-$40
S.W. TX

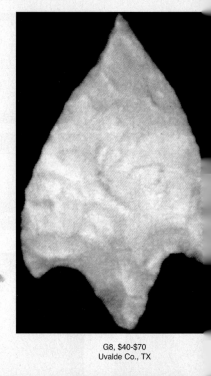

G9, $125-$200
Waco, TX

G8, $40-$70
Uvalde Co., TX

ANDICE - Early Archaic, 8000 - 5000 B. P.

(Also see Bell, Calf Creek and Little River)

Barb &
base nick

Resharpened
many times

Barbs lost in
resharpening

G4, $35-$60
Crane Co., TX

G7, $650-$1200
Dewitt Co., TX

G8, $800-$1500
Travis Co., TX

Base
nick

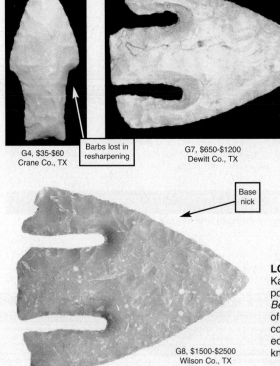

G8, $1500-$2500
Wilson Co., TX

LOCATION: Southern to Central Texas, Oklahoma and Kansas. **DESCRIPTION:** A broad, thin, large, triangular point with very deep, parallel basal notches. Larger than *Bell* or *Calf Creek* Points. Barbs reach the base. Because of the deep notches, barbs were easily broken off making complete, unbroken specimens rare. Found in a cave hafted to a wooden handle with pitch adhesive; used as a knife. **I.D. KEY:** Location and deep parallel basal notches.

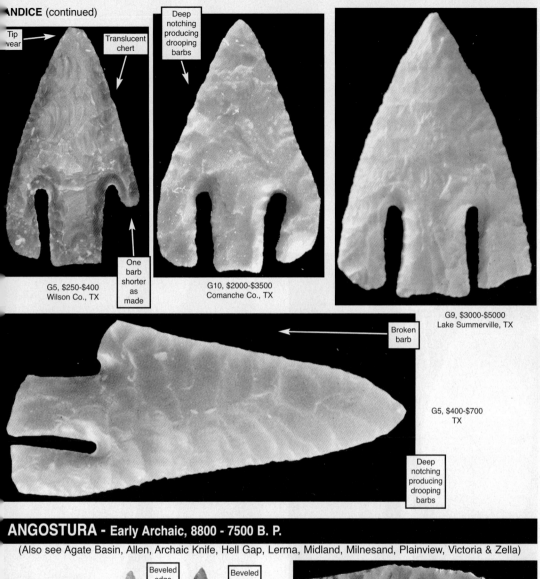

Tip wear

Translucent chert

Deep notching producing drooping barbs

One barb shorter as made

G5, $250-$400
Wilson Co., TX

G10, $2000-$3500
Comanche Co., TX

G9, $3000-$5000
Lake Summerville, TX

Broken barb

G5, $400-$700
TX

Deep notching producing drooping barbs

S C

ANGOSTURA - Early Archaic, 8800 - 7500 B. P.

(Also see Agate Basin, Allen, Archaic Knife, Hell Gap, Lerma, Midland, Milnesand, Plainview, Victoria & Zella)

Beveled edge

Beveled edge

G8, $125-$200
TX

Beveled edge

G6, $80-$150
Bexar Co., TX

G4, $25-$40
Angelina Co., TX

G8, $65-$125
Bell Co., TX

G6, $40-$75
Taylor Co., TX

Beveled edge

LOCATION: Midwest to Western states. **DESCRIPTION:** A medium to large size, lanceolate blade with a contracting, concave, straight or convex base. Both broad and narrow forms occur. Flaking can be parallel oblique to random. Blades are commonly steeply beveled on one side of each face; some are serrated and most have basal grinding. Formerly called Long points. **I.D. KEY:** Basal form, flaking on blade which can be beveled.

ANGOSTURA (continued)

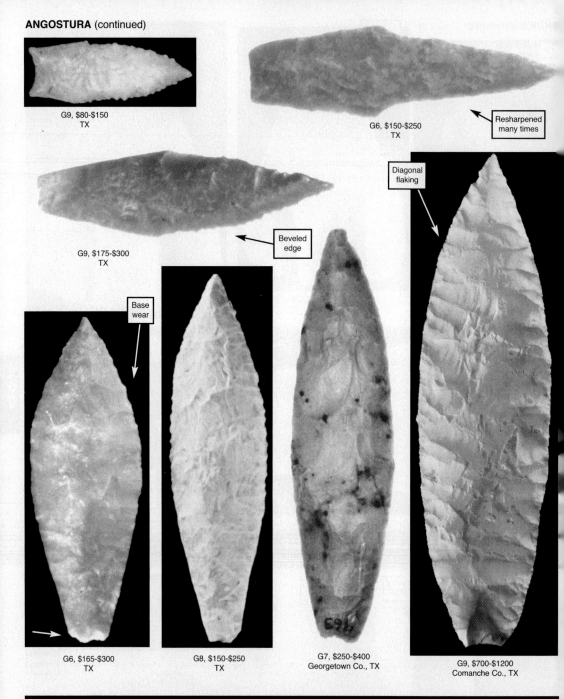

G9, $80-$150
TX

G6, $150-$250
TX

Resharpened
many times

Diagonal
flaking

G9, $175-$300
TX

Beveled
edge

Base
wear

G6, $165-$300
TX

G8, $150-$250
TX

G7, $250-$400
Georgetown Co., TX

G9, $700-$1200
Comanche Co., TX

ANTLER - Mississippian, 1300 - 400 B. P.

(Also see Angostura, Golondrina, Midland, Pelican and Plainview)

G4, $5-$10
Saline Co., AR

View from
the base

G7, $12-$20
Saline Co., AR

LOCATION: Most of United States.
DESCRIPTION: A medium size, conical shaped point made from deer antler.

ARCHAIC KNIFE - Transitional Paleo, 10,000 - 5000 B. P.

(Also see Angostura, Darl Stemmed, Early Stemmed and Victoria)

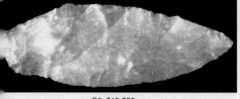
G6, $15-$25
Comal Co., TX

G6, $15-$30
Comal Co., TX

LOCATION: Texas, Oklahoma and Arkansas. **DESCRIPTION:** A medium to large size, lanceolate point with a contracting basal area. Shoulders are weakly tapered to non-existant.

ARENOSA   (See Langtry-Arenosa)

ARKABUTLA - Transitional Paleo, 10,000 - 8000 B. P.

(Also see Angostura, Coldwater, Golondrina, Midland, Pelican, Plainview, Rodgers Side Hollowed and San Patrice)

G7, $135-$250
Mineola, TX

G8, $175-$325
Cent. TX

G9, $275-$500
AR

LOCATION: AR, LA, MS, TN. **DESCRIPTION:** A small to medium size, broad, thin, lanceolate point with expanded auricles. Blade edges recurve into the base which is concave. **I.D. KEY:** Eared basal form.

AXTEL - Early-mid Archaic 7,000 - 3500 B. P.

(Also see Godley, Lajita, Palmillas and Williams)

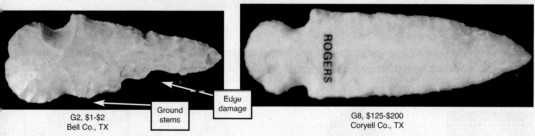
G2, $1-$2
Bell Co., TX
Ground stems
Edge damage
ROGERS
G8, $125-$200
Coryell Co., TX

LOCATION: Central Texas. **DESCRIPTION:** A medium size, narrow point with barbed shoulders and a bulbous stem. Called "Penny Points" by local collectors. Stem edges are usually ground. **I.D. KEY:** Bulbous stem that is ground. See Prewitt, p.90, Tex. Arc. Society 66, 1995 and *Field Guide to Stone Artifacts of Texas*, Turner & Hester, p.75, 1993

BAKER - Early Archaic, 7500 - 6000 B. P.

(Also see Bandy, Pedernales and Uvalde)

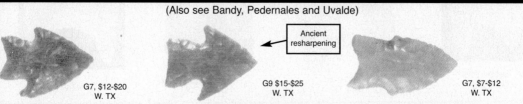
Ancient resharpening
G7, $12-$20
W. TX
G9 $15-$25
W. TX
G7, $7-$12
W. TX

S
C

527

BAKER (continued)

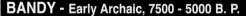

G8, $55-$100
Val Verde Co., TX

G2, $1-$3
Brewster Co., TX

Broken tip

LOCATION: W. Texas into New Mexico. **DESCRIPTION:** A small size, thin dart point with a short to long expanding stem that is bifurcated to concave. Tips are sharp and shoulders are barbed. Some basal areas can be ground. **I.D. KEY:** Base extended and bifurcated, early flaking.

BANDY - Early Archaic, 7500 - 5000 B. P.

(Also see Baker, Marcos, Marshall and Martindale)

G9, $65-$125
McCulloch Co., TX

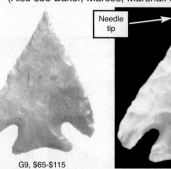

G9, $65-$115
TX

Needle tip

G10, $125-$200
Austin, TX

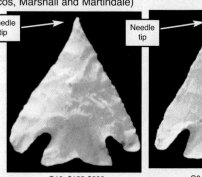

Needle tip

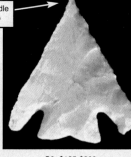

G9, $125-$200
Comanche Co., TX

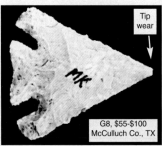

Tip wear

G8, $55-$100
McCulluch Co., TX

LOCATION: Southern Texas. **DESCRIPTION:** A small sized *Martindale* more commonly found in southern Texas. A corner notched to expanded stemmed point. The base is usually formed by two curves meeting at the center but can be straight to concave. **I.D. KEY:** Basal form, early flaking.

G7, $65-$125
Uvalde Co., TX

BARBER - Transitional Paleo, 10,000 - 9000 B. P.

(Also see Allen, Angostura, Clovis, Golondrina, Goshen, Kinney, McKean and Plainview)

G5, $65-$125
Llano Co., TX

G5, $80-$150
Cent. TX

G6, $150-$250
Kerr Co., TX

Ground basal area

G1, $35-$60
Llano Co., TX

528

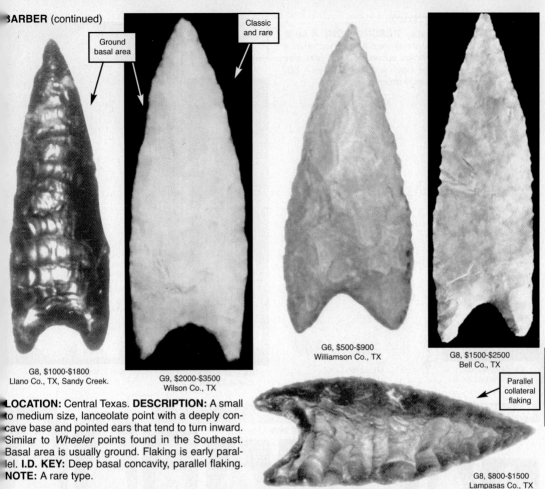

Ground basal area

Classic and rare

Parallel collateral flaking

S C

G8, $1000-$1800
Llano Co., TX, Sandy Creek.

G9, $2000-$3500
Wilson Co., TX

G6, $500-$900
Williamson Co., TX

G8, $1500-$2500
Bell Co., TX

G8, $800-$1500
Lampasas Co., TX

LOCATION: Central Texas. **DESCRIPTION:** A small to medium size, lanceolate point with a deeply concave base and pointed ears that tend to turn inward. Similar to *Wheeler* points found in the Southeast. Basal area is usually ground. Flaking is early parallel. **I.D. KEY:** Deep basal concavity, parallel flaking. **NOTE:** A rare type.

BASE TANG KNIFE - Late Archaic to Woodland, 4000 - 2000 B. P.

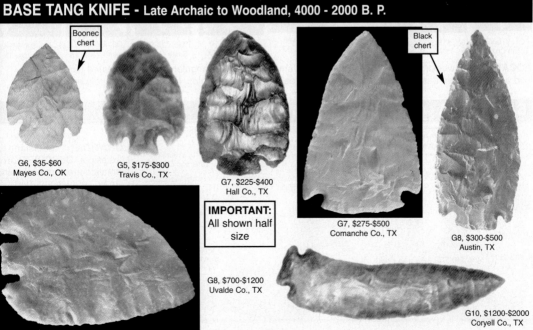

Boonec chert

Black chert

G6, $35-$60
Mayes Co., OK

G5, $175-$300
Travis Co., TX

G7, $225-$400
Hall Co., TX

IMPORTANT:
All shown half size

G7, $275-$500
Comanche Co., TX

G8, $300-$500
Austin, TX

G8, $700-$1200
Uvalde Co., TX

G10, $1200-$2000
Coryell Co., TX

529

BASE TANG KNIFE (continued)

LOCATION: Central Texas. **DESCRIPTION:** A large size, broad, blade with small basal notches and a straight base. Most examples curve more on one side and are believed to have been used as knives. **I.D. KEY:** Large size, small basal notches.

IMPORTANT: All shown half size

G9, $1000-$1700
Comanche Co., TX

G10, $700-$1200
Gillespie Co., TX

G9, $800-$1500
Coryell Co., TX

G8, $1500-$2500
Dardanelle, AR

BASSETT - Mississippian, 800 - 400 B. P.

(Also see Cliffton, Perdiz, Rockwall and Steiner)

Tip nick

Needle tip

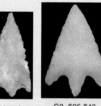

G7, $15-$25
Smith Co., TX

G7, $15-$25
TX

G8, $25-$40
Zapata Co., TX

G8, $25-$40
Smith Co., TX

G8, $30-$50
Smith Co., TX

G8, $35-$60
Smith Co., TX

G9, $80-$150
Emanuel Co., TX

G9, $90 $175
Smith Co., TX

LOCATION: Midwestern states. **DESCRIPTION:** A small size, thin, triangular point with pointed tangs and a small pointed base. High quality flaking is evident on most examples. **I.D. KEY:** Small pointed base.

BAYOGOULA - Mississippian, 800 - 400 B. P.

(Also see Edwards, Friley)

Ear wear

Serrated edge

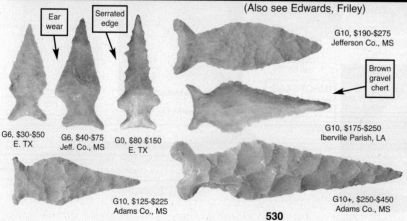

G10, $190-$275
Jefferson Co., MS

Brown gravel chert

G6, $30-$50
E. TX

G6, $40-$75
Jeff. Co., MS

G0, $80 $150
E. TX

G10, $175-$250
Iberville Parish, LA

G10, $125-$225
Adams Co., MS

G10+, $250-$450
Adams Co., MS

LOCATION: Louisianna, Mississippi. **DESCRIPTION:** A small to medium size, thin, narrow, arrowpoint with a bulbous mid-section, tapered shoulders and a short, expanded, concave base that forms ears. Distal ends are acute with long, sharp tips. This type has also been found at the Cahokia Mound site (See North Central Section). **I.D. KEY:** Eared base, tapered shoulders.

BELL - Middle Archaic, 7000 - 5000 B. P.

(Also see Andice and Calf Creek).

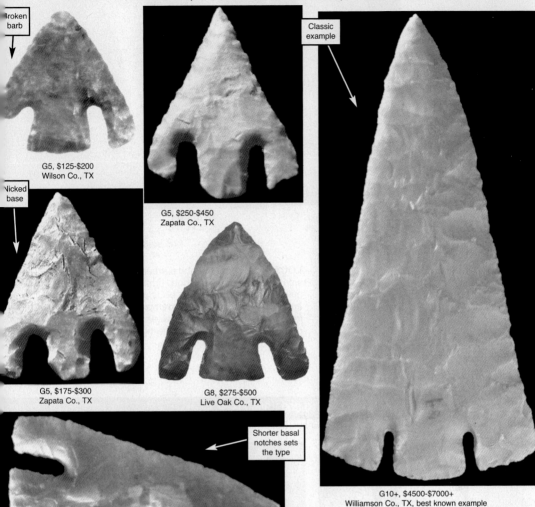

Broken barb

G5, $125-$200
Wilson Co., TX

Nicked base

G5, $250-$450
Zapata Co., TX

Classic example

G5, $175-$300
Zapata Co., TX

G8, $275-$500
Live Oak Co., TX

Shorter basal notches sets the type

Base nick

G7, $650-$1200
Lee Co., TX

G10+, $4500-$7000+
Williamson Co., TX, best known example

LOCATION: Central Texas. **DESCRIPTION:** A small to medium size point with medium-deep parallel basal notches, but not as deep as in *Andice*. Larger examples usually would fall under *Andice*. Found primarily in Texas. Barbs can turn inward at the base. **I.D. KEY:** Shorter barbs and notching.

BIG CREEK - Late Archaic to early Woodland, 3500 - 2500 B. P.

(Also see Ellis, Grand, Kings, Marcos and Williams)

Conglomerate

G4, $2-$4
AR

G6, $5-$8
Saline Co., AR

G6, $5-$8
AR

BIG CREEK (continued)

G5, $8-$15
AR

G5, $12-$20
Saline Co., AR

Novacaculite

G6, $15-$25
Saline Co., AR

G9, $45-$85
AR

G9, $25-$45
AR

LOCATION: Arkansas and surrounding states. **DESCRIPTION:** A small to medium size, short, broad, corner notched point with a bulbous base. Believed to be related to *Marcos* points. The tips are needle sharp on some examples, similar to *Mud Creek* points from Alabama. Barbs can be weak to very long. Small *Big Sloughs* of the Southeast would be indistinguishable to this type. **I.D. KEY:** Rounded base and barbs drop.

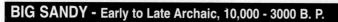

BIG SANDY - Early to Late Archaic, 10,000 - 3000 B. P.

(Also see Cache River, Ensor, Frio, Hickory Ridge and Savage Cave)

G5, $5-$10
Starr Co., TX

G5, $5-$10
Val Verde Co., TX

G5, $5-$10
Brewster Co., TX

G5, $5-$10
Coahuila, MX

Petrified wood

G5, $5-$10
Val Verde Co., TX

G5, $5-$10
Val Verde Co., TX

G5, $8-$15
Saline Co., AR

G7, $20-$35
Trinity Co., TX

G9, $150-$250
E. TX

LOCATION: Eastern Texas eastward. **DESCRIPTION:** A small to medium size, side notched point with early forms showing basal grinding, serrations and horizontal flaking. Bases are straight to concave. Deeply concave bases form ears. **I.D. KEY:** Basal form.

BLEVINS - Mississippian, 1200 - 600 B. P.

(Also see Hayes, Howard and Sequoyah)

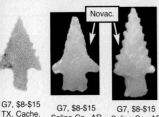

G8, $35-$60
W. AR.

LOCATION: Midwestern states. **DESCRIPTION:** A small size, narrow spike point with two or more notches on each blade side. The base is diamond shaped. A cross between *Hayes* and *Howard*. **I.D. KEY:** Diamond shaped base.

BONHAM - Woodland to Mississippian, 1200 - 600 B. P.

(Also see Alba, Bulbar Stemmed, Cuney, Hayes, Moran, Perdiz, Rockwall & Sabinal)

Novac.

G7, $8-$15
TX. Cache.

G7, $8-$15
Saline Co., AR

G7, $8-$15
Saline Co., AR

G8, $35-$60
AR

G8, $35-$60
Comanche Co., TX

G8, $35-$60
McCulloch Co., TX

G9, $45-$85
AR

G9, $35-$60
TX. Cache

G8, $45-$85
TX

Needle barbs

Slight tip nick

Fine serrations

G9, $35-$60
Comanche Co., TX

G9, $90-$150
Gaines Co., TX

G7, $45-$85
TX, cache point

G9, $90-$175
Cent. TX

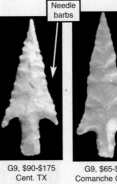

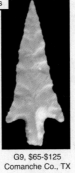

G9, $65-$125
Comanche Co., TX

3.

G9, $90-$175
TX

G10, $275-$500
Comanche Co., TX

S C

LOCATION: Texas and Oklahoma. **DESCRIPTION:** A small to medium size, thin, well made triangular point with a short to long squared or rounded, narrow stem. Many examples are finely serrated. Blade edges are straight, concave, or convex or recurved. Shoulders are squared to barbed. **I.D. KEY:** Long straight base, expanded barbs.

BRAZOS   (See Darl Stemmed)

BREWERTON EARED - Middle to Late Archaic, 6000 - 4000 B. P.

(Also see Rice Shallow Side Notched)

G4, $1-$2
Nuevo Leon, MX

G4, $1-$2
Saline Co., AR

G7, $3-$15
Coleman Co., TX

G7, $3-$5
AR

LOCATION: Northeast Texas eastward. **DESCRIPTION:** A small size, triangular point with shallow side notches and a concave base.

BREWERTON SIDE NOTCHED - Middle to Late Archaic,   6000 - 4000 B. P.

(Also see Big Sandy)

LOCATION: Northeast Texas eastward. **DESCRIPTION:** A small size, triangular point with shallow side notches and a concave base.

G2, $1-$2
Friendship Co., AR

G6, $2-$3
Waco, TX

BROWNS VALLEY - Transitional Paleo, 10,000 - 8000 B. P.

(Also see Agate Basin, Allen, Angostura, Barber, Clovis, Firstview, Midland and Plainview)

Note oblique flaking

Note oblique flaking

Ground basal area

G10, $500-$900
Terry Co., TX

Orange/red jasper

G9, $1000-$1800
N.E. AR. Translucent patinated Knife River flint. Classic example.

Knife River flint

LOCATION: A Minnesota type that has been found in Arkansas and W. Texas. **DESCRIPTION:** A medium to large thin, lanceolate blade with usually oblique to horizontal transverse flaking and a concave to straight base which can be ground. A very rare type. **I.D. KEY:** Paleo transverse flaking.

BULVERDE - Middle Archaic to Woodland, 5000 - 1000 B. P.

(Also see Carrolton, Delhi and Wells)

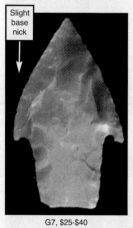

Slight base nick

G7, $25-$40
Bell Co., TX

G7, $30-$50
Burnett Co., TX

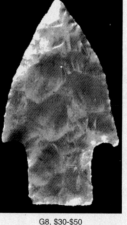

G8, $30-$50
Comanche Co., TX

G8, $35-$60
Llano, TX

G6, $35-$60
Bell Co., TX

LOCATION: Texas. **DESCRIPTION:** A medium to large size, long, rectangular stemmed point with usually barbed shoulders. Believed to be related to Carrolton. **I.D. KEY:** Long, squared base and barbed shoulders.

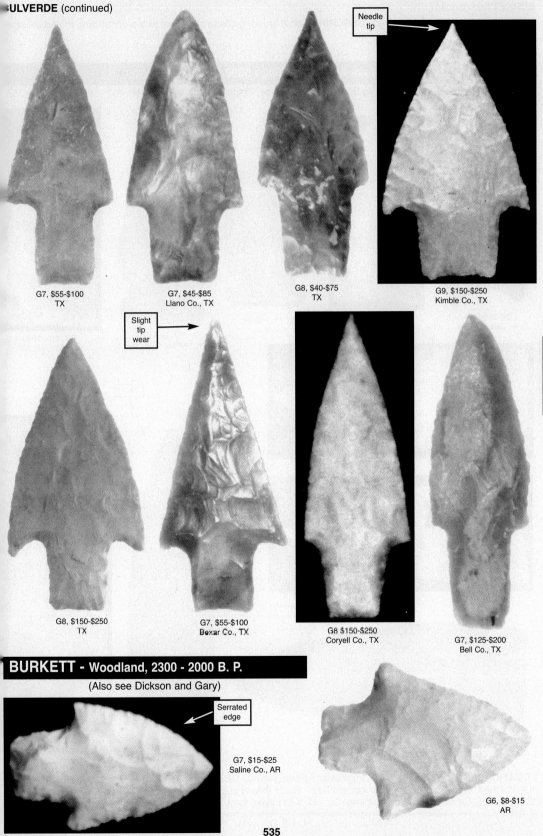

G7, $55-$100
TX

G7, $45-$85
Llano Co., TX

G8, $40-$75
TX

Needle tip

G9, $150-$250
Kimble Co., TX

Slight tip wear

G8, $150-$250
TX

G7, $55-$100
Bexar Co., TX

G8 $150-$250
Coryell Co., TX

G7, $125-$200
Bell Co., TX

S C

BURKETT - Woodland, 2300 - 2000 B. P.

(Also see Dickson and Gary)

Serrated edge

G7, $15-$25
Saline Co., AR

G6, $8-$15
AR

535

BURKETT (continued)

LOCATION: Arkansas into Missouri. **DESCRIPTION:** A broad, medium size point with a contracting to parallel side stem and barbed to horizontal shoulders.

CACHE RIVER - Early to Late Archaic, 10,000 - 5000 B. P.

(Also see Big Sandy, Hickory Ridge, Knight Island and White River)

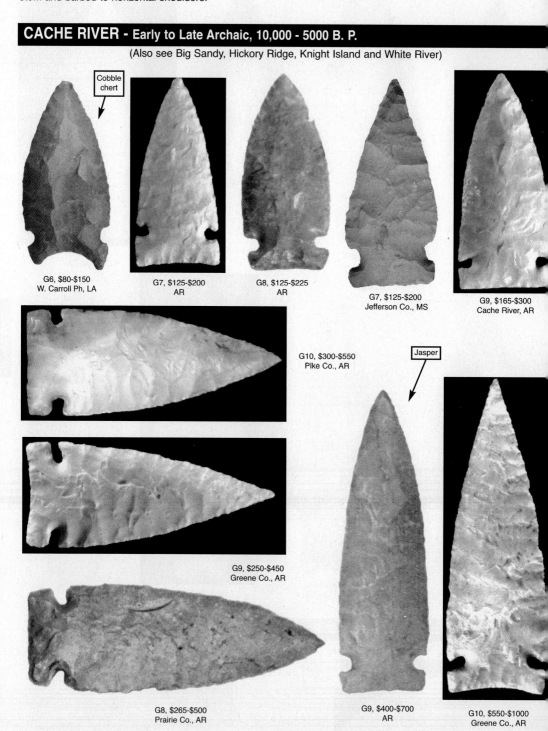

Cobble chert

G6, $80-$150
W. Carroll Ph, LA

G7, $125-$200
AR

G8, $125-$225
AR

G7, $125-$200
Jefferson Co., MS

G9, $165-$300
Cache River, AR

G10, $300-$550
Pike Co., AR

Jasper

G9, $250-$450
Greene Co., AR

G8, $265-$500
Prairie Co., AR

G9, $400-$700
AR

G10, $550-$1000
Greene Co., AR

LOCATION: Arkansas to Ohio, West Virginia and Pennsylvania. **DESCRIPTION:** A small to medium size, fairly thin side-notched, triangular point with a concave base. Blade flaking is of the early parallel type. Could be related to *Big Sandy* points. Called *Kessell* in West Virginia. **I.D. KEY:** Base form, narrow notched & flaking of blade.

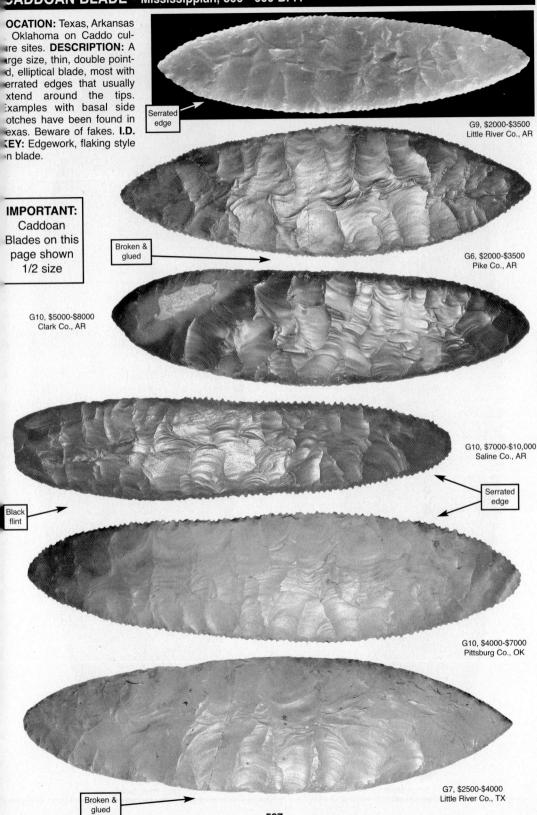

LOCATION: Texas, Arkansas & Oklahoma on Caddo culture sites. **DESCRIPTION:** A large size, thin, double pointed, elliptical blade, most with serrated edges that usually extend around the tips. Examples with basal side notches have been found in Texas. Beware of fakes. **I.D. KEY:** Edgework, flaking style on blade.

IMPORTANT: Caddoan Blades on this page shown 1/2 size

Serrated edge

G9, $2000-$3500
Little River Co., AR

Broken & glued

G6, $2000-$3500
Pike Co., AR

G10, $5000-$8000
Clark Co., AR

G10, $7000-$10,000
Saline Co., AR

Serrated edge

Black flint

G10, $4000-$7000
Pittsburg Co., OK

Broken & glued

G7, $2500-$4000
Little River Co., TX

S C

Serrated edge

Red & pink chert

Serrated edge

IMPORTANT:
Caddoan Blades on this page are shown FULL size

G10, $4500-$8000
Clark Co., AR

G10, $4500-$8000
Pike Co., AR

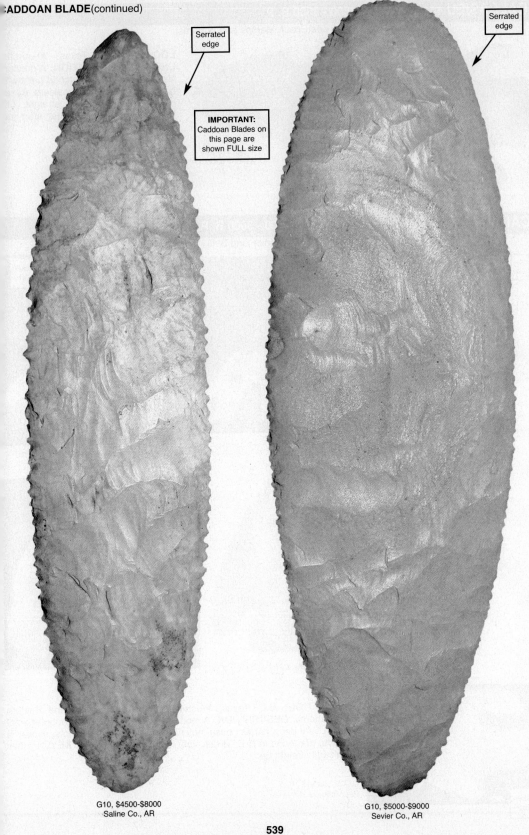

Serrated edge

Serrated edge

IMPORTANT:
Caddoan Blades on
this page are
shown FULL size

S
C

G10, $4500-$8000
Saline Co., AR

G10, $5000-$9000
Sevier Co., AR

CALCASIEU - Late Archaic, 4500 - 3000 B. P.

(Also see Ensor, Marcos and Williams)

LOCATION: E. Texas, Arkansas Louisiana. **DESCRIPTION:** A medium size, corner to side notched point with barbed to horizontal shoulders. Bases are slightly convex to straight. **I.D. KEY:** Corner notches that start just above the base.

G8, $25-$45
St. Francis Co., AR

G6, $12-$20
Vernon Parrish, LA

CALF CREEK - Early to Middle Archaic, 8000 - 5000 B. P.

(Also see Andice and Bell)

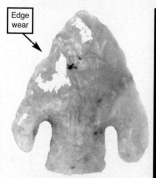

Edge wear

G6, $150-$250
Marshall Co., OK

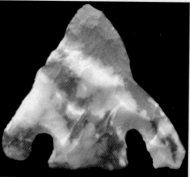

G5, $55-$100
Saline Co., AR

Broken barb

G5, $125-$200
Yell Co., AR

G7, $175-$300
TX/AR

G5, $175-$300
AR

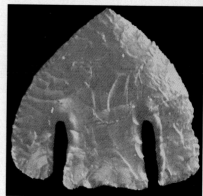

G8, $700-$1200
Searcy Co., AR

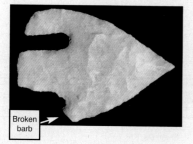

Broken barb

G3, $30-$50
Val Verde Co., TX

LOCATION: N.E. Texas, Western Arkansas, Missouri and eastern Oklahoma. **DESCRIPTION:** A medium to large size thin, triangular point with very deep parallel basal notches. *Andice* and *Bell* points, similar in form, are found in N.E. Texas. Very rare in type area. **I.D. KEY:** Notches almost straight up.

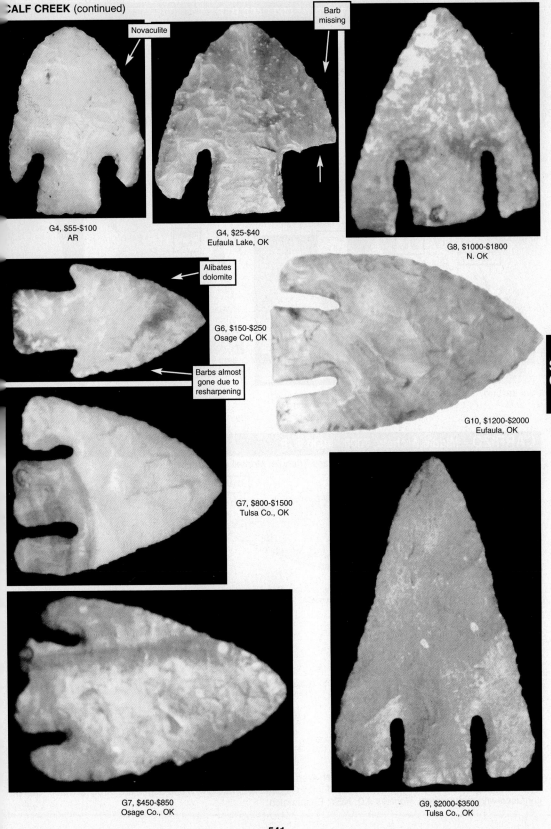

Novaculite

Barb missing

G4, $55-$100
AR

G4, $25-$40
Eufaula Lake, OK

G8, $1000-$1800
N. OK

Alibates
dolomite

G6, $150-$250
Osage Col, OK

Barbs almost
gone due to
resharpening

S
C

G10, $1200-$2000
Eufaula, OK

G7, $800-$1500
Tulsa Co., OK

G7, $450-$850
Osage Co., OK

G9, $2000-$3500
Tulsa Co., OK

CARACARA - Mississippian to Historic, 600 - 400 B. P.

(Also see Huffaker, Reed and Washita)

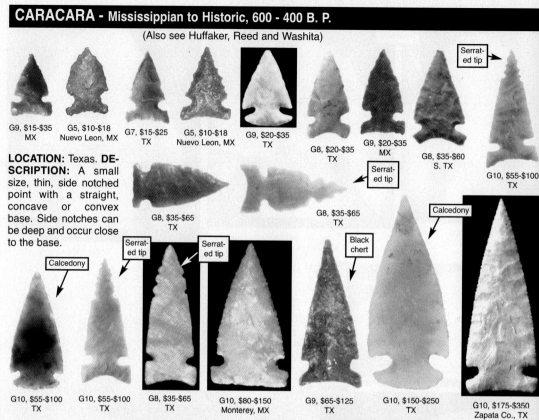

LOCATION: Texas. **DESCRIPTION:** A small size, thin, side notched point with a straight, concave or convex base. Side notches can be deep and occur close to the base.

G9, $15-$35 MX

G5, $10-$18 Nuevo Leon, MX

G7, $15-$25 TX

G5, $10-$18 Nuevo Leon, MX

G9, $20-$35 TX

G8, $20-$35 TX

G9, $20-$35 MX

G8, $35-$60 S. TX

Serrated tip

G10, $55-$100 TX

Serrated tip

G8, $35-$65 TX

G8, $35-$65 TX

Calcedony

Serrated tip

Serrated tip

Black chert

Calcedony

G10, $55-$100 TX

G10, $55-$100 TX

G8, $35-$65 TX

G10, $80-$150 Monterey, MX

G9, $65-$125 TX

G10, $150-$250 TX

G10, $175-$350 Zapata Co., TX

CARRIZO - Middle Archaic, 7000 - 4000 B. P.

(Also see Early Triangle, Montell and Tortugas)

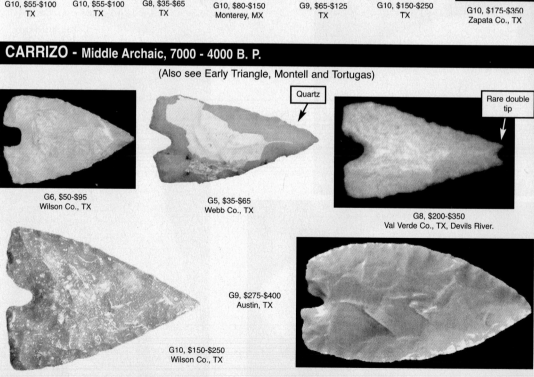

Quartz

Rare double tip

G6, $50-$95 Wilson Co., TX

G5, $35-$65 Webb Co., TX

G8, $200-$350 Val Verde Co., TX, Devils River.

G9, $275-$400 Austin, TX

G10, $150-$250 Wilson Co., TX

LOCATION: Texas to Colorado. **DESCRIPTION:** A small to medium size, triangular point with a deep single notch or a concave indention in the center of the base. Flaking is parallel to random. Blade edges are rarely serrated. Can be confused with resharpened *Montells.* **I.D. KEY:** Basal notch.

CARROLTON - Middle to Late Archaic, 5000 - 3000 B. P.

(Also see Adena, Bulverde, Dallas, Morrill and Wells)

G3, $2-$4
Bexar Co., TX

G6, $5-$10
Titus Co., TX

G7, $15-$30
Coryell Co., TX

G6, $12-$20
Comanche Co., TX

G6, $12-$20
Bell Co., TX

G7, $25-$40
Central TX

LOCATION: North Texas. **DESCRIPTION:** A medium to large size, long parallel stemmed point with a square base. Shoulders are usually tapered. Workmanship is crude to medium grade. Believed to be related to *Bulverde* points.

CASTROVILLE - Late Archaic to Woodland, 4000 - 1500 B. P.

(Also see Lange, Marcos, Marshall and San Jacinto)

G8, $12-$20
I X

G8, $15-$30
TX

G7, $30-$55
Comanche Co., TX

G7, $50-$95
TX

G7, $30-$50
Comanche Co., TX

G8, $70-$125
Lampassas, TX

S C

G7, $50-$95
Bell Co., TX

G8, $70-$125
Comal Co., TX

G9, $125-$225
Bandera Co., TX

G9, $125-$200
Williamson Co., TX

G7, $125-$200
Coryell Co., TX

G9, $150-$275
Kimble Co., TX

Slight tip wear

G7, $55-$100
Williamson Co., TX

G10, $300-$500
Kendall Co., TX

Perfect symmetry

G7, $125-$225
Lampassas Co., TX

G8, $165-$300
TX

G9, $250-$450
Kerr Co., TX

S C

Needle tip

G8, $275-$500
Kimble Co., TX

G7, $275-$500
Coryell Co., TX

G8 $275-$500
Comanche Co., TX

LOCATION: Texas to Colorado. **DESCRIPTION:** A medium to large size, broad, corner notched point with an expanding stem and prominent barbs that can reach the basal edge. The base can be straight to convex and is usually broader than in *Lange* and *Marshall*. **I.D. KEY:** Broad base, corner notches.

CATAHOULA - Mississippian, 800 - 400 B. P.

(Also see Friley, Rockwall and Scallorn)

G6, $25-$40
Cat. Lake, LA

G6, $30-$50
Cat. Lake, LA

G6, $35-$50
AR

G7, $35-$65
AR

Brown chert

G8, $40-$75
AR

G6, $35-$60
Cat. Lake, LA

G9, $70-$135
Cat. Lake, LA

G5, $20-$35
AR

G9, $65-$125
AR

White chert

G8, $40-$75
AR

G8, $65-$125
AR

Tan chert

G7, $30-$55
AR

Red chert

G8, $40-$75
AR

Red jasper

G7, $40-$75
Cat. Lake, LA

G9, $40-$75
TX

G7, $35-$60
Cat. Lake, LA

Petrified palmwood

Heat treated pertrified palmwood

One of best known

G8, $80-$150
Catahoula Ph, LA

G10, $135-$250
AR

Tan chert

G8, $40-$75
AR

G9, $165-$300
Cat. Parish, LA

G10+, $600-$1000
Catahoula Lake, LA

LOCATION: East Texas, Louisiana to Arkansas. **DESCRIPTION**: A small size, thin, point with broad, flaring, squared tangs. The stem is parallel sided to expanding. The base is straight to convex. **I.D. KEY:** Expanded barbs.

CATAN - Late Archaic to Mississippian, 4000 - 300 B. P.

(Also see Abasolo, Matamoros and Young)

G5, $.50-$1
Nuevo Leon, MX

G5, $1-$2
Nuevo Leon, MX

G5, $1-$2
Nuevo Leon, MX

G6, $1-$3
Nuevo Leon, MX

G5, $1-$2
Coahuila, MX

G6, $1-$3
Starr Co., TX

G9, $4-$8
Nuevo Leon, MX

G9, $4-$8
TX

G8, $4-$8
Starr Co., TX

G7, $4-$8
TX

G8, $5-$10
Nuevo Leon, MX

LOCATION: Southern Texas and New Mexico. **DESCRIPTION**: A small, thin, lanceolate point with a rounded base. Large examples would fall under the *Abasolo* type.

CHARCOS - Woodland, 3000 - 2000 B. P.

(Also see Duran, Evans and Sinner)

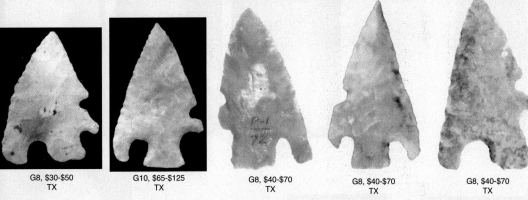

G8, $30-$50
TX

G10, $65-$125
TX

G8, $40-$70
TX

G8, $40-$70
TX

G8, $40-$70
TX

G7, $35-$60
TX

LOCATION: Northern Mexico into south Texas & Colorado. **DESCRIPTION:** A small size, thin, single barbed point with a notch near the opposite shoulder. Stem is rectangular. **I.D. KEY:** Asymmetrical form. Some are double notched. Beware of resharpened *Shumla* points with notches added in modern times to look like *Charcos.*

CHOPPER - Paleo to Archaic, 11,500 - 6000 B. P.

(Also see Kerrville Knife)

LOCATION: Paleo sites everywhere. **DESCRIPTION**: A medium to large size, thick, ovoid hand axe made from local creek or river stones. Used in the butchering process. Also known as Butted knife.

Chopper shown half size

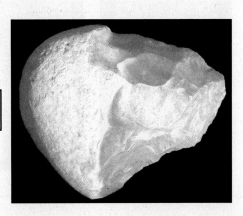

G8, $125-$200
Kimble Co., TX

CLIFFTON - Mississippian, 1200 - 500 B. P.

(Also see Bassett)

LOCATION: Central Texas.
DESCRIPTION: A small size, crude point that is usually made from a flake and is uniface. The base is sharply contracting to pointed. Preforms for *Perdiz*?

G9, $5-$10
TX

G1, $.50-$1
Waco, TX

G6, $4-$8
TX

G6, $1-$2
TX

CLOVIS - Early Paleo, 11,500 - 10,600 B. P.

(Also see Allen, Angostura, Barber, Browns Valley, Dalton, Golondrina and Plainview)

G6, $250-$400
TX

G5, $250-$400
Comanche Co., TX

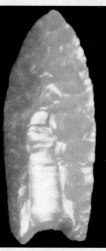

G8, $700-$1200
OK

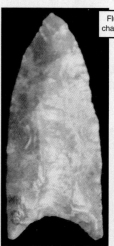

G7, $350-$650
OK

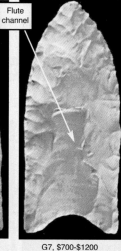

Flute channel

G7, $700-$1200
Comanche Co., TX

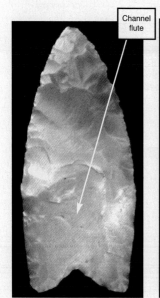

Channel flute

G8, $800-$1400
Childress Co., TX

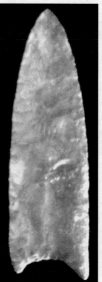

G7, $800-$1500
TX

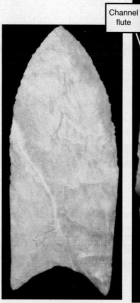

G9, $800-$1500
Wilson Co., TX

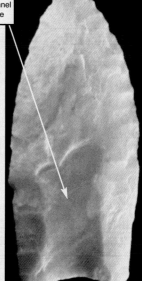

Channel flute

G8, $1500-$2500
Dawson, TX

548

Flute channel

G10, $1200-$2000
TX

Edwards Plateau flint

Siltstone

Flute channel

Translucent

Flute channel

Tip wear

Edge wear

G8, $700-$1200
Harris Co., TX

G6, $400-$750
Wilson Co., TX

S
C

G6, $275-$500
Comanche Co., TX

G6, $1200-$2000
Brown Co., TX

G8, $2500-$4500
Bastrop Co., TX

G10, $7000-$12,000+
Bexar Co., TX

LOCATION: All of North America. **DESCRIPTION:** A medium to large size, auriculate, fluted, lanceolate point with convex sides and a concave base that is ground. Most examples are fluted on both sides about 1/3 the way up from the base. The flaking can be random to parallel. *Clovis* is the earliest point type in the hemisphere. There is no pre-*Clovis* evidence here in the U.S.(no crude forms that pre-date *Clovis*). The origin of *Clovis* is unknown. It may have developed from earlier forms brought here from the old world. *Clovis*-like fluted points have been reported found in China dating to 11-12,000 B.P. *Clovis* has also been found in Alaska and southern Chile in South America. **I.D. KEY:** Paleo flaking, shoulders, batan fluting instead of indirect style. Basal form and fluting.

COAHUILA - Late Archaic to Woodland, 4000 - 2000 B. P.

(Also see Adena, Gary, Hidden Valley and Langtry)

G5, $12-$20
Val Verde Co., TX

G7, $35-$60
TX

G8, $40-$75
Comanche Co., TX

G7, $12-$20
Comanche Co., TX

LOCATION: Central Texas. **DESCRIPTION:** A medium to large size, narrow point with tapered shoulders and a long, pointed, contracting stem. A scarce type. **I.D. KEY:** Long, pointed stem. Rare type. Also known as *Jora* points.

CODY KNIFE   (See Red River Knife)

COLBERT - Mississippian, 1100 - 800 B. P.

(Also see Alba, Homan, Hughes and Keota)

Serrated edges

Serrated edges

Green flint

G7, $25-$40
TX

G5, $2-$4
Ellis Co., TX

G8, $12-$20
TX

G5, $3-$6
Ellis Co., TX

G6, $5-$10
Ellis Co., TX

G6, $30-$55
AR

G5, $3-$6
Saline Co., AR

LOCATION: Louisiana to E. Oklahoma. **DESCRIPTION:** A small to medium size, arrow point with wide corner notches. Stems expand and bases can be straight to rounded. Reported to be related to *Alba* points. Also known as *Massard* points.

COLDWATER - Trans. Paleo, 10,000 - 8000 B. P.

(Also see Arkabutla, Pelican and San Patrice)

LOCATION: East Texas into Arkansas & Louisiana. **DESCRIPTION:** A medium size, Lanceolate point with a longer waist than *Pelican* and a straight to concave base which is ground. The blade expands up from the base.

G10, $700-$1200
San Augustine Co., TX

Petrified wood

CONEJO - Late Archaic, 4000 - 3000 B. P.

(Also see Bandy, Ellis, Fairland and Marshall)

CONEJO (continued)

G5, $8-$15
Schleicher Co., TX

G10, $45-$85
TX

G4, $3-$5
Comanche Co., TX

G6, $15-$25
Austin, TX

LOCATION: Texas and New Mexico **DESCRIPTION:** A medium size, corner notched point with an expanding, concave base and shoulder tangs that turn towards the base.

CORNER TANG KNIFE - Late Archaic to Woodland, 4000 - 2000 B. P.

(Also see Base Tang, Crescent Knife and Mid-Back Tang Knife)

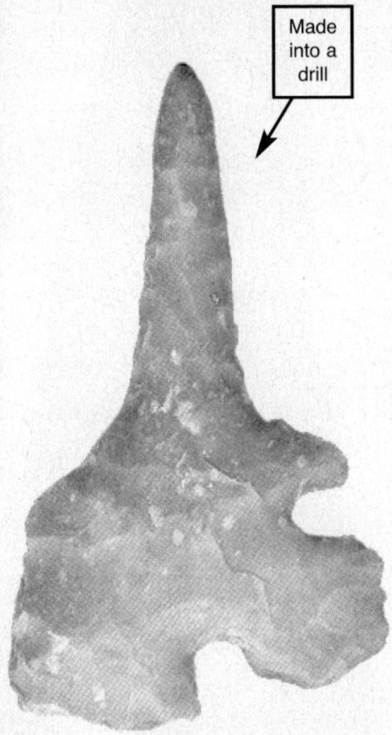

Made into a drill

S
C

Dog log form

G6, $350-$600
Kerr Co., TX

G7, $350-$600
Wilson Co., TX

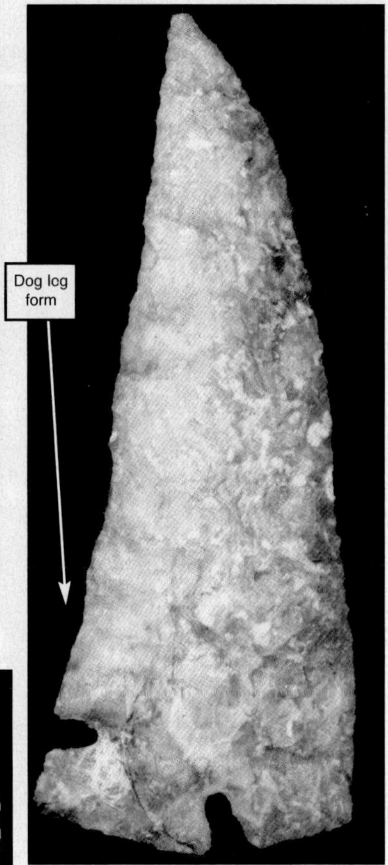

G9, $1700-$3000
Kerr Co., TX

G7, $600-$1100
Kerr Co., TX

LOCATION: Texas to Oklahoma. **DESCRIPTION:** This knife is notched producing a tang at a corner for hafting to a handle. Tang knives are very rare and have been reproduced in recent years. **I.D. KEY:** Angle of hafting.

$150-$250
Comal Co., TX,
restored

Rare double tang
knife; only three
known

G9, $700-$1200
Coryell Co., TX

G10, $1200-$2200
Kerr Co., TX

G9, $1700-$3000
Coryell Co., TX

G10, $3500-$6000
Waco, TX

COSOTAT RIVER - Early Archaic, 9500 - 8000 B. P.

(Also see Ensor Split Base, Frio & Rice Lobbed)

G10, $450-$800
AR

G8, $125-$200
Lake Eufaula, OK

LOCATION: Texas into Oklahoma, Arkansas and Missouri. **DESCRIPTION:** A medium to large size, thin, usually serrated, widely corner notched point with large round to square ears and a shallow to deep notch in the center of the base. Bases are usually ground. **I.D. KEY:** Basal notching and early Archaic flaking.

CORYELL - Middle Archaic, 7000 - 5000 B. P.

(Also see Searcy and Wells)

First stage form; Heiner Lake tan Coryell Co. heat treated chert

Heat treated brown Coryell Co. chert

Extreme resharpening; tan Coryell Co. non-heat treated chert

ROGERS

Ground stem

G8, $150-$250
Coryell Co., TX

G5 $125-$200
Coryell Co., TX

G10, $250-$400
Coryell Co., TX

G7, $150-$250
Bell Co., TX

Gray & white Coryell Co. non-heat treated chert

G9, $200-$350
Coryell Co., TX

LOCATION: Eastern Texas with type area in Coryell Co. **DESCRIPTION:** A medium to large size, serrated stemmed point with a large stem that usually tapers towards the base. Stems are usually ground. Serrations are not a product of resharpening. Shoulders are tapered to horizontal. Formerly known as "large stem Wells." This type has been found (in some camps) with Early Triangles in Coryell & Bell Co. with both types made from heat treated "Heiner Lake" tan chert. Similar to the *Searcy* point from Arkansas. **I.D. KEY:** Long stem and serrated blade edges. **NOTE:** Named "**Texas Kirk**" in Perino's book.

553

COVINGTON - Late Archaic, 4000 - 3000 B. P.

(Also see Crescent Knife, Friday, Gahagan, Sabine, San Saba and San Gabriel)

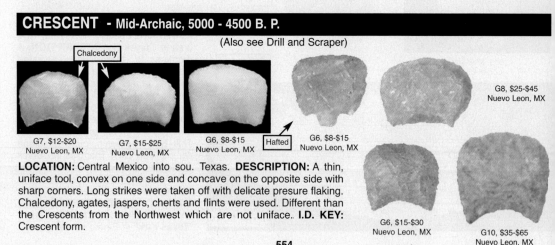

G6, $20-$30
Hill Co., TX

G7, $25-$45
Austin, TX

G6, $30-$50
TX

G6, $35-$65
Williamson Co., TX

G6, $35-$60
Concho Co., TX

G7, $125-$225
Coryell Co., TX

G6, $50-$80
Travis Co., TX

IMPORTANT:
All Covingtons
shown 50% actual size.

G7, $25-$45
Saline Co., AR

G7, $30-$50
TX

G8, $125-$225
Kimble Co., TX

G8, $75-$145
TX

G9, $250-$400
TX

LOCATION: Texas into Oklahoma. **DESCRIPTION:** A medium to large size, thin, lanceolate blade with a broad, rounded base.

CRESCENT - Mid-Archaic, 5000 - 4500 B. P.

(Also see Drill and Scraper)

Chalcedony

G7, $12-$20
Nuevo Leon, MX

G7, $15-$25
Nuevo Leon, MX

G6, $8-$15
Nuevo Leon, MX

Hafted

G6, $8-$15
Nuevo Leon, MX

G8, $25-$45
Nuevo Leon, MX

G6, $15-$30
Nuevo Leon, MX

G10, $35-$65
Nuevo Leon, MX

LOCATION: Central Mexico into sou. Texas. **DESCRIPTION:** A thin, uniface tool, convex on one side and concave on the opposite side with sharp corners. Long strikes were taken off with delicate presure flaking. Chalcedony, agates, jaspers, cherts and flints were used. Different than the Crescents from the Northwest which are not uniface. **I.D. KEY:** Crescent form.

CRESCENT KNIFE - Trans. Paleo to Early Archaic, 10,200 - 8000 B. P.

(Also see Base Tang, Corner Tang, Covington)

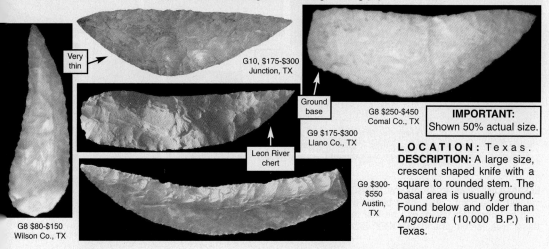

Very thin

G10, $175-$300
Junction, TX

Ground base

G8 $250-$450
Comal Co., TX

G9 $175-$300
Llano Co., TX

Leon River chert

G9 $300-$550
Austin, TX

G8 $80-$150
Wilson Co., TX

IMPORTANT:
Shown 50% actual size.

LOCATION: Texas.
DESCRIPTION: A large size, crescent shaped knife with a square to rounded stem. The basal area is usually ground. Found below and older than *Angostura* (10,000 B.P.) in Texas.

CUNEY - Historic, 400 - 200 B. P.

(Also see Bonham, Edwards, Morris, Perdiz, Rockwall and Scallorn)

G6, $18-$30
AR

Broken barb & ear

G5, $12-$20
Comanche Co., TX

G2, $1-$3
Titus Co., TX

G9, $40-$75
Comanche Co., TX

G6, $15-$30
Ellis Co., TX

G5, $12-$20
Comanche Co., TX

G7, $30-$50
Comanche Co., TX

G10, $60-$100
AR. Tan chert.

LOCATION: Midwestern states. **DESCRIPTION:** A small size, well made, barbed, triangular point with a very short, small, expanding base that is bifurcated.

CUPP - Late Woodland to Mississippian, 1500 - 600 B. P.

(Also see Epps, Gibson, Grand and Motley)

Stone material sparkles with mica

Classic "textbook" example

G9, $275-$500
Osage Co., OK

LOCATION: Northern Texas, Arkansas Missouri, and Oklahoma. **DESCRIPTION:** A medium to large size, narrow barbed point with a short, expanding stem, broad corner notches and a convex base. Basal corners can be asymmetrical. Similar to *Motley*, but the base stem is shorter. *Epps* has square to tapered shoulders, otherwise is identical to *Motley*.

DALLAS - Late Archaic to Woodland, 4000 - 1500 B. P.

(Also see Carrolton, Dawson, Elam, Kent, Travis and Wells)

S C

DALLAS (continued)

G3, $1-$2
Waco, TX

G3, $1-$2
Waco, TX

Knife form

G4, $1-$3
Waco, TX

G4, $1-$3
Waco, TX

G8, $25-$40
TX

G5, $3-$6
Comanche Co., TX

G5, $3-$6
Waco, TX

G5, $3-$6
Comanche Co., TX

LOCATION: Texas to Oklahoma. **DESCRIPTION:** A small to medium size point with a short blade, weak shoulders, and a long squared stem. Stem can be half the length of the point. Basal area can be ground. **I.D. KEY:** Size, squared stem.

DALTON-BRECKENRIDGE - Early Archaic, 10,000 - 9200 B. P.

(Also see Dalton Classic and Meserve)

G4, $20-$35
AR

LOCATION: Midwestern states, **DESCRIPTION:** A medium to large size, auriculate point with an obvious bevel extending the entire length of the point from tip to base. Similar in form to the *Dalton-Greenbrier*. Basal area is usually ground.

DALTON CLASSIC - Early Archaic, 10,000 - 9200 B. P.

(Also see Angostura, Barber, Clovis, Golondrina, Meserve, Plainview and San Patrice)

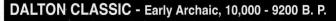

Made into a drill

Serrated edge

Tip wear

G7, $25-$45
AR

G8, $40-$75
Hot Spring Co., AR

G8, $40-$75
N. E. AR

G7, $35-$60
Clark Co., AR

G5, $25-$45
Van Zandt Co., TX

Flute channel

G8, $125-$225
N.E. AR

G8, $125-$200
Coke Co., TX

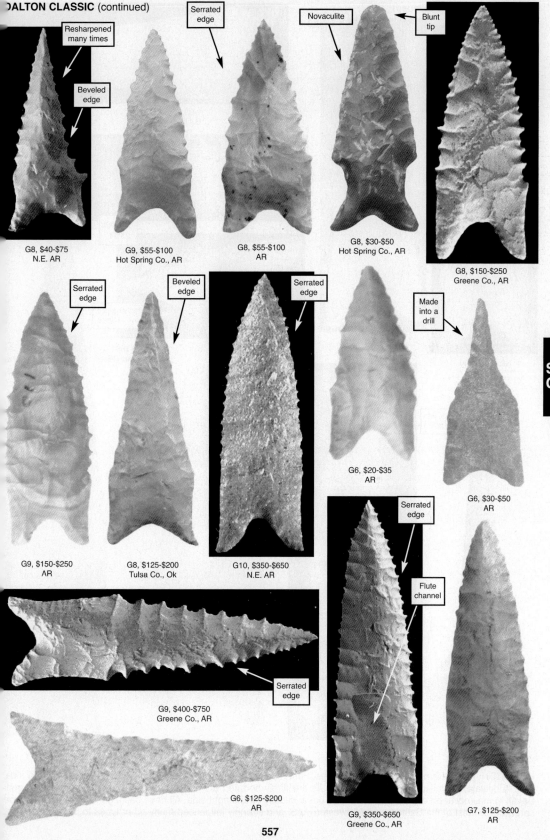

Resharpened many times

Beveled edge

G8, $40-$75
N.E. AR

Serrated edge

G9, $55-$100
Hot Spring Co., AR

Serrated edge

G8, $55-$100
AR

Novaculite

Blunt tip

G8, $30-$50
Hot Spring Co., AR

G8, $150-$250
Greene Co., AR

S C

Serrated edge

Beveled edge

Serrated edge

Made into a drill

G6, $20-$35
AR

G6, $30-$50
AR

G9, $150-$250
AR

G8, $125-$200
Tulsa Co., Ok

G10, $350-$650
N.E. AR

Serrated edge

G9, $400-$750
Greene Co., AR

G6, $125-$200
AR

Serrated edge

Flute channel

G9, $350-$650
Greene Co., AR

G7, $125-$200
AR

557

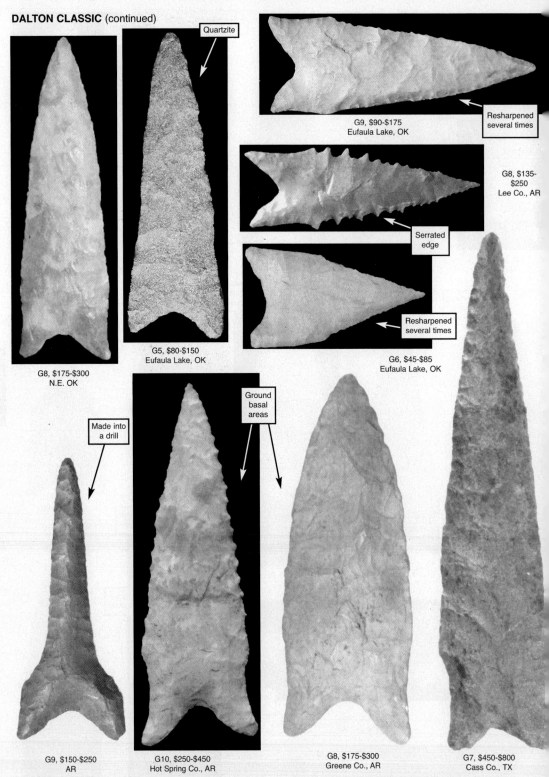

Quartzite

G9, $90-$175
Eufaula Lake, OK

G8, $135-$250
Lee Co., AR

Serrated edge

Resharpened several times

Resharpened several times

G6, $45-$85
Eufaula Lake, OK

G8, $175-$300
N.E. OK

G5, $80-$150
Eufaula Lake, OK

Made into a drill

Ground basal areas

G9, $150-$250
AR

G10, $250-$450
Hot Spring Co., AR

G8, $175-$300
Greene Co., AR

G7, $450-$800
Cass Co., TX

LOCATION: Midwestern to Southeastern states. First recognized in Missouri. **DESCRIPTION:** A small to large size, thin, auriculate, fishtailed point. Many examples are finely serrated and exhibit excellent flaking. Some are fluted. Beveling may occur on one side of each face but is usually on the right side. All have basal grinding. This early type spread over most of the Eastern and Midwestern U.S. and strongly influenced many other types to follow.

DALTON-COLBERT - Early Archaic, 10,000 - 9200 B. P.

(Also see Beaver Lake, Dalton-Nuckolls, Plainview and Searcy)

G7, $40-$75
AR

G6, $55-$100
AR

LOCATION: Midwestern to Southeastern states. **DESCRIPTION:** A medium size, auriculate form with a squared base and a weakly defined hafting area which is ground. Some examples are serrated and exhibit parallel flaking of the highest quality. **I.D. KEY:** Squarish basal area.

DALTON-GREENBRIER - Early Archaic, 10,000 - 9200 B. P.

(Also see Dalton Breckenridge, Golondrina, Meserve, Pelican and Plainview)

S
C

G4, $18-$30
Saline Co., AR

G7, $25-$50
Van Zandt Co., TX

G7, $20-$35
AR

G6, $20-$35
Hot Spring Co., AR

G8, $25-$50
N.E. AR

G7, $65-$125
E. TX

G6, $25-$40
AR

G7, $25-$50
N.E. AR

G7, $30-$50
N.E. AR

G5, $20-$35
AR

G7, $25-$50
Van Zandt Co., TX

G7, $30-$50
AR

G8, $25-$50
AR

LOCATION: Midwestern to Eastern states and Florida. **DESCRIPTION:** A medium to large size, auriculate form with a concave base and drooping to expanding auricles. Many examples are serrated, some are fluted on both sides, and all have basal grinding. Resharpened examples are usually beveled on the right side of each face although left side beveling does occur. Thinness and high quality flaking is evident on many examples. This early variation developed in the Arkansas/Kentucky/Tennessee area. **I.D. KEY:** Expanded auricles.

Fluting channel

G7, $60-$100
Greene Co., AR

G5, $45-$80
Comanche Co., TX

Quartzite

Beveled edge

LOCATION: Midwestern to Eastern states. **DESCRIPTION:** A medium to large size point with expanded auricles and horizontal, tapered to weak shoulders. Blade edges are usually serrated and bases are ground. In later times, this variant developed into the *Hemphill* point. **I.D. KEY:** Straightened extended shoulders.

G8, $275-$500
AR/MO

Novaculit

G7, $275-$350
Saline Co., AR

Serrated edge

G9, $400-$750
Ozark Co., AR

Basal thinning

G10, $3000-$5500
OK

G8, $275-$500
Saline Co., AR

Diagonal flaking

Stems are heavily ground

S C

G7, $450-$850
S. E. OK

G9, $600-$1000
OK

G10+, $4500-$7000+
Dardanelle, AR

DALTON-HEMPSTEAD - Early Archaic, 10,000 - 9200 B. P.

(Also see Dalton Breckenridge and Meserve)

G6, $45-80
Saline Co., AR

LOCATION: Arkansas.
DESCRIPTION: A medium size, narrow, auriculate, fish-tailed point with wide side notches and a hafting area that is shorter than the classic *Dalton*. The base is concave and is ground. Blade edges can be serrated.

DALTON-KISATCHIE - Early Archaic, 10,000 - 9200 B. P.

(Also see Breckenridge, Dalton Classic, and Meserve)

561

DALTON-KISATCHIE (continued)

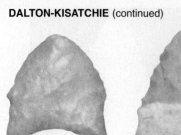

G5, $35-$60
LA

G3, $35-$60, LA

G8, $55-$100, LA

G7, $125-$200
LA

LOCATION: Louisiana into E. Texas, Arkansas & Oklahoma. **DESCRIPTION:** A medium size, fishtailed point with a shorter hafting area than the traditional *Dalton*. Stem sides and bases are ground. Blade edges can be serrated. The base is concave and can be thinned. **I.D. KEY:** Shorter hafting area.

G8, $80-$150
LA

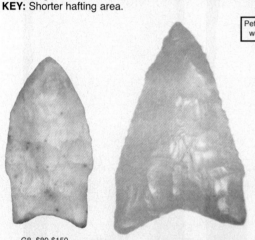

Petrified wood

G7, $175-$300
Smith Co., TX

G8, $200-$350
Vernon Parrish, LA

G6, $150-$250
Angelina Co., TX

DARDANELLE - Mississippian, 600 - 400 B. P.

(Also see Agee, Keota and Nodena)

G10, $265-$500
Spiro Mound, OK

G5, $30-$50
TX

G10, $125-$200
Spiro Mound, OK

G8, $125-$200
Spiro Mound, OK

G10, $175-$300
Yell Co., OK

G10, $175-$300
Spiro Mound, OK

G10, $175-$300
OK

G10, $265-$500
Spiro Mound, OK

G10, $265-$500
Spiro Mound, OK

G10, $265-$500
Spiro Mound, OK

LOCATION: Arkansas to Oklahoma. **DESCRIPTION:** A small to medium size, narrow, thin, serrated, corner or side notched arrow point. Bases can be rounded or square. A *Nodena* variant form with basal notches. This type has been found in caches from the Spiro mound in Oklahoma and from Arkansas. **I.D. KEY:** Basal form.

(Also see Darl Stemmed, Dawson, Hoxie, kent & Zephyr)

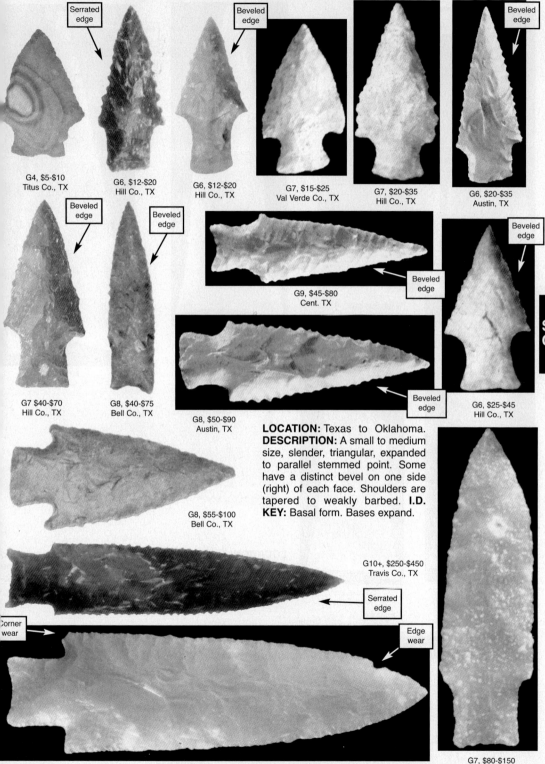

Serrated edge

G4, $5-$10
Titus Co., TX

G6, $12-$20
Hill Co., TX

Beveled edge

G6, $12-$20
Hill Co., TX

G7, $15-$25
Val Verde Co., TX

G7, $20-$35
Hill Co., TX

Beveled edge

G6, $20-$35
Austin, TX

Beveled edge

Beveled edge

G7 $40-$70
Hill Co., TX

G8, $40-$75
Bell Co., TX

Beveled edge

Beveled edge

G9, $45-$80
Cent. TX

G8, $50-$90
Austin, TX

Beveled edge

Beveled edge

Beveled edge

G6, $25-$45
Hill Co., TX

S C

LOCATION: Texas to Oklahoma.
DESCRIPTION: A small to medium size, slender, triangular, expanded to parallel stemmed point. Some have a distinct bevel on one side (right) of each face. Shoulders are tapered to weakly barbed. **I.D. KEY:** Basal form. Bases expand.

G8, $55-$100
Bell Co., TX

G10+, $250-$450
Travis Co., TX

Serrated edge

Corner wear

Edge wear

G8, $200-$350
Bastrop Co., TX

G7, $80-$150
Bastrop Co., TX

563

DARL BLADE - Woodland, 2500 - 1000 B. P.

(Also see Covington, Friday, Gahagan and Kinney)

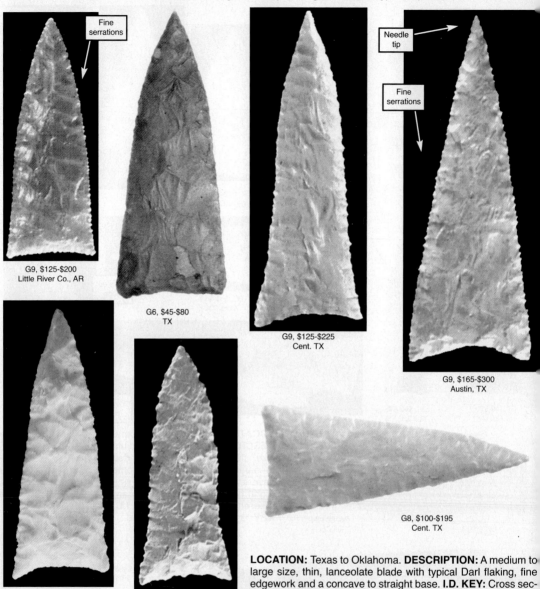

Fine serrations

G9, $125-$200
Little River Co., AR

G6, $45-$80
TX

Needle tip

Fine serrations

G9, $125-$225
Cent. TX

G9, $165-$300
Austin, TX

G6, $65-$125
Williamson Co., TX

G5, $35-$65
Austin, TX

G8, $100-$195
Cent. TX

LOCATION: Texas to Oklahoma. **DESCRIPTION:** A medium to large size, thin, lanceolate blade with typical Darl flaking, fine edgework and a concave to straight base. **I.D. KEY:** Cross section thinness and fine secondary flaking on blade edges.

DARL FRACTURED BASE - Woodland, 2500 - 1000 B. P.

(Also see Darl Stemmed, Dawson, Hoxie & Zephyr)

Sugar quartz

G6, $25-$40
Cent. TX

Fractured from basal corners

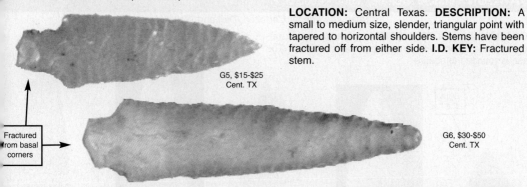

LOCATION: Central Texas. **DESCRIPTION:** A small to medium size, slender, triangular point with tapered to horizontal shoulders. Stems have been fractured off from either side. **I.D. KEY:** Fractured stem.

G5, $15-$25
Cent. TX

G6, $30-$50
Cent. TX

Fractured from basal corners

DARL STEMMED - Early Archaic, 8000 - 5000 B. P.

(Formerly Brazos; also see Darl, Hoxie, and Zephyr)

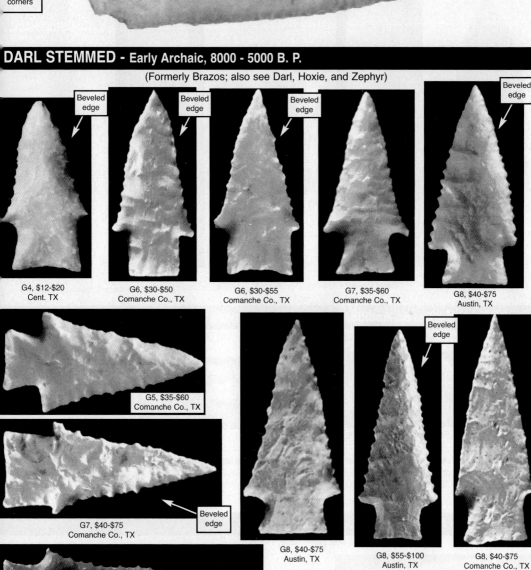

Beveled edge

G4, $12-$20
Cent. TX

G6, $30-$50
Comanche Co., TX

G6, $30-$55
Comanche Co., TX

G7, $35-$60
Comanche Co., TX

G8, $40-$75
Austin, TX

S C

G5, $35-$60
Comanche Co., TX

G7, $40-$75
Comanche Co., TX

G8, $40-$75
Austin, TX

G8, $55-$100
Austin, TX

G8, $40-$75
Comanche Co., TX

G9, $165-$300
Austin, TX

LOCATION: Central Texas. **DESCRIPTION:** A medium to large size, narrow point with horizontally barbed shoulders and an expanding to square stem. The blades on most examples are steeply beveled on one side of each face. Flaking is early parallel and is of much higher quality than *Darl*. **I.D. KEY:** Early flaking, straight base.

565

DAWSON - Middle Archaic, 7000 - 4000 B. P.

(Also see Adena, Carrolton, Darl and Wells)

LOCATION: Texas. **DESCRIPTION:** A medium size, narrow, stemmed point with strong, tapered shoulders. The base is rounded to square.

Black chert

G8, $60-$100
TX

G8, $65-$125
Saline Co., AR

G8, $80-$150
N.E. OK

G9, $150-$250
Austin, TX

G9, $125-$200
Tulsa Co., OK

DEADMAN'S - Desert Traditions-Developmental Phase, 1600 - 1300 B. P.

(Also see Perdiz, Rockwall and Scallorn)

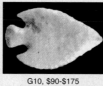

G8, $55-$100
TX

G9, $75-$145
TX

G9, $75-$145
TX

G9, $40-$75
TX

G10, $90-$175
TX

G10, $150-$250
TX

LOCATION: Southeastern Arizona, southern New Mexico and western Texas. **DESCRIPTION:** A small arrow point with very deep basal notches creating a long, straight to slightly bulbous stem with a rounded basal edge. The blade is triangular. **I.D. KEY:** Long stem and barbs.

DELHI - Late Archaic, 3500 - 2000 B. P.

(Also see Darl, Kent, Pogo and Pontchartrain)

G6, $25-$40
Comanche Co., TX

G6, $25-$40
TX

566

Gravel chert

G7, $35-$65
Comanche Co., TX

G7, $40-$75
LA

G7, $55-$100
Adams Co., MS

G7, $55-$100
Richland, Ph, LA, Macon Ridge

S C

G8, $65-$125
Comanche Co., TX

G7, $80-$150
E. TX

G10, $175-$300
LA

G8, $80-$150
Comanche Co., TX

G6, $30-$50
E. TX

G9, $150-$250
Austin, TX

LOCATION: Louisiana into E. Texas. **DESCRIPTION:** A medium to large size, narrow, stemmed point with strong, barbed shoulders. The stem can be square or expands and the base is straight to slightly convex.

DESMUKE - Late Archaic to Woodland, 4000 - 2000 B. P.

(Also see Lerma)

G5, $2-$5
Nuevo Leon, MX

G5, $3-$6
Nuevo Leon, MX

G5, $4-$8
Val Verde Co., TX

G6, $4-$8
Hill Co., TX

LOCATION: Central to southern Texas. **DESCRIPTION:** A medium size lanceolate point with a recurved to convex blade and a contracting stem that is usually rounded. **I.D. KEY:** Stem form.

Petrified wood

Chert

Ground base

G8, $6-$12
S. TX

G9, $12-$20
Webb Co., TX

G10, $25-$40
Austin, TX

DICKSON - Late Archaic to Woodland, 2500 - 1600 B. P.

(Also see Adena, Adena Robbins, Burkett, Gary, Hidden Valley and Morrow Mountain)

G9, $80-$150
N. OK

LOCATION: Midwestern states. **DESCRIPTION:** A medium to large size point with tapered shoulders and a contracting stem. High quality flaking and thinness is evident on most examples. **I.D. KEY:** Basal form.

G5, $15-$25
Saline Co., AR

G5, $15-$25
AR

G8, $650-$1200
AR

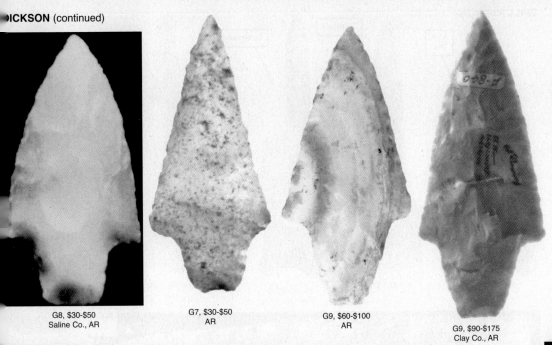

G8, $30-$50
Saline Co., AR

G7, $30-$50
AR

G9, $60-$100
AR

G9, $90-$175
Clay Co., AR

DOUBLE TIP (Occurs in Carrizo and Pedernales types)

DOVETAIL (See St. Charles)

S
C

DRILL - Paleo to Historic, 11,500 - 200 B. P.

(Also see Perforator and Scraper)

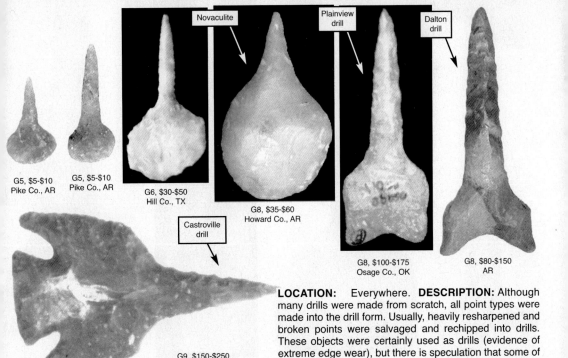

Novaculite

Plainview
drill

Dalton
drill

G5, $5-$10
Pike Co., AR

G5, $5-$10
Pike Co., AR

G6, $30-$50
Hill Co., TX

Castroville
drill

G8, $35-$60
Howard Co., AR

G8, $100-$175
Osage Co., OK

G8, $80-$150
AR

G9, $150-$250
Kimble Co., TX

LOCATION: Everywhere. **DESCRIPTION:** Although many drills were made from scratch, all point types were made into the drill form. Usually, heavily resharpened and broken points were salvaged and rechipped into drills. These objects were certainly used as drills (evidence of extreme edge wear), but there is speculation that some of these forms may have been used as pins for clothing, ornaments, ear plugs and other uses.

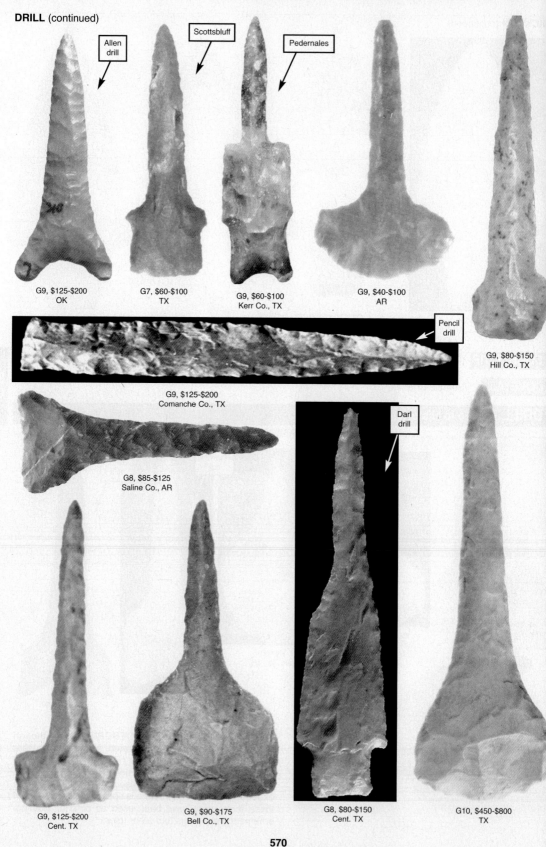

Allen drill

Scottsbluff

Pedernales

G9, $125-$200
OK

G7, $60-$100
TX

G9, $60-$100
Kerr Co., TX

G9, $40-$100
AR

Pencil drill

G9, $80-$150
Hill Co., TX

G9, $125-$200
Comanche Co., TX

G8, $85-$125
Saline Co., AR

Darl drill

G9, $125-$200
Cent. TX

G9, $90-$175
Bell Co., TX

G8, $80-$150
Cent. TX

G10, $450-$800
TX

DURAN - Woodland, 3000 - 2000 B. P.

(Also see Charcos, Evans and Sinner)

G5, $8-$15
TX

G9, $45-$85
TX

G5, $12-$20
Coahila, MX

G6, $15-$30
Nuevo Leon, MX

G10, $50-$90
TX

G8, $25-$45
TX

G9, $40-$70
TX

Translucent

Barb nick

G10, $45-$85
TX

G7, $15-$25
TX

G6, $25-$45
TX

G9, $25-$90
Val Verde Co., TX

G5, $15-$25
W. TX

G10, $55-$100
W. TX

G9, $45-$85
TX

S C

LOCATION: Texas. **DESCRIPTION:** A small size, narrow, stemmed point with double notches on each side. Base can be parallel sided to tapered. **I.D. KEY:** Double notches.

EARLY STEMMED - Early Archaic, 9000 - 7000 B. P.

(Also see Castroville, Darl Stemmed, King, Lange, Scottsbluff and Zephyr)

G6, $80-$150
Burnet Co., TX

G9, $175-$300
Wilson Co., TX

G5, $35-$60
Bell Co., TX

G5, $65-$125
Angelina Co., TX

G5, $65-$125
Wilson Co., TX

Barb nick

LOCATION: Texas to Oklahoma. **DESCRIPTION:** A medium to large size, broad point with a medium to long expanded stem and shoulder barbs. Stems are ground. Often confused with *Lange* points which do not have ground stems. Also known as *Wilson* points from the Wilson-Leonard site in Bell Co.

571

EARLY STEMMED LANCEOLATE - Early Archaic, 9000 - 7000 B. P.

(Also see Angostura, Archaic Knife, Castroville, Darl Stemmed, Pontchartrain, Rio Grande, Victoria & Zephyr)

G5, $12-$20
TX

G6, $40-$75
Wilson Co., TX

G9, $55-$100
TX

G6, $55-$100
Bell Co., TX

G6, $40-$75
Bell Co., TX

G6, $40-$75
Bell Co., TX

G6, $40-$75
Bell Co., TX

LOCATION: Texas to Oklahoma. **DESCRIPTION:** A medium to large size, narrow lanceolate stemmed point with weak, tapered shoulders.

EARLY TRIANGULAR - Early Archaic, 9000 - 7000 B. P.

(Also see Angostura, Carrizo, Clovis, Kinney and Tortugas)

Long thinning strikes from base

G8, $25-$40
Webb Co., TX

G6, $15-$30
Bexar Co., TX

G6, $25-$40
TX

G6, $25-$40
Comanche Co., TX

Ground base

LOCATION: Texas. **DESCRIPTION:** A medium to large size, broad, triangle that is usually serrated. The base is either fluted or has long thinning strikes. Quality is excellent with early oblique transverse flaking and possible right hand beveling. **I.D. KEY:** Basal thinning and edgework.

G8, $110-$195
Bee Co., TX

572

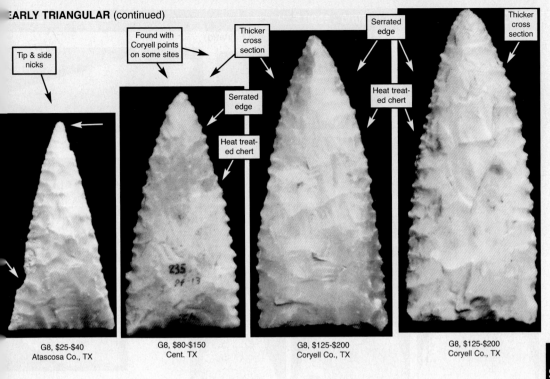

Tip & side nicks

Found with Coryell points on some sites

Thicker cross section

Serrated edge

Heat treated chert

Serrated edge

Heat treated chert

Thicker cross section

G8, $25-$40
Atascosa Co., TX

G8, $80-$150
Cent. TX

G8, $125-$200
Coryell Co., TX

G8, $125-$200
Coryell Co., TX

ECCENTRIC   (See Exotic Forms)

EDEN - Early Archaic, 10,000 - 8000 B. P.
(Also see Firstview and Scottsbluff)

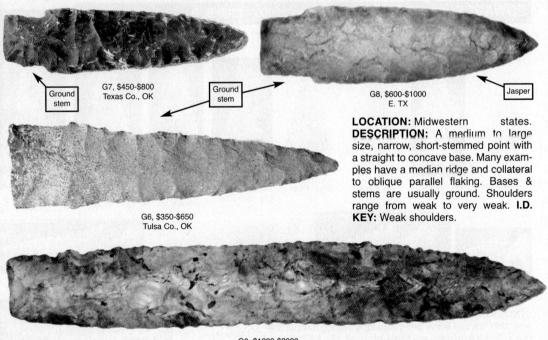

Ground stem

G7, $450-$800
Texas Co., OK

Ground stem

G8, $600-$1000
E. TX

Jasper

G6, $350-$650
Tulsa Co., OK

LOCATION: Midwestern states. **DESCRIPTION:** A medium to large size, narrow, short-stemmed point with a straight to concave base. Many examples have a median ridge and collateral to oblique parallel flaking. Bases & stems are usually ground. Shoulders range from weak to very weak. **I.D. KEY:** Weak shoulders.

G8, $1200-$2000
Bailey Co., TX

573

EDGEWOOD - Woodland, 3000 - 1500 B. P.

(Also see Ellis and Fairland)

G6, $5-$10
Saline Co., AR

G3, $1-$3
Saline Co., AR

G7 $15-$30
McIntosh Co., OK

G7, $12-$20
Saline Co., AR

G8, $25-$45
McIntosh Co., OK

G6, $3-$5
Saline Co., AR

G6, $12-$20
McCulloch Co., TX

G7, $12-$20
Comanche Co., TX

G6, $5-$8
Comanche Co., TX

LOCATION: Texas to Oklahoma. **DESCRIPTION:** A small to medium size, expanded stem point with a concave base. Shoulders are barbed to tapered and the base is usually as wide as the shoulders.

EDWARDS - Woodland to Mississippian, 2000 - 1000 B. P.

(Also see Bayogoula, Cuney, Haskell and Sallisaw)

Tip nick

G10, $20-$35
TX

G8, $65-$125
Spiro Mound, OK

G9, $20-$35
TX

G5, $15-$25
TX

G8, $65-$125
Spiro Mound, OK

G8, $65-$125
Comanche Co., TX

G9, $150-$250
Spiro Mound, OK

G10+, $450-$850
Comanche Co., TX

G4, $12-$20
Coman. Co., TX

G8, $65-$125
Spiro Mound, OK

G10, $150-$250
TX

G9, $125-$200
Spiro Mound, OK

LOCATION: Texas to Oklahoma. **DESCRIPTION:** A small size, thin, barbed arrow point with long, flaring ears at the base. Some examples are finely serrated. **I.D. KEY:** Basal form and flaking.

G10 $165-$300
Spiro Mound, OK

ELAM - Late Archaic to Woodland, 4000 - 2000 B. P.

(Also see Dallas, Darl and Ellis)

G6, $3-$5
Comanche Co., TX

G4, $3-$5
Comanche Co., TX

G4, $3-$5
Waco, TX

G4, $3-$5
Waco, TX

LOCATION: Texas. **DESCRIPTION:** A small size exhausted point with a squared base and weak shoulders. A resharpened point almost to exhaustion.

ELLIS - Late Archaic, 4000 - 2000 B. P.

(Also see Edgewood, Ensor, Godley, Marcos and Scallorn)

G4, $1-$3
S. TX

G3, $1-$3
Concho Co., TX

G4, $3-$5
Comanche Co., TX

G8, $12-$15
TX

G4, $3-$5
Hill Co., TX

G4, $3-$5
Saline Co., AR

LOCATION: Texas, Arkansas to Oklahoma. **DESCRIPTION:** A small to medium size, expanded stemmed to corner notched point with tapered to barbed shoulders. Bases are convex to straight.

Cobble chert

Cobble chert

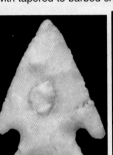
G8, $8-$15
Saline Co., AR

G6, $8-$15
McCulloch Co., TX

G5, $5-$10
Saline Co., AR

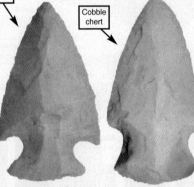
G9, $30-$50
Beauregard Parish, LA

G8 $25-$40
Jackson Parish, LA

ENSOR - Late Archaic to Early Woodland, 4000 - 1500 B. P.

(Also see Calcasieu, Ellis, Frio, Marcos, Marshall and San Jacintol)

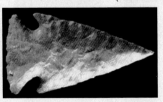
G9, $25-$40
Austin, TX

Tip nick

G6, $15-$30
Comanche Co., TX

G6, $20-$35
Comanche Co., TX

LOCATION: Texas. **DESCRIPTION:** A medium to large size, thin, well made corner-notched point with a concave, convex or straight base. Some examples are serrated and sharply barbed and tipped. **I.D. KEY:** Thinness, sharp barbs and edgework.

S C

575

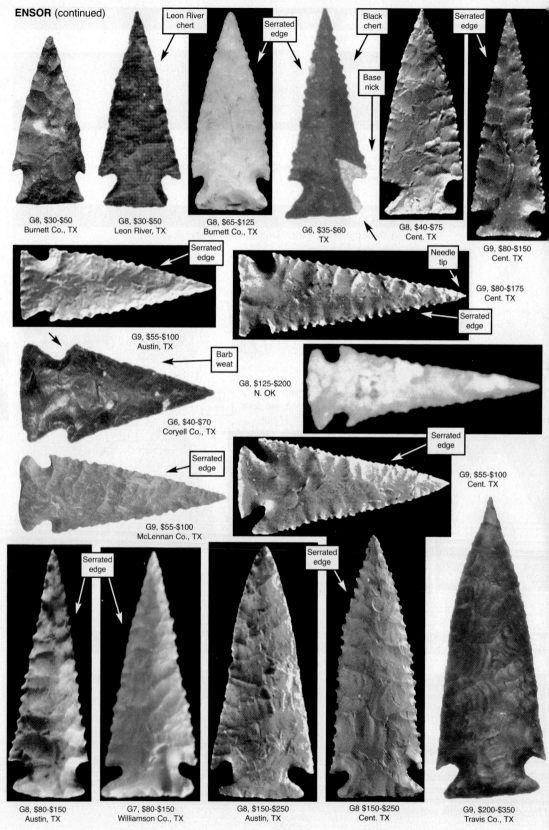

ENSOR (continued)

Leon River chert

Serrated edge

Black chert

Serrated edge

Base nick

Needle tip

Serrated edge

Serrated edge

Barb weat

Serrated edge

Serrated edge

Serrated edge

Serrated edge

Serrated edge

G8, $30-$50
Burnett Co., TX

G8, $30-$50
Leon River, TX

G8, $65-$125
Burnett Co., TX

G6, $35-$60
TX

G8, $40-$75
Cent. TX

G9, $80-$150
Cent. TX

G9, $55-$100
Austin, TX

G9, $80-$175
Cent. TX

G8, $125-$200
N. OK

G6, $40-$70
Coryell Co., TX

G9, $55-$100
Cent. TX

G9, $55-$100
McLennan Co., TX

G8, $80-$150
Austin, TX

G7, $80-$150
Williamson Co., TX

G8, $150-$250
Austin, TX

G8 $150-$250
Cent. TX

G9, $200-$350
Travis Co., TX

576

ENSOR BLADE - Late Archaic to Early Woodland, 4000 - 1500 B. P.

(Also see Covington, Darl Blade, Gahagan, Kinney)

LOCATION: Texas. **DESCRIPTION:** A medium to large size, thin, well made un-notched blade. Bases are straight to slightly concave. Blade edges can be serrated. look for typical *Ensor* edgework on the finished blade. **I.D. KEY:** Thin-ness, *Ensor* edgework.

G8, $150-$250
Bell Co., TX

G10, $250-$400
Cent. TX

ENSOR SPLIT-BASE - Late Archaic to Early Woodland, 4000 - 1500 B. P.

(Also see Cosotat River, Edgewood, Frio and Martindale)

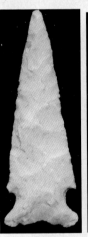

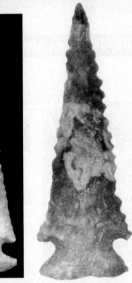

G8, $50-$90
Gillespie Co., TX

G6, $35-$65
Burnett Co., TX

G6, $35-$65
Austin, TX

G10+, $200-$350
Kerr Co., TX

G10, $150-$275
Coryell Co., TX

LOCATION: Texas. **DESCRIPTION:** Identical to *Ensor* except for the bifurcated base. Look for *Ensor* flaking style. A cross type linking *Frio* with *Ensor*. **I.D. KEY:** Sharp barbs, thinness, edgework and split base.

G9, $125-$200
Austin, TX

G8, $150-$250
Comanche Co., TX

577

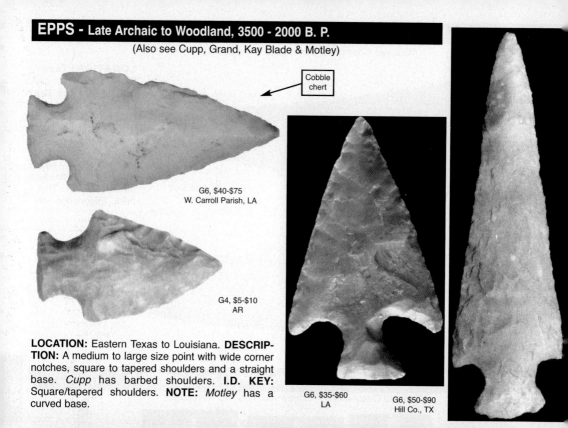

EPPS - Late Archaic to Woodland, 3500 - 2000 B. P.
(Also see Cupp, Grand, Kay Blade & Motley)

Cobble chert

G6, $40-$75
W. Carroll Parish, LA

G4, $5-$10
AR

LOCATION: Eastern Texas to Louisiana. **DESCRIPTION:** A medium to large size point with wide corner notches, square to tapered shoulders and a straight base. *Cupp* has barbed shoulders. **I.D. KEY:** Square/tapered shoulders. **NOTE:** *Motley* has a curved base.

G6, $35-$60
LA

G6, $50-$90
Hill Co., TX

EVANS - Late Archaic To Woodland, 4000 - 2000 B. P.
(Also see Charcos, Duran and Sinner)

Novaculite

Yellow jasper

G5, $12-$20
Saline Co., AR

G6, $25-$40
Bossier Parish, LA

G6, $25-$40
TX

G7, $55-$100
E. TX

G6, $45-$85
Pike Co., AR

G7, $55-$100
Saline Co., AR

G7, $65-$125
Saline Co., AR

Novaculite

578

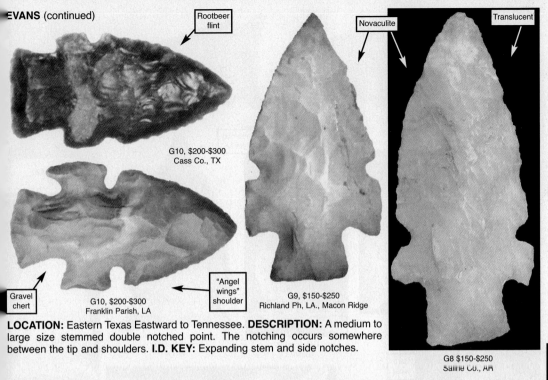

Rootbeer flint

G10, $200-$300
Cass Co., TX

Novaculite

Translucent

Gravel chert

"Angel wings" shoulder

G10, $200-$300
Franklin Parish, LA

G9, $150-$250
Richland Ph, LA., Macon Ridge

G8 $150-$250
Saline Co., AR

LOCATION: Eastern Texas Eastward to Tennessee. **DESCRIPTION:** A medium to large size stemmed double notched point. The notching occurs somewhere between the tip and shoulders. **I.D. KEY:** Expanding stem and side notches.

S
C

EXOTIC FORMS - Mid Archaic to Mississippian, 5000 - 1000 B. P.

(Also see Double Tip)

Exotic Marshall point

Ground stem

G9, $125-$200
Kerr Co., TX

G7, $25-$40
Kimble Co., TX

G7, $25-$40
Bandera Co., TX

LOCATION: Everywhere **DESCRIPTION:** The forms illustrated here are very rare. Some are definitely effigy forms while others may be no more than the result of practicing how to notch, or unfinished and unintentional doodles.

FAIRLAND - Woodland, 3000 - 1500 B. P.

(Also see Edgewood, Ellis, Marcos and Marshall)

FAIRLAND (continued)

G5, $3-$5
TX

G8, $40-$75
Williamson Co., TX

G6, $40-$75
Cent. TX

G7, $12-$20
TX

Resharpened
many times

G7, $25-$45
TX

G6, $15-$30
Tom Green Co., TX

G9, $40-$75
Austin, TX

G9, $40-$75
E. TX

G9, $40-$75
Burnett Co., TX

Barb
wear

G8, $100-$175
Bell Co., TX

G8, $200-$350
Austin, TX

G10, $265-$500
Travis Co., TX

G6, $45-$80
Killeen, TX

LOCATION: Texas, Arkansas to Oklahoma. **DESCRIPTION:** A small to medium size, thin, expanded stem point with a concave base that is usually thinned. Shoulders can be weak and tapered to slightly barbed. The base is broad. **I.D. KEY:** Basal form, systematic form of flaking.

FIGUEROA - Woodland, 3000 - 1500 B. P.

(Also see Big Sandy, Brewerton, Ensor, Gibson and Zorra)

LOCATION: Texas. **DESCRIPTION:** A small to medium size side notched to expanded base point with a convex to straight base. Basal corners are sharp to rounded. **I.D. KEY:** Basal form, wide notches.

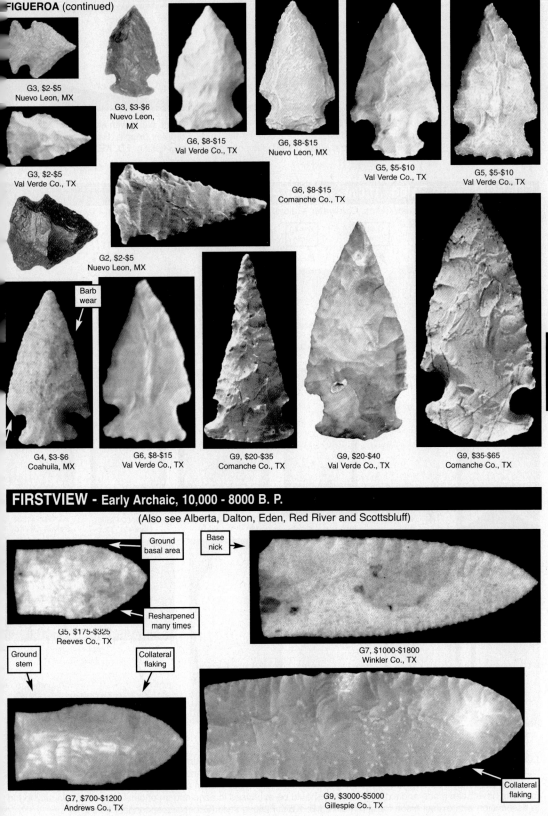

FIGUEROA (continued)

G3, $2-$5
Nuevo Leon, MX

G3, $3-$6
Nuevo Leon,
MX

G6, $8-$15
Val Verde Co., TX

G6, $8-$15
Nuevo Leon, MX

G5, $5-$10
Val Verde Co., TX

G5, $5-$10
Val Verde Co., TX

G3, $2-$5
Val Verde Co., TX

G6, $8-$15
Comanche Co., TX

G2, $2-$5
Nuevo Leon, MX

Barb
wear

G4, $3-$6
Coahuila, MX

G6, $8-$15
Val Verde Co., TX

G9, $20-$35
Comanche Co., TX

G9, $20-$40
Val Verde Co., TX

G9, $35-$65
Comanche Co., TX

S
C

FIRSTVIEW - Early Archaic, 10,000 - 8000 B. P.

(Also see Alberta, Dalton, Eden, Red River and Scottsbluff)

Ground
basal area

Base
nick

Resharpened
many times

G5, $175-$325
Reeves Co., TX

G7, $1000-$1800
Winkler Co., TX

Ground
stem

Collateral
flaking

G7, $700-$1200
Andrews Co., TX

G9, $3000-$5000
Gillespie Co., TX

Collateral
flaking

FIRSTVIEW (continued)

G10, $7000-$12,000
Winkler Co., TX

Ground stem →

Collateral flaking

LOCATION: Texas to Colorado. **DESCRIPTION:** A medium to large size lanceolate blade with early paleo flaking and very weak shoulders. A variant of the *Scottsbluff* type made by the Cody Complex people. Bases are straight and stem sides are parallel. Many examples are median ridged with collateral, parallel flaking. **I.D. KEY:** Broad base, weak shoulders.

FOLSOM - Late Paleo, 11,000 - 10,000 B. P.

(Also see Arkabutla, Clovis, Coldwater, Golondrina, Goshen, McKean, Midland and Plainview)

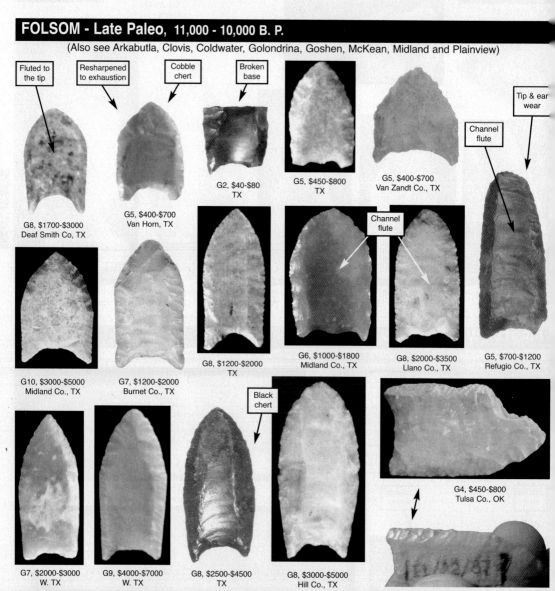

Fluted to the tip

Resharpened to exhaustion

Cobble chert

Broken base

Tip & ear wear

Channel flute

G2, $40-$80
TX

G5, $450-$800
TX

G5, $400-$700
Van Zandt Co., TX

G8, $1700-$3000
Deaf Smith Co, TX

G5, $400-$700
Van Horn, TX

Channel flute

G10, $3000-$5000
Midland Co., TX

G7, $1200-$2000
Burnet Co., TX

G8, $1200-$2000
TX

G6, $1000-$1800
Midland Co., TX

G8, $2000-$3500
Llano Co., TX

G5, $700-$1200
Refugio Co., TX

Black chert

G7, $2000-$3000
W. TX

G9, $4000-$7000
W. TX

G8, $2500-$4500
TX

G8, $3000-$5000
Hill Co., TX

G4, $450-$800
Tulsa Co., OK

LOCATION: Texas to Montana to Canada. **DESCRIPTION:** A small to medium size, very thin, high quality, fluted point with contracted, pointed auricles and a concave base. Fluting usually extends the entire length of each face. Blade flaking is extremely fine. The hafting area is ground. A very rare type, even in area of highest incidence. Modern reproductions have been made and extreme caution should be exercised in acquiring an original specimen. Usually found in association with extinct bison fossil remains. **I.D. KEY:** Flaking style (Excessive secondary flaking)

G7, $4500-$8000
OK

G9, $7000-$12,000
N. OK

Jasper

Long flute channel

Ear wear

Diagonal flaking

G9, $7000-$12,000
Custer Co., OK

Tip nick

G2, $80-$150
Gaines Co., TX

Broken back

G5, $3000-$5000
Lake Limestone, TX

Tip lost while being fluted

FREDERICK - Late Paleo-Early Archaic, 9000 - 8000 B. P.

(Also see Angostura, Clovis, Dalton, Golondrina, and Plainview)

Ground stem

G10, $700-$1200
N.E. OK

G8, $350-$600
Osage Co., OK

LOCATION: Texas, Oklahoma, Montana, Nebraska and Kansas. **DESCRIPTION:** A medium size, thin, lanceolate blade with early diagonal to collateral flaking and a concave base. Basal area is ground. **I.D. KEY:** Broad base, deep concavity.

FRESNO - Mississippian, 1200 - 250 B. P.

(Also see Bassett, Friley, Huffaker, Maud and Talco)

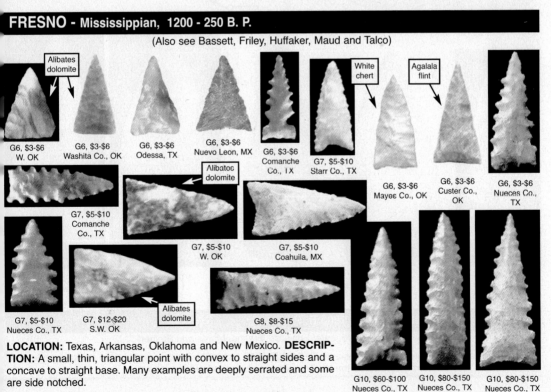

Alibates dolomite

G6, $3-$6
W. OK

G6, $3-$6
Washita Co., OK

G6, $3-$6
Odessa, TX

G6, $3-$6
Nuevo Leon, MX

G6, $3-$6
Comanche Co., TX

G7, $5-$10
Starr Co., TX

White chert

Agalala flint

G6, $3-$6
Mayes Co., OK

G6, $3-$6
Custer Co., OK

G6, $3-$6
Nueces Co., TX

G7, $5-$10
Comanche Co., TX

Alibates dolomite

G7, $5-$10
W. OK

G7, $5-$10
Coahuila, MX

G7, $5-$10
Nueces Co., TX

G7, $12-$20
S.W. OK

Alibates dolomite

G8, $8-$15
Nueces Co., TX

G10, $60-$100
Nueces Co., TX

G10, $80-$150
Nueces Co., TX

G10, $80-$150
Nueces Co., TX

LOCATION: Texas, Arkansas, Oklahoma and New Mexico. **DESCRIPTION:** A small, thin, triangular point with convex to straight sides and a concave to straight base. Many examples are deeply serrated and some are side notched.

S
C

583

(Also see Covington, Gahagan, Pandora, Sabine and San Gabriel)

Chert

G6, $65-$125
Tom Green Co., TX

G6, $40-$75
Montell, TX

G8, $55-$100
TX

G7, $80-$150
Coryell Co., TX

G9, $150-$250
Webb Co., TX

G7, $80-$150
Concho Co., TX

G7, $65-$125
TX

Black chert

LOCATION: Texas to Oklahoma.
DESCRIPTION: A medium to large, thin, lanceolate blade with recurved to straight sides, sharp corners and a straight base. Flaking quality is excellent. Many examples have a long triangular form.

IMPORTANT:
All Fridays shown
half size

G9, $200-$350
Coryell Co., TX

G9, $200-$350
TX

G8, $80-$150
Waco, TX

G7, $65-$125
TX

G8, $150-$275
Coryell Co., TX

Black chert

G8, $200-$350
Lampasos Co., TX

G9, $200-$350
Travis Co., TX

G9, $250-$400
TX

G10, $500-$900
Kerr Co., TX

G9, $350-$650
Belll Co., TX

(Also see Bayogoula, Edwards, Fresno, Morris and Steiner)

LOCATION: East Texas, Arkansas to Louisiana. **DESCRIPTION:** A small size, thin, triangular point with exaggerated shoulders that flare outward and towards the tip. The base can be rounded to eared.

FRILEY (continued)

G6, $25-$40 AR

G6, $25-$40 Comanche Co., TX

Yellow jasper

Needle tip & barbs

G8, $55-$100 AR

G8, $55-$100 AR

G10, $80-$150 AR

G10+, $250-$400 LA

G7, $90-$175 Comanche Co., TX

G10+, $450-$700 Vernon Parish, LA

FRIO - Middle Archaic to Woodland, 5000 - 1500 B. P.

(Also see Big Sandy, Cosotat River, Ensor Split-Base, Fairland, Montell and Uvalde)

S C

Resharpened many times

Barb wear

G3, $5-$10 Comanche Co., TX

G4, $15-$25 TX

G5, $15-$25 Kimble Co., TX

G7, $35-$60 TX

G5, $60-$100 Bell Co., TX

Broken barb

G5, $8-$15 TX

Edge wear

Broken barb

Novaculite

Broken tip

G4, $20-$35 TX

G3, $1-$3 Coleman Co., TX

G5, $25-$45 Comanche Co., TX

G7, $40-$75 AR

LOCATION: Texas to Oklahoma. **DESCRIPTION:** A small to medium size, side to corner-notched point with a concave to notched base that has squared to rounded ears that flare. Some examples can be confused with *Big Sandy Auriculate* forms. **I.D. KEY:** Flaring ears.

585

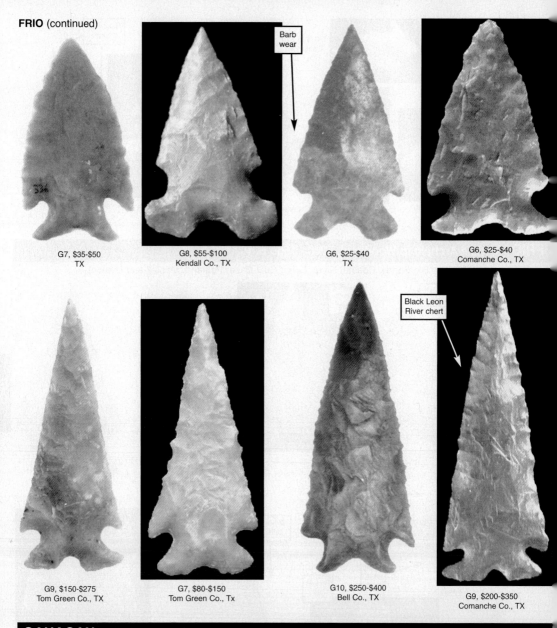

Barb wear

G7, $35-$50
TX

G8, $55-$100
Kendall Co., TX

G6, $25-$40
TX

G6, $25-$40
Comanche Co., TX

Black Leon
River chert

G9, $150-$275
Tom Green Co., TX

G7, $80-$150
Tom Green Co., Tx

G10, $250-$400
Bell Co., TX

G9, $200-$350
Comanche Co., TX

GAHAGAN - Woodland, 4000 - 1500 B. P.

(Also see Covington, Darl Blade, Friday, Kinney, Mineral Springs, Sabine and San Gabriel)

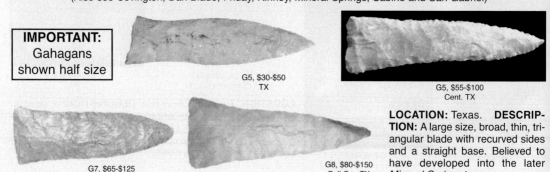

IMPORTANT:
Gahagans
shown half size

G5, $30-$50
TX

G5, $55-$100
Cent. TX

G7, $65-$125
Bell Co., TX

G8, $80-$150
Bell Co., TX

LOCATION: Texas. **DESCRIPTION:** A large size, broad, thin, triangular blade with recurved sides and a straight base. Believed to have developed into the later *Mineral Springs* type.

GAHAGAN (continued)

G8, $250-$400
Cent. OK

G10, $1500-$2500
Little River Co., AR

IMPORTANT: Gahagans shown half size

G8, $300-$550
Travis Co., TX

G8, $250-$400
Cent. TX

GAR SCALE - Late Woodland to Mississippian, 1800 - 400 B. P.

G5, $1-$2
LA/TX

G5, $1-$2
LA/TX

G5, $1-$2
LA/TX

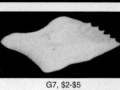

G7, $2-$5
LA/TX

G7, $1-$2
LA/TX

LOCATION: Sites along large rivers in the Southeast such as the Tennessee River and the Mississippi. **DESCRIPTION:** Scales from Garfish were utilized as arrow points. These scales are hard and are naturally bipointed which was easily adapted as tips for arrows. Some examples altered into more symmetrical forms by the Indians.

S
C

GARY - Late Archaic to early Woodland, 3200 - 1000 B. P.

(Also see Adena, Almagre, Burkett, Dickson, Hidden Valley, Kent, Langtry, Morrow Mountain and Waubesa)

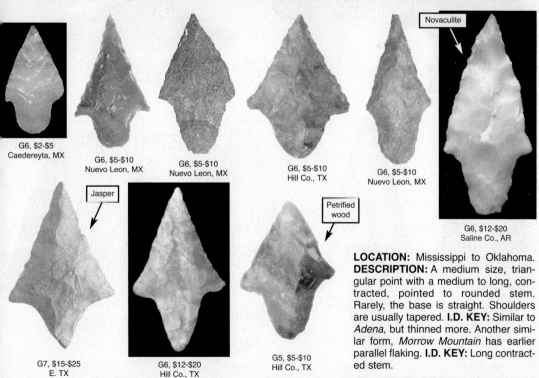

G6, $2-$5
Caedereyta, MX

G6, $5-$10
Nuevo Leon, MX

G6, $5-$10
Nuevo Leon, MX

G6, $5-$10
Hill Co., TX

G6, $5-$10
Nuevo Leon, MX

Novaculite

G6, $12-$20
Saline Co., AR

Jasper

G7, $15-$25
E. TX

G6, $12-$20
Hill Co., TX

Petrified wood

G5, $5-$10
Hill Co., TX

LOCATION: Mississippi to Oklahoma. **DESCRIPTION:** A medium size, triangular point with a medium to long, contracted, pointed to rounded stem. Rarely, the base is straight. Shoulders are usually tapered. **I.D. KEY:** Similar to *Adena,* but thinned more. Another similar form, *Morrow Mountain* has earlier parallel flaking. **I.D. KEY:** Long contracted stem.

GARY (continued)

G5, $2-$5
LA

G6, $3-$6
Hopkins Co., TX

G6, $5-$10
Bolivar Co., MS

G9, $15-$30
TX

G6, $15-$30
AR

G8, $40-$75
Austin, TX

G5, $15-$25
Hill Co., TX

G8, $25-$40
AR

G7, $15-$30
AR

G65, $12-$20
AR

G6, $15-$30
OK

G8, $35-$60
TX

Novaculite

G7, $25-$45
TX

Quartzite

Fossil chert

Black quartzite

G7, $35-$65
McIntosh Co.,
OK

G7, $45-$85
Eufaula Lake, OK

G7, $40-75
OK

G9, $125-$200
Waco, TX

S
C

Novaculite

G8, $125-$200
Eufaula Lake, OK

G9, $165-$300
Haskell Co., OK

G8, $200-$350
AR

GARY (continued)

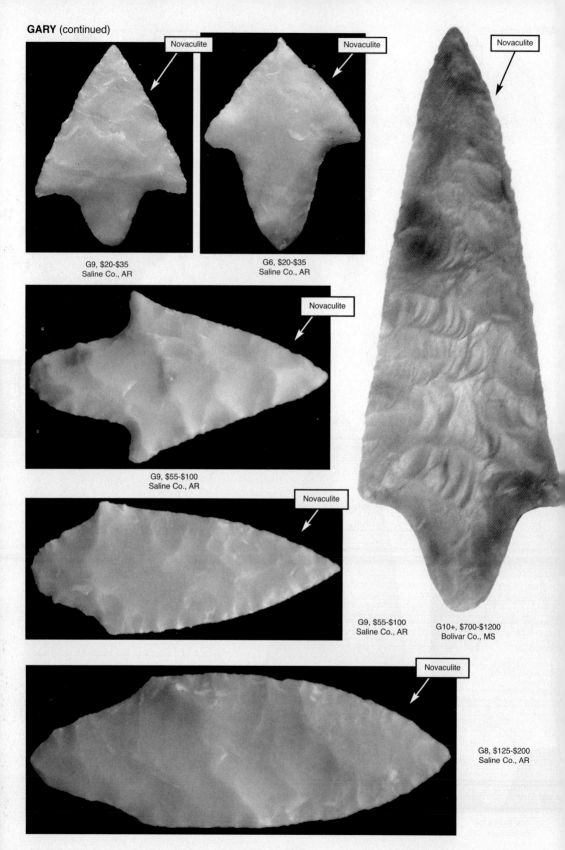

Novaculite

Novaculite

Novaculite

G9, $20-$35
Saline Co., AR

G6, $20-$35
Saline Co., AR

Novaculite

G9, $55-$100
Saline Co., AR

Novaculite

G9, $55-$100
Saline Co., AR

G10+, $700-$1200
Bolivar Co., MS

Novaculite

G8, $125-$200
Saline Co., AR

590

GARZA - Mississippian to Historic, 500 - 300 B. P.

(Also see Harrell, Lott, Starr and Toyah)

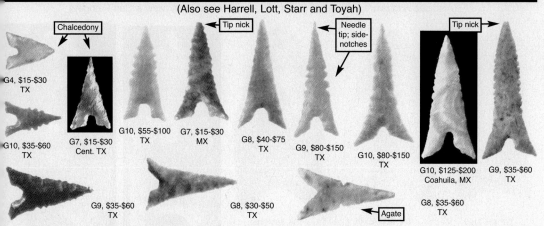

Chalcedony

Tip nick

Needle tip; side-notches

Tip nick

G4, $15-$30
TX

G10, $35-$60
TX

G7, $15-$30
Cent. TX

G10, $55-$100
TX

G7, $15-$30
MX

G8, $40-$75
TX

G9, $80-$150
TX

G10, $80-$150
TX

G10, $125-$200
Coahuila, MX

G9, $35-$60
TX

G9, $35-$60
TX

G8, $30-$50
TX

Agate

G8, $35-$60
TX

LOCATION: Northern Mexico to Oklahoma. **DESCRIPTION:** A small size, thin, triangular point with concave to convex sides and base that has a single notch in the center. Many examples are serrated. See *Soto* in SW Section.

GIBSON - Mid to Late Woodland, 2000 - 1500 B. P.

(Also see Cupp, Epps, Grand, Motley and St. Charles)

G8, $50-$90
AR

LOCATION: Midwestern to Eastern states**. DESCRIPTION:** A medium to large size side to corner notched point with a large, convex base.

S
C

GODLEY - Woodland, 2500 - 1500 B. P.

(Also see Ellis and Palmillas)

G6, $12-$20
AR

G5, $12-$20
Williamson Co., TX

G6, $15-$30
Williamson Co., TX

G6, $15-$30
Williamson Co., TX

LOCATION: Texas. **DESCRIPTION:** A small to medium size point with broad, expanding side-notches, tapered shoulders and a convex base. Basal area can be ground. Many specimens show unique beveling at the stem, usually from the same side.

GOLONDRINA - Transitional Paleo, 9000 - 7000 B. P.

(Also see Angostura, Arkabutla, Dalton, Midland, Pelican, Plainview & San Patrice)

G7, $65-$125
Coryell Co., TX

G6, $135-$250
San Angelo, TX

G6, $65-$125
Williamson Co., TX

G6, $135-$250
Craighead, AR

G8, $165-$300
Craighead, AR

G7, $165-$300
Comanche Co., TX

G9, $350-$600
TX

G8, $250-$400
Webbl Co., TX

G7, $185-$350
TX

G8, $350-$600
Wilson Co., TX

G7, $225-$400
Abilene, TX

LOCATION: Texas, Arkansas to Oklahoma. **DESCRIPTION:** A medium to large size auriculate unfluted point with rounded ears that flare and a deeply concave base. Basal areas are ground. Believed to be related to *Dalton*. **I.D. KEY:** Expanded ears, paleo flaking.

G8, $400-$700
Dyersburg, TN

GOSHEN - Late Paleo, 11,250 - 9500 B. P.

(Also see Clovis, Midland, Milnesand)

G6, $80-$150
TX

LOCATION: Oklahoma to Montana. **DESCRIPTION:** A small to medium size, very thin, auriculate point with a concave base. Basal corners slope inward and are rounded. Flaking is oblique to horizontal transverse. A rare type. **I.D. KEY:** Thinness, auricles.

Blunt tip

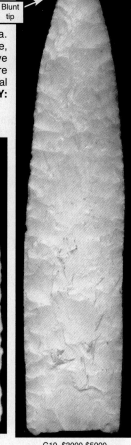

Red jasper

Yellow jasper

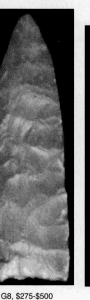

S
C

G8, $650-$1200
Osage Co., OK

G8, $275-$500
N. OK

G9, $1000-$1800
N. OK

G7, $350-$600
N. OK

G10, $3000-$5000
Comanche Co., TX

GOWER - Early Archaic, 8000 - 5000 B. P.

(Also see Barber, Jetta, Pedernales and Uvalde)

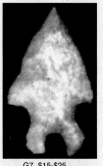

G9, $150-$265
Cent. TX

G5, $12-$20
Comanche Co., TX

G7, $15-$25
Cent. TX

G5, $12-$20
Comanche Co., TX

G10, $175-$325
Williamson Co., TX

GOWER (continued)

G6, $15-$30
Comanche Co., TX

G8, $175-$300
Austin, TX

LOCATION: Texas. **DESCRIPTION:** A medium size, narrow point with weak shoulders and a long, deeply bifurcat stem. One or both basal ears turn inward on some examples or flare outward on others. **I.D. KEY:** Narrowness, ba form.

GRAHAM CAVE - Early to Middle Archaic, 9000 - 5000 B. P.

(Also see Big Sandy, Hickory Ridge and White River)

Edge wear

Serrated edge

G6, $25-$40
Hot Spring Co., AR

G3, $3-$5
Saline Co., AR

G6, $25-$40
Saline Co., AR

G7, $125-$200
Eufaula Lake, OK

G6, $150-$250
Eufaula Lake, OK

G6, $65-$125
Hot Spring Co., AR

G6, $20-$35
Saline Co., AR

G6, $35-$65
Hot Spring Co., AR

G7, $25-$40
Saline Co., AR

LOCATION: Midwestern states. **DESCRIPTION:** A medium to large size, narrow, side-notched point with recurved excurvate sides, pointed basal ears, and a concave base. Some examples are serrated. Bases are ground. **I.D. KE** Drooping basal ears.

594

GRAND - Mid-Woodland, 1800 - 1600 B. P.

(Also see Big Creek, Cupp, Epps, Gibson and Motley)

G9, $150-$250
Cherokee Co., OK

G6, $30-$50
N.E. OK

LOCATION: Oklahoma into Kansas. **DESCRIPTION:** A medium sized, broad, corner notched point with barbed shoulders and an expanding, convex base. Basal corners can be sharp. **I.D. KEY:** Width of blade, corner notches.

GRAVER - Paleo to Archaic, 11,500 - 4000 B. P.

(Also see Drill, Perforator and Scraper)

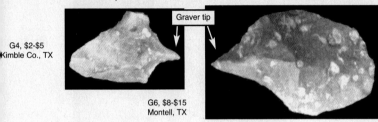

Graver tip

G4, $2-$5
Kimble Co., TX

G6, $8-$15
Montell, TX

LOCATION: Early man sites everywhere. **DESCRIPTION:** An irregular shaped uniface tool with sharp, pointed projections used for puncturing, incising, tattooing, etc. Some examples served a dual purpose for scraping as well. In later times.

S
C

GUERRERO - Historic, 300 - 100 B. P.

(Also see Maud and Nodena)

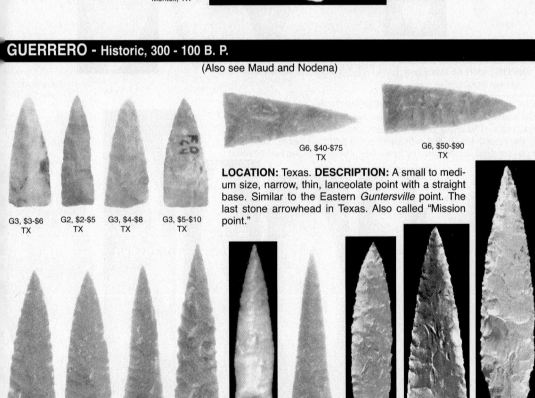

G6, $40-$75
TX

G6, $50-$90
TX

LOCATION: Texas. **DESCRIPTION:** A small to medium size, narrow, thin, lanceolate point with a straight base. Similar to the Eastern *Guntersville* point. The last stone arrowhead in Texas. Also called "Mission point."

G3, $3-$6
TX

G2, $2-$5
TX

G3, $4-$8
TX

G3, $5-$10
TX

G7, $65-$125
TX

G8, $80-$150
TX

G7, $65-$125
TX

G6, $50-$90
TX

G9, $150-$250
Coke Co., TX

G6, $50-$90
TX

G9, $65-$125
Coman. Co., TX

G9, $90-$175
Miss. Co., AR

G9, $150-$250
Coman. Co., TX

595

HALE (Bascom) - Late Archaic, 4000 - 3500 B. P.

(Also see Peisker Diamond)

LOCATION: Arkansas into Mississippi. **DESCRIPTION:** A large size, broad point with shoulders tapering to the base which is straight to rounded. Similar to the *Bascom* form found in Alabama and Georgia.

G7, $55-$100
AR

HARAHEY - Mississippian, 700 - 400 B. P.

(Also see Covington, Friday, Lerma and Refugio)

Alibates dolomite

G6, $65-$250
Deaf Smith Co., TX

G6, $65-125
Cent. TX

Quartzite

G5, $55-$100
Tarrant Co., TX

G8, $80-$150
Texas Co., OK

G8, $80-$150
Coryell Co., TX

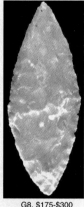

G8, $175-$300
TX

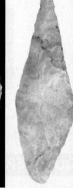

G7, $150-$250
Bexar Co., TX

IMPORTANT: All Haraheys shown 50% actual size

LOCATION: Texas to Colorado. **DESCRIPTION:** A large size, double pointed knife that is usually beveled on one or all four sides of each face. The cross section is rhomboid. The true buffalo skinning knife. Found associated with small arrow points in Texas. **I.D. KEY:** Four beveled double pointed form. See *Neosho* for the two beveled form.

Alibates dolomite

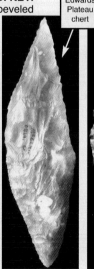

Edwards Plateau chert

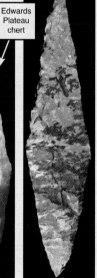

G9, $250-$450
Mayes Co., OK

G10, $400-$750
N. W. OK

G8, $200-$350
N. OK

G8, $250-$400
McClair Co., OK

G9, $350-$600
N.E. OK

G10, $450-$800
TX

596

(Also see Alberta, Kirk, Ocala, St. Charles and Scottsbluff)

G4, $8-$15
AR

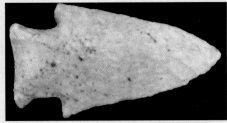

G6, $45-$80
AR

LOCATION: Midwestern to Eastern states. **DESCRIPTION:** A large size, well made triangular barbed point with an expanded base that is usually ground. Resharpened examples have one beveled edge on each face. *Hardin* points are believed to have evolved from the *Scottsbluff* type. **I.D. KEY:** Notches and stem form.

G7, $80-$150
Angelina Co., TX

G7, $150-$250
Austin, TX

G7, $175-$300
Milam Co., TX

Beveled edge

G8, $200-$350
N. E. AR

S C

G7, $150-$250
AR

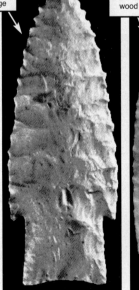

Serrated edge

G8, $200-$350
Greene Co., AR

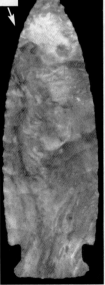

Petrified wood

G9, $400-$750
Angelina Co., TX

G7, $90-$175
AR

597

HARE BIFACE - Late Archaic to Woodland, 3000 - 2000 B. P.

(Also see Covington, Friday, Pandora and San Gabriel)

LOCATION: Texas. **DESCRIPTION:** A medium to large size knife with excurvate sides and a rounded base. Made primarily by the percussion flake method. Bases can be beveled to thinned.

Petrified wood

G6, $12-$20
TX

HARRELL - Mississippian to Historic, 900 - 500 B. P.

(Also see Toyah and Washita)

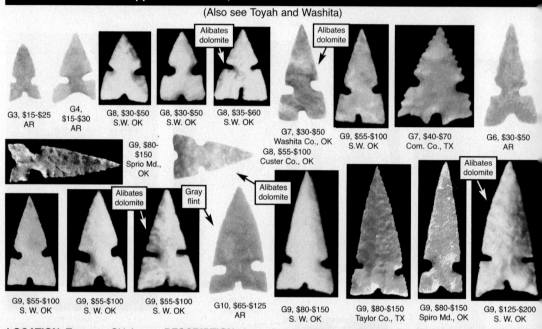

G3, $15-$25 AR

G4, $15-$30 AR

G8, $30-$50 S.W. OK

G8, $30-$50 S.W. OK

G8, $35-$60 S.W. OK

Alibates dolomite

Alibates dolomite

G7, $30-$50 Washita Co., OK
G8, $55-$100 Custer Co., OK

G9, $55-$100 S.W. OK

G7, $40-$70 Com. Co., TX

G6, $30-$50 AR

G9, $80-$150 Spiro Md., OK

Alibates dolomite

Gray flint

Alibates dolomite

Alibates dolomite

G9, $55-$100 S. W. OK

G9, $55-$100 S. W. OK

G9, $55-$100 S. W. OK

G10, $65-$125 AR

G9, $80-$150 S. W. OK

G9, $80-$150 Taylor Co., TX

G9, $80-$150 Spiro Md., OK

G9, $125-$200 S. W. OK

LOCATION: Texas to Oklahoma. **DESCRIPTION:** A small size, thin, triangular arrow point with side and a basal notch. Basal lobes are squared.

HASKELL - Mississippian to Historic, 800 - 600 B. P.

(Also see Edwards, Huffaker, Reed, Toyah and Washita)

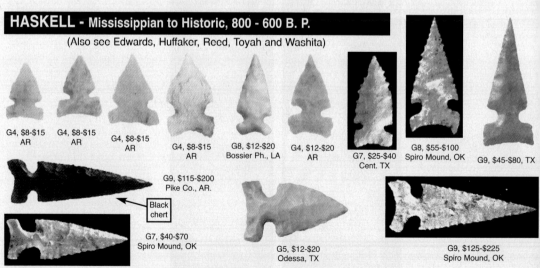

G4, $8-$15 AR

G4, $8-$15 AR

G4, $8-$15 AR

G4, $8-$15 AR

G8, $12-$20 Bossier Ph., LA

G4, $12-$20 AR

G7, $25-$40 Cent. TX

G8, $55-$100 Spiro Mound, OK

G9, $45-$80, TX

G9, $115-$200 Pike Co., AR.

Black chert

G7, $40-$70 Spiro Mound, OK

G5, $12-$20 Odessa, TX

G9, $125-$225 Spiro Mound, OK

LOCATION: Oklahoma to Arkansas. **DESCRIPTION:** A small size, thin, narrow, triangular, side notched point with a concave base. Rarely, basal tangs are notched.

(Also see Alba, Blevins, Homan, Howard, Perdiz, Sequoya and Turner)

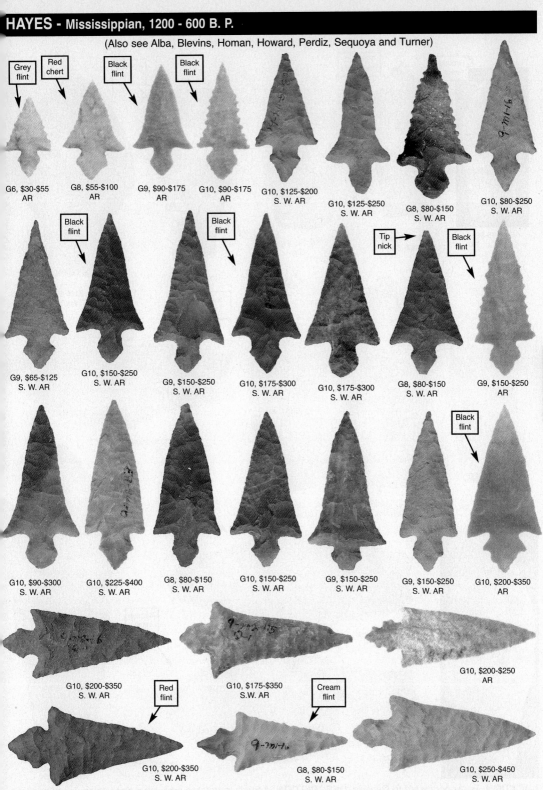

Grey flint · Red chert · Black flint · Black flint

G6, $30-$55 AR

G8, $55-$100 AR

G9, $90-$175 AR

G10, $90-$175 AR

G10, $125-$200 S. W. AR

G10, $125-$250 S. W. AR

G8, $80-$150 S. W. AR

G10, $80-$250 S. W. AR

Black flint · Black flint · Tip nick · Black flint

G9, $65-$125 S. W. AR

G10, $150-$250 S. W. AR

G9, $150-$250 S. W. AR

G10, $175-$300 S. W. AR

G10, $175-$300 S. W. AR

G8, $80-$150 S. W. AR

G9, $150-$250 AR

S C

Black flint

G10, $90-$300 S. W. AR

G10, $225-$400 S. W. AR

G8, $80-$150 S. W. AR

G10, $150-$250 S. W. AR

G9, $150-$250 S. W. AR

G9, $150-$250 S. W. AR

G10, $200-$350 AR

G10, $200-$350 S. W. AR

Red flint

G10, $175-$350 S.W. AR

Cream flint

G10, $200-$250 AR

G10, $200-$350 S. W. AR

G8, $80-$150 S. W. AR

G10, $250-$450 S. W. AR

LOCATION: Louisiana to Oklahoma. **DESCRIPTION:** A small to medium size, narrow, expanded barb arrow point with a turkeytail base. Blade edges are usually strongly recurved forming sharp pointed barbs. Base is pointed and can be double notched. Some examples are serrated. Has been found in caches with *Alba* points. **I.D. KEY:** Diamond shaped base and flaking style.

599

(Also see Agate Basin, Angostura, Midland, Pelican and Rio Grande)

Ground stem

G5, $35-$60
Llano Co., TX

Petrified Palmwood

G6, $70-$125
Webb Co., TX

G6, $80-$150
TX

Foraker flint

G7, $150-$250
Osage Co., OK

G6, $165-$300
S. W. TX

Needle tip

G10, $350-$600
TX

G5, $65-$125
Osage Co., OK

G3, $40-$70
Osage Co., OK

G5, $80-$150
Osage Co., OK

Ground stem

G6, $135-$250
Travis Co., TX

Alibates flint

G7, $175-$325
TX

G9, $800-$1500
Woodward Co., OK

G9, $550-$1000
Tulsa Co., OK

LOCATION: Texas northward to Canada. **DESCRIPTION:** A medium to large size, lanceolate point with a long, contracting stem. The widest part of the blade is above mid-section. The base is straight to slightly concave and the stem edges are usually ground. **I.D. KEY:** Very high up blade stems.

HEMPHILL - Middle Archaic, 7000 - 4000 B. P.

(Also see Big Sandy, Dalton-Hemphill, Graham Cave, Hemphill and Hickory Ridge)

LOCATION: Missouri, Illinois into Wisconsin. **DESCRIPTION:** A medium to large size side-notched point with a concave base and parallel to convex sides. These points are usually thinner and of higher quality than the similar *Osceola* type found in Wisconsin.

G4, $15-$30
Jonesboro, AR

HICKORY RIDGE - Middle Archaic, 7000 - 4000 B. P.

(Also see Big Sandy, Cache River and Hemphill)

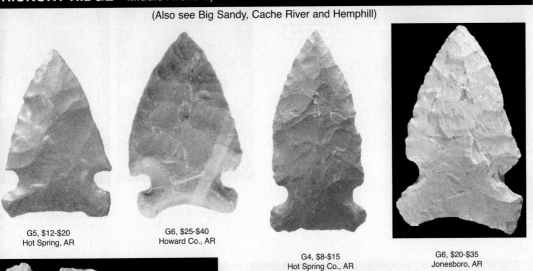

G5, $12-$20
Hot Spring, AR

G6, $25-$40
Howard Co., AR

G4, $8-$15
Hot Spring Co., AR

G6, $20-$35
Jonesboro, AR

S
C

G4, $8-$15
Jonesboro, AR

G6, $35-$65
Jonesboro, AR

G6, $35-$65
Jonesboro, AR

G9, $150-$250
Greene Co., AR

LOCATION: Arkansas. **DESCRIPTION:** A medium to large size side-notched point. The base is straight to concave and early forms are ground. Basal corners are rounded to square. Side notches are usually wide. **I.D. KEY:** Broad, large side notched point.

601

HIDDEN VALLEY - Early to Middle Archaic, 8000 - 6000 B. P.

(Also see Burkett, Dickson, Gary, Langtry and Morrow Mountain)

G6, $50-$90
Craighead, AR

Novaculite

G6, $45-$80
Pike Co., AR

G7, $40-$70
Craighead, AR

G6, $50-$90
Craighead, AR

LOCATION: Arkansas to Wisconsin. **DESCRIPTION:** A medium size point with square to tapered shoulders and a contracting base that can be pointed to straight. Flaking is earlier and more parallel than on *Gary* points. Called *Rice Contracted Stemmed* in Missouri.

HOLLAND - Early Archaic, 10,000 - 7500 B. P.

(Also see Alberta, Dalton, Eden, Hardin and Scottsbluff)

G9, $175-$300
AR

G8, $150-$250
N. OK

G8, $200-$350
N. OK

G6, $150-$250
N. OK

G7, $80-$150
AR

G9, $250-$450
N. OK

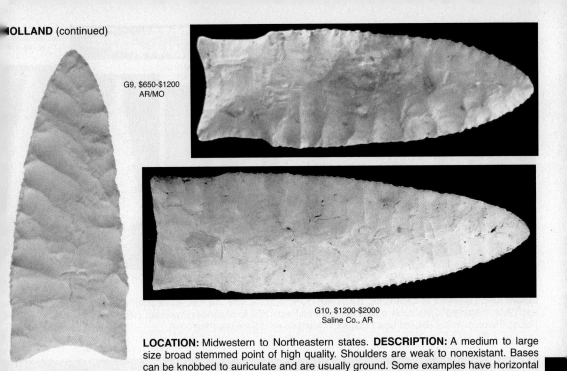

G9, $650-$1200
AR/MO

G10, $1200-$2000
Saline Co., AR

G8, $200-$375
Bowie Co., TX

LOCATION: Midwestern to Northeastern states. **DESCRIPTION:** A medium to large size broad stemmed point of high quality. Shoulders are weak to nonexistant. Bases can be knobbed to auriculate and are usually ground. Some examples have horizontal to oblique transverse flaking. **I.D. KEY:** Weak shoulders, concave base.

S
C

HOMAN - Mississippian, 1000 - 700 B. P.

(Also see Agee, Alba, Colbert, Hayes, Hughes, Keota, Perdiz and Scallorn)

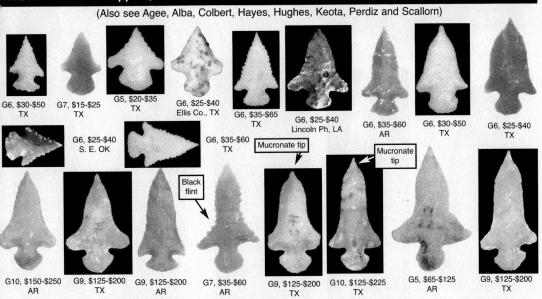

G6, $30-$50
TX

G7, $15-$25
TX

G5, $20-$35
TX

G6, $25-$40
Ellis Co., TX

G6, $35-$65
TX

G6, $25-$40
Lincoln Ph, LA

G6, $35-$60
AR

G6, $30-$50
TX

G6, $25-$40
TX

G6, $25-$40
S. E. OK

G6, $35-$60
TX

Mucronate tip

Mucronate tip

Black flint

G10, $150-$250
AR

G9, $125-$200
TX

G9, $125-$200
AR

G7, $35-$60
AR

G9, $125-$200
TX

G10, $125-$225
TX

G5, $65-$125
AR

G9, $125-$200
TX

LOCATION: Oklahoma to Arkansas. **DESCRIPTION:** A small size expanded barbed arrow point with a bulbous stem. Some tips are mucronate or apiculate. **I.D. KEY:** Bulbous stem.

HOWARD - Mississippian, 700 - 500 B. P.

(Also see Blevins, Hayes and Sequoyah)

HOWARD (continued)

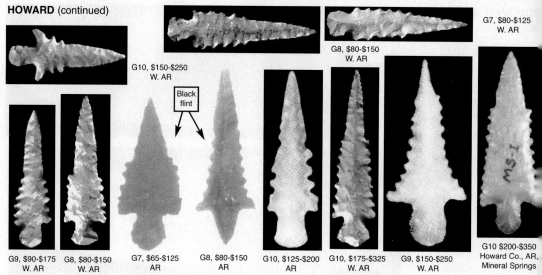

G10, $150-$250
W. AR

G7, $80-$125
W. AR

G8, $80-$150
W. AR

Black flint

G9, $90-$175
W. AR

G8, $80-$150
W. AR

G7, $65-$125
AR

G8, $80-$150
AR

G10, $125-$200
AR

G10, $175-$325
W. AR

G9, $150-$250
W. AR

G10 $200-$350
Howard Co., AR,
Mineral Springs

LOCATION: Louisiana to Oklahoma. **DESCRIPTION:** A small size, narrow, spike point with two or more barbs on each side, restricted to the lower part of the point and a parallel to expanding, rounded stem. A diamond shaped base places the point in the *Blevins* type. **I.D. KEY:** Multiple serrations near the base.

HOXIE - Early Archaic, 8000 - 5000 B. P.

(Also see Bulverde, Darl, Darl Stemmed, Early Stemmed Lanceolate, Gower and Zephyr)

G6, $12-$20
Comal Co., TX

Translucent

Black chert

G6, $35-$60
Cent. TX

G7, $35-$75
Comanche Co., TX

G8, $125-$200
Austin, TX

G8, $150-$250
Austin, TX

G8, $200-$350
Hood Co., TX

LOCATION: Texas. **DESCRIPTION:** A medium to large size, narrow point with weak shoulders and a parallel sided, concave stem that is ground. Believed to be an early form of *Darl*.

HUFFAKER - Mississippian, 1000 - 500 B. P.

(Also see Duran, Evans, Fresno, Harrell, Haskell, Sinner and Washita)

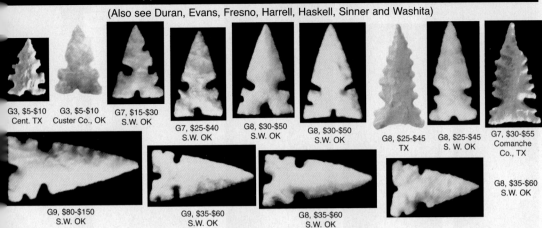

G3, $5-$10
Cent. TX

G3, $5-$10
Custer Co., OK

G7, $15-$30
S.W. OK

G7, $25-$40
S.W. OK

G8, $30-$50
S.W. OK

G8, $30-$50
S.W. OK

G8, $25-$45
TX

G8, $25-$45
S. W. OK

G7, $30-$55
Comanche
Co., TX

G8, $35-$60
S.W. OK

G9, $80-$150
S.W. OK

G9, $35-$60
S.W. OK

G8, $35-$60
S.W. OK

LOCATION: Texas northward to Canada. **DESCRIPTION:** A small size triangular point with a straight to concave base and double side notches. Blade edges can be heavily barbed. Bases can have a single notch. **I.D. KEY:** Double notches.

HUGHES - Mississippian, 1200 - 600 B. P.

(Also see Alba, Colbert, Hayes, Homan, Keota)

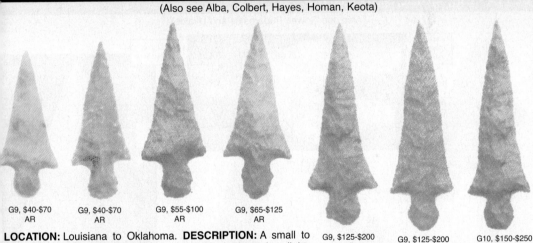

G9, $40-$70
AR

G9, $40-$70
AR

G9, $55-$100
AR

G9, $65-$125
AR

G9, $125-$200
AR

G9, $125-$200
AR

G10, $150-$250
AR

LOCATION: Louisiana to Oklahoma. **DESCRIPTION:** A small to medium size, thin, narrow point with a sharp tip, horizontal to slightly barbed shoulders and an expanding, bulbous stem. **I.D. KEY:** Bulbous stem.

JAKIE STEMMED - Early Archaic, 8000 - 5000 B. P.

(Also see Cosatot River, Gower, Pedernales, Rice Lobbed and Uvalde)

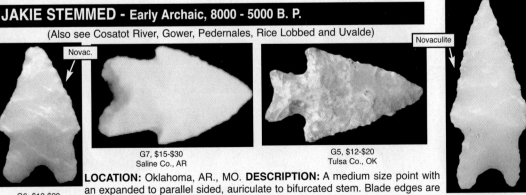

Novac.

Novaculite

G7, $15-$30
Saline Co., AR

G5, $12-$20
Tulsa Co., OK

G6, $12-$20
Saline Co., AR

G6, $15-$30
Saline Co., AR

LOCATION: Oklahoma, AR., MO. **DESCRIPTION:** A medium size point with an expanded to parallel sided, auriculate to bifurcated stem. Blade edges are serrated and the base is ground with rounded lobes.

JAKIE STEMMED (continued)

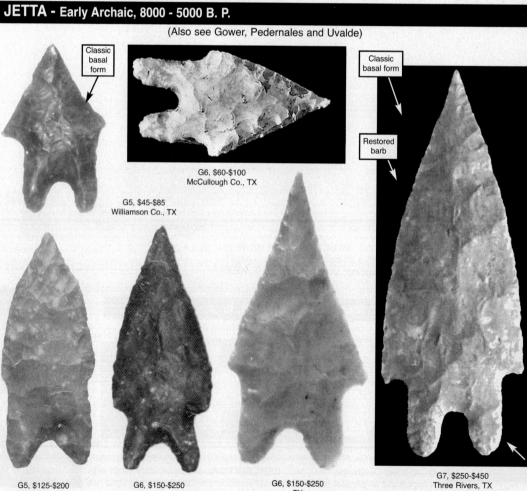

Impact fracture

Side wear

G6, $15-$25
Washington Co., AR

G5, $15-$25
Tulsa Co., OK

G7, $30-$50
Tulsa Co., OK

G8, $35-$65
Tulsa Co., OK

G5, $20-$35
MO

JETTA - Early Archaic, 8000 - 5000 B. P.

(Also see Gower, Pedernales and Uvalde)

Classic basal form

Classic basal form

Restored barb

G6, $60-$100
McCullough Co., TX

G5, $45-$85
Williamson Co., TX

G5, $125-$200
Travis Co., TX

G6, $150-$250
TX

G6, $150-$250
TX

G7, $250-$450
Three Rivers, TX

LOCATION: Texas to Oklahoma. **DESCRIPTION:** A medium to large size point with tapered, horizontal or short point-ed shoulders and a deeply notched base. Basal tangs are rounded and the stem is more squared and wider than *Pedernalis.* A very rare type.

JOHNSON - Early to Middle Archaic, 9000 - 5000 B. P.

(Also see Bulverde and Savannah River)

G5, $12-$20
AR

G6, $20-$35
Pike Co., AR

Novaculite

G8, $30-$50
Hot Spring, AR

G10, $175-$300
Saline Co., AR

S
C

Novaculite

G9, $55-$100
Hot Spring Co., AR

G9, $35-$65
Saline Co., AR

G6, $20-$35
Hot Spring, AR

G8, $30-$55
Hot Spring, AR

Novaculite

G9, $80-$150
Cent. AR. Novaculite.

LOCATION: Mississippi to Oklahoma. **DESCRIPTION:** A medium size, thick, well made, expanded stem point with a broad, short, concave base. Bases are usually thinned and grinding appears on some specimens. Shoulders can be slight and are roughly horizontal. **I.D. KEY:** Broad stem that is thinned.

607

JORA (see Coahuila)

KAY BLADE - Mississippian, 1000 - 600 B. P.

(Also see Cupp, Epps, Motley)

LOCATION: Oklahoma into mid-western states. **DESCRIPTION:** A medium to large size corner notched point with a long expanding stem and barbed shoulders. Bases are straight to almost convex. Used by the Mississippian, Caddoan people. **I.D. KEY:** Broad corner notches.

G8, $200-$350
N. OK

G8, $200-$350
N. OK

KEITHVILLE (See San Patrice - Keithville)

KENT- Woodland, 3000 - 2800 B. P.

(Also see Adena-Robbins, Dallas, Darl, Delhi, Gary, Morrill, Travis)

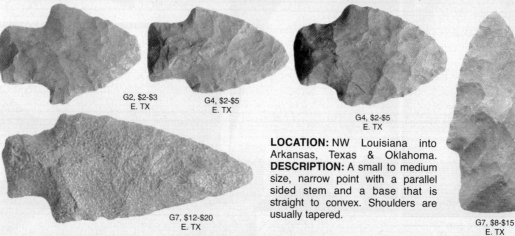

G2, $2-$3
E. TX

G4, $2-$5
E. TX

G4, $2-$5
E. TX

G7, $12-$20
E. TX

LOCATION: NW Louisiana into Arkansas, Texas & Oklahoma. **DESCRIPTION:** A small to medium size, narrow point with a parallel sided stem and a base that is straight to convex. Shoulders are usually tapered.

G7, $8-$15
E. TX

KEOTA - Mississippian, 800 - 600 B. P.

(Also see Agee, Alba, Colbert, Dardanelle, Hayes, Homan, Hughes and Sequoyah)

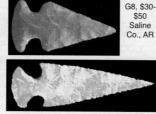

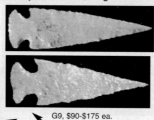

G8, $30-$50
Saline Co., AR

LOCATION: Texas, Arkansas to Oklahoma. **DESCRIPTION:** A small size, thin, triangular, side to corner-notched point with a rounded, bulbous base. The basal area is large on some specimens. **I.D. KEY:** Large bulbous base.

G3, $5-$10
Comanche Co., TX

G9, $80-$140
TX

G9, $90-$175 ea.
Spiro Mound, OK

608

KERRVILLE KNIFE - Middle to Late Archaic, 5000 - 3000 B. P.

(Also see Chopper and Scraper)

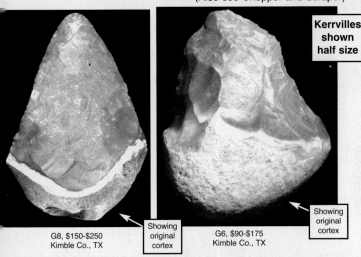

Kerrvilles shown half size

G5, $65-$125
TX

LOCATION: Midwestern states. **DESCRIPTION:** A large size, thick, triangular cutting or chopping tool with straight to slightly convex edges. The original rind occurs at the base. Also called fist axes.

G8, $150-$250
Kimble Co., TX

Showing original cortex

G6, $90-$175
Kimble Co., TX

Showing original cortex

KINGS - Middle Archaic, 5000 - 2000 B. P.

(Also see Big Creek, Cupp, Epps and Motley)

LOCATION: Arkansas, Oklahoma into Missouri and Kansas. **DESCRIPTION:** A medium to large size, corner notched point with strong, sharp shoulders and an expanding base. Bases are straight, concave or convex.

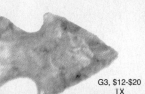

G3, $12-$20
TX

G4, $5-$10
Saline Co., AR

tip wear

S
C

G9, $125-$200
N.E. OK

KINNEY - Middle Archaic-Woodland, 5000 - 2000 B. P.

(Also see Darl Blade, Early Triangular, Gahagan, Pandora and Tortugas)

G3, $8-$15
Comanche Co., TX

G7, $35-$65
TX

LOCATION: Texas. **DESCRIPTION:** A medium to large size, thin, broad, lanceolate, well made blade with convex to straight blade edges and a concave base. Basal corners are pointed to rounded. **I.D. KEY:** Broad, concave base.

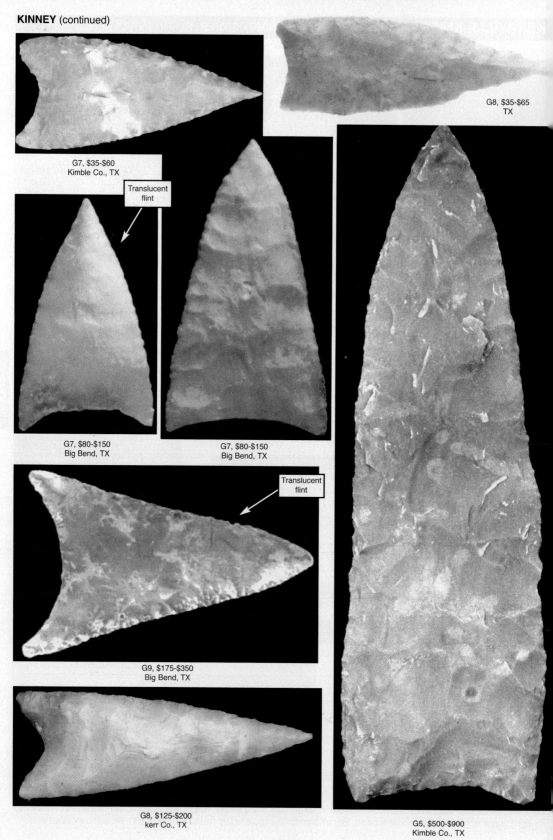

G8, $35-$65
TX

G7, $35-$60
Kimble Co., TX

Translucent
flint

G7, $80-$150
Big Bend, TX

G7, $80-$150
Big Bend, TX

Translucent
flint

G9, $175-$350
Big Bend, TX

G8, $125-$200
kerr Co., TX

G5, $500-$900
Kimble Co., TX

KNIGHT ISLAND - Late Woodland, 1500 - 1000 B. P.

(Also see Brewerton, Cache River, Hickory Ridge, Reed, Schustorm and White River)

LOCATION: Arkansas to South- eastern states. **DESCRIPTION:** A small to medium size, very thin, narrow, side-notched point with a straight base. Longer examples can have a pentagonal appearance. Called *Racoon Creek* in Ohio. A side-notched Jacks Reef. **I.D. KEY:** Thinness, basal form. Made by the small triangle point people.

G8, $65-$125
N.E., AR

LA JITA - Middle Archaic, 7000 - 4000 B. P.

(Also see Axtel, Palmillas and Williams)

S
C

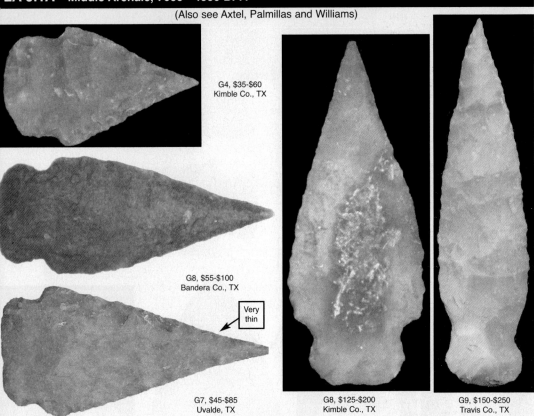

G4, $35-$60
Kimble Co., TX

G8, $55-$100
Bandera Co., TX

Very thin

G7, $45-$85
Uvalde, TX

G8, $125-$200
Kimble Co., TX

G9, $150-$250
Travis Co., TX

LOCATION: Texas. **DESCRIPTION:** A medium to large size, broad point with weak shoulders and a broad, bulbous base that expands and has rounded basal corners. **I.D. KEY:** Large bulbous base.

LAMPASAS (See Zephyr)

LANGE - Middle Archaic to Woodland, 6000 - 1000 B. P.

(Also see Bulverde, Castorville, Morrill, Nolan and Travis)

LOCATION: Louisiana to Texas to Oklahoma. **DESCRIPTION:** A medium to large size, narrow, expanded stem dart point with tapered to horizontal, barbed shoulders and a straight to convex base. **I.D. KEY:** Expanding base, tapered to horizontal shoulders.

G3, $5-$10
Comanche Co., TX

G6, $20-$35
Comanche Co., TX

G6, $20-$35
Austin, TX

G9, $35-$65
Burnett Co., TX

G8, $65-$125
TX

G7, $35-$65
Comal Co., TX

G6, $40-$75
Bossier Ph., LA

Brown quartzite

G6, $25-$45
Bell Co., TX

Black chert

G7, $55-$100
Comanche Co., TX

G8, $150-$150
Comanche Co., TX

G10, $200-$350
Eufaula Lake, OK

G9, $150-$250
Austin, TX

(Also see Almagre, Gary, Hidden Valley, Morrow Mountain and Val Verde)

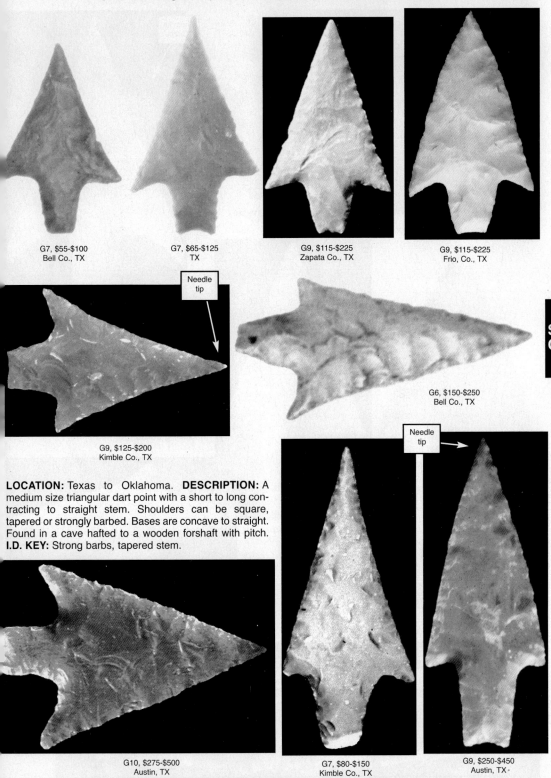

G7, $55-$100
Bell Co., TX

G7, $65-$125
TX

G9, $115-$225
Zapata Co., TX

G9, $115-$225
Frio, Co., TX

Needle tip

S C

G9, $125-$200
Kimble Co., TX

G6, $150-$250
Bell Co., TX

Needle tip

LOCATION: Texas to Oklahoma. **DESCRIPTION:** A medium size triangular dart point with a short to long contracting to straight stem. Shoulders can be square, tapered or strongly barbed. Bases are concave to straight. Found in a cave hafted to a wooden forshaft with pitch. **I.D. KEY:** Strong barbs, tapered stem.

G10, $275-$500
Austin, TX

G7, $80-$150
Kimble Co., TX

G9, $250-$450
Austin, TX

LANGTRY-ARENOSA - Middle Archaic to Woodland, 5000 - 2000 B. P.

(Also see Almagre, Coahuila, Gary and Val Verde)

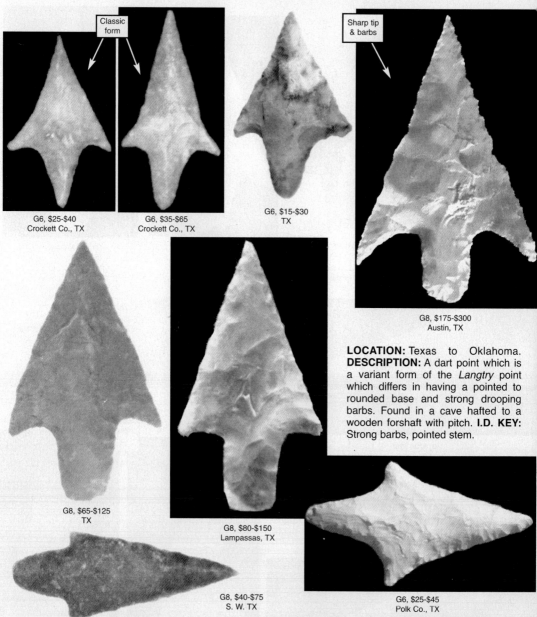

Classic form

Sharp tip & barbs

G6, $25-$40
Crockett Co., TX

G6, $35-$65
Crockett Co., TX

G6, $15-$30
TX

G8, $175-$300
Austin, TX

G8, $65-$125
TX

G8, $80-$150
Lampassas, TX

G8, $40-$75
S. W. TX

G6, $25-$45
Polk Co., TX

LOCATION: Texas to Oklahoma.
DESCRIPTION: A dart point which is a variant form of the *Langtry* point which differs in having a pointed to rounded base and strong drooping barbs. Found in a cave hafted to a wooden forshaft with pitch. **I.D. KEY:** Strong barbs, pointed stem.

LEFLORE BLADE - Mississippian-Historic, 500 - 250 B. P.

(Also see Agate Basin, Caddoan Blade, Lerma)

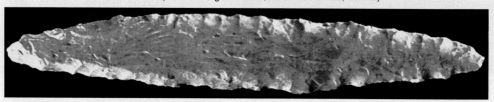

G8, $175-$300
McIntosh Co., OK

LOCATION: Oklahoma to N. Texas and Kansas. **DESCRIPTION:** A large size, narrow lanceolate, bi-pointed blade. Blade edges are usually smoothed. Much more narrow than *Lerma* points. Believed to be *Caddoan Blades* used as skinning knives. These blades having lost their utilitarian use due to excessive resharpening have been found in caches. **I.D. KEY:** Narrow width in relation to length, ground edges.

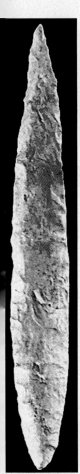

G8, $200-$350
McIntosh Co., OK

G9, $350-$600
Cass Co., TX

G9, $450-$800
Cass Co., TX

G10, $800-$1500
Cass Co., TX

S
C

LERMA POINTED BASE - Early Archaic, 9000 - 8000 B. P.

(Also see Agate Basin, Angostura, Desmuke, Harahey & LeFlore Blade)

LERMA POINTED BASE (continued)

G6, $80-$150
Burnet Co., TX

G8, $80-$150
Burnet Co., TX

LOCATION: Siberia to Alaska, Canada, Mexico South America and across the U.S. **DESCRIPTION:** A large size, narrow, lanceolate blade with a pointed base. Most are fairly thick in cross section but finer examples can be thin. Flaking tends to be collateral. Basal areas can be ground. Western forms are beveled on one side of each face. Similar forms have been found in Europe and Africa dating back to 20,000 - 40,000 B.P., but didn't enter the U.S. until after the advent of *Clovis*.

NOTE: Lerma may be much older.

G9, $175-$325
Comanche Co., TX

LERMA ROUNDED BASE - Early Archaic, 9000 - 8000 B. P.

(Also see Agate Basin, Angostura, Covington and Harahey)

G4, $10-$20
Hill Co., TX

Resharpened many times

G4, $15-$25
Comanche Co., TX

G3, $10-$20
Comanche Co., TX

Tip wear

G8, $35-$65
Webb Co., TX

G9, $300-$500
Kimble Co., TX

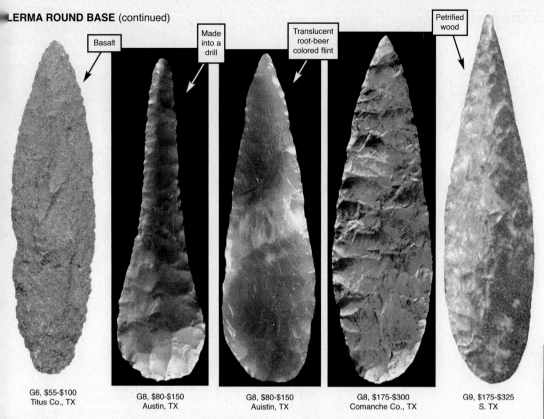

Basalt

Made into a drill

Translucent root-beer colored flint

Petrified wood

G6, $55-$100
Titus Co., TX

G8, $80-$150
Austin, TX

G8, $80-$150
Auistin, TX

G8, $175-$300
Comanche Co., TX

G9, $175-$325
S. TX

LOCATION: Same as pointed base Lerma. **DESCRIPTION:** A large size, narrow, thick, lanceolate blade with a rounded base. Some Western examples are beveled on one side of each face. Flaking tends to be collateral and finer examples are thin in cross section.

LITTLE RIVER - Mid to Late Archaic, 5000 -3000 B. P.

(Also see Smith & Ouachita)

Novaculite

G8, $450-$800
AR

G9, $350-$600
Calhoun Co., AR, Moro
Bayou. One of a cache of
four.

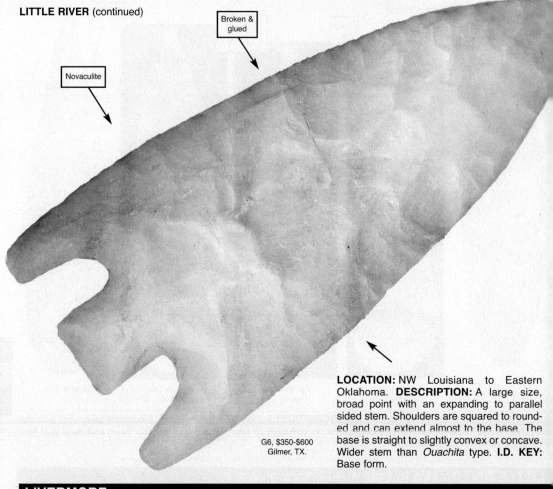

Broken & glued

Novaculite

G6, $350-$600
Gilmer, TX.

LOCATION: NW Louisiana to Eastern Oklahoma. **DESCRIPTION:** A large size, broad point with an expanding to parallel sided stem. Shoulders are squared to rounded and can extend almost to the base. The base is straight to slightly convex or concave. Wider stem than *Ouachita* type. **I.D. KEY:** Base form.

LIVERMORE - Mississippian, 1200 - 600 B. P.

(Also see Bassett, Drill, Howard and Sequoyah)

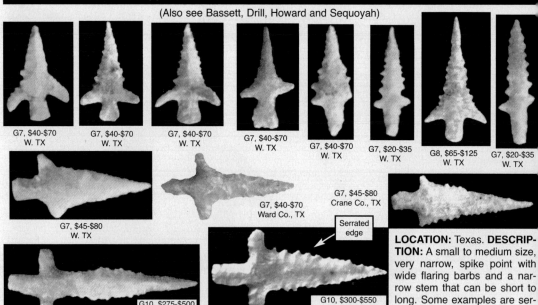

G7, $40-$70
W. TX

G7, $40-$70
W. TX

G7, $40-$70
W. TX

G7, $40-$70
W. TX

G7, $40-$70
W. TX

G7, $20-$35
W. TX

G8, $65-$125
W. TX

G7, $20-$35
W. TX

G7, $45-$80
W. TX

G7, $40-$70
Ward Co., TX

G7, $45-$80
Crane Co., TX

Serrated edge

G10, $275-$500
W. TX

G10, $300-$550
Culberson Co., TX

LOCATION: Texas. **DESCRIPTION:** A small to medium size, very narrow, spike point with wide flaring barbs and a narrow stem that can be short to long. Some examples are serrated. **I.D. KEY:** Extreme narrowness of blade.

618

LOTT - Mississippian to Historic, 500 - 300 B. P.

(Also see Garza and Harrell)

G9, $200-$350
Garza Co., TX

G10, $275-$500
Garza Co., TX

LOCATION: Texas to Arizona. A rare type. **DESCRIPTION:** A medium size, weakly barbed, thin, arrow point with a bifurcated base. Ears can be long and flare outward. Basal sides and the base are usually straight. **I.D. KEY:** Form of ears.

MAHAFFEY - Transitional Paleo-Early Archaic, 10,500 - 8000 B. P.

(Also see Agate Basin and Angostura)

S
C

G8, $55-$100
N.E. OK

G8, $175-$300
N. OK

G8, $65-$125
N.E. OK

G9, $200-$350
Wilson Co., TX

G9, $200-$375
TX

LOCATION: Texas, Arkansas to Oklahoma. **DESCRIPTION:** A medium size, ovate point with a rounded base. Widest near the tip, the basal area is usually ground. Believed to be related to the Agate Basin point. **I.D. KEY:** Blade form.

MARCOS - Late Archaic to Woodland, 3500 - 1800 B. P.

(Also see Calcasieu, Castroville, Ensor, Fairland, Marshall and San Jacinto)

G7, $65-$125
Austin, TX

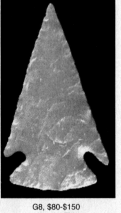

G8, $80-$150
Austin, TX

G7, $80-$150
TX

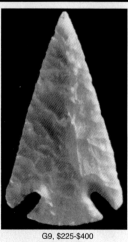

G9, $225-$400
Austin, TX

LOCATION: Texas to Oklahoma. **DESCRIPTION:** A small to medium size, broad, corner notched point with an expanded stem. The blade edges are straight to recurved. Many examples have long barbs and a sharp pointed tip. Bases are convex, straight or concave. **I.D. KEY:** Angle of corner notches.

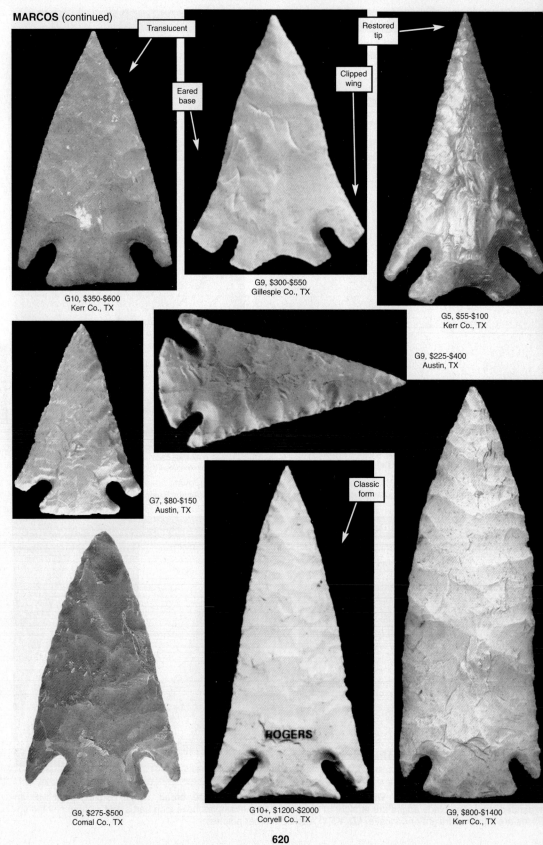

MARCOS (continued)

Translucent

Eared base

Restored tip

Clipped wing

G10, $350-$600
Kerr Co., TX

G9, $300-$550
Gillespie Co., TX

G5, $55-$100
Kerr Co., TX

G9, $225-$400
Austin, TX

G7, $80-$150
Austin, TX

Classic form

ROGERS

G9, $275-$500
Comal Co., TX

G10+, $1200-$2000
Coryell Co., TX

G9, $800-$1400
Kerr Co., TX

620

MARSHALL - Middle Archaic to Woodland, 6000 - 2000 B. P.

(Also see Castroville, Ensor, Marcos and San Jacinto)

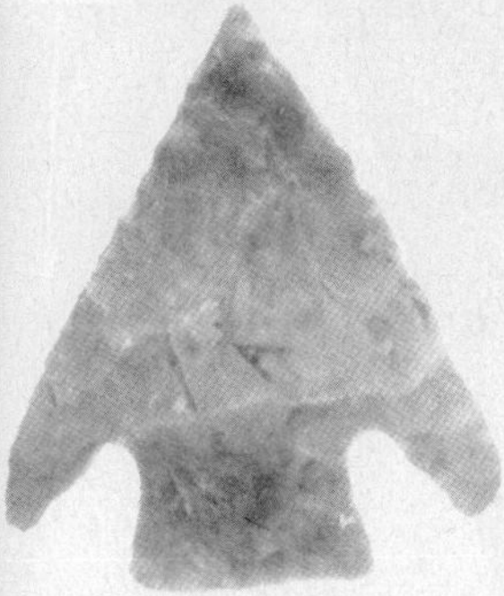
G5, $25-$45
TX

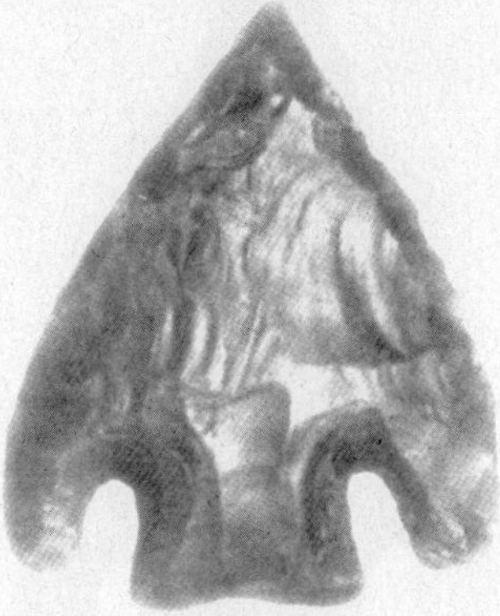
G5, $45-$85
Bell Co., TX

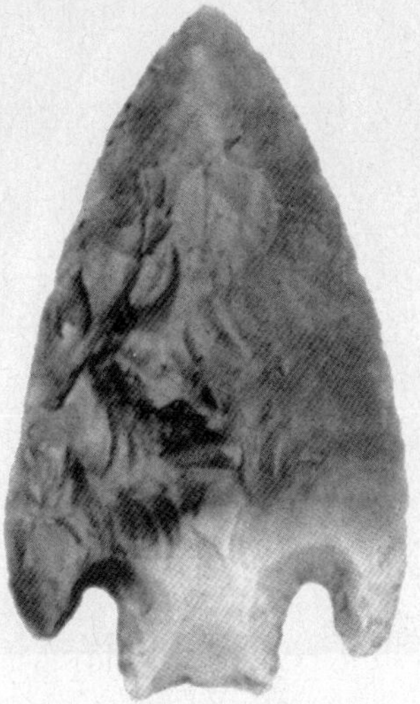
G5, $125-$200
Burnet Co., TX

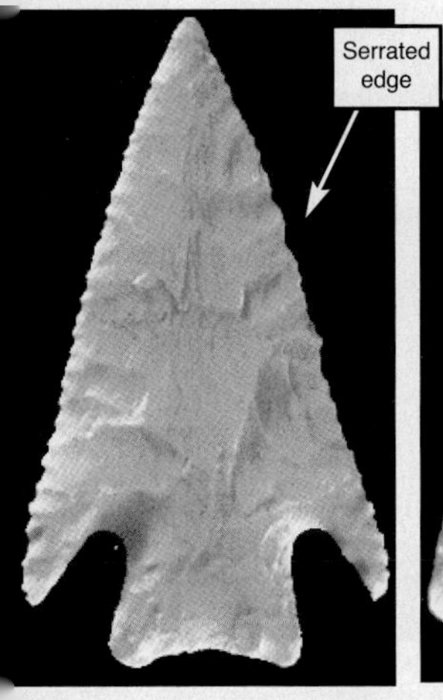
Serrated edge
G8, $150-$250
Comanche Co., TX

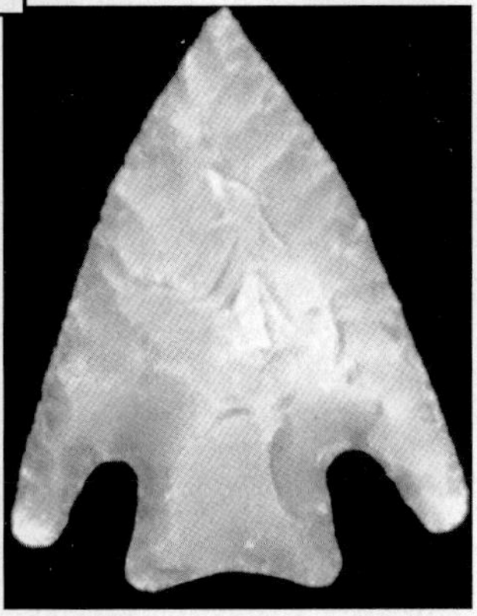
G8, $80-$150
Kimble Co., TX

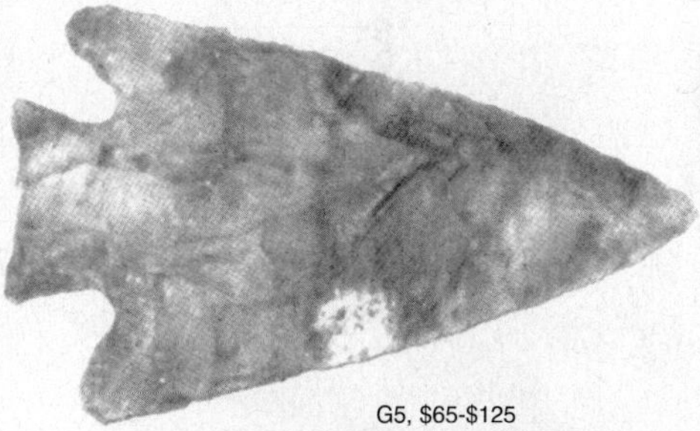
G5, $65-$125
Coryell Co., TX

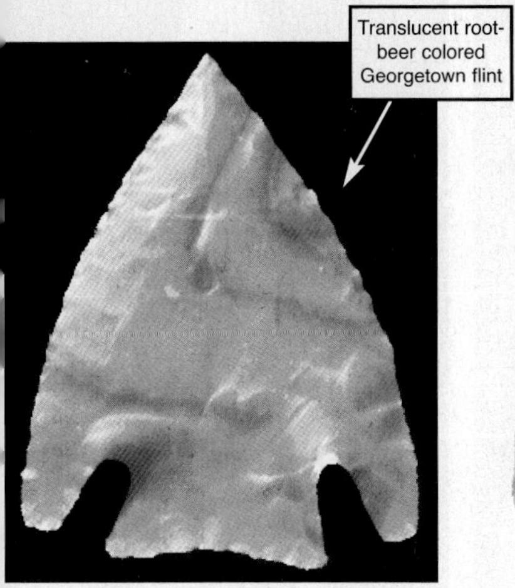
Translucent root-beer colored Georgetown flint
G7, $125-$200
Austin, TX

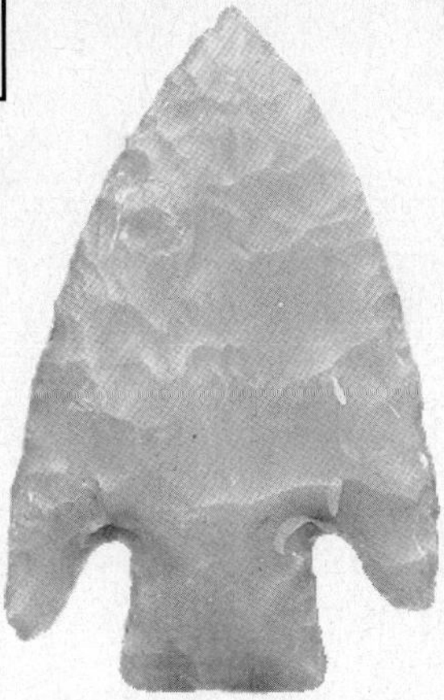
G8, $150-$250
Kerr Co., TX

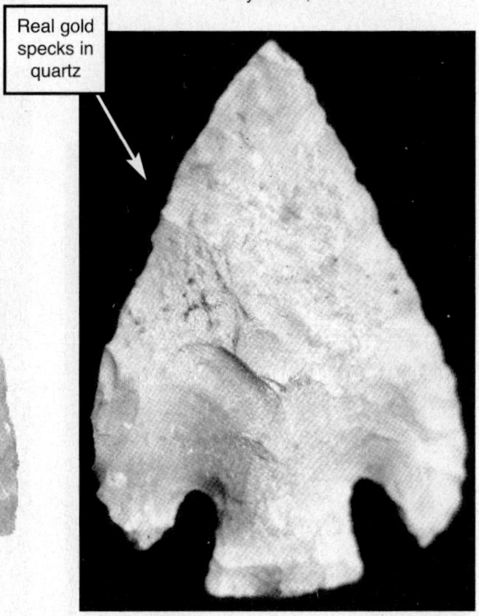
Real gold specks in quartz
G5, $80-$150
Hill Co., TX

LOCATION: Texas to Colorado. **DESCRIPTION:** A medium to large size, broad, high quality, corner to basal notched point with long barbs that turn inward towards the base. Notching is less angled than in *Marcos.* Bases are straight to concave to bifurcated. **I.D. KEY:** Drooping tangs.

G7,$150-$250
Coryell Co., TX

G8, $250-$300
Kimble Co., TX

Clipped
wing

G7, $200-$350
TX

G8, $200-$350
Kerr Co., TX

G9, $200-$350
Austin, TX

Needle
tip

G8, $200-$350
Uvalde Co., TX

G8, $250-$400
Kerr Co., TX

G8, $250-$400
Bandera Co., TX

MARTINDALE - Early Archaic, 8000 - 5000 B. P.

(Also see Bandy, Marcos and Marshall)

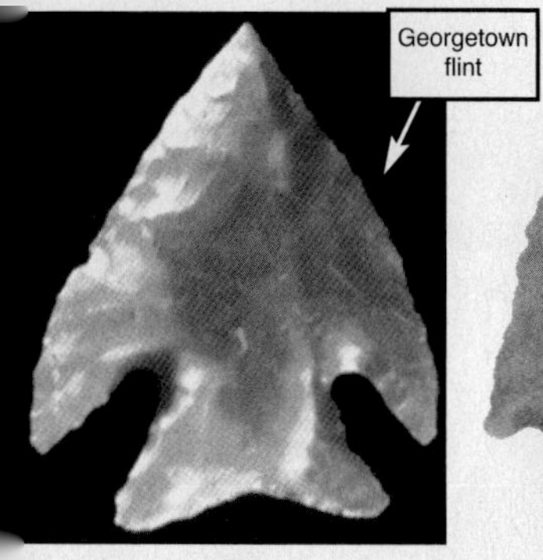

Georgetown flint

G7, $40-$70
Austin, TX

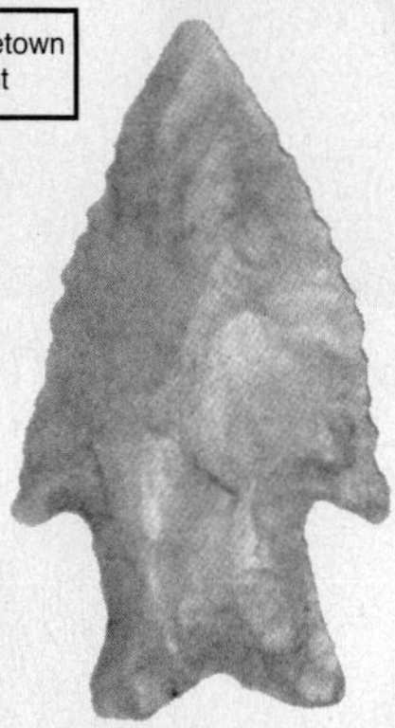

G6, $30-$50
Bell Co, TX

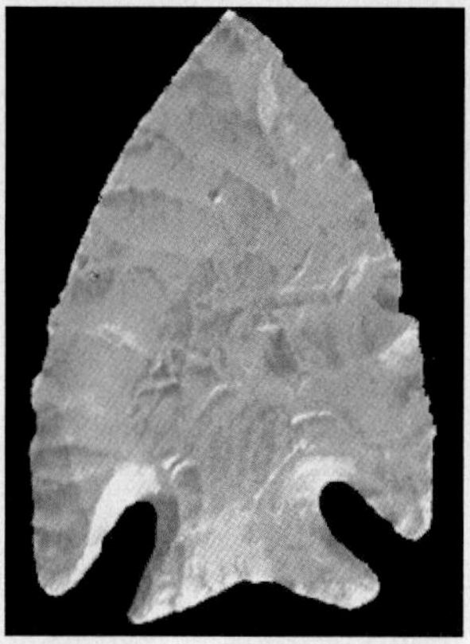

G7, $45-$85
Austin, TX

G7, $30-$50
Austin, TX

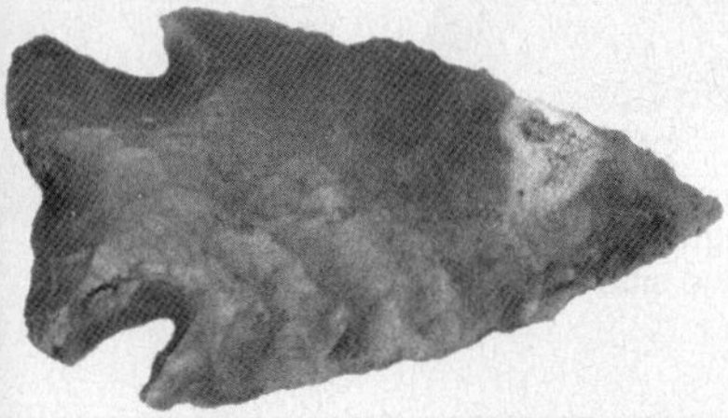

G5, $30-$50
Bell Co, TX

Black chert

Note typical "fishtailed" base

Caliche on surface

Minor side and barb damage

G8, $150-$275
TX

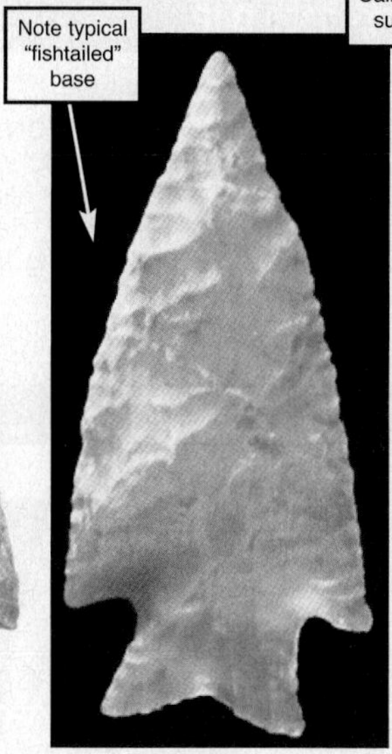

G7, $80-$150
Austin, TX

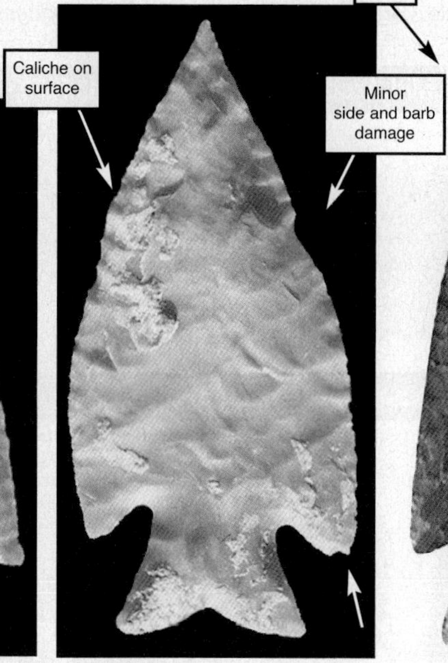

G8, $175-$300
Williamson Co., TX

G10, $400-$700
Austin, TX

LOCATION: Texas to Oklahoma. **DESCRIPTION**: A medium size corner notched to expanded stem point. The base is unique in that it is formed by two curves meeting at the center. Called *Bandy* in southern Texas. **I.D. KEY**: Basal form, early flaking.

MASSARD   (see Colbert)

MATAMOROS - Late Archaic to Mississippian, 3000 - 300 B. P.

(Also see Abasolo, Catan and Tortugas)

MATAMOROS (continued)

G7, $3-$6
Nuevo Leon, MX

G7, $3-$6
Nuevo Leon, MX

G8, $4-$8
Nuevo Leon, MX

G6, $4-$8
Starr Co., TX

G6, $4-$8
S. TX

G7, $6-$12
S. TX

G7, $6-$12
S. TX

G7, $5-$10
Nuevo Leon, MX

G7, $6-$12
Nuevo Leon, MX

G8, $6-$12
S. TX

G8, $8-$15
Nuevo Leon, MX

LOCATION: Texas. **DESCRIPTION**: A small to medium size, broad, triangular point with concave, straight, or convex base. On some examples, beveling occurs on one side of each face as in *Tortugas* points. Larger points would fall under the *Tortugas* type.

MATANZAS - Mid-Archaic to Mississippian, 4500 - 3000 B. P.

(Also see Palmillas)

G7, $30-$50
AR

LOCATION: Arkansas to Missouri. **DESCRIPTION:** A medium size, narrow, side notched dart point with an expanding stem and a straight base.

MAUD - Mississippian, 800 - 500 B. P.

(Also see Fresno, Starr and Talco)

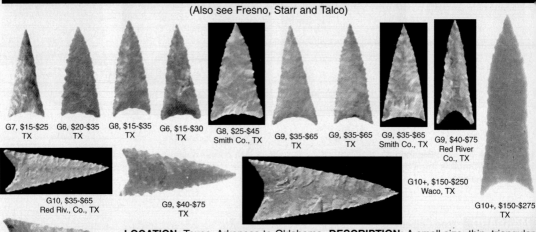

G7, $15-$25
TX

G6, $20-$35
TX

G8, $15-$35
TX

G6, $15-$30
TX

G8, $25-$45
Smith Co., TX

G9, $35-$65
TX

G9, $35-$65
TX

G9, $35-$65
Smith Co., TX

G9, $40-$75
Red River
Co., TX

G10, $35-$65
Red Riv., Co., TX

G9, $40-$75
TX

G10+, $150-$250
Waco, TX

G10+, $150-$275
TX

G9, $45-$85
TX

LOCATION: Texas, Arkansas to Oklahoma. **DESCRIPTION:** A small size, thin, triangular arrow point with straight to convex sides and a concave base. Basal corners are sharp. Associated with the Caddo culture in the Midwest. Blades are usually very finely serrated. **I.D. KEY:** Convex sides, sharp basal corners.

MCKEAN - Middle to Late Archaic, 4500 - 2500 B. P.

(Also see Angostura, Folsom, Goshen)

G9, $250-$450
N. OK

LOCATION: N. Plains into Oklahoma. **DESCRIPTION:** A small to medium size, narrow, basal notched point. No basal grinding is evident. Similar to the much earlier *Wheeler* points of the Southeast. Basal ears are rounded to pointed. Flaking is more random although earlier examples can have parallel flaking. **I.D. KEY:** Narrow lanceolate with notched base.

MERKLE - Mid-Archaic to Mississippian, 4500 - 3000 B. P.

(Also see Duran, Evans, Sinner)

G6, $25-$50
Saline Co., AR

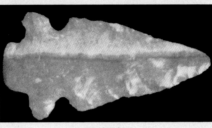

G7, $35-$60
N. OK

LOCATION: Arkansas to Missouri. **DESCRIPTION:** A medium size, side notched dart point with a short stem formed by corner notches. The base is straight. **I.D. KEY:** Straight base and double notches.

S
C

MESERVE - Early Archaic, 9500 - 4000 B. P.

(Also see Angostura, Dalton and Plainview)

G5, $25-$40
TX

G5, $15-$25
TX

Alibates dolomite

G6, $90-$175
OK

Beveled edge

G5, $35-$65
Abilene, TX

G5, $80-$150
N.E. OK

Beveled edge

G8, $150-$275
N. OK

G7, $65-$125
Tulsa Co., OK

Drill form

G6, $40-$75
Dickens, CO

Beveled edge

LOCATION: Texas westward to Arizona and northward to Montana. **DESCRIPTION:** A medium size, auriculate point with a blade that is beveled on one side of each face. Beveling extends into the basal area. This type is the western form of *Dalton* points.

625

MESERVE (continued)

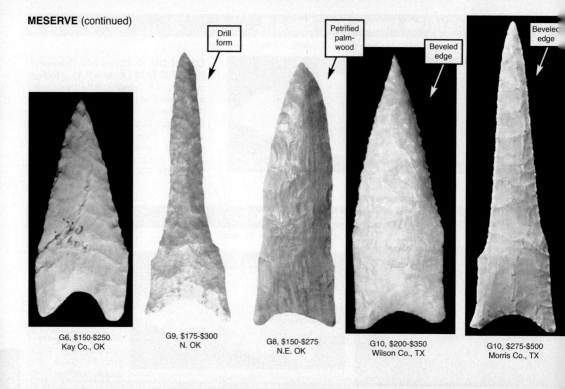

Drill form

Petrified palm-wood

Beveled edge

Beveled edge

G6, $150-$250
Kay Co., OK

G9, $175-$300
N. OK

G8, $150-$275
N.E. OK

G10, $200-$350
Wilson Co., TX

G10, $275-$500
Morris Co., TX

MID-BACK TANG - Late Archaic to Woodland, 4000 - 2000 B. P.

(Also see Base Tang Knife and Corner Tang)

Classic form

Leon River chert

G6, $200-$350
Coleman Co., TX

G7, $350-$600
Coryell Co., TX.

LOCATION: Texas. **DESCRIPTION:** A variation of the corner tang knife with the hafting area occuring near the center of one side of the blade. A very rare type.

MIDLAND - Late Paleo, 11,000 - 10,000 B. P.

(Also see Angostura, Arkabutla, Clovis, Folsom, Goshen, Milnesand and Plainview)

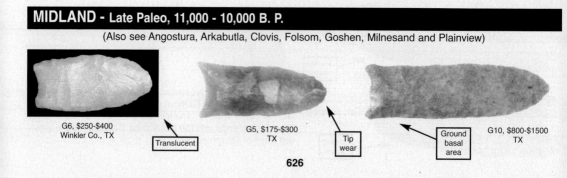

G6, $250-$400
Winkler Co., TX

Translucent

G5, $175-$300
TX

Tip wear

Ground basal area

G10, $800-$1500
TX

Side wear

Black chert

Brown agate

Small piece restored

G6, $175-$300
OK

G6, $250-$450
Dawson Co., TX

G5, $125-$200
Lubbock, TX

G6, $175-$300
OK

G6, $200-$350
TX

Diagonal flaking

G6, $650-$1200
Wheeler Co., TX

Translucent flint

Collateral flaking

G5, $250-$400
Plainview, TX

G7, $400-$700
Crane Co., TX

Tip wear

Tip impact

G6, $250-$400
Midland Co., TX

G9, $700-$1200
Andrews Co., TX

G5, $225-$400
Midland Co., TX

G7, $450-$800
TX

G6, $450-$800
Edwards, TX

G10, $1500-$2700
Lubbock, TX

S C

LOCATION: Texas northward to Canada. **DESCRIPTION:** An unfluted *Folsom*. A small to medium size, thin, unfluted lanceolate point with parallel to convex sides. Basal thinning is weak and the blades exhibit fine micro edgework. Bases usually have a shallow concavity and are ground most of the way to the tip.

MILNESAND - Late Paleo, 11,000 - 10,000 B. P.

(Also see Agate Basin, Angostura, Browns Valley, Firstview, Hell Gap and Rio Grande)

Ground base & sides

Tip wear

Collateral flaking

G7, $165-$300
Comanche Co., TX

G4, $40-$75
TX

LOCATION: Texas, New Mexico, northward to Canada and Alaska. **DESCRIPTION:** A medium size unfluted lanceolate point that becomes thicker and wider towards the tip. The base is basically square and ground. Thicker than *Midland*. **I.D. KEY:** Square base and Paleo flaking.

G8, $350-$600
Crosby Co., TX

627

MILNESAND (continued)

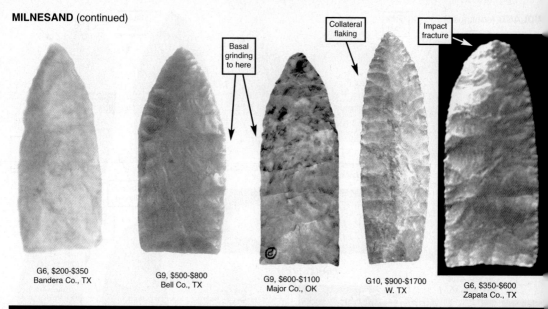

Basal grinding to here

Collateral flaking

Impact fracture

G6, $200-$350
Bandera Co., TX

G9, $500-$800
Bell Co., TX

G9, $600-$1100
Major Co., OK

G10, $900-$1700
W. TX

G6, $350-$600
Zapata Co., TX

MINERAL SPRINGS - Mississippian, 1300 - 1000 B. P.

(Also see Gahagan)

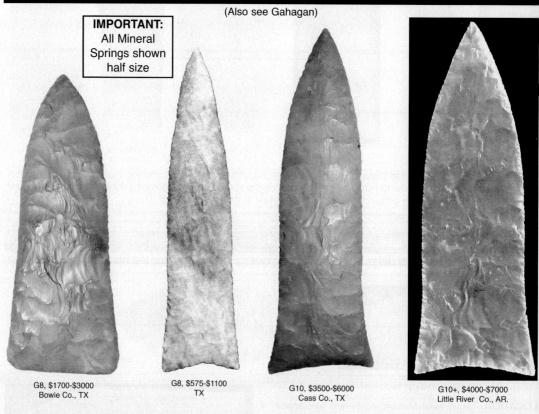

IMPORTANT:
All Mineral Springs shown half size

G8, $1700-$3000
Bowie Co., TX

G8, $575-$1100
TX

G10, $3500-$6000
Cass Co., TX

G10+, $4000-$7000
Little River Co., AR.

LOCATION: Texas, Oklahoma, Arkansas and Louisiana. **DESCRIPTION:** A broad, large size knife with recurved sides, sharp basal corners to rounded corners and a concave base. Some examples have notches at the basal corners. Believed to be related to the earlier *Gahagan* Blade.

MONTELL - Mid-Archaic to late Woodland, 5000 - 1000 B. P.

(Also see Ensor Split-Base and Uvalde)

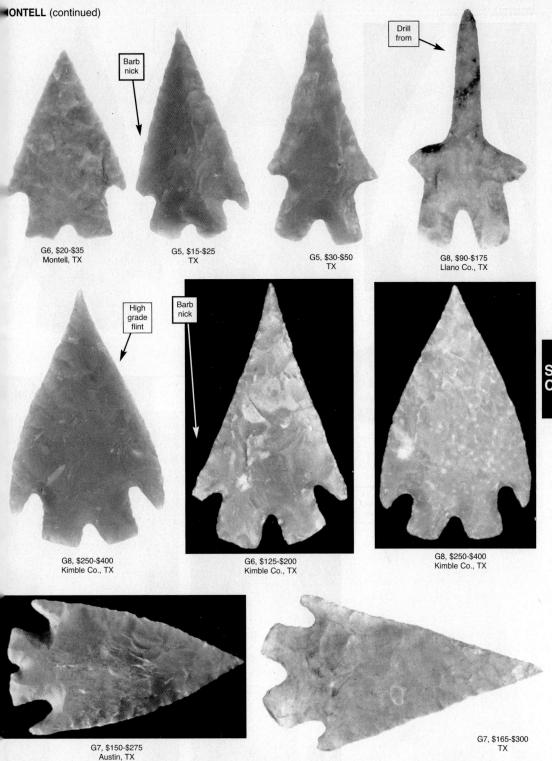

Barb nick

Drill from

G6, $20-$35
Montell, TX

G5, $15-$25
TX

G5, $30-$50
TX

G8, $90-$175
Llano Co., TX

High grade flint

Barb nick

S
C

G8, $250-$400
Kimble Co., TX

G6, $125-$200
Kimble Co., TX

G8, $250-$400
Kimble Co., TX

G7, $150-$275
Austin, TX

G7, $165-$300
TX

LOCATION: Midwestern states. **DESCRIPTION:** A small to medium size, bifurcated point with barbed shoulders. The ears are usually squared and some examples are beveled on one side of each face and are serrated. The deep basal notch "buck tooth" form is the preferred style. **I.D. KEY:** Square basal lobes.

629

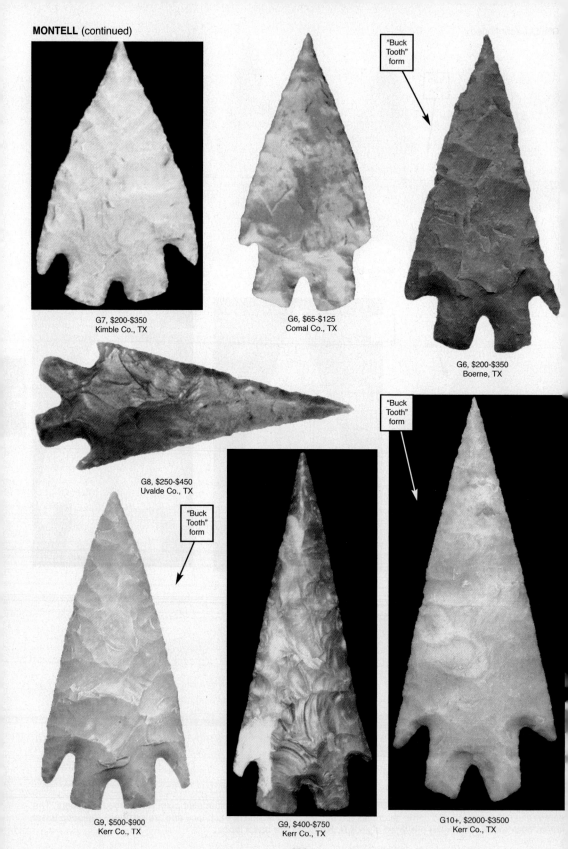

"Buck Tooth" form

G7, $200-$350
Kimble Co., TX

G6, $65-$125
Comal Co., TX

G6, $200-$350
Boerne, TX

G8, $250-$450
Uvalde Co., TX

"Buck Tooth" form

"Buck Tooth" form

G9, $500-$900
Kerr Co., TX

G9, $400-$750
Kerr Co., TX

G10+, $2000-$3500
Kerr Co., TX

MORAN - Woodland-Mississippian, 1200 - 600 B. P.

(Also see Bonham, Colbert, Rockwall, Sabinal and Scallorn)

G9, $30-$50
TX

G8, $65-$125
S. W. TX

LOCATION: Central Texas. **DESCRIPTION:** A small, thin, barbed arrow point with a narrow, rectangular base. Shoulder barbs are usually sharp. Very limited distributional area.

MORHISS - Late Archaic to Woodland, 4000 - 1000 B. P.

(Also see Adena, Bulverde, Carrolton and Morrill)

G3, $2-$4
Hill Co., TX

G3, $2-$4
Nuevo Leon, MX

G5, $20-$35
Comanche Co., TX

Petrified wood

G9, $125-$200
E. TX

G6, $25-$40
N. E. TX

G9, $150-$250
Calhoun Co., TX

LOCATION: Texas to Oklahoma. **DESCRIPTION:** A medium to large size, thick, long stemmed point with weak shoulders and a convex base.

S
C

MORRILL - Woodland, 3000 - 1000 B. P.

(Also see Carrolton, Kent, Lange, Morhiss, Pontchartrain, Wells and Yarbrough)

Novaculite

G8, $20-$35
Saline Co., AR

G5, $8-$15
Coryell Co., TX

LOCATION: Texas. **DESCRIPTION:** A medium size, thick, narrow, triangular point with weak, squared shoulders and a long rectangular stem. Bases are usually straight.

MORRILL (continued)

Made into a perforator

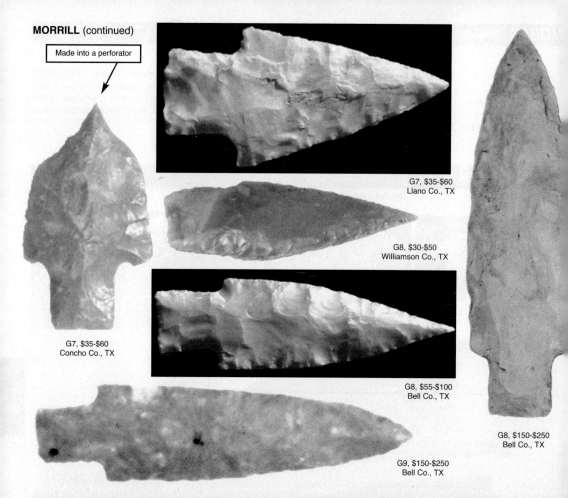

G7, $35-$60
Llano Co., TX

G8, $30-$50
Williamson Co., TX

G7, $35-$60
Concho Co., TX

G8, $55-$100
Bell Co., TX

G8, $150-$250
Bell Co., TX

G9, $150-$250
Bell Co., TX

MORRIS - Mississippian, 1200 - 400 B. P.

(Also see Cuney, Friley and Sallisaw)

G4, $6-$12
TX

G5, $25-$40
Spiro Mound,
OK

G4, $15-$30
AR

    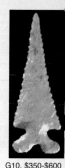

LOCATION: Texas to Oklahoma. **DESCRIPTION:** A small size, thin, barbed point with a bifurcated base and rounded ears. Blade edges can be serrated. **I.D. KEY:** Rounded basal ears.

G6, $25-$40
Spiro Mound,
OK

G6, $30-$50
Comanche Co.,
TX

G7, $40-$75
Saline Co.,
AR

G7, $40-$75
McCurtain Co.,
OK

G10, $350-$600
Spiro Mound,
OK

MORROW MOUNTAIN (See Hale and Peisker Diamond)

MOTLEY - Middle Archaic to Woodland, 4500 - 2500 B. P.

(Also see Cupp, Epps, Gibson, Grand and Kings)

LOCATION: Eastern Texas into Arkansas and Louisiana. **DESCRIPTION:** A medium to large size, expanded stemmed to widely corner notched point with strong barbs. The blade edges are convex. Bases are convex to straight. **I.D. KEY:** Long, expanding base, convex base.

G3, $8-$15
Waco, TX

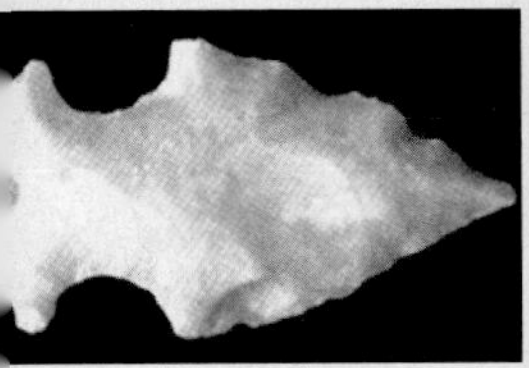

G3, $8-$15
Val Verde Co., TX

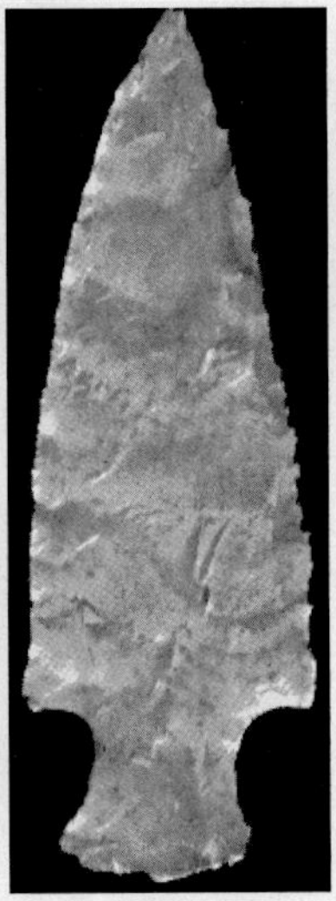

G5, $25-$40
Comanche Co., TX

G9, $150-$250
E. TX

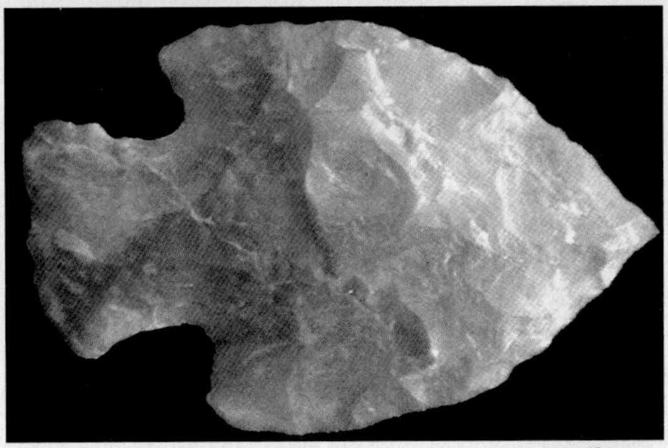

G5, $20-$35
Saline Co., AR

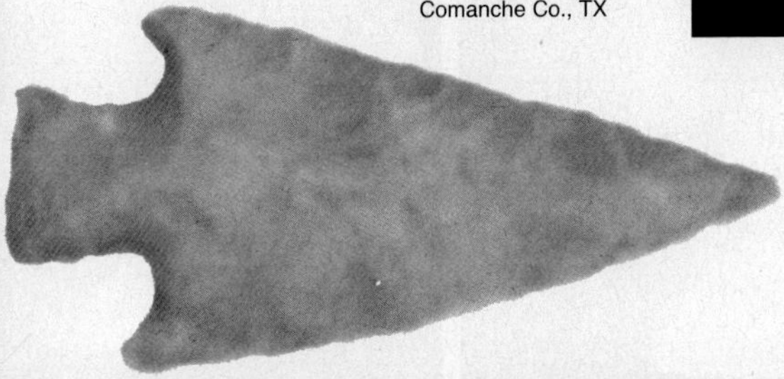

G5, $30-$50
Williamson Co., TX

S
C

Dover
chert

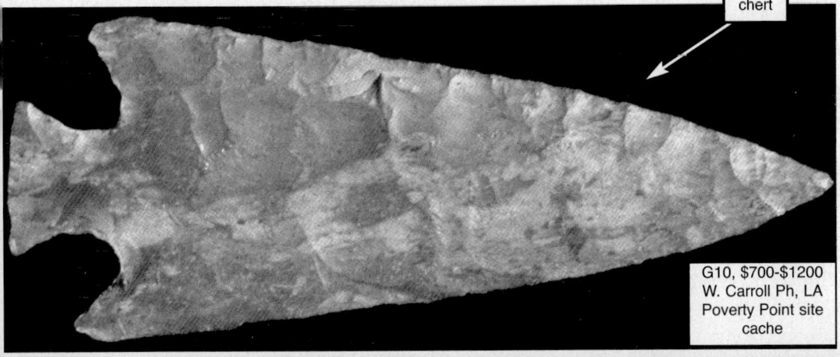

G10, $700-$1200
W. Carroll Ph, LA
Poverty Point site
cache

G6, $40-$75
TX

Patinated
gray flint

G10, $1500-$2700
W. Carroll Ph, LA,
Poverty Point site
cache. Bayou
Macon River

This cache
was plowed
up in 1948

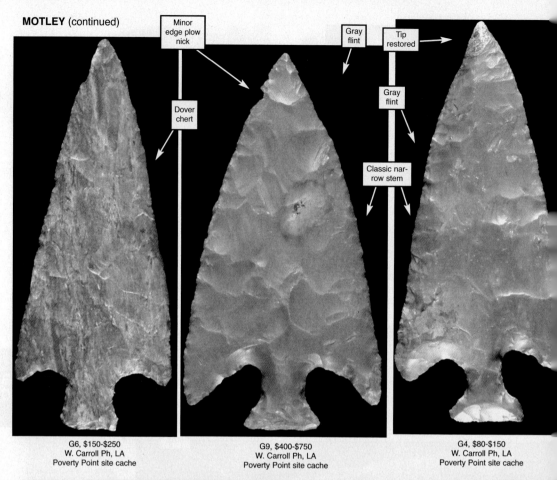

Minor edge plow nick

Dover chert

Gray flint

Tip restored

Gray flint

Classic narrow stem

G6, $150-$250
W. Carroll Ph, LA
Poverty Point site cache

G9, $400-$750
W. Carroll Ph, LA
Poverty Point site cache

G4, $80-$150
W. Carroll Ph, LA
Poverty Point site cache

NEOSHO - Late Archaic, 400 - 250 B. P.

(Also see Palmillas)

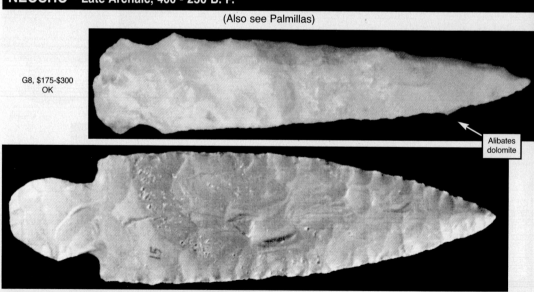

G8, $175-$300
OK

Alibates dolomite

G7, $165-$300, Cache Riv., AR, Harrison form.

LOCATION: Texas, Colorado, Oklahoma, into Arkansas & Missouri. **DESCRIPTION:** A large size, narrow knife form with broad to narrow side notches and a short, convex to a long tapered stem that can be pointed to rounded. Related to the *Harahey* Knife.

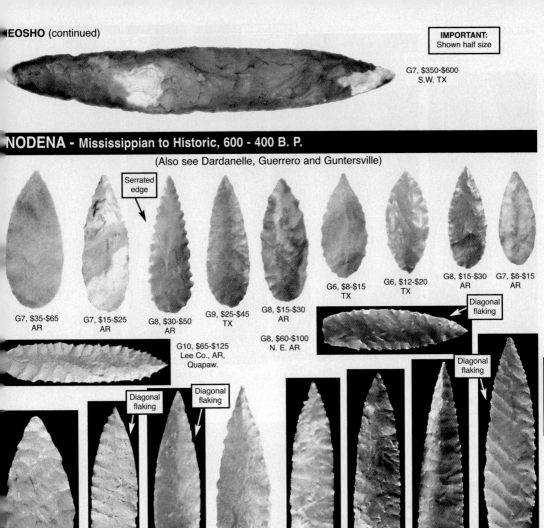

IMPORTANT:
Shown half size

G7, $350-$600
S.W. TX

NODENA - Mississippian to Historic, 600 - 400 B. P.

(Also see Dardanelle, Guerrero and Guntersville)

Serrated edge

G6, $8-$15
TX

G6, $12-$20
TX

G8, $15-$30
AR

G7, $8-$15
AR

G7, $35-$65
AR

G7, $15-$25
AR

G8, $30-$50
AR

G9, $25-$45
TX

G8, $15-$30
AR

Diagonal flaking

G10, $65-$125
Lee Co., AR,
Quapaw.

G8, $60-$100
N. E. AR

Diagonal flaking

Diagonal flaking

Diagonal flaking

G8, $45-$80
Saline Co., AR

G8, $65-$125
AR

G10, $80-$150
AR

G9, $80-$150
TX

G9, $80-$150
AR

G10, $80-$150
AR

G10, $125-$200
AR

G7, $80-$150
AR

S C

LOCATION: Arkansas and Tennessee. **DESCRIPTION:** A small to medium size, narrow, thin, elliptical shaped arrow point with a pointed to rounded base. Some examples have oblique, parallel flaking. Called *Tampa* in Florida. Used by the Quapaw Indians.

NOLAN - Mid-Archaic, 6000 - 4000 B. P.

(Also see Bulverde, Lange, Travis and Zorra)

Tip wear

G3, $8-$15
Comal Co., TX

Beveled stem on opposite faces

G6, $20-$35
Cent. TX

635

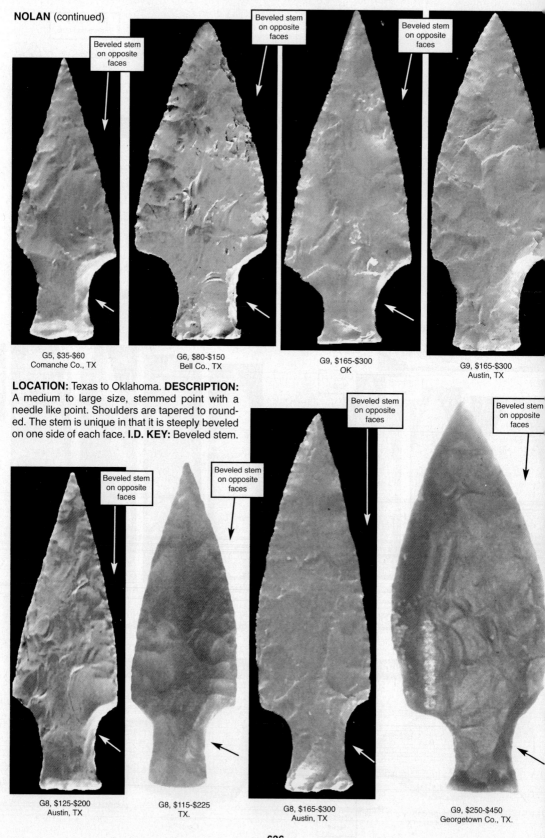

Beveled stem on opposite faces

Beveled stem on opposite faces

Beveled stem on opposite faces

Beveled stem on opposite faces

G5, $35-$60
Comanche Co., TX

G6, $80-$150
Bell Co., TX

G9, $165-$300
OK

G9, $165-$300
Austin, TX

LOCATION: Texas to Oklahoma. **DESCRIPTION:** A medium to large size, stemmed point with a needle like point. Shoulders are tapered to rounded. The stem is unique in that it is steeply beveled on one side of each face. **I.D. KEY:** Beveled stem.

Beveled stem on opposite faces

Beveled stem on opposite faces

Beveled stem on opposite faces

Beveled stem on opposite faces

G8, $125-$200
Austin, TX

G8, $115-$225
TX.

G8, $165-$300
Austin, TX

G9, $250-$450
Georgetown Co., TX.

OCALA - Early Archaic, 9500 - 8000 B. P.

(Also see Hardin, St. Charles)

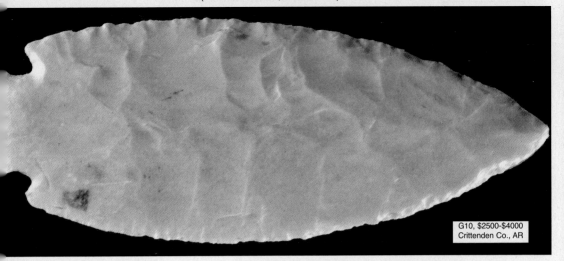

G10, $2500-$4000
Crittenden Co., AR

LOCATION: Arkansas, Illinois, Missouri, Kentucky into Tennessee and Florida. **DESCRIPTION:** A large corner notched point with strong barbs and a convex base. Stems are ground and blades are convex. Perino states this is a rare type. May be related to *St. Charles* and *Hardin* points. **I.D. KEY:** Beveled stem.

OAUCHITA - Mid-Archaic, 5000 - 3000 B. P.

(Also see Base Tang, Little River, Pontchartrain and Smith)

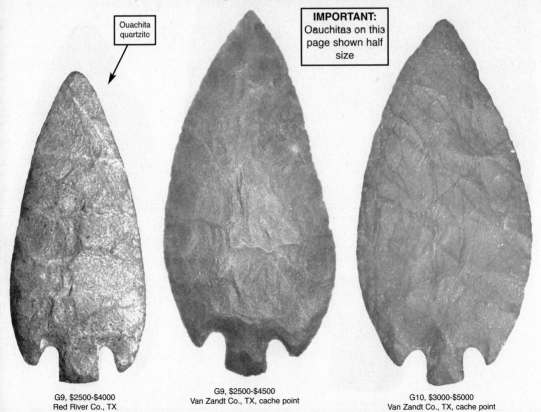

Ouachita
quartzite

IMPORTANT:
Ouachitas on this
page shown half
size

G9, $2500-$4000
Red River Co., TX

G9, $2500-$4500
Van Zandt Co., TX, cache point

G10, $3000-$5000
Van Zandt Co., TX, cache point

LOCATION: Texas. **DESCRIPTION:** A large, broad, knife point with a short parallel stem and drooping shoulders that are sharp. has been found in caches. Related to the *Little River* point from the same area.

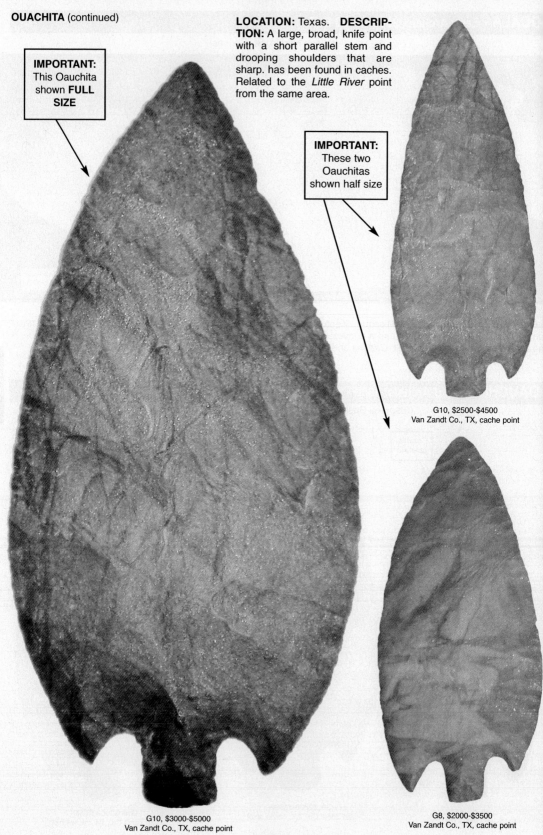

IMPORTANT: This Oauchita shown **FULL SIZE**

IMPORTANT: These two Oauchitas shown half size

G10, $2500-$4500
Van Zandt Co., TX, cache point

G10, $3000-$5000
Van Zandt Co., TX, cache point

G8, $2000-$3500
Van Zandt Co., TX, cache point

PAISANO - Mid-Archaic, 6000 - 5000 B. P.

(Also see Big Sandy, Dalton, San Patrice)

LOCATION: Texas. **DESCRIPTION:** A medium size point with broad side notches forming a squared to auriculate base that is concave. Some examples have notched/serrated edges.

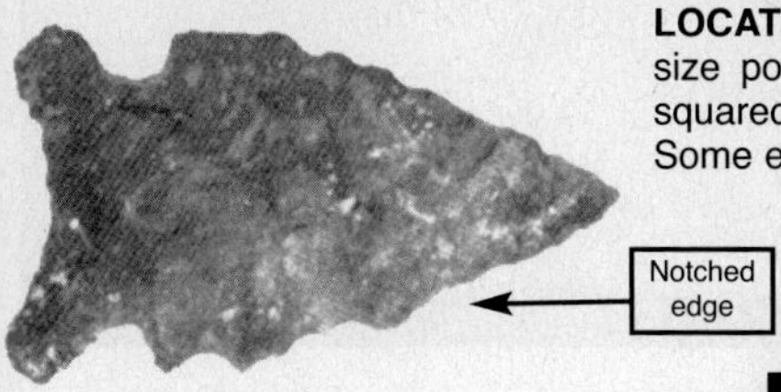

Notched edge

G6, $30-$50
W. TX

G5, $15-$30
W. TX

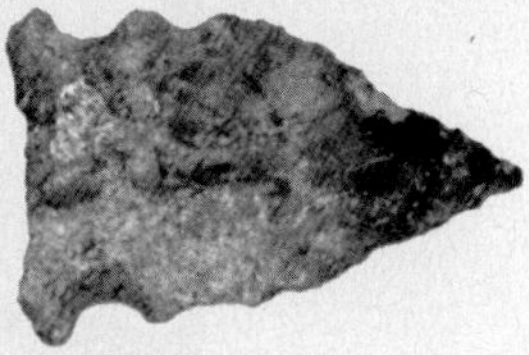

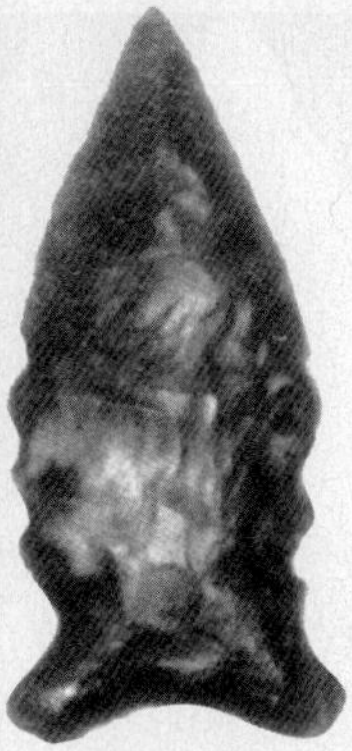

G6, $25-$40
Pecos Co., TX

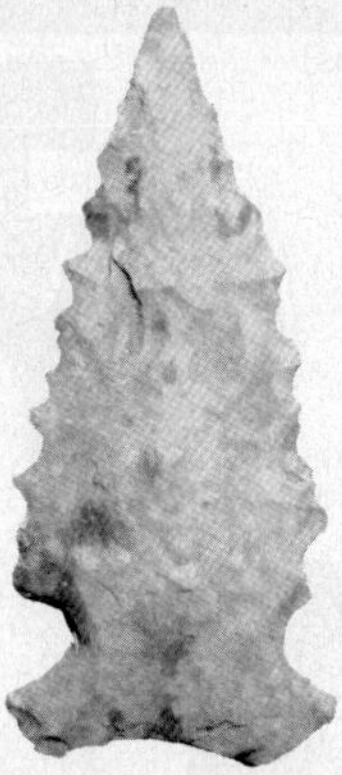

G7, $30-$50
Val Verde Co., TX

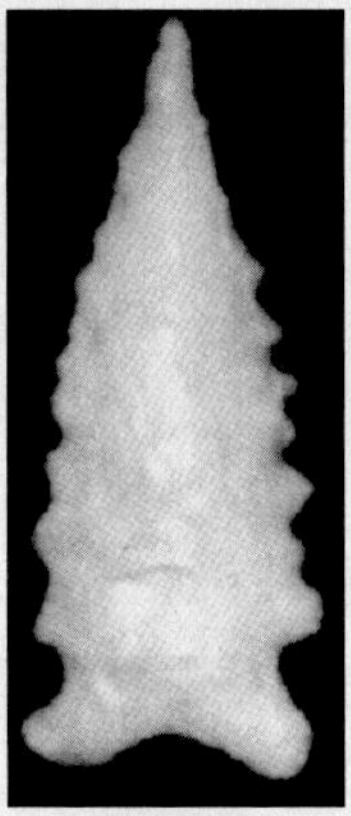

G8, $80-$150
Reeves Co., TX

Notched edge
Needle tip

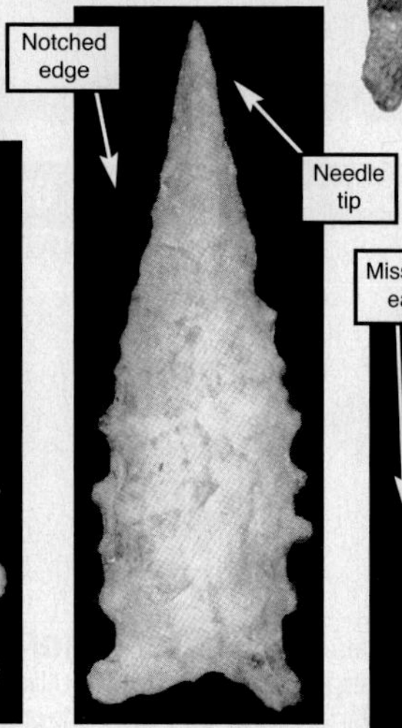

G9, $150-$250
Val Verde Co., TX

Missing ear

G2, $15-$25
Ward Co., TX

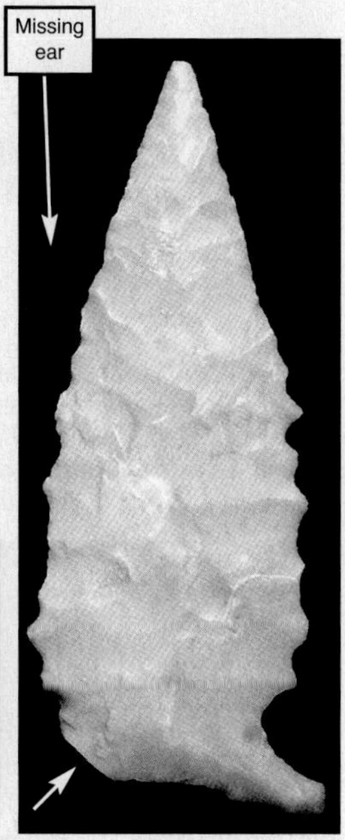

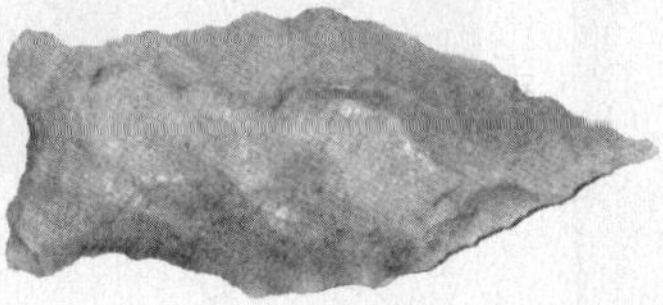

G7, $30-$50
W. TX

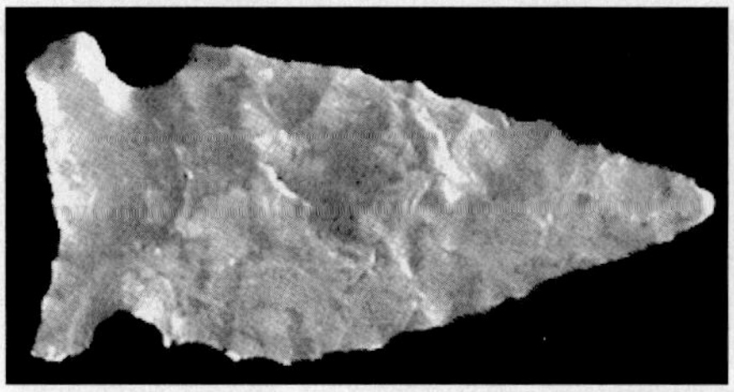

G6, $25-$40
Comanche Co., TX

PALEO KNIFE - Transitional Paleo, 10,000 - 8000 B. P.

(Also see Scraper, Round-End Knife and Square Knife)

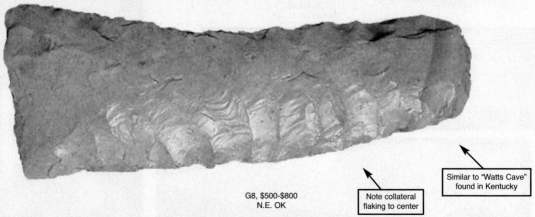

Note collateral flaking to center
Similar to "Watts Cave" found in Kentucky

G8, $500-$800
N.E. OK

LOCATION: All of North America. **DESCRIPTION:** A large size lanceolate blade finished with broad parallel flakes. These are found on Paleo sites and were probably used as knives.

PALEO KNIFE (continued)

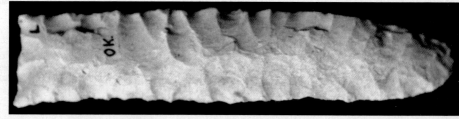

G7, $225-$400
Cherokee Co., OK

PALMILLAS - Middle to Late Archaic, 6000 - 3000 B. P.

(Also see Axtel, Godley and Williams)

Novaculite

G6, $5 $10
LA

G6, $8-$15
Hill Co., TX

LOCATION: Texas to Oklahoma. **DESCRIPTION:** A small to medium size triangular point with a bulbous stem. Shoulders are prominent and can be horizontal to barbed or weak and tapered. Stems expand and are rounded. **I.D. KEY:** Bulbous stem.

Novaculite

G6, $8-$15
AR

G7, $30-$50
Saline Co., AR

G7, $15-$25
Comanche Co., TX

G7, $15-$25
Saline Co., AR

G6, $25-$40
Saline Co., AR

G6, $35-$60
Bell Co., TX

G5, $20-$35
Saline Co., AR

640

PANDALE - Middle Archaic, 6000 - 3000 B. P.

(Also see Darl and Travis)

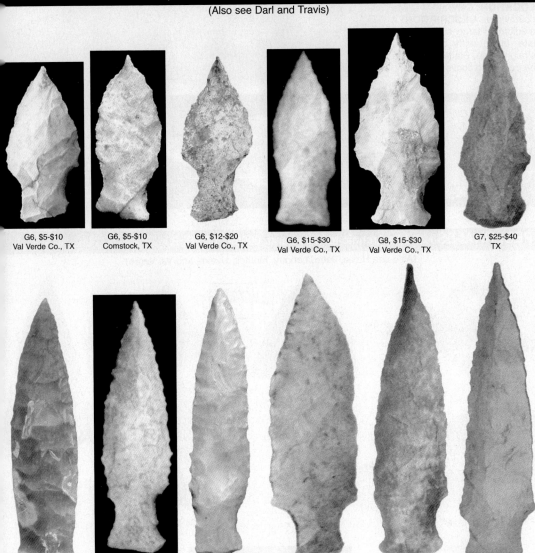

G6, $5-$10
Val Verde Co., TX

G6, $5-$10
Comstock, TX

G6, $12-$20
Val Verde Co., TX

G6, $15-$30
Val Verde Co., TX

G8, $15-$30
Val Verde Co., TX

G7, $25-$40
TX

S
C

G9, $65-$125
Burnett Co., TX

G8, $65-$125
Val Verde Co., TX

G7, $35-$60
Lynn Co., TX

G8 $65-$125
S. W. TX

G9, $125-$200
TX

G8, $90-$175
Val Verde Co., TX

LOCATION: Texas. **DESCRIPTION:** A medium size, narrow, stemmed point or spike with a steepy beveled or torque blade. Some examples show oblique parallel flaking.

PANDORA - Late Archaic to Woodland, 4000 - 1000 B. P.

(Also see Adena Blade, Friday, Kinney and Refugio)

G5, $12-$20
Val Verde Co., TX

G9, $35-$60
Comanche Co., TX

Classic form

PANDORA (continued)

LOCATION: Central Texas southward. **DESCRIPTION:** A medium to large size, lanceolate blade with basically a straight base. Blade edges can be parallel to convex.

G7, $45-$85
Bell Co., TX

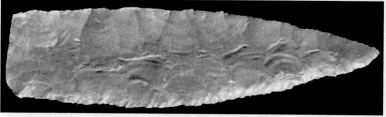

G8, $65-$125
Cent. TX

PEDERNALES - Middle Archaic to Woodland, 6000 - 2000 B. P.

(Also see Hoxie, Jetta, Langtry, Montell, Uvalde and Val Verde)

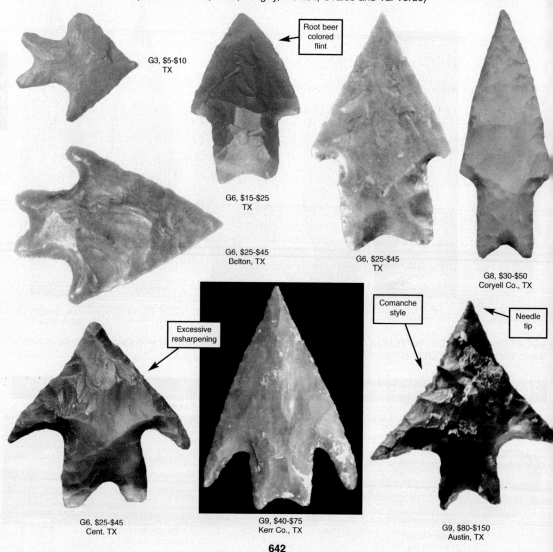

G3, $5-$10
TX

Root beer colored flint

G6, $15-$25
TX

G6, $25-$45
Belton, TX

G6, $25-$45
TX

G8, $30-$50
Coryell Co., TX

Excessive resharpening

Comanche style

Needle tip

G6, $25-$45
Cent. TX

G9, $40-$75
Kerr Co., TX

G9, $80-$150
Austin, TX

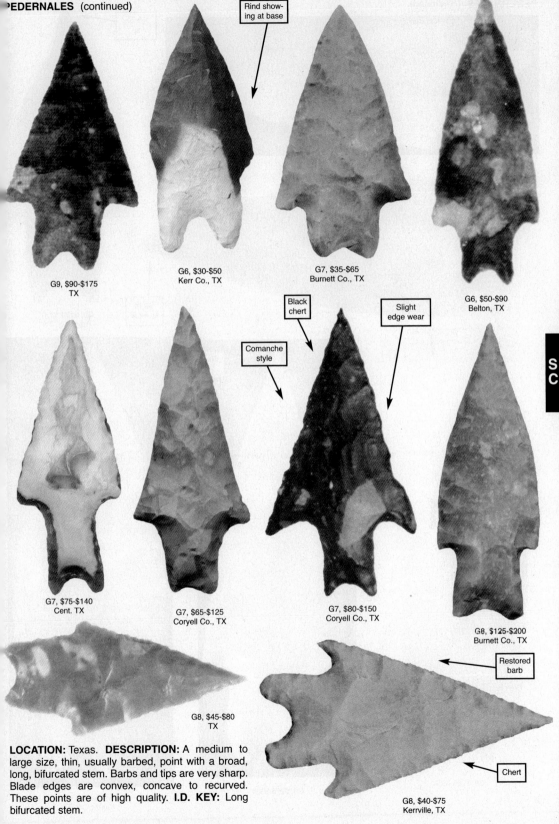

PEDERNALES (continued)

Rind showing at base

G9, $90-$175
TX

G6, $30-$50
Kerr Co., TX

G7, $35-$65
Burnett Co., TX

G6, $50-$90
Belton, TX

Black chert

Comanche style

Slight edge wear

G7, $75-$140
Cent. TX

G7, $65-$125
Coryell Co., TX

G7, $80-$150
Coryell Co., TX

G8, $125-$200
Burnett Co., TX

Restored barb

G8, $45-$80
TX

Chert

G8, $40-$75
Kerrville, TX

LOCATION: Texas. **DESCRIPTION:** A medium to large size, thin, usually barbed, point with a broad, long, bifurcated stem. Barbs and tips are very sharp. Blade edges are convex, concave to recurved. These points are of high quality. **I.D. KEY:** Long bifurcated stem.

S C

Needle tip

G8, $175-$300
Cent. TX

G8, $250-$450
Georgetown Co., TX

Slight tip wear

Needle tip

G9, $150-$250
Travis Co., TX

G9, $200-$350
TX

G9, $275-$500
TX

G9, $275-$500
Kimble Co., TX

PEISKER DIAMOND - Woodland, 2500 - 2000 B. P.

(Also see Gary and Hale)

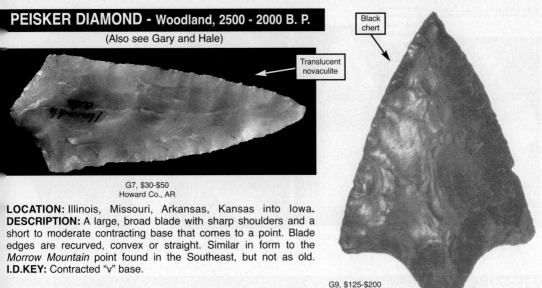

Translucent novaculite

Black chert

G7, $30-$50
Howard Co., AR

G9, $125-$200
OK

LOCATION: Illinois, Missouri, Arkansas, Kansas into Iowa. **DESCRIPTION:** A large, broad blade with sharp shoulders and a short to moderate contracting base that comes to a point. Blade edges are recurved, convex or straight. Similar in form to the *Morrow Mountain* point found in the Southeast, but not as old. **I.D.KEY:** Contracted "v" base.

PELICAN - Transitional Paleo to Early Archaic, 10,000 - 8000 B. P.

(Also see Arkabutla, Coldwater, Golondrina, Hell Gap, Midland, Rio Grande and San Patrice)

S C

Heavily resharpened

G8, $80-$150
TX

G6, $55-$100
AR

G5, $30-$50
TX

G6, $80-$150
TX

G9, $125-$200
AR

Flute channel

Red novaculite

Cobble chert

G8, $125-$200
AR

G7, $125-$200
Jasper Co., TX

G9, $200-$325
N. E. TX

G8, $150-$250
Angelina Co., TX

Ear wear

G7, $150-$275
AR

LOCATION: West Tennessee to Texas. **DESCRIPTION:** A short, broad, usually auriculate point with basal grinding. Shoulders taper into a long contracting stem. Some examples are basally thinned or fluted. **I.D. KEY:** Basal contraction, small size.

645

PELICAN (continued)

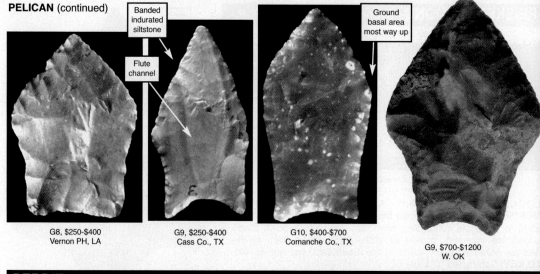

Banded indurated siltstone

Flute channel

Ground basal area most way up

G8, $250-$400
Vernon PH, LA

G9, $250-$400
Cass Co., TX

G10, $400-$700
Comanche Co., TX

G9, $700-$1200
W. OK

PERDIZ - Mississippian, 1000 - 500 B. P.

(Also see Alba, Bassett, Bonham, Cliffton, Cuney, Hayes, Homan and Keota)

G5, $6-$10
Hill Co., TX

G6, $12-$20
Comanche Co., TX

G6, $25-$45
Hill Co., TX

G9, $35-$60
TX

G8, $40-$70
Comanche Co., TX

G8, $35-$60
Ellis Co., TX

G9, $40-$70
Hill Co. TX

G9, $60-$115
Comanche Co., TX

G9, $55-$100
Ward Co., TX

G9, $60-$115
Comanche Co., TX

G9, $65-$125
Emanuel Co., TX

G8, $65-$125
Comanche Co., TX

G8, $65-$125
TX

G10, $125-$225
Hill Co., TX

LOCATION: Texas to Oklahoma. **DESCRIPTION:** A small to medium size, thin, narrow, triangular arrow point with pointed barbs and a long, pointed to near pointed stem. Some examples are serrated. Barbs and tips are sharp. **I.D. KEY:** Long pointed stem and barbs.

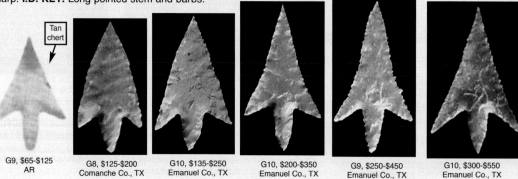

Tan chert

G9, $65-$125
AR

G8, $125-$200
Comanche Co., TX

G10, $135-$250
Emanuel Co., TX

G10, $200-$350
Emanuel Co., TX

G9, $250-$450
Emanuel Co., TX

G10, $300-$550
Emanuel Co., TX

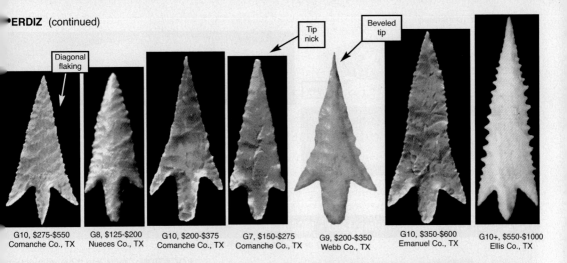

Diagonal flaking

Tip nick

Beveled tip

G10, $275-$550
Comanche Co., TX

G8, $125-$200
Nueces Co., TX

G10, $200-$375
Comanche Co., TX

G7, $150-$275
Comanche Co., TX

G9, $200-$350
Webb Co., TX

G10, $350-$600
Emanuel Co., TX

G10+, $550-$1000
Ellis Co., TX

PERFORATOR - Archaic to Mississippian, 9000 - 400 B. P.

(Also see Drill, Graver and Scraper)

G3, $1-$3
Nuevo Leon, MX

G5, $5-$10
Bell Co., TX

G6, $8-$15
Comanche Co., TX.

S C

G6, $15-$25
AR

G6, $5-$10
Saline Co., AR

Made from a Pedernales point

G6, $15-$25
TX

LOCATION: Archaic and Woodland sites everywhere. **DESCRIPTION:** A jabbing projection at the tip would qualify for the type. It is believed that *perforators* were used for tattooing, incising or to punch holes in leather or other materials or objects. Paleo peoples used *Gravers* for the same purpose. All Archaic and Woodland cultures converted their points into this type. Therefore, most point types could occur in this form.

PIKE COUNTY - Early Archaic, 10,000 - 9200 B. P.

(Also see Dalton and Plainview)

PIKE COUNTY (continued)

IMPORTANT:
All shown half size

G9, $250-$450
McIntosh Co., OK

Agate

G9+, $1700-$3000
Osage Co., OK

Classic form

G10, $800-$1500
AR

LOCATION: Oklahoma, Arkansas into Missouri and Illinois
DESCRIPTION: A large size, lanceolate blade with an eared, concave base. Basal area is ground. Related To *Dalton.* **I.D. KEY:** Fishtailed base.

PIPE CREEK - Mississippian, 1200 - 1000 B. P.

(Also see Corner Tang Knife)

G9, $50-$90
TX

G4, $8-$15
Pike Co., AR

G8, $40-$75
S. W. TX

G1, $.50-$1
Webb Co., TX

Broken tip

LOCATION: Texas into the southeastern states. **DESCRIPTION:** An unusual knife form having a single corner notch at one basal corner. The base is straight to slightly convex and can be lopsided. Perino and others speculate that this tool was used by early arrow makers in preparing feathers for use on arrow shafts. **I.D. KEY:** Single notch at base.

PLAINVIEW - Late Paleo, 11,250 - 9500 B. P.

(Also see Angostura, Barber, Brown's Valley, Clovis, Dalton, Frederick, Golondrina, Gosen and Midland)

Yellow chalcedony

Chalcedony

G6, $65-$125
Lampasas, TX

G6, $80-$150
Hico, TX

G6, $125-$225
Tulsa Co., OK

G7, $175-$300
Comanche Co., TX

G8, $250-$400
Polk Co., TX

G8, $250-$400
Llano Co., TX

G6, $150-$275
Dawson Co., TX

G7, $200-$350
Irion, TX

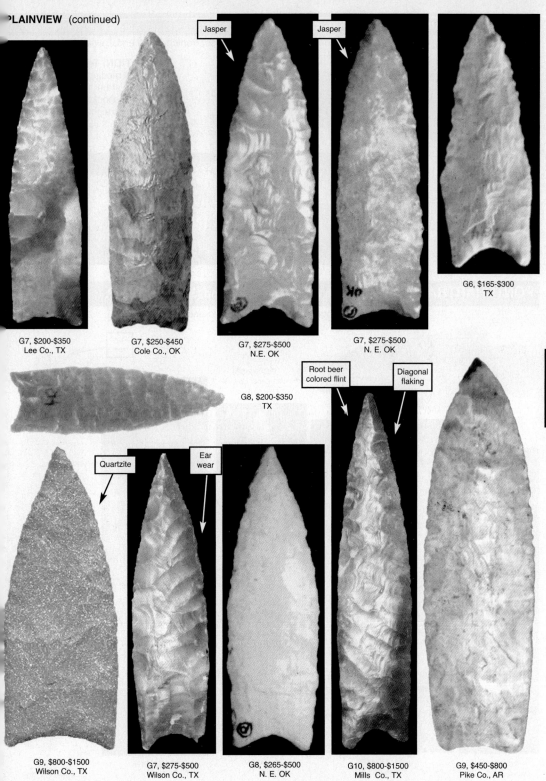

Jasper

Jasper

G6, $165-$300
TX

G7, $200-$350
Lee Co., TX

G7, $250-$450
Cole Co., OK

G7, $275-$500
N.E. OK

G7, $275-$500
N. E. OK

G8, $200-$350
TX

Root beer
colored flint

Diagonal
flaking

S
C

Quartzite

Ear
wear

G9, $800-$1500
Wilson Co., TX

G7, $275-$500
Wilson Co., TX

G8, $265-$500
N. E. OK

G10, $800-$1500
Mills Co., TX

G9, $450-$800
Pike Co., AR

LOCATION: Mexico northward to Canada and Alaska. **DESCRIPTION:** A medium size, thin, lanceolate point with usually parallel sides and a concave base that is ground. Some examples are thinned or fluted and is believed to be related to the earlier *Clovis* and contemporary *Dalton* type. Flaking is of high quality and can be collateral to oblique transverse.

POGO - Woodland to Mississippian, 2000 - 500 B. P.

(Also see Darl, Dickson, Hidden Valley, Lange, Morhiss, Pontchartrain and Travis)

LOCATION: Texas. **DESCRIP-TION:** A medium to large size con-tracted stem point with small tapered shoulders. The base is usually straight. Also known as *Morhiss*.

G9, $90-$175
Montgomery Co., TX

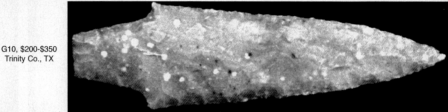

G10, $200-$350
Trinity Co., TX

PONTCHARTRAIN (Type I) - Late Archaic to Woodland, 3400 - 2000 B. P.

(Also see Lange, Morrill, Morhiss, Pogo and Travis)

G5, $12-$20
Van Zandt Co., TX

Tip wear

G6, $15-$30
Comanche Co., TX

G8, $80-$150
Saline Co., AR

G6, $30-$50
Austin, TX

G9, $65-$125
E. TX

G5, $30-$50
Waller Co., TX

LOCATION: Alabama to Texas. **DESCRIPTION:** A medium to large size, thick, narrow, stemmed point with weak, tapered or barbed shoulders. The stem is parallel sided with a convex to straight base. Some examples are finely ser-rated and are related and similar to the *Flint Creek* type.

PONTCHARTRAIN (Type II) - Late Archaic to Woodland, 3400 - 2000 B. P.

(Also see Lange, Morrill and Morhiss)

Burlington chert

Gravel chert

G7, $45-$85
St. Mary Parish, LA

G5, $15-$30
LA

LOCATION: Alabama to Texas. **DESCRIPTION:** A medium to large size, thick, broad, stemmed point with barbed shoulders. The stem is parallel sided to tapered with a convex to straight base.

G7, $65-$125
Van Zandt Co., TX

G7, $95-$175
AR

S C

RED RIVER KNIFE - Early Archaic, 9500 - 7000 B. P.

(Also see Albany Knife, Alberta, Eden, Firstview and Scottsbluff)

Beveled edge

Novaculite

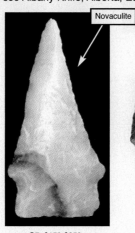

Bround stem

G7, $175-$300
LeFlore Co., OK

G7, $150-$250
Harrison Co., TX

G8, $550-$1000
Osage Co., OK

LOCATION: Texas to Colorado. **DESCRIPTION:** A medium size, asymmetrical blade with weak shoulders and a short, expanding to squared stem. Bases are straight to slightly convex. It has been reported that these knifes were made by the Cody Complex people from *Scottsbluff* points. Look for early parallel flaking and stem grinding.

G8, $200-$350
Dallas Co., TX

REED - Woodland to Mississippian, 1500 - 500 B. P.

(Also see Haskell, Knight Island, Schustorm and Washita)

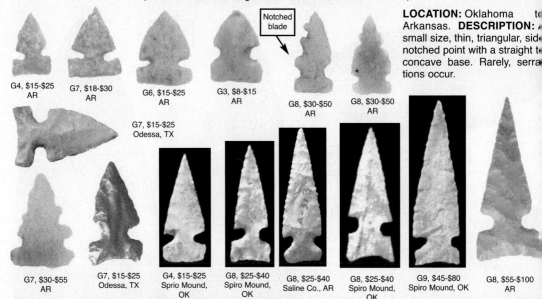

LOCATION: Oklahoma to Arkansas. **DESCRIPTION:** A small size, thin, triangular, side notched point with a straight to concave base. Rarely, serrations occur.

Notched blade

G4, $15-$25
AR

G7, $18-$30
AR

G6, $15-$25
AR

G3, $8-$15
AR

G8, $30-$50
AR

G8, $30-$50
AR

G7, $15-$25
Odessa, TX

G7, $30-$55
AR

G7, $15-$25
Odessa, TX

G4, $15-$25
Sprio Mound, OK

G8, $25-$40
Spiro Mound, OK

G8, $25-$40
Saline Co., AR

G8, $25-$40
Spiro Mound, OK

G9, $45-$80
Spiro Mound, OK

G8, $55-$100
AR

REFUGIO - Late Archaic, 4000 - 2000 B. P.

(Also see Gahagan, Pandora and Sabine)

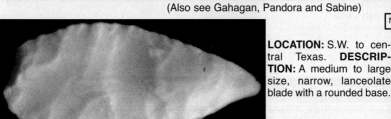

LOCATION: S.W. to central Texas. **DESCRIPTION:** A medium to large size, narrow, lanceolate blade with a rounded base.

G5, $8-$15
Saline Co., AR

Novaculite

G6, $40-$75
Comanche Co., TX

G4, $8-$15
Saline Co., AR

RICE CONTRACTED STEM

RICE LOBBED - Early Archaic, 9000 - 5000 B. P.

(Also see Uvalde)

LOCATION: Oklahoma to Missouri. **DESCRIPTION:** A medium to large size bifurcated to lobed base point with serrated blade edges. The base has a shallow indentation compared to the other bifurcated types. Shoulders are sharp and prominent. Called *Culpepper Bifurcate* in Virginia.

Serrated edge

Serrated edge

Novaculite

G6, $8-$15
Saline Co., AR

G7, $20-$35
Hot Spring Co., AR

G6, $20-$35
Hot Spring Co., AR

Novaculite

Serrated edge

Novaculite

G6, $25-$45
Hot Spring Co., AR

Tip wear

Serrated edge

G9, $35-$65
Saline Co., AR

G8, $25-$45
Saline Co., AR

G8, $35-$65
Hot Spring Co., AR

G4, $5-$10
Hot Spring Co., AR

Serrated edge

Note early parallel flaking

Bixby flint

Tip wear

G7, $45-$85
Hot Spring Co., AR

G6, $15-$30
Newton Co., AR

G8, $35-$65
Tulsa Co., OK

G4, $8-$15
Saline Co., AR

S
C

RICE SHALLOW SIDE NOTCHED - Woodland, 1600 - 1400 B. P.

(Also see Brewerton Eared & Jakie Stemmed)

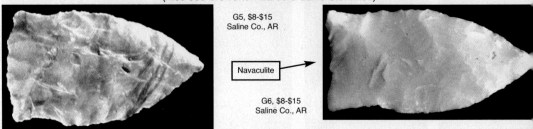

G5, $8-$15
Saline Co., AR

Navaculite

G6, $8-$15
Saline Co., AR

LOCATION: Oklahoma to Missouri. **DESCRIPTION:** A medium size, broad point with shallow side notches and a convex base.

RIO GRANDE - Early Archaic, 7500 - 6000 B. P.

(Also see Agate Basin, Angostura, Hell Gap and Pelican)

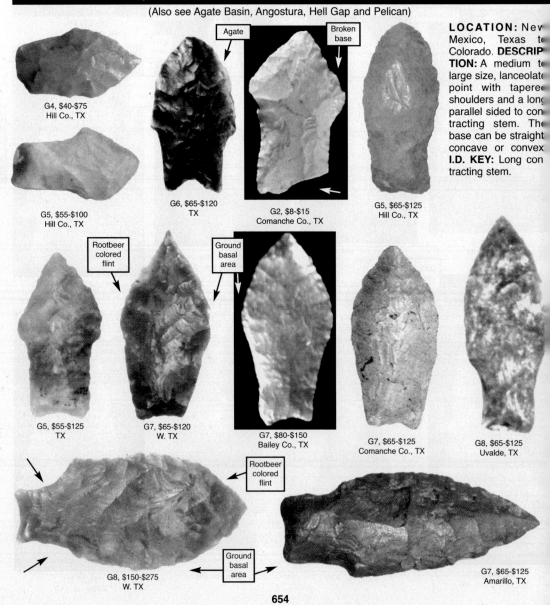

Agate

Broken base

LOCATION: New Mexico, Texas to Colorado. **DESCRIPTION:** A medium to large size, lanceolate point with tapered shoulders and a long parallel sided to contracting stem. The base can be straight, concave or convex. **I.D. KEY:** Long contracting stem.

G4, $40-$75
Hill Co., TX

G5, $55-$100
Hill Co., TX

G6, $65-$120
TX

G2, $8-$15
Comanche Co., TX

G5, $65-$125
Hill Co., TX

Rootbeer colored flint

Ground basal area

G5, $55-$125
TX

G7, $65-$120
W. TX

G7, $80-$150
Bailey Co., TX

G7, $65-$125
Comanche Co., TX

G8, $65-$125
Uvalde, TX

Rootbeer colored flint

G8, $150-$275
W. TX

Ground basal area

G7, $65-$125
Amarillo, TX

654

ROCKWALL - Late Woodland, 1400 - 1000 B. P.

(Also see Alba, Colbert, Moran, Sabinal, Scallorn and Shumla)

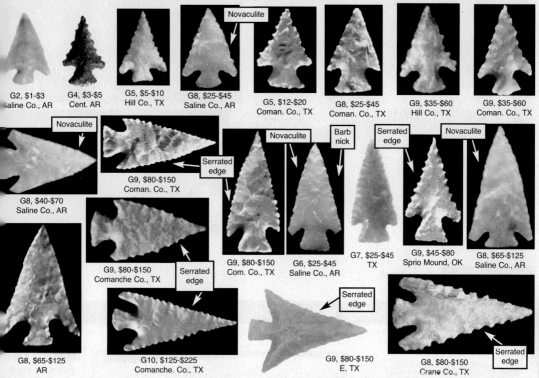

G2, $1-$3
Saline Co., AR

G4, $3-$5
Cent. AR

G5, $5-$10
Hill Co., TX

G8, $25-$45
Saline Co., AR

Novaculite

G5, $12-$20
Coman. Co., TX

G8, $25-$45
Coman. Co., TX

G9, $35-$60
Hill Co., TX

G9, $35-$60
Coman. Co., TX

Novaculite

Serrated edge

G9, $80-$150
Coman. Co., TX

G8, $40-$70
Saline Co., AR

Novaculite

Barb nick

Serrated edge

Novaculite

G9, $80-$150
Comanche Co., TX

Serrated edge

G9, $80-$150
Com. Co., TX

G6, $25-$45
Saline Co., AR

G7, $25-$45
TX

G9, $45-$80
Sprio Mound, OK

G8, $65-$125
Saline Co., AR

G8, $65-$125
AR

G10, $125-$225
Comanche. Co., TX

Serrated edge

Serrated edge

G9, $80-$150
E. TX

Serrated edge

G8, $80-$150
Crane Co., TX

LOCATION: Louisiana to Oklahoma. **DESCRIPTION:** A small, thin, triangular arrow point with corner notches. Shoulders are barbed and usually extend almost to the base. Many examples are serrated. Tips and barbs are sharp. **I.D. KEY:** Broad corner notches

RODGERS SIDE HOLLOWED - Early Archaic, 10,000 - 8000 B. P.

(Also see Arkabutla, Dalton, Golondrina, Pelican and San Patrice)

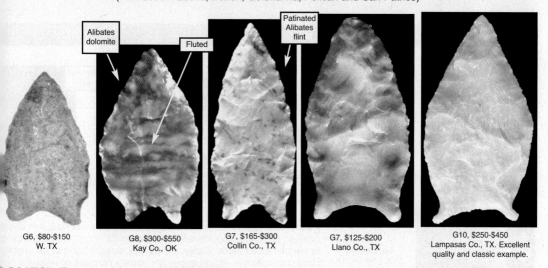

Alibates dolomite

Fluted

Patinated Alibates flint

G6, $80-$150
W. TX

G8, $300-$550
Kay Co., OK

G7, $165-$300
Collin Co., TX

G7, $125-$200
Llano Co., TX

G10, $250-$450
Lampasas Co., TX. Excellent quality and classic example.

LOCATION: Texas into Arkansas. **DESCRIPTION:** A medium size, broad, unfluted auriculate point which is a variant form of the *San Patrice* type. Also known as *Brazos Fishtail*. Base is concave and is ground. Some examples are fluted. **I.D. KEY:** Expanding auricles.

RODGERS SIDE HOLLOWED (continued)

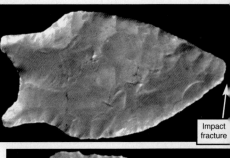

G7, $175-$300
Comanche, TX

Ear
damage

G5, $40-$75
Tom Green Co., TX

Impact
fracture

Fluted

G9, $200-$350
AR

G6, $125-$200
Austin, TX

ROSS COUNTY (See Clovis)

ROUND-END KNIFE - Historic 1000 - 300 B. P.

(Also see Archaic Knife, Paleo Knife and Square-End Knife)

IMPORTANT:
Shown half
size

G7, $60-$100
Victoria, TX

G9, $275-$500
Travis Co., TX

LOCATION: Texas. **DESCRIPTION:** A large, narrow knife form with rounded ends. This form was hafted along one side leaving a cutting edge on the opposite side.

SABINAL - Mississippian, 1000 - 700 B. P.

(Also see Bonham & Rockwall)

Serrated
edge

Serrated
edge

Serrated
edge

Serrated
edge

G9 $40-$70
Le Flore Co., OK

G7, $30-$55
Le Flore Co., OK

G9, $40-$70
Le Flore Co.,
OK

G9, $30-$50
Le Flore Co., OK

G8, $40-$70
Spiro Mound, OK

G6, $25-$45
Ellis Co., TX

G9, $65-$125
Comanche Co., TX

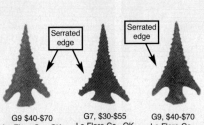

G9, $65-$125
Comanche Co., TX

LOCATION: Southern Texas. **DESCRIPTION:** A small size, thin basal notched point with shoulders that flare outward and a short expanding to parallel sided stem. Bases are usually straight but can be slightly convex or concave. Blade edges are usually concave or recurved but can be straight. **I.D. KEY:** Flaring barbs.

Classic form

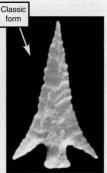

G7, $45-$80
TX

G9, $55-$100
TX

G8, $25-$45
TX

G5, $15-$30
Comanche Co., TX

G10+, $350-$650
Comanche Co., TX

G8, $80-$150
TX

SABINE - Late Archaic to Woodland, 4000 - 2000 B. P.

(Also see Covington, Friday, Gahagan, Refugio and San Gabriel)

G6, $25-$40
Comanche Co., TX

LOCATION: Midwestern states. **DESCRIPTION:** A medium to large size, thin, lanceolate blade with a contracting, rounded to "V" base. Blade edges can be serrated.

S
C

ST. CHARLES - Early Archaic, 9500 - 8000 B. P.

(Also see Gibson, Ocala and Thebes)

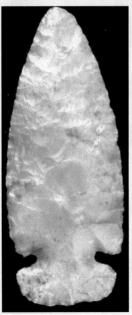

G3, $5-$10
Saline Co., AR

G5, $20-$35
Saline Co., AR

G6, $275-$500
Cherokee Co., TX

G9, $450-$800
Taylor Co., TX

Rarity in area
increases value

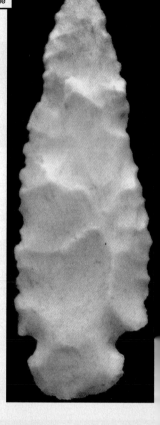

G9, $800-$1500
Cass Co., TX

G8, $200-$375
AR

LOCATION: East Texas Eastward. **DESCRIPTION:** Also known as *Dovetail* medium to large size, corner notched, dovetailed base point. The blade is beveled on one side of each face on resharpened examples. Bases are ground and can be fractured on both sides or center notched on some examples as found in Ohio. **I.D. KEY:** Dovetailed base, early flaking.

G5, $20-$35
Saline Co., AR

SALLISAW - Mississippian, 800 - 600 B. P.

(Also see Edwards, Haskell and Morris)

G8, $65-$125
Spiro Mound, OK

G9, $200-$350
Le Flore Co., OK

G10+, $600-$1000
Comanche Co., TX. very thin and excellent quality.

LOCATION: Oklahoma to Arkansas and Texas. **DESCRIPTION:** A small size, thin, serrated, barbed point with long drooping basal tangs and a deeply concave base. A very rare type. **I.D. KEY:** Long drooping ears.

SAN GABRIEL - Woodland 2000 - 1500 B. P.

(Also see Covington, Friday, Gahagan, Kinney and Sabine)

G10, $450-$800
Coryell Co., TX

IMPORTANT:
All San Gabriels
shown half size

G7, $200-$350
Bell Co., TX

LOCATION: Central Texas. **DESCRIPTION:** A large size, broad blade with a straight to slightly convex base.

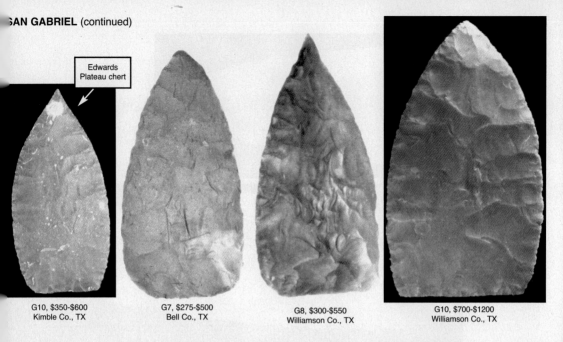

Edwards Plateau chert

G10, $350-$600
Kimble Co., TX

G7, $275-$500
Bell Co., TX

G8, $300-$550
Williamson Co., TX

G10, $700-$1200
Williamson Co., TX

SAN JACINTO - Mid-Archaic, 6000 - 4000 B. P.

(Also see Castroville, Ensor, Marcos and Marshall)

S
C

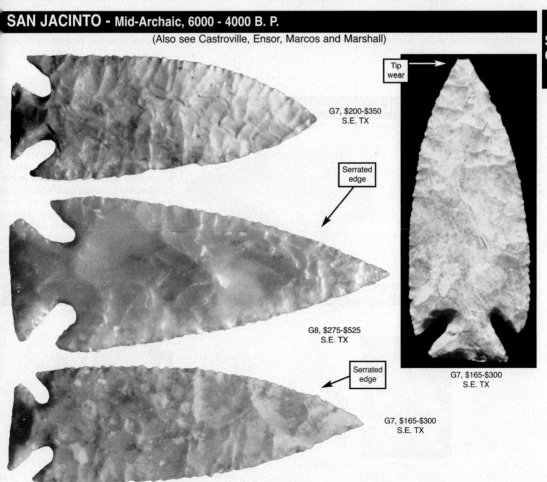

G7, $200-$350
S.E. TX

Serrated edge

Tip wear

Serrated edge

G8, $275-$525
S.E. TX

G7, $165-$300
S.E. TX

G7, $165-$300
S.E. TX

SAN JACINTO (continued)

G9, $350-$600
S.E. TX

G8, $300-$550
S.E. TX

LOCATION: Texas S.E. Gulf Coast and Coastal Plain areas. **DESCRIPTION:** A medium to large size, thin, corner notched knife with a straight base. Notches are deep and angular creating a broad expanding stem. Base width is less than shoulder width. Some examples are finely serrated. **I.D. KEY:** Deep corner notches. Named by Dwain Rogers.

SAN PATRICE-GENEILL - Early Archaic, 10,000 - 8000 B. P.

(Also see Dalton, Palmer, Pelican and Rodgers Side Hollowed)

Red chert

G5, $60-$100
AR

G8, $150-$275
TX

LOCATION: Louisiana to Oklahoma. **DESCRIPTION:** A scarce, small size, thin, stemmed point with a short, expanding concave base that forms small ears. Shoulders can be strong and sharp. Some examples are thinned from the base. Basal area is usually ground. **I.D. KEY:** Extended auriculate base and small size.

SAN PATRICE-HOPE VARIETY - Early Archaic, 10,000 - 8000 B. P.

(Also see Coldwater, Dalton, Hinds, Palmer, Pelican, Rodgers Side Hollowed and Zephyr)

Yellow jasper

Petrified wood

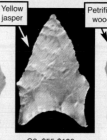

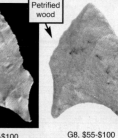

G3, $25-$45
Vernon Ph, LA

G6, $35-$60
San Augustine Co., TX

G6, $40-$70
E. TX

G6, $40-$70
Lufkin, TX

G8, $55-$100
E. TX

G8, $55-$100
E. TX

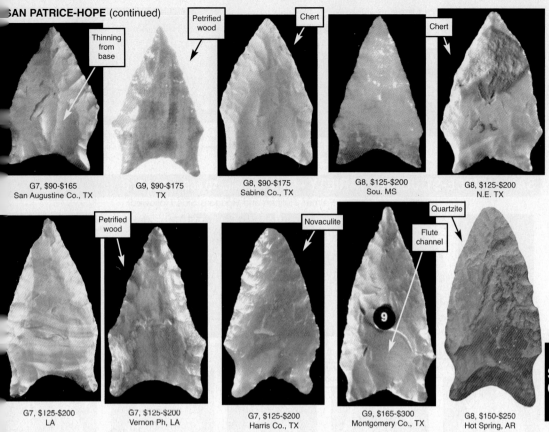

Thinning from base

Petrified wood

Chert

Chert

Petrified wood

Novaculite

Flute channel

Quartzite

9

G7, $90-$165
San Augustine Co., TX

G9, $90-$175
TX

G8, $90-$175
Sabine Co., TX

G8, $125-$200
Sou. MS

G8, $125-$200
N.E. TX

G7, $125-$200
LA

G7, $125-$200
Vernon Ph, LA

G7, $125-$200
Harris Co., TX

G9, $165-$300
Montgomery Co., TX

G8, $150-$250
Hot Spring, AR

LOCATION: Louisiana to Oklahoma. **DESCRIPTION:** A small size, thin, auriculate point with a concave base. Some examples are thinned from the base. Basal area is longer than the "St. Johns" variety and is usually ground. **I.D. KEY:** Extended auriculate base and small size.

SAN PATRICE-KEITHVILLE - Early Archaic, 10,000 - 8000 B. P.

(Also see Albany Knife, Dalton, Palmer, Pelican and Rodgers Side Hollowed)

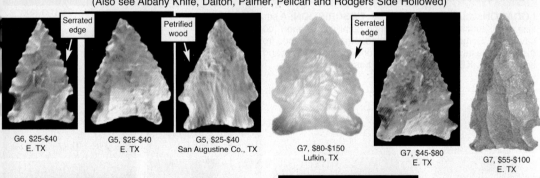

Serrated edge

Petrified wood

Serrated edge

G6, $25-$40
E. TX

G5, $25-$40
E. TX

G5, $25-$40
San Augustine Co., TX

G7, $80-$150
Lufkin, TX

G7, $45-$80
E. TX

G7, $55-$100
E. TX

G6, $50-$90
Lincoln Parish, LA

G7, $90-$175
Lufkin, TX

G6, $40-$75
Val Verde, TX

LOCATION: Louisiana to Oklahoma. **DESCRIPTION:** A small size, thin, auriculate to side notched point forming a lobed base. Basal area is usually ground. Blade edges can be serrated. **I.D. KEY:** Lobbed base.

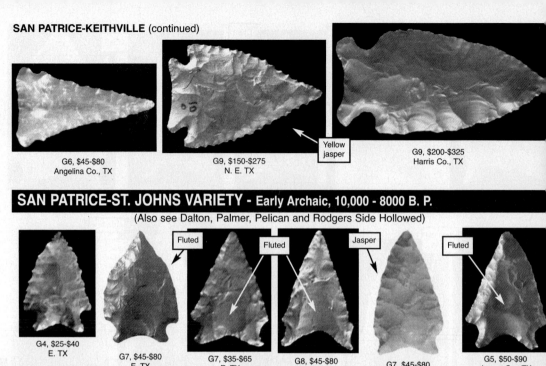

G6, $45-$80
Angelina Co., TX

G9, $150-$275
N. E. TX

Yellow jasper

G9, $200-$325
Harris Co., TX

SAN PATRICE-ST. JOHNS VARIETY - Early Archaic, 10,000 - 8000 B. P.

(Also see Dalton, Palmer, Pelican and Rodgers Side Hollowed)

G4, $25-$40
E. TX

Fluted

G7, $45-$80
E. TX

Fluted

G7, $35-$65
E. TX

G8, $45-$80
E. TX

Jasper

G7, $45-$80
Bowie Co., TX

Fluted

G5, $50-$90
Jasper Co., TX

Fluted

G8, $150-$225
San Augustine Co., TX

Petrified wood

G8 $125-$200
Sabine Parish, LA

Jasper

G7, $80-$150
Sabine Co., TX

G7, $50-$90
Montgomery Co., TX

Chert

G8, $125-$200
S. W. AR

LOCATION: Louisiana to Oklahoma. **DESCRIPTION:** A small size, thin, auriculate to side notched point with a short, concave base. Some examples are fluted, others are thinned from the base. Basal area is usually ground. Blade edges can be serrated. **I.D. KEY:** Short auriculate base and small size.

G7, $125-$200
E. TX

G10, $165-$300
LA

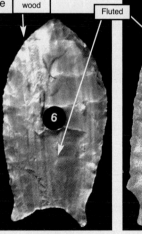

Petrified wood

Fluted

G8, $275-$500
Vernon Parish, LA

Fluted

G10+, $3500-$6000
E. TX

(Also see Base Tang, Corner Tang and Mid-Back Tang)

G6, $150-$250
Coryell Co., TX

Made into
a drill

G9, $450-$850
Austin, TX

G8, $276-$500
TX

Leon
River
chert

S
C

G10, $400-$700
Comanche Co., TX

G8, $250-$400
Cent. TX

LOCATION: Texas. **DESCRIPTION:** A large size, triangular blade with shallow, narrow, basal notches. Bases usually are straight. **I.D. KEY:** Small basal notches.

663

SAVAGE CAVE - Early to Middle Archaic, 7000 - 4000 B. P.

(Also see Big Sandy, Cache River, Hemphill, Hickory Ridge and White River)

G6, $8-$15
Jonesboro, AR

G7, $15-$25
N.E. AR

G3, $3-$6
N.E. AR

LOCATION: Kentucky, Tennessee to Arkansas. **DESCRIPTION:** A medium to large size, broad, side notched poin' that is usually serrated. Bases are generally straight but can be slightly concave or convex.

SAVANNAH RIVER - Middle Archaic to Woodland, 5000 - 2000 B. P.

(Also see Johnson)

G5, $15-$25
Jonesboro, AR

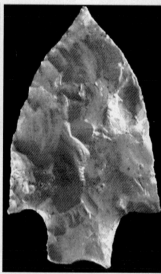

LOCATION: Arkansas to Eastern states. **DESCRIPTION:** A medium to large size, straight to contracting stemmed point with a Straight or concave to bifurcated base. The shoulders are tapered to square. The stems are narrow to broad. Believed to be related to the earlier *Stanly* point. **I.D. KEY:** Broad, concave base.

G5, $12-$20
Jonesboro, AR

G6, $20-$35
Greene, Co., AR

SCALLORN - Woodland to Mississippian, 1300 - 500 B. P.

(Also see Alba, Catahoula, Cuney, Ellis, Homan, Keota, Rockwall, Sequoyah and Steiner)

Tan
chert

G5, $8-$15
Ellis Co., TX

G6, $15-$25
TX

G8, $25-$45
Comanche
Co., TX

G8, $25-$45
AR

G6, $15-$25
Ellis Co., TX

G6, $15-$25
TX

G9, $15-$35
TX

G8, $25-$45
AR

G8, $25-$45
Comanche
Co., TX

LOCATION: Texas, Oklahoma. **DESCRIPTION:** A small size, corner notched arrow point with a flaring stem. Bases and blade edges are straight, concave or convex and many examples are serrated. Not to be confused with *Sequoyah* not found in Texas. **I.D. KEY:** Small corner notched point with sharp barbs and tip.

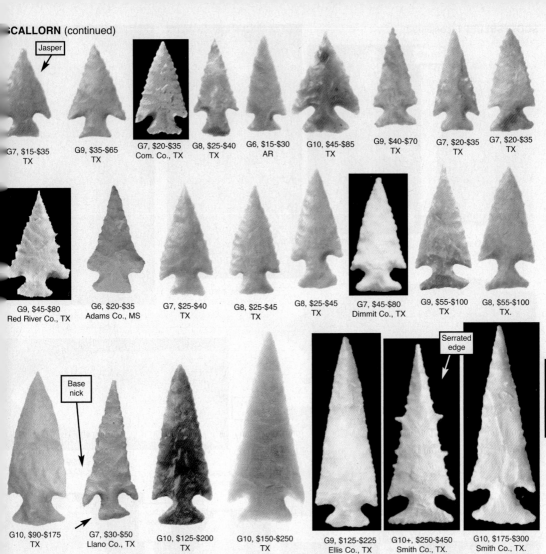

Jasper

G7, $15-$35
TX

G9, $35-$65
TX

G7, $20-$35
Com. Co., TX

G8, $25-$40
TX

G6, $15-$30
AR

G10, $45-$85
TX

G9, $40-$70
TX

G7, $20-$35
TX

G7, $20-$35
TX

G9, $45-$80
Red River Co., TX

G6, $20-$35
Adams Co., MS

G7, $25-$40
TX

G8, $25-$45
TX

G8, $25-$45
TX

G7, $45-$80
Dimmit Co., TX

G9, $55-$100
TX

G8, $55-$100
TX.

Base nick

Serrated edge

G10, $90-$175
TX

G7, $30-$50
Llano Co., TX

G10, $125-$200
TX

G10, $150-$250
TX

G9, $125-$225
Ellis Co., TX

G10+, $250-$450
Smith Co., TX.

G10, $175-$300
Smith Co., TX.

S
C

SCHUSTORM - Mississippian, 1200 - 600 B. P.

(Also see Knight Island, Reed and Washita)

G9, $60-$100
AΠ., Dowman site.

LOCATION: Arkansas into Texas. **DESCRIPTION:** A small size, thin, triangular arrow point with small, weak side notches high up from the base. The base is concave **I.D. KEY:** Weak notches.

SCOTTSBLUFF I - Early Archaic, 10,000 - 8000 B. P.

(Also see Alberta, Cody Knife, Eden, Hardin, Holland and Red River)

LOCATION: Louisiana to New Mexico to Canada and the Northwest coast. **DESCRIPTION:** A medium to large size, broad stemmed point with convex to parallel sides and weak shoulders. The stem is parallel to expanding. The basal area is ground. Most examples have horizontal to oblique parallel flaking and are of high quality and thinness. Made by the Cody Complex people. Believed to have evolved into *Hardin* in later times. **I.D. KEY:** Broad stem, weak shoulders, collateral flaking.

Tip nick

G4, $80-$150
N. E. OK

G6, $125-$200
Leflore Co., OK

G8, $250-$450
Wood Co., TX

G7, $350-$600
Little River Co., AR

G8 $250-$450
Sabine Co., TX

Collateral flaking

G8, $350-$600
Angelina Co., TX

G5, $175-$300
Leflore Co., OK

Collateral flaking

Minor base nick

G8, $450-$800
Wilson Co., TX

G6, $300-$550
Colorado Co., TX

G6, $275-$500
Cass Co., TX

G7, $400-$700
Angelina Co., TX

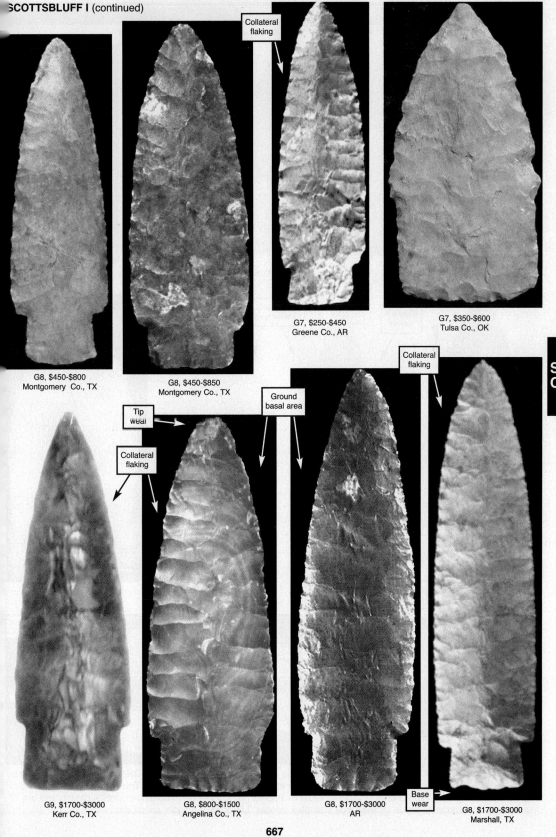

Collateral flaking

G7, $250-$450
Greene Co., AR

G7, $350-$600
Tulsa Co., OK

S
C

G8, $450-$800
Montgomery Co., TX

G8, $450-$850
Montgomery Co., TX

Ground basal area

Collateral flaking

Tip wear

Collateral flaking

Base wear

G9, $1700-$3000
Kerr Co., TX

G8, $800-$1500
Angelina Co., TX

G8, $1700-$3000
AR

G8, $1700-$3000
Marshall, TX

(Also see Alberta, Cody Knife, Eden, Hardin, Holland and Red River)

Quartzite

G5, $55-$100
Cass Co., TX

G3, $40-$75
N. E. OK

G4, $65-$125
Athens, TX

G4, $45-$85
Osage Co., OK

G8, $200-$350
Montgomery Co., TX

Collateral flaking

Ground basal area

Basal corner wear

G8, $500-$900
Osage Co., OK

Ground basal area

G6, $150-$275
Haskle Co., OK

G6, $150-$250
Angelina Co., TX

G4, $175-$300
Angelina Co., TX

G7, $200-$350
Cent. TX

G8, $450-$800
AR

Collateral flaking

LOCATION: Louisiana to New Mexico to Canada to the Northwest coast. **DESCRIPTION:** A medium to large size, broad stemmed point with convex to parallel sides and stronger shoulders than type I. The stem is parallel sided to slightly expanding. The hafting area is ground. Most examples have horizontal to oblique parallel flaking and are of high quality and thinness. Made by the Cody Complex people. **I.D. KEY:** Stronger shoulders.

Tip wear

Edge wear

G8, $500-$900
Angelina Co., TX

G9, $1000-$1800
N. Cent. AR

G7, $650-$1200
Harris Co., TX

G6, $350-$600
N. E. OK

S
C

SCRAPER - Paleo to Archaic, 11,500 - 5000 B. P.

(Also see Drill, Graver, Perforator and Paleo Knife)

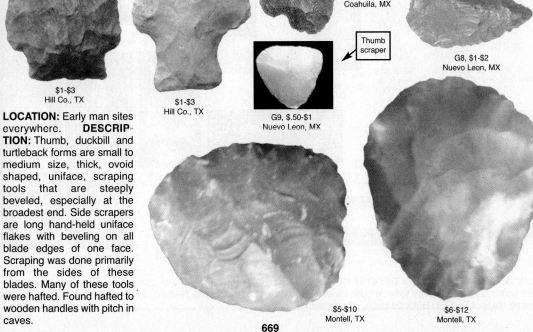

Hafted

Thumb scraper

G8, $1-$2
Coahuila, MX

Thumb scraper

G8, $1-$2
Nuevo Leon, MX

$1-$3
Hill Co., TX

$1-$3
Hill Co., TX

G9, $.50-$1
Nuevo Leon, MX

LOCATION: Early man sites everywhere. **DESCRIPTION:** Thumb, duckbill and turtleback forms are small to medium size, thick, ovoid shaped, uniface, scraping tools that are steeply beveled, especially at the broadest end. Side scrapers are long hand-held uniface flakes with beveling on all blade edges of one face. Scraping was done primarily from the sides of these blades. Many of these tools were hafted. Found hafted to wooden handles with pitch in caves.

$5-$10
Montell, TX

$6-$12
Montell, TX

SEARCY - Early to Middle Archaic, 7000 - 5000 B. P.

(Also see Coryell, Dalton, Early Stemmed, Hoxie, Rio Grande, Victoria & Wells)

Classic example from type county

G7, $50-$90
Searcy Co., AR

Classic example

G8, $80-$150
Morris Co., TX

G8, $80-$150
AR

Classic example

G10, $150-$250
Benton Co., AR

G9, $80-$150
Type site, Searcy Co. AR, Calf Creek Cave.

LOCATION: Texas, Oklahoma to Missouri to Tennessee. **DESCRIPTION:** A small to medium size, thin, lanceolate point with a squared hafting area. Blade edges are serrated. The base is straight to concave and is usually ground. **I.D. KEY:** Long squared stem, serrations.

SEQUOYAH - Mississippian, 1000 - 600 B. P.

(Also see Alba, Blevins, Hayes, Homan, Livermore, Scallorn and Steiner)

G5, $8-$15
Red River Co., TX

G5, $8-$15
Red River Co., TX

G5, $8-$15
Red River Co., TX

G6, $12-$20
Spiro Mound, OK

G6, $15-$25
Red River Co., TX

G9, $55-$100
Spiro Mound, OK

Serrated edge

Serrated edge

G8, $30-$50
Red River Co., TX

Black flint

G9, $45-$80
Spiro Mound, OK

G9, $35-$65
LeFlore Co., OK

G7, $25-$40
Saline Co., AR

G9, $80-$150
Spiro Mound, OK

G8, $30-$50
AR

Serrated edge

G9, $125-$200
LeFlore Co., OK

G8, $165-$300
Spiro Mound, OK

LOCATION: IL, OK, AR, MO. **DESCRIPTION:** A small size, thin, narrow point with coarse serrations and an expanded, bulbous stem. Believed to have been made by Caddo and other people. Named after the famous Cherokee of the same name. **I.D. KEY:** Bulbous base, coarse serrations.

SHUMLA - Woodland, 3000 - 1000 B. P.

(Also see Bell, Calf Creek, Marshall and Rockwall)

G6, $15-$25
Starr Co., TX

G7, $25-$50
TX

G8, $65-$125
TX

G9, $80-$150
Caedereyta, MX

Serrated edge

G10, $150-$250
Austin, TX

G8, $80-$150
MX

G9, $125-$200
TX

G10, $150-$275
Zapata Co., TX

G10, $150-$275
Zapata Co., TX

LOCATION: Texas to Oklahoma. **DESCRIPTION:** A small size, basal notched point with convex, straight or recurved sides. Barbs turn in towards and usually extend to the base.

SINNER - Woodland, 3000 - 2000 B. P.

(Also see Charcos, Duran, Evans and Huffaker)

G3, $1-$3
Lincoln Parrish, LA

G4, $3-$6
LA

G5, $8-$15
Lincoln Parish, LA

G6, $12-$20
Lincoln Parrish, LA

G5, $5-$10
Lincoln Parrish, LA

G5, $5-$10
Lincoln Parrish, LA

G8, $20-$35
TX

G5, $8-$15
Lincoln Parrish, LA

G8, $15-$25
Maverick Co., TX

LOCATION: Louisianna to Texas. **DESCRIPTION:** A medium size, expanded stemmed point with several barbs occurring above the shoulders. **I.D. KEY:** Barbed edges.

SMITH - Late Archaic, 4000 - 3000 B. P.

(Also see Bell, Castroville, Calf Creek, Little River, San Saba, Shumla)

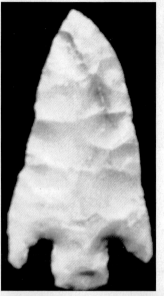

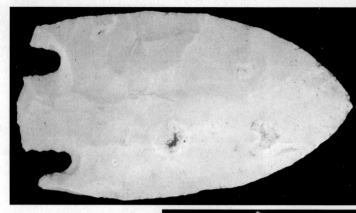

G8, $150-$250
Saline Co., AR

G5, $25-$40
Saline Co., AR

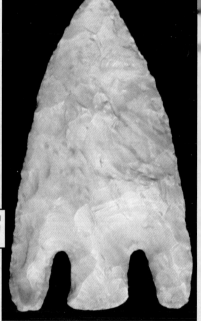

Unusual notched ears

LOCATION: Arkansas into Missouri and Illinois.
DESCRIPTION: A very large size, broad, point with long parallel shoulders and a squared to slightly expanding base. Some examples may appear to be basally notched due to the long barbs.

G7, $250-$400
N. E. OK

G9, $200-$350
S. W. AR

SPOKESHAVE - Woodland, 3000 -1500 B. P.

(Also see Scraper)

LOCATION: Tennessee, Kentucky, Ohio, Indiana into Texas. **DESCRIPTION:** A medium to large size stemmed tool used for scraping. The blade is asymmetrical with one edge convex or notched and the other concave.

G10, $55-$100
TX

SQUARE-END KNIFE (See Round-End Knife)

672

STARR - Mississippian to Historic, 1000 - 250 B. P.

(Also see Maud and Talco)

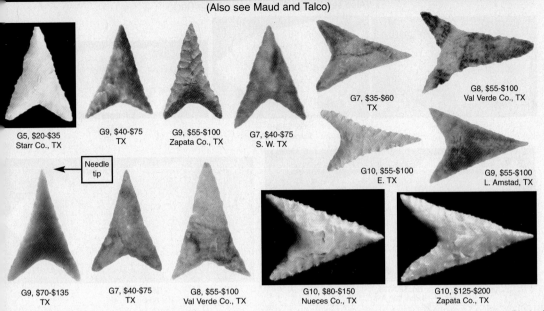

G5, $20-$35
Starr Co., TX

G9, $40-$75
TX

G9, $55-$100
Zapata Co., TX

G7, $40-$75
S. W. TX

G7, $35-$60
TX

G8, $55-$100
Val Verde Co., TX

G10, $55-$100
E. TX

G9, $55-$100
L. Amstad, TX

Needle tip

G9, $70-$135
TX

G7, $40-$75
TX

G8, $55-$100
Val Verde Co., TX

G10, $80-$150
Nueces Co., TX

G10, $125-$200
Zapata Co., TX

LOCATION: Texas westward. **DESCRIPTION:** A small size, thin, triangular point with a "V" base concavity. Blade edges can be concave to straight. An eccentric form of Starr is call "New Form" found near the Mexican border. **I.D. KEY:** "V" base.

S
C

STEINER - Mississippian, 1000 - 400 B. P.

(Also see Friley, Scallorn and Sequoyah)

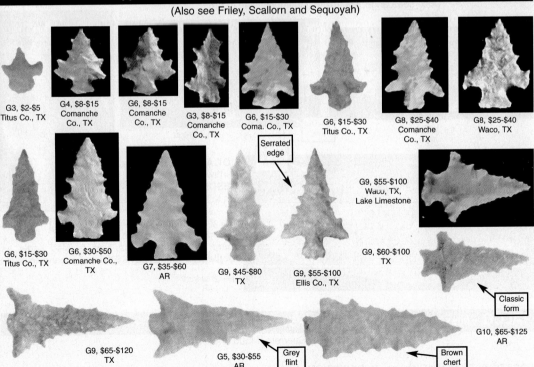

G3, $2-$5
Titus Co., TX

G4, $8-$15
Comanche Co., TX

G6, $8-$15
Comanche Co., TX

G3, $8-$15
Comanche Co., TX

G6, $15-$30
Coma. Co., TX

G6, $15-$30
Titus Co., TX

G8, $25-$40
Comanche Co., TX

G8, $25-$40
Waco, TX

Serrated edge

G9, $55-$100
Waco, TX,
Lake Limestone

G6, $15-$30
Titus Co., TX

G6, $30-$50
Comanche Co., TX

G7, $35-$60
AR

G9, $45-$80
TX

G9, $55-$100
Ellis Co., TX

G9, $60-$100
TX

Classic form

G9, $65-$120
TX

G5, $30-$55
AR

Grey flint

Brown chert

G10, $65-$125
AR

LOCATION: Mexico, E. Texas into Arkansas. **DESCRIPTION:** A small to medium size, thin, barbed arrow point with strong shoulders. The stem is short and may be horizontal or expanded to bifurcated. Believed to be related to the *Friley* point. **I.D. KEY:** Strong barbs.

673

STEUBEN - Woodland, 2000 - 1000 B. P.

(Also see Lange, Palmillas and Table Rock)

G4, $4-$8
Saline Co., AR

G5, $5-$10
Saline Co., AR

G7, $12-$20
AR

G6, $20-$35
Saline Co., AR

G6, $20-$35
Hot Spring Co., AR

LOCATION: Arkansas to Illinois. **DESCRIPTION:** A medium to large size, narrow, expanded stem point. shoulders can be tapered to straight. The base is straight to convex. This type is very similar to *Bakers Creek* in the Southeast.

TABLE ROCK - Late Archaic, 4000 - 3000 B. P.

(Also see Lange, Matanzas, Motley and Steuben)

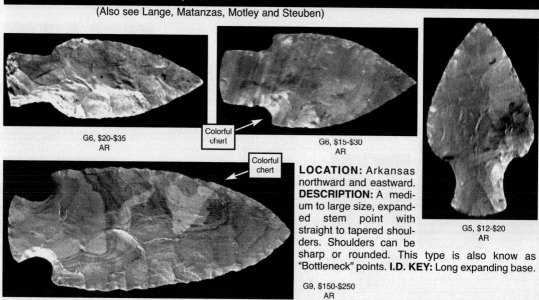

G6, $20-$35
AR

Colorful chert

G6, $15-$30
AR

Colorful chert

G5, $12-$20
AR

LOCATION: Arkansas northward and eastward. **DESCRIPTION:** A medium to large size, expanded stem point with straight to tapered shoulders. Shoulders can be sharp or rounded. This type is also know as "Bottleneck" points. **I.D. KEY:** Long expanding base.

G9, $150-$250
AR

TALCO - Mississippian to Historic, 800 - 500 B. P.

(Also see Guerrero, Maud and Starr)

LOCATION: Texas to Oklahoma. **DESCRIPTION:** A small to medium size, thin, narrow, triangular arrow point with recurved sides and a concave base. Blade edges are very finely serrated. On classic examples, tips are more angled than *Maud*. Tips and corners are sharp. This type is found on Caddo and related sites. **I.D. KEY:** Angled tip.

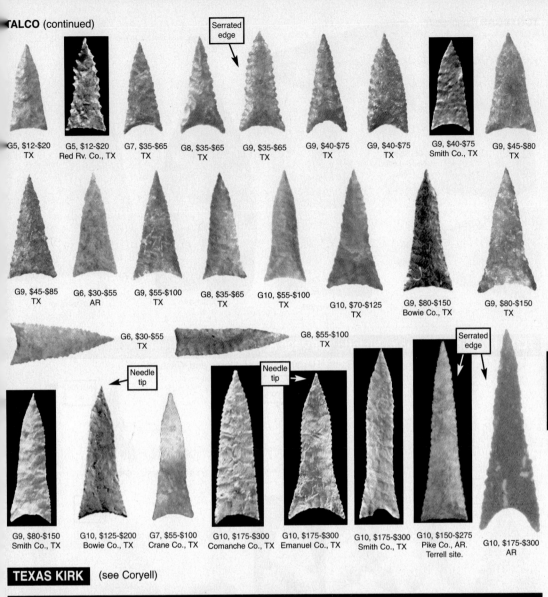

Serrated edge

G5, $12-$20
TX

G5, $12-$20
Red Rv. Co., TX

G7, $35-$65
TX

G8, $35-$65
TX

G9, $35-$65
TX

G9, $40-$75
TX

G9, $40-$75
TX

G9, $40-$75
Smith Co., TX

G9, $45-$80
TX

G9, $45-$85
TX

G6, $30-$55
AR

G9, $55-$100
TX

G8, $35-$65
TX

G10, $55-$100
TX

G10, $70-$125
TX

G9, $80-$150
Bowie Co., TX

G9, $80-$150
TX

G6, $30-$55
TX

G8, $55-$100
TX

Serrated edge

S C

Needle tip

Needle tip

G9, $80-$150
Smith Co., TX

G10, $125-$200
Bowie Co., TX

G7, $55-$100
Crane Co., TX

G10, $175-$300
Comanche Co., TX

G10, $175-$300
Emanuel Co., TX

G10, $175-$300
Smith Co., TX

G10, $150-$275
Pike Co., AR.
Terrell site.

G10, $175-$300
AR

TEXAS KIRK (see Coryell)

TORTUGAS - Middle Archaic to Woodland, 6000 - 1000 B. P.

(Also see Kinney, Early Triangular and Matamoros)

G4, $1-$3
Starr Co., TX

G5, $2-$4
Nuevo Leon, MX

G7, $8-$15
TX

G6, $5-$10
Zapata Co., TX

Petrified wood

G6, $6-$12
Zapata Co., TX

LOCATION: Oklahoma to Tennessee. **DESCRIPTION:** A medium size, fairly thick, triangular point with straight to convex sides and base. Some examples are beveled on one side of each face. Bases are usually thinned. Smaller examples would fall in the *Matamoros* type.

675

TORTUGAS (continued)

G8, $15-$25
S. TX

G6, $8-$15
Nuevo Leon,
MX

G7, $8-$15
Zapata Co., TX

G8, $15-$25
TX

G7, $25-$40
S. W. TX

G9, $50-$90
S. TX

TOYAH - Mississippian to Historic, 600 - 400 B. P.

(Also see Garza, Harrell, Huffaker, Morris and Washita)

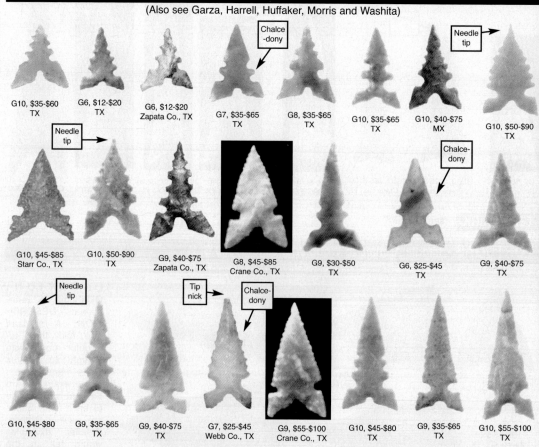

G10, $35-$60
TX

G6, $12-$20
TX

G6, $12-$20
Zapata Co., TX

Chalce
-dony

G7, $35-$65
TX

G8, $35-$65
TX

G10, $35-$65
TX

Needle tip

G10, $40-$75
MX

G10, $50-$90
TX

Needle
tip

G10, $45-$85
Starr Co., TX

G10, $50-$90
TX

G9, $40-$75
Zapata Co., TX

G8, $45-$85
Crane Co., TX

G9, $30-$50
TX

Chalce-
dony

G6, $25-$45
TX

G9, $40-$75
TX

Needle
tip

G10, $45-$80
TX

G9, $35-$65
TX

G9, $40-$75
TX

Tip
nick

G7, $25-$45
Webb Co., TX

Chalce-
dony

G9, $55-$100
Crane Co., TX

G10, $45-$80
TX

G9, $35-$65
TX

G10, $55-$100
TX

LOCATION: Northern Mexico to Texas. **DESCRIPTION:** A small size, thin, triangular point with expanded barbs and one or more notches on each side and a basal notch. **I.D. KEY:** Has drooping, pointed barbs.

TRADE POINTS - Historic, 400 - 170 B. P.

IMPORTANT: All Trades shown half size

Iron

Notched base

G8, $45-$80
W. TX

G8, $65-$125
TX Panhandle

G8, $80-$150
Colorado City, TX

G8, $90-$175
Mitchell Co., TX

LOCATION: All of North America. **DESCRIPTION:** These points were made of copper, iron and steel and were traded to the Indians by the French, British and others from the 1600s to the 1800s.

TRAVIS - Middle-Archaic to Woodland, 5500 - 1000 B. P.

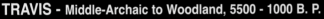

(Also see Darl, Gary, Kent, Lange, Nolan and Pandale)

S C

G6, $5-$10
Coryell Co., TX

G8, $12-$20
Comal Co., TX

G6, $8-$15
Hill Co., TX

G6, $8-$15
Austin, TX

G6, $12-$20
Hill Co., TX

G6, $15-$30
Comal Co., TX

G9, $25-$45
TX

Side wear

G6, $25-$45
TX

G8, $35-$65
Comanche Co., TX

G7, $25-$45
Cent. TX

LOCATION: Texas to Oklahoma. **DESCRIPTION:** A small to medium size, narrow point with weak, tapered shoulders and a parallel sided to expanded or contracting stem. The base is straight to convex. Some examples have sharp needle-like tips. **I.D. KEY:** Weak, tapered shoulders.

677

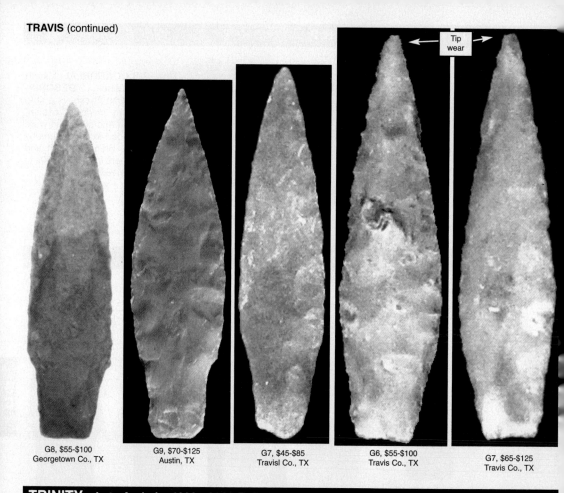

Tip wear

G8, $55-$100
Georgetown Co., TX

G9, $70-$125
Austin, TX

G7, $45-$85
Travisl Co., TX

G6, $55-$100
Travis Co., TX

G7, $65-$125
Travis Co., TX

TRINITY - Late Archaic, 4000 - 2000 B. P.

(Also see Ellis, Godley and Travis)

G6, $5-$10
Van Zandt Co., TX

G4, $1-$2
Comanche Co., TX

G4, $1-$3
Waco, TX

G4, $5-$10
Hopkins Co., TX

G7, $12-$20
Waco, TX

G7, $12-$20
Van Zandt Co.,
TX

G7, $8-$15
Comanche Co., TX

G7, $5-$10
Hopkins Co., TX

LOCATION: Texas to Oklahoma. **DESCRIPTION:** A small to medium size point with broad side notches, weak shoulders and a broad convex base which is usually ground.

TURNER - Mississippian, 1000 - 800 B. P.

(Also see Alba, Blevins, Hayes, Homan, Howard, Perdiz and Sequoyah)

G9, $125-$200
AR

Incup tip

G8, $80-$150
TX

Incup tip

Incup tip

G9, $150-$250
AR

LOCATION: Louisiana to Oklahoma. **DESCRIPTION:** Related to *Hayes* points and is a later variety. A small size, narrow, expanded barb arrow point with a turkeytail base. The tip is inset about 1/4th the distance. Blade edges are usually incurved forming sharp, "squarish" pointed barbs. Base is pointed and can be double notched. Some examples are serrated. Has been found in caches. **I.D. KEY:** Diamond shaped base and flaking style.

UVALDE - Middle Archaic to Woodland, 6000 - 1500 B. P.

(Also see Frio, Hoxie, Langtry, Pedernales, Rice Lobbed and Val Verde)

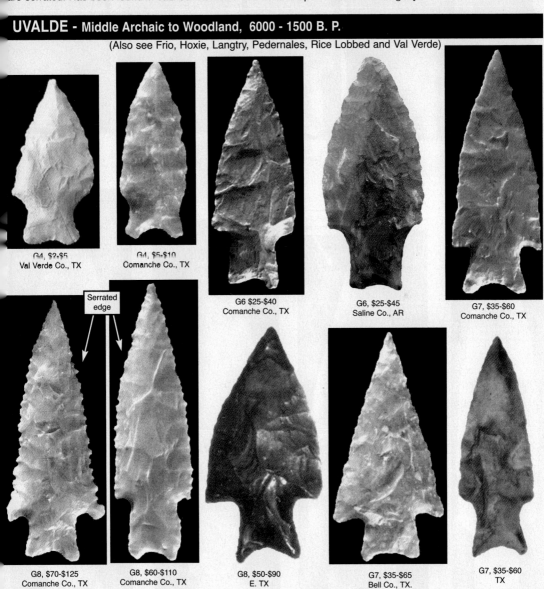

G4, $2-$5
Val Verde Co., TX

G4, $5-$10
Comanche Co., TX

G6 $25-$40
Comanche Co., TX

G6, $25-$45
Saline Co., AR

G7, $35-$60
Comanche Co., TX

Serrated edge

G8, $70-$125
Comanche Co., TX

G8, $60-$110
Comanche Co., TX

G8, $50-$90
E. TX

G7, $35-$65
Bell Co., TX.

G7, $35-$60
TX

LOCATION: Texas to Oklahoma. **DESCRIPTION:** A medium size, bifurcated stemmed point with barbed to tapered shoulders. Some examples are serrated. The *Frio* point is similar but is usually broader and the ears flare outward more than this type. **I.D. KEY:** Narrow bifurcated stem.

G7, $80-$150
Bell Co., TX

G6, $35-$65
Saline Co., AR

G8, $70-$125
Comanche Co., TX

G7, $50-$90
Llano Co., TX

G7, $50-$90
Comanche Co., TX

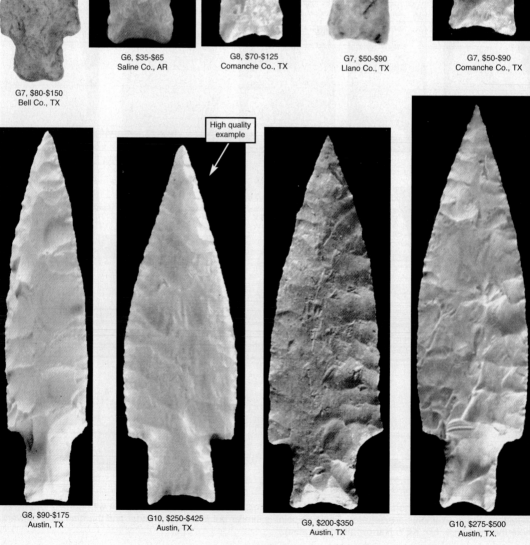

High quality
example

G8, $90-$175
Austin, TX

G10, $250-$425
Austin, TX.

G9, $200-$350
Austin, TX

G10, $275-$500
Austin, TX.

(Also see Langtry, Pedernales and Uvalde)

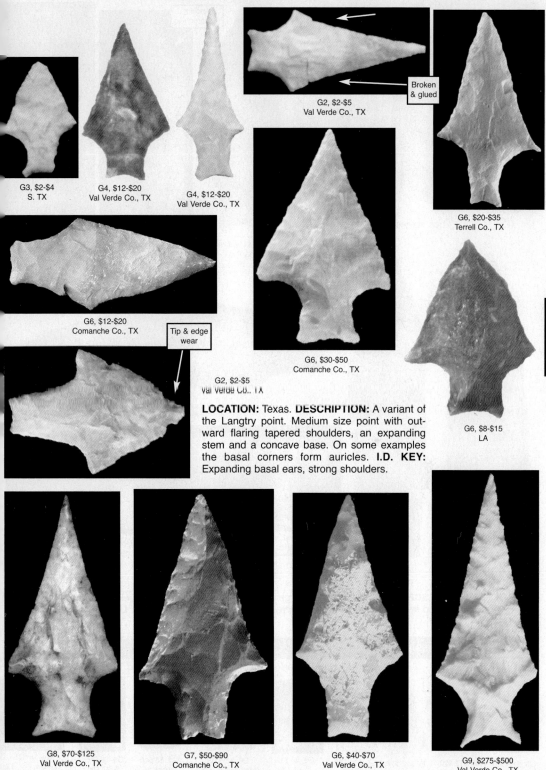

G3, $2-$4
S. TX

G4, $12-$20
Val Verde Co., TX

G4, $12-$20
Val Verde Co., TX

G2, $2-$5
Val Verde Co., TX

Broken & glued

G6, $20-$35
Terrell Co., TX

G6, $12-$20
Comanche Co., TX

Tip & edge wear

G6, $30-$50
Comanche Co., TX

G2, $2-$5
Val Verde Co., TX

G6, $8-$15
LA

LOCATION: Texas. **DESCRIPTION:** A variant of the Langtry point. Medium size point with outward flaring tapered shoulders, an expanding stem and a concave base. On some examples the basal corners form auricles. **I.D. KEY:** Expanding basal ears, strong shoulders.

S C

G8, $70-$125
Val Verde Co., TX

G7, $50-$90
Comanche Co., TX

G6, $40-$70
Val Verde Co., TX

G9, $275-$500
Val Verde Co., TX

VICTORIA - Early Archaic, 8000 - 6000 B. P.

(Also see Angostura, Early Stemmed Lanceolate, Hell Gap, Rio Grande and Searcy)

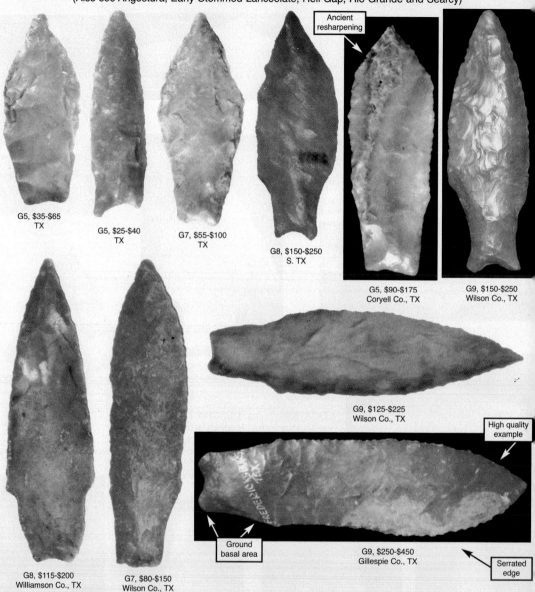

G5, $35-$65
TX

G5, $25-$40
TX

G7, $55-$100
TX

G8, $150-$250
S. TX

Ancient resharpening

G5, $90-$175
Coryell Co., TX

G9, $150-$250
Wilson Co., TX

G9, $125-$225
Wilson Co., TX

High quality example

G8, $115-$200
Williamson Co., TX

G7, $80-$150
Wilson Co., TX

Ground basal area

G9, $250-$450
Gillespie Co., TX

Serrated edge

LOCATION: Texas. **DESCRIPTION:** A medium to large size, narrow, lanceolate blade with an incurvate base. The hafting area is separated from the blade by weak, tapered shoulders. Bases are ground. **I.D. KEY:** Base form.

WASHITA - Mississippian, 800 - 400 B. P.

(Also see Harrell, Haskell, Keota, Reed, Schustorm and Toyah)

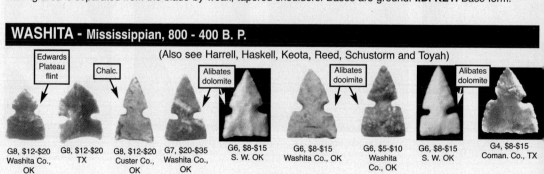

Edwards Plateau flint

Chalc.

Alibates dolomite

Alibates dooimite

Alibates dolomite

G8, $12-$20
Washita Co., OK

G8, $12-$20
TX

G8, $12-$20
Custer Co., OK

G7, $20-$35
Washita Co., OK

G6, $8-$15
S. W. OK

G6, $8-$15
Washita Co., OK

G6, $5-$10
Washita Co., OK

G6, $8-$15
S. W. OK

G4, $8-$15
Coman. Co., TX

VASHITA (continued)

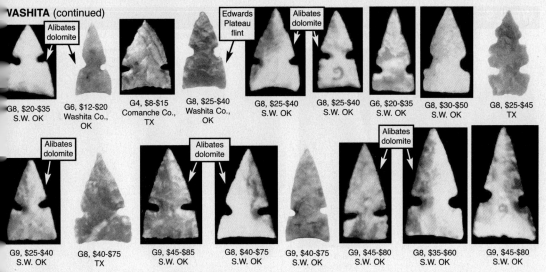

G8, $20-$35 S.W. OK — Alibates dolomite

G6, $12-$20 Washita Co., OK

G4, $8-$15 Comanche Co., TX

G8, $25-$40 Washita Co., OK — Edwards Plateau flint

G8, $25-$40 S.W. OK — Alibates dolomite

G8, $25-$40 S.W. OK

G6, $20-$35 S.W. OK

G8, $30-$50 S.W. OK

G8, $25-$45 TX

G9, $25-$40 S.W. OK — Alibates dolomite

G8, $40-$75 TX

G9, $45-$85 S.W. OK — Alibates dolomite

G8, $40-$75 S.W. OK

G9, $40-$75 S.W. OK

G9, $45-$80 S.W. OK — Alibates dolomite

G8, $35-$60 S.W. OK

G9, $45-$80 S.W. OK

LOCATION: Texas to Oklahoma. **DESCRIPTION:** A small size, thin, triangular side notched arrow point with a con-cave to straight base. Basal area is usually large in proportion to the blade size. Similar forms occur in the Southwest and Plains states under different names. Concave base forms are called "Peno." **I.D. KEY:** Small triangle with side notches high up from base.

WASHITA-PENO - Mississippian, 800 - 400 B. P.

(Also see Harrell, Keota, Reed and Toyah)

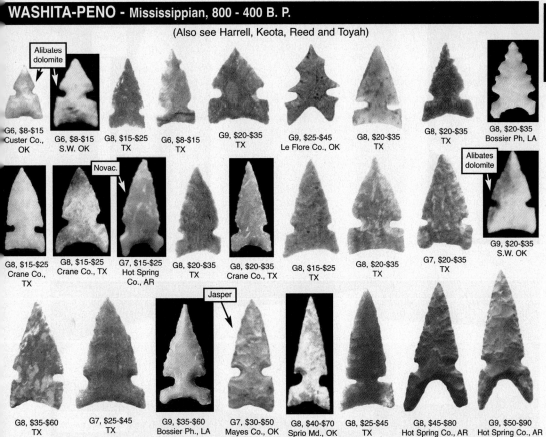

G6, $8-$15 Custer Co., OK — Alibates dolomite

G6, $8-$15 S.W. OK

G8, $15-$25 TX

G6, $8-$15 TX

G9, $20-$35 TX

G9, $25-$45 Le Flore Co., OK

G8, $20-$35 TX

G8, $20-$35 TX

G8, $20-$35 Bossier Ph, LA

G8, $15-$25 Crane Co., TX

G8, $15-$25 Crane Co., TX — Novac.

G7, $15-$25 Hot Spring Co., AR

G8, $20-$35 TX

G8, $20-$35 Crane Co., TX

G8, $15-$25 TX

G8, $20-$35 TX

G7, $20-$35 TX

G9, $20-$35 S.W. OK — Alibates dolomite

G8, $35-$60 TX

G7, $25-$45 TX

G9, $35-$60 Bossier Ph., LA — Jasper

G7, $30-$50 Mayes Co., OK

G8, $40-$70 Sprio Md., OK

G8, $25-$45 TX

G8, $45-$80 Hot Spring Co., AR

G9, $50-$90 Hot Spring Co., AR

LOCATION: Texas to Oklahoma. **DESCRIPTION:** A variant form with side notches one third to one half the distance up from the base and the base is concave to eared. Basal concavity can be slight to very deep. **I.D. KEY:** Base form and notch placement.

(Also see Adena, Bulverde, Carrolton, Coryell, Dawson & Searcy)

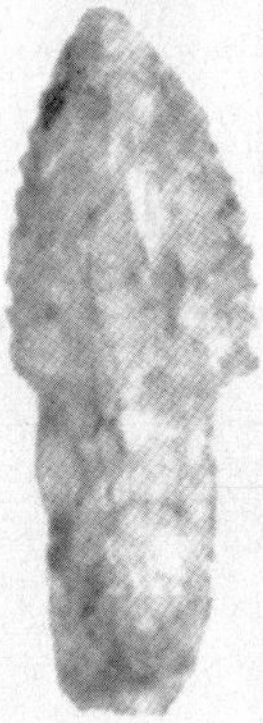

G4, $8-$15
Comanche Co., TX

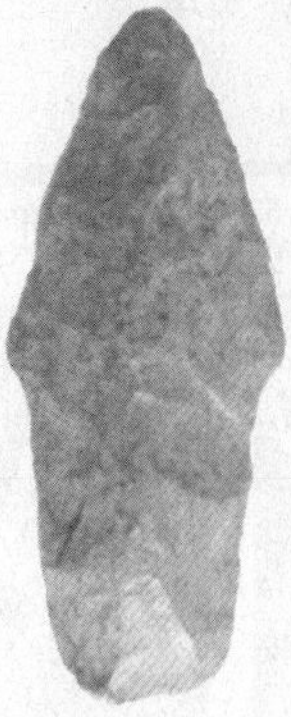

G5, $8-$15
Hill Co., TX

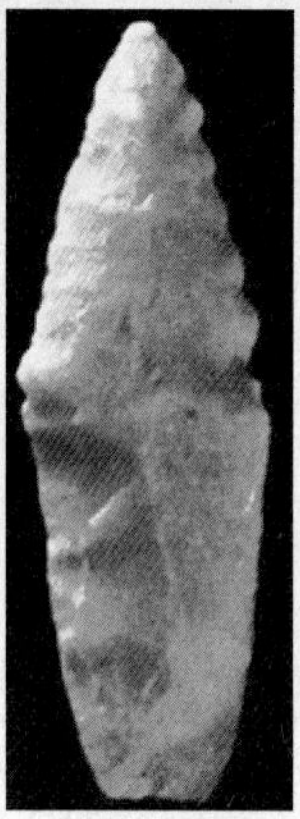

G5, $12-$20
Comanche, TX

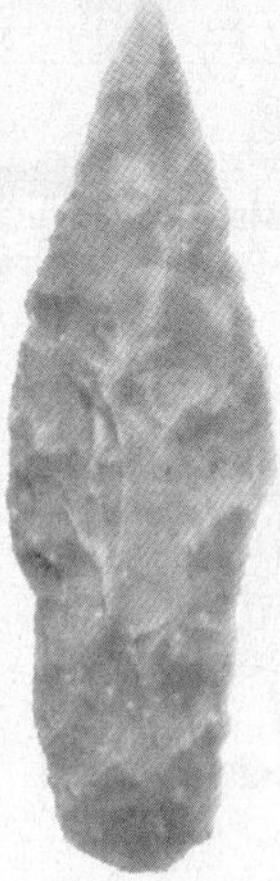

G7, $15-$30
TX

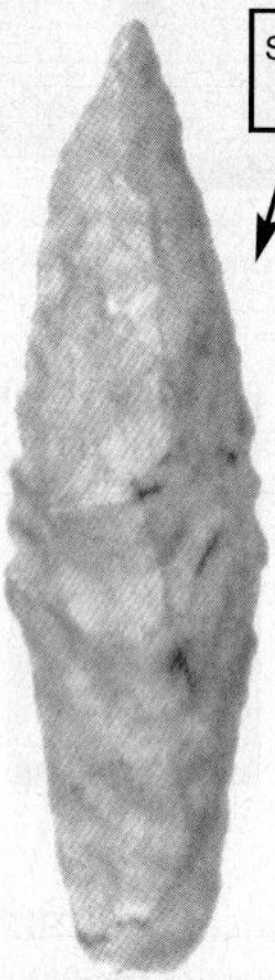

Serrated edge

G7, $30-$50
Austin, TX

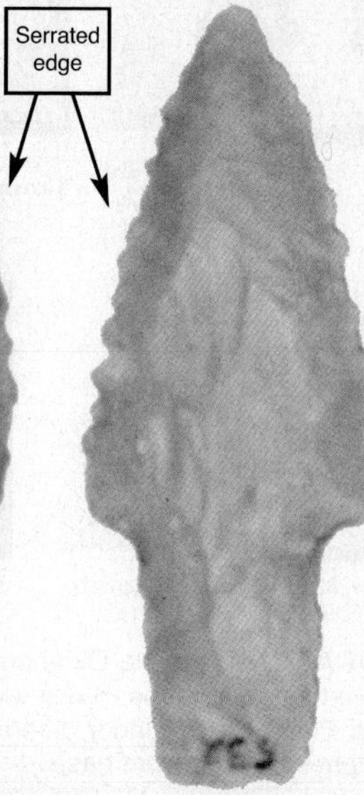

G8, $65-$125
Bell Co., TX

Serrated edge

G8, $45-$85
Bell Co., TX

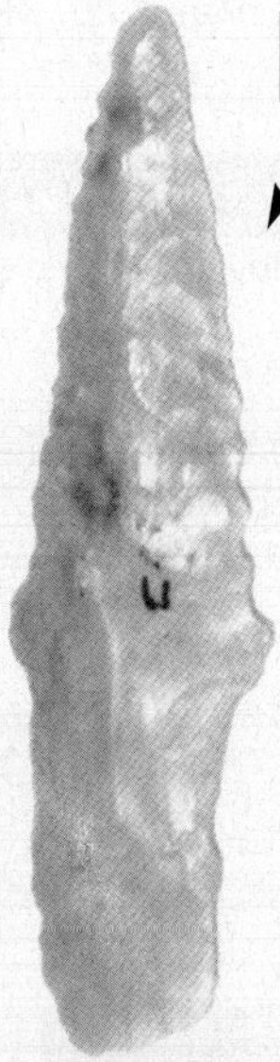

G7, $30-$50
Travis Co., TX

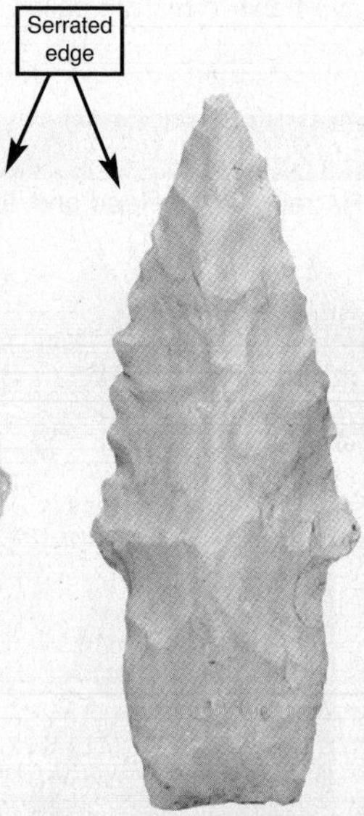

G7, $30-$50
Cent. TX

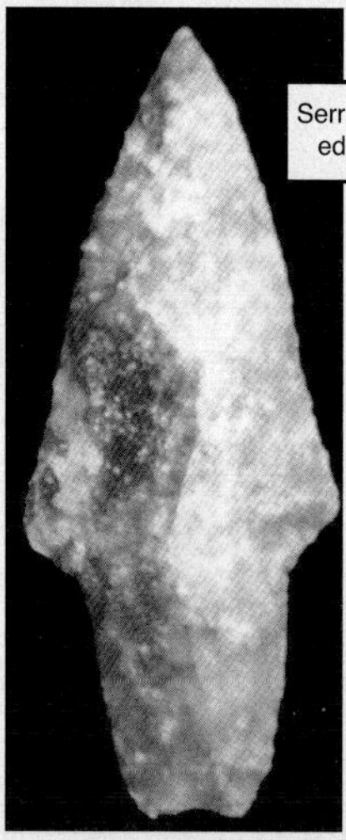

G7, $35-$00
Llano Co., TX

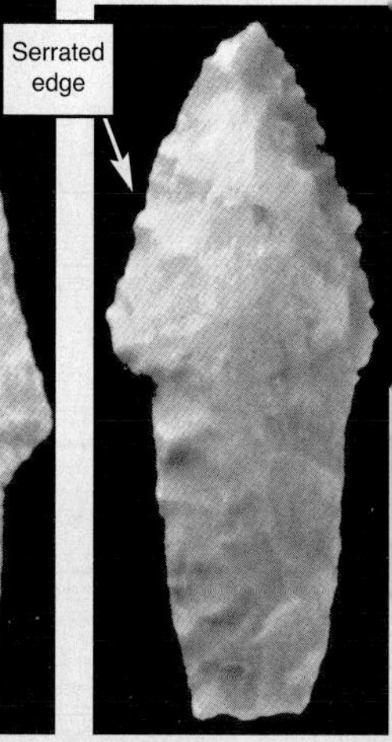

Serrated edge

G0, $30-$50
Comanche Co., TX

G9, $350-$650
Comanche Co., TX

LOCATION: Eastern Texas and Oklahoma. **DESCRIPTION:** A medium to large size, thin, usually serrated point with a long, narrow, contracting to parallel stem that has a rounded to straight base. Shoulders are weak and can be tapered, horizontal or barbed. **I.D. KEY:** Basal form, extended and squared up. Early flaking style.

Basalt

G7, $40-$75
Titus Co., TX

G7, $80-$150
Bell Co., TX

G6, $45-$85
Saline Co., AR

G7, $80-$150
Comanche Co., TX

G7, $80-$150
Williamson Co., TX

S
C

WHITE RIVER - Middle Archaic to Woodland, 6000 - 1000 B. P.

(Also see Big Sandy and Hickory Ridge)

Beveled
edge

Beveled
edge

G7, $35-$65
AR

G8, $40-$75
AR

LOCATION: Arkansas, Missouri. **DESCRIPTION:** A medium to large size, narrow, side notched point with a straight to concave base. Blade edges are beveled and serrated. Ground base and notches. **I. D. KEY:** *Graham Cave* style points with a beveled edge.

G8, $125-$200
AR

G8, $150-$250
Greene Co., AR

(Also see Axtel, Castroville, Marcos, Marshall, Palmillas and Shumla)

LOCATION: Texas to Oklahoma. **DESCRIPTION:** A medium to large size, corner notched, point with an expanded, rounded base. Shoulders are barbed and extend downwards. Resharpened examples can have tapered shoulders. **I.D. KEY:** Base form, barbs.

G8, $12-$20
TX

G8, $20-$35
Comanche Co., TX

G8, $25-$45
Tulsa Co., OK

G8, $35-$60
Belton, TX

G8, $30-$50
N. OK

G8, $80-$150
TX

Black chert

G9, $70-$135
Lampasas, TX

G9, $70-$135
Bell Co., TX

G7, $125-$200
Austin, TX

G9, $175-$300
Georgetown Co., TX

Black chert

G6, $35-$65
Comanche Co., TX

G8, $40-$75
TX

G6 $15-$25
Coryell Co., TX

G9, $175-$300
Travis Co., TX

YARBROUGH - Woodland, 2500 - 1000 B. P.

(Also see Darl, Hoxie, Lange, Travis and Zorra)

S
C

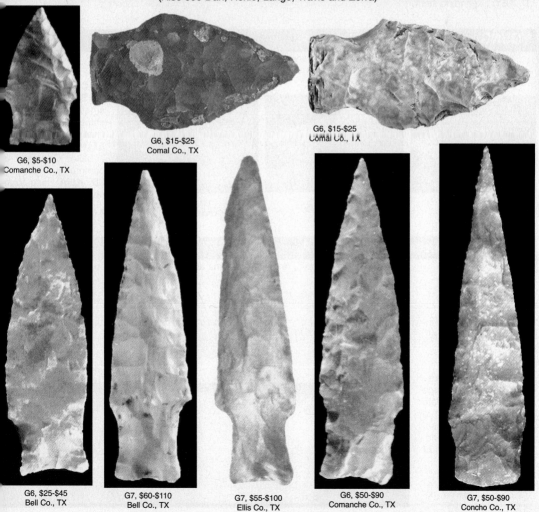

G6, $15-$25
Comal Co., TX

G6, $15-$25
Comal Co., TX

G6, $5-$10
Comanche Co., TX

G6, $25-$45
Bell Co., TX

G7, $60-$110
Bell Co., TX

G7, $55-$100
Ellis Co., TX

G6, $50-$90
Comanche Co., TX

G7, $50-$90
Concho Co., TX

YARBROUGH (continued)

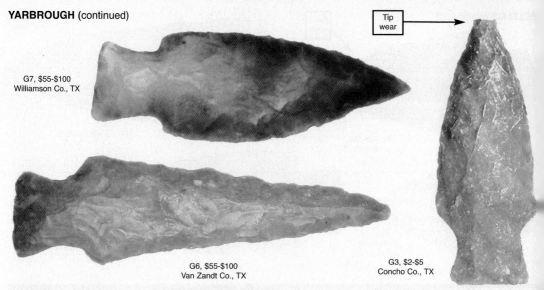

Tip wear

G7, $55-$100
Williamson Co., TX

G6, $55-$100
Van Zandt Co., TX

G3, $2-$5
Concho Co., TX

LOCATION: Texas to Oklahoma. **DESCRIPTION:** A medium size, narrow point with a long, expanding, rectangula stem that has slightly concave sides. The shoulders are very weak and tapered. The stem edges are usually ground **I.D. KEY:** Expanding stem.

YOUNG - Mississippian, 1000 - 400 B. P.

(Also see Catan and Clifton)

G1, $.50-$1
Waco, TX

G5, $.50-$1
Comanche Co., TX

G3, $.50-$1
Comanche Co., TX

LOCATION: Texas **DESCRIPTION:** A small size, crudely chipped, elliptica shaped, usually round base point made from a flake. One side is commonly uniface **I.D. KEY:** Base form uniface.

ZELLA - Early Archaic, 8500 - 7500 B. P.

(Also see Agate Basin, Angostura, Lerma and Mahaffey)

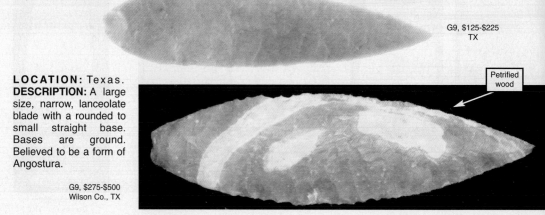

G9, $125-$225
TX

Petrified wood

LOCATION: Texas. **DESCRIPTION:** A large size, narrow, lanceolate blade with a rounded to small straight base. Bases are ground. Believed to be a form of Angostura.

G9, $275-$500
Wilson Co., TX

688

(Formerly Lampasos; also see Darl Stemmed, Darl, Hoxie and Uvalde)

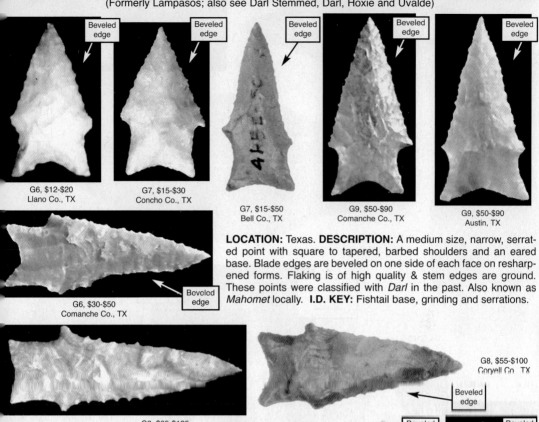

G6, $12-$20
Llano Co., TX

G7, $15-$30
Concho Co., TX

G7, $15-$50
Bell Co., TX

G9, $50-$90
Comanche Co., TX

G9, $50-$90
Austin, TX

G6, $30-$50
Comanche Co., TX

LOCATION: Texas. **DESCRIPTION:** A medium size, narrow, serrated point with square to tapered, barbed shoulders and an eared base. Blade edges are beveled on one side of each face on resharpened forms. Flaking is of high quality & stem edges are ground. These points were classified with *Darl* in the past. Also known as *Mahomet* locally. **I.D. KEY:** Fishtail base, grinding and serrations.

G8, $65-$125
Comanche Co., TX

G8, $55-$100
Coryell Co., TX

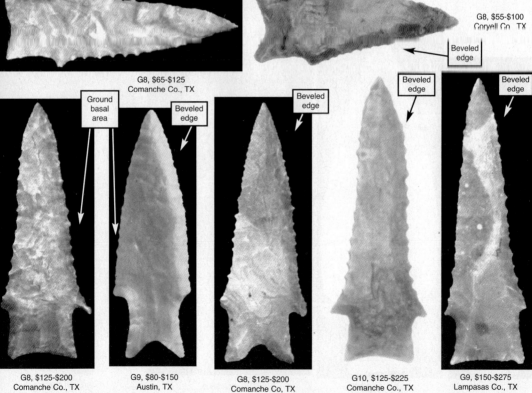

G8, $125-$200
Comanche Co., TX

G9, $80-$150
Austin, TX

G8, $125-$200
Comanche Co., TX

G10, $125-$225
Comanche Co., TX

G9, $150-$275
Lampasas Co., TX

(Also see Darl, Lange, Nolan and Travis)

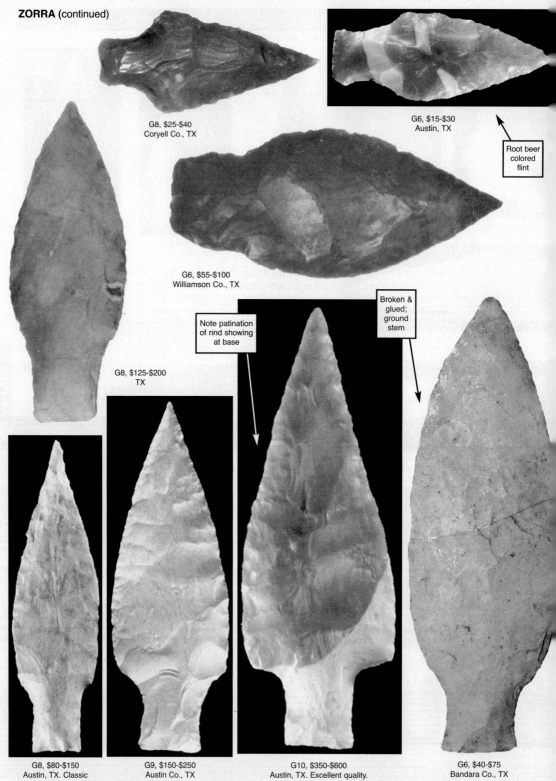

G8, $25-$40
Coryell Co., TX

G6, $15-$30
Austin, TX

Root beer
colored
flint

G6, $55-$100
Williamson Co., TX

G8, $125-$200
TX

Note patination
of rind showing
at base

Broken &
glued;
ground
stem

G8, $80-$150
Austin, TX. Classic

G9, $150-$250
Austin Co., TX

G10, $350-$600
Austin, TX. Excellent quality.

G6, $40-$75
Bandara Co., TX

LOCATION: Texas. **DESCRIPTION:** A medium to large size point with tapered shoulders and stem that is usually flat on one face and beveled on both sides of the opposite face. Otherwise identical to *Nolan*. Most have needle tips and good quality flaking. **I.D. KEY:** Base beveling.

NORTHERN CENTRAL SECTION:

This section includes point types from the following states:
Eastern Colorado, Kansas, Illinois, Iowa, Minnesota, Missouri, Nebraska and Wisconsin.

The points in this section are arranged in alphabetical order and are shown **actual size**. All types are listed that were available for photographing. Any missing types will be added to future editions as photographs become available. We are always interested in receiving sharp, black and white or color glossy photos, color slides or high resolution (300 pixels/inch) digital pictures of your collection. Be sure to include a ruler in the photograph so that proper scale can be determined.

Lithics: Materials employed in the manufacture of point types from this region include: agate, Burlington, chalcedony, chert, conglomerate, crystal, flint, jasper, kaolin, Knife River, hornstone, novaculite, petrified wood, quartzite, silicified sandstone and vein quartz.

Regional Consultants:
Roy Motley and Dave Church

Special Advisors:
Tom Davis, Bill Jackson
Glenn Leesman, Floyd Ritter,
Larry Troman, Michael Troman, Brian Wrage

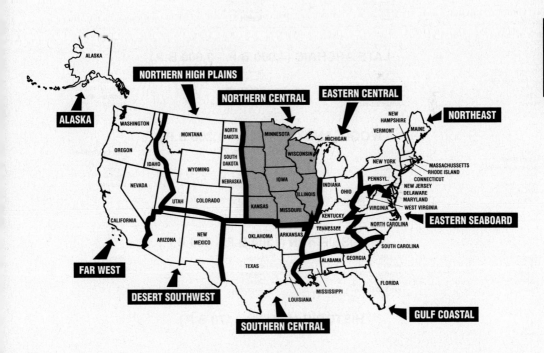

NORTHERN CENTRAL
(Archaeological Periods)

PALEO-LATE PALEO (11,500 B.P. - 10,000 B.P.)

Beaver Lake	Cumberland	Goshen
Clovis	Cumberland Unfluted	Plainview
Clovis-Hazel	Drill	Redstone
Clovis-St. Louis	Folsom	

TRANSITIONAL PALEO (11,000 B.P. - 9,000 B.P.)

Agate Basin	Early Ovoid Knife	Paleo Knife	Wheeler
Allen	Eden	Pelican	
Angostura	Hell Gap	Quad	
Browns Valley	Hi-Lo	Scottsbluff Type 1 & 2	

EARLY ARCHAIC (10,000 B.P. - 7,000 B.P.)

Allen	Decatur	Johnson	St. Charles
Angostura	Dovetail	Kirk Corner Notched	Standlee Contracting Stemmed
Burroughs	Firstview	Lake Erie	Stilwell
Cache River	Fox Valley	Lerma	Tennessee River
Calf Creek	Graham Cave	Lost Lake	Thebes
Cobbs Triangular	Greenbrier	Meserve	Turin
Cossatot River	Hardin	Nebo Hill	Warrick
Dalton Breckenridge	Heavy Duty	Neuberger	
Dalton Classic	Hickory Ridge	Osceola	
Dalton-Colbert	Hidden Valley	Pike County	
Dalton-Hemphill	Holland	Pine Tree Corner Notched	
Dalton-Nuckolls	Hollenberg Stemmed	Rice Lobbed	
Dalton-Sloan	Howard County	Rochester	

MIDDLE ARCHAIC (7,000 B.P. - 4,000 B.P.)

Afton	Hemphill	Munker's Creek	Smith
Benton	Kings	Raddatz	Stone Square Stem
Epps	Lamine Knife	Ramey Knife	
Exotic Forms	Matanzas	Red Ochre	
Ferry	Motley	Sedalia	

LATE ARCHAIC (4,000 B.P. - 3,000 B.P.)

Copena Classic	Gary	Mehlville	Table Rock
Corner Tang Knife	Godar	Merkle	Turkeytail-Fulton
Delhi	Hatten Knife	Pelican Lake	Turkeytail-Harrison
Etley	Helton	Robinson	Turkeytail-Hebron
Evans	Knight Island	Square-End Knife	Wadlow

WOODLAND (3,000 B.P. - 1,300 B.P.)

Adena	Collins	Kampsville	Rice Side-Notched
Adena Blade	Cupp	Kramer	Ross
Adena-Narrow Stem	Dickson	Lehigh	Snyders
Alba	Gibson	Mason	Steuben
Apple Creek	Grand	Morse Knife	Waubesa
Burkett	Hopewell	North	
Carter	Jacks Reef Corner Notched	Peisker Diamond	

MISSISSIPPIAN (1300 B.P. - 400 B.P.)

Agee	Haskell	Lundy	Washita
Bayogoula	Hayes	Madison	
Cahokia	Homan	Nodena	
Harahey	Huffaker	Scallorn	
Harrell	Kay Blade	Sequoyah	

HISTORIC (450 B.P. - 170 B.P.)

Neosho

NORTHERN CENTRAL
THUMBNAIL GUIDE SECTION

The following references are provided to aid the collector in easier and quicker identification of point types. All photos are exactly 30% of actual size and are proportional to each other. Each point pictured in this section represents classic form for the type. When a match is found, go to the alphabetical location of that type for more examples in actual size.

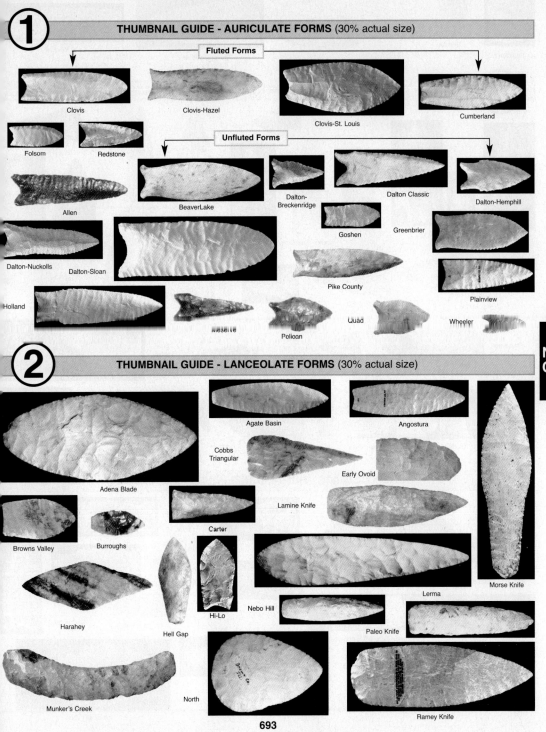

① THUMBNAIL GUIDE - AURICULATE FORMS (30% actual size)

Fluted Forms

Clovis

Clovis-Hazel

Clovis-St. Louis

Cumberland

Folsom

Redstone

Unfluted Forms

Allen

BeaverLake

Dalton-Breckenridge

Dalton Classic

Dalton-Hemphill

Dalton-Nuckolls

Dalton-Sloan

Goshen

Greenbrier

Pike County

Plainview

Holland

Meserve

Poloan

Quad

Wheeler

② THUMBNAIL GUIDE - LANCEOLATE FORMS (30% actual size)

Agate Basin

Angostura

Cobbs Triangular

Early Ovoid

Adena Blade

Lamine Knife

Carter

Morse Knife

Browns Valley

Burroughs

Lerma

Harahey

Hi-Lo

Nebo Hill

Paleo Knife

Hell Gap

Munker's Creek

North

Ramey Knife

693

THUMBNAIL GUIDE - Lanceolate forms (continued)

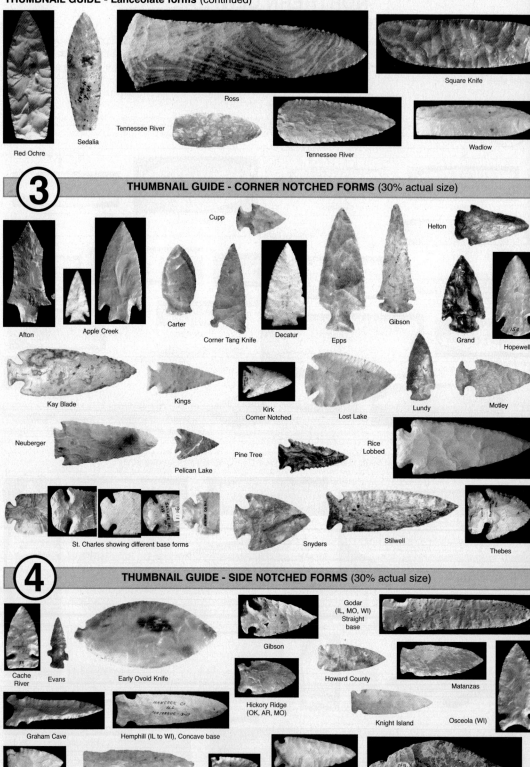

Red Ochre

Sedalia

Tennessee River

Ross

Square Knife

Tennessee River

Wadlow

(3) THUMBNAIL GUIDE - CORNER NOTCHED FORMS (30% actual size)

Cupp

Helton

Afton

Apple Creek

Carter

Corner Tang Knife

Decatur

Epps

Gibson

Grand

Hopewell

Kay Blade

Kings

Kirk Corner Notched

Lost Lake

Lundy

Motley

Neuberger

Pelican Lake

Pine Tree

Rice Lobbed

St. Charles showing different base forms

Snyders

Stilwell

Thebes

(4) THUMBNAIL GUIDE - SIDE NOTCHED FORMS (30% actual size)

Godar (IL, MO, WI) Straight base

Gibson

Cache River

Evans

Early Ovoid Knife

Howard County

Matanzas

Hickory Ridge (OK, AR, MO)

Knight Island

Osceola (WI)

Graham Cave

Hemphill (IL to WI), Concave base

Raddatz (WI)

Rice Side-Notched

Robinson (MO, IL, IN)

Turin

Turkeytail-Fulton

694

Neosho

Turkeytail-Harrison

Warrick

⑤ THUMBNAIL GUIDE - STEMMED FORMS (30% of actual size)

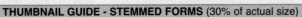

Expanded Base

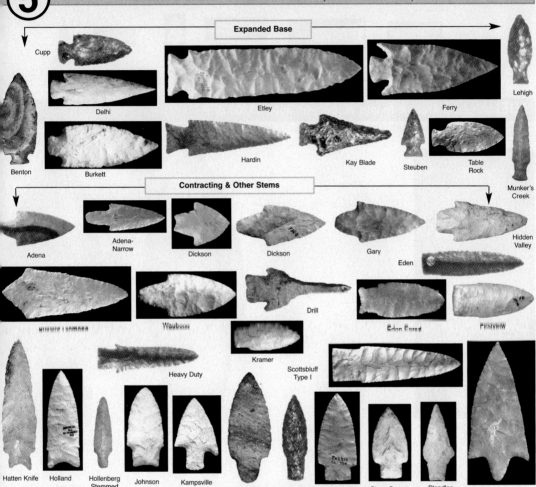

Cupp

Delhi

Etley

Ferry

Lehigh

Benton

Burkett

Hardin

Kay Blade

Steuben

Table Rock

Munker's Creek

Contracting & Other Stems

Adena

Adena-Narrow

Dickson

Dickson

Gary

Hidden Valley

Eden

Drill

Eden Eared

Waubesa

Kramer

Scottsbluff Type I

N C

Hatten Knife

Holland

Hollenberg Stemmed

Johnson

Kampsville

Heavy Duty

Mason

Rochester

Scottsbluff Type II

Stone Square Stem

Standlee Contracting

Turkeytail-Hebron

⑥ THUMBNAIL GUIDE - STEMMED-BIFURCATED FORMS (30% of actual size)

Fox Valley

Lake Erie

Cossatot River

⑦ THUMBNAIL GUIDE - BASAL NOTCHED FORMS (30% of actual size)

Calf Creek

Mehlville

Smith

8 THUMBNAIL GUIDE - ARROW POINTS (30% of actual size)

Agee
Alba
Bayogoula
Cahokia
Collins
Harrell
Haskell
Hayes
Homan
Huffaker
Jacks Reef
Corner Notched
Madison
Madison-Titterington
Nodena
Scallorn
Sequoyah
Washita

ADENA - Late Archaic to late Woodland, 3000 - 1200 B. P.

(see Burkett, Dickson, Gary, Kramer, Hidden Valley, Rochester and Waubesa)

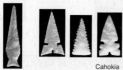

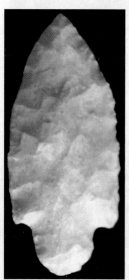

G4, $20-$35
S. W. IL

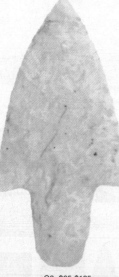

G9, $65-$125
MO

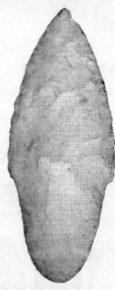

G7, $45-$85
MO

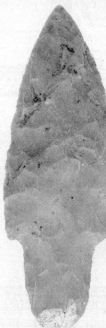

G7, $65-$125
Alexandra Co., IL

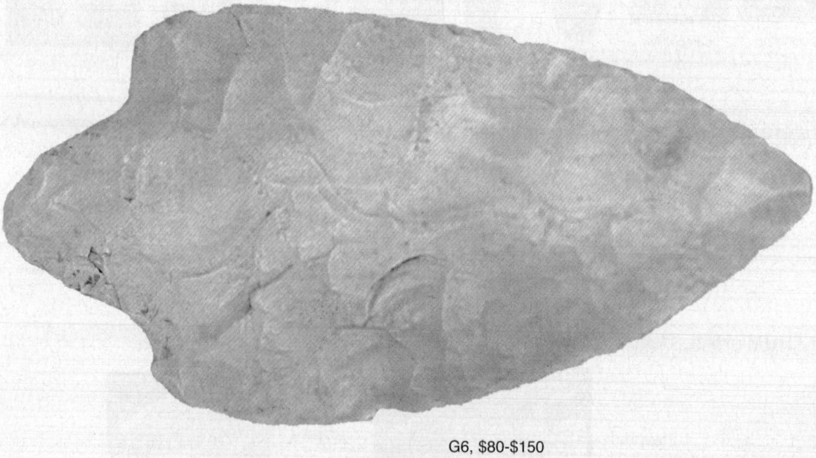

G6, $80-$150
Madison Co., IL

LOCATION: Eastern to Southeastern states. **DESCRIPTION:** A medium to large, thin, narrow, triangular blade that is sometimes serrated, and with a medium to long, narrow to broad rounded "beaver tail" stem. Most examples are from average to excellent quality. Base can be ground. **I.D. KEY:** Rounded base, Woodland random flaking.

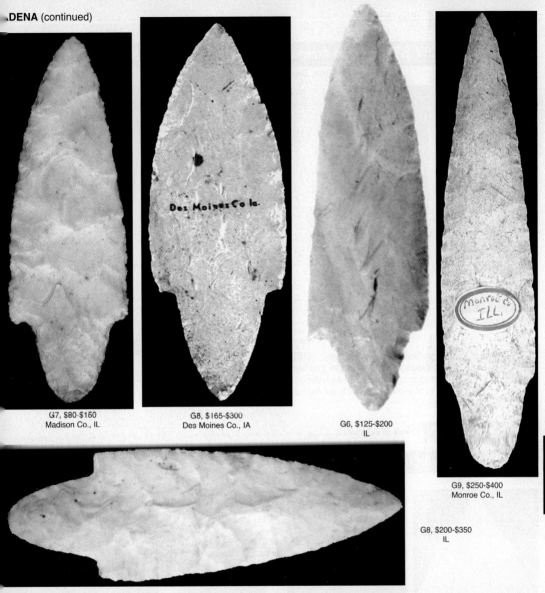

G7, $80-$150
Madison Co., IL

G8, $165-$300
Des Moines Co., IA

G6, $125-$200
IL

G9, $250-$400
Monroe Co., IL

G8, $200-$350
IL

ADENA BLADE - Late Archaic to Woodland, 3000 - 1200 B. P.

(Also see Lerma, North, Red Ochre & Stenfield)

LOCATION: Midwestern to Eastern states. **DESCRIPTION:** A large size, thin, broad, ovate blade with a rounded base and is often found in caches. **I.D. KEY:** Random flaking.

G8, $275-$500
McLean Co., IL

IMPORTANT:
Shown half
size

697

ADENA-DICKSON (See Dickson)

ADENA-NARROW STEM - Late Archaic to Woodland, 3000 - 1200 B. P.

(Also see Adena, Dickson, Rochester and Waubesa)

G4, $4-$8
IL

G3, $3-$5
N. E. OK

G5, $12-$20
Macoupin Co., IL

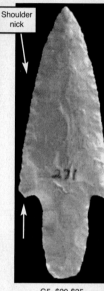

Shoulder nick

G6, $45-$80
Pettis Co., MO

G5, $20-$35
IL

LOCATION: Eastern to Southeastern states. **DESCRIPTION:** A medium to large, thin, narrow triangular blade that is sometimes serrated, and a medium to long, narrow, rounded stem. Most examples are well made. **I.D. KEY:** Narrow rounded base with more secondary work than ordinary Adena.

ADENA-WAUBESA (See Waubesa)

AFTON - Middle Archaic to early Woodland, 5000 - 2000 B. P.

(Also see Apple Creek, Ferry and Helton)

G8, $80-$150
Cooper Co., MO

G5, $30-$50
MO

G8, $175-$300
MO

Barb wear

G6, $65-$125
Cooper Co., MO

Translucent Mozarkite chert

G9, $450-$850
Saline Co., MO

LOCATION: Midwestern states and is rarely found in some Eastern and Southeastern states. **DESCRIPTION:** A medium to large size pentagonal shaped point with a flaring or corner notched stem. Some examples are base notched and some are stemmed. **I.D. KEY:** Blade form.

698

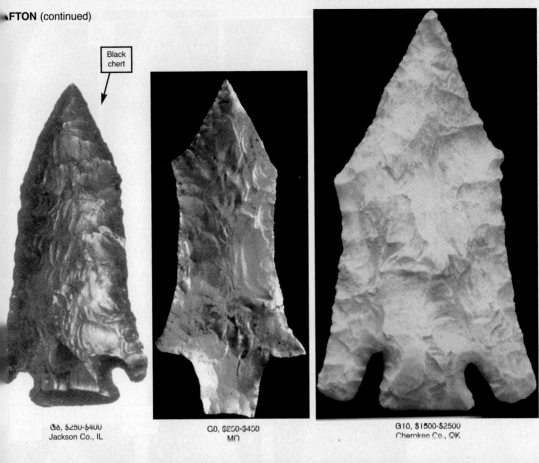

Black
chert

G8, $250-$400
Jackson Co., IL

G9, $250-$450
MO

G10, $1500-$2500
Cherokee Co., OK

AGATE BASIN - Transitional Paleo to Early Archaic, 10,200 - 8500 B. P.

(Also see Allen, Angostura, Burroughs, Eden, Lerma, Nebo Hill and Sedalia)

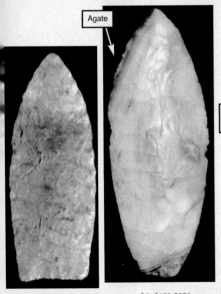

Agate

G6, $70-$125
MO.

G6, $150-$250
W. IA

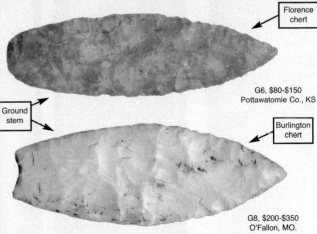

Florence
chert

G6, $80-$150
Pottawatomie Co., KS

Ground
stem

Burlington
chert

G8, $200-$350
O'Fallon, MO.

LOCATION: Midwestern states. **DESCRIPTION:** A medium to large size lanceolate blade of unusually high quality. Bases are either convex, concave or straight, and are usually ground. Some examples are median ridged and have random to parallel flaking. **I.D. KEY:** Basal form and flaking style.

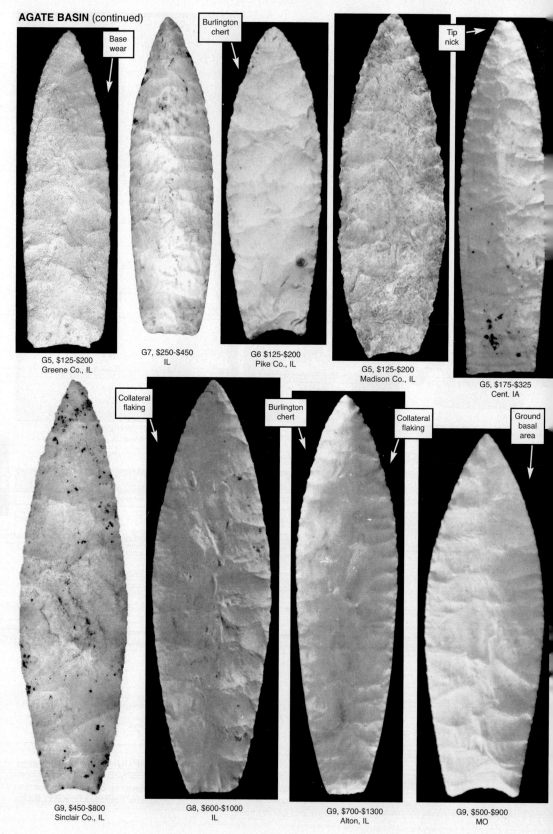

AGATE BASIN (continued)

Base wear

G5, $125-$200
Greene Co., IL

G7, $250-$450
IL

Burlington chert

G6 $125-$200
Pike Co., IL

G5, $125-$200
Madison Co., IL

Tip nick

G5, $175-$325
Cent. IA

G9, $450-$800
Sinclair Co., IL

Collateral flaking

G8, $600-$1000
IL

Burlington chert

Collateral flaking

G9, $700-$1300
Alton, IL

Ground basal area

G9, $500-$900
MO

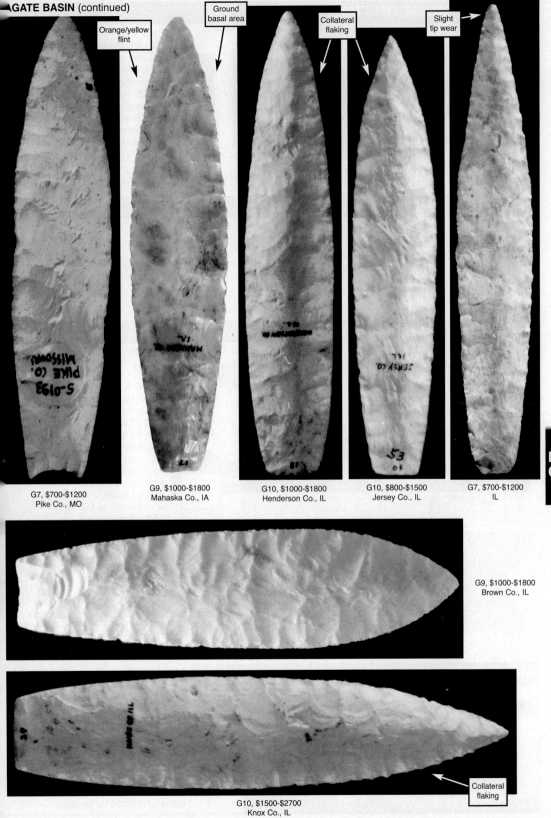

Orange/yellow flint

Ground basal area

Collateral flaking

Slight tip wear

G7, $700-$1200
Pike Co., MO

G9, $1000-$1800
Mahaska Co., IA

G10, $1000-$1800
Henderson Co., IL

G10, $800-$1500
Jersey Co., IL

G7, $700-$1200
IL

N C

G9, $1000-$1800
Brown Co., IL

Collateral flaking

G10, $1500-$2700
Knox Co., IL

701

AGEE - Mississippian, 1200 - 700 B. P.

(Also see Alba, Hayes, Homan)

Needle tip →

Shoulder nick →

LOCATION: Arkansas; rarely into Missouri and Illinois. **DESCRIPTION:** A small to medium size, narrow, expanded barbed, corner notched point. Tips are needle sharp. Some examples are double notched at the base. A rare type **I.D. KEY:** Basal form and barb expansion.

G5, $90-$150 Cent., MO

G6, $125-$200 Cent., MO

G5, $165-$300 Cent., MO

G6, $165-$300 Cent., MO

G6, $165-$300 Cent., MO

G6, $125-$200 Cent., MO

ALBA - Woodland to Mississippian, 2000 - 400 B. P.

(Also see Agee, Hayes, Homan and Sequoyah)

LOCATION: Louisiana, Arkansas into Oklahoma; rarely into Illinois. **DESCRIPTION:** A small to medium size, narrow, well made point with prominent tangs, a recurved blade and a bulbous stem. Some examples are serrated. **I.D. KEY:** Rounded base and expanded barbs.

G9, $80-$150 IL

ALLEN - Early Archaic, 8,500 - 7500 B. P.

(Also see Angostura, Browns Valley, Clovis, Goshen and Plainview)

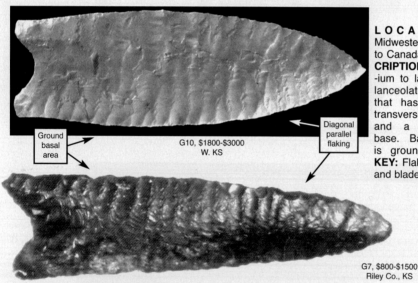

Ground basal area →

Diagonal parallel flaking

G10, $1800-$3000 W. KS

LOCATION: Midwestern states to Canada. **DESCRIPTION:** A medium to large size lanceolate point that has oblique transverse flaking and a concave base. Basal area is ground. **I.D. KEY:** Flaking style and blade form.

G7, $800-$1500 Riley Co., KS

G5, $250-$450 Pottowatomie Co., K

ANGOSTURA - Early to Middle Archaic, 8,800 - 7500 B. P.

(Also see Agate Basin, Allen, Eden & Wheeler Excurvate)

G9, $350-$600 Sou. Platt Riv., NB

LOCATION: Midwest to Western states. **DESCRIPTION:** A medium to large size lanceolate blade with a contracting, concave, straight or convex base. Both broad and narrow forms occur. Flaking can be parallel oblique to random. Blades are commonly steeply beveled on one side of each face; some are serrated and most have basal grinding. Formerly called *Long* points. **I.D. KEY:** Basal form, flaking on blade which can be beveled.

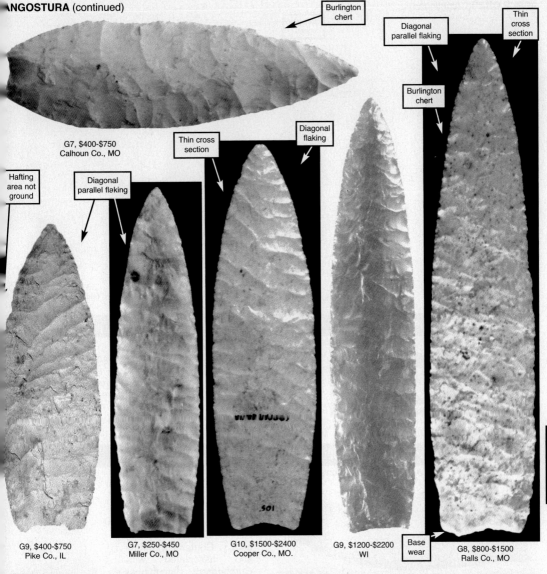

Burlington chert

Diagonal parallel flaking

Thin cross section

Burlington chert

Diagonal flaking

Thin cross section

G7, $400-$750
Calhoun Co., MO

Hafting area not ground

Diagonal parallel flaking

G9, $400-$750
Pike Co., IL

G7, $250-$450
Miller Co., MO

G10, $1500-$2400
Cooper Co., MO.

G9, $1200-$2200
WI

Base wear

G8, $800-$1500
Ralls Co., MO

N C

APPLE CREEK - Late Woodland, 1700 - 1500 B. P.

(Also see Helton, Jacks Reef, Kirk Corner Notched, Lundy and Pine Tree)

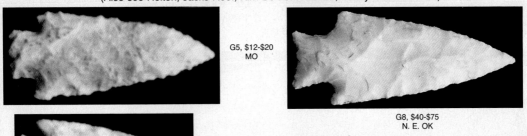

G5, $12-$20
MO

G8, $40-$75
N. E. OK

G8, $35-$50
Cherokee Co., KS

LOCATION: Kansas, Missouri & Illinois. **DESCRIPTION**: A medium to large size, broad, corner notched point with an expanded stem. Barbs are short to moderate. Bases are convex, straight or concave. **I.D. KEY**: Angle of corner notches.

703

APPLE CREEK (continued)

Burlington chert

G6, $20-$35
Miller Co., MO

G5, $40-$75
Greene Co., IL

G8, $80-$150
Madison Co., IL

G9, $125-$200
Madison Co., IL

BAYOGOULA - Mississippian, 800 - 400 B. P.

(Also see Cahokia, Madison)

Restored base

This point was brought up to Cahokia from Louisianna, possibly on a trading trip

G1, $40-$70
Cahokia Mound site, IL

LOCATION: Louisiana. **DESCRIPTION:** A small to medium size, thin, narrow, arrowpoint with tapered shoulders and a short, expanded base that is concave. A Louisiana type that has been found at Cahokia Mound site.

BEAVER LAKE - Paleo, 11,250 - 8000 B. P.

(Also see Clovis, Cumberland, Greenbrier, Pike County and Quad)

G7, $120-$200
MO/IL

G6, $85-$165
MO

LOCATION: Alabama, Tennessee into Illinois and Missouri. **DESCRIPTION:** A medium to large size lanceolate blade with flaring ears. Contemporaneous and associated with *Cumberland,* but thinner than unfluted *Cumberlands.* Bases are ground and blade edges are recurved. **I.D. KEY:** Paleo flaking, shoulder area.

G8, $500-$800
Fulton Co. IL

G10, $2000-$3500
MO

BENTON - Middle Archaic, 6000 - 4000 B. P.

(Also see Etley)

Mozarkite

Bottle-neck form

G8, $275-$500
MO

LOCATION: Mississippi River into Tennessee and Kentucky. **DESCRIPTION:** A medium to very large size, broad, stemmed point with straight to convex sides. Bases can be corner or side notched, double notched, knobbed, bifurcated or expanded. Some examples show parallel oblique flaking. All four edges are beveled and basal corners usually have barbs. **I. D. KEY:** Wide squared, eared or notched base.

BLACK SAND   (Now typed as Godar)

BRECKENRIDGE   (See Dalton-Breckenridge)

BREWERTON CORNER NOTCHED - Mid-late Archaic, 6000 - 4000 B. P.

(Also see Apple Creek, Helton, Kirk, Lundy)

G5, $12-$20
MO

G6, $15-$25
MO

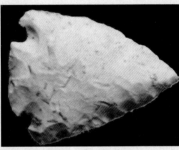

G5, $15-$30
MO

LOCATION: Midwestern states into the Northeast. **DESCRIPTION:** A small size triangular point with faint corner notches and a convex base. Called *Freeheley* in Michigan.

BREWERTON SIDE NOTCHED - Mid-late Archaic, 6000 - 4000 B. P.

(Also see Godar, Graham Cave, Hickory Ridge, Howard County, Raddatz and Robinson)

LOCATION: Midwestern states into the Northeast. **DESCRIPTION:** A small to medium size, triangular point with weak side notches and a concave to straight base.

G5, $12-$20
MO

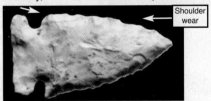

Shoulder wear

BROWNS VALLEY - Transitional Paleo, 10,000 - 8000 B. P.

(Also see Agate Basin, Allen, Angostura, Burroughs, Clovis, Plainview and Sedalia)

Diagonal flaking

G7, $350-$650
Cent. IL. Note oblique parallel flaking which is characteristic of the type.

LOCATION: Upper Midwestern states. **DESCRIPTION:** A medium to large, thin, lanceolate blade with usually oblique to horizontal transverse flaking and a concave to straight base which can be ground. **I.D. KEY:** Paleo transverse flaking.

BURKETT - Woodland, 2300 - 1800 B. P.

(Also see Adena, Dickson, Gary, Mason)

LOCATION: Missouri into Arkansas. **DESCRIPTION:** A medium to large size point with a short rectangular to contracting stem. The base can be straight to rounded. Shoulders can be tapered to barbed. Possibly part of the *Adena* culture.

G7, $65-$125
Stockton Lake, MO

BURROUGHS - Early Archaic, 8000 - 6000 B. P.

(Also see Agate Basin and Browns Valley

LOCATION: Northern Midwestern states. **DESCRIPTION:** A small to medium size, lanceolate point with convex sides and a straight to slightly concave base.

G6, $45-$80
Riley Co., KS

CACHE RIVER - Early to Middle Archaic, 10,000 - 5000 B. P.

(Also see Godar, Graham Cave, Hickory Ridge, Howard County, Raddatz and Robinson)

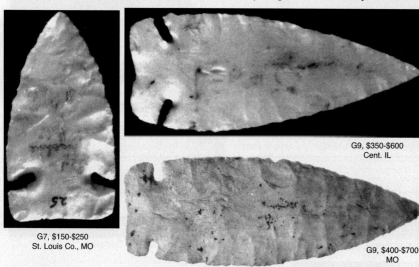

G9, $350-$600
Cent. IL

G7, $150-$250
St. Louis Co., MO

G9, $400-$700
MO

G7, $80-$150
Alexander Co., IL

LOCATION: Midwestern states. **DESCRIPTION:** A small to medium size, fairly thin, side-notched, triangular point with a concave base. Could be related to *Big Sandy* points.
I.D. KEY: Base form, narrow notched & flaking of blade.

CAHOKIA - Mississippian, 1000 - 500 B. P.

(Also see Harrell, Huffaker, Madison and Washita)

G8, $40-$70
MO

G8, $80-$150
St. Clair Co., IL

Very thin

Four notches

G9, $125-$200
IL

706

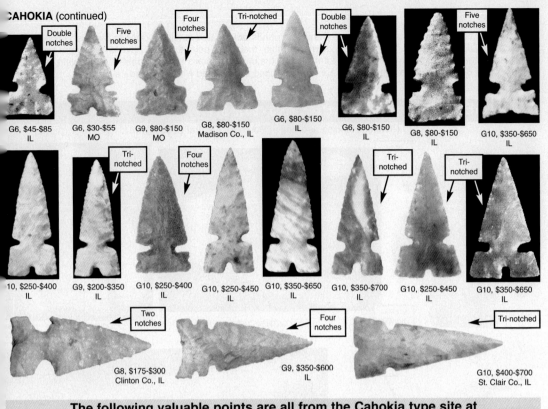

Double notches
G6, $45-$85 IL

Five notches
G6, $30-$55 MO

G9, $80-$150 MO

Four notches
G8, $80-$150 Madison Co., IL

Tri-notched
G6, $80-$150 IL

Double notches
G6, $80-$150 IL

G8, $80-$150 IL

Five notches
G10, $350-$650 IL

10, $250-$400 IL

Tri-notched
G9, $200-$350 IL

Four notches
G10, $250-$400 IL

G10, $250-$450 IL

G10, $350-$650 IL

Tri-notched
G10, $350-$700 IL

Tri-notched
G10, $250-$450 IL

G10, $350-$650 IL

Two notches
G8, $175-$300 Clinton Co., IL

Four notches
G9, $350-$600 IL

Tri-notched
G10, $400-$700 St. Clair Co., IL

The following valuable points are all from the Cahokia type site at the Cahokia Mounds location in St. Clair Co., IL

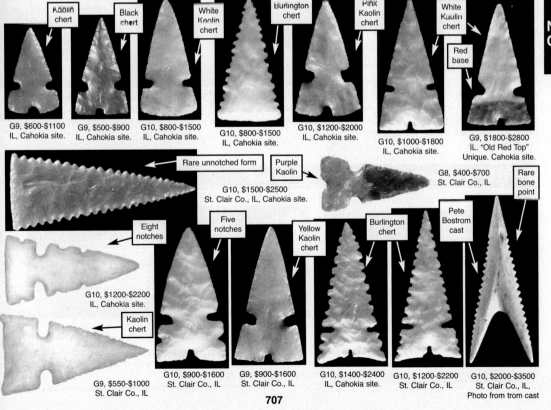

Kaolin chert
G9, $600-$1100 IL, Cahokia site.

Black chert
G9, $500-$900 IL, Cahokia site.

White Kaolin chert
G10, $800-$1500 IL, Cahokia site.

G10, $800-$1500 IL, Cahokia site.

Burlington chert
G10, $1200-$2000 IL, Cahokia site.

Pink Kaolin chert
G10, $1000-$1800 IL, Cahokia site.

White Kaolin chert
Red base
G9, $1800-$2800 IL. "Old Red Top" Unique. Cahokia site.

Rare unnotched form
G10, $1500-$2500 St. Clair Co., IL, Cahokia site.

Purple Kaolin

G8, $400-$700 St. Clair Co., IL

Rare bone point
Pete Bostrom cast

Eight notches
G10, $1200-$2200 IL, Cahokia site.

Kaolin chert
G9, $550-$1000 St. Clair Co., IL

Five notches
G10, $900-$1600 St. Clair Co., IL

Yellow Kaolin chert
G9, $900-$1600 St. Clair Co., IL

Burlington chert
G10, $1400-$2400 IL, Cahokia site.

G10, $1200-$2200 St. Clair Co., IL

G10, $2000-$3500 St. Clair Co., IL, Photo from trom cast

N C

LOCATION: Midwestern states. The famous Cahokia mounds are located in Illinois close to the Mississippi River in St. Clair Co. **DESCRIPTION:** A small to medium size, thin, triangular point that can have one or more notches on each blade edge. A rare unnotched serrated form also occurs on the Cahokia site. The base is either plain, has a center notch or is deeply concave. Rarely, they are made of bone. Associated with the Caddo culture.

CALF CREEK - Early to Middle Archaic, 8000 - 5000 B. P.

(Also see Andice and Bell in Southern Central Section)

Kay County flint

Broken shoulder

G3, $45-$80
Kay Co., OK

G6, $250-$400
Manhattan, KS

G3, $200-$350
Cherokee Co., KS

Broken shoulder

Kay County flint

Barb lost in resharpening

G4, $125-$200
Kay Co., OK

G10, $2500-$4000
Riley Co., KS

LOCATION: Texas into Oklahoma, Arkansas, Kansas and Missouri. The type site is in Searcy Co., Arkansas. **DESCRIPTION:** A medium to large size thin, broad, triangular point with very deep parallel basal notches. Related to the *Andice* and *Bell* points found in Texas. Tangs on first-stage examples extended to the base. Very rare in type area. **I.D. KEY:** Notches almost straight up.

CARTER (Hopewell) - Woodland, 2500 - 1500 B. P.

(Also see Grand and Snyders)

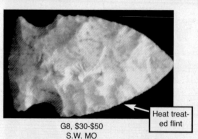

Heat treated flint

G8, $30-$50
S.W. MO

Blade form

G5, $25-$45
Madison Co., IL

LOCATION: Illinois. **DESCRIPTION:** A medium to large size, narrow, wide corner to side notched point with a convex base. Shoulders are rounded, weak to non-existent. The Blade form has no shoulders and is similar in appearance to *Copena* found in Tennessee and Alabama. Related to the *Snyders* point.

CARTER (continued)

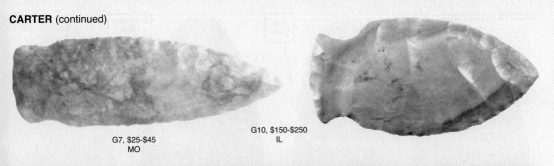

G7, $25-$45
MO

G10, $150-$250
IL

CLOVIS - Early Paleo, 11,500 - 10,600 B. P.

(Also see Allen, Angostura, Browns Valley, Cumberland, Dalton, Folsom and Plainview)

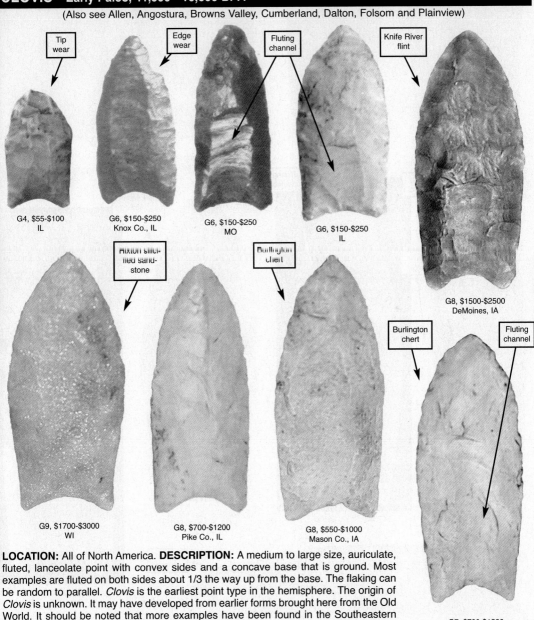

Tip wear

Edge wear

Fluting channel

Knife River flint

G4, $55-$100
IL

G6, $150-$250
Knox Co., IL

G6, $150-$250
MO

G6, $150-$250
IL

Hixton silici-fied sand-stone

Burlington chert

G8, $1500-$2500
DeMoines, IA

N
C

Burlington chert

Fluting channel

G9, $1700-$3000
WI

G8, $700-$1200
Pike Co., IL

G8, $550-$1000
Mason Co., IA

LOCATION: All of North America. **DESCRIPTION:** A medium to large size, auriculate, fluted, lanceolate point with convex sides and a concave base that is ground. Most examples are fluted on both sides about 1/3 the way up from the base. The flaking can be random to parallel. *Clovis* is the earliest point type in the hemisphere. The origin of *Clovis* is unknown. It may have developed from earlier forms brought here from the Old World. It should be noted that more examples have been found in the Southeastern U.S. than anywhere else. *Clovis* is known from South America as well. **I.D. KEY:** Paleo flaking, shoulders, billet or baton fluting instead of indirect style.

G7, $700-$1200
Nemaha Co., KS

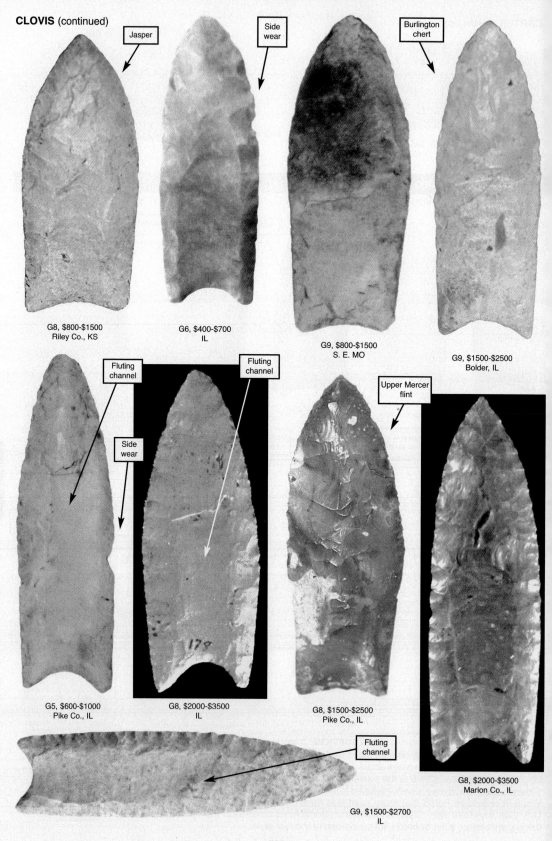

CLOVIS (continued)

Jasper

Side wear

Burlington chert

G8, $800-$1500
Riley Co., KS

G6, $400-$700
IL

G9, $800-$1500
S. E. MO

G9, $1500-$2500
Bolder, IL

Fluting channel

Fluting channel

Side wear

Upper Mercer flint

G5, $600-$1000
Pike Co., IL

G8, $2000-$3500
IL

G8, $1500-$2500
Pike Co., IL

G8, $2000-$3500
Marion Co., IL

Fluting channel

G9, $1500-$2700
IL

710

CLOVIS-HAZEL - Early Paleo, 11,500 - 10,600 B. P.

Flute channel

G8, $1000-$1800
IL

Classic form

G9, $2000-$3500
MO

G8, $900-$1700
IL

LOCATION: Midwestern states eastward. **DESCRIPTION:** A small to large size auriculate point with recurved blade edges and a fishtailed base that is concave. **I.D. KEY:** Fishtailed base.

CLOVIS-ST. LOUIS - Early Paleo, 11,500 - 10,600 B. P.

Early form

Ear nick

G8, $2000-$3500
MO

N
C

LOCATION: The Dakotas, Wisconsin southward to Arkansas and eastward to Michigan. **DESCRIPTION:** A large size, broad, auriculate, fluted, lanceolate point with convex sides and a concave base that is ground. Most examples are fluted on both sides 1/3 or more up from the base. The flaking can be random to parallel. One of the Earliest *Clovis* forms. **I.D. KEY:** Size and broadness.

COBBS TRIANGULAR - Early Archaic, 8000 - 5000 B. P.

(Also see Decatur, Dovetail, Lerma and Lost Lake)

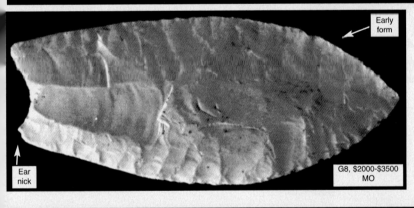

Silicified sandstone

Beveled edge

IMPORTANT:
All Cobbs
shown half size

Beveled edge

G9, $125-$200
AR

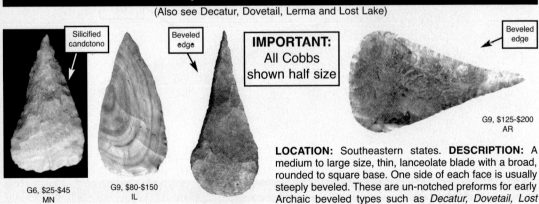

G6, $25-$45
MN

G9, $80-$150
IL

G9, $125-$200
Kay Co., OK

LOCATION: Southeastern states. **DESCRIPTION:** A medium to large size, thin, lanceolate blade with a broad, rounded to square base. One side of each face is usually steeply beveled. These are un-notched preforms for early Archaic beveled types such as *Decatur, Dovetail, Lost Lake,* etc.

COBBS (continued)

IMPORTANT:
All Cobbs
shown half size

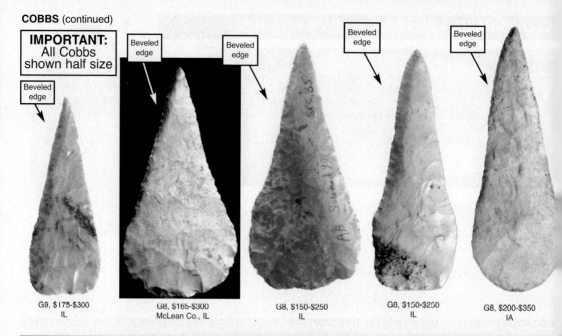

Beveled edge

Beveled edge

Beveled edge

Beveled edge

Beveled edge

G9, $175-$300
IL

G8, $165-$300
McLean Co., IL

G8, $150-$250
IL

G8, $150-$250
IL

G8, $200-$350
IA

COLLINS - Woodland, 1500 - 1200 B. P.

(Also see Haskell, Scallorn)

G8, $35-$65
Cherokee
Co., KS

LOCATION: Arkansas into Kansas. **DESCRIPTION:**
A small, narrow arrowpoint with broad side notches.
Bases can be straight, to eared to convex.

CORNER TANG KNIFE - Late Archaic to Woodland, 4000 - 2000 B. P.

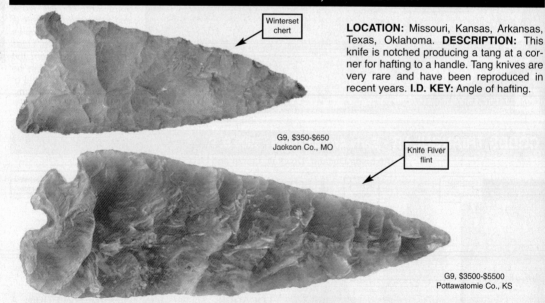

Winterset chert

LOCATION: Missouri, Kansas, Arkansas,
Texas, Oklahoma. **DESCRIPTION:** This
knife is notched producing a tang at a corner for hafting to a handle. Tang knives are
very rare and have been reproduced in
recent years. **I.D. KEY:** Angle of hafting.

G9, $350-$650
Jackson Co., MO

Knife River flint

G9, $3500-$5500
Pottawatomie Co., KS

COSSATOT RIVER - Early Archaic, 9500 - 8000 B. P.

(Also see Fox Valley and Lake Erie)

G4, $12-$20
Logan Co., IL

G6, $15-$30
Madison Co., IL

G8, $15-$30
Logan Co., IL

G7, $30-$55
Logan Co., IL

G6, $25-$45
Cherokee Co., KS

Serrated edge

G9, $65-$125, Logan Co., IL.

G8, $40-$75
Logan Co., IL

LOCATION: Illinois, Missouri into Oklahoma. **DESCRIPTION:** A medium to large size, thin, usually serrated, widely corner notched point with large round to square ears and a deep notch in the center of the base. Bases are usually ground. **I.D. KEY:** Basal notching, early Archaic flaking.

CRESCENT KNIFE (see Munker's Creek)

CUMBERLAND - Paleo, 11,250 - 10,000 B. P.

(Also see Beaver Lake, Clovis, Dalton and Quad)

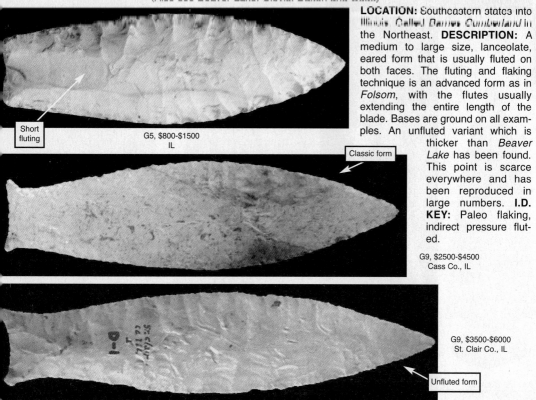

Short fluting

G5, $800-$1500
IL

Classic form

G9, $2500-$4500
Cass Co., IL

G9, $3500-$6000
St. Clair Co., IL

Unfluted form

LOCATION: Southeastern states into Illinois. Called *Barnes Cumberland* in the Northeast. **DESCRIPTION:** A medium to large size, lanceolate, eared form that is usually fluted on both faces. The fluting and flaking technique is an advanced form as in *Folsom*, with the flutes usually extending the entire length of the blade. Bases are ground on all examples. An unfluted variant which is thicker than *Beaver Lake* has been found. This point is scarce everywhere and has been reproduced in large numbers. **I.D. KEY:** Paleo flaking, indirect pressure fluted.

N
C

(Also see Epps, Helton, Kay Blade, Lundy, Motley, Snyders, Steuben, Table Rock)

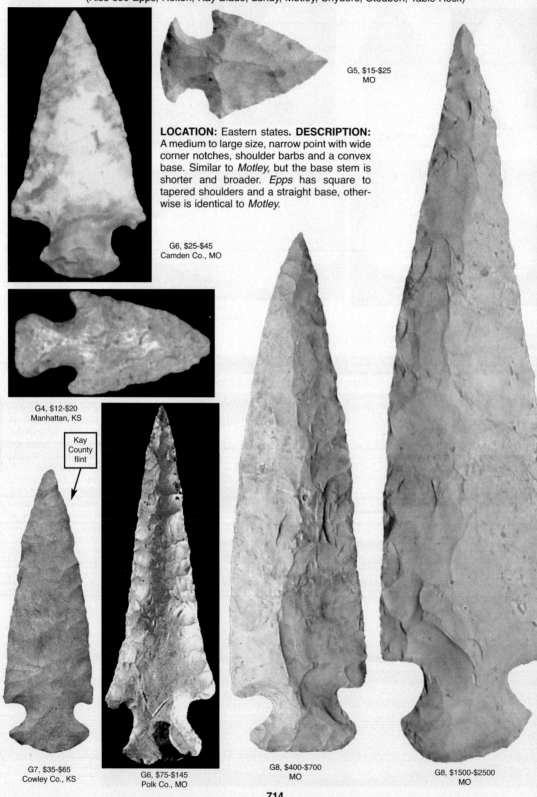

G5, $15-$25
MO

LOCATION: Eastern states. **DESCRIPTION:** A medium to large size, narrow point with wide corner notches, shoulder barbs and a convex base. Similar to *Motley,* but the base stem is shorter and broader. *Epps* has square to tapered shoulders and a straight base, otherwise is identical to *Motley.*

G6, $25-$45
Camden Co., MO

G4, $12-$20
Manhattan, KS

Kay County flint

G7, $35-$65
Cowley Co., KS

G6, $75-$145
Polk Co., MO

G8, $400-$700
MO

G8, $1500-$2500
MO

DALTON-BRECKENRIDGE - Early Archaic, 10,00 - 9200 B. P.

(Also see Dalton and Meserve)

G6, $30-$50
MO

Beveled edge

Woodford flint

Tip wear

G5, $35-$65
Kay Co., OK

G9, $150-$275
MO/KY

Beveled edge

Woodford flint

G6, $70-$125
Kay Co., OK

LOCATION: Midwestern states, **DESCRIPTION:** A medium to large size, auriculate point with an obvious bevel extending the entire length of the point from tip to base. Similar in form to the *Dalton-Greenbrier*. Basal area is usually ground.

DALTON CLASSIC - Early Archaic, 10,000 - 9200 B. P.

(Also see Beaver Lake, Greenbrier, Holland, Meserve, Pelican, Plainview and Quad)

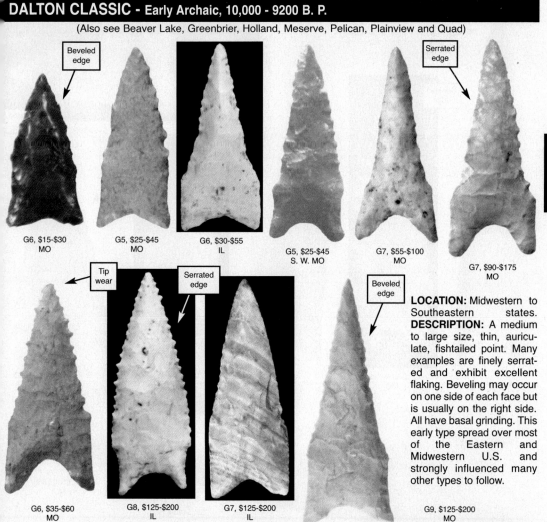

N
C

Beveled edge

Serrated edge

G6, $15-$30
MO

G5, $25-$45
MO

G6, $30-$55
IL

G5, $25-$45
S. W. MO

G7, $55-$100
MO

G7, $90-$175
MO

Tip wear

Serrated edge

Beveled edge

G6, $35-$60
MO

G8, $125-$200
IL

G7, $125-$200
IL

G9, $125-$200
MO

LOCATION: Midwestern to Southeastern states. **DESCRIPTION:** A medium to large size, thin, auriculate, fishtailed point. Many examples are finely serrated and exhibit excellent flaking. Beveling may occur on one side of each face but is usually on the right side. All have basal grinding. This early type spread over most of the Eastern and Midwestern U.S. and strongly influenced many other types to follow.

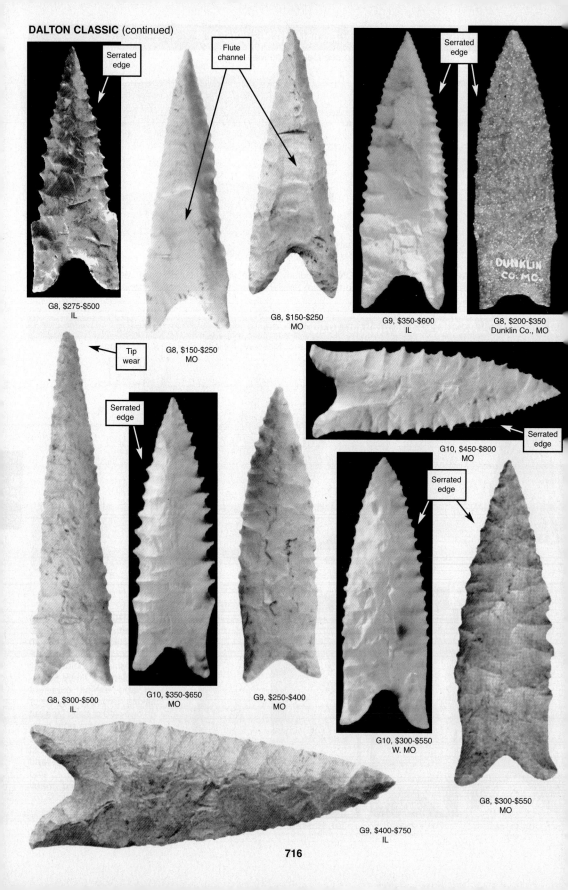

Serrated edge

Flute channel

Serrated edge

Serrated edge

Tip wear

Serrated edge

Serrated edge

Serrated edge

G8, $275-$500
IL

G8, $150-$250
MO

G8, $150-$250
MO

G9, $350-$600
IL

G8, $200-$350
Dunklin Co., MO

DUNKLIN CO. MO.

G10, $450-$800
MO

G8, $300-$500
IL

G10, $350-$650
MO

G9, $250-$400
MO

G10, $300-$550
W. MO

G8, $300-$550
MO

G9, $400-$750
IL

716

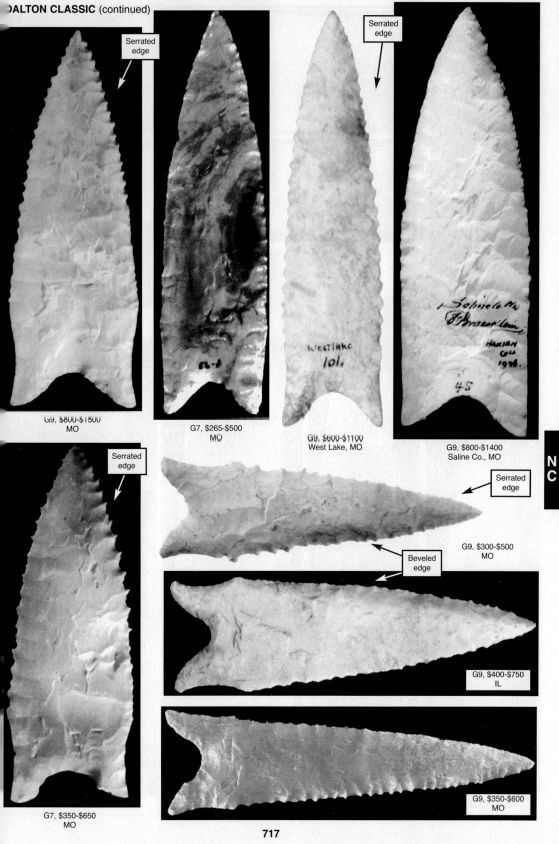

Serrated edge

G9, $800-$1500
MO

G7, $265-$500
MO

Serrated edge

G9, $600-$1100
West Lake, MO

G9, $800-$1400
Saline Co., MO

Serrated edge

G7, $350-$650
MO

Serrated edge

G9, $300-$500
MO

Beveled edge

G9, $400-$750
IL

G9, $350-$600
MO

N
C

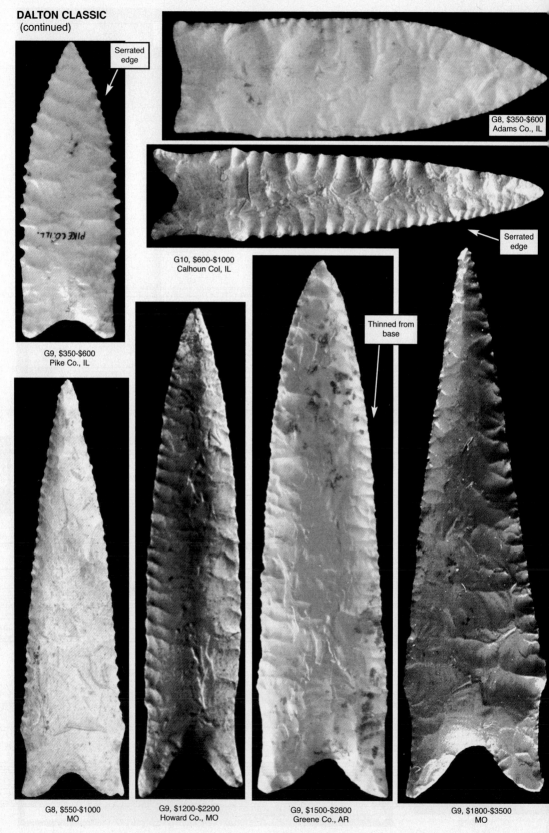

Serrated edge

G8, $350-$600
Adams Co., IL

G10, $600-$1000
Calhoun Col, IL

Serrated edge

Thinned from base

G9, $350-$600
Pike Co., IL

PIKE CO. ILL.

G8, $550-$1000
MO

G9, $1200-$2200
Howard Co., MO

G9, $1500-$2800
Greene Co., AR

G9, $1800-$3500
MO

DALTON-COLBERT - Early Archaic, 10,000 - 9200 B. P.

(Also see Beaver Lake, Greenbrier, Meserve)

Serrated

Black agate

LOCATION: Midwestern to Eastern states. **DESCRIPTION:** A medium size auriculate form with a squared stem and a weakly defined hafting area which is ground. Some examples are serrated and exhibit parallel flaking of the highest quality. **I.D. KEY:** Squarish basal area.

G7, $200-$350
N.E. KS

DALTON-HEMPHILL - Early Archaic, 10,000 - 9200 B. P.

(Also see Holland and Scottsbluff)

Serrated edge

Mozarkite chert

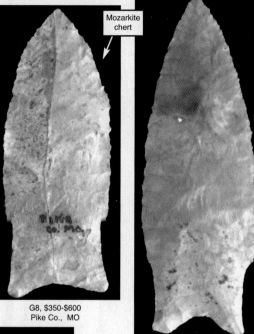

G7, $150-$275
South Cent. IA.

G8, $175-$300
MO/IL

G8, $350-$600
Pike Co., MO

G8, $300-$550
Sou. IL

LOCATION: Midwestern to Eastern states. **DESCRIPTION:** A medium to large size point with expanded auricles and horizontal, tapered to weak shoulders. Blade edges are usually serrated and bases are ground. In later times, this variant developed into the *Hemphill* point. **I.D. KEY:** Straightened extended shoulders.

G8, $350-$600
MO/IL

DALTON-NUCKOLLS - Early Archaic, 10,000 - 9200 B. P.

(Also see Dalton and Holland)

N
C

DALTON-NUCKOLLS (continued)

LOCATION: Midwestern to Southeastern states. **DESCRIPTION:** A medium to large size variant form, probably occurring from resharpening the *Greenbrier Dalton*. Bases are squared to lobbed to eared, and have a shallow concavity. **I.D. KEY:** Broad base and shoulders, flaking on blade.

G8, $250-$400
Graves Co., IL

Collateral flaking

DALTON-SLOAN - Early Archaic, 10,000 - 9200 B. P.

(Also see Allen, Angostura, Dalton, Greenbrier, Holland and Plainview)

IMPORTANT:
All Sloans shown half size

LOCATION: Midwestern states. **DESCRIPTION:** A large size variant of the *Dalton* point. This point is usually serrated, lacking shoulders and has a concave, fishtail base. Flaking is typically of the Dalton parallel style. **I.D. KEY:** No shoulders, serrations, fishtail base.

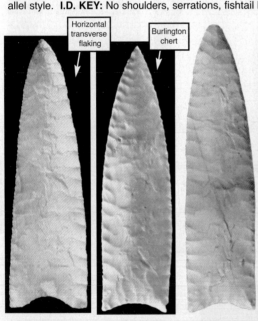

Horizontal transverse flaking

Burlington chert

Burlington chert

Burlington chert

Burlington chert

St. Clair Co. Ill. Sarnovsky coll.

G8, $1500-$2800
St. Louis Co., MO

G9, $2000-$3500
Scott Co., IL

G8, $2500-$4200
Boone Co., MO

G9, $3500-$6500
Warren Co., MO

G10, $4000-$7500
St. Clair Co., IL

G10+, $5500-$10,000
Bloomfield, MO

DECATUR - Early Archaic, 9000 - 3000 B. P.

(Also see Cobbs Triangular, Hardin, Kirk, Lost Lake and St. Charles)

Tip nick

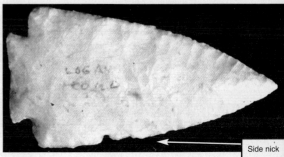

Side nick

G4, $35-$65
Fulton Co., IL

G7, $125-$225
Logan Co., IL

DECATUR (continued)

LOCATION: Eastern to Midwestern States. **DESCRIPTION:** A small to medium size, serrated, corner notched point that is usually beveled on one side of each face. The base is usually broken off (fractured) by a blow inward from each corner of the stem. Sometimes the sides of the stem and backs of the tangs are also fractured, and in rare cases, the tip may be fractured by a blow on each side directed towards the base. Bases are usually ground and flaking is of high quality. Basal fracturing also occurs in *Kirk, Motley, St. Charles* and *Snyders*.

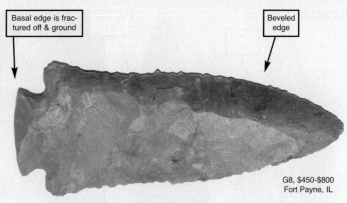

Basal edge is fractured off & ground

Beveled edge

G8, $450-$800
Fort Payne, IL

DELHI - Late Archaic; 3500 - 2000 B. P.

(Also see Helton)

G8, $65-$125
Cooper Co., MO

G9, $90-$150
Cooper Co., MO

LOCATION: Louisiana into Missouri. **DESCRIPTION:** A medium to large size, narrow, stemmed point with a long blade and strong, barbed shoulders. The stem can be square but usually expands and the base is straight to slightly convex. **I.D. KEY:** Base form, narrowness of blade.

DICKSON - Woodland,   2500 - 1600 B. P.

(Also see Adena, Burkett, Gary, Hidden Valley and Waubesa)

G5, $15-$25
MO

G5, $15-$35
Kay Co., OK

G8, $15-$45
MO

G9, $30-$50
AR

DICKSON (continued)

Pink chert

Florence flint

G8, $40-$75
MO

G6, $35-$65
Riley Co., KS

G7, $45-$85
MO

G8, $65-$125
MO

Foraker flint

Colorful Mozarkite

G6, $35-$65
MO

G6, $35-$65
Riley Co., KS

G7, $55-$100
MO

G7, $125-$200
Cooper Co., MO

Novaculite

LOCATION: Midwestern states. **DESCRIPTION:** Associated with the Hopewell culture. A medium to large size point with tapered shoulders and a contracting stem. High quality flaking and thinness is evident on most examples. **I.D. KEY:** Basal form.

G8, $48-$150
AR

G9, $250-$450
MO

G7, $150-
$250
IL

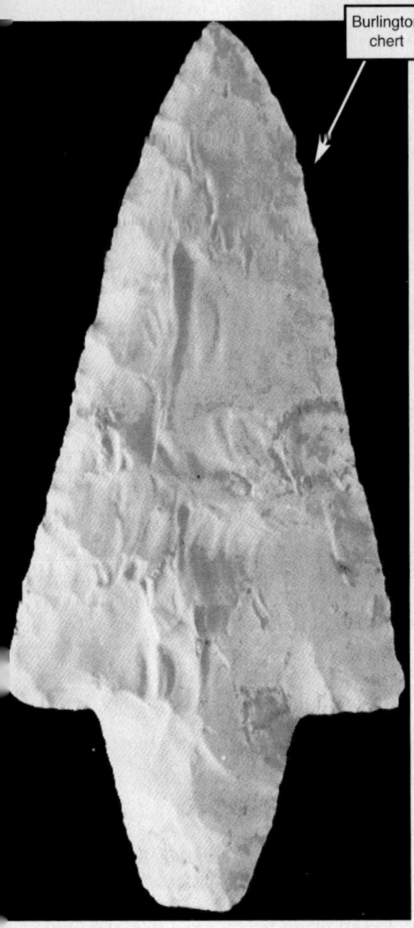

Heat treated
Burlington
chert

Burlington
chert

N
C

G9, $350-$600
IL

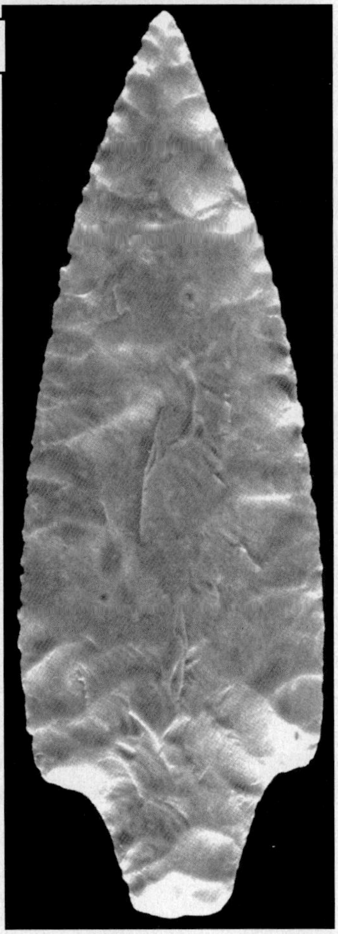

G9, $250-$450
Schuyler Co., IL

G10, $1200-$2200
Logan Co., IL

DOVETAIL (See St. Charles)

DRILL - Paleo to Historic, 11,500 - 200 B. P.

(Also see Scraper)

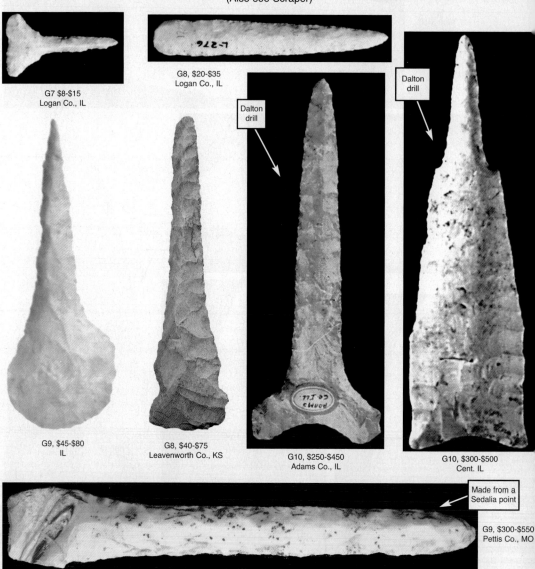

G7 $8-$15
Logan Co., IL

G8, $20-$35
Logan Co., IL

G9, $45-$80
IL

G8, $40-$75
Leavenworth Co., KS

Dalton drill

G10, $250-$450
Adams Co., IL

Dalton drill

G10, $300-$500
Cent. IL

Made from a
Sedalia point

G9, $300-$550
Pettis Co., MO

LOCATION: Everywhere. **DESCRIPTION:** Although many drills were made from scratch, all point types were made into the drill form. Usually, heavily resharpened and broken points were salvaged and rechipped into drills. These objects were certainly used as drills (evidence of extreme edge wear), but there is speculation that some of these forms may have been used as pins for clothing, ornaments, ear plugs and other uses.

EARLY OVOID KNIFE - Trans. Paleo-Early Archaic, 11,000 - 9000 B. P.

(Also see Turkeytail)

Burlington chert

G9, $450-$850
Fulton Co., IL. Rare
Shown 1/2 size

LOCATION: Arkansas, Missouri to Wisconsin. **DESCRIPTION:** A medium to large size, broad, thin, flat ovoid knife. Usually occurs as a double pointed blade but examples have been found with a small, notched stem. A very rare type. **I.D. KEY:** Broad blade, small stem to ovoid shape.

724

ARLY OVOID KNIFE (continued)

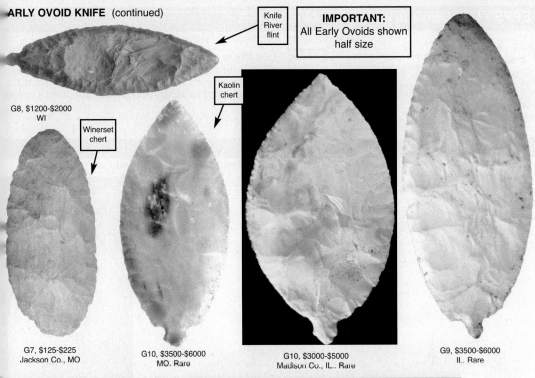

Knife River flint

IMPORTANT:
All Early Ovoids shown half size

Kaolin chert

G8, $1200-$2000
WI

Winerset chert

G7, $125-$225
Jackson Co., MO

G10, $3500-$6000
MO, Rare

G10, $3000-$5000
Madison Co., IL., Rare

G9, $3500-$6000
IL. Rare

EDEN - Transitional Paleo, 10,000 - 8000 B. P.

(Also see Agate Basin, Angostura, Hardin, Holland, Hollenberg Stemmed, Nebo Hill, Scottsbluff)

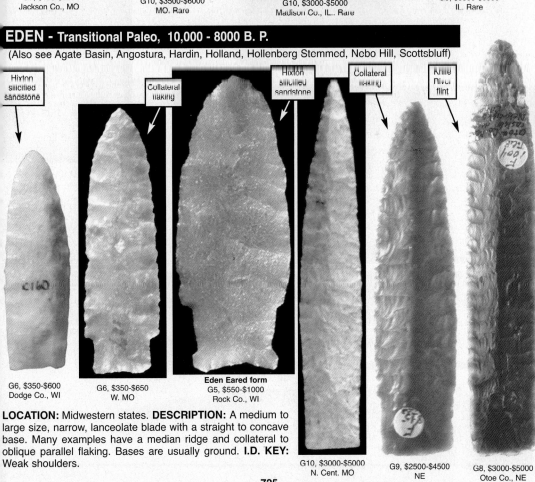

Hixton silicified sandstone

Collateral flaking

Hixton silicified sandstone

Collateral flaking

Knife River flint

N
C

G6, $350-$600
Dodge Co., WI

G6, $350-$650
W. MO

Eden Eared form
G5, $550-$1000
Rock Co., WI

G10, $3000-$5000
N. Cent. MO

G9, $2500-$4500
NE

G8, $3000-$5000
Otoe Co., NE

LOCATION: Midwestern states. **DESCRIPTION:** A medium to large size, narrow, lanceolate blade with a straight to concave base. Many examples have a median ridge and collateral to oblique parallel flaking. Bases are usually ground. **I.D. KEY:** Weak shoulders.

EPPS - Late Archaic to Woodland, 3500 - 2000 B. P.

(Also see Cupp, Kay Blade and Motley)

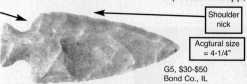

Shoulder nick

Acgtural size = 4-1/4"

G5, $30-$50
Bond Co., IL

LOCATION: Louisiana, Arkansas into Illinois. **DESCRIP-TION:** A medium to large broadly corner notched to expand ed stemmed point. Base is straight. Shoulders are not a strongly barbed as *Motley* points which also have a conve base.

ETLEY - Late Archaic, 4000 - 2500 B. P.

(Also see Hardin, Mehlville, Smith, Stilwell, Stone Square Stem and Wadlow)

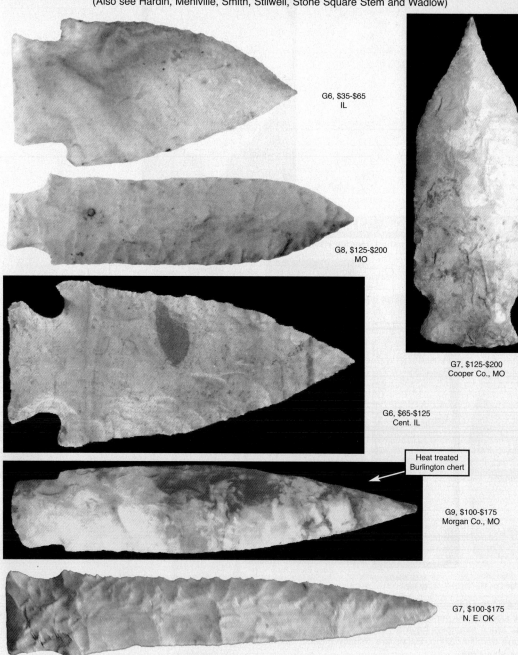

G6, $35-$65
IL

G8, $125-$200
MO

G7, $125-$200
Cooper Co., MO

G6, $65-$125
Cent. IL

Heat treated
Burlington chert

G9, $100-$175
Morgan Co., MO

G7, $100-$175
N. E. OK

726

G7, $175-$300
S. E. MO

G6, $125-$200
MO

G8, $250-$400
Greene Co., IL

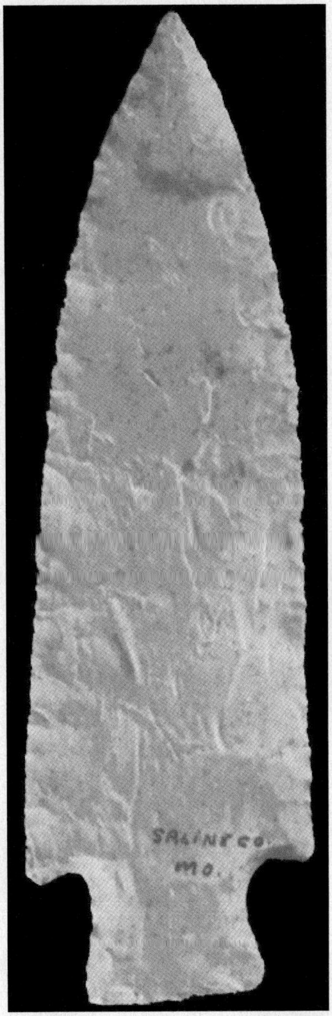

237

SALINE CO.
MO.

G8, $250-$450
Saline Co., MO

N
C

G8, $250-$400
MO

727

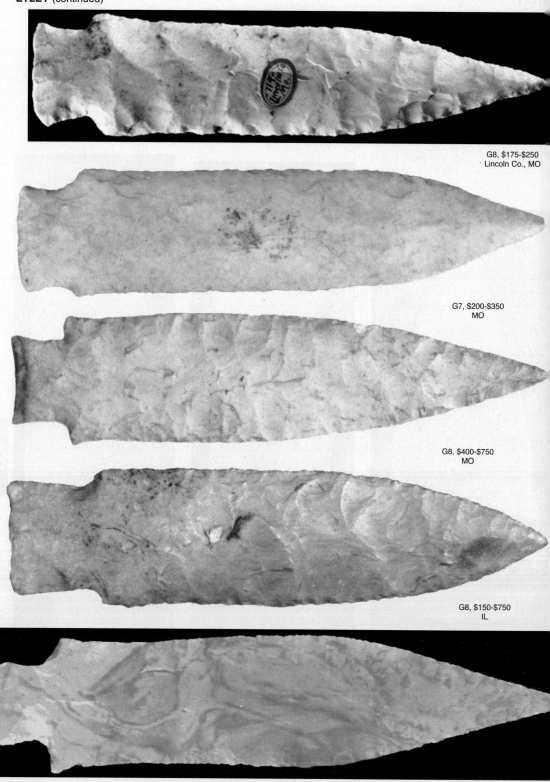

G8, $175-$250
Lincoln Co., MO

G7, $200-$350
MO

G8, $400-$750
MO

G8, $150-$750
IL

G8, $500-$900
Lincoln Co., MO

LOCATION: Midwestern states. The Etley site is in Calhoun Co., IL. Many *Wadlow* points were found there which is the pre-form for this type. **DESCRIPTION:** A large, narrow, blade with an angular point, recurved blade edges, a short, expanded stem and a straight to slightly convex base. Shoulders usually expand but have a tendency to point inward towards the base. **I.D. KEY:** Large size, barbs, narrow blade.

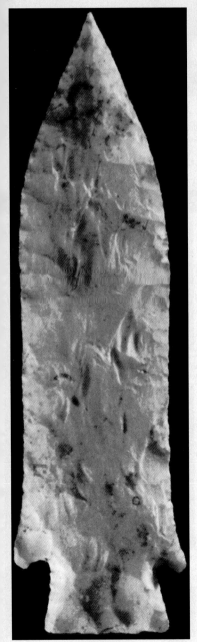

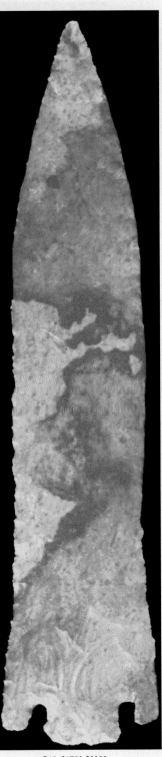

Tip wear

N C

G9, $650-$1200
Boone Co., MO

G10, $1700-$3000
Livingston, MO

G8, $450-$800
MO

EVANS - Late Archaic to Woodland, 4000 - 2000 B. P.

(Also see Hickory Ridge, Merkle and Turkeytail)

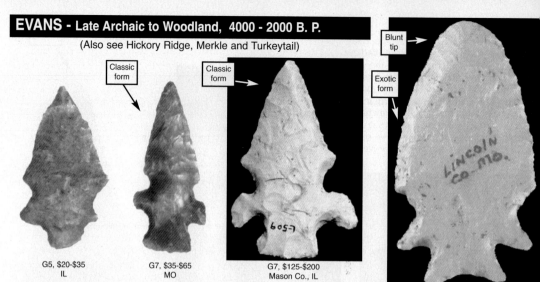

Classic form

Classic form

Blunt tip

Exotic form

LINCOLN CO. MO.

G5, $20-$35
IL

G7, $35-$65
MO

G7, $125-$200
Mason Co., IL

G8, $200-$350
Lincoln Co., MO

LOCATION: Midwestern to Southeastern states. **DESCRIPTION:** A medium to large size stemmed point that is notched on each side somewhere between the point and shoulders. A similar form is found in Ohio and called *Ohio Double-Notched.*

EXOTIC FORMS - Archaic-Mississippian, 5000 - 1000 B. P.

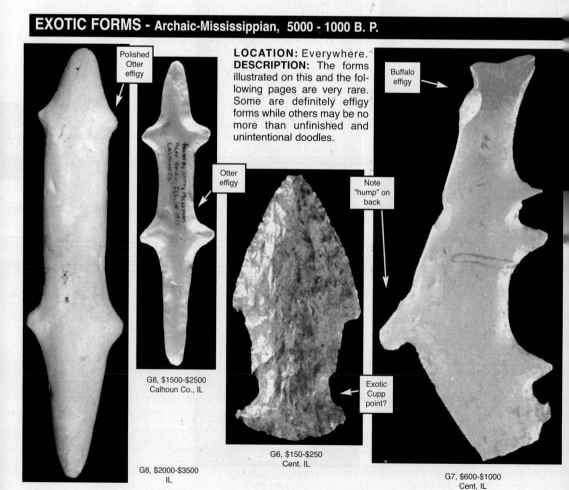

Polished Otter effigy

Otter effigy

Buffalo effigy

Note "hump" on back

Exotic Cupp point?

LOCATION: Everywhere. **DESCRIPTION:** The forms illustrated on this and the following pages are very rare. Some are definitely effigy forms while others may be no more than unfinished and unintentional doodles.

G8, $1500-$2500
Calhoun Co., IL

G6, $150-$250
Cent. IL

G8, $2000-$3500
IL

G7, $600-$1000
Cent. IL

FERRY - Middle to late Archaic, 5500 - 4500 B. P.

(Also see Grand, Hardin, Kay Blade, Kirk Corner Notched and Stilwell)

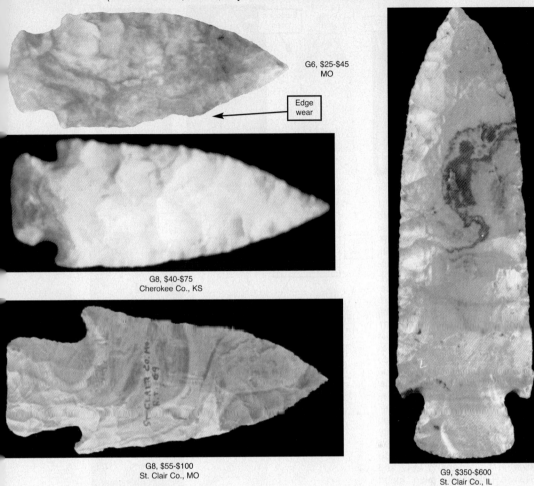

G6, $25-$45
MO

Edge
wear

G8, $40-$75
Cherokee Co., KS

G8, $55-$100
St. Clair Co., MO

G9, $350-$600
St. Clair Co., IL

LOCATION: Illinois and Missouri. **DESCRIPTION:** A medium to large size, broad, stemmed point with a bulbous base and sharp tips. The blade is convex to recurved. The shoulders are barbed. **I.D. KEY:** Basal form and barbs.

FIRSTVIEW - Transitional Paleo, 10,000 - 8000 B. P.

(Also see Agate Basin, Angostura, Eden, Holland, Nebo Hill, Scottsbluff)

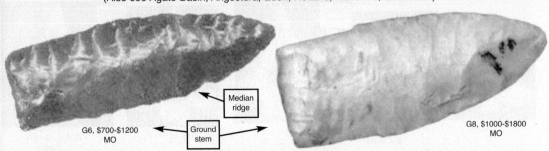

Median
ridge

G6, $700-$1200
MO

Ground
stem

G8, $1000-$1800
MO

LOCATION: Missouri into Texas to Colorado. **DESCRIPTION:** A medium to large size lanceolate blade with early collateral flaking and very weak shoulders. A variant of the *Scottsbluff* type made by the Cody Complex people. Bases are straight and stem sides are parallel. Many examples are median ridged with collateral, parallel flaking. **I.D. KEY:** Broad base, weak shoulders.

FOLSOM - Paleo, 11,000 - 10,000 B. P.

(Also see Clovis, Cumberland and Goshen)

Fully fluted

Flint

Burlington chert

Fully fluted

G8, $700-$1200
Logan Co., IL

G8, $1600-$3000
MN

G8, $1800-$3200
Jackson Co., MO

G8, $1800-$3400
Greene Co., IL

G8, $2000-$3600
Jersey Co., IL

G9, $2500-$4200
Knox Co., IL

LOCATION: N. Indiana Westward to Texas, northward to the Dakotas and West to Montana. **DESCRIPTION:** A small to medium size, thin, high quality, fluted point with contracted to slightly expanding, pointed auricles and a concave base. Fluting usually extends the entire length of each face. Blade flaking is extremely fine. The hafting area is ground. A very rare type, even in area of highest incidence. Modern reproductions have been made and extreme caution should be exercised in acquiring an original specimen. Often found in association with extinct bison fossil remains. **I.D. KEY:** Thinness and flaking style (Excessive secondary flaking). **NOTE:** A *Folsom* site was recently found on the Tippecanoe River in N. Indiana. *Clovis* and *Beaver Lake* were also found there.

Fully fluted

A "Barnes" Folsom, believed by experts to be a little older than the traditional folsom

Burlington chert

Silicified sandstone

Fully fluted

Knife River flint

G9, $2500-$4800
WI

G9, $3000-$5500
Greene Co., IL

G10+, $12,000-$20,000
S.W. WI; photo from a cast by Pete Bostrom

G10, $10,000 $18,000
N. IA

FOX VALLEY - Early to Middle Archaic, 9000 - 4000 B. P.

(Also see Kirk, Lake Erie and Cossatot River)

Classic form

Classic form

G5, $30-$50
IL

G9, $65-$125
IL. Classic.

G8, $65-$125
Will Co., IL

G8, $60-$100
Will Co., IL

G10, $150-$275
IL. Classic.

LOCATION: Midwestern states. **DESCRIPTION:** A small size, triangular point with flaring shoulders and a short bifurcated stem. Shoulders are sometimes clipped winged and have a tendency to turn towards the tip. Blades exhibit early parallel flaking and the edges are usually serrated. An identical point is found in TN, KY to WV to New York known as *Kanawha Stemmed*. **I.D. KEY:** Bifurcated base and barbs.

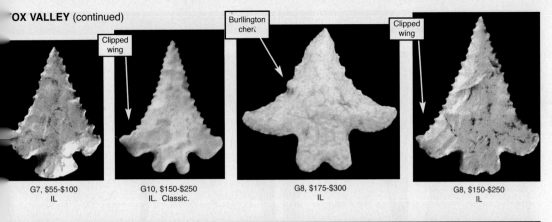

Clipped wing

Burllington chert

Clipped wing

G7, $55-$100
IL

G10, $150-$250
IL. Classic.

G8, $175-$300
IL

G8, $150-$250
IL

GARY - Late Archaic to Early Woodland, 3200 - 300 B. P.

(Also see Adena, Burkett, Dickson, Hidden Valley, Peisker Diamond and Waubesa)

G4, $2-$5
Clinton Co., IL

Mozarkite

N
C

G5, $8-$15
N. E. OK

G4, $8-$15
N. E. OK

G6, $15-$25
N. E. OK

G8, $35-$60
MO

G9, $250-$450
MO

G8, $40-$70
N. E. OK

LOCATION: Midwestern to Southwestern states. **DESCRIPTION:** A medium size, triangular point with a medium to long, contracted, pointed to rounded base. Shoulders are usually tapered. **I.D. KEY:** Similar to *Adena*, but thinned more.

GIBSON - Mid to late Woodland, 2000 - 1500 B. P.

(Also see Cupp, Grand, Motley and St. Charles)

G8, $80-$175
IA

G8, $65-$125
IL

G8, $65-$125
Blackjack, MO

G9, $150-$250
Lee Co., IA

G6, $40-$75
Walworth Co., WI

LOCATION: Midwestern to Eastern states. Gibson Mound group (1969), type site in Calhoun Co., IL. **DESCRIPTION:** A medium to large size side to corner notched point with a large, convex base.

GODAR - Late Archaic, 4500 - 3500 B. P.

(Also see Hemphill, Hickory Ridge, Osceola and Raddatz)

Heat treated Burlington chert

G6, $25-$45
Cooper Co., MO

G7, $50-$80
Madison Co., IL

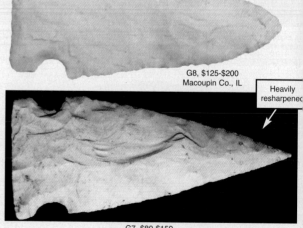

Burlington chert

G8, $125-$200
Macoupin Co., IL

Heavily resharpened

G7, $80-$150
Morgan Co., MO

734

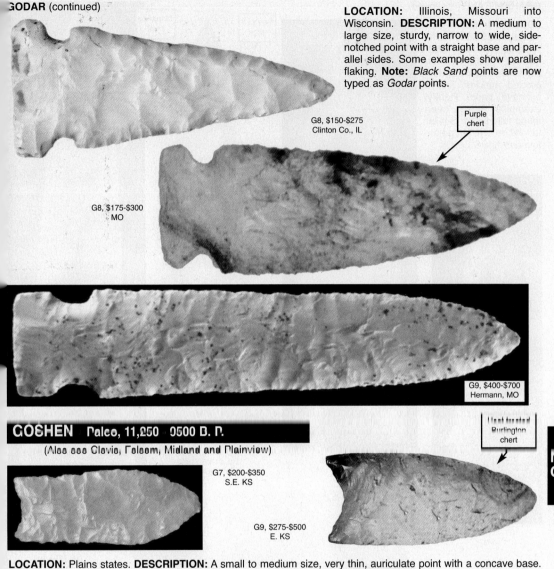

GODAR (continued)

LOCATION: Illinois, Missouri into Wisconsin. **DESCRIPTION:** A medium to large size, sturdy, narrow to wide, side-notched point with a straight base and parallel sides. Some examples show parallel flaking. **Note:** *Black Sand* points are now typed as *Godar* points.

G8, $150-$275
Clinton Co., IL

Purple chert

G8, $175-$300
MO

G9, $400-$700
Hermann, MO

Heat treated
Burlington chert

N
C

GOSHEN Paleo, 11,250 - 9500 B. P.

(Also see Clovis, Folsom, Midland and Plainview)

G7, $200-$350
S.E. KS

G9, $275-$500
E. KS

LOCATION: Plains states. **DESCRIPTION:** A small to medium size, very thin, auriculate point with a concave base. Basal corners range from being rounded to pointed. Blade edges are parallel sided to recurved. Basal area is ground. Flaking is oblique to horizontal transverse. A very rare type. **I.D. KEY:** Thinness, auricles

GRAHAM CAVE - Early to Middle Archaic, 9000 - 5000 B. P.

(Also see Godar, Hemphill, Howard County, Osceola and Raddatz)

G5, $45-$80
IL

G10, $250-$475
Morgan Co., MO

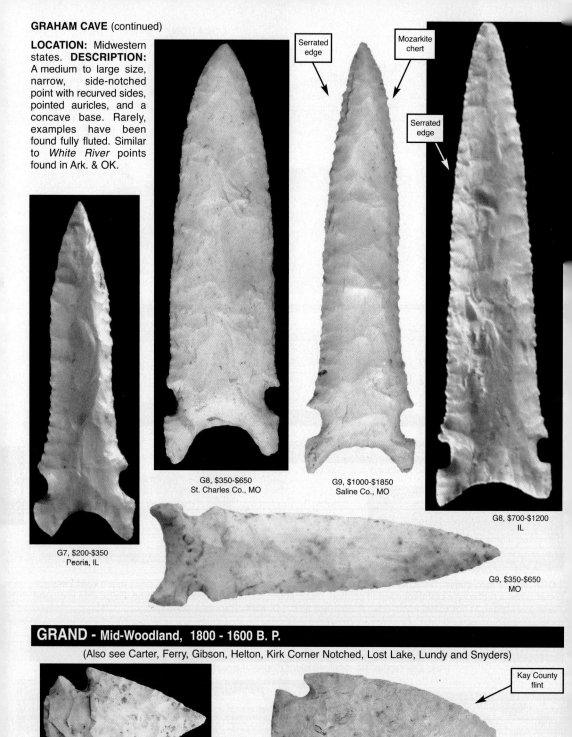

GRAHAM CAVE (continued)

LOCATION: Midwestern states. **DESCRIPTION:** A medium to large size, narrow, side-notched point with recurved sides, pointed auricles, and a concave base. Rarely, examples have been found fully fluted. Similar to *White River* points found in Ark. & OK.

Serrated edge

Mozarkite chert

Serrated edge

G8, $350-$650
St. Charles Co., MO

G9, $1000-$1850
Saline Co., MO

G8, $700-$1200
IL

G7, $200-$350
Peoria, IL

G9, $350-$650
MO

GRAND - Mid-Woodland, 1800 - 1600 B. P.

(Also see Carter, Ferry, Gibson, Helton, Kirk Corner Notched, Lost Lake, Lundy and Snyders)

Kay County flint

G8, $15-$25
N. E. OK

G7, $25-$40
Cowley Co., KS

LOCATION: Oklahoma, Kansas. **DESCRIPTION:** A medium sized, broad, corner notched point with barbed shoulders and an expanding, convex base. Basal corners can be sharp. **I.D. KEY:** Width of blade, corner notching.

G6, $25-$40
Burlington, IL

G5, $15-$25
MO

G10, $65-$125
MO

G8, $65-$125
Riley Co., KS

Kay
County
flint

G6, $8-$15
Cowley Co., KS

G7, $80-$150
Cowley Co., KS

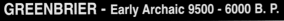

N
C

GREENBRIER - Early Archaic 9500 - 6000 B. P.

(Also see Dalton, Pike County and Pine Tree)

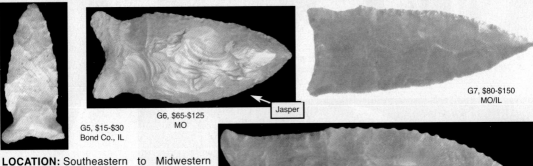

G5, $15-$30
Bond Co., IL

G6, $65-$125
MO

Jasper

G7, $80-$150
MO/IL

G10, $800-$1500
IL

LOCATION: Southeastern to Midwestern states. **DESCRIPTION:** A medium to large size, auriculate point with tapered shoulders and broad, weak side notches. Blade edges are usually finely serrated. The base can be concave, lobbed, eared, straight or bifurcated and is ground. Early examples can be fluted. This type developed from the *Dalton* point and later evolved into other types such as the *Pine Tree* point. **I.D. KEY:** Heavy grinding in shoulders, good secondary edgework.

737

GREENBRIER (continued)

Banded chert

G10, $250-$450
MO

G8, $500-$900
Adams Co., IL

HARAHEY - Mississippian, 700 - 350 B. P.

(Also see Lerma and Morse Knife)

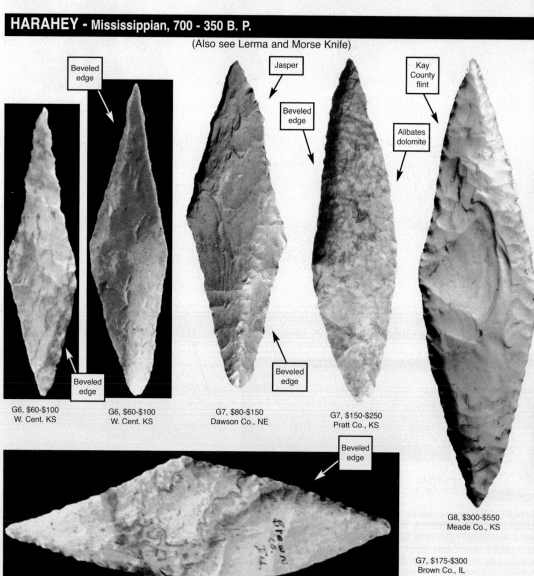

Beveled edge

Beveled edge

Jasper

Beveled edge

Kay County flint

Alibates dolomite

G6, $60-$100
W. Cent. KS

G6, $60-$100
W. Cent. KS

Beveled edge

G7, $80-$150
Dawson Co., NE

Beveled edge

G7, $150-$250
Pratt Co., KS

Beveled edge

G8, $300-$550
Meade Co., KS

G7, $175-$300
Brown Co., IL

LOCATION: Midwestern states to Texas. **DESCRIPTION:** A large size, double pointed knife that is beveled on all four sides of each face when resharpened forming a rhomboid cross section. **I.D. KEY:** Rhomboid cross section, four beveled form. For two beveled form see *Neosho.*

738

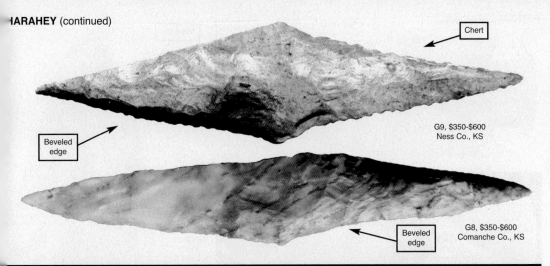

Chert

Beveled edge

G9, $350-$600
Ness Co., KS

Beveled edge

G8, $350-$600
Comanche Co., KS

HARDIN - Early Archaic, 9000 - 6000 B. P.

(Also see Ferry, Kirk, Lost Lake, St. Charles, Scottsbluff and Stilwell)

Serrated edge

Hixton silicified sandstone

Barb wear

G6, $55-$100
Cent. IL

G6, $90-$175
St. Clair Co., IL

G7, $40-$125
Cent. IL

Fulton Co. Ill.

G7, $275-$500
Fulton Co., IL

Serrated edge

Burlington chert

Burlington chert

58.

G6, $175-$300
Cent. IL

G9, $200-$350
Fulton Co., IL

G8, $350-$600
Madison Co., IL

LOCATION: Midwestern to Eastern states. **DESCRIPTION:** A large size, well made triangular barbed point with an expanded base that is usually ground. Resharpened examples have one beveled edge on each face. This type is believed to have evolved from the *Scottsbluff* type. Examples have occurred with fluted bases **I.D. KEY:** Notches and stem form.

Burlington chert

Mozarkite

G9, $300-$550
Harrison Co., MO

Serrated edge

G9, $700-$1200
St. Louis Co., MO

G9, $275-$500
IL

Serrated edge

Serrated edge

Serrated edge

G9, $300-$550
IL

Serrated, beveled edge

G9, $500-$950
Scott Co., IL

G7, $450-$850
Jersey Co., IL

G9, $1200-$2000
IL

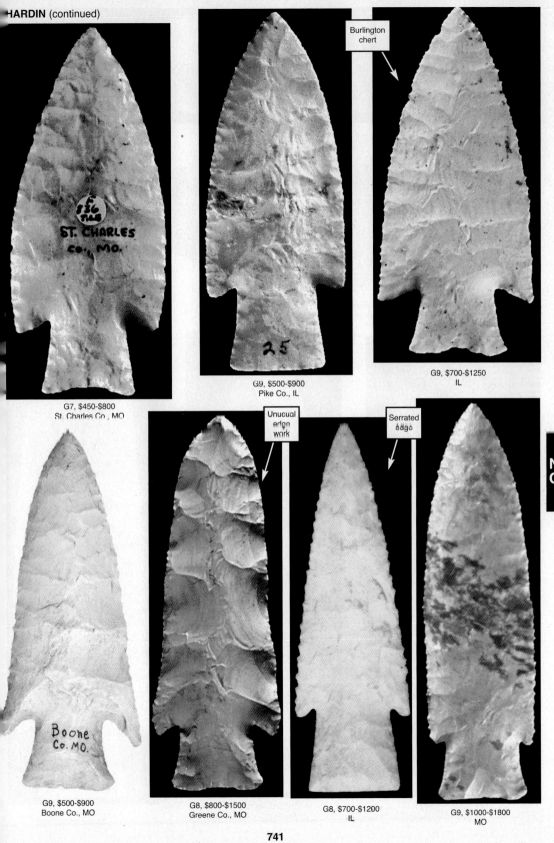

Burlington chert

G7, $450-$800
St. Charles Co., MO

G9, $500-$900
Pike Co., IL

G9, $700-$1250
IL

Unusual edge work

Serrated edge

N
C

G9, $500-$900
Boone Co., MO

G8, $800-$1500
Greene Co., MO

G8, $700-$1200
IL

G9, $1000-$1800
MO

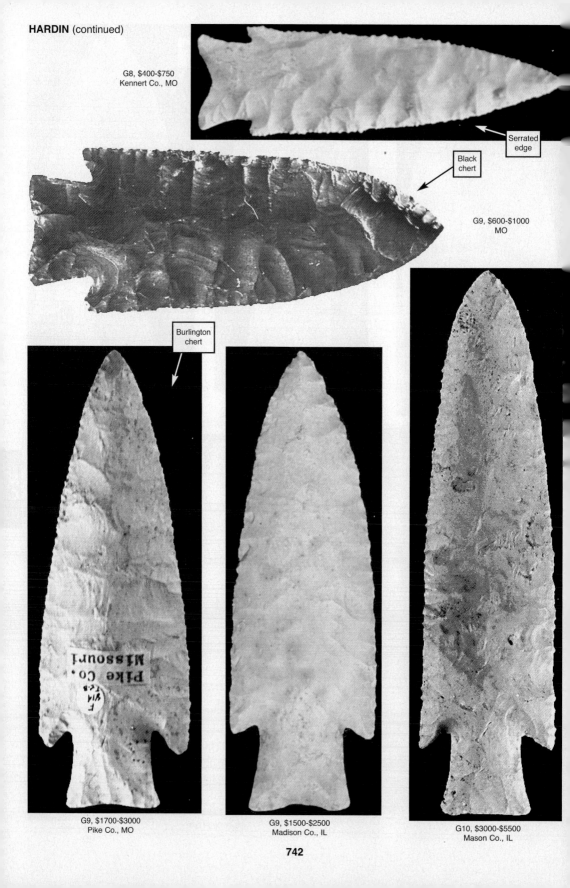

HARDIN (continued)

G8, $400-$750
Kennert Co., MO

Serrated edge

Black chert

G9, $600-$1000
MO

Burlington chert

G9, $1700-$3000
Pike Co., MO

G9, $1500-$2500
Madison Co., IL

G10, $3000-$5500
Mason Co., IL

HARRELL - Mississippian, 900 - 500 B. P.

(Also see Cahokia, Huffaker and Washita)

G5, $25-$40
IL

G5, $25-$40
IL

G8, $50-$95
Pottowatomie Co., KS

G4, $25-$40
IL

G4, $15-$25
IL

Tip damage

G7, $45-$80
Howard Co., MO

G7, $45-$80
Riley Co., KS

LOCATION: Midwestern states. **DESCRIPTION:** A small, thin, triangular arrow point with side and basal notches. Basal ears can be pointed. Bases are usually slightly concave with a basal notch. **I.D. KEY:** Triple notching.

HASKELL - Mississippian to Historic, 800 - 600 B. P.

(Also see Bayogoula, Collins and Washita)

G6, $20-$35
Cherokee Co., KS

G7, $25-$45
Cherokee Co., KS

G9, $35-$60
IL

G9, $65-$125
IL

LOCATION: Midwestern states. **DESCRIPTION:** A small, thin, triangular arrow point with upward sloping side notches. The base is concave and on some examples, basal ears can be extreme. **I.D. KEY:** Broad basal ears.

HATTEN KNIFE - Late Archaic, 3000 - 1800 B. P.

(Also see Hardin)

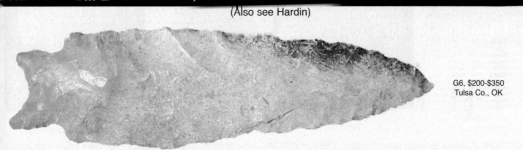

G6, $200-$350
Tulsa Co., OK

N
C

LOCATION: Oklahoma into Wisconsin. **DESCRIPTION:** A large size, narrow, stemmed knife with short shoulders that can be horizontal to slightly barbed and side notches angled in towards the tip. Bases are concave and the stem is usually ground. **I.D. KEY:** Small side notches.

HAYES - Mississippian, 1200 - 600 B. P.

(Also see Alba, Homan and Sequoyah)

G7, $65-$125
Central, MO

Serrated edge

G9, $350-$550
IL

Serrated edge

G10, $250-$400
IL

LOCATION: Midwestern states. **DESCRIPTION:** A small to medium size, narrow, expanded tang point with a turkey-tail base. Blade edges are usually strongly recurved forming sharp pointed barbs. Base is pointed and can be double notched. Some examples are serrated. **I.D. KEY:** Pointed base and flaking style.

HAYES (continued)

G9, $400-$700
IL

G10, $400-$750
IL

Mucronate tip

G9, $125-$225
IL

HEAVY DUTY - Early to Middle Archaic, 7000 - 5000 B. P.

(Also see Rochester, Stone Square Stem)

Bifurcated base

BUREAU Co. IL.

G9, $150-$250
Adams Co., IL

G6, $175-$300
Dewitt Co., IL

G9, $150-$250
Cent. IL

G8, $175-$300
Bureau Co., IL

LOCATION: Eastern to Midwestern states. **DESCRIPTION:** A medium to large size, thick, serrated point with a parallel stem and a straight to slightly concave base. **I.D. KEY:** Base, thickness, flaking.

HELL GAP - Transitional Paleo, 10,300 - 9500 B. P.

(Also see Agate Basin, Angostura and Burroughs)

LOCATION: Midwestern to Western states. **DESCRIPTION:** A medium to large size, lanceolate point with a long, contracting stem. The widest part of the blade is above the midsection. The base is straight to slightly concave and the stem edges are usually ground. **I.D. KEY:** Early flaking and base form.

G8, $200-$350
MO

Westerville chert

G10, $800-$1500
Clay Co., MO

Edge wear

Florence chert

Edge wear

G4, $65-$125
S. E. KS

G7, $265-$500
S.E. KS

HELTON - Late Archaic to early Woodland, 4000 - 2500 B. P.

(Also see Apple Creek, Delhi, Kay Blade, Lehigh, Lundy and Motley)

Toronto flint

N
C

G8, $30-$50
Cherokee Co., KS

G7, $35-$60
Atchison Co., KS

G6, $25-$40
Riley Co., KS

G6, $30-$50
Cherokee Co., KS

LOCATION: Midwestern states. **DESCRIPTION:** A medium to large size, broad point with a short, expanding stem. Shoulders are horizontal to barbed, and the base is convex. **I.D. KEY:** Base form.

HEMPHILL - Mid to Late Archaic, 7000 - 5000 B. P.

(Also see Godar, Graham Cave, Howard County, Osceola, Raddatz and Turin)

G5, $12-$20
Bond Co., IL

LOCATION: Illinois, Missouri into Wisc. Type site-Brown Co., IL. Associated with the Old Copper & Red Ochre culture. **DESCRIPTION:** A medium to large size side-notched point with a concave base and parallel to convex sides. These points are usually thinner and of higher quality than the similar *Osceola* type.

745

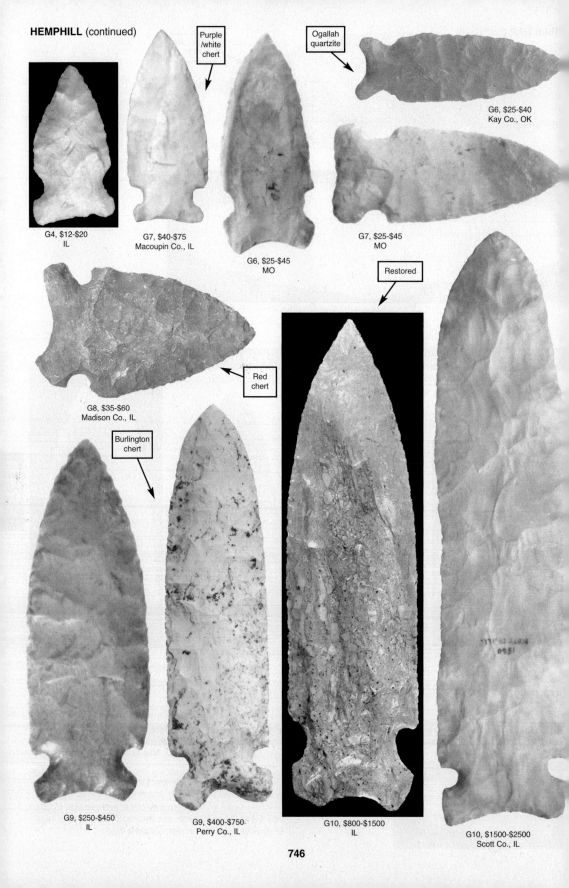

HEMPHILL (continued)

Purple /white chert

Ogallah quartzite

G4, $12-$20
IL

G7, $40-$75
Macoupin Co., IL

G6, $25-$45
MO

G6, $25-$40
Kay Co., OK

G7, $25-$45
MO

Restored

Red chert

G8, $35-$60
Madison Co., IL

Burlington chert

G9, $250-$450
IL

G9, $400-$750
Perry Co., IL

G10, $800-$1500
IL

G10, $1500-$2500
Scott Co., IL

Ground
ears &
notches

G10, $2700-$5000
Osage Co., MO

HI-LO - Transitional Paleo, 10,000 - 8000 B. P.

(Also see Angostura, Browns Valley and Burroughs)

G7, $150-$275
MO

LOCATION: Midwestern states. **DESCRIPTION:** A medium to large size, broad, eared, lanceolate point with a concave base. Believed to be related to *Plainview* and *Dalton* points.

HICKORY RIDGE - Early Archaic, 7000 - 5000 B.P.

(Also see Godar, Hemphill, Osceola, Raddatz, Robinson and Turin)

N
C

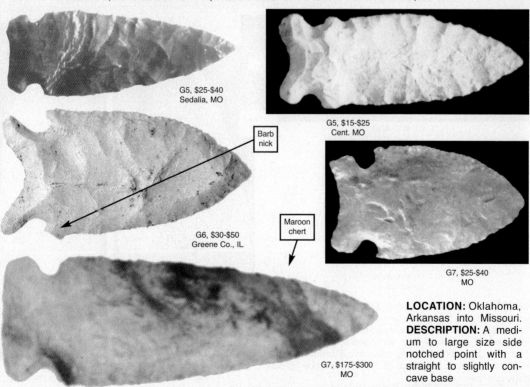

G5, $25-$40
Sedalia, MO

G5, $15-$25
Cent. MO

Barb
nick

Maroon
chert

G6, $30-$50
Greene Co., IL

G7, $25-$40
MO

G7, $175-$300
MO

LOCATION: Oklahoma, Arkansas into Missouri. **DESCRIPTION:** A medium to large size side notched point with a straight to slightly concave base

HIDDEN VALLEY - Early to mid-Archaic, 8500 - 7000 B. P.

(Also see Adena, Dickson, Gary and Waubesa)

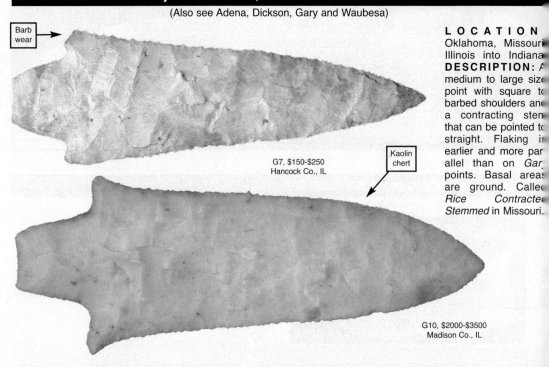

Barb wear

G7, $150-$250
Hancock Co., IL

Kaolin chert

G10, $2000-$3500
Madison Co., IL

LOCATION
Oklahoma, Missouri
Illinois into Indiana
DESCRIPTION: A
medium to large size
point with square to
barbed shoulders and
a contracting stem
that can be pointed to
straight. Flaking is
earlier and more parallel than on *Gary*
points. Basal areas
are ground. Called
*Rice Contracted
Stemmed* in Missouri.

HOLLAND - Early Archaic, 10,000 - 9000 B. P.

(Also see Dalton, Dalton-Sloan, Eden, Hardin, Johnson, Pike County and Scottsbluff)

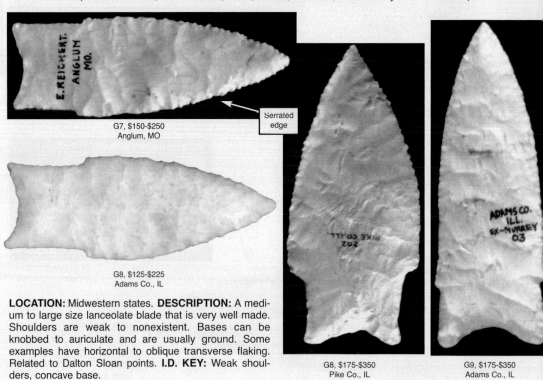

E. REICHERT.
ANGLUM
MO.

G7, $150-$250
Anglum, MO

Serrated edge

G8, $125-$225
Adams Co., IL

G8, $175-$350
Pike Co., IL

G9, $175-$350
Adams Co., IL

LOCATION: Midwestern states. **DESCRIPTION:** A medium to large size lanceolate blade that is very well made. Shoulders are weak to nonexistent. Bases can be knobbed to auriculate and are usually ground. Some examples have horizontal to oblique transverse flaking. Related to Dalton Sloan points. **I.D. KEY:** Weak shoulders, concave base.

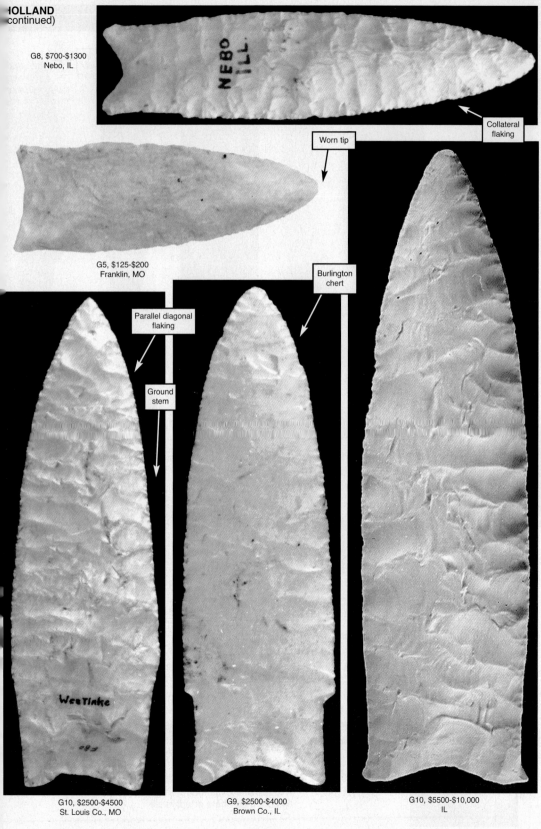

G8, $700-$1300
Nebo, IL

NEBO ILL.

Collateral flaking

Worn tip

G5, $125-$200
Franklin, MO

Burlington chert

Parallel diagonal flaking

Ground stem

WeeTinke

N
C

G10, $2500-$4500
St. Louis Co., MO

G9, $2500-$4000
Brown Co., IL

G10, $5500-$10,000
IL

HOLLENBERG STEMMED - Early Archaic, 9000 - 7500 B. P.

(Also see Eden, Munker's Creek and Scottsbluff)

Tip wear →

G7, $55-$100
Washington Co., KS

G7, $55-$100
Jefferson Co., NE

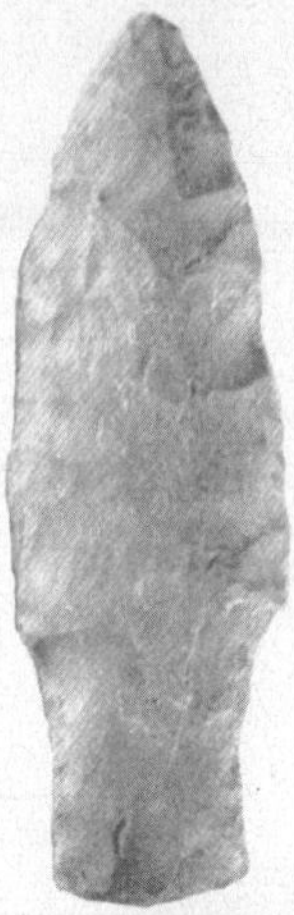

G6, $55-$100
Washington Co., KS

G7, $80-$150
Washington Co., KS

G6, $80-$150
Jefferson Co., KS

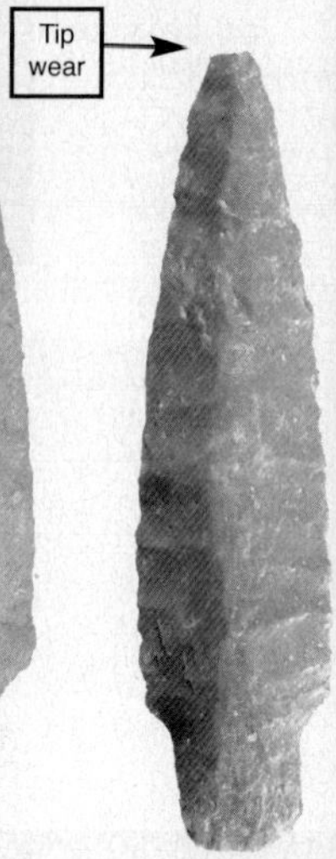

G5, $40-$75
Washington Co., KS

Edge wear ↓

Tip wear →

G8, $150-$250
Washington Co., KS

G6, $55-$100
Washington Co., KS

G7, $125-$200
Jefferson Co., NE

G6, $55-$100
Gage Co., NE

G8, $150-$250
Washington Co., KS

G8, $150-$250
Nuckolls Co., NE

LOCATION: Central to Eastern Nebraska and Kansas. **DESCRIPTION:** A medium to large size, narrow, stemmed point with tapered shoulders and a straight to convex base. Related to *Eden* and *Eden Eared*. Stem sides are parallel to slightly expanding and are ground.

HOMAN - Mississippian, 1000 - 700 B. P.

(Also see Agee, Alba, Hayes and Sequoyah)

G9, $125-$200
IL

LOCATION: Northwest to Midwestern states. **DESCRIPTION:** A small size expanded barb point with a bulbous stem. Some tips are mucronate or apiculate.

750

(Also see Carter, Dickson, Gibson, Motley, North, St. Charles, Snyders & Waubesa)

G5, $50-$80
IL

G6, $20-$35
Jackson Co., IL

G8, $150-$250
MO

G7, $150-$250
Springfield, MO

G5, $55-$100
IL

G8, $150-$275
Cooper Co., MO

G5, $55-$100
Jefferson Co., KS

N C

LOCATION: Midwestern to Eastern states. **DESCRIPTION:** A large size, broad, corner notched point that is similar to *Snyders*. Made by the Hopewell culture.

HOWARD COUNTY - Early Archaic, 7500 - 6500 B. P.

(Also see Cache River, Gibson, Grand, Helton, St. Charles)

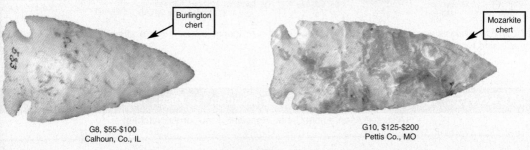

Burlington chert

Mozarkite chert

G8, $55-$100
Calhoun, Co., IL

G10, $125-$200
Pettis Co., MO

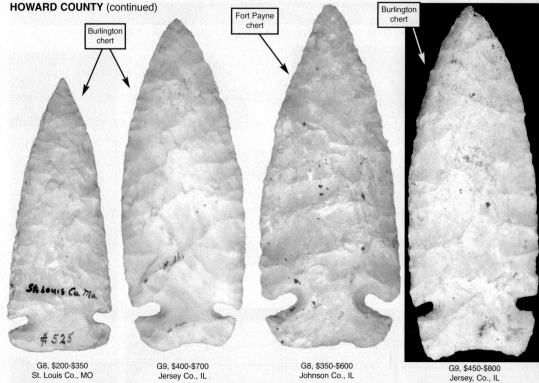

Burlington chert

Fort Payne chert

Burlington chert

Burlington chert

G8, $200-$350 St. Louis Co., MO	G9, $400-$700 Jersey Co., IL	G8, $350-$600 Johnson Co., IL	G9, $450-$800 Jersey, Co., IL

LOCATION: Illinois and Missouri. **DESCRIPTION:** A small to medium size, thin, well-made point. The blade is long and triangular with slightly convex edges. Notches are narrow and fairly low on the sides, entering at a slight diagonally upward angle. The basal edge may range from slightly incurvate to slightly convex. It has squared basal corners on straight-based points and rounded basal corners on convex-based points. Basal edge has light grinding to none. If grinding is absent, light crushing of the basal edge is noted. A peculiarity of this point is that it has been recognized primarily for its like-new, unused condition with little to no evidence of resharpening, as has been noted on *Cache River* and *Kessel* points. For years this has been an un-named variant of the *Cache River* points. **I.D. KEY:** Lack of basal grinding and resharpening. Can be much larger than *Cache River* or *Kessel* points.

HUFFAKER - Mississippian, 1000 - 500 B. P.

(Also see Cahokia, Evans and Washita)

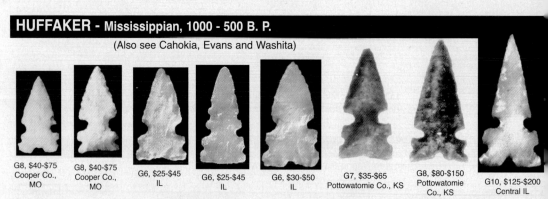

G8, $40-$75 Cooper Co., MO	G8, $40-$75 Cooper Co., MO	G6, $25-$45 IL	G6, $25-$45 IL	G6, $30-$50 IL	G7, $35-$65 Pottowatomie Co., KS	G8, $80-$150 Pottowatomie Co., KS	G10, $125-$200 Central IL

LOCATION: Midwestern states. **DESCRIPTION:** A small size triangular point with a straight to concave base and double side notches. Bases can have a single notch.

JACKS REEF CORNER NOTCHED - Late Woodland to Miss., 1500 - 1000 B. P.

(Also see Afton, Apple Creek, Hopewell, Kirk Corner Notched)

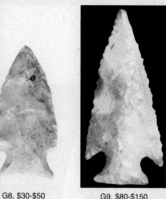

Pentagonal form

G8, $30-$50
Madison Co., IL

G9, $80-$150
Cooper Co., MO

G9, $70-$120
Cooper Co., MO

G8, $40-$75
Madison Co., IL

G9, $80-$150
MO

LOCATION: Midwestern to Eastern states. **DESCRIPTION:** A small to medium size, thin, corner notched point that is well made. The blade is convex to pentagonal. Some examples are widely corner notched and appear to be expanded stem points with barbed shoulders. Rarely, they are basal notched. The *pentagonal form* also exists as a variation of the type. **I.D. KEY:** Thinness, made by the birdpoint people.

JOHNSON - Early to Middle Archaic, 9000 - 5000 B. P.

(Also see Hidden Valley, Holland and Stone Square Stem)

N C

G7, $35-$65
Cherokee Co., KS

G8, $45-$85
N. E. OK

G9, $65-$125
Washington Co., KS

LOCATION: Mississippi to Kansas. **DESCRIPTION:** A medium size, thick, well made, expanded to contracting stem point with a broad, short, concave base. Bases are usually thinned and grinding appears on some specimens. Shoulders can be slight and are roughly horizontal. **I.D. KEY:** Broad stem that is thinned.

KAMPSVILLE - Late Archaic to Woodland, 3000 - 2500 B. P.

(Also see Cupp, Helton, Kings, Kramer, Lundy, Lehigh and Motley)

LOCATION: Midwestern states. **DESCRIPTION:** A medium to large size, point with broad corner notches producing a parallel stem and barbed shoulders. Similar to *Buck Creek* found in Kentucky.

G6, $45-$85
Pettis Co., MO

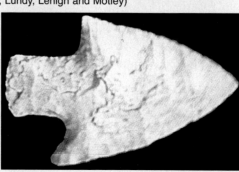

753

(Also see Cupp, Epps, Helton, Kramer, Lundy, Lehigh and Motley)

G9, $80-$150
N.E. OK

Toronto flint

G6, $35-$60
Leavenworth Co., KS

LOCATION: Midwestern states.
DESCRIPTION: A medium to large size point with a long expanding stem and barbed shoulders. Used by the Mississippian, Caddoan people.

G6, $35-$60
Douglas Co., KS

G7, $200-$350
St. Louis Co., MO

G10, $2700-$5000
Greene Co., MO

KINGS - Middle Archaic to Woodland, 4500 - 2500 B. P.

(Also see Apple Creek, Hopewell, Kampsville, Kirk Corner and Motley)

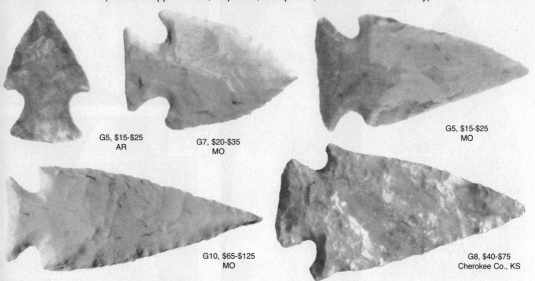

G5, $15-$25
AR

G7, $20-$35
MO

G5, $15-$25
MO

G10, $65-$125
MO

G8, $40-$75
Cherokee Co., KS

LOCATION: Midwestern states. **DESCRIPTION:** A medium size corner notched point with an expanding stem and barbed shoulders. Barbs and basal corners are sharp. Base can be convex, straight or concave.

KIRK CORNER NOTCHED - Early to Middle Archaic, 9000 - 6000 B. P.

(Also see Apple Creek, Decatur, Lost Lake, Pine Tree, St. Charles & Stilwell)

Kay County flint

All have ground basal areas

G7, $40-$75
Chautauqua Co., KS

G6, $55-$100
WI

G9, $65-$125
Cooper Co. MO

G6, $30-$50
IL

G9, $150-$250, IL

G5, $15-$25
IL

LOCATION: Midwestern to Southeasten states. **DESCRIPTION:** A medium to large size, corner notched point. Blade edges can be convex to recurved and are finely serrated on many examples. The base can be convex, concave, straight or auriculate. Points that are beveled on one side of each face would fall under the *Lost Lake* type. **I.D. KEY:** Secondary edgework.

755

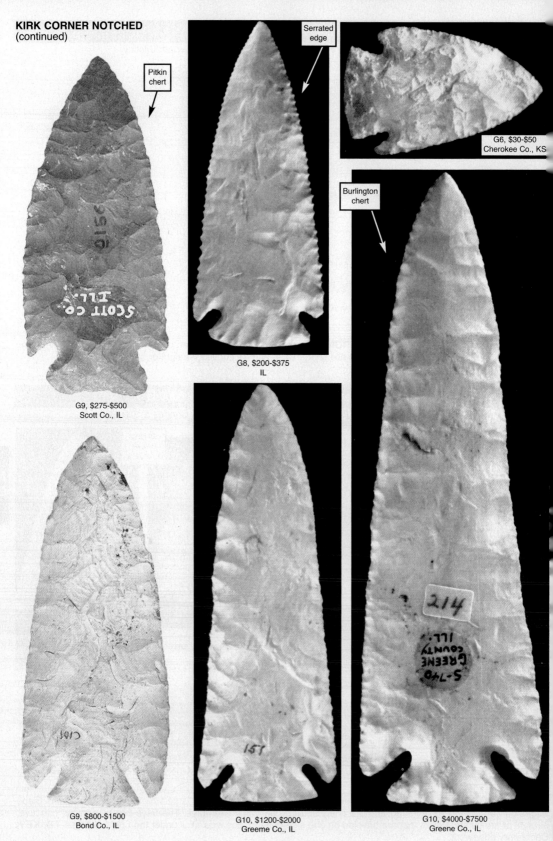

KIRK CORNER NOTCHED
(continued)

Pitkin chert

Serrated edge

G6, $30-$50
Cherokee Co., KS

Burlington chert

G9, $275-$500
Scott Co., IL

G8, $200-$375
IL

G9, $800-$1500
Bond Co., IL

G10, $1200-$2000
Greeme Co., IL

G10, $4000-$7500
Greene Co., IL

KNIGHT ISLAND - LATE Woodland, 1500 - 1000 B. P.

(Also see Cache River, Jacks Reef and Robinson)

G9, $150-$250
Scott Co., IL

LOCATION: Tennessee, Alabama, Kentucky into Illinois. **DESCRIPTION:** A small to medium size, very thin, narrow, side-notched point with a straight base. Longer examples can have a pentagonal appearance. Called *Raccoon Creek* in Ohio. A side-notched *Jacks Reef.* **I.D. KEY:** Thinness, basal form.

KRAMER - Woodland, 3000 - 2500 B. P.

(Also see Helton, Lehigh, Rochester and Stone Square Stem)

G6, $15-$25
N. E. OK

G7, $20-$35
Miller Co., MO

G7, $20-$35
N. E. OK

G7, $66 $100
MO

LOCATION: Midwest. **DESCRIPTION:** A medium size, narrow point with weak shoulders that are tapered to horizontal and a long rectangular stem. Stems are usually ground. **I.D. KEY:** Rectangular stem.

G7, $80-$150
St. Clair Co., IL

LAKE ERIE - Early to Middle Archaic, 9000 - 5000 B. P.

(Also see Cossatot River and Fox Valley)

G5, $3-$6
IL

G5, $8-$15
IL

G6, $12-$20
IL

G5, $8-$15
IL

G7, $15-$25
IL

LOCATION: Northeastern states. **DESCRIPTION:** A small to medium size, thin, deeply notched or serrated, bifurcated stemmed point. The basal lobes are parallel with a tendency to turn inward and are pointed. The outward sides of the basal lobes are usually fractured from the base towards the tip and can be ground. Similar to *LeCroy* found further south.

LAMINE KNIFE - Archaic, 5000 - 3000 B. P.

(Also see Morse Knife, Munker's Creek, Ramey Knife, Sedalia and Wadlow)

LOCATION: Missouri and adjacent area. **DESCRIPTION:** A large size, narrow knife with an assymmetrical blade with one edge curved more towards the tip. Stem form varies from rounded to expanded. Believed to have been used for cutting thatch since most examples show a polish, usually along the curved, cutting edge. **I.D. KEY:** Size and form.

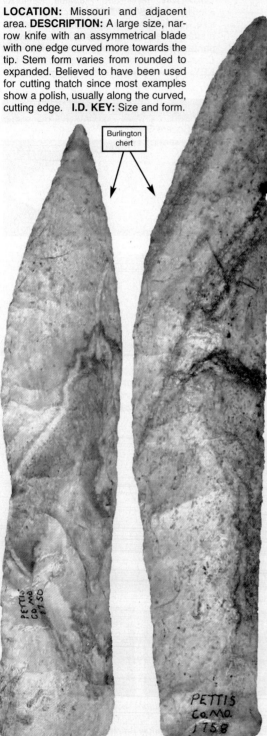

Burlington chert

G7 $300-$575
Pettis Co., MO

G10, $700-$1200
Pettis Co., MO

LEHIGH - Woodland, 2500 - 1500 B. P.

(Also see Helton, Kay Blade, Kramer, Lundy an Steuben)

G6, $25-$40
Pottowatomie Co., KS

LOCATION: Midwest. **DESCRIPTION:** A medium t large size, narrow point with tapered shoulders and long expanding stem. Bases are straight. **I.D. KEY** Long expanding stem.

LERMA - Early to Middle Archaic, 10,000 - 5000 B. P.

(Also see Agate Basin, Burroughs and Sedalia)

G8, $150-$250
Fulton Co., IL

G7, $200-$350
MO

IMPORTANT:
All Lermas shown half size

G10, $400-$750
Cent. MO

LOCATION: Siberia to Alaska, Canada, Mexico, South America and across the U.S. **DESCRIPTION:** A large size, narrow, lanceolate blade with a pointed base. Most are fairly thick in cross section but finer examples can be thin. Flaking tends to be collateral. Basal areas can be ground. Western forms are beveled on one side of each face. Similar forms have been found in Europe and Africa dating back to 20,000 - 40,000 B.P., but didn't appear in the U.S. until after the advent of *Clovis*.

LOST LAKE - Early Archaic, 9000 - 6000 B. P.

(Also see Hardin, Kirk Corner Notched, St. Charles and Thebes)

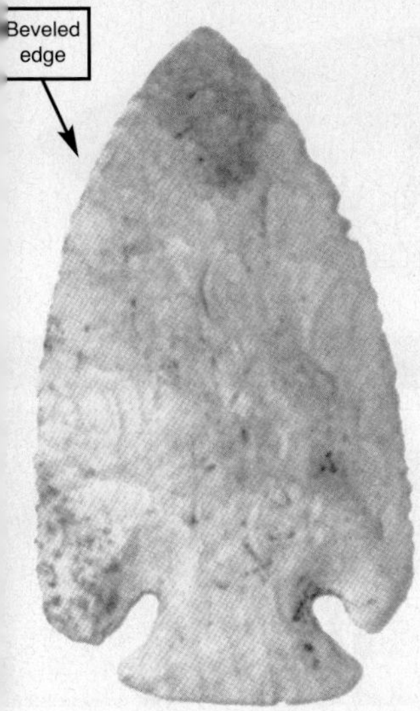

Beveled edge

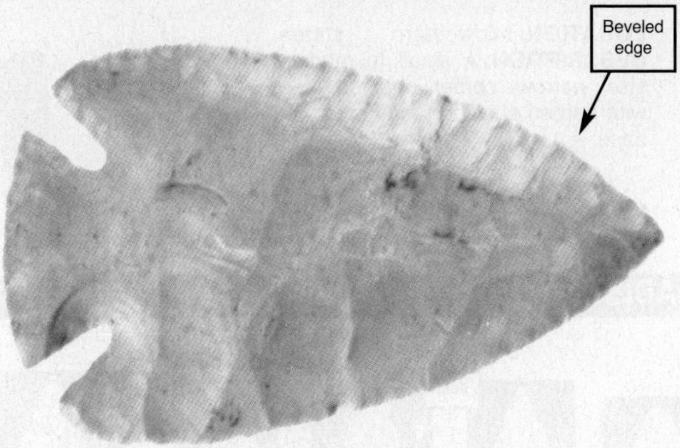

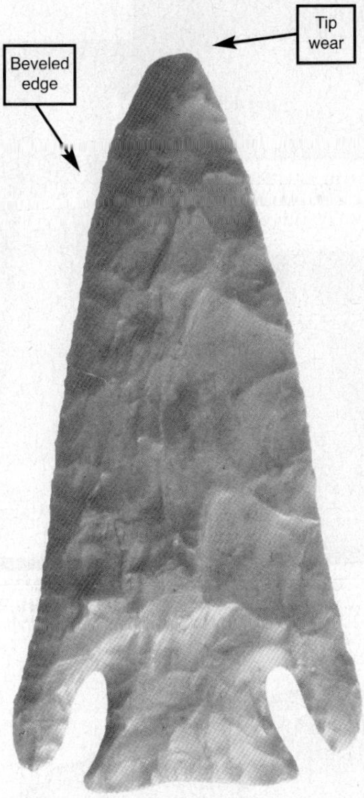

G7, $250-$400
St. Clair Co., IL

Beveled edge

G9, $1000-$1800
IL

Beveled edge
Tip wear

G7, $250-$450
Webster, MO

Beveled edge

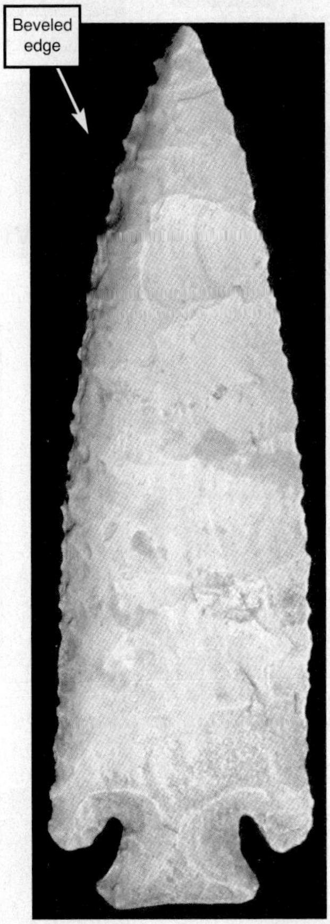

G9, $1200-$2000
Madison Co., IL

Slight tip wear
Beveled edge
Pink/red jasper

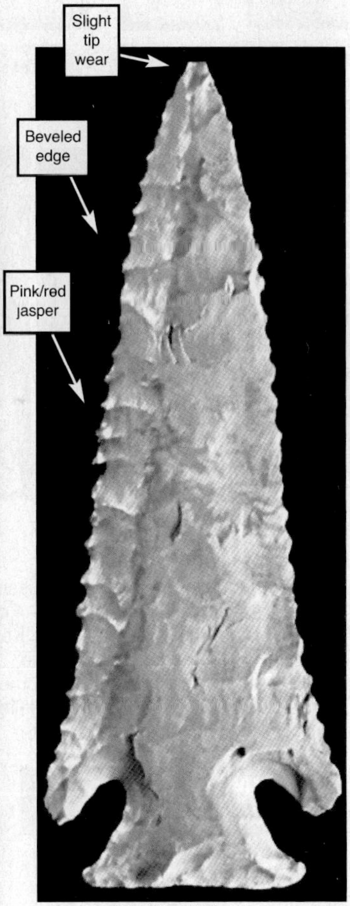

G8, $800-$1500
Pemiscot Co., MO

LOCATION: DESCRIPTION: A medium to large size, broad, corner notched point that is beveled on one side of each face. The beveling continues when resharpened and creates a flat rhomboid cross section. Most examples are finely serrated and exhibit high quality flaking and symmetry. **I.D. KEY:** Notching, secondary edgework is always opposite creating at least slight beveling on one side of each face.

LUNDY - Late Caddoan, 800 - 600 B. P.

(Also see Helton, Kay Blade, Lehigh, Motley, Steuben and Table Rock)

LOCATION: Midwestern states.
DESCRIPTION: A small to medium size, narrow, corner notched point with barbed shoulders and a convex base.

G6, $15-$30
Geary Co., KS

MADISON - Mississippian, 1100 - 200 B. P.

(Also see Cahokia)

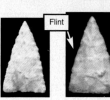

Flint

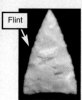

Flint

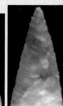

G3, $1-$2
Rogers Co.,
OK

G6, $4-$8
Rogers Co.,
OK

G3, $4-$8
MN

G6, $4-$8
Rogers Co.,
OK

G6, $5-$10
Minn.

G8, $12-$20
Macoupin Co., IL

G5, $5-$10
Clinton Co., IL

G6, $12-$20
Madison Co.,
IL

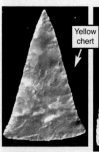

Yellow chert

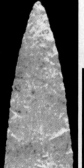

Gray flint

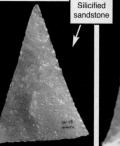

Silicified sandstone

G10, $275-$500
Cahokia Mound site.
St. Clair Co., IL

G8, $20-$35
MO

Note: Gem points from the Cahokia Mound site are very rare and valuable.

G8, $30-$50
Cent. IL

G8, $15-$25
Cooper Co., MO

G10, $250-$450
IL, Cahokia Mound site.
Titterington form.

G10, $700-$1300
Cahokia Mound site.
St. Clair Co., IL

G10+, $1200-$2300, IL
Cahokia site. Finest known
Titterington form.

LOCATION: Coincides with the Mississippian culture in the Eastern states. Type site-St. Clair Co., IL. Found at Cahokia mounds. Un-notched *Cahokias*. Used by the Kaskaskia tribe into the 1700s.
DESCRIPTION: A small to medium size, thin, triangular point with usually straight sides and base. Some examples are notched on two to three sides. Many are of high quality and some are finely serrated.

MASON - Late Woodland, 3000 - 2500 B. P.

(Also see Adena, Dickson & Waubesa)

G7, $250-$400
Saline Co., MO

LOCATION: Illinois, Missouri, Wisconsin. **DESCRIPTION:** A medium to large point with a rounded stem that contracts. This point has a ground stem and is earlier than Adena points which are similar. Unlike Adenas, this point is widest above the shoulders. **I. D. KEY:** Contracting stem that is convex.

MATANZAS - Mid-Archaic to Woodland, 4500 - 2500 B. P.

(Also see Carter, Cupp, Hickory Ridge, Kirk Corner Notched)

G5, $5-$10
Clinton Co., IL

G4, $8-$15
WI

G6, $8-$15
Clinton Co., IL

G5, $12-$20
Madison Co., IL

G6, $25-$45
Morgan Co., MO

G6, $25-$45
Cooper Co., MO

G6, $35-$60
Cass Co., IL

LOCATION: Midwestern states. Type site is in Fulton Co., IL. **DESCRIPTION:** A small to medium size, usually thick, narrow, side notched point with a convex to straight base.

MEHLVILLE - Late Archaic, 4000 - 3000 B. P.

(Also see Etley and Smith)

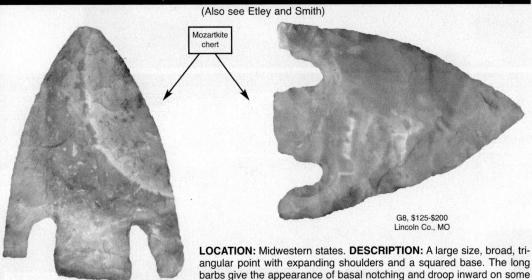

Mozartkite
chert

G8, $125-$200
Lincoln Co., MO

G7, $80-$150
Cooper Co., MO

LOCATION: Midwestern states. **DESCRIPTION:** A large size, broad, triangular point with expanding shoulders and a squared base. The long barbs give the appearance of basal notching and droop inward on some examples. **I.D. KEY:** Expanding barbs.

761

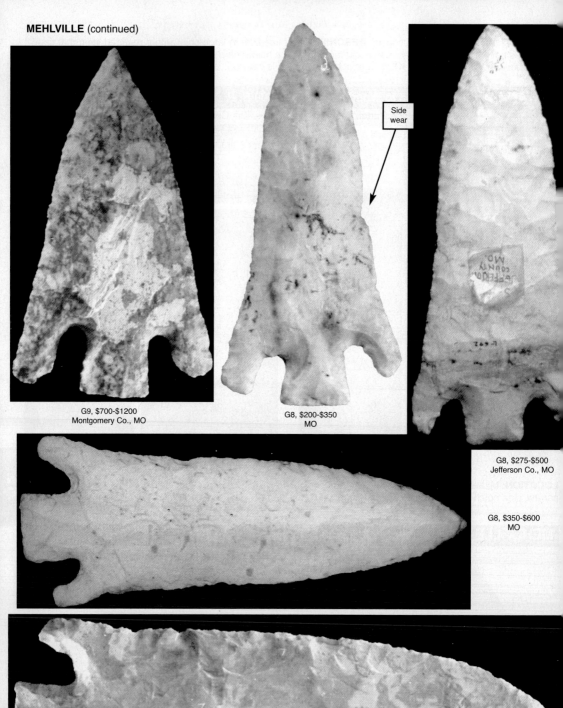

Side wear

G9, $700-$1200
Montgomery Co., MO

G8, $200-$350
MO

G8, $275-$500
Jefferson Co., MO

G8, $350-$600
MO

G9, $800-$1500
Craighead Co., AR

MERKLE - Late Archaic to Woodland, 4000 - 2000 B. P.

(Also see Evans)

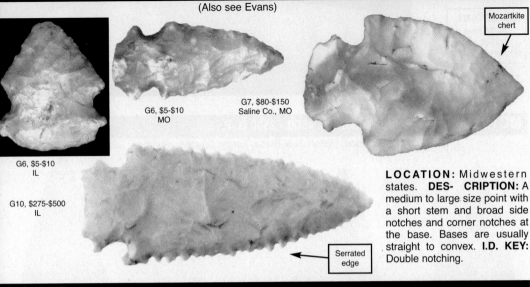

Mozartkite chert

G6, $5-$10
MO

G7, $80-$150
Saline Co., MO

G6, $5-$10
IL

G10, $275-$500
IL

Serrated edge

LOCATION: Midwestern states. **DES- CRIPTION:** A medium to large size point with a short stem and broad side notches and corner notches at the base. Bases are usually straight to convex. **I.D. KEY:** Double notching.

MESERVE - Early Archaic, 9500 - 4000 B. P.

(Also see Dalton, Greenbrier and Plainview)

LOCATION: Midwestern states to Texas and west to Montana. **DESCRIPTION:** A medium size auriculate point with a blade that is beveled on one side of each face. Beveling extends into the basal area. Related to *Dalton* points. **I.D. KEY:** Beveling into the base.

G8, $80-$150
Manhattan, KS

MORSE KNIFE - Woodland, 3000 - 1500 B. P.

(Also see Harahey, Lerma, Ramey Knife and Red Ochre)

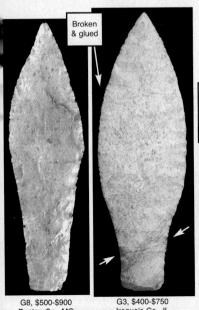

Broken & glued

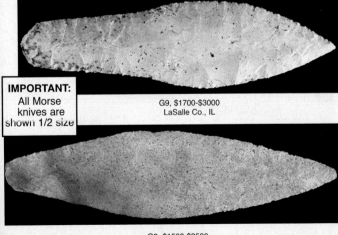

IMPORTANT: All Morse knives are shown 1/2 size

G9, $1700-$3000
LaSalle Co., IL

G9, $1500-$2500
Calhoun Co., IL

G8, $500-$900
Benton Co., MO

G3, $400-$750
Iroquois Co., IL

LOCATION: Midwestern states. **DESCRIPTION:** A large lanceolate blade with a long contracting stem and a rounded base. The widest part of the blade is towards the tip.

763

MORSE KNIFE
(continued)

IMPORTANT:
All Morse knives are shown 1/2 size

G10, $3500-$6000
IL

Heat treated Burlington chert

MOTLEY - Late Archaic-Woodland, 4500 - 2500 B. P.

(Also see Cupp, Epps, Helton, Kay Blade, Lundy, Snyders, Steuben, Table Rock)

G7, $80-$150
N. E. OK

G8, $125-$200
Lee Co. IA

G6, $55-$100
Madison Co., IL

Heat treated Burlington chert

G8, $175-$325
Boone Co., MO

G9, $225-$400
Pettis Co., MO

G6, $125-$200
Bond Co., IL

LOCATION: Iowa, Missouri, Illinois, Kentucky into the southeast. **DESCRIPTION:** A medium to large size, expanded stemmed to widely corner notched point with strong barbs. The blade edges and the base are convex to straight. Has been found associated with *Wade* points in caches. Similar to *Epps* found in Louisiana which has a straight base; *Motleys* are more barbed than *Epps*. **I.D. KEY:** Large corner notches.

MUNKER'S CREEK - Early Archaic, 5400 - 3300 B. P.

(Also see Hollenberg Stemmed, Lamine Knife & Tablerock)

LOCATION: Central to eastern Kansas and Nebraska. **DESCRIPTION: Curved Knife:** A large size, thick, curved knife with rounded base and tip. Both knives and points are found together.

DESCRIPTION: Dart/knife form: A medium to large size, narror, stemmed point with a long parallel sided to expanding stem. Bases are straight to slightly concave or convex. Shoulders are weak and tapered. Blade edges are slightly convex to parallel sided.

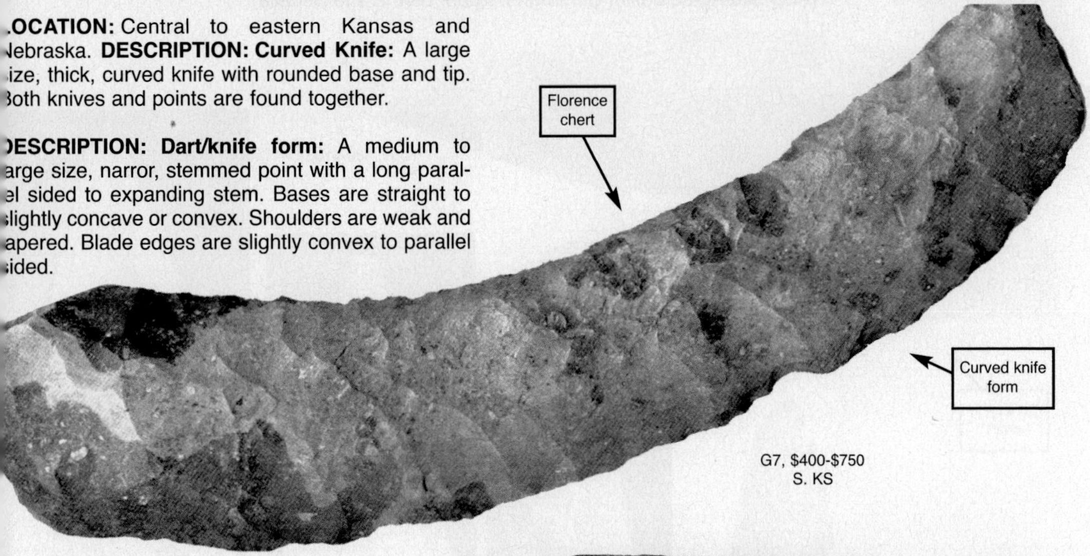

Florence chert
Curved knife form

G7, $400-$750
S. KS

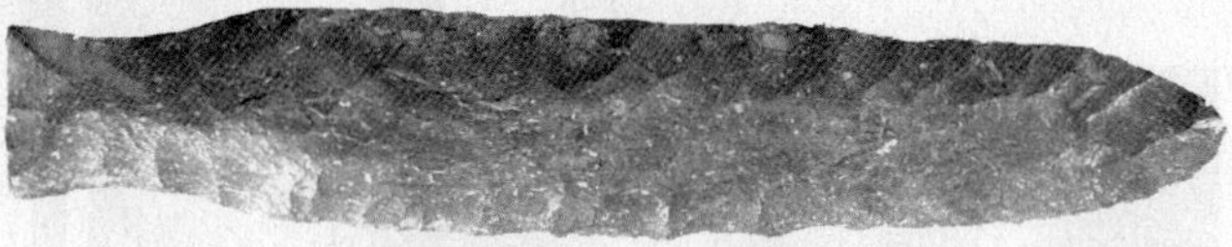

G9, $65-$125
Washington Co., KS

Florence chert

G6, $33-$50
ashington Co., KS

G8, $40-$75
Washington Co., KS

G8, $40-$75
Washington Co., KS

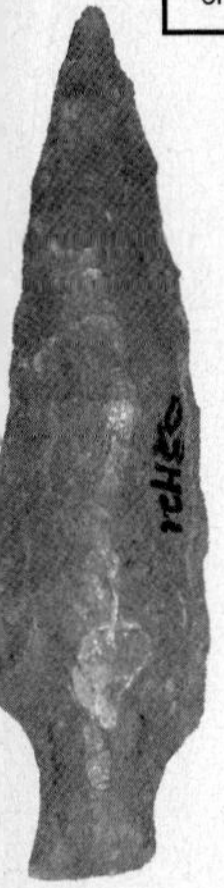

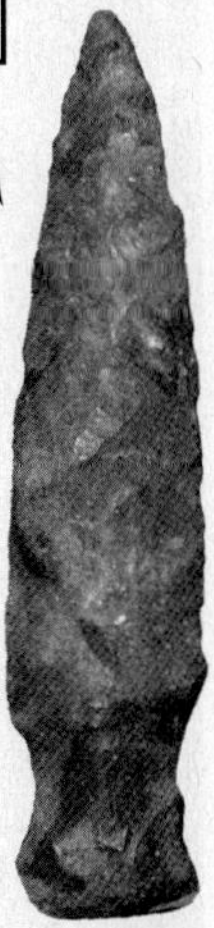

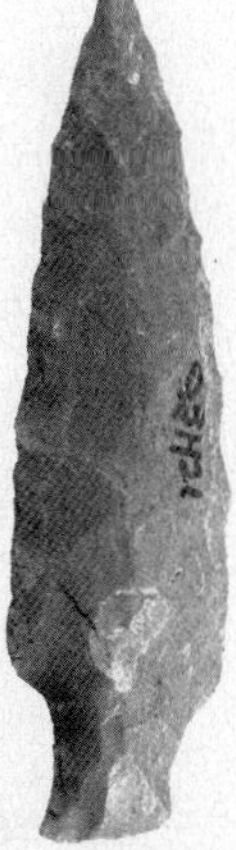

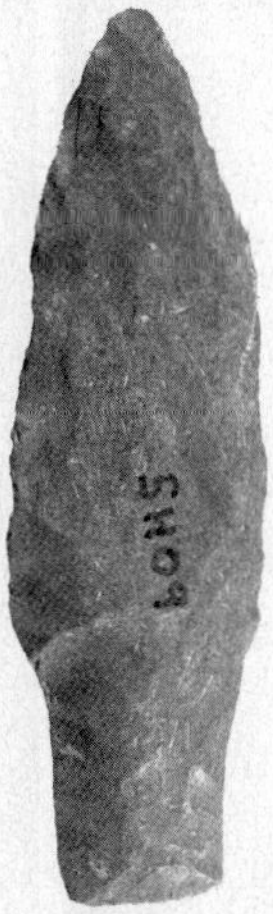

G7, $40-$75
Washington Co., KS

G8, $40-$75
Washington Co., KS

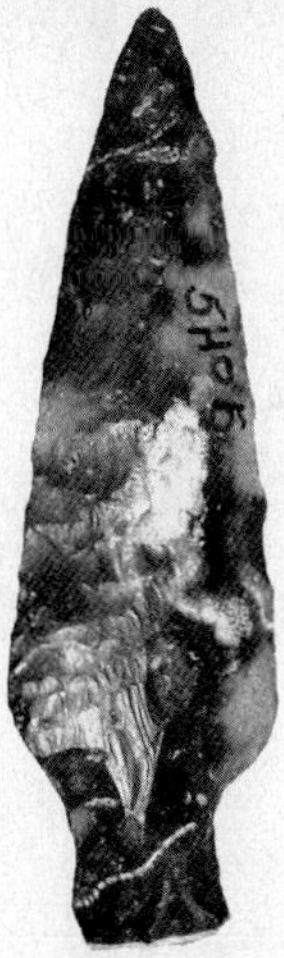

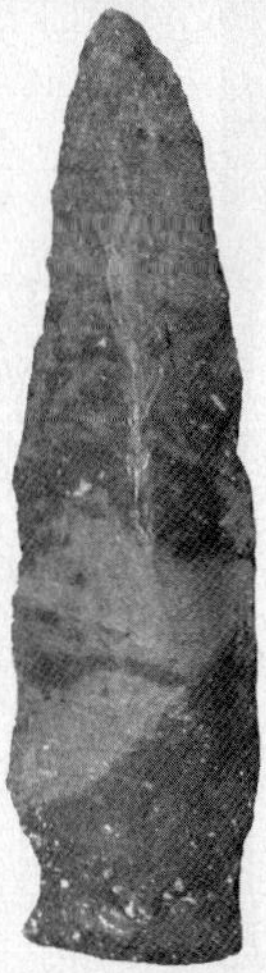

G5, $30-$50
Washington Co., KS

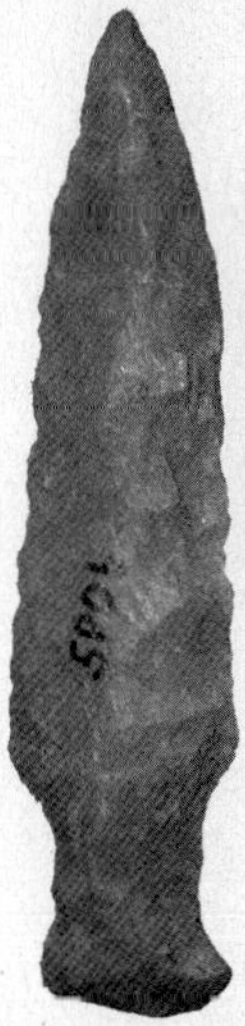

G7, $65-$125
Washington Co., KS

G5, $35-$65
Washington Co., KS

G8, $65-$125
Washington Co., KS

G5, $20-$35
Jefferson Co., NE

G6, $125-$200
Washington Co., KS

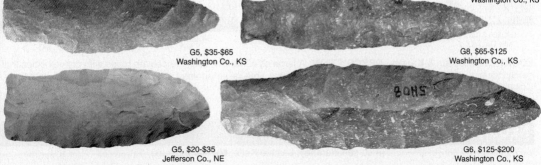

NEBO HILL - Early Archaic, 7500 - 6000 B. P.

(Also see Agate basin, Burroughs, Eden, Lerma and Sedalia)

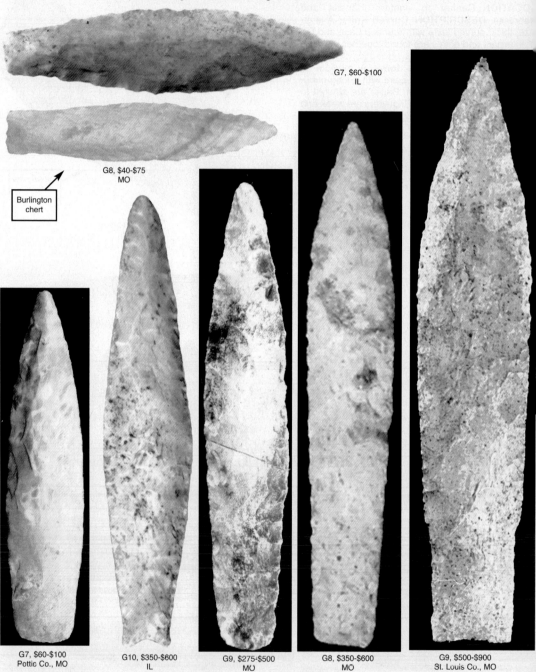

G7, $60-$100
IL

G8, $40-$75
MO

Burlington
chert

G7, $60-$100
Pottic Co., MO

G10, $350-$600
IL

G9, $275-$500
MO

G8, $350-$600
MO

G9, $500-$900
St. Louis Co., MO

LOCATION: Missouri & Kansas. **DESCRIPTION:** A large size, narrow, thick, lanceolate blade with convex sides that gently taper to the base. On some examples, the basal area is determined by the presence of slight shoulders. Collateral flaking does occur on some examples.

NEOSHO - Early Archaic, 400 - 250 B. P.

(Also see Harahey, Lamine Knife, Munker's Creek)

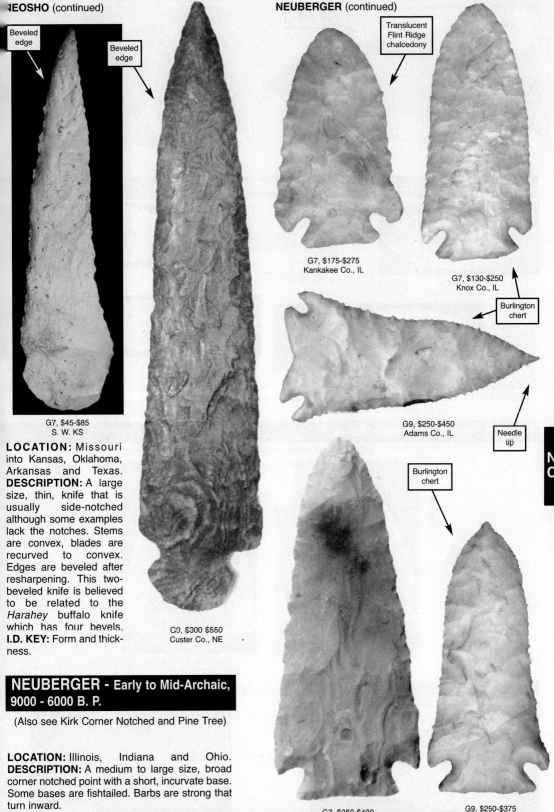

Beveled edge

Beveled edge

G7, $45-$85
S. W. KS

LOCATION: Missouri into Kansas, Oklahoma, Arkansas and Texas. **DESCRIPTION:** A large size, thin, knife that is usually side-notched although some examples lack the notches. Stems are convex, blades are recurved to convex. Edges are beveled after resharpening. This two-beveled knife is believed to be related to the *Harahey* buffalo knife which has four bevels. **I.D. KEY:** Form and thickness.

NEUBERGER - Early to Mid-Archaic, 9000 - 6000 B. P.

(Also see Kirk Corner Notched and Pine Tree)

LOCATION: Illinois, Indiana and Ohio. **DESCRIPTION:** A medium to large size, broad corner notched point with a short, incurvate base. Some bases are fishtailed. Barbs are strong that turn inward.

C9, $300 $550
Custer Co., NE

Translucent Flint Ridge chalcedony

G7, $175-$275
Kankakee Co., IL

G7, $130-$250
Knox Co., IL

Burlington chert

G9, $250-$450
Adams Co., IL

Needle tip

Burlington chert

N
C

G7, $250-$400
IL

G9, $250-$375
Jersey Co., IL

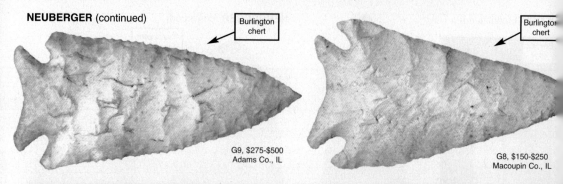

NEUBERGER (continued)

Burlington chert

Burlington chert

G9, $275-$500
Adams Co., IL

G8, $150-$250
Macoupin Co., IL

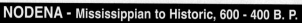

NODENA - Mississippian to Historic, 600 - 400 B. P.

G7, $30-$50
Pemiscot Co., MO

G7, $30-$50
Washington Co., IL

G7, $35-$60
Pemiscot Co., MO

G7, $40-$75
Pemiscot
Co., MO

G7, $65-$125
IL

LOCATION: Midwestern states. **DESCRIPTION:** A small to medium size, narrow, thin elliptical shaped arrow point with a pointed to rounded base. Some examples have oblique, parallel flaking.

NORTH - Woodland, 2200 - 1600 B. P.

(Also see Hopewell, Snyders and Stenfield)

Photo from a cast by Pete Bostrom

G6, $45-$85
MO

G9, $500-$900
Osage Co., MO

G10, $600-$1000
Madison Co., IL

G7, $55-$100
IL

IMPORTANT:
All Norths shown 1/2 size

G7, $150-$250
Scott Co., IL

G10, $600-$1000
Pike Co., IL

G9, $350-$650
MO

G8, $250-$400
Logan Co., IL

G7, $275-$500
Calhoun Co., IL

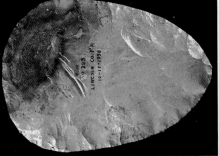

G8, $275-$500
Lincoln Co., MO

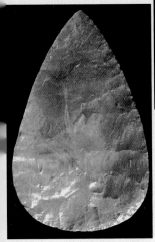

G10, $600-$1000
Lincoln Co., MO

LOCATION: Midwestern to Eastern states. **DESCRIPTION:** A large, thin, elliptical, broad, well made blade with a convex base. This type is usually found in caches and is related to the *Snyders* point of the Hopewell culture. Believed to be unnotched *Snyders* points.

IMPORTANT:
All Norths shown 1/2 size

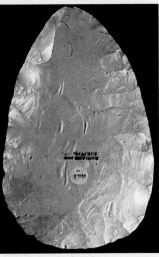

G8, $350-$600
Camden Co., MO

N
C

OSCEOLA - Early to Middle Archaic, 7000 - 5000 B. P.

(Also see Cache River, Godar, Graham Cave, Hemphill, Raddatz and Turin)

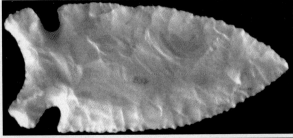

LOCATION: Wisconsin into Iowa. **DESCRIPTION:** A large size, narrow, side notched point with parallel sides on longer examples and a straight to concave to notched base which could be ground. **I.D. KEY:** Always has early flaking to the middle of the blade.

G9, $150-$250
MO

G8, $275-$500
Bourbon Co., KS

G8, $250-$450
Keokuk Co., IA

Coral

G8, $275-$500
IL

G10, $700-$1200
Calhoun Co., IL

G9, $1200-$2000
Jersey Co., IL

OVOID (see Early Ovoid Knife)

PALEO KNIFE - Transitional Paleo, 10,000 - 8000 B. P.

(Also see Scraper and Square Knife)

PALEO KNIFE (continued)

LOCATION: All of North America.
DESCRIPTION: A large size lanceolate blade finished with broad parallel flakes. These are found on Paleo sites and were probably used as knives.

> **IMPORTANT:** All Paleo Knives shown half size

G9, $800-$1400
Stark Co., IL

PEISKER DIAMOND - Woodland, 2500 - 2000 B. P.

(Also see Adena and Gary)

Mozarkite chert

Classic example

G7, $55-$100
Hooker Co., NE

G7, $150-$250
Lincoln Co., MO

G6, $65-$125
Custer Co., NE

G9, $450-$800
IL

Burlington chert

G9, $450-$800
Saline Co., MO

PEISKER DIAMOND (continued)

LOCATION: Illinois, Missouri, Kansas into Iowa. **DESCRIPTION:** A large, broad blade with sharp shoulders and a short to moderate contracting base that comes to a point. Blade edges are recurved, convex or straight. Similar in form to the Morrow Mountain point found in the Southeast, but not as old. **I.D.KEY:** Contracted base, pointed base.

This shorter base is not typical of type

G9, $250-$400
Cherokee Co., KS

PELICAN - Transitional Paleo, 10,000 - 6000 B. P.

(Also see Beaver Lake, Dalton, Greenbrier and Holland)

Ear restored

G4, $125-$200
Douglas Co., KS

LOCATION: Louisiana, Texas, Arkansas into Kansas. **DESCRIPTION:** A medium size auriculate point with recurved sides. The base is concave with edge grinding. **I.D. KEY:** Basal contraction.

PELICAN LAKE - Late Archaic to Woodland, 3500 - 2200 B. P.

(Also see Apple Creek, Kirk Corner Notched and Pine Tree)

G5, $18-$30
E. NE

Tip wear

G7, $35-$65
E. NE

Winterset chert

G10, $150-$250
Clay Co., MO

LOCATION: Plains states into Missouri. **DESCRIPTION:** A medium size, thin, corner notched dart point with a straight to concave to convex, expanding base. Tangs are usually pointed. Grinding may occur in notches and around base.

PIKE COUNTY - Early Archaic, 9500 - 7500 B. P.

(Also see Beaver Lake, Dalton, Greenbrier and Holland)

LOCATION: Midwestern states. **DESCRIPTION:** A medium to large size, lanceolate blade with an eared, fishtail base. Basal area is ground. Related to *Dalton*.

G8, $300-$500
Pike Co., MO

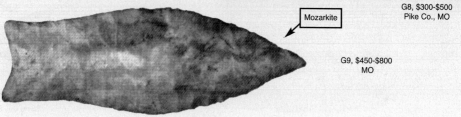

Mozarkite

G9, $450-$800
MO

772

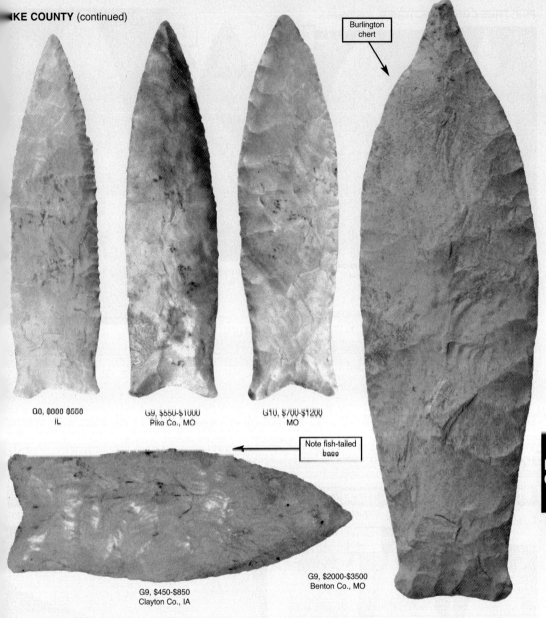

Burlington chert

G0, 0000 0550
IL

G9, $550-$1000
Pike Co., MO

G10, $700-$1200
MO

Note fish-tailed base

G9, $450-$850
Clayton Co., IA

G9, $2000-$3500
Benton Co., MO

N
C

PINE TREE CORNER NOTCHED - Early Archaic, 8000 - 5000 B. P.

(Also see Kirk and Lost Lake and Stilwell)

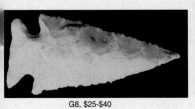

G8, $25-$40
Cooper Co., MO

G9, $60-$100
Cooper Co., MO

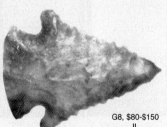

G8, $80-$150
IL

PINE TREE CORNER NOTCHED (continued)

Serrated edge

Needle tip

Serrated edge

G8, $125-$200
Morgan Co., MO

G9, $250-$450
MO

G8, $165-$300
IL

G6, $35-$65
MO

G8, $250-$450
Adams Co., IL

LOCATION: DESCRIPTION: A small to medium size, thin, corner notched point with a concave, convex, straight, bifurcated or auriculate base. Blade edges are usually serrated and flaking is parallel to the center of the blade. The shoulders expand and are barbed. The base is ground. Small examples would fall under the *Palmer* type. **I.D. KEY:** Archaic flaking to the center of each blade.

PLAINVIEW - Late Paleo, 11,250 - 9500 B. P.

(Also see Angostura, Browns Valley, Clovis, Cumberland and Dalton)

Diagonal flaking

Florence chert

AVONDALE
6·3·70

G8, $300-$550
Platt Co., MO

G4, $65-$125
Geary Co., KS

G8, $400-$700
Cent. IA

G8, $250-$450
MO

G8, $350-$600
Alexander Co., IL

LOCATION: Midwestern states and Canada. **DESCRIPTION:** A medium size, thin, lanceolate point with usually parallel sides and a concave base that is ground. Some examples are thinned or fluted and is believed to be related to the earlier *Clovis* and contemporary *Dalton* type. Flaking is of high quality and can be collateral to oblique transverse.

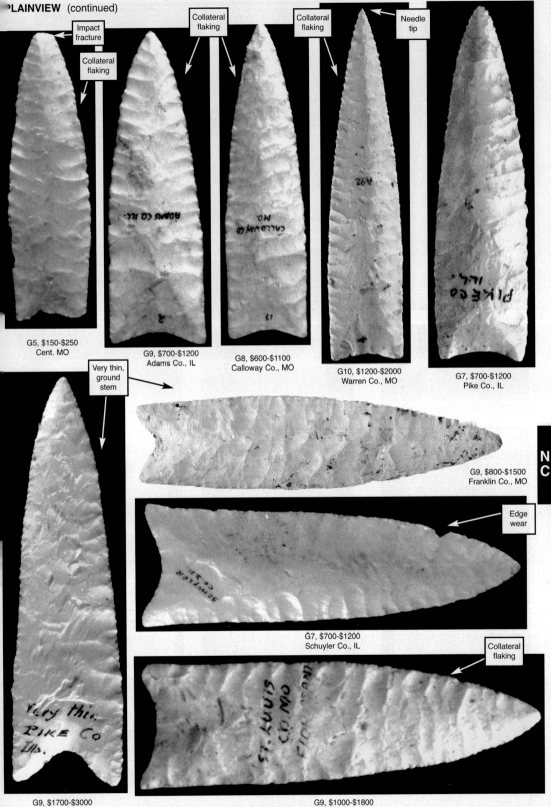

Impact fracture

Collateral flaking

Collateral flaking

Collateral flaking

Collateral flaking

Needle tip

G5, $150-$250
Cent. MO

G9, $700-$1200
Adams Co., IL

G8, $600-$1100
Calloway Co., MO

G10, $1200-$2000
Warren Co., MO

G7, $700-$1200
Pike Co., IL

Very thin, ground stem

NC

G9, $800-$1500
Franklin Co., MO

Edge wear

G7, $700-$1200
Schuyler Co., IL

Collateral flaking

G9, $1700-$3000
Pike Co., IL

G9, $1000-$1800
St. Louis Co., MO

775

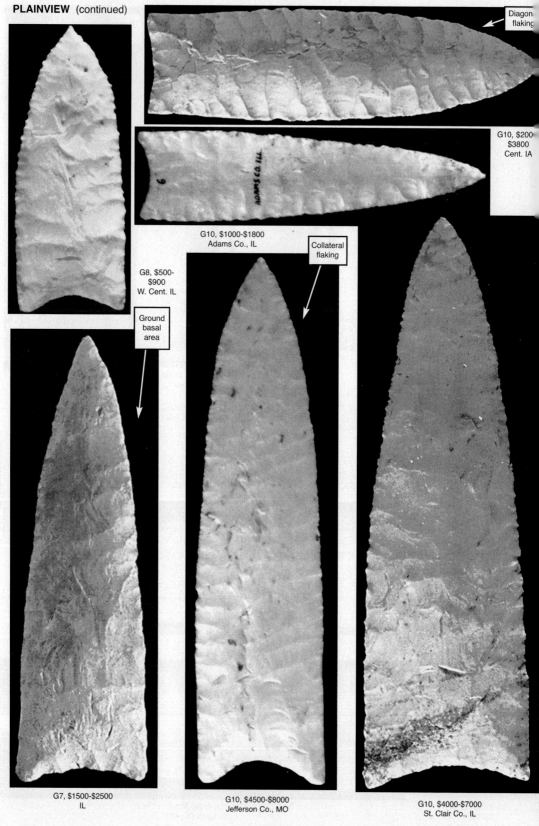

Diagonal flaking

G10, $2000-$3800
Cent. IA

G10, $1000-$1800
Adams Co., IL

Collateral flaking

G8, $500-$900
W. Cent. IL

Ground basal area

G7, $1500-$2500
IL

G10, $4500-$8000
Jefferson Co., MO

G10, $4000-$7000
St. Clair Co., IL

QUAD - Transitional Paleo, 10,000 - 6000 B. P.

(Also see Beaver Lake, Clovis, Gosen and Cumberland)

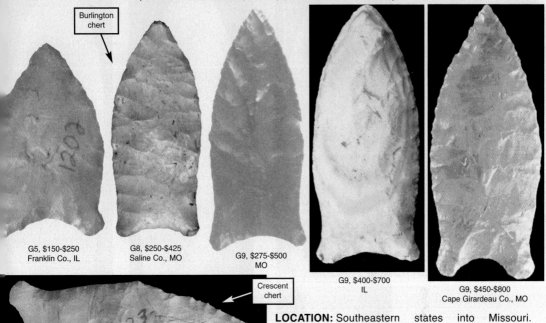

Burlington chert

G5, $150-$250
Franklin Co., IL

G8, $250-$425
Saline Co., MO

G9, $275-$500
MO

G9, $400-$700
IL

G9, $450-$800
Cape Girardeau Co., MO

Crescent chert

G8, $500-$900
Pettis Co., MO

LOCATION: Southeastern states into Missouri. **DESCRIPTION:** A medium to large size lanceolate point with flaring "squared" auricles and a concave base which is ground. Most examples show basal thinning and some are fluted. Believed to be related to the earlier *Cumberland* point. **I.D. KEY:** Paleo flaking, squarish auricles.

RADDATZ - Mid-Archaic to Woodland, 5000 - 2000 B. P.

(Also see Godar, Graham Cave, Hemphill, Hickory Ridge and Osceola)

Chert

G4, $8-$15
WI

G5, $18-$30
MN

Flintridge flint

Hixton silicified sandstone

G6, $20-$35
WI

G6, $20-$35
WI, E-Notch.

Flint

LOCATION: Wisconsin & Minnesota. **DESCRIPTION:** A medium size, side notched point with a concave to straight base. Similar in outline to *Hickory Ridge* points centered in Arkansas.

RAMEY KNIFE - Mid-Archaic, 5000 - 4000 B. P.

(Also see Lerma, Morse Knife and Red Ochre)

LOCATION: Midwestern states. **DESCRIPTION:** A large size, broad, lanceolate blade with a rounded base and high quality flaking.

RAMEY KNIFE (continued)

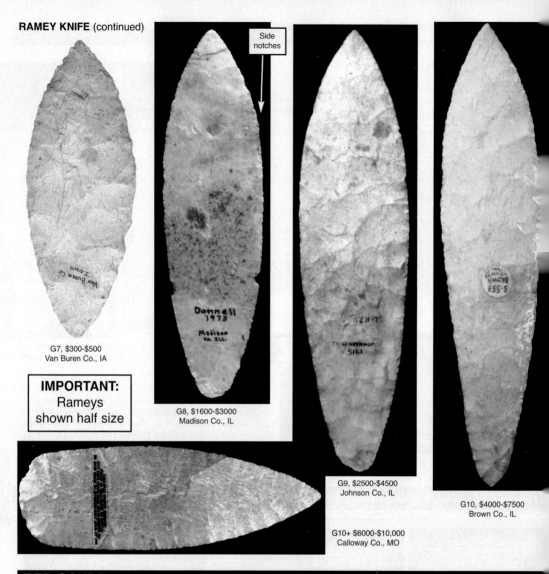

Side notches

G7, $300-$500
Van Buren Co., IA

IMPORTANT:
Rameys
shown half size

G8, $1600-$3000
Madison Co., IL

G9, $2500-$4500
Johnson Co., IL

G10+ $6000-$10,000
Calloway Co., MO

G10, $4000-$7500
Brown Co., IL

RED OCHRE - Mid to Late Archaic, 5000 - 3000 B. P.

(Also see Adena Blade, Sedalia and Wadlow)

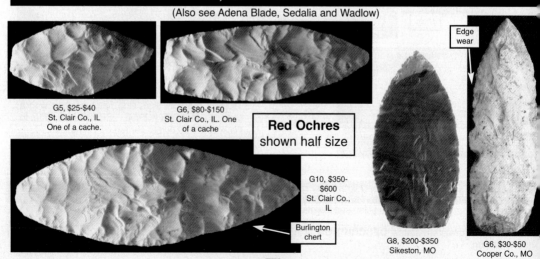

G5, $25-$40
St. Clair Co., IL
One of a cache.

G6, $80-$150
St. Clair Co., IL. One
of a cache

Red Ochres
shown half size

G10, $350-
$600
St. Clair Co.,
IL

Burlington
chert

Edge
wear

G8, $200-$350
Sikeston, MO

G6, $30-$50
Cooper Co., MO

778

RED OCHRE (continued)

LOCATION: Midwestern states. Type site-St. Louis MO. Named by Scully ('51)-Red Ochre Mound in Fulton Co., MO.
DESCRIPTION: A large, thin, broad blade with a contracting basal area. The base is convex to straight. Very similar to *Wadlow* which has the parallel sides. Possibly related to the *Turkeytail* type.

REDSTONE - Paleo, 11,500 - 10,600 B. P.

(Also see Allen, Angostura, Clovis, Cumberland, Dalton, Folsom & Plainview)

Flute channel

G8, $450-$850
MO

LOCATION: Midwestern to Southeastern states.
DESCRIPTION: A medium to large size, thin, auriculate, fluted point with convex sides expanding to a wide, deeply concave base. The hafting area is ground. This point is widest at the base. Fluting can extend most of the way down each face. Multiple flutes are usual. **I.D. KEY:** Baton or billet fluted, edgework on the hafting area. Very Rare.

RICE LOBBED - Early Archaic, 9000 - 5000 B. P.

(Also see Grand, Helton and Lundy)

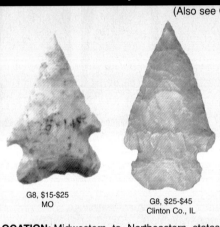

G8, $15-$25
MO

G8, $25-$45
Clinton Co., IL

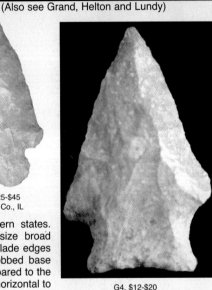

LOCATION: Midwestern to Northeastern states.
DESCRIPTION: A medium to large size broad point with a straight to lobbed base. Blade edges can be serrated and beveled. The lobbed base variety has a shallow indentation compared to the other bifurcated types. Shoulders are horizontal to tapered and basal corners are rounded.

G4, $12-$20
Stone Co., MO

G8, $40-$70
MO

N
C

RICE SIDE-NOTCHED - Late Woodland, 1600 - 1400 B. P.

(Also see Carter, Lehigh, Mantanzas and Steuben)

G5, $15-$25
MO

G7, $35-$60
Pettis Co., MO

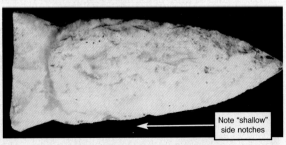

Note "shallow" side notches

LOCATION: Arkansas into Missouri and Kansas. **DESCRIPTION:** A medium to large size, narrow, point with broad side notches to an expanding stem and weak shoulders. The base is straight but can be slightly concave. **I.D. KEY:** Basal form.

RICE SIDE-NOTCHED
(continued)

G8, $125-$200
Boone Co., MO

ROBINSON - Late Archaic, 4000 - 3000 B. P.

(Also see Cache River, Hickory Ridge, Knight Island and Raddatz)

LOCATION: Missouri & Illinois. **DESCRIPTION:** A small to medium size, narrow, side-notched point with a straight to concave base. **I.D. KEY:** Size, small basal notches.

G4, $2-$5
Clinton Co., IL

G6, $12-$20
Clinton Co., IL

G5, $6-$12
Clinton Co., IL

G6, $15-$25
MO

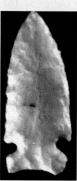

G6, $25-$40
MO

G8, $60-$100
Cooper Co., MO

ROCHESTER - Early Archaic, 8000 - 6000 B. P.

(Also see Kramer)

G5, $20-$35
Marion Co., KS

Blunt tip

G6, $35-$50
Pottowatomie Co., KS

LOCATION: Midwestern states. **DESCRIPTION:** A medium to large size, narrow point with weak, tapered shoulders and a long rectangular stem.

G6, $50-$90
Riley Co., KS

ROSS- Woodland, 2500 - 1500 B. P.

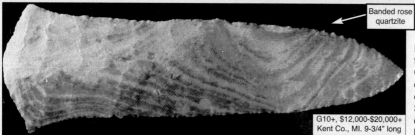

Banded rose quartzite

G10+, $12,000-$20,000+
Kent Co., MI. 9-3/4" long

IMPORTANT:
Shown half size

LOCATION: Midwestern to Eastern states. **DESCRIPTION:** A large size ceremonial blade with an expanded, rounded base. Some examples have a contracting "V" shaped base.

ST. CHARLES - Early Archaic, 9500 - 8000 B. P.

(Also see Gibson, Grand, Helton, Kirk Corner Notched and Lost Lake)

Beveled edge

G4, $8-$15
Clinton Co., IL

Beveled edge

G6, $40-$75
IL

Beveled edge

G6, $50-$90
Fayette Co., IL

Beveled edge

G7, $80-$150
Logan Co., IL

Beveled edge

G6, $90-$175
Cass Co., IL

Beveled edge

G8, $250-$450
IL

Edge nick

Beveled edge

G7, $250-$400
Sangamon Co., IL

G8, $250-$400
Peoria Co., IL

G7, $250-$450
MO

LOCATION: Midwestern to Eastern states. **DESCRIPTION:** Also known as *Dovetail*. A medium to large size, broad, thin, elliptical, corner notched point with a dovetail base. Blade edges are beveled on opposite sides when resharpened. The base is convex and most examples exhibit high quality flaking. There is a rare variant that has the barbs clipped (clipped wing) as in the *Decatur* type. There are many variations on base style from bifurcated to eared, rounded or squared. Base size varies from small to very large. **I.D. KEY:** Dovetailed base.

N
C

G8, $200-$350
MO

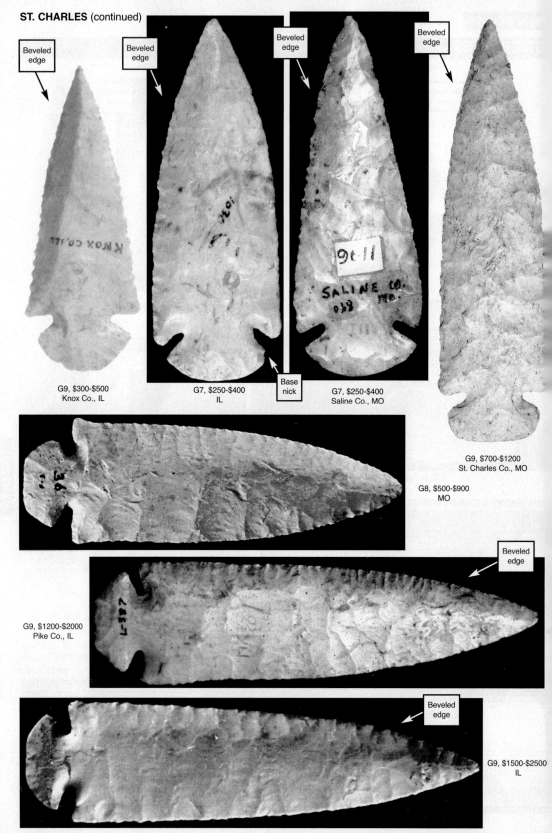

Beveled edge

Beveled edge

Beveled edge

Beveled edge

G9, $300-$500
Knox Co., IL

G7, $250-$400
IL

Base nick

G7, $250-$400
Saline Co., MO

G9, $700-$1200
St. Charles Co., MO

G8, $500-$900
MO

G9, $1200-$2000
Pike Co., IL

Beveled edge

Beveled edge

G9, $1500-$2500
IL

782

Collateral flaking

Tip wear

G8, $1000-$1800
Nebo, IL

Beveled edge

G10, $2500-$4000
St. Louis Co., MO

G9, $2500-$4000
Calhoun Co., IL

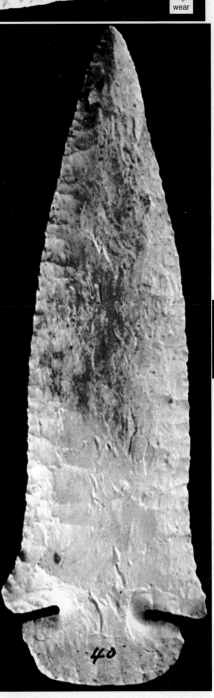

G10, $6000-$10,000
Perry Co., MO

N
C

SCALLORN - Woodland to Mississippian, 1300 - 500 B. P.

(Also see Alba, Collins, Haskell, Jacks Reef and Sequoyah)

Toronto flint

G3, $2-$5
Leavenworth Co., KS

G6, $12-$20
Leavenworth Co., KS

Toronto flint

G8, $50-$80
Cooper Co., MO

G9, $80-$15?
MO

G8, $15-25
Lawrence Co., MO

G8, $20-35
Cooper Co., MO

G6, $5-$10
Leavenworth Co., KS

Tip wear

G8, $50-$95
Cooper Co., MO

LOCATION: Texas, Oklahoma, Arkansas into Missouri. **DESCRIPTION:** A small size, corner notched arrow point with a flaring stem. Bases and bladed edges are straight, concave or convex and many examples are serrated. **I.D. KEY.** Small corner notched point with sharp barbs and tip.

SCOTTSBLUFF I - Transitional Paleo, 10,000 - 8000 B. P.

(Also see Eden, Hardin, Holland, Hollenberg Stemmed and Stone Square Stem)

Edge wear

Mozarkite chert

Diagonal flaking

G6, $150-$250
MO

G4, $150-$250
Riley Co., KS

G6, $200-$350
MO

G10, $800-$1500
Johnson Co., MO

G8, $250-$400
MO

Burlington chert

G9, $500-$900
Douglas Co., MO

G8, $275-$500
MO

LOCATION: Midwestern states. **DESCRIPTION:** A medium to large size, broad stemmed point with convex to parallel sides and weak shoulders. The stem is parallel sided to expanding. The hafting area is ground. Made by the Cody Complex people. Contemporary with *Hardins*. Most examples have horizontal to oblique parallel flaking and are of high quality and thinness.

784

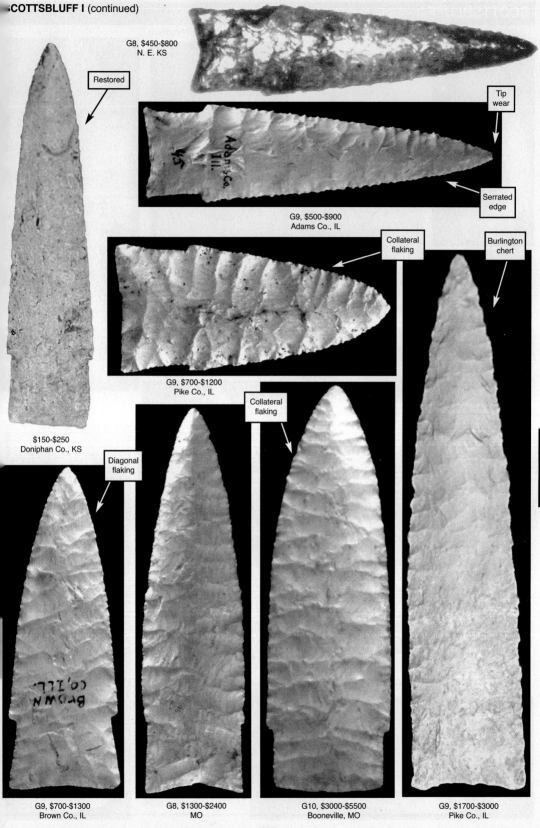

G8, $450-$800
N. E. KS

Restored

Tip wear

Serrated edge

G9, $500-$900
Adams Co., IL

Collateral flaking

Burlington chert

G9, $700-$1200
Pike Co., IL

$150-$250
Doniphan Co., KS

Collateral flaking

Diagonal flaking

N C

G9, $700-$1300
Brown Co., IL

G8, $1300-$2400
MO

G10, $3000-$5500
Booneville, MO

G9, $1700-$3000
Pike Co., IL

SCOTTSBLUFF II - Early Archaic, 9500 - 7000 B. P.

(Also see Hardin, Holland and Hollenberg Stemmed)

Diagonal flaking

G5, $80-$150
Moro, IL

G6, $175-$300
MO

G8, $350-$650
Pettis Co., MO

Pettis
Co. Mo.

G8, $800-$1500
Jackson Co., MO

G8, $350-$650
MO

G5, $175-$300
MO

G6, $350-$600
MO

G9, $600-$1000
Kansas City, MO.

G9, $1600-$3000
Cooper Co., MO

LOCATION: Midwestern states.
DESCRIPTION: A medium to large size triangular point with shoulders a little stronger than on Type I and a broad parallel sided/expanding stem.

G5, $175-$300
WI, Mississippi Riv.

Hand held to show size and form

Permian chert

Knife form

G6, $350-$600
KS

Edge wear

G8, $6000-$10,000
Moniteau Co,. MO

N
C

SEDALIA - Mid-Late Archaic, 5000 - 3000 B. P.

(Also see Agate Basin, Burroughs, Lerma, Nebo Hill and Red Ochre)

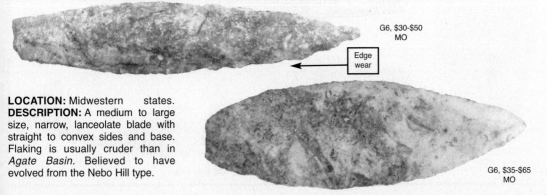

G6, $30-$50
MO

Edge wear

LOCATION: Midwestern states.
DESCRIPTION: A medium to large size, narrow, lanceolate blade with straight to convex sides and base. Flaking is usually cruder than in *Agate Basin.* Believed to have evolved from the Nebo Hill type.

G6, $35-$65
MO

G7, $150-$250
Cooper Co., MO

G7, $125-$200
MO

G6, $90-$175
Cooper Co., MO

G9, $250-$450
MO

G8, $200-$350
IL

G10, $350-$650
Cooper Co., MO

G7, $150-$250
MO

G9, $350-$600
MO

G8, $250-$450
MO

Buffalo River chert

G6, $90-$175
MO

N
C

G7, $175-$300
MO

G6, $150-$250
Cole Co., MO

COLE CO.
MO.

G10, $400-$750
Schuyler Co., IL

G10, $1200-$2000
MO

SEQUOYAH - Mississippian, 1000 - 600 B. P.

(Also see Alba, Hayes and Homan)

Serrated edges

Serrated edge

Notched edge

Tip nick

G5, $15-$25
St. Louis Co.,
MO

G5, $15-$25
St. Louis Co.,
MO

G8, $40-$70
Cooper Co.,
MO

G9, $45-$80
Cooper Co.,
MO

G6, $25-$40
Pulaski Co.,
MO

G8, $50-$90
IL

G9, $45-$80
Cooper Co.,
MO

G9, $150-$250
IL

G8, $80-$150
IL

LOCATION: IL, OK, AR, MO.
DESCRIPTION: A small size, thin, narrow point with coarse serrations and an expanded, bulbous stem. Believed to have been made by Caddo and other people. Associated with Mississippian Caddo culture sites. Named after the famous Cherokee chief of the same name. **I.D. KEY:** Bulbous base, coarse serrations.

SMITH - Middle Archaic, 7000 - 4000 B. P.

(Also see Etley and Mehlville)

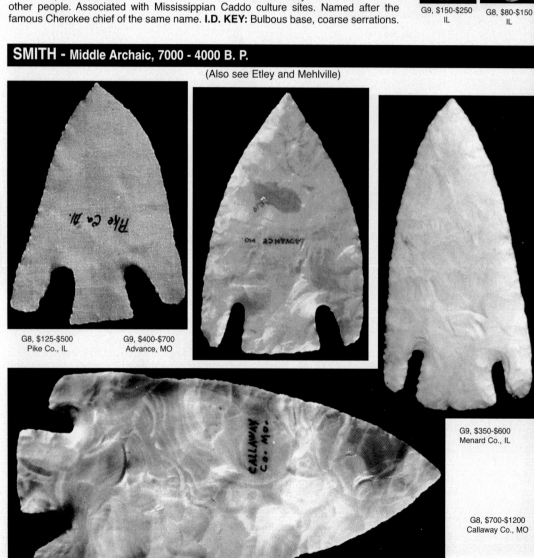

G8, $125-$500
Pike Co., IL

G9, $400-$700
Advance, MO

G9, $350-$600
Menard Co., IL

G8, $700-$1200
Callaway Co., MO

LOCATION: Midwestern States. **DESCRIPTION:** A very large size, broad, point with long parallel shoulders and a squared to slightly expanding base. Some examples may appear to be basally notched due to the long barbs.

Burlington chert

G8, $350-$600
MO

Indiana hornstone

G8, $125-$200
Cooper Co., MO

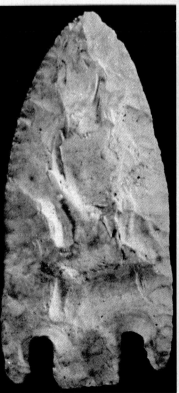

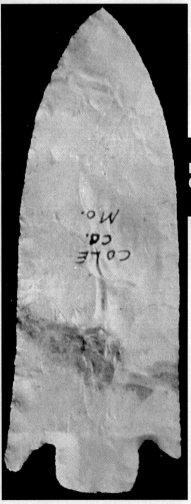

N
C

G7, $150-$250
Macoupin Co., IL

G8, $400-$750
Howard Co., MO

G9, $950-$1750
Cole Co., MO

791

G8, $55-$100
IL

G8, $175-$300
MO

G9, $200-$350
Lincoln Co., MO

Angel Fish
form

G8, $150-$250
Lincoln Co., MO

G7, $80-$150
Cent. IL

G7, $175-$300
IL

Red/cream
chert

G8, $200-$350
Peoria Co., IL

G10, $300-$500
IL

LOCATION: Midwestern to Eastern states. Type site located in Calhoun Co., IL. **DESCRIPTION:** A medium to large size, broad, thin wide corner notched point of high quality. Blade edges and base are convex. Many examples have intentional fractured bases. Made by the Hopewell culture. This point has been reproduced in recent years. **I.D KEY:** Size and broad corner notches.

Base
nick

G8, $150-$250
IL

G10, $650-$1200
IL

G10, $450-$800
Quincy Co., IL

N
C

G10, $450-$800
IL

G8, $800-$1500
Greene Co., IL

793

SQUARE KNIFE - Late Archaic to Historic, 3500 - 400 B. P.

(Also see Angostura, Red Ochre and Wadlow)

G6, $150-$250
Morris Co., KS

G10, $800-$1500
Douglas Co., KS. Classic. Cache blade.

G6, $65-$120
Morgan Co., MO

G9, $350-$600
Madison Co., IL

LOCATION: Midwestern states. **DESCRIPTION:** A medium to large size squared blade with rounded corners.

IMPORTANT:
All shown half size

STANFIELD (see Tennessee River)

STANDLEE CONTRACTING STEMMED - Woodland, 7500 - 7000 B. P.

(Also see Dickson, Langtry in Texas & Searcy in Arkansas)

LOCATION: Arkansas,Missouri,Oklahoma. **DESCRIPTION:** A medium size, contracting stemmed point with tapered shoulders. Bases are straight to concave. Blade edges are convex, recurved to pentagonal. **I.D. KEY:** Long contracting stem.

G5, $12-$20
Lawrence Co., MO

STEUBEN - Woodland, 2000 - 1000 B. P.

(Also see Carter, Ferry, Hardin, Lehigh, Matanzas, Motley, Rice Side Notched and Table Rock)

G5, $1-$3
Clinton Co., IL

G6, $8-$15
N.E. KS

G6, $8-$15
Madison Co., IL

G4, $8-$15
Miller Co., MO

G6, $12-$20
N. E. OK

G6, $15-$25
Miller Co., MO

G6, $25-$45
Washington Co., KS

794

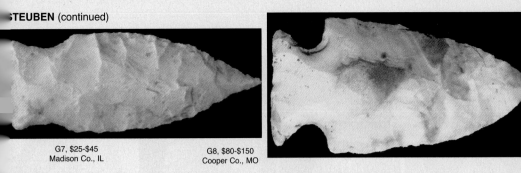

G7, $25-$45
Madison Co., IL

G8, $80-$150
Cooper Co., MO

LOCATION: Midwestern states. **DESCRIPTION:** A medium to large size, narrow point with tapered to horizontal shoulders and a medium to long expanding stem. The base is straight. Convex base places it under the *Snyder* type. **I.D. KEY:** Long expanded stem.

STILWELL - Early Archaic, 9000 - 7000 B. P.

(Also see Kirk Corner Notched and Pine Tree)

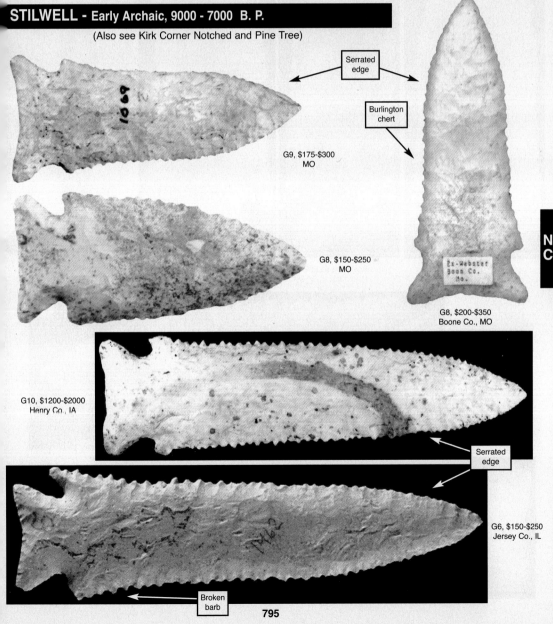

Serrated edge

G9, $175-$300
MO

Burlington chert

G8, $150-$250
MO

Ex-Webster
Boon Co.
Mo.

G8, $200-$350
Boone Co., MO

N
C

G10, $1200-$2000
Henry Co., IA

Serrated edge

G6, $150-$250
Jersey Co., IL

Broken barb

795

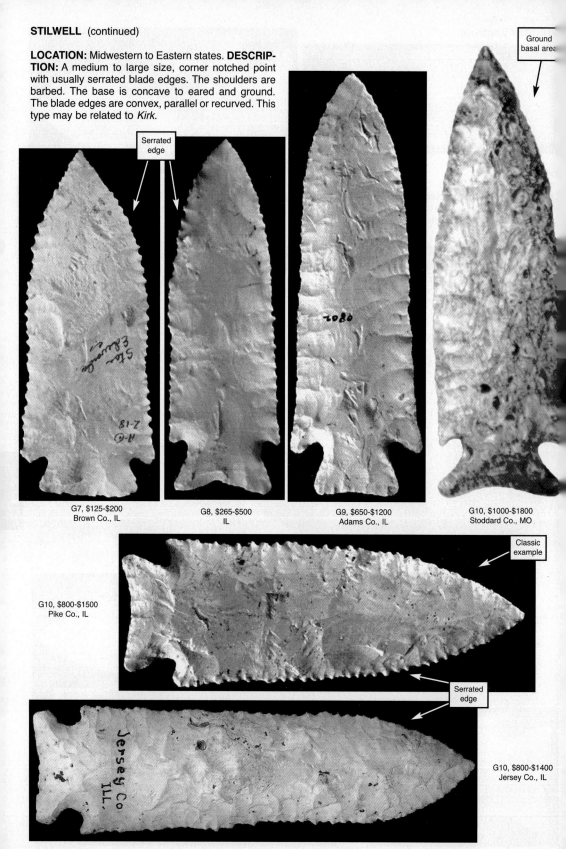

STILWELL (continued)

LOCATION: Midwestern to Eastern states. **DESCRIPTION:** A medium to large size, corner notched point with usually serrated blade edges. The shoulders are barbed. The base is concave to eared and ground. The blade edges are convex, parallel or recurved. This type may be related to *Kirk*.

Ground basal area

Serrated edge

G7, $125-$200
Brown Co., IL

G8, $265-$500
IL

G9, $650-$1200
Adams Co., IL

G10, $1000-$1800
Stoddard Co., MO

G10, $800-$1500
Pike Co., IL

Classic example

Serrated edge

G10, $800-$1400
Jersey Co., IL

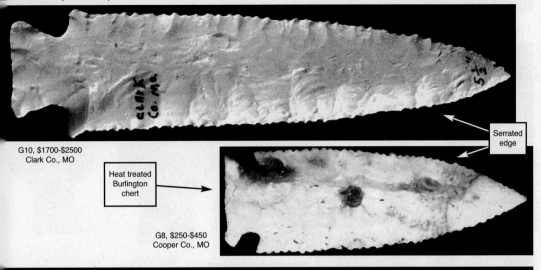

G10, $1700-$2500
Clark Co., MO

Serrated edge

Heat treated Burlington chert

G8, $250-$450
Cooper Co., MO

STONE SQUARE STEM - Middle Archaic, 6000 - 4000 B. P.

(Also see Etley, Heavy Duty, Johnson, Kramer and Rochester)

N
C

G6, $25-$45
Cherokee Co., KS

G6, $15-$25
Clinton Co., IL

G6, $25-$40
Lawrence Co., MO

G5, $20-$35
Morgan Co., MO

G9, $250-$400
Cent. IL

LOCATION: Midwestern states. Type site is in Stone Co., MO. **DESCRIPTION:** A medium to large size, broad stemmed point. Blade edges are convex to recurved. The shoulders are horizontal to barbed and the base is square to slightly expanding with a prominent, short stem. **I.D. KEY:** Short, square stem.

(Also see Kay Blade, Lehigh, Motley, Munker's Creek and Steuben)

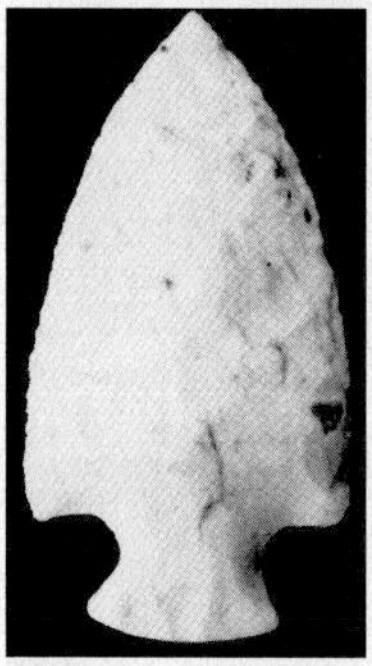

Kay County flint

Winterset flint

Kay County flint

G7, $30-$50
Cooper Co., MO

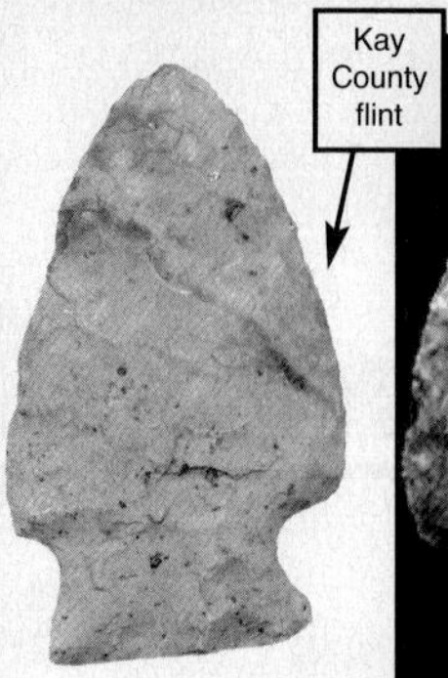

G5, $15-$25
Cowley Co., KS

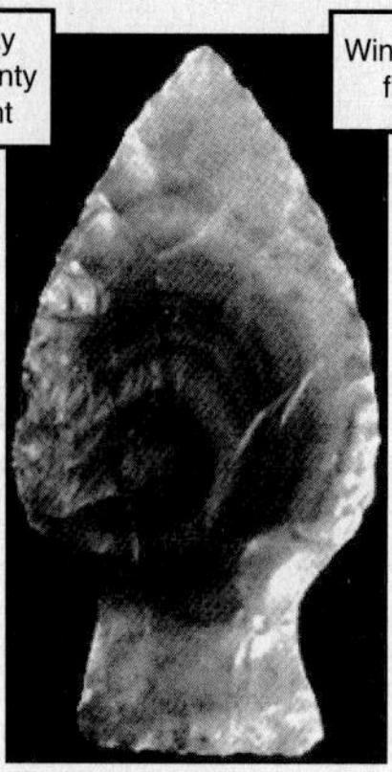

G6, $30-$50
MO

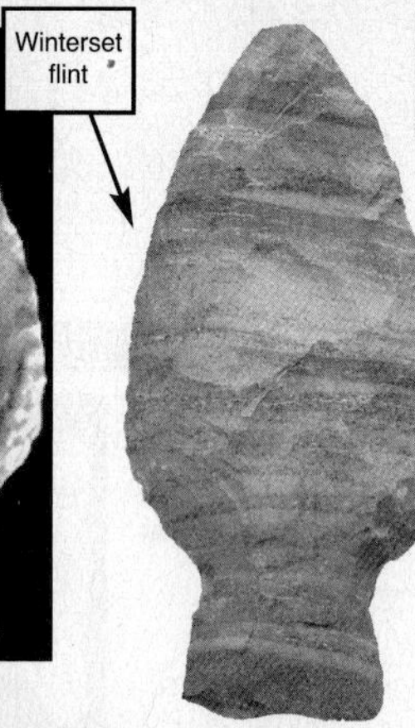

G6, $30-$50
Leavenworth Co., KS

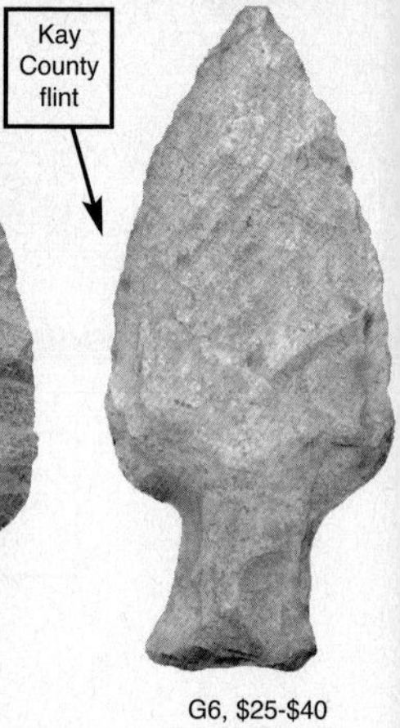

G6, $25-$40
Cowley Co., KS

G9, $125-$200
IL

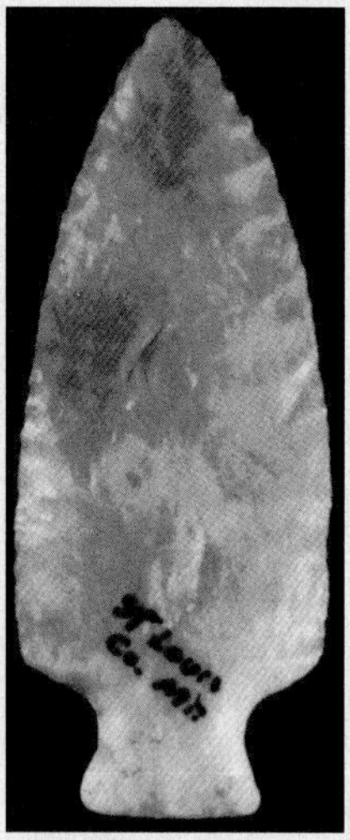

G8, $90-$175
St. Louis Co., MO

G8, $70-$135
IL

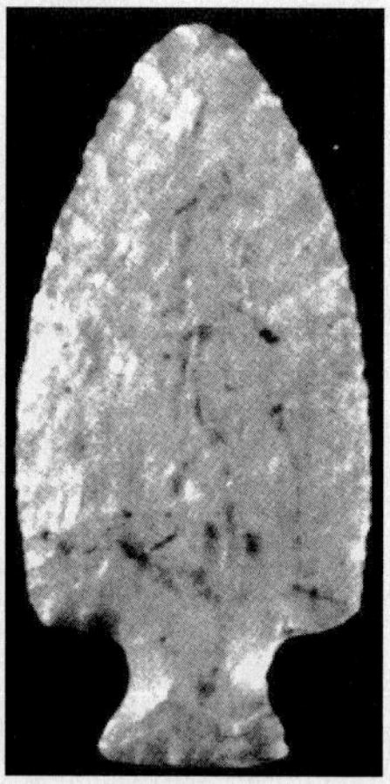

G6, $25-$50
MO

G6, $20-$35
MO

LOCATION: Midwestern to Northeastern states.
DESCRIPTION: A medium to large size, expanded stem point with straight to tapered shoulders. Shoulders can be sharp or rounded. This type is also known as a "Bottleneck" point.

G7, $80-$150
IL

G8, $175-$300
St. Charles Co., MO

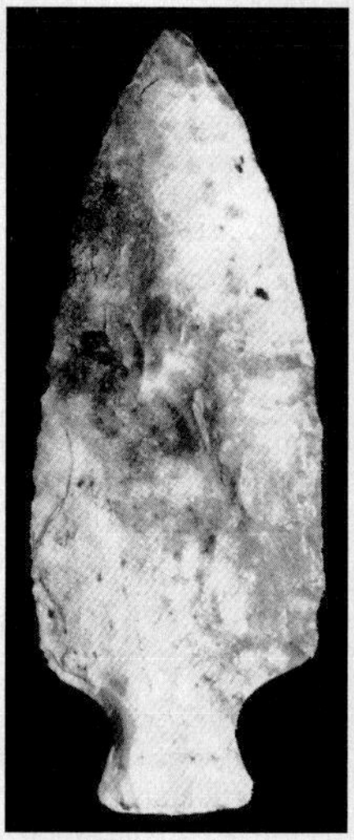

G8, $125-$200
Cooper Co., MO

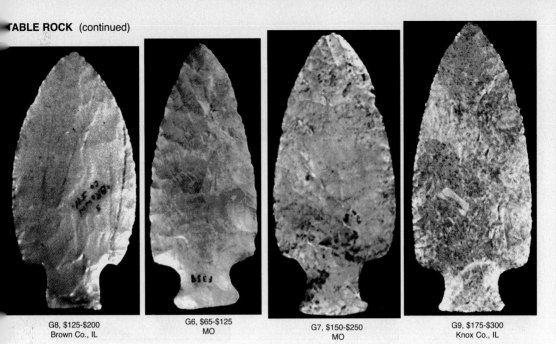

G8, $125-$200
Brown Co., IL

G6, $65-$125
MO

G7, $150-$250
MO

G9, $175-$300
Knox Co., IL

TENNESSEE RIVER - Early Archaic, 9000 - 6000 B. P.

(Also see Adena Blade, Cobbs Triangular, Kirk, Red Ochre and Stanfield)

G8, $65-$125
Pemiscott Co., MO

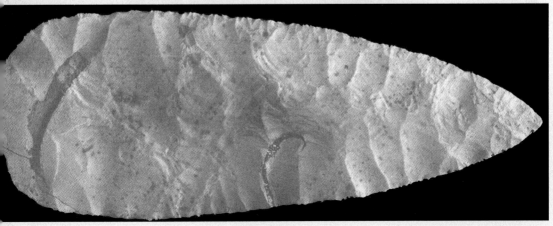

G10, $700-$1200
MO

LOCATION: Midwestern to Southeastern states. **DESCRIPTION:** These are unnotched preforms for early Archaic types such as *Kirk, Eva*, etc. and would have the same description as that type without the notches. Bases can be straight, concave or convex. **I.D. KEY:** Archaic style edgework. **NOTE:** This type has been confused with the *Stanfield* point which is a medium size, narrow, thicker point. A beveled edge would place your point under the *Cobbs Triangular* type.

THEBES - Early Archaic, 10,000 - 8000 B. P.

(Also see Lost Lake, St. Charles and Stilwell)

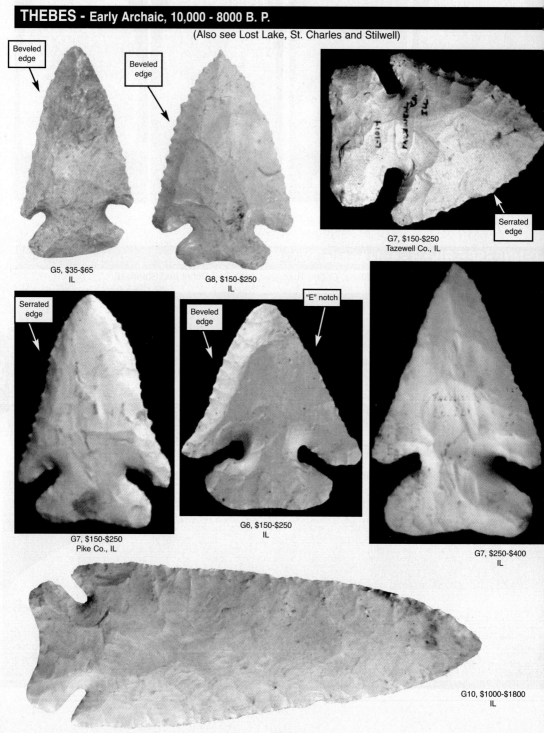

Beveled edge

Beveled edge

Serrated edge

G7, $150-$250
Tazewell Co., IL

G5, $35-$65
IL

G8, $150-$250
IL

Serrated edge

Beveled edge

"E" notch

G7, $150-$250
Pike Co., IL

G6, $150-$250
IL

G7, $250-$400
IL

G10, $1000-$1800
IL

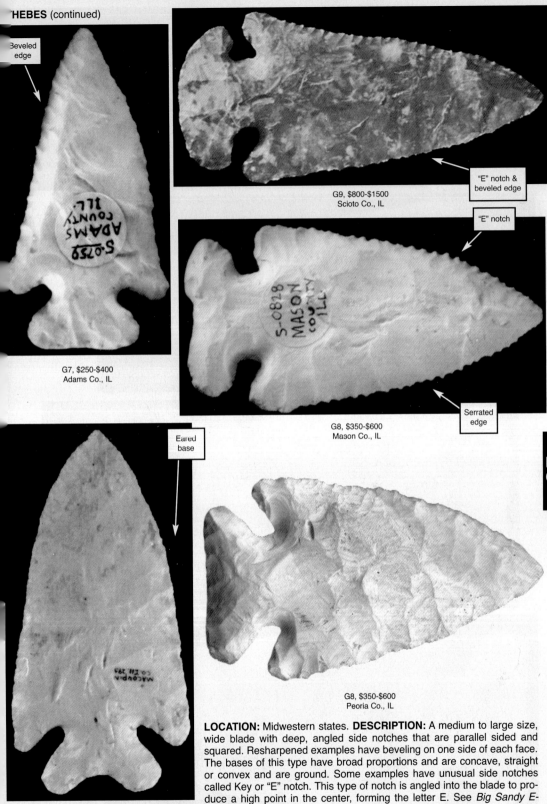

Beveled edge

"E" notch & beveled edge

G9, $800-$1500
Scioto Co., IL

"E" notch

Serrated edge

G8, $350-$600
Mason Co., IL

G7, $250-$400
Adams Co., IL

Eared base

N
C

G8, $350-$600
Peoria Co., IL

G9, $800-$1400
Macoupin Co., IL

LOCATION: Midwestern states. **DESCRIPTION:** A medium to large size, wide blade with deep, angled side notches that are parallel sided and squared. Resharpened examples have beveling on one side of each face. The bases of this type have broad proportions and are concave, straight or convex and are ground. Some examples have unusual side notches called Key or "E" notch. This type of notch is angled into the blade to produce a high point in the center, forming the letter E. See *Big Sandy E-Notched*.

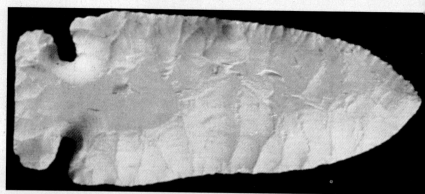

G7, $400-$700
Fulton Co., IL

Beveled
edge

G8, $700-$1200
Pike Co., IL

G8, $700-$1200
Pike Co., MO

Serrated
edge

G8, $700-$1200
Pike Co., IL

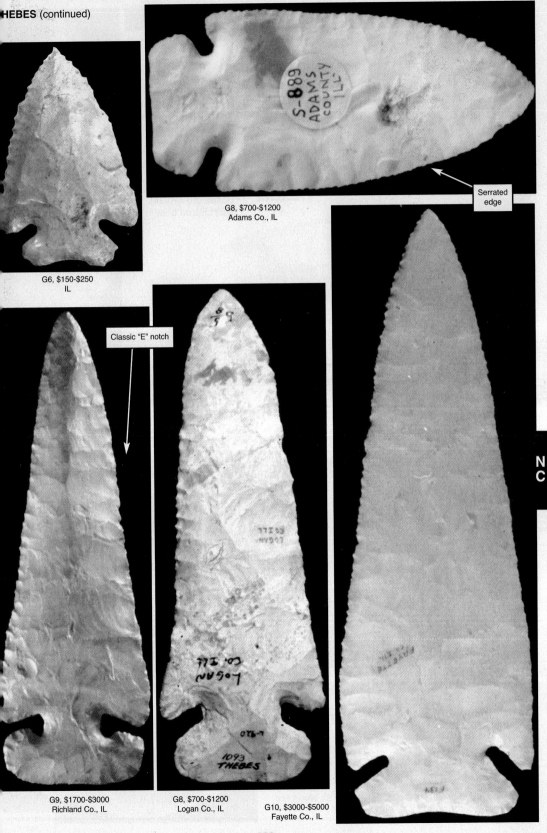

Serrated edge

G8, $700-$1200
Adams Co., IL

G6, $150-$250
IL

Classic "E" notch

G9, $1700-$3000
Richland Co., IL

G8, $700-$1200
Logan Co., IL

G10, $3000-$5000
Fayette Co., IL

N
C

TURIN - Early Archaic, 8500 - 7500 B. P.

(Also see Godar, Graham Cave, Hemphill, Hickory Ridge, Osceola, Raddatz and Robinson)

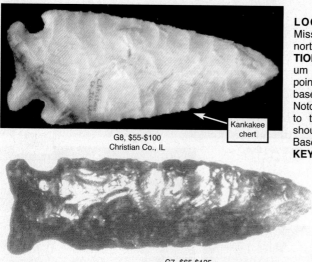

Kankakee chert

G8, $55-$100
Christian Co., IL

G7, $65-$125
Pottowatomie Co., KS

LOCATION: Illinois, Missouri, Nebraska northward. **DESCRIPTION:** A small to medium size side-notched point with an auriculate base that is concave. Notching occurs close to the base and the shoulders are barbed. Bases are ground. **I.D. KEY:** Eared base.

G6, $125-$200
S.E. KS

TURKEYTAIL-FULTON - Late Archaic to Woodland, 4000 - 2500 B. P.

(Also see Early Ovoid Knife)

From a large cache

G8, $800-$1400
St. Charles Co., MO

G8, $800-$1400
St. Charles Co., MO

G7, $350-$600
N. E. OK

G6, $400-$700
MO. Titterington cache.

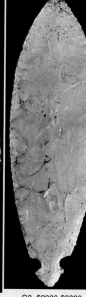

G9, $2000-$3800
Morgan Co., IL

LOCATION: Midwestern to Eastern states. **DESCRIPTION:** A medium to large size, wide, thin, elliptical blade with shallow notches very close to the base. This type is usually found in caches and has been reproduced in recent years. Made by the Adena culture. An earlier form was found in *Benton* caches in Mississippi carbon dated to about 4700 B.P.

IMPORTANT:
All Turkeytails shown half size

G8, $900-$1600
St. Charles Co., MO

From a large cache

TURKEYTAIL-HARRISON - Late Archaic to Woodland, 4000 - 2500 B. P.

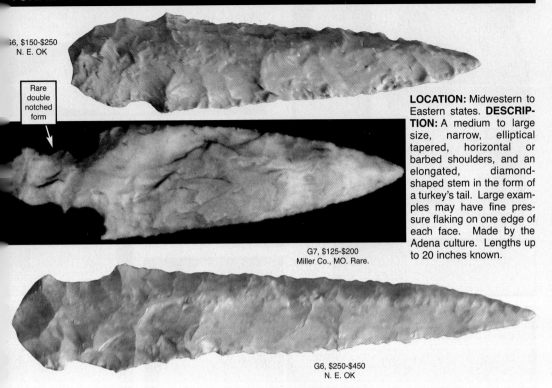

G6, $150-$250
N. E. OK

Rare double notched form

G7, $125-$200
Miller Co., MO. Rare.

LOCATION: Midwestern to Eastern states. **DESCRIPTION:** A medium to large size, narrow, elliptical tapered, horizontal or barbed shoulders, and an elongated, diamond-shaped stem in the form of a turkey's tail. Large examples may have fine pressure flaking on one edge of each face. Made by the Adena culture. Lengths up to 20 inches known.

G6, $250-$450
N. E. OK

TURKEYTAIL-HEBRON - Late Archaic to Woodland, 3500 - 2500 B. P.

(Also see Waubesa)

G10, $1500-$2500
Cairo., IL

LOCATION: Around the great lakes region from Wisconsin to New York. **DESCRIPTION:** A medium to large size blade with barbed shoulders, and a narrow, contracting stem with a convex base. Made by the *Adena* culture.

WADLOW - Late Archaic, 4000 - 2500 B. P.

(Also see Cobbs Triangular, Etley and Red Ochre)

WADLOW (continued)

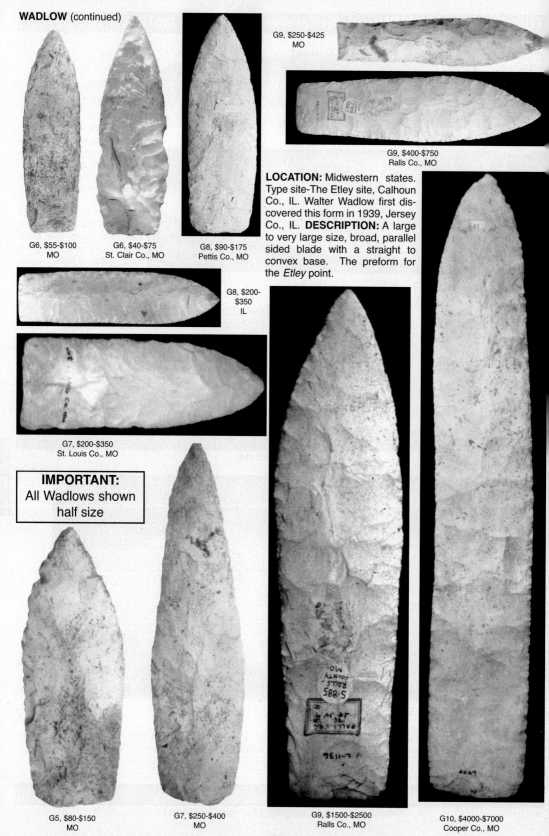

G6, $55-$100
MO

G6, $40-$75
St. Clair Co., MO

G8, $90-$175
Pettis Co., MO

G9, $250-$425
MO

G9, $400-$750
Ralls Co., MO

LOCATION: Midwestern states. Type site-The Etley site, Calhoun Co., IL. Walter Wadlow first discovered this form in 1939, Jersey Co., IL. **DESCRIPTION:** A large to very large size, broad, parallel sided blade with a straight to convex base. The preform for the *Etley* point.

G8, $200-$350
IL

G7, $200-$350
St. Louis Co., MO

IMPORTANT:
All Wadlows shown
half size

G5, $80-$150
MO

G7, $250-$400
MO

G9, $1500-$2500
Ralls Co., MO

G10, $4000-$7000
Cooper Co., MO

IMPORTANT:
All Wadlows
shown half size

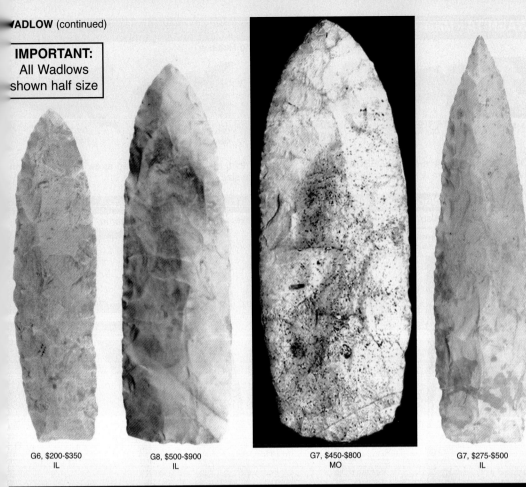

G6, $200-$350
IL

G8, $500-$900
IL

G7, $450-$800
MO

G7, $275-$500
IL

WARRICK - Early Archaic, 9000 - 5000 B. P.

(Also see St. Charles)

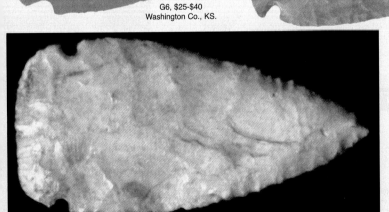

G6, $25-$40
Washington Co., KS.

G8, $135-$250
Washington Co., KS.

LOCATION: Midwestern states. **DESCRIPTION:** A medium to large size, sturdy, side to corner notched point. Notching is close to the base which is ground. Flaking is of high quality.

G8, $275-$500
Camden Co., MO

WASHITA - Mississippian, 800 - 400 B. P.

(Also see Cahokia and Huffaker)

G5, $12-$20
IL

G9, $65-$125
Garden City, KS

Alibates
dolomite

G9, $50-$95
Pottowatomie Co., KS

G10, $150-$250
Garden City, KS

Alibates
dolomite

G9, $150-$250
Hooker Co., NE

LOCATION: Midwestern states. **DESCRIPTION:** A small size, thin, triangular side notched arrow point with a con
cave base. Basal area is usually large in proportion to the blade size.

WAUBESA - Woodland, 2500 - 1500 B. P.

(Also see Adena, Dickson, Gary, Hidden Valley, Mason & Turkeytail-Hebron)

Hixton slicified
sandstone

Colorful
chert

G5, $15-$25
Kay Co., OK

Knife River
flint

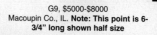

G5, $25-$50
WI

G9, $65-$125
AR

LOCATION: Midwestern to Southeastern United States. **DESCRIPTION:** Associated with the Hopewell culture. A medium to large, narrow, thin, well made point with a contracting stem that is rounded or pointed. Some examples exhibit unusually high quality flaking and saw-tooth serrations. Blades are convex to recurved. Shoulders are squared to barbed. **I.D. KEY:** Basal form pointed or near pointed. Good secondary flaking and thin.

G9, $5000-$8000
Macoupin Co., IL. **Note: This point is 6-
3/4" long shown half size**

G9, $160-$300
Sedalia, MO

WHEELER EXCURVATE - Transitional Paleo, 10,000 - 8000 B. P.

(Also see Angostura)

G9, $150-$250
S.W. MO

LOCATION: Southeastern states. Rare in Illinois and Missouri. **DESCRIPTION:** A small to medium size, lanceolate point with a deep concave base that is steeply beveled. Some examples are fluted, others are finely serrated and show excellent quality collateral flaking. Most bases are deeply notched but some examples have a more shallow concavity. Basal grinding is usually absent. The ears on some examples turn inward. Blade edges are excurvate. **I.D. KEY:** Base form and flaking style.

DESERT SOUTHWEST SECTION:

This section includes point types from the following states: Arizona, Colorado, Nevada, New Mexico, Texas, Utah and from Mexico

The points in this section are arranged in alphabetical order and are shown **actual size**. All types are listed that were available for photographing. Any missing types will be added to future editions as photographs become available. We are always interested in receiving sharp, black and white or color glossy photos, color slides or high resolution (300 pixels/inch) digital pictures of your collection. Be sure to include a ruler in the photograph so that proper scale can be determined.

Lithics: Materials employed in the manufacture of projectile points from this region are: agate, basalt, chalcedony, chert, jasper, obsidian, petrified wood, quartzite, siltstone.

Important sites: Clovis (Paleo), Blackwater Draw, NM. Folsom (Paleo), Folsom NM. Sandia (Paleo), Sandia Cave, NM.

Special Senior Advisor
Vern Crites

Special advisors:
John Byrd, Jim Hogue, Alan L. Phelps,
Art Tatum

In memory of Charles D. Meyer who was instrumental in establishing this section of the guide with his advice, descriptions, and photographs.

DESERT SOUTHWEST POINT TYPES
(Archaeological Periods)

PALEO (13,200 B.P - 9,000 B.P.)

Belen	Folsom	Lake Mohave	Midland
Clovis	Goshen	Lancet	Milnesand
Drill	Graver	Madden Lake	Sandia

EARLY ARCHAIC (10,300 B.P - 5,000 B.P.)

Abasolo	Bell	Escobas	Pelona	Texcoco
Agate Basin	Circular Uniface Knife	Firstview	Perforator	Tortugas
Allen	Cody Knife	Golondrina	Pinto Basin	Uvalde
Angostura	Cruciform I	Hell Gap	Plainview	Ventana-Amargosa
Archaic Knife	Cruciform II	Jay	Rio Grande	Zephyr
Augustin	Darl Stemmed	Lancet	Round-Back Knife	Zorra
Augustin Snapped Base	Datil	Meserve	San Jose	
Bajada	Early Leaf	Mount Albion	Scottsbluff	
Baker	Early Triangular	Moyote	Scraper	
Barreal	Eden	Northern Side Notched	Silver Lake	
Bat Cave	Embudo	Palmillas	Sudden Series	

MIDDLE ARCHAIC (5,100 B.P - 3,300 B.P.)

Ahumada	Dagger	Green River	Neff
Catan	Disc	Gypsum Cave	Refugio
Chiricahua	Duncan	Hanna	San Rafael
Corner Tang Knife	Durango	Kinney	Squaw Mountain
Cortero	Frio	Lerma	Ventana Side Notched
Crescent	Frio Transitional	Manzano	

LATE ARCHAIC (3,400 B.P - 2,300 B.P.)

Acatita	Conejo	Gobernadora	Shumla
Amaragosa	Duran	Maljamar	Socorro
Basal Double Tang	Early Stemmed	Martis	Triangular Knife
Carlsbad	Elko Corner Notched	Matamoros	Yavapai
Charcos	Elko Eared	San Pedro	
Cienega	Exotic	Saw	

DESERT TRADITIONS:
TRANSITIONAL (2,300 B.P - 1600 B.P.)

Black Mesa Narrow Neck	Figueroa	Guadalupe	Humboldt

DEVELOPMENTAL (1600 - 700 B.P)

Awatovi Side Notched	Dry Prong	Point Of Pines Side Notched	Snaketown
Basketmaker	Gatlin Side Notched	Pueblo Alto Side Notched	Snaketown Side Notched
Bonito Notched	Gila River Corner Notched	Pueblo Del Arroyo Side Notched	Snaketown Triangular
Bull Creek	Hodges Contracting Stem	Pueblo Side Notched	Soto
Chaco Corner Notrched	Hohokam Knife	Rose Springs Corner Notched	Temporal
Citrus Side Notched	Kin Kletso Side Notched	Rose Springs Stemmed	Truxton
Cohonina Stemmed	Mimbre	Sacaton	Walnut Canyon Side Notched
Convento	Nawthis	Salado	
Deadman's	Padre	Salt River Indented Base	
Dolores	Parowan	Santa Cruz	

CLASSIC PHASE (700 - 400 B.P)

Aguaje	Cow's Skull	Desert-Sierra	Sobaipuri
Buck Taylor Notched	Del Carmen	Garza	Toyah
Caracara	Desert-Delta	Harahey	White Mountain Side Notched
Cottonwood Leaf	Desert-General	Mescal Knife	
Cottonwood Triangle	Desert-Redding	San Bruno	

HISTORIC (400 B.P - Present)

Glass	Trade

DESERT SOUTHWEST
THUMBNAIL GUIDE SECTION

The following references are provided to aid the collector in easier and quicker identification of point types. All photos are exactly 30% of actual size and are proportional to each other. Each point pictured in this section represents a classic form for the type. When a match is found, go to the alphabetical location of that type for more examples in true actual size.

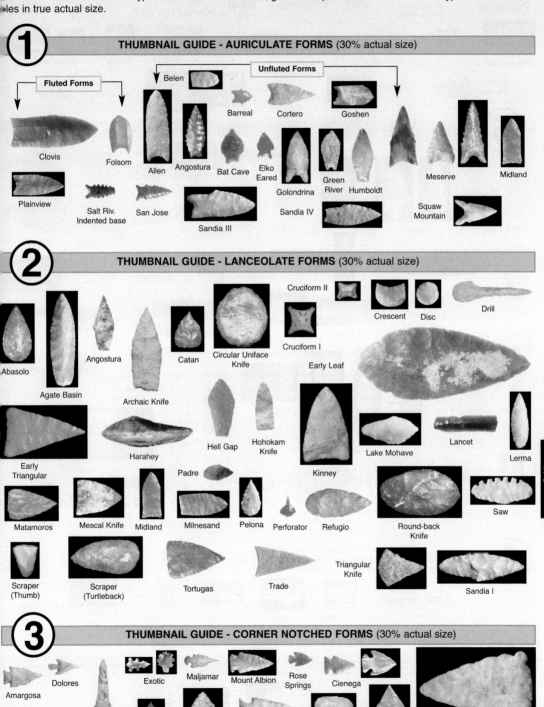

① THUMBNAIL GUIDE - AURICULATE FORMS (30% actual size)

Fluted Forms

Belen

Unfluted Forms

Clovis

Folsom

Allen

Angostura

Barreal

Cortero

Goshen

Bat Cave

Elko Eared

Green River

Humboldt

Golondrina

Meserve

Midland

Plainview

Salt Riv. Indented base

San Jose

Sandia III

Sandia IV

Squaw Mountain

② THUMBNAIL GUIDE - LANCEOLATE FORMS (30% actual size)

Abasolo

Agate Basin

Angostura

Archaic Knife

Catan

Circular Uniface Knife

Cruciform II

Crescent

Disc

Drill

Cruciform I

Early Leaf

Harahey

Hell Gap

Hohokam Knife

Lake Mohave

Lancet

Lerma

Early Triangular

Kinney

Matamoros

Mescal Knife

Midland

Milnesand

Pelona

Perforator

Refugio

Padre

Round-back Knife

Saw

Scraper (Thumb)

Scraper (Turtleback)

Tortugas

Trade

Triangular Knife

Sandia I

S W

③ THUMBNAIL GUIDE - CORNER NOTCHED FORMS (30% actual size)

Amargosa

Dolores

Exotic

Maljamar

Mount Albion

Rose Springs

Cienega

Elko Corner Notched

Drill

Frio

Moyote

San Pedro

Scraper (Blunt)

Texcoco

Corner Tang

811

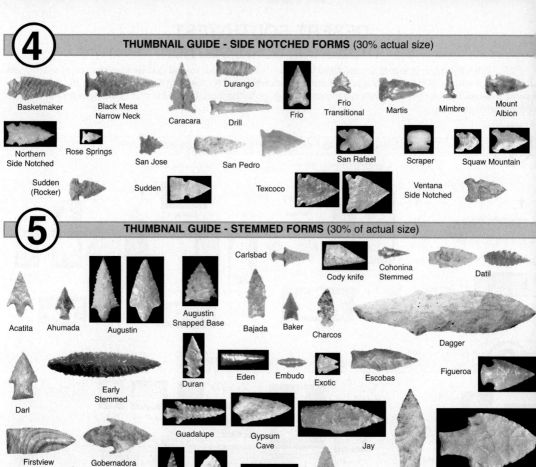

④ THUMBNAIL GUIDE - SIDE NOTCHED FORMS (30% actual size)

Basketmaker

Black Mesa Narrow Neck

Caracara

Durango

Drill

Frio

Frio Transitional

Martis

Mimbre

Mount Albion

Northern Side Notched

Rose Springs

San Jose

San Pedro

San Rafael

Scraper

Squaw Mountain

Sudden (Rocker)

Sudden

Texcoco

Ventana Side Notched

⑤ THUMBNAIL GUIDE - STEMMED FORMS (30% of actual size)

Carlsbad

Cody knife

Cohonina Stemmed

Datil

Acatita

Ahumada

Augustin

Augustin Snapped Base

Bajada

Baker

Charcos

Dagger

Darl

Early Stemmed

Duran

Eden

Embudo

Exotic

Escobas

Figueroa

Firstview

Gobernadora

Guadalupe

Gypsum Cave

Jay

Lake Mohave

Madden Lake

Maljamar

Manzano

Neff

Palmillas

Rio Grande

San Jose

San Pedro

Scottsbluff

Truxton

Silver Lake

Socorro

Trade

Trade

Uvalde

Ventana-Amargosa

Yavapai

Zephyr

Zorra

⑥ THUMBNAIL GUIDE - STEMMED-BIFURCATED FORMS (30% of actual size)

Barreal

Chiricauha

Conejo

Duncan

Hanna

San Jose

⑦ THUMBNAIL GUIDE - BASAL NOTCHED FORMS (30% of actual size)

Bell

Basal Double Tang

Moyote

Parowan

Shumla

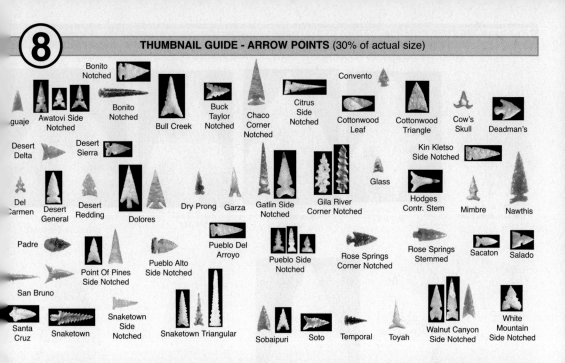

Bonito Notched

guaje

Awatovi Side Notched

Bonito Notched

Bull Creek

Buck Taylor Notched

Chaco Corner Notched

Citrus Side Notched

Convento

Cottonwood Leaf

Cottonwood Triangle

Cow's Skull

Deadman's

Desert Delta

Desert Sierra

Del Carmen

Desert General

Desert Redding

Dolores

Dry Prong

Garza

Gatlin Side Notched

Gila River Corner Notched

Glass

Kin Kletso Side Notched

Hodges Contr. Stem

Mimbre

Nawthis

Padre

Point Of Pines Side Notched

Pueblo Alto Side Notched

Pueblo Del Arroyo

Pueblo Side Notched

Rose Springs Corner Notched

Rose Springs Stemmed

Sacaton

Salado

San Bruno

Santa Cruz

Snaketown

Snaketown Side Notched

Snaketown Triangular

Sobaipuri

Soto

Temporal

Toyah

Walnut Canyon Side Notched

White Mountain Side Notched

ABASOLO - Early to Middle Archaic, 7000 - 5000 B. P.

(Also see Catan, Matamoros, Padre and Refugio)

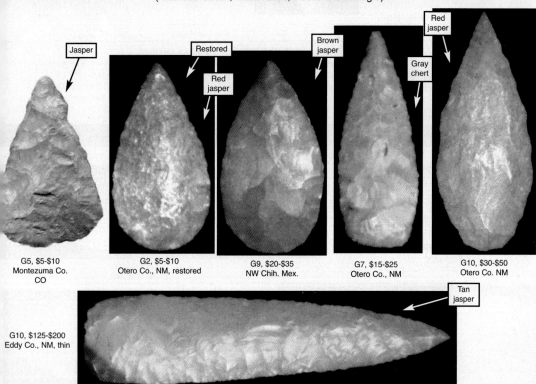

Jasper

Restored

Red jasper

Brown jasper

Red jasper

Gray chert

S W

G5, $5-$10
Montezuma Co. CO

G2, $5-$10
Otero Co., NM, restored

G9, $20-$35
NW Chih. Mex.

G7, $15-$25
Otero Co., NM

G10, $30-$50
Otero Co. NM

Tan jasper

G10, $125-$200
Eddy Co., NM, thin

LOCATION: Southern Texas into Mexico and New Mexico. **DESCRIPTION:** A medium to large size, broad, lanceolate point with a rounded base. The blade can be beveled on one side of each face and the base can be thinned. **I.D. KEY:** Early form of flaking on blade with good secondary edgework and rounded base.

ACATITA - Late Archaic, 3000 - 2600 B.P.

(Also see Augustine, Gobernadora, Gypsum Cave, Manzano, Socorro and Shumla)

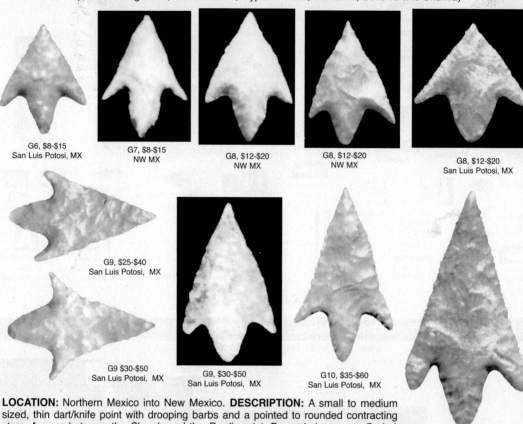

G6, $8-$15
San Luis Potosi, MX

G7, $8-$15
NW MX

G8, $12-$20
NW MX

G8, $12-$20
NW MX

G8, $12-$20
San Luis Potosi, MX

G9, $25-$40
San Luis Potosi, MX

G9 $30-$50
San Luis Potosi, MX

G9, $30-$50
San Luis Potosi, MX

G10, $35-$60
San Luis Potosi, MX

LOCATION: Northern Mexico into New Mexico. **DESCRIPTION:** A small to medium sized, thin dart/knife point with drooping barbs and a pointed to rounded contracting stem. A cross between the *Shumla* and the *Perdiz* point. Formerly known as *Cedral*; given the name *Acatita* by Perino in his Vol. 3. **I.D. KEY:** Barbs and base form.

G10, $70-$135
San Luis Potosi, MX

AGATE BASIN - Early Archaic, 10,200 - 8,500 B.P.

(Also see Allen, Angostura, Archaic Knife, Lerma and Sandia)

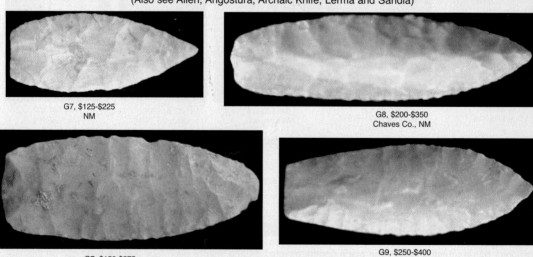

G7, $125-$225
NM

G8, $200-$350
Chaves Co., NM

G7, $150-$275
W. TX

G9, $250-$400
W. TX

G9, $200-$375
AZ

LOCATION: New Mexico eastward to Pennsylvania. **DESCRIPTION:** A medium to large size lanceolate blade of high quality. Bases are either convex, concave or straight and are usually ground. Some examples are median ridged. **I.D. KEY:** Basal form and flaking style.

AGUAJE - Classic Phase, 600 - 550 B.P.

(Also see Bull Creek, Cottonwood and Sobaipuri)

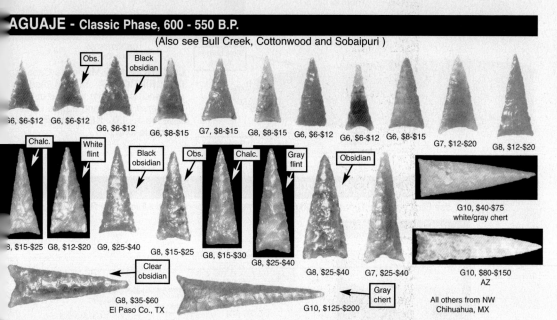

G6, $6-$12   G6, $6-$12   G6, $6-$12   G6, $8-$15   G7, $8-$15   G8, $8-$15   G6, $6-$12   G6, $6-$12   G6, $8-$15   G7, $12-$20   G8, $12-$20

Obs.   Black obsidian

Chalc.   White flint   Black obsidian   Obs.   Chalc.   Gray flint   Obsidian

G8, $15-$25   G8, $12-$20   G9, $25-$40   G8, $15-$25   G8, $15-$30   G8, $25-$40   G8, $25-$40   G7, $25-$40

G10, $40-$75
white/gray chert

Clear obsidian

G8, $35-$60
El Paso Co., TX

Gray chert

G10, $125-$200

G10, $80-$150
AZ

All others from NW
Chihuahua, MX

LOCATION: Northwest Chihuahua, MX. into Sou. New Mexico and far West Texas. **DESCRIPTION:** A small, thin triangular arrow point with a straight to concave base. This type has needle tips and sharp basal corners. Some examples have basal ears. **I.D. KEY:** Small, narrow triangle.

AHUMADA - Mid-Late Archaic, 4000 - 2500 B.P.

(Also see Carlsbad, Cienega, Dolores, Guadalupe, Maljamar, Neff and Truxton)

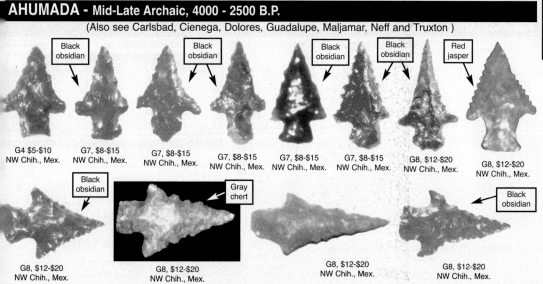

Black obsidian   Black obsidian   Black obsidian   Black obsidian   Red jasper

G4 $5-$10
NW Chih., Mex.   G7, $8-$15
NW Chih., Mex.   G7, $8-$15
NW Chih., Mex.   G7, $8-$15
NW Chih., Mex.   G7, $8-$15
NW Chih., Mex.   G7, $8-$15
NW Chih., Mex.   G8, $12-$20
NW Chih., Mex.   G8, $12-$20
NW Chih., Mex.

Black obsidian   Gray chert   Black obsidian

G8, $12-$20
NW Chih., Mex.   G8, $12-$20
NW Chih., Mex.   G8, $12-$20
NW Chih., Mex.   G8, $12-$20
NW Chih., Mex.

S
W

815

AHUMADA (continued)

LOCATION: Arizona, New Mexico and N.W. Chihuahua, MX. **DESCRIPTION:** A corner notched dart point with a tri angular blade; almost always serrated and with an expanding stem. McNish reported that most examples are from Villa Ahumada in N.W. Chihuahua, MX. **I.D. KEY:** Fan shaped stem and serrations.

ALLEN - Early Archaic, 8,500 - 7500 B.P.

(Also see Angostura, Clovis, Cortero, Goshen, Humboldt, Meserve, Plainview)

Quartzite

G6, $250-$400
Alamosa Co., CO

G8, $275-$550
Chaves Co., NM

Note oblique flaking

LOCATION: New Mexico to Canada. **DESCRIPTION:** A small to medium size lanceolate point that has oblique transverse flaking and a ground concave base. **I.D. KEY:** Flaking style and blade form.

G2, $150-$250
NM

Restored tip reduces value

AMARGOSA - Middle Archaic, 3000 - 2000 B.P.

(Also see Basketmaker, Cienega, Elko Corner Notched, Figueroa, Mt. Albion, San Pedro)

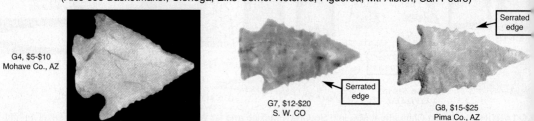

G4, $5-$10
Mohave Co., AZ

Serrated edge

G7, $12-$20
S. W. CO

Serrated edge

G8, $15-$25
Pima Co., AZ

LOCATION: Southeastern California into W. Arizona and W. Nevada. **DESCRIPTION:** A small size, corner notched dart/knife point with a needle tip and sharp tangs. Some examples are serrated. Bases are straight to slightly convex or concave. **I.D. KEY:** Sharp tangs and corners, needle tip.

ANGOSTURA - Early Archaic, 8,800 - 7500 B.P.

(Also see Agate Basin, Allen, Archaic Knife, Clovis and Humboldt)

Diagonal flaking

Purple/white chert

Restored tip

G2, $15-$30
Otero Co., NM, ground stem sides and base. Thick.

Agate

G7, $30-$50
S. W. CO

G7, $30-$50
S. W. CO

G6, $35-$60
S. W. CO

G7, $30-$50
Pima Co., AZ

G8, $150-$250
NM

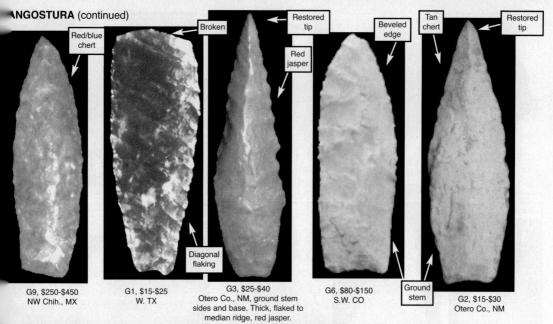

Red/blue chert

Broken

Restored tip

Red jasper

Beveled edge

Tan chert

Restored tip

Diagonal flaking

Ground stem

G9, $250-$450
NW Chih., MX

G1, $15-$25
W. TX

G3, $25-$40
Otero Co., NM, ground stem
sides and base. Thick, flaked to
median ridge, red jasper.

G6, $80-$150
S.W. CO

G2, $15-$30
Otero Co., NM

LOCATION: Southwestern states. **DESCRIPTION:** A medium to large size lanceolate blade of unusually high quality. Bases are either convex, concave or straight and are usually ground. Most examples have oblique transverse flaking. **I.D. KEY:** Basal form and flaking style.

G8, $250-$450
El Paso Co., TX

ARCHAIC KNIFE - Early to Mid Archaic, 6000 - 4000 B.P.

(Also see Angostura and Early Triangular)

Broken & glued

Base nick

G2, $15-$30
Pima Co., AZ

LOCATION: Arizona into Plains states. **DESCRIPTION:** A medium to large size triangular blade with a concave to straight base. **I.D. KEY:** Large triangle with early flaking.

S W

AUGUSTIN - Early to Middle Archaic, 7000- 5000 B.P.

(Also see Acatita, Gypsum Cave, Manzano and Santa Cruz)

Basalt

G4, $8-$15
Yavapai Co., AZ

G8, $25-$40
S. W. CO

G8, $25-$40
S. W. CO

LOCATION: The southern portion of the southwestern states and northern Mexico. **DESCRIPTION:** A small to medium sized dart/knife point with a broad triangular blade and a contracting, rounded to pointed stem and obtuse shoulders. The *Gypsum Cave* point may be a westerly and northerly extension of this point. **I.D. KEY:** Contracting base.

AUGUSTIN (continued)

G5, $15-$30
Cochise Co., AZ

G4, $12-$20
Hildago Co., NM

G5, $15-$30
S. AZ

Drill

G6, $15-$30
Yavapai Co., AZ

Red jasper, serrated

Pink jasper

G8, $40-$75
NW Chih., Mex., thin, not ground.

Restored barb

G2, $12-$20
Otero Co., NM

White quartz

Restored barb

Serrated

Chert

Gray chert

G8, $40-$75
NW Chih., Mex.

G2, $12-$20
Otero Co., NM

G6, $25-$40
S. AZ

G8, $60-$110
Otero Co., NM, ground stem.

G9, $60-$110
Luna Co., NM

Pink jasper, serrated.

Red jasper, serrated

G9, $95-$185
NW Chih, Mex, ground stem, thin.

G9, $95-$185
SW CO

Ground stem

G7, $55-$100
NW Chih, Mex.

G10, $250-$450
NW Chih, Mex., thin.

818

AUGUSTIN-SNAPPED BASE - Early to Mid-Archaic, 7000 - 5000 B.P.

(Also see Gypsum Cave)

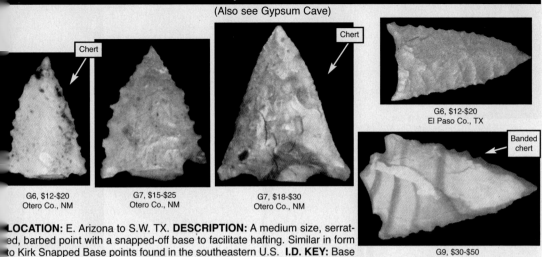

G6, $12-$20
Otero Co., NM

G7, $15-$25
Otero Co., NM

G7, $18-$30
Otero Co., NM

G6, $12-$20
El Paso Co., TX

G9, $30-$50
NW Chih, Mex., flat on reverse side

LOCATION: E. Arizona to S.W. TX. **DESCRIPTION:** A medium size, serrated, barbed point with a snapped-off base to facilitate hafting. Similar in form to Kirk Snapped Base points found in the southeastern U.S. **I.D. KEY:** Base snapped off.

AWATOVI SIDE NOTCHED - Develop. to Classic Phase, 750 - 600 B.P.

(Also see Buck Taylor Notched, Dell Carmen, Desert Sierra, Pueblo Side, White Mountain)

G4, $2-$5
Otero Co., NM

G5, $12-$20
NW Chih., MX

G8, $12-$20
S. W. CO

G9, $30-$50
Montez. Co., CO

G5, $12-$20
NW Chih., MX

G6, $15-$30
NW Chih., MX

G5, $12-$20
NW Chih., MX

G5, $12-$20
NW Chih., MX

G9, $25-$40
S. W. CO

G8, $25-$40
NW Chih., MX

G8, $25-$40
Coconino Co., AZ

G7, $25-$40
NW Chih., MX

G7, $18-$30
Mojave Co., AZ

G10, $35-$65
NM

G10, $45-$80
NW Chih., MX

G9, $30-$50
S. W. CO

G9, $45-$80
NW Chih., Mex.

G9, $60-$100
NW Chih., Mex.

G7, $20-$35
Yavapai Co., AZ

G9, $45-$80
Montez. Co., CO

G9, $45-$80
S. W. CO

G8, $25-$45
S. W. CO

LOCATION: Arizona, New Mexico, northern Mexico, southern Utah and S.W. Colorado. **DESCRIPTION:** A small size, narrow, triple-notched, triangular arrow point. Side notches can occur high up from the base. Part of the *Pueblo Side Notched* cluster and similar to the *Harrell* point of the southern Plains. **I.D. KEY:** Tri-notches.

BAJADA - Late Archaic to Developmental Phase, 6000 - 5000 B.P.

(Also see Conejo, Duncan, Escobas, Hanna, Jay and Rio Grande)

LOCATION: Northern Arizona to New Mexico, Sou. Colorado & Utah. **DESCRIPTION:** A medium sized birfurcated, stemmed point with weak shoulders and serrated blade edges. Related to the earlier *Escobas* point. **I.D. KEY:** Long concave stem.

S
W

BAJADA (continued)

G6, $12-$20
S. W. CO

G6, $15-$30
Yavapai Co., AZ

G6, $12-$20
S. W. CO

G6, $15-$30
NM

G6, $15-$30
S. W. CO

Alibates dolomite

Ground stem

Restored tip

G8, $30-$50
S. W. CO

Obsidian

G8, $200-$350
E. CO

G3, $12-$20
Otero Co., NM

G5, $20-$35
S. W. CO

G4, $12-$20
Alamosa, CO

G8, $45-$85
S. W. CO

G8, $40-$70
S. W. CO

Ground stem

G8, $55-$100
S. W. CO

G10, $80-$150
Montezuma Co., CO

Ground stem

G9, $85-$165
S. W. CO

Note side notches

G8, $80-$175
Navajo Co., AZ

Basalt

G10+, $350-$600
Alamosa Co., CO

BAKER - Early Archaic, 7500 - 6000 B. P.

(Also see Bajada, Darl, Datil, San Jose, Uvalde and Zephyr)

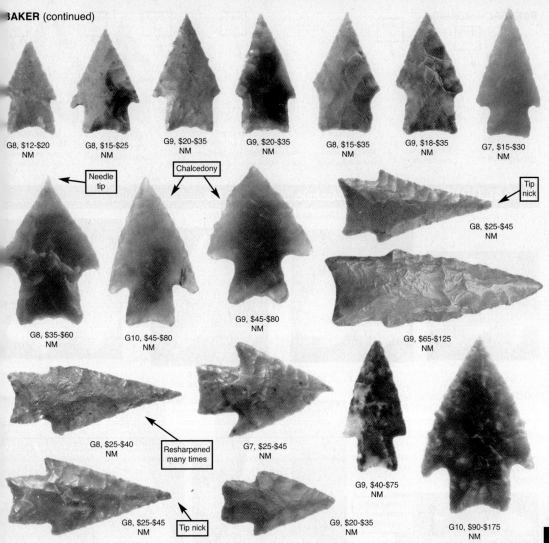

G8, $12-$20 NM

G8, $15-$25 NM

G9, $20-$35 NM

G9, $20-$35 NM

G8, $15-$35 NM

G9, $18-$35 NM

G7, $15-$30 NM

Needle tip

Chalcedony

Tip nick

G8, $25-$45 NM

G8, $35-$60 NM

G10, $45-$80 NM

G9, $45-$80 NM

G9, $65-$125 NM

G8, $25-$40 NM

Resharpened many times

G7, $25-$45 NM

G9, $40-$75 NM

G8, $25-$45 NM

Tip nick

G9, $20-$35 NM

G10, $90-$175 NM

S
W

LOCATION: Western Texas into New Mexico. **DESCRIPTION:** A small to medium size, thin, point with a sharp tip and a bifurcated to concave base. Barbs are sharp and the stem expands. The stem length varies from short to long. Similar to the *Bandy* point found in southern Texas. **I.D. KEY:** Base extended and bifurcated or concave.

BARREAL - Early Archaic, 9000 - 7200 B.P.

(Also see Duncan, Hanna, San Jose, Squaw Mountain)

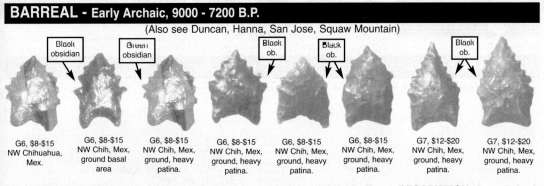

Black obsidian

Green obsidian

Black ob.

Black ob.

Black ob.

G6, $8-$15 NW Chihuahua, Mex.

G6, $8-$15 NW Chih, Mex, ground basal area

G6, $8-$15 NW Chih, Mex, ground, heavy patina.

G6, $8-$15 NW Chih, Mex, ground, heavy patina.

G6, $8-$15 NW Chih, Mex, ground, heavy patina.

G6, $8-$15 NW Chih, Mex, ground, heavy patina.

G7, $12-$20 NW Chih, Mex, ground, heavy patina.

G7, $12-$20 NW Chih, Mex, ground, heavy patina.

LOCATION: N.W. Chihuahua, Mexico into southern New Mexico and far west Texas. **DESCRIPTION:** A small sized, thin, serrated dart point with projecting ears and a concave base. The stem sides are straight to concave. Basal area is usually ground. Shoulders are weak to non-existent. **I.D. KEY:** Basal form and serrations.

BARREAL (continued)

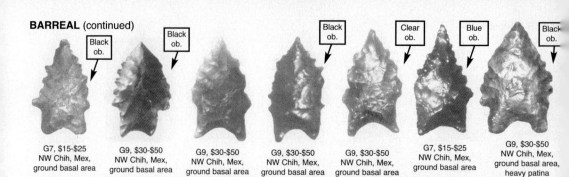

Black ob.   Black ob.   Black ob.   Clear ob.   Blue ob.   Black ob.

G7, $15-$25
NW Chih, Mex,
ground basal area

G9, $30-$50
NW Chih, Mex,
ground basal area

G9, $30-$50
NW Chih, Mex,
ground basal area

G9, $30-$50
NW Chih, Mex,
ground basal area

G9, $30-$50
NW Chih, Mex,
ground basal area

G7, $15-$25
NW Chih, Mex,
ground basal area

G9, $30-$50
NW Chih, Mex,
ground basal area,
heavy patina

BASAL DOUBLE TANG - Late Archaic, 3500 - 2300 B.P.

(Also see Bell and Parowan)

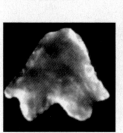

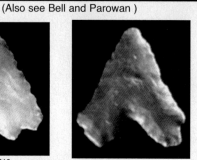

G3, $4-$8
San Luis Potosi, MX

G3, $5-$10
San Luis Potosi, MX

G3, $5-$10
San Luis Potosi, MX

G4, $15-$30
San Luis Potosi, MX

LOCATION: Sou. Arizona, New Mexico and northern Mexico. **DESCRIPTION:** A medium sized dart/knife point which is baseally notched, and then with the stem bifurcated. Worn out examples appear as a lanceolate blade with a notched basal edge. **I.D. KEY:** Triple basal notches.

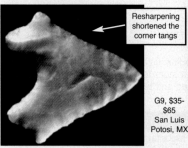

Resharpening shortened the corner tangs

G9, $35-$65
San Luis Potosi, MX

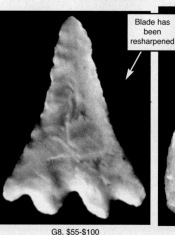

Blade has been resharpened

G8, $55-$100
San Luis Potosi, MX

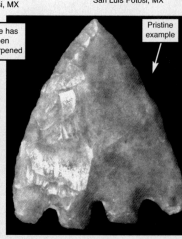

Pristine example

G10, $150-$250
Pinal Co., AZ

BASKETMAKER - Developmental, 1500 - 1300 B.P.

(Also see Amargosa, Black Mesa, Carlsbad, Cienega, Dolores, Elko Corner Notched, Figueroa, Mount Albion)

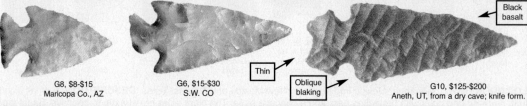

Black basalt

Thin

Oblique blaking

G8, $8-$15
Maricopa Co., AZ

G6, $15-$30
S.W. CO

G10, $125-$200
Aneth, UT, from a dry cave; knife form.

LOCATION: Southern Utah into northern Arizona & N.W. New Mexico. **DESCRIPTION:** A small to medium size, thin, dart/knife point that is side to corner notched. **I.D. KEY:** Corner notching.

BAT CAVE - Early Archaic, 9000 - 8000 B.P.

(Also see Humboldt)

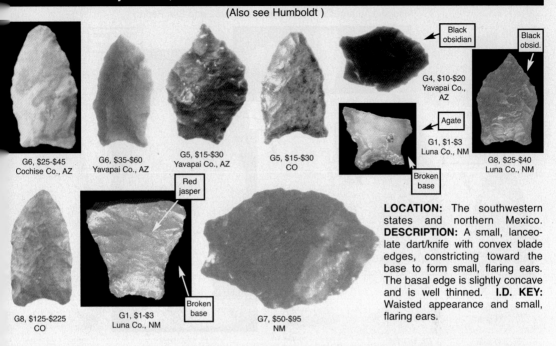

G6, $25-$45
Cochise Co., AZ

G6, $35-$60
Yavapai Co., AZ

G5, $15-$30
Yavapai Co., AZ

G5, $15-$30
CO

Black obsidian

G4, $10-$20
Yavapai Co., AZ

Black obsid.

Agate

G1, $1-$3
Luna Co., NM

Broken base

G8, $25-$40
Luna Co., NM

Red jasper

Broken base

G8, $125-$225
CO

G1, $1-$3
Luna Co., NM

G7, $50-$95
NM

LOCATION: The southwestern states and northern Mexico. **DESCRIPTION:** A small, lanceolate dart/knife with convex blade edges, constricting toward the base to form small, flaring ears. The basal edge is slightly concave and is well thinned. **I.D. KEY:** Waisted appearance and small, flaring ears.

BELEN - Paleo, 10,500 - 8000 B.P.

(Also see Folsom, Midland, Milnesand)

Base nick

G4, $45-$80
W. TX

Tip wear

G3, $30-$50
W. TX

LOCATION: E. New Mexico into W. Texas. **DESCRIPTION:** A small, thin lanceloate point with ground stem sides and a straight to concave base. Similar to *Midland* points but differ in that *Belen* points have one basal ear that is more prominent. **I.D. KEY:** Thinness, prominent single basal ear.

S
W

BELL - Middle Archaic, 7000 - 5000 B.P.

(Also see Basal Double Tang, Moyote and Parowan)

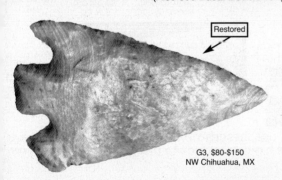

Restored

G3, $80-$150
NW Chihuahua, MX

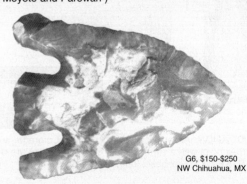

G6, $150-$250
NW Chihuahua, MX

LOCATION: Cent. Texas into N. Mexico. **DESCRIPTION:** A small to medium size point with medium-deep parallel basal notches, but not as deep as in Andice. Larger examples usually would fall under Andice. Found primarily in Texas. Barbs turn inward at the base. **I.D. KEY:** Shorter barbs and notching.

BLACK MESA NARROW NECK - Trans.-Developmental Phase, 2000 - 1200 B.P.

(Also see Amargosa, Basketmaker, Figueroa and San Pedro)

Broken back

Multi-colored chalcedony

Gray basalt

G1, $1-$2
Pima Co., AZ

Basalt

G6, $20-$35
Chinle, AZ

Gray chert

Mottled blue chert

Red/brown jasper

G8, $30-$55
Big Bend, TX

G8, $50-$90
NM

G7, $30-$55
Pima Co., AZ

G10, $350-$650
S.E. CA

G10+, $250-$450
Pima Co., AZ

LOCATION: Sou. California into Arizona and New Mexico. **DESCRIPTION:** A medium to large deeply corner notched dart point with a narrow neck and an expanding stem. Bases are straight to convex. **I.D. KEY:** Very narrow neck.

BONITO NOTCHED - Developmental, 1050 - 850 B.P.

(Also see Chaco Corner Notched, Convento, Desert, Dry Prong, Rose Springs & Temporal)

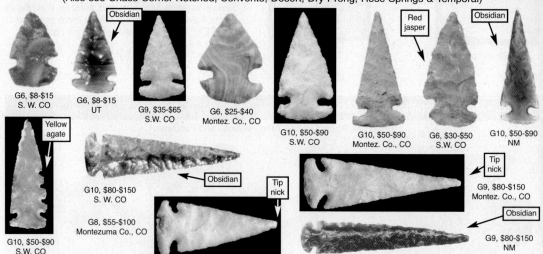

Obsidian

Red jasper

Obsidian

G6, $8-$15
S. W. CO

G6, $8-$15
UT

G9, $35-$65
S.W. CO

G6, $25-$40
Montez. Co., CO

G10, $50-$90
S.W. CO

G10, $50-$90
Montez. Co., CO

G6, $30-$50
S.W. CO

G10, $50-$90
NM

Yellow agate

Obsidian

Tip nick

Tip nick

G10, $80-$150
S. W. CO

G9, $80-$150
Montez. Co., CO

G8, $55-$100
Montezuma Co., CO

Obsidian

G10, $50-$90
S.W. CO

G9, $80-$150
NM

LOCATION: Arizona, New Mexico, S.W. Colorado, sou. Utah. **DESCRIPTION:** A small size, narrow, side notched arrow point with a convex base. Some examples are double or triple notched on one side. Part of the Chaco cluster. **I.D. KEY:** Convex base, long, narrow blade.

BUCK TAYLOR NOTCHED - Classic to Historic Phase, 600 - 200 B.P.

(Also see Awatovi Side Notched, Desert, Dell Carmen, Walnut Canyon, Sobaipuri, White Mtn.)

BUCK TAYLOR NOTCHED (continued)

Clear obsidian

Black obsidian

Clear obsidian

Obsidian

G7, $20-$35
Pima Co.,
AZ.

G6, $8-$15
Maricopa Co.,
AZ

G5, $8-$15
Mohave Co.,
AZ

G4, $6-$12
Mohave Co.,
AZ

G6, $12-$20
Mohave Co., AZ

G6, $18-$30
NW Chihuahua,
Mex.

G5, $8-$15
Yavapai Co., AZ

G6, $15-$30
Mohave Co., AZ

G7, $8-$15
Maricopa Co.,
AZ

LOCATION: Arizona. **DESCRIPTION:** A small, triangular, tri-notched arrow point including a deep basal notch. Part of the *Pueblo Side Notched* cluster. Formerly known as *Red Horn*. **I.D. KEY:** Very narrow neck.

BULL CREEK - Desert Traditions-Developmental Phase, 950 - 700 B.P.

(Also see Aguaje, Cottonwood, Desert, Pueblo Side Notched & Snaketown Triangular)

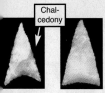

Chalcedony

G6, $5-$10
Pima Co., AZ

G7, $30-$55
Pima Co., AZ

G7, $30-$55
AZ

G5, $25-$45
AZ

G7, $30-$55
AZ

G8, $35-$65
AZ

G8, $35-$65
AZ

G10, $50-$90
AZ

G8, $35-$65
Yavapai Co., AZ

G10, $65-$125
AZ

G10, $65-$125
AZ

Jasper

G7, $35-$60
Mohave Co., AZ

G8, $35-$65
AZ

G10, $150-$250
AZ

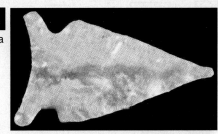

Red agate

G9, $80-$150
Pima Co., AZ

G10, $175-$300
San Juan Co., UT

LOCATION: Northern Arizona, southern Utah and northeastern Nevada. **DESCRIPTION:** A long, thin triangular arrow point with a deeply concave basal edge. They are sometimes serrated. Some examples have been shortened by resharpening. **I.D. KEY:** Isosceles triangle shape and concave base.

CARACARA - Mississippian to Historic, 600 - 400 B.P.

(Also see Desert, Frio, Hohokam, Martis, Sacaton, Salado, Ventana Side Notched)

LOCATION: Texas into N.W. Chihuaha, MX. **DESCRIPTION:** A small size, thin, side notched arrow point with a straight, concave or convex base. Shoulders can be tapered to horizontal to barbed. Side notches are shallow to deep.

G10, $80-$150
NM

S W

CARLSBAD - Late Archaic-Transitional, 3000 - 1700 B.P.

(Also see Amargosa, Basketmaker, Black Mesa, Cienega, Dolores and Guadalupe)

Red basalt

Broken tip

Basalt

Basalt

Worn tip

G1, $2-$5
Pima Co., AZ

G6, $20-$35
Alamosa, CO

G3, $15-$25
Pima Co., AZ

825

LOCATION: Sou. New Mexico into Mexico and Arizona. **DESCRIPTION:** Part of the *Cienega* cluster. A small size deep basal to corner notched point and a convex base. Most examples have been resharpened to exhaustion reducing the shoulders significantly. Stem sides are concave and expanding.

CATAN - Late Archaic to Mississippian, 4000 - 300 B. P.

(Also see Abasolo, Matamoros & Padre)

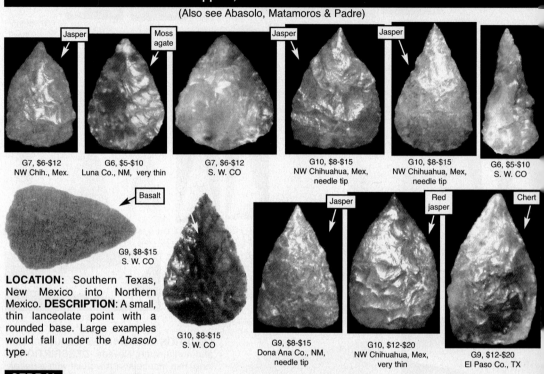

G7, $6-$12
NW Chih., Mex.

G6, $5-$10
Luna Co., NM, very thin

G7, $6-$12
S. W. CO

G10, $8-$15
NW Chihuahua, Mex,
needle tip

G10, $8-$15
NW Chihuahua, Mex,
needle tip

G6, $5-$10
S. W. CO

G9, $8-$15
S. W. CO

LOCATION: Southern Texas, New Mexico into Northern Mexico. **DESCRIPTION:** A small, thin lanceolate point with a rounded base. Large examples would fall under the *Abasolo* type.

G10, $8-$15
S. W. CO

G9, $8-$15
Dona Ana Co., NM,
needle tip

G10, $12-$20
NW Chihuahua, Mex,
very thin

G9, $12-$20
El Paso Co., TX

CEDRAL (see Acatita)

CHACO CORNER NOTCHED - Developmental, 1250 - 1050 B.P.

(Also see Bonito Notched, Convento, Dolores and Rose Springs)

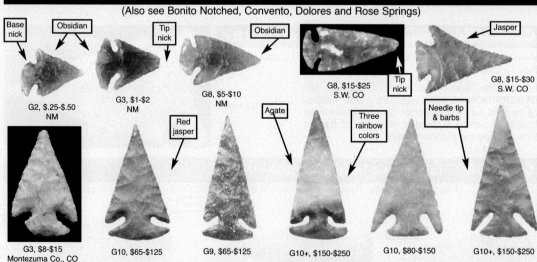

G2, $.25-$.50
NM

G3, $1-$2
NM

G8, $5-$10
NM

G8, $15-$25
S.W. CO

G8, $15-$30
S.W. CO

G3, $8-$15
Montezuma Co., CO

G10, $65-$125

G9, $65-$125

G10+, $150-$250

G10, $80-$150

G10+, $150-$250

All above five points to right from a cache, Montezuma Co., CO

LOCATION: Arizona, New Mexico, S.W. Colorado, sou. Utah. **DESCRIPTION:** A small to medium size, thin, corner notched arrow point with a wide convex base. Notches turn upward toward the tip. **I.D. KEY:** Broad convex base, deep, upward sloping notches.

Agate

G10+, $150-$250
Montezuma Co., CO, cache point

Knife/dart
form

G10, $200-$350
S.W. CO

CHARCOS - Late Archaic-Trans., 3000 - 2000 B.P.

Jasper

G6, $12-$20
Alamosa Co., CO

G5, $12-$20
S.W. CO

LOCATION: N. Mexico into New Mexico, Texas and Colorado. **DESCRIPTION:** A small size, thin, single barbed point with a notch near the opposite shoulder. Stem is rectangular or expanding. **I.D. KEY:** Asymmetrical form. Some are double notched.

CHIRICAHUA - Middle Archaic, 5000 - 4000 B.P.

(Also see Duncan, Frio-Transitional, Hanna, San Jose, Squaw Mountain and Ventana Side Notched)

Basalt

G3, $2-$4
Alamosa Co., CO

G4, $2-$5
Cochise Co., AZ

G6, $8-$15
Cochise Co., AZ

G5, $6-$12
Cochise Co., AZ

G6, $10-$20
Cochise Co., AZ

Basalt

G5, $12-$20
S.W. CO

G4, $5-$10
Cochise Co., AZ

Basalt

G5, $25-$45
Cochise Co., AZ

Double tip

G8, $25-$45
AZ

G6, $8-$15
Mohave Co., AZ

Dinged

G9, $35-$60
Cochise Co., AZ

LOCATION: New Mexico, Arizona, southern California and northern Mexico. **DESCRIPTION:** A small to medium sized dart/knife point with side notches and a concave base, producing an eared appearance. **I.D. KEY:** Generally ears are "rounded" in appearance.

S W

CIENEGA - Late Archaic-Transitional, 2800 - 1800 B.P.

(Also see Amargosa, Basketmaker, Black Mesa, Carlsbad, Dolores, Guadalupe and San Pedro)

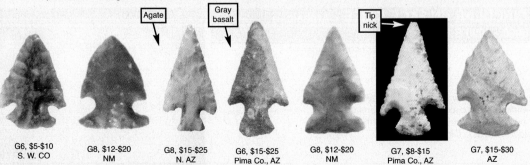

Agate

Gray basalt

Tip nick

G6, $5-$10
S. W. CO

G8, $12-$20
NM

G8, $15-$25
N. AZ

G6, $15-$25
Pima Co., AZ

G8, $12-$20
NM

G7, $8-$15
Pima Co., AZ

G7, $15-$30
AZ

CIENEGA (continued)

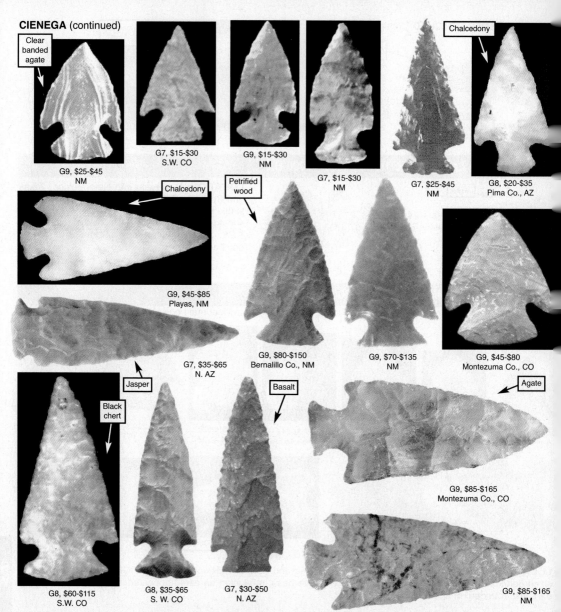

Clear banded agate

G9, $25-$45
NM

G7, $15-$30
S.W. CO

G9, $15-$30
NM

G7, $15-$30
NM

G7, $25-$45
NM

Chalcedony

G8, $20-$35
Pima Co., AZ

Chalcedony

G9, $45-$85
Playas, NM

Petrified wood

G9, $80-$150
Bernalillo Co., NM

G9, $70-$135
NM

G9, $45-$80
Montezuma Co., CO

Jasper

G7, $35-$65
N. AZ

Black chert

G8, $60-$115
S.W. CO

G8, $35-$65
S. W. CO

Basalt

G7, $30-$50
N. AZ

Agate

G9, $85-$165
Montezuma Co., CO

G9, $85-$165
NM

LOCATION: Arizona into New Mexico. **DESCRIPTION:** A small to medium sized dart/knife point with corner notches, shoulder barbs and a convex base, producing an expanded stem. **I.D. KEY:** Narrow stems and broad corner notches. Illustrated points are called *Tularosa Corner Notched* which are part of the Cienega cluster.

CIRCULAR UNIFACE KNIFE - Archaic, 6000 - 4000 B.P.

(Also see Disc, Lancet, Scraper)

LOCATION: New Mexico. **DESCRIPTION:** A medium sized circular knife that is uniface on one side and steeply flaked on the other side. **I.D. KEY:** Circular uniface.

G10, $12-$20
NM, knife.

(Also see Desert, Gatlin Side Notched, Salado)

G7, $35-$60
AZ

Tip nick

G9, $55-$100
AZ

LOCATION: Arizona **DESCRIPTION:** A small size, very thin, triangular, side notched *Hohokam* arrow point with a straight to slightly convex base which is the widest part of the point. Blade edges are concave, tips are long and slender. **I.D. KEY:** Long, needle tips

---

CLOVIS - Early Paleo, 11,500 - 10,600 B.P.

(Also see Allen, Angostura, Folsom, Golondrina, Goshen, Madden Lake, Meserve and Sandia)

Brown/beige banded chert

Gray chert

Not fluted

G4, $175-$300
NM

Red jasper

Tip wear

G8, $200-$350
Eddy Co., NM,
ground basal area.

G3, $125-$200
Hudspeth Co., TX,
ground basal.

G4, $125-$200
Garfield Co., UT

Tip wear

Ear wear

Tan/gray chert

Fluting channel

Fluting channel

Tip wear

Fluting channel

Side restoration

G6, $500-$900
NM

G5, $500-$900
NW Chih, Mex,
flint, ground basal area.
Restored small side piece.

G8, $1200-$2000
Lehner site, AZ

Ground basal area

G9, $1200-$2000
Clovis, NM

S W

829

CLOVIS (continued)

G8, $1800-$3400,
Curry Co., NM,
Blanco Creek.
Colorful chert.

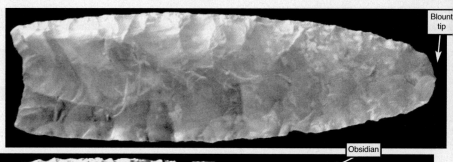

Blount tip

Obsidian

Fluting channel

Side wear

G4, $1500-$2500
AZ

LOCATION: All of North America. Named after Clovis, New Mexico near where these fluted projectile points were found. **DESCRIPTION:** A medium to large size, auriculate, fluted, lanceolate point with a concave base that is ground. Most examples are fluted on both sides about 1/3 the way up from the base. *Clovis* is the earliest known point type in the hemisphere. The first *Clovis* find associated with Mastodons was in 1979 at Mastodon State Park, Jefferson Co., MO. in the Kimmswick bone bed dated to 11,500 B.P. The origin of Clovis is a mystery as there is no pre-*Clovis* evidence here (crude forms that pre-date Clovis). **I.D. KEY:** Paleo flaking, basal ears, baton or billet fluting instead of indirect style.

CODY KNIFE - Early to Middle Archaic, 10,000 - 8000 B. P.

(Also see Base-Tang Knife, Corner Tang, Eden, Mid-Back Tang and Scottsbluff)

G5, $150-$250
Luna Co., NM, snapped base,
not ground

LOCATION: Northern Plains states. **DESCRIPTION:** A medium to large size asymmetrical blade with one or two shoulders and a medium to short stem. Stem edges are ground on early examples. Made by the Cody complex people who made *Scottsbluff* points. Flaking is similar to the *Scottsbluff* type and some examples were made from *Scottsbluff* points. **I.D. KEY:** Paleo flaking, asymmetrical form.

COHONINA STEMMED - Developmental Phase, 1300 - 900 B.P.

(Also see Rose Springs)

G4, $2-$4
Coconino Co., AZ

G5, $4-$8
Coconino Co., AZ

G6, $8-$15
Coconino Co., AZ

G7, $8-$15
Coconino Co., AZ

LOCATION: Northern Arizona. **DESCRIPTION:** A small size, narrow, stemmed to corner notched point with tapered shoulders and an expanding stem.

CONEJO - Late Archaic, 3500 - 2300 B.P.

(Also see Bell, Duncan)

CONEJO (continued)

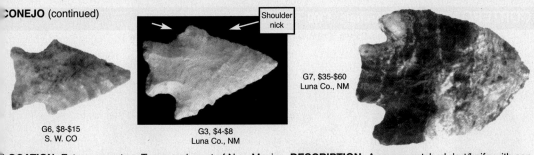

G6, $8-$15
S. W. CO

Shoulder nick

G3, $4-$8
Luna Co., NM

G7, $35-$60
Luna Co., NM

LOCATION: Extreme western Texas and most of New Mexico. **DESCRIPTION:** A corner notched dart/knife with convex blade edges, short barbs and a short, straight stem. The basal edge may be straight or concave.

CONVENTO - Developmental Phase, 950 - 850 B. P.

(Also see Chaco Corner Notched, Rose Springs)

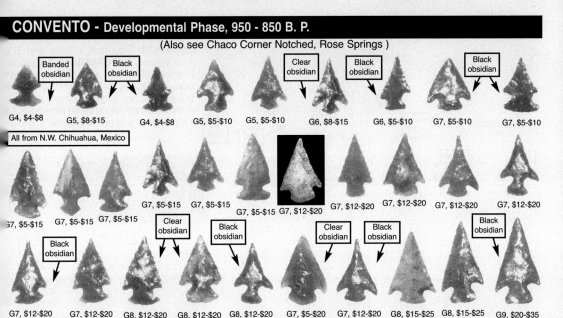

Banded obsidian

Black obsidian

Clear obsidian

Black obsidian

Black obsidian

G4, $4-$8   G5, $8-$15   G4, $4-$8   G5, $5-$10   G5, $5-$10   G6, $8-$15   G6, $5-$10   G7, $5-$10   G7, $5-$10

All from N.W. Chihuahua, Mexico

G7, $5-$15   G7, $5-$15   G7, $5-$15   G7, $5-$15   G7, $12-$20   G7, $12-$20   G7, $12-$20   G7, $12-$20   G7, $12-$20

Black obsidian

Clear obsidian

Black obsidian

Clear obsidian

Black obsidian

Black obsidian

G7, $12-$20   G7, $12-$20   G8, $12-$20   G8, $12-$20   G8, $12-$20   G7, $5-$20   G7, $12-$20   G8, $15-$25   G8, $15-$25   G9, $20-$35

LOCATION: N.W. Chihuahua, MX into southern New Mexico and far west Texas. **DESCRIPTION:** A small, thin, barbed, corner notched arrow point with an expanding stem and a convex base. **I.D. KEY:** Barbs and base form.

CORNER TANG - Late Archaic to Woodland, 4000 - 2000 B.P.

S W

LOCATION: Texas, Oklahoma, New Mexico. **DESCRIPTION:** This knife is notched producing a tang at a corner for hafting to a handle. Tang knives are very rare and have been reproduced in recent years. **I.D. KEY:** Angle of hafting.

G6, $300-$500
San Juan Co., NM

831

CORTERO - Mid to Late Archaic, 4300 - 2300 B. P.

(Also see Clovis, Cottonwood, Golondrina, Goshen, Plainview)

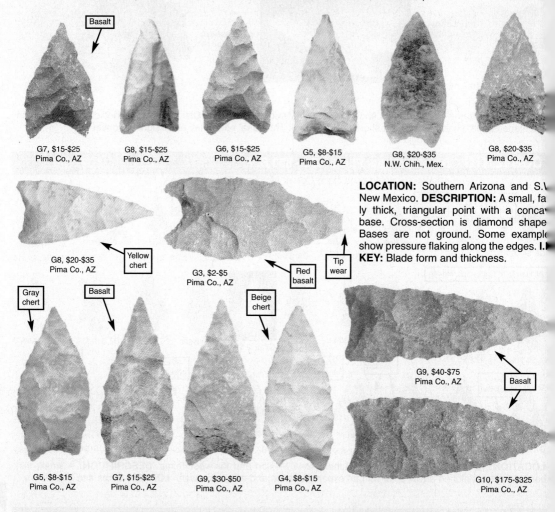

Basalt

G7, $15-$25
Pima Co., AZ

G8, $15-$25
Pima Co., AZ

G6, $15-$25
Pima Co., AZ

G5, $8-$15
Pima Co., AZ

G8, $20-$35
N.W. Chih., Mex.

G8, $20-$35
Pima Co., AZ

G8, $20-$35
Pima Co., AZ

Yellow chert

G3, $2-$5
Pima Co., AZ

Red basalt

Tip wear

LOCATION: Southern Arizona and S.\
New Mexico. **DESCRIPTION:** A small, fa\
ly thick, triangular point with a conca\
base. Cross-section is diamond shape\
Bases are not ground. Some example\
show pressure flaking along the edges. I.\
KEY: Blade form and thickness.

Gray chert

Basalt

Beige chert

G9, $40-$75
Pima Co., AZ

Basalt

G5, $8-$15
Pima Co., AZ

G7, $15-$25
Pima Co., AZ

G9, $30-$50
Pima Co., AZ

G4, $8-$15
Pima Co., AZ

G10, $175-$325
Pima Co., AZ

COTTONWOOD LEAF - Desert Traditions-Classic/Historic Phases, 700 - 200 B.P.

(Also see Catan, Datil, Padre and Pelona)

G7, $15-30
Apache Co., AZ

G2, $.50-$1
Mohave Co., AZ

G8, $30-$50
Pima Co., AZ

G3, $2-$4
Pima Co., AZ

G6, $5-$10
Pima Co., AZ

G7, $20-$40
Yavapai Co., AZ

LOCATION: Arizona and westward into California and Nevada. **DESCRIPTION:** A small, thin, leaf shaped arrow point that resembles a long tear-drop. The base is rounded. **I.D. KEY:** Size and blade form.

COTTONWOOD TRIANGLE - Desert Traditions-Classic and Historic Phases, 700 - 200 B.P.

(Also see Aguaje, Bull Creek, Cottonwood Leaf, Desert, Pueblo Side Notched, Sobaipuri)

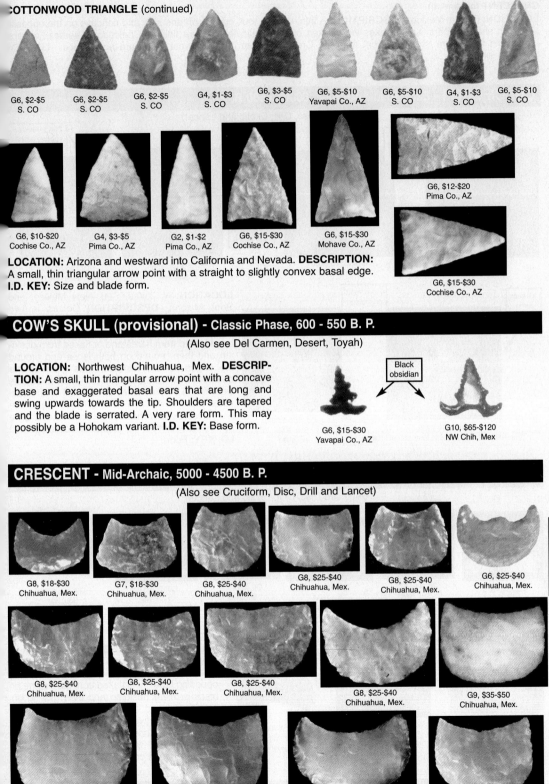

G6, $2-$5
S. CO

G6, $2-$5
S. CO

G6, $2-$5
S. CO

G4, $1-$3
S. CO

G6, $3-$5
S. CO

G6, $5-$10
Yavapai Co., AZ

G6, $5-$10
S. CO

G4, $1-$3
S. CO

G6, $5-$10
S. CO

G6, $10-$20
Cochise Co., AZ

G4, $3-$5
Pima Co., AZ

G2, $1-$2
Pima Co., AZ

G6, $15-$30
Cochise Co., AZ

G6, $15-$30
Mohave Co., AZ

G6, $12-$20
Pima Co., AZ

G6, $15-$30
Cochise Co., AZ

LOCATION: Arizona and westward into California and Nevada. **DESCRIPTION:** A small, thin triangular arrow point with a straight to slightly convex basal edge. **I.D. KEY:** Size and blade form.

COW'S SKULL (provisional) - Classic Phase, 600 - 550 B. P.

(Also see Del Carmen, Desert, Toyah)

LOCATION: Northwest Chihuahua, Mex. **DESCRIPTION:** A small, thin triangular arrow point with a concave base and exaggerated basal ears that are long and swing upwards towards the tip. Shoulders are tapered and the blade is serrated. A very rare form. This may possibly be a Hohokam variant. **I.D. KEY:** Base form.

Black obsidian

G6, $15-$30
Yavapai Co., AZ

G10, $65-$120
NW Chih, Mex

CRESCENT - Mid-Archaic, 5000 - 4500 B. P.

(Also see Cruciform, Disc, Drill and Lancet)

S W

G8, $18-$30
Chihuahua, Mex.

G7, $18-$30
Chihuahua, Mex.

G8, $25-$40
Chihuahua, Mex.

G8, $25-$40
Chihuahua, Mex.

G8, $25-$40
Chihuahua, Mex.

G6, $25-$40
Chihuahua, Mex.

G8, $25-$40
Chihuahua, Mex.

G8, $25-$40
Chihuahua, Mex.

G8, $25-$40
Chihuahua, Mex.

G8, $25-$40
Chihuahua, Mex.

G9, $35-$50
Chihuahua, Mex.

G10, $40-$75
Chihuahua, MX

Chalcedony

G10, $35-$65
Chihuahua, MX

G10, $30-$50
Chihuahua, Mex.

G8, $25-$40
N. Chihuahua, MX.,

CRESCENT (continued)

LOCATION: Central Mexico. **DESCRIPTION:** A thin, uniface tool, convex on one side and concave on the opposite side with sharp corners. Long strikes were taken off with delicate pressure flaking. Chalcedony, agates, jaspers, cherts and flints were used. Different than the Crescents from the Northwest which are not uniface. **I.D. KEY** Crescent form.

CRUCIFORM I - Early to Mid-Archaic, 6000 - 4500 B. P.

(Also see Disc, Drill, Exotic and Lancet)

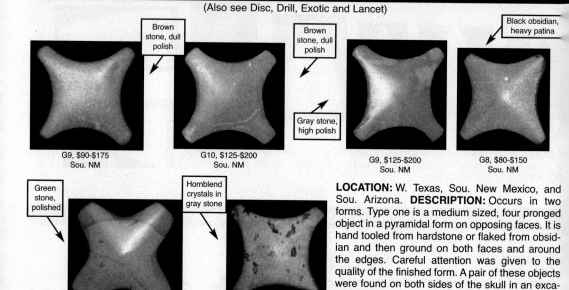

Brown stone, dull polish

Brown stone, dull polish

Gray stone, high polish

Black obsidian, heavy patina

G9, $90-$175
Sou. NM

G10, $125-$200
Sou. NM

G9, $125-$200
Sou. NM

G8, $80-$150
Sou. NM

Green stone, polished

Hornblend crystals in gray stone

G10, $125-$200
Sou. NM, flattened pyramid form on each face

G9, $90-$175
Sou. NM, polished

LOCATION: W. Texas, Sou. New Mexico, and Sou. Arizona. **DESCRIPTION:** Occurs in two forms. Type one is a medium sized, four pronged object in a pyramidal form on opposing faces. It is hand tooled from hardstone or flaked from obsidian and then ground on both faces and around the edges. Careful attention was given to the quality of the finished form. A pair of these objects were found on both sides of the skull in an excavated grave in Arizona. It is believed that these were used as ear ornaments. These objects were named due to their resemblance to cruciforms. **I.D. KEY:** Form.

CRUCIFORM II - Late to Transitional, 3000 - 2000 B. P.

(Also see Disc, Drill, Exotic and Lancet)

G3, $40-$75
Lordsberg, NM

G6, $40-$75
Sou. NM, clear obsidian, ground, heavy patina

G6, $50-$90
Sou. NM, clear obsidian, ground, heavy patina

G6, $50-$90
Sou. NM, black obsidian, ground, heavy patina

G8, $55-$100
Sou. NM, clear obsidian, ground, heavy patina

G9, $55-$100
Sou. NM, black obsidian, flaked and not yet ground.

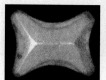 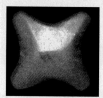

G9 $55-$100
Sou. NM, black obsidian, ground, heavy patina

G10, $55-$100
Sou. NM, clear obsidian, ground, heavy patina

G10, $55-$100
Sonora, MX, basalt, ground.

LOCATION: W. Texas, Sou. New Mexico, and Sou. Arizona. **DESCRIPTION:** Occurs in two forms. Type two is a small sized, four pronged object in a slanted roof form on opposing faces. It is flaked from hard stone or black or clear obsidian and then ground on both faces and around the edges. Careful attention was given to the quality of the finished form. These objects' actual use is unknown and were named due to their resemblance to cruciforms. **I.D. KEY:** Form.

DAGGER- Mid-Archaic, 4000 - 2500 B. P.

(Also see Disc, Drill, Early Stemmed and Lancet)

AGGER (continued)

LOCATION: Mexico. **DESCRIPTION:** A large size lanceolate knife with a recurved blade, expanding, tapered tangs and a long contracting stem. Probably hafted to a handle in use. **I.D. KEY:** Size and form.

Shown half size

G9, $300-$575
MX

DARL STEMMED - Early Archaic, 8000 - 5000 B. P.

(Also see Ahumada, Datil, San Pedro and Ventana Amargosa)

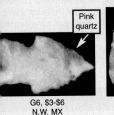

Pink quartz

G6, $3-$6
N.W. MX

G6, $5-$10
Otero Co., NM

G6, $5-$10
Otero Co., NM

G7, $12-$20
Otero Co., NM

LOCATION: Central Texas into New Mexico and Northern Mexico. **DESCRIPTION:** A medium to large size point with horizontally barbed shoulders and an expanding to square stem. The blades can be steeply beveled on one side of each face. Flaking is early parallel and is of much higher quality than *Darl*. **I.D. KEY:** Early flaking, straight base.

DATIL - Early Archaic, 7000 - 6000 B. P.

(Also see Cottonwood Leaf, Darl, Embudo, Lerma, Pelona, San Pedro and Truxton)

basalt

Basalt

G4, $2-$5
Cochise Co., AZ

G5, $12-$20
S. W. CO

G6, $12-$20
Yavapai Co., AZ

G5, $12-$20
Cochise Co., AZ

G7, $15-$30
Chihuahua, Mex.

G6, $15-$25
Pima Co., AZ

G7, $25-$40
Yavapai Co., AZ

Basalt

Orange chert

Banded purple chert

Basalt

G7, $30-$50
Yavapai Co., AZ

G7, $30-$50
Pima Co., AZ

G9, $80-$150
San Juan Co., NM

G5, $12-$20
Pima Co., AZ
trans. point.

G5, $12-$20
S. W. CO

G6, $15-$30
Pima Co., AZ

G4, $5-$10
Yavapai Co., AZ

S W

835

DATIL (continued)

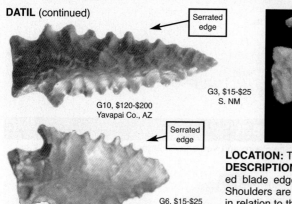

Serrated edge

G10, $120-$200
Yavapai Co., AZ

G3, $15-$25
S. NM

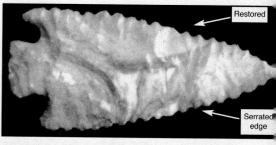

Restored

Serrated edge

Serrated edge

G6, $15-$25
S. W. CO

LOCATION: The southern portion of the southwestern states **DESCRIPTION:** A small dart/knife with long, narrow, heavily serrated blade edges. The stem is short and rectangular to rounded Shoulders are straight to obtuse and are very small to non-existent in relation to the overall size of the point.

DEADMAN'S - Desert Traditions-Developmental Phase, 1600 - 1300 B. P.

(Also see Hodges Contracting Stem, Gila Butte, Perdiz and Rose Springs)

Tang nick

G5, $5-$10
Luna Co., NM

G7, $15-$30
Cochise Co., AZ

Bulbous base

G6, $10-$20
Cochise Co., AZ

Bulbous base

G7, $15-$30
Cochise Co., AZ

G8, $25-$40
Cochise Co., AZ

LOCATION: Southeastern Arizona, southern New Mexico and western Texas. **DESCRIPTION:** A small arrow point with very deep basal notches creating a long, straight to slightly bulbous stem with a rounded basal edge. The blade is triangular. **I.D. KEY:** Bulbous stem and barbs.

DEL CARMEN - Classic Phase, 550 B. P.

(Also see Awatovi Side Notched, Buck Taylor Notched, Desert, Pueblo Side, Soto, Toyah)

All others from N.W. Chihuahua, MX

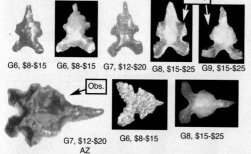

Chalcedony

Chalcedony

Chert

Clear obsidian

Chalcedony

G6, $8-$15   G6, $8-$15   G7, $12-$20   G8, $15-$25   G9, $15-$25   G9, $18-$30   G8, $15-$25   G7, $12-$20   G6, $12-$20   G9, $20-$35

Obs.

G7, $12-$20
AZ

G6, $8-$15

G8, $15-$25

LOCATION: N.W. Chihuahua, MX. into sou. New Mexico. **DESCRIPTION:** A small, thin, arrow point with an elongated tip, side notches, expanding ears and a concave base. Some examples are double notched. **I.D. KEY:** Barbs always flare out beyond the base.

DESERT DELTA - Desert Traditions-Classic to Historic, 700 - 200 B. P.

(Also see Pueblo Side Notched, Sacaton, Salado, Temporal, Walnut Canyon)

Single notch

Jasper

Moss agate

Clear obsidian

G3, $2-$5
S.W. CO

G5, $3-$6
S. W. COl

G5, $2-$5
AZ

G5, $5-$10
Apache Co., AZ

G6, $5-$10
S. W. COl

G5, $5-$10
NM

G6, $8-$15
S.W. CO

G6, $8-$15
S.W. CO

G7, $25-$40
AZ

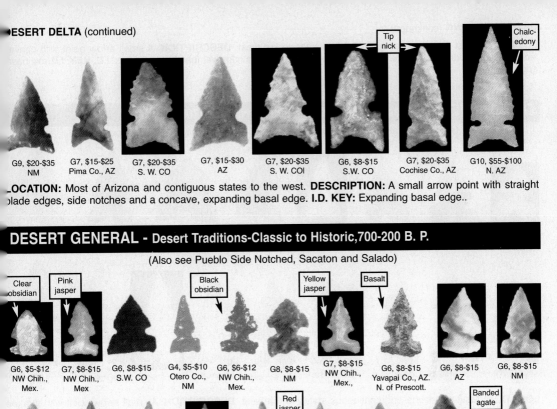

| G9, $20-$35 NM | G7, $15-$25 Pima Co., AZ | G7, $20-$35 S. W. CO | G7, $15-$30 AZ | G7, $20-$35 S.W. CO | G6, $8-$15 S.W. CO | G7, $20-$35 Cochise Co., AZ | G10, $55-$100 N. AZ |

Tip nick / Chalcedony

LOCATION: Most of Arizona and contiguous states to the west. **DESCRIPTION:** A small arrow point with straight blade edges, side notches and a concave, expanding basal edge. **I.D. KEY:** Expanding basal edge..

DESERT GENERAL - Desert Traditions-Classic to Historic,700-200 B. P.

(Also see Pueblo Side Notched, Sacaton and Salado)

Clear obsidian / Pink jasper / Black obsidian / Yellow jasper / Basalt

| G6, $5-$12 NW Chih., Mex. | G7, $8-$15 NW Chih., Mex | G6, $8-$15 S.W. CO | G4, $5-$10 Otero Co., NM | G6, $6-$12 NW Chih., Mex. | G8, $8-$15 NM | G7, $8-$15 NW Chih., Mex., | G6, $8-$15 Yavapai Co., AZ. N. of Prescott. | G6, $8-$15 AZ | G6, $8-$15 NM |

Red jasper / Banded agate

| G7, $15-$30 AZ | G8, $30-$50 NM | G8, $30-$50 NM | G8, $25-$40 S. W. CO | G8, $25-$40 NM | G8, $25-$40 San Juan Co., NM | G7, $15-$25 NM | G8, $20-$35 NM | G8, $12-$20 NM |

Clear / Obsidian

| G8, $30-$50 E.W. CO | G8, $30-$50 Montez. Co., CO | G7, $25-$40 Yuma Co., AZ | G7, $25-$40 AZ | G9, $35-$60 S.W. CO | G8, $35-$60 Cochise Co., AZ | G8, $35-$60 S.W. CO | G10, $55-$100 NM | G9, $55-$100 NM |

S W

LOCATION: Most of Arizona and contiguous states to the west. **DESCRIPTION:** A small arrow point with convex blade edges, side notches and a straight to slightly concave basal edge. **I.D. KEY:** Straight to concave base.

DESERT REDDING - Desert Traditions-Classic to Historic, 700-200 B. P.

(Also see Mimbre, Pueblo Side Notched, Sacaton, Salado and Temporal)

| G4, $5-$10 NM | G6, $8-$15 NM | G5, $6-$10 Pima Co., AZ | G7, $12-$25 Pima Co., AZ | G8, $18-$30 NW Chih., Mex., chalc. | G8, $25-$45 S.W. CO |

DESERT REDDING (continued)

LOCATION: Most of Arizona and contiguous states to the west. **DESCRIPTION:** A small arrow point with conve~ sides, diagonal side notches and a concave basal edge which is narrower than the shoulders. **I.D. KEY:** Narrow basε edge.

DESERT SIERRA - Desert Traditions-Classic to Historic, 700-200 B. P.

(Also see Awatovi, Buck Taylor, Notched, Del Carmen, Sacaton, White Mountain)

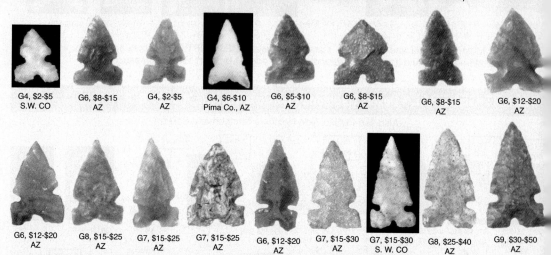

G4, $2-$5
S.W. CO

G6, $8-$15
AZ

G4, $2-$5
AZ

G4, $6-$10
Pima Co., AZ

G6, $5-$10
AZ

G6, $8-$15
AZ

G6, $8-$15
AZ

G6, $12-$20
AZ

G6, $12-$20
AZ

G8, $15-$25
AZ

G7, $15-$25
AZ

G7, $15-$25
AZ

G6, $12-$20
AZ

G7, $15-$30
AZ

G7, $15-$30
S. W. CO

G8, $25-$40
AZ

G9, $30-$50
AZ

LOCATION: Most of Arizona and contiguous states to the west. **DESCRIPTION:** A small arrow point with straight sides, a straight basal edge, side notches and a basal notch. **I.D. KEY:** Triangular tri-notched point.

DISC - Mid-Archaic, 5000 - 4500 B.P.

(Also see Crescent, Cruciform and Exotic)

All from San Luis Potosi, MX

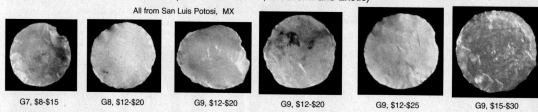

G7, $8-$15

G8, $12-$20

G9, $12-$20

G9, $12-$20

G9, $12-$25

G9, $15-$30

LOCATION: Central Mexico. **DESCRIPTION:** A small circular object pressure flaked to an edge on each face. The purpose of these objects is unknown. These were in use about the same time as the *Crescents*. Examples show good patination. **I.D. KEY:** Circular form.

DOLORES - Developmental Phase, 1300 - 1100 B.P.

(Also see Amargosa, Basketmaker, Carlsbad, Cienega, Guadalupe)

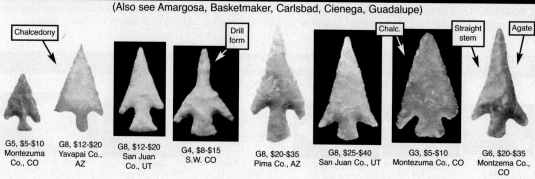

Chalcedony

Drill form

Chalc.

Straight stem

Agate

G5, $5-$10
Montezuma
Co., CO

G8, $12-$20
Yavapai Co.,
AZ

G8, $12-$20
San Juan
Co., UT

G4, $8-$15
S.W. CO

G8, $20-$35
Pima Co., AZ

G8, $25-$40
San Juan Co., UT

G3, $5-$10
Montezuma
Co., CO

G6, $20-$35
Montzema Co.,
CO

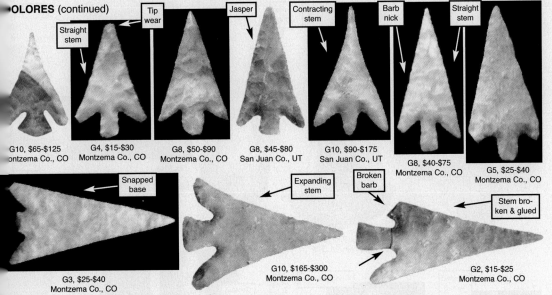

OLORES (continued)

Straight stem — Tip wear — Jasper — Contracting stem — Barb nick — Straight stem

G10, $65-$125
ontzema Co., CO

G4, $15-$30
Montzema Co., CO

G8, $50-$90
Montzema Co., CO

G8, $45-$80
San Juan Co., UT

G10, $90-$175
San Juan Co., UT

G8, $40-$75
Montzema Co., CO

G5, $25-$40
Montzema Co., CO

Snapped base — Expanding stem — Broken barb — Stem broken & glued

G3, $25-$40
Montzema Co., CO

G10, $165-$300
Montzema Co., CO

G2, $15-$25
Montzema Co., CO

LOCATION: Northern Arizona & New Mexico into southern Utah and S.W. Colorado. Type area is in S.W. Colorado. **DESCRIPTION:** A small, barbed arrow point with a medium to long, narrow expanding to parallel to slightly contracting stem. Blade edges are concave to recurved and can be serrated. Found in late Basketmaker or early Pueblo I sites in four corners area. **I.D. KEY:** Barbs and narrow stem.

DRILL - Paleo to Historic, 11,500 - 850 B.P.

(Also see Circular Uniface Knife, Lancet and Scraper)

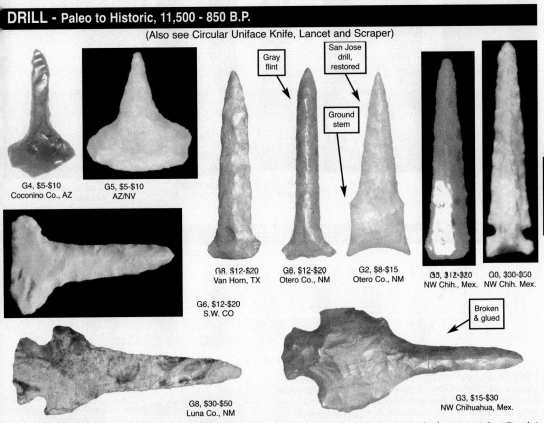

Gray flint — San Jose drill, restored — Ground stem

G4, $5-$10
Coconino Co., AZ

G5, $5-$10
AZ/NV

G8, $12-$20
Van Horn, TX

G8, $12-$20
Otero Co., NM

G2, $8-$15
Otero Co., NM

G5, $12-$20
NW Chih., Mex.

G8, $00-$50
NW Chih. Mex.

G6, $12-$20
S.W. CO

Broken & glued

G8, $30-$50
Luna Co., NM

G3, $15-$30
NW Chihuahua, Mex.

LOCATION: Throughout North America. **DESCRIPTION:** Although many drills were made from scratch, all point types were made into the drill form. Usually, heavily resharpened and broken points were salvaged and rechipped into drills. **I.D. KEY:** Narrow blade form.

S
W

DRILL (continued)

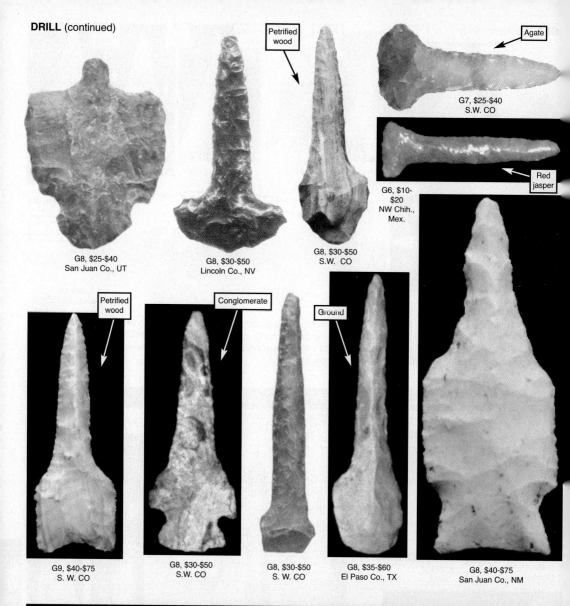

Agate

G7, $25-$40
S.W. CO

Petrified
wood

Red
jasper

G6, $10-
$20
NW Chih.,
Mex.

G8, $25-$40
San Juan Co., UT

G8, $30-$50
Lincoln Co., NV

G8, $30-$50
S.W. CO

Petrified
wood

Conglomerate

Ground

G9, $40-$75
S. W. CO

G8, $30-$50
S.W. CO

G8, $30-$50
S. W. CO

G8, $35-$60
El Paso Co., TX

G8, $40-$75
San Juan Co., NM

DRY PRONG - Desert Traditions, 1000 - 850 B.P.

(Also see Desert, Mimbre, Pueblo Side Notched, Sacaton and Temporal)

Obsidian

Obsidian

G5-6 average, Apache Co., AZ. 6 point cache. Value of cache of 6 points $200.

LOCATION: East central Arizona and west central New Mexico. **DESCRIPTION:** A small, narrow triangular arrow point with side notches and one or two additional side notches on one side of the blade. Some examples do not have the extra notch(es) and must be found in association with the extra notch variety to be typed as *Dry Prong* points. **I.D. KEY:** The extra side notch(es).

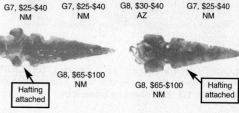

G7, $25-$40
NM

G7, $25-$40
NM

G8, $30-$40
AZ

G7, $25-$40
NM

G8, $65-$100
NM

G8, $65-$100
NM

Hafting
attached

Hafting
attached

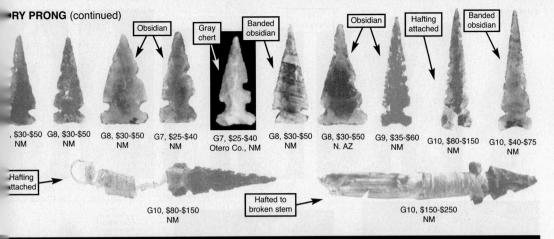

, $30-$50
NM

G8, $30-$50
NM

Obsidian

G8, $30-$50
NM

G7, $25-$40
NM

Gray chert

G7, $25-$40
Otero Co., NM

Banded obsidian

G8, $30-$50
NM

Obsidian

G8, $30-$50
N. AZ

Hafting attached

G9, $35-$60
NM

G10, $80-$150
NM

Banded obsidian

G10, $40-$75
NM

Hafting attached

G10, $80-$150
NM

Hafted to broken stem

G10, $150-$250
NM

DUNCAN - Middle to Late Archaic, 4500 - 2850 B. P.

(Also see Bajada, Barreal, Chiricahua, Escobas, Hanna and San Jose)

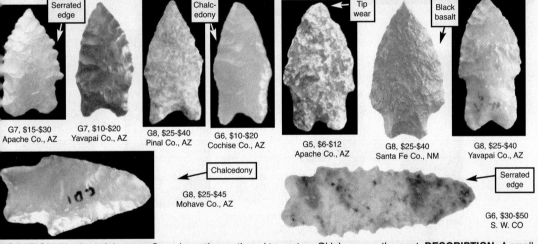

Serrated edge

G7, $15-$30
Apache Co., AZ

G7, $10-$20
Yavapai Co., AZ

Chalcedony

G8, $25-$40
Pinal Co., AZ

G6, $10-$20
Cochise Co., AZ

Tip wear

G5, $6-$12
Apache Co., AZ

G8, $25-$40
Santa Fe Co., NM

Black basalt

G8, $25-$40
Yavapai Co., AZ

Chalcedony

G8, $25-$45
Mohave Co., AZ

Serrated edge

G6, $30-$50
S. W. CO

LOCATION: Northern Arizona to Canada on the north and to eastern Oklahoma on the east. **DESCRIPTION:** A small to medium sized dart/knife point with a triangular blade and angular shoulders. The stem is straight with a V-shaped notch in the basal edge. Stem edges are usually ground. **I.D. KEY:** Straight stem edges.

S
W

DURAN - Late Archaic to Transitional Phase, 3000 - 2000 B. P.

(Also see Guadalupe, Maljamar, Neff and Truxton)

G8, $15-$25
NW Chih., Mex.

G6, $20-$35
Apache Co., AZ

G6, $15-$30
S.W. CO

G7, $25-$40
Apache Co., AZ

G6, $15-$25
Otero Co., NM

G7, $20-$35
Dona Ana Co., NM

G7, $25-$40
NW Chih., Mex.

LOCATION: Texas into Mexico. **DESCRIPTION:** A small size, narrow, stemmed point with double to multiple notches on each side. Base can be parallel sided to tapered with rounded basal corners. Similar to *Contra Costa* found in California. **I.D. KEY:** Double notches, round base.

DURAN (continued)

Flint

Clear chalcedony

G8, $25-$45
NW Chih., Mex.

G8, $30-$50
NW Chih., Mex.

G6, $25-$40
San Luis Potosi, Mex.

G6, $30-$50
NW Chih., Mex.

G8, $25-$40
San Luis Potosi, Mex.

G8, $35-$60
NW Chih., Mex.

G9, $35-$60
NW Chihuahua, M

G9, $70-$135
NW Chih., Mex.

Obsidian

G9, $65-$125
NM

Yellow jasper

Pink agate; restored

Barb nick

G7, $40-$75
Otero Co., NM

G8, $30-$50
NW Chih., Mex.

G9, $55-$100
Chaves Co., NM

G10, $40-$70
W. TX

G2, $10-$20
NW Chih., Mex.

G8, $150-$250
NW Chih., Mex.

DURANGO - Mid to LateArchaic, 4500 - 2500 B. P.

(Also see Basketmaker and San Pedro)

Washington Pass red agate

G9, $30-$50
S.W. CO

G9, $25-$40
S.W. CO

G6, $12-$20
S.W. CO

LOCATION: Type site in Durango, Colorado. **DESCRIPTION:** A small size, narrow point with shallow side notches near the base. Most examples are serrated and the base is either convex or straight. **I.D. KEY:** Weak notches near the base.

EARLY LEAF - Early to Middle Archaic, 8000 - 5000 B. P.

(Also see Early Stemmed, Refugio, Round-back Knife)

Obsidian

G3, $55-$100
N. MX

IMPORTANT: Only this point shown half size

Broken & glued

LOCATION: Mexico. **DESCRIPTION:** A large size, thin, ovoid blade with a pointed base. Early parallel flaking is evident on many examples.

Black obsidian

G9, $175-$300
N. MX

EARLY STEMMED - Late Archaic to Woodland, 3500 - 2300 B. P.

(Also see Augustin, Early Leaf, Escobas)

G4, $30-$50
Albequerque, NM

Diagonal flaking

Obsidian

Obsidian

G9, $80-$150
MX

LOCATION: Mexico. **DESCRIPTION:** A medium size point with sloping shoulders. Stems are straight to contracting to a straight to convex base. Shoulders are weak and sloping. Stem sides are sometimes ground. Flaking is oblique transverse and the cross section is elliptical. **I.D. KEY:** Base form and size.

EARLY TRIANGULAR - Early Archaic, 9000 - 7000 B. P.

(Also see Angostura, Clovis, Kinney, Mescal Knife, Tortugas & Triangular Knife)

S
W

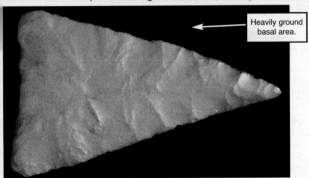

Heavily ground basal area.

LOCATION: New Mexico into Texas. **DESCRIPTION:** A medium to large size, broad, thin, trianglular blade that can be serrated. The base is either fluted or has long thinning strikes. Quality is excellent with early oblique transverse and possible right hand beveling when resharpened. Basal areas are ground. **I.D. KEY:** Basal thinning and edgework.

G10, $125-$225
Otero Co., NM
Thin.

EDEN - Early Archaic, 9500 - 7500 B. P.

(Also see Firstview and Scottsbluff)

EDEN (continued)

Agate

Broken half

Ground stem

Petrified wood

Base nick

G1, $30-$50
El Paso Co., TX

Broken half

G6, $65-$120
Far West TX.
Base is finished & not ground.

G1, $30-$50
Luna Co., NM

G1, $25-$40
Mohave Co., AZ

G8, $900-$1700
Navajo Co., AZ

Diagonal flaking

LOCATION: Southwest to northern and midwestern states. **DESCRIPTION:** A medium to large size, narrow, lanceolate blade with a straight to concave base and almost unnoticable shoulders. Many examples have a median ridge and collateral oblique parallel flaking. Bases are usually ground. **I.D. KEY:** Narrowness, weak shoulders.

ELKO CORNER NOTCHED - Mid-Archaic to Developmental Phase, 3500 - 1200 B.P.

(Also see Amargosa, Cienega, Mount Albion, San Pedro)

Yellow agate

Gray chert

G6, $5-$10
Yavapai Co., AZ

G8, $15-$25
S.W. CO

G3, $2-$5
AZ

G8, $30-$50
Otero Co., NM

LOCATION: Great Basin into Arizona. **DESCRIPTION:** A small to large size, thin, corner notched dart point with shoulder barbs and a convex, concave or auriculate base. Shoulders and tips are sharp. Some examples exhibit excellent parallel flaking on blade edges which can be serrated. **I.D. KEY:** Corner notches, sharp barbs.

ELKO EARED - Mid-Archaic to Developmental Phase, 3500 - 1200 B.P.

(Also see Eastgate, Hanna and San Jose)

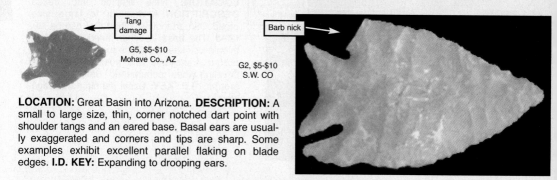

Tang damage

G5, $5-$10
Mohave Co., AZ

G2, $5-$10
S.W. CO

Barb nick

LOCATION: Great Basin into Arizona. **DESCRIPTION:** A small to large size, thin, corner notched dart point with shoulder tangs and an eared base. Basal ears are usually exaggerated and corners and tips are sharp. Some examples exhibit excellent parallel flaking on blade edges. **I.D. KEY:** Expanding to drooping ears.

EMBUDO - Early Archaic, 7000 - 6000 B. P.

(Also see Cohonina Stemmed, Datil, Embudo and Pelona)

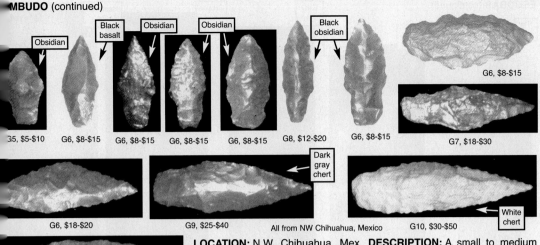

Obsidian

Black basalt

Obsidian

Obsidian

Black obsidian

G5, $5-$10

G6, $8-$15

G6, $8-$15

G6, $8-$15

G6, $8-$15

G8, $12-$20

G6, $8-$15

G6, $8-$15

G7, $18-$30

Dark gray chert

G6, $18-$20

G9, $25-$40

All from NW Chihuahua, Mexico

G10, $30-$50

White chert

Gray basalt

G9, $25-$40

LOCATION: N.W. Chihuahua, Mex. **DESCRIPTION:** A small to medium sized, narrow, spike dart point with weak, sloping shoulders and a contracting, straight to bulbous stem. Blade edges can have fine serrations. Stem sides are usually ground. Bases are usually convex but can be incurvate to straight. **I.D. KEY:** Spike-like form.

ESCOBAS - Mid-Archaic, 6500 - 5000 B. P.

(Also see Bajada, Duncan, Hanna, Jay, Rio Grande and San Jose)

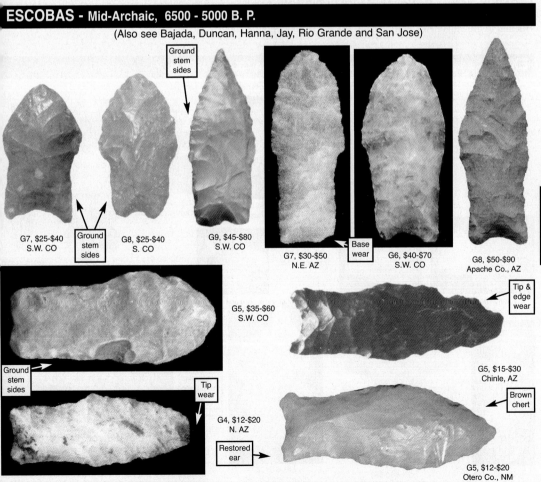

Ground stem sides

G7, $25-$40
S.W. CO

Ground stem sides

G8, $25-$40
S. CO

G9, $45-$80
S.W. CO

Base wear

G7, $30-$50
N.E. AZ

G6, $40-$70
S.W. CO

G8, $50-$90
Apache Co., AZ

S W

G5, $35-$60
S.W. CO

Tip & edge wear

G5, $15-$30
Chinle, AZ

Ground stem sides

Tip wear

G4, $12-$20
N. AZ

Restored ear

Brown chert

G5, $12-$20
Otero Co., NM

845

ESCOBAS (continued)

Tip wear

Restored tip & left ear

Tan chert

Gray chert

Ground stem sides

Restored tip

G5, $15-$30
Otero Co., NM, chert

G5, $15-$30
Otero Co., NM, thick. ground stem and base.

G9, $60-$120
Otero Co., NM, ground stem sides. thick. gray chert flaked to a median ridge.

G3, $15-$30
Otero Co., NM

G3, $15-$30
Otero Co., NM, ground ste sides. thick. flaked to a me an ridge.

LOCATION: Arizona into New Mexico. **DESCRIPTION:** A medium size, thick, long stemmed point with weak shoulders and a concave base. Basal areas are ground. Flaking is to a median ridge. Develops into the *Bajada* point Related to the earlier *Rio Grande* type. **I.D. KEY:** Long straight stem; concave base.

EXOTIC - Late Archaic to Developmental Phase, 3000 - 1000 B. P.

(Also see Crescent, Cruciform and Disc)

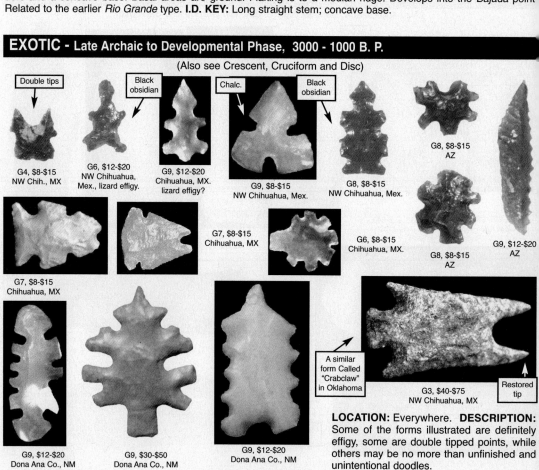

Double tips

Black obsidian

Chalc.

Black obsidian

G4, $8-$15
NW Chih., MX

G6, $12-$20
NW Chihuahua, Mex., lizard effigy.

G9, $12-$20
Chihuahua, MX. lizard effigy?

G9, $8-$15
NW Chihuahua, Mex.

G8, $8-$15
NW Chihuahua, Mex.

G8, $8-$15
AZ

G7, $8-$15
Chihuahua, MX

G6, $8-$15
Chihuahua, MX.

G8, $8-$15
AZ

G9, $12-$20
AZ

G7, $8-$15
Chihuahua, MX

A similar form Called "Crabclaw" in Oklahoma

Restored tip

G3, $40-$75
NW Chihuahua, MX

G9, $12-$20
Dona Ana Co., NM

G9, $30-$50
Dona Ana Co., NM

G9, $12-$20
Dona Ana Co., NM

LOCATION: Everywhere. **DESCRIPTION:** Some of the forms illustrated are definitely effigy, some are double tipped points, while others may be no more than unfinished and unintentional doodles.

846

FIGUEROA - Transitional Phase, 2200 B. P.

(Also see Amargosa, Black Mesa Narrow Neck, Cienega, Mount Albion, San Pedro)

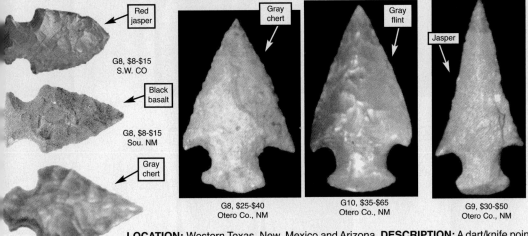

Red jasper

G8, $8-$15
S.W. CO

Black basalt

G8, $8-$15
Sou. NM

Gray chert

G6, $15-$25
NW Chih., Mex.

Gray chert

Gray flint

Jasper

G8, $25-$40
Otero Co., NM

G10, $35-$65
Otero Co., NM

G9, $30-$50
Otero Co., NM

LOCATION: Western Texas, New Mexico and Arizona. **DESCRIPTION:** A dart/knife point with medium-wide side notches, an expanding stem and a convex basal edge. Similar to the *Motley* point found in Louisiana. **I.D. KEY:** Wide side notches, convex base.

FIRSTVIEW - Late Paleo, 10,000 - 8000 B. P.

(Also see Eden, Escobas and Scottsbluff)

Collateral flaking

G9, $450-$800
Chaves Co., NM

Tiger chert

Collateral flaking

Very small tip piece & base chip restored

G7, $1600-$2800
El Paso Co., TX

LOCATION: Extreme W. Texas into New Mexico and Sou. Colorado. **DESCRIPTION:** A lanceolate point with slightly convex edges, slight shoulders and a rectangular stem. Shoulders are sometimes absent from resharpening. It generally exhibits parallel-transverse flaking. **I.D. KEY:** A diamond shaped cross-section.

FOLSOM - Paleo, 11,000 - 10,000 B. P.

(Also see Allen, Belen, Angostura, Clovis, Goshen, Green River and Midland)

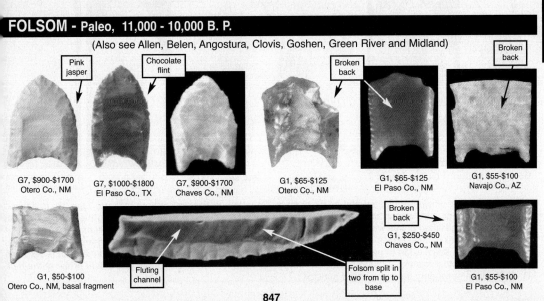

Pink jasper

Chocolate flint

Broken back

Broken back

G7, $900-$1700
Otero Co., NM

G7, $1000-$1800
El Paso Co., TX

G7, $900-$1700
Chaves Co., NM

G1, $65-$125
Otero Co., NM

G1, $65-$125
El Paso Co., NM

G1, $55-$100
Navajo Co., AZ

Fluting channel

Folsom split in two from tip to base

Broken back

G1, $250-$450
Chaves Co., NM

G1, $50-$100
Otero Co., NM, basal fragment

G1, $55-$100
El Paso Co., NM

847

FOLSOM (continued)

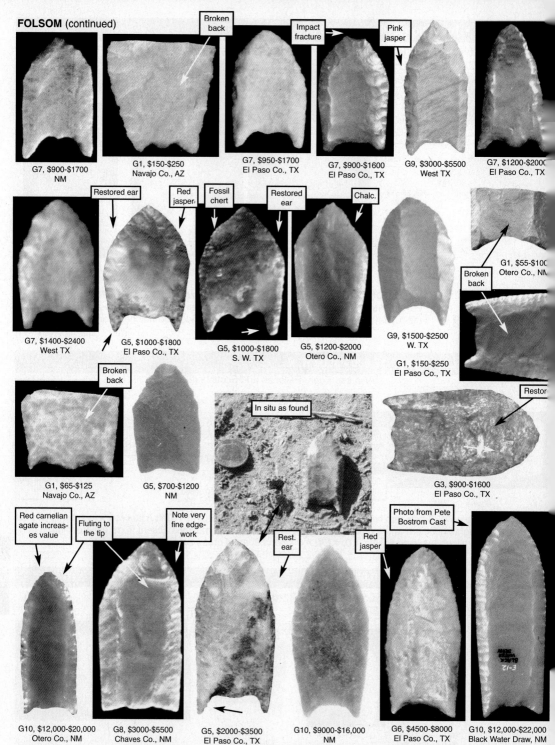

Broken back

Impact fracture

Pink jasper

G7, $900-$1700
NM

G1, $150-$250
Navajo Co., AZ

G7, $950-$1700
El Paso Co., TX

G7, $900-$1600
El Paso Co., TX

G9, $3000-$5500
West TX

G7, $1200-$2000
El Paso Co., TX

Restored ear

Red jasper

Fossil chert

Restored ear

Chalc.

G7, $1400-$2400
West TX

G5, $1000-$1800
El Paso Co., TX

G5, $1000-$1800
S. W. TX

G5, $1200-$2000
Otero Co., NM

G9, $1500-$2500
W. TX

G1, $55-$100
Otero Co., NM

Broken back

G1, $150-$250
El Paso Co., TX

Broken back

G1, $65-$125
Navajo Co., AZ

G5, $700-$1200
NM

In situ as found

Restor

G3, $900-$1600
El Paso Co., TX

Red carnelian agate increases value

Fluting to the tip

Note very fine edge-work

Rest. ear

Red jasper

Photo from Pete Bostrom Cast

G10, $12,000-$20,000
Otero Co., NM

G8, $3000-$5500
Chaves Co., NM

G5, $2000-$3500
El Paso Co., TX

G10, $9000-$16,000
NM

G6, $4500-$8000
El Paso Co., TX

G10, $12,000-$22,000
Black Water Draw, NM

LOCATION: The southwestern states and as far north as Canada and east to northern Indiana. Type site is a bison kill site near Folsom, NM, where 24 fluted *Folsom* points were excavated in 1926-1928. Being the first fluted point named, for years all fluted points were called *Folsom*. **DESCRIPTION:** A very thin, small to medium sized, lanceolate point with convex to parallel edges and a concave basal edge creating sharp ears or basal corners. Most examples are fluted from the basal edge to nearly the tip of the point. They do rarely occur unfluted. Workmanship is very fine and outstanding. Most examples found have worn out tips or were rebased from longer points that broke at the haft. **I.D. KEY:** Micro secondary flaking, pointed auricles.

FRIO - Early to Middle Archaic, 5000 - 1500 B. P.

(Also see Caracara, Uvalde, Squaw Mountain, Ventana Side Notched)

Clear obsidian — G6, $12-$20 NW Chih., Mex.

Very thin — G8, $18-$30 NW Chih., Mex, needle tip and tangs

G9, $18-$30 S. NM

G6, $12-$20 S. NM

Gray flint — G7, $12-$20 NW Chih., Mex, very thin

Black obsidian — G10, $40-$70 NW Chih., Mex, very thin

Red basalt — G8, $25-$45 NW Chih., Mex.,

G10, $85-$165 NW Chih., Mex, very thin

Agate; pink base, beige tip

G10, $70-$135 NW Chih., Mex, very thin, ground base

LOCATION: N.W. Chihuhhua, Mexico into Texas and Oklahoma. **DESCRIPTION:** A small to medium size, side to corner-notched point with a concave to notched base that has squared to rounded ears that flare. Some examples are similar to *Big Sandy Auriculate* forms from Tennessee. **I.D. KEY:** Flaring ears.

FRIO-TRANSITIONAL - Late Archaic to Trans., 3000 - 2000 B. P.

(Also see Barreal, Chiricahua)

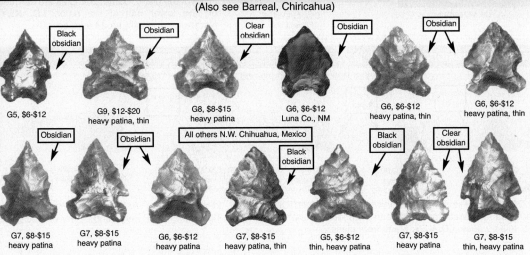

Black obsidian — G5, $6-$12

Obsidian — G9, $12-$20 heavy patina, thin

Clear obsidian — G8, $8-$15 heavy patina

Obsidian — G6, $6-$12 Luna Co., NM

Obsidian — G6, $6-$12 heavy patina, thin

Obsidian — G6, $6-$12 heavy patina, thin

Obsidian — G7, $8-$15 heavy patina

Obsidian — G7, $8-$15 heavy patina

G6, $6-$12 heavy patina

All others N.W. Chihuahua, Mexico

Black obsidian — G7, $8-$15 heavy patina, thin

G5, $6-$12 thin, heavy patina

Black obsidian — G7, $8-$15 heavy patina

Clear obsidian — G7, $8-$15 thin, heavy patina

LOCATION: N.W. Chihuahua, Mexico. **DESCRIPTION:** A small size dart point with side notches and an eared base. Serrations and basal grinding occur. Ears are usually rounded. Shoulders are tapered to horizontal and can be sharp. Very similar to the *Chiricahua* point found in Arizona but not as old. **I.D. KEY:** Short stubby point with flaring ears.

GARZA - Desert Traditions-Classic Phase, 500 - 300 B.P.

(Also see Buck Taylor Notched, Snaketown Triangular, Soto and Toyah)

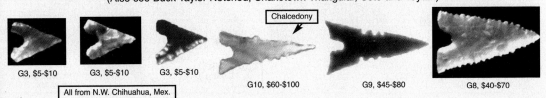

G3, $5-$10

G3, $5-$10

G3, $5-$10

Chalcedony

All from N.W. Chihuahua, Mex.

G10, $60-$100

G9, $45-$80

G8, $40-$70

S W

849

GARZA (continued)

LOCATION: NW Chihuahua, Mexico. **DESCRIPTION:** A small, thin, triangular arrow point. Blade edges vary from convex to concave and can be serrated. The basal edge is deeply concave and notched, creating long, thin ears.

GATLIN SIDE NOTCHED - Devel. to Classic Phase, 800 - 600 B. P.

(Also see Pueblo Side Notched, Snaketown Triangular)

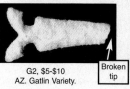
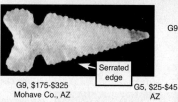

G2, $5-$10
AZ. Gatlin Variety.

Broken tip

G9, $175-$325
Mohave Co., AZ

Serrated edge

G5, $25-$45
AZ

G9, $125-$225
AZ

Tip nick

LOCATION: Sou. California into Arizona. **DESCRIPTION:** A medium size, thin, triangular *Hohokam* arrow point with broad side notches, a long needle tip and a wide base that can be deeply concave. Some examples are serrated. Basal corners are sharp to rounded. **I.D. KEY:** Long needle tip.

GILA BUTTE   (see Hodges Contracting Stem)

GILA RIVER CORNER NOTCHED - Devel. Phase, 1350-1000 B. P.

(Also see Snaketown)

G9, $125-$200
AZ

G10, $140-$265
Phoenix, AZ

LOCATION: Arizona. **DESCRIPTION:** A very rare form of *Hohokam* arrow point. The stem is straight to expanded and sometimes concave to bifurcated and has large serrations on both sides of the blade. Some examples are serrated on the lower half of the point. **I.D. KEY:** Narrowness, length, broad serrations.

GLASS - Historic, 400 - 100 B. P.

(Also see Bull Creek, Cottonwood, Sobaipuri and Trade)

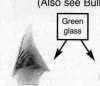

Green glass

Green glass

Amber glass

G3, $5-$10
Pima Indian,
Maricopa Co., AZ

G3, $8-$15
Pima Indian,
Maricopa Co., AZ

G6, $20-$25
Pima IIndian,
Maricopa Co., AZ

G6, $20-$25
Pima Indian,
Maricopa Co., AZ

G8, $20-$35
Pima Indian, Maricopa Co., AZ

LOCATION: Historic sites everywhere. **DESCRIPTION:** A small, thin arrow point that can be triangular or side notched fashioned from bottle and telephone insulator glass. Such tribes as Pima, Papago and others utilized glass for this purpose. **I.D. KEY:** Made from glass.

GOBERNADORA - Late Archaic, 3000 B. P.

(Also see Acatita, Augustin, Gypsum Cave and Socorro)

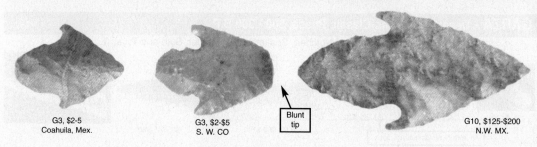

G3, $2-5
Coahuila, Mex.

G3, $2-$5
S. W. CO

Blunt tip

G10, $125-$200
N.W. MX.

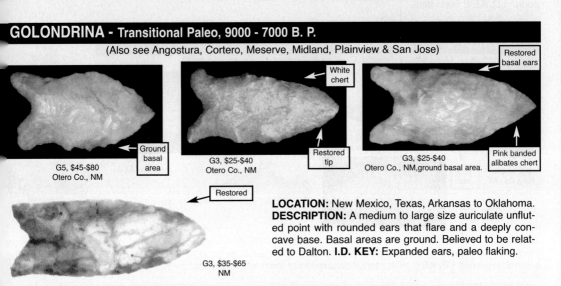

G9, $90-$175
N.W. MX.

G9, $150-$250
N.W. MX.

LOCATION: S.E. Arizona into southern New Mexico and N.E. Mexico. **DESCRIPTION:** A medium sized, thin, dart/knife with inward-sloping tangs and a long contracting turkeytail stem. **I.D. KEY:** Stem form.

GOLONDRINA - Transitional Paleo, 9000 - 7000 B. P.

(Also see Angostura, Cortero, Meserve, Midland, Plainview & San Jose)

Restored basal ears

White chert

Ground basal area

Restored tip

G5, $45-$80
Otero Co., NM

G3, $25-$40
Otero Co., NM

G3, $25-$40
Otero Co., NM, ground basal area.

Pink banded alibates chert

Restored

G3, $35-$65
NM

LOCATION: New Mexico, Texas, Arkansas to Oklahoma. **DESCRIPTION:** A medium to large size auriculate unfluted point with rounded ears that flare and a deeply concave base. Basal areas are ground. Believed to be related to Dalton. **I.D. KEY:** Expanded ears, paleo flaking.

GOSHEN - Paleo, 11,250 - 9,500 B. P.

(Also see Clovis, Folsom, Green River, Meserve, Midland, Milnesand)

Resharpened many times

Restored right ear

G4, $125-$200
El Paso Co., NM

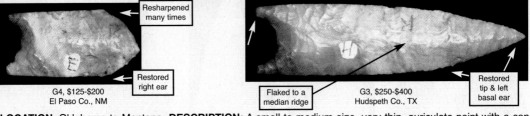

Flaked to a median ridge

G3, $250-$400
Hudspeth Co., TX

Restored tip & left basal ear

S W

LOCATION: Oklahoma to Montana. **DESCRIPTION:** A small to medium size, very thin, auriculate point with a concave base. Basal corners slope inward and are rounded. Flaking is oblique to horizontal transverse. A rare type. **I.D. KEY:** Thinness, auricles.

GRAVER - Paleo to Archaic, 14,000 - 4000 B. P.

(Also see Drill, Perforator and Scraper)

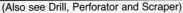

Graver tip

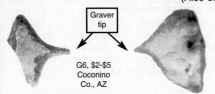

G6, $4-$8
Coconino Co., AZ

G6, $2-$5
Coconino Co., AZ

LOCATION: Paleo and Archaic sites everywhere. **DESCRIPTION:** An irregular shaped uniface took with one or more sharp, pointed projections used for puncturing, incising, tattooing, etc. Some examples served a dual purpose for scraping as well. **I.D. KEY:** Stem form.

GREEN RIVER - Mid-Archaic, 4500 - 4200 B. P.

(Also see Allen, Bat Cave, Folsom, Goshen, Humboldt and Midland)

G4, $8-$15
Mohave Co., AZ

G6, $25-$40
Mohave Co., AZ

G6, $25-$40
Mohave Co., AZ

G6, $30-$50
Mohave Co., AZ

LOCATION: Central Arizona to Wyoming, Colorado, Montana, New Mexico and Nebraska. **DESCRIPTION:** A small size auriculate point with a concave base. Auricles turn inward and are rounded. Similar to *McKean* found further north. **I.D. KEY:** Stem form.

GUADALUPE - Transitional-Developmental, 1900 - 1200 B. P.

(Also see Ahumada, Carlsbad, Cienega, Dolores and Neff)

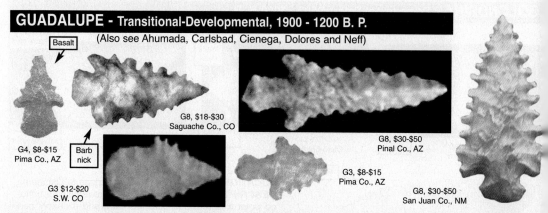

Basalt

G4, $8-$15
Pima Co., AZ

Barb nick

G3 $12-$20
S.W. CO

G8, $18-$30
Saguache Co., CO

G3, $8-$15
Pima Co., AZ

G8, $30-$50
Pinal Co., AZ

G8, $30-$50
San Juan Co., NM

LOCATION: Arizona, New Mexico into N. Mexico. **DESCRIPTION:** A medium size, barbed, corner notched dart/arrow point with an expanding stem. Blades are serrated and bases are straight to convex. Believed to be part of the Livermore cluster. **I.D. KEY:** Wild serrations, expanded stem with corner notches.

GYPSUM CAVE - Middle Archaic, 5000 - 3300 B. P.

(Also see Augustin, Manzano, Parowan and Santa Cruz)

Basalt

G8, $25-$40
Mohave Co., AZ

G8, $25-$40
S. W. CO

G7, $30-$50
Mohave Co., AZ

G6, $15-$30
Virgin River, NV

G8, $35-$60
San Juan Co., UT

G7, $25-$45
Pima Co., AZ

G7, $30-$50
Otero Co., NM

LOCATION: Northwestern Arizona and into contiguous states to the west and north. Type site is Gypsum Cave, NV. **DESCRIPTION:** A medium sized dart/knife with straight blade edges and a short stem which contracts to a rounded point. The shoulders are obtuse. This point may be a northerly and westwardly extension of the *Augustin* point, though, in general, it seems to have better workmanship. **I.D. KEY:** Stubby stem.

852

Preform

Basalt

Black obsidian

G6, $15-$30
Mohave Co., AZ

G5, $5-$10
Pima Co., AZ

G7, $25-$40
Cohonina Co., AZ

G9, $30-$65
Mexico

G7, $25-$40
Otero Co., NM

G6, $15-$30
S.W. TX

G9, $35-$60
Garfield Co., UT

G3, $8-$15
Yavapa Co., AZ

G8, $45-$80
Mohave Co., AZ

G4, $50-$90
Alamosa Co., CO

Knife form

G8, $175-$300
San Juan Co., UT

Red jasper

S
W

HANNA - Middle to Late Archaic, 4500 - 2850 B. P.

(Also see Barreal, Chiricahua, Duncan and Squaw Mountain)

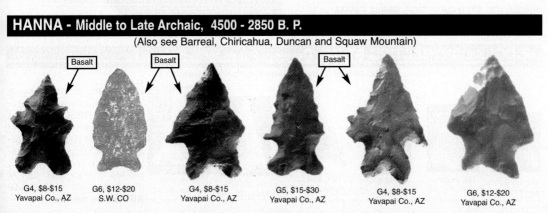

Basalt

Basalt

Basalt

G4, $8-$15
Yavapai Co., AZ

G6, $12-$20
S.W. CO

G4, $8-$15
Yavapai Co., AZ

G5, $15-$30
Yavapai Co., AZ

G4, $8-$15
Yavapai Co., AZ

G6, $12-$20
Yavapai Co., AZ

HANNA (continued)

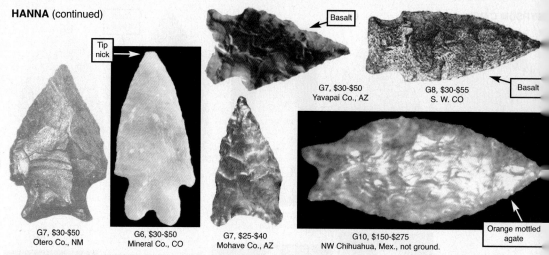

Tip nick →

Basalt

G7, $30-$50
Yavapai Co., AZ

G8, $30-$55
S. W. CO

Basalt ←

G7, $30-$50
Otero Co., NM

G6, $30-$50
Mineral Co., CO

G7, $25-$40
Mohave Co., AZ

G10, $150-$275
NW Chihuahua, Mex., not ground.

Orange mottled agate →

LOCATION: Southwestern states and north as far as Canada and east as far as Nebraska. **DESCRIPTION:** A small dart/knife with obtuse shoulders and an expanding stem which is notched to produce diagonally projecting ears. **I.D. KEY:** Expanding stem.

HARAHEY - Classic Phase, 700 - 400 B. P.

(Also see Archaic Knife)

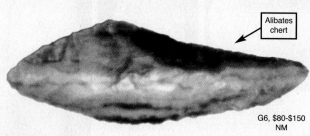

Alibates chert ←

LOCATION: Texas to Colorado. **DESCRIPTION:** A large size, double pointed knife that is usually beveled on one of all four sides of each face. The cross section is rhomboid. The true buffalo skinning knife. Found in association with small arrow points in Texas. **I.D. KEY:** Four beveled double pointed form.

G6, $80-$150
NM

HARRELL (see Awatovi)

HELL GAP - Late Paleo, 10,300 - 8500 B. P.

(Also see Agate Basin, Angostura, Escobas, Jay, Lake Mohave, Rio Grande)

LOCATION: Colorado northward to the Dakotas and Canada and eastward to Texas. **DESCRIPTION:** A medium size lanceolate point with a long, contracting basal stem and a short, stubby tip. Bases are generally straight and are ground. High quality flaking. **I.D. KEY:** Long stem.

Basalt →

G7, $175-$300
S.W., CO

HODGES CONTRACTING STEM - Develop. Phase,1500 - 1300 B. P.

(Also see Gila River, Santa Cruz and Snaketown)

LOCATION: Arizona ranging into adjacent parts of contiguous states. **DESCRIPTION:** A small *Hohokam* arrow point with basal notching which creates barbs ranging from shallow to deep. The stem may be pointed or truncated. part of the *Snaketown* cluster. **I.D. KEY:** Basal notches.

G8, $18-$30
Mohave Co., AZ

G6, $5-$10
Mohave Co., AZ

G4, $5-$10
Mohave Co., AZ

G4, $8-$15
Yavapai Co., AZ

G4, $8-$15
Hildago Co., NM

G6, $12-$20
Navajo Co., AZ

854

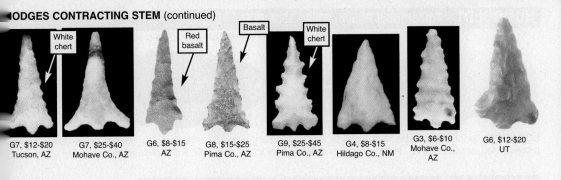

White chert — G7, $12-$20 Tucson, AZ

G7, $25-$40 Mohave Co., AZ

Red basalt — G6, $8-$15 AZ

G8, $15-$25 Pima Co., AZ

Basalt — White chert — G9, $25-$45 Pima Co., AZ

G4, $8-$15 Hildago Co., NM

G3, $6-$10 Mohave Co., AZ

G6, $12-$20 UT

HOHOKAM (see Awatovi Side Notched, Buck Taylor Notched, Citrus Side Notched, Gatlin Side Notched, Gila River Corner Notched, Hodges Contracted Stem, Pueblo Side Notched, Salt River Indented Base, Snaketown Triangular, Sobaipuri, Walnut Canyon Side Notched)

HOHOKAM KNIFE - Desert Trad.-Develop. Phase, 1200 - 1000 B. P.

(Also see Abasolo, Archaic Knife)

Pink/beige chert

G7, $20-$35 Pima Co., AZ

LOCATION: Most of Arizona. **DESCRIPTION:** A medium to large size blade that can be parallel sided to convex and can be side notched. Bases are straight. Random flaking was used.

Ground slate, hafted

Basalt

G6, $25-$45 Pima Co., AZ

G8, $35-$60 AZ.

Tchamahia form of Hohokam knife

Purple quartzite

G8, $55-$100 AZ.

S W

HUMBOLDT - Transitional Phase, 2000 - 1500 B. P.

(Also see Allen, Angostura)

G6, $15-$30
Mohave Co., AZ

Obsidian

G7, $40-$70
NM

LOCATION: Great Basin states, esp. Nevada. **DESCRIPTION:** A small to medium size, narrow, lanceolate point with a constricted, concave base. Basal concavity can be slight to extreme. **I.D. KEY:** Base form.

JAY - Early Archaic, 8000 - 6800 B. P.

(Also see Bajada, Hell Gap, Lake Mohave, Rio Grande, Silver Lake)

Basalt

G8, $65-$125
Catron Co., NM

G7, $65-$125
NM

G9, $125-$225
Otero Co., NM, ground stem
sides & base.

G9, $250-$450
NM

LOCATION: Southern Arizona. **DESCRIPTION:** A medium to large size, narrow, long stemmed point with tapered shoulders. The base is convex. Stem sides and base are ground. Similar to the *Hell Gap* point found further east. **I.D. KEY:** Broad, concave base.

KIN KLETSO SIDE NOTCHED - Late Archaic to Classic Phase, 900 - 750 B. P.

(Also see Bonito, Chaco & Pueblo Alto & Pueblo Del Arroyo Side Notched)

Chalc.

G9, $12-$20
S. W. CO

G8, $15-$30
S. W. CO

Yellow agate

G8, $25-$40
S. W. CO

G10, $60-$100
NM

LOCATION: Chaco Canyon and four corners area. **DESCRIPTION:** A small, thin, side notched arrow point with a straight to slightly concave base. Notching is very narrow. **I.D. KEY:** Triangular form.

KINNEY - Middle Archaic-Woodland, 5000 - 2000 B. P.

(Also see Early Triangular, Matamoros, Mescal Knife and Tortugas)

KINNEY (continued)

LOCATION: Texas into northern Mexico.
DESCRIPTION: A medium to large size, thin, broad, lanceolate, well made blade with convex to straight blade edges and a concave base. Basal corners are pointed to rounded. **I.D. KEY:** Broad, concave base.

G8, $80-$150
NW Chihuahua, Mex.,
thin

White/orange chert

LAKE MOHAVE - Paleo, 13,200 - 10,000 B.P.

(Also see Hell Gap, Jay, Rio Grande, Silver Lake)

Conglomerate

Ground stem

G7, $45-$80
S.W. CO

Blunt tip

Ground stem

G5, $40-$75
Luna Co., NM

G9, $65-$125
S.W. CO

Ground stem

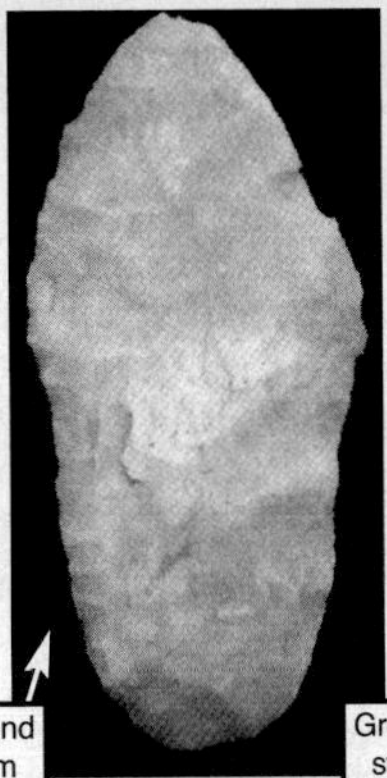

G7, $55-$100
Navajo Co., AZ

Ground stem

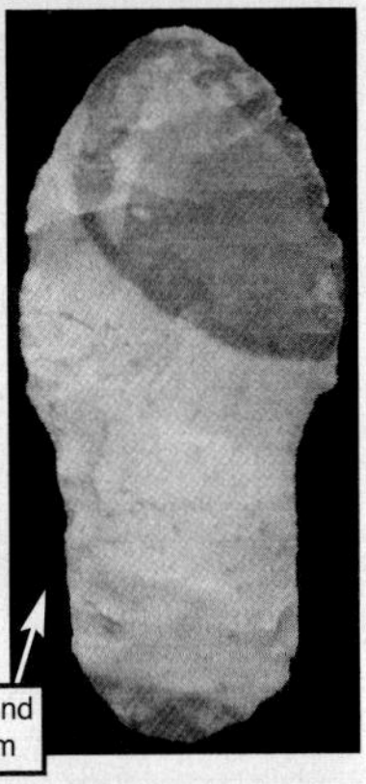

G8, $65-$125
Navajo Co., AZ

Resharpened many times

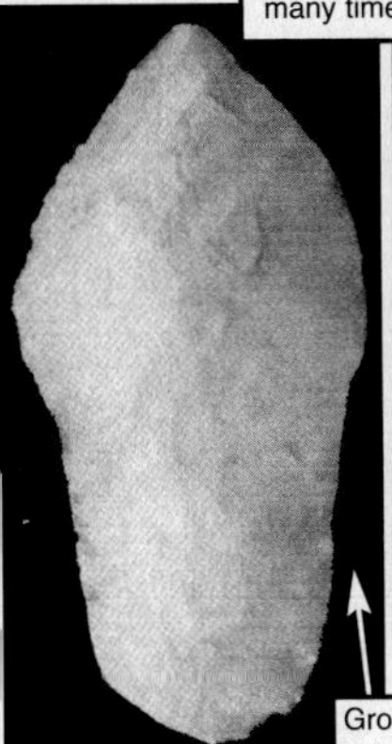

Ground stem

G7, $65-$125
Navajo Co., AZ

Ground stem

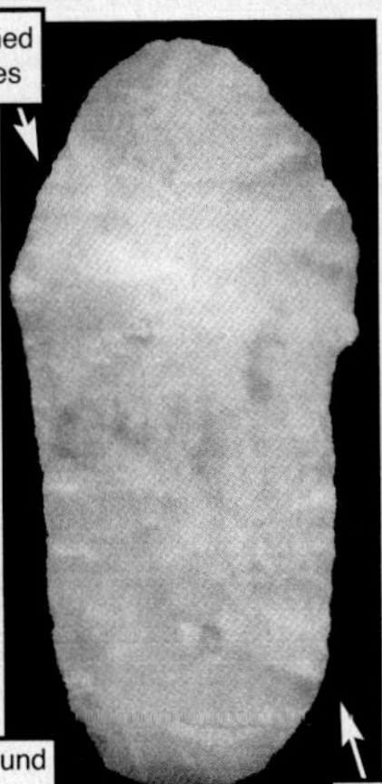

G8, $90-$175
Navajo Co., AZ

Ground stem

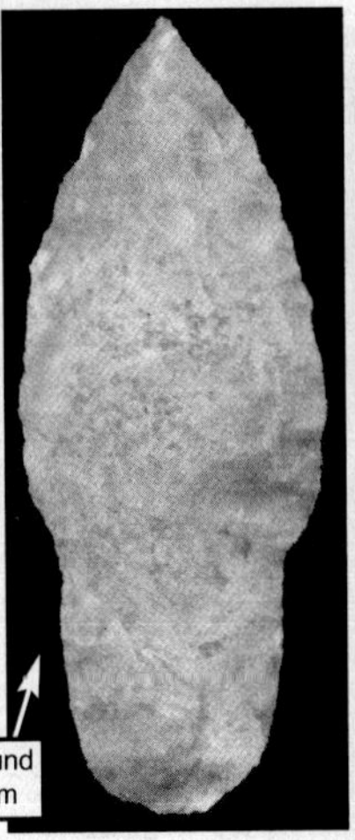

G9, $125-$200
Navajo Co., AZ

Tip wear

Ground stem

G8 $165-$300
Navajo Co., AZ

Ground stem

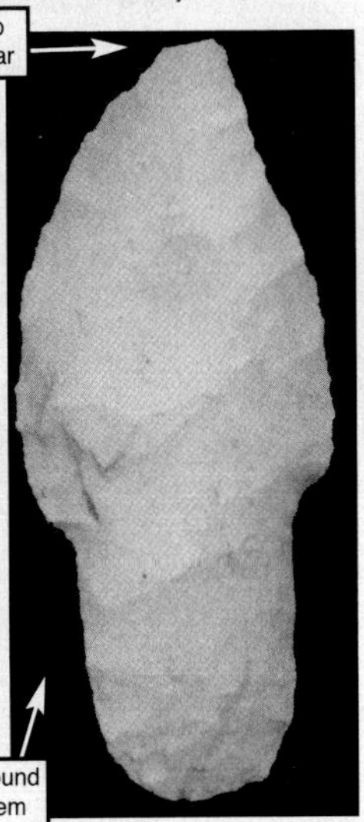

G7, $55-$100
San Juan Co., UT

Ground stem

G9, $250-$450
Navajo Co., AZ

S W

LAKE MOHAVE (continued)

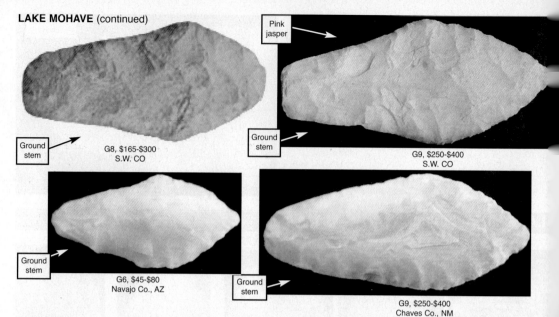

Pink jasper

Ground stem
G8, $165-$300
S.W. CO

Ground stem
G9, $250-$400
S.W. CO

Ground stem
G6, $45-$80
Navajo Co., AZ

Ground stem
G9, $250-$400
Chaves Co., NM

LOCATION: Southern California into Arizona and the Great Basin. **DESCRIPTION:** A medium sized, narrow, parallel to contracting stemmed point with weak, tapered to no shoulders. Stem is much longer than the blade and are ground. Conflicting data on the age which ranges over 5000 years. **I.D. KEY:** Long stem, very short blade.

LANCET - All Periods from Paleo to Historic

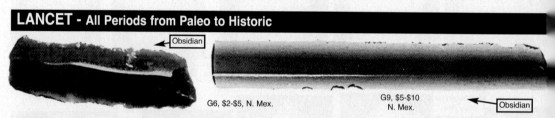

Obsidian

G6, $2-$5, N. Mex.

G9, $5-$10
N. Mex.

Obsidian

LOCATION: Over the entire U.S. **DESCRIPTION:** This artifact is also known as a lammeler flake blade and was produced by knocking a flake or spall off a parent stone. Most of the western examples are of obsidian. Perhaps the best known of the type were those made and used by the Hopewell people in the midwest. **I.D. KEY:** Double uniface and the presence, generally, of the parent stone showing on one face.

LERMA - Middle to Late Archaic, 4000 - 1000 B. P.

(Also see Abasolo, Agate Basin, Angostura, Catan, Datil, Embudo, Padre and Pelona)

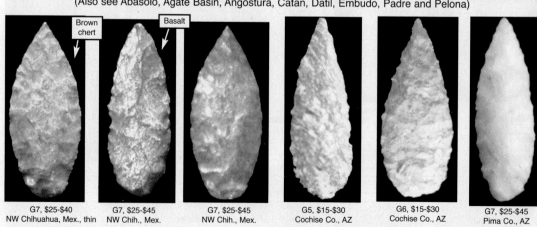

Brown chert

Basalt

G7, $25-$40
NW Chihuahua, Mex., thin

G7, $25-$45
NW Chih., Mex.

G7, $25-$45
NW Chih., Mex.

G5, $15-$30
Cochise Co., AZ

G6, $15-$30
Cochise Co., AZ

G7, $25-$45
Pima Co., AZ

LOCATION: From central Texas westward through New Mexico, N.W. Chihuahua, Mexico and into eastern Arizona. Examples of *Lerma* points from further east are, most likely, Guilford points. **DESCRIPTION:** A long ovoid with a rounded to somewhat pointed basal edge.

858

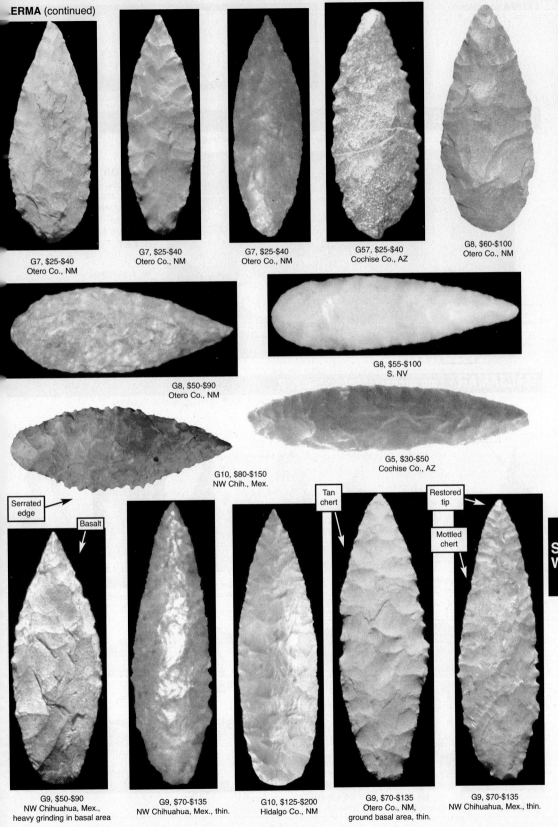

G7, $25-$40
Otero Co., NM

G7, $25-$40
Otero Co., NM

G7, $25-$40
Otero Co., NM

G57, $25-$40
Cochise Co., AZ

G8, $60-$100
Otero Co., NM

G8, $55-$100
S. NV

G8, $50-$90
Otero Co., NM

G5, $30-$50
Cochise Co., AZ

G10, $80-$150
NW Chih., Mex.

Serrated edge

Basalt

Tan chert

Restored tip

Mottled chert

G9, $50-$90
NW Chihuahua, Mex.,
heavy grinding in basal area

G9, $70-$135
NW Chihuahua, Mex., thin.

G10, $125-$200
Hidalgo Co., NM

G9, $70-$135
Otero Co., NM,
ground basal area, thin.

G9, $70-$135
NW Chihuahua, Mex., thin.

SW

LERMA (continued)

G7, $65-$125
Cochise Co., AZ

MADDEN LAKE - Paleo, 10,700 B. P.

(Also see Clovis, Rio Grande, San Jose and Sandia)

Shoulder nick

Ground stem

Flute channel

Tip nick

LOCATION: Panama to southern South America. **DESCRIPTION:** A medium to large size, fluted stemmed point with horizontal to tapered shoulders. Bases are fishtailed and ground. **I.D. KEY:** Fishtail stem.

G6, $1800-$3000
N. Belize, Fells Creek

This example is large for type

MALJAMAR - Late Archaic, 3500 - 2300 B. P.

(Also see Ahumada, Duran, Mount Albion, Neff, San Jose and Truxton)

Barbed edges

Dark gray flint

Basalt

G8, $40-$75
Otero Co., NM

G8, $40-$75
Gaines Co., TX

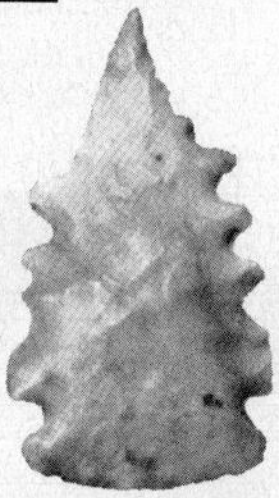

G6, $30-$50
NW Chih., Mex.

G6, $30-$50
Ward Co., TX

G6, $30-$50
Ward Co., TX

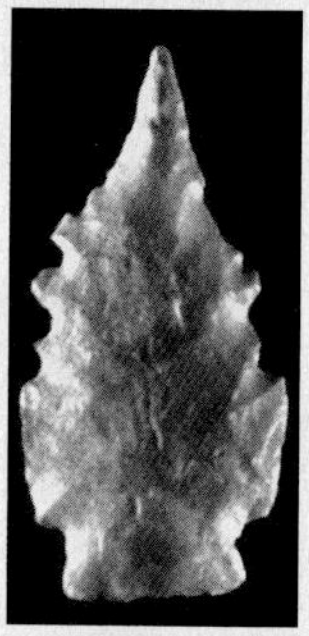

G6, $30-$50
Ward Co., TX

G9, $80-$150
Otero Co., NM

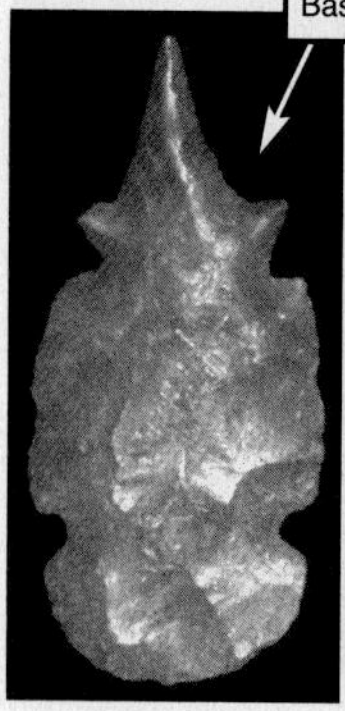

Basalt

Barbed edges

Gray chert

Gray flint

G10, $150-$250
Otero Co., NM

Barbed edges

White chert

G8, $40-$70
Otero Co., NM

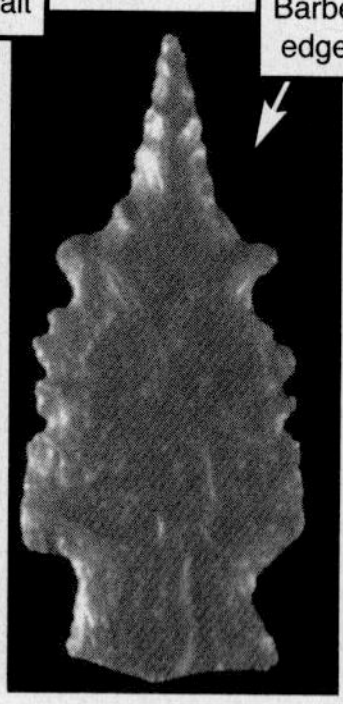

G8, $55-$100
Otero Co., NM

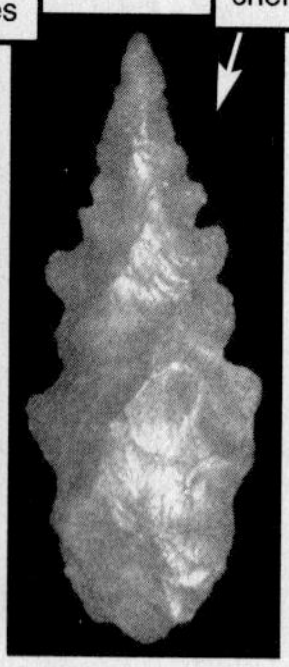

G6, $33-$60
Otero Co., NM

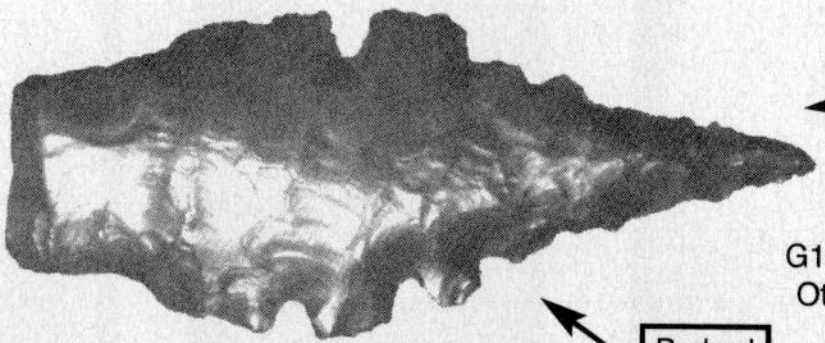

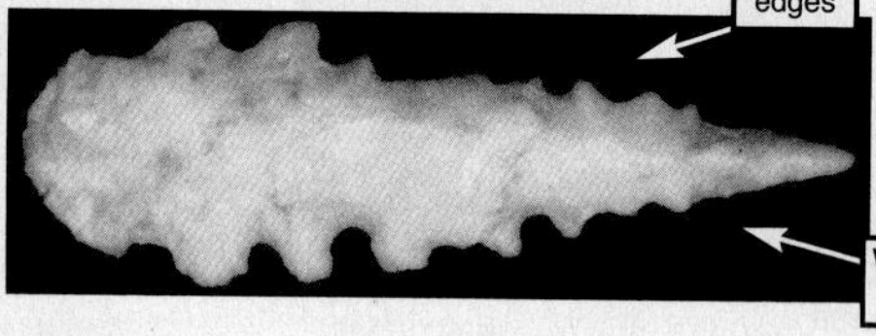

G8, $80-$150
NW Chihuahua, Mex.

860

LOCATION: N.W. Chihuahua, Mexico, Southeastern New Mexico and extreme western Texas. **DESCRIPTION:** A small side notched dart point with a rounded to pointed stem. They are serrated, sometimes heavily, and can acquire extra notches along the blade edges. Similar to *Duran* and *Sinner* found in Texas. **I.D. KEY:** Multiple notching.

MANZANO - Mid to Late Archaic, 5000 - 3000 B. P.

(Also see Augustin, Gypsum Cave and Santa Cruz)

Beveled edge

G8, $25-$40
N.W. NM

G6, $25-$40
Yavapai Co., AZ

LOCATION: N.W. New Mexico into Arizona. **DESCRIPTION:** A medium size, broad, triangular point with a short, contracting, rounded stem. Shoulders are prominent and slightly barbed. Opposite edges are beveled. Related to the *Gypsum Cave* type. **I.D. KEY:** Blade beveling, short stem.

MARTIS - Late Archaic, 3000 - 1500 B. P.

(Also see Northern, San Rafael, Ventana Side Notched)

Red jasper

G6, $20-$35
NW Chihuahua,
Mex, thick

G6, $18-$30
NW Chihuahua,
Mex.

White chert

G6, $15-$25
NW Chihuahua, Mex.

Clear obsidian

G6, $18-$30
NW Chihuahua, Mex.

Gray chert

G8, $30-$50
S. W. TX

S
W

LOCATION: W. Arizona into the Great Basin. **DESCRIPTION:** A small to medium size side notched point with a straight to concave base. Shoulders are tapered to horizontal.

MATAMOROS - Late Archaic to Classic Phase, 3000 - 400 B. P.

(Also see Abasolo, Catan, Early Triangular, Mescal Knife and Triangular Knife)

G8, $25-$40
Mohave Co., AZ

G8, $15-$30
Cochise Co., AZ

G7, $12-$25
W. TX

MATAMOROS (continued)

Brown petrified Palmwood

Black chert

Banded red jasper

G5, $18-$30
Otero Co., NM

G8, $18-$30
Otero Co., NM

G10, $35-$60
N.W. Chihuahua, Mex.

LOCATION: Western Texas into Arizona. **DESCRIPTION:** A small to medium size, broad, triangular point with concave, straight, or convex base. On some examples, beveling occurs on one side of each face as in *Tortugas* points. **I.D. KEY:** Triangular form.

MESCAL KNIFE - Desert Traditions- Classic and Historic Phases, 700 B. P. to historic times

(Also see Matamoros, Kinney and Triangular Knife)

LOCATION: Southwestern states. **DESCRIPTION:** A well made triangular blade which was hafted horizontally along one edge.

G9, $120-$200
Yavapai Co., AZ

MESERVE - Early Archaic, 9500 - 8500 B.P.

(Also see Allen, Angostura, Midland and San Jose)

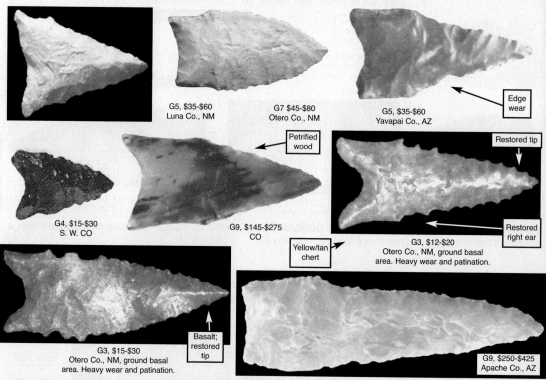

G5, $35-$60
Luna Co., NM

G7 $45-$80
Otero Co., NM

G5, $35-$60
Yavapai Co., AZ

Edge wear

Petrified wood

G4, $15-$30
S. W. CO

G9, $145-$275
CO

Restored tip

Restored right ear

Yellow/tan chert

G3, $12-$20
Otero Co., NM, ground basal area. Heavy wear and patination.

Basalt; restored tip

G3, $15-$30
Otero Co., NM, ground basal area. Heavy wear and patination.

G9, $250-$425
Apache Co., AZ

LOCATION: Throughout the U.S. from the Rocky Mountains to the Mississippi River. **DESCRIPTION:** A member of the *Dalton* Family. Blade edges are straight to slightly concave with a straight to very slightly concave sided stem. They are basally thinned and most examples are beveled and have light serrations on the blade edges. The basal edge is concave. **I.D. KEY:** Squared, concave base.

MIDLAND - Paleo, 10,700 - 10,400 B. P.

(Also see Belen, Folsom, Goshen, Mescal Knife and Milnesand)

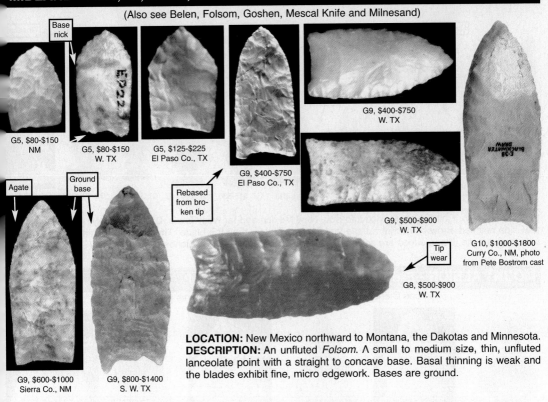

Base nick

G5, $80-$150
NM

G5, $80-$150
W. TX

G5, $125-$225
El Paso Co., TX

G9, $400-$750
El Paso Co., TX

Rebased from broken tip

G9, $400-$750
W. TX

G9, $500-$900
W. TX

Tip wear

G8, $500-$900
W. TX

G10, $1000-$1800
Curry Co., NM, photo
from Pete Bostrom cast

Agate

Ground base

G9, $600-$1000
Sierra Co., NM

G9, $800-$1400
S. W. TX

LOCATION: New Mexico northward to Montana, the Dakotas and Minnesota.
DESCRIPTION: An unfluted *Folsom*. A small to medium size, thin, unfluted lanceolate point with a straight to concave base. Basal thinning is weak and the blades exhibit fine, micro edgework. Bases are ground.

MILNESAND - Transitional Paleo, 11,000 - 8000 B. P.

(Also see Folsom, Goshen and Midland)

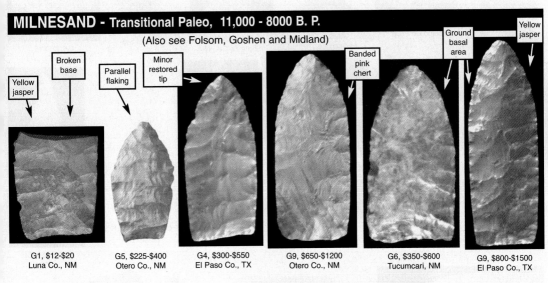

Yellow jasper

Broken base

Parallel flaking

Minor restored tip

Banded pink chert

Ground basal area

Yellow jasper

G1, $12-$20
Luna Co., NM

G5, $225-$400
Otero Co., NM

G4, $300-$550
El Paso Co., TX

G9, $650-$1200
Otero Co., NM

G6, $350-$600
Tucumcari, NM

G9, $800-$1500
El Paso Co., TX

LOCATION: Texas, New Mexico northward to Canada. **DESCRIPTION:** Medium size unfluted lanceolate point that becomes thicker and wider towards the tip. The base is basically square and ground. Thicker than *Midland*. A scarce type. **I.D. KEY:** Square base and Paleo parallel flaking.

Ground stem sides & base

G8, $700-$1200
Chihuahua, MX

Yellow jasper

S W

863

MIMBRE - Developmental Phase, 800 B. P.

(Also see Del Carmen, Desert, Dry Prong, Nawthis and Sacaton)

Obsidian

G7, $15-$25

Obsidian

G6, $12-$20

G6, $12-$20

Obsidian

G6, $12-$20

G6, $12-$20

Black basalt

Red jasper

Black basalt

Red jasper

Black obsidian

Black obsidian

G6, $15-$25   G7, $15-$30   G8, $25-$40

G8, $25-$40   G7, $18-$30   G7, $15-$30   G8, $25-$40   G7, $15-$30   G9, $30-$50   G9, $30-$50

All from N.W. Chihuahua, Mexico

LOCATION: N.W. Chihuahua, Mexico into Sou. New Mexico and far west Texas. **DESCRIPTION:** A small size, narrow, side notched arrow point with a base that flares out wider than the blade. The base is straight to slightly incurvate to excurvate. Blade edges are serrated. **I.D. KEY:** Broad base, wide notches.

MOUNT ALBION - Early to Middle Archaic, 5800 - 5350 B. P.

(Also see Cienega, Elko Corner Notched, Figueroa, Martis and San Pedro)

Tip wear

G6, $5-$10
NM

G5, $8-$15
Hidalgo Co., NM

G8, $20-$35
Hidalgo Co., NM

G7, $12-$20
Santa Fe Co., NM

G7, $25-$45
S. W. CO

G5, $8-$15
Cochise Co., AZ

G8, $30-$55
NM

G8, $30-$55
NM

G8, $30-$55
NM

G6, $20-$35
Luna Co., NM

G7, $25-$45
AZ

G8, $25-$45
NM

G7, $25-$45
NM

G7, $15-$30
Cochise Co., AZ

G8, $25-$45
Cochise Co., AZ

LOCATION: Northeastern Arizona, southeastern Utah, northern New Mexico and southern Colorado. **DESCRIP-TION:** A medium sized dart/knife with small side to corner notches, an expanded stem and convex blade edges. The basal edge is convex. **I.D. KEY:** Large expanded, convex base

---

MOYOTE - Early to Mid-Archaic, 7000 - 4500 B. P.

(Also see Bell, Cienega, Elko Corner Notched, Figueroa, Marshall, Shumla)

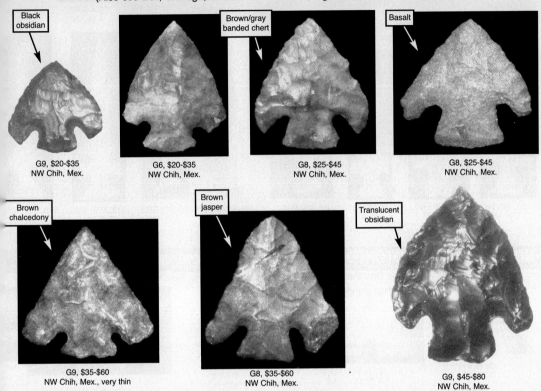

Black obsidian

G9, $20-$35
NW Chih, Mex.

G6, $20-$35
NW Chih, Mex.

Brown/gray banded chert

G8, $25-$45
NW Chih, Mex.

Basalt

G8, $25-$45
NW Chih, Mex.

Brown chalcedony

G9, $35-$60
NW Chih, Mex., very thin

Brown jasper

G8, $35-$60
NW Chih, Mex.

Translucent obsidian

G9, $45-$80
NW Chih, Mex.

LOCATION: N.W. Chihuahua, Mex. **DESCRIPTION:** A medium size, thin, broad, corner notched point with an expanding stem. Blade edges can be straight to convex. Base is mostly convex but can be straight. Barbs are broad and squarrish and some examples show a clipped wing on at least one barb. **I.D. KEY:** Broadness and angle of notching.

NAWTHIS - Developmental Phase, 1100 - 700 B.P.

(Also see Buck Taylor Side Notched, Desert, Mimbre and Sacaton)

LOCATION: Northern New Mexico into Colorado. **DESCRIPTION:** A well made, side notched arrow point. It is triangular in shape with deep, narrow notches placed low on the blade. **I.D. KEY:** Low, deep and narrow side notches.

G8, $15-$30
NM

NEFF - Late Archaic, 3500 - 2300 B. P.

(Also see Ahumada, Duran, Escobas, Maljamar and San Jose)

LOCATION: Eastern New Mexico and western Texas. **DESCRIPTION:** A small to medium sized dart/knife with an expanded stem, drooping shoulders and multiple notches between the shoulders and tip. Another variation similar to *Duran, Sinner* and *Livermore* found in Texas. **I.D. KEY:** Large expanded, convex base.

S W

NEFF (continued)

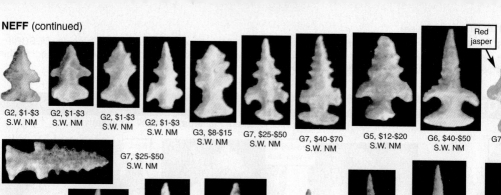

G2, $1-$3 S.W. NM	G2, $1-$3 S.W. NM	G2, $1-$3 S.W. NM

Red jasper

G2, $1-$3 S.W. NM

G3, $8-$15 S.W. NM

G7, $25-$50 S.W. NM

G7, $40-$70 S.W. NM

G5, $12-$20 S.W. NM

G6, $40-$50 S.W. NM

G7, $25-$4 AZ

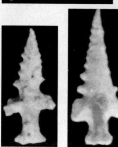

G7, $25-$50 S.W. NM

G7, $45-$80 S.W. NM

G8, $60-$115 S.W. NM

G8, $50-$90 S.W. NM

G8, $60-$115 S.W. NM

G8, $60-$115 S.W. NM

G9, $95-$185 S.W. NM

G10, $150-$265 S.W. NM

G10, $150-$265 S.W. NM

NORTHERN SIDE NOTCHED - Early to Late Archaic, 9000 - 3000 B. P.

(Also see San Pedro, San Rafael, Sudden, Ventana Side Notched,)

G6 $8-$15 S. W. CO

G6 $8-$15 S. W. CO

G7, $12-$20 NM

G9, $25-$40 NW Chih, Mex.

Red jaspe

Fiery red plume agate with black; unique

LOCATION: Great Basin states into Utah, Arizona and N. Mexico. **DESCRIPTION:** A medium to large size, narrow side-notched point with early forms showing basal grinding and parallel flaking. Bases are usually concave to eared. Shoulders are tapered to horizontal. **I.D. KEY:** Broad side notched point.

G10+ $2500-$4500+ San Juan Co., UT

PADRE - Developmental to Classic Phase, 800 - 400 B.P.

(Also see Cottonwood, Embudo & Pelona)

All from N.W. Chihuahua, MX, $5-10 ea.

LOCATION: N.W. Chihuahua, Mex. **DESCRIPTION:** A small size, thin, lonzenge to ovoid shapped arrow point. Fine serrations can occur on some examples. Bases are convex. Generally smaller than Pelona points found in Arizona. **I.D. KEY:** Tear drop form.

PALMILLAS - Middle to Late Archaic, 6000 - 3000 B. P.

(Also see Axtel, Godley, Williams, Yavapai)

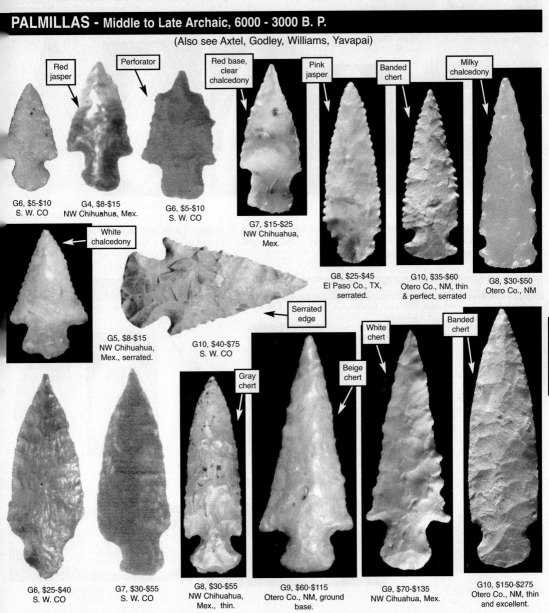

Red jasper

Perforator

Red base, clear chalcedony

Pink jasper

Banded chert

Milky chalcedony

G6, $5-$10
S. W. CO

G4, $8-$15
NW Chihuahua, Mex.

G6, $5-$10
S. W. CO

G7, $15-$25
NW Chihuahua, Mex.

G8, $25-$45
El Paso Co., TX, serrated.

G10, $35-$60
Otero Co., NM, thin & perfect, serrated

G8, $30-$50
Otero Co., NM

White chalcedony

Serrated edge

G5, $8-$15
NW Chihuahua, Mex., serrated.

G10, $40-$75
S. W. CO

White chert

Banded chert

Gray chert

Beige chert

G6, $25-$40
S. W. CO

G7, $30-$55
S. W. CO

G8, $30-$55
NW Chihuahua, Mex., thin.

G9, $60-$115
Otero Co., NM, ground base.

G9, $70-$135
NW Cihuahua, Mex.

G10, $150-$275
Otero Co., NM, thin and excellent.

S W

PALMILLAS (continued)

LOCATION: Texas to Oklahoma. **DESCRIPTION:** A small to medium size triangular point with a bulbous stem. Shoulders are prominent and can be horizontal to barbed or weak and tapered. Stems expand and are rounded. **I.D KEY:** Bulbous stem.

PAROWAN - Desert Traditions-Developmental Phase, 1300 - 800 B. P.

(Also see Augustin, Basal Double Tang, Hodges Contracting and Santa Cruz)

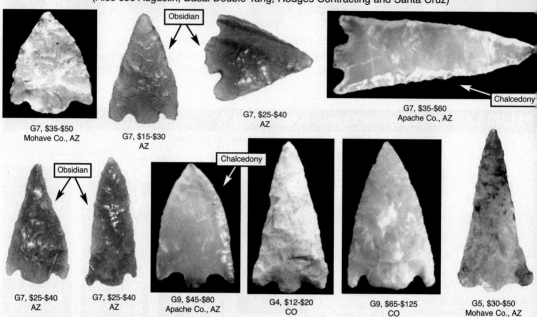

LOCATION: Southern Utah, northern Arizona and into Nevada & Colorado. **DESCRIPTION**: A medium to large triangular arrowpoint with two shallow basal notches creating a short straight to contracting stem. **I.D. KEY:** Stem and barbs are the same length when pristine.

PELONA - Early to Middle Archaic, 6000 - 4000 B. P.

(Also see Abasolo, Catan, Cottonwood, Datil, Embudo, Lerma, Padre and Refugio)

868

| G8, $25-$45 Luna Co., NM | G8, $25-$45 Dona Ana Co., NM | G7, $20-$35 Dona Ana Co., NM | G7, $25-$45 Apache Co., AZ | G7, $30-$55 Luna Co., NM | G9, $35-$65 Apache Co., AZ |

LOCATION: Southern Arizona, southwestern New Mexico and southeastern California. **DESCRIPTION:** Ranges from lozenge to ovoid in shape. It may have serrations on the blade, or, less frequently, on the hafting area, or, in most cases, not serrated.

PERFORATOR - Archaic to Historic, 9000 - 400 B. P.

(Also see Drill, Graver and Scraper)

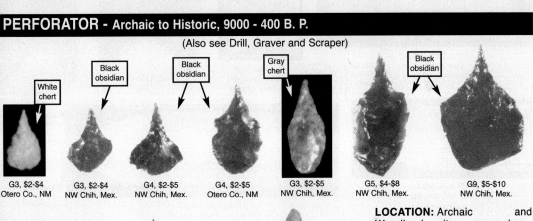

| G3, $2-$4 Otero Co., NM | G3, $2-$4 NW Chih, Mex. | G4, $2-$5 NW Chih, Mex. | G4, $2-$5 Otero Co., NM | G3, $2-$5 NW Chih, Mex. | G5, $4-$8 NW Chih, Mex. | G9, $5-$10 NW Chih, Mex. |

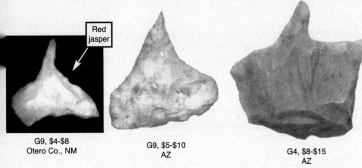

| G9, $4-$8 Otero Co., NM | G9, $5-$10 AZ | G4, $8-$15 AZ |

LOCATION: Archaic and Woodland sites everywhere. **DESCRIPTION:** A jabbing projection at the tip would qualify for the type. It is believed that *perforators* were used for tattooing, incising or punching holes in leather or other materials or objects. Paleo peoples used *Gravers* for the same purpose. All Archaic and Woodland cultures converted their points into this type. Therefore, most point types could occur in this form.

S
W

PINTO BASIN - Early to Late Archaic, 8000 - 3000 B. P.

(Also see Duncan and Hanna)

| G4, $2-$4 S. W. CO | G4, $8-$15 Apache Co., AZ | G5, $8-$15 S. W. CO | G4, $4-$8 S. W. CO |

PINTO BASIN (continued)

LOCATION: Arizona, New Mexico into E. California, Utah, Nevada, Idaho and Oregon. **DESCRIPTION**: A medium size auriculate point. Shoulders can be tapered, horizontal or barbed. Bases are either deeply bifurcated with parallel to expanding ears or tapered with a concave basal edge. **I.D. KEY:** Bifurcated base.

PLAINVIEW - Late Paleo, 10,000 - 7000 B. P.

(Also see Allen, Angostura, Clovis, Golondrina, Goshen)

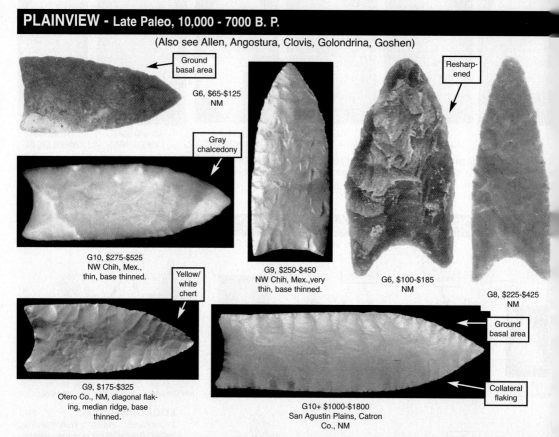

Ground basal area

G6, $65-$125 NM

Gray chalcedony

Resharpened

G10, $275-$525 NW Chih, Mex., thin, base thinned.

Yellow/ white chert

G9, $250-$450 NW Chih, Mex.,very thin, base thinned.

G6, $100-$185 NM

G8, $225-$425 NM

Ground basal area

G9, $175-$325 Otero Co., NM, diagonal flaking, median ridge, base thinned.

Collateral flaking

G10+ $1000-$1800 San Agustin Plains, Catron Co., NM

LOCATION: Mexico northward to Canada. **DESCRIPTION:** A medium to large size, thin, lanceolate point with usually parallel sides and a concave base that is ground. Some examples are thinned or fluted and is believed to be related to the earlier *Clovis* and contemporary *Dalton* type. Flaking is of high quality and can be collateral to oblique transverse. **I.D. KEY:** Base form, thinness.

POINT OF PINES SIDE NOTCHED - Dev. Phase, 850 - 700 B. P.

(Also see Kin Kletso, Pueblo Side notched, Salado, Snaketown Triangular & Walnut Canyon)

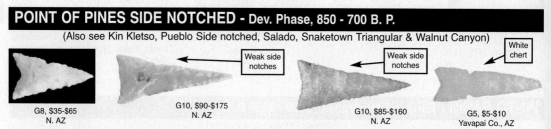

White chert

Weak side notches

Weak side notches

G8, $35-$65 N. AZ

G10, $90-$175 N. AZ

G10, $85-$160 N. AZ

G5, $5-$10 Yavapai Co., AZ

LOCATION: Arizona. **DESCRIPTION**: A small size, thin, triangular, arrow point with a concave base, needle tip and weak side notches. Notches occur about half way up from the base. Basal corners are sharp. **I.D. KEY:** Triangular form with weak side notches.

PUEBLO ALTO SIDE NOTCHED - Developmental Phase, 1000 - 800 B. P.

(Also see Awatovi Side Notched, Bonito, Desert, Pueblo Arroyo, Temporal)

PUEBLO ALTO SIDE NOTCHED (continued)

LOCATION: S.W. colorado into Utah, Arizona & New Mexico. **DESCRIPTION:** A small, thin, triangular arrow point with side notches. Bases are mostly convex, rarely straight with rounded corners

G9, $15-$30
Apache Co., AZ

Shoulder wear

G6, $5-$10
Apache Co., AZ

PUEBLO DEL ARROYO SIDE NOTCHED - Developmental Phase, 1000 - 800 B. P.

(Also see Bonito, Desert, Pueblo Alto, Pueblo Side Notched)

Chalc.

G8, $25-$40
S.W. CO

G10, $40-$75
Montez. Co., CO

G9, $35-$60
Montez. Co., CO

LOCATION: S.W. Colorado into Utah, Arizona & New Mexico. **DESCRIPTION:** A small, thin, triangular arrow point with side notches that are close to the base and are angled upward toward the tip. Bases are straight with square corners.

PUEBLO SIDE NOTCHED - Dev. to Classic Phase, 850 - 500 B. P.

(Also see Awatovi Side Notched, Buck Taylor Notched, Desert, Salado, Walnut Canyon)

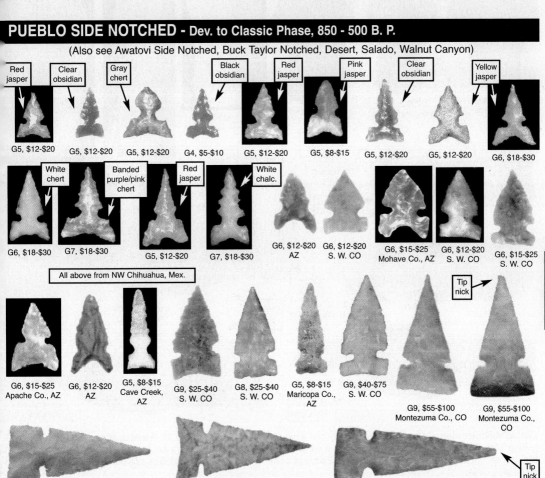

Red jasper — G5, $12-$20

Clear obsidian — G5, $12-$20

Gray chert — G5, $12-$20

G4, $5-$10

Black obsidian — G5, $12-$20

Red jasper — G5, $8-$15

Pink jasper — G5, $12-$20

Clear obsidian — G5, $12-$20

Yellow jasper — G6, $18-$30

White chert — G6, $18-$30

G7, $18-$30

Banded purple/pink chert — G5, $12-$20

Red jasper — G7, $18-$30

White chalc. — G6, $12-$20

G6, $12-$20 AZ

G6, $15-$25 Mohave Co., AZ

G6, $12-$20 S. W. CO

G6, $15-$25 S. W. CO

All above from NW Chihuahua, Mex.

G6, $15-$25 Apache Co., AZ

G6, $12-$20 AZ

G5, $8-$15 Cave Creek, AZ

G9, $25-$40 S. W. CO

G8, $25-$40 S. W. CO

G5, $8-$15 Maricopa Co., AZ

G9, $40-$75 S. W. CO

Tip nick

G9, $55-$100 Montezuma Co., CO

G9, $55-$100 Montezuma Co., CO

G10, $80-$150 Montezuma Co., CO

G10, $80-$150 S. W. CO

G9, $65-$125 Montezuma Co., CO

Tip nick

S W

LOCATION: Sou. California into Arizona, New Mexico and N. Mex. **DESCRIPTION**: A small size, thin, triangular, side notched arrow point with a straight to concave base. Notches can occur one fourth to half way up from the base. Basal corners can be squared to eared. **I.D. KEY:** Triangular form with side notches.

RED HORN (see Buck Taylor Notched and White Mountain Side Notched)

REFUGIO - Middle Archaic, 5000 - 2000 B. P.

(Also see Abasolo, Lerma, Pelona)

LOCATION: New Mexico into Texas.
DESCRIPTION: A medium to large size, narrow, lanceolate blade with a rounded base.

G7, $20-$35
Otero Co., NM

RIO GRANDE - Early Archaic, 7500 - 6000 B. P.

(Also see Agate Basin, Angostura, Bajada, Escobas, Hell Gap, Jay, Lake Mohave, Madden Lake)

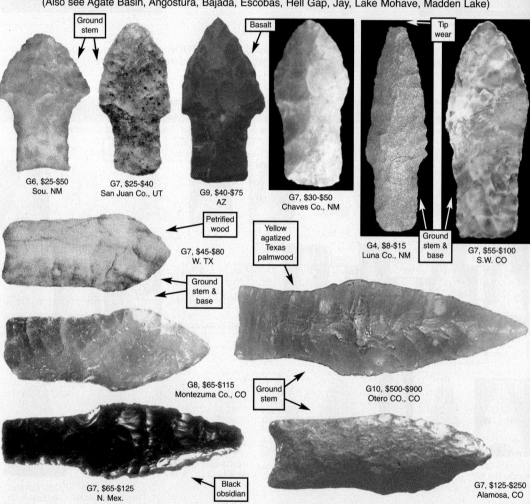

Ground stem

Basalt

Tip wear

G6, $25-$50
Sou. NM

G7, $25-$40
San Juan Co., UT

G9, $40-$75
AZ

G7, $30-$50
Chaves Co., NM

G4, $8-$15
Luna Co., NM

Ground stem & base

G7, $55-$100
S.W. CO

Petrified wood

G7, $45-$80
W. TX

Yellow agatized Texas palmwood

Ground stem & base

G8, $65-$115
Montezuma Co., CO

Ground stem

G10, $500-$900
Otero CO., CO

G7, $65-$125
N. Mex.

Black obsidian

G7, $125-$250
Alamosa, CO

LOCATION: Southern Colorado, New Mexico and western Texas. **DESCRIPTION:** A lanceolate point with a relatively long stem formed by obtuse shoulders. The stem contracts slightly and stem edges are ground. Developed from the earlier *Jay* point and related to the later *Escobas* point. **I.D. KEY:** The shoulders are more pronounced than on *Hell Gap* points.

ROSE SPRINGS CORNER NOTCHED - Developmental Phase, 1600 - 700 B. P.

(Also see Chaco Corner Notched, Convento, Bonito and Desert)

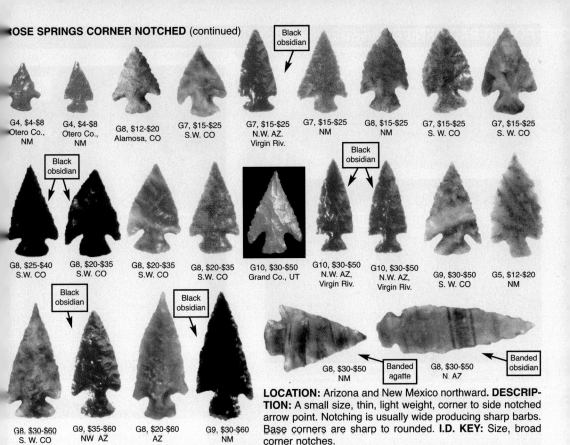

Black obsidian

G4, $4-$8
Otero Co.,
NM

G4, $4-$8
Otero Co.,
NM

G8, $12-$20
Alamosa, CO

G7, $15-$25
S.W. CO

G7, $15-$25
N.W. AZ.
Virgin Riv.

G7, $15-$25
NM

G7, $15-$25
NM

G8, $15-$25
NM

G7, $15-$25
S. W. CO

G7, $15-$25
S. W. CO

Black obsidian

Black obsidian

G8, $25-$40
S.W. CO

G8, $20-$35
S.W. CO

G8, $20-$35
S.W. CO

G8, $20-$35
S.W. CO

G10, $30-$50
Grand Co., UT

G10, $30-$50
N.W. AZ,
Virgin Riv.

G10, $30-$50
N.W. AZ,
Virgin Riv.

G9, $30-$50
S. W. CO

G5, $12-$20
NM

Black obsidian

Black obsidian

Banded agatte

Banded obsidian

G8, $30-$50
NM

G8, $30-$50
N. AZ

G8, $30-$60
S. W. CO

G9, $35-$60
NW AZ

G8, $20-$60
AZ

G9, $30-$60
NM

LOCATION: Arizona and New Mexico northward. **DESCRIPTION:** A small size, thin, light weight, corner to side notched arrow point. Notching is usually wide producing sharp barbs. Base corners are sharp to rounded. **I.D. KEY:** Size, broad corner notches.

ROSE SPRINGS STEMMED - Developmental Phase, 1600 - 700 B. P.

(Also see Cohonina Stemmed & Snaketown)

G7, $8-$15
AZ

G7, $25-$40
Alamosa, CO

G6, $20-$35
Costilla Co., CO

G5, $15-$25
Costilla Co., CO

Quartzite

Agate

G7, $35-$70
Alamosa, CO

Finely serrated

G7, $12-$20
AZ

G10+, $175-$300
S.W. CO

G9, $125-$200
Elko Co., NV

G6, $12-$20
NM

S W

LOCATION: Arizona and New Mexico northward. **DESCRIPTION:** A small to medium size, thin, narrow, light weight, stemmed arrow point. Stems are parallel sided to tapered to expanding. Bases are incurvate to rounded. Larger examples are dart/knives. **I.D. KEY:** Thinness and narrowness.

(Also see Agate Basin, Early Leaf, Lerma, Refugio)

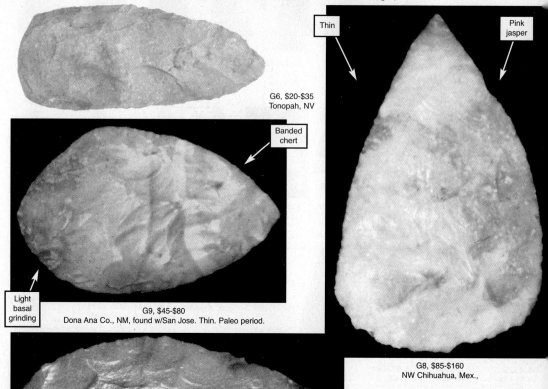

G6, $20-$35
Tonopah, NV

Thin

Pink jasper

Banded chert

Light basal grinding

G9, $45-$80
Dona Ana Co., NM, found w/San Jose. Thin. Paleo period.

G8, $85-$160
NW Chihuahua, Mex.,

LOCATION: Arizona into N.W. Chihuahua, Mexico. **DESCRIPTION:** A large size lanceolate blade with a convex base. Some examples are very thin and well made. **I.D. KEY:** Convex base.

G8, $40-$75
NW Chihuahua, Mex.,

G8, $150-$250
S. W. CO

SACATON - Desert Traditions-Developmental Phase, 1100 - 900 B. P.

(Also see Desert, Dry Prong, Mimbre and Temporal)

Clear obsidian

G8, $25-$40
NM

G8, $25-$40
NM

G7, $15-$30
Apache Co., AZ

G6, $8-$15
Mohave Co., AZ

LOCATION: Arizona and central and southwestern New Mexico. **DESCRIPTION:** A small, triangular arrow point with relatively large side notches placed close to the basal edge. The base is the widest part of the point and is slightly concave. **I.D. KEY:** Wide base.

SALADO - Developmental-Classic Phase, 850 - 500 B.P.

(Also see Desert, Pueblo Side Notched and Walnut Canyon Side Notched)

G6, $15-$25
Cedar
Ridge, AZ

G5, $15-$25
AZ

G8, $25-$45
AZ

G8, $25-$45
NW Chih., MX

G8, $25-$45
Cedar Ridge, AZ

G8, $25-$45
Cedar Ridge,
AZ

G8, $25-$45
Cedar Ridge,
AZ

G7, $25-$45
AZ

G8, $40-$70
AZ

G9, $35-$65
Cedar Ridge,
AZ

G8, $25-$45
Gila River, AZ.

G8, $30-$55
NW Chih., MX

G7, $30-$55
AZ

G6, $25-$45
AZ

G6, $20-$35
N. AZ

G9, $80-$150
AZ

G7, $35-$65
AZ

G10, $80-$150
AZ

G10, $125-$200
AZ

G10, $80-$150
AZ

G9, $65-$125
AZ

G9, $80-$150
AZ

G10, $90-$180
AZ

G10, $90-$180
AZ

LOCATION: Arizona to California. **DESCRIPTION:** A small, thin, arrow point with a straight to concave base and tiny side notches set well up from the base. Related to *Hohokam*. Given this name in Perino #3. Also known as *Pueblo Side Notched*; see Justice, 2002. **I.D. KEY:** Large basal area.

SALT RIVER INDENTED BASE - Developmental, 1150 - 1000 B. P.

(Also see Gila River Corner Notched, Snaketown Side Notched)

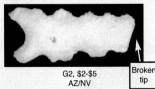

G8, $20-$35
Pima Co., AZ

Red
basalt

G2, $1-$3
AZ/NV

Broken
tip

G3, $2-$5
Yavapai Co., AZ

Broken
tip

G2, $2-$5
AZ/NV

Broken
tip

LOCATION: Arizona and New Mexico. **DESCRIPTION:** A medium size, narrow, spike, auriculate Hohokam arrow point with multiple barbs that are larger close to the base. The base is eared and deeply concave. **I.D. KEY:** Exaggerated barbs and auriculate base.

SAN BRUNO - Classic to Historic Phase, 600 - 200 B. P.

(Also see Desert, Gatlin, Gila River, Pueblo Side Notched, Rose Springs & Snaketown)

SAN BRUNO (continued)

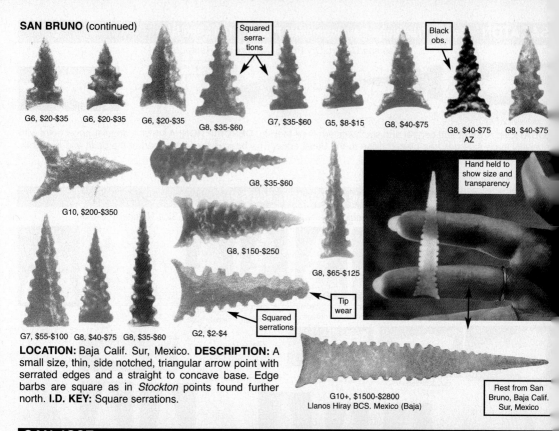

G6, $20-$35

G6, $20-$35

G6, $20-$35

G8, $35-$60 — Squared serrations

G7, $35-$60

G5, $8-$15

G8, $40-$75

G8, $40-$75 AZ — Black obs.

G8, $40-$75

G10, $200-$350

G8, $35-$60

G8, $150-$250

G8, $65-$125

G7, $55-$100

G8, $40-$75

G8, $35-$60

G2, $2-$4 — Squared serrations

Tip wear

Hand held to show size and transparency

G10+, $1500-$2800
Llanos Hiray BCS. Mexico (Baja)

Rest from San Bruno, Baja Calif. Sur, Mexico

LOCATION: Baja Calif. Sur, Mexico. **DESCRIPTION:** A small size, thin, side notched, triangular arrow point with serrated edges and a straight to concave base. Edge barbs are square as in *Stockton* points found further north. **I.D. KEY:** Square serrations.

SAN JOSE - Early Archaic, 9000 - 6000 B. P.

(Also see Bajada, Baker, Barreal, Chiricahua, Duncan, Escobas, Hanna, Maljamar, Meserve, Neff, Snake- town, Soto and Uvalde)

G3, $5-$10
Yavapai Co., AZ

G3, $2-$5
Yavapai Co., AZ

G3, $2-$5
Yavapai Co., AZ

G6, $5-$10
Yavapai Co., AZ

G6, $5-$10
Luna Co., NM — Basalt

G6, $8-$15
Apache Co., AZ

G8, $8-$15
Navajo Co., AZ

G6, $12-$20
Yavapai Co., AZ

G5, $15-$25
Otero Co., NM

G6, $25-$40
NM — Obsidian

G6, $25-$40
San Juan Co., UT — Serrated edge

G6, $25-$40
Otero Co., NM

G8 $35-$60
N.W. Mex. — Serrated edge

LOCATION: Arizona, New Mexico, sou. Utah, Nevada and Colorado. **DESCRIPTION:** A small to medium size dart/knife with wide, shallow side notches creating an auriculate base. The shoulders are obtuse and the blade edges always have relatively large serrations. Stem and base edges are usually ground. Similar to the *Barreal* point of the same age. **I.D. KEY:** Auriculate base.

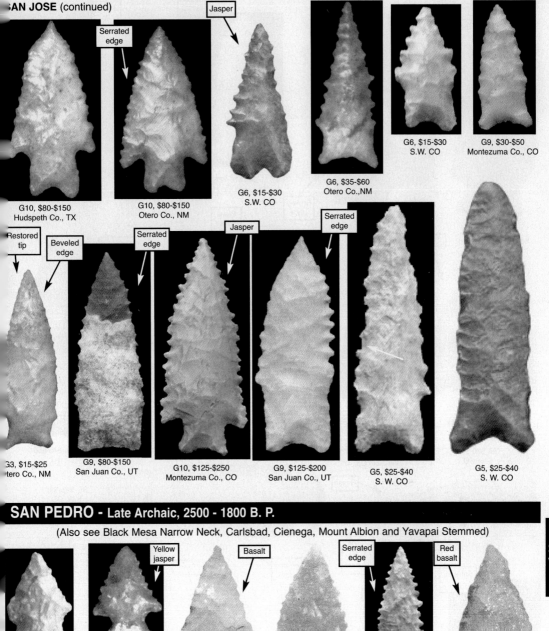

SAN JOSE (continued)

Jasper

Serrated edge

G10, $80-$150
Hudspeth Co., TX

G10, $80-$150
Otero Co., NM

G6, $15-$30
S.W. CO

G6, $35-$60
Otero Co.,NM

G6, $15-$30
S.W. CO

G9, $30-$50
Montezuma Co., CO

Restored tip

Beveled edge

Serrated edge

Jasper

Serrated edge

G3, $15-$25
Otero Co., NM

G9, $80-$150
San Juan Co., UT

G10, $125-$250
Montezuma Co., CO

G9, $125-$200
San Juan Co., UT

G5, $25-$40
S. W. CO

G5, $25-$40
S. W. CO

SAN PEDRO - Late Archaic, 2500 - 1800 B. P.

(Also see Black Mesa Narrow Neck, Carlsbad, Cienega, Mount Albion and Yavapai Stemmed)

Yellow jasper

Basalt

Serrated edge

Red basalt

G3, $2-$5
Cochise Co., AZ

G6, $8-$15
NW Chih., Mex.

G5, $15-$25
Pima Co., AZ

G5, $12-$20
Pima Co., AZ

G10, $25-$40
S.W. CO

G6, $20-$35
Pima Co., AZ

G7, $20-$35
S. W. CO

G7, $20-$35
Navajo Co., AZ

G9, $25-$45
S. W. CO

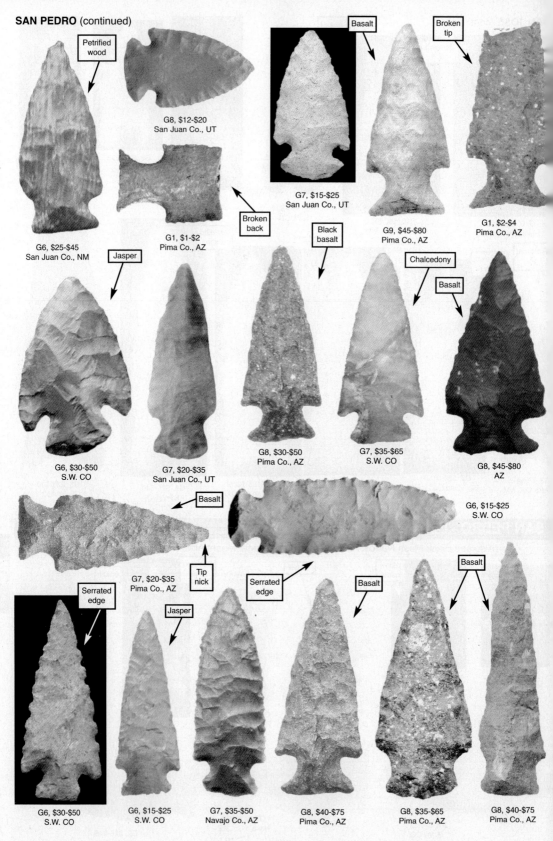

Petrified wood

G8, $12-$20
San Juan Co., UT

Basalt

Broken tip

G6, $25-$45
San Juan Co., NM

Broken back

G1, $1-$2
Pima Co., AZ

G7, $15-$25
San Juan Co., UT

Black basalt

G9, $45-$80
Pima Co., AZ

G1, $2-$4
Pima Co., AZ

Jasper

Chalcedony

Basalt

G6, $30-$50
S.W. CO

G7, $20-$35
San Juan Co., UT

G8, $30-$50
Pima Co., AZ

G7, $35-$65
S.W. CO

G8, $45-$80
AZ

Basalt

G6, $15-$25
S.W. CO

G7, $20-$35
Pima Co., AZ

Tip nick

Serrated edge

Basalt

Basalt

Serrated edge

Jasper

G6, $30-$50
S.W. CO

G6, $15-$25
S.W. CO

G7, $35-$50
Navajo Co., AZ

G8, $40-$75
Pima Co., AZ

G8, $35-$65
Pima Co., AZ

G8, $40-$75
Pima Co., AZ

G7, $30-$50
Cochise Co., AZ

G8, $40-$75
S.W. CO

G7, $25-$45
S. W. CO

G5, $20-$35
Yavapai Co., AZ

G5, $12-$20
Yavapai Co., AZ

Chalcedony

G8, $40-$75
S.W. CO

G6, $35-$65
S.W. CO

Chert

G6, $35-$65
Sou. CA

G6, $35-$65
Montezuma Co., CO

Gray
basalt

Serrated
edge

G9, $80-$165
Pima Co., AZ

G8, $65-$125
San Juan Co., UT

S
W

LOCATION: New Mexico, Arizona and northern Mexico. **DESCRIPTION:** A small to medium sized dart/knife made on a triangular preform and having side notches which begin at the basal corners and range from shallow to as deep as wide. Blade edges may be lightly serrated and the basal edge is straight to slightly convex. This type has been found hafted to foreshafts with sinew and pitch in Utah and New Mexico.

SAN PEDRO (continued)

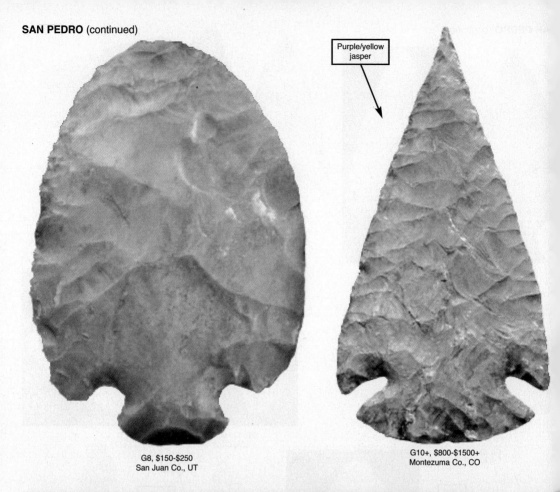

Purple/yellow jasper

G8, $150-$250
San Juan Co., UT

G10+, $800-$1500+
Montezuma Co., CO

SAN RAFAEL - Middle Archaic, 4,400 - 3500 B. P.

(Also see Frio, Martis, Northern Side Notched and Ventana Side Notched)

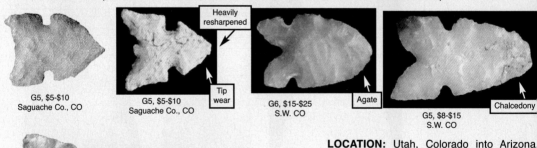

Heavily resharpened

Tip wear

G5, $5-$10
Saguache Co., CO

G5, $5-$10
Saguache Co., CO

G6, $15-$25
S.W. CO

Agate

Chalcedony

G5, $8-$15
S.W. CO

G10, $175-$300
S.W. CO

LOCATION: Utah, Colorado into Arizona.
DESCRIPTION: A medium size, broad, side-notched point with usually a deeply concave to eared base. Some examples include a small notch at the center of the basal concavity. Side notches occur high up from the base and the cross section is very thin. Similar in form to *Mallory* found in the northern plains. **I.D. KEY:** High-up side notches, eared base, thinness.

SANDIA I-III - Paleo, 11,500? - 10,000 B. P.

(Also see Clovis, Folsom and Madden Lake)

SANDIA I-III (continued)

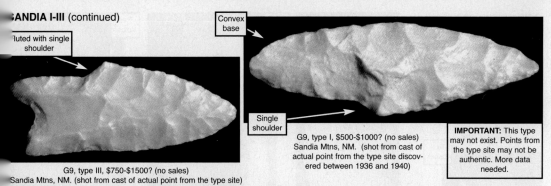

luted with single shoulder

Convex base

Single shoulder

G9, type III, $750-$1500? (no sales)
Sandia Mtns, NM. (shot from cast of actual point from the type site)

G9, type I, $500-$1000? (no sales)
Sandia Mtns, NM. (shot from cast of actual point from the type site discovered between 1936 and 1940)

IMPORTANT: This type may not exist. Points from the type site may not be authentic. More data needed.

Base nick

G6, type II, $350-$700? (no sales)
Sandia Mtns, NM.
(shot from cast of actual point from the type site)

LOCATION: Type site is Sandia Mtns., New Mexico, south of Albuquerque. **DESCRIPTION:** This point was reported to occur in three forms: The first form is a narrow, elliptical shape with only one shoulder and a rounded base. The second form has a slightly concave base, otherwise it is the same as the first form. The third form has a deeply concave base with drooping auricles. This, as well as the second form, have been found fluted on one or both faces. **If the type exists, and it probably doesn't,** it may be later than *Clovis*. Another site with datable context has not yet been found. Originally (questionably?) carbon dated to 20,000 B.P. **I.D. KEY:** Single shoulder.

SANDIA IV (provisional) - Paleo, 11,500? - 10,000 B. P.

(Also see Clovis and Folsom)

Fluting channel

Ground basal area

G9, $1200-$2000
Colfax Co., NM.

LOCATION: This point is found in New Mexico with very few examples known. **DESCRIPTION:** Thin with flaking in the *Folsom* style. This authenticated point is very thin, single shouldered and fluted on both sides. Percussion flaked with fine pressure flaking. Basal area is ground. The classic *Sandia* form, but is thinner and better made than Sandia I-III points which lack the fine pressure flaking. **I.D. KEY:** Single shoulder, fine retouch.

SANTA CRUZ - Desert Traditions-Developmental Phase, 1400-600 B. P.

(Also see Augustin, Gypsum Cave, Hodges Contr. Stem, Manzano and Truxton)

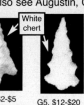

White chert

G7, $25-$40
Apache Co., AZ

G5 $8-$15
Cochise Co., AZ

G5, $12-$20
Coconino Co., AZ

G3, $2-$5
Apache Co., AZ

G3, $2-$5
Apache Co., AZ

G5, $12-$20
Tucson, AZ

G3, $2-$5
Mohave Co., AZ

G5, $8-$15
Apache Co., AZ

LOCATION: Arizona and contiguous parts of adjoining states. **DESCRIPTION:** A small, triangular arrow point with straight to obtuse shoulders and a short, tapering stem. These may prove to be small *Hodges Contracting Stem* points. **I.D. KEY:** Tiny, triangular stem.

SAW - Late Archaic, 3500 - 3000 B. P.

(Also see Drill, Perforator, Scraper)

Beige chert

Gray chert

G5, $2-$5
Otero Co., NM

G4, $1-$3
Otero Co., NM

LOCATION: New Mexico into Texas. **DESCRIPTION:** A small to large size double uniface tool made from a flake with at least on edge with saw-tooth serrations for sawing.

S W

SAW (continued)

Quartz

G6, $5-$10
Otero Co., NM

Red
jasper

G9, $35-$60
Montezuma Co., CO

Beige
chert

G9, $30-$50
Montezuma Co., CO

Red
jasper

G9, $40-$75
Montezuma Co., CO

G9, $35-$60
Montezuma Co., CO

G9, $50-$90
Montezuma
Co., CO

G9, $35-$60
Montezuma Co., CO

G9, $35-$60
Montezuma Co., CO

G9, $40-$70
Montezuma Co., CO

G9, $80-$150
Montezuma Co., CO

SCOTTSBLUFF II - Early Archaic, 9500 - 8500 B. P.

(Also see Bajada, Eden and Firstview)

LOCATION: Midwestern states. **DESCRIP-TION:** A medium to large size triangular point with shoulders a little stronger than on Type I and a broad parallel sided/expanding stem.

Red
jasper

G5, $150-$250
Montezuma Co., CO

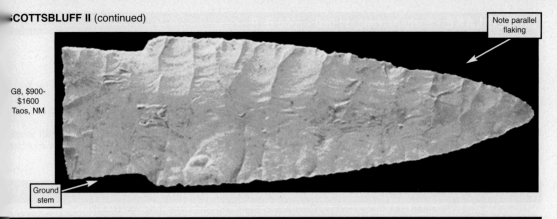

Note parallel flaking

G8, $900-$1600
Taos, NM

Ground stem

SCRAPER - Archaic, 8000 - 2300 B. P.

(Also see Drill, Lancet and Saw)

All NM & TX Thumb scrapers found on a Folsom site

Gray chert

Jasper

Jasper

Jasper

G6, $1-$2
Luna Co., NM

G6, $1-$2
Otero Co., NM

G6, $1-$2
Luna Co., NM

G9, $2-$5
El Paso Co., TX

G5, $1-$2
S. CO

G10, $2-$5
N.W. Chihuahua, MX

G10, $2-$5
N.W. Chihuahua, MX

G5, $1-$2
N.W. Chihuahua, MX

G5, $1-$2
N.W. Chihuahua, MX

All hafted

G5, $1-$2
S. CO

G5, $1-$2
S. CO

G5, $1-$3
S. CO

S W

LOCATION: All of the United States. **DESCRIPTION:** A small to large size scraping tool either made from spent points or fresh from scratch. Thumb and Turtleback scrapers are uniface with steeply beveled edges. Many were hafted while others were hand-held in use.

SHUMLA - Woodland, 3000 - 1000 B. P.

(Also see Acatita, Marshall, Parowan)

G6, $15-$25
San Luis Potosi, MX

LOCATION: Northern Mexico to Oklahoma. **DESCRIPTION:** A small size, basal notched point with convex, straight or recurved sides. Basal corners can be rounded to sharp. Bases are straight to slightly convex. Barbs turn in towards and usually extend to the base. Related to *Acatita* in Mexico?

SILVER LAKE - Early Archaic, 11,000 - 7000 B. P.

(Also see Early Stemmed, Firstview, Lake Mohave and Yavapai)

G9, $85-$150
Yavapai Co., AZ

G6, $30-$50
NV

LOCATION: Arizona, Nevada to California. **DESCRIPTION:** A medium to large size, stemmed point with weak tapered shoulders and usually a serrated edge. The stem can be up to half its length. The base is usually rounded and ground. **I.D. KEY:** Long stem, weak shoulders.

SNAKETOWN - Desert Traditions-Developmental Phase, 1200-1050 B. P.

(Also see Gila River, Hodges Contracting Stem and Salt River Indented Base)

G10, $150-$250
Kearny, AZ

Serrated edge

LOCATION: Arizona. **DESCRIPTION:** A very rare, form of *Hohokam* arrow point. The stem is straight to expanded and sometimes concave to bifurcated and has large serrations on both sides of the blade. Some examples are serrated on the lower half of the point. **I.D. KEY:** Narrowness, length, broad serrations.

SNAKETOWN SIDE NOTCHED - Dev.-Classic Phase, 800-600 B. P.

(Also see Bonito Notched, Gatlin, Gila River, Pueblo Side Notched)

G6, $5-$10
Yavapai Co., AZ

G5, $12-$20
Apache Co., AZ

G9, $25-$45
Pima Co., AZ

G6, $15-$30
Apache Co., AZ

G9, $35-$50
Yavapai Co., AZ

LOCATION: Southern California into Arizona and New Mexico. **DESCRIPTION:** A small, serrated, side notched, *Hohokam* triangular arrow point with a concave to straight base. Basal corners are wide and rounded. Notches are broad. **I.D. KEY:** Broad notches.

G6 $15-$30
S. W. CO

SNAKETOWN TRIANGULAR - Developmental Phase, 1050-850 B. P.

(Also see Bull Creek, Salt River Indented Base, Sobaipuri, Soto)

Black obsidian

Gray basalt

White chert

Straight base form

G7, $15-$25
Pima Co., AZ

G7, $15-$25
Pima Co., AZ

G7, $15-$25
Maricopa Co., AZ

G7, $15-$25
Cedar Ridge, AZ

G7, $15-$30
Pima Co., AZ

G6, $8-$15
Yavapai Co., AZ.

G7, $15-$25
Cedar Ridge, AZ

G6, $8-$15
Cedar Ridge, AZ

G7, $15-$25
Cave Cr., AZ

Red basalt

Gray basalt

Straight base form

Broken tip

Drill form

Dacite

G8, $20-$35
AZ

G8, $15-$25
Pinal Co., AZ

G7, $8-$15
Maricopa Co., AZ

G8, $30-$55
Apache Co., AZ

G9, $25-$40
AZ

G9, $30-$50
AZ

G9, $40-$70
Gila River, AZ

G8, $40-$75
Pima Co., AZ

G3, $5-$10
AZ

Straight base form

G10, $250-$450
AZ

NAKETOWN TRIANGULAR (continued)

G7, $15-$30
Cedar Ridge, AZ

G10, $25-$40, Pinal Co., AZ

White chert

LOCATION: Southern California into Arizona and New Mexico. **DESCRIPTION:** A small, serrated, triangular *Hohokam* arrow point with a concave to straight base. Made by the Hohokam people. **I.D. KEY:** Wild barbs.

SOBAIPURI - Classic to Historic Phase, 500 - 200 B. P.

(Also see Aguaje, Bull Creek, Cottonwood, Salt River Indented Base and Snaketown)

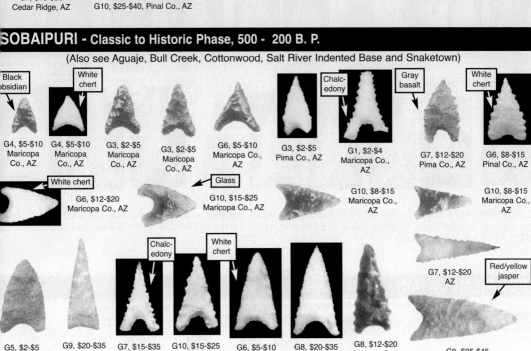

Black obsidian

White chert

G4, $5-$10 Maricopa Co., AZ

G4, $5-$10 Maricopa Co., AZ

G3, $2-$5 Maricopa Co., AZ

G3, $2-$5 Maricopa Co., AZ

G6, $5-$10 Maricopa Co., AZ

G3, $2-$5 Pima Co., AZ

Chalcedony

G1, $2-$4 Maricopa Co., AZ

Gray basalt

G7, $12-$20 Pima Co., AZ

White chert

G6, $8-$15 Pinal Co., AZ

White chert

G6, $12-$20 Maricopa Co., AZ

Glass

G10, $15-$25 Maricopa Co., AZ

G10, $8-$15 Maricopa Co., AZ

G10, $8-$15 Maricopa Co., AZ

Chalcedony

White chert

G5, $2-$5 Maricopa Co., AZ

G9, $20-$35 Yavapai Co., AZ

G7, $15-$35 Maricopa Co., AZ

G10, $15-$25 Maricopa Co., AZ

G6, $5-$10 Maricopa Co., AZ

G8, $20-$35 Maricopa Co., AZ

G8, $12-$20 Mohave Co., AZ

G7, $12-$20 AZ

Red/yellow jasper

G9, $25-$45 Pima Co., AZ, diagonal flaking.

LOCATION: Southern Arizona, New Mexico and northern Mexico. **DESCRIPTION:** A small triangular, finely serrated, arrow point with convex sides and a deep, concave basal notch. **I.D. KEY:** Small triangular point with serrations.

SOCORRO - Late Archaic, 3000 B. P.

(Also see Acatita, Cienega and Gobernadora, Yavapai)

Needle tip & barbs

G9, $65-$125 NM

G9, $75-$140 NM

G10, $85-$165 NM

G10, $90-$175 NM

G10, $90-$175 NM

LOCATION: Northern Mexico into New Mexico. **DESCRIPTION:** A medium size dart/knife point with a long needle tip and sharp, drooping barbs that can turn inward. Stems are generally long and expanding to slightly contracting with a straight to bulbous base.

SOTO - Classic Phase to Early Historic, 1000-700 B. P.

(Also see Awatovi, Del Carmen, Garza, Pueblo Side Notched, San Jose and Toyah)

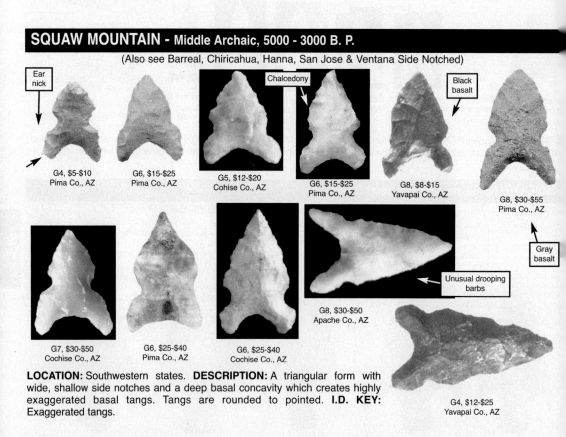

Black basalt

G6, $10-$20 G6, $8-$15 G7, $15-$25 G7, $12-$20 Otero Co., NM G6, $10-$20 G6, $15-$25

White agate Red agate

G6, $15-$30 G6, $10-$20 G7, $20-$30 G8, $20-$35

All others from N.W. Chihuahua, Mexico

Yel/red jasper

Yellow jasper Fine serrations Pink jasper

G8, $20-$35 G8, $25-$40 G9, $25-$40 ea. G9, $25-$40 G9, $25-$40 G9, $30-$50 G9, $30-$50

LOCATION: NW Chihuahua Mexico. **DESCRIPTION:** A small, serrated arrow point with expanding ears, weak shoulders and a concave base. Most are made of agate and jasper. Similar to Garza & Toyah. Named by Alan Phelps. **I.D. KEY:** Thinness, drooping ears.

SQUAW MOUNTAIN - Middle Archaic, 5000 - 3000 B. P.

(Also see Barreal, Chiricahua, Hanna, San Jose & Ventana Side Notched)

Ear nick

Chalcedony Black basalt

G4, $5-$10 Pima Co., AZ G6, $15-$25 Pima Co., AZ G5, $12-$20 Cohise Co., AZ G6, $15-$25 Pima Co., AZ G8, $8-$15 Yavapai Co., AZ G8, $30-$55 Pima Co., AZ

Gray basalt

Unusual drooping barbs

G8, $30-$50 Apache Co., AZ

G7, $30-$50 Cochise Co., AZ G6, $25-$40 Pima Co., AZ G6, $25-$40 Cochise Co., AZ

G4, $12-$25 Yavapai Co., AZ

LOCATION: Southwestern states. **DESCRIPTION:** A triangular form with wide, shallow side notches and a deep basal concavity which creates highly exaggerated basal tangs. Tangs are rounded to pointed. **I.D. KEY:** Exaggerated tangs.

SUDDEN SERIES - Early to Mid Archaic, 6300 - 4180 B. P.

(Also see Northern Side Notch, San Rafael & Ventana Side Notched)

"Rocker" form

Black basalt

Straight base form

G9, $25-$45
S. W. CO

G8, $35-$60
UT

G9, $35-$65
S. W. CO

G7, $25-$45
S. W. CO

G7, $25-$45
S. W. CO

G9, $45-$80
S. W. CO

"Rocker" form

Stripped agate

"Rocker" form

G5, $25-$40
S.E. UT., regular
"Sudden" side-notch.

G10, $65-$125
S. W. CO

G9, $60-$115
Montezuma Co., CO

G8, $45-$80
S. W. CO

G8, $60-$115
S. W. CO

Banded quartz

Red material

Shoulder wear

G6, $35-$60
S. W. CO

Red jasper

G9, $80-$150
S. W. CO

G6, $40-$75
S. W. CO

G6, $40-$75
San Juan Co., NM

G6, $40-$75
S. W. CO

S W

LOCATION: SE Utah, S.W. Colorado into Arizona. **DESCRIPTION:** A medium size side notched dart/knife point that comes in two forms. Side notches are high up from the base. The regular form has a large basal area and a straight to concave base. The "Rocker" form has a convex base.

TEMPORAL - Desert Traditions-Developmental Phase, 1000 - 800 B. P.

(Also see Bonito Notched, Desert, Dry Prong and Sacaton)

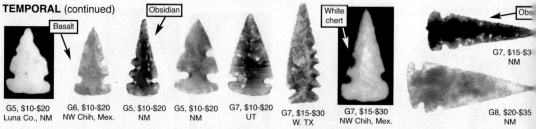

Basalt — Obsidian — White chert — Obs

G5, $10-$20
Luna Co., NM

G6, $10-$20
NW Chih, Mex.

G5, $10-$20
NM

G5, $10-$20
NM

G7, $10-$20
UT

G7, $15-$30
W. TX

G7, $15-$30
NW Chih, Mex.

G7, $15-$3
NM

G8, $20-$35
NM

LOCATION: New Mexico, Arizona and western Texas. **DESCRIPTION:** A small side notched arrow point with one o two extra notches on one side. It is triangular with straight sides and a convex basal edge. Notches are narrow and deeper than they are wide. **I.D. KEY:** Rounded or rocker like basal edge.

TEXCOCO - Late Archaic, 6000 - 5000 B.P.

(Also see Elko Corner Notched, Mount Albion and San Pedro)

Straight base — Concave base — Straight base

G4, $3-$5

G4, $3-$5

G5, $6-$10

G7, $12-$20

G7, $15-$25

Straight base

All from San Luis Potosi, Mexico

Concave base

Straight base

Concave base

G7, $25-$45

G7, $30-$55

G8, $35-$60

G9, $40-$70

Concave base

Concave base

Concave base

G7, $35-$60

G5, $15-$25

Ear wear

G8, $35-$60

LOCATION: Central Mexico. **DESCRIPTION:** A triangular, wide based, thin, flat, corner to side notched point. The base is straight to concave. **I.D. KEY:** Width and thinness.

TORTUGAS - Middle Archaic to Woodland, 6000 - 1000 B. P.

(Also see Early Triangular, Kinney, Matamoros, Mescal & Trangular Knife)

LOCATION: New Mexico, Northern Mexico, Oklahoma to Tennessee. **DESCRIPTION:** A medium size, fairly thick, triangular point with straight to convex sides and base. Some examples are beveled on one side of each face. Bases are usually thinned. Smaller examples would fall in the *Matamoros* type.

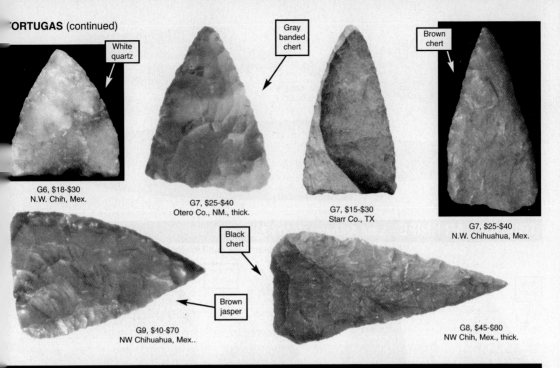

White quartz

Gray banded chert

Brown chert

G6, $18-$30
N.W. Chih, Mex.

G7, $25-$40
Otero Co., NM., thick.

G7, $15-$30
Starr Co., TX

G7, $25-$40
N.W. Chihuahua, Mex.

Black chert

Brown jasper

G9, $40-$70
NW Chihuahua, Mex..

G8, $45-$80
NW Chih, Mex., thick.

TOYAH - Desert Traditions-Late Classic Phase, 600 - 400 B. P.

(Also see Awatovi Side Notched, Del Carmen, Desert , Pueblo Side notched and Soto)

Restored

G5, $5-$10
S.W. CO

G9, $25-$45
W. TX

G5, $15-$25
S. NM

LOCATION: Western Texas. **DESCRIPTION:** A small triangular arrow point with straight blade edges, side notches, and a concave base which often has a further central notch. Variations of this point may have multiple sets of side notches.

TRADE - Historic, 400 - 170 B. P.

(Also see Glass)

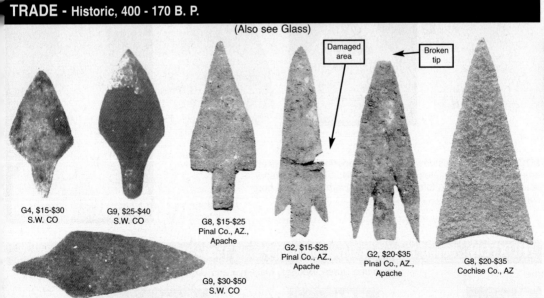

Damaged area

Broken tip

S
W

G4, $15-$30
S.W. CO

G9, $25-$40
S.W. CO

G8, $15-$25
Pinal Co., AZ.,
Apache

G2, $15-$25
Pinal Co., AZ.,
Apache

G2, $20-$35
Pinal Co., AZ.,
Apache

G8, $20-$35
Cochise Co., AZ

G9, $30-$50
S.W. CO

LOCATION: All over North America. **DESCRIPTION:** These points were made of copper, iron, and steel and were traded to the Indians by the French, British and others from the 1600s to the 1800s. Examples have been found all over the United States. Steel knives were usually resharpened with opposing bevels on the blade edges.

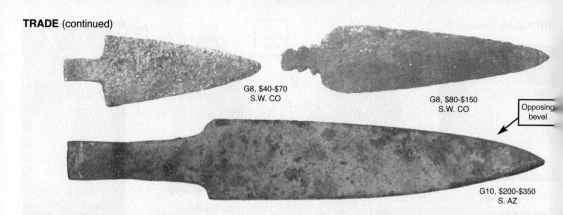

G8, $40-$70
S.W. CO

G8, $80-$150
S.W. CO

Opposing bevel

G10, $200-$350
S. AZ

TRIANGULAR KNIFE - Late Archaic, 3500 - 2300 B. P.

(Also see Early Triangular, Matamoros and Mescal Knife)

Gray chert

Jasper

Brown chert

Beveled all four edges

Yellow jasper

G9, $40-$70
NW Chih., Mex.

G7, $10-$20
Otero Co., NM, thin.

G5, $8-$15
S. CO

G8, $25-$40
Otero Co., NM, thin.

Red chert

G7, $15-$25
N. AZ

G7, $25-$40
N.W. Chih., Mex.

LOCATION: Northwestern Arizona and, possibly, into adjacent areas of contiguous states. **DESCRIPTION**: A large, asymmetrical to triangular knife form which may have been hafted horizontally. The blade is very thin and flat for its size.

G8, $35-$60
Otero Co., NM

G6, $25-$40
Mohave Co., AZ

TRUXTON - Desert Traditions-Developmental Phase, 1500 - 1000 B. P.

(Also see Duran, Hodges, Maljamar and Santa Cruz)

G4, $6-$12
Mohave Co., AZ

G4, $8-$15
Mohave Co., AZ

G6, $25-$40
Mohave Co., AZ

RUXTON (continued)

G5, $12-$25
Mohave Co., AZ

G4, $5-$10
Navajo Co., AZ

G7, $25-$40
Apache Co., AZ

LOCATION: Northern Arizona and possibly into adjacent states. **DESCRIPTION:** A small arrow point with a short stem, most often with a convex basal edge. The central portion of the blade has multiple notches and the tip of the blade is straight-sided converging to a sharply pointed tip.

TULAROSA CORNER NATCHED (see Cienega)

UVALDE - Middle Archaic to Woodland, 6000 - 1500 B. P.

(Also see Frio, Hanna, San Jose and Zephyr)

G10 $275-$500
Otero Co., NM

LOCATION: Texas to Oklahoma and New Mexico. **DESCRIPTION:** A medium size, bifurcated stemmed point with barbed to tapered shoulders. Some examples are serrated. The *Frio* point is similar but is usually broader and the ears flare outward more than this type. **I.D. KEY:** Narrow bifurcated stem.

VENTANA-AMARGOSA - Early Archaic, 7000 - 5000 B. P.

(Also see Yavapai Stemmed)

Obsidian   Rhyolite

G3, $3-$6
Cochise Co., AZ

G7, $15-$25
NW Chihuahua, Mex.

G5, $8-$15
Yavapai Co., AZ

G6, $20-$35
Pima Co., AZ

G6, $20-$35
Pima Co., AZ

G7, $25-$40
Coconino Co., AZ

G4, $5-$10
Yavapai Co., AZ

S W

LOCATION: Arizona and contiguous parts of adjacent states. **DESCRIPTION:** A small to medium sized dart/knife with a triangular blade with straight to slightly convex edges and straight to angular shoulders. The stem is parallel sided and rectangular to square. The basal edge is straight to rounded. **I.D. KEY:** A very square appearing stem.

VENTANA SIDE NOTCHED - Mid-Archaic, 5500 - 4800 B. P.

(Also see Basketmaker, Northern Side Notched, San Rafael, Sudden)

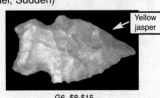

Yellow
jasper

G4, $3-$6
Sou. NM

Black
obsidian

G6, $5-$10
S. W. CO

G6, $5-$10
S. W. CO

G6, $8-$15
NW Chuahua, Mex.,
not ground

VENTANA SIDE NOTCHED (continued)

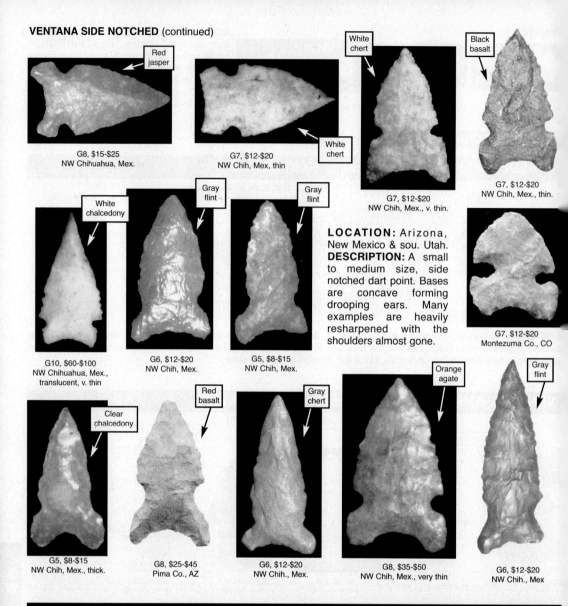

Red jasper

G8, $15-$25
NW Chihuahua, Mex.

White chert

G7, $12-$20
NW Chih, Mex, thin

White chert

G7, $12-$20
NW Chih, Mex., v. thin.

Black basalt

G7, $12-$20
NW Chih, Mex., thin.

White chalcedony

Gray flint

Gray flint

LOCATION: Arizona, New Mexico & sou. Utah. **DESCRIPTION:** A small to medium size, side notched dart point. Bases are concave forming drooping ears. Many examples are heavily resharpened with the shoulders almost gone.

G10, $60-$100
NW Chihuahua, Mex., translucent, v. thin

G6, $12-$20
NW Chih, Mex.

G5, $8-$15
NW Chih, Mex.

G7, $12-$20
Montezuma Co., CO

Clear chalcedony

Red basalt

Gray chert

Orange agate

Gray flint

G5, $8-$15
NW Chih, Mex., thick.

G8, $25-$45
Pima Co., AZ

G6, $12-$20
NW Chih., Mex.

G8, $35-$50
NW Chih, Mex., very thin

G6, $12-$20
NW Chih., Mex

WALNUT CANYON SIDE NOTCHED - Dev. to Classic Phase 850 - 700 B. P.

(Also see Awatovi Side Notched, Desert, Gatlin Side Notched, Point Of Pines, Pueblo Side Notched & Salado)

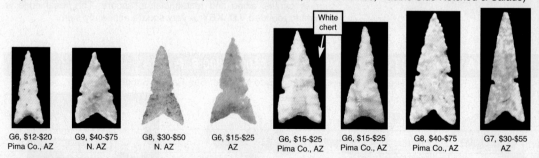

White chert

G6, $12-$20
Pima Co., AZ

G9, $40-$75
N. AZ

G8, $30-$50
N. AZ

G6, $15-$25
AZ

G6, $15-$25
Pima Co., AZ

G6, $15-$25
Pima Co., AZ

G8, $40-$75
Pima Co., AZ

G7, $30-$55
AZ

LOCATION: Arizona into New Mexico. **DESCRIPTION:** A small, narrow, side notched, triangular *Hohokam* arrow point with a deeply concave base. Notches occur high up from the base below mid-section. Basal corners are rounded to sharp. **I.D. KEY:** Narrowness and large basal area.

WALNUT CANYON SIDE NOTCHED (continued)

Agate

G9, $65-$125
AZ

G10, $100-$195
AZ

G10, $125-$225
AZ

G10, $125-$200
AZ

G10, $125-$200
AZ

G10, $125-$200
AZ

G10, $125-$200
Cedar Ridge, AZ

WHITE MOUNTAIN SIDE NOTCHED - Classic-Historic, 600 - 200 B. P.

(Also see Del Carmen, Desert and Rose Springs Side Notched)

LOCATION: Most of Arizona, southern New Mexico, S.W. Texas and northern Mexico. **DESCRIPTION:** A small, triangular arrow point with a deep basal notch and multiple side notches, most often with two pairs of side notches but examples with three pairs are not uncommon. Blade edges are generally straight. **I.D. KEY:** Multiple side notches.

G6, $12-$25
Navajo Co., AZ

G8, $25-$50
Navajo Co., AZ

YAVAPAI - Late Archaic to Transitional, 3300 - 1000 B. P.

(Also see Darl, Ventana-Amargosa)

S
W

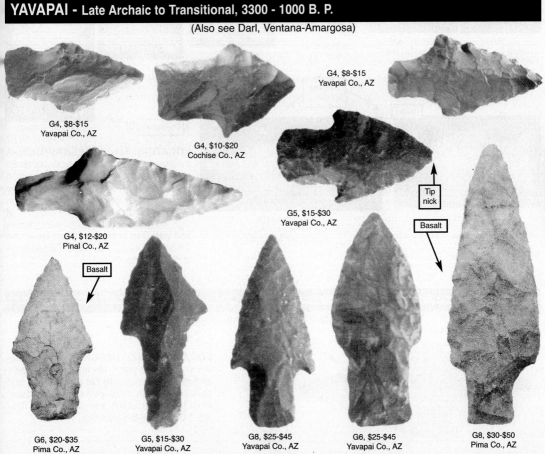

G4, $8-$15
Yavapai Co., AZ

G4, $8-$15
Yavapai Co., AZ

G4, $10-$20
Cochise Co., AZ

G4, $12-$20
Pinal Co., AZ

Basalt

G5, $15-$30
Yavapai Co., AZ

Tip
nick

Basalt

G6, $20-$35
Pima Co., AZ

G5, $15-$30
Yavapai Co., AZ

G8, $25-$45
Yavapai Co., AZ

G6, $25-$45
Yavapai Co., AZ

G8, $30-$50
Pima Co., AZ

893

Basalt

G7, $45-$85
Pima Co., AZ, torque blade.

LOCATION: Arizona and contiguous areas of adjacent states. **DESCRIPTION:** A medium sized dart point with a triangular blade and obtuse to lightly barbed shoulders. The stem is rectangular to slightly tapering or slightly expanding and longer than wide. The basal edge is straight to slightly concave or convex. **I.D. KEY:** Stem longer than wide.

ZEPHYR - Early Archaic, 9000 - 6000 B. P.

(Formerly Lampasos; also see San Jose and Uvalde)

White chert | Restored tip | Brown jasper | Jasper | Brown jasper | Restored tip | Red jasper | Chalcedony

G2, $8-$15
Otero Co., NM, ground basal area, serrated.

G3, $12-$20
Otero Co., NM, ground basal area, serrated.

G9, $60-$115
S.W. CO

G8, $60-$115
Otero Co., NM, ground basal area

G3, $15-$30
NW Chih, Mex. red jasper. ground basal area, serrated.

G10, $200-$350
S.W. CO

Serrated edge

Jasper

White chert

G7, $40-$75
Otero Co., NM, ground basal area, serrated.

G9, $90-$175
Otero Co., NM, ground basal area, serrated.

LOCATION: Texas. **DESCRIPTION:** A medium to large size, narrow, serrated point with square to tapered, barbed shoulders and an eared base. Blade edges are beveled on one side of each face on resharpened forms. Flaking is of high quality. These points were classified with *Darl* in the past. Also known as *Mahomet* locally. **I.D. KEY:** Fishtail base and serrations.

ZORRA - Middle Archaic, 6000 - 4000 B. P.

(See Augustin, Gypsum Cave, Yavapai)

Basalt

G8, $25-$40
W. TX

LOCATION: Texas. **DESCRIPTION:** A medium to large size point with tapered shoulders and stem that is usually flat on one face and beveled on both sides ot the opposite face. Most have needle tips and good quality flaking. **I.D. KEY:** Base beveling.

NORTHERN HIGH PLAINS SECTION:

This section includes point types from the following states:
Colorado, Idaho, Kansas, Montana, Nebraska, North Dakota,
South Dakota, Utah and Wyoming

The points in this section are arranged in alphabetical order and are shown **actual size**. All types are listed that were available for photographing. Any missing types will be added to future editions as photographs become available. We are always interested in receiving sharp, black and white or color glossy photos, color slides or high resolution (300 pixels/inch) digital pictures of your collection. Be sure to include a ruler in the photograph so that proper scale can be determined.

Lithics: Materials employed in the manufacture of projectile points from this region are: agate, basalt, chert, Dendritic chert, Flat Top chert, Flint, Knife River flint, obsidian, petrified wood, porcellanite, siltstone, Swan River chert and quartzite.

Regional Consultant:
John Byrd

Special Advisors:
Jerry Cubbuck, Jeb Taylor, Greg Truesdell

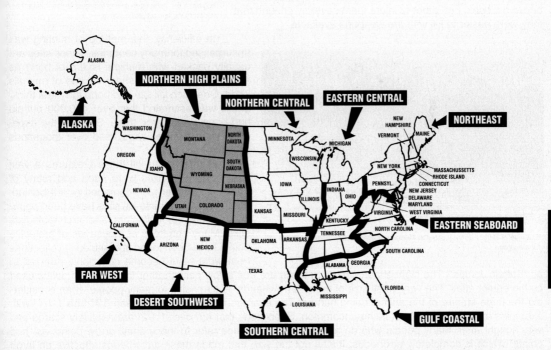

N
P

HUNTING THE BUFFALO JUMPS
By John Byrd

Throughout all of the 14,000 plus years that prehistoric peoples lived in the geographical area now known as Montana, hunting has been the primary subsistence base. The open prairie grass lands and abundant water found in the eastern three quarters of this region provided an ideal habitat for all manner of grazing herd animals. Chief among these were the bison and later the buffalo, both of which were favorite prey for these early hunters.

To a limited degree, mass kills of these herds by coordinated communal hunting techniques were employed from the earliest of times. However, the sheer number of these kill sites dramatically increased around 1,200 to 1,300 years ago. Interestingly enough, this fits the time period when the bow and arrow technology was replacing the atlatl and a number of these kill sites will show evidence of use with both weapon types. The systematic use of this hunting method continued up until the 1600s when horses finally became readily available to the Indian population.

The technique employed was usually very similar from one location to another. Small groups of between 10 and 100 animals were gathered from their grazing areas or intercepted going to or from water. They were then driven or stampeded to the site chosen as the kill area (no small task given the nature of these animals). This actual kill would either be a low cliff 10 to 50 feet high or more frequently a steep bank or low lying depression. In the later cases, a stout corral was built to contain the herd long enough to complete the slaughter. The intent was not necessarily to kill the animals from the drop over a cliff or down a bank, but rather to injure them severely enough that they were easier to kill with the weapons available.

Digging in the bone beds of this Montana Buffalo Jump has yielded many fine projectile points.

In efficiency, this method of hunting was unsurpassed for many centuries. These sites are usually packed with multiple layers of bone as silent testimony to the sheer volume of animals killed. One such kill site had bone forty feet thick, and it was estimated that over 400,000 buffalo had been slaughtered there. Some of the especially strategic sites were used over thousands of years.

Of course, to kill these creatures a vast number of projectiles were used and many of these were either lost, damaged or left behind. Since the 1930s these kill sites have been popular locations for collectors and archaeologists alike. Many hundreds of thousands of projectile points have been found and placed in collections from what have become commonly referred to

Example of Buffalo Jump located in Montana. Animals were driven over this cliff for slaughter.

as "Buffalo Jumps". The highest percentage of these are true arrow points rather than the dart points used by the earlier atlatl. The very small size of these "arrowheads" is surprising to many people when considering the large stature of the animal being hunted. The average length will be between 3/4" and 1 1/4" with examples as small as 1/4" not being uncommon. Specimens that are over 1 1/2" are relatively scarce and very sought after. Many people who do not know the difference refer to these small arrow points as "bird points" which is completely erroneous. It was not the size that made these arrowheads effective on large animals but rather their ability to penetrate into the vital organs.

NORTHERN HIGH PLAINS POINT TYPES
(Archaeological Periods)(Carbon dates shown)

PLAINS PALEO (11,500 B. P. - 7,500 B. P.)

Agate Basin	Crescent Knife	Graver	Plainview
Alberta	Drill	Hell Gap	Red River Knife
Anderson	Eden	Lancet	San Jose
Browns Valley	Firstview	Meserve	Scottsbluff I & II
Clovis	Folsom	Midland	Scraper
Clovis-Colby	Frederick	Milnesand	
Cody Knife	Goshen	Paleo Knife	

TRANSITIONAL PALEO (9,000 B. P. - 7,200 B. P.)

Allen	Angostura	Lusk

MOUNTAIN PALEO (9,400 B. P. - 6,000 B. P.)

Alder Complex	Frederick	Lovell	Pryor Stemmed

EARLY ARCHAIC (8,000 B. P. - 5,000 B. P.)

Archaic Knife	Logan Creek	Plains Knife
Archaic Triangle	Lookingbill	Simonsen
Hawken	Mount Albion	

MIDDLE ARCHAIC (5,100 B. P. - 3,300 B. P.)

Duncan	Hanna-Northern	Oxbow
Green River	Mallory	Wray
Hanna	McKean	Yonkee

LATE ARCHAIC (3,400 B. P. - 1,000 B. P.)

Base Tang Knife	Corner Tang Knife	Mid-Back Tang	Samantha Dart
Besant	Exotic Forms	Pelican Lake	Sonota
Besant Knife	Hafted Knife	Plains Side Notched	

LATE PREHISTORIC (1,900 B. P. - 150 B. P.)

Avonlea-Carmichael	Glendo Arrow	Mummy Cave	Stott
Avonlea-Classic	Glendo Dart	Nanton	Swift Current
Avonlea-Gull Lake	Harahey	Paskapoo	Tompkins
Avonlea-Timber Ridge	Harrell	Pekisko	Washita
Billings	High River	Pipe Creek	Washita Northern
Buffalo Gap	Hog Back	Plains Side Notched	
Cottonwood Leaf	Horse Fly	Prairie Side Notched	
Cottonwood Triangle	Huffaker	Samantha-Arrow	
Emigrant	Irvine	Sattler	
Galt	Lewis	Side Knife	

N P

PROTOHISTORIC (300 B. P. - 100 B.P.)

Bone Point	Cut Bank Jaw Notched	Plains Triangular	Trade Points

NORTHERN HIGH PLAINS
THUMBNAIL GUIDE SECTION

The following references are provided to aid the collector in easier and quicker identification of point types. All photos are exactly 30% of actual size and are proportional to each other. Each point pictured in this section represent a classic form for the type. When a match is found, go to the alphabetical location of that type for more examples in actual size.

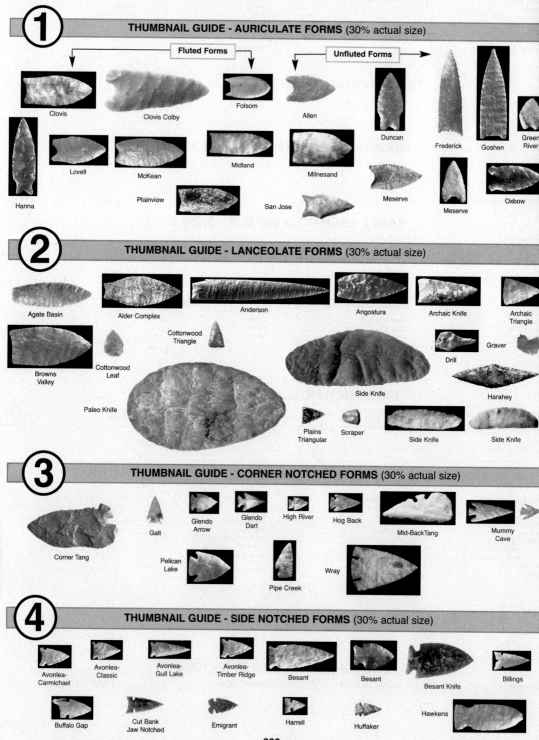

① THUMBNAIL GUIDE - AURICULATE FORMS (30% actual size)

Fluted Forms   Unfluted Forms

Clovis · Clovis Colby · Folsom · Allen · Duncan · Frederick · Goshen · Green River
Lovell · McKean · Midland · Milnesand · Meserve · Oxbow
Hanna · Plainview · San Jose · Meserve

② THUMBNAIL GUIDE - LANCEOLATE FORMS (30% actual size)

Agate Basin · Alder Complex · Anderson · Angostura · Archaic Knife · Archaic Triangle
Browns Valley · Cottonwood Triangle · Cottonwood Leaf · Graver · Drill
Paleo Knife · Side Knife · Harahey
Plains Triangular · Scraper · Side Knife · Side Knife

③ THUMBNAIL GUIDE - CORNER NOTCHED FORMS (30% actual size)

Galt · Glendo Arrow · Glendo Dart · High River · Hog Back · Mid-BackTang · Mummy Cave
Corner Tang · Pelican Lake · Pipe Creek · Wray

④ THUMBNAIL GUIDE - SIDE NOTCHED FORMS (30% actual size)

Avonlea-Carmichael · Avonlea-Classic · Avonlea-Gull Lake · Avonlea-Timber Ridge · Besant · Besant · Besant Knife · Billings
Buffalo Gap · Cut Bank Jaw Notched · Emigrant · Harrell · Huffaker · Hawkens

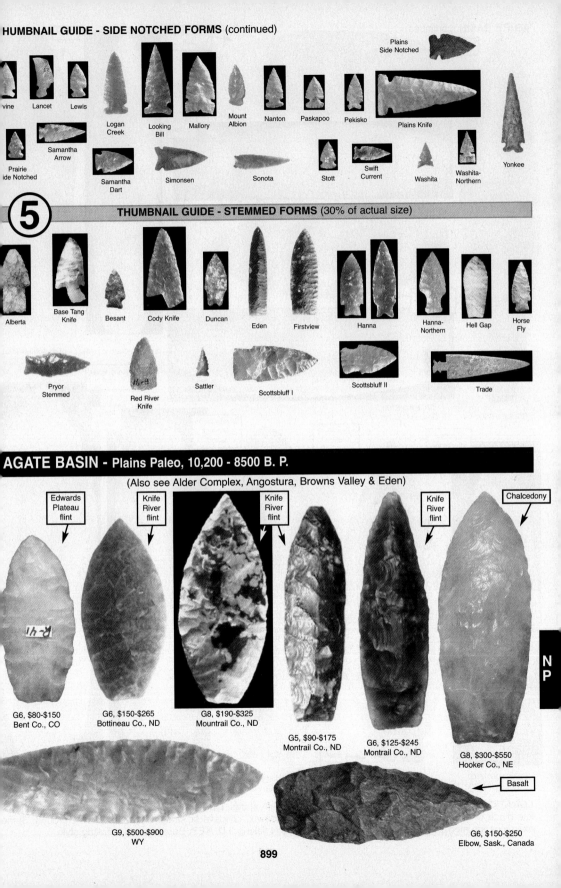

HUMBNAIL GUIDE - SIDE NOTCHED FORMS (continued)

vine Lancet Lewis Logan Creek Looking Bill Mallory Mount Albion Nanton Paskapoo Pekisko Plains Side Notched Plains Knife

Prairie ide Notched Samantha Arrow Samantha Dart Simonsen Sonota Stott Swift Current Washita Washita-Northern Yonkee

⑤ THUMBNAIL GUIDE - STEMMED FORMS (30% of actual size)

Alberta Base Tang Knife Besant Cody Knife Duncan Eden Firstview Hanna Hanna-Northern Hell Gap Horse Fly

Pryor Stemmed Red River Knife Sattler Scottsbluff I Scottsbluff II Trade

AGATE BASIN - Plains Paleo, 10,200 - 8500 B. P.

(Also see Alder Complex, Angostura, Browns Valley & Eden)

Edwards Plateau flint

Knife River flint

Knife River flint

Knife River flint

Chalcedony

G6, $80-$150
Bent Co., CO

G6, $150-$265
Bottineau Co., ND

G8, $190-$325
Mountrail Co., ND

G5, $90-$175
Montrail Co., ND

G6, $125-$245
Montrail Co., ND

G8, $300-$550
Hooker Co., NE

Basalt

G9, $500-$900
WY

G6, $150-$250
Elbow, Sask., Canada

N
P

899

AGATE BASIN (continued)

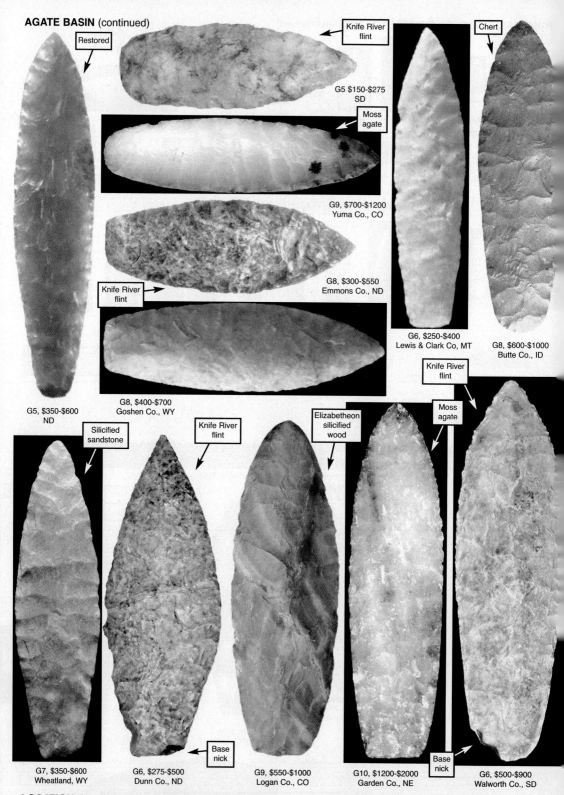

Restored

Knife River flint

G5 $150-$275
SD

Moss agate

G9, $700-$1200
Yuma Co., CO

Chert

Knife River flint

G8, $300-$550
Emmons Co., ND

G5, $350-$600
ND

G8, $400-$700
Goshen Co., WY

G6, $250-$400
Lewis & Clark Co, MT

G8, $600-$1000
Butte Co., ID

Knife River flint

Silicified sandstone

Knife River flint

Elizabetheon silicified wood

Moss agate

Base nick

Base nick

G7, $350-$600
Wheatland, WY

G6, $275-$500
Dunn Co., ND

G9, $550-$1000
Logan Co., CO

G10, $1200-$2000
Garden Co., NE

G6, $500-$900
Walworth Co., SD

LOCATION: Northern states from Pennsylvania to western states. **DESCRIPTION:** A medium to large size lanceolate blade of unusually high quality. Bases are either convex, concave or straight, and are usually ground. Some examples are median ridged and have random to parallel flaking. **I.D. KEY:** Basal form and flaking style.

900

(Also see Cody Knife, Eden, Rio Grande and Scottsbluff)

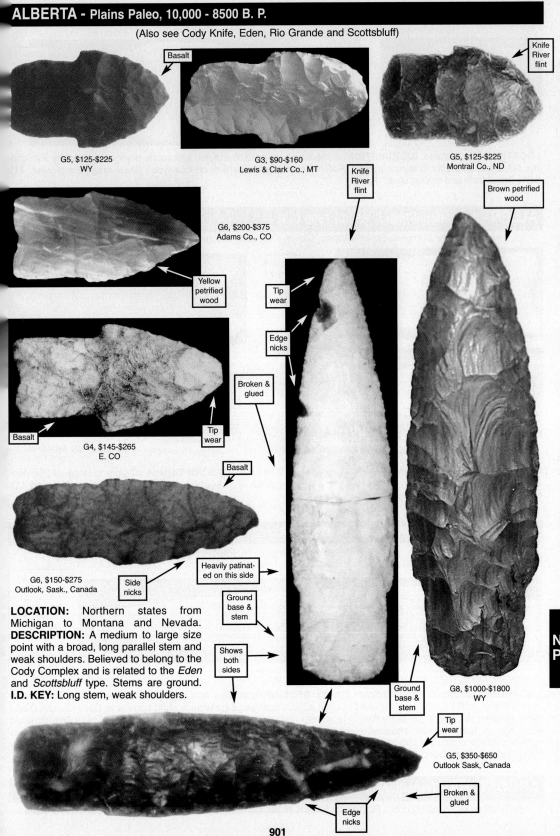

Basalt

G5, $125-$225
WY

G3, $90-$160
Lewis & Clark Co., MT

Knife River flint

G5, $125-$225
Montrail Co., ND

G6, $200-$375
Adams Co., CO

Knife River flint

Brown petrified wood

Yellow petrified wood

Basalt

Tip wear

G4, $145-$265
E. CO

Tip wear

Edge nicks

Broken & glued

Basalt

G6, $150-$275
Outlook, Sask., Canada

Side nicks

Heavily patinated on this side

Ground base & stem

Shows both sides

Ground base & stem

G8, $1000-$1800
WY

LOCATION: Northern states from Michigan to Montana and Nevada.
DESCRIPTION: A medium to large size point with a broad, long parallel stem and weak shoulders. Believed to belong to the Cody Complex and is related to the *Eden* and *Scottsbluff* type. Stems are ground.
I.D. KEY: Long stem, weak shoulders.

Tip wear

G5, $350-$650
Outlook Sask, Canada

Broken & glued

Edge nicks

N
P

ALDER COMPLEX - Mountain Paleo, 9400 B. P.

(Also see Agate Basin, Browns Valley, Clovis, Green River, Lovell and Meserve)

G3, $60-$110
Lewis & Clark Co., MT

G8, $400-$650
Park Co., MT

Oblique flaking

LOCATION: Plains states. **DESCRIPTION:** A medium to large size unfluted lanceolate point of high quality with convex sides and a straight to concave base. Flaking is usually the parallel oblique type. Basal areas are ground. **I.D KEY:** Basal form and flaking style.

ALLEN - Transitional Paleo, 8500 - 7500 B. P.

(Also see Alder Complex, Browns Valley, Clovis, Frederick, Goshen, Green River, Lovell & Meserve)

Agate

G6, $275-$500
E. CO

G8, $400-$650
Morgan Co., CO

Oblique parallel flaking

G6, $250-$425
E. CO

Chalcedony

G8, $400-$700
Washington Co., KS

LOCATION: Plains states. Named after Jimmy Allen of Wyoming. **DESCRIPTION:** A medium to large size lanceolate point that has oblique tranverse flaking and a concave base with usually rounded ears. Basal area is ground. **I.D. KEY:** Basal form and flaking style.

ANDERSON - Plains Paleo, 9000 - 8000 B. P.

(Also see Allen, Angostura, Plainview)

Intentional burinated base

G10, $5,000-$10,000+
Yuma Co., CO

Oblique flaking

Famous point found by Perry Anderson published as 1st Yuma point; later named Allen or Angostura and recently named Anderson after its finder.

LOCATION: Colorado, Wyoming & South Dakota. **DESCRIPTION:** Very rare. A long slender lanceolate form exhibiting a uniform profile that is very thin with straight edges; stem edge grinding is short (similar to Cody Complex) and basal grinding is present; pressure flaking is superb and serial, parallel oblique. **Note:** This type was first identified years ago as *Yuma* and later changed to *Allen, Angostura* and other types. Recently it has been determined that this type is unique and different enough to have its own distinct name which has been proposed by Jeb Taylor. Named for Perry Anderson who found the first well known example.

ANGOSTURA - Transitional Paleo, 8800 - 7500 B. P.

(Also see Alder Complex, Allen, Anderson, Archaic Knife, Browns Valley, Clovis, Frederick, Goshen and Lusk)

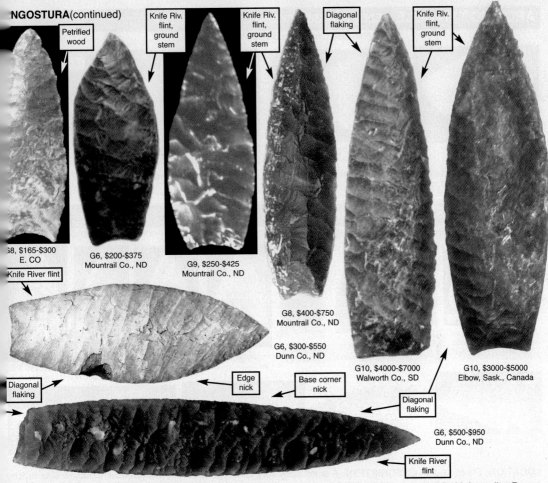

NGOSTURA (continued)

Petrified wood

Knife Riv. flint, ground stem

Knife Riv. flint, ground stem

Diagonal flaking

Knife Riv. flint, ground stem

G8, $165-$300
E. CO

G6, $200-$375
Mountrail Co., ND

G9, $250-$425
Mountrail Co., ND

Knife River flint

G8, $400-$750
Mountrail Co., ND

G6, $300-$550
Dunn Co., ND

Diagonal flaking

Edge nick

Base corner nick

G10, $4000-$7000
Walworth Co., SD

G10, $3000-$5000
Elbow, Sask., Canada

Diagonal flaking

G6, $500-$950
Dunn Co., ND

Knife River flint

LOCATION: Plains states. **DESCRIPTION:** A medium to large size lanceolate blade of unusually high quality. Bases are either convex, concave or straight and are usually ground. Most examples have oblique transverse flaking. **I.D. KEY:** Basal form and flaking style.

ARCHAIC KNIFE - Early Archaic, 8000 - 5000 B. P.

(Also see Angostura, Harahey, Plains Knife, Plains Triangular & Side Knife)

G5, $12-$20
E. CO

G3, $2-$4
Morton Co., ND

N
P

knife River flint

G10, $3000-$5000
SD

LOCATION: Plains states. **DESCRIPTION:** A medium to large triangular blade with a concave to straight base. **I.D. KEY:** Large triangle with early flaking.

903

ARCHAIC TRIANGLE - Early to Middle Archaic, 6000 - 4000 B. P.

(Also see Cottonwood and Plains Triangular)

G6, $8-$15
Custer Co., NE

G6, $12-$20
Lewis & Clark Co., MT

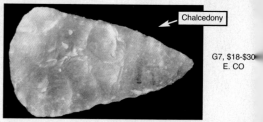

Chalcedony

G7, $18-$30
E. CO

LOCATION: Plains states. **DESCRIPTION:** A small size triangular point that shows early flaking. **I.D. KEY:** Triangle with early flaking.

AVONLEA-CARMICHAEL - Late Prehistoric, 1800 - 1300 B. P.

(Also see Galt, High River, Irvine, Lewis, Nanton, Pekisko, Swift Current and Tompkins)

G5, $20-$35
Cascade Co., MT

G5, $20-$35
Cascade Co., MT

G5, $20-$35
Choteau Co., MT

G8, $40-$70
Elbow, Sask., Canada

G6, $40-$75
Choteau Co., MT

G8, $40-$75
Meagher Co., MT

G7, $40-$75
Cascade Co., MT

G7, $40-$75
MeagherCo., MT

G8, $45-$80
Saco, MT

G7, $40-$75
Cascade Co., MT

G7, $40-$75
Choteau Co., MT

G8, $50-$90
Meagher Co., MT

G7, $40-$75, Teton Co., MT

LOCATION: Plains states. **DESCRIPTION:** A small size, very thin, high quality arrow point with shallow side notches close to the base which is concave. The blade is constructed with broad, parallel flakes that extend to the center. Quality is slightly lower than the other forms of this type. Frequently found on Bison kill sites. **I.D. KEY:** Low side notches, very thin.

AVONLEA-CLASSIC - Late Prehistoric, 1800 - 1230 B. P.

(Also see Galt, High River, Irvine, Lewis, Nanton, Pekisko, Swift Current and Tompkins)

G6, $20-$35
Custer Co., NE

G6, $20-$35
Choteau Co., MT

G6, $20-$35
Meagher Co., MT

G6, $20-$35
Meagher Co., MT

G6, $20-$35
Meagher Co., MT

G8, $30-$55
Meagher Co., MT

G6, $20-$35
Phillips Co., MT

G6, $25-$45
Meagher Co., MT

G8, $30-$55
Meagher Co., MT

G8, $35-$65
Meagher Co., MT

G8, $35-$65
Cascade Co., MT

G8, $50-$90
Teton Co., MT

LOCATION: Plains states. **DESCRIPTION:** A small size, very thin, high quality arrow point with shallow side notches close to the base which is concave. High quality parallel flaking is evident on the blade. Found at Bison kill sites. The first true Arrowpoint of the high plains along with Galt. **I.D. KEY:** Low side notches, very thin.

(Also see Besant, Galt, High River, Irvine, Lewis, Nanton, Pekisko, Swift Current & Tompkins)

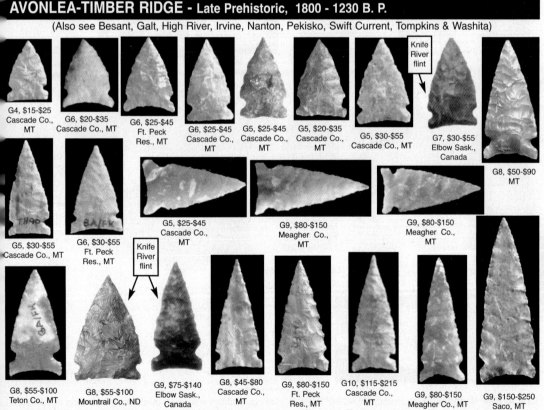

Obsidian

Parallel flaking

G5, $20-$35 Meagher Co., MT.

G9, $45-$80 Meacher Co., MT

G7, $40-$70 Meagher Co., MT.

G8, $50-$90 Phillips Co., MT

G10, $150-$250 Cascade Co., MT

G9, $80-$150 Meagher Co., MT

G8, $75-$140 Meagher Co., MT

G9, $90-$165 Meagher Co., MT

G10, $100-$190 Cascade Co., MT.

Parallel flaking

G9, $75-$140 Meagher Co., MT

G8, $80-$150 Meagher Co., MT.

G10, $250-$425 Meagher Co., MT. Best known example.

G10, $250-$400 Meagher Co., MT

LOCATION: Plains states. **DESCRIPTION:** A small to medium size, thin, high quality point with shallow notches located close to the base. The earliest form for the type. Carefully controlled parallel flaking was used in the construction. Some examples have basal grinding. The earliest forms of this variety were dart points changing into arrow points at a later time. Believed to be related to the *Besant* type. **I.D. KEY:** Basal form and flaking style.

AVONLEA-TIMBER RIDGE - Late Prehistoric, 1800 - 1230 B. P.

(Also see Besant, Galt, High River, Irvine, Nanton, Pekisko, Swift Current, Tompkins & Washita)

Knife River flint

G4, $15-$25 Cascade Co., MT

G6, $20-$35 Cascade Co., MT

G6, $25-$45 Ft. Peck Res., MT

G6, $25-$45 Cascade Co., MT

G5, $25-$45 Cascade Co., MT

G5, $20-$35 Cascade Co., MT

G5, $30-$55 Cascade Co., MT

G7, $30-$55 Elbow Sask., Canada

G8, $50-$90 MT

G5, $25-$45 Cascade Co., MT

G9, $80-$150 Meagher Co., MT

G9, $80-$150 Meagher Co., MT

G5, $30-$55 Cascade Co., MT

G6, $30-$55 Ft. Peck Res., MT

Knife River flint

G8, $55-$100 Teton Co., MT

G8, $55-$100 Mountrail Co., ND

G9, $75-$140 Elbow Sask., Canada

G8, $45-$80 Cascade Co., MT

G9, $80-$150 Ft. Peck Res., MT

G10, $115-$215 Cascade Co., MT

G9, $80-$150 Meagher Co., MT

G9, $150-$250 Saco, MT

N P

LOCATION: Northern Plains states. **DESCRIPTION:** A small size, very thin, narrow, arrow point with shallow side notches close to the base. Bases can be straight to concave. Corners of ears are sharper than the other varieties.

BASE TANG KNIFE - Late Archaic, 3200 - 1500 B. P.

(Also see Cody Knife, Corner Tang and Mid-Back Tang)

Petrified wood

G6, $60-$115
E. CO.

G6, $60-$115
E. CO.

G5, $35-$65
Bent Co., CO

LOCATION: Northern Plains states. **DESCRIPTION:** Two forms. First: A medium to large size shouldered point with a long stem meeting the base a a sharp angle. Second: A large size ovoid double pointed blade with a smal side notched base. **I.D. KEY:** Asymmetrical form.

BESANT - Late Archaic, 1900 - 1500 B. P.

(Also see Avonlea, Glendo Dart, Pelican Lake, Samantha and Sonata)

Silicified sandstone

G3, $2-$5
CO

G5, $15-$30
Liberty Co., MT

G5, $15-$30
Liberty Co., MT

G5, $15-$30
Mandan, ND

G6, $25-$40
Meagher Co., MT

G6, $25-$40
Dodge City, KS

G8, $35-$60
Birsay, Sask., Canada

Knife River flint

G5, $25-$40
Zortman, MT

G6, $35-$60
Elbow, Sask., Canada

G6, $35-$65
Elbow, Sask., Canada

G6, $45-$85
Elbow, Sask., Canada

G6, $80-$150
Meagher Co., MT

Broken & glued

G6, $45-$85
Elbow, Sask., Canada

LOCATION: Northern Plains states. **DESCRIPTION:** A small to medium size, high quality corner to side notched dart point. Notches occur close to the base. The base is straight to convex. Believed to be related to the *Avonlea* type and the earlier *Pelican Lake* type. Shoulders are tapered to straight.

Crystal quartz

G8, $90-$175
Meagher Co., MT

G8, $90-$175
W. KS

G8, $95-$185
Meagher Co., MT

G8, $90-$175
Lewis & Clark Co., MT

G8, $90-$175
Meagher Co., MT

G7, $80-$175
Meagher Co., MT

Knife
River flint

Silicified
sandstone

Petrified
wood

Knife
River flint

G6, $45-$85
Elbow, Sask., Canada

G9, $125-$200
McLain Co., ND

G6, $65-$125
Elbow Sask, Canada

G6, $55-$100
Brisay, Sask., Canada

G9, $125-$200
Elbow, Sask., Canada

Knife
River flint

Broken
& glued

Knife
River flint

Best known
example

G9, $150-$275
Mountrail Co., ND

G9, $250-$400
Birsay, Sask., Canada

G6, $90-$175
Meagher Co., MT

G8, $200-$350
Birsay, Sask., Canada

G10, $250-$450
Meagher Co., MT

N
P

BESANT KNIFE - Late Archaic, 1900 - 1500 B. P.

(Also see Plains Knife)

LOCATION: Northern Plains states. **DESCRIPTION:** A medium to large size asymmetrical knife with wide corner to side notches. On some examples the blade leans heavily to one side. **I.D.KEY:** Symmetry of blade and notches.

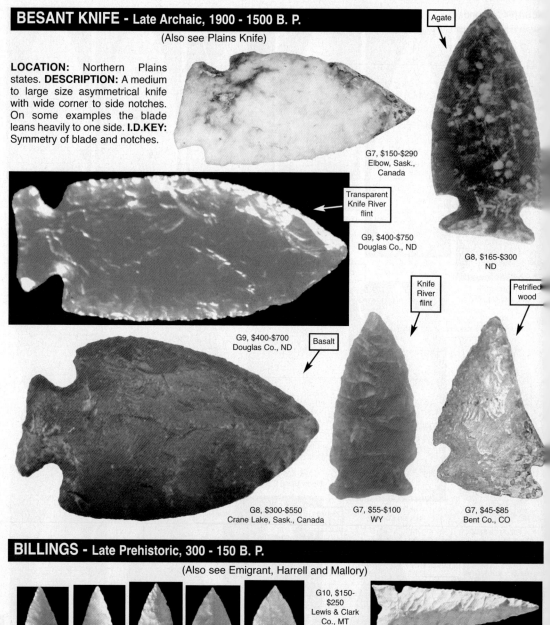

Agate

G7, $150-$290
Elbow, Sask.,
Canada

Transparent
Knife River
flint

G9, $400-$750
Douglas Co., ND

G8, $165-$300
ND

Knife
River
flint

Petrified
wood

G9, $400-$700
Douglas Co., ND

Basalt

G8, $300-$550
Crane Lake, Sask., Canada

G7, $55-$100
WY

G7, $45-$85
Bent Co., CO

BILLINGS - Late Prehistoric, 300 - 150 B. P.

(Also see Emigrant, Harrell and Mallory)

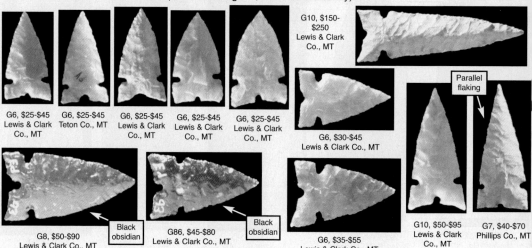

G6, $25-$45
Lewis & Clark
Co., MT

G6, $25-$45
Teton Co., MT

G6, $25-$45
Lewis & Clark
Co., MT

G6, $25-$45
Lewis & Clark
Co., MT

G6, $25-$45
Lewis & Clark
Co., MT

G10, $150-
$250
Lewis & Clark
Co., MT

Parallel
flaking

G6, $30-$45
Lewis & Clark Co., MT

G8, $50-$90
Lewis & Clark Co., MT

Black
obsidian

G86, $45-$80
Lewis & Clark Co., MT

Black
obsidian

G6, $35-$55
Lewis & Clark Co., MT

G10, $50-$95
Lewis & Clark
Co., MT

G7, $40-$70
Phillips Co., MT

LLINGS (continued)

LOCATION: Northern Plains states. **DESCRIPTION:** A small, thin, tri-notched point with a straight to convex base. lade edges can be serrated. Basal corners are sharp to pointed. Widest at the base, this point has excellent flaking, usually of the oblique transverse variety. If basal corners are rounded the type would be *Emigrant*.

BITTERROOT (see Lookingbill for points found east of the Great Basin area)

BONE POINT - Proto Historic, 300 - 150 B. P.

(Also see Hafted Knife and Side Knife)

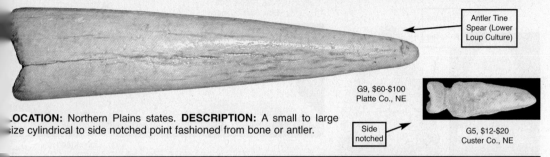

Antler Tine Spear (Lower Loup Culture)

G9, $60-$100
Platte Co., NE

LOCATION: Northern Plains states. **DESCRIPTION:** A small to large size cylindrical to side notched point fashioned from bone or antler.

Side notched

G5, $12-$20
Custer Co., NE

BROWNS VALLEY - Plains Paleo, 10,000 - 8000 B. P.

(Also see Agate Basin, Alder Complex, Allen, Angostura, Goshen and Lovell)

Diagonal flaking

G8, $165-$300
Mountrail Co., ND

Knife River flint

Petrified wood

G8, $400-$700
Cascade Co., MT

Diagonal flaking

G9, $400-$700
Lewis & Clark Co., MT

LOCATION: Midwest to Northern Plains states. **DESCRIPTION:** A medium to large, thin, lanceolate blade with usually oblique to horizontal transverse flaking and a concave to straight base which can be ground. **I.D. KEY:** Paleo transverse flaking.

BUFFALO GAP - Late Prehistoric, 1900 - 1000 B. P.

(Also see Lookingbill & Washita)

Knife River flint

Asymmetrical base

Plate chalcedony

G6, $25-$40
Mountrail Co., ND

G3, $12-$20
Teton Co., MT

G10+, $500-$900
Walworth Co., SD

LOCATION: Northern Plains states. **DESCRIPTION:** A medium size, thin, side notched triangular point with a concave base. Basal corners are asymmetrical with one higher than the other, called a "single spur" base. **I.D. KEY:** Asymmetrical basal corners.

909

(Also see Alder Complex, Allen, Angostura, Folsom, Goshen and Plainview)

Knife River flint

$30-$50
Mountrail Co., ND

Channel flake

G8, $800-$1500
Elbo, Sask., Canada

G6, $250-$450
Elbow, Sask., Canada

Patinated Knife River flint

Tan chert

Tip wear

G7, $1000-$1800
E. CO

G6, $250-$475
Teton Co., MT

G8, $1500-$2500
ND

Side nick

G7, $800-$1500
CO

Petrified wood

Agate

Flute channel

Butterscotch agate

Jasper

G10, $3000-$5500
Alamosa, CO

G6, $1500-$2500
E. CO

G8, $1500-$2500
CO

G6, $800-$1500
San Luis Valley, CO

LOCATION: All of North America. **DESCRIPTION:** A medium to large size, auriculate, fluted, lanceolate point with convex sides and a concave base that is ground. Most examples are fluted on both sides about 1/3 the way up from the base. The flaking can be random to parallel. Clovis is the earliest point type in the hemisphere. The origin of Clovis is unknown. It may have developed from earlier forms brought here from the Old World. The first Clovis find associated with Mastodon was in 1979 at Mastodon State Park, Jefferson Co., MO. in the Kimmswick bone bed carbon dated to 11,500 B.P. or approx. 14,000 actual years. **I.D. KEY:** Paleo flaking, shoulders, baton or billet fluting instead of indirect style.

Ear damage

Agate

Patinated Knife River flint

Flute channel

Outré passé over-shot flaking

Honey agate w/jasper-agate tip

G5, $800-$1500
MT

G9, $6500-$10,000
CO. Cache point

G10+, $9000-$15,000+
Walworth Co., SD, AKA "Bull Moose"

G8, $7000-$12,000
Logan Co., CO

CLOVIS-COLBY - Plains Paleo, 11,500 - 10,600 B. P.

(Also see Alder Complex, Allen, Angostura, Folsom, Goshen, Midland and Plainview)

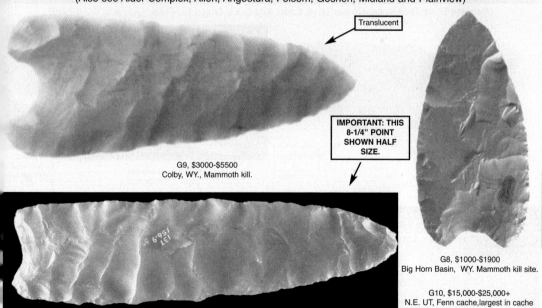

Translucent

IMPORTANT: THIS 8-1/4" POINT SHOWN HALF SIZE.

G9, $3000-$5500
Colby, WY., Mammoth kill.

G8, $1000-$1900
Big Horn Basin, WY. Mammoth kill site.

G10, $15,000-$25,000+
N.E. UT, Fenn cache, largest in cache

N
P

LOCATION: Northern Plains states. **DESCRIPTION:** Rebased *Clovis* points. A later form for the type. A medium to large size, auriculate, fluted, lanceolate point with convex sides and a deep, concave base that is ground. Most examples are fluted on both sides up to about 1/3 the way from the base. The flaking can be random to parallel. Has been found associated with bison and mammoth remains. *Clovis* is the earliest point type in the hemisphere. **I.D. KEY:** Paleo flaking, shoulders, baton or billet fluting instead of indirect style.

CLOVIS-COLBY (continued)

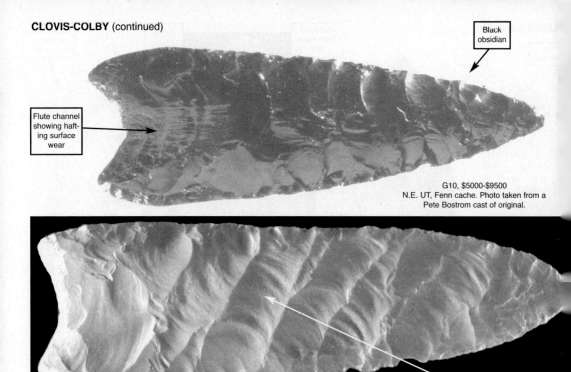

Black obsidian

Flute channel showing hafting surface wear

G10, $5000-$9500
N.E. UT, Fenn cache. Photo taken from a Pete Bostrom cast of original.

Outré Passé over-shot flaking

G10, $8500-$15,000+
N.E. UT, Fenn cache.

CODY KNIFE - Plains Paleo, 10,000 - 8000 B. P.

(Also see Base-Tang Knife, Corner Tang, Eden, Mid-Back Tang, Red River Knife and Scottsbluff)

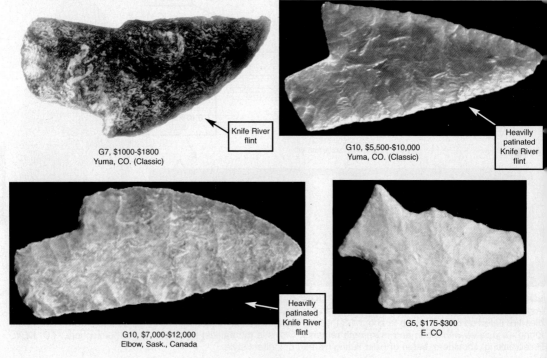

Knife River flint

G7, $1000-$1800
Yuma, CO. (Classic)

Heavilly patinated Knife River flint

G10, $5,500-$10,000
Yuma, CO. (Classic)

Heavilly patinated Knife River flint

G10, $7,000-$12,000
Elbow, Sask., Canada

G5, $175-$300
E. CO

CODY KNIFE (continued)

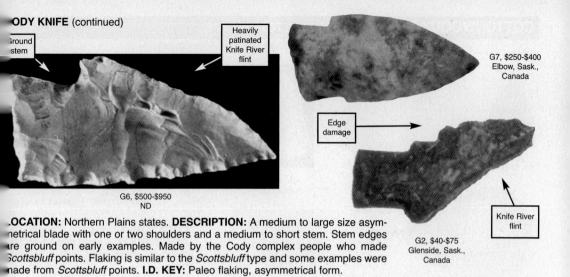

Ground stem

Heavily patinated Knife River flint

G6, $500-$950
ND

G7, $250-$400
Elbow, Sask.,
Canada

Edge damage

Knife River flint

G2, $40-$75
Glenside, Sask.,
Canada

LOCATION: Northern Plains states. **DESCRIPTION:** A medium to large size asymmetrical blade with one or two shoulders and a medium to short stem. Stem edges are ground on early examples. Made by the Cody complex people who made *Scottsbluff* points. Flaking is similar to the *Scottsbluff* type and some examples were made from *Scottsbluff* points. **I.D. KEY:** Paleo flaking, asymmetrical form.

CORNER TANG KNIFE - Late Archaic, 3400 - 1000 B. P.

(Also see Base-Tang Knife, Cody & Mid-Back Tang)

Exotic form

Alibates dolomite

G6, $200-$375
WY

Knife River flint

G5, $200-$375
Mountrail Co., ND

G9, $700-$1200
Otero Co., CO

Basalt

G7, $250-$450
Alamosa, CO

N
P

LOCATION: Arizona northward. **DESCRIPTION:** A medium to large size knife that is notched at one corner producing a tang for hafting to a handle. Tang knives are rare and have been reproduced in recent years. **I.D. KEY:** Angle of hafting.

G6, $200-$375
CO

COTTONWOOD LEAF - Late Prehistoric, 700 - 150 B. P.

(Also see Archaic Triangle and Plains Triangular)

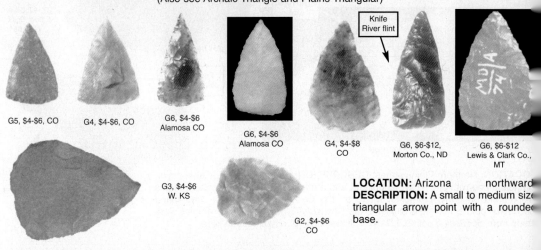

G5, $4-$6, CO

G4, $4-$6, CO

G6, $4-$6
Alamosa CO

G6, $4-$6
Alamosa CO

G4, $4-$8
CO

Knife
River flint

G6, $6-$12,
Morton Co., ND

G6, $6-$12
Lewis & Clark Co.,
MT

G3, $4-$6
W. KS

G2, $4-$6
CO

LOCATION: Arizona northward
DESCRIPTION: A small to medium size
triangular arrow point with a rounded
base.

COTTONWOOD TRIANGLE - Late Prehistoric, 700 - 150 B. P.

(Also see Archaic Triangle and Plains Triangular)

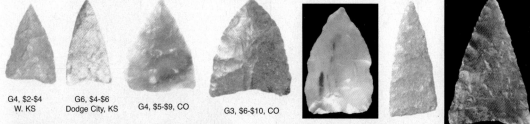

G4, $2-$4
W. KS

G6, $4-$6
Dodge City, KS

G4, $5-$9, CO

G3, $6-$10, CO

G2, $4-$6
Weld Co., CO

G4, $4-$6, CO

G8, $12-$20
Standing Rock Res., SD

LOCATION: Arizona northward. **DESCRIPTION:** A small to medium size triangular arrow point with a straight, slightly convex or
concave base. Basal corners tend to be sharp.

CUT BANK JAW-NOTCHED - Proto Historic, 300 - 150 B. P.

(Also see Buffalo Gap, Emigrant, Paskapoo, Pekisko, Plains Side Notched & Washita)

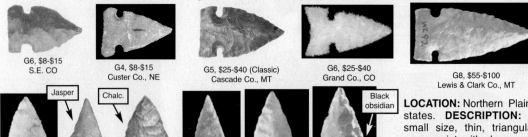

G6, $8-$15
S.E. CO

G4, $8-$15
Custer Co., NE

G5, $25-$40 (Classic)
Cascade Co., MT

G6, $25-$40
Grand Co., CO

G8, $55-$100
Lewis & Clark Co., MT

Jasper

Chalc.

Black
obsidian

G7, $25-$40
Lewis & Clark
Co., MT

G6, $25-$40
San Luis
Valley, CO

G6, $20-$35
S.E. CO

G9, $80-$150
Weld Co., CO

G8, $40-$75
Teton Co., MT

G8, $50-$80
Lewis & Clark
Co., MT

LOCATION: Northern Plains
states. **DESCRIPTION:** A
small size, thin, triangular
arrow point with deep, narrow side notches that expand
towards the center of the
blade. Base can be straight
to concave. Flaking is of high
quality, usually oblique parallel struck from the edge to
the center of the blade.

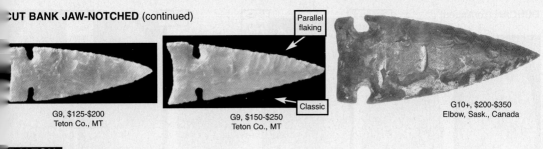

Parallel flaking

Classic

G9, $125-$200
Teton Co., MT

G9, $150-$250
Teton Co., MT

G10+, $200-$350
Elbow, Sask., Canada

DALTON (See Meserve)

DESERT-GENERAL (See Washita for the correct type in the Northern Plains)

DESERT-SIERRA (See Harrell for the correct type in the Northern Plains)

DRILL - Plains Paleo to Historic Phase, 11,500 - 15 0 B. P.

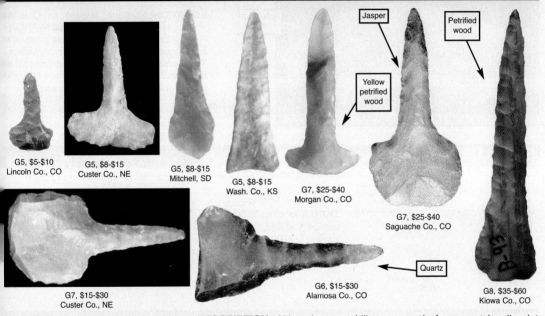

Jasper

Petrified wood

Yellow petrified wood

Quartz

G5, $5-$10
Lincoln Co., CO

G5, $8-$15
Custer Co., NE

G5, $8-$15
Mitchell, SD

G5, $8-$15
Wash. Co., KS

G7, $25-$40
Morgan Co., CO

G7, $25-$40
Saguache Co., CO

G7, $15-$30
Custer Co., NE

G6, $15-$30
Alamosa Co., CO

G8, $35-$60
Kiowa Co., CO

LOCATION: Throughout North America. **DESCRIPTION:** Although many drills were made from scratch, all point types were made into the drill form. Usually, heavily resharpened and broken points were salvaged and rechipped into drills. **I.D. KEY:** Narrow blade form.

DUNCAN - Middle to Late Archaic, 4600 - 3500 B. P.

(Also see Hanna, Meserve and San Jose)

Jasper

G4, $8-$15
Lincoln Co., CO

G4, $8-$15
Sundance, WY

G4, $8-$15
Lincoln Co., CO

G5, $12-$20
Bent Co., CO

G5, $12-$20
Alamosa Co., CO

G5, $35-$60
Lewis & Clark Co., MT

G5, $25-$45
Dillon, MT

DUNCAN (continued)

G7, $35-$65
Elbow, Sask., Canada

G9, $45-$85
Elbow, Sask., Canada

G8, $70-$135
Lewis & Clark Co., MT

G8, $50-$90
Montrail Co., ND

G8, $70-$125
Mountrail Co., ND

G8, $60-$110
Mountrail Co., ND

Knife River flint

LOCATION: Northern Arizona to Canada and to eastern Oklahoma. **DESCRIPTION:** A small to medium size dart/knife point with a triangular blade and angular shoulders. The stem is straight with a V-shaped notch in the basal edge. Stem edges are usually ground. **I.D. KEY:** Straight stem edges.

G9, $250-$400
Jamestown, ND

EARLY TRIANGULAR - Early Archaic, 9000 - 7000 B. P.

(Also see Angostura, Triangular Knife)

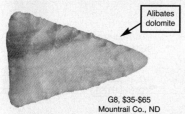

Alibates dolomite

LOCATION: New Mexico into Colorado and W. Texas. **DESCRIPTION:** A medium to large size , broad, thin, triangular blade that can be serrated. The base is either flutaed or has long thinning strikes. Quality is excellent with early oblique transverse and possible right hand beveling when resharpened. Basal areas are gound. **I.D. KEY:** Basal thinning and edgework.

G8, $35-$65
Mountrail Co., ND

EDEN - Plains Paleo, 10,000 - 8000 B. P.

(Also see Agate Basin, Alberta, Alder Complex, Angostura, Browns Valley and Scottsbluff)

G6, $200-$350
Bent Co., CO

G6, $200-$350
Cent. ND

G8, $450-$800
Cheyenne Co., CO

G4, $150-$250
Otero Co., CO

G3, $150-$250
E. CO

G8, $450-$800
Upton, WY

G8, $650-$1200
Renville Co., ND

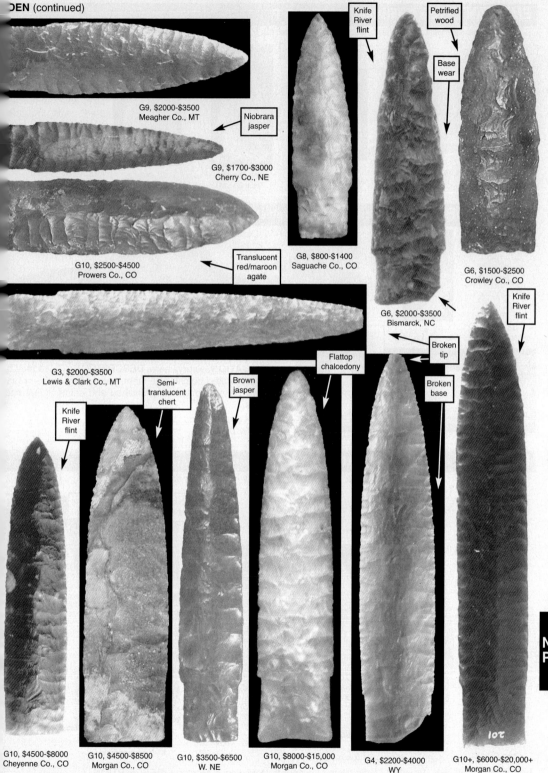

G9, $2000-$3500
Meagher Co., MT

Niobrara jasper

G9, $1700-$3000
Cherry Co., NE

Knife River flint

Petrified wood

Base wear

Translucent red/maroon agate

G10, $2500-$4500
Prowers Co., CO

G8, $800-$1400
Saguache Co., CO

G6, $1500-$2500
Crowley Co., CO

G6, $2000-$3500
Bismarck, NC

Knife River flint

Broken tip

Flattop chalcedony

Broken base

G3, $2000-$3500
Lewis & Clark Co., MT

Semi-translucent chert

Brown jasper

Knife River flint

G10, $4500-$8000
Cheyenne Co., CO

G10, $4500-$8500
Morgan Co., CO

G10, $3500-$6500
W. NE

G10, $8000-$15,000
Morgan Co., CO

G4, $2200-$4000
WY

G10+, $6000-$20,000+
Morgan Co., CO

NP

LOCATION: Northern Plains to Midwestern states. **DESCRIPTION:** A medium to large size, narrow, stemmed point with very weak shoulders and a straight to convex base. Basal sides are parallel to slightly expanding. Many examples have a median ridge and collateral to oblique parallel flaking. Bases are usually ground. A Cody Complex point. **I.D. KEY:** Paleo flaking, narrowness.

EMIGRANT - Late Prehistoric, 900 - 400 B. P.

(Also see Billings, Buffalo Gap, Cut Bank, Harrell, Plains Side Notched, Swift Current & Washita)

Classic form

Obsidian

G6, $12-$20
Cascade Co., MT

G7, $25-$45
MT

G9, $40-$75
Meagher Co., MT

G9, $50-$90
Teton Co., MT

G9, $40-$75
Teton Co., MT

LOCATION: Norther Plains states. **DESCRIPTION:** A sma size, thin, tri-notche point with rounde basal corners. If bas corners are pointe the type would b Billings. **I.D. KEY** Rounded basal co ners.

EXOTIC FORMS - Late Archaic to Late Prehistoric, 3000 - 1000 B. P.

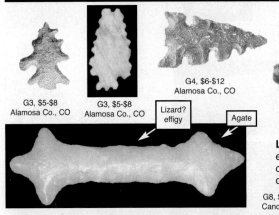
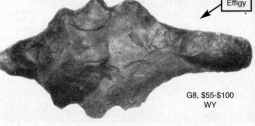

Effigy

G3, $5-$8
Alamosa Co., CO

G3, $5-$8
Alamosa Co., CO

G4, $6-$12
Alamosa Co., CO

G8, $55-$100
WY

Lizard? effigy

Agate

G8, $200-$350
Canon City, CO

LOCATION: Everywhere. **DESCRIPTION:** These may b exaggerated notching on other types, effigy forms or ma only be no more than unfinished and unintentional doc dles.

FIRSTVIEW - Plains Paleo, 10,00 - 8000 B. P.

(Also see Alberta, Alder Complex, Cody Knife, Eden and Scottsbluff)

Chalcedony

Knife River flint

Knife River flint

Broken Base

Collateral flaking

Jasp

G10, $1000-$1800
Otero Co., CO

G6, $250-$400
Dunn Co., ND

G8, $1200-$2000
Lincoln Co., CO

G1, $80-$150
McLean Co., ND

G7, $350-$600
McLean Co., ND
silicified sandstone

G9, $1700-$3000
Cheyenne Co., CO

LOCATION: Colorado, Western Texas, New Mexico into Wyoming & Montana. **DESCRIPTION:** A medium to large size lanceolate point with slightly convex blade edges, slight shoulders and a rectangular stem. Shoulders are sometimes absent from resharpening. It generally exhibits parallel-transverse flaking. A variant form of the *Scottsbluff* type made by Cody Complex people. **I.D. KEY:** Weak shoulders, diamond shaped cross-section.

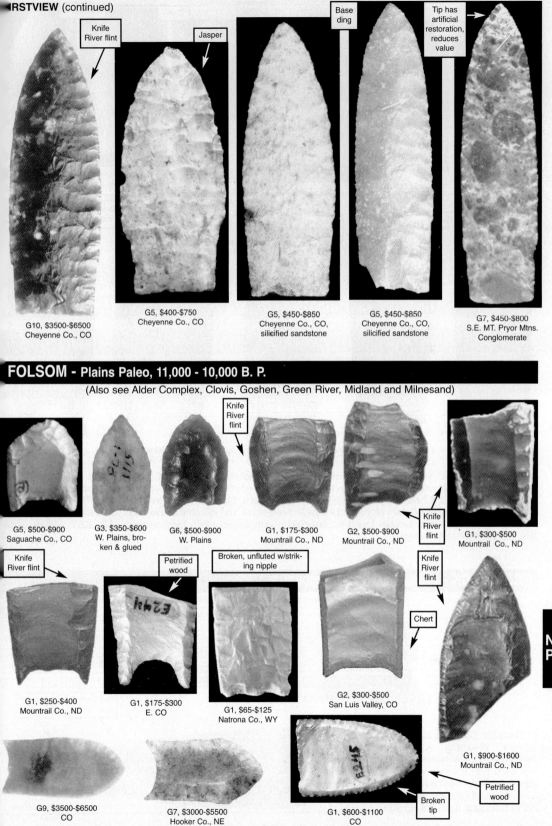

Knife River flint

Jasper

Base ding

Tip has artificial restoration, reduces value

G10, $3500-$6500
Cheyenne Co., CO

G5, $400-$750
Cheyenne Co., CO

G5, $450-$850
Cheyenne Co., CO,
silicified sandstone

G5, $450-$850
Cheyenne Co., CO,
silicified sandstone

G7, $450-$800
S.E. MT. Pryor Mtns.
Conglomerate

FOLSOM - Plains Paleo, 11,000 - 10,000 B. P.

(Also see Alder Complex, Clovis, Goshen, Green River, Midland and Milnesand)

Knife River flint

G5, $500-$900
Saguache Co., CO

G3, $350-$600
W. Plains, bro-
ken & glued

G6, $500-$900
W. Plains

G1, $175-$300
Mountrail Co., ND

G2, $500-$900
Mountrail Co., ND

Knife River flint

G1, $300-$500
Mountrail Co., ND

Knife River flint

Petrified wood

Broken, unfluted w/strik-
ing nipple

Knife River flint

Chert

N
P

G1, $250-$400
Mountrail Co., ND

G1, $175-$300
E. CO

G1, $65-$125
Natrona Co., WY

G2, $300-$500
San Luis Valley, CO

G1, $900-$1600
Mountrail Co., ND

Petrified wood

G9, $3500-$6500
CO

G7, $3000-$5500
Hooker Co., NE

G1, $600-$1100
CO

Broken tip

919

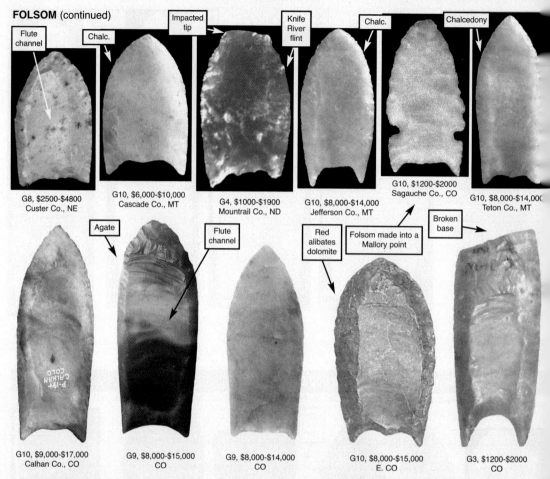

Flute channel — Chalc. — Impacted tip — Knife River flint — Chalc. — Chalcedony

G8, $2500-$4800
Custer Co., NE

G10, $6,000-$10,000
Cascade Co., MT

G4, $1000-$1900
Mountrail Co., ND

G10, $8,000-$14,000
Jefferson Co., MT

G10, $1200-$2000
Sagauche Co., CO

G10, $8,000-$14,000
Teton Co., MT

Agate — Flute channel — Red alibates dolomite — Folsom made into a Mallory point — Broken base

G10, $9,000-$17,000
Calhan Co., CO

G9, $8,000-$15,000
CO

G9, $8,000-$14,000
CO

G10, $8,000-$15,000
E. CO

G3, $1200-$2000
CO

LOCATION: Canada to the Southwestern states and to N. Indiana. **DESCRIPTION:** A very thin, small to medium sized lanceolate point with convex edges and a concave basal edge creating sharp ears or basal corners. Most examples are fluted from the basal edge to nearly the tip of the point. Blade flaking is extremely fine. The hafting area is ground. A very rare type. Modern reproductions have been made and extreme caution should be exercised in acquiring an original specimen. Usually found in association with extinct bison fossil remains. **I.D. KEY:** Flaking style (Excessive secondary flaking).

FREDERICK - Plains Paleo, 9000 - 8000 B. P.

(Also see Allen, Anderson, Angostura, Goshen, Lovell, Lusk)

Oblique parallel flaking

G9, $400-$650
CO

Oblique parallel flaking — Agatized wood

LOCATION: Colorado, Montana, North & South Dakota, Wyoming, Kansas & Nebraska. **DESCRIPTION:** A medium to large size lanceolate point with a concave base. Flaking is random to oblique transverse. Bases are thinned and are usually the widest part of the point. **I.D. KEY:** Triangular form, flaking style.

G9, $1500-$2800
Walworth Co., SD

(Also see Besant, Avonlea, Glendo)

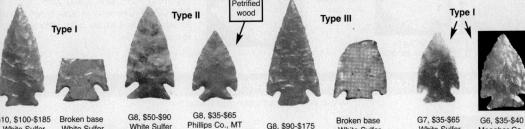

Type I

Type II

Petrified wood

Type III

Type I

G10, $100-$185
White Sulfer
Springs, MT

Broken base
White Sulfer
Springs, MT

G8, $50-$90
White Sulfer
Springs, MT

G8, $35-$65
Phillips Co., MT

G8, $90-$175
White Sulfer
Springs, MT

Broken base
White Sulfer
Springs, MT

G7, $35-$65
White Sulfer
Springs, MT

G6, $35-$40
Meagher Co.,
MT

Type II

Type I

G7, $40-$70
White Sulfer
Springs, MT

Type I

G8, $65-$125
Meagher Co., MT

Type II

G10, $125-$200
White Sulfer
Springs, MT

Type II

G6, $25-$40
White Sulfer
Springs, MT

Type I

G9, $80-$150
Meagher Co., MT

Type I **Type II**

Type II

Type I

Tip nick

Type II **Type I** **Type II**

G10, $80-$150
White Sulfer
Springs, MT

G8, $45-$80
White Sulfer
Springs, MT

G8, $45-$80
White Sulfer
Springs, MT

G8, $45-$80
Dodge City, KS

G3, $5-$10
Meagher Co., MT

G8, $45-$85
White Sulfer
Springs, MT

G8, $45-$80
Ulm, MT

G8, $45-$80
White Sulfer
Springs, MT

G10, $175-$300
White Sulfer
Springs, MT

LOCATION: North central Montana to northern half of Wyoming. **DESCRIPTION:** A small to medium size, thin, extremely well made, delicate arrow point. Flaking is random. Delicate "U" shaped angled notches that are deeper than those found on *Avonlea* points. Bases are straight to slightly concave. The high plains first true "arrow point" along with *Avonlea*. **Galt Type I** are corner notched removing equal portions of the basal and lateral blade edges. **Galt Type II** points start at the basal corner and remove the notch on the lateral edge. **Galt Type III** points are basal notched with the notch starting at the basal corner.

GALT (Hastings Var.) - Late Prehistoric, 1500 - 900 B. P.

(Also see Avonlea, Besant, Glendo)

LOCATION: North central Montana to northern half of Wyoming. **DESCRIPTION:** Similar to the regular *Galt* point but with a decidedly convex base, type I corner notches, and are slightly thicker than the classic type.

G7, $35-$60
Ulm, MT

G8, $50-$90
Ulm, MT

GLENDO ARROW - Late Prehistoric, 1500 - 800 B. P.

(Also see Pelican Lake)

N
P

GLENDO ARROW (continued)

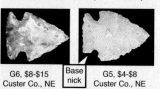

G6, $8-$15
Custer Co., NE

Base nick

G5, $4-$8
Custer Co., NE

G8, $25-$40
Bent/Crowler Co., CO

LOCATION: New Mexico into Colorado Wyoming, southern Idaho and Montana **DESCRIPTION:** A small size, broad, corne to side notched arrow point with a straigh to convex base.

GLENDO DART - Late Prehistoric, 1700 - 1200 B. P.

(Also see Pelican Lake and Besant)

G5, $5-$10
Custer Co., NE

G6, $20-$35
Bent Co., CO

G6, $25-$40
El Paso Co., CO

G7, $30-$55
Teller Co., CO

LOCATION: New Mexico into Colorado, Wyoming, southern Idaho and Montana. **DESCRIPTION:** A medium to large size, broad, corner to side notched dart point with a straight to convex base. Some examples have a concave base producing ears. Believed to be related to the *Besant* point.

G6, $15-$25
Custer Co., NE

G9, $45-$85
Custer Co., NE

GOSHEN - Plains Paleo, 11,250 - 9500 B. P.

(Also see Alder Complex, Clovis, Folsom, Green River, Midland and Milnesand)

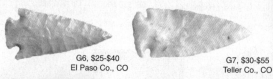

Pet. wood

G1, $25-$40
Mountrail Co., ND

Broken base

Alibates dolomite

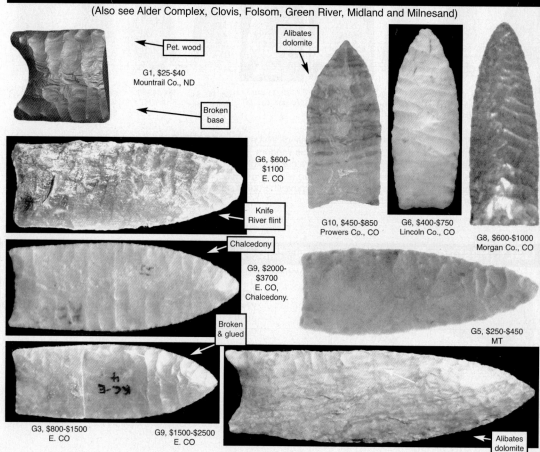

G6, $600-$1100
E. CO

Knife River flint

Chalcedony

G9, $2000-$3700
E. CO, Chalcedony.

G10, $450-$850
Prowers Co., CO

G6, $400-$750
Lincoln Co., CO

G8, $600-$1000
Morgan Co., CO

G5, $250-$450
MT

Broken & glued

G3, $800-$1500
E. CO

G9, $1500-$2500
E. CO

Alibates dolomite

922

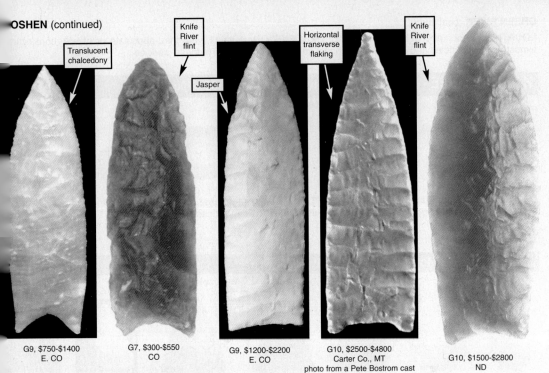

Translucent chalcedony

Knife River flint

Jasper

Horizontal transverse flaking

Knife River flint

G9, $750-$1400
E. CO

G7, $300-$550
CO

G9, $1200-$2200
E. CO

G10, $2500-$4800
Carter Co., MT
photo from a Pete Bostrom cast

G10, $1500-$2800
ND

Broken & glued

Jasper

G5, $1200-$2000
Logan Co., CO

LOCATION: Northern Plains states. **DESCRIPTION:** A small to medium size, very thin, auriculate dart point with a concave base. Basal corners are rounded to sharp. Basal area is ground. Flaking is oblique to horizontal transverse or random. Same as *Plainview* found in Texas. **I.D. KEY:** Thinness, auricles.

GRAVER - Plains Paleo to Archaic, 11,500 - 4000 B. P.

(Also see Scraper)

Graver points

G6, $5-$10 ea.
Alamosa, CO, Folsom site.

G6, $5-$10
Prowers Co., CO

LOCATION: Early man sites everywhere. **DESCRIPTION:** An irregular shaped uniface tool with sharp, pointed projections used for puncturing, incising, tattooing, etc.

N P

GREEN RIVER - Mid-Archaic, 4500 - 4200 B.P.

(Also see Alder Complex, Clovis, Folsom, Green River, Midland and Milnesand)

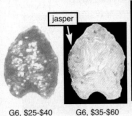

jasper

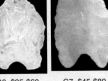

jasper

G6, $25-$40
N. UT

G6, $35-$60
E. CO

G7, $45-$80
Red Desert, WY

G1, $5-$10
Casper, WY.
Broken Back.

G8, $60-$110
Otero Co., CO
Kay County chert

G1, $8-$15
Casper, WY,
Tip damage.

G7, $65-$125
ID

GREEN RIVER (continued)

LOCATION: Mont., WY, CO, NE, NM & AZ. **DESCRIPTION:** A small, very thin, auriculate point with contractin~ almost pointed auricles and a small, deep basal concavity. **I.D. KEY:** Thinness, auricles.

HAFTED KNIFE - Late Archaic to Late Prehistoric - 2300 - 400 B.P.

(Also see Side Knife)

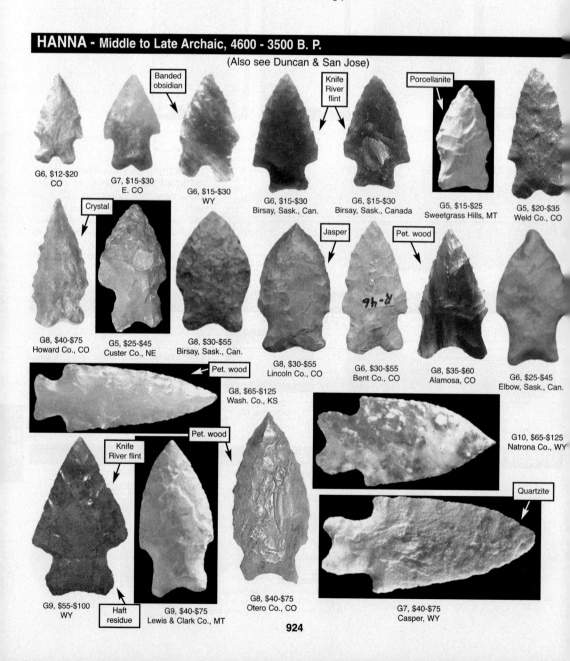

Knife shown 3/4th actual size

G8, $450-$800
Custer Co., NE

LOCATION: Northern Plains states. **DES- CRIPTION:** A medium to large size blade hafted into a wooden, antler c bone handle. Usually asphaltum and fiber were used in the hafting process.

HANNA - Middle to Late Archaic, 4600 - 3500 B. P.

(Also see Duncan & San Jose)

Banded obsidian

Knife River flint

Porcellanite

G6, $12-$20
CO

G7, $15-$30
E. CO

G6, $15-$30
WY

G6, $15-$30
Birsay, Sask., Can.

G6, $15-$30
Birsay, Sask., Canada

G5, $15-$25
Sweetgrass Hills, MT

G5, $20-$35
Weld Co., CO

Crystal

Jasper

Pet. wood

G8, $40-$75
Howard Co., CO

G5, $25-$45
Custer Co., NE

G8, $30-$55
Birsay, Sask., Can.

G8, $30-$55
Lincoln Co., CO

G6, $30-$55
Bent Co., CO

G8, $35-$60
Alamosa, CO

G6, $25-$45
Elbow, Sask., Can.

Pet. wood

G8, $65-$125
Wash. Co., KS

G10, $65-$125
Natrona Co., WY

Pet. wood

Knife River flint

Quartzite

G9, $55-$100
WY

Haft residue

G9, $40-$75
Lewis & Clark Co., MT

G8, $40-$75
Otero Co., CO

G7, $40-$75
Casper, WY

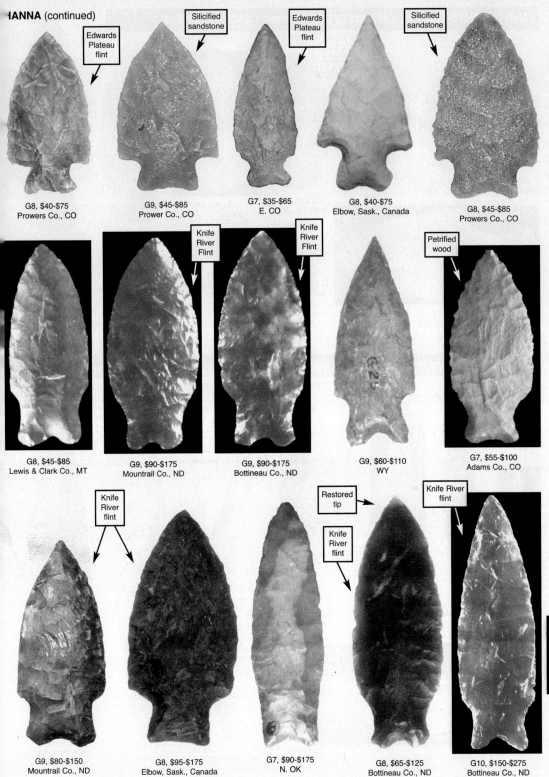

Edwards Plateau flint

Silicified sandstone

Edwards Plateau flint

Silicified sandstone

G8, $40-$75
Prowers Co., CO

G9, $45-$85
Prower Co., CO

G7, $35-$65
E. CO

G8, $40-$75
Elbow, Sask., Canada

G8, $45-$85
Prowers Co., CO

Knife River Flint

Knife River Flint

Petrified wood

G8, $45-$85
Lewis & Clark Co., MT

G9, $90-$175
Mountrail Co., ND

G9, $90-$175
Bottineau Co., ND

G9, $60-$110
WY

G7, $55-$100
Adams Co., CO

Knife River flint

Restored tip

Knife River flint

Knife River flint

Knife River flint

G9, $80-$150
Mountrail Co., ND

G8, $95-$175
Elbow, Sask., Canada

G7, $90-$175
N. OK

G8, $65-$125
Bottineau Co., ND

G10, $150-$275
Bottineau Co., ND

N P

LOCATION: Nebraska to Canada and as far south as the Southwestern states. **DESCRIPTION:** A small to medium size, narrow, bifurcated stemmed dart/knife point with tapered to horizontal shoulders and an expanding stem which is notched to produce diagonally projecting rounded "ears". **I.D. KEY:** Expanding stem.

925

HANNA NORTHERN - Middle to Late Archaic , 4600 - 3500 B. P.

(Also see Duncan)

Basalt

Basalt

G4, $5-$10
Bent Co., CO

G4, $5-$10
Bent Co., CO

G8, $15-$25
Birsay, Sask.,
Canada

G5, $12-$20
Bent Co., CO

G5, $12-$20
Custer Co., NE

G6, $25-$45
N. Lincoln Co., CO

G6, $35-$65
WY

G6, $30-$55
Alberta, Canada

G6, $25-$40
Lincoln Co., CO

LOCATION: Northern Plains states to Canada. **DESCRIPTION:** A small to medium size, narrow, long stemmed point with tapered to horizontal shoulders. Stem can be bifurcated.

HARAHEY - Late Prehistoric, 700 - 300 B. P.

(Also see Archaic Knife and Neosho)

Beveled on 4 sides

Chert

Beveled on 4 sides

ALL HARAHEYS SHOWN HALF SIZE

Beveled on 4 sides

Jasper

Alibates dolomite

Beveled on 4 sides

G8, $45-$80
SD

G9, $170-$325
KS

G5, $150-$275
Prowers Co., CO

G8, $200-$375
Bent Co., CO

Alibates dolomite

Beveled on 4 sides

G9, $450-$800
Hamilton Co., KS

G10, $450-$850
Baca Co., CO

G10, $275-$500
Elbert Co., CO

G10, $350-$600
Natrona Co., WY

LOCATION: Northern Plains states to Texas to Illinois to Canada. **DESCRIPTION:** A large size, double pointed buffalo knife that is beveled on all four edges. The cross section is rhomboid. See *Neosho* for the two beveled form. **I.D. KEY:** Rhomboid cross section.

HARRELL- Late Prehistoric, 900 - 500 B. P.

(Also see Billings, Emigrant and Washita)

G9, $15-$30
Sherman Co., NE

G6, $12-$20
Bismark, ND

G9, $30-$50
Sherman Co., NE

G9, $30-$50
Buffalo Co., NE

G9, $40-$70
Custer Co., NE

LOCATION: Eastern Colorado, Arkansas, Oklahoma, Kansas, Nebraska and Missouri. **DESCRIPTION:** A small size, thin, triangular arrow point with side notches and a basal notch. Bases are slightly concave to straight.

HAWKEN - Early to Middle Archaic, 6500 - 6200 B. P.

(Also see Besant, Logan Creek and Lookingbill)

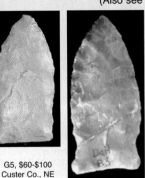

G5, $60-$100
Custer Co., NE

G7, $130-$225
Teton Co., MT

G8, $125-$200
E. SD

G6, $100-$175
Meagher Co., MT

G7, $150-$265
Meagher Co., MT

Tip nick

G8, $300-$550
Meagher Co., MT

LOCATION: Northern Plains state. Type site is in Wyoming. **DESCRIPTION:** A small to medium size, narrow point with broad, shallow side notches and an expanding stem. Blade flaking is of high quality and is usually the oblique to horizontal parallel type. Along with *Logan Creek* and *Lookingbill* this is one of the earliest side-notched points of the Plains states. **I.D. KEY:** Broad side notches, expanding base.

HELL GAP - Plains Paleo, 10,300 - 9500 B. P.

(Also see Agate Basin, Angostura, Bajada, Browns Valley, Pryor Stemmed and Rio Grande)

G6, $40-$75
CO

G5, $100-$180
Weld Co., CO

G5, $100-$180
Washington Co., CO

G7, $175-$300
Morgan Co., CO

G7, $250-$400
E. CO

Alibates dolomite

Jasper

LOCATION: Northern Plains states to Canada. **DESCRIPTION:** A medium to large size, narrow, long stemmed point with weak, tapered shoulders. Base can be concave, convex or straight. The basal area is usually ground. **I.D. KEY:** Early flaking and base form. Can be easily confused with *Rio Grande* Points found in southern Colorado southward through New Mexico.

927

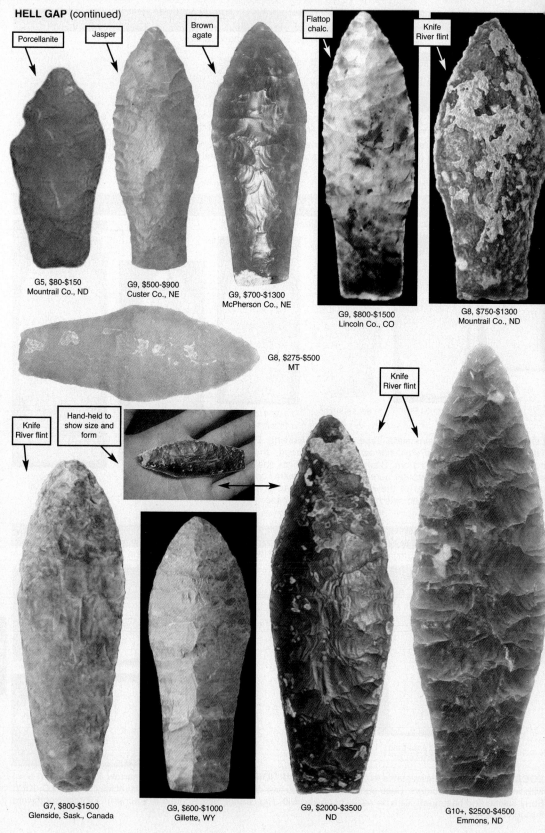

Porcellanite

Jasper

Brown agate

Flattop chalc.

Knife River flint

G5, $80-$150
Mountrail Co., ND

G9, $500-$900
Custer Co., NE

G9, $700-$1300
McPherson Co., NE

G9, $800-$1500
Lincoln Co., CO

G8, $750-$1300
Mountrail Co., ND

G8, $275-$500
MT

Knife River flint

Hand-held to show size and form

Knife River flint

G7, $800-$1500
Glenside, Sask., Canada

G9, $600-$1000
Gillette, WY

G9, $2000-$3500
ND

G10+, $2500-$4500
Emmons, ND

HIGH RIVER - Late Prehistoric, 1300 - 800 B. P.

(Also see Avonlea, Hog Back, Pelican Lake and Samantha)

G4, $4-$7
Chouteau Co., MT

G4, $6-$10
Meagher Co., MT

G4, $4-$7
Ft. Peck Res., MT

G7, $8-$15
Meagher Co., MT

G7, $8-$15
Lewis & Clark Co., MT

G8, $15-$20
Meagher Co., MT

G4, $5-$10
Chouteau Co., MT

G4, $4-$7
Lincoln Co., CO

LOCATION: Northern Plains states to Canada. **DESCRIPTION:** A small, thin, corner notched triangular arrow point with a straight to convex base. Basal grinding is evident on some specimens. **I.D. KEY:** Small corner notched point.

HOG BACK - Late Prehistoric, 1000 - 600 B. P.

(Also see Camel Back, High River, Mummy Cave, Pelican Lake & Samantha)

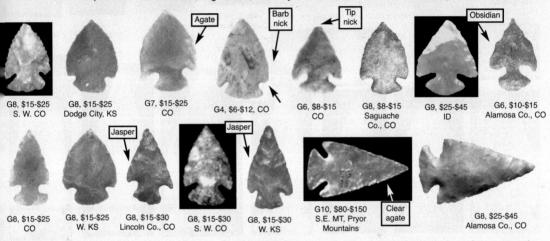

Agate
Barb nick
Tip nick
Obsidian

G8, $15-$25
S. W. CO

G8, $15-$25
Dodge City, KS

G7, $15-$25
CO

G4, $6-$12, CO

G6, $8-$15
CO

G8, $8-$15
Saguache Co., CO

G9, $25-$45
ID

G6, $10-$15
Alamosa Co., CO

Jasper
Jasper

G8, $15-$25
CO

G8, $15-$25
W. KS

G8, $15-$30
Lincoln Co., CO

G8, $15-$30
S. W. CO

G8, $15-$30
W. KS

G10, $80-$150
S.E. MT, Pryor Mountains

Clear agate

G8, $25-$45
Alamosa Co., CO

LOCATION: Northern Plains states to Canada. **DESCRIPTION:** A small, thin, corner notched triangular arrow point with barbed shoulders and a convex base. The preform is ovoid and blade edges can be serrated. **I.D. KEY:** Small corner notched point, barbs.

HORSE FLY - Late Prehistoric, 1500 - 1000 B. P.

(Also see High River and Lewis)

G8, $30-$50
Prowers Co., CO

G7, $18-$30
E. CO. Petrified wood.

Quartzite

Edwards Plateau flint

LOCATION: Colorado. **DESCRIPTION:** A medium to large size, narrow, stemmed point with a short, expanding stem and a straight to slightly convex base. Shoulders are horizontal to slightly barbed. **I.D. KEY:** Short, expanding stem.

G7, $25-$40
Crowley Co., CO

HUFFAKER - Late Prehistoric, 1000 - 500 B. P.

(Also see Harrell & Washita)

HUFFAKER (continued)

G6, $15-$25
Bismark, ND

G6, $15-$25
Lincoln Co., CO

G6, $15-$25
Bent Co., CO

LOCATION: Midwest to Northern Plains states. **DESCRIPTION:** A small size, thin arrowpoint with a straight to concave base and double side notches. Bases can have a single notch. **I.D. KEY:** Double side notches.

IRVINE - Late Prehistoric, 1400 - 800 B. P.

(Also see Avonlea, Emigrant, Lookingbill, Plains Side Notched, Samantha & Washita)

Petrified wood

Petrified wood

Knife River flint

G5, $12-$20
Phillips Co., MT

G3, $7-$12
Meagher Co., MT

G6, $15-$30
Meagher Co., MT

G6, $25-$45
Phillips Co., MT

G5, $15-$30
Cascade Co., MT

G8, $35-$60
Phillips Co., MT

G6, $30-$50
Cascade Co., MT

G6, $30-$50
Meagher Co., M

G6, $25-$40
Malta, MT

G5, $40-$70
Cascade Co., MT

Parallel flaking

Obliquel flaking

G9, $65-$120
Saco, MT, Milk Riv

G9, $65-$120
Meagher Co., MT

G9, $65-$120
Cascade Co., MT

G10, $70-$125
Meagher Co., MT

G8, $50-$80
Bent Co., CO

G10, $80-$150
Meagher Co., MT

G10, $80-$150
Meagher Co., MT

LOCATION: Northern Plains states. **DESCRIPTION:** A small size, thin, side notched arrow point with a concave base. The notching is distinct forming squarish basal ears. **I.D. KEY:** Square basal ears.

LANCET - Plains Paleo to Historic Phase, 11,500 - 200 B. P.

(Also see Drill and Scraper)

G7, $8-$12 ea. (All hafted)
Lewis & Clark Co., MT

LOCATION: Everywhere. **DESCRIPTION:** Also known as a lammeler flake blade, it was produced by striking a flake or spall off a parent stone and was used as a knife for cutting. Some examples are notched for hafting. Recent experiments proved that these knives were sharper than a surgeon's scalpel. Similar to *burins* which are fractured at one end to produce a sharp point.

930

LEWIS - Late Prehistoric, 1400 - 400 B. P.

(Also see Avonlea, High River, Irvine, Nanton, Paskapoo, Swift Current and Tompkins)

Knife River flint

G5, $5-$10
Lewis & Clark Co., MT

G6, $6-$12
Phillips Co., MT

G8, $15-$30
Meagher Co., MT

G6, $15-$30
MT

G10, $45-$85
Mountrail Co., ND

LOCATION: Midwestern to Northern Plains states. **DESCRIPTION:** A small to medium size, thin, side notched point with a convex to concave base. The width of the base is less than the shoulders and the basal corners are rounded. Some specimens have basal grinding.

LOGAN CREEK - Early Archaic, 7000 - 5000 B. P.

(Also see Hawken, Lookingbill, Mallory, Plains Side Notched and Simonsen)

G6, $15-$25
W. KS

G6, $20-$35
Washington Co., KS

G8, $35-$65
Jefferson Co., NE

G6, $25-$45
Jefferson Co., NE

G8, $35-$65
Washington Co., NE

G7, $35-$65
Washington Co., KS

Knife River flint

Oblique flaking

G6, $25-$45
Washington Co., KS

G7, $35-$65
Washington Co., KS

G8, $50-$90
Jefferson Co., KS

G7, $35-$65
Washington Co., KS

G8, $100-$195
Douglas Co., ND

G6, $35-$60
Washington Co., KS

G7, $40-$75
Washington Co., KS

LOGAN CREEK S.D.

G9, $165-$300
S.D

LOCATION: NE, IA, WY, MT, SD, KS. **DESCRIPTION:** A medium to large size, broad side-notched point with a straight, concave or convex base. Along with *Hawken* and *Lookingbill* , this is one of the earliest side-notched points of the Plains states. Oblique to horizontal blade flaking is evident on some examples. **I.D. KEY:** Broad side-notches close to the base, early flaking.

N
P

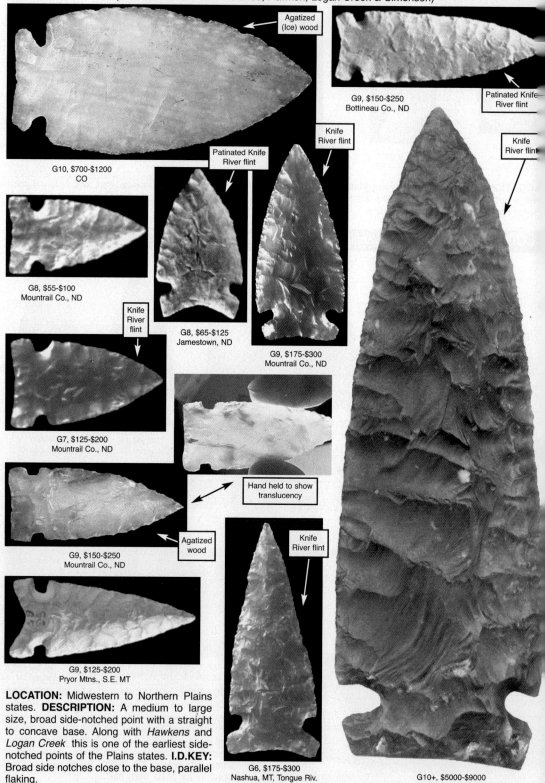

LOOKINGBILL - Early to Middle Archaic, 7200 - 6900 B. P.

(Also see Archaic Side Notched, Hawken, Logan Creek & Simonsen)

Agatized (Ice) wood

G10, $700-$1200
CO

G9, $150-$250
Bottineau Co., ND

Patinated Knife River flint

Knife River flint

Patinated Knife River flint

G8, $55-$100
Mountrail Co., ND

G8, $65-$125
Jamestown, ND

Knife River flint

G9, $175-$300
Mountrail Co., ND

Knife River flint

G7, $125-$200
Mountrail Co., ND

Hand held to show translucency

Agatized wood

G9, $150-$250
Mountrail Co., ND

Knife River flint

G9, $125-$200
Pryor Mtns., S.E. MT

LOCATION: Midwestern to Northern Plains states. **DESCRIPTION:** A medium to large size, broad side-notched point with a straight to concave base. Along with *Hawkens* and *Logan Creek* this is one of the earliest side-notched points of the Plains states. **I.D.KEY:** Broad side notches close to the base, parallel flaking.

G6, $175-$300
Nashua, MT, Tongue Riv.

G10+, $5000-$9000
McKenzie Co., ND

LOVELL - Mountain Paleo, 8400 - 7800 B. P.

(Also see Agate Basin, Alder Complex, Clovis, Folsom, Goshen and Green River)

G7, $45-$85
Brookings Co., SD

Knife River flint

Ground base

G6, $45-$85
Mountrail Co., ND

Ground base

Oblique flaking

G6, $65-$125
Lewis & Clark Co., MT

G6, $55-$100
ND, Knife River flint

G5, $200-$350
Lewis & Clark Co., MT

Ground base

G10, $400-$750
Broadwater Co., MT

LOCATION: Northern Plains states. **DESCRIPTION:** A small to medium size, narrow, unfluted lanceolate point with a straight to concave base. Blade edges recurve towards the base on most examples. Random to oblique or horizontal parallel flaking occurs. **I.D. KEY:** Form and basal constriction.

G10, $500-$900
WY

LUSK - Transitional Paleo, 8500 - 7400 B. P.

(Also see Angostura)

G8, $175-$300
Mountrail Co., ND

G8, $275-$350
Washington Co., CO

LOCATION: ND, SD, CO, NE, KS, WY. **DESCRIPTION:** A medium to large size, point with a contracting stem. Bases are usually concave and thinned. Related to *Angostura* points. **I.D.KEY:** Lanceolate point with contracting stem.

MALLORY - Middle Archaic, 4600 - 3500 B. P.

(Also see Billings, Emigrant, Logan Creek and Lookingbill)

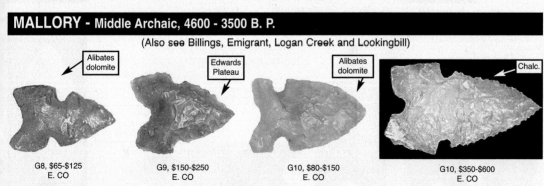

Alibates dolomite

Edwards Plateau

Alibates dolomite

Chalc.

G8, $65-$125
E. CO

G9, $150-$250
E. CO

G10, $80-$150
E. CO

G10, $350-$600
E. CO

LOCATION: Northern Plains states. **DESCRIPTION:** A small to medium size, broad, tri-notched to side notched point with a concave base and sharp basal corners. Side notches occur high up from the base. **I.D. KEY:** Size and tri-notching.

933

MALLORY (continued)

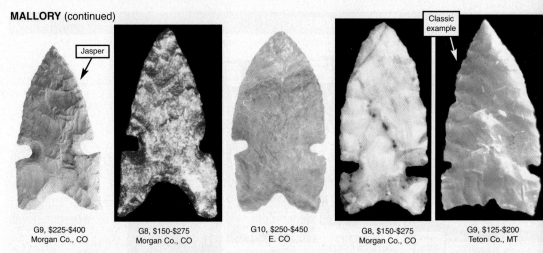

Jasper

Classic example

G9, $225-$400
Morgan Co., CO

G8, $150-$275
Morgan Co., CO

G10, $250-$450
E. CO

G8, $150-$275
Morgan Co., CO

G9, $125-$200
Teton Co., MT

MCKEAN - Middle Archaic, 4600 - 3500 B. P.

(Also see Folsom, Goshen, Green River and Lovell)

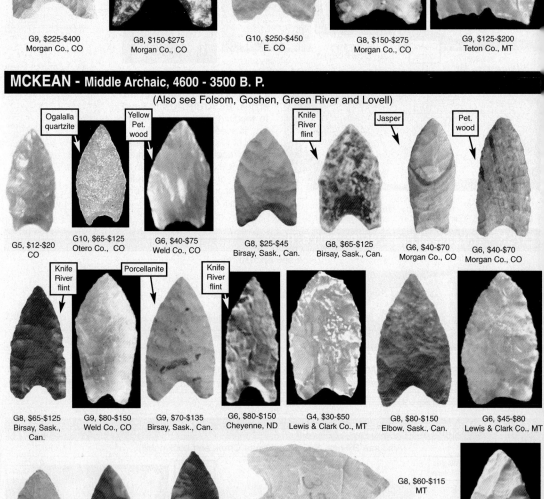

Ogalalla quartzite

Yellow Pet. wood

Knife River flint

Jasper

Pet. wood

G5, $12-$20
CO

G10, $65-$125
Otero Co., CO

G6, $40-$75
Weld Co., CO

G8, $25-$45
Birsay, Sask., Can.

G8, $65-$125
Birsay, Sask., Can.

G6, $40-$70
Morgan Co., CO

G6, $40-$70
Morgan Co., CO

Knife River flint

Porcellanite

Knife River flint

G8, $65-$125
Birsay, Sask., Can.

G9, $80-$150
Weld Co., CO

G9, $70-$135
Birsay, Sask., Can.

G6, $80-$150
Cheyenne, ND

G4, $30-$50
Lewis & Clark Co., MT

G8, $80-$150
Elbow, Sask., Can.

G6, $45-$80
Lewis & Clark Co., MT

G8, $60-$115
MT

Found in two pieces. Note patination difference

Knife River flint

G9, $90-$175
Mountrail Co., ND

G9, $90-$175
Elbow, Sask., Can.

G9, $125-$225
Elbow, Sask., Can.

G5, $45-$85
Elbow, Sask., Can.

G8, $70-$135
Lewis & Clark Co., MT

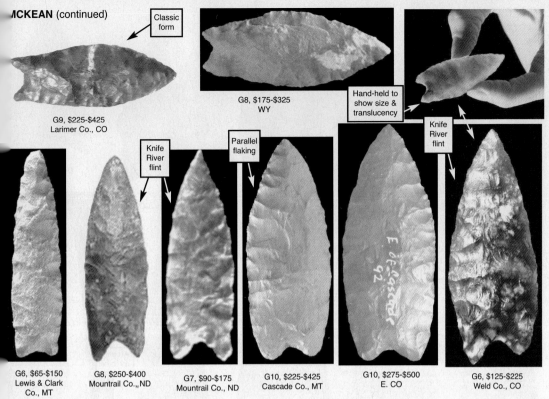

MCKEAN (continued)

Classic form

G9, $225-$425
Larimer Co., CO

G8, $175-$325
WY

Hand-held to show size & translucency

Knife River flint

Knife River flint

Parallel flaking

G6, $65-$150
Lewis & Clark Co., MT

G8, $250-$400
Mountrail Co., ND

G7, $90-$175
Mountrail Co., ND

G10, $225-$425
Cascade Co., MT

G10, $275-$500
E. CO

G6, $125-$225
Weld Co., CO

LOCATION: Northern Plains states. Type site is in N.E. Wyoming. **DESCRIPTION:** A small to medium size, narrow, basal notched point. No basal grinding is evident. Similar to the much earlier *Wheeler* points of the Southeast. Basal ears are rounded to pointed. Flaking is more random although earlier examples can have parallel flaking. **I.D. KEY:** Narrow lanceolate with notched base.

MERKLE - Late Archaic to Woodland, 4000 - 2000 B. P.

(Also see Huffakerl)

LOCATION: Mid-western states northward into Canada. **DESCRIPTION:** A medium to large size point with a short stem and broad side notches and corner notches at the base. Bases are usually straight to convex. **I.D. KEY:** Double notching.

Quartzite

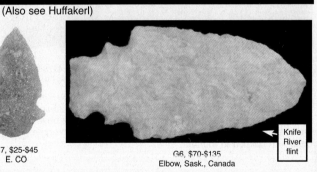

G7, $25-$45
E. CO

Knife River flint

G6, $70-$135
Elbow, Sask., Canada

N
P

MESERVE - Plains Paleo, 9500 - 8500 B. P.

(Also see Clovis, Folsom, Goshen, Lovell and San Jose)

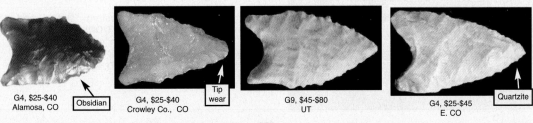

G4, $25-$40
Alamosa, CO

Obsidian

G4, $25-$40
Crowley Co., CO

Tip wear

G9, $45-$80
UT

G4, $25-$45
E. CO

Quartzite

MESERVE (continued)

Knife River flint

G9, $145-$275
CO

G9, $200-$350
Glenside, Sask., Canada

G6, $45-$85
El Paso Co., CO

G6, $85-$165
CO

G8, $175-$325
Weld Co., CO

Brown jasper

Yellow petrified wood

Knife River flint

Beveled edge

Beveled edge

Alibates dolomite

G10, $400-$750
WY

G8, $225-$425
CO

G9, $275-$525
Weld Co., CO

G9, $400-$700
Mitchell, SD

G10+, $600-$1000
E. CO

LOCATION: Co, SD, ND, MT, WY. **DESCRIPTION:** The Plains extension of the *Dalton* family. Blade edges are straight to slightly concave with a straight to very slightly concave sided stem. They are basally thinned and most examples are beveled and have light serrations on the blade edges. Beveling extends to the basal area on some examples. **I.D. KEY:** Concave base with pointed to rounded ears.

MID-BACK TANG - Late Archaic, 3400 - 1000 B. P.

(Also see Base Tang Knife, Cody Knife and Corner Tang)

Quartzite

G7, $250-$450
E. CO

LOCATION: Midwestern states and Canada. **DESCRIPTION:** A variation fo the corner tang knife with the hafting area occurring near the center of one side of the blade. **I.D. KEY:** Tang in center of blade.

936

Agate

G10, $1800-$3500
WY

MIDLAND - Plains Paleo, 10,900 - 10,200 B. P.

(Also see Alder Complex, Clovis, Folsom, Goshen and Milnesand)

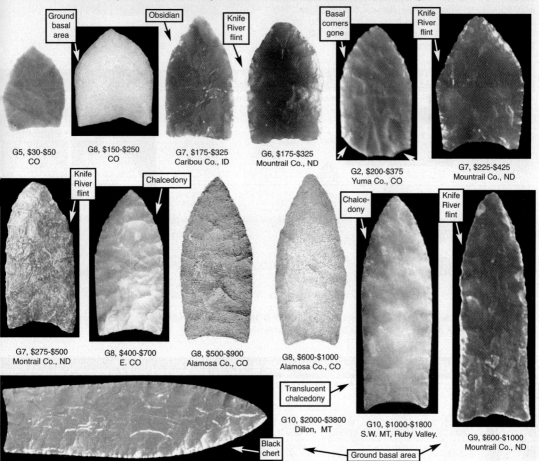

Ground basal area

Obsidian

Knife River flint

Basal corners gone

Knife River flint

G5, $30-$50
CO

G8, $150-$250
CO

G7, $175-$325
Caribou Co., ID

G6, $175-$325
Mountrail Co., ND

G2, $200-$375
Yuma Co., CO

G7, $225-$425
Mountrail Co., ND

Knife River flint

Chalcedony

Chalcedony

Knife River flint

G7, $275-$500
Montrail Co., ND

G8, $400-$700
E. CO

G8, $500-$900
Alamosa Co., CO

G8, $600-$1000
Alamosa Co., CO

Translucent chalcedony

G10, $2000-$3800
Dillon, MT

G10, $1000-$1800
S.W. MT, Ruby Valley.

G9, $600-$1000
Mountrail Co., ND

Black chert

Ground basal area

LOCATION: Texas to the Northern Plains states. **DESCRIPTION:** A small to medium size, very thin, unfluted lance-olate point with the widest part near the tip. Believed to be unfluted *Folsoms*. Bases have a shallow concavity. Basal thinning is weak and the blades exhibit fine micro-edgework. **I.D. KEY:** Form and thinness.

MILNESAND - Plains Paleo, 11,000 - 9500 B. P.

(Also see Alder Complex and Midland)

MILNESAND (continued)

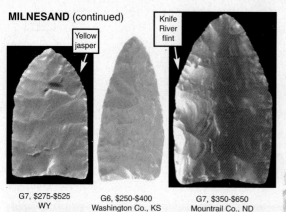

Knife River flint

Yellow jasper

G7, $275-$525
WY

G6, $250-$400
Washington Co., KS

G7, $350-$650
Mountrail Co., ND

Alibates dolomite

G7, $450-$800
E. CO

Obsidian

G9, $800-$1500
Marshall Co., KS

LOCATION: North Dakota to Colorado to west Texas and eastern New Mexico. **DESCRIPTION:** A lanceolate point with parallel to very slightly convex blade edges. The basal edge is straight and is beveled and ground, as are the stem edges. Thicker than *Midland*. **I.D. KEY:** Thickness and Paleo parallel flaking.

MOUNT ALBION - Early Archaic, 5900 - 5600 B. P.

(Also see Besant & Samantha)

G3, $3-$6
Weld Co., CO

Alibates dolomite

G4, $2-$5
CO

G3, $3-$6
Weld Co., CO

G3, $3-$6
Weld Co., CO

G3, $4-$8
Weld Co., CO

G6, $6-$12
E. CO

G6, $8-$15
Lincoln Co., CO

G9, $45-$80
E. CO

G7, $12-$20
E. CO

LOCATION: Southwestern states to Colorado. **DESCRIPTION:** A small to medium size, narrow, broad side notched point with a convex base. Shoulders are tapered. Basal corners are rounded.

MUMMY CAVE - Late Prehistoric, 1400 - 1200 B. P.

(Also see Hog Back and Pelican Lake)

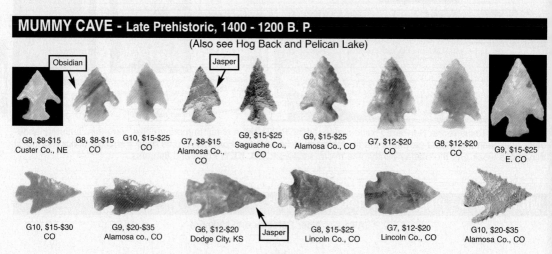

Obsidian

Jasper

G8, $8-$15
Custer Co., NE

G8, $8-$15
CO

G10, $15-$25
CO

G7, $8-$15
Alamosa Co., CO

G9, $15-$25
Saguache Co., CO

G9, $15-$25
Alamosa Co., CO

G7, $12-$20
CO

G8, $12-$20
CO

G9, $15-$25
E. CO

G10, $15-$30
CO

G9, $20-$35
Alamosa co., CO

G6, $12-$20
Dodge City, KS

Jasper

G8, $15-$25
Lincoln Co., CO

G7, $12-$20
Lincoln Co., CO

G10, $20-$35
Alamosa Co., CO

MUMMY CAVE (continued)

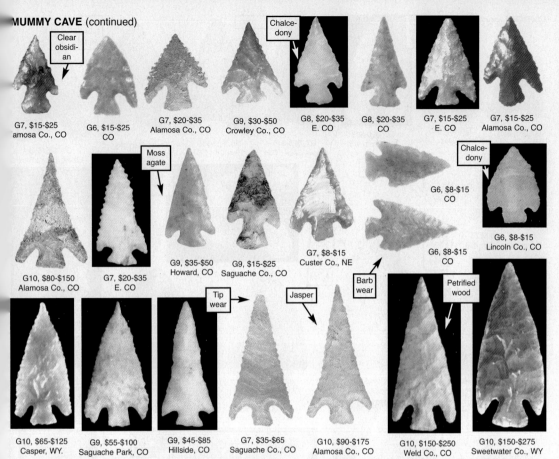

Clear obsidian

G7, $15-$25
amosa Co., CO

G6, $15-$25
CO

G7, $20-$35
Alamosa Co., CO

Chalcedony

G9, $30-$50
Crowley Co., CO

G8, $20-$35
E. CO

G8, $20-$35
CO

G7, $15-$25
E. CO

G7, $15-$25
Alamosa Co., CO

Moss agate

Chalcedony

G6, $8-$15
CO

G6, $8-$15
Lincoln Co., CO

G10, $80-$150
Alamosa Co., CO

G7, $20-$35
E. CO

G9, $35-$50
Howard, CO

G9, $15-$25
Saguache Co., CO

G7, $8-$15
Custer Co., NE

G6, $8-$15
CO

Barb wear

Tip wear

Jasper

Petrified wood

G10, $65-$125
Casper, WY.

G9, $55-$100
Saguache Park, CO

G9, $45-$85
Hillside, CO

G7, $35-$65
Saguache Co., CO

G10, $90-$175
Alamosa Co., CO

G10, $150-$250
Weld Co., CO

G10, $150-$275
Sweetwater Co., WY

LOCATION: Northern Plains states. **DESCRIPTION:** A small size, thin, corner notched dart point with sharp, pointed barbs and an expanding base. Blade edges can be serrated. Similar to *Rose Springs* found in the Great Basin. **I.D. KEY:** Thinness, sharp tangs, early flaking.

NANTON - Late Prehistoric, 1400 - 300 B. P.

(Also see Avonlea, Cut Bank, Pekisko, Irvine and Swift Current)

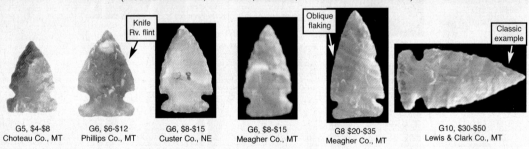

Knife Rv. flint

Oblique flaking

Classic example

G5, $4-$8
Choteau Co., MT

G6, $6-$12
Phillips Co., MT

G6, $8-$15
Custer Co., NE

G6, $8-$15
Meagher Co., MT

G8 $20-$35
Meagher Co., MT

G10, $30-$50
Lewis & Clark Co., MT

LOCATION: Northern Plains states. **DESCRIPTION:** A small to medium size, thin, narrow, side-notched point with rounded basal ears. Basal grinding occurs on some examples.

OXBOW - Middle Archaic, 5200 - 5100 B. P.

(Also see Meserve, San Jose, McKean)

LOCATION: Northern Plains states and Canada. **DESCRIPTION:** A small to medium size, side notched, auriculate point with a concave to bifurcated base that may be ground. Ears are squared to rounded and extend outward or downward from the base. Flaking is random to parallel oblique. **I.D. KEY:** Basal form.

N
P

OXBOW (continued)

Knife River flint

G7, $15-$25
Weld Co., CO

G7, $15-$25
Elbow, Sask., Can.

G7, $20-$35
Moorcroft, WY

Pet. wood

G7, $25-$45
Elbow, Sask., Can.

G6, $20-$35
Bent Co., CO

G7, $40-$75
Birsay, Sask., Can.

Knife River flint

G7, $50-$95
Elbow, Sask., Can.

Agate

G6, $80-$135
Jamestown, ND

Knife River flint

G10, $90-$175
Mountrail Co., ND

Knife River flint

Knife River flint

Yellow petrified wood

Knife River flint

G10, $100-$185
Mountrail Co., ND

G9, $125-$200
Birsay, Sask., Can.

Agate

G8, $125-$200
Devide Co., ND

G8, $100-$185
Birsay, Sask., Canada

G8, $80-$150
Mountrail Co., ND

G6, $50-$90
Broadwater Co., MT

Knife River flint

Knife River flint

One of the best known

G9, $150-$275
Mountrail Co., ND

G10, $250-$450
Meagher Co., MT

G10, $200-$350
Bottineau Co., ND

Agatized wood

Knife River flint

Petrified wood

Patinated Knife River flint

G10, $150-$250
MT

G8, $150-$250
Broadus, MT

G10, $200-$350
Mountrail Co., ND

G10+, $350-$650
Bottineau Co., ND

G10+, $1500-$2500+
Walworth Co., SD

PALEO KNIFE - Plains Paleo, 11,500 - 10,600 B. P.

(Also see Clovis, Crescent Knife)

Patinated
Knife River flint

G10, $4000-$7000
ND

LOCATION: Clovis sites everywhere. **DESCRIPTION:** A large size, ovoid knife form that have been associat-ed with Clovis points on known Clovis occupation sites. **I.D. KEY:** Large size and large parallel percussion scars.

PASKAPOO - Late Prehistoric, 1000 - 400 B. P.

(Also see Cut Bank, Irvine, Nanton, Pekisko and Plains Side Notched)

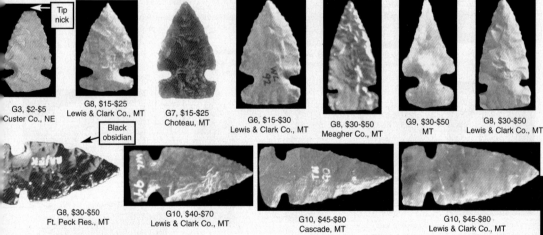

Tip
nick

G3, $2-$5
Custer Co., NE

G8, $15-$25
Lewis & Clark Co., MT

G7, $15-$25
Choteau, MT

G6, $15-$30
Lewis & Clark Co., MT

G8, $30-$50
Meagher Co., MT

G9, $30-$50
MT

G8, $30-$50
Lewis & Clark Co., MT

Black
obsidian

G8, $30-$50
Ft. Peck Res., MT

G10, $40-$70
Lewis & Clark Co., MT

G10, $45-$80
Cascade, MT

G10, $45-$80
Lewis & Clark Co., MT

LOCATION: Northern Plains states. **DESCRIPTION:** A small to medium size, thin arrow point with side-notches that occur higher up from the base than other Plains forms. The base is straight with rounded corners and are usually ground.

PEKISKO - Late Prehistoric, 800 - 400 B. P.

(Also see Buffalo Gap, Cut Bank, Nanton, Paskapoo & Washita)

LOCATION: Northern Plains states. **DESCRIPTION:** A small to medium size, thin, triangular arrow point with v-notch-es on both sides above the base. Bases are concave to straight and are as wide as the shoulders. **I.D.KEY:** V-notch-es.

941

PEKISKO (continued)

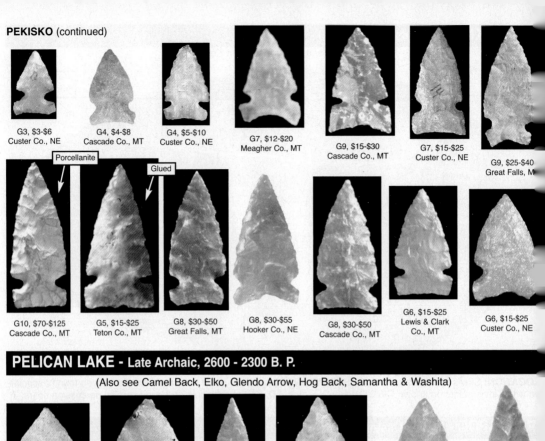

G3, $3-$6
Custer Co., NE

G4, $4-$8
Cascade Co., MT

G4, $5-$10
Custer Co., NE

G7, $12-$20
Meagher Co., MT

G9, $15-$30
Cascade Co., MT

G7, $15-$25
Custer Co., NE

G9, $25-$40
Great Falls, M

Porcellanite

Glued

G10, $70-$125
Cascade Co., MT

G5, $15-$25
Teton Co., MT

G8, $30-$50
Great Falls, MT

G8, $30-$55
Hooker Co., NE

G8, $30-$50
Cascade Co., MT

G6, $15-$25
Lewis & Clark
Co., MT

G6, $15-$25
Custer Co., NE

PELICAN LAKE - Late Archaic, 2600 - 2300 B. P.

(Also see Camel Back, Elko, Glendo Arrow, Hog Back, Samantha & Washita)

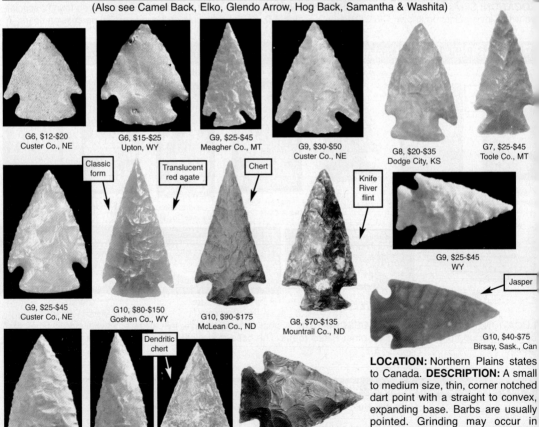

G6, $12-$20
Custer Co., NE

G6, $15-$25
Upton, WY

G9, $25-$45
Meagher Co., MT

G9, $30-$50
Custer Co., NE

G8, $20-$35
Dodge City, KS

G7, $25-$45
Toole Co., MT

Classic
form

Translucent
red agate

Chert

Knife
River
flint

G9, $25-$45
WY

Jasper

G9, $25-$45
Custer Co., NE

G10, $80-$150
Goshen Co., WY

G10, $90-$175
McLean Co., ND

G8, $70-$135
Mountrail Co., ND

G10, $40-$75
Birsay, Sask., Can

Dendritic
chert

Knife
River
flint

G8, $30-$55
Meagher Co., MT

G8, $25-$45
Meagher Co., MT

G9, $25-$45
Mountrail Co., ND

G8, $35-$65
Custer Co., NE

LOCATION: Northern Plains states to Canada. **DESCRIPTION:** A small to medium size, thin, corner notched dart point with a straight to convex, expanding base. Barbs are usually pointed. Grinding may occur in notches and around base. Believed to have evolved into the *Samantha Dart* point. **I.D. KEY:** Sharp barbs.

942

Petrified wood

G9, $90-$175
E. CO

Basalt

G6, $80-$150
Bent Co., CO

Classic form

Knife River flint

G7, $90-$175
McLean Co., ND

G9, $80-$150
Custer Co., NE

Tip nick

G8, $150-$250
Lewis & Clark Co., MT

Knife River flint

G7, $80-$150
Mountrail Co., ND

G10, $200-$350
Douglas Co., ND

Petrified wood

G10, $200-$350
WY

Agate

G7, $45-$80
NE

Knife River flint

G8, $200-$350
Mountrail Co., ND

G9, $150-$250
Casper, WY

G9, $125-$200
N. OK

Dendritic chert

G10, $250-$450
Montrail Co., ND

Knife River flint

G10, $300-$575
Mountrail Co., ND

G9, $200-$350
N. OK

Knife River flint

G10, $350-$650
Emmons Co., ND

Knife River flint

G10, $400-$700
Bottineau Co., ND

N
P

943

PIPE CREEK - Late Prehistoric, 1200 - 1000 B. P.

(Also see Corner Tang Knife)

G5, $5-$10
Custer Co., NB

G6, $12-$20
Weld Co., CO

LOCATION: Colorado into Texas and Tennessee. **DESCRIPTION:** A medium size knife with a notch in one basal corner. Bases can be straight to sloping. **I.D. KEY:** Single corner notch.

PLAINS KNIFE - Early to Middle Archaic, 6000 - 4000 B. P.

(Also see Archaic Knife, Archaic Side, Logan Creek, Lookingbill and Mallory)

Black obsidian

G8, $70-$135
Lewis & Clark Co., MT

LOCATION: Northern Plains states. **DESCRIPTION:** A medium to large size, triangular, side-notched point with a straight to concave base. Flaking is horizontal transverse. The widest part of the point is at the basal corners. Bases are ground. **I.D. KEY:** Size, wide base.

G9, $165-$300
Lewis & Clark Co., MT

Broken & glued

G4, $80-$150
Phillips Co., MT

Knife River flint

G10+, $3000-$5000
WI

944

(Also see Bitterroot, Buffalo Gap, Cut Bank, Desert, Nanton, Paskapoo, Pekisko & Washita)

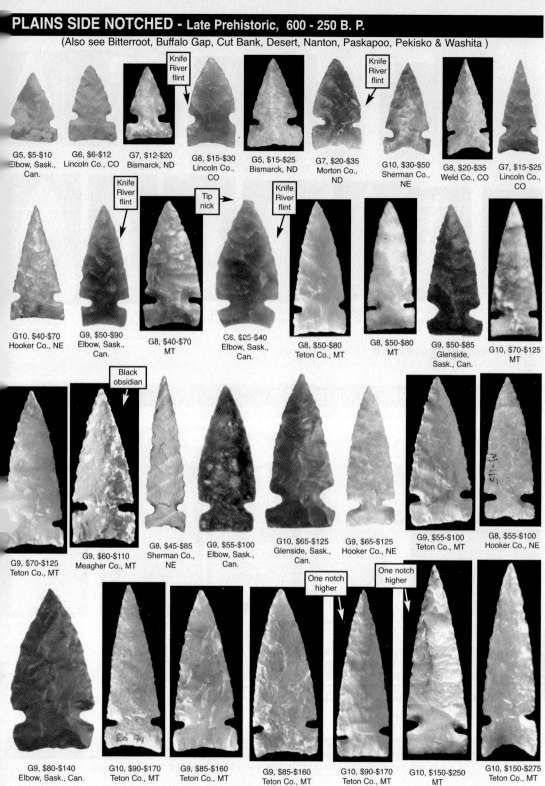

Knife River flint

Knife River flint

G5, $5-$10
Elbow, Sask., Can.

G6, $6-$12
Lincoln Co., CO

G7, $12-$20
Bismarck, ND

G8, $15-$30
Lincoln Co., CO

G5, $15-$25
Bismarck, ND

G7, $20-$35
Morton Co., ND

G10, $30-$50
Sherman Co., NE

G8, $20-$35
Weld Co., CO

G7, $15-$25
Lincoln Co., CO

Knife River flint

Tip nick

Knife River flint

G10, $40-$70
Hooker Co., NE

G9, $50-$90
Elbow, Sask., Can.

G8, $40-$70
MT

G6, $25-$40
Elbow, Sask., Can.

G8, $50-$80
Teton Co., MT

G8, $50-$80
MT

G9, $50-$85
Glenside, Sask., Can.

G10, $70-$125
MT

Black obsidian

G9, $70-$125
Teton Co., MT

G9, $60-$110
Meagher Co., MT

G8, $45-$85
Sherman Co., NE

G9, $55-$100
Elbow, Sask., Can.

G10, $65-$125
Glenside, Sask., Can.

G9, $65-$125
Hooker Co., NE

G9, $55-$100
Teton Co., MT

G8, $55-$100
Hooker Co., NE

One notch higher

One notch higher

G9, $80-$140
Elbow, Sask., Can.

G10, $90-$170
Teton Co., MT

G9, $85-$160
Teton Co., MT

G9, $85-$160
Teton Co., MT

G10, $90-$170
Teton Co., MT

G10, $150-$250
MT

G10, $150-$275
Teton Co., MT

N P

LOCATION: Northern Plains states. **DESCRIPTION:** A small to medium size, thin, triangular, side-notched arrow point with a concave base. Notches are narrow and occur high up from the base. Basal corners are usually sharp and blade edges are not serrated. Many have been dug in buffalo kill sites. **I.D. KEY:** Notches.

PLAINS TRIANGULAR - Proto Historic, 200 - 150 B. P.

(Also see Archaic Triangle, Cottonwood)

G3, $2-$5
Bent Co., CO

G6, $5-$10
Custer Co., NE

G7, $8-$15
Bismarck, ND

Alibates dolomite

G9, $15-$30
Prowers Co., CO

G8, $12-$20
Custer Co., NE

G9, $20-$35
Bismarck, ND

Moss agate

G9, $20-$35
Bismarck, ND

G9, $15-$25
Bismarck, ND

G7, $12-$20
Custer Co., NE

G10, $25-$45
Bismarck, ND

G8, $15-$30
Swan Creek, SD

G8, $25-$45
Elbow, Sask., Can.

G9, $25-$45
NE

G10, $30-$55
Bismarck, ND

G8, $25-$40
S.E. MT, Pryor Mtns.

G8, $25-$40
Custer Co., NE

LOCATION: Northern Plains states. **DESCRIPTION:** A small size, thin, triangular arrow point with a straight to concave base and sharp basal ears. **I.D. KEY:** Small triangle

PLAINVIEW - Plains Paleo, 11,250 - 9500 B. P.

(Also see Clovis, Folsom, Goshen, Lovell, Midland, Milnesand)

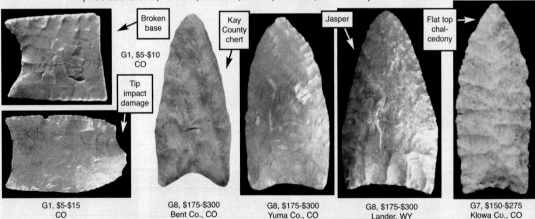

Broken base

G1, $5-$10
CO

Tip impact damage

Kay County chert

Jasper

Flat top chalcedony

G1, $5-$15
CO

G8, $175-$300
Bent Co., CO

G8, $175-$300
Yuma Co., CO

G8, $175-$300
Lander, WY

G7, $150-$275
Kiowa Co., CO

LOCATION: Colorado into Texas. **DESCRIPTION:** A medium to large size, thin, lanceolate point with usually parallel sides and a concave base that is ground. Some examples are thinned or fluted and are believed to be related to the earlier *Clovis* and contemporary *Dalton/Merserve* types. Examples found further north are called *Goshen* which is the same type. Flaking is of high quality and can be collateral to oblique transverse. A cross type between *Clovis* and *Dalton*. **I.D. KEY:** Basal form and parallel flaking.

PRAIRIE SIDE NOTCHED - Late Prehistoric, 1300 - 620 B. P.

(Also see Irvine, Nanton, Paskapoo, Pekisko, Plains Side Notched & Washita)

LOCATION: Northern Plains states. **DESCRIPTION:** A medium size triangular arrow point with broad side notches. Bases are straight to slightly concave.

PRARIE SIDE NOTCHED (continued)

Knife River flint

G5, $6-$10
Mitchell, SD

G5, $7-$12
Mitchell, SD

G6, $12-$20
Mitchell, SD

Knife River flint

G5, $12-$20
Phillips Co., MT

Knife River flint

G5, $6-$10
Phillips Co., MT

G6, $15-$25
Mitchell, SD

G5, $12-$20
Phillips Co., MT

Knife River flint

G6, $15-$25
Mitchell, SD

G6, $12-$20
Lewis & Clark Co., MT

G5, $12-$20
Phillips Co., MT

Knife River flint

G5, $12-$20
Phillips Co., MT

G5, $12-$20
Elbow, Sask., Can.

G6, $15-$25
Lewis & Clark Co., MT

G6, $15-$25
Phillips Co., MT

G7, $20-$35
Lewis & Clark Co., MT

G7, $15-$25
Lewis & Clark Co., MT

PRYOR STEMMED - Mountain Paleo, 8500 - 7500 B. P.

(Also see Eden eared and Hell Gap)

Oblique transverse flaking

G7, $50-$90
WY

Quartz

G7, $90-$175
CO/NE border

LOCATION: Northern Plains states into W. Oregon. **DESCRIPTION:** A medium size, short stemmed point with slight, tapered shoulders, a concave base and rounded basal corners. Flaking is usually oblique transverse. Stems are ground.

RED RIVER KNIFE - Plains Paleo, 10,000 - 8000 B. P.

(Also see Alberta, Cody Knife, Eden, Firstview and Scottsbluff)

LOCATION: Texas to Colorado. **DESCRIPTION:** A medium size, asymmetrical blade with weak shoulders and a short, expanding stem. Bases are straight to slightly convex. It has been reported that these knives were made by the Cody Complex people from *Scottsbluff* points. Look for early parallel flaking and stem grinding.

Spanish Diggins quartzite

G9, $250-$400
Bent Co., CO

SAMANTHA-ARROW - Late Prehistoric, 1500 - 1200 B. P.

(Also see Avonlea, High River, Lewis and Tompkins)

LOCATION: Canada to the Northern Plains states. **DESCRIPTION:** A small to medium size, narrow, thin, corner to side-notched arrow point. Flaking is random to oblique transverse. Related and developed from the earlier *Samantha Dart* point. Shoulders are tapered and the stem expands to a straight to slightly concave base.

SAMANTHA ARROW
(continued)

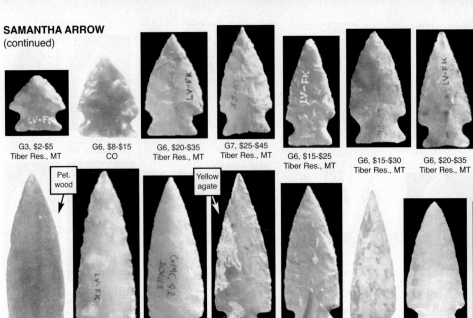

G3, $2-$5
Tiber Res., MT

G6, $8-$15
CO

G6, $20-$35
Tiber Res., MT

G7, $25-$45
Tiber Res., MT

G6, $15-$25
Tiber Res., MT

G6, $15-$30
Tiber Res., MT

G6, $20-$35
Tiber Res., MT

G7, $30-$50
Meagher Co., M

Pet. wood

Yellow agate

G10, $90-$175
Mountrail Co., ND

G10, $80-$150
Tiber Res., MT

G10, $80-$150
Meagher Co., MT

G10, $135-$250
Lewis & Clark Co., MT

G9, $55-$100
Tiber Res., MT

G9, $45-$85
Elbow, Sask., Can.

G8, $35-$65
E. CO

G6, $30-$50
Tiber Res., MT

SAMANTHA-DART - Late Archaic, 2200 - 1500 B. P.

(Also see Besant, Mount Albion and Pelican Lake)

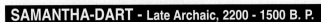

G7, $12-$20
CO

G8, $20-$35
CO

Gem

G5, $12-$20
Lewis & Clark Co., MT

G5, $12-$20
Lewis & Clark Co., MT

G5, $12-$20
Lewis & Clark Co., MT

Knife River flint

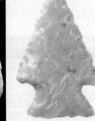

G6, $20-$35
Lewis & Clark Co., MT

G6, $15-$25
WY

G7, $15-$25
Custer Co., NE

G6, $20-$35
Mandan, ND

G8, $25-$45
CO

G7, $25-$45
Sweetgrass Hills, MT

G9, $45-$85
Elbow, Sask., Can.

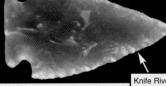

G8, $30-$50
Meagher Co., MT

G8, $70-$135
Renville Co., ND

Knife River flint

LOCATION: Canada to the Northern Plains states. **DESCRIPTION:** A medium to large size, corner to side-notched dart point with with horizontal, tapered or slightly barbed shoulders. Believed to have evolved from the *Pelican Lake* type changing into the *Besant* type at a later time.

Edge wear

G7, $45-$80
Lewis & Clark Co., MT

Knife River flint

G7, $40-$70
S. E. MT

G8, $50-$90
Harding Co., SD

G8, $30-$55
Zortman, MT

G8, $45-$80
Pollack, SD

Quartzite

Knife River Flint

Knife River Flint

G8, $80-$150
Mountrail Co., ND

Petrified wood

G9, $200-$350
Sublette, So., WY

G10, $250-$425
Adams Co., CO

G10, $250-$425
SD

G5, $40-$75
Elbow, Sask., Canada

SAN JOSE - Plains Paleo - Transitional Paleo, 9000 - 6000 B. P.

(Also see Bajada, Clovis, Folsom, Goshen, Hanna, Lovell and Meserve)

G3, $2-$5
Dodge City, KS

G10, $15-$30
Conejos Co., CO

Basalt

G6, $20-$35
Conejos Co., CO

G8, $50-$95
Crowley Co., CO

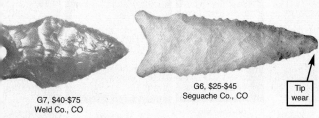

G7, $40-$75
Weld Co., CO

G6, $25-$45
Seguache Co., CO

Tip wear

LOCATION: Arizona, Colorado, Nevada, New Mexico, Sou. Utah. **DESCRIPTION:** A small to medium size dart/knife point with wide, shallow side notches creating an auriculate base. The shoulders are obtuse and the blade edges always have serrations. Stem and base edges are usually ground. **I.D. KEY:** Auriculate base.

N
P

949

SATTLER - Late Prehistoric, 1400 - 400 B. P.

(Also see Hog Back)

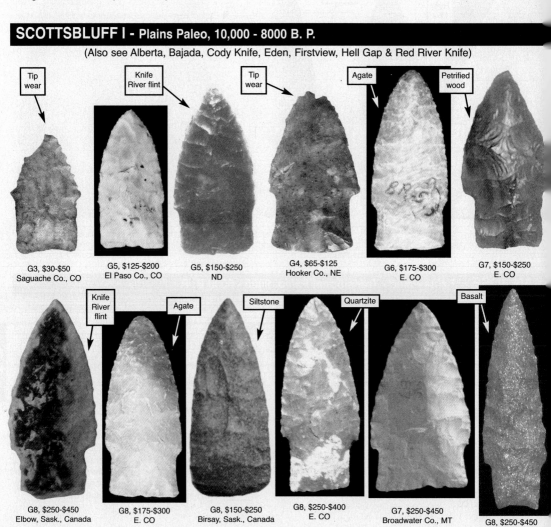

Basalt

Basalt

Basalt

Tip nick

Basalt

Basalt

Basalt

Basalt

Basalt

G5, $5-$10
Alamosa, CO

G65, $8-$15
Alamosa, CO

G5, $5-$10
Saguache Co.,
CO

G4, $5-$10
Alamosa, CO

G6, $8-$15
Alamosa, CO

G5, $8-$15
Alamosa, CO

G6, $12-$20
Alamosa, CO

G5, $12-$20
Alamosa, CO

G6, $12-$20
Alamosa, CO

G6, $12-$20
Alamosa, CO

G6, $12-$20
Alamosa, CO

Basalt

G8, $15-$30
Alamosa, CO

Basalt

G6, $12-$20
Seguache Co., CO

G8, $12-$20
Costilla Co., CO

LOCATION: Sou. Colorado. **DESCRIPTION:** A small size, thin, serrated arrow point with an expanded base. Base is straight to concave. Tips are sharp.

SCOTTSBLUFF I - Plains Paleo, 10,000 - 8000 B. P.

(Also see Alberta, Bajada, Cody Knife, Eden, Firstview, Hell Gap & Red River Knife)

Tip wear

Knife River flint

Tip wear

Agate

Petrified wood

G3, $30-$50
Saguache Co., CO

G5, $125-$200
El Paso Co., CO

G5, $150-$250
ND

G4, $65-$125
Hooker Co., NE

G6, $175-$300
E. CO

G7, $150-$250
E. CO

Knife River flint

Agate

Siltstone

Quartzite

Basalt

G8, $250-$450
Elbow, Sask., Canada

G8, $175-$300
E. CO

G8, $150-$250
Birsay, Sask., Canada

G8, $250-$400
E. CO

G7, $250-$450
Broadwater Co., MT

G8, $250-$450
Weld Co., CO

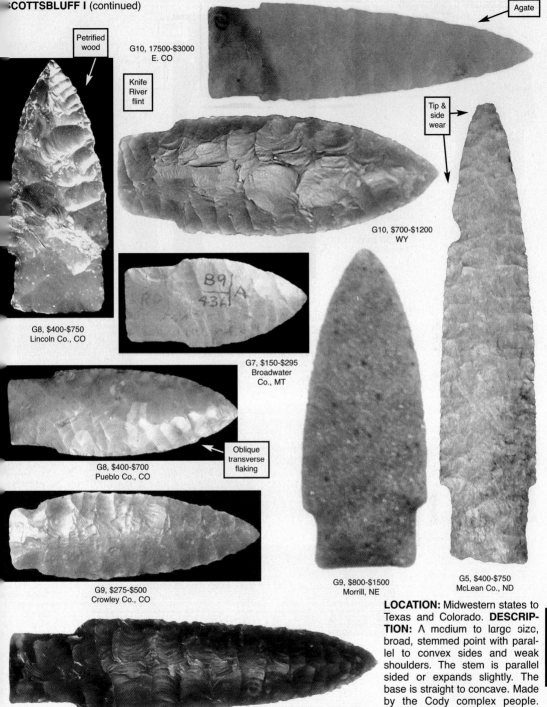

Petrified wood

Agate

G10, 17500-$3000
E. CO

Knife River flint

Tip & side wear

G10, $700-$1200
WY

G8, $400-$750
Lincoln Co., CO

89
A
436

G7, $150-$295
Broadwater
Co., MT

Oblique transverse flaking

G8, $400-$700
Pueblo Co., CO

G9, $275-$500
Crowley Co., CO

G9, $800-$1500
Morrill, NE

G5, $400-$750
McLean Co., ND

LOCATION: Midwestern states to Texas and Colorado. **DESCRIPTION:** A medium to large size, broad, stemmed point with parallel to convex sides and weak shoulders. The stem is parallel sided or expands slightly. The base is straight to concave. Made by the Cody complex people. Flaking is of the high quality parallel horizontal to oblique transverse type. Bases are ground. **I.D. KEY:** Broad stem, weak shoulders.

N
P

G9, $1600-$3000
Elbow, Saskatchewan, CA

Knife River flint

SCOTTSBLUFF II - Plains Paleo, 10,000 - 8000 B. P.

(Also see Alberta, Bajada, Cody Knife, Eden, Hell Gap & Red River Knife)

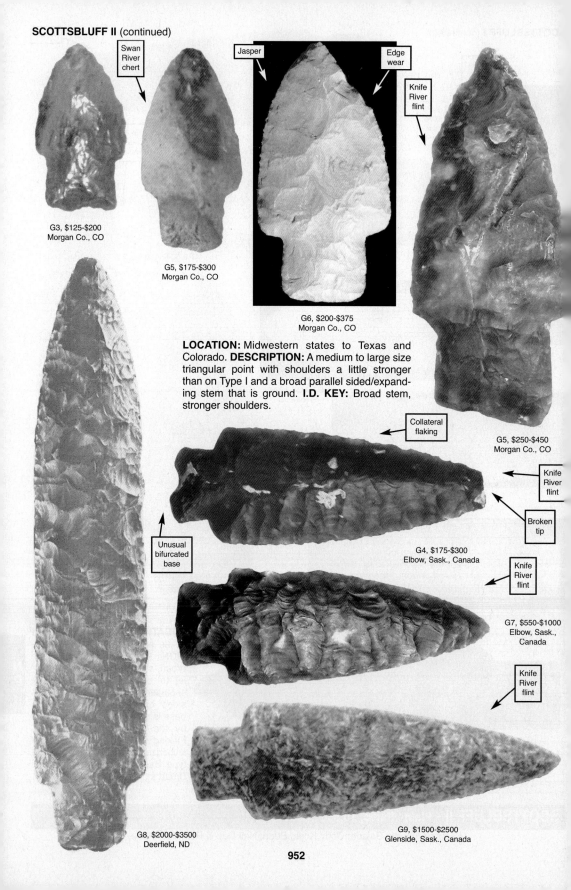

Swan River chert

Jasper

Edge wear

Knife River flint

G3, $125-$200
Morgan Co., CO

G5, $175-$300
Morgan Co., CO

G6, $200-$375
Morgan Co., CO

LOCATION: Midwestern states to Texas and Colorado. **DESCRIPTION:** A medium to large size triangular point with shoulders a little stronger than on Type I and a broad parallel sided/expanding stem that is ground. **I.D. KEY:** Broad stem, stronger shoulders.

Collateral flaking

G5, $250-$450
Morgan Co., CO

Knife River flint

Broken tip

G4, $175-$300
Elbow, Sask., Canada

Unusual bifurcated base

Knife River flint

G7, $550-$1000
Elbow, Sask., Canada

Knife River flint

G8, $2000-$3500
Deerfield, ND

G9, $1500-$2500
Glenside, Sask., Canada

952

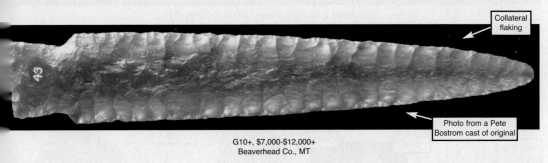

Collateral flaking

Photo from a Pete Bostrom cast of original

G10+, $7,000-$12,000+
Beaverhead Co., MT

SCRAPER - Plains Paleo to Middle Archaic, 11,500 - 5000 B. P.

(Also see Drill, Hafted Knife, Paleo Knife and Side knife)

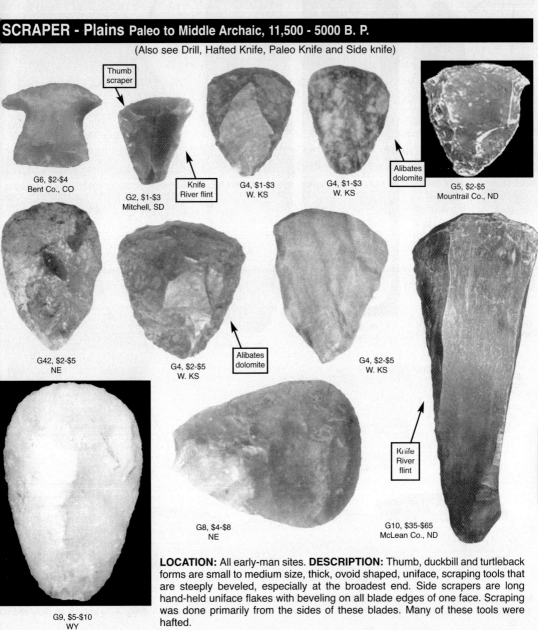

Thumb scraper

G6, $2-$4
Bent Co., CO

G2, $1-$3
Mitchell, SD

Knife River flint

G4, $1-$3
W. KS

G4, $1-$3
W. KS

Alibates dolomite

G5, $2-$5
Mountrail Co., ND

G42, $2-$5
NE

G4, $2-$5
W. KS

Alibates dolomite

G4, $2-$5
W. KS

Knife River flint

G10, $35-$65
McLean Co., ND

G9, $5-$10
WY

G8, $4-$8
NE

N
P

LOCATION: All early-man sites. **DESCRIPTION:** Thumb, duckbill and turtleback forms are small to medium size, thick, ovoid shaped, uniface, scraping tools that are steeply beveled, especially at the broadest end. Side scrapers are long hand-held uniface flakes with beveling on all blade edges of one face. Scraping was done primarily from the sides of these blades. Many of these tools were hafted.

(Also see Crescent, Hafted Knife & Scraper)

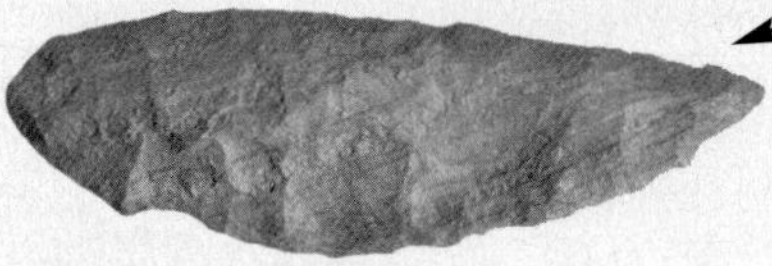

Petrified wood

G7, $35-$60
Lincoln Co., CO

G6, $25-$45
Bent Co., CO

Knife River flint

Broken & glued

Quartzite

Knife River flint

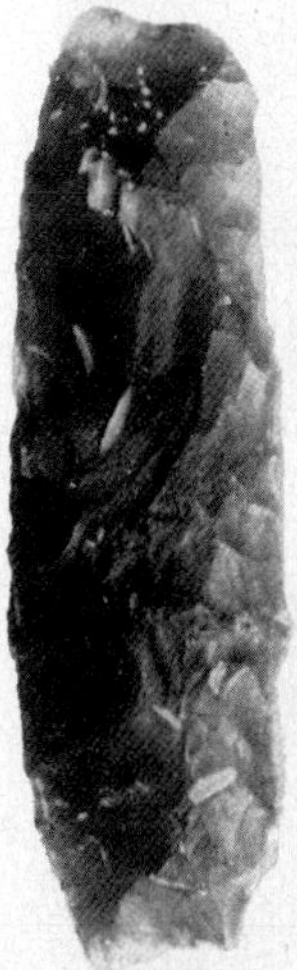

G6, $40-$70
Morton Co., ND

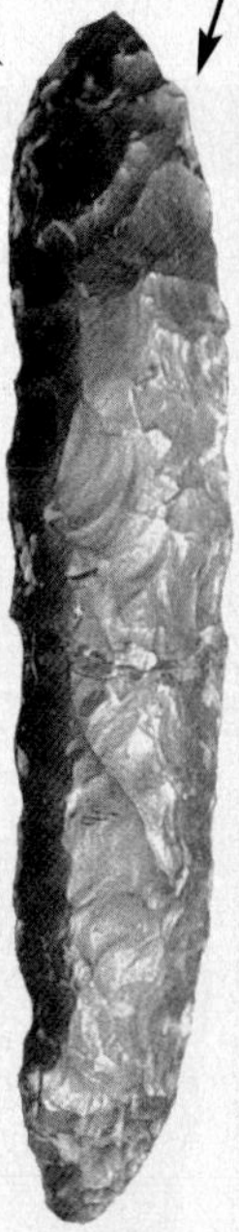

G4, $25-$40
Mountrail Co., ND

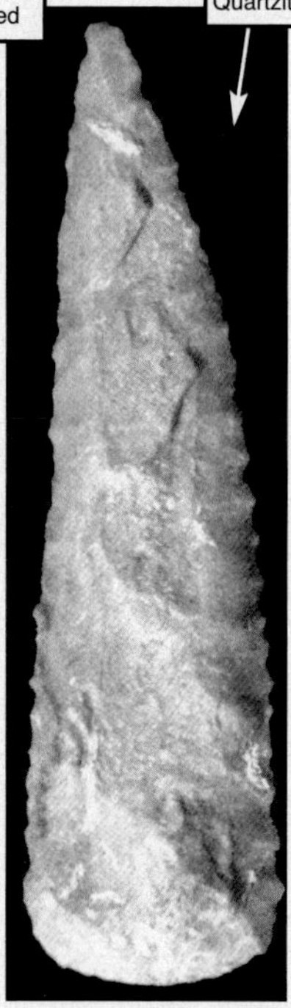

G6, $45-$85
Alamosa, CO

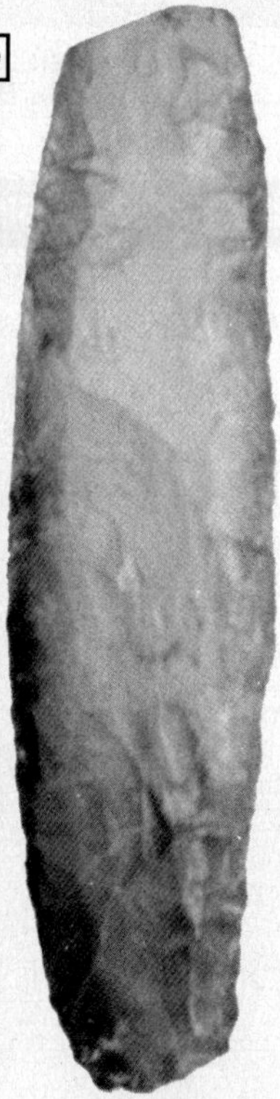

G8, $55-$100
E. CO

F-56

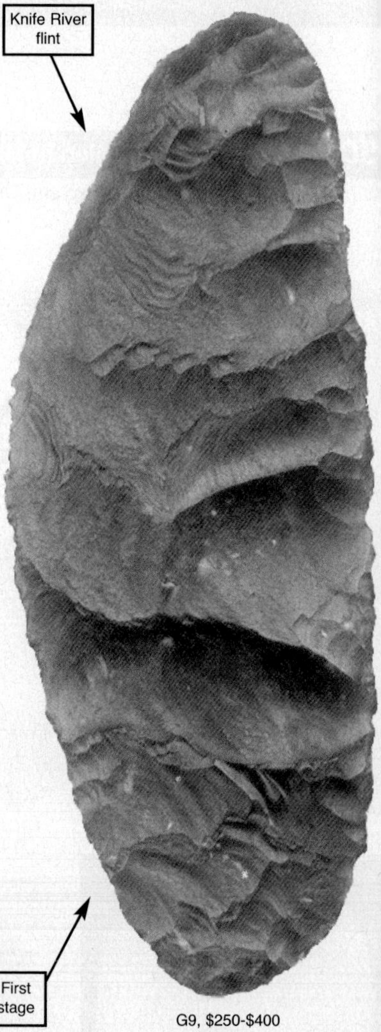

First stage

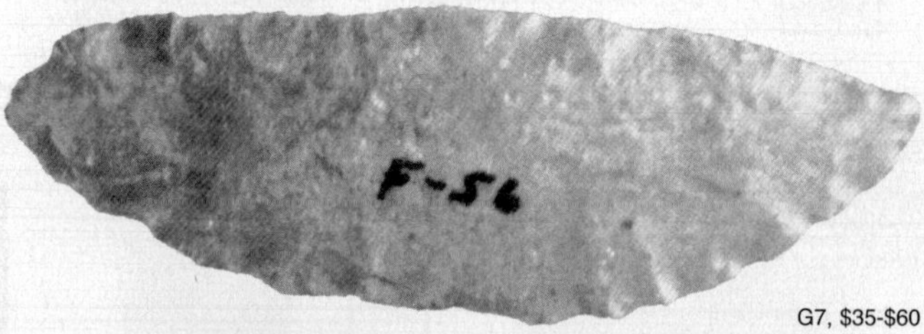

G7, $35-$60
SD

G9, $250-$400
ND

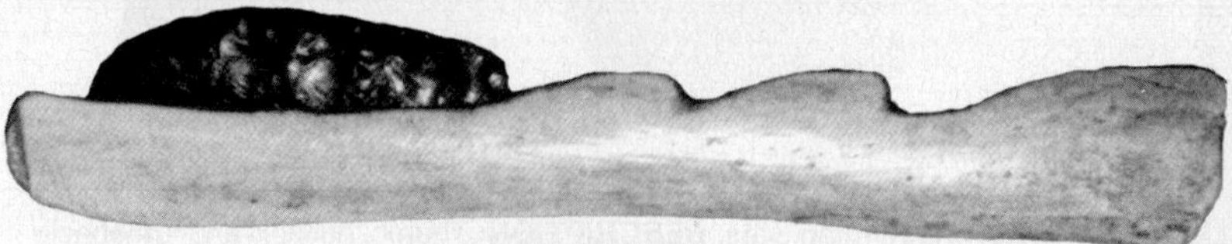

G10, $550-$1000
ND. 500-800 years old.

Very rare examples of hafted knives, both in a bone handle and found perfectly preserved. Asphaltum or pitch was used as an adhesive to glue the stone tool in the handle.

LOCATION: Northern Plains states. **DESCRIPTION:** Side Knives were generally hafted into bison rib-bone handles as illustrated below. Gut and plant fibers were also used when needed to bind the hafting. Also known as *Round-End Knife.*

G10, $800-$1500
E. CO. Bone handle, stone blade.

G6, $40-$70
Morton Co., ND

SIDE NOTCH (See Archaic Side Notch)

SIMONSEN - Early Archaic, 6800 - 6400 B. P.

(Also see Besant and Bitterroot)

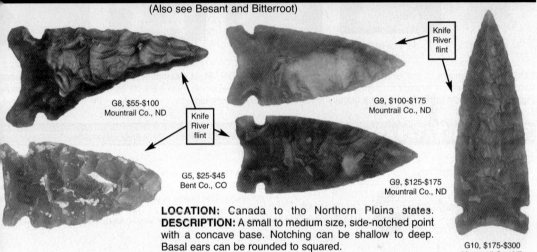

G8, $55-$100
Mountrail Co., ND

Knife River flint

G5, $25-$45
Bent Co., CO

Knife River flint

Knife River flint

G9, $100-$175
Mountrail Co., ND

G9, $125-$175
Mountrail Co., ND

LOCATION: Canada to the Northern Plains states.
DESCRIPTION: A small to medium size, side-notched point with a concave base. Notching can be shallow to deep. Basal ears can be rounded to squared.

G10, $175-$300
Mountrail Co., ND

SONOTA - Late Archaic, 1900 - 1500 B. P.

(Also see Besant and Bitterroot)

hand-held to show flaking pattern

Broken tip

Knife River flint

Very thin

side wear

Clasic example

Broken ear

Knife River flint

Broken tip

Knife River flint

Knife River flint

G2, $5-$10
Mountrail Co., ND

G8, $35-$60
Mountrail Co., ND

G3, $10-$20
Mountrail Co., ND

G8, $70-$125
Mountrail Co., ND

G6, $30-$50
Mountrail Co., ND

G10, $250-$400
Mountrail Co., ND

G6, $40-$75
Mountrail Co., ND

N
P

955

SONOTA (continued)

| G10, $250-$450 Bottineau Co., ND | G8, $150-$275 Mountrail Co., ND | G8, $150-$275 Lewis & Clark Co., MT | G10, $275-$500 McKenzie Co., ND | G9, $250-$450 McClean Co., ND |

LOCATION: Canada to the Northern Plains states. **DESCRIPTION:** Most examples are small, thin, side to corner notched points with a straight to slightly concave base. Basal corners can form ears on some examples and notching is usually close to the base. Base usually is not as wide as the shoulders.

SPOKESHAVE - Late Archaic, 3000 - 1500 B. P.

(Also see Scraper)

G7, $15-$25
Mountrail Co., ND

LOCATION: Canada to the Northern Plains states. **DESCRIPTION:** A medium to large size tool used for scraping. The blade is asymmetrical with one edge convex and the other concave.

STOTT - Late Prehistoric, 1300 - 600 B. P.

(Also see Besant, Bitterroot, Nanton, Paskapoo, Pekisko and Tompkins)

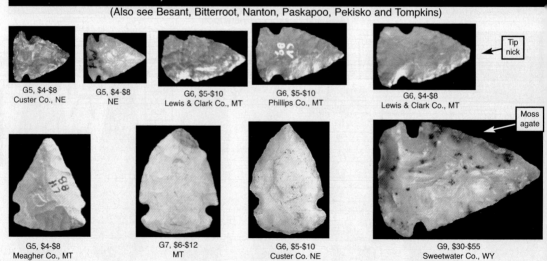

| G5, $4-$8 Custer Co., NE | G5, $4-$8 NE | G6, $5-$10 Lewis & Clark Co., MT | G6, $5-$10 Phillips Co., MT | G6, $4-$8 Lewis & Clark Co., MT |

| G5, $4-$8 Meagher Co., MT | G7, $6-$12 MT | G6, $5-$10 Custer Co. NE | G9, $30-$55 Sweetwater Co., WY |

LOCATION: Canada to the Northern Plains states. **DESCRIPTION:** A small size, v-notched point with a convex base. Size of base is large in proportion to the blade size. **I.D. KEY:** V-notches, large base.

SWIFT CURRENT - Late Prehistoric, 1300 - 800 B. P.

(Also see Avonlea, Cut Bank, Irvine and Pekisko)

G6, $15-$30
Lewis & Clark Co., MT

G6, $12-$20
Lewis & Clark Co., MT

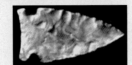

G6, $35-$60
Saco, MT, Milk Rv.

G6, $15-$25
Phillips Co., MT

From a Buffalo jump kill site

G6, $35-$60
Nelson Res., MT

G7, $25-$45
Lewis & Clark Co., MT

G6, $20-$35
Saco, MT

G7, $25-$45
Cascade Co., MT

G7, $25-$45
Lewis & Clark Co., MT

G8, $25-$45
Lewis & Clark Co., MT

G7, $30-$55
Lewis & Clark Co., MT

G7, $20-$35
Great Falls, MT

G7, $30-$55
Lewis & Clark Co., MT

G9, $40-$70
Phillips Co,, MT

Classic form

G8, $40-$70
Lewis & Clark Co., MT

G9, $30-$50
Fort Peck Res., MT

G8, $30-$55
Lewis & Clark Co., MT

G9, $35-$65
Elbow, Sask., Can.

LOCATION: Northern Plains states. **DESCRIPTION:** A small size, thin, side notched arrow point with a concave base. Blade edges can be serrated. Ancient buffalo jump kill sites have been discovered in the Plains states where this type is found. Early man drove the buffalo over cliffs and into corrals for easy killing. **I.D. KEY:** Drooping ears.

TOMPKINS - Late Prehistoric, 1200 - 800 B. P.

(Also see Cut Bank, High River, Irvine, Nanton, Pekisko, Paskapoo, Prairie Side Notched and Swift Current)

G6, $4-$8
Choteau Co., MT

G6, $4-$8
Phillips Co., MT

G6, $5-$10
Phillips Co., MT.

Knife River flint

LOCATION: Northern Plains states. **DESCRIPTION:** A small size, thin, serrated, side to corner notched arrow point with a concave base. On some examples, one notch is from the corner and the other definitely from the side. Some have basal grinding. Found on ancient Buffalo jump kill sites.

N P

TRADE POINTS - Proto Historic, 300 - 100 B. P.

G6, $25-$40
McLean Co., ND

Brass

Silver alloy

G6, $30-$50
Bent Co., CO

G7, $25-$40
Custer Co., NE

Copper

G9, $45-$85
Mountrail Co., ND

TRADE (continued)

Note: All points with * were probably blacksmith made trade points.

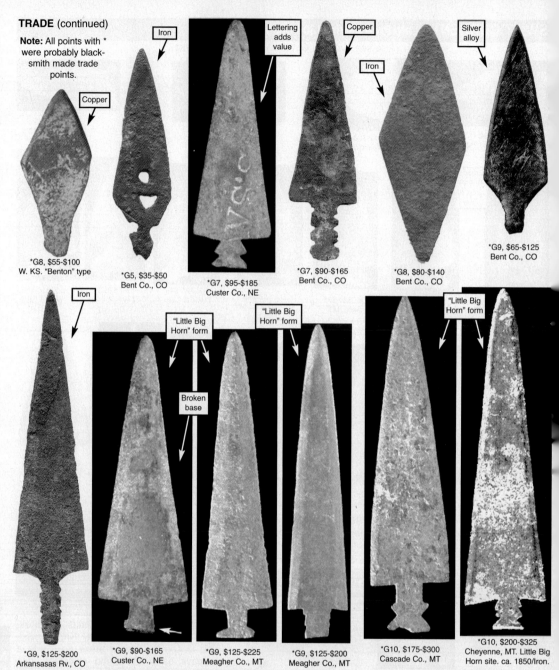

Copper

Iron

Lettering adds value

Copper

Iron

Silver alloy

Iron

*G8, $55-$100
W. KS. "Benton" type

*G5, $35-$50
Bent Co., CO

*G7, $95-$185
Custer Co., NE

*G7, $90-$165
Bent Co., CO

*G8, $80-$140
Bent Co., CO

*G9, $65-$125
Bent Co., CO

"Little Big Horn" form

"Little Big Horn" form

Broken base

"Little Big Horn" form

*G9, $125-$200
Arkansas Rv., CO

*G9, $90-$165
Custer Co., NE

*G9, $125-$225
Meagher Co., MT

*G9, $125-$200
Meagher Co., MT

*G10, $175-$300
Cascade Co., MT

*G10, $200-$325
Cheyenne, MT. Little Big Horn site. ca. 1850/Iron.

These points were made of copper, iron, and steel and were traded to the Indians by the French, British and others from the 1600s to the 1800s. Examples have been found all over the United States. **NOTE:** All points with * were probably blacksmith made trade points.

VENTANNA-AMARGOSA - Early Archaic, 7000 - 5000 B. P.

(Also see Base Tang Knife, Mount Albion, Pelican Lake and Samantha Dart)

G6, $5-$10
W. KS

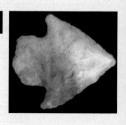

G8, $12-$20
W. KS

LOCATION: Arizona eastward to Kansas. **DESCRIPTION:** A small to medium sized dart/knife with a triangular blade with straight to slightly convex edges and straight to angular shoulders. The stem is parallel sided and rectangular to square. The basal edge is straight to rounded. **I.D. KEY:** A very square appearing stem.

WASHITA - Late Prehistoric, 800 - 400 B. P.

(Also see Harrell and Toyah)

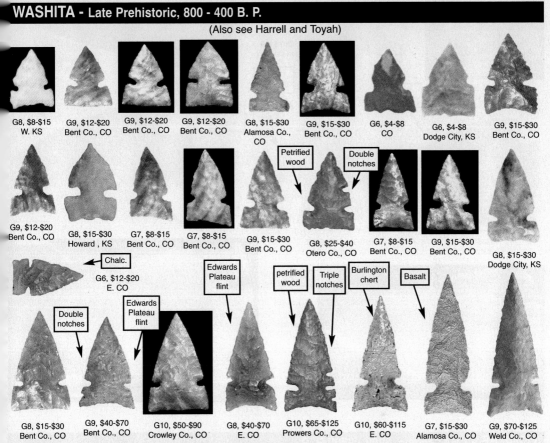

G8, $8-$15
W. KS

G9, $12-$20
Bent Co., CO

G9, $12-$20
Bent Co., CO

G9, $12-$20
Bent Co., CO

G8, $15-$30
Alamosa Co., CO

G9, $15-$30
Bent Co., CO

G6, $4-$8
CO

G6, $4-$8
Dodge City, KS

G9, $15-$30
Bent Co., CO

G9, $12-$20
Bent Co., CO

G8, $15-$30
Howard , KS

G7, $8-$15
Bent Co., CO

Petrified wood

Double notches

G7, $8-$15
Bent Co., CO

G9, $15-$30
Bent Co., CO

G8, $25-$40
Otero Co., CO

G7, $8-$15
Bent Co., CO

G9, $15-$30
Bent Co., CO

G8, $15-$30
Dodge City, KS

Chalc.

G6, $12-$20
E. CO

Edwards Plateau flint

petrified wood

Triple notches

Burlington chert

Basalt

Double notches

Edwards Plateau flint

G8, $15-$30
Bent Co., CO

G9, $40-$70
Bent Co., CO

G10, $50-$90
Crowley Co., CO

G8, $40-$70
E. CO

G10, $65-$125
Prowers Co., CO

G10, $60-$115
E. CO

G7, $15-$30
Alamosa Co., CO

G9, $70-$125
Weld Co., CO

LOCATION: Kansas, E. Colorado northward into the Dakotas. **DESCRIPTION:** A small size, thin, side notched arrow point with a concave base and sharp basal corners. Notches usually occur far up from the base. Can be confused with the Desert series.

WASHITA-NORTHERN - Late Prehistoric, 800 - 400 B. P.

(Also see Harrell & Toyah)

G6, $25-$45
Cascade Co., MT

G7, $10-$20
ND

Knife River flint

G6, $30-$50
Bismark, ND

G6, $35-$60
Lewis & Clark Co., MT

G6, $35-$60
Cascade Co., MT

Classic form

LOCATION: Northern Plains states. **DESCRIPTION:** A small size, thin, triangular side notched arrow point with a concave base. Basal area is usually large in proportion to the blade size. Basal corners are sharp. Notches are narrow.

WRAY - Mid-Archaic, 5000 - 3500 B. P.

(Also see Base Tang Knife, Mount Albion, Pelican Lake and Samantha Dart)

LOCATION: Northern Plains states to Canada. **DESCRIPTION:** A broad, medium size basal notched point with a convex base. Shoulders are sharp to squared and the base that is usually ground is convex.

N
P

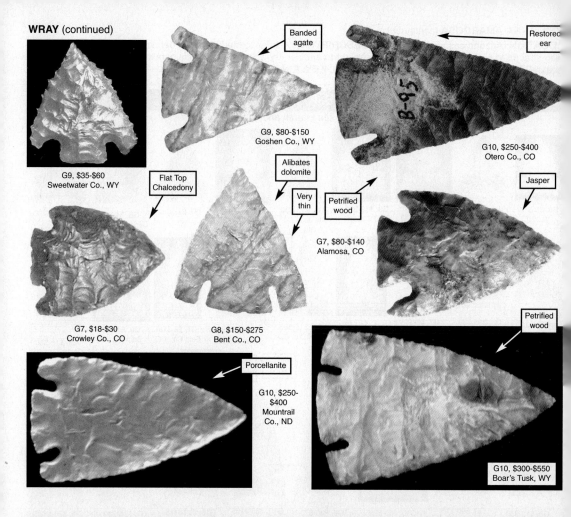

Banded agate

G9, $80-$150
Goshen Co., WY

Restored ear

B-95

G10, $250-$400
Otero Co., CO

G9, $35-$60
Sweetwater Co., WY

Flat Top Chalcedony

Alibates dolomite

Very thin

Petrified wood

Jasper

G7, $80-$140
Alamosa, CO

G7, $18-$30
Crowley Co., CO

G8, $150-$275
Bent Co., CO

Petrified wood

Porcellanite

G10, $250-$400
Mountrail Co., ND

G10, $300-$550
Boar's Tusk, WY

YONKEE - Late Archaic, 3200 - 2500 B. P.

(Also see Besant and Bitterroot)

Knife River flint

Classic form

Classic form

G9, $350-$600
Powers-Yonkee type site.
Montana/Wyoming border

G7, $35-$60
Mountrail Co., ND

G7, $40-$75
Lewis & Clark Co., MT

G9, $350-$600
Powers-Yonkee type site.
Montana/Wyoming border

LOCATION: Northern Plains states. Type site is on the Montana/Wyoming border and is known as the Powers-Yonkee type site. **DESCRIPTION:** A medium size, narrow point that is corner or side-notched. The stem expands and the base is convex and bifurcated forming ears. Shoulders are barbed to horizontal. Related to *Samantha* points. **I.D. KEY:** Lobed ears.

FAR WEST SECTION:

This section includes point types from the following states:
Great Basin, California, W. Idaho, W. Utah, Nevada, Oregon, Washington,
and British Columbia and Saskatchewan, Canada

The points in this section are arranged in alphabetical order and are shown **actual size**. All types are listed that were available for photographing. Any missing types will be added to future editions as photographs become available. We are always interested in receiving sharp, black and white, color glossy photos or high resolution (300 pixels/inch) digital images of your collection. Be sure and include a ruler in the photograph so that proper scale can be determined.

Lithics: Materials employed in the manufacture of projectile points from this region are: obsidian, basalt, dacite and ignimbrite with lesser amounts of agate, jasper, chert, chalcedony, nephrite, opal, petrified wood & silicified sandstone.

Important sites: Clovis: Borax Lake, N. California, Wenatchee Clovis cache, WA.

Note: This section contains many new types marked "provisional" which indicates the names and descriptions are subject to change depending on future research. These types appear to be new types and are included here for informational purposes only. Consult Perino, Noel Justice and others for published information about these types.

Regional Consultants:
John Byrd, Jim Hogue

Special Advisors:
Mark Berreth, Tony Hardie, Bill & Donna Jackson,
Randy McNeice, Rodney Michel, Gregory J. Truesdell

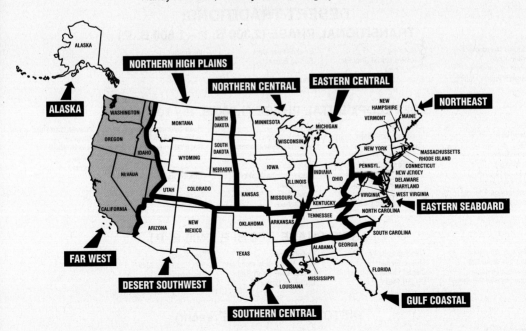

F
W

FAR WEST POINT TYPES
(Archaeological Periods)
PALEO (13,200 B. P. - 8,000 B. P.)

Agate Basin
Alder Complex
Black Rock Concave
Cecilo Falls I
Cecilo Falls II

Folsom
Kennewick
Lake Mohave
Lancet
Lind Coulee

Midland
Milnesand
Owl Cave
Paleo Knife
Pieces Esquillees

Plainview
Scraper
Silver Lake
Spedis I
Spedis II

Spedis Fishtail
Spedis Triangular Knife
Tulare Lake
Windust
Windust-Alberta

Windust Contracting
Stem
Windust-Hatwai

EARLY ARCHAIC (10,500 B. P. - 5,500 B. P.)

Alberta
Albion-Head Side Notched
Atlatl Valley Triangular
Base Tang Knife
Bitterroot
Borax Lake
Cascade
Cascade Knife
Cascade Shouldered
Chilcotin Plateau

Cody Complex Knife
Cordilleran
Diablo Canyon Side
Notched
Early Eared
Early Leaf
Eden
Firstview
Humboldt Basal Notched
Humboldt Constricted

Base
Humboldt Triangular
Jalama Side Notched
Kelsey Creek Barbed
Mahkin Shouldered Lance.
Nightfire
Northern Side Notched
Okanogan Knife
Parman
Perforator

Pinto Basin
Pinto Basin Sloping
Shoulder
Pluvial Lakes Side
Notched
Pryor Stemmed
Salmon River
Scottsbluff I
Scottsbluff II
Scottsbluff Knife

Sierra Contracting
Stemmed
Sudden Series
Tulare Lake Bi-Point
Wendover
Wildcat Canyon
Youngs River Stemmed

MIDDLE ARCHAIC (5,500 B. P. - 3,300 B. P.)

Big Valley Stemmed
Bullhead
Cold Springs
Coquille Broadneck
Coquille Knife
Coquille Side Notched

Corner Tang Knife
Crump Lake Eared
Fish Gutter
Gatecliff
Gatecliff Split-Stem
Gold Hill

Gypsum Cave
High Desert Knife
Houx Contracting Stem
Mayacmas Corner
Notched
McGillivray Expanding

Stem
McKee Uniface
Mendocino Concave
Base
Rossi Square-Stemmed
Steamboat Lanceolate

Surprise Valley
Triple "T"
Vandenberg Contracting
Stem
Willits Side Notched

LATE ARCHAIC (3,500 B. P. - 2,300 B. P.)

Ahsahka
Año Nuevo
Buchanan Eared
Burin
Combat Wand Blade
Contra Costa

Elko Cor. Notched
Elko Eared
Elko Split-Stem
Elko Wide-Notch
Excelsior
Exotic Forms

Fountain Bar
Harpoon
Hendricks
Lady Island Pent.
Martis
Merrybell, Var. I

Merrybell, Var. II
Merrybell, Var. III
Need Stemmed
Lanceolate
Ochoco Stemmed
Point Sal Barbed

Priest Rapids
Quilomene Bar
Shaniko Stemmed
Spedis III
Square-End Knife
Tuolumne Notched

Wooden Dart/Arrow

DESERT TRADITIONS:
TRANSITIONAL PHASE (2,300 B. P. - 1,600 B. P.)

Coquille Narrowneck
Hafted Knife
Rabbit Island Dart
Sauvie's Island Hafting

Notched
Sauvie's Island Shoulder
Notched
Sizer

Snake River Dart
Strong Barbed
Auriculate
Three-Piece Fish Spear

Vendetta

DEVELOPMENTAL PHASE (1,600 B. P. - 700 B. P.)

Alkali
Bear River
Bliss
Bone Arrow
Calapooya
Calapooya Knife
Cottonwood Leaf
Cottonwood Triangle
Dagger

Eastgate
Eastgate Split-Stem
Emigrant Springs
Freemont Triangular
Gunther Barbed
Gunther Triangular
Hell's Canyon Basal
Notched
Hell's Canyon Corner

Notched
Malaga Cove Leaf
Malaga Cover Stemmed
One-Que
Parowan
Rose Springs Corner
Notched
Rose Springs Side
Notched

Rose Springs Sloping
Shoulder
Rose Springs Stemmed
Side Knife
Stockton
Timponogus Blade
Trojan
Uinta
Wahmuza

Wallula Gap Rect. Stem
Washoe
Wealth Blade
Wintu
Yana

CLASSIC PHASE (700 B. P. - 400 B. P.)

Canalino Triangular
Columbia Mule Ear
Columbia Plateau
Columbia Riv. Pin Stem

Deschutes Knife
Desert Delta
Desert General
Desert Redding

Desert Sierra
Lake Rivier Side Notched
Lewis River Short Stem
Miniature Blade

Nez Perce
NW Four-Way Knife
Piquinin
Plateau Pentagonal

HISTORIC (400 B. P. - Present)

Diamond Back
Ground Stone

Ishi
Klickitat

Nottoway
Panoche

Trade Points
Ulu

FAR WEST
THUMBNAIL GUIDE SECTION

The following references are provided to aid the collector in easier and quicker identification of point types. All photos are exactly 30% of actual size and are proportional to each other. Each point pictured in this section represents a classic form for the type. When a match is found, go to the alphabetical location of that type for more examples in true actual size.

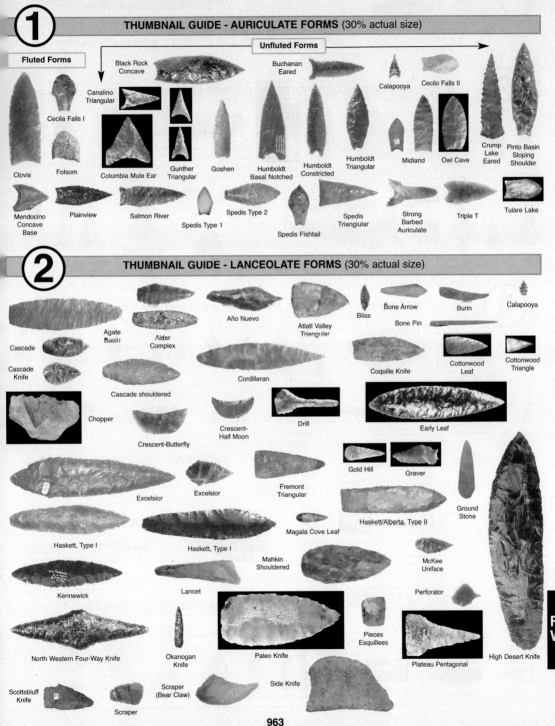

① **THUMBNAIL GUIDE - AURICULATE FORMS** (30% actual size)

Unfluted Forms

Fluted Forms

Black Rock Concave · Buchanan Eared · Calapooya · Cecilo Falls II · Canalino Triangular · Cecila Falls I · Clovis · Folsom · Columbia Mule Ear · Gunther Triangular · Goshen · Humboldt Basal Notched · Humboldt Constricted · Humboldt Triangular · Midland · Owl Cave · Crump Lake Eared · Pinto Basin Sloping Shoulder · Mendocino Concave Base · Plainview · Salmon River · Spedis Type 1 · Spedis Type 2 · Spedis Fishtail · Spedis Triangiular · Strong Barbed Auriculate · Triple T · Tulare Lake

② **THUMBNAIL GUIDE - LANCEOLATE FORMS** (30% actual size)

Cascade · Agate Basin · Alder Complex · Año Nuevo · Atlatl Valley Triangular · Bliss · Bone Arrow · Bone Pin · Burin · Calapooya · Cascade Knife · Cascade shouldered · Cordilleran · Coquille Knife · Cottonwood Leaf · Cottonwood Triangle · Chopper · Crescent-Butterfly · Crescent-Half Moon · Drill · Early Leaf · Excelsior · Excelsior · Fremont Triangular · Gold Hill · Graver · Ground Stone · Haskett, Type I · Haskett, Type I · Magala Cove Leaf · Haskett/Alberta, Type II · McKee Uniface · Kennewick · Lancet · Mahkin Shouldered · Perforator · North Western Four-Way Knife · Okanogan Knife · Paleo Knife · Pieces Esquillees · Plateau Pentagonal · High Desert Knife · Scottsbluff Knife · Scraper · Scraper (Bear Claw) · Side Knife

FW

963

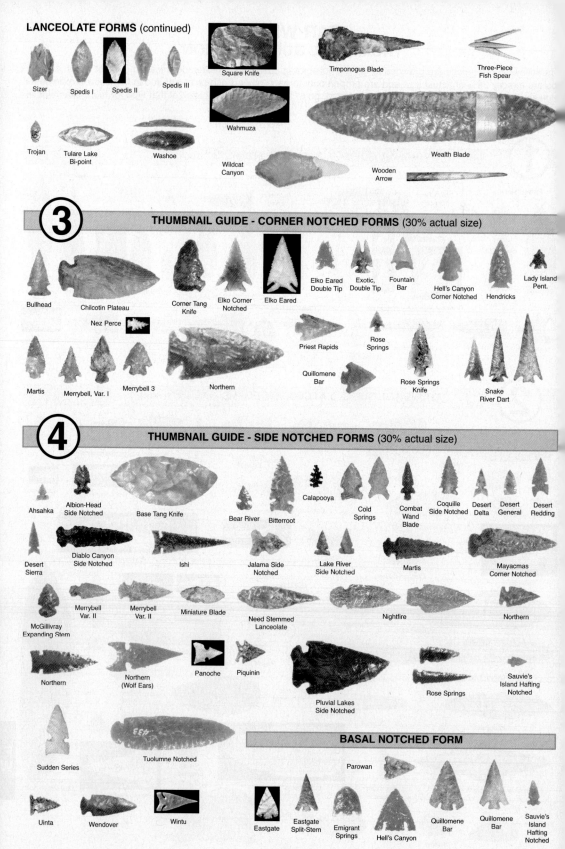

LANCEOLATE FORMS (continued)

Sizer
Spedis I
Spedis II
Spedis III
Square Knife
Timponogus Blade
Three-Piece Fish Spear

Trojan
Tulare Lake Bi-point
Washoe
Wahmuza
Wildcat Canyon
Wooden Arrow
Wealth Blade

③ THUMBNAIL GUIDE - CORNER NOTCHED FORMS (30% actual size)

Bullhead
Chilcotin Plateau
Corner Tang Knife
Elko Corner Notched
Elko Eared
Elko Eared Double Tip
Exotic, Double Tip
Fountain Bar
Hell's Canyon Corner Notched
Hendricks
Lady Island Pent.

Nez Perce

Martis
Merrybell, Var. I
Merrybell 3
Northern
Priest Rapids
Rose Springs
Quillomene Bar
Rose Springs Knife
Snake River Dart

④ THUMBNAIL GUIDE - SIDE NOTCHED FORMS (30% actual size)

Ahsahka
Albion-Head Side Notched
Base Tang Knife
Bear River
Bitterroot
Calapooya
Cold Springs
Combat Wand Blade
Coquille Side Notched
Desert Delta
Desert General
Desert Redding

Desert Sierra
Diablo Canyon Side Notched
Ishi
Jalama Side Notched
Lake River Side Notched
Martis
Mayacmas Corner Notched

McGillivray Expanding Stem
Merrybell Var. II
Merrybell Var. II
Miniature Blade
Need Stemmed Lanceolate
Nightfire
Northern

Northern
Northern (Wolf Ears)
Panoche
Piquinin
Pluvial Lakes Side Notched
Rose Springs
Sauvie's Island Hafting Notched

Sudden Series
Tuolumne Notched

BASAL NOTCHED FORM

Parowan

Uinta
Wendover
Wintu
Eastgate
Eastgate Split-Stem
Emigrant Springs
Hell's Canyon
Quillomene Bar
Quillomene Bar
Sauvie's Island Hafting Notched

⑤

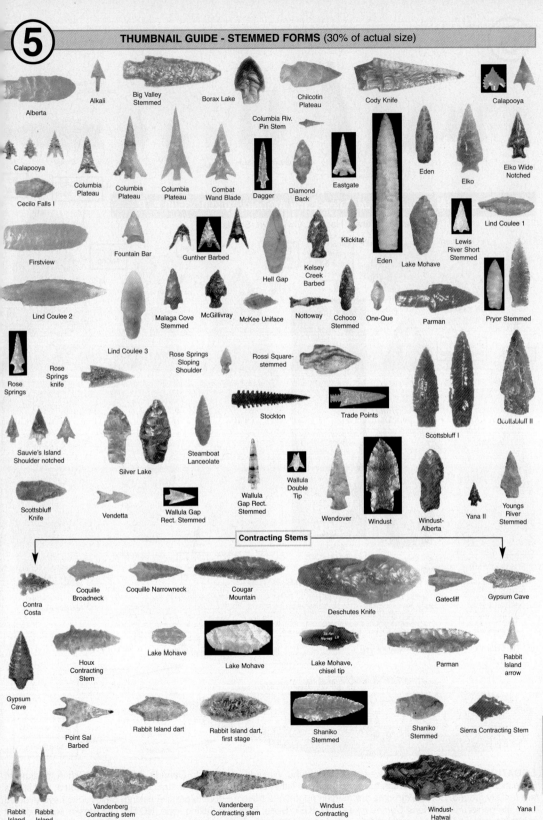

Alberta

Alkali

Big Valley Stemmed

Borax Lake

Chilcotin Plateau

Cody Knife

Calapooya

Columbia Riv. Pin Stem

Calapooya

Columbia Plateau

Cecilo Falls I

Columbia Plateau

Columbia Plateau

Combat Wand Blade

Dagger

Diamond Back

Eastgate

Eden

Elko

Elko Wide Notched

Firstview

Fountain Bar

Gunther Barbed

Hell Gap

Kelsey Creek Barbed

Klickitat

Eden

Lake Mohave

Lewis River Short Stemmed

Lind Coulee 1

Lind Coulee 2

Lind Coulee 3

Malaga Cove Stemmed

McGillivray

McKee Uniface

Nottoway

Cchoco Stemmed

One-Que

Parman

Pryor Stemmed

Rose Springs

Rose Springs knife

Rose Springs Sloping Shoulder

Rossi Square-stemmed

Sauvie's Island Shoulder notched

Silver Lake

Steamboat Lanceolate

Stockton

Trade Points

Scottsbluff I

Scottsbluff II

Scottsbluff Knife

Vendetta

Wallula Gap Rect. Stemmed

Wallula Gap Rect. Stemmed

Wallula Double Tip

Wendover

Windust

Windust-Alberta

Yana II

Youngs River Stemmed

Contracting Stems

Contra Costa

Coquille Broadneck

Coquille Narrowneck

Cougar Mountain

Deschutes Knife

Gatecliff

Gypsum Cave

Gypsum Cave

Houx Contracting Stem

Lake Mohave

Lake Mohave

Lake Mohave, chisel tip

Parman

Rabbit Island arrow

Point Sal Barbed

Rabbit Island dart

Rabbit Island dart, first stage

Shaniko Stemmed

Shaniko Stemmed

Sierra Contracting Stem

Rabbit Island arrow

Rabbit Island dart

Vandenberg Contracting stem

Vandenberg Contracting stem

Windust Contracting

Windust-Hatwai

Yana I

F
W

965

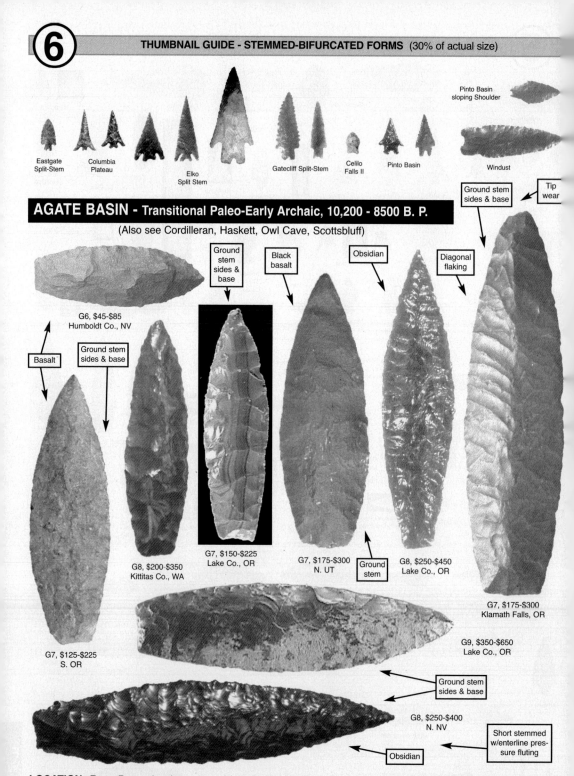

Eastgate Split-Stem

Columbia Plateau

Elko Split Stem

Gatecliff Split-Stem

Celilo Falls II

Pinto Basin

Pinto Basin sloping Shoulder

Windust

AGATE BASIN - Transitional Paleo-Early Archaic, 10,200 - 8500 B. P.

(Also see Cordilleran, Haskett, Owl Cave, Scottsbluff)

Ground stem sides & base

Tip wear

Ground stem sides & base

Black basalt

Obsidian

Diagonal flaking

G6, $45-$85 Humboldt Co., NV

Basalt

Ground stem sides & base

G8, $200-$350 Kittitas Co., WA

G7, $150-$225 Lake Co., OR

G7, $175-$300 N. UT

Ground stem

G8, $250-$450 Lake Co., OR

G7, $175-$300 Klamath Falls, OR

G9, $350-$650 Lake Co., OR

G7, $125-$225 S. OR

Ground stem sides & base

G8, $250-$400 N. NV

Short stemmed w/enterline pressure fluting

Obsidian

LOCATION: From Pennsylvania westward into Idaho, Nevada, Oregon to Canada. **DESCRIPTION:** A medium to large size lanceolate blade of high quality. Bases are either convex, concave or straight, are often beveled, and stems are usually ground. Some examples are median ridged and have random to parallel flaking. Believed to have evolved from the earlier *Haskett/Lind Coulee types.* **I.D. KEY:** Basal form and flaking style. **NOTE:** The Alaska *Mesa* point is a similar form and has been reportedly dated to 13,700 years B.P., but more data is needed to verify this extreme age.

AHSAHKA - Late Archaic-Classic Phase, 3,000 - 500 B. P.

(Also see Cold Springs, Desert, Lake River Side, Northern Side, Piqunin & Sauvie's Island)

G3, $1-$3 N. ID

G3, $1-$3 N. ID

G5, $2-$5 Spokane, WA

G5, $2-$5 Spokane, WA

G4, $2-$5 Spokane, WA

G6, $3-$6 Snake River, ID

G6, $4-$8 Snake River, ID

LOCATION: Northern Idaho & Washington. **DESCRIPTION:** A medium size dart point with shallow side notches and a straight to convex base. A descendent of *Hatwai* which is a descendent of *Cold Springs*. **I.D. KEY:** Shallow side notches.

ALBERTA - Early Archaic, 10,000 - 8500 B. P.

(Also see Big Valley, Cody Complex Knife, Eden, Firstview, Lind Coulee, Parman, Scottsbluff & Windust)

LOCATION: Northern States from Michigan to Montana to Nevada and Oregon. **DESCRIPTION:** A medium to large size point with a broad, long parallel stem that is ground and weak shoulders. Developed from the *Haskett, Lind Coulee* in the Great Basin and later changed into the Cody Complex and is related to the *Eden* and *Scottsbluff* types. **I.D. KEY:** Long, broad rectangular stem, weak shoulders, serial flaking.

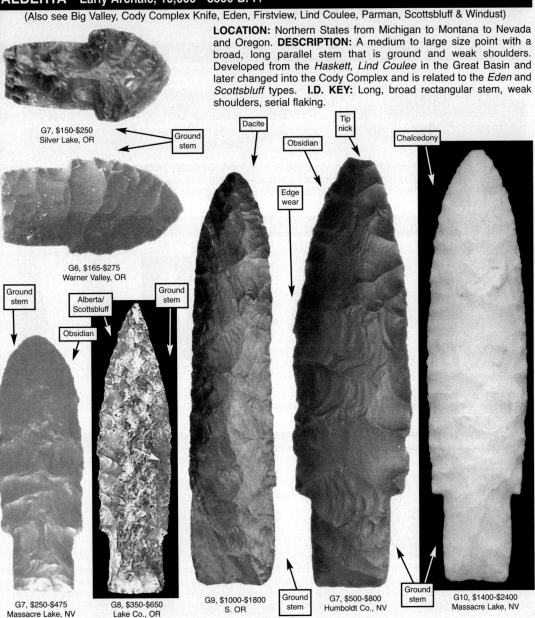

G7, $150-$250 Silver Lake, OR

Ground stem

G6, $165-$275 Warner Valley, OR

Dacite

Obsidian

Tip nick

Chalcedony

Edge wear

Ground stem

Alberta/ Scottsbluff

Ground stem

Obsidian

G7, $250-$475 Massacre Lake, NV

G8, $350-$650 Lake Co., OR

G9, $1000-$1800 S. OR

Ground stem

G7, $500-$800 Humboldt Co., NV

Ground stem

G10, $1400-$2400 Massacre Lake, NV

F W

967

ALBERTA (continued)

G9, $900-$1600
Massacre Lake, NV

Ground stem →

ALBION-HEAD SIDE NOTCHED - Early Archaic to Transitional, 6500 - 2000 B. P.

(Also see Cold Springs, Northern and Rose Springs)

Rare double tip

G7, $8-$15
Bethel Isle, CA

LOCATION: N. California. **DESCRIPTION:** A medium size dart point with side notches and a concave base with rounded ears.

ALDER COMPLEX - Late Paleo, 9,500 - 8000 B. P.

(Also see Agate Basin, Cascade, Haskett, Owl Cave and Pryor Stemmed)

Collateral flaking

G7, $15-$25
S. E. OR

Diagonal flaking

Tip wear

G5, $5-$10
S. E. OR

LOCATION: S. E. Oregon into Idaho, Utah, Wyoming and Montana. **DESCRIPTION:** A medium to large size unfluted lanceolate point of high quality with convex sides and a straight to concave base. Flaking is usually the parallel oblique type. Basal areas are ground. **I.D. KEY:** Basal form and flaking style.

ALKALI - Developmental to Classic Phase, 1500 - 500 B. P.

(Also see Eastgate, Elko and Rose Springs)

Yellow agate

Serrated edge

G7, $2-$5
Col. Riv. OR

G8, $8-$15
S. E. OR

G8, $8-$15
Lake Co., OR

G8, $8-$15
Lake Co., OR

G8, $8-$15
Lake Co., OR

G8, $15-$25
Columbia Riv., OR

G10, $25-$40
Columbia Riv., OR

G10, $25-$45
Lake Co., OR

LOCATION: California to Canada. **DESCRIPTION:** A small size, barbed arrow point with a long parallel sided stem. This type was included with *Rose Springs* in early reports. **I.D. KEY:** Flaking style and long stem.

AÑO NUEVO - Late Archaic, 2950 - 2500 B. P.

(Also see Cougar Mountain, Deschutes Knife, Lind Coulee, Parman and Wildcat Canyon)

Apiculate tip

G8, $15-$25
Coastal CA

Monterey chert

G8, $45-$80
Mendocino Co., CA

LOCATION: Type site is in San Mateo Co., CA. **DESCRIPTION:** A medium to large size point with a long, tapered stem and weak tapered shoulders. The base is convex and stem sides are not ground. The distal end can be apiculate and flaking is random. Thicker than *Cougar Mountain* points. Made almost exclusively of Monterey Chert which is rootbeer colored, similar to Knife River flint from the Dakotas. **I.D. KEY:** Tip style and long stem.

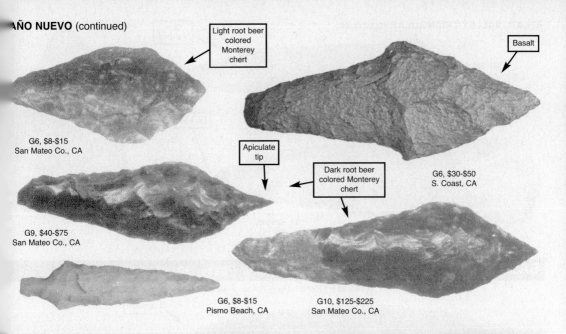

Light root beer colored Monterey chert

Basalt

G6, $8-$15
San Mateo Co., CA

Apiculate tip

Dark root beer colored Monterey chert

G6, $30-$50
S. Coast, CA

G9, $40-$75
San Mateo Co., CA

G6, $8-$15
Pismo Beach, CA

G10, $125-$225
San Mateo Co., CA

ATLATL VALLEY TRIANGULAR - Early to late Archaic, 7000 - 3500 B. P.

(Also see Coquille Knife, Cottonwood, Fremont Triangular, Plateau Pentagonal)

Black pitchstone

Beveled base

G5, $2-$5
The Dalles, OR

G8, $5-$10
OR

G8, $12-$20
Columbia Riv., OR

G8, $12-$20
Columbia Plateau, WA

Beveled edge

Dark brown/red jasper with inclusions

Beveled base

G10, $175-$300
Jefferson Co., ID

G8, $40-$75
OR

F
W

LOCATION: Snake River in the East to the Cowlitz River in W. Oregon. **DESCRIPTION:** A small to medium size triangular knife with an occasional bevel on one side of each face. Some are uniface. Bases are straight to convex and are well thinned to beveled. Some bases are beveled half way across, then change at the midway point to an opposing bevel. These are never hafted & are resharpened all the way to the basal corners. Smaller examples have been found with *Rabbit Island* points. **I.D. KEY:** Beveling and blade form.

ATLATL VALLEY TRIANGULAR (continued)

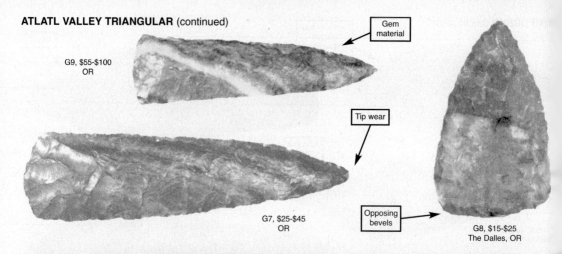

Gem material

G9, $55-$100
OR

Tip wear

G7, $25-$45
OR

Opposing bevels

G8, $15-$25
The Dalles, OR

BASE TANG KNIFE - Early Archaic to Transitional Phase, 10,000 - 2000 B. P.

(Also see Corner Tang Knife, Paleo Knife)

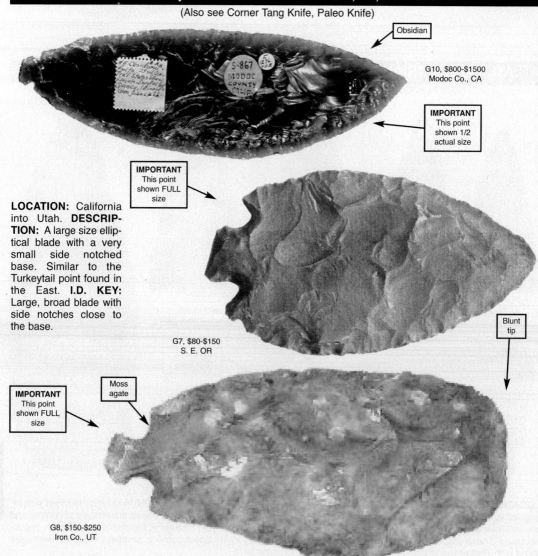

Obsidian

G10, $800-$1500
Modoc Co., CA

IMPORTANT
This point shown 1/2 actual size

IMPORTANT
This point shown FULL size

LOCATION: California into Utah. **DESCRIPTION:** A large size elliptical blade with a very small side notched base. Similar to the Turkeytail point found in the East. **I.D. KEY:** Large, broad blade with side notches close to the base.

G7, $80-$150
S. E. OR

Blunt tip

IMPORTANT
This point shown FULL size

Moss agate

G8, $150-$250
Iron Co., UT

BEAR RIVER - Developmental to Classic Phase, 1300 - 400 B. P.

(Also see Desert, Emigrant, Lake River, Rose Spring, Sauvie's Island Side)

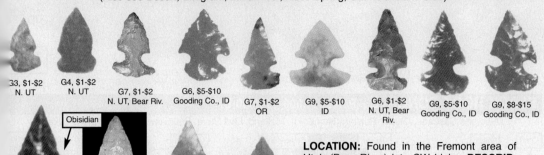

G3, $1-$2
N. UT

G4, $1-$2
N. UT

G7, $1-$2
N. UT, Bear Riv.

G6, $5-$10
Gooding Co., ID

G7, $1-$2
OR

G9, $5-$10
ID

G6, $1-$2
N. UT, Bear
Riv.

G9, $5-$10
Gooding Co., ID

G9, $8-$15
Gooding Co., ID

Obsidian

G9, $8-$15
ID

G8, $8-$15
N. UT, Bear Riv.

G10, $15-$30
OR

G6, $6-$12
N. ID

LOCATION: Found in the Fremont area of Utah (Bear River) into SW Idaho. **DESCRIPTION:** A small size, thin, side-notched arrow point with deep notches. The base is large in relation to its overall size. Basal corners are rounded. **I.D. KEY:** Large base, small overall size.

BIG VALLEY STEMMED - Middle Archaic, 4000 - 3500 B. P.

(Also see Alberta, Cody Complex, Lind Coulee, Mayacmas Corner, Parman and Silver Lake)

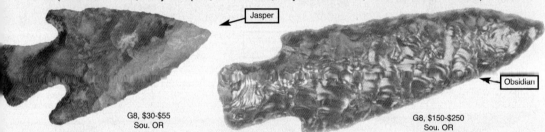

Jasper

Obsidian

G8, $30-$55
Sou. OR

G8, $150-$250
Sou. OR

LOCATION: Northern California into southern Cascades, Oregon. **DESCRIPTION:** A medium to large size, long stemmed point with rounded basal corners. Shoulders are horizontal and bases are straight. **I.D. KEY:** Large stem. See Noel Justice, 2002.

BITTERROOT - Early to middle Archaic, 7500 - 5000 B. P.

(See Ahsahka, Desert, Emigrant, Nightfire, Northern Side Notched & Salmon River)

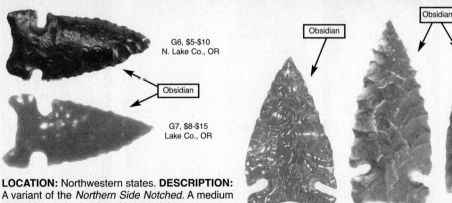

G6, $5-$10
N. Lake Co., OR

Obsidian

G7, $8-$15
Lake Co., OR

Obsidian

Obsidian

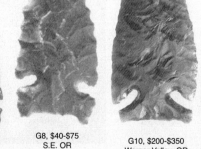

LOCATION: Northwestern states. **DESCRIPTION:** A variant of the *Northern Side Notched*. A medium size side-notched point with a straight, concave or convex base. Notches are placed at an angle into each side of the blade. Early Archaic flaking is evident on many examples.

G9, $50-$90
Lake Co., OR

G8, $40-$75
S.E. OR

G10, $200-$350
Warner Valley, OR

F
W

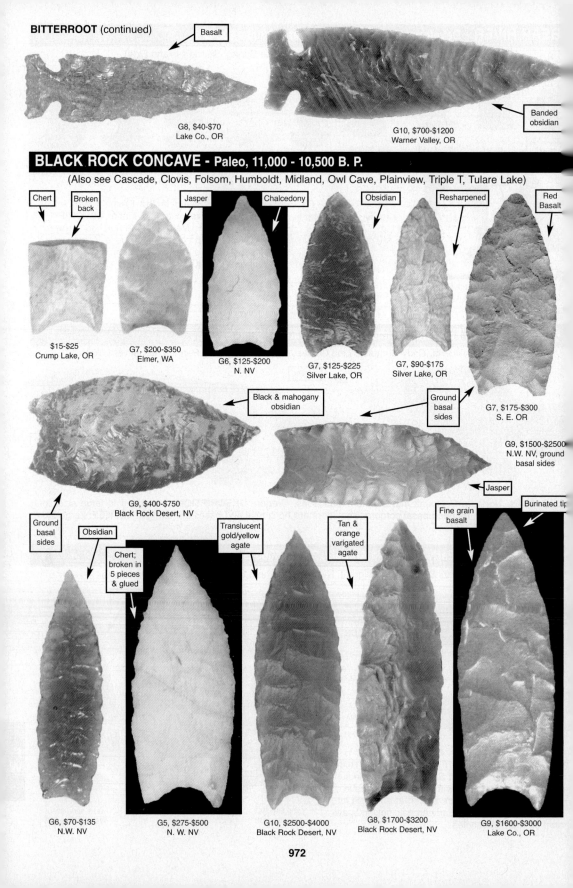

BITTERROOT (continued)

Basalt

G8, $40-$70
Lake Co., OR

Banded obsidian

G10, $700-$1200
Warner Valley, OR

BLACK ROCK CONCAVE - Paleo, 11,000 - 10,500 B. P.

(Also see Cascade, Clovis, Folsom, Humboldt, Midland, Owl Cave, Plainview, Triple T, Tulare Lake)

Chert

Broken back

Jasper

Chalcedony

Obsidian

Resharpened

Red Basalt

$15-$25
Crump Lake, OR

G7, $200-$350
Elmer, WA

G6, $125-$200
N. NV

G7, $125-$225
Silver Lake, OR

G7, $90-$175
Silver Lake, OR

G7, $175-$300
S. E. OR

Black & mahogany obsidian

Ground basal sides

G9, $1500-$2500
N.W. NV, ground basal sides

G9, $400-$750
Black Rock Desert, NV

Jasper

Fine grain basalt

Burinated tip

Ground basal sides

Obsidian

Chert; broken in 5 pieces & glued

Translucent gold/yellow agate

Tan & orange varigated agate

G6, $70-$135
N.W. NV

G5, $275-$500
N. W. NV

G10, $2500-$4000
Black Rock Desert, NV

G8, $1700-$3200
Black Rock Desert, NV

G9, $1600-$3000
Lake Co., OR

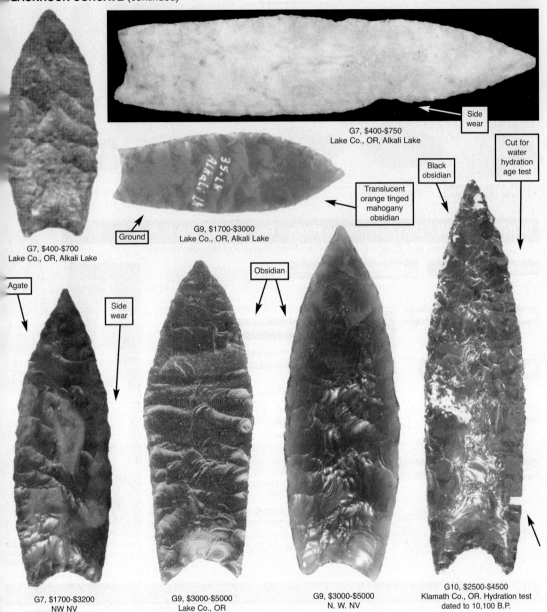

G7, $400-$750
Lake Co., OR, Alkali Lake

Side wear

Cut for water hydration age test

Black obsidian

Translucent orange tinged mahogany obsidian

Ground

G9, $1700-$3000
Lake Co., OR, Alkali Lake

G7, $400-$700
Lake Co., OR, Alkali Lake

Agate

Side wear

Obsidian

G7, $1700-$3200
NW NV

G9, $3000-$5000
Lake Co., OR

G9, $3000-$5000
N. W. NV

G10, $2500-$4500
Klamath Co., OR. Hydration test
dated to 10,100 B.P.

LOCATION: NW Nevada and SE Oregon. An extremely rare type with few complete examples known. **DESCRIPTION:** A medium size, thin, lanceolate point with a concave base. Basal edges are usually ground. Blade flaking is horizontal transverse. Similar in flaking style and form to *Midland* and *Goshen* points and is considered to be the unfluted *Folsom* of the Great Basin. **I.D. KEY:** Micro secondary flaking, ground basal sides, thinness.

BLISS (provisional) - Developmental to Historic Phase, 900 - 350 B. P.

(Also see Spedis III)

F
W

G4, $2-$3
S.W. ID

G4, $2-$4
S.W. ID

Chalc.

G4, $2-$5
S.W. ID

Chalc.

G4, $2-$5
S.W. ID

LOCATION: SW Idaho into SE Oregon border area. **DESCRIPTION:** A small size lanceolate point that is found in two forms: Bipointed, widest near the center, and with a rounded to straight base, widest near the tip. Blade edges are convex. Thicker than *Spedis*, has been found hafted to a wooden foreshaft of an arrow.

BLISS (continued)

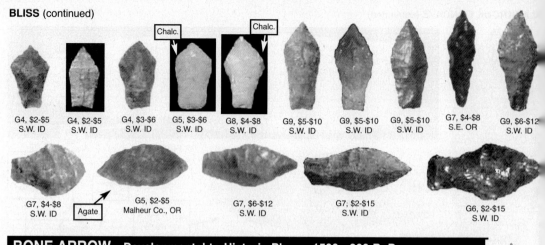

G4, $2-$5 S.W. ID

G4, $2-$5 S.W. ID

G4, $3-$6 S.W. ID

Chalc.
G5, $3-$6 S.W. ID

Chalc.
G8, $4-$8 S.W. ID

G9, $5-$10 S.W. ID

G9, $5-$10 S.W. ID

G9, $5-$10 S.W. ID

G7, $4-$8 S.E. OR

G9, $6-$12 S.W. ID

G7, $4-$8 S.W. ID

Agate

G5, $2-$5 Malheur Co., OR

G7, $6-$12 S.W. ID

G7, $2-$15 S.W. ID

G6, $2-$15 S.W. ID

BONE ARROW - Developmental to Historic Phase, 1500 - 200 B. P.

(Also see Bone Pin, Three-Piece Fish Spear and Wooden Arrow)

G8, $12-$20 OR coast

G9, $15-$25 OR coast

G8, $15-$30 Columbia Plateau, WA

G8, $15-$25 OR coast

G8, $12-$20 Astoria, OR

G9, $15-$25 OR coast

G8, $15-$25 OR coast

G8, $12-$20 OR coast

G9, $50-$90 Clearwater Riv., ID

G8, $12-$20 OR coast

G10, $40-$70 OR

G8, $15-$25 OR coast

G10, $40-$70 OR

LOCATION: Oregon into Alaska.
DESCRIPTION: A long narrow foreshaft and point crafted from bone or ivory.

G10, $90-$175 CA coast Circa: 1860-1880

G10, $250-$325 CA coast. Hafted, Circa: 1860-1880

BONE PIN - Paleo, 11,500- 10,000 B. P.

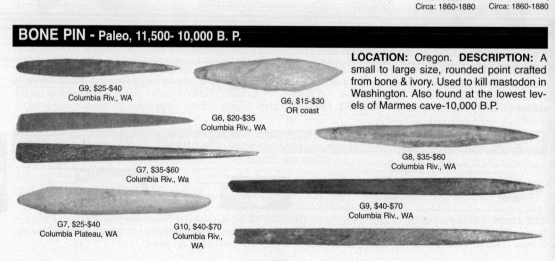

LOCATION: Oregon. **DESCRIPTION:** A small to large size, rounded point crafted from bone & ivory. Used to kill mastodon in Washington. Also found at the lowest levels of Marmes cave-10,000 B.P.

G9, $25-$40 Columbia Riv., WA

G6, $15-$30 OR coast

G6, $20-$35 Columbia Riv., WA

G7, $35-$60 Columbia Riv., Wa

G8, $35-$60 Columbia Riv., WA

G7, $25-$40 Columbia Plateau, WA

G10, $40-$70 Columbia Riv., WA

G9, $40-$70 Columbia Riv., WA

ONE PIN (continued)

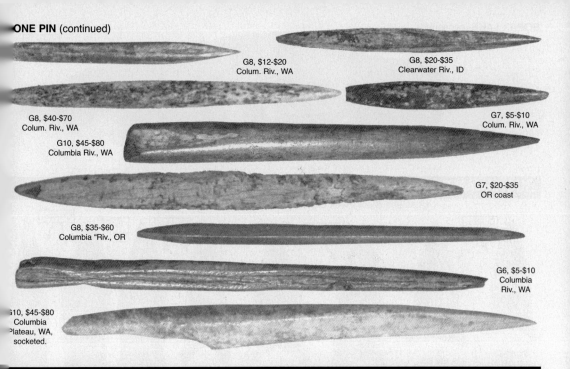

G8, $12-$20
Colum. Riv., WA

G8, $20-$35
Clearwater Riv., ID

G8, $40-$70
Colum. Riv., WA

G7, $5-$10
Colum. Riv., WA

G10, $45-$80
Columbia Riv., WA

G7, $20-$35
OR coast

G8, $35-$60
Columbia "Riv., OR

G6, $5-$10
Columbia
Riv., WA

G10, $45-$80
Columbia
Plateau, WA,
socketed.

BORAX LAKE - Early Archaic, 8000 - 5000 B. P.

(Also see Houx Contracting Stem, Scottsbluff)

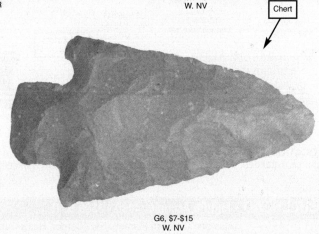

Jasper

Translucent
obsidian

Chert

G6, $3-$5
N. W. NV

G8, $35-$60
OR

G6, $5-$10
W. NV

Chert

LOCATION: N. California into S. Oregon.
DESCRIPTION: This type has an elongat-ed, triangular blade when pristine with a wide, approximately square stem. Stem sides are often ground. Bases are straight to slightly convex. A very similar point with a concave base is called the *Stanislaus Broad Stem*. There are narrower versions of both types and they range from the cen-tral valley of California to the Pacific Ocean, north into southern Oregon, and sporadi-cally into W. Nevada. Have been found with Crescents. **I.D. KEY:** Strong Hertzican core scars in notches, wide, thin primary flake removal on pristine specimens, and chevron pattern resharpening on worn-out pieces. See Noel Justice, 2002.

G6, $7-$15
W. NV

F
W

975

BORAX LAKE (continued)

Obsidian

G8, $150-$250
Sou. OR

BUCHANAN EARED - Late Archaic to Developmental Phase, 3000 - 1300 B. P.

(Also see Black Rock Concave, Early Eared, Humboldt and Strong)

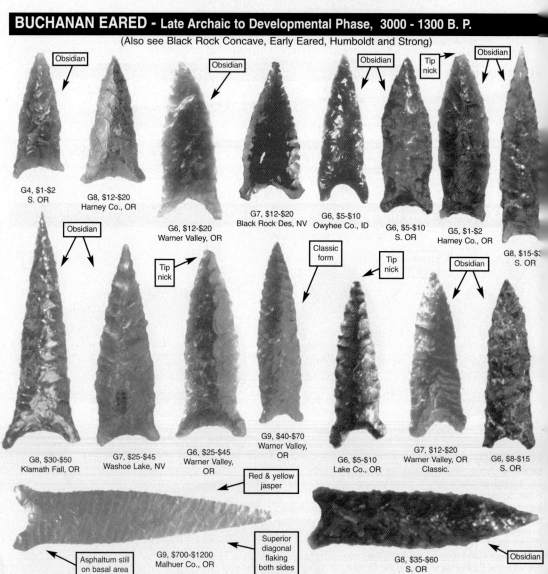

Obsidian

Obsidian

Obsidian

Tip nick

Obsidian

G4, $1-$2
S. OR

G8, $12-$20
Harney Co., OR

G6, $12-$20
Warner Valley, OR

G7, $12-$20
Black Rock Des, NV

G6, $5-$10
Owyhee Co., ID

G6, $5-$10
S. OR

G5, $1-$2
Harney Co., OR

G8, $15-$3
S. OR

Obsidian

Tip nick

Classic form

Tip nick

Obsidian

G8, $30-$50
Klamath Fall, OR

G7, $25-$45
Washoe Lake, NV

G6, $25-$45
Warner Valley, OR

G9, $40-$70
Warner Valley, OR

G6, $5-$10
Lake Co., OR

G7, $12-$20
Warner Valley, OR
Classic.

G6, $8-$15
S. OR

Red & yellow jasper

Asphaltum still on basal area

G9, $700-$1200
Malheur Co., OR

Superior diagonal flaking both sides

G8, $35-$60
S. OR

Obsidian

LOCATION: Great Basin states, esp. N.W. Nevada. **DESCRIPTION:** A small to medium size, narrow, lanceolate point with an expanded, eared, concave base. Some examples show excellent parallel flaking. A later form of *Humboldt*.

BULLHEAD - Middle Archaic, 4000 - 3500 B. P.

(Also see Chilcotin Plateau, Elko Corner, Hell's Canyon, Hendricks, Merrybell)

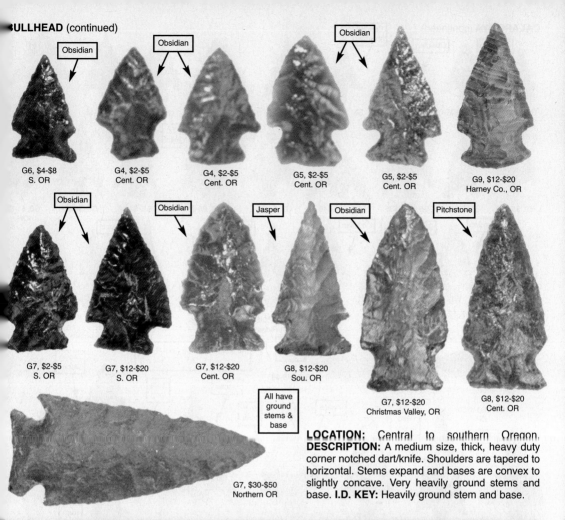

Obsidian

G6, $4-$8
S. OR

Obsidian

G4, $2-$5
Cent. OR

G4, $2-$5
Cent. OR

Obsidian

G5, $2-$5
Cent. OR

G5, $2-$5
Cent. OR

G9, $12-$20
Harney Co., OR

Obsidian

G7, $2-$5
S. OR

G7, $12-$20
S. OR

Obsidian

G7, $12-$20
Cent. OR

Jasper

G8, $12-$20
Sou. OR

Obsidian

G7, $12-$20
Christmas Valley, OR

Pitchstone

G8, $12-$20
Cent. OR

All have ground stems & base

G7, $30-$50
Northern OR

LOCATION: Central to southern Oregon.
DESCRIPTION: A medium size, thick, heavy duty corner notched dart/knife. Shoulders are tapered to horizontal. Stems expand and bases are convex to slightly concave. Very heavily ground stems and base. **I.D. KEY:** Heavily ground stem and base.

BURIN - Late Archaic to Historic Phase, 2500 - 200 B. P.

(Also see Chopper, Drill, Graver, Lancet, Perforator, Paleo Knife and Scraper)

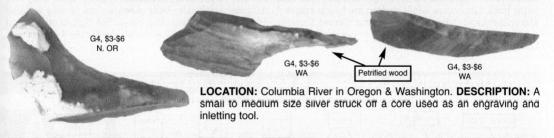

G4, $3-$6
N. OR

G4, $3-$6
WA

Petrified wood

G4, $3-$6
WA

LOCATION: Columbia River in Oregon & Washington. **DESCRIPTION:** A small to medium size sliver struck off a core used as an engraving and inletting tool.

CALAPOOYA - Developmental to Historic Phase, 1000 - 200 B. P.

(Also see Columbia Plateau, Gunther, Wallula and Wintu)

F
W

G4, $2-$5   G6, $2-$5   G9, $6-$12   G7, $6-$12
OR   G6, $6-$12   G8, $6-$12   G8, $6-$12   G6, $5-$10
N. OR   G9, $8-$15

All others from Fern Ridge, OR

CALAPOOYA (continued)

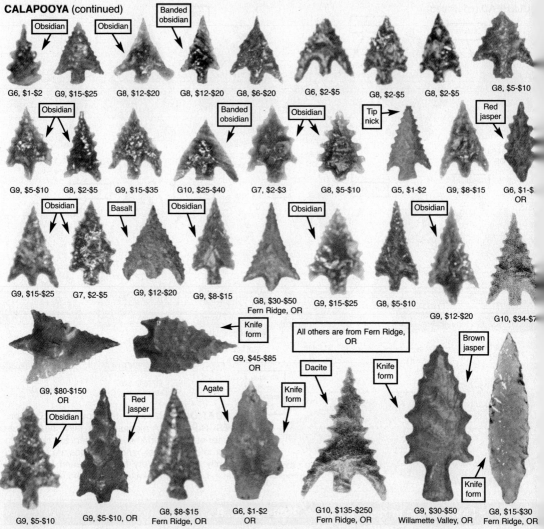

Obsidian — G6, $1-$2
Obsidian — G9, $15-$25
G8, $12-$20
Banded obsidian — G8, $12-$20
G8, $6-$20
G6, $2-$5
G8, $2-$5
G8, $2-$5
G8, $5-$10

Obsidian — G9, $5-$10
G8, $2-$5
G9, $15-$35
Banded obsidian — G10, $25-$40
Obsidian — G7, $2-$3
G8, $5-$10
Tip nick — G5, $1-$2
G9, $8-$15
Red jasper — G6, $1-$ OR

Obsidian — G9, $15-$25
G7, $2-$5
Basalt — G9, $12-$20
Obsidian — G9, $8-$15
G8, $30-$50 Fern Ridge, OR
Obsidian — G9, $15-$25
G8, $5-$10
Obsidian — G9, $12-$20
G10, $34-$7

Knife form — G9, $45-$85 OR

All others are from Fern Ridge, OR

G9, $80-$150 OR

Obsidian

Red Jasper

Agate

Knife form

Dacite

Knife form

Brown jasper

Knife form

G9, $5-$10
G9, $5-$10, OR
G8, $8-$15 Fern Ridge, OR
G6, $1-$2 OR
G10, $135-$250 Fern Ridge, OR
G9, $30-$50 Willamette Valley, OR
G8, $15-$30 Fern Ridge, OR

LOCATION: Willamette Valley, Oregon between the Columbia and Rogue rivers. **DESCRIPTION:** A small size, thin, arrow point that occurs either as stemmed, side notched, triangular and ovate. Most examples are heavily serrated and imitate local styles such as *Gunther, Desert, Columbia Plateau, Wallula* and other types. The barbed edge, short stemmed variant is locally called a *Fern Leaf* point. This type has three spellings: Calapooya, Calapooia & Kalapooya. **I.D. KEY:** Wild serrations.

CANALINO TRIANGULAR - Classic to Historic Phase, 700 - 200 B. P.
(Also see Bull Creek, Cottonwood, Gold Hill, Gunther Triangular)

Jasper agate — G8, $8-$15 Ventura Co., CA
Agate — G9, $12-$20 Ventura Co., CA
Quartz — G6, $1-$2 Santa Barbara Co., CA.
Fused shale — G8, $8-$15 Ventura Co., CA Green Chalc.
Moss agate — G6, $1-$2 Santa Barbara Co., CA.
Fused shale — G10, $15-$25 Ventura Co., CA
G7, $5-$10 Santa Barbara Co., CA.
Monterey chert — G7, $8-$15 Los Angeles Co., CA.

LOCATION: California. **DESCRIPTION:** A small size, thin, triangular arrow point with a shallow to deep concave base. Some are serrated. Also known as *Coastal Cottonwood*. See Noel Justice, 2002.

ANALINO TRIANGULAR (continued)

G7, $20-$35
Santa Barbara Co., CA.

G8, $5-$10
Ventura Co., CA.

Fused shale

G9, $30-$50
Mendocino Co., CA

Agate

G9, $35-$60
Los Angeles Co., CA.

Monterey chert

Fused shale

G10, $35-$60
Ventura Co., CA.

G10, $30-$50
Ventura Co., CA.

G10, $40-$75
Santa Barbara Co., CA.

CASCADE - Early Archaic, 8000 - 4000 B. P.

(Also see Agate Basin, Cordilleran, Early Leaf, Excelsior, Gold Hill, Haskett, Kennewick, Mankin Shouldered, Need Stemmed, NW Four-Way Knife, Owl Cave, Parman, Steamboat, and Windust)

Jasper

Basalt

Obsidian

Agate

Obsidian

Jasper

G6, $8-$15
N. OR

G3, $5-$10
OR

G6, $8-$15
N. OR

G6, $8-$15
S. OR

G6, $8-$15
N. ID

G6, $8-$15
N. ID

G5, $2-$5
S. OR

G7, $15-$30
Columb. Riv., OR

Basalt

Serrated edge

Jasper

Obsidian

Obsidian

Basalt

G6, $12-$20
N. ID

G6, $12-$20
N. ID

G9, $35-$60
N. ID

G8, $20-$35
WA

G6 $8-$15
WA

G6, $8-$15
WA

G9, $35-$60
N. ID

Obsidian

Diagonal flaking

Diagonal flaking

Obsidian

G9, $40-$70
OR

G8, $35-$60
Lake Co., OR

F
W

LOCATION: Great Basin to Washington. **DESCRIPTION:** A medium to large size, narrow, thin, blade that can exhibit oblique parallel flaking. Base can be convex to pointed. Early forms have ground basal areas. The famous Paulina Creek Dietz Cascade cache of 2130 blades was found in Oregon in 1961. **I.D. KEY:** Narrow, lanceolate form.

979

CASCADE (continued)

Obsidian

Obsidian

Jasper

Obsidian

G8, $35-$60
S. OR

G7, $20-$35
S. OR

G7, $20-$35
Lake Co., OR

G7, $25-$40
Columb. Riv., OR

G9, $125-$200
Lake Co., OR

G10, $1
$250
Lake C
OR

Obsidian

Early form;
ground basal
area

Obsidian

Tip nick

Obsidian

Dacite

G9, $125-$200
Lake Co., OR

G10, $175-$300
Deschutes Co., OR

G7, $40-$65
OR

G9, $125-$225
Lake Co., OR

G8, $100-
$185
Cent. OR

Early form;
ground basal
area

Obsidian

G10, $400-$750
OR

Diagonal flaking

Obsidian

Jasper

G9, $65-$125
N. NV

G8, $40-$75
S. OR

G9, $65-$125
S. OR

Obsidian
with alkali
around
edges

Obsidian

Obsidian

G9, $150-$250
S. OR

G10, $350-$600
Lake Co., OR

G10, $400-$750
OR

F
W

981

CASCADE (continued)

NOTE: There is a difference between the *Cascade base-notched* and the *Humboldt* points. The *Humboldt* point usually has a straight more visible hafting area than the *Cascade*. The *Cascade* hafting area tapers to the base, while the *Humboldt* usually expands slightly near the base. Most *Humboldts* have wider base notches than the *Cascades*. The *Cascade* base-notch appears to be a field improvisation while the *Humboldt* notch is preplanned and usually has multiple strokes. While approximately 90% of *Humboldt* stems are ground, less than 10% of the Cascades have ground stems. Completely worn out or damaged specimens could be mistaken for one another.

CASCADE KNIFE - Early Archaic, 8000 - 4000 B. P.

(Also see Cascade Knife, Cascade Shouldered, Early Leaf, Excelsior, Haskett, High Desert Knife, Kennewick, and NW Four-Way Knife)

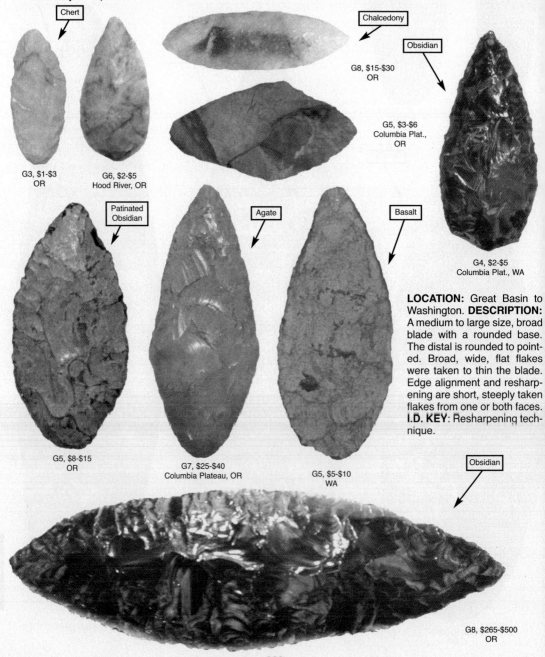

Chert

G3, $1-$3
OR

G6, $2-$5
Hood River, OR

Chalcedony

G8, $15-$30
OR

Obsidian

G5, $3-$6
Columbia Plat.,
OR

Obsidian

G4, $2-$5
Columbia Plat., WA

Patinated
Obsidian

Agate

Basalt

G5, $8-$15
OR

G7, $25-$40
Columbia Plateau, OR

G5, $5-$10
WA

LOCATION: Great Basin to Washington. **DESCRIPTION:** A medium to large size, broad blade with a rounded base. The distal is rounded to pointed. Broad, wide, flat flakes were taken to thin the blade. Edge alignment and resharpening are short, steeply taken flakes from one or both faces. **I.D. KEY:** Resharpening technique.

Obsidian

G8, $265-$500
OR

982

Jasper

G8, $200-$350
Lake Co., OR

Basalt

G7, $30-$50
N. ID

Chalcedony

Chalcedony

G9, $250-$400
N. OR

Base wear

G9, $350-$650
Columbia River, OR

G10, $400-$750
Warner Valley, OR

F W

CASCADE KNIFE (continued)

Jasper

G10, $250-$450
Iron Co., UT

Obsidian

Knife form

G10, $450-$850
Warner Valley, OR

G10, $600-$1000
Warner Valley, OR

G10, $800-$1500
Lake Co., OR

Also see Cascade, Cascade Knife, Early Leaf, Excelsior, Harahey, Haskett, Kennewick, Mahkin Shouldered, NW Four-Way Knife, Parman, Shaniko Stemmed and Windust)

Basalt

Obsidian

Agate

Obsidian

G5, $4-$8
Cent. OR

G6, $4-$8
Coastal OR

G6, $4-$8
S. OR

G6, $12-$20
N. OR

G8, $8-$15
Coastal OR

G9, $50-$90
OR

Obsidian

Ignimbrite

Obsidian

Agate

Obsidian

G7, $15-$30
Lake Co., OR

G5, $8-$15
OR

G7, $25-$40
Lake Co., OR

G6, $15-$25
WA

G8, $15-$30
S. OR

Ground
stem

G8, $80-$150
Columb. Rv., OR

G8, $40-$75
S. OR

Obsidian

G10, $300-$550
S. OR

LOCATION: Great Basin to Washington. **DESCRIPTION:** A medium to large size, narrow, thin, blade that can exhibit oblique parallel flaking. Base can be convex to pointed. A faint shoulder occurs on one or both sides that contracts to the base. Early forms have ground basal areas. **I.D. KEY:** Slight shoulder on one or both sides.

F
W

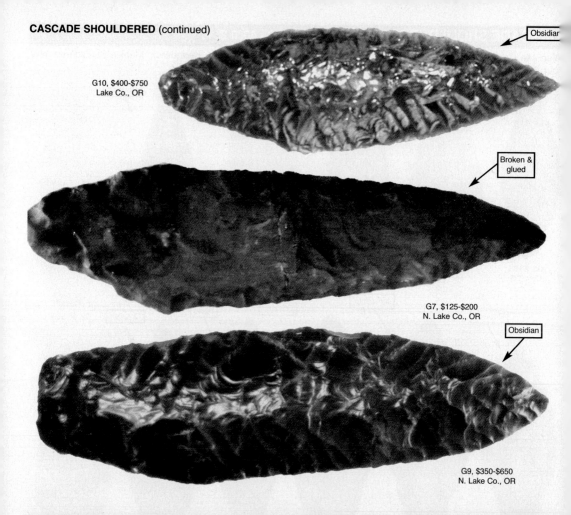

Obsidian

G10, $400-$750
Lake Co., OR

Broken &
glued

G7, $125-$200
N. Lake Co., OR

Obsidian

G9, $350-$650
N. Lake Co., OR

CELILO FALLS I (provisional) - Paleo, 10,800 - 10,100 B. P.

(Also see Midland, Spedis)

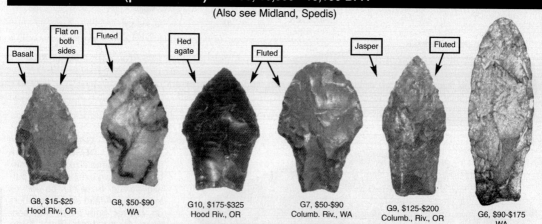

Basalt

Flat on
both
sides

Fluted

Hed
agate

Fluted

Jasper

Fluted

G8, $15-$25
Hood Riv., OR

G8, $50-$90
WA

G10, $175-$325
Hood Riv., OR

G7, $50-$90
Columb. Riv., WA

G9, $125-$200
Columb., Riv., OR

G6, $90-$175
WA

LOCATION: Great Basin westward. **DESCRIPTION:** Early knives are strongly shouldered and have one, two or no flutes. Flutes vary in length, but usually pass the shoulders into the blade. Stems are ground or smoothed into the shoulders and stem sides are incurvate to straight, rarely contracting. Most, but not all, bases have delicate auricles, giving these points the nickname "fishtail." There is a small or unfluted, basally thinned variety made on spalled flakes, that can be flat on one or both sides, with minimal retouch edge alignment. **I.D. KEY:** Auriculate stem, strong shoulders.

CECILO FALLS II (provisional) - Paleo, 9500 - 8600 B. P.

(Also see Midland, Pryor Stemmed & Spedis)

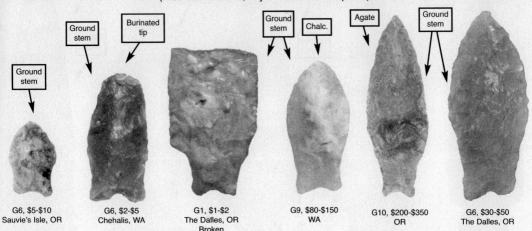

Ground stem — G6, $5-$10 Sauvie's Isle, OR

Ground stem — G6, $2-$5 Chehalis, WA

Burinated tip — G1, $1-$2 The Dalles, OR Broken

Ground stem · Chalc. — G9, $80-$150 WA

Agate — G10, $200-$350 OR

Ground stem — G6, $30-$50 The Dalles, OR

LOCATION: Oregon & Washington. **DESCRIPTION:** This point is a well flaked, small to medium sized dart knife previously identified as *Pryor* or *Pryor*-like. Location (N.W.) and basal thinning technique separate the two types. This point is basally thinned by steeply flaking one side of the basal and then using that platform to drive one or more longer flakes from the opossing side. This technique occurs on some *Midland* and some *Spedis* points. This type has a bifurcated or "eared" base and stem that is usually incurvate and well ground. Cross sections are lenticular. Blade shoulders can be obtuse to barbed. These points are not well-known in North America but are probably related to the somewhat earlier *Spedis Fishtail* point. *Pryor* or *Pryor*-like are found in the Snake River drainage in W. Idaho & S.E. Oregon. I.D. KEY: Long hafting area; ground auriculate stem.

CHILCOTIN PLATEAU - Early Archaic, 8000 - 5000 B. P.

(See Bullhead, Elko Corner, Hell's Canyon, Hendricks, Northern Side Notched, Snake River & Wendover)

Agate — G7, $12-$20 British Colum., CA

Basalt — G7, $8-$15 Sou. OR

Agate — G7, $5-$10 Harney Co., OR

— G10, $175-$300 WA

Basalt — G6, $8-$15 Sou. OR

Asymmetrical base · Tip wear

Jasper — G10, $300-$550 Yakima Co., WA

G5, $30-$50 Lake Co., OR

F
W

Basalt

Red jasper

Ground base

Basalt

Diagonal flaking

Yellow jasper

G6, $8-$15
Harney Co., OR

G8, $35-$65
OR

G6, $12-$20
Hood Riv., OR

G6, $30-$50
Union Co., OR

G10+, $800-$1500
Lake Co., OR

Brown petrified wood

Jassper

G10, $275-$525
The Dalles, OR

Perfect base example, round & beveled

G7, $125-$225
Wendover, NV

G10, $250-$475
Klamath Co., OR

LOCATION: Oregon. **DESCRIPTION:** A medium to large size, corner notched, barbed point with a straight to convex base and expanding stem. The cross section is lenticular (fairly thick at times, but occasionally flat). Blade edges are convex and rarely are resharpened by beveling. Stem sides are ground while bases are only occassionally ground. **I.D. KEY**: Grinding on stem sides, rounded or convex base that is beveled.

CHOPPER - Paleo, 11,500 - 10,000 B. P.

(Also see Hand Axe and Scraper)

LOCATION: California. **DESCRIPTION:** A medium to large size, thick, early chopping and pounding tool. Most are irregular shaped to oval to circular.

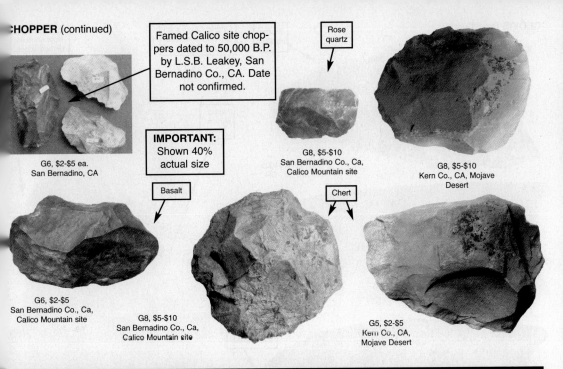

CHOPPER (continued)

Famed Calico site choppers dated to 50,000 B.P. by L.S.B. Leakey, San Bernadino Co., CA. Date not confirmed.

G6, $2-$5 ea.
San Bernadino, CA

IMPORTANT:
Shown 40% actual size

Rose quartz

G8, $5-$10
San Bernadino Co., Ca,
Calico Mountain site

G8, $5-$10
Kern Co., CA, Mojave Desert

Basalt

G6, $2-$5
San Bernadino Co., Ca,
Calico Mountain site

G8, $5-$10
San Bernadino Co., Ca,
Calico Mountain site

Chert

G5, $2-$5
Kern Co., CA,
Mojave Desert

CLOVIS - Paleo, 11,500 - 10,600 B. P.

(Also see Black Rock Concave, Cascade, Folsom, Humboldt, Midland, Plainview, Tulare Lake & Windust)

Obsidian

G5, $150-$250
S. OR, glued

G6, $300-$500
Lake Co., OR

Scraper

G1, $50-$100
WA

Glued

G5, $175-$300
WA

Flute channel

G8, $350-$650
Owyhee Co., ID

Black obsidian

Resharpened many times

G6, $450-$800
OR, Rebased from a longer point

Obsidian

G8, $400-$700
Lane Co., OR

F
W

LOCATION: All of North America. **DESCRIPTION:** A small to large size, auriculate, fluted, lanceolate point with convex sides and a concave base that is ground. Most examples have multiple flutes, usually on both sides. The basal concavity varies from shallow to deep. The oldest known point in North America. This point has been found associated with extinct mammoth & bison remains in several western states. **I.D. KEY:** Lanceolate form, baton fluting instead of indirect style.

989

CLOVIS (continued)

Banded obsidian

Largest Clovis point known. Actual size is 9-1/2" long

Note unusual barbed edges

Long channel flute

G7, $600-$1000
Lake Co., OR

G6, $650-$1200
Malhuer Co., OR

Fine-grained black basalt

G9, $1500-$2800
WA

Obsidian

Flute channel

G10, $1800-$3000
Lake Co., OR

G8, $2000-$3500
Double O Flats, OR

G10+, $50,000+, Douglas Co., WA. Obsidian. This point was probably used as a knife. It was found next to an extinct bison trail close to where the Wenatchee Clovis site is located. Picture from a Pete Bostrom cast of original. **Shown almost full size.**

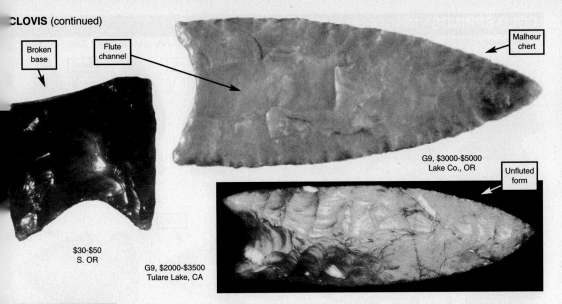

Broken base

Flute channel

Malheur chert

G9, $3000-$5000
Lake Co., OR

Unfluted form

$30-$50
S. OR

G9, $2000-$3500
Tulare Lake, CA

CODY COMPLEX   (see Eden and Scottsbluff)

CODY COMPLEX KNIFE - Early Archaic, 10,000 - 8000 B. P.

(Also see Eden, Firstview, Scottsbluff and Scottsbluff Knife)

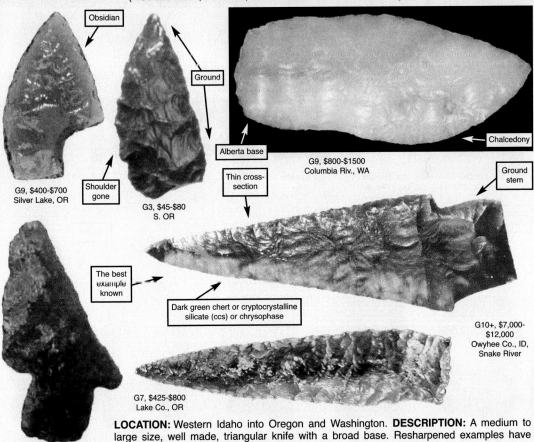

Obsidian

Ground

Alberta base

Thin cross-section

Chalcedony

G9, $800-$1500
Columbia Riv., WA

Ground stem

G9, $400-$700
Silver Lake, OR

Shoulder gone

G3, $45-$80
S. OR

The best example known

Dark green chert or cryptocrystalline silicate (ccs) or chrysophase

G10+, $7,000-$12,000
Owyhee Co., ID, Snake River

G7, $425-$800
Lake Co., OR

G5, $65-$125
S.W. ID

F
W

LOCATION: Western Idaho into Oregon and Washington. **DESCRIPTION:** A medium to large size, well made, triangular knife with a broad base. Resharpened examples have prominent shoulders forming a pentagonal form. The classic blade form has a diagonal slant. **I.D. KEY:** Early flaking, diagonal slant.

COLD SPRINGS - Middle Archaic, 5000 - 4000 B. P.

(Also see Ahsahka, Bear River, Bitterroot, Diablo Canyon, Jalama Side, Nightfire and Northern Side Notched)

Basalt

"Fox ear"

Basalt

Basalt

Basalt

G5, $5-$10
WA

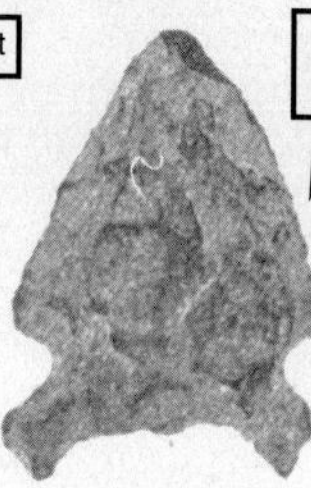

G5, $5-$10
OR, fox ear form

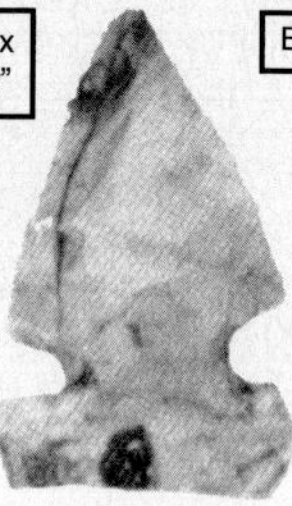

G6, $8-$15
Priest Rapids, OR

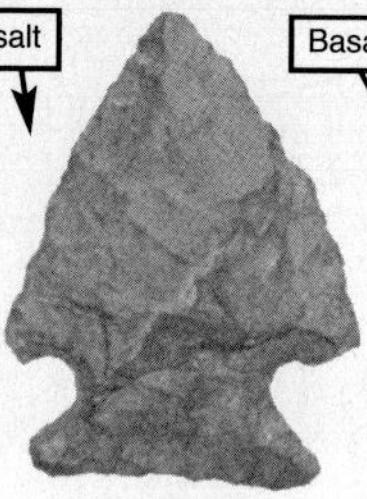

G6, $8-$15
WA

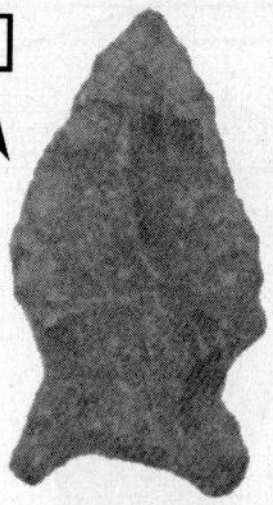

G6, $8-$15
Columb. Riv., WA

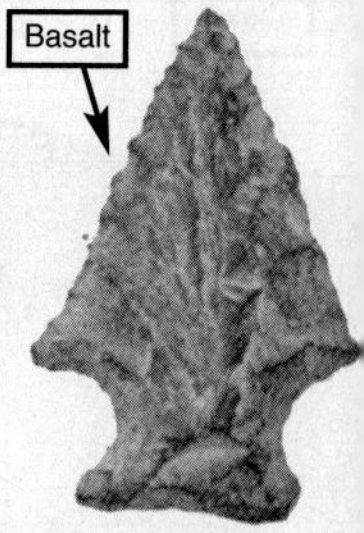

G6, $8-$15
WA

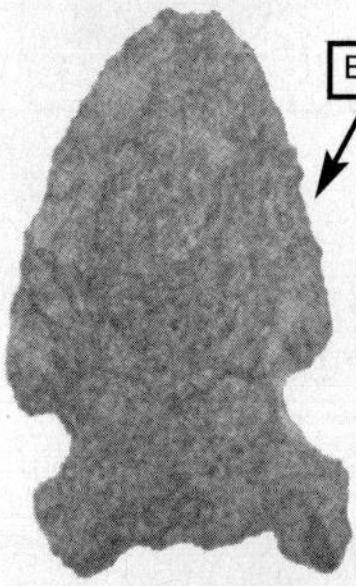

Basalt

"Fox ear"

Basalt

Agate

G6, $6-$12
Priest Rapids, OR

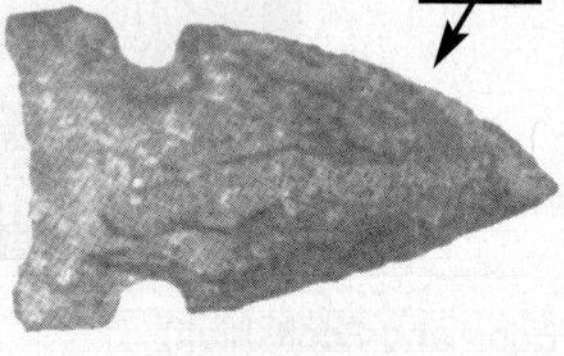

G8, $12-$20
Snake River, WA

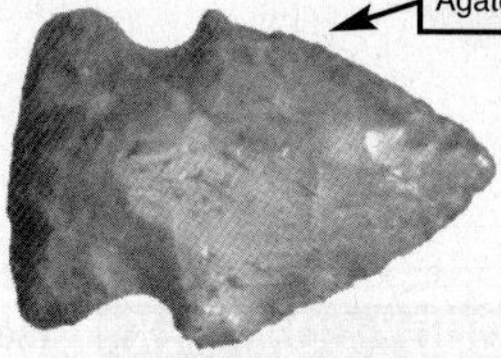

G6, $12-$20
WA

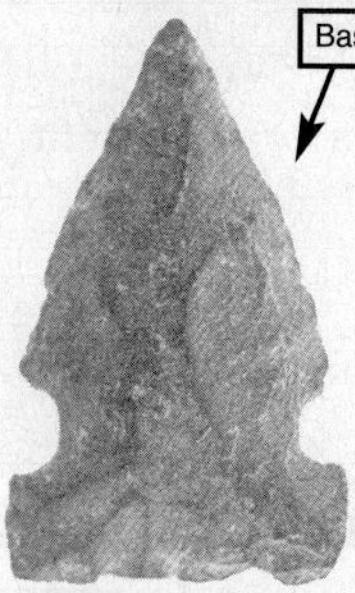

G5, $5-$10
WA

Basalt

Fox Ear form

Basalt

Obsidian

Basalt

Agate

G8, $12-$20
Harney Co., OR

G7, $12-$20
Hood Riv., OR

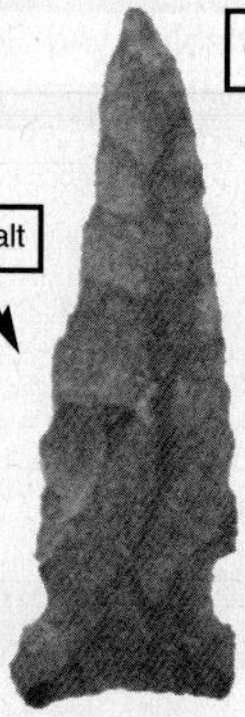

G6, $12-$20
WA

G7, $12-$20
OR

G7, $15-$25
WA

G8, $20-$35
Columb. Riv., OR

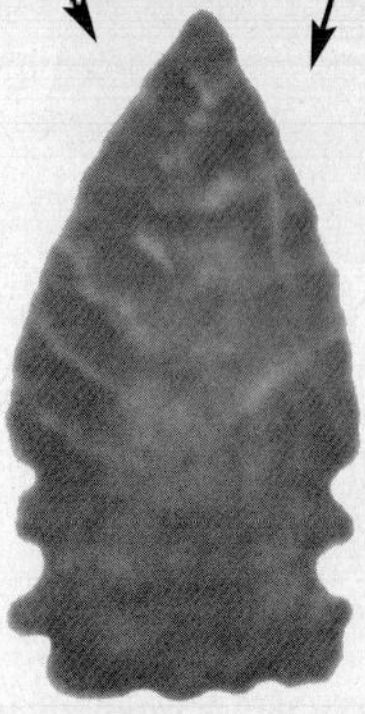

Exotic, double, triple notched

Jasper

Basalt

Agate

Obsidian

G7, $50-$90
Columbia Riv., OR

G7, $15-$30
Harney Co., OR

G7, $35-$60
Clearwater Riv., ID

G8, $35-$60
Columbia Riv., OR

G8, $30-$50
Fort Rock Valley, OR

992

Basalt

Basalt

Dacite

Basalt

Obsidian

Base wear

G9, $40-$75
Union Co., OR

G7, $15-$30
Union Co., OR

G9, $70-$135
Union Co., OR

G9, $80-$150
Union Co., OR

G9, $125-$200
Priest Rapids, OR

G8, $125-$200
Union Co., OR

LOCATION: Idaho, Oregon & Washington. **DESCRIPTION:** A small to medium size broadly side to corner notched point with a straight to concave base. Hafting areas can vary considerably from "Fox Ear" forms to auriculate bases. Most are made from Basalt. **I.D. KEY:** Point of origin.

COLUMBIA MULE EAR - Classic Phase, 700 - 400 B. P.

(Also see Plateau Pentagonal and Strong)

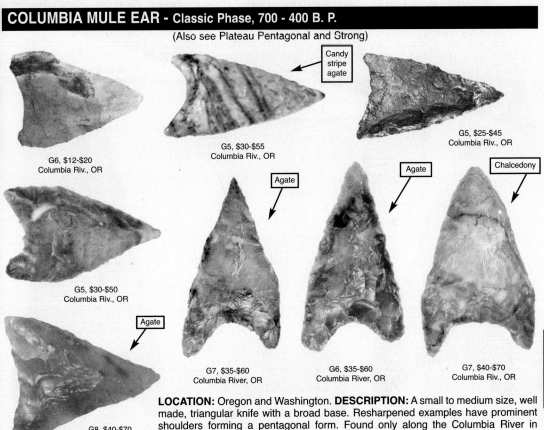

Candy stripe agate

Agate

Agate

Chalcedony

G6, $12-$20
Columbia Riv., OR

G5, $30-$55
Columbia Riv., OR

G5, $25-$45
Columbia Riv., OR

G5, $30-$50
Columbia Riv., OR

Agate

G8, $40-$70
WA

G7, $35-$60
Columbia River, OR

G6, $35-$60
Columbia River, OR

G7, $40-$70
Columbia Riv., OR

F
W

LOCATION: Oregon and Washington. **DESCRIPTION:** A small to medium size, well made, triangular knife with a broad base. Resharpened examples have prominent shoulders forming a pentagonal form. Found only along the Columbia River in Washington & Oregon. **I.D. KEY:** Pentagonal form and prominent auricles.

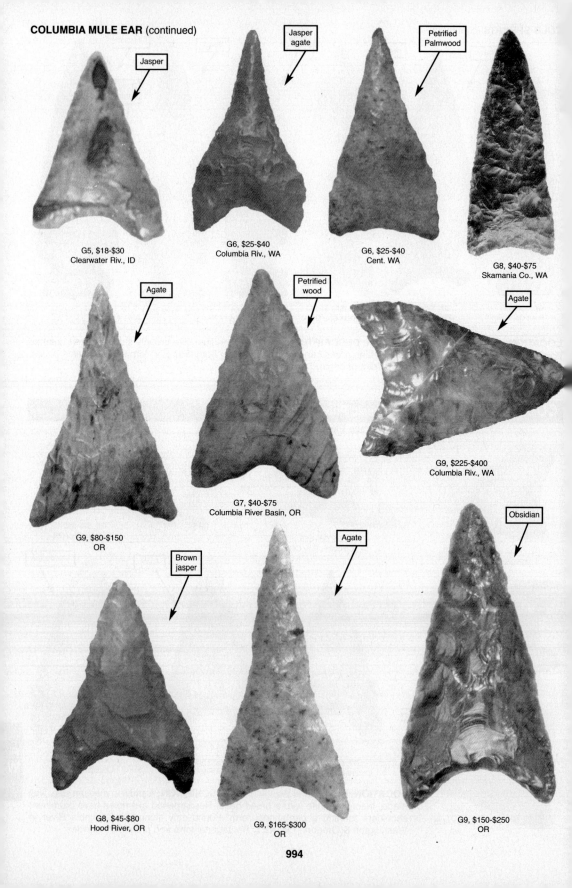

COLUMBIA MULE EAR (continued)

Jasper

Jasper agate

Petrified Palmwood

G5, $18-$30
Clearwater Riv., ID

G6, $25-$40
Columbia Riv., WA

G6, $25-$40
Cent. WA

G8, $40-$75
Skamania Co., WA

Agate

Petrified wood

Agate

G9, $80-$150
OR

G7, $40-$75
Columbia River Basin, OR

G9, $225-$400
Columbia Riv., WA

Brown jasper

Agate

Obsidian

G8, $45-$80
Hood River, OR

G9, $165-$300
OR

G9, $150-$250
OR

(Also see Eastgate, Gatecliff, Gunther, Rose Springs, Sauvies Island and Wallula)

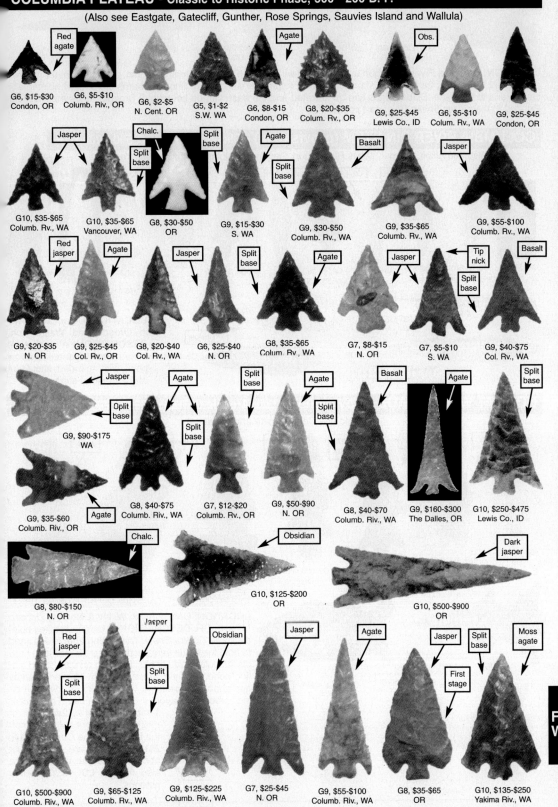

Red agate

G6, $15-$30
Condon, OR

G6, $5-$10
Columb. Riv., OR

G6, $2-$5
N. Cent. OR

G5, $1-$2
S.W. WA

Agate

G6, $8-$15
Condon, OR

G8, $20-$35
Colum. Rv., OR

Obs.

G9, $25-$45
Lewis Co., ID

G6, $5-$10
Colum. Rv., WA

G9, $25-$45
Condon, OR

Jasper

Chalc.

Split base

Split base

Agate

Basalt

Jasper

G10, $35-$65
Columb. Rv., WA

G10, $35-$65
Vancouver, WA

G8, $30-$50
OR

G9, $15-$30
S. WA

G9, $30-$50
Columb. Rv., WA

G9, $35-$65
Columb. Rv., WA

G9, $55-$100
Columb. Rv., WA

Red jasper

Agate

Jasper

Split base

Agate

Jasper

Tip nick

Split base

Basalt

G9, $20-$35
N. OR

G9, $25-$45
Col. Rv., OR

G8, $20-$40
Col. Rv., WA

G6, $25-$40
N. OR

G8, $35-$65
Colum. Rv., WA

G7, $8-$15
N. OR

G7, $5-$10
S. WA

G9, $40-$75
Col. Rv., WA

Jasper

Oplit base

Agate

Split base

Split base

Agate

Split base

Basalt

Agate

Split base

G9, $90-$175
WA

G9, $35-$60
Columb. Riv., OR

Agate

G8, $40-$75
Columb. Riv., WA

G7, $12-$20
Columb. Rv., OR

G9, $50-$90
N. OR

G8, $40-$70
Columb. Riv., WA

G9, $160-$300
The Dalles, OR

G10, $250-$475
Lewis Co., ID

Chalc.

Obsidian

Dark jasper

G8, $80-$150
N. OR

G10, $125-$200
OR

G10, $500-$900
OR

Red jasper

Jasper

Split base

Obsidian

Jasper

Agate

Jasper

Split base

Moss agate

Split base

First stage

G10, $500-$900
Columb. Riv., WA

G9, $65-$125
Columb. Rv., WA

G9, $125-$225
Columb. Riv., WA

G7, $25-$45
N. OR

G9, $55-$100
Columb. Riv., WA

G8, $35-$65
OR

G10, $135-$250
Yakima Riv., WA

F
W

COLUMBIA PLATEAU (continued)

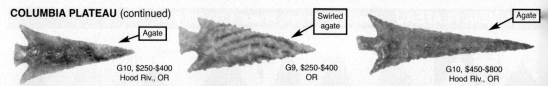

G10, $250-$400
Hood Riv., OR

G9, $250-$400
OR

G10, $450-$800
Hood Riv., OR

LOCATION: Columbia River in Oregon and Washington. **DESCRIPTION:** A small size, thin, triangular corner notched arrow point with strong barbs and a short, expanding to parallel sided stem. Shoulder barbs are usually pointed and can extend to the base. Blade edges can be serrated and the base can be bifurcated. Broader tangs than Wallula. Related to the earlier *Snake River* dart points.

COLUMBIA RIVER PIN STEM (provisional) - Classic to Historic, 500 - 200 B. P.

(Also see Alkali, Dagger, Lewis River Short Stemmed, Rabbit Island, Wallula, Yana)

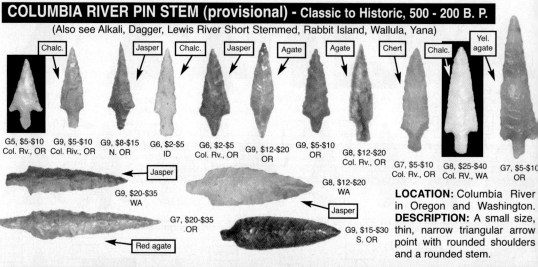

G5, $5-$10
Col. Rv., OR

G9, $5-$10
Col. Riv., OR

G9, $8-$15
N. OR

G6, $2-$5
ID

G6, $2-$5
Col. Rv., OR

G9, $12-$20
OR

G9, $5-$10
OR

G8, $12-$20
Col. Rv., OR

G7, $5-$10
Col. Rv., OR

G8, $25-$40
Col. RV., WA

G7, $5-$1(
OR

G9, $20-$35
WA

G7, $20-$35
OR

G8, $12-$20
WA

G9, $15-$30
S. OR

LOCATION: Columbia River in Oregon and Washington. **DESCRIPTION:** A small size, thin, narrow triangular arrow point with rounded shoulders and a rounded stem.

COMBAT WAND BLADE (provisional) - Late Archaic to Trans., 2500 - 2000 B. P.

(Also see Contra Costa and Vendetta)

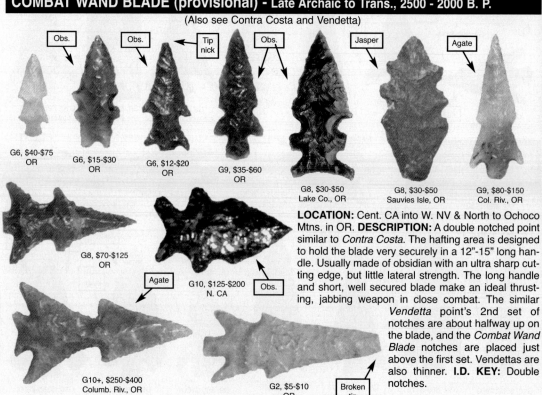

G6, $40-$75
OR

G6, $15-$30
OR

G6, $12-$20
OR

G9, $35-$60
OR

G8, $30-$50
Lake Co., OR

G8, $30-$50
Sauvies Isle, OR

G9, $80-$150
Col. Riv., OR

G8, $70-$125
OR

G10, $125-$200
N. CA

G10+, $250-$400
Columb. Riv., OR

G2, $5-$10
OR

LOCATION: Cent. CA into W. NV & North to Ochoco Mtns. in OR. **DESCRIPTION:** A double notched point similar to *Contra Costa*. The hafting area is designed to hold the blade very securely in a 12"-15" long handle. Usually made of obsidian with an ultra sharp cutting edge, but little lateral strength. The long handle and short, well secured blade make an ideal thrusting, jabbing weapon in close combat. The similar *Vendetta* point's 2nd set of notches are about halfway up on the blade, and the *Combat Wand Blade* notches are placed just above the first set. Vendettas are also thinner. **I.D. KEY:** Double notches.

CONTRA COSTA - Late Archaic to Developmental Phase, 2500 - 1500 B. P.

(Also see Combat Wand Blade, Coquille, Gypsum Cave, Point Sal Barbed, Vandenberg Contracting Stem)

G8, $65-$125
Warner Valley, OR

Basalt

Broken & glued

Mouse obsidian

G4, $80-$150
CA/OR line

Broken barb

G4, $8-$15
Crump Lake, OR

G4, $5-$10
N. Lake Co., OR

G4, $2-$5
CA coast

LOCATION: Central California Coastal area. **DESCRIPTION:** A medium size, dart/knife with a contracting stem and double side notches. Shoulders droop towards base. See Noel Justice, 2002.

COQUILLE BROADNECK - Mid-Archaic to Trans. Phase, 4500 - 2200 B. P.

(Also see Contra Costa, Gatecliff, Gypsum Cave, Rabbit Island, Sierra Contracting, Vandenberg Contracting)

Red jasper

Barbed edge

Jasper

Classic example

G4, $2-$5
Curry Co., OR

G5, $5-$10
Curry Co., OR

G5, $5-$10
Curry Co., OR

G5, $5-$10
S.W. OR

G7, $15-$25
Curry Co., OR

G10, $35-$65
Coos Co., OR

G6, $8-$15
S.W. OR

Brown jasper

Dark red jasper

G7, $35-$60
Curry Co., OR

Basalt

G7, $15-$25
Curry Co., OR

Serrated edge

G7, $15-$25
S.W. OR

G10, $40-$75
Curry Co., OR

G7, $12-$20
OR

F
W

997

COQUILLE BROADNECK (continued)

Serrated edge

Agate

Serrated edge

Classic example

G9, $65-$125
Coquille Riv., OR

Barbed edge

Serrated edge

G7, $15-$30
Curry Co., OR

G7, $15-$25
Coquille Riv., OR

G9, $35-$65
Coquille Riv., OR

G8, $65-$125
Coquille Riv., OR

G10, $125-$200
Josephine Co., OR

G10, $125-$225
S. OR

LOCATION: Coos & Curry Co. OR & N.W. California. **DESCRIPTION:** A medium size, triangular dart/knife with a convex to straight blade edge. The stem is broad and triangular to tapering and rounded. Shoulders are barbed to horizontal. Many are serrated. Named by Dr. Thomas & Connolly, et al at the Standly Site. **I.D. KEY:** Broad, tapering to rounded stem.

COQUILLE KNIFE - Mid-Archaic to Transitional Phase, 4500 - 400 B. P.

(Also see Cascade, Mahkin Shouldered)

Red jasper

Red jasper

G8, $15-$25
Curry Co., OR

Broken tip

G7, $3-$7
Rogue Riv., OR

LOCATION: Coos & Curry Co. OR. **DESCRIPTION:** A medium sized lanceolate knife with a straight base. **I.D. KEY:** Medium lanceolate form.

G6, $1-$2
Rogue Riv., OR

G3, $1-$2
Rogue Riv., OR

Basalt

COQUILLE NARROWNECK - Transition Phase, 2200 - 400 B. P.

(Also see Gatecliff, Gold Hill, Rabbit Island, Rose Springs Sloping Shoulder, Sierra Contracting)

Jasper

Green chert

G5, $2-$5
OR

G6, $5-$10
OR

G7, $3-$6
Rogue Riv., OR

G7, $5-$10
Rogue Riv., OR

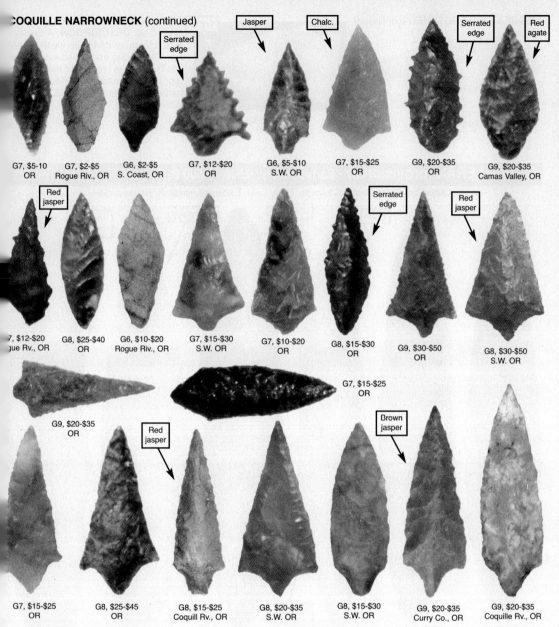

Jasper

Chalc.

Serrated edge

Red agate

G7, $5-10
OR

G7, $2-$5
Rogue Riv., OR

G6, $2-$5
S. Coast, OR

G7, $12-$20
OR

G6, $5-$10
S.W. OR

G7, $15-$25
OR

G9, $20-$35
OR

G9, $20-$35
Camas Valley, OR

Red jasper

Serrated edge

Red jasper

7, $12-$20
Rgue Rv., OR

G8, $25-$40
OR

G6, $10-$20
Rogue Riv., OR

G7, $15-$30
S.W. OR

G7, $10-$20
OR

G8, $15-$30
OR

G9, $30-$50
OR

G8, $30-$50
S.W. OR

G7, $15-$25
OR

G9, $20-$35
OR

Red jasper

Brown jasper

G7, $15-$25
OR

G8, $25-$45
OR

G8, $15-$25
Coquill Rv., OR

G8, $20-$35
S.W. OR

G8, $15-$30
S.W. OR

G9, $20-$35
Curry Co., OR

G9, $20-$35
Coquille Rv., OR

LOCATION: Coos Co. & Curry Co. OR. & N.W. California. **DESCRIPTION:** A medium size, triangular dart/knife with a convex to straight blade edge. The stem is narrow and triangular to tapering and rounded. Shoulders are barbed to horizontal. Many are serrated. **I.D. KEY:** Narrow, tapering to rounded stem.

COQUILLE SIDE NOTCHED - Mid-Archaic to Trans., 4500 - 2200 B. P.

(Also see Cold Springs, Merrybell & Rose Springs Side Notched)

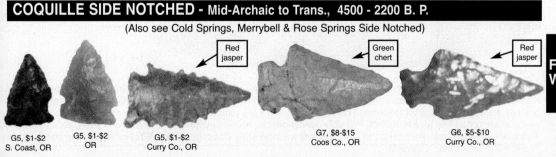

Red jasper

Green chert

Red jasper

G5, $1-$2
S. Coast, OR

G5, $1-$2
OR

G5, $1-$2
Curry Co., OR

G7, $8-$15
Coos Co., OR

G6, $5-$10
Curry Co., OR

F
W

COQUILLE SIDE NOTCHED (continued)

G6, $5-$10
Curry Co., OR

Crystal

G6, $15-$25
S. OR

LOCATION: Coos & Curry Co. OR.
N.W. Calif. **DESCRIPTION:** A medium
size, triangular dart/knife wiath a convex blade edge and broad side notch
es. The stem is broad and triangular to
tapering and rounded. Shoulders ar
barbed to tapered. **I.D. KEY:** Broad
side notches.

CORDILLERAN (provisional) - Early Archaic, 9,500 - 7,500 B. P.

(Also see Agate Basin, Cascade, Early Leaf, Excelsior, Haskett, Kennewick)

Basalt

Obsidian

Chalcedony

Side wear

G7, $55-$100
OR

G6, $150-$250
OR

G9, $175-$300
S. W. Canada

Diagonal
flaking

G8, $65-$125
OR

Cordilleran/
Haskett
cross type

G10, $275-$500
Hood Riv., WA

Ground
stem

G7, $80-$150
S. OR

Dacite

G9, $250-$400
OR

LOCATION: Great Basin states northward. **DESCRIPTION:** A usually large, mostly bi-pointed lanceolate spear or dart/knife with parallel and occasionally oblique flaking. Basal configuration is always contracting and can be dully pointed, rounded or straight with rounded corners. Stem sides are usually ground and blade cross-sections are lenticular and are not as thin as *Kennewick*. Possible descendant of *Haskett* points and later evolving into *Cascade* points. This point is transitional overlapping the late *Hasketts* with the early *Cascades*. **I.D. KEY:** Hafting area is shorter than *Haskett* but longer than *Cascade*.

Red basalt

Diagonal flaking

Beveled on opposite edges

Cordilleran/ Haskett cross type

Obsidian

Stem grinding

Basalt

Stem grinding

G9, $250-$400
N. UT

G7, $165-$300
S. OR

G7, $350-$600
Sou. OR

G9, $400-$700
WA

CORNER TANG KNIFE - Late Archaic, 3,400 -1000 B. P.

(Also see Base Tang and Paleo Knife)

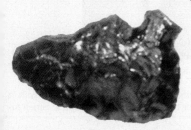

LOCATION: Texas northward. **DESCRIPTION:** A medium to large size knife that is notched at one corner producing a tang for hafting to a handle. Tang knives are rare, especially in this area. **I.D. KEY:** Angle of hafting.

G4, $12-$20
S.E. OR, obsidian

F
W

COTTONWOOD LEAF - Developmental to Historic Phase, 1100 - 200 B. P.

(Also see Canalino, Cascade, Cottonwood Triangle, Gold Hill, Magala Cove Leaf and Trojan)

G5, $.50-$1
NV

G6, $1-$3
OR

G6, $1-$2
Humboldt Co.,
NV

G6, $1-$3
Lake Co., OR

Obsidian

G8, $2-$5
S. OR

Basalt

G5, $1-$3
NV

Obsidian

G6, $2-$5
Humboldt Co., NV

Jasper

G8, $8-$15
S. OR

Agate

G8, $12-$20
CA

Obsidian

G5, $2-$5
S. W. OR

Obsidian

G6, $5-$10
Colum. Riv., OR.

G7, $12-$20
S. W. OR

Petrified wood

G9, $35-$60
OR

LOCATION: Great Basin states northward. **DESCRIPTION:** A small size, thin, ovoid point with a convex base. Similar to the *Nodena* type from Arkansas. **I.D. KEY:** Small ovoid form.

COTTONWOOD TRIANGLE - Developmental to Historic Phase, 1100 - 200 B. P.

(Also see Bull Creek, Canalino Triangular, Cottonwood Leaf, Desert & Gunther Triangular)

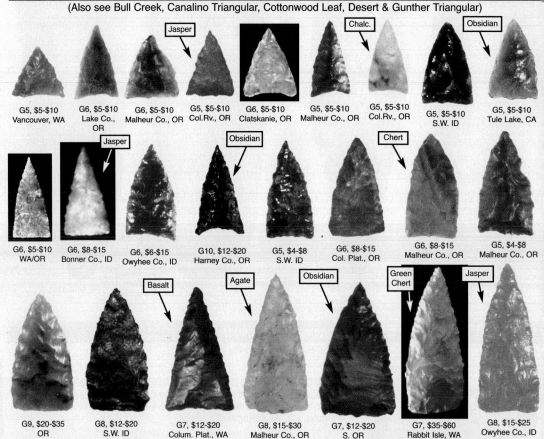

G5, $5-$10
Vancouver, WA

G6, $5-$10
Lake Co.,
OR

Jasper

G6, $5-$10
Malheur Co., OR

G5, $5-$10
Col.Rv., OR

G6, $5-$10
Clatskanie, OR

G5, $5-$10
Malheur Co., OR

Chalc.

G5, $5-$10
Col.Rv., OR

G5, $5-$10
S.W. ID

Obsidian

G5, $5-$10
Tule Lake, CA

Jasper

G6, $5-$10
WA/OR

G6, $8-$15
Bonner Co., ID

G6, $6-$15
Owyhee Co., ID

Obsidian

G10, $12-$20
Harney Co., OR

G5, $4-$8
S.W. ID

G6, $8-$15
Col. Plat., OR

Chert

G6, $8-$15
Malheur Co., OR

G5, $4-$8
Malheur Co., OR

G9, $20-$35
OR

G8, $12-$20
S.W. ID

Basalt

G7, $12-$20
Colum. Plat., WA

Agate

G8, $15-$30
Malheur Co., OR

Obsidian

G7, $12-$20
S. OR

Green Chert

G7, $35-$60
Rabbit Isle, WA

Jasper

G8, $15-$25
Owyhee Co., ID

LOCATION: Great Basin states northward. **DESCRIPTION:** A small to medium size, thin, triangular point with a straight to concave base. Basal corners are sharp to rounded. The preform for the *Desert* series. **I.D. KEY:** Small triangle form.

Also see Agate Basin, Año Nuevo, Cody Complex, Haskett, Lake Mohave, Lind Coulee and Parman, Shaniko Stemmed and Wildcat Canyon)

Yellow agate

Red jasper

Red and blue on one side, green on the other

Obsidian

Ground stem

G7, $200-$350
S. Cent. OR

G7, $150-$275
S. OR

Ground stem

Ground stem

G7, $150-$275
S. Cent. OR

Ground stem

G8, $350-$600
CA/OR state line

Ground stem

Dacite

Resharpened into a scraper

G8, $425-$800
Tule Lake, CA

Ground stem

Ground stem

Ground stem

Ground stem

G8, $700-$1200
S. OR

G6, $450-$800
S. OR

G3, $200-$350
S. OR

G6, $175-$300
Warner Valley, OR

F
W

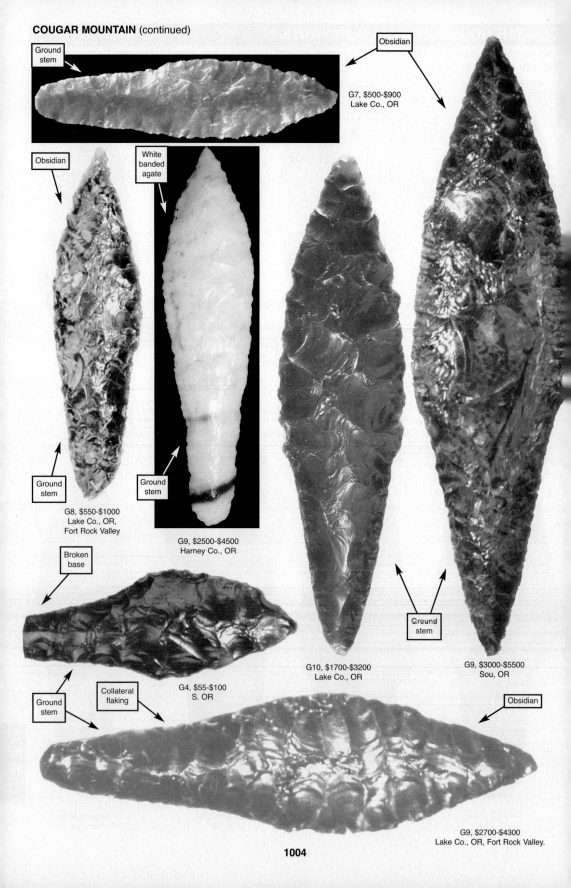

Ground stem

Obsidian

G7, $500-$900
Lake Co., OR

Obsidian

Obsidian

White banded agate

Ground stem

Ground stem

G8, $550-$1000
Lake Co., OR,
Fort Rock Valley

Ground stem

G9, $2500-$4500
Harney Co., OR

Broken base

Ground stem

Collateral flaking

G4, $55-$100
S. OR

Ground stem

G10, $1700-$3200
Lake Co., OR

G9, $3000-$5500
Sou, OR

Obsidian

G9, $2700-$4300
Lake Co., OR, Fort Rock Valley.

Black obsidian

Obsidian

Ground stem

G10, $2500-$4000
Lake Co., OR

LOCATION: Southern Oregon, N.W. Nevada. **DESCRIPTION:** A large size, long stemmed form with weak tapered shoulders and a convex base. Basal area is ground. Associated with *Haskett* points found on the same sites. Among the earliest points found at Cougar Mountain Cave in Southern Oregon. Very rare. **I.D. KEY:** Long tapered stem & obtuse shoulders.

Oolitic jasper

Used as a knife

Beveled edge

Gray obsidian

Ground stem

Ground stem to here

G8, $1600-$3000
Harney Co., OR, Malheur Lake

G10+, $3500-$6500
Lake Co., OR

G10+, $4500-$8500+
Lake Co., OR

F
W

1005

(Also see Black Rock Concave)

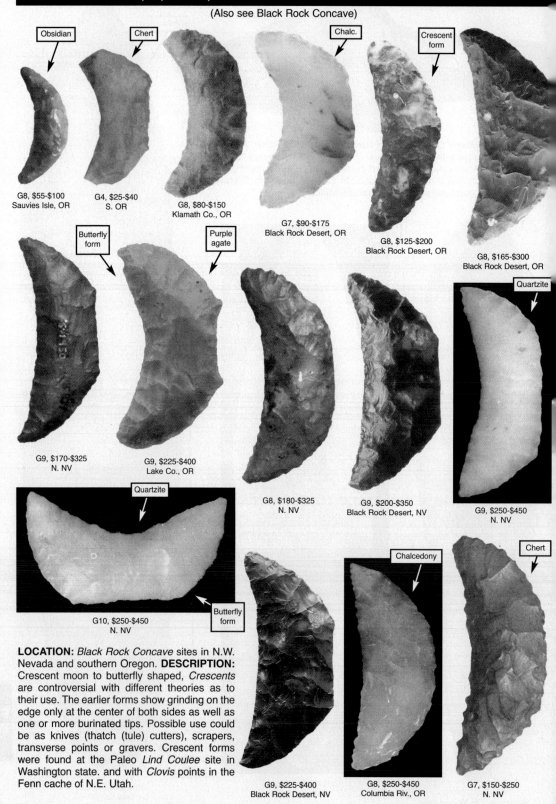

Obsidian

Chert

Chalc.

Crescent form

G8, $55-$100
Sauvies Isle, OR

G4, $25-$40
S. OR

G8, $80-$150
Klamath Co., OR

G7, $90-$175
Black Rock Desert, OR

G8, $125-$200
Black Rock Desert, OR

G8, $165-$300
Black Rock Desert, OR

Butterfly form

Purple agate

Quartzite

G9, $170-$325
N. NV

G9, $225-$400
Lake Co., OR

G8, $180-$325
N. NV

G9, $200-$350
Black Rock Desert, NV

G9, $250-$450
N. NV

Quartzite

Butterfly form

G10, $250-$450
N. NV

Chalcedony

Chert

LOCATION: *Black Rock Concave* sites in N.W. Nevada and southern Oregon. **DESCRIPTION:** Crescent moon to butterfly shaped, *Crescents* are controversial with different theories as to their use. The earlier forms show grinding on the edge only at the center of both sides as well as one or more burinated tips. Possible use could be as knives (thatch (tule) cutters), scrapers, transverse points or gravers. Crescent forms were found at the Paleo *Lind Coulee* site in Washington state. and with *Clovis* points in the Fenn cache of N.E. Utah.

G9, $225-$400
Black Rock Desert, NV

G8, $250-$450
Columbia Riv., OR

G7, $150-$250
N. NV

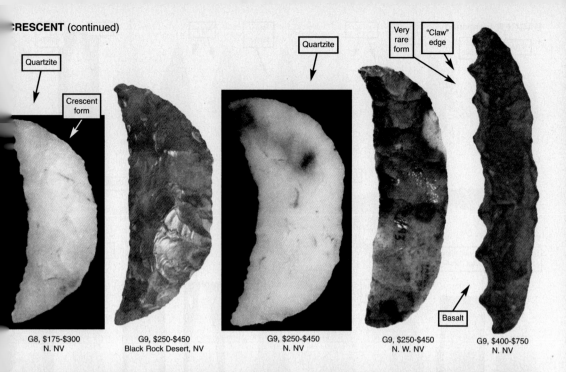

Quartzite

Crescent form

Quartzite

Very rare form

"Claw" edge

Basalt

G8, $175-$300
N. NV

G9, $250-$450
Black Rock Desert, NV

G9, $250-$450
N. NV

G9, $250-$450
N. W. NV

G9, $400-$750
N. NV

CRUMP LAKE EARED (provisional) - Mid-Archaic, 5000-3000 B. P.

(Also see Cascade, Early Leaf, Excelsior, Mahkin Shouldered)

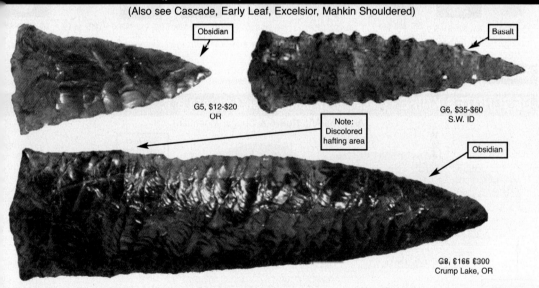

Obsidian

Basalt

G5, $12-$20
OR

G6, $35-$60
S.W. ID

Note: Discolored hafting area

Obsidian

G8, $165-$300
Crump Lake, OR

LOCATION: N. Great Basin in Oregon N. to Yakima Wash. and E. to Idaho. **DESCRIPTION:** A knife form with everted auricles. The auricles or "ears" extend plus/minus 90 degrees from the center line of the stem. Bases can be symmetrically convex, or have a conspious "bump" in the center of the base. Both stem sides and bases are ground. Finish flaking can be parallel, parallel oblique or random. Cross sections are thin lenticular to plano-convex. Found occasionally with *Northern Side Notch* points.

DAGGER - Developmental to Classic Phase, 1200 - 400 B. P.

(Also see Columbia River Pin Stem, Diamond Back, Klickitat and Nottoway)

LOCATION: Columbia River basin along the Columbia River. **DESCRIPTION:** A small size, narrow, thin, barbed point or knife. Bases with dagger like handles (stems) vary from expanded to contracted. Diamond shaped bases would place point in *Klickitat* type. **I.D. KEY:** Dagger-like handles.

F
W

DAGGER (continued)

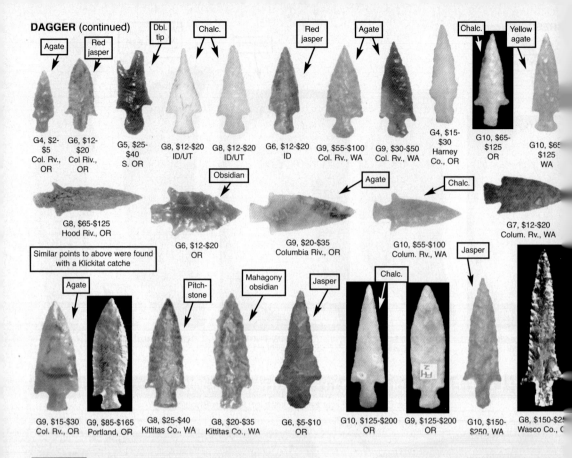

Agate
Red jasper
Dbl. tip
Chalc.
Red jasper
Agate
Chalc.
Yellow agate

G4, $2-$5 Col. Rv., OR

G6, $12-$20 Col Riv., OR

G5, $25-$40 S. OR

G8, $12-$20 ID/UT

G8, $12-$20 ID/UT

G6, $12-$20 ID

G9, $55-$100 Col. Rv., WA

G9, $30-$50 Col. Rv., WA

G4, $15-$30 Harney Co., OR

G10, $65-$125 OR

G10, $65-$125 WA

Obsidian
Agate
Chalc.

G8, $65-$125 Hood Riv., OR

G6, $12-$20 OR

G9, $20-$35 Columbia Riv., OR

G10, $55-$100 Colum. Rv., WA

G7, $12-$20 Colum. Rv., WA

Similar points to above were found with a Klickitat catche

Agate
Pitch-stone
Mahagony obsidian
Jasper
Chalc.
Jasper

G9, $15-$30 Col. Rv., OR

G9, $85-$165 Portland, OR

G8, $25-$40 Kittitas Co., WA

G8, $20-$35 Kittitas Co., WA

G6, $5-$10 OR

G10, $125-$200 OR

G9, $125-$200 OR

G10, $150-$250, WA

G8, $150-$2?? Wasco Co., O?

DAGGER (see Klickitat)

DESCHUTES KNIFE - Classic to Historic Phase, 500 - 250 B. P.

(Also see Año Nuevo & Cougar Mountain)

Root beer colored flint

G8, $165-$300 Lake Co., OR

Must have notch in base

LOCATION: Mid-Columbia River basin in Oregon. **DESCRIPTION:** Very rare. A large size, long stemmed to lanceolate knife with slight to tapered shoulders and a concave base. Length can be 4 to 9". There is edge grinding on the stem. This blade had a wrapped handle and was held as a knife. **I.D. KEY:** Size, basal notch & blade form.

DESERT CORNER NOTCHED (see Elko Corner Notched)

DESERT DELTA - Classic to Historic Phase, 700 - 200 B. P.

(Also see Bitterroot, Cold Spring, Panoche, Piquinin, Uinta)

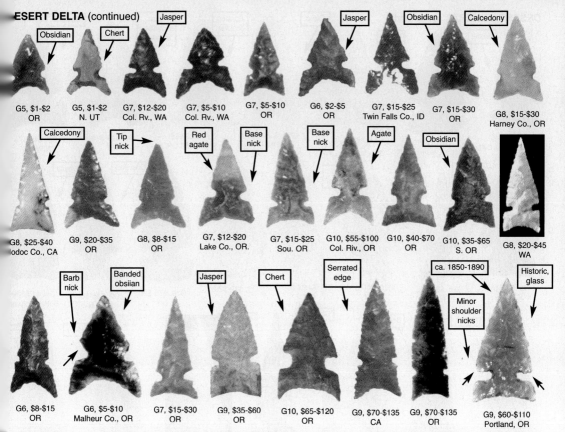

Obsidian

G5, $1-$2
OR

Chert

G5, $1-$2
N. UT

Jasper

G7, $12-$20
Col. Rv., WA

Jasper

G7, $5-$10
Col. Rv., WA

G7, $5-$10
OR

Jasper

G6, $2-$5
OR

Obsidian

G7, $15-$25
Twin Falls Co., ID

Calcedony

G7, $15-$30
OR

G8, $15-$30
Harney Co., OR

Calcedony

G8, $25-$40
Modoc Co., CA

G9, $20-$35
OR

Tip
nick

G8, $8-$15
OR

Red
agate

G7, $12-$20
Lake Co., OR.

Base
nick

G7, $15-$25
Sou. OR

Base
nick

G10, $55-$100
Col. Riv., OR

Agate

G10, $40-$70
OR

Obsidian

G10, $35-$65
S. OR

G8, $20-$45
WA

Barb
nick

G6, $8-$15
OR

Banded
obsiian

G6, $5-$10
Malheur Co., OR

Jasper

G7, $15-$30
OR

Chert

G9, $35-$60
OR

Serrated
edge

G10, $65-$120
OR

G9, $70-$135
CA

ca. 1850-1890

Minor
shoulder
nicks

G9, $70-$135
OR

Historic,
glass

G9, $60-$110
Portland, OR

LOCATION: Great Basin westward. **DESCRIPTION:** A small, thin, triangular, side notched arrow point with a deeply concave base, straight blade edges and expanded, pointed ears making the base the widest part of the point. Blade edges can be serrated. **I.D. KEY:** Small triangle, side notched form.

DESERT GENERAL - Classic to Historic Phase, 700 - 200 B. P.

(Also see Ahsahka, Bear River, Bitterroot, Cold Spring, Panoche, Piqunin, Rose, Uinta & Wintu)

Basalt

G4, $2-$4
Gooding Co.,
ID

G7, $8-$15
Owyhee Co.,
ID

G7, $15-$25
OR

Red
jasper

G7, $8-$15
OR

G7, $10-$15
OR

G7, $12-$20
OR

Obsidian

G8, $15-$25
Humboldt Co., NV

Gem

G5, $6-$12
N. OR

G6, $6-$12
S. OR

Obsidian

G9, $15-$25
S.W. ID

Banded
obsidian

G9, $20-$35
OR

Double
notched

G8, $30-$50
WA

G6, $12-$20
N. OR

Serrated

G7, $15-$30
Humboldt Co.,
NV

Chalc.

G8, $20-$35
Columbia
Riv., WA

G9, $25-$45
OR

Double
notched

G9, $40-$70
WA

Basalt

G7, $12-$20
British Colum.,
CAN

F
W

LOCATION: Calif. coastal to E. Rockies, N. into Canada & S. to Mexico. **DESCRIPTION:** A small, thin, side notched arrow point with a straight to slightly concave base. Blade edges can be serrated. Similar to the *Reed* point found in Oklahoma. The Desert series was named for the Calif. section of the Great Basin (Delta). Many groups adopted this point into Historic times.

DESERT GENERAL (continued)

Basalt

G6, $8-$15
British Colum., CAN

Basalt

G6, $5-$10
British Colum., CAN

G8, $12-$20
Columbia Riv., WA

Clear

G10, $35-$60
OR

Banded obsidian

G7, $20-$35
Sou. Cent. OR

Rare snowflake obsidian

G9, $40-$75
OR

Obsidian

G9, $40-$75
N.W. NV

Obsidian

G6, $8-$15
S.W. ID

G6, $8-$15
N.W. NV

Clear Chalc.

G10, $40-$70
OR

G8, $12-$20
OR

G8, $12-$20
OR

G10, $50-$90
OR

Obsidian

G9, $35-$60
N.W. NV

Basalt

G8, $15-$30
British Colum. CAN

Obsidian

G8, $12-$20
S. OR

Basalt

G7, $8-$15
British Colum., CAN

Obsidian

G8, $12-$20
Gooding Co., ID

G8, $25-$40
OR

Double notched

G10, $90-$175
WA

Obsidian

G10, $35-$60
OR

Bone

G9, $40-$75
S. OR

Still hafted to arrow shaft with asphaltum

G10, $150-$275
N. UT, Hogup cave,
30" long & complete
w/agate point

LOCATION: Great Basin westward. **DESCRIPTION:** A small, thin, side notched arrow point with a straight to slightly concave base. Blade edges can be serrated. Similar to the *Reed* point found in Oklahoma. Used by many different groups into the Historic period.

DESERT REDDING - Classic to Historic Phase, 700 - 200 B. P.

(Also see Bear River, Bitterroot, Cold Spring, Panoche, Piquinin)

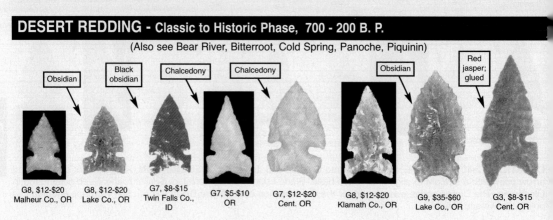

Obsidian

G8, $12-$20
Malheur Co., OR

Black obsidian

G8, $12-$20
Lake Co., OR

Chalcedony

G7, $8-$15
Twin Falls Co., ID

Chalcedony

G7, $5-$10
OR

G7, $12-$20
Cent. OR

Obsidian

G8, $12-$20
Klamath Co., OR

G9, $35-$60
Lake Co., OR

Red jasper; glued

G3, $8-$15
Cent. OR

OCATION: Great Basin westward. **DESCRIPTION:** A small, thin, side notched arrow point with a concave base. ade edges curve into the base and can be serrated. Used by different groups into the Historic period.

DESERT - SIERRA VARIETY - Classic to Historic Phase, 700 - 200 B. P.

(Also see Bitterroot, Cold Spring and Panoche)

Jasper   Jasper   Mah. obs.   Obs.   Jasper   Obs.   Agate

6, $5-$10 ol. Rv., WA	G8, $8-$15 Col. Riv., WA	G10, $12-$20 Condon, OR	G10, $12-$20 OR	G8, $8-$15 Col. Rv., OR	G8, $8-$15 S. OR	G9, $8-$15 Col. Rv., WA	G9, $8-$15 Haarney Co., OR	G8, $15-$25 Sou. OR	G6, $15-$25 Col. Riv. OR

Obsidian   Gem   Obsidian   Black obsidian   Red jasper

G7, $15-$30 Owhyee Co., ID	G8, $15-$25 OR	G8, $30-$50 OR	G6, $5-$10 Malheur Co., OR	G8, $35-$65 OR	G8, $35-$65 Sou. OR	G10, $80-$150 WA	G8, $40-$75 Col. Rv., OR	G9, $40-$75 Harney Co., OR

Chalcedony   Obsidian   Chert   Obsidian   Jasper

0, $55-$100 olumbia Riv., WA	G9, $30-$50 OR S. coast	G9, $50-$90 S. OR	G8, $55-$100 Central OR	G9, $55-$100 S. OR	G9, $50-$90 Sou. OR	G9, $55-$100 OR	G7, $12-$20 OR	G7, $15-$25 OR

Banded obsidian   Obsidian   Obsidian   Obsidian   Mahagony obsidian   Obsidian

G8, $30-$50 OR	G8, $30-$50 Central OR	G10, $65-$125 Central OR	G10, $125-$200 Lake Co., OR	G8, $30-$50 Lake Co. OR	G9, $30-$50 Warner Val., OR	G9, $55-$100 Warner Valley, OR	G9, $55-$100 Warner Val., OR

LOCATION: Great Basin westward. **DESCRIPTION:** A small size, thin, triangular side and basal notched arrow point with distinctive basal pointed barbs and a basal notch. **I.D. KEY:** Triple notches, pointed basal corners.

DIABLO CANYON SIDE NOTCHED - Early to Mid-Archaid, 8000 - 5500 B. P.

(Also see Ahsahka, Bitterroot, Cold Springs, Jalama Side Notched, Nightfire, Northern Side Notch)

G6, $12-$20 S. OR coast

G7, $8-$15 S. OR coast

LOCATION: California Coast. **DESCRIPTION:** A medium size, narrow, broadly side-notched point with a convex base. **I.D. KEY:** Broad notches. See Noel Justice, 2002.

F W

DIAMOND-BACK (provisional) - Historic Phase, 300 - 160 B. P.

(Also see Klickitat, One-Que)

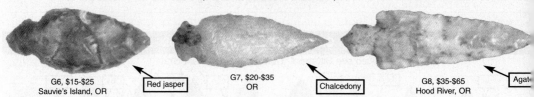

G6, $15-$25
Sauvie's Island, OR

Red jasper

G7, $20-$35
OR

Chalcedony

G8, $35-$65
Hood River, OR

Agate

LOCATION: Columbia River basin. **DESCRIPTION:** A small, thin, arrow point with a diamond shaped stem. Shoulders are horizontal to tapered. Bases are pointed to rounded. The knife form of *Klickitat Daggers*. More utilitarian, lacking the refinements of true daggers. This point, in dart form, appears in the early to middle levels at Sauvie's Island. The type fades away and appears to come back as *Klickitat*. See site reports of Ron Butler at Cash Dollar Site, an OAS sanctioned dig.

DRILL - Paleo to Historic Phase, 11,500 - 200 B. P.

(Also see Chopper, Graver, Hand Axe, Lancet, Perforator and Scraper)

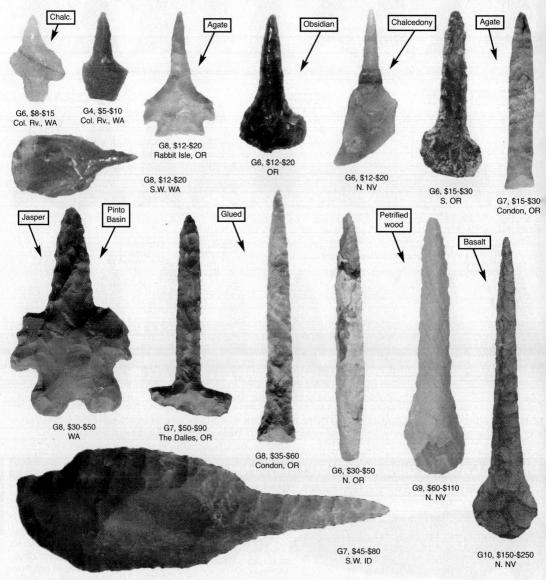

Chalc.

G6, $8-$15
Col. Rv., WA

G4, $5-$10
Col. Rv., WA

Agate

G8, $12-$20
Rabbit Isle, OR

G8, $12-$20
S.W. WA

Obsidian

G6, $12-$20
OR

Chalcedony

G6, $12-$20
N. NV

Agate

G6, $15-$30
S. OR

G7, $15-$30
Condon, OR

Jasper

Pinto
Basin

G8, $30-$50
WA

G7, $50-$90
The Dalles, OR

Glued

G8, $35-$60
Condon, OR

Petrified
wood

G6, $30-$50
N. OR

G9, $60-$110
N. NV

Basalt

G7, $45-$80
S.W. ID

G10, $150-$250
N. NV

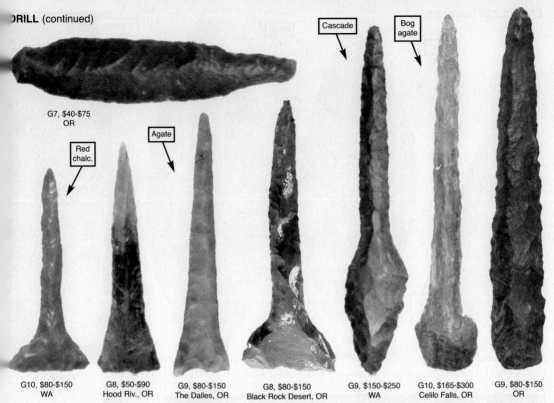

G7, $40-$75
OR

Red chalc.

Agate

Cascade

Bog agate

G10, $80-$150
WA

G8, $50-$90
Hood Riv., OR

G9, $80-$150
The Dalles, OR

G8, $80-$150
Black Rock Desert, OR

G9, $150-$250
WA

G10, $165-$300
Celilo Falls, OR

G9, $80-$150
OR

LOCATION: Everywhere. **DESCRIPTION:** Although many drills were made from scratch, all point types were made into the drill form. Usually, heavily resharpened and broken points were salvaged and rechipped into drills. These objects were certainly used as drills (evidence of extreme edge wear), but there is speculation that some of these forms may have been used as pins for clothing, ornaments, ear plugs and other uses.

EARLY EARED (provisional) - Early to middle Archaic, 8000 - 5000 B. P.

(Also see Goshen, Humboldt Expanded Base, Midland, Pryor Stemmed and Shaniko Stemmed)

Tip nick

Franciscan chert

Both have Pryor-like forms

Tip nick

G5, $15-$25
OR

G8, $40-$70
Nixon, NV

LOCATION: Great Basin westward. **DESCRIPTION:** A medium size, thin, lanceolate point with broad, shallow side notches expanding into rounded ears that may be ground. The base is straight to concave. These haven't been officially named yet.

EARLY LEAF - Early to middle Archaic, 8000 - 5000 B. P.

(Also see Agate Basin, Cascade, Cordilleran, Excelsior, High Desert Knife, Kennewick, Shaniko Stemmed and Wildcat Canyon)

G6, $15-$25
S. OR

Basalt

F W

1013

Diagonal flaking

Basalt

Basalt

Diagonal flaking

Diagonal flaking

Side nicks

G6, $15-$25
S.E. OR

G7, $55-$100
British Colum.,
Canada

G6, $20-$35
N. NV

Probably Clovis or Windust knife

G8, $65-$125
S.E. OR

G8, $80-$150
Harney Co., OR

Basalt

Found with Windust points

Obsidian

G9, $165-$300
Warner Valey, OR

NOTE: Early Leaf points are currently being re-classified. The points shown on this page will in the future fall under various types such as *Cascade, Clovis Knife, Cordilleran, High Desert Knife, Windust Knife* and other types.

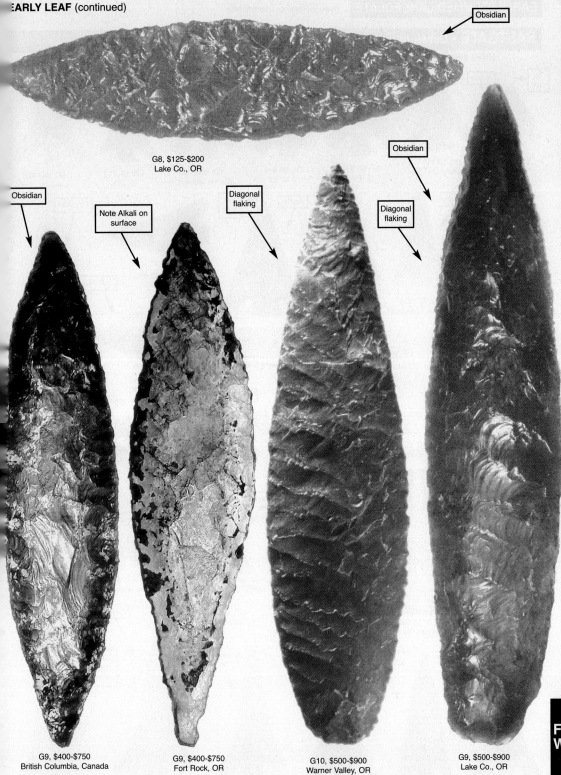

Obsidian

G8, $125-$200
Lake Co., OR

Obsidian

Obsidian

Note Alkali on
surface

Diagonal
flaking

Diagonal
flaking

G9, $400-$750
British Columbia, Canada

G9, $400-$750
Fort Rock, OR

G10, $500-$900
Warner Valley, OR

G9, $500-$900
Lake Co., OR

F
W

LOCATION: Great Basin to Washington. **DESCRIPTION:** A medium to large size lanceolate point or blade with a convex, pointed or straight base. Early parallel flaking is evident on many examples. These haven't been officially named yet and could be early *Cascade* forms.

EASTGATE - Developmental to Classic Phase, 1500 - 400 B. P.

(Also see Columbia Plateau, Eastgate, Elko, Emigrant Springs, Gunther, Rose Springs, Wallula)

Tip nick

Jasper

Chert

Obsidian

Carnelian agate

Obsidian

G4, $2-$5
N. OR

G6, $8-$15
Owhyee Co., ID

G7, $5-$10
S. OR

G6, $8-$15
S.W. ID

G8, $30-$50
Warner Valley, OR

G6, $8-$15
E. OR

G9, $45-$80
Lake Co., OR

Obsidian

Agate

Tip nick

Obsidian

Obsidian

G8, $25-$40
Col. Rv., WA

G7, $12-$20
Warner Valley, OR

G8, $30-$50
Warner Valley, OR

G8, $25-$40
S. OR

G6,, $15-$25
Col. Rv., WA

LOCATION: Great Basin westward. **DESCRIPTION:** A small, thin, triangular corner-notched arrow point with a short parallel sided to expanded stem. Barbs can be pointed or squared and usually extend to base.

Agate

Basalt

G7, $35-$60
Warner Valley, OR

G9, $80-$150
Warner Valey, OR

Obsidian

G10, $200-$350
Humboldt Co., NV

G9, $30-$50
S. OR

G9, $80-$150
OR

G9, $90-$175
Humboldt Co., NV

Agate

Chalc.

Jasper

Jasper

G9, $55-$100
Humboldt Sink, NV

Jasper

One of best known

G10, $250-$400
Harney Co., OR

G9, $125-$225
Humboldt Riv., NV

G9, $150-$275
Columbia Riv., OR

G9, $150-$250
Columbia Riv. OR

Tip nick

Obsidian

Glued

Obsidian

G10, $250-$400
The Dalles, OR

G6, $15-$25
S. OR

G4, $15-$25
Malheur Co., OR

G8, $35-$60
S. OR

G10+, $250-$450
The Dalles, OR

G10+, $1000-$1800
Owyhee Riv., OR

(Also see Columbia Plateau, Gunther, Wallula)

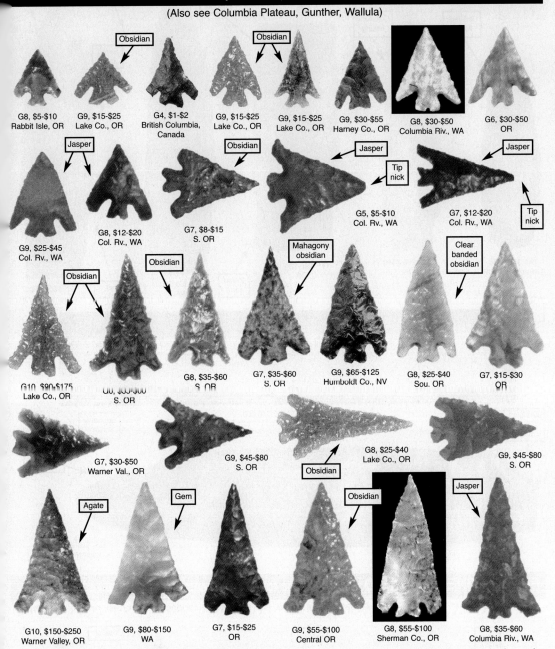

G8, $5-$10
Rabbit Isle, OR

G9, $15-$25
Lake Co., OR

Obsidian

G4, $1-$2
British Columbia,
Canada

Obsidian

G9, $15-$25
Lake Co., OR

G9, $15-$25
Lake Co., OR

G9, $30-$55
Harney Co., OR

G8, $30-$50
Columbia Riv., WA

G6, $30-$50
OR

Jasper

G9, $25-$45
Col. Rv., WA

G8, $12-$20
Col. Rv., WA

Obsidian

G7, $8-$15
S. OR

Jasper

Tip
nick

G5, $5-$10
Col. Rv., WA

Jasper

Tip
nick

G7, $12-$20
Col. Rv., WA

Obsidian

Obsidian

G10, $90-$175
Lake Co., OR

G0, $JJJ-J00
S. OR

Mahagony
obsidian

Clear
banded
obsidian

G8, $35-$60
S. OR

G7, $35-$60
S. OR

G9, $65-$125
Humboldt Co., NV

G8, $25-$40
Sou. OR

G7, $15-$30
OR

G7, $30-$50
Warner Val., OR

G9, $45-$80
S. OR

Obsidian

G8, $25-$40
Lake Co., OR

G9, $45-$80
S. OR

Agate

Gem

Obsidian

Obsidian

Jasper

G10, $150-$250
Warner Valley, OR

G9, $80-$150
WA

G7, $15-$25
OR

G9, $55-$100
Central OR

G8, $55-$100
Sherman Co., OR

G8, $35-$60
Columbia Riv., WA

LOCATION: Great Basin westward. **DESCRIPTION:** A small, thin, triangular arrow point with expanding barbs and a small bifurcated base. Blade edges are usually finely serrated.

EDEN - Early Archaic, 10,000 - 8000 B. P.

(Also see Alberta, Cody Knife, Firstview, Shaniko Stemmed, Scottsbluff & Windust)

LOCATION: Midwest into the Plains states and the Great Basin to Oregon and Washington. **DESCRIPTION:** A medium to large size, narrow, short-stemmed point with a straight to concave base. Most examples have a median ridge and collateral to oblique parallel flaking. Shoulders are very weak and are not as prominent as in the *Scottsbluff* type. Bases can be eared and are usually ground. Stems are Usually parallel sided. **I. D. KEY:** Diamond cross-section, median ridge on both faces, and have 3-4 layers of serial flaking.

F
W

EDEN (continued)

Collateral flaking

Collateral flaking

Broken half

Median ridge

Snapped stem

Obsidian

Eared form

Median ridge

Eared form

G6, $55-$100
Columb. Riv., OR

G7, $265-$500
OR

G1, $35-$60
S. OR

G6, $350-$600
WA

Weak shoulders

G7, $500-$900
Warner Valley, OR

Ground stem

G10, $6000-$10,000
OR

Burinated, socketed base

Weak shoulders

Burinated tip

Obsidian

G5, $165-$300
Cougar Mtn., OR

ELKO CORNER NOTCHED - Late Archaic to Developmental Phase, 3500 - 1200 B. P.

(Also see Chilcotin Plateau, Columbia Plateau, Eastgate, Hell's Canyon, Hendricks, Merrybell, and Snake River)

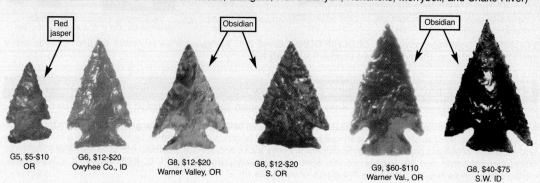

Red jasper

Obsidian

Obsidian

G5, $5-$10
OR

G6, $12-$20
Owyhee Co., ID

G8, $12-$20
Warner Valley, OR

G8, $12-$20
S. OR

G9, $60-$110
Warner Val., OR

G8, $40-$75
S.W. ID

Obsidian

G9, $80-$175
Warner Val., OR

G7, $20-$35
S. OR

Obsidian

G8, $25-$45
S. W. ID

Obsidian

G9, $55-$100
Warner Valley, OR

Serrated edge

G7, $15-$25
Warner Valley, OR

Obsidian

G9, $125-$225
Warner Valley, OR

Obsidian

G7, $35-$60
OR

Serrated edge

G10, $125-$200
Warner Valley, OR

Jasper

G10, $150-$250
Bend, OR

Tip & edge wear

G5, $12-$20
Cent. OR

Clear banded obsidian

Obsidian

Serrated edge

G10+, $275-$500
Warner Valley, OR

Obsidian

G10, $80-$150
Warner Valley, OR

Mahagony obsidian

G6, $15-$25
Warner Valley, OR

Red Jasper

G9, $150-$250
OR

G9, $175-$325
Silver Lake, OR

Obsidian

G9, $250-$450
Lake Co., OR

Agate

G9, $200-$350
Twin Fall Co., ID

Barb wear

G8, $100-$185
S. OR

Mahagony obsidian

LOCATION: Great Basin westward. **DESCRIPTION:** A small to large size, thin, corner notched dart point with shoulder tangs and a convex, concave or auriculate base. Shoulders and tips are sharp. Some examples exhibit excellent parallel flaking on blade edges.

F
W

ELKO CORNER NOTCHED (continued)

Obsidian

Obsidian

Obsidian

Obsidian

G9, $95-$175
S. OR

G10, $300-$550
Warner Valley, OR

G10, $250-$400
Warner Valley, OR

Mahagony
obsidian

G8, $95-$175
Lake Co., OR

G7, $25-$40
Lake Co., OR

G6, $65-$125
Fort Rock Valley, OR

Obsidian

Obsidian

G7, $40-$75
Warner Valley, OR

Unused
"blob" tip

G10+, $800-$1500+
Sou. OR

Obsidian

Edge
wear

G8, $250-$450
Sou. OR

(Also see Eastgate, Elko Corner Notched and Merrybell)

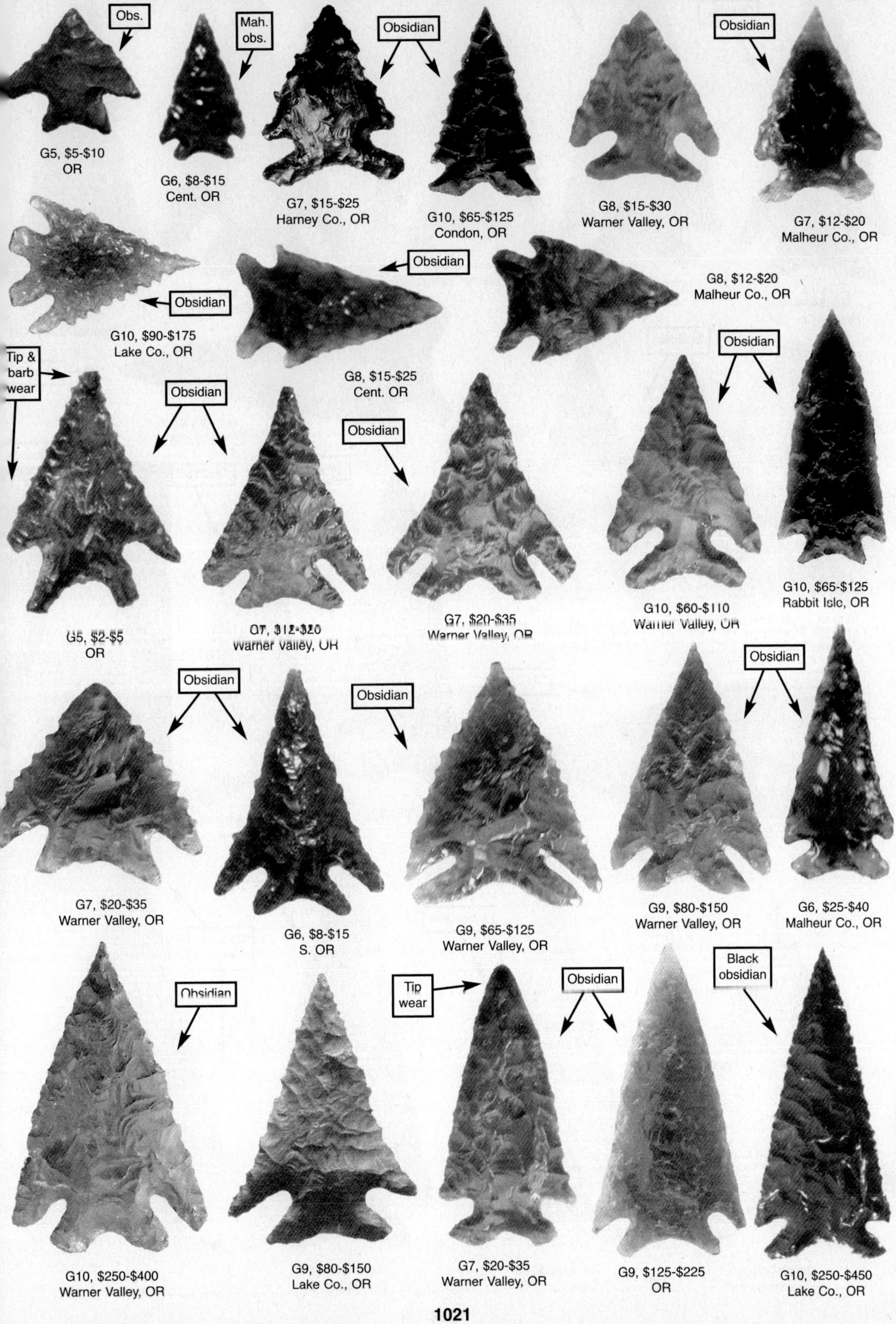

Obs.

G5, $5-$10
OR

Mah.
obs.

G6, $8-$15
Cent. OR

Obsidian

G7, $15-$25
Harney Co., OR

G10, $65-$125
Condon, OR

G8, $15-$30
Warner Valley, OR

Obsidian

G7, $12-$20
Malheur Co., OR

Obsidian

G10, $90-$175
Lake Co., OR

Obsidian

G8, $15-$25
Cent. OR

G8, $12-$20
Malheur Co., OR

Obsidian

Tip &
barb
wear

Obsidian

Obsidian

Obsidian

G5, $2-$5
OR

G7, $12-$20
Warner Valley, OR

G7, $20-$35
Warner Valley, OR

G10, $60-$110
Warner Valley, OR

G10, $65-$125
Rabbit Isle, OR

Obsidian

Obsidian

Obsidian

G7, $20-$35
Warner Valley, OR

G6, $8-$15
S. OR

G9, $65-$125
Warner Valley, OR

G9, $80-$150
Warner Valley, OR

G6, $25-$40
Malheur Co., OR

Obsidian

Tip
wear

Obsidian

Black
obsidian

G10, $250-$400
Warner Valley, OR

G9, $80-$150
Lake Co., OR

G7, $20-$35
Warner Valley, OR

G9, $125-$225
OR

G10, $250-$450
Lake Co., OR

F
W

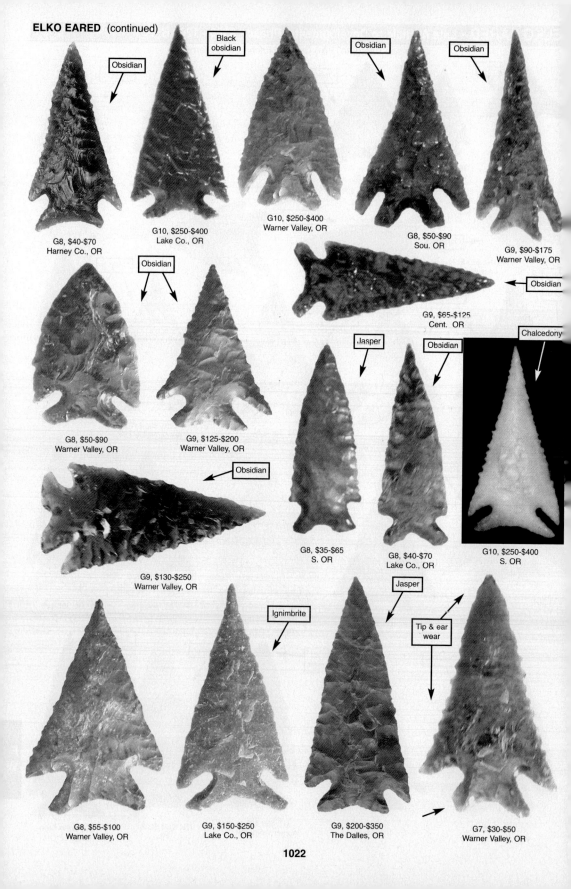

ELKO EARED (continued)

Obsidian

Black obsidian

Obsidian

Obsidian

G8, $40-$70
Harney Co., OR

G10, $250-$400
Lake Co., OR

G10, $250-$400
Warner Valley, OR

G8, $50-$90
Sou. OR

G9, $90-$175
Warner Valley, OR

Obsidian

Obsidian

G9, $65-$125
Cent. OR

G8, $50-$90
Warner Valley, OR

G9, $125-$200
Warner Valley, OR

Jasper

Obsidian

Chalcedony

Obsidian

G8, $35-$65
S. OR

G8, $40-$70
Lake Co., OR

G10, $250-$400
S. OR

G9, $130-$250
Warner Valley, OR

Ignimbrite

Jasper

Tip & ear
wear

G8, $55-$100
Warner Valley, OR

G9, $150-$250
Lake Co., OR

G9, $200-$350
The Dalles, OR

G7, $30-$50
Warner Valley, OR

ELKO EARED (continued)

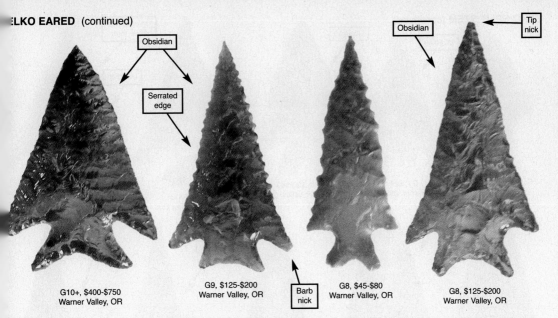

G10+, $400-$750
Warner Valley, OR

G9, $125-$200
Warner Valley, OR

Barb
nick

G8, $45-$80
Warner Valley, OR

G8, $125-$200
Warner Valley, OR

LOCATION: Great Basin westward. **DESCRIPTION:** A small to large size corner notched dart point with shoulder barbs and an eared base. Basal ears are usually exaggerated, and corners and tips are sharp. Some examples exhibit excellent parallel flaking on blade faces.

ELKO SPLIT-STEM (provisional) - Late Archaic to Developmental, 3500 - 1200 B. P.

(Also see Eastgate, Elko Corner Notched, Elko Eared, Gatecliff Split-Stem)

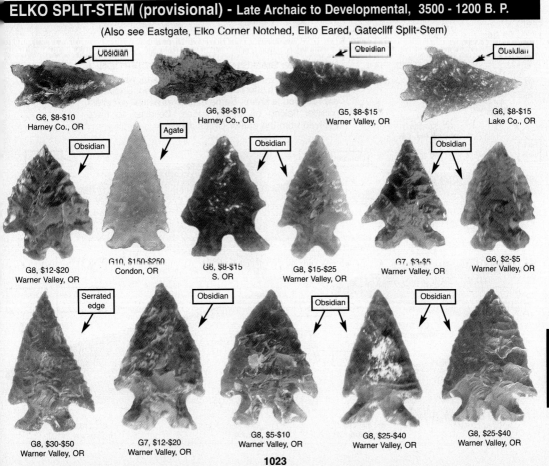

G6, $8-$10
Harney Co., OR

G6, $8-$10
Harney Co., OR

G5, $8-$15
Warner Valley, OR

G6, $8-$15
Lake Co., OR

G8, $12-$20
Warner Valley, OR

G10, $150-$250
Condon, OR

G6, $8-$15
S. OR

G8, $15-$25
Warner Valley, OR

G7, $3-$5
Warner Valley, OR

G6, $2-$5
Warner Valley, OR

G8, $30-$50
Warner Valley, OR

G7, $12-$20
Warner Valley, OR

G8, $5-$10
Warner Valley, OR

G8, $25-$40
Warner Valley, OR

G8, $25-$40
Warner Valley, OR

F
W

1023

ELKO SPLIT STEM (continued)

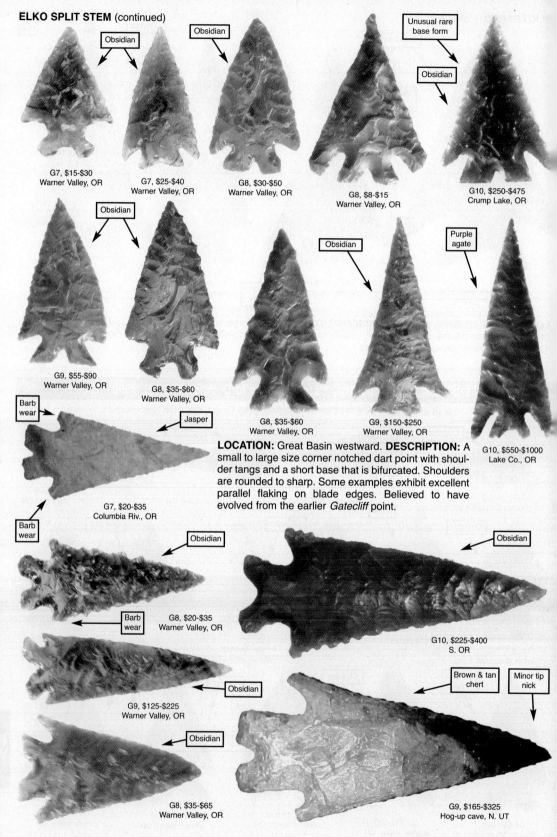

Obsidian

G7, $15-$30
Warner Valley, OR

Obsidian

G7, $25-$40
Warner Valley, OR

Obsidian

G8, $30-$50
Warner Valley, OR

G8, $8-$15
Warner Valley, OR

Unusual rare base form

Obsidian

G10, $250-$475
Crump Lake, OR

Obsidian

G9, $55-$90
Warner Valley, OR

G8, $35-$60
Warner Valley, OR

Obsidian

Purple agate

G8, $35-$60
Warner Valley, OR

G9, $150-$250
Warner Valley, OR

G10, $550-$1000
Lake Co., OR

Barb wear

Jasper

G7, $20-$35
Columbia Riv., OR

Barb wear

LOCATION: Great Basin westward. **DESCRIPTION:** A small to large size corner notched dart point with shoulder tangs and a short base that is bifurcated. Shoulders are rounded to sharp. Some examples exhibit excellent parallel flaking on blade edges. Believed to have evolved from the earlier *Gatecliff* point.

Obsidian

Barb wear

G8, $20-$35
Warner Valley, OR

Obsidian

G10, $225-$400
S. OR

Obsidian

G9, $125-$225
Warner Valley, OR

Obsidian

Brown & tan chert

Minor tip nick

G8, $35-$65
Warner Valley, OR

G9, $165-$325
Hog-up cave, N. UT

1024

ELKO WIDE NOTCH (provisional) - Late Archaic to Developmental, 3500 - 1200 B. P.

(Also see Eastgate, Elko, Elko Corner Notched and Elko Eared)

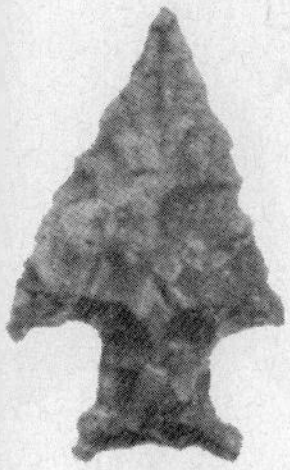

G7, $12-$20
Lake Co., OR

Obsidian

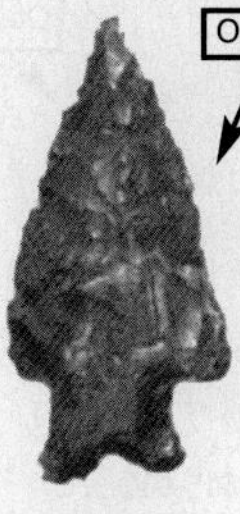

G6, $8-$15
S. OR

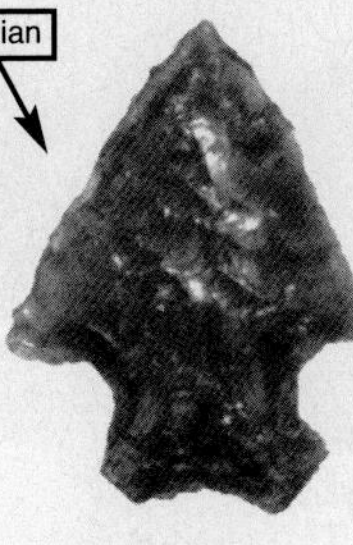

G6, $15-$20
S. OR

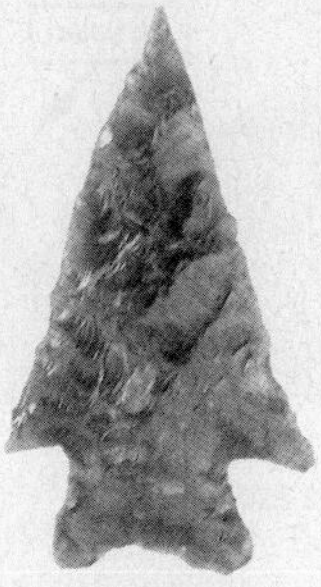

G8, $25-$40
Warner Valley, OR

Obsidian

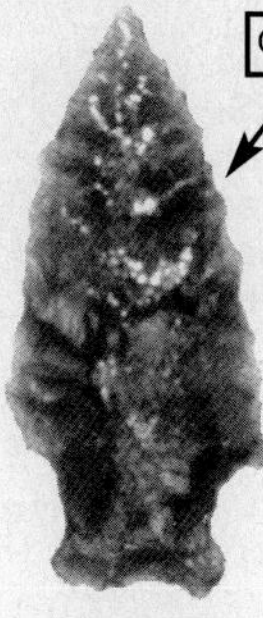

G6, $8-$15
Lake Co., OR

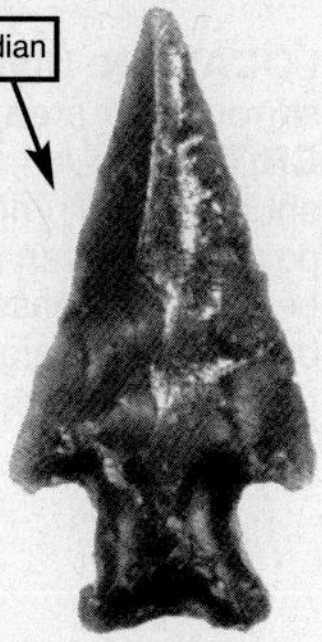

G7, $12-$20
S. OR

Obsidian

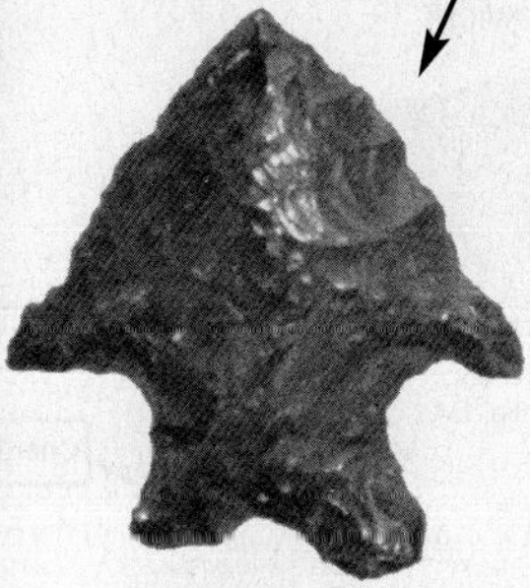

G8, $15-$25
Cent. OR

Basalt

G7, $15-$25
Lake Co., OR

Tip wear

G6, $5-$10
OR

Serrated edge

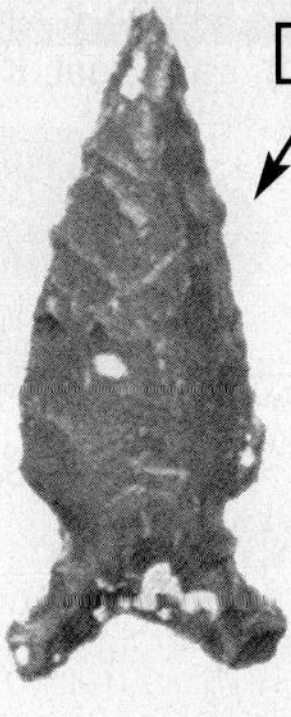

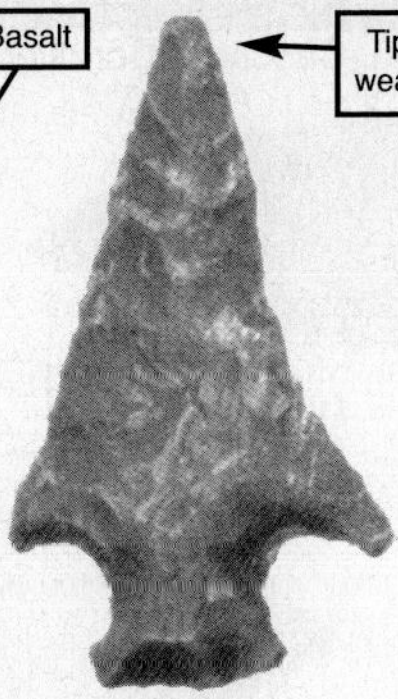

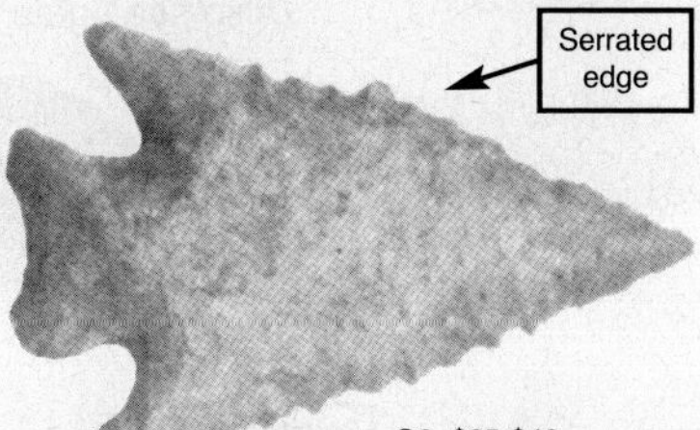

G8, $25-$40
N.W. NV

Obsidian

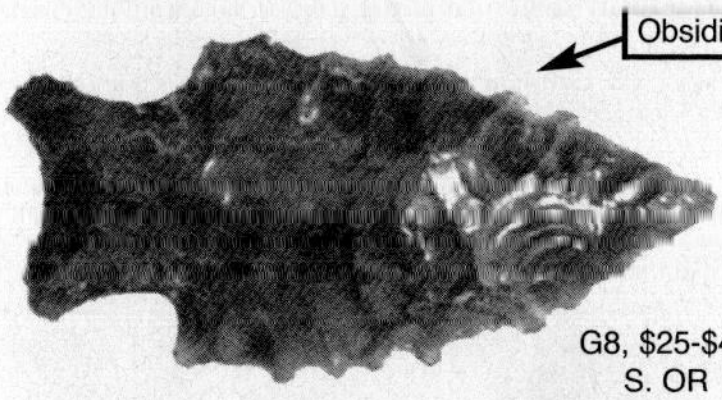

G8, $25-$40
S. OR

Black obsidian

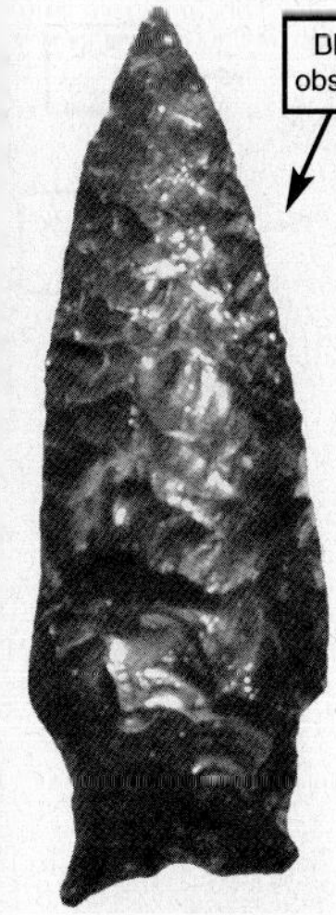

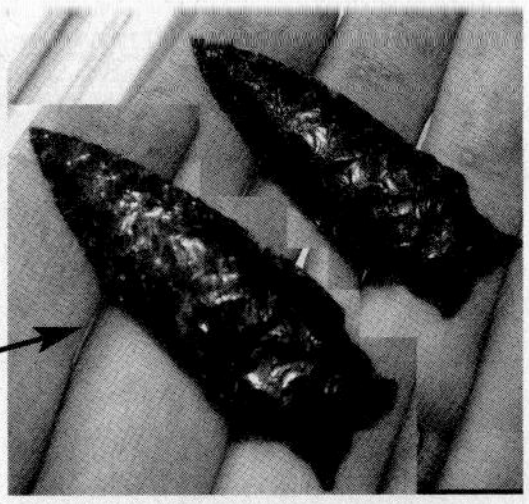

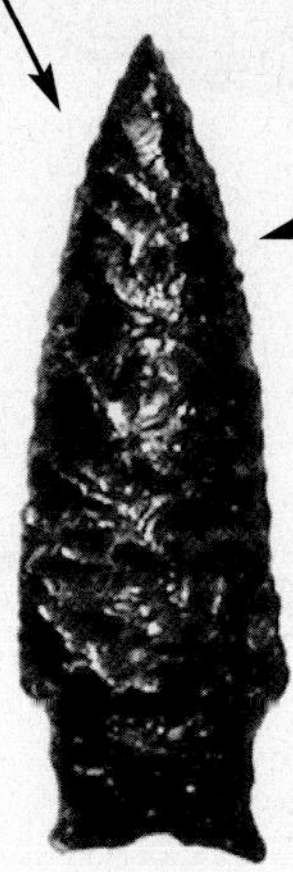

G7, $35-$65
E. OR

G9, $55-$100
E. OR

Hand held to show
size & form

LOCATION: Great Basin westward. **DESCRIPTION:** A medium size knife with broad corner to side notches and a concave base. Shoulders are usually barbed and bases are eared. It appears to be a knife-only variant and is made from existing Elko types. All have been resharpened several times.

Obsidian

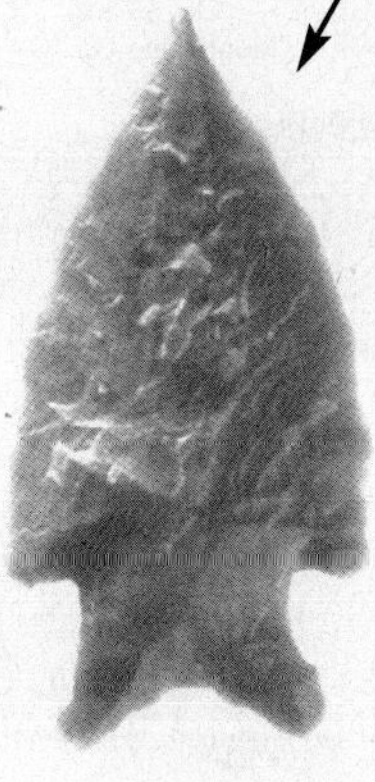

G9, $40-$70
Warner Valley, OR

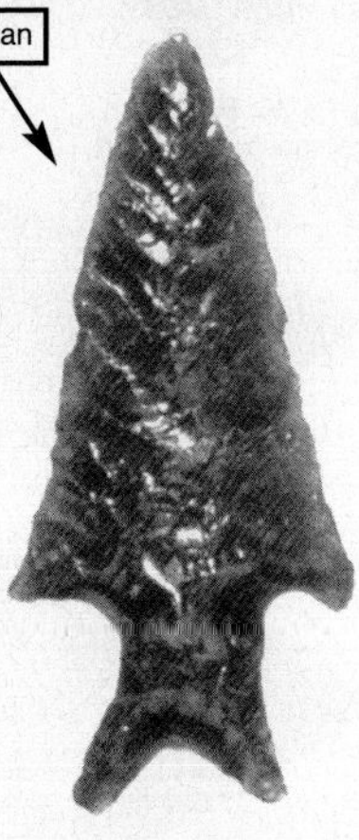

G5, $8-$15
S. OR

G9, $25-$45
OR

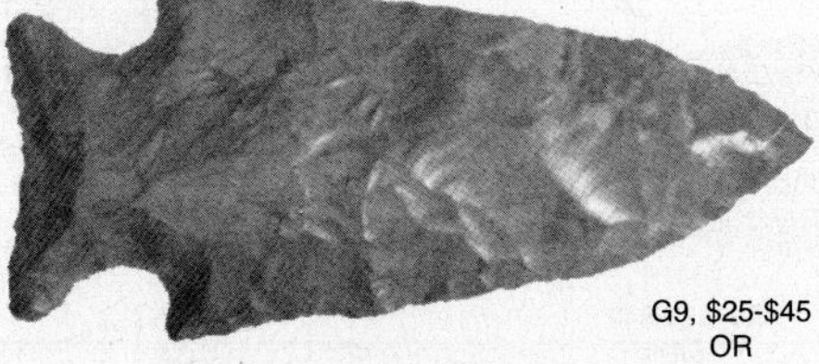

Mahagony obsidian

G7, $20-$35
Warner Valley, OR

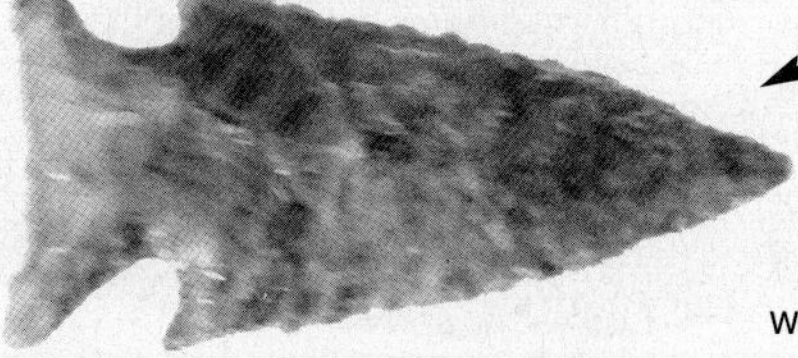

EMIGRANT SPRINGS (provisional) - Developmental Phase, 1200 - 1000 B. P.

(Also see Hell's Canyon Basal and Eastgate)

LOCATION: Utah and surrounding area. **DESCRITION:** A broad, short basal notched point. Tangs can extend beyond the base. The base is straight to rounded. Shoulders are rounded.

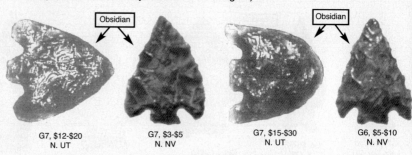

Obsidian

Obsidian

G7, $12-$20
N. UT

G7, $3-$5
N. NV

G7, $15-$30
N. UT

G6, $5-$10
N. NV

EXCELSIOR - Late Archaic to Transitional Phase, 3000 - 1700 B. P.

(Also see Agate Basin, Cascade, Cordilleran, Early Leaf, Kennewick)

G5, $5-$10
OR

G6, $12-$25
CA

Serrated edge

G4, $2-$5
Susanville, CA

Obsidian

Chert

Serrated edge

G10, $200-$350
Ventura Co., CA

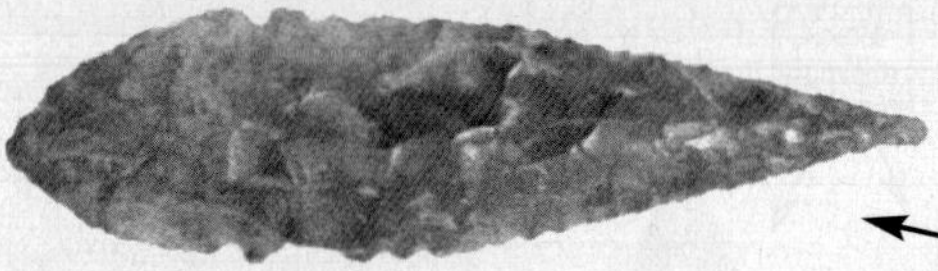

Red jasper

Serrated edge

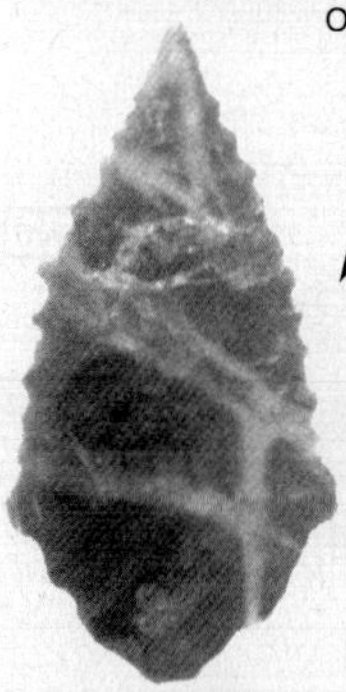

G6, $8-$15
Mendocino Co., CA

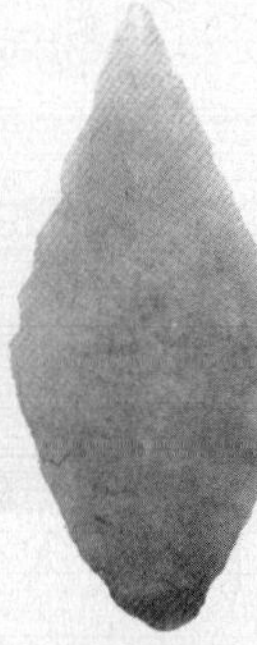

G5, $5-$10
Mendocino Co., CA

G7, $8-$15
CA

Yellow jasper

G10, $200-$350
Tiburon, CA

Obsidian

Obsidian

G10, $200-$350
Marin Co., CA

Serrated edge

Obsidian

G6, $25-$40
CA

G8, $30-$55
CA

EXCELSIOR (continued)

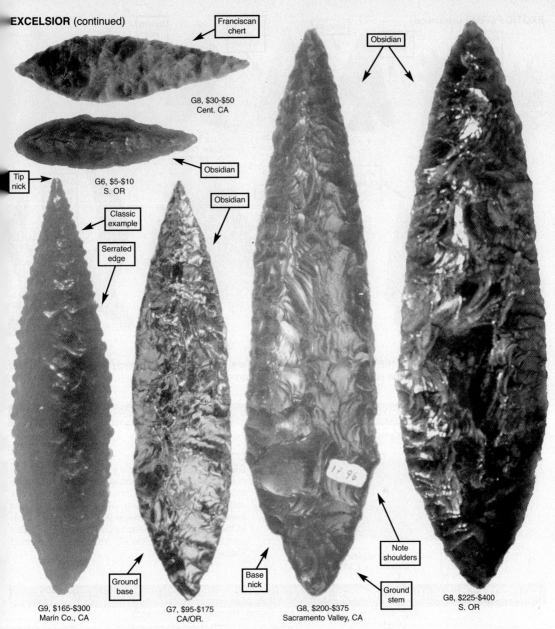

Franciscan chert

G8, $30-$50
Cent. CA

Obsidian

Obsidian

Tip nick

G6, $5-$10
S. OR

Classic example

Obsidian

Serrated edge

Ground base

G9, $165-$300
Marin Co., CA

G7, $95-$175
CA/OR.

Base nick

Note shoulders

Ground stem

G8, $200-$375
Sacramento Valley, CA

G8, $225-$400
S. OR

LOCATION: Northern California and Sou. Oregon. **DESCRIPTION:** A medium to large size, narrow, lanceolate, double pointed blade. Some examples are serrated. Basal areas are usually ground. See Perino, vol. 3, 2002.

EXOTIC FORMS - Late Archaic to Developmental Phase, 3000 - 1000 B. P.

(Also see Stockton and Vendetta)

Chert

Double notch

G6, $5-$10
N. UT

G6, $8-$15
Col. Rv. WA

G6, $8-$15
N. UT

G6, $5-$10
NI UT

G9, $55-$100
Sou. OR

G9, $55-$100
Sauvies Isle, OR

F
W

EXOTIC FORMS (continued)

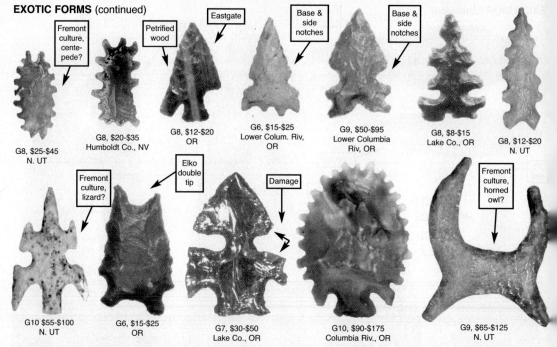

Fremont culture, centepede?

G8, $25-$45
N. UT

G8, $20-$35
Humboldt Co., NV

Petrified wood

G8, $12-$20
OR

Eastgate

G6, $15-$25
Lower Colum. Riv,
OR

Base & side notches

G9, $50-$95
Lower Columbia
Riv, OR

Base & side notches

G8, $8-$15
Lake Co., OR

G8, $12-$20
N. UT

Fremont culture, lizard?

G10 $55-$100
N. UT

Elko double tip

G6, $15-$25
OR

G7, $30-$50
Lake Co., OR

Damage

G10, $90-$175
Columbia Riv., OR

Fremont culture, horned owl?

G9, $65-$125
N. UT

LOCATION: Everywhere. **DESCRIPTION:** The forms illustrated are rare. Some are definitely effigy forms or exotic point designs while others may be no more than unfinished and unintentional doodles.

FIRSTVIEW - Early Archaic, 10,000 - 8000 B. P.

(Also see Alberta, Cody Complex, Eden and Scottsbluff)

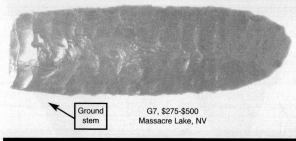

Ground stem

G7, $275-$500
Massacre Lake, NV

LOCATION: Great Basin into the Plains states. **DESCRIPTION:** A rare, medium to large size lanceolate point with slight shoulders and a rectangular stem that is ground. Shoulders are sometimes absent from resharpening. Most examples exhibit excellent parallel transverse flaking. A variant form of the *Scottsbluff* type made by the Cody Complex people. **I.D. KEY:** Weak shoulders, diamond shaped cross-section.

FOLSOM - Paleo, 11.000 - 10,000 B. P.

(Also see Black Rock Concave, Clovis, Humboldt and Midland)

Broken base

Resharpened many times

Fully fluted

G1, $15-$30
Blue Creek, UT

G4, $350-$600
NV

G6, $600-$1000
Stinking Pig Site, WA

LOCATION: Canada into Southwestern states and eastward to N. Indiana. **DESCRIPTION:** A very thin, small to medium sized lanceolate point with convex to straight sides and a convex basal edge creating sharp ears or basal corners. Most examples are fluted from the basal edge to nearly the tip of the point. Blade flaking is extremely fine and the hafting area is ground. Very Rare for the area. **I.D. KEY:** Thinness and form.

FOUNTAIN BAR (provisional) - Late Archaic, 3000 B. P.

(Also see Rose Springs Single Shoulder)

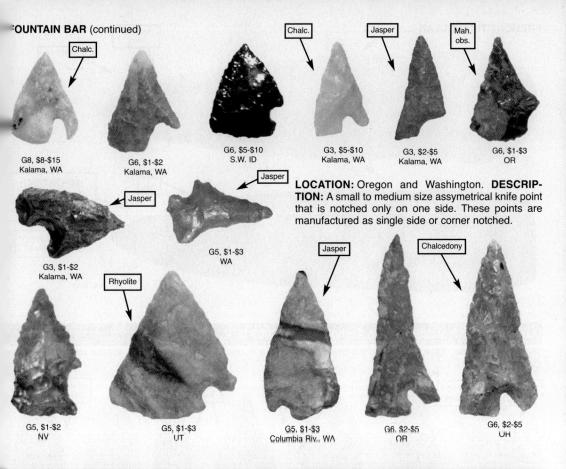

Chalc.

G8, $8-$15
Kalama, WA

G6, $1-$2
Kalama, WA

Chalc.

G6, $5-$10
S.W. ID

Jasper

G3, $5-$10
Kalama, WA

Jasper

G3, $2-$5
Kalama, WA

Mah. obs.

G6, $1-$3
OR

Jasper

G3, $1-$2
Kalama, WA

Jasper

G5, $1-$3
WA

LOCATION: Oregon and Washington. **DESCRIPTION:** A small to medium size assymetrical knife point that is notched only on one side. These points are manufactured as single side or corner notched.

Rhyolite

G5, $1-$2
NV

G5, $1-$3
UT

Jasper

G5, $1-$3
Columbia Riv., WA

G6, $2-$5
OR

Chalcedony

G6, $2-$5
OR

FREMONT TRIANGULAR (provisional) - Developmental Phase, 1600 - 800 B. P.

(Also see Plateau Pentagonal)

Carnelian agate

Quartzite

Edge wear

Quartzite

G6, $3-$5
Central UT

G6, $3-$5
W. Utah Lake, UT

G7, $5-$10
W. Utah Lake, UT

G3, $1-$2
N. UT

G8, $35-$60
N. UT

F
W

LOCATION: Southern to Northern Utah into Nevada where the Fremont culture lived. **DESCRIPTION:** A large, thin, narrow, triangular knife with a straight to convex base. There are three variants: Square base, rounded base and unfinished base. Some examples were notched to facilitate hafting.

FREMONT TRIANGULAR (continued)

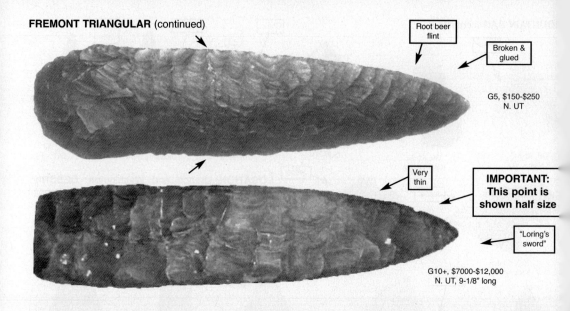

Root beer flint

Broken & glued

G5, $150-$250
N. UT

Very thin

IMPORTANT: This point is shown half size

"Loring's sword"

G10+, $7000-$12,000
N. UT, 9-1/8" long

GATECLIFF - Middle to Late Archaic, 5000 - 3000 B. P.

(Also see Coquille, Eastgate, Elko Split-Stem, Gypsum Cave, Houx Contracting Stem, Rabbit Isle, Vandenberg Contracting Stem)

Chalc.

Straight base

Obsidian

Red jasper

Straight base

Straight base

G9, $20-$35
Colum. Riv., OR

G6, $5-$10
Lake Co., OR

G5, $.50-$20
Harney Co., OR

G6, $3-$5
Harney Co., OR

G6, $1-$2
Humbolt Co., NV

G8, $25-$40
OR

G6, $3-$5
Owhyee Co., ID

Straight base

Red jasper

Straight base

Obsidian

Straight base

Agate

G6, $5-$10
N. Lake Co., OR

G6, $25-$45
Black Rock Desert, NV

G6, $2-$5
Harney Co., OR

G6, $12-$20
OR

G6, $2-$5
Lake Co., OR

G7, $5-$10
OR

Straight base

G6, $5-$10
Lake Co., OR

LOCATION: Great Basin westward. **DESCRIPTION:** A medium to large size dart point with horizontal to barbed shoulders and a contracted stem. Bases are straight to rounded. Blade edges are convex to recurved. Most of the contracting stem points are known as *Gypsum Cave* further south. Parallel, oblique flaking does occur on this type. **I.D. KEY:** Tapered stem.

Jasper

Tip nick

Obsidian

Obsidian

Petrified wood

Straight base

G8, $35-$65
N. W. NV

G6, $5-$10
Bend, OR

G6, $5-$10
Cent. OR

G7, $15-$25
Lake Co., OR

G8, $20-$35
S. OR

G8, $35-$60
OR

Obsidian

Obsidian

Agate

G10, $150-$250
Silver Lake, OR

G8, $20-$35
Harney Co., OR

G8, $20-$35
S. OR

G9, $40-$75
Klamath Falls, OR

G8, $90-$175
OR

Agate

Basalt

Straight base

Obsidian

G10, $165-$300
Lake Co., OR

G7, $15-$30
Clearwater Riv., ID

G10, $150-$250
N. NV

G10, $250-$450
Deschutes Co;., OR

G8, $150-$250
S. E. OR

F
W

1031

(Also see Coquille, Eastgate, Elko Split-Stem, Pinto Basin, Rabbit Island & Vandenberg Contracting Stem)

Obsidian

Obsidian

Basalt

Obsidian

G6, $2-$5
Sou. OR.

G8, $12-$20
Sou. OR.

G6, $2-$5
Harney Co., OR

G5, $2-$5
S.W. ID.

G4, $8-$15
Sou. OR.

G7, $5-$10
S.W. ID.

G7, $15-$25
S.W. ID

Obsidian

Orange jasper

Obsidian

White agate

Obsidian

G6, $8-$15
Warner Valley, OR

G8, $20-$35
Bend, OR

G7, $15-$30
S. OR.

G10, $40-$75
S. OR

G8, $20-$35
Cent. OR

G9, $35-$65
Warner Valley, OR

Obsidian

Obsidian

Oblique flaking

Obsidian

Basal ears clipped

Obsidian

Serrate edge

G9, $80-$150
N.W. NV

G6, $12-$20
S.OR

G7, $30-$55
Tule Lake, CA

G5, $15-$30
S.W. ID

G6, $15-$30
Cent. OR

G9, $200-$375
Warner Valley, OR

LOCATION: Great Basin westward. **DESCRIPTION:** A medium to large size stemmed, bifurcated dart point that is usually serrated with horizontal to barbed shoulders. Believed to have evolved into *Elko* points. The *Gatcliff* usually has a longer stem and a shallower base notch than *Pinto Basin* of which it was a part. Parallel, oblique blade flaking does occur. Slightly contracting or expanding is acceptable. **I.D. KEY:** Shallow bifurcated stem.

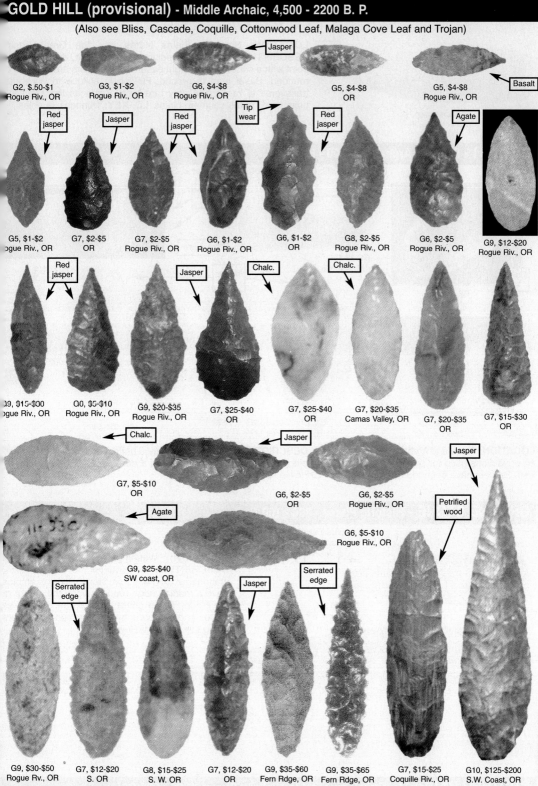

(Also see Bliss, Cascade, Coquille, Cottonwood Leaf, Malaga Cove Leaf and Trojan)

G2, $.50-$1
Rogue Riv., OR

G3, $1-$2
Rogue Riv., OR

Jasper

G6, $4-$8
Rogue Riv., OR

G5, $4-$8
OR

G5, $4-$8
Rogue Riv., OR

Basalt

Red jasper

Jasper

Red jasper

Tip wear

Red jasper

Agate

G5, $1-$2
Rogue Riv., OR

G7, $2-$5
OR

G7, $2-$5
Rogue Riv., OR

G6, $1-$2
Rogue Riv., OR

G6, $1-$2
OR

G8, $2-$5
Rogue Riv., OR

G6, $2-$5
Rogue Riv., OR

G9, $12-$20
Rogue Riv., OR

Red jasper

Jasper

Chalc.

Chalc.

G9, $15-$30
Rogue Riv., OR

G0, $5-$10
Rogue Riv., OR

G9, $20-$35
Rogue Riv., OR

G7, $25-$40
OR

G7, $25-$40
OR

G7, $20-$35
Camas Valley, OR

G7, $20-$35
OR

G7, $15-$30
OR

Chalc.

Jasper

Jasper

G7, $5-$10
OR

G6, $2-$5
OR

G6, $2-$5
Rogue Riv., OR

Petrified wood

Agate

G6, $5-$10
Rogue Riv., OR

G9, $25-$40
SW coast, OR

Serrated edge

Jasper

Serrated edge

G9, $30-$50
Rogue Rv., OR

G7, $12-$20
S. OR

G8, $15-$25
S. W. OR

G7, $12-$20
OR

G9, $35-$60
Fern Rdge, OR

G9, $35-$65
Fern Rdge, OR

G7, $15-$25
Coquille Riv., OR

G10, $125-$200
S.W. Coast, OR

F W

LOCATION: S.W. Oregon and N.W. Calif. **DESCRIPTION:** A descendant of the *Cascade* type. A small to medium size lanceolate dart point with a rounded base. Named by Dr. Luther S. Cressman, Univ. of Oregon. See Noel Jusice, 2002 & Perino, vol. 3, 2002.

GOSHEN - Paleo, 11,250 - 9,500

(Also see Alder Complex, Folsom, Midland, Milnesand, Plainview & Spedis)

Agate

LOCATION: Northern Plains states into the Great Basin **DESCRIPTION:** A small to medium size, very thin, auriculate dart point with a concave to straight base. Basal corners are squared to rounded. Basal area is ground. Flaking is oblique to horizontal, transverse to random. A very rare type. Same as the *Plainview* point found in the southern plains. **I.D. KEY:** Thinness, auricles.

G9, $165-$300
Warner Valley, OR

GRAVER - Paleo to Archaic, 11,500 - Historic

(Also see Drill, Lancet, Perforator, Scraper & Sizer)

Graver
tip

Graver
tip

Graver
tips

Agate

Graver
tips

G6, $8-$15
Lady Island, WA

G6, $8-$15
Lake Co., OR

Red
agate

Graver
tips

G6, $12-$20
N.W. NV

Graver
tip

G6, $8-$15
Lake Co., OR

G6, $8-$15
Sou. OR

G10, $25-$40
Columbia River, OR

LOCATION: Paleo and Archaic sites everywhere. **DESCRIPTION:** An irregular shaped uniface tool with sharp, pointed projections used for puncturing, incising, tattooing, etc. Some examples served a dual purpose for scraping as well. Gravers have been found on *Black Rock Concave* sites in the Great Basin.

GROUND STONE - Historic Phase, 300 - 100 B. P.

(Also see Cascade & Side Knife)

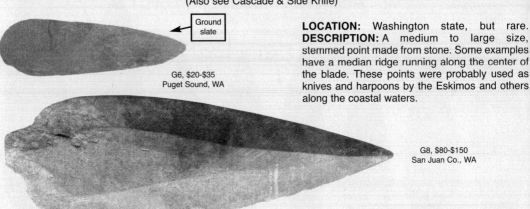

Ground
slate

LOCATION: Washington state, but rare. **DESCRIPTION:** A medium to large size, stemmed point made from stone. Some examples have a median ridge running along the center of the blade. These points were probably used as knives and harpoons by the Eskimos and others along the coastal waters.

G6, $20-$35
Puget Sound, WA

G8, $80-$150
San Juan Co., WA

GUNTHER BARBED - Developmental to Historic Phase, 1000 - 200 B. P.

(Also see Calapooya, Columbia Plateau, Point Sal Barbed, Rabbit Island and Wallula)

G6, $12-$20
Jackson Co., OR

G6, $15-$30
Jackson Co., OR

G8, $20-$35
Jackson Co., OR

Serrated edge

G9, $80-$150
Jackson Co., OR

Agate

G10, $250-$450
Sou. OR

Agate

Agate

G10, $275-$500
Sou. OR

G10, $175-$300
Jackson Co., OR

Chalc.

G7, $30-$50
Coos Co., OR

Basalt

G6, $20-$35
S.W. OR

Agate

G6, $15-$25
S. coast, OR

Basalt

G10, $150-$250
The Dalles, OR

Serrated edge

G6, $35-$60
S. coast, OR

Tip nick

G10, $350-$650
Coos Co., OR

Serrated edge

G6, $5-$10
S. coast, OR

Green chert

G9, $150-$275
Coos Co., OR

G10, $150-$275
Coos Co., OR

Serrated edge

G10, $200-$350
Coos Co., OR

Agate

G10, $200-$350
Coos Co., OR

Tip nick

G9, $80-$150
Coos Co., OR

Jasper

Serrated edge

G9, $75-$140
Klamath Co., OR

Chalc.

G9, $125-$200
Coos Co., OR

Serrated edge

G10, $250-$475
Jackson Co., OR

Serrated edge

G10, $150-$250
Klamath Falls, OR

G7, $15-$30
Jackson Co., OR

Serrated edge

G10, $80-$150
Klamath Falls, OR

Serrated edge

G10, $200-$350
Jackson Co., OR

Serrated edge

G10, $275-$500
Coos Co., OR

G9, $165-$300
Coos Co., OR

G9, $80-$150
OR

G10, $55-$100
Coos Co., OR

G10, $125-$200
Coos Co., OR

F W

GUNTHER BARBED (continued)

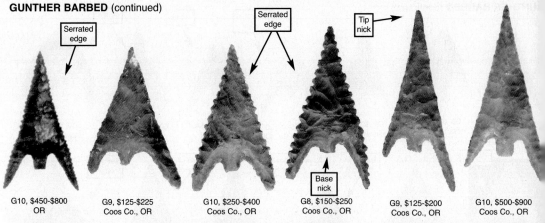

Serrated edge

Serrated edge

Tip nick

Base nick

G10, $450-$800
OR

G9, $125-$225
Coos Co., OR

G10, $250-$400
Coos Co., OR

G8, $150-$250
Coos Co., OR

G9, $125-$200
Coos Co., OR

G10, $500-$900
Coos Co., OR

LOCATION: Great Basin westward. **DESCRIPTION:** A small to medium size, thin, broad, triangular arrow point with long barbs that extend to and beyond the base. The blade sides are straight to concave and the stem is parallel sided to slightly contracting or expanding. These points exhibit high quality flaking. Other local names used for this type are "Camas Valley," "Mad River," "Molalla," "Rogue River," and "Shasta."

GUNTHER TRIANGULAR - Developmental to Historic Phase, 1000 - 200 B. P.

(Also see Canalino Triangular and Cottonwood)

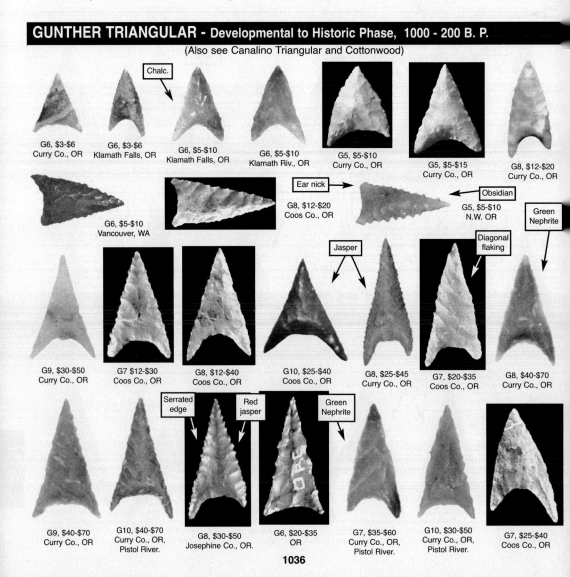

Chalc.

G6, $3-$6
Curry Co., OR

G6, $3-$6
Klamath Falls, OR

G6, $5-$10
Klamath Falls, OR

G6, $5-$10
Klamath Riv., OR

G5, $5-$10
Curry Co., OR

G5, $5-$15
Curry Co., OR

G8, $12-$20
Curry Co., OR

G6, $5-$10
Vancouver, WA

Ear nick

G8, $12-$20
Coos Co., OR

Obsidian

G5, $5-$10
N.W. OR

Green Nephrite

Jasper

Diagonal flaking

Green Nephrite

G9, $30-$50
Curry Co., OR

G7 $12-$30
Coos Co., OR

G8, $12-$40
Coos Co., OR

G10, $25-$40
Coos Co., OR

G8, $25-$45
Curry Co., OR

G7, $20-$35
Coos Co., OR

G8, $40-$70
Curry Co., OR

Serrated edge

Red jasper

Green Nephrite

G9, $40-$70
Curry Co., OR

G10, $40-$70
Curry Co., OR,
Pistol River.

G8, $30-$50
Josephine Co., OR.

G6, $20-$35
OR

G7, $35-$60
Curry Co., OR,
Pistol River.

G10, $30-$50
Curry Co., OR,
Pistol River.

G7, $25-$40
Coos Co., OR

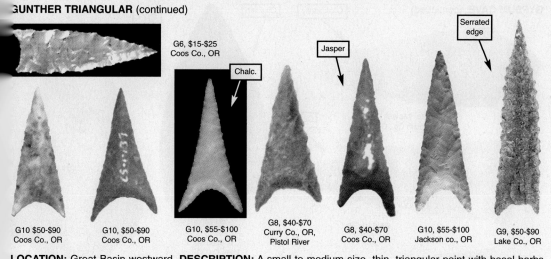

G6, $15-$25
Coos Co., OR

Chalc.

Jasper

Serrated edge

G10 $50-$90
Coos Co., OR

G10, $50-$90
Coos Co., OR

G10, $55-$100
Coos Co., OR

G8, $40-$70
Curry Co., OR,
Pistol River

G8, $40-$70
Coos Co., OR

G10, $55-$100
Jackson co., OR

G9, $50-$90
Lake Co., OR

LOCATION: Great Basin westward. **DESCRIPTION:** A small to medium size, thin, triangular point with basal barbs that can be asymmetrical with one longer than the other. The basal ears have a tendency to turn in towards the base which is concave. Early forms are called U-Back locally. Usually made from jasper, agate, green chert, rarely from obsidian.

GYPSUM CAVE - Middle Archaic, 5000 - 3300 B. P.

(Also see Coquille, Gatecliff, Parowan, Rabbit Island, Sierra Contracting, Vandenberg)

Obsidian

Obsidian

Obsidian

Agate

Obsidian

G6, $1-$2
Harney Co., OR

G5, $1-$2
Harney Co., OR

G6, $1-$2
OR

G5, $5-$10
S. OR

G7, $20-$35
Harney Co., OR

G7, $30-$55
Lake Co., OR

Tip wear

Obsidian

Diagonal flaking

Obsidian

G6, $1-$2
S. OR

G8, $35-$60
Lake Co., OR

G9, $35-$65
Lake Co., OR

G9, $45-$80
Silver Lake, OR

G9, $65-$125
N. NV

G7, $15-$30
Silver Lake, OR

G7, $12-$20
S. OR

F
W

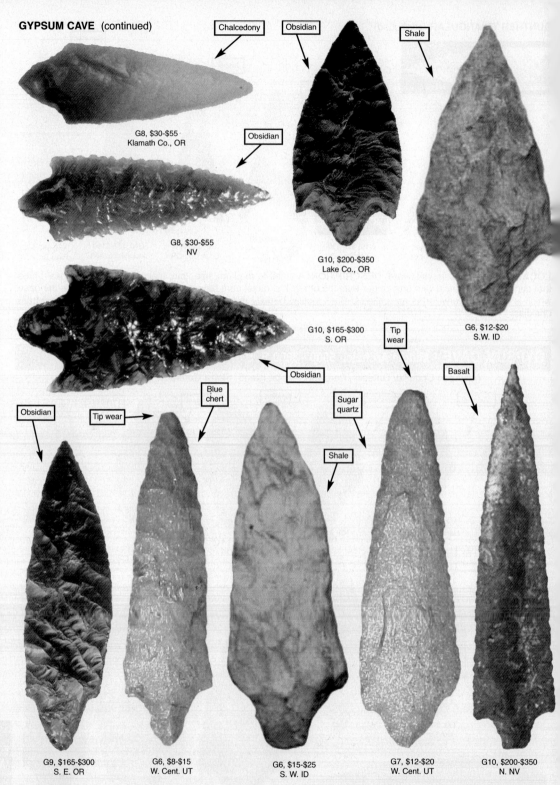

GYPSUM CAVE (continued)

Chalcedony

Obsidian

Shale

G8, $30-$55
Klamath Co., OR

Obsidian

G8, $30-$55
NV

G10, $200-$350
Lake Co., OR

G10, $165-$300
S. OR

Tip wear

G6, $12-$20
S.W. ID

Obsidian

Basalt

Obsidian

Tip wear

Blue chert

Sugar quartz

Shale

G9, $165-$300
S. E. OR

G6, $8-$15
W. Cent. UT

G6, $15-$25
S. W. ID

G7, $12-$20
W. Cent. UT

G10, $200-$350
N. NV

LOCATION: Type site is Gypsum Cave, Nev. Found in ID, E. CA, E. OR, N. AZ, W. UT **DESCRIPTION:** A medium sized dart/knife with straight blade edges and a short stem which contracts to a rounded or pointed base. The shoulders are obtuse. this point may be related to the *Augustin* point found further south and the Gatecliff point from Oregon, though, in general, it seems to have better workmanship. **I.D. KEY:** Stubby stem.

(Also see Hafted Knife in Northern High Plains section)

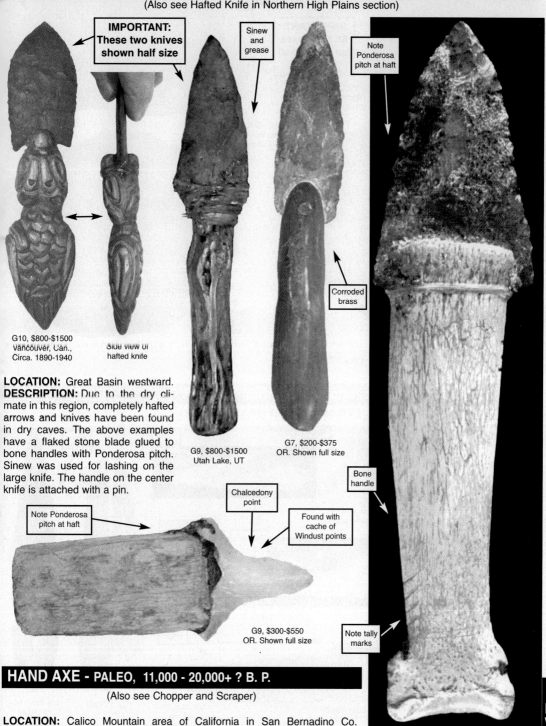

IMPORTANT: These two knives shown half size

Sinew and grease

Note Ponderosa pitch at haft

Corroded brass

G10, $800-$1500
Vancouver, Can.,
Circa. 1890-1940

Side view of hafted knife

LOCATION: Great Basin westward.
DESCRIPTION: Due to the dry climate in this region, completely hafted arrows and knives have been found in dry caves. The above examples have a flaked stone blade glued to bone handles with Ponderosa pitch. Sinew was used for lashing on the large knife. The handle on the center knife is attached with a pin.

G9, $800-$1500
Utah Lake, UT

G7, $200-$375
OR. Shown full size

Bone handle

Note Ponderosa pitch at haft

Chalcedony point

Found with cache of Windust points

G9, $300-$550
OR. Shown full size

Note tally marks

(Also see Chopper and Scraper)

LOCATION: Calico Mountain area of California in San Bernadino Co.
DESCRIPTION: Irregular percussion shaped axes used for cutting and chopping. This site is famed for producing very early man-made objects that were questionable dated by L. S. B. Leakey to 50,000 years ago. This age remains controversial waiting a corroborative date from another site which has yet to be found.

G10, $1500-$2500
Fort Rock Desert, Sou. Cent.
OR, cave site. Shown full size

F
W

HAND AXE (continued)

Paleo flaking

Chert

IMPORTANT: All hand axes are shown half size

G6, $2-$5
San Bernadino Co., CA, Calico Mountains,

G9, $5-$10
San Bernadino Co., CA
Calico Mountains

Jasper

G9, $5-$10
San Bernadino Co., CA, Calico Mountains

G8, $5-$10
San Bernadino Co., CA, Calico Mountains

HARAHEY (see Northwestern 4-Way Knife)

HARPOON - Late Archaic to Historic Phase, 3000 - 200 B. P.

(Also see Harpoons in Alaska Section)

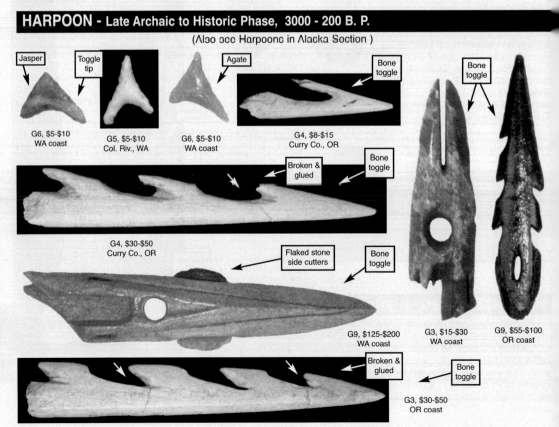

Jasper

Toggle tip

Agate

Bone toggle

Bone toggle

G6, $5-$10
WA coast

G5, $5-$10
Col. Riv., WA

G6, $5-$10
WA coast

G4, $8-$15
Curry Co., OR

Broken & glued

Bone toggle

G4, $30-$50
Curry Co., OR

Flaked stone side cutters

Bone toggle

G9, $125-$200
WA coast

G3, $15-$30
WA coast

G9, $55-$100
OR coast

Broken & glued

Bone toggle

G3, $30-$50
OR coast

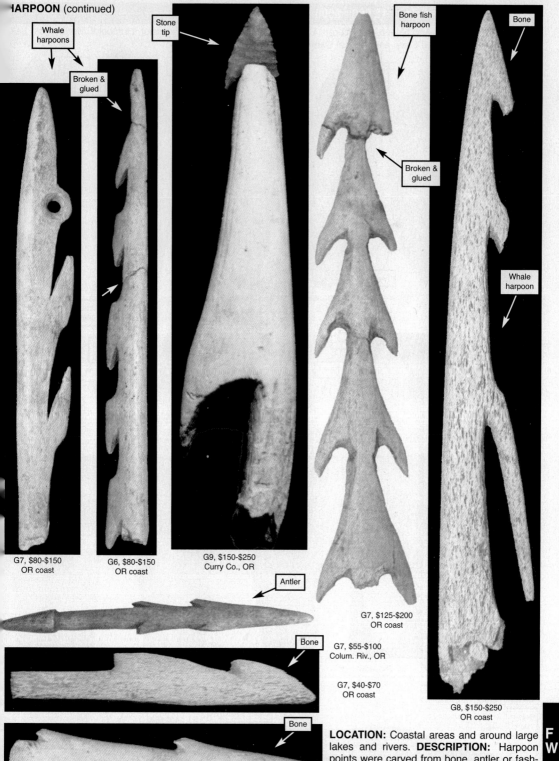

Whale harpoons

Broken & glued

Stone tip

Bone fish harpoon

Broken & glued

Bone

Whale harpoon

Antler

Bone

Bone

G7, $80-$150
OR coast

G6, $80-$150
OR coast

G9, $150-$250
Curry Co., OR

G7, $125-$200
OR coast

G7, $55-$100
Colum. Riv., OR

G7, $40-$70
OR coast

G7, $30-$50
OR coast

G8, $150-$250
OR coast

LOCATION: Coastal areas and around large lakes and rivers. **DESCRIPTION:** Harpoon points were carved from bone, antler or fashioned from metal. They were used in fishing. Some have stone tips and were hafted either directly to the shaft or inserted as a foreshaft.

F
W

HASKETT - Late Paleo, 12,000 - 8000 B. P.

(Also see Agate Basin, Año Nuevo, Cordilleran, Cougar Mountain, Cascade, Excelsior, Humboldt, Kennewick, Lake Mojave, Lind Coulee, Owl Cave and Wildcat Canyon)

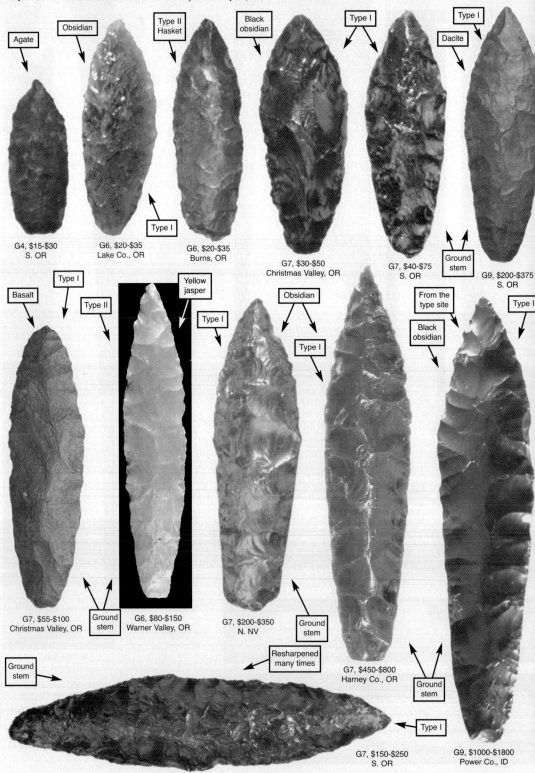

Agate

Obsidian

Type II Hasket

Black obsidian

Type I

Type I

Dacite

Type I

Ground stem

G4, $15-$30
S. OR

G6, $20-$35
Lake Co., OR

G6, $20-$35
Burns, OR

G7, $30-$50
Christmas Valley, OR

G7, $40-$75
S. OR

G9, $200-$375
S. OR

Basalt

Type I

Type II

Yellow jasper

Type I

Obsidian

Type I

From the type site

Black obsidian

Type I

G7, $55-$100
Christmas Valley, OR

Ground stem

G6, $80-$150
Warner Valley, OR

G7, $200-$350
N. NV

Ground stem

G7, $450-$800
Harney Co., OR

Ground stem

Ground stem

Resharpened many times

Type I

G7, $150-$250
S. OR

G9, $1000-$1800
Power Co., ID

1042

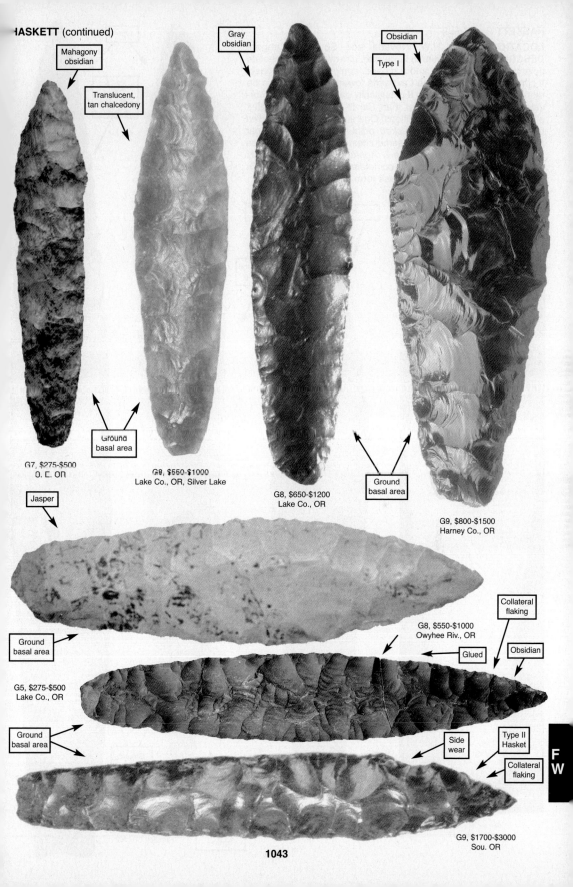

Mahagony obsidian

Translucent, tan chalcedony

Gray obsidian

Obsidian

Type I

Ground basal area

G7, $275-$500
O. E. OR

G8, $550-$1000
Lake Co., OR, Silver Lake

G8, $650-$1200
Lake Co., OR

Ground basal area

G9, $800-$1500
Harney Co., OR

Jasper

Ground basal area

G8, $550-$1000
Owyhee Riv., OR

Collateral flaking

Glued

Obsidian

G5, $275-$500
Lake Co., OR

Ground basal area

Side wear

Type II Hasket

Collateral flaking

G9, $1700-$3000
Sou. OR

F
W

HASKETT (continued)

LOCATION: Idaho, N.W. Nevada and Southern Oregon.
DESCRIPTION: A medium to large size, narrow, thick, lanceolate point with parallel flaking and a ground, convex to straight base. It comes in two types: **Type I** expands towards the tip (Could be resharpened **type IIs**). **Type II** is basically parallel sided to excurvate. Consistantly dated older than *Clovis* from hydration dates obtained from controlled conditions. One such test dated *Haskett* to 12,100 years old. The *Haskett* point is related to *Cougar Mountain* points found on the same sites. *Haskett /Lind Coulee* points later evolved into *Alberta* & *Agate Basins*. An extremely rare type with only a few dozen complete examples known. **I.D. KEY:** Early parallel flaking and base form.

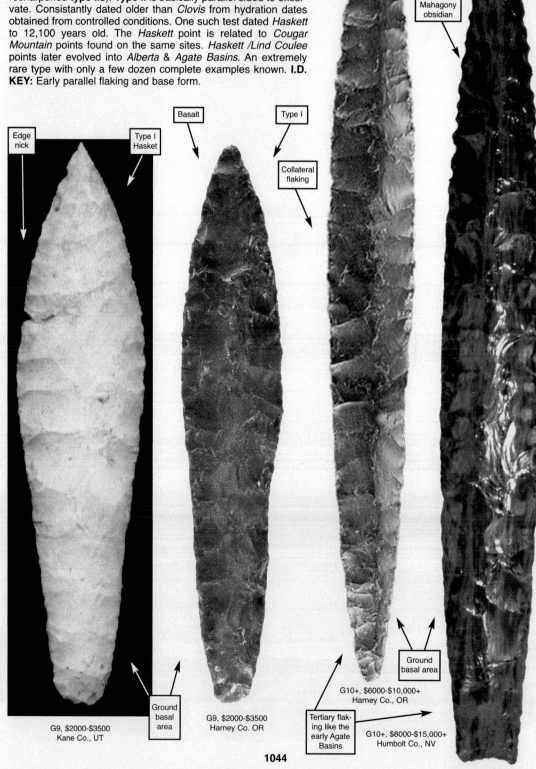

Edge nick

Type I Hasket

Basalt

Type I

Collateral flaking

Type II

Red & black Mahagony obsidian

Ground basal area

Ground basal area

G9, $2000-$3500
Kane Co., UT

G9, $2000-$3500
Harney Co. OR

G10+, $6000-$10,000+
Harney Co., OR

Tertiary flaking like the early Agate Basins

G10+, $8000-$15,000+
Humbolt Co., NV

HELL GAP (provisional) - Late Paleo, 10,300 - 9500 B. P.

(Also see Agate Basin, Cascade Shouldered, Lake Mohave, Mahkin Shouldered, Silver Lake, Windust)

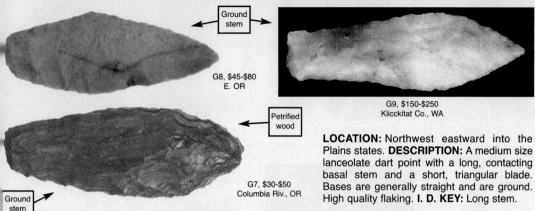

Ground stem

G8, $45-$80
E. OR

G9, $150-$250
Klicckitat Co., WA

Petrified wood

G7, $30-$50
Columbia Riv., OR

Ground stem

LOCATION: Northwest eastward into the Plains states. **DESCRIPTION:** A medium size lanceolate dart point with a long, contacting basal stem and a short, triangular blade. Bases are generally straight and are ground. High quality flaking. **I. D. KEY:** Long stem.

HELL'S CANYON BASAL NOTCHED - Developmental to Historic Phase, 1200 - 200 B. P.

(Also see Eastgate, Elko Corner Notched, Emigrant Springs, Fountain Bar and Quillomene Bar)

Agate

Agate

G6, $15-$20
Harney Co., OR

G6, $15-$20
OR

G8, $25-$40
OR

G5, $12-$20
OR

G5, $12-$20
Harney Co., OR

G5, $15-$30
OR

Mahagony obsidian

Basalt

Black obsidian

G7, $50-$90
Columb. Riv., OR

G8, $40-$70
Umatilla, OR

G6, $35-$65
Umatilla Co., OR

G8, $125-$200
Lake Co., OR

Petrified wood

Basalt

G9, $200-$375
Priest Rapids, WA

G9, $275-$500
WA/OR

G7, $125-$200
Chehalis, WA

F
W

1045

HELL'S CANYON BASAL NOTCHED (continued)

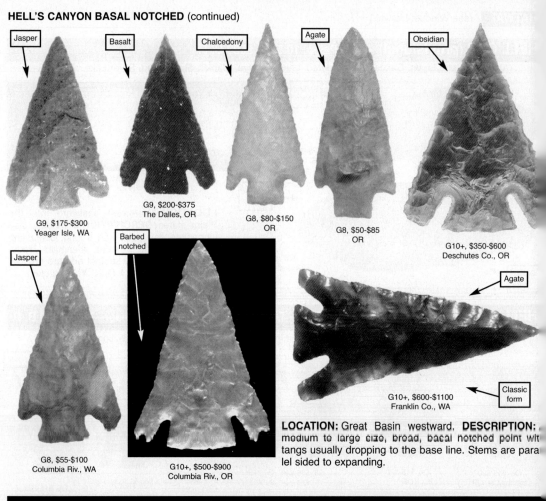

Jasper
G9, $175-$300
Yeager Isle, WA

Basalt
G9, $200-$375
The Dalles, OR

Chalcedony
G8, $80-$150
OR

Agate
G8, $50-$85
OR

Obsidian
G10+, $350-$600
Deschutes Co., OR

Jasper
G8, $55-$100
Columbia Riv., WA

Barbed notched
G10+, $500-$900
Columbia Riv., OR

Agate

Classic form
G10+, $600-$1100
Franklin Co., WA

LOCATION: Great Basin westward. **DESCRIPTION:** medium to large size, broad, basal notched point with tangs usually dropping to the base line. Stems are parallel sided to expanding.

HELL'S CANYON CORNER NOTCHED - Develop. to Historic, Phase, 1200 - 200 B. P.

(Also see Bullhead, Elko Corner Notched & Quillomene Bar, Wendover)

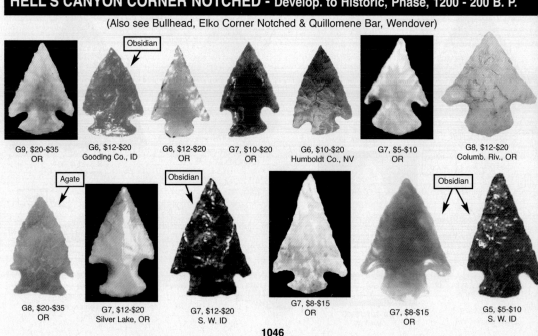

G9, $20-$35
OR

Obsidian
G6, $12-$20
Gooding Co., ID

G6, $12-$20
OR

G7, $10-$20
OR

G6, $10-$20
Humboldt Co., NV

G7, $5-$10
OR

G8, $12-$20
Columb. Riv., OR

Agate
G8, $20-$35
OR

G7, $12-$20
Silver Lake, OR

Obsidian
G7, $12-$20
S. W. ID

G7, $8-$15
OR

G7, $8-$15
OR

Obsidian
G5, $5-$10
S. W. ID

Obsidian

Obsidian

Chalcedony

Obsidian

Chalcedony

G8, $12-$20
OR

G6, $2-$5
OR

G7, $15-$25
OR

G5, $2-$5
Gooding Co., ID

G5, $5-$10
S. W. ID

G6, $12-$20
OR

Obsidian

Obsidian

Tip nick

G5, $2-$5
S. W, ID

G6, $2-$5
S. W, ID

G8, $15-$30
S. W, ID

G5, $1-$2
S. W. ID

G6, $15-$25
S. W. ID

LOCATION: Great Basin westward. **DESCRIPTION:** A medium to large size, broad, corner notched point with barbed shoulders and an expanding stem. Shoulder barbs are rounded. First recognized and found on Hell's Canyon Reservoir in Idaho.

HENDRICKS (provisional) - Late Archaic to Woodland, 3500 - 1500 B. P.

(Also see Elko Corner Notched, Merrybell and Snake River)

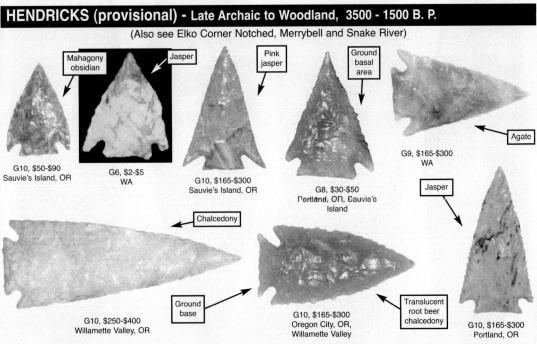

Mahagony obsidian

Jasper

Pink jasper

Ground basal area

G10, $50-$90
Sauvie's Island, OR

G6, $2-$5
WA

G10, $165-$300
Sauvie's Island, OR

G8, $30-$50
Portland, OR, Sauvie's Island

Agate

G9, $165-$300
WA

Jasper

Chalcedony

Ground base

G10, $250-$400
Willamette Valley, OR

G10, $165-$300
Oregon City, OR,
Willamette Valley

Translucent root beer chalcedony

G10, $165-$300
Portland, OR

LOCATION: Northern Willamette Valley in Oregon. **DESCRIPTION:** A medium sized corner notched point with fine blade serrations. Basal corners and barbs are sharp. Bases are straight and are usually ground. Similar to the *Snake River* point which mostly have concave bases. **I.D. KEY:** Location and straight bases and quality.

F
W

IMPORTANT: High Desert Knives shown **HALF** size.

Obsidian

G8, $350-$600
Harney Co., OR

Obsidian

G9, $450-$800
Lake Co., OR

Banded obsidian

Obsidian

G6, $50-$80
S. OR

Black obsidian

Obsidian

Banded obsidian

G10, $550-$1000
Harney Co., OR

G10+, $650-$1200
Harney Co., OR

G9, $800-$1500
Lake Co., OR

G10, $2000-$3500
Lake Co., OR

LOCATION: Columbia River in Washington, E. Calif. and all of Nevada. **DESCRIPTION:** A very large biface knife blade with excurvate sides and a rounded to pointed base. Flaking quality is usually very high. This knife was made by several pre-historic groups in the Great Basin, Columbia Plateau and adjoining territory. Formational flaking, pressure flaking, blade edge alignment and silhouette profiles are a close approximation of each other. Until there is a manufacturing formulation, these blades cannot be assigned to any one culture or group unless found in situ.

HOUX CONTRACTING STEM - Mid-Archaic to Developmental, 4500 - 1500 B. P.

(Also see Coquille, Gatecliff, Gypsum Cave & Sierra Contracting Stem)

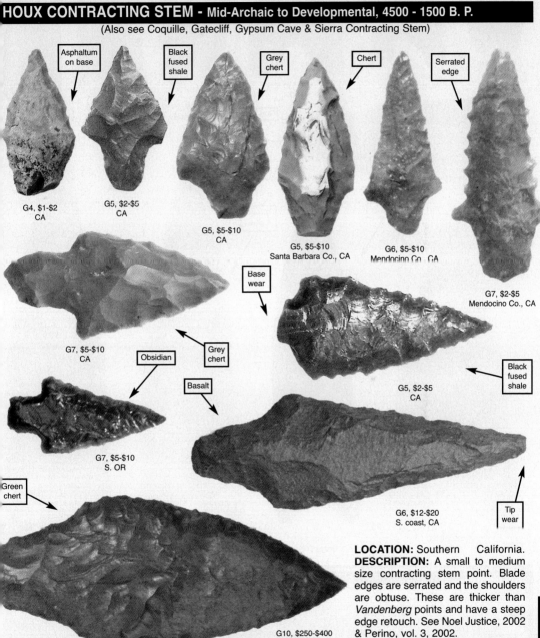

Asphaltum on base

G4, $1-$2
CA

G5, $2-$5
CA

Black fused shale

G5, $5-$10
CA

Grey chert

G5, $5-$10
Santa Barbara Co., CA

Chert

G6, $5-$10
Mendocino Co. CA

Serrated edge

G7, $2-$5
Mendocino Co., CA

G7, $5-$10
CA

Obsidian

Grey chert

Basalt

Base wear

G5, $2-$5
CA

Black fused shale

G7, $5-$10
S. OR

Green chert

G6, $12-$20
S. coast, CA

Tip wear

G10, $250-$400
S. Oregon coast

LOCATION: Southern California. **DESCRIPTION:** A small to medium size contracting stem point. Blade edges are serrated and the shoulders are obtuse. These are thicker than *Vandenberg* points and have a steep edge retouch. See Noel Justice, 2002 & Perino, vol. 3, 2002.

F
W

HUMBOLDT-BASAL NOTCHED - Early to mid-Archaic, 8000 - 5000 B. P.

(Also see Black Rock Concave, Buchanan Eared, Clovis, Pinto Basin)

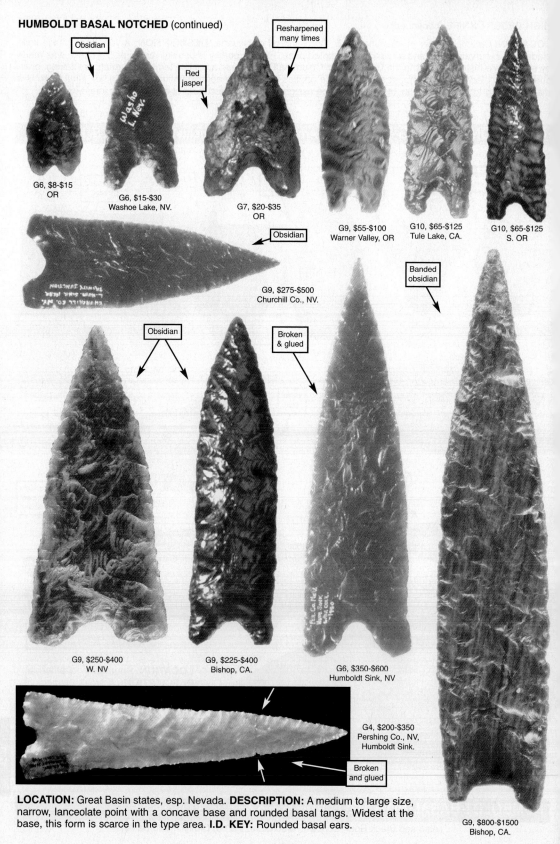

Obsidian

G6, $8-$15
OR

Washo L. Nev.

G6, $15-$30
Washoe Lake, NV.

Red jasper

G7, $20-$35
OR

Resharpened many times

G9, $55-$100
Warner Valley, OR

G10, $65-$125
Tule Lake, CA.

G10, $65-$125
S. OR

Obsidian

G9, $275-$500
Churchill Co., NV.

Banded obsidian

Obsidian

G9, $250-$400
W. NV

Broken & glued

G9, $225-$400
Bishop, CA.

G6, $350-$600
Humboldt Sink, NV

G4, $200-$350
Pershing Co., NV,
Humboldt Sink.

Broken and glued

G9, $800-$1500
Bishop, CA.

LOCATION: Great Basin states, esp. Nevada. **DESCRIPTION:** A medium to large size, narrow, lanceolate point with a concave base and rounded basal tangs. Widest at the base, this form is scarce in the type area. **I.D. KEY:** Rounded basal ears.

HUMBOLDT-CONSTRICTED BASE - Early to mid-Archaic, 7000 - 5000 B. P.

(Also see Buchanan Eared, Early Leaf, Pinto Basin and Pryor Stemmed)

Obs. Obs.
G6, $1-$2
S. W. ID

Basalt
G6, $1-$2
S. W. ID

Obs.
G6, $1-$2
S. W. ID

G6, $5-$10
S. OR

Obs.
G6, $5-$10
S. W. ID

Obs.
G6, $12-$20
S. W. ID

Basalt
G6, $5-$10
S. W. ID

Obs.
G6, $15-$30
S. W. ID

Mahagony obsidian

Obsidian

Obsidian

Obsidian

G8, $20-$35
S. OR

G8, $35-$60
Warner Val.,
OR

G8, $20-$35
Warner Val.,
OR

G7, $12-$20
Cent. OR

G6, $12-$20
S. W. ID

G8, $12-$20
S. W. ID

G5, $5-$10
S. W. ID

Obsidian

G9 $55-$100
Warner Valley, OR

Obsidian

G6, $20-$30
Cent. OR

Black obsidian

Excellent oblique flaking & clear obsidian with black bands

Obsidian

Obsidian

G8, $25-$40
S. OR

G9, $90-$175
Warner Valley, OR

G10, $90-$175
S. W. ID

G10, $600-$1000
Modoc Co., CA

G10+, $1800-$3000
Warner Valley, OR

G7, $80-$150
Modoc Co., CA

F
W

LOCATION: Great Basin states, esp. Nevada. **DESCRIPTION:** A small to medium size, narrow, lanceolate point with a constricted, concave, eared base. Some examples have faint shoulders. Parallel, oblique flaking occurs on many examples.

HUMBOLDT EXPANDED BASE (see Buchanan Eared)

HUMBOLDT-TRIANGULAR - Mid to late Archaic, 7000 - 5000 B. P.

(Also see Black Rock Concave, Cascade, Clovis, Early Leaf and Owl Cave)

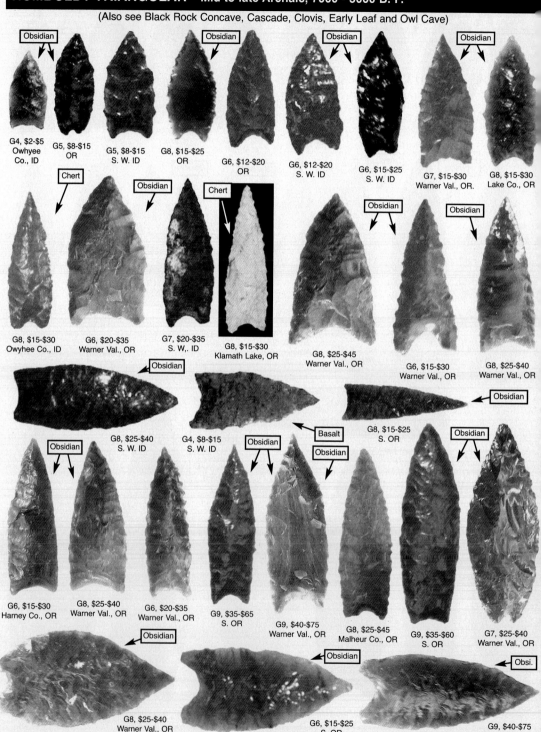

G4, $2-$5
Owhyee Co., ID

G5, $8-$15
OR

G5, $8-$15
S. W. ID

G8, $15-$25
OR

G6, $12-$20
OR

G6, $12-$20
S. W. ID

G6, $15-$25
S. W. ID

G7, $15-$30
Warner Val., OR.

G8, $15-$30
Lake Co., OR

G8, $15-$30
Owyhee Co., ID

G6, $20-$35
Warner Val., OR

G7, $20-$35
S. W,. ID

G8, $15-$30
Klamath Lake, OR

G8, $25-$45
Warner Val., OR

G6, $15-$30
Warner Val., OR

G8, $25-$40
Warner Val., OR

G8, $25-$40
S. W. ID

G4, $8-$15
S. W. ID

G8, $15-$25
S. OR

G6, $15-$30
Harney Co., OR

G8, $25-$40
Warner Val., OR

G6, $20-$35
Warner Val., OR

G9, $35-$65
S. OR

G9, $40-$75
Warner Val., OR

G8, $25-$45
Malheur Co., OR

G9, $35-$60
S. OR

G7, $25-$40
Warner Val., OR

G8, $25-$40
Warner Val., OR

G6, $15-$25
S. OR

G9, $40-$75
Warner Val., OR

LOCATION: Great Basin states, esp. Nevada. **DESCRIPTION:** A small to medium size, narrow, lanceolate point with a tapered, concave base. Basal concavity can be slight to extreme. Many examples have high quality oblique parallel flaking.

Obsidian

Obsidian

Obsidian

Obsidian

Obsidian

G9, $45-$80
S. OR

G7, $30-$50
Owyhee Co., ID

G8, $40-$70
Humboldt Co., NV

G6, $25-$40
S. OR

G9, $65-$125
S. OR

G7, $30-$50
Crump Lake, OR

G8, $55-$100
S. OR

Obsidian

Obsidian

G7 $20-$35
S. OR

G7, $15-$30
S. OR

Obsidian

Obsidian

Obsidian

Jasper

G7, $35-$60
S. OR

G8, $50-$90
S. OR

G8, $50-$90
S. OR

G7, $20-$35
S. OR

G10, $700-$1300
Lake Co., OR

G10, $700-$1300
Humboldt Co., NV

Obsidian

Diagonal
flaking

G10+, $1200-$2000
CA

FW

ISHI - Historic Phase, 100 - 80 B.P.

(Also see Glass)

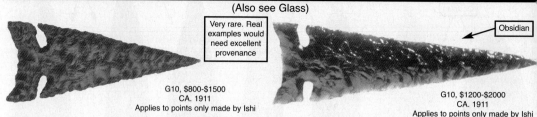

Very rare. Real examples would need excellent provenance

Obsidian

G10, $800-$1500
CA. 1911
Applies to points only made by Ishi

G10, $1200-$2000
CA. 1911
Applies to points only made by Ishi

LOCATION: Northern California. **DESCRIPTION:** A medium size, thin, corner to side notched point with deep notches set close to the base. Bases vary from concave to convex. Ishi, known as the last wild Indian in North America and the last survivor of his tribe, in fear for his life, turned himself in to the local authorities in Oroville, California. The year was 1911. The University of California museum offered him sanctuary for the rest of his life. While there, he knapped arrowpoints which were given to friends and acquaintances he met at the museum. For more information, read "Ishi in Two Worlds", 1963, University of Calif. Press at Berkeley.

JALAMA SIDE NOTCHED - Early to mid-Archaic, 6000 - 4500 B. P.

(Also see Bitterroot, Cold Springs, Diablo Canyon, Northern Side Notched, Pluvial Lakes Side)

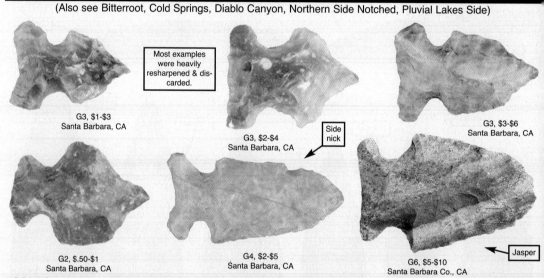

Most examples were heavily resharpened & discarded.

G3, $1-$3
Santa Barbara, CA

G3, $2-$4
Santa Barbara, CA

Side nick

G3, $3-$6
Santa Barbara, CA

G2, $.50-$1
Santa Barbara, CA

G4, $2-$5
Santa Barbara, CA

G6, $5-$10
Santa Barbara Co., CA

Jasper

LOCATION: Pacific coast of southern California. **DESCRIPTION:** A medium to large side notched point with straight to concave bases. Notches are close to the base and are deep and broad producing basal ears on some examples. Shoulders are horizontal to tapered. Grinding in the hafting area is rare. **I.D. KEY:** Broad notches, eared base. See Noel Justice, 2002.

KELSEY CREEK BARBED - Early to mid-Archaic, 6000 - 4500 B. P.

(Also see Big Valley Stemmed and Mayacmas Corner Notched, McGillivray)

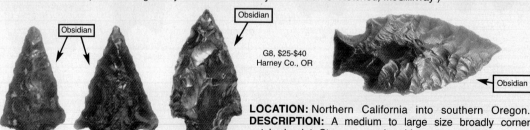

Obsidian

Obsidian

G8, $25-$40
Harney Co., OR

Obsidian

G5, $8-$15
N. CA

G6, $12-$20
N. CA

G8, $25-$40
Napa Valley, CA

LOCATION: Northern California into southern Oregon. **DESCRIPTION:** A medium to large size broadly corner notched point. Stems expand and bases are straight to convex. Basal corners are sharp to rounded. Shoulders are horizontal to strongly barbed. Stems can be fairly long on some examples. See Noel Justice, 2002.

KELSEY CREEK BARBED (continued)

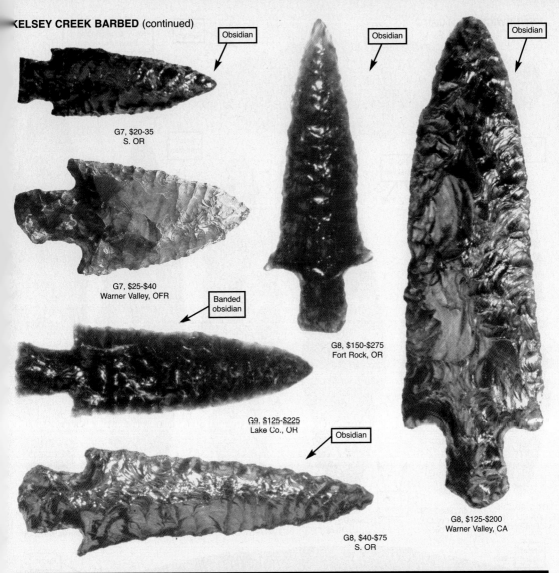

Obsidian

G7, $20-35
S. OR

Obsidian

G7, $25-$40
Warner Valley, OFR

Banded obsidian

G9, $125-$225
Lake Co., OR

Obsidian

G8, $150-$275
Fort Rock, OR

Obsidian

G8, $40-$75
S. OR

G8, $125-$200
Warner Valley, CA

KENNEWICK (provisional)- Paleo, 11,000 - 9000 B.P.

(Also see Cascade, Cordilleran, Cougar Mountain, Early Leaf, Lind Coulee, Parman & Windust)

G10, $375-$700
Lake Co., OR

Ground stem

LOCATION: Columbia Plateau in Washington, south into Oregon, Nevada and Utah. **DESCRIPTION:** The lanceolate form of *Windust* or *Lind Coulee*. A medium to large size, thin, double pointed lanceolate blade with convex sides. The basal end is usually a little more rounded than the tip. Flaking is to a median ridge with a very thin to medium thin cross-section. Stem sides are heavily ground for hafting. Previously known as part of the *Cordilleran Cascade* group, it was usually identified as a willow leaf. **I.D. KEY:** Basal grinding and double pointed form. A similar point was found in the hip of "Kennewick Man," a 9300 year old Caucasoid. Named by Jim Hogue and John Cockrell. Similar points were found at the lowest levels in Cougar Mtn. Cave.

F
W

Orange jasper

Heavy edge grinding all the way to the tip

G5, $55-$100
S. OR

Basal area is ground

Black obsidian

Black obsidian

Edge wear

Black obsidian

G7, $125-$225
Lake Co., OR, Fort Rock

G7, $90-$175
Lake Co., OR, Fort Rock

Ground stem

G8, $200-$325
Lake Co., OR, Fort Rock

G7, $125-$200
S.W. OR

Ground stem

G9, $250-$400
Lake Co., OR, Fort Rock

Basal fluting

G9, $350-$600
Warner Valley, OR

Ground stem

Basalt

G8, $275-$500
N. NV

KLICKITAT - Historic Phase, 300 - 160 B.P.

(Also see Dagger, Diamond-Back, Nottoway and One-Que)

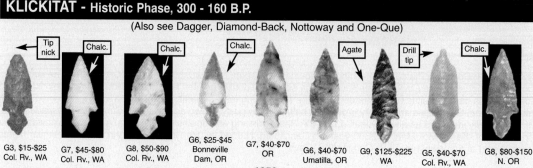

Tip nick

Chalc.

Chalc.

Chalc.

Agate

Drill tip

Chalc.

G3, $15-$25
Col. Rv., WA

G7, $45-$80
Col. Rv., WA

G8, $50-$90
Col. Rv., WA

G6, $25-$45
Bonneville Dam, OR

G7, $40-$70
OR

G6, $40-$70
Umatilla, OR

G9, $125-$225
WA

G5, $40-$70
Col. Rv., WA

G8, $80-$150
N. OR

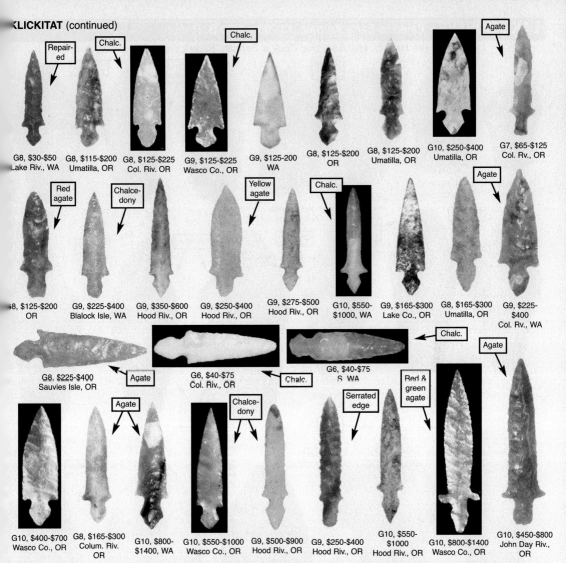

Repaired

Chalc.

Chalc.

Agate

G8, $30-$50
Lake Riv., WA

G8, $115-$200
Umatilla, OR

G8, $125-$225
Col. Riv. OR

G9, $125-$225
Wasco Co., OR

G9, $125-200
WA

G8, $125-$200
OR

G8, $125-$200
Umatilla, OR

G10, $250-$400
Umatilla, OR

G7, $65-$125
Col. Rv., OR

Red agate

Chalcedony

Yellow agate

Chalc.

Agate

8, $125-$200
OR

G9, $225-$400
Blalock Isle, WA

G9, $350-$600
Hood Riv., OR

G9, $250-$400
Hood Riv., OR

G9, $275-$500
Hood Riv., OR

G10, $550-$1000, WA

G9, $165-$300
Lake Co., OR

G8, $165-$300
Umatilla, OR

G9, $225-$400
Col. Rv., WA

G8, $225-$400
Sauvies Isle, OR

Agate

G6, $40-$75
Col. Riv., OR

Chalc.

G6, $40-$75
S WA

Chalc.

Agate

Agate

Chalcedony

Serrated edge

Red & green agate

Agate

G10, $400-$700
Wasco Co., OR

G8, $165-$300
Colum. Riv. OR

G10, $800-$1400, WA

G10, $550-$1000
Wasco Co., OR

G9, $500-$900
Hood Riv., OR

G9, $250-$400
Hood Riv., OR

G10, $550-$1000
Hood Riv., OR

G10, $800-$1400
Wasco Co., OR

G10, $450-$800
John Day Riv., OR

LOCATION: The Columbia River in Oregon and Washington. **DESCRIPTION:** A rare, small size, narrow, thin, lance-olate, barbed arrow point with a usually diamond shaped base. Bases can also be rectangular with horizontal barbs. Some examples have excellent oblique, parallel flaking. Other base forms would fall under the Dagger type.

LADY ISLAND PENTAGONAL (provisional) - Late Archaic to Classic, 2500 - 400 B. P.

(Also see Merrybell)

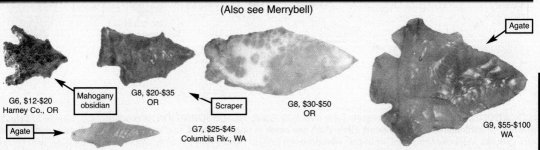

Agate

G6, $12-$20
Harney Co., OR

Mahogany obsidian

G8, $20-$35
OR

Scraper

G8, $30-$50
OR

Agate

G7, $25-$45
Columbia Riv., WA

G9, $55-$100
WA

F
W

LOCATION: Type site is Lady Island, Columbia River. Oregon and Washington. **DESCRIPTION:** All points are under-cut at the shoulder to form a single serration cutter. A "shoulder" is formed in the blade by resharpening. This modification can be found on dart and arrow points in the lower Columbia and other parts of the northwest.

(Also see Haskett, Hell Gap, Lind Coulee, Parman, Silver Lake and Windust)

G3, $2-$5
Iron Co., UT

G3, $12-$20
Iron Co., UT

G5, $20-$35
Lake Co., OR

Ground stem

G5, $20-$35
Owens Valley, CA

Ground stem

G4, $15-$25
Lake Co., OR

G6, $15-$25
S. OR

Obsidian

G6, $25-$40
S. OR

Obsidian

G6, $8-$15
Lake Co., OR

G6, $5-$10
S. OR

Chisel tip

G5, $15-$25
S. OR

Obsidian

Obsidian

Ground stem

G6, $25-$40
Black Rock Desert, NV

G5, $12-$20
Lake Co., OR

Basalt

G5, $12-$20
S. W. ID

Basalt

Chisel tip

Obsidian

G7, $40-$70
Humboldt Co., NV

Ground stem

G8, $150-$250
S. OR

Ground stem

G7, $40-$70
S. OR

Obsidian

Chert

Obsidian

G6, $40-$70
San Bernadino Co., CA

Ground stem

G8, $35-$65
S. OR

Classic example

Obsidian

G7, $75-$140
Lake Co., OR

G6, $65-$120
Lake Co., OR

LOCATION: S.E. Calif. to Sou. Oregon. Type site: S.E. California. **DESCRIPTION:** A medium size, narrow to broad, parallel to contracting stemmed point. Shoulders are weak to none. Stem is much longer than the blade. Basal sides are ground. Most examples are worn-out, resharpened points. Found with *Butterfly Crescents*. Associated with Bison hunting. One of the oldest dated projectile point types in the Great Basin. Carbon dated to 13,200 B.P. Variants exist where a burin was removed from opposite sides of the tip, called chisel tips. This type may prove to be worn-out *Parmans*.

AKE MOHAVE (continued)

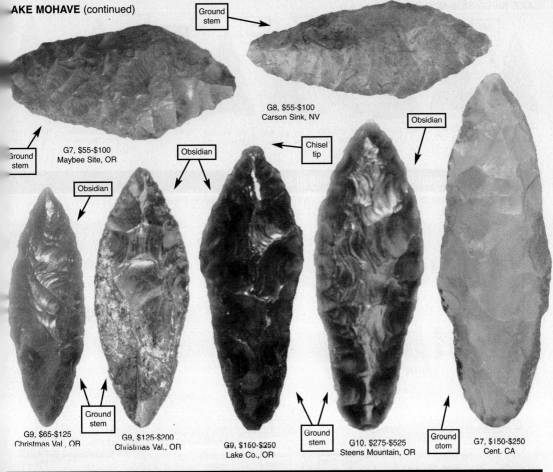

Ground stem

G8, $55-$100
Carson Sink, NV

Obsidian

Ground stem

G7, $55-$100
Maybee Site, OR

Obsidian

Obsidian

Chisel tip

Ground stem

G9, $65-$125
Christmas Val., OR

G9, $125-$200
Christmas Val., OR

G9, $150-$250
Lake Co., OR

Ground stem

Ground stem

G10, $275-$525
Steens Mountain, OR

Ground stem

G7, $150-$250
Cent. CA

LAKE RIVER SIDE NOTCHED (provisional) - Classic to Historic, 700 - 200 B. P.

(Also see Ahsahka, Bear River, Desert, Panoche, Rose Springs, Sauvie's Island Side Notched)

Jasper

Chalc.

Agate

G4, $2-$4
Lewis Riv., WA

G4, $2-$4
Col. Riv., OR

G4, $2-$4
OR

G3, $2-$4
N. OR

G5, $2-$5
WA

G5, $2-$5
N. W. OR

G7, $2-$5
OR

G5, $3-$6
Vancouver, WA

G7, $3-$6
N. W. OR

Red jasper

Agate

Agate

Red jasper

Agate

Jasper

G6, $5-$10
OR

G8, $4-$8
OR

G8, $5-$10
N. OR

G8, $5-$10
Col. Riv., WA

G8, $5-$10
OR

G7, $5-$10
OR

G8, $4-$8
Col. Rv., OR

G7, $4-$8
Vancouver, WA

G7, $2-$4
Col. Rv., OR

LOCATION: Lower Columbia River and some tributaries near the name site, Lake River near Vancouver, Wash.
DESCRIPTION: A small triangular arrow point that has low placed side notches that vary in depth and width. The bases are convex to concave with straight being dominant. These points are made on narrow to widely triangular pre-forms and flakes. This type is smaller, on average, than the *Desert Side Notched* series, but is a localized variant of that type. Despite the great deal of variation in the silhouette of these points, they were found together in caches. This point was found in situ with late era trade beads. Defined and named in 2001 by A. Erickson, J.L. Hogue and R. Snyder.

F W

LAKE RIVER SIDE NOTCHED (continued)

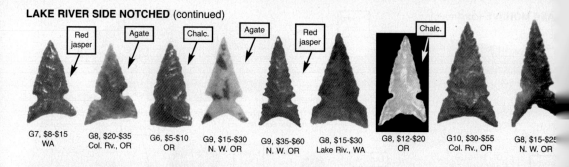

Red jasper

Agate

Chalc.

Agate

Red jasper

Chalc.

G7, $8-$15
WA

G8, $20-$35
Col. Rv., OR

G6, $5-$10
OR

G9, $15-$30
N. W. OR

G9, $35-$60
N. W. OR

G8, $15-$30
Lake Riv., WA

G8, $12-$20
OR

G10, $30-$55
Col. Rv., OR

G8, $15-$25
N. W. OR

LANCET - Paleo to Archaic, 11,500 - 5000 B. P.

(Also see Burin, Chopper, Drill, Graver, Hand Axe, Perforator, Paleo Knife and Scraper)

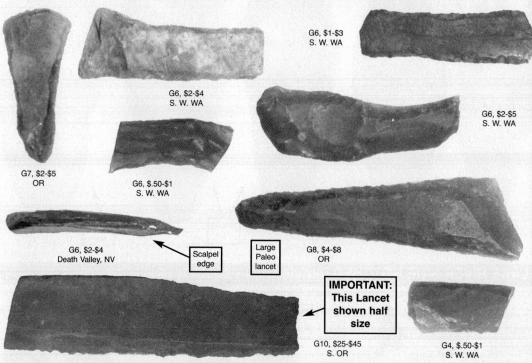

G6, $1-$3
S. W. WA

G6, $2-$4
S. W. WA

G6, $2-$5
S. W. WA

G7, $2-$5
OR

G6, $.50-$1
S. W. WA

G6, $2-$4
Death Valley, NV

Scalpel edge

Large Paleo lancet

G8, $4-$8
OR

IMPORTANT: This Lancet shown half size

G10, $25-$45
S. OR

G4, $.50-$1
S. W. WA

LOCATION: Great Basin westward. **DESCRIPTION:** A medium to large size sliver used as a knife for cutting. Recent experiments proved that these knives were sharper than a surgeon's scalpel. Similar to *Burins* which are fractured at one end to produce a sharp point.

LEWIS RIVER SHORT STEMMED (provisional) - Classic to Historic, 700 - 200 B. P.

(Also see Columbia River Pin Stem, Gunther, Rabbit Island, Rose Springs Stemmed)

Agate

G6, $1-$3
OR

G6, $1-$3
N. OR

G6, $1-$3
Col. Rv., OR

G6, $2-$4
S. OR coast

G8, $2-$4
Lewis Riv., WA

G5, $2-$4
Lewis Riv., WA

G5, $2-$4
Lewis Riv., WA

G8, $2-$4
Lewis Riv., WA

G6, $2-$4
Lewis Riv., WA

Agate

G10, $12-$20
N. OR

Chalc.

G8, $6-$12
Lewis Riv., WA

G8, $5-$10
John Day
Riv., OR

G5, $2-$4
Lewis Riv.,
WA

LEWIS RIVER SHORT STEMMED (continued)

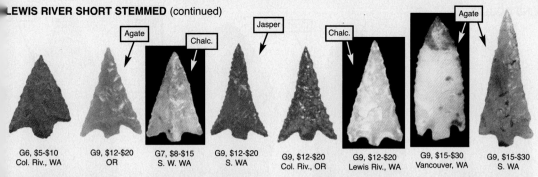

G6, $5-$10
Col. Riv., WA

G9, $12-$20
OR

G7, $8-$15
S. W. WA

G9, $12-$20
S. WA

G9, $12-$20
Col. Riv., OR

G9, $12-$20
Lewis Riv., WA

G9, $15-$30
Vancouver, WA

G9, $15-$30
S. WA

LOCATION: Lower Columbia River and tributaries in Oregon and Washington. **DESCRIPTION:** This point is a small triangular arrow point with straight to slightly convex blade edges. The shoulders are straight to slightly barbed. The stems are short, square or occasionally contracting to a rounded base. Many bases are truncated and finished with short steep strokes. Found in situ with late era trade beads. Defined and named by Jim Hogue in 2000.

LIND COULEE - Late Paleo, 11,000 - 10,500 B.P.

(Also see Año Nuevo, Cougar Mountain, Early Stemmed, Haskett, Hell Gap, Kennewick, Lake Mohave, Parman, Silver Lake and Windust)

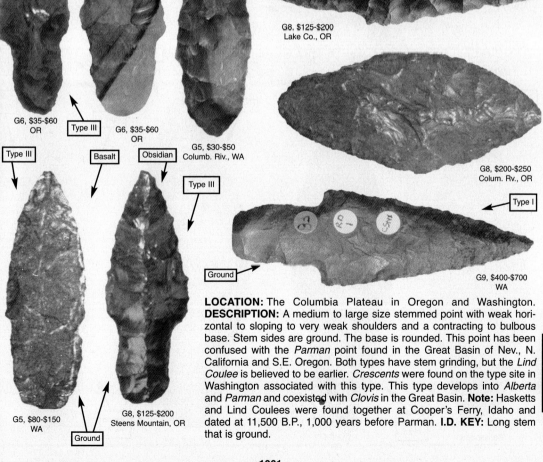

G6, $35-$60
OR

G6, $35-$60
OR

G5, $30-$50
Columb. Riv., WA

G8, $125-$200
Lake Co., OR

G8, $200-$250
Colum. Rv., OR

G9, $400-$700
WA

G5, $80-$150
WA

G8, $125-$200
Steens Mountain, OR

LOCATION: The Columbia Plateau in Oregon and Washington. **DESCRIPTION:** A medium to large size stemmed point with weak horizontal to sloping to very weak shoulders and a contracting to bulbous base. Stem sides are ground. The base is rounded. This point has been confused with the *Parman* point found in the Great Basin of Nev., N. California and S.E. Oregon. Both types have stem grinding, but the *Lind Coulee* is believed to be earlier. *Crescents* were found on the type site in Washington associated with this type. This type develops into *Alberta* and *Parman* and coexisted with *Clovis* in the Great Basin. **Note:** Hasketts and Lind Coulees were found together at Cooper's Ferry, Idaho and dated at 11,500 B.P., 1,000 years before Parman. **I.D. KEY:** Long stem that is ground.

F
W

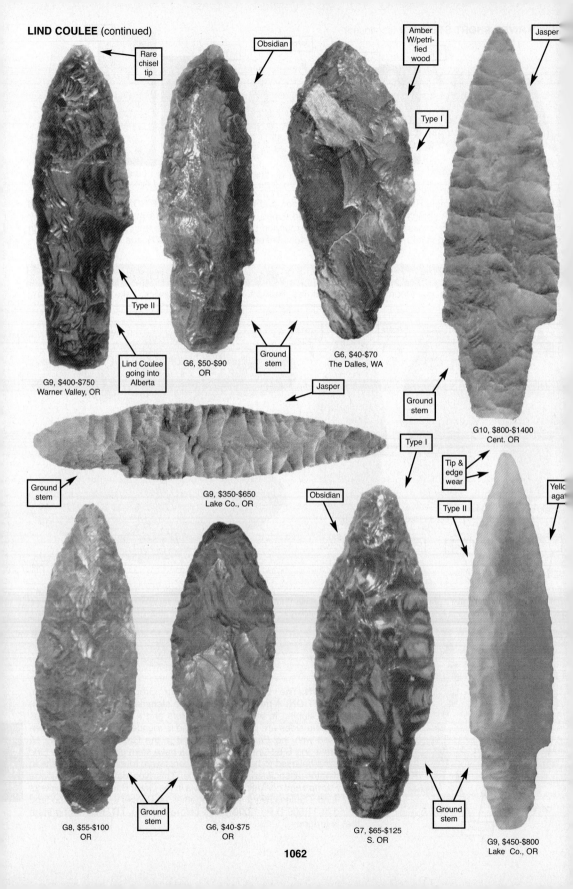

LIND COULEE (continued)

Rare chisel tip

Obsidian

Amber W/petrified wood

Jasper

Type I

Type II

Lind Coulee going into Alberta

G9, $400-$750
Warner Valley, OR

Ground stem

G6, $50-$90
OR

G6, $40-$70
The Dalles, WA

Jasper

Ground stem

G10, $800-$1400
Cent. OR

Ground stem

G9, $350-$650
Lake Co., OR

Type I

Obsidian

Tip & edge wear

Type II

Yellow agate

Ground stem

G8, $55-$100
OR

Ground stem

G6, $40-$75
OR

G7, $65-$125
S. OR

Ground stem

G9, $450-$800
Lake Co., OR

1062

G7, $175-$300
Warner Valley, OR

Ground stem

Jasper

Ground

G9, $250-$450
Coqwlitz Co., WA

Tip wear

First stage with only one resharpening

Obsidian

Type III

Reef agate

Obsidian

Found with a Haskett

Ground stem

Ground stem & base

G9, $275-$500
S. ID/N. UT

G10, $500-$900
Cent. OR

G9, $650-$1200
N. Central OR

F
W

G9, $350-$650
Lake Co., OR

MAHKIN SHOULDERED LANCEOLATE (provisional) - Early Archaic, 6500 - 5000 B. P.

(Also see Cascade Shouldered, Fish Gutter, Hell Gap, Plateau Pentagonal, Wahmuza & Windust/Mahkin)

Agate

Red jasper

Obsidian

Basalt

G4, $12-$20
Columb. Plat., WA

G6, $20-$35
Clearwater Riv., ID

G6, $15-$30
OR

Bog agate

G9, $35-$65
Lake Co., OR

G8, $55-$100
OR

Basalt

G6, $35-$65
OR

G8, $55-$100
WA

Obsidian

G8, $30-$50
N. OR

G6, $25-$40
S. OR

LOCATION: Oregon & Washington. **DESCRIPTION:** A medium to large size lanceolate point with a rounded base and very weak, but definite shoulders. Stems are usually ground. A very rare type as part of the *Cascade* series.

(Also see Cascade, Cottonwood, Gold Hill, and Trojan)

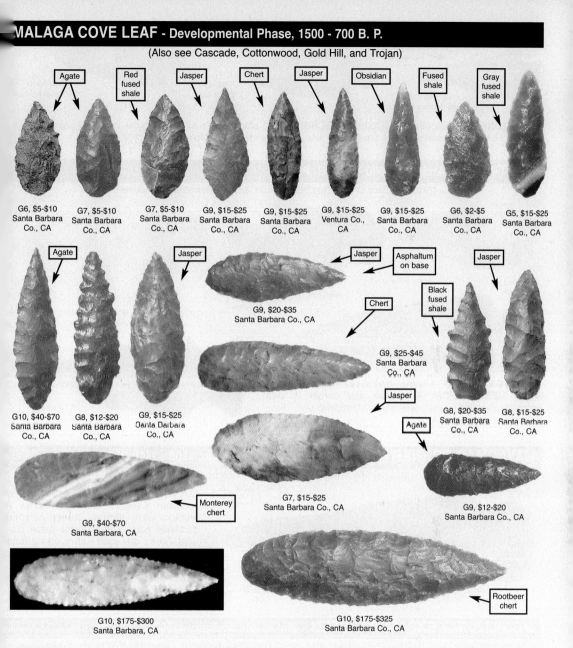

Agate

Red fused shale

Jasper

Chert

Jasper

Obsidian

Fused shale

Gray fused shale

G6, $5-$10
Santa Barbara
Co., CA

G7, $5-$10
Santa Barbara
Co., CA

G7, $5-$10
Santa Barbara
Co., CA

G9, $15-$25
Santa Barbara
Co., CA

G9, $15-$25
Santa Barbara
Co., CA

G9, $15-$25
Ventura Co.,
CA

G9, $15-$25
Santa Barbara
Co., CA

G6, $2-$5
Santa Barbara
Co., CA

G5, $15-$25
Santa Barbara
Co., CA

Agate

Jasper

Jasper

Asphaltum on base

Jasper

Chert

Black fused shale

G9, $20-$35
Santa Barbara Co., CA

G9, $25-$45
Santa Barbara
Co., CA

Jasper

G10, $40-$70
Santa Barbara
Co., CA

G8, $12-$20
Santa Barbara
Co., CA

G9, $15-$25
Santa Barbara
Co., CA

G8, $20-$35
Santa Barbara
Co., CA

G8, $15-$25
Santa Barbara
Co., CA

Agate

Monterey chert

G7, $15-$25
Santa Barbara Co., CA

G9, $12-$20
Santa Barbara Co., CA

G9, $40-$70
Santa Barbara, CA

G10, $175-$300
Santa Barbara, CA

Rootbeer chert

G10, $175-$325
Santa Barbara Co., CA

LOCATION: Coastal southern California. **DESCRIPTION:** A small to medium size lanceolate point with a rounded to pointed base. Some examples are serrated. Similar to the *Gold Hill* point found in Oregon. Also known as the *Coastal Cottonwood* point. See Noel Justice, 2002.

(Also see Columbia Plateau, Rose Springs, Steamboat Lanceolate, Wallula Gap)

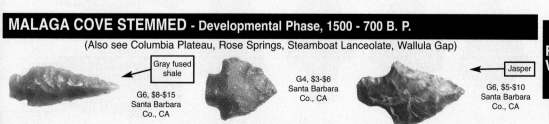

Gray fused shale

Jasper

G6, $8-$15
Santa Barbara
Co., CA

G4, $3-$6
Santa Barbara
Co., CA

G6, $5-$10
Santa Barbara
Co., CA

F
W

MALAGA COVE STEMMED (continued)

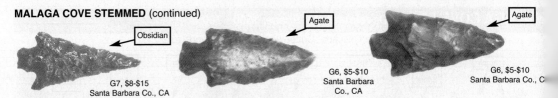

G7, $8-$15
Santa Barbara Co., CA

G6, $5-$10
Santa Barbara Co., CA

G6, $5-$10
Santa Barbara Co., C

LOCATION: Coastal southern California. **DESCRIPTION:** A small size, narrow, triangular stemmed point with ho[r]izontal to barbed shoulders. Stems are parallel sided to expanding. See Noel Justice, 2002.

MARTIS - Late Archaic, 3000 - 1500 B. P.

(Also see Elko Corner Notched, Hell's Canyon, Merrybell, Wendover)

G6, $5-$10
OR

G6, $5-$10
Harney Co., OR

Red jasper

G6, $8-$15
Susanville, CA

G9, $20-$35
S. OR

LOCATION: Western Arizona northward into the Great Basin. **DESCRIPTION:** A medium size corner to side notched point with small tapered to horizontal shoulders. Bases are often asymmetrical.

G7, $15-$20
S. OR

MAYACMAS CORNER NOTCHED - Mid to late Archaic, 4500 - 2500 B. P.

(Also see Big Valley and Kelsey Creek barbed & McGillivray)

Obsidian

LOCATION: Northern California into southern Oregon. **DESCRIPTION:** A medium size, narrow, corner notched dart/knife point with rounded basal corners. Stems are short with notching from the basal corners. Shoulders are usually horizontal and barbed but can be rounded. Edges can be serrated. Related to the *Big Valley* point. See Noel Justice, 2002.

G8, $35-$60
OR

MCGILLIVRAY EXPANDING STEM - Mid to late Archaic, 4500 - 2500 B. P.

(Also see Base Tang, Kelsey Creek, Mayacmas, Need Stemmed, Nightfire, Tuolumne, Wendover, Willits Side)

Obsidian

Obsidian

Red jaspe[r]

G7, $5-$10
Harney Co., OR

G4, $1-$2
N. CA

G5, $1-$3
Humboldt Co., NV

G5, $1-$3
N. CA

G5, $2-$5
N. CA

G6, $7-$15
N. CA

Obsidian

MCGILLIVRAY EXPANDING STEM (continued)

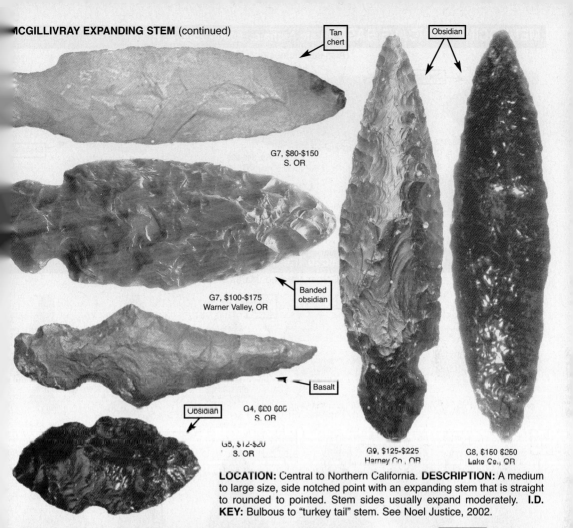

Tan chert

Obsidian

G7, $80-$150
S. OR

G7, $100-$175
Warner Valley, OR

Banded obsidian

Basalt

Obsidian

G4, $20-$35
S. OR

G5, $12-$20
S. OR

G9, $125-$225
Harney Co., OR

G8, $150-$250
Lake Co., OR

LOCATION: Central to Northern California. **DESCRIPTION:** A medium to large size, side notched point with an expanding stem that is straight to rounded to pointed. Stem sides usually expand moderately. **I.D. KEY:** Bulbous to "turkey tail" stem. See Noel Justice, 2002.

MCKEE UNIFACE - Middle Archaic, 5000 - 4000 B. P.

(Also see Cascade, Excelsior, Marybelle & Washoe)

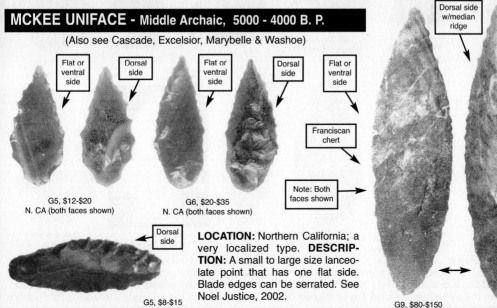

Flat or ventral side

Dorsal side

Flat or ventral side

Dorsal side

Flat or ventral side

Dorsal side w/median ridge

Franciscan chert

Note: Both faces shown

G5, $12-$20
N. CA (both faces shown)

G6, $20-$35
N. CA (both faces shown)

Dorsal side

G5, $8-$15
Susanville, CA

LOCATION: Northern California; a very localized type. **DESCRIPTION:** A small to large size lanceolate point that has one flat side. Blade edges can be serrated. See Noel Justice, 2002.

G9, $80-$150
N. CA

F
W

1067

MENDOCINO CONCAVE BASE - Late Archaic, 5000 - 2500 B. P.

(Also see Humboldt & Triple T)

Obsidian

G5, $12-$20
S. OR

Basalt

G9, $40-$75
OR

Obsidian

G5, $12-$20
Beatty, NV

Obsidian

G5, $12-$20
Cent. OR

LOCATION: Southern to northern California.
DESCRIPTION: A medium size, eared lanceolate dart point with a concave base. A California variant of the *Humboldt* point. See Noel Justice, 2002.

MERRYBELL, VAR. I - Late Archaic to Transitional Phase, 2500 - 1750 B.P.

(Also see Elko Corner Notched, Martis and Snake River)

Agate

Chalc.

Yellow agate

G5, $3-$5
Sauvies, Isle, OR

G7, $4-$7
S. W. WA

G4, $3-$5
Col. Rv., OR

G6, $5-$10
Col. Riv., OR

G6, $5-$10
Col. Rv., OR

G4, $3-$5
OR

G4, $3-$5
OR

Barb nick

Agate

Made into a perforator

Amber agate

Petrified wood

G2, $.50-$1
OR

G6, $7-$15
Vancouver, WA

G8, $15-$25
Portland, OR, Sauvie's Island

G8, $15-$25
OR

G8, $12-$20
OR

G5, $5-$10
OR

Petrified wood

Chalc.

Pearl chalcedony

Quartzite

G8, $15-$25
Columb. Riv., OR

G5, $8-$15
Clatskanie, OR

G4, $4-$8
OR

G4, $4-$8
OR

G8, $15-$25
Columb. Riv., WA

G6, $15-$20
N. OR

LOCATION: Oregon and Washington coasts. Type site is the Merrybell farm on Sauvie's Island near Portland, Oregon. **DESCRIPTION:** A small to medium sized corner notched point with a straight to convex edge. Shoulders become modified with resharpenings. Bases are straight to convex and can be ground. Cross sections are lenticular. Blade edges are sometimes serrated. First published by Ken Matsen in 1968 in the Oregon Archaeological Society's "Screenings," Vol., 17 #7.

Jasper

Carnelian agate

Chalcedony

Agate

Jasper

G6, $8-$15
N. OR

G6, $15-$25
Chehalis, WA

G7, $12-$20
Fern Ridge Res., OR

G6, $8-$15
Sauvie's Isle, OR

G4, $5-$10
N. OR

Basalt

Chalcedony

Jasper

Jasper

Chalc.

G9, $20-$35
Sauvie's Isle, OR

Jasper

G4, $3-$6
N. OR

G6, $15-$30
Columb. Riv., OR

G4, $5-$10
Vancouver, WA

G1, $5-$10
N. OR

G7, $25-$40
N. OR

Agate

Carnelian agate

Merrybell farm, type site,

Agate

G9, $45-$80
Columbia Riv., OR,
Priest Rapid

Agate

Merrybell farm, type site, Portland, OR.

G10, $25-$40
Sauvie's Isle, OR

G8, $25-$40
Sauvie's Isle, OR

G9, $30-$55
Sauvie's Isle, OR

G7, $35-$65
Columbia Riv., OR

MERRYBELL, VAR. II - Late Archaic to Transitional Phase, 2500 - 1750 B.P.

(Also see Cold Springs, Uinta and Wendover)

Agate

F
W

G3, $1-$2
Col. Rv., OR, agate

G3, $1-$2
OR

G3, $1-$2
N. OR, agate

G4, $1-$3
OR

G4, $3-$5
OR

LOCATION: Oregon and Washington coasts. **DESCRIPTION:** A small to medium sized widely side-notched point with a convex base. Stem sides and base can be ground. Blade edges are convex to incurvate and can be serrated.

MERRYBELL, VAR. II (continued)

G3, $1-$3
OR

G5, $2-$5
OR

Agate

G4, $3-$7
Sauvie's Isle, OR

G5, $4-$8
Clatskanie Riv., OR

G6, $5-$10
Sauvie's Isle, OR

Red
jasper

G6, $6-$10
OR

Agate

G8, $8-$20
OR

G7, $12-$2
Col. Rv., O

G5, $6-$1
OR

G5, $6-$10
Portland, OR

G7, $12-$20
Cent. OR

Red
obsidian

Ground
basal

Tip
nick

Chalcedony

Jasper

G7, $12-$20
OR

G9, $30-$50
OR

G9, $45-$80
OR

G7, $20-$35
OR

G10, $40-$75
Columbia Riv., OR

G9, $30-$50
OR

MERRYBELL, VAR. III - Late Archaic to Transitional Phase, 2500 - 1750 B.P.

(Also see Elko Corner Notched, Elko Eared)

Chalc.

Agate

Red
jasper

G6, $5-$10
Sauvie's Isle, OR

G8, $8-$15
Sauvie's Isle, OR

G8, $8-$15
Sauvie's Isle, OR

G7, $8-$15
OR

G7, $8-$15
OR

G9, $15-$30
Sauvie's Isle, OR

G9, $30-$50
Lower Columbia
Riv., OR

LOCATION: Oregon and Washington coasts. **DESCRIPTION:** A small to medium sized corner notched point with a convex to concave edge. Corner notches are usually wide and start at or slightly above the corner. Bases are concave to notched and almost always smoothed. Cross sections are lenticular. Blade edges are sometimes serrated. **I.D. KEY:** Basal treatment is only significant difference from the type I

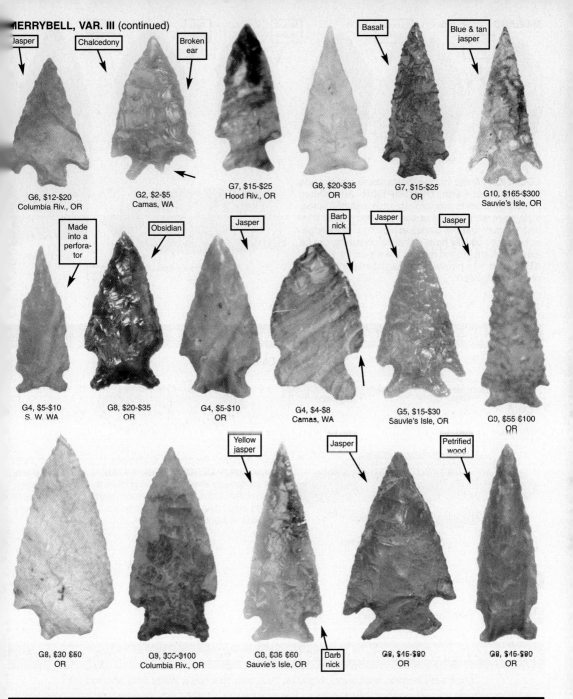

Jasper

Chalcedony

Broken ear

Basalt

Blue & tan jasper

G6, $12-$20
Columbia Riv., OR

G2, $2-$5
Camas, WA

G7, $15-$25
Hood Riv., OR

G8, $20-$35
OR

G7, $15-$25
OR

G10, $165-$300
Sauvie's Isle, OR

Made into a perforator

Obsidian

Jasper

Barb nick

Jasper

Jasper

G4, $5-$10
S. W. WA

G8, $20-$35
OR

G4, $5-$10
OR

G4, $4-$8
Camas, WA

G5, $15-$30
Sauvie's Isle, OR

G0, $55 $100
OR

Yellow jasper

Jasper

Petrified wood

G8, $30 $50
OR

O9, $55-$100
Columbia Riv., OR

G8, $35 $60
Sauvie's Isle, OR

Barb nick

G8, $45-$80
OR

G8, $45-$80
OR

MIDLAND - Transitional Paleo, 10,900 - 10,200 B. P.

(Also see Celilo Falls, Folsom, Goshen, Milnesand, Plainview and Spedis)

G4, $12-$20
OR

G10, $225-$400
WA

G7, $40-$70
OR

G6, $30-$50
Col. Riv., OR

G4, $35-$60
OR

F W

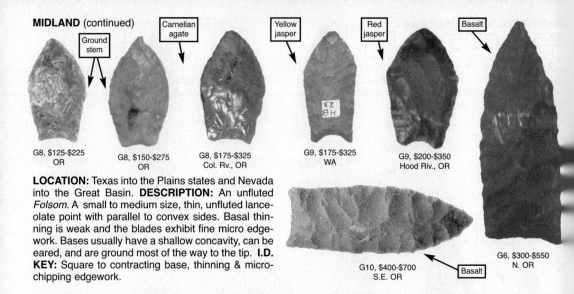

MIDLAND (continued)

Ground stem

Carnelian agate

Yellow jasper

Red jasper

Basalt

G8, $125-$225
OR

G8, $150-$275
OR

G8, $175-$325
Col. Rv., OR

G9, $175-$325
WA

G9, $200-$350
Hood Riv., OR

G10, $400-$700
S.E. OR

Basalt

G6, $300-$550
N. OR

Basalt

LOCATION: Texas into the Plains states and Nevada into the Great Basin. **DESCRIPTION:** An unfluted *Folsom*. A small to medium size, thin, unfluted lanceolate point with parallel to convex sides. Basal thinning is weak and the blades exhibit fine micro edgework. Bases usually have a shallow concavity, can be eared, and are ground most of the way to the tip. **I.D. KEY:** Square to contracting base, thinning & microchipping edgework.

MINIATURE BLADE - Classic to Historic Phase, 500 - 100 B. P.

(Also see Cascade)

G9, $15-$25 ea.
Coastal WA

G9, $30-$50
Coastal OR

LOCATION: Northern California into Oregon and Washington. **DESCRIPTION:** A small size, double pointed lanceolate blade made in miniature to possibly symbolize the larger dance or Wealth blades. These objects could also have been used as buttons to fasten garmets or nose ornaments.

G9, $55-$100
Lake Co., OR

MOLALLA (See Gunther)

MULE EAR (See Columbia Mule Ear)

NEED STEMMED LANCEOLATE - Late Archaic to Developmental , 2500 - 1500 B. P.

(Also see Cascade, McGillivray, Nightfire, Tuolumne Notched & Willits Side Notched)

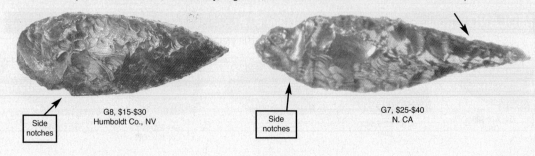

Side notches

G8, $15-$30
Humboldt Co., NV

Side notches

G7, $25-$40
N. CA

NEED STEMMED LANCEOLATE (Continued)

LOCATION: Northern California into Sou. Oregon. **DESCRIPTION:** A medium to large size, narrow leaf shaped point with shallow side notches, and random flaking, that is occasionally oblique. Cross sections are varied, flattened to oval to plano-convex. Bases are tapered to round or straight and somewhat bulbous **I.D. KEY:** Weak side notches and round bulbous base. See Noel Justice, 2002.

Obsidian

Jasper

G8, $150-$250
OR

G9, $400-$750
S. OR

NEWBERRY (See Rabbit Island)

NEZ PERCE (provisional) - Late Prehistoric , 700 - 400 B. P.

(Also see Rose Spring)

NEZ PERCE (continued)

G9, $25-$45
Lewis Co., ID

G9, $25-$45
Lewis Co., ID

G9, $25-$45
Lewis Co., ID

LOCATION: W. Idaho. **DESCRIPTION:** A small, serrated arrowpoint with strong shoulder barbs and an expanded stem. Bases are basically straight. **I.D. KEY:** Size and serrations.

NIGHTFIRE - Early to mid-Archaic, 7000 - 4000 B. P.

(Also see Bitterroot, Cold Springs, Need Stemmed Lanceolate, McGillvray, Northern Side Notched, Tuolumne Notched and Willits Side Notched)

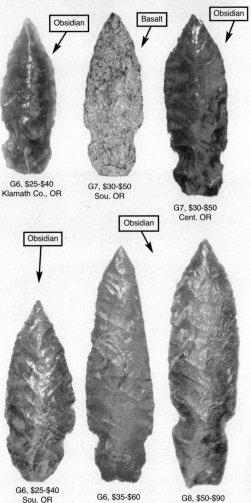

Obsidian

Basalt

Obsidian

G6, $25-$40
Klamath Co., OR

G7, $30-$50
Sou. OR

G7, $30-$50
Cent. OR

Obsidian

Obsidian

G6, $25-$40
Sou. OR

G6, $35-$60
N. CA

G8, $50-$90
OR

F
W

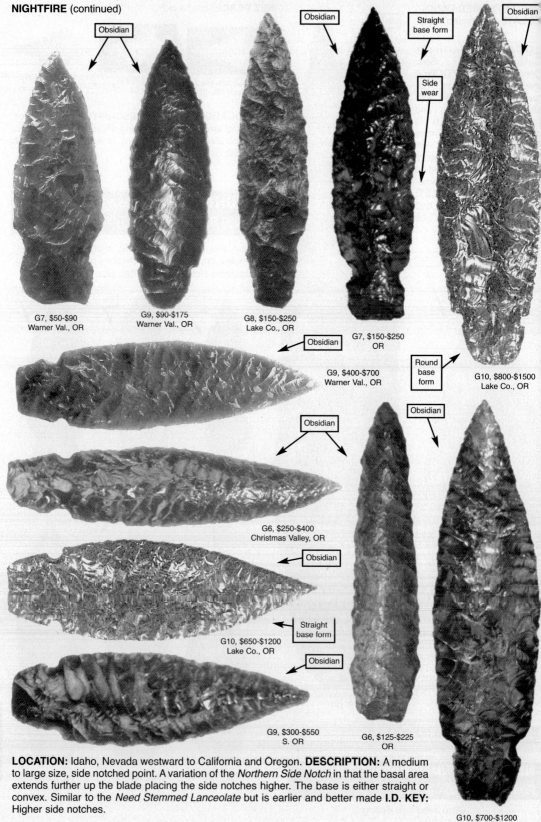

Obsidian

Obsidian

Obsidian

Straight base form

Side wear

Obsidian

G7, $50-$90
Warner Val., OR

G9, $90-$175
Warner Val., OR

G8, $150-$250
Lake Co., OR

G7, $150-$250
OR

Obsidian

G9, $400-$700
Warner Val., OR

Round base form

G10, $800-$1500
Lake Co., OR

Obsidian

Obsidian

G6, $250-$400
Christmas Valley, OR

Obsidian

G10, $650-$1200
Lake Co., OR

Straight base form

Obsidian

G9, $300-$550
S. OR

G6, $125-$225
OR

LOCATION: Idaho, Nevada westward to California and Oregon. **DESCRIPTION:** A medium to large size, side notched point. A variation of the *Northern Side Notch* in that the basal area extends further up the blade placing the side notches higher. The base is either straight or convex. Similar to the *Need Stemmed Lanceolate* but is earlier and better made **I.D. KEY:** Higher side notches.

G10, $700-$1200
Lake Co., OR

Obsidian

Obsidian

"Fox Ear" form

Obsidian

Obsidian

G6, $12-$20
OR

G9, $90-$175
Warner Valley, OR

G7, $25-$40
Warner Valley, OR

G6, $15-$30
Lake Co., OR

G6, $12-$20
OR

G7, $35-$60
S. OR

Serrated edge

"Fox Ear" form

G9, $150-$250
Warner Valley, OR

Obsidian

G8, $125-$225
Warner Valley, OR

G8, $80-$150
Warner Valley, OR

G7, $40-$75
Warner Valley, OR

G9, $175-$300
Warner Valley, OR

Tip nick

G8, $55-$100
Warner Valley, OR

Obsidian

"Fox Ear" form

Obsidian

Obsidian

G8, $150-$250
Warner Valley, OR

G7, $125-$200
Warner Valley, OR

G9, $200-$350
Warner Valley, OR

G9, $200-$350
Warner Valley, OR

G7, $80-$150
OR

G8, $250-$400
OR

LOCATION: Great Basin westward and south into Arizona. **DESCRIPTION:** A medium to large size, narrow, side-notched dart/knife point with early forms showing basal grinding and parallel flaking. Bases are usually concave to eared. Shoulders are tapered to horizontal. **I.D. KEY:** Broad side notched point.

"Fox Ear" form

Banded obsidian

Obsidian

Red obsidian

Obsidian

Serrated edge

G9, $250-$450
Warner Valley, OR

G8, $80-$150
Warner Valley, OR

G7, $90-$175
Warner Valley, OR

G8, $90-$175
Warner Valley, OR

G8, $150 $250
Warner Valley, OR

"Fox Ear" form

Tip wear

Banded obsidian

G7, $65-$125
Lake Co., OR

G9, $125-$225
Warner Valley, OR

Obsidian

Petrified wood

Obsidian

G9, $275-$500
Warner Valley, OR

G9, $450-$800
Lake Co., OR

G9, $350-$600
S. OR

G9, $450-$800
Lake Co., OR

Obsidian

Ledge agate

Serrated edge

G10+, $800-$1500
Warner Valley, OR

Obsidian

Obsidian

G10+, $650-$1200
OR

Serrated edge

G9, $250-$450
N. NV

G10, $400-$750
OR

G10+, $700-$1300
Lake Co., OR

Obsidian

Obsidian

G8, $450-$800
Harney Co., OR

G8, $500-$900
Warner Valley, OR

G9, $1200-$2000
Werner Valley, OR

F
W

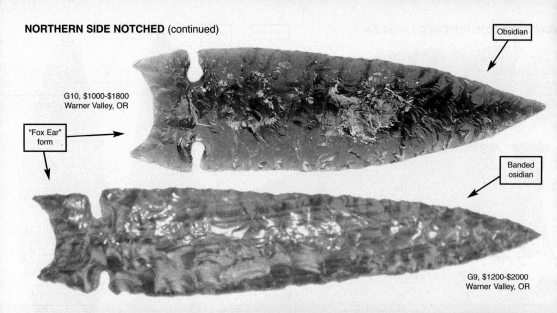

Obsidian

G10, $1000-$1800
Warner Valley, OR

"Fox Ear" form

Banded osidian

G9, $1200-$2000
Warner Valley, OR

NORTHWESTERN FOUR-WAY KNIFE - Classic Phase, 700 - 400 B. P.

(Also see Cascade, Cordilleran, Early Leaf, Excelsior, High Desert Knife, Mahkin Shouldered, Wahmuza)

Jasper

Obsidian

G9, $150-$250
Lake Co., OR

Obsidian

G8, $150-$275
Cent. OR

G7, $40-$75
OR

LOCATION: N. California into S. Oregon. **DESCRIPTION:** A large size double pointed knife that is usually beveled on one or all four sides of each face. The cross section is rhomboid. The true skinning knife. **I.D. KEY:** Two and four beveled double pointed form. **NOTE:** This form is known as the *Harahey knife* in the mid west where it is found from Wyoming, Colorado and Texas into Kansas, Illinois, Kentucky, Tennessee and Georgia. Believed to be the resharpened form of bipointed knives such as the *High Desert knife* and others.

Obsidian

G9, $350-$600
S. OR

Four-way bevel

Obsidian

Two bevels

Edge wear

G8, $125-$200
Atlatl Valley, Wa

Obsidian

Red basalt

G9, $175-$300
Snowville, UT

G9, $275-$500
Lake Co., OR

G10, $550-$1000
Warner Valley, OR

G9, $700-$1200
Sou. OR

F
W

NOTTOWAY - Historic Phase, 300 - 160 B. P.

(Also see Merrybell, Rose Springs)

G6, $15-$25
Malheur Co., OR

White
chalcedony

G8, $20-$35
Sou. OR

Red
chalcedony

G8, $25-$45
OR

Chalcedony

Red Jasper

G8, $20-$35
Columbia Riv., OR

G8, $20-$35
Columbia Riv., OR

G10, $90-$165
Sou. OR

Obsidian

LOCATION: Great Basin westward. **DESCRIPTION:** A small to medium size, narrow, thin, arrowpoint with tapered shoulders and a long, expanded stem. **I.D. KEY:** Large basal area.

OCHOCO STEMMED (provisional) - Late Archaic to Devel. Phase, 2500 - 1500 B.P.

(Also see Parman and Rabbit Island)

Drill

Jasper

Obsidian

Chalc.

G8, $5-$10
OR

G8, $8-$15
N. OR

G8, $8-$15
S. OR

G7, $5-$10
Col. Plat., OR

G7, $15-$30
OR

G6, $12-$20
Sou. OR

G8, $15-$30
Lake Co., OR

G6, $15-$30
S. OR

Obsidian

G6, $15-$25
Cent. OR

G6, $25-$40
S. OR

Obsidian

G8, $25-$40
Sou. OR

G8, $30-$50
S. OR

LOCATION. John Day River watershed in Oregon. **DESCRIPTION:** A medium size point with an elongated, triangular blade. Stem is straight sided to slightly contracting to bulbous. Looks like late *Parmans*, but slightly later in age. Possibly related to the *Rabbit Island* point.

OKANOGAN KNIFE (provisional) - Early to mid-Archaic, 8000 - 4000 B. P.

(Also see Coquille Knife & Paleo Knife)

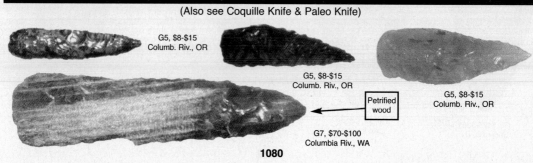

G5, $8-$15
Columb. Riv., OR

G5, $8-$15
Columb. Riv., OR

G5, $8-$15
Columb. Riv., OR

Petrified
wood

G7, $70-$100
Columbia Riv., WA

LOCATION: (Great Basin westward. **DESCRIPTION:** A small to large size, narrow, lanceolate knife with a convex base. Stems are unusually long and heavily ground. **I.D. KEY:** The slight single shoulder on pristine specimens. Resharpened shoulderless points can be identified by the length of the ground stem.

ONE-QUE (provisional) - Developmental to Historic Phase, 1320 - 1000 B. P.

(Also see Dagger, Diamond Back and Klickitat)

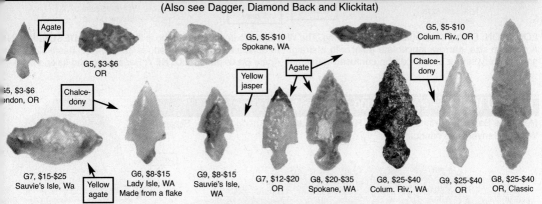

Agate

G5, $3-$6
OR

Chalce-
dony

G5, $3-$6
ondon, OR

Yellow
jasper

Agate

G5, $5-$10
Spokane, WA

G5, $5-$10
Colum. Riv., OR

Chalce-
dony

G7, $15-$25
Sauvie's Isle, Wa

Yellow
agate

G6, $8-$15
Lady Isle, WA
Made from a flake

G9, $8-$15
Sauvie's Isle,
WA

G7, $12-$20
OR

G8, $20-$35
Spokane, WA

G8, $25-$40
Colum. Riv., WA

G9, $25-$40
OR

G8, $25-$40
OR, Classic

LOCATION: Lower Columbia River in Oregon. **DESCRIPTION:** A small to medium size, arrow point with side notches. The base is diamond shaped, similar to Klikitat but rougher made. **I.D. KEY:** Diamond shaped base.

OWL CAVE - Late Paleo, 9500 - 8000 B. P.

(Also see Alder Complex, Cody Complex, Haskett, Humboldt Triangular, Pryor Stemmed)

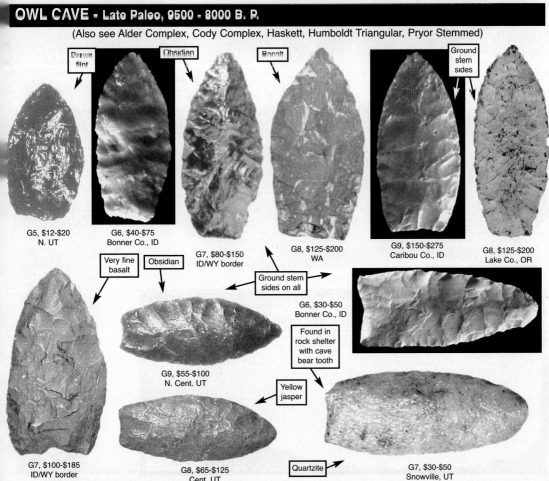

Brown
flint

Obsidian

Basalt

Ground
stem
sides

G5, $12-$20
N. UT

G6, $40-$75
Bonner Co., ID

G7, $80-$150
ID/WY border

G8, $125-$200
WA

G9, $150-$275
Caribou Co., ID

G8, $125-$200
Lake Co., OR

Very fine
basalt

Obsidian

Ground stem
sides on all

G6, $30-$50
Bonner Co., ID

Found in
rock shelter
with cave
bear tooth

G7, $100-$185
ID/WY border

G9, $55-$100
N. Cent. UT

Yellow
jasper

G8, $65-$125
Cent. UT

Quartzite

G7, $30-$50
Snowville, UT

F
W

OWL CAVE (continued)

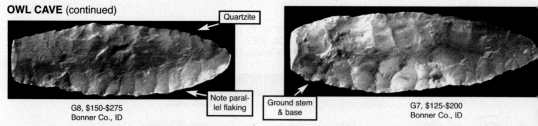

Quartzite

Note parallel flaking

G8, $150-$275
Bonner Co., ID

Ground stem & base

G7, $125-$200
Bonner Co., ID

LOCATION: Oregon, Nevada, Idaho, Wyoming. The Wasden Site in southern Idaho is the type area. **DESCRIPTION** A medium size, narrow, lanceolate point with a straight to concave base. Blade edges are convex. Basal sides are ground. Very similar to and can be confused with small *Agate Basin* points. **I.D. KEY:** Basal form and flaking style.

PALEO KNIFE - Paleo, 10,000 - 8000 B. P.

(Also see Base Tang Knife, Chopper, Hand Axe, Lancet, Okanogan Knife, Scraper, Wildcat Canyon and Windust)

Jasper

G8, $40-$75
Warner Valley, OR

G8, $40-$75
Lake Co., OR

Fluted on this side

Petrified wood

G8, $20-$35
OR

Fluted on this side

G7, $65-$125
Cortez, CA

G7, $25-$45
Lake Co., OR

LOCATION: Great Basin westward. **DESCRIPTION:** A medium to large size, broad, lanceolate blade with a rounded base. Look for parallel horizontal flaking and large thinning flakes.

PANOCHE - Historic, 300 - 200 B. P.

(Also see Bear River, Cold Springs, Desert, Lake River, Sauvie's Island, Uinta)

G5, $2-$5

G5, $5-$10

G6, $8-$15

All Monterey Co., CA

G6, $12-$20

LOCATION: Panoche Reservoir in Fresno Co., California. **DESCRIPTION:** A small size, thin side notched arrow point with a straight to concave base. Notches are larger than other *Desert Side Notched* forms that they are related. Similar to *Salado* found further East. See Noel Justice, 2002.

PARMAN - Early Archaic, 10,500 - 9000 B. P.

(Also see Cougar Mountain, Early Stemmed, Lake Mohave, Lind Coulee & Silver Lake)

Obsidian

Obsidian

Basalt

Chisel tip

Obsidian

OR

OR

G6, $15-$30
OR

G7, $30-$50
Silver Lake, OR

G5, $15-$25
S. OR

G5, $25-$45
OR

G5, $30-$50
OR

Obsidian

Obsidian

Obsidian

G6, $35-$65
N. Lake Co., OR

G8, $55-$100
OR

G7, $55-$100
Warner Valley, OR

G6, $40-$75
Cent. OR

G5, $40-$75
Warner Vall., OR

G5, $35-$65
S. E. OR

F
W

LOCATION: N.W. Nevada and southern Oregon. **DESCRIPTION:** A medium size, medium to long contracted stemmed point with tapered to squared shoulders. The Basal area is rounded to square and is ground on early examples. Flaking is random. Heavily resharpened examples may be the same as *Lake Mohave* points. A very rare type. Occurs in chisel tip along with *Lake Mohave* and *Windust*. Believed to have evolved from the earlier *Lind Coulee*. **I.D. KEY:** Long stem with straight to convex base.

PARMAN (continued)

Ground stem

Obsidian

Rare chisel tip

Black obsidian

G10, $400-$700
N. Idaho (photo from Pete
Bostrom cast)

Ground stem

Basalt

G9, $300-$550
Lake Co., OR

G5, $65-$125
OR

G5, $65-$125
OR

Obsidian

Black obsidian

Rare first stage form

G9, $500-$900
Lake Co., OR

Ground stem

G8, $400-$750
Lake Co., OR

G8, $250-$450
N. Lake Co., OR

Ground stem

G10+, $700-$1300
Lake Co., OR

Tip wear

G9, $350-$600
Lake Co., OR

Ground stem

G8, $225-$425
Salton City, CA

Obsidian

Red basalt

Black basalt

Very thin

Ground stem

Ground stem

G9, $550-$1000
Cent. OR

G9, $450-$800
OR

G6, $200-$350
E. OR

F
W

PAROWAN - Developmental Phase, 1300 - 800 B. P.

(Also see Gatecliff, Gypsum Cave, Rabbit Island)

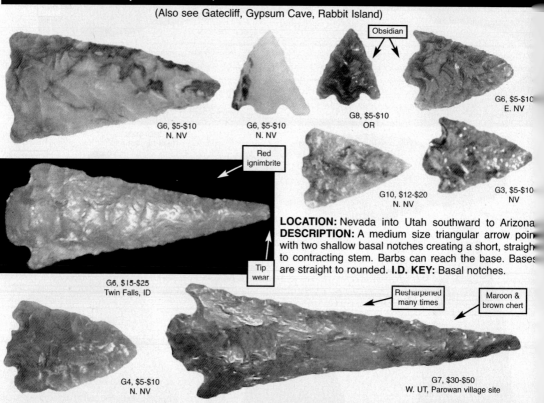

Obsidian

G6, $5-$10
N. NV

G6, $5-$10
N. NV

G8, $5-$10
OR

G6, $5-$10
E. NV

G10, $12-$20
N. NV

G3, $5-$10
NV

Red
ignimbrite

Tip
wear

G6, $15-$25
Twin Falls, ID

LOCATION: Nevada into Utah southward to Arizona
DESCRIPTION: A medium size triangular arrow point
with two shallow basal notches creating a short, straight
to contracting stem. Barbs can reach the base. Bases
are straight to rounded. **I.D. KEY:** Basal notches.

Resharpened
many times

Maroon &
brown chert

G4, $5-$10
N. NV

G7, $30-$50
W. UT, Parowan village site

PERFORATOR - Archaic to Historic, 9000 - 400 B. P.

(Also see Drill, Graver and Scraper)

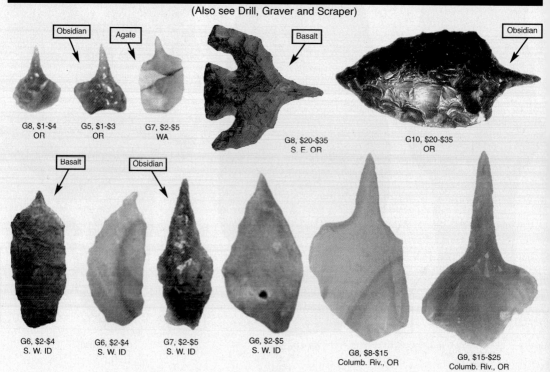

Obsidian

Agate

Basalt

Obsidian

G8, $1-$4
OR

G5, $1-$3
OR

G7, $2-$5
WA

G8, $20-$35
S. E. OR

G10, $20-$35
OR

Basalt

Obsidian

G6, $2-$4
S. W. ID

G6, $2-$4
S. W. ID

G7, $2-$5
S. W. ID

G6, $2-$5
S. W. ID

G8, $8-$15
Columb. Riv., OR

G9, $15-$25
Columb. Riv., OR

1086

PERFORATOR (continued)

LOCATION: Archaic and Woodland sites everywhere. **DESCRIPTION:** A jabbing projection at the tip would qualify for the type. It is believed that *perforators* were used for tattooing, incising or to punch holes in leather or other materials or objects. Paleo peoples used Gravers for the same purpose. All Archaic and Woodland cultures converted their points into this type. Therefore, most point types could occur in this form, although many examples were made from scratch. **I.D. KEY:** Long , slender tip.

PIECES ESQUILLEES - Paleo to Historic, 10,000 - 400 B. P.

(Also see Drill, Graver and Scraper)

Red/brown jasper

Basalt

Blade edge

G5, $1-$2
WA

Basalt

G6, $1-$2
Vancouver, WA

Hammer strokes

G6, $2-$4
Columbia Riv., OR

G6, $2-$4
Chehalis, WA

LOCATION: Oregon & Washington **DESCRIPTION:** A splitting wedge. Some in the old world may be 30,000 years old. The bottom cutting edge should be beveled or V shaped. The opposing edge or hammering surface should be flattened or knobbed enough to receive a hammer blow. The larger pieces could be used to split house timbers or planks, or perhaps spear shafts and foreshafts. The smaller pieces could be used to split bone for needles and arrow or small dart points. Look for hammer scars on the edge opposing the "V" or beveled edge. **I.D. KEY:** Wedge form.

PINTO BASIN - Early to late Archaic, 8000 - 2650 B. P.

(Also see Eastgate Bifurcated, Elko, Gatecliff, Humboldt and Rose Valley)

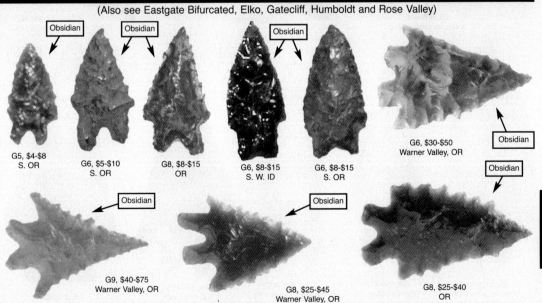

Obsidian

Obsidian

Obsidian

G5, $4-$8
S. OR

G6, $5-$10
S. OR

G8, $8-$15
OR

G6, $8-$15
S. W. ID

G6, $8-$15
S. OR

G6, $30-$50
Warner Valley, OR

Obsidian

Obsidian

Obsidian

Obsidian

G9, $40-$75
Warner Valley, OR

G8, $25-$45
Warner Valley, OR

G8, $25-$40
OR

F
W

1087

PINTO BASIN (continued)

Jasper

Obsidian

Obsidian

Obsidian

G6, $8-$15
OR

G9, $25-$40
Warner Valley, OR

G8, $25-$40
Warner Valley, OR

G8, $25-$45
Cent. OR

G8, $25-$45
Warner Valley, OR

G7, $25-$30
S. OR

Obsidian

Obsidian

Obsidian

G6, $30-$50
Warner Valley, OR

G9, $35-$65
Warner Valley, OR

G8, $30-$50
Warner Valley, OR

G7, $30-$50
Cent. OR

G7, $30-$50
Warner Valley, OR

G8, $40-$75
S. OR

Obsidian

Obsidian

Red obsidian

G7, $25-$45
Warner Valley, OR

G9, $35-$65
S. OR

G8, $35-$65
Lake Co., OR

Obsidian

Obsidian

Basalt

G8, $125-$200
Warner Valley, OR

G8, $65-$125
Warner Valley, OR

G8, $35-$60
Warner Valley, OR

G6, $40-$75
Lake Co., OR

G5, $15-$30
S. W. ID

Obsidian

Obsidian

Mahagony obsidian

Obsidian

G9, $35-$65
Warner Valley, OR

G8, $55-$100
Warner Valley, OR

G7, $25-$45
Warner Valley, OR

G8, $40-$75
Lake Co., Or

G7, $25-$45
Warner Valley, OR

Obsidian

Tip wear

Tip nick

Obsidian

Obsidian

Shale

G7, $35-$65
Warner Valley, OR

G5, $15-$25
S. W. ID

G8, $40-$75
Lake Co., OR

G8, $65-$125
Warner Valley, OR

G10, $450-$800
Humboldt Co., NV

LOCATION: Great Basin states. **DESCRIPTION:** A medium to large sized, narrow, auriculate point. Shoulders can be tapered, horizontal or barbed. Bases are either deeply bifurcated with parallel to expanding ears or tapered with a concave basal edge. The bifurcated form may prove to be *Gatecliff* forms. Most examples show excellent flaking. **I.D. KEY:** Long pointed ears; tapered base.

PINTO BASIN SLOPING SHOULDER - Early to late Archaic 8000 - 3000 B. P.

(Also see Eastgate Bifurcated, Elko, Gatecliff, Humboldt and Windust)

Basalt

Obsidian

G6, $20-$35
Duck Flat, OR

G9, $25-$45
Lake Co., OR

F
W

PINTO BASIN-SLOPING SHOULDER (continued)

Obsidian

Hafting notches

G7, $25-$45
Warner Valley, OR

G6, $15-$25
Warner Valley, OR

Obsidian

G9, $55-$100
Warner Valley, OR

Obsidian

G8, $25-$45
Warner Valley, OR

Obsidian

G8, $20-$35
S. OR

Obsidian

G9, $20-$35
Warner Valley, OR

Obsidian

G7, $15-$30
Humboldt Co., NV

Obsidian

Ear wear

Dacite

Red jasper

G6, $12-$20
S. OR

G8, $30-$50
S. OR

G8, $90-$175
Cent. OR

G7, $40-$70
Warner Valley, OR

Black obsidian

Obsidian

Obsidian

G10, $250-$400
Warner Valley, OR

G9, $150-$275
Warner Valley, Or

G10+, $275-$500
Lake Co., OR

G9, $150-$250
Lake Co., OR

G9, $165-$300
Warner Valley, Or

Obsidian

Obsidian

Black
obsidian

G9, $225-$400
Harney Co., OR

G6, $25-$45
Lake Co., OR

G9, $65-$125
Lake Co., OR

LOCATION: Great Basin states. **DESCRIPTION:**
The typical *Pinto Basin* point, but with a distinctive
single shoulder on one side and a convex blade
edge on the opposite side. **Note:** This may later
prove to be a late *Windust* cross-type.

PIQUNIN (provisional) - Classic to Historic Phase, 700 - 150 B. P.

(Also see Cold Springs, Elko Eared, Merrybell, Panoche and Sauvie's Island)

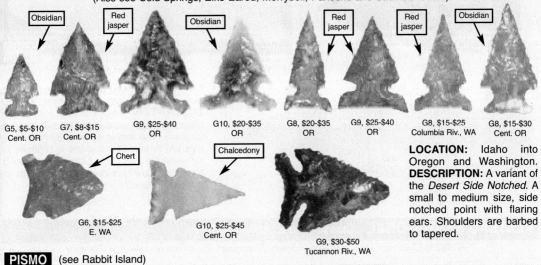

Obsidian

Red
jasper

Obsidian

Red
jasper

Red
jasper

Obsidian

G5, $5-$10
Cent. OR

G7, $8-$15
Cent. OR

G9, $25-$40
OR

G10, $20-$35
OR

G8, $20-$35
OR

G9, $25-$40
OR

G8, $15-$25
Columbia Riv., WA

G8, $15-$30
Cent. OR

Chert

Chalcedony

G6, $15-$25
E. WA

G10, $25-$45
Cent. OR

G9, $30-$50
Tucannon Riv., WA

LOCATION: Idaho into
Oregon and Washington.
DESCRIPTION: A variant of
the *Desert Side Notched*. A
small to medium size, side
notched point with flaring
ears. Shoulders are barbed
to tapered.

PISMO (see Rabbit Island)

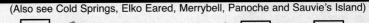

PLAINVIEW - Late Paleo, 10,000 - 7000 B. P.

(Also see Alder Complex, Black Rock Concave, Clovis, Goshen, Midland, Milnesand, Spedis)

Basalt

G6, $55-$100
Columbia Riv., OR

G6, $40-$75
WA

G8, $55-$100
Columbia Riv., WA

Petrified
wood

Obsidian

G9, $350-$600
Columbia Riv., OR

G9, $125-$200
S. OR

F
W

PLAINVIEW (continued)

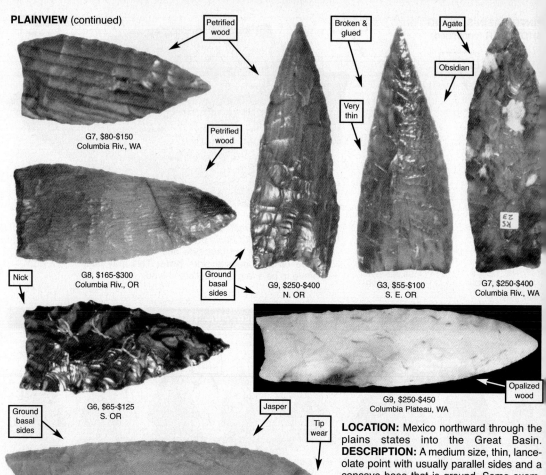

Petrified wood

G7, $80-$150
Columbia Riv., WA

Petrified wood

G8, $165-$300
Columbia Riv., OR

Nick

Ground basal sides

G6, $65-$125
S. OR

Ground basal sides

Ground basal sides

G9, $250-$400
N. OR

Broken & glued

Very thin

G3, $55-$100
S. E. OR

Agate

Obsidian

G7, $250-$400
Columbia Riv., WA

G9, $250-$450
Columbia Plateau, WA

Opalized wood

Jasper

Tip wear

G9, $265-$500
OR

LOCATION: Mexico northward through the plains states into the Great Basin. **DESCRIPTION:** A medium size, thin, lanceolate point with usually parallel sides and a concave base that is ground. Some examples are thinned or fluted and is believed to be related to the earlier *Clovis* type. Flaking is of high quality and can be collateral to oblique transverse.

PLATEAU PENTAGONAL - Classic Phase, 600 - 400 B. P.

(Related to Columbia Mule Ear; see Fremont Triangular, Wahmuza and Wildcat Canyon)

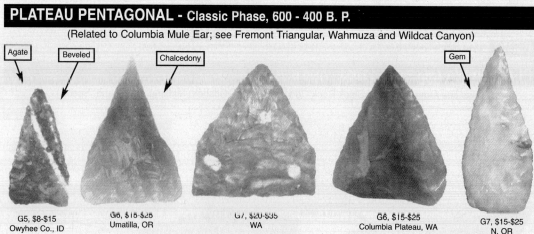

Agate

Beveled

Chalcedony

Gem

G5, $8-$15
Owyhee Co., ID

G6, $15-$25
Umatilla, OR

G7, $20-$35
WA

G6, $15-$25
Columbia Plateau, WA

G7, $15-$25
N. OR

LOCATION: Great Basin westward. **DESCRIPTION:** A medium to large size lanceolate blade with a squarish base. The blade expands into the base. Parallel flaking is usually evident. Basal sides are square to tapered with usuallly a straight blade. Most of these were hafted to a handle and resharpened back to the haft. **I.D. KEY:** Boxed stem.

Jasper

Agate

G6, $15-$25
WA

G6, $15-$30
OR

G7, $40-$70
Columbia Riv., OR

G7, $30-$30
Columbia Riv., WA

G7, $25-$40
Umatilla, OR

Purple &
white agate

G8, $55-$100
N. UT

Jasper

G7, $35-$60
Umatilla, OR

G7, $35-$65
N. OR

G7, $30-$50
Col. Riv., OR

Chalcedony

G7, $55-$100
WA

Yellow
jasper

G9, $150-$275
WA

First
stage

Agate

Agate

G7, $50-$90
Columbia Riv., OR

G6, $30-$50
Wasco Co., OR

G8, $55-$100
Wasco Co., OR

G9, $65-$125
OR

F
W

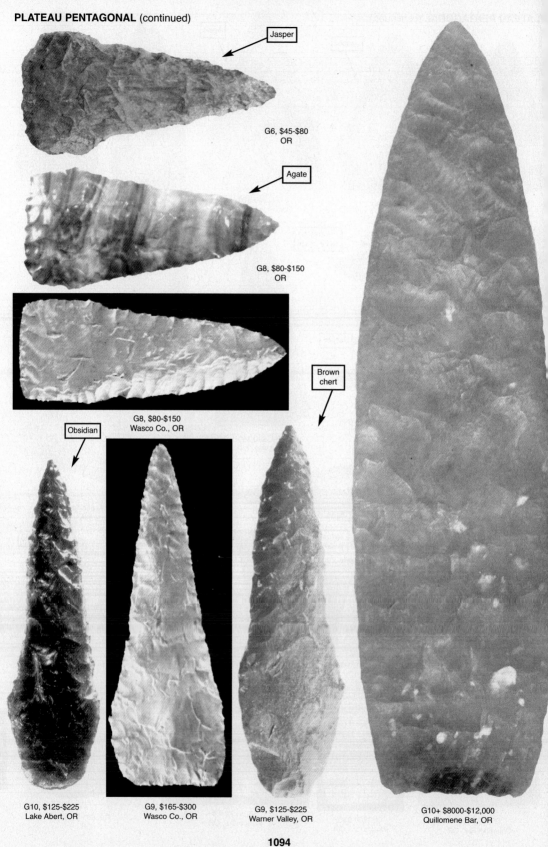

PLATEAU PENTAGONAL (continued)

Jasper

G6, $45-$80
OR

Agate

G8, $80-$150
OR

G8, $80-$150
Wasco Co., OR

Brown
chert

Obsidian

G10, $125-$225
Lake Abert, OR

G9, $165-$300
Wasco Co., OR

G9, $125-$225
Warner Valley, OR

G10+ $8000-$12,000
Quillomene Bar, OR

(Also see Bitterroot, Northern Side Notch)

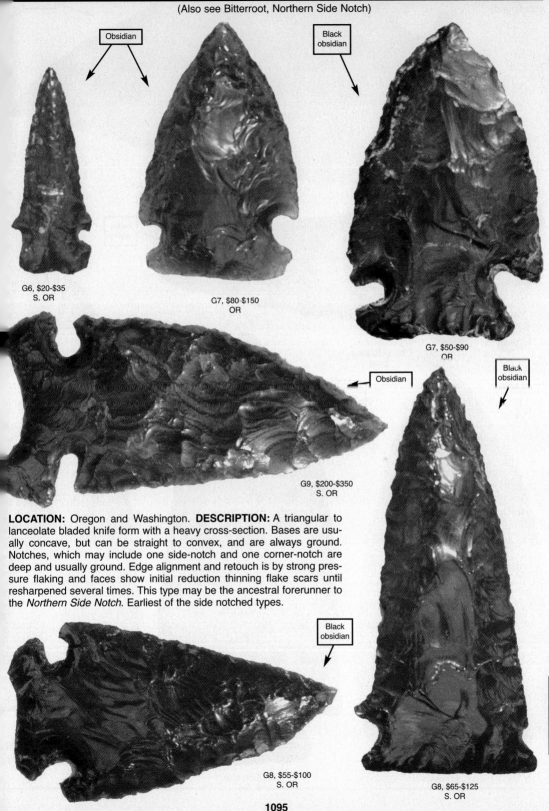

Obsidian

Black obsidian

G6, $20-$35
S. OR

G7, $80-$150
OR

G7, $50-$90
OR

Obsidian

Black obsidian

G9, $200-$350
S. OR

LOCATION: Oregon and Washington. **DESCRIPTION:** A triangular to lanceolate bladed knife form with a heavy cross-section. Bases are usually concave, but can be straight to convex, and are always ground. Notches, which may include one side-notch and one corner-notch are deep and usually ground. Edge alignment and retouch is by strong pressure flaking and faces show initial reduction thinning flake scars until resharpened several times. This type may be the ancestral forerunner to the *Northern Side Notch*. Earliest of the side notched types.

Black obsidian

G8, $55-$100
S. OR

G8, $65-$125
S. OR

F W

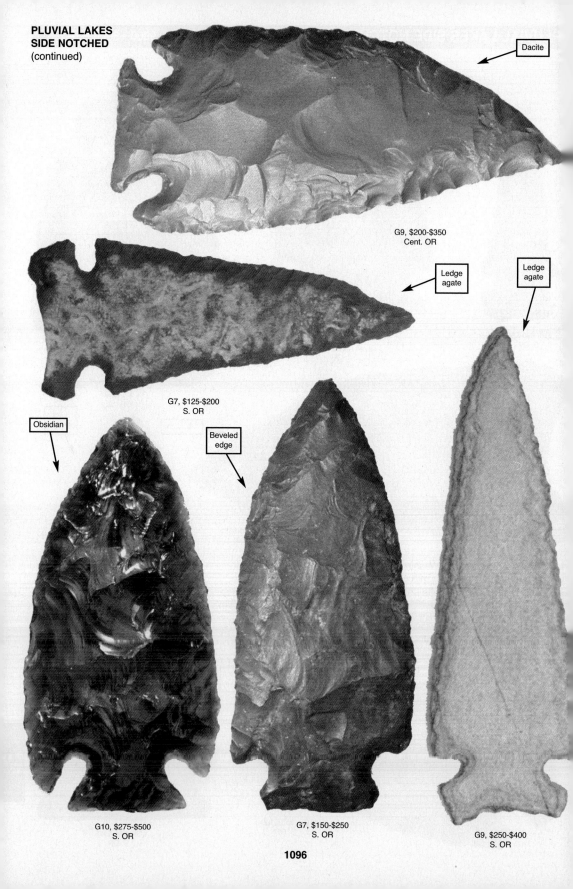

**PLUVIAL LAKES
SIDE NOTCHED**
(continued)

Dacite

G9, $200-$350
Cent. OR

Ledge
agate

Ledge
agate

G7, $125-$200
S. OR

Obsidian

Beveled
edge

G10, $275-$500
S. OR

G7, $150-$250
S. OR

G9, $250-$400
S. OR

Knife form

Chert

Chert

G8, $150-$250
N. W. UT

G10, $1200-$2000
Warner Valley, OR

G7, $200-$350
Black Rock Desert, OR

Obsidian

G9, $550-$1000
Lake Co., OR

F
W

POINT SAL BARBED - Late Archaic to Developmental Phase, 3500 - 1500 B. P.

(Also see Columbia Plateau, Contra Costa, Coquille, Gunther, Rabbit Island, Sierra Contracting Stem & Yana)

LOCATION: California coast. **DESCRIPTION:** A medium to large size, triangular point with drooping barbs and a narrow, contracting stem that is rounded to pointed. Blade edges are recurved. The distal end is acuminate. See Noel Justice, 2002.

G9, $80-$150
Santa Barbara Co., CA

PRIEST RAPIDS (provisional) - Late Archaic to Trans. Phase, 3000 - 1750 B.P.

(Also see Hell's Canyon, Merrybell, Quilomene Bar)

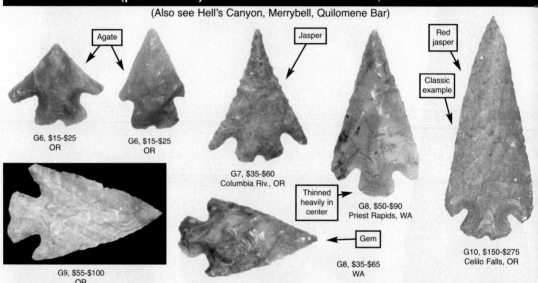

Agate

Jasper

Red jasper

Classic example

G6, $15-$25
OR

G6, $15-$25
OR

G7, $35-$60
Columbia Riv., OR

Thinned heavily in center

G8, $50-$90
Priest Rapids, WA

Gem

G8, $35-$65
WA

G9, $55-$100
OR

G10, $150-$275
Celilo Falls, OR

LOCATION: Columbia River basin, Oregon & Priest Rapids, WA **DESCRIPTION:** A medium size, short stemmed to basal notched point with drooping shoulders that turn inward and a rounded stem that is notched or well-thinned. A very rare type with only a few examples known. See Perino Vol. 3, 2002.

PRYOR STEMMED (provisional) - Early Archaic, 8000 - 7000 B. P.

(Also see Alder Complex, Celilo Falls, Eden, Humboldt Constricted, Owl Cave, Parman, Shaniko Stemmed)

Tip wear

Possible Lovel point

Gem

Ground stem

Very thin w/ground stem

Tip nick

Possible Lovel point

Broken & glued ear

G6, $35-$60
Hogup Cave, N.W. UT, dated to 9755 B.P.

G9, $125-$200
Lake Pend Oreill, ID

G4, $15-$30
Lake Co., OR

G7, $35-$60
Caribou Co., ID

G7, $125-$200
Hogup Cave, N.W. UT, dated to 9755 yrs. old

G7, $35-$65
Lake Co., OR

RYOR STEMMED (continued)

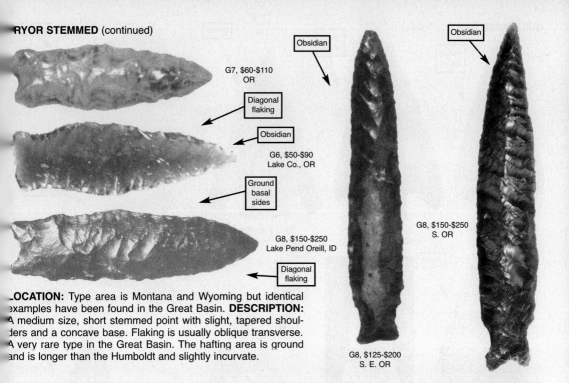

G7, $60-$110
OR

Diagonal flaking

Obsidian

Obsidian

G6, $50-$90
Lake Co., OR

Obsidian

Ground basal sides

G8, $150-$250
Lake Pend Oreill, ID

Diagonal flaking

G8, $150-$250
S. OR

G8, $125-$200
S. E. OR

LOCATION: Type area is Montana and Wyoming but identical examples have been found in the Great Basin. **DESCRIPTION:** A medium size, short stemmed point with slight, tapered shoulders and a concave base. Flaking is usually oblique transverse. A very rare type in the Great Basin. The hafting area is ground and is longer than the Humboldt and slightly incurvate.

QUILOMENE BAR - Late Archaic to Transitional Phase, 3000 - 2000 B. P.

(Also see Elko Corner Notched & Hell's Canyon)

Resharpened form

Agate

Petrified wood

Red jasper

G6, $12-$20
OR

G5, $15-$30
Columbia Riv., OR

G9, $90-$175
Columbia Riv., OR

G9, $45-$85
Priest Rapids, WA

G8, $35-$65
OR

G10, $250-$400
Wasco Co., OR

Jasper

Obsidian

Agate

Agate

G10, $150-$275
Columbia Riv., OR

G10, $175-$325
OR

G9, $150-$250
Columbia Riv., OR

G9, $150-$250
OR

G8, $125-$200
OR

F W

LOCATION: Columbia River in Oregon and Washington. **DESCRIPTION:** A medium size base to corner notched point. The classic form has a convex base but can be straight to slightly concave. The stem is straight to expanded & the shoulders are squared

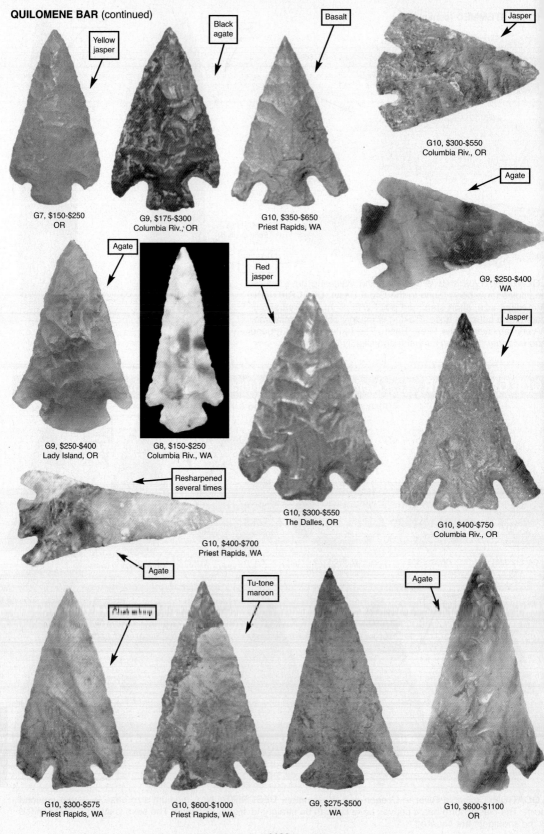

QUILOMENE BAR (continued)

Yellow jasper

Black agate

Basalt

Jasper

G10, $300-$550
Columbia Riv., OR

G7, $150-$250
OR

G9, $175-$300
Columbia Riv., OR

G10, $350-$650
Priest Rapids, WA

Agate

G9, $250-$400
WA

Agate

Red jasper

Jasper

G9, $250-$400
Lady Island, OR

G8, $150-$250
Columbia Riv., WA

Resharpened several times

G10, $300-$550
The Dalles, OR

G10, $400-$750
Columbia Riv., OR

G10, $400-$700
Priest Rapids, WA

Agate

Tu-tone maroon

Agate

G10, $300-$575
Priest Rapids, WA

G10, $600-$1000
Priest Rapids, WA

G9, $275-$500
WA

G10, $600-$1100
OR

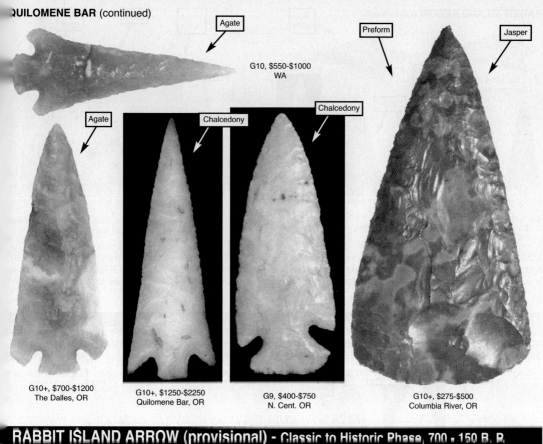

Agate

G10, $550-$1000
WA

Preform

Jasper

Agate

Chalcedony

Chalcedony

G10+, $700-$1200
The Dalles, OR

G10+, $1250-$2250
Quilomene Bar, OR

G9, $400-$750
N. Cent. OR

G10+, $275-$500
Columbia River, OR

RABBIT ISLAND ARROW (provisional) - Classic to Historic Phase, 700 - 150 B. P.

(Also see Columbia Riv. Pin Stem, Coquille, Gatecliff, Gypsum Cave, Sauvie's Island Shoulder Notched, Rose Springs & Yana)

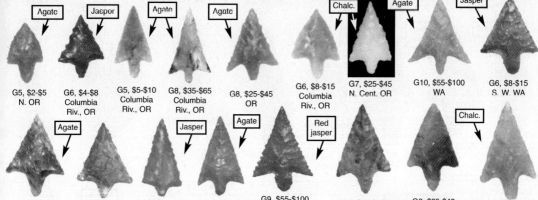

Agate

Jasper

Agate

Agate

Chalc.

Agate

Jasper

G5, $2-$5
N. OR

G6, $4-$8
Columbia
Riv., OR

G5, $5-$10
Columbia
Riv., OR

G8, $35-$65
Columbia
Riv., OR

G8, $25-$45
OR

G6, $8-$15
Columbia
Riv., OR

G7, $25-$45
N. Cent. OR

G10, $55-$100
WA

G6, $8-$15
S. W. WA

Agate

Jasper

Agate

Red
jasper

Chalc.

G9, $35-$60
Col. Rv., OR

G6, $30-$50
S. W. WA

G6, $25-$40
Col. Rv., OR

G9, $40-$70
WA

G9, $55-$100
S. W. WA

G7, $35-$60
S. W. WA

G6, $25-$40
Snake Rv., WA

G8, $55-$100
N. OR

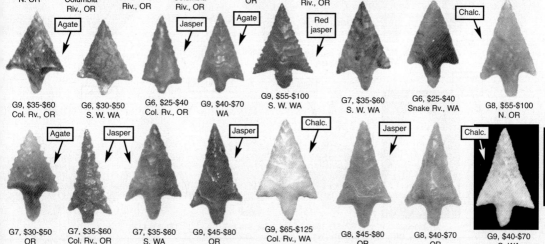

Agate

Jasper

Jasper

Chalc.

Jasper

Chalc.

G7, $30-$50
OR

G7, $35-$60
Col. Rv., OR

G7, $35-$60
S. WA

G9, $45-$80
OR

G9, $65-$125
Col. Rv., WA

G8, $45-$80
OR

G8, $40-$70
OR

G9, $40-$70
S. WA

F
W

1101

RABBIT ISLAND ARROW (continued)

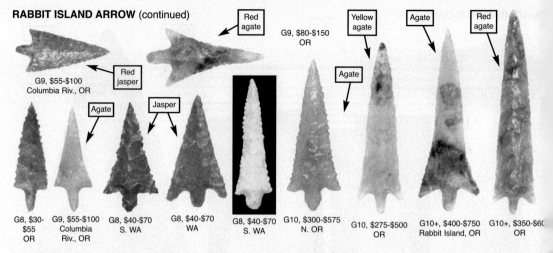

G9, $55-$100
Columbia Riv., OR — Red jasper

Red agate

G9, $80-$150
OR

Yellow agate

Agate

Agate

Red agate

Agate — G8, $30-$55 OR

G9, $55-$100
Columbia Riv., OR

Jasper — G8, $40-$70 S. WA

G8, $40-$70 WA

G8, $40-$70 S. WA

G10, $300-$575 N. OR

G10, $275-$500 OR

G10+, $400-$750 Rabbit Island, OR

G10+, $350-$60 OR

LOCATION: Columbia River of Oregon and Washington. **DESCRIPTION:** A small to medium size, thin, barbed point with a short, tapered base that can be pointed, to rounded. **Note:** This type is similar to the *Wallula* point which has a square stem; this type has a tapered stem. Evolved from the earlier dart point and was used to historic times.

RABBIT ISLAND DART - Transitional to Classic Phase, 2000 - 700 B. P.

(Also see Coquille, Gatecliff, Gypsum Cave, Point Sal Barbed, Rose Springs, Sauvie's Island Shoulder Notched, Sierra Contracting Stem & Yana)

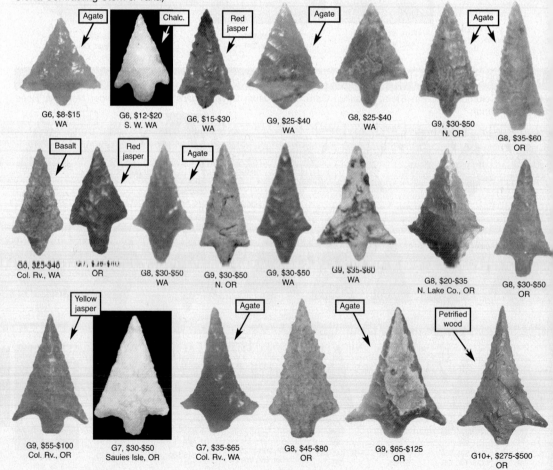

Agate — G6, $8-$15 WA

Chalc. — G6, $12-$20 S. W. WA

Red jasper — G6, $15-$30 WA

Agate — G9, $25-$40 WA

Agate — G8, $25-$40 WA

Agate — G9, $30-$50 N. OR

G8, $35-$60 OR

Basalt — G6, $25-$40 Col. Rv., WA

Red jasper — G7, $15-$10 OR

Agate — G8, $30-$50 WA

G9, $30-$50 N. OR

G9, $30-$50 WA

G9, $35-$60 WA

G8, $20-$35 N. Lake Co., OR

G8, $30-$50 OR

Yellow jasper — G9, $55-$100 Col. Rv., OR

G7, $30-$50 Sauies Isle, OR

G7, $35-$65 Col. Rv., WA

Agate — G8, $45-$80 OR

Agate — G9, $65-$125 OR

Petrified wood — G10+, $275-$500 OR

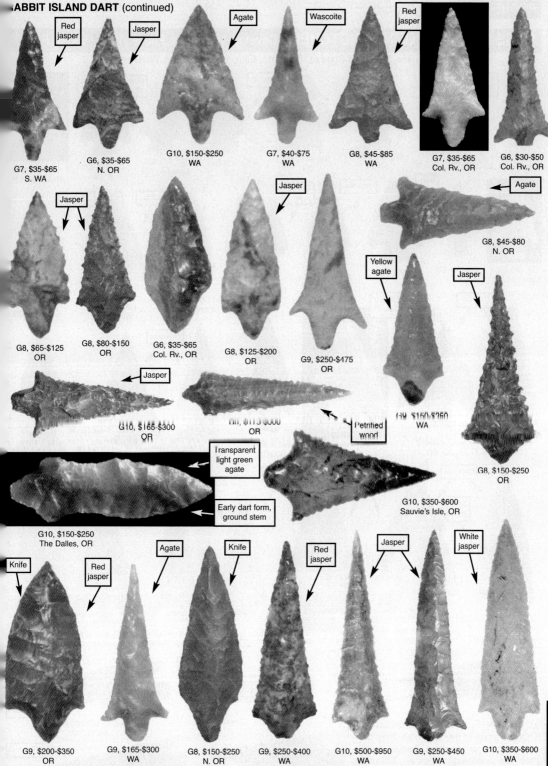

Red jasper

Jasper

Agate

Wascoite

Red jasper

G7, $35-$65
S. WA

G6, $35-$65
N. OR

G10, $150-$250
WA

G7, $40-$75
WA

G8, $45-$85
WA

G7, $35-$65
Col. Rv., OR

G6, $30-$50
Col. Rv., OR

Jasper

Jasper

Agate

G8, $45-$80
N. OR

Yellow agate

Jasper

G8, $65-$125
OR

G8, $80-$150
OR

G6, $35-$65
Col. Rv., OR

G8, $125-$200
OR

G9, $250-$475
OR

Jasper

Jasper

Petrified wood

G10, $165-$300
OR

G8, $175-$300
OR

G9, $150-$250
WA

G8, $150-$250
OR

Transparent light green agate

Early dart form, ground stem

G10, $150-$250
The Dalles, OR

G10, $350-$600
Sauvie's Isle, OR

Knife

Red jasper

Agate

Knife

Red jasper

Jasper

White jasper

G9, $200-$350
OR

G9, $165-$300
WA

G8, $150-$250
N. OR

G9, $250-$400
WA

G10, $500-$950
WA

G9, $250-$450
WA

G10, $350-$600
WA

F
W

LOCATION: Columbia River of Oregon and Washington. **DESCRIPTION:** A medium size, contracted stemmed point with tapered to horizontal, pointed shoulders and a short base that can be pointed or rounded. Early forms have a tapered stem with a straight base. Blade edges can be serrated. Also known as *Pismo*. **Note:** This type evolves into an arrow point in later times and lasted to the historic period.

ROSE SPRINGS CORNER NOTCHED - Develop. to Classic Phase, 1600 - 600 B. P.

(Also see Columbia Plateau, Eastgate, Elko, Snake River & Wendover)

Banded obsidian

G8, $20-$35
Owyhee Co., ID

G10, $40-$70
Clearwater Co., ID

G9, $30-$45
OR

Obsidian

G9, $30-$55
OR

G8, $25-$45
OR

Mah. obs.

G7, $20-$35
Lake Co., OR

G7, $15-$25
S. OR

G10, $30-$55
Grand Co., UT

G8, $15-$25
Lake Co., OR

G8, $25-$20
UT

Mah. obs.

Obsidian

G7, $15-$30
Lake Co., OR

G7, $15-$30
OR

Double tip

G8, $35-$60
S. OR

G8, $35-$60
Warner Val., OR

Obsidian

G9, $40-$70
Lake Co., OR

Obsidian

G7, $30-$50
Lake Co., OR

Obsidian

G8, $40-$70
S. OR

G8, $40-$70
S. OR

Chalce-dony

Knife

G8, $40-$70
OR

G8, $25-$40
S. OR

G9, $40-$70
Warner Val., OR

Obsidian

G7, $30-$50
Warner Val., OR

G8, $40-$70
S. OR

Obsidian

Dart/knife

G7, $35-$60
Humboldt Co., NV

G8, $45-$80
Sou. OR

Dart/knife

G6, $30-$50
S. OR

Arrow

G7, $45-$80
Sou. OR

Obsidian

G10, $150-$275
Oregon desert

Yellow jasper

G7, $40-$75
Warner Val., OR

G7, $35-$65
S. OR

G9, $200-$375
OR

Arrow

Obsidian

G10, $250-$400
Oregon desert

Obsidian

G10, $275-$500
Lake Co., OR

Obsidian

LOCATION: S. OR into NV. **DESCRIP-TION:** A small to medium size, thin, corner notched arrow point. Larger examples are knives/dart points. Shoulder tangs can be sharp to rounded. Same as *Columbia Plateau* points except where found.

G9, $125-$200
Lake Co., OR

Obsidian

G9, $65-$125
Warner Val., OR

Obsidian

Yellow chert

G7, $35-$65
S. OR

Agate

Agate

Obsidian

Obsidian

Obsidian

G9, $65-$125
OR

G9, $65-$125
Warner Val., OR

G7, $40-$70
Warner Val., OR

G8, $65-$125
Warner Val., OR

G9, $125-$200
Lake Co., OR

G10, $150-$250
S. OR

Obsidian

Obsidian

Knife

Obsidian

10, $250-$400
Lake Co., OR

G8, $65-$125
Warner Val., OR

Mahaony
obsidian

G8, $75-$140
OR

G8, $75-$140
Warner Valley, OR

G6, $40-$70
S. OR

G9, $125-$200
S. OR

G8, $150-$250
S. OR

G9, $165-$300
Cent. OR

ROSE SPRINGS SIDE NOTCHED - Developmental to Classic Phase, 1600 - 600 B. P.

(Also see Albion-Head, Coquille, Eastgate, Elko, Nottoway, Piqunin, & Wendover)

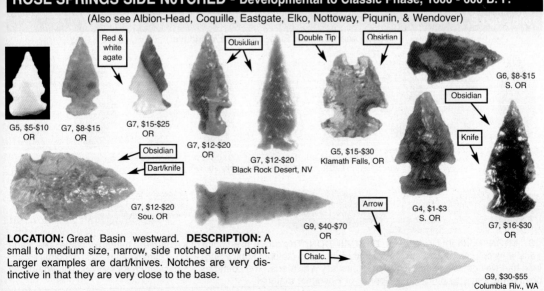

Red & white agate

Obsidian

Double Tip

Obsidian

Obsidian

G6, $8-$15
S. OR

G5, $5-$10
OR

G7, $8-$15
OR

G7, $15-$25
OR

G7, $12-$20
OR

G7, $12-$20
OR

G5, $15-$30
Klamath Falls, OR

Obsidian

Knife

Obsidian

Dart/knife

G7, $12-$20
Sou. OR

G9, $40-$70
OR

Arrow

G4, $1-$3
S. OR

G7, $16-$30
OR

Chalc.

G7, $12-$20
Black Rock Desert, NV

G9, $30-$55
Columbia Riv., WA

LOCATION: Great Basin westward. **DESCRIPTION:** A small to medium size, narrow, side notched arrow point. Larger examples are dart/knives. Notches are very distinctive in that they are very close to the base.

F
W

ROSE SPRINGS SIDE NOTCHED (continued)

G5, $8-$15
S. OR

G5, $8-$15
S. OR

G6, $15-$30
S. OR

Obsidian
Crystal
Knife

G7, $40-$75
Washoe Lake, NV

G7, $15-$30
Harney Co., OR

Obsidian

G6, $5-$10
S. OR

G6, $8-$15
S. OR

White quartzite

Dart/knife

G7, $15-$30
Warnor Valley, OR

Tip nick

G7, $15-$30
Columbia Riv., WA

G7, $20-$35
S. OR

G7, $15-$30
OR

G8, $25-$40
Cent. OR

G8, $25-$45
OR

G8, $30-$50
Lake Co., OR

G8, $30-$50
OR

G10+, $400-$700
N.W. UT

ROSE SPRINGS SLOPING SHOULDER (provisional) - Developmental to Classic, 1600 - 600 B. P.

(Also see Eastgate, Elko, Wallula & Wendover)

G8, $5-$10
S. E. OR

G7, $5-$10
Humboldt Co., NV

G5, $4-$8
Humboldt Co., NV

G8, $5-$10
S. E. OR

G8, $8-$15
Lake Co., OR

G7, $5-$10
Lake Co., OR

G5, $4-$8
Harney Co., OR

G8, $6-$12
S. E. OR

G6, $8-$15
Lake Co., OR

G6, $6-$12
Lake Co., OR

G7 $12-$20
S. W. ID

G6, $16-$30
S. E. OR

LOCATION: Northern Great Basin. **DESCRIPTION:** This arrow sized point has a barbless triangular blade. The blade transitions smoothly into a straight, slightly expanding (seldom contracting) stem. Approximately 90% of points examined had well ground stems. This type is usually well made. The point has a lenticular cross section. The age of the point is the same as other Rose Springs or Rosegate material.

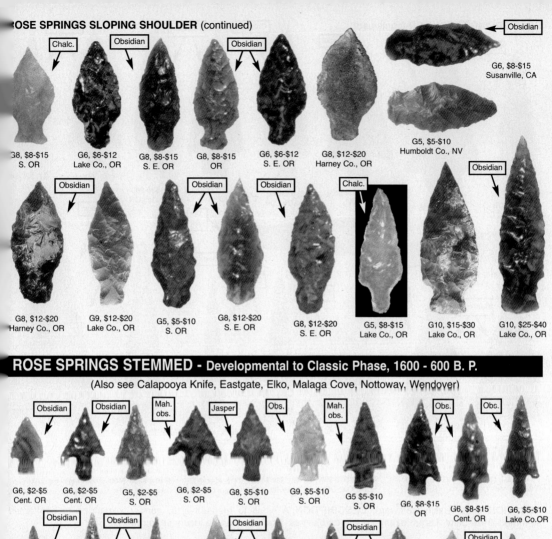

Chalc.

Obsidian

Obsidian

Obsidian

G8, $8-$15
S. OR

G6, $6-$12
Lake Co., OR

G8, $8-$15
S. E. OR

G8, $8-$15
OR

G6, $6-$12
S. E. OR

G8, $12-$20
Harney Co., OR

Obsidian

G6, $8-$15
Susanville, CA

G5, $5-$10
Humboldt Co., NV

Obsidian

Obsidian

Obsidian

Chalc.

Obsidian

G8, $12-$20
Harney Co., OR

G9, $12-$20
Lake Co., OR

G5, $5-$10
S. OR

G8, $12-$20
S. E. OR

G8, $12-$20
S. E. OR

G5, $8-$15
Lake Co., OR

G10, $15-$30
Lake Co., OR

G10, $25-$40
Lake Co., OR

ROSE SPRINGS STEMMED - Developmental to Classic Phase, 1600 - 600 B. P.

(Also see Calapooya Knife, Eastgate, Elko, Malaga Cove, Nottoway, Wendover)

Obsidian

Obsidian

Mah. obs.

Jasper

Obs.

Mah. obs.

Obs.

Obs.

G6, $2-$5
Cent. OR

G6, $2-$5
Cent. OR

G5, $2-$5
S. OR

G6, $2-$5
S. OR

G8, $5-$10
S. OR

G9, $5-$10
S. OR

G5 $5-$10
S. OR

G6, $8-$15
OR

G6, $8-$15
Cent. OR

G6, $5-$10
Lake Co.OR

Obsidian

Obsidian

Obsidian

Obsidian

Obsidian

G9, $12-$20
Harney Co., OR

G9, $25-$40
OR

G9, $25-$40
Malheur Co., OR

G8, $20-$35
Colum. Riv.,
Basin, OR

G6, $12-$20
OR

G6, $8-$15
Lake Co.OR

G8, $12-$20
S. OR

G6, $12-$20
Cent. OR

G6, $8-$15
S. OR

Obsidian

Obs.

Mah. obs.

Obsidian

Obsidian

Obsidian

G6, $8-$15
OR

G6, $8-$15
S. OR

G9, $15-$30
Lake Co., OR

G9, $15-$30
Lake Co., OR

G8, $12-$20
OR

G10, $200-$375
Lake Co., OR

G8, $20-$35
S. OR

G8, $20-$35
OR

G7, $35-$60
Harney Co., OR

F
W

ROSE SPRINGS STEMMED (continued)

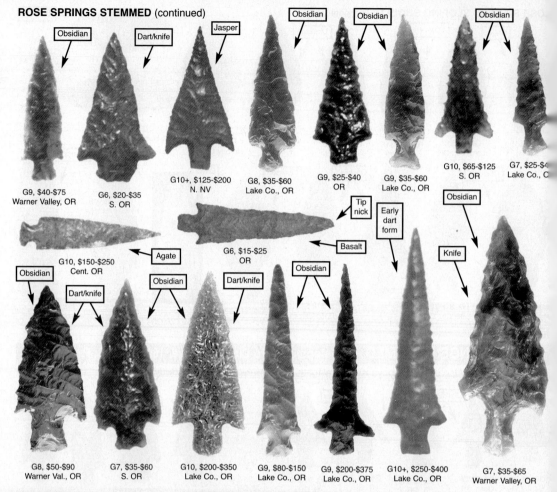

Obsidian

Obsidian

Dart/knife

Jasper

Obsidian

Obsidian

Obsidian

Obsidian

G9, $40-$75
Warner Valley, OR

G6, $20-$35
S. OR

G10+, $125-$200
N. NV

G8, $35-$60
Lake Co., OR

G9, $25-$40
OR

G9, $35-$60
Lake Co., OR

G10, $65-$125
S. OR

G7, $25-$4[
Lake Co., C

Tip nick

Early dart form

Obsidian

Agate

G10, $150-$250
Cent. OR

G6, $15-$25
OR

Basalt

Knife

Obsidian

Dart/knife

Obsidian

Dart/knife

Obsidian

G8, $50-$90
Warner Val., OR

G7, $35-$60
S. OR

G10, $200-$350
Lake Co., OR

G9, $80-$150
Lake Co., OR

G9, $200-$375
Lake Co., OR

G10+, $250-$400
Lake Co., OR

G7, $35-$65
Warner Valley, OR

LOCATION: Great Basin westward. **DESCRIPTION:** A small to medium size, narrow, expanded to contracted stemmed arrow point. Larger examples are dart/knives. The base can be incurvate to rounded.

ROSSI SQUARE-STEMMED - Mid-Archaic-Transitional Phase, 4000 - 2000 B. P.

(Also see Shaniko Stemmed)

LOCATION: San Mateo Co., California and surrounding area into central and sou. coastal California. Usually made of Monterey Chert. **DESCRIPTION:** A medium size, square stemmed dart/knife point with horizontal shoulders. See Noel Justice, 2002.

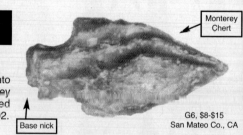

Monterey Chert

Base nick

G6, $8-$15
San Mateo Co., CA

SALMON RIVER - Early Archaic, 8000 - 5800 B. P.

(Also see Bitterroot, Shaniko Stemmed & Wendover)

Basalt

G6, $15-$20
Humboldt Co., NV

G8, $20-$35
S.E. OR

Basalt

G6, $15-$25
WA

Basalt

G6, $15-$25
WA

Basalt

Worn tip

G5, $15-$25
Union Co., OR

Basalt

G9, $125-$225
Black Rock Desert, NV

LOCATION: Oregon and Washington state. **DESCRIPTION:** A *Bitterroot* variant. A medium size, narrow, dart point with weak, tapered shoulders, an expanding stem and a straight base. Basal corners are sharp to rounded. Stems can be short to long.

SAUVIE'S ISLAND HAFTING-NOTCHED (provisional) - Trans. to Classic Phase., 1750 - 400 B. P.

(Also see Columbia Plateau, Combat Wand Blade, Rabbit Island, Vendetta and Wallula)

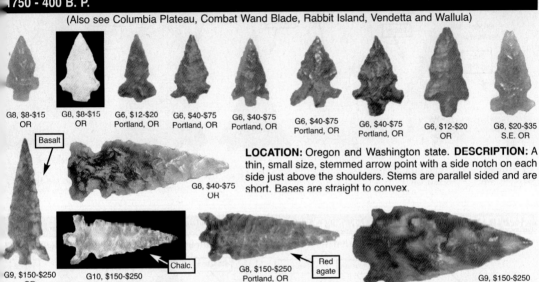

G8, $8-$15
OR

G8, $8-$15
OR

G6, $12-$20
Portland, OR

G6, $40-$75
Portland, OR

G6, $40-$75
Portland, OR

G6, $40-$75
Portland, OR

G6, $40-$75
Portland, OR

G6, $12-$20
OR

G8, $20-$35
S.E. OR

Basalt

G8, $40-$75
OR

LOCATION: Oregon and Washington state. **DESCRIPTION:** A thin, small size, stemmed arrow point with a side notch on each side just above the shoulders. Stems are parallel sided and are short. Bases are straight to convex.

G9, $150-$250
OR

Chalc.

G10, $150-$250
Columbia Riv., OR

G8, $150-$250
Portland, OR

Red agate

G9, $150-$250
WA

SAUVIE'S ISLAND SHOULDER NOTCHED (provisional) - Trans. to Classic Phase., 1750 - 400 B. P.

(Also see Columbia Plateau, Rabbit Island and Wallula)

Agate

Basalt

Red agate

Agate

Jasper

G6, $15-$30
OR

G8, $25-$40
Vacouver, WA

G10, $25-$45
Vancouver, WA

G6, $25-$45
Sauvies Isle, OR

G8, $35-$60
Portland, OR

G10, $35-$60
Portland, OR

G10, $40-$75
Vancouver, WA

G7, $25-$45
Sauvies Isle, OR

G9, $35-$60
Vancouver, WA

Basalt

Jasper

Chalc.

LOCATION: Oregon and Washington state. **DESCRIPTION:** A thin, small size, stemmed arrow point with one or both shoulders that contain a notch. These are consistently *Rabbits* & *Wallula Gaps* with shoulder notches. Shoulders can be tapered to barbed. Bases are straight to convex. Stems are short and are either squared or tapered. Named by Jim Hogue.

G10, $40-$70
OR

G10, $40-$70
Vancouver, WA

G9, $40-$70
Vancouver, WA.

F W

1109

SAUVIE'S ISLAND SHOULDER NOTCHED (continued)

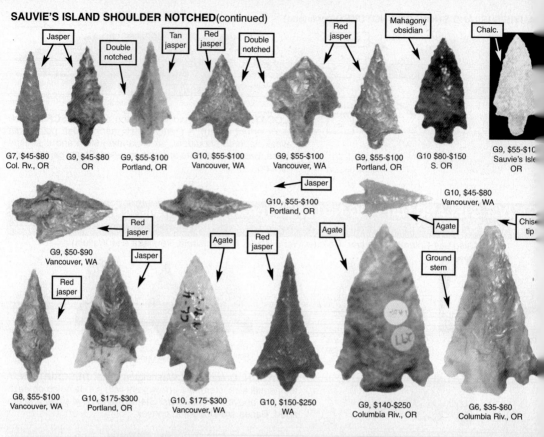

Jasper

Double notched

Tan jasper

Red jasper

Double notched

Red jasper

Mahagony obsidian

Chalc.

G7, $45-$80
Col. Rv., OR

G9, $45-$80
OR

G9, $55-$100
Portland, OR

G10, $55-$100
Vancouver, WA

G9, $55-$100
Vancouver, WA

G9, $55-$100
Portland, OR

G10 $80-$150
S. OR

G9, $55-$10
Sauvie's Isle
OR

Jasper

G10, $55-$100
Portland, OR

G10, $45-$80
Vancouver, WA

Agate

Chis tip

Red jasper

G9, $50-$90
Vancouver, WA

Jasper

Agate

Red jasper

Agate

Ground stem

Red jasper

G8, $55-$100
Vancouver, WA

G10, $175-$300
Portland, OR

G10, $175-$300
Vancouver, WA

G10, $150-$250
WA

G9, $140-$250
Columbia Riv., OR

G6, $35-$60
Columbia Riv., OR

SCOTTSBLUFF I - Early Archaic, 10,000 - 8000 B. P.

(Also see Alberta, Cody Knife, Eden, Firstview, Lind Coulee, Parman, Shaniko Stemmed & Windust)

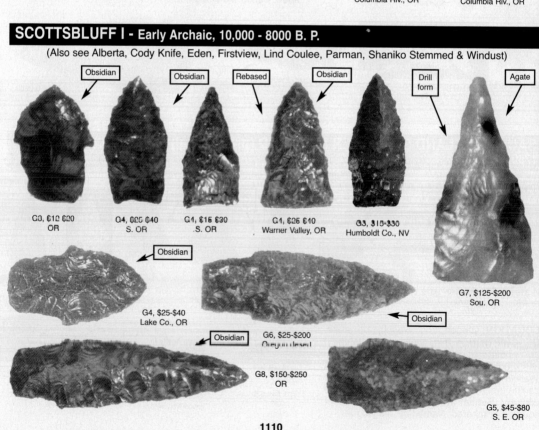

Obsidian

Obsidian

Rebased

Obsidian

Drill form

Agate

G3, $10-$20
OR

G4, $25-$40
S. OR

G1, $15-$30
.S. OR

G1, $25-$40
Warner Valley, OR

G3, $15-$30
Humboldt Co., NV

G7, $125-$200
Sou. OR

Obsidian

G4, $25-$40
Lake Co., OR

Obsidian

Obsidian

G6, $25-$200
Oregon desert

G8, $150-$250
OR

G5, $45-$80
S. E. OR

1110

Obsidian

Red/gray agate

Agate

Obsidian

G6, $80-$150
WA

G6, $80-$150
Columb. Plat., WA

G7, $125-$200
Lake Co., OR

Ground stem

G6, $150-$250
Henry's Lake, ID

Obsidian

Obsidian

Mahagony obsidian

G8, $265-$500
Lake Co., OR

Petrified wood

Red chalcedony

G6, $300-$150
Lake Co., OR

G6, $175-$300
Columb. Riv., OR

G10+, $1200-$2000
S. E. OR

Ground stem

G7, $450-$800
Crook Co., OR

Ground stem

G6, $125-$200
OR

Obsidian

G8, $400-$700
S. OR

Ground stem

G6, $265-$500
Wasco Co., OR

LOCATION: Western Washington & Oregon into Idaho, Nevada, Utah, Montana & Wyoming. **DESCRIPTION:** A medium to large size, broad, stemmed point with weak shoulders and a broad parallel sided to expanding stem that is ground. Developed from earlier *Alberta* points. *Cody* points in this area have shorter and more variable stems (including miniatures) than anywhere else in the country. The concave based *Scottsbluff* are described in the "Claypool Study" republished in part by George Frisson in "Prehistoric Hunters of the High Plains." Stems are burinated and flaked to fit into sockets for a solidly hafted knife or spear. Flaking is usually the horizontal to oblique style. Chisel tips are known. **I.D. KEY:** Early flaking, square stem that is ground.

F
W

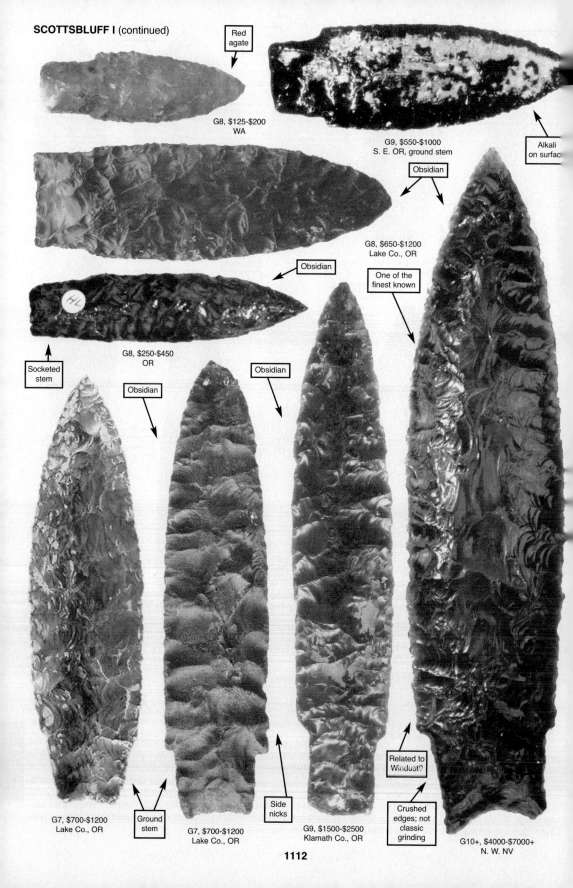

SCOTTSBLUFF I (continued)

Red agate

G8, $125-$200
WA

G9, $550-$1000
S. E. OR, ground stem

Alkali on surface

Obsidian

G8, $650-$1200
Lake Co., OR

One of the finest known

Obsidian

G8, $250-$450
OR

Socketed stem

Obsidian

Obsidian

G7, $700-$1200
Lake Co., OR

Ground stem

G7, $700-$1200
Lake Co., OR

Side nicks

G9, $1500-$2500
Klamath Co., OR

Related to Windust?

Crushed edges; not classic grinding

G10+, $4000-$7000+
N. W. NV

(Also see Alberta, Cody Knife, Eden, Firstview, Lind Coulee, Parman, Shaniko Stemmed & Windust)

Obsidian

G6, $300-$550
S. OR

Socketed
stem

Basalt

Minor
nicks

Ear
nick

G5, $300-$550
S. OR

Ground
stem

G7, $150-$250
Lake Co., OR

G6, $125-$200
Columbia Riv., OR

Ground
stem

G7, $350-$600
LaPine, OR

G8, $350-$650
Lake Co., OR

Black
obsidian

Obsidian

Broken
half

LOCATION: Western Oregon into Idaho, Nevada and Montana.
DESCRIPTION: A medium to large size, broad, stemmed point with stronger shoulders and a broad parallel sided to expanding stem that is ground. Developed from earlier *Alberta* points. *Cody* points in this area have shorter and longer stems than anywhere else in the country. Flaking is usually the horizontal to oblique style. Chisel tips are known. The concave based form is described in the "Claypool Study," republished in part by Geo. Frisson in "Prehistoric Hunters Of The High Plains & Horner, The Cody Site."
I.D. KEY: Early flaking, square stem that is ground.

Obsidian

Larson
type

Ground
stem

Ground
stem

G7, $125-$200
S. ID

G7, $275-$500
OR

G7, $350-$600
S. OR

G1, $35-$65
N. NV

F
W

1113

SCOTTSBLUFF II (continued)

Made into a scraper

G3, $30-$50
OR

Classic "High Plains" style Scottsbluff

Jasper

Obsidian

Eared knife form

G9, $550-$1000
Portland, OR

Ground "socketed" stem

G8, $1500-$2800
S. OR

Ground stem

G8, $1500-$2500
N. NV

Base nick

SCOTTSBLUFF KNIFE - Early Archaic, 10,000 - 8000 B. P.

(Also see Cody Knife)

Obsidian

G6, $80-$150
Deschutes Co.,
OR, miniature

G6, $15-$30
OR

Red jasper

G7, $15-$30
WA

COTTSBLUFF KNIFE (continued)

G7, $40-$75
OR, miniature — Chalcedony

Ground stem

G6, $40-$70
Columbia Riv., WA

Well ground stem

Obs.

G6, $65-$125
Bend, OR

LOCATION: Western Oregon into Idaho, Nevada and Montana. **DESCRIPTION:** These are reworked Scottsbluff points where the blade was resharpened at an angle, unlike the traditional Cody Complex knife that was designed and made from scratch.

SCRAPER - Paleo to Developmental Phase, 11,500 - 1000 B. P.

(Also see Chopper, Drill, Graver, Hand Axe, Lancet, Paleo Knife, Perforator and Sizer)

Scraping edge

Basalt

G4, $1-$2
S. WA

G6, $2-$5
S. WA

G6, $2-$5
S. OR

G6, $4-$7
Malheur Co., OR

Agate

G6, $1-$3
Malheur Co., OR

Scraping edge

G4 $1-$3
OR

G8, $5-$10
S. WA

G8, $5-$10
Harney Co., OR

G8, $5-$10
S. W. ID

Chert

G8, $5-$10
S. WA

G6, $2-$5
S. W. ID

G6, $2-$5
S. E. OR

Mah. obs.

G8, $5-$10
Malheur Co., OR

F
W

SCRAPER (continued)

Paleo

G6, $8-$15
OR

LOCATION: All early-man sites. **DESCRIPTION:** Thumb, duckbill, claw and turtleback forms are small to medium size, thick, ovoid shaped, uniface, scraping tools that are steeply beveled, especially at the broadest end. Side scrapers are long to oval hand-held uniface flakes with beveling on the edges intended for use. Scraping was done primarily from the sides of these blades. Some of these tools were hafted.

SHANIKO STEMMED - Late Archaic to Woodland, 3500 - 2300 B. P.

(Also see Cascade, Eden, Lake Mohave, Lind Coulee, Owl Cave, Parman, Pryor Stemmed, Rossi Square-Stemmed Scottsbluff, Sierra Contracting Stem, Silver Lake and Windust)

Obsidian

Jasper

Chalcedony

Basalt

G6, $15-$25
S. W. ID

G8, $25-$40
S. OR

G7, $25-$40
OR

G7, $30-$50
OR

G7, $30-$50
OR

G6, $25-$40
S. W. ID

Dark yellow/red agate

Basalt

G0, $66-$125
WA

G7, $15-$30
Plymouth, OR

Jaopor

G7, $12-$20
Columb. Riv., OR

Black basalt

Basalt

Ground stem

G10, $150-$250
Umatilla, OR

Back-lit to show translucency

G8, $20-$35
OR

G6, $5-$10
S. W. ID

G8, $45-$80
OR

1116

Petrified wood

Obsidian

G7, $80-$150
WA

G9, $200-$350
Lake Co., OR

Jasper/agate

Ground stem

Agate

Well ground stem

G8, $55-$100
Columbia Riv., WA

G8, $80-$150
WA

G8, $120-$225
Deschutes Co., OR

G9, $125-$200
Columbia Riv., WA

Obsidian

G8, $90-$175
Jefferson Co., OR

G9, $150-$250
OR

G8, $150-$250
Lake Co., OR

LOCATION: Mid-Columbia River area in Oregon. **DESCRIPTION:** A medium size point with sloping to slightly barbed shoulders. Stems are straight to contracting to a straight to convex base. Stem sides are sometimes ground and bases can be thinned. Flaking is random and the cross section is flat. Named by A.R. Snyder and J.L. Hogue in April, 2000. Formerly called *Early Stemmed*. **I.D. KEY:** Base form and size.

SIDE KNIFE - Devlopmental to Historic Phase, 1000 - 300 B. P.

(Also Scraper, Square-End Knife)

Chalcedony

LOCATION: Great Basin westward. **DESCRIPTION:** A large size blade made for hafting along one side. Gut and plant fibers were used when needed to bind the hafting. Pitch or asphaltum were used as an adhesive to glue the stone tool in the handle.

F
W

G7, $20-$35
Hood Riv., OR

SIERRA CONTRACTING STEM (provisional) - Early to Late Archaic, 6000 - 3000 B. P.

(Also see Coquille, Houx Contracting Stem, Rabbit Island, Shaniko, Silver Lake)

Basalt

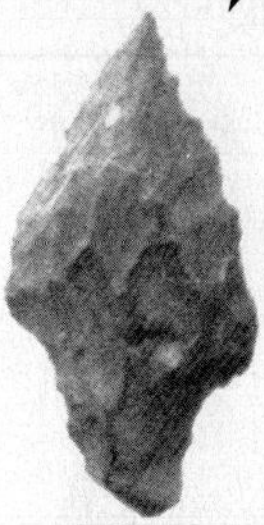

Obsidian

Classic

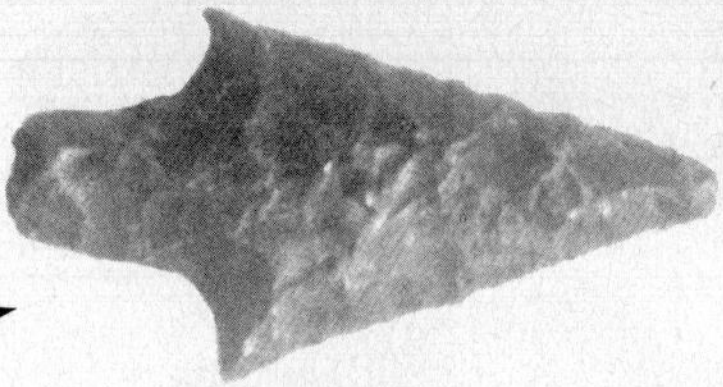

G7, $5-$10
Mendocino Co., CA

Obsidian

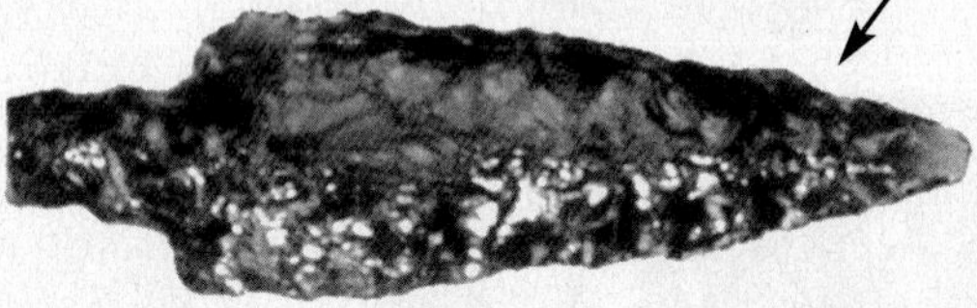

G7, $2-$5
NV

G7, $8-$15
California desert

G7, $2-$5
CA

Classic

G6, $12-$20
Warner Mountains, CA

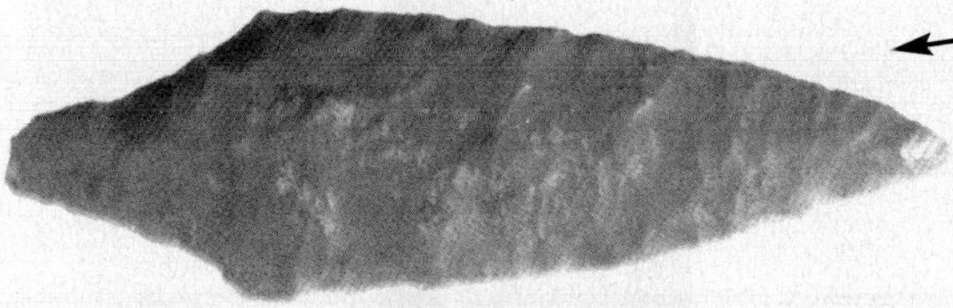

G10, $50-$90
CA

Classic

Tip
nick

Obsidian

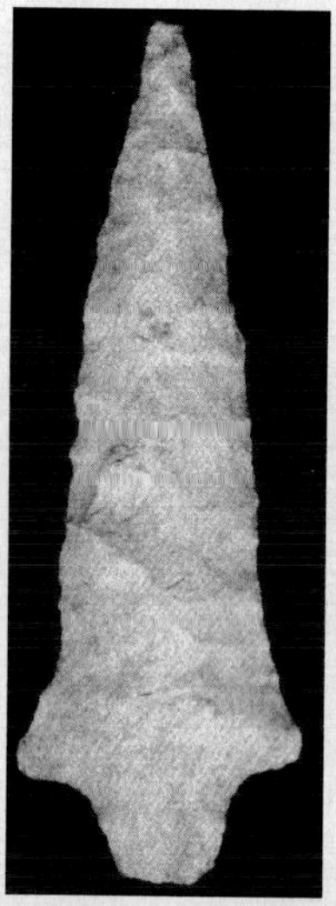

G6, $8-$15
San Bernadino Co., CA

G6, $20-$35
S. OR

G7, $35-$65
Warner Mountains, CA

G7, $35-$60
Warner Mountains, CA

G9, $250-$400
Cent. CA

LOCATION: Northern Calif. southward into Arizona. **DESCRIPTION:** A narrow triangular dart point/knife with horizontal to tapered barbs and a contracting, rounded to pointed stem, although stems do occur parallel sided. Stem edges can be serrated. Stem width varies from narrow to wide. Blade edges are convex, recurved or straight. **I.D. KEY:** Base form and size. See Noel Justice, 2002 & Perino, Vol. 3, 2002.

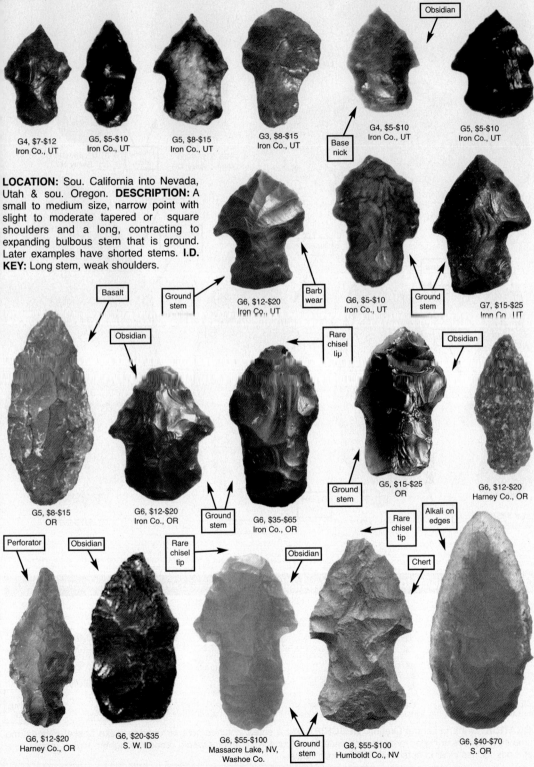

SILVER LAKE - Late Paleo to Early Archaic, 11,000 - 7000 B. P.

(Also see Borax Lake, Eden, Hell Gap, Lake Mohave, Lind Coulee, Parman, Rose Valley, Scottsbluff, Shaniko, Sierra Stemmed)

Obsidian

G4, $7-$12
Iron Co., UT

G5, $5-$10
Iron Co., UT

G5, $8-$15
Iron Co., UT

G3, $8-$15
Iron Co., UT

Base nick

G4, $5-$10
Iron Co., UT

G5, $5-$10
Iron Co., UT

LOCATION: Sou. California into Nevada, Utah & sou. Oregon. **DESCRIPTION:** A small to medium size, narrow point with slight to moderate tapered or square shoulders and a long, contracting to expanding bulbous stem that is ground. Later examples have shorted stems. **I.D. KEY:** Long stem, weak shoulders.

Ground stem

Barb wear

Ground stem

G6, $12-$20
Iron Co., UT

G6, $5-$10
Iron Co., UT

G7, $15-$25
Iron Co., UT

Basalt

Obsidian

Rare chisel lip

Obsidian

Ground stem

G5, $15-$25
OR

G6, $12-$20
Harney Co., OR

G5, $8-$15
OR

G6, $12-$20
Iron Co., OR

Ground stem

G6, $35-$65
Iron Co., OR

Perforator

Obsidian

Rare chisel tip

Obsidian

Rare chisel tip

Alkali on edges

Chert

G6, $12-$20
Harney Co., OR

G6, $20-$35
S. W. ID

G6, $55-$100
Massacre Lake, NV, Washoe Co.

Ground stem

G8, $55-$100
Humboldt Co., NV

G6, $40-$70
S. OR

F
W

1119

SILVER LAKE (continued)

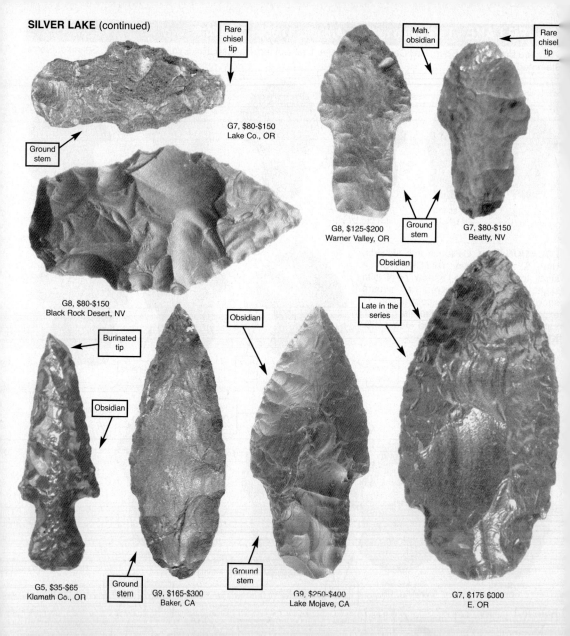

Rare chisel tip

G7, $80-$150
Lake Co., OR

Ground stem

Mah. obsidian

Rare chisel tip

G8, $125-$200
Warner Valley, OR

Ground stem

G7, $80-$150
Beatty, NV

G8, $80-$150
Black Rock Desert, NV

Obsidian

Obsidian

Late in the series

Burinated tip

Obsidian

G5, $35-$65
Klamath Co., OR

Ground stem

G9, $165-$300
Baker, CA

Ground stem

G9, $250-$400
Lake Mojave, CA

G7, $175 $300
E. OR

SIZER - Transitional to Historic Phase, 2,300 - 200 B. P.

(Also see Drill, Graver and Scraper)

G6, $1-$2
OR

G5, $1-$2
OR

G10, $2-$5
OR, fully flaked

G4, $1-$2
OR

G4, $1-$2
Cowlitz Co., WA

G5, $2-$5
Lake Co., OR

Sinew splitting size

LOCATION: North to central Oregon. **DESCRIPTION:** A small, notched scraper used to make basket material the same size. Spruce or cedar roots vary considerably. A uniform diameter would produce a tighter, higher quality basket. Look for use wear in notch. **I.D. KEY:** Small notch.

(Also see Columbia Plateau, Eastgate, Elko, Hendricks, Rose Springs, Sauvie's Island, Wallula)

Petrified wood

Serrated edge

Agate

Chalcedony

Serrated edge

Jasper

G8, $35-$65
Umatilla, OR

G9, $65-$125
Columbia Riv., OR

G9, $125-$200
Columbia Riv., OR

G10, $165-$300
Columbia Riv., OR

G6, $20-$35
OR

G7, $30-$50
OR

G9, $80-$150
N. E. OR

Serrated edge

Agate

Drill

Chalcedony

G8, $40-$75
WA

G8, $40-$75
WA

G6, $30-$50
OR

G0, 000 050
OR

G9, $150-$250
Columbia Riv., OR

G10, $265-$500
Columbia Riv., OR

Obsidian

G10, $325-$600
Columbia Riv., OR

Agate

Basalt

Agate

Serrated edge

Agate

G10, $250-$450
Columbia Riv., OR

G9, $250-$450
Priest Rapids, WA

G9, $250-$450
Rabbit Island, OR

G6, $55-$100
Clearwater Riv., ID

G7, $65-$125
OR

G10, $175-$300
Cascade Lock, WA

Yellow agate

G10, $250-$450
Blalock Isle, WA

Serrated edge

G9, $150-$250
Columbia Riv., OR

**F
W**

LOCATION: Great Basin westward. **DESCRIPTION:** A small to medium size barbed, corner notched dart point. Blade edges can be serrated. Bases are usually straight to concave to auriculate. Evolves into the arrow point at a later time and also believed to have evolved into *Columbia Plateau* arrow points.

SNAKE RIVER DART (continued)

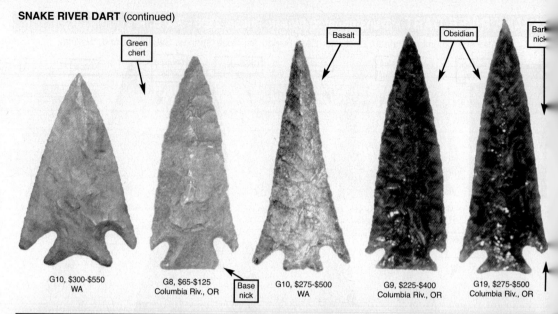

Green chert

Basalt

Obsidian

Barb nick

G10, $300-$550
WA

G8, $65-$125
Columbia Riv., OR

Base nick

G10, $275-$500
WA

G9, $225-$400
Columbia Riv., OR

G19, $275-$500
Columbia Riv., OR

SPEDIS I - Paleo, 10,000 - 8000 B. P.

(Also see Cascade, Celilo Falls, Gypsum Cave, Haskett, Midland & Rabbit Island)

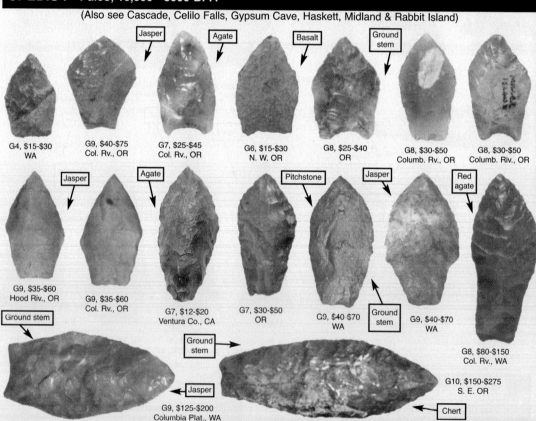

Jasper

Agate

Basalt

Ground stem

G4, $15-$30
WA

G9, $40-$75
Col. Rv., OR

G7, $25-$45
Col. Rv., OR

G6, $15-$30
N. W. OR

G8, $25-$40
OR

G8, $30-$50
Columb. Rv., OR

G8, $30-$50
Columb. Riv., OR

Jasper

Agate

Pitchstone

Jasper

Red agate

G9, $35-$60
Hood Riv., OR

G9, $35-$60
Col. Rv., OR

G7, $12-$20
Ventura Co., CA

G7, $30-$50
OR

G9, $40-$70
WA

Ground stem

G9, $40-$70
WA

G8, $80-$150
Col. Rv., WA

Ground stem

Ground stem

Jasper

G10, $150-$275
S. E. OR

G9, $125-$200
Columbia Plat., WA

Chert

LOCATION: Oregon and Washington, Columbia River basin. **DESCRIPTION:** A small to medium size, thin, narrow, lanceolate dart/knife point with a distinctive "pumpkin seed" shape. The stems are contracting and have straight to slightly concave sides and are ground. The bases are straight, truncated, diagonally biased or notched and are usually smoothed. Single shoulder examples occur. Usually exotic materials were employed. They are thinned by a combination of percussion and pressure. The cross sections are flattened to lenticular. **I.D. KEY:** "Pumpkin seed" bladeform. Usually thinner than Spedis II.

(See Cascade, Celilo Falls, Gypsum Cave, Haskett, Midland, Rabbit Island)

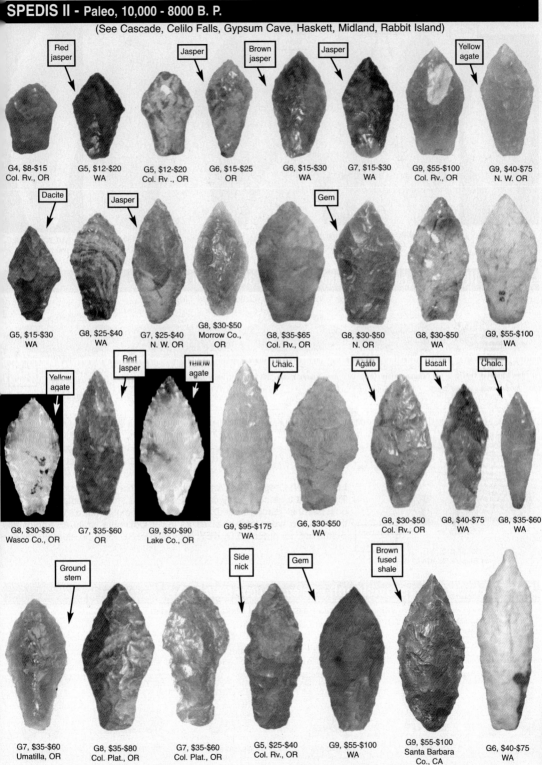

Red jasper

Jasper

Brown jasper

Jasper

Yellow agate

G4, $8-$15
Col. Rv., OR

G5, $12-$20
WA

G5, $12-$20
Col. Rv ., OR

G6, $15-$25
OR

G6, $15-$30
WA

G7, $15-$30
WA

G9, $55-$100
Col. Rv., OR

G9, $40-$75
N. W. OR

Dacite

Jasper

Gem

G5, $15-$30
WA

G8, $25-$40
WA

G7, $25-$40
N. W. OR

G8, $30-$50
Morrow Co.,
OR

G8, $35-$65
Col. Rv., OR

G8, $30-$50
N. OR

G8, $30-$50
WA

G9, $55-$100
WA

Yellow agate

Red jasper

Yellow agate

Chalc.

Agate

Basalt

Chalc.

G8, $30-$50
Wasco Co., OR

G7, $35-$60
OR

G9, $50-$90
Lake Co., OR

G9, $95-$175
WA

G6, $30-$50
WA

G8, $30-$50
Col. Rv., OR

G8, $40-$75
WA

G8, $35-$60
WA

Ground stem

Side nick

Gem

Brown fused shale

G7, $35-$60
Umatilla, OR

G8, $35-$80
Col. Plat., OR

G7, $35-$60
Col. Plat., OR

G5, $25-$40
Col. Rv., OR

G9, $55-$100
WA

G9, $55-$100
Santa Barbara
Co., CA

G6, $40-$75
WA

F
W

LOCATION: Oregon and Washington, Columbia River basin. **DESCRIPTION:** Has the same "pumpkin seed" shaped blade, but the stems are slightly longer and narrower. The stem sides contract to a straight base with rounded corners. Both stem sides and base are usually ground. **I.D. KEY:** "Pumpkin seed" form with longer stem.

SPEDIS II (continued)

G9, $80-$150
S. OR

Chalc.

G9, $125-$200
Morrow Co., OR

Red jasper

G10, $200-$350
Morrow Co., OR

Ground stem

G8, $125-$200
WA

G10, $150-$275
WA

Yellow agate

G10, $200-$375
Wasco Co., OR

SPEDIS III - Late Archaic to Transitional Phase, 3000 - 2000 B. P.

(Also see Bliss, Cascade, Gold Hill and Trojan)

G4, $2-$5
Sauvie's Isle, OR

G6, $12-$20
Sauvie's Isle, OR

G6, $4-$8
Sauvie's Isle, OR

G4, $3-$6
Sauvie's Isle, OR

Tip wear

G9, $15-$25
Sauvie's Isle, OR

Red jasper

G6, $8-$15
Bonneville, OR

G8, $12-$20
Col. Plat., WA

G6, $15-$25
Col. Plat., WA

G9, $20-$35
OR

Root beer agate

G8, $5-$10
Santa Barbara Co., CA

LOCATION: Oregon and Washington, Columbia River basin. **DESCRIPTION:** This type commonly called "Spedis" is a small Woodland point that only has the "pumpkin seed" silhouette. This point is not as well made as the first two types and qualifies as lower Columbia types #5 and/or #6. Stems are not ground. **I.D. KEY:** "Pumpkin seed" form, no stem grinding.

SPEDIS FISHTAIL (provisional) - Paleo, 10,000 - 8000 B. P.

(Also see Cecilo Falls, Goshen, Midland and Spedis)

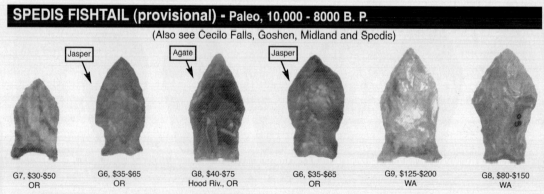

Jasper

Agate

Jasper

G7, $30-$50
OR

G6, $35-$65
OR

G8, $40-$75
Hood Riv., OR

G6, $35-$65
OR

G9, $125-$200
WA

G8, $80-$150
WA

LOCATION: Oregon and Washington, Columbia River basin. **DESCRIPTION:** A small to medium size, thin, lanceolate dart/knife point with most having expanded auricles and a recurved blade producing a waist. Bases are generally concave and are usually ground. This type is separated from the *Pay Paso* type by basal thinning technique. **I.D. KEY:** Eared base.

SPEDIS FISHTAIL (continued)

Yellow agate

Red jasper

Rootbeer agate

G9, $125-$200
OR

G8, $55-$100
Columb. Riv., OR

G9, $125-$200
WA

G8, $125-$200
WA

G9, $150-$250
OR

G10, $175-$300
WA

G9, $175-$300
OR

SPEDIS TRIANGULAR KNIFE - Paleo, 10,000 - 8000 B. P.

(Also see Cecilo Falls, Goshen, Humboldt, Owl Cave, Plainview, Triple T, Tulare Lake)

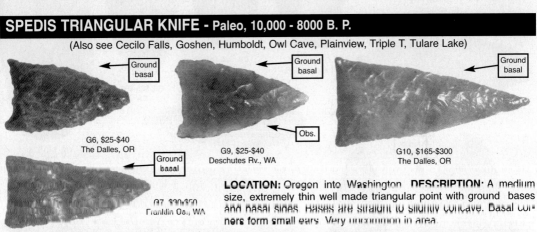

Ground basal

Ground basal

Ground basal

Obs.

G6, $25-$40
The Dalles, OR

G9, $25-$40
Deschutes Rv., WA

G10, $165-$300
The Dalles, OR

Ground basal

G7, $30-$50
Franklin Co., WA

LOCATION: Oregon into Washington **DESCRIPTION:** A medium size, extremely thin well made triangular point with ground bases and basal sides. Bases are straight to slightly concave. Basal corners form small ears. Very uncommon in area.

SQUARE-END KNIFE · Late Archaic to Historic, 3500 - 400 B. P.

(Also see Drill, Hand Axe, Scraper, Paleo Knife & Side Knife)

LOCATION: Great Basin westward. **DESCRIPTION:** A medium to large size squared blade that is beveled on all four sides for cutting. **I.D. KEY:** Squared form.

G6, $10-$20
Lake Co., OR,
Christmas Lake.

G6, $12-$20
Lake Co., OR

Obs.

White chert

G6, $12-$20
S. OR

Early form

G8, $30-$50
Lake Co., OR

Basalt

F
W

STEAMBOAT LANCEOLATE - Mid to late Archaic, 5000 - 2500 B. P.

(Also see Cascade, Cordilleran, Malaga Cove Leaf, Sierra Contracting Stem)

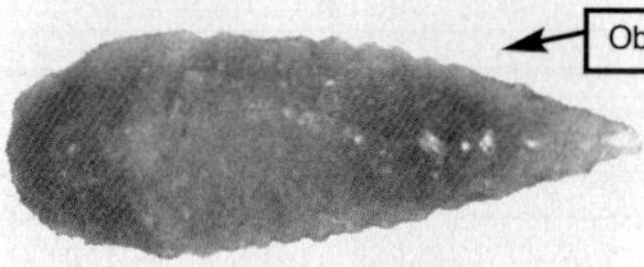

Obsidian

G7, $15-$30
CA

G7, $20-$35
OR

G7, $20-$35
OR

Basalt

G7, $25-$45
Lake Co., OR

G8, $25-$45
CA

Obsidian

G8, $35-$60
CA

G9, $40-$75
CA

G8, $15-$30
CA

Jasper

G6, $12-$20
OR

G6, $30-$50
CA

Jasper

G6, $25-$40
CA

G5, $20-$35
CA

G9, $200-$375
CA

LOCATION: Northern California, Western Nevada into southern Oregon. **DESCRIPTION:** A medium to large size, narrow to broad, lanceolate dart/knife point with a rounded, pointed or straight base. Some examples show stem grinding. See Noel Justice, 2002.

(Also see Exotic and Vendetta)

Black obsidian

G6, $65-$120
Holt, CA

Unique double notch

G6, $55-$100
Bethel Isle, CA

G5, $45-$85
Holt, CA

Black obsidian

G3, $25-$40
Bethel Isle, CA

G8, $40-$75
Diablo Mtn., CA

G7, $175-$300
San Joaquin Co., CA

G5, $35-$60
Diablo Mtn., CA

Black obsidian

Black obsidian

G7, $450-$100
Holt, CA

G8, $275-$500
Holt, CA

G7, $150-$250
Mt. Diablo, CA

G7, $125-$200
Sacramento Valley, CA

Black obsidian

"Squared" notches

Edge wear

G8, $400-$700
Holt, CA

G8, $400-700
Holt, CA

G4, $40-$75
Holt, CA

Note rare and unique notching

G10, $900-$1600
Holt, CA

Green Franciscan chert

G7, $175-$300
W. NV

Black obsidian

Classic form

G9, $1200-$2000
Holt, CA

"Squared" notches

G9, $450-$800
Holt, CA

Broken tip

Black obsidian

G8, $650-$1000
Holt, CA

G2, $30-$50
Sacramento Valley, CA

F
W

LOCATION: Stockton, California area. Very rare. **DESCRIPTION:** A small to large size, thin, narrow, point that has exaggerated, squared barbs along the blade edges. Believed to have been used for sawing as well as an arrow point. Forms vary from stemmed to auriculate to corner notched. **I.D. KEY:** Deep square barbs. **Warning:** Reproductions exist in the market today. Credible provenience is recommended before acquiring a specimen.

Black obsidian

Restored ear

Tip and right ear are broken & glued

"Squared" notches

G6, $1500-$2700
Holt, CA

STRONG BARBED AURICULATE - Transitional to Classic Phase, 1750 - 700 B. P.

(Also see Columbia Mule Ear, Humboldt and Triple T)

Note: Absolute authentication of this rare type is necessary as modern reproductions may exist.

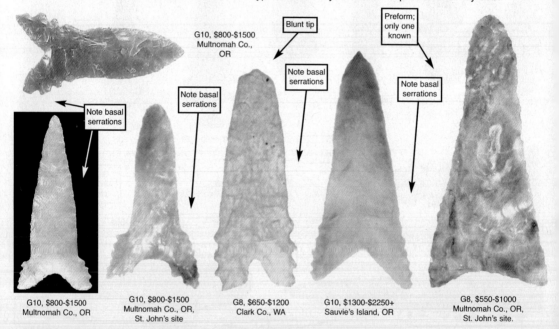

G10, $800-$1500
Multnomah Co., OR

Blunt tip

Preform; only one known

Note basal serrations

Note basal serrations

Note basal serrations

Note basal serrations

Note basal serrations

G10, $800-$1500
Multnomah Co., OR

G10, $800-$1500
Multnomah Co., OR,
St. John's site

G8, $650-$1200
Clark Co., WA

G10, $1300-$2250+
Sauvie's Island, OR

G8, $550-$1000
Multnomah Co., OR,
St. John's site.

LOCATION: Sauvie's Island, Oregon and adjacent areas. **DESCRIPTION:** A very rare type with only 15 examples known. A medium size auriculate point with a concave, notched to v-shaped base and an obtuse to apiculate tip. The basal ears are serrated. **I.D. KEY:** Basal ears serrated. **Note:** Unique; none have been sold and value will be determined when sales data becomes available. See Perino Vol. 3, 2002.

SUDDEN SERIES - Early to Mid-Archais, 6300 - 4180 B. P.

(Also see Bitterroot, Northern Side Notched)

Chert

G8, $25-$40
Cent. UT

LOCATION: Cent. Utah into SW Colorado and Arizona. **DESCRIPTION:** A medium size side notched dart/knife point that comes in two forms. Side notches are high up from the base. The regular form has a large basal area and a straight to concave base. The "Rocker" form has a convex. base. See Noel Justice, 2002.

SURPRISE VALLEY - Mid-Archaic, 4000 - 700 B. P.

(Also see Bitterroot, Northern Side Notched)

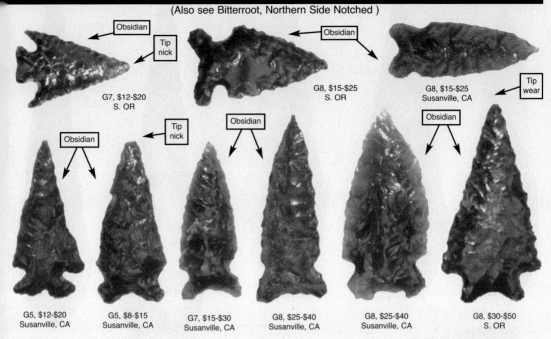

Obsidian
Tip nick
G7, $12-$20
S. OR

Obsidian
G8, $15-$25
S. OR

Obsidian
G8, $15-$25
Susanville, CA
Tip wear

Tip nick
Obsidian
G5, $12-$20
Susanville, CA

G5, $8-$15
Susanville, CA

Obsidian
G7, $15-$30
Susanville, CA

G8, $25-$40
Susanville, CA

Obsidian
G8, $25-$40
Susanville, CA

G8, $30-$50
S. OR

LOCATION: Northern California **DESCRIPTION:** A broad, concave basal, eared, low quality and fairly thick, side-notched point. Named after Surprise Valley located in Lassen Co., CA. Shoulders are tapered to barbed. See Noel Justice, 2002.

THREE-PIECE FISH SPEAR - Transitional to Historic Phase, 2300 - 200 B.P.

(Also see Harpoon)

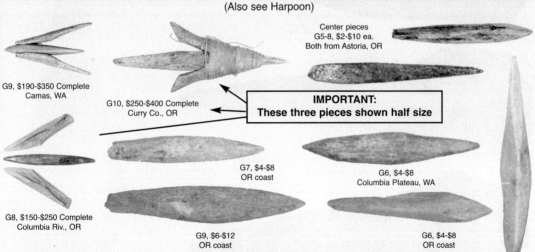

G9, $190-$350 Complete
Camas, WA

G10, $250-$400 Complete
Curry Co., OR

Center pieces
G5-8, $2-$10 ea.
Both from Astoria, OR

IMPORTANT:
These three pieces shown half size

G7, $4-$8
OR coast

G6, $4-$8
Columbia Plateau, WA

G8, $150-$250 Complete
Columbia Riv., OR

G9, $6-$12
OR coast

G6, $4-$8
OR coast

G8, $5-$10
OR coast

LOCATION: East & west coast into Canada. **DESCRIPTION:** A small size bone point consisting of two flanges and a short center shaft. The flanges comprise the barbs and a portion of the point. The flanges are grooved at one end to fit over the center shaft. They were tied together to form the point. This point was then hafted over a spear shaft. Rarely found complete. **I.D. KEY:** Widely extended barbs.

F
W

TIMPONOGUS BLADE (provisional) - Transitional to Historic Phase, 800 - 200 B.P.

(Also see Cascade, Mahkin Shouldered, Wahmuza, Wildcat Canyon)

TIMPONOGUS BLADE (continued)

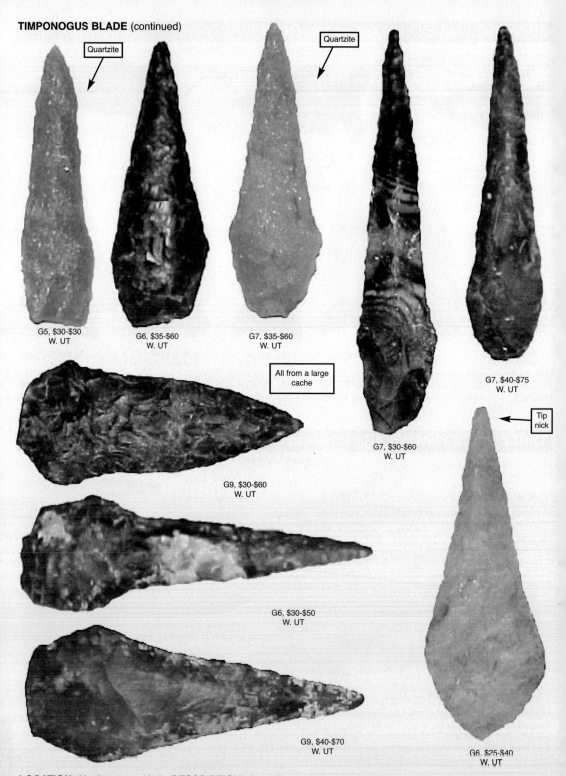

Quartzite

Quartzite

G5, $30-$30
W. UT

G6, $35-$60
W. UT

G7, $35-$60
W. UT

All from a large cache

G7, $40-$75
W. UT

G7, $30-$60
W. UT

G9, $30-$60
W. UT

Tip nick

G6, $30-$50
W. UT

G9, $40-$70
W. UT

G6, $25-$40
W. UT

LOCATION: Northwestern Utah. **DESCRIPTION:** A medium to large size blade that occurs in caches in two forms. The stemmed form has an enlarged basal area that contracts to a straight, pointed or rounded base. Blade edges can vary. The stem area can be short to very long. The side-notched form has shallow notches placed on either side of the stem creating small tapered shoulders. Similar in outline to the *Wahmuza* point found in the Northwest.

1130

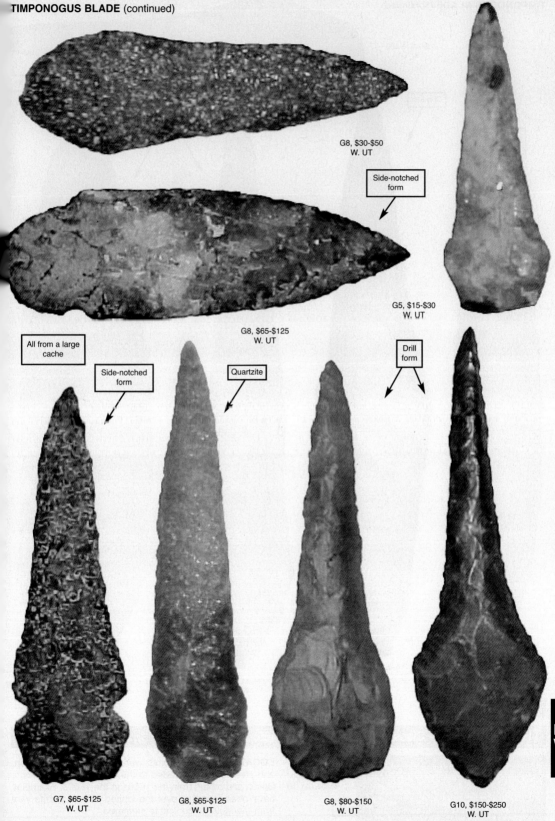

G8, $30-$50
W. UT

Side-notched
form

G5, $15-$30
W, UT

G8, $65-$125
W. UT

All from a large
cache

Side-notched
form

Quartzite

Drill
form

G7, $65-$125
W. UT

G8, $65-$125
W. UT

G8, $80-$150
W. UT

G10, $150-$250
W. UT

F
W

TIMPONOGUS BLADE (continued)

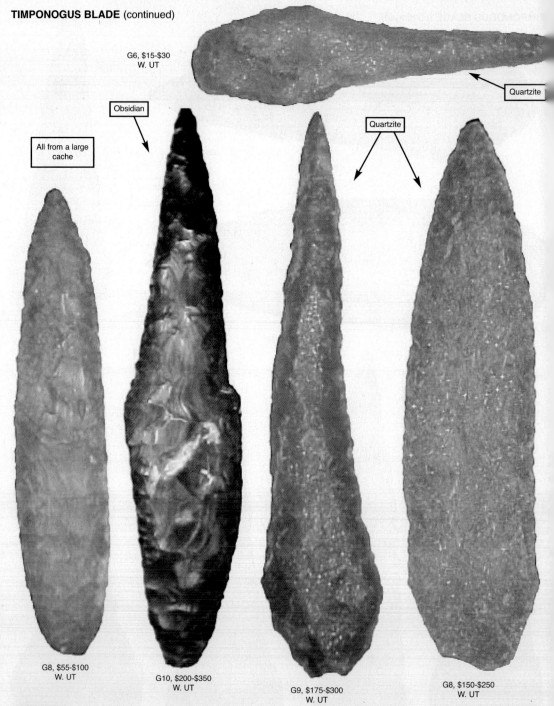

G6, $15-$30
W. UT

Quartzite

Obsidian

Quartzite

All from a large cache

G8, $55-$100
W. UT

G10, $200-$350
W. UT

G9, $175-$300
W. UT

G8, $150-$250
W. UT

TOGGLE (See Harpoon)

TRADE POINTS - Classic to Historic Phase, 400 - 170 B.P.

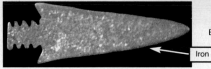

G8, $50-$90
Bonner Co., ID

Iron

LOCATION: These points were made of copper, iron, and steel and were traded to the Indians by the French, British and others from the 1600s to the 1800s. Examples have been found all over the United States. Forms vary from triangular to conical to stemmed.

TRIPLE "T" - Middle Archaic, 5500 - 5000 B. P.

(Also see Black Rock Concave, Cascade, Humboldt, Mendocino Concave Base and Strong)

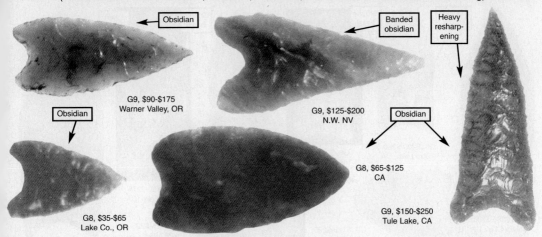

Obsidian

Banded obsidian

Heavy resharp-ening

G9, $90-$175
Warner Valley, OR

Obsidian

G9, $125-$200
N.W. NV

Obsidian

Obsidian

G8, $35-$65
Lake Co., OR

G8, $65-$125
CA

G9, $150-$250
Tule Lake, CA

LOCATION: Great Basin westward. **DESCRIPTION:** A medium size, lanceolate point with rounded basal corners and a concave base. Blade edges curve from point to base. Another variation of the *Humboldt* series.

TROJAN (provisional) - Developmental to Classic Phase, 1320 - 300 B. P.

(Also see Cottonwood, Gold Hill, Magala Cove Leaf)

Jasper

Agate

Agate

Triangular form

Jasper

$1-$5 ea.
Trojan Point, OR, Type site.

Knife

G6, $1-$3
S.W. WA

G6, $1-$3
OR

G6, $1-$3
OR

G9, $1-$3
WA

Chisel tip

Knife

Knife

Jasper

Agate

$1-$3 ea.
Trojan Point, OR, Type site.

$2-$4 ea.
Trojan Point, OR, Type site.

F
W

LOCATION: Lower Columbia River from Portland to Astoria. **DESCRIPTION:** A small, thin, triangular to ovate arrow point. Many are made from flakes with unfinished bases and minimal retouch. Over 2200 were found at the Trojan site. Possible use as tips in bone harpoons for hunting seal and fish.

1133

TULARE LAKE - Paleo, 11,200 - 10,000 B. P.

(Also see Black Rock Concave, Clovis, Humboldt and Mendocino Concave Base)

Thinning strikes

Ground basal

Ground basal

Chert

G6, $200-$350
Tulare Lake, CA

G6, $200-$350
Tulare Lake, CA

G6, $200-$350
Tulare Lake, CA

Chert

G5, $265-$500
Tulare Lake, CA

G5, $125-$200
CA

G6, $150-$275
Tulare Lake, CA

G5, $125-$225
Tulare Lake, CA

G10, $450-$800
Kern Co., CA

LOCATION: Central California. **DESCRIPTION:** A late *Clovis* variant. A small to medium size unfluted, auriculate point with a concave base. Basal area is ground. Some bases are thinned. Basal area is usually over half the length of the point. Has been found with *Crescents* and unfluted *Clovis* points at the Witt site. See Perino, vol. 3, 2002.

TULARE LAKE BI-POINT (provisional) - Early Archaic, 8,000 - 6,000 B. P.

(Also see Cascade, Cordilleran, Early Leaf, Excelsior, Kennewick, Wildcat Canyon)

G2, $1-$3
Tulare Lake, CA

G4, $8-$15
Tulare Lake, CA

G6, $12-$20
Tulare Lake, CA

G6, $15-$30
Tulare Lake, CA

G6, $25-$40
Tulare Lake, CA

G8, $35-$60
Tulare Lake, CA

LOCATION: Central California. **DESCRIPTION:** A medium to large size double pointed lanceolate blade found on the Clovis Witt site in California.

TUOLUMNE NOTCHED (provisional) - Late Archaic, 3100 - 2500 B. P.

(Also see McGillivray, Need Stemmed Lanceolate, Nightfire & Willits Side Notched)

LOCATION: Central Northern California. **DESCRIPTION:** A large corner to side notched point with a convex, bulbous base. Some examples have excellent oblique, parallel flaking on the blade faces. Similar to but later than the Nightfire point found further North. **I.D. KEY:** Bulbous base. See Noel Justice, 2002.

G8, $125-$200
Fort Rock Valley, OR

Obsidian

1134

UOLUMNE NOTCHED (continued)

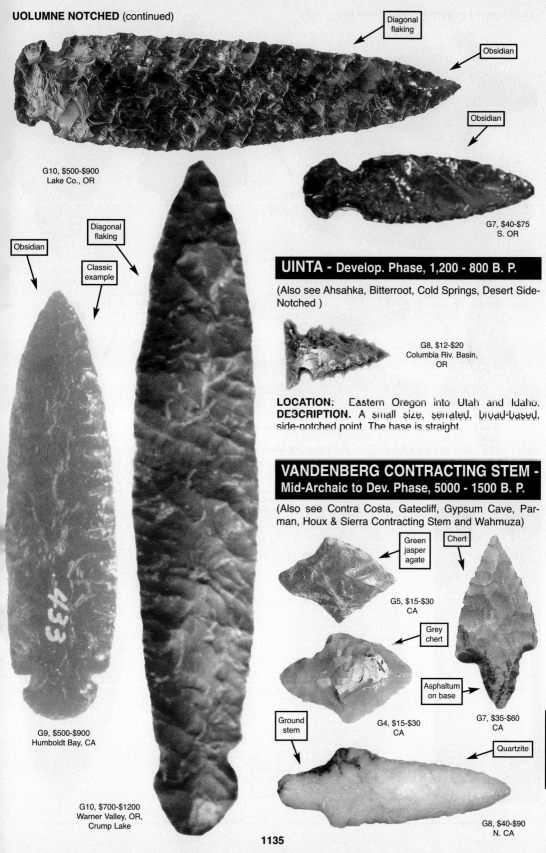

Diagonal flaking

Obsidian

Obsidian

G10, $500-$900
Lake Co., OR

G7, $40-$75
S. OR

Obsidian

Diagonal flaking

Classic example

UINTA - Develop. Phase, 1,200 - 800 B. P.

(Also see Ahsahka, Bitterroot, Cold Springs, Desert Side-Notched)

G8, $12-$20
Columbia Riv. Basin, OR

LOCATION: Eastern Oregon into Utah and Idaho.
DESCRIPTION. A small size, serrated, broad-based, side-notched point. The base is straight.

VANDENBERG CONTRACTING STEM - Mid-Archaic to Dev. Phase, 5000 - 1500 B. P.

(Also see Contra Costa, Gatecliff, Gypsum Cave, Parman, Houx & Sierra Contracting Stem and Wahmuza)

Green jasper agate

Chert

G5, $15-$30
CA

Grey chert

Asphaltum on base

G7, $35-$60
CA

Ground stem

G4, $15-$30
CA

G9, $500-$900
Humboldt Bay, CA

Quartzite

G10, $700-$1200
Warner Valley, OR,
Crump Lake

G8, $40-$90
N. CA

F
W

VANDENBERG CONTRACTING STEM (continued)

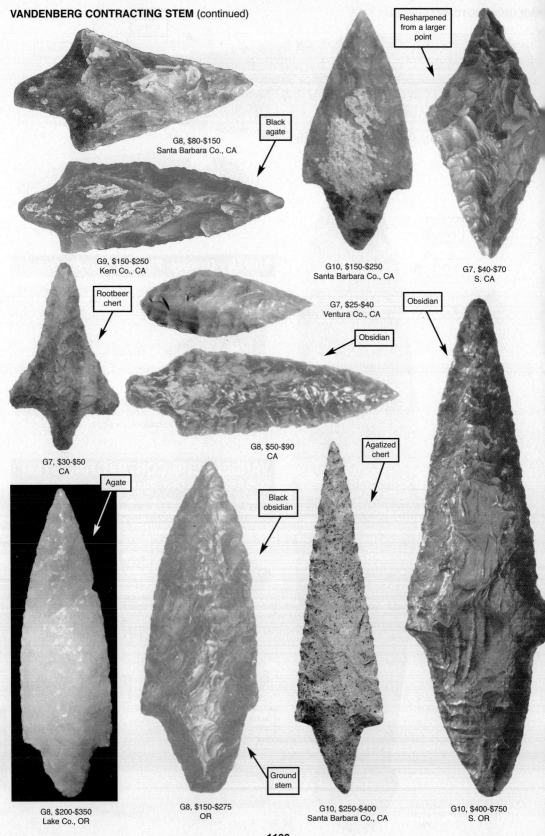

G8, $80-$150
Santa Barbara Co., CA

Black agate

G9, $150-$250
Kern Co., CA

Rootbeer chert

Resharpened from a larger point

G10, $150-$250
Santa Barbara Co., CA

G7, $40-$70
S. CA

G7, $25-$40
Ventura Co., CA

Obsidian

Obsidian

G8, $50-$90
CA

G7, $30-$50
CA

Agate

Agatized chert

Black obsidian

Ground stem

G8, $200-$350
Lake Co., OR

G8, $150-$275
OR

G10, $250-$400
Santa Barbara Co., CA

G10, $400-$750
S. OR

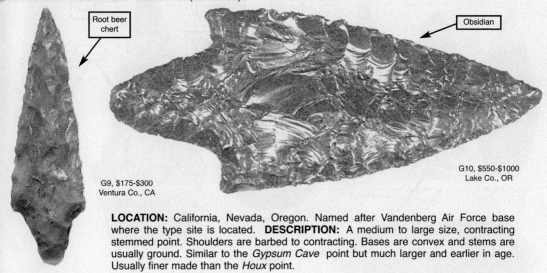

Root beer chert

Obsidian

G9, $175-$300
Ventura Co., CA

G10, $550-$1000
Lake Co., OR

LOCATION: California, Nevada, Oregon. Named after Vandenberg Air Force base where the type site is located. **DESCRIPTION:** A medium to large size, contracting stemmed point. Shoulders are barbed to contracting. Bases are convex and stems are usually ground. Similar to the *Gypsum Cave* point but much larger and earlier in age. Usually finer made than the *Houx* point.

VENDETTA (provisional) - Transitional to Classic Phase, 1750 - 200 B. P.

(Also see Combat Wand Blade, Dagger, Exotic & Sauvie's Island Shoulder)

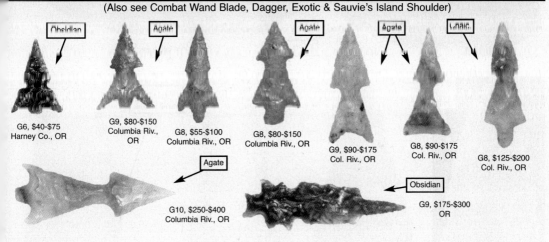

Obsidian

Agate

Agate

Agate

Chalc.

G6, $40-$75
Harney Co., OR

G9, $80-$150
Columbia Riv.,
OR

G8, $55-$100
Columbia Riv., OR

G8, $80-$150
Columbia Riv., OR

G9, $90-$175
Col. Riv., OR

G8, $90-$175
Col. Riv., OR

G8, $125-$200
Col. Riv., OR

Agate

Obsidian

G10, $250-$400
Columbia Riv., OR

G9, $175-$300
OR

LOCATION: Columbia River Basin, Oregon. Researched and described by Jim Hogue and Del Greer in 1998. **DESCRIPTION:** A small to medium size barbed-notched triangular blade that has had a second set of notches flaked into the blade halfway between the shoulders and the tip. This style is usually made on larger sized *Wallula Gap* and/or *Rabbit Islands*, although other types are sometimes used. The cross section is flattened lenticular. The depth of the second set of barbs varies, and triple notches do occur. These points are well made and usually of gem material, and were locally called "*Vendetta*" points as they were designed to snap at the weakened halfway point, on contact with bone, cartilage or heavy muscle. **I.D. KEY:** Double shoulders.

WAHMUZA - Developmenal to early Historic Phase, 1500 - 500 B. P.

F
W

(Also see Cascade, Gypsum Cave, Owl Cave, Plateau Pent., Vandenberg Contracting Stem & Wildcat Canyon)

LOCATION: Great Basin area. **DESCRIPTION:** A medium size lanceolate point with a recurved edge and a long, straight-sided, tapered stem that is ground. The basal edge is short and straight to rounded. **I.D. KEY:** Pronounced contracting stem.

WAHMUZA (continued)

Chalcedony

Ground basal sides

Tip wear

Jasper

G4, $12-$20
Lake Co., OR

G4, $12-$20
OR

G7, $25-$45
Lake Co., OR

G8, $40-$75
OR

Agate

G6, $30-$55
Sou. OR

G8, $50-$90
Five Mile Locks, OR

G8, $35-$65
Malheur Co., OR

Obsidian

G7, $30-$50
OR

G9, $65-$125
W. UT

Ground basal sides

Note parallel blade strikes

G8, $65-$125
Caribou Co., ID

G8, $55-$100
OR

G8, $110-$200
OR

Petrified wood

G9, $200-$350
WA

G10, $250-$400
Sherman Co., OR

1138

Obsidian

Obsidian

G10, $200-$350
Warner Valley, OR

Obsidian

G6, $125-$200
Warner Valley, OR

Jasper

Well
ground
basal
area

Obsidian

G8, $150-$250
Warner Valley, OR

Obsidian

Obsidian

G6, $150-$250
Warner Valley, OR

G9, $250-$400
Warner Valley, OR

G9, $275-$500
Sou. OR

G10, $500-$900
Columbia River, OR

F
W

1139

WALLULA GAP RECTANGULAR STEMMED - Dev. to Historic Phase, 1000 - 200 B. P.

(Also see Columbia Plateau, Eastgate, Rabbit Island, Rose Spring & Sauvie's Island)

Jasper
G6, $12-$20
S. WA

G7, $15-$30
OR

G9, $15-$30
Condon, OR

G7, $15-$30
N. OR

Agate / Chalc.
G5, $8-$15
Col. Rv., OR

G9, $25-$40
S. WA

Agate
G10, $45-$80
N. OR

Agate
G10, $55-$100
WA

Jasper
G8, $15-$3
OR

Jasper
G8, $25-$40
OR

G10, $50-$90
OR

Black jasper
G8, $35-$60
Condon, OR

Agate
G9, $35-$65
John Day Rv., OR

Candy stripe agate
G9, $45-$80
Col. Rv., WA

Agate
G8, $30-$50
OR

G6, $20-$35
OR

Agate
G7, $35-$65
Col.. Ri., WA

Agate
G9, $50-$90
WA

G10, $65-$125
John Day Riv., OR

G7, $35-$65
Col. Rv., OR

G10, $65-$125
Condon, OR

Jasper
G7, $25-$45
Col. Rv., OR

Agate
G6, $15-$30
Col. Rv., OR

Jasper
G6, $15-$30
Col. Rv., OR

G7, $25-$40
Col. Rv., WA

Agate
G6, $30-$50
S. WA

G9, $75-$140
Col. Rv., WA

Jasper
G6, $12-$20
Col. Rv., OR

Agate
G9, $25-$45
WA

Agate
G9, $25-$45
S. WA

Agate / Chalc.
G8, $15-$30
Col. Rv., WA

Jasper
G8, $25-$40
OR

Agate
G9, $30-$55
OR

Agate
G9, $65-$1
Col. Rv., O

Agate
G6, $30-$50
S. WA

Obs.
G9, $45-$80
OR

Agate
G10, $65-$125
N. OR

Agate
G9, $25-$45
WA

Chalc.
G8, $15-$30
WA

Basalt
G6, $15-$30
Col. Rv., WA

Agate
G9, $50-$95
S. WA

Hed jasper
G9, $35-$60
OR

Agate
G6, $45-$80
OR

Opalized wood
G6, $25-$50
OR

Agate
G8, $35-$60
S. W. WA

G8, $40-$70
WA

Agate
G9, $45-$80
WA

G9, $65-$125
WA

Red jasper
G8, $35-$60
S. WA

Agate
G9, $65-$125
S. WA

LOCATION: Columbia River basin of Oregon and Washington. **DESCRIPTION:** A small size, thin, stemmed, arrow point usually with barbs. Blades are more narrow and barbs are not as prominent as on *Columbia Plateau* points. The stem can be slightly expanding or contracting or bulbous but is usually rectangular. Shoulders barbed to horizontal. Blade edges can be serrated. A contracting stem would place the point in the *Rabbit Island* type.

Red jasper

Candy agate

Agate

Tip nick

G6, $12-$20
OR

G10, $350-$600
WA

G10, $165-$300
Col. Rv., OR

G4, $25-$40
WA

Petrified wood

Jasper

Chalc.

Tip nick

Chalc.

Yel. jasper

G8, $45-$80
OR

G8, $45-$80
Col. Rv ., OR

G9, $125-$200
Columb. Rv., WA

G9, $65-$125
Columb. Rv., OR

G9, $125-$200
OR

G8, $55-$100
Col. Rv., WA

G10, $125-$200
OR

G9, $40-$75
Umtilla, OR

Tip nick

Agate

Chalc.

Jasper

Red jasper

Chalc.

Agate

G7, $40-$70
S. WA

G10, $150-$250
S. WA

G9, $80-$150
Col. Rv., WA

G9, $80-$150
Col. Rv., WA

G7, $45-$80
WA

G10, $150-$275
Col. Rv., OR

G9, $65-$125
Col. Rv., WA

G9, $35-$65
S. WA

Arrow

Knife

Jasper

Tip nick

Agate

Jasper

Knife

Yellow agate

Jasper

G8, $55-$100
Col. Rv., WA

G5, $15-$30
Col. Rv., WA

G9, $125-$200
Colum. Rv., WA

G8, $50-$90
OR

G10, $150-$275
WA

G9, $80-$150
Col. Rv., OR

G9, $80-$150
Col. Rv., WA

G9, $90-$165
Col. Rv., WA

Red jasper

Arrow

Dart

Knife

Knife

Red jasper

Obsidian

Knife

G6, $15-$30
OR

G9, $125-$200
WA

G8, $100-$175
WA

G7, $35-$65
N. OR

G8, $140-$250
OR

G6, $55-$100
OR

F
W

WASHOE (provisional) - Developmental to Present, 1200 B.P. - Present

(Also see Cascade, Early Leaf & McKee Uniface)

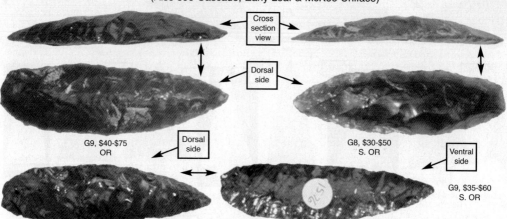

Cross section view

Dorsal side

G9, $40-$75
OR

Dorsal side

G8, $30-$50
S. OR

Ventral side

G9, $35-$60
S. OR

LOCATION: Southern Oregon. **DESCRIPTION:** A medium to large size elliptical bladelet with a dorsal ridge on one side and flat on the ventral side. Bases are pointed, straight to rounded. **I.D. KEY:** Uniface bladelet. See Justice, 2002.

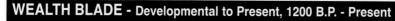

WEALTH BLADE - Developmental to Present, 1200 B.P. - Present

(Also see Cascade, Early Leaf)

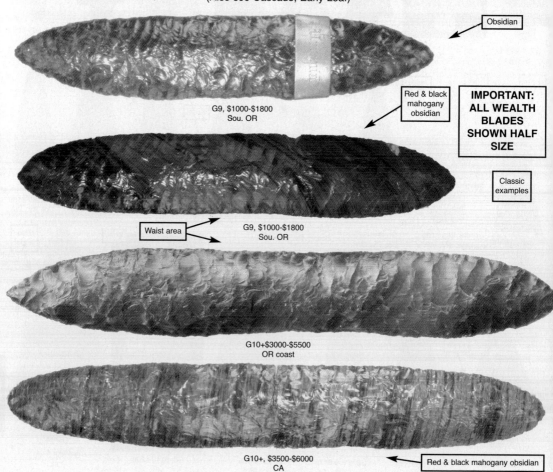

Obsidian

G9, $1000-$1800
Sou. OR

Red & black mahogany obsidian

IMPORTANT: ALL WEALTH BLADES SHOWN HALF SIZE

Classic examples

Waist area

G9, $1000-$1800
Sou. OR

G10+$3000-$5500
OR coast

G10+, $3500-$6000
CA

Red & black mahogany obsidian

1142

SHOWN HALF SIZE

Broken & glued

WENDOVER - Early to middle Archaic, 7000 - 5000 B. P.

(Also see Bitterroot, Bullhead, Chilcotin Plateau, Eastgate, Hell's Canyon, Merrybell and Rose Springs)

Basalt

G6, $12-$20
Black Rock Des., OR

G7, $12-$20
Wallowa Co., OR

G5, $10-$20
Pyramid Lake, NV

Obsidian

Red agate

G6, $15-$25
Sou. OR

G7, $15-$30
OR

G10, $125-$200
Umatilla Co., OR

G7, $2500-$4000
S.OR

LOCATION: N.W. California & S.W. Oregon near the Pacific coast. **DESCRIPTION:** A large to very large size lanceolate, double pointed blade. Some examples have a waist in the center of the blade to facilitate holding. Recent examples have been used in dance ceremonies. The classic examples are 11"–16" long, well made, generally always waisted. **I.D. KEY:** Extreme size.

Obsidian

Basalt

Obsidian

G8, $25-$40
Sou. OR

G9, $15-$30
Harney Co., OR

G9, $35-$60
Cent. OR

F
W

WENDOVER (continued)

G10, $80-$150
Lake Co., OR

G5, $10-$20
S. W. ID

LOCATION: Great Basin westward. **DESCRIPTION:** A medium size, narrow, expanded stem to side notched dart point with a convex base. Shoulders can be slightly tapered to barbed. Base corners are sharp to rounded. Found on buffalo jump sites in Owyhee Co., ID.

G8, $80-$150
S. E. OR

G6, $40-$75
S. W. ID

G9, $225-$400
N.W. UT, Hogup Mountains,

G9, $150-$250
OR

WILDCAT CANYON (provisional) - Early Archaic, 9000 - 7500 B. P.

(Also see Cascade, Early Leaf, Paleo Knife, Plateau Pentagonal & Wahmuza)

G8, $65-$120
Columbia Riv., WA

LOCATION: Found in Wildcat Canyon near The Dalles, Oregon.
DESCRIPTION: A large, broad, lanceolate knife with a convex base. Most basal areas are ground where they were hafted. Blades are usually beveled when resharpened. *Cascades* do not have this beveling.

G10, $55-$100
OR

1144

Chert

Beveled edge

Beveled edge

G8, $30-$50
Columbia Riv., WA

Chert

Beveled edge

G9, $45-$80
Columbia Riv., WA

Basalt

Well ground stem

G6, $20-$35
OR

Beveled edge

G9, $55-$100
OR

G9, $55-$100
WA

Beveled edge

Chert

G9, $150-$275
Columbia River, WA

G8, $65-$125
WA

G8, $65-$125
WA

F
W

G9, $200-$375
Columbia River, WA

G9, $200-$350
Columbia Riv., OR

G6, $150-$250
Columbia Riv., OR

WILLITS SIDE NOTCHED - Mid-Archaic, 4000 - 1500 B. P.

(See Kelsey Creek, Mayacmas, McGillivray, Need Stemmed Lanceolate, Nightfire & Tuolumne Notched)

Basalt

Obsidian

Obsidian

Heavily
resharpened

Obsidian

G7, $35-$60
Silver Lake, OR

G7, $35-$75
Lake Co., OR

G5, $12-$20
Humboldt Co., NV

G6, $20-$35
Sou. CA coast

G7, $30-$50
CA

Basalt

G1, $2-$5
OR

Broken
tip

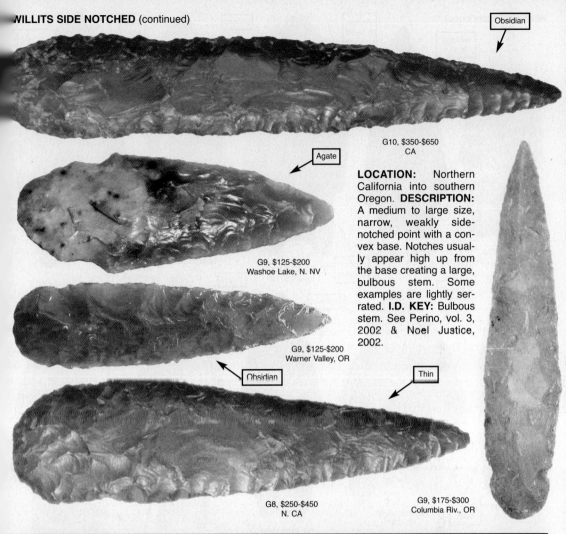

Obsidian

G10, $350-$650
CA

Agate

G9, $125-$200
Washoe Lake, N. NV

G9, $125-$200
Warner Valley, OR

Obsidian

Thin

G8, $250-$450
N. CA

G9, $175-$300
Columbia Riv., OR

LOCATION: Northern California into southern Oregon. **DESCRIPTION:** A medium to large size, narrow, weakly side-notched point with a convex base. Notches usually appear high up from the base creating a large, bulbous stem. Some examples are lightly serrated. **I.D. KEY:** Bulbous stem. See Perino, vol. 3, 2002 & Noel Justice, 2002.

WINDUST - Paleo to Early Archaic, 10,500 - 8000 B. P.

(See Eden, Hell Gap, Lake Mohave, Lind Coulee, Owl Cave, Parman, Scottsbluff, Shaniko Stemmed, Silver Lake & Youngs River)

Obsidian

Mahagony obsidian

Obsidian

G6, $40-$75
Sou. OR

G6, $40-$75
N. Lake Co., OR

Ground stem

G6, $55-$100
Lake Co., OR

G6, $40-$75
Sou. OR

Ground stem

G7, $40-$75
Gooding Co., ID

F
W

LOCATION: Oregon and Washington. **DESCRIPTION:** A medium size, broad point that has weak shoulders and a stemmed, concave basal area. Basal concavity can be shallow to deep and rarely can be fluted. Some examples are non-stemmed with a concave base. Basal area can be ground. Chisel tips occur along with *Lake Mojave* and *Parman* points. This point co-existed with *Clovis*.

WINDUST (continued)

Windust/Scott. I

Broken & glued

Jasper

Side wear

Obsidian

G8, $125-$200
Harney Co., OR

G3, $15-$30
OR

Basal grinding

G9, $200-$350
Lake Co., OR

Jasper

G5, $90-$175
Lake Co., OR

Basal grinding

G9, $250-$400
Warner Valley, OR

Basalt

Obsidian

Basalt

G8, $125-$200
OR

Ground stem

G8, $150-$250
E. OR

G9, $150-$250
E. OR

G9, $250-$450
WA

Basal grinding

G0, $175 $300
Lake Co., OR, Christmas Lake

Monterey chert

G9, $165-$300
Cent. CA

Yellow jasper

Tip wear

Obsidian

G9, $175-$300
WA

Obsidian

Ground stem

G9, $175-$300
WA

G7, $150-$250
WA

G4, $30-$50
WA

1148

Obsidian

Windust/
Cody

Obsidian

Classic
form

G9, $300-$500
Lake Co., OR

G9, $325-$450
Lake Co., OR

G7, $275-$500
Sou. OR

G10, $400-$750
S. OR

Obsidian

Classic
form

Ground
stem

Thinning
strikes at
base

Obsidian

Windust/
Scottsbluff II

G7, $275-$500
Lake Co., OR

G9, $400-$700
S.E. OR. Classic form.

G8, $350-$600
S. E. OR

G6, $200-$350
Rye patch, NV

F
W

Obsidian

Basalt

Basal grinding

G9, $250-$450
S. W. ID

G6, $65-$125
OR

G9, $350-$650
S. OR

G8, $400-$700
Lake Co., OR

Ground stem

Ground stem

Banded obsidian

Basalt

G9, $450-$800
Lake Co., OR

G10, $550-$1000
Lake Co., OR

G9, $650-$1200
Lake Co., OR

G9, $550-$1000
Lake Co., OR

Obsidian

G9, $550-$1000
Warner Valley, OR

WINDUST-ALBERTA (provisional) - Paleo to Early Archaic, 10,500 - 9000 B. P.

(See Alberta, Lake Mohave, Lind Coulee, Owl Cave, Parman, Scottsbluff, Shaniko Stemmed and Silver Lake)

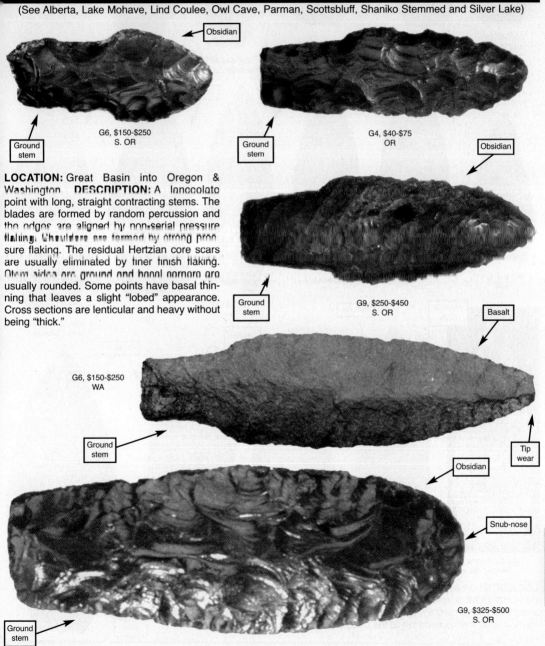

Obsidian

Ground
stem

G6, $150-$250
S. OR

Ground
stem

G4, $40-$75
OR

Obsidian

LOCATION: Great Basin into Oregon & Washington. **DESCRIPTION:** A lanceolate point with long, straight contracting stems. The blades are formed by random percussion and the edges are aligned by non-serial pressure flaking. Shoulders are formed by strong pressure flaking. The residual Hertzian core scars are usually eliminated by finer finish flaking. Stem sides are ground and basal corners are usually rounded. Some points have basal thinning that leaves a slight "lobed" appearance. Cross sections are lenticular and heavy without being "thick."

Ground
stem

G9, $250-$450
S. OR

Basal

G6, $150-$250
WA

Ground
stem

Obsidian

Tip
wear

Snub-nose

Ground
stem

G9, $325-$500
S. OR

F
W

1151

WINDUST CONTRACTING STEM - Paleo to Early Archaic, 10,500 - 8000 B. P.

(See Lake Mohave, Lind Coulee, Owl Cave, Parman, Shaniko Stemmed and Silver Lake)

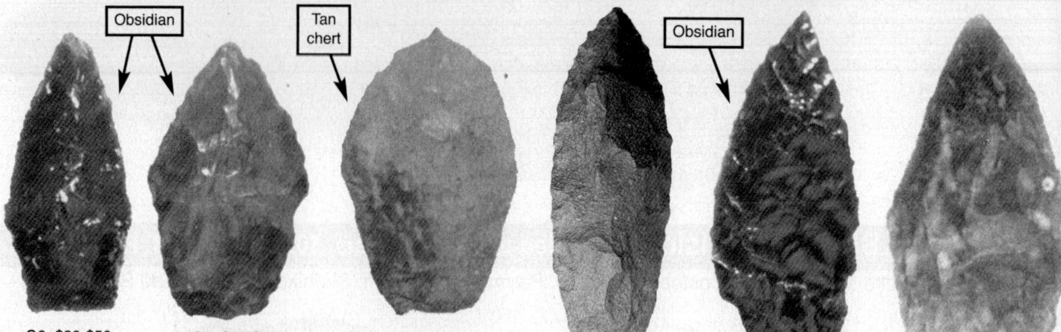

Obsidian
Tan chert
Obsidian

G6, $30-$50 Xmas Vall., OR

G5, $25-$40 OR

G5, $25-$40 Columbia Riv., OR

G6, $35-$65 Humboldt Co., NV

G6, $15-$30 OR

G5, $25-$40 OR

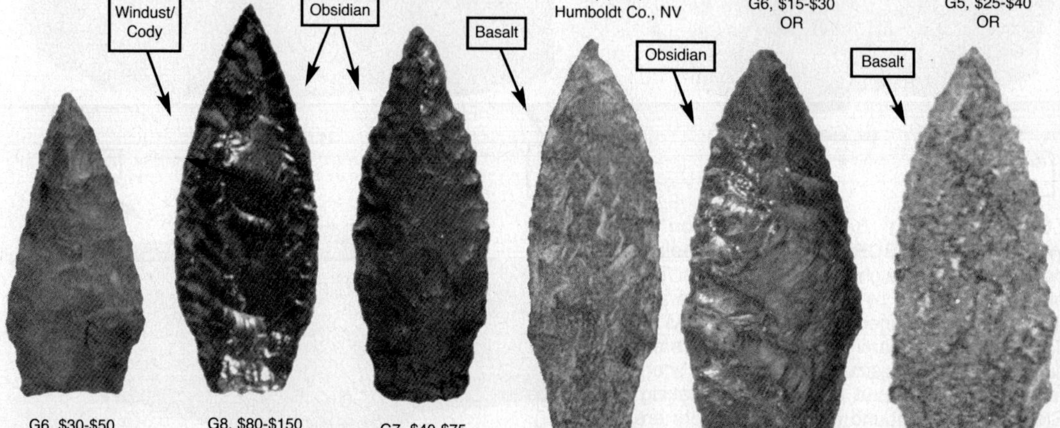

Windust/ Cody
Obsidian
Basalt
Obsidian
Basalt

G6, $30-$50 WA

G8, $80-$150 Sou. OR

G7, $40-$75 OR

G7, $55-$100 Snake River, ID

G8, $80-$150 OR

G6, $125-$200 Snake River, WA

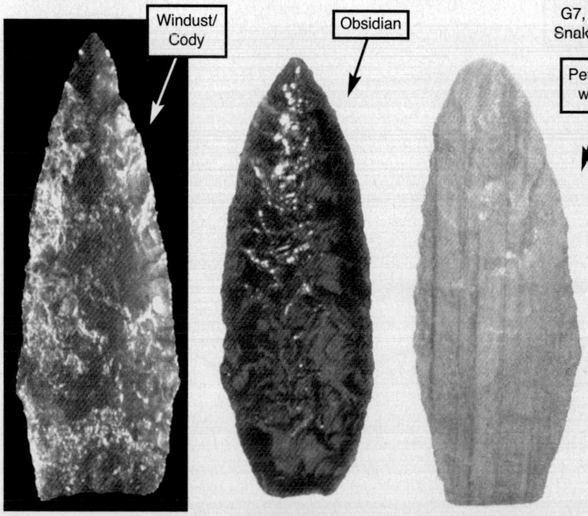

Windust/ Cody
Obsidian
Petrified wood

G6, $125-$200 Lake Co., OR

G8, $80-$150 S. E. OR

G4, $25-$40 Col. Rv., OR

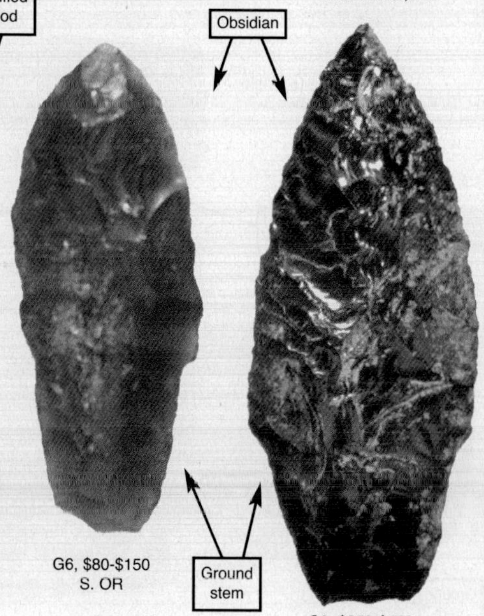

Obsidian
Ground stem

G6, $80-$150 S. OR

G9, $250-$400 OR

LOCATION: Great Basin into Oregon & Washington. **DESCRIPTION:** A medium size, broad point that has weak shoulders and a contracting stem. This style of *Windust* has many characteristics common to the Cody Complex.

Obsidian

Obsidian

G9, $250-$400
Lake Co., OR

Obsidian

Obsidian

Ground
stem

G10, $250-$450
Cent. OR

G9, $275-$500
S. Cent. OR

G7, $80-$150
OR

Agate

Ignumbrite

Ground
stem

Ground
stem

Ground
stem

G9, $275-$500
WA

G8, $250-$400
E. WA

G10, $650-$1200
S. Cent. OR

F
W

WINDUST-HATWAI (provisional) - Paleo to Early Archaic, 10,500 - 8000 B. P.

(See Lake Mohave, Lind Coulee, Owl Cave, Parman, Shaniko Stemmed and Silver Lake)

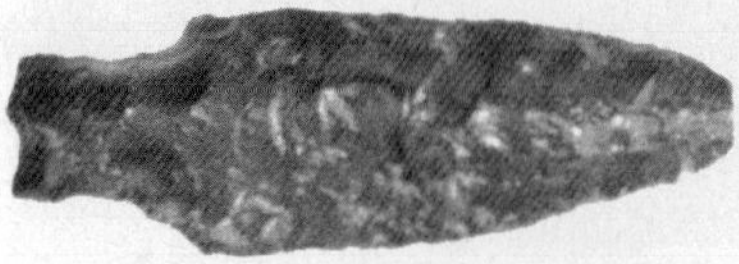
Tip wear

G5, $25-$40
OR

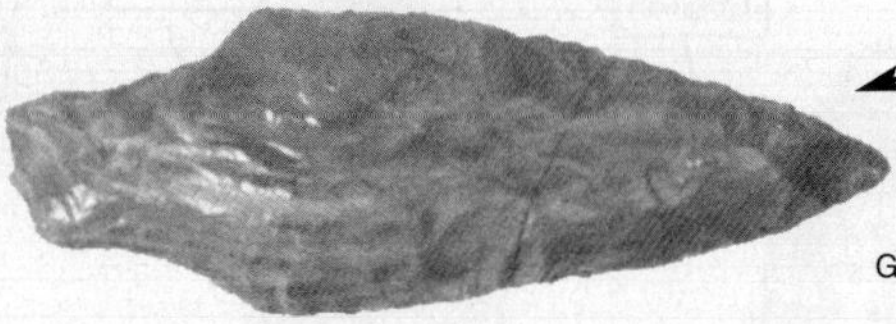
Jasper

G8, $65-$125
OR

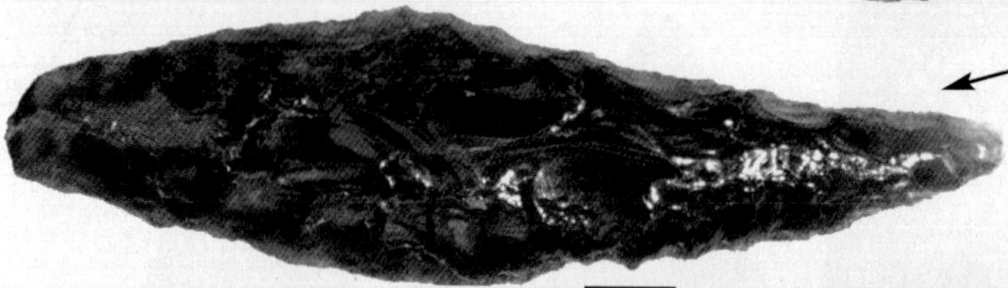
Obsidian

G6, $65-$125
S. OR

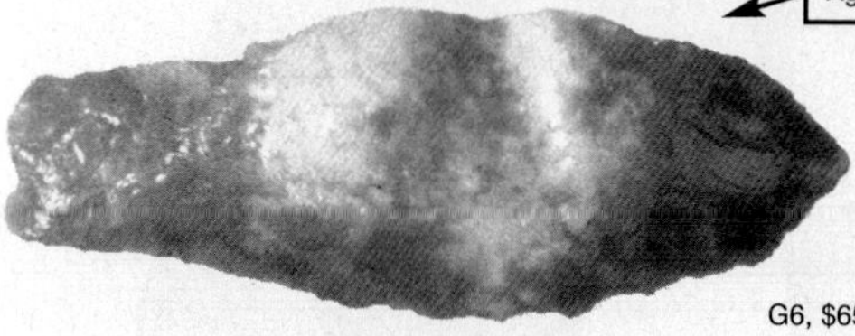
Agate

G6, $65-$125
WA

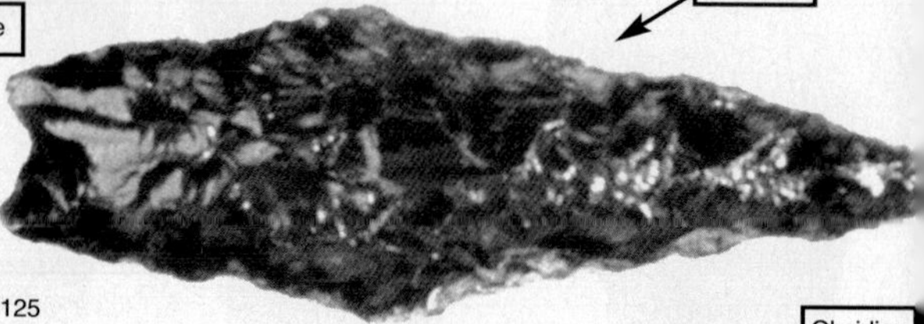
Obsidian

G8, $125-$200
Steens Mtn., OR

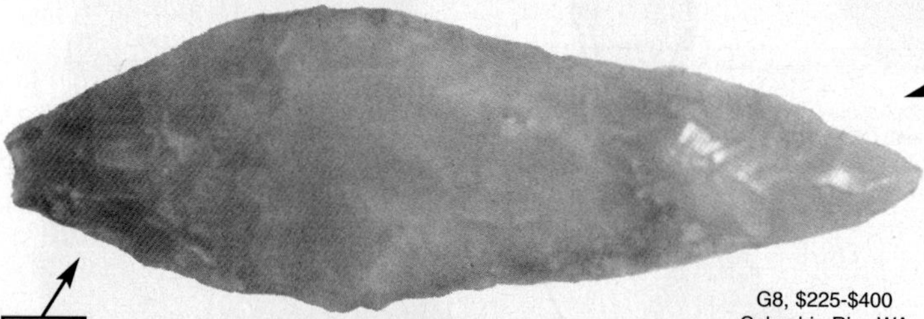
Chalcedony
Ground stem

G8, $225-$400
Columbia Riv., WA

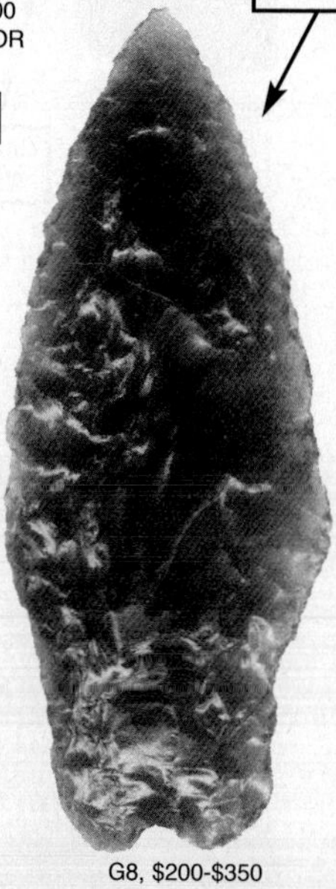
Obsidian

G8, $200-$350
Lake Co., OR

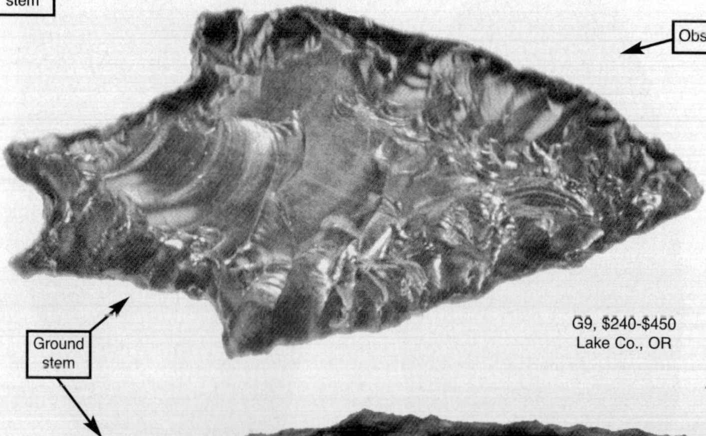
Obsidian
Ground stem

G9, $240-$450
Lake Co., OR

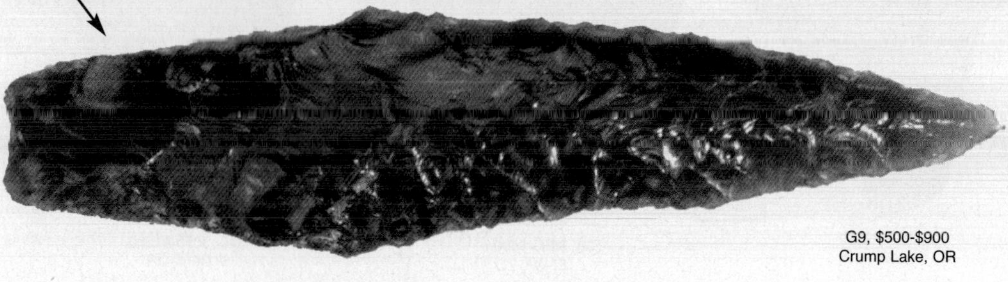
Obsidian

G9, $500-$900
Crump Lake, OR

Obsidian

Windust/plane

Obsidian

G8, $165-$300
Crump Lake, OR

Ground stem

Obsidian

G8, $225-$400
OR

G8, $80-$150
OR

Agate

LOCATION: Great Basin into Oregon & Washington.
DESCRIPTION: A medium to large size dart/knife that has a long, contracting, bifurcated stem. Shoulders are obtuse to horizontal to barbed. Stem edges are ground. Basal concavity usually shows a strong hertzian cone of percussion that is often off-center

G8, $40-$75
OR

Obsidian

Blunt tip

Ear nick

Ground stem

Ear nick

Ground stem

G5, $25-$40
Warner Valley, OR

G7, $40-$75
Warner Valley, OR

G9, $265-$500
Crump Lake, OR

F
W

Obsidian

Base wear

Ground stem

Obsidian

Obsidian

G5, $20-$35
Cent. OR

Obsidian

Ground stem

Ground stem

Ground stem

G9, $150-$250
Warner Valley, OR

G9, $265-$500
OR

G7, $55-$100
Warner Valley, OR

Obsidian

Ground stem

G9, $350-$600
Crump Lake, OR

Obsidian

Hatwai bse

Ground stem

G10, $500-$900
S. OR

WINTU - Developmental to Historic Phase, 1000 - 200 B. P.

(Also see Desert Side Notched and Piquinin)

Obsidian

Serrated edge

G10+, $275-$500
Redding, CA, from a Pete Bostrom cast

G10, $250-$400
Warner Valley, OR

G10++, $700-$1200
Modoc Co., CA

LOCATION: Central California to sou. Oregon. **DESCRIPTION:** A rare, thin, needle tipped point with unique upward sloping, narrow side notches and a concave base. Usually made of jasper and obsidian. See Noel Justice, 2002.

WOODEN DART/ARROW - Late Archaic to Transitional Phase, 3500 - 2000 B. P.

(Also see Bone Arrow, Bone Pin)

G9, $15-$25
N. UT, Hogup Cave
6" long, dated to 2200 B.P.
made of willow wood

G9, $15-$25, N. UT, Hogup
Cave, 6" long, dated to 2200 B.P.

G8, $15-$25
N. UT, Hogup Cave
Atlatl tip made of grease
wood. Dated to 3500 B.P.

LOCATION: Utah. **DESCRIPTION:** Fashioned from sand bar willow wood and grease wood, these dart/arrows were carved and polished to sharp tips. Stone tips were not utilized. These were carbon dated to 3,500 & 2,200 years old.

YANA - Developmental to Historic Phase, 1500 - 400 B. P.

(Also see Coquille, Gatecliff, Gunther, Gypsum Cave, Point Sal Barbed, Rabbit Island and Wallula)

Obs.

Jasper

Basalt

G4, $1-$3
N. CA

G6, $4-$8
S. OR

G5, $2-$5
S. OR

G6, $5-$10
S. OR

G9, $25-$45
Shasta Co., CA,
Redding, CA

G8, $40-$75
Mendocino Co., CA

All above examples are type 1

F
W

YANA (continued)

LOCATION: Northern California. **DESCRIPTION:** A rare, thin, small to medium size, barbed point that occurs in two different forms. **Type 1** has a short to long tapered stem. Shoulders are barbed and blade edges can be serrated. **Type 2** has a short, expanding stem. Shoulders are horizontal to barbed. Bases are straight to concave. A rare type. Part of the *Gunther* cluster. **I.D. KEY:** Stem form. See Perino, vol. 3, 2002.

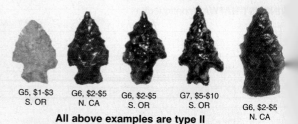

G5, $1-$3
S. OR

G6, $2-$5
N. CA

G6, $2-$5
S. OR

G7, $5-$10
S. OR

All above examples are type II

G6, $2-$5
N. CA

YOUNGS RIVER STEMMED (provisional) - Early Archaic, 8000 - 6000 B. P.

(Also see Windust)

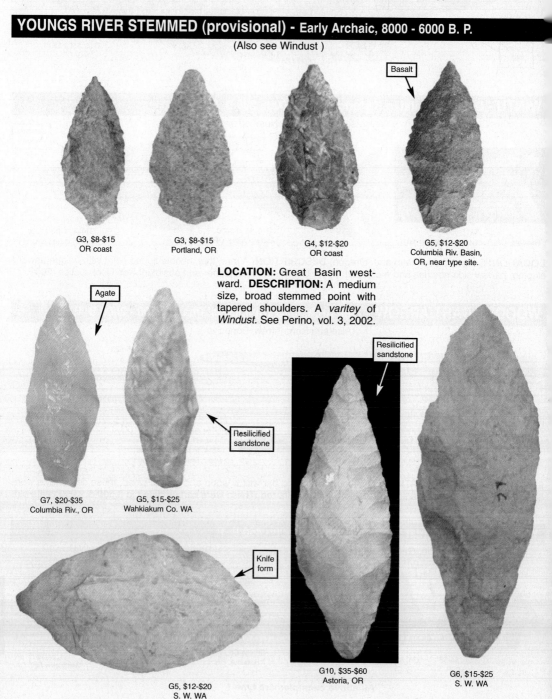

G3, $8-$15
OR coast

G3, $8-$15
Portland, OR

G4, $12-$20
OR coast

Basalt

G5, $12-$20
Columbia Riv. Basin,
OR, near type site.

LOCATION: Great Basin westward. **DESCRIPTION:** A medium size, broad stemmed point with tapered shoulders. A *varitey* of *Windust*. See Perino, vol. 3, 2002.

Agate

Resilicified
sandstone

G7, $20-$35
Columbia Riv., OR

G5, $15-$25
Wahkiakum Co. WA

Knife
form

Resilicified
sandstone

G10, $35-$60
Astoria, OR

G5, $12-$20
S. W. WA

G6, $15-$25
S. W. WA

ALASKA THE FAR NORTH SECTION:

This section includes artifact types from the following regions:
St. Lawrence Island, Bering Sea - southward into the Aleutian Islands, Northern Slope
and eastward.

With a few exceptions, archaeological sites in the Northern Reaches are either sparse or involve shallow multiple occupations, often over large areas, that are disturbed and mixed through frost action. Organic materials are seldom preserved except in late sites.

Lithics: Material employed in the manufacture of projectile points and related artifacts from these regions are: Basalt, chalcedony, chert, Jadeite, jasper, nephrite, obsidian, slate.

Important sites: Anangula, Broken Mammoth, Gerstle River Quarry, Healy Lake, Lime Hills, Mesa, Onion Portage.

Note: Many of the points in this section are also found in contiguous parts of Canada and may be known by other names.

Regional Consultant:
Joel Castanza

Special Advisors:
Mark Berreth, Jim Hogue

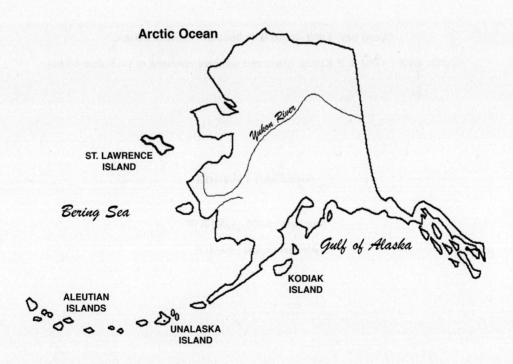

A
K

ALASKAN CULTURAL PERIODS

Including: Aleutian Islands, Kodiak Region, Bering Sea Region, Siberia, Northern Alaska, Canada

Bering Sea Region, Siberia, Northern Alaska, Canada

Paleo-Arctic – 10,000 - 7,000 years B. P.

Northern Archaic: 6,500 - 4,000 B. P.

Arctic Small Tool: 6,000 - 4,200 B. P.

Norton Tradition: 3,000 - 1,200 B. P.

Dorset Tradition: 3,000 - 1000 B. P.

Thule Tradition: 2,500 - 1000 B. P. Includes the Old Bering Sea, Okvik, Punuk, Birnirk

Inuit/Eskimo: 2,800 B.P. - Historic

Athapaskan: 2,000 B.P. - Historic

Kodiak Region

Ocean Bay: 6,000 - 3,000 B. P. Southern coast of Alaska

Kodiak: 6,000 - 1,000 B. P. Kodiak Island and adjacent mainland of southeast Alaska

Aleutian Islands

Anangula: 9,000 - 5,000 B .P.

Aleutian: 5,000 - 200 B.P.

ALEUTIAN REGION

The artifacts from Chignik are all site points.

CHIGNIK DART - Aleutian Tradition, 5000 - 200 B. P.

(Also see Dutch Harbor Stemmed, Kotzebue Dart and Whale)

Basalt

LOCATION: Lower Alaskan peninsula. **DESCRIPTION:** A medium size, broad point with rounded, tapered shoulders and a rounded stem.

G9, $65-$120
Chignik Lake Outlet, Aleutian Peninsula.
Very rare

CHIGNIK LANCEOLATE - Aleutian Tradition, 5000 - 200 B. P.

(Also see Dutch Harbor Lanceolate and Independence)

LOCATION: Lower Alaskan peninsula. **DESCRIPTION:** A medium size, lanceolate projectile with a tapering hafting area and a straight to convex base.

Basalt

G7, $20-$35
Aleutian Peninsula

G10, $80-$150
Aleutian Peninsula

CHIGNIK LEAF - Aleutian Tradition, 5000 - 200 B. P.

(Also see Dutch Harbor Lanceolate, Naknek & St. Michael Leaf)

G10, $40-$75
Aleutian Peninsula

Basalt

LOCATION: Lower Alaskan peninsula. **DESCRIPTION:** A medium size, narrow, lanceolate point with a convex base.

G9, $55-$100
Aleutian Peninsula

CHIGNIK STEMMED - Aleutian Tradition, 5000 - 200 B. P.

(Also see Kayuk, Kotzebue Bay, Portage, Ugashik & Unalaska)

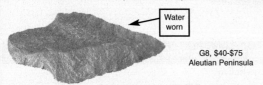

Water worn

G8, $40-$75
Aleutian Peninsula

LOCATION: Lower Alaskan peninsula. **DESCRIPTION:** A medium size, stemmed point with medium, tapered shoulders. The stem tapers into a rounded base.

DUTCH HARBOR BI-POINT - Aleutian Tradition, 5000 - 200 B. P.

(Also see Chignik Lanceolate, Chignik Leaf, Mesa & Portage & Cascade in Far West Section)

LOCATION: Lower Alaskan peninsula islands. **DESCRIPTION:** A medium to large size, bipointed blade with excurvate edges.

AK

**DUTCH HARBOR
BI-POINT** (continued)

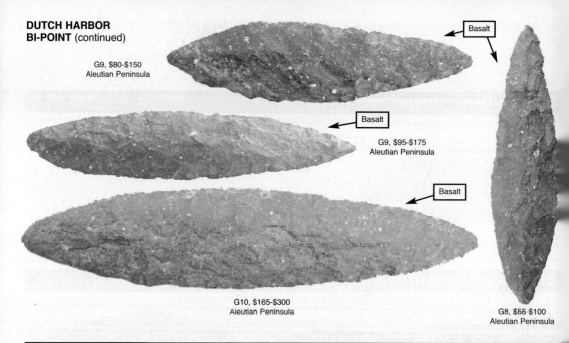

G9, $80-$150
Aleutian Peninsula

Basalt

Basalt

G9, $95-$175
Aleutian Peninsula

Basalt

G10, $165-$300
Aleutian Peninsula

G8, $55 $100
Aleutian Peninsula

DUTCH HARBOR LARGE STEMMED - Aleutian Tradition, 5000 - 200 B. P.

(Also see Dutch Harbor Stemmed)

Basalt

G7, $55-$100
Peninsula Islands, Alaska

LOCATION: Lower Alaskan peninsula islands. **DESCRIPTION:** A medium to large size, narrow point with a medium-long, tapering stem. Shoulders are tapered and the base is straight to convex.

Black chalcedony

G10, $180-$350
Black Chalcedony
Peninsula Islands, Alaska

Andesite

Three sided lance

G8, $200-$300
Peninsula Islands, Alaska

DUTCH HARBOR SIDE NOTCHED - Aleutian Tradition, 5000 - 200 B. P.

(Also see Kotzebue Bay)

Chert

LOCATION: Lower Alaskan peninsula islands. **DESCRIPTION:** A medium size point with shallow side notches. Base can be convex to concave.

G9, $20-$35
Peninsula Islands, Alaska

Glassy basalt

G9, $35-$60
Peninsula Islands, Alaska

DUTCH HARBOR STEMMED - Aleutian Tradition, 5000 - 200 B. P.

(Also see Chignik Dart and Point Hope)

Basalt

G6, $25-$45
Peninsula Islands, Alaska

Basalt

Basalt

G10, $80-$150
Unalaska Captain's Cove, Alaska
Lower Alaskan Peninsula Islands

G8, $35-$60
Peninsula Islands, Alaska

G8, $35-$60
Unalaska Island, AK

G10, $80-$150
Peninsula Islands, Alaska

LOCATION: Lower Alaskan peninsula islands. **DESCRIPTION:** A medium size, broad point with a short to median, tapering stem. Shoulders are tapered and the base is straight to convex.

UNALASKA (Dutch Harbor) - Aleutian Tradition, 5000 - 200 B. P.

(Also see Chignik Stemmed)

Banded
chalcedony

G6, $8-$15
Aleutian Peninsula, AK

Brown
chalcedony

Basalt

G8, $15-$30
Aleutian Peninsula, AK

Basalt

Tip
wear

G4, $8-$15
Aleutian Peninsula, AK

G9, $40-$75
Aleutian Peninsula, AK

Basalt

Basalt

Tip
wear

G4, $12-$20
Aleutian Peninsula, AK

Tip
wear

G7, $35-$60
Aleutian Peninsula, AK

LOCATION: Lower Alaskan peninsula islands. **DESCRIPTION:** A medium to large size, narrow, auriculate, stemmed point with broad side notches to an expanding stem. Bases are straight to concave.

AK

ARCTIC ESKIMO REGION

BEAR-TYPE 1 (Under 2") - Norton Tradition, 3000 B.P. - Inuit/Eskimo - Historic
(Also see Kavik, Kayuk, Point Hope & Unalakleet)

Tip nick

Gray chert

Gray/brown flint

Chert

Chert

Shovel-nose tip

G4, $30-$50
Alaska

Gray cher

G4, $5-$10
High Arctic,
Alaska

G4, $5-$10
Point Hope,
Alaska

G6, $12-$20
Alaska

G5, $12-$20
Alaska

G5, $5-$10
Utkiavwin, AK

G6, $20-$35
High Arctic,
Alaska

G5, $15-$30
Point Hope, Alaska

Tip wear

LOCATION: Bear points are found mostly along the North Alaskan coast and St. Lawrence and Punuk Island
DESCRIPTION: A small size, narrow point with weak, tapered shoulders and a short parallel stem. Flaking is collateral on the better-made specimens. Bear points were inserted into a bone, antler or ivory shaft and were used in hunting walrus, seals, caribou & other large animals and in war. **Note:** Dating has been difficult. The Yupuk of the St. Lawrence Island have been digging archaeological sites for at least 300 years due to demand for fossil ivory which has destroyed the archaeological record on most sites. This type may date to 5,000-6,000 B.P.

BEAR-TYPE 2 (2"-3") - Norton Tradition, 3000 B.P. - Inuit/Eskimo - Historic
(Also see Kavik, Kayuk, Point Hope & Unalakleet)

Tip wear

Collateral flaking to a median ridge

Gray chert

Dark chalc.

Gray chert

G4, $8-$15
St. Lawrence,
Island, Alaska

G6, $25-$40
Alaska

black chert

G8, $40-$75
Nuwuk, Alaska

Black chalc.

G6, $30-$50
Alaska

G6, $35-$65
Alaska

G7, $65-$125
Alaska

G5, $25-$45
Alaska

Bifurcated base

G8, $65-$125
Alaska

Chalcedony

LOCATION: Same as type 1. **DESCRIPTION:** A medium size (2"-3"), narrow point with horizontal shoulders and a medium-length, parallel stem. Base is straight to slightly convex. Blade edges can be serrated. Cross section forms a median ridge with usually collateral flaking. **I.D. KEY:** Long, narrow stemmed point.

Green chert w/red streak

G8, $75-$140
Alaska

G6, $80-$150
Alaska

Collateral flaking to a median ridge

BEAR-TYPE 3 (Over 3") - Norton Tradition, 3000 B. P. - Inuit/Eskimo - Historic

(Also see Kavik, Kayuk, Point Hope & Unalakleet)

Black chert

Translucent chalcedony

Gray chert

Green/gray chert

Collateral flaking to a median ridge

Black chert

Base fracture

Material flaw

G9, $125-$200
Alaska

G5, $150-$250
Alaska

G9, $200-$350
Alaska

G10, $175-$300
Alaska

G10+, $250-$400
Alaska

LOCATION: See type 1. **DESCRIPTION:** A large size, narrow point with horizontal shoulders and a medium-length, parallel stem. Base is straight to slightly convex. Blade edges can be serrated. Cross section forms a median ridge. **I.D. KEY:** Long, narrow stemmed point.

BEAR-TYPE 4 - Norton Tradition, 3000 B. P. - Inuit/Eskimo - Historic

(Also see Kayuk, Point Hope, Unalaklett)

Gray chert

Fired chert

G4, $20-$35
Alaska

G7, $65-$125
Alaska

Green/gray chert

Gray chert

G8, $35-$65
Alaska

G6, $60-$110
Alaska

1165

A
K

BEAR-TYPE 4 (continued)

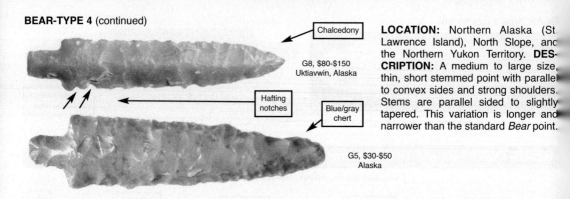

Chalcedony

G8, $80-$150
Uktiavwin, Alaska

Hafting
notches

Blue/gray
chert

G5, $30-$50
Alaska

LOCATION: Northern Alaska (St Lawrence Island), North Slope, and the Northern Yukon Territory. **DESCRIPTION:** A medium to large size, thin, short stemmed point with parallel to convex sides and strong shoulders. Stems are parallel sided to slightly tapered. This variation is longer and narrower than the standard *Bear* point.

BIRD ARROW-BLUNT - Inuit/Eskimo, 2800 B. P. - Historic

(Also see Bone Arrow and Harpoon)

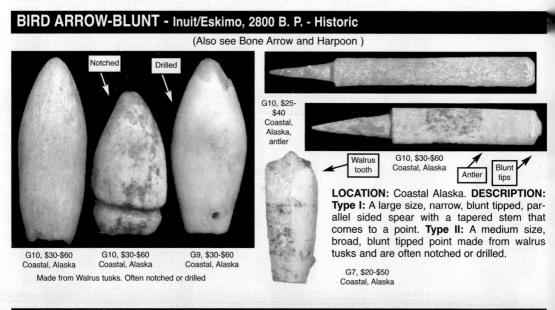

Notched

Drilled

G10, $25-$40
Coastal, Alaska, antler

Walrus tooth

G10, $30-$60
Coastal, Alaska

Antler

Blunt tips

G10, $30-$60
Coastal, Alaska

G10, $30-$60
Coastal, Alaska

G9, $30-$60
Coastal, Alaska

Made from Walrus tusks. Often notched or drilled

G7, $20-$50
Coastal, Alaska

LOCATION: Coastal Alaska. **DESCRIPTION: Type I:** A large size, narrow, blunt tipped, parallel sided spear with a tapered stem that comes to a point. **Type II:** A medium size, broad, blunt tipped point made from walrus tusks and are often notched or drilled.

BIRD SPEAR - Inuit/Eskimo, 2800 B. P. - Historic

(Also see Bone Arrow and Harpoon)

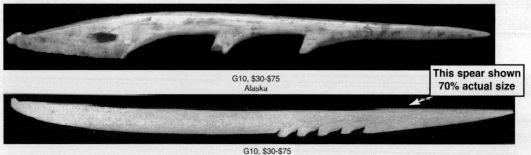

G10, $30-$75
Alaska

This spear shown 70% actual size

G10, $30-$75
Alaska

LOCATION: Coastal Alaska. **DESCRIPTION:** A large size, narrow spear with barbs. Made from bone or antler.

BONE ARROW - Inuit/Eskimo, 2800 B. P. - Historic

(Also see Harpoon)

LOCATION: Bering Sea Region. **DESCRIPTION:** A long, narrow foreshaft and point crafted from fossilized ivory, tusk and antler.

BONE ARROW (continued)

G9, $30-$50
AK

G10, $40-$70
AK

All long arrows are made from ivory

G10, $35-$60
AK

G6, $30-$50
AK

Deer arrow. Deer arrows have a long trihedral pile of antler from 4-8" long, with a sharp thin-edged point slightly concaved on the faces like the point of a bayonet. Two of the edges are rounded, but the third is sharp and cut into one or more simple barbs. Behind the barb the pile takes the form of a rounded shank, ending in a shoulder and a sharp rounded tang a little enlarged above the point. Ref: 9th Annual Report, 1887-88 Bureau of Etnology.

All points on this page made from fossilized ivory, bone, tusk and antler

Bone

G6, $30-$50
AK

Bone

G7, $55-$100
AK

All points on this page shown Actual Size

G7, $55-$100
AK

Ivory

Bone

G7, $55-$100
AK

Antler

G6, $55-$100
AK

G10, $80-$150
AK

Leg bone of large bird. Very rare

BONE ARROW w/Metal or Stone points - Inuit/Eskimo, 2800 B. P. - Historic

(Also see Hafted Knife, Harpoon, Unalakleet)

Unalakleet point tip

G10, $200-$350 (complete)
AK

(see Unalakleet page for price of point only

BONE ARROW with metal or stone points (continued)

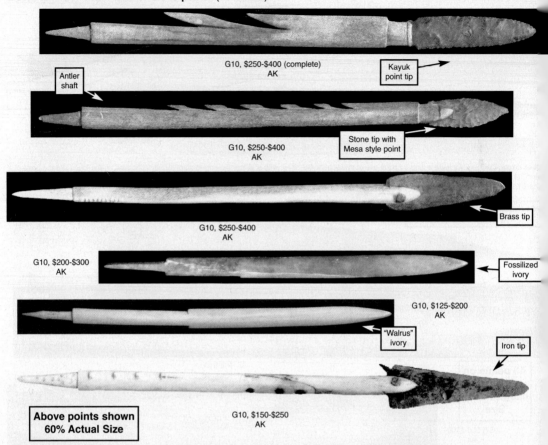

G10, $250-$400 (complete)
AK

Antler shaft

Kayuk point tip

G10, $250-$400
AK

Stone tip with Mesa style point

G10, $250-$400
AK

Brass tip

G10, $200-$300
AK

Fossilized ivory

G10, $125-$200
AK

"Walrus" ivory

Iron tip

Above points shown
60% Actual Size

G10, $150-$250
AK

LOCATION: Bering Sea Region. **DESCRIPTION:** A large size, narrow, parallel sided spear with a tapered, pointed stem that that inserts into the main shaft. Made from fossilized ivory, tusk and antler. Metal or stone points were used as tips.

CHINDADN - Paleo-Arctic Tradition, 11,300 - 11,000 B. P.

(Also see Mesa and Sub-Triangular)

G8, $25-$50
Nenana Valley, AK

Picture from a cast made by Pete Bostrom

LOCATION: Alaska. **DESCRIPTION:** A small size, broad, thin, ovate point made from a flake that has a convex base. Made during the Nenana occupation. **I.D. KEY:** Broad, ovate form.

DORSET TRIANGULAR - The Dorset Tradition, 2500 - 1000 B. P.

(Also see Chignik Leaf)

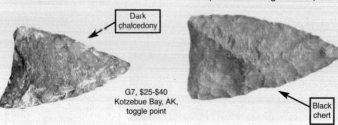

Dark chalcedony

LOCATION: Bering Sea Region, Canadian Arctic. **DESCRIPTION:** A medium sized, thin, triangular point with a concave base.

G9, $25-$40
Yupuk-Eskimo, AK
Bering Sea Region, Canadian Arctic

G7, $25-$40
Kotzebue Bay, AK,
toggle point

Black chert

DRILL - Paleo-Arctic Tradition - Historic, 10,000 - 200 B. P.

(Also see Hafted Knife, Scraper)

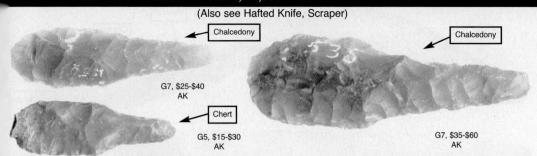

Chalcedony

G7, $25-$40
AK

Chalcedony

Chert

G5, $15-$30
AK

G7, $35-$60
AK

LOCATION: Everywhere. **DESCRIPTION:** Although many drills were made from scratch, all point types were made into the drill form. Usually, heavily resharpened and broken points were salvaged and rechipped into drills. These objects were certainly used as drills (evidence of extreme edge wear), but there is speculation that some of these forms may have been used as pins for clothing, ornaments, ear plugs and other uses.

FIRSTVIEW - Paleo-Arctic to Northern Archaic Tradition, 10,000 - 8000 B. P.

(Also see Mesa and Eden, Firstview & Scottsbluff In Northern Plains Section)

Gray chert

Ground stem

G9, $165-$300
Alaska

LOCATION: Alaska. **DESCRIPTION:** A small to medium sized stemmed projectile with weak shoulders and a straight to convex base. Basal sides are parallel, median ridged and collateral to oblique parallel flaking. stem is often ground. Made by the Cody Complex people.

FLAKING TOOL - INUIT/ESKIMO, 2800 B. P. - Historic

(Also see Drill, Hafted Knife, Scraper)

Flaking Tool shown 65% Actual Size

G10, $125-$200
Alaska. Eskimo flint flaker with 5-7/8" long channeled antler handle and an accompanying 4-3/4" long antler rod

LOCATION: Alaska. **DESCRIPTION:** A large hand tool for knapping stone into projectiles and other tools.

HAFTED KNIFE - INUIT/ESKIMO, 2800 B.P. - Historic

(Also see Arrow, Bone Arrow, Drill, Scraper)

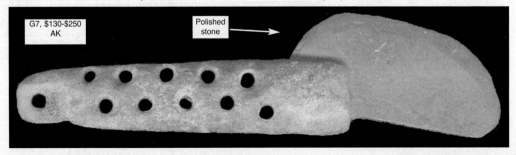

G7, $130-$250
AK

Polished stone

LOCATION: Alaska. **DESCRIPTION:** Hafting handles were crafted from wood, fossilized ivory, tusk or bone and were affixed to the blade with pitch or other adhesive. Flaked and polished stone were used as cutting blades.

HAFTED KNIFE (continued)

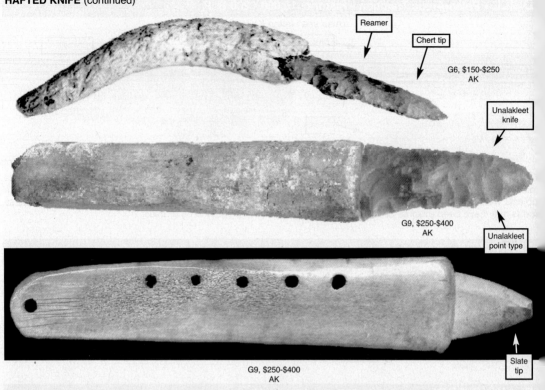

Reamer

Chert tip

G6, $150-$250
AK

Unalakleet knife

G9, $250-$400
AK

Unalakleet point type

Slate tip

G9, $250-$400
AK

HARPOON - Inuit/Eskimo - Historic, 3000 - 200 B. P.

(Also see Bird Spear, Hafted Knife)

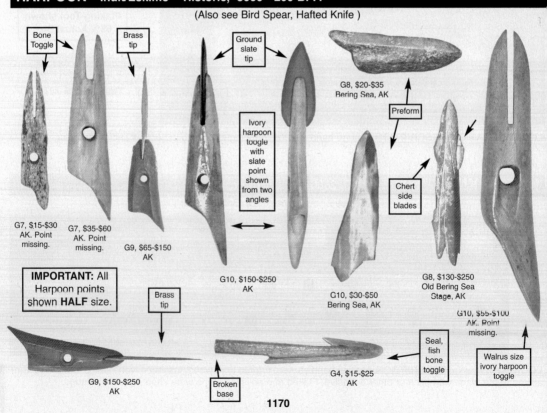

Bone Toggle

Brass tip

Ground slate tip

G8, $20-$35
Bering Sea, AK

Preform

Ivory harpoon toogle with slate point shown from two angles

Chert side blades

G7, $15-$30
AK. Point missing.

G7, $35-$60
AK. Point missing.

G9, $65-$150
AK

IMPORTANT: All Harpoon points shown **HALF** size.

G10, $150-$250
AK

G10, $30-$50
Bering Sea, AK

G8, $130-$250
Old Bering Sea Stage, AK

G10, $55-$100
AK. Point missing.

Brass tip

Brass tip

Seal, fish bone toggle

Walrus size ivory harpoon toggle

G9, $150-$250
AK

Broken base

G4, $15-$25
AK

1170

HARPOON (continued)

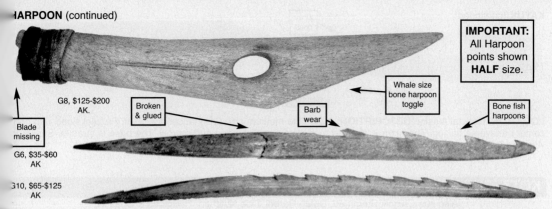

IMPORTANT:
All Harpoon points shown **HALF** size.

G8, $125-$200
AK.

Broken & glued

Barb wear

Whale size bone harpoon toggle

Bone fish harpoons

Blade missing

G6, $35-$60
AK

G10, $65-$125
AK

LOCATION: Coastal areas and around large lakes and rivers, Bering Sea Region. **DESCRIPTION:** Harpoon points were carved from bone, antler or fashioned from metal. They were used in fishing. Some have stone tips and were hafted either directly to the shaft or inserted as a foreshaft.

INDEPENDENCE - Arctic Small Tool Tradition, 6000 - 4200 B. P.

(Also see Chignik Lanceolate)

Petrified wood

G10, $130-$250
AK

LOCATION: Alaska. **DESCRIPTION:** A medium size lanceolate to pentagonal point with a tapered stem and a straight base.

KAVIK - Historic Phase, 300 - 200 B.P.

(Also see Bear and Unalakleet)

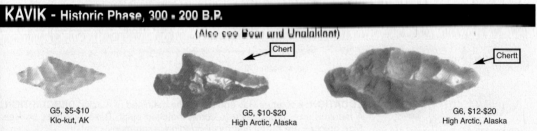

Chert

Chertt

G5, $5-$10
Klo-kut, AK

G5, $10-$20
High Arctic, Alaska

G6, $12-$20
High Arctic, Alaska

LOCATION: Alaska. **DESCRIPTION:** A medium size stemmed point with the blade expanding towards the base. Shoulders are horizontal and the stem is narrow and parallel sided. Base is straight to convex. **I.D. KEY:** Base and shoulder form.

KAYUK - Northern Archaic Tradition, 6500 - 4000 B. P.

(Also see Bear, Chignik Stemmed)

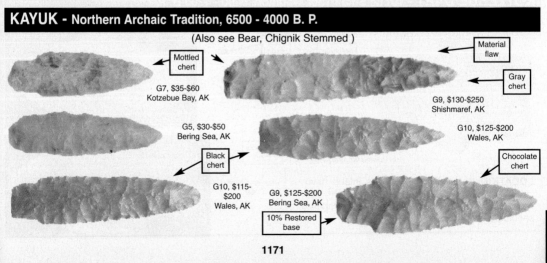

Mottled chert

Material flaw

Gray chert

G7, $35-$60
Kotzebue Bay, AK

G9, $130-$250
Shishmaref, AK

G5, $30-$50
Bering Sea, AK

G10, $125-$200
Wales, AK

Black chert

Chocolate chert

G10, $115-$200
Wales, AK

G9, $125-$200
Bering Sea, AK

10% Restored base

AK

KAYUK (continued)

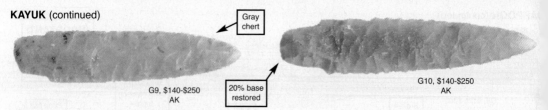

Gray chert

20% base restored

G9, $140-$250
AK

G10, $140-$250
AK

LOCATION: Coastal Alaska. **DESCRIPTION:** A small to medium size (2"+) lanceolate point. Parallel sided with horizontal transverse flaking. The stem is short to moderate, parallel sided and narrow. The base is straight. Similar to *Alberta, Eden, First View* and *Scottsbluff* types.

KOTZEBUE BAY - Arctic Small Tool Tradition, 6000 - 4200 B. P.

(Also see Chignik Stemmed, Dutch Harbor Side Notched, Palisades & Ugashik)

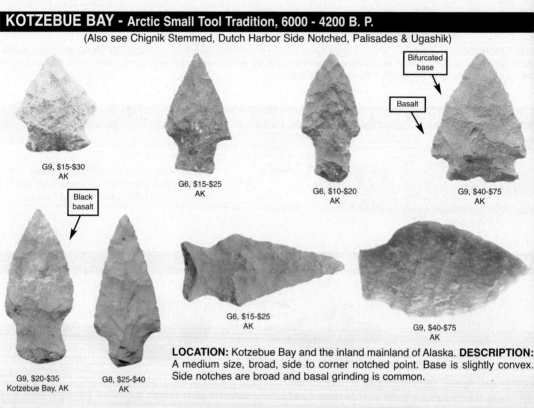

Bifurcated base

Basalt

G9, $15-$30
AK

G6, $15-$25
AK

G6, $10-$20
AK

G9, $40-$75
AK

Black basalt

G6, $15-$25
AK

G9, $40-$75
AK

G9, $20-$35
Kotzebue Bay, AK

G8, $25-$40
AK

LOCATION: Kotzebue Bay and the inland mainland of Alaska. **DESCRIPTION:** A medium size, broad, side to corner notched point. Base is slightly convex. Side notches are broad and basal grinding is common.

KOTZEBUE DART - Arctic Small Tool Tradition, 6000 - 4200 B. P.

(Also see Chignik Dart and Whale)

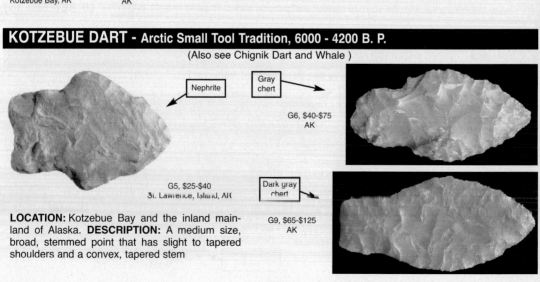

Nephrite

Gray chert

G6, $40-$75
AK

G5, $25-$40
St. Lawrence, Island, AK

Dark gray chert

G9, $65-$125
AK

LOCATION: Kotzebue Bay and the inland mainland of Alaska. **DESCRIPTION:** A medium size, broad, stemmed point that has slight to tapered shoulders and a convex, tapered stem

Olive
chert

G7, $65-$125
Aleutian Peninsula, AK

MESA - Paleo-Arctic Tradition, 10,000 - 7000 B. P.

(Also see Chindadn, Firstview, Sub-Triangular and Agate Basin, Scottsbluff in Great Basin section)

Blue/green
chert

Black
chert

Basalt

Cast of original by Bostrom

Cast of original by Bostrom

G6, $80-$150
N. AK

G7, $90-$175
N. AK

G6, $125-$200
N. Slope, AK

G7, $175-$300
N. AK

Tip
wear

Collateral
flaking

G9, $300-$550
N. AK

G7, $300-$500
N. AK

G8, $350-$600
N. AK

Collateral
flaking

LOCATION: Alaska. **DESCRIPTION:** A medium to large size lanceolate blade of high quality. Bases are either convex, concave or straight, and stems are usually ground. Some examples are median ridged and have random to parallel flaking. **I.D. KEY:** Basal form and flaking style. **Note:** The *Agate Basin* point, found in southern Canada into the western United States, is similar in form but not as old. The *Mesa* point has been reportedly dated to 13,700 years B.P., but more data is needed to verify this extreme age.

NAKNEK - Arctic Small Tool Tradition, 6000 - 4200 B. P.

(Also see Chignik Leaf, Dutch Harbor Lanceolate and Portage)

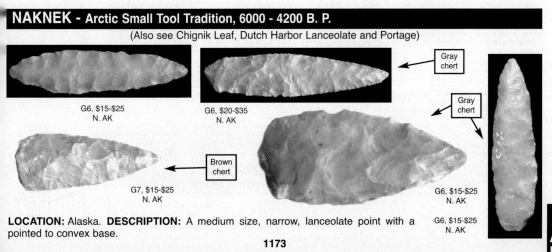

G6, $15-$25
N. AK

G6, $20-$35
N. AK

Gray
chert

Gray
chert

Brown
chert

G7, $15-$25
N. AK

G6, $15-$25
N. AK

G6, $15-$25
N. AK

LOCATION: Alaska. **DESCRIPTION:** A medium size, narrow, lanceolate point with a pointed to convex base.

1173

A
K

PALISADES - Late Northern Archaic Tradition, 7000 - 4000 B. P.

(Also see Kotzebue Bay)

G7, $12-$20
AK

LOCATION: Alaska. **DESCRIPTION:** Northern extension of the *Snake River* type. A small to medium size dart point with an expanding stem that is concave. Shoulders are horizontal to slightly barbed. Blade edges are convex. Basal corners are pointed to rounded. Notches and stem edges are ground.

POINT HOPE - Bear (type 5) - Norton Tradition, 3000 - Inuit/Eskimo - Historic

(Also see Bear, Dutch Harbor Stemmed and Unalakleet)

Basalt

G10, $115-$200
AK

Green chert

G10, $130-$250
AK

Black chert

Siberian point not typed

G10, $165-$300
Point Hope, AK

LOCATION: Northern Alaska. **DESCRIPTION:** A medium to large size, broad, dart/knife stemmed point that is parallel sided and median ridged. Shoulders are rounded. Stem is parallel sided with a convex base. This point is broader than the other *Bear* forms.

POLISHED STONE - The Thule Tradition, 2000 - 400 B. P.

(Also see Snow Knife & Ulu)

Toggle point

Ground slate

G7, $12-$20
AK

G7, $15-$25
AK

G7, $15-$30
AK

G7, $15-$30
AK

G4, $10-$20
AK

G8, $30-$50
AK

Ground slate

Knife

G5, $15-$30
AK

G5, $15-$25
AK

Ground slate

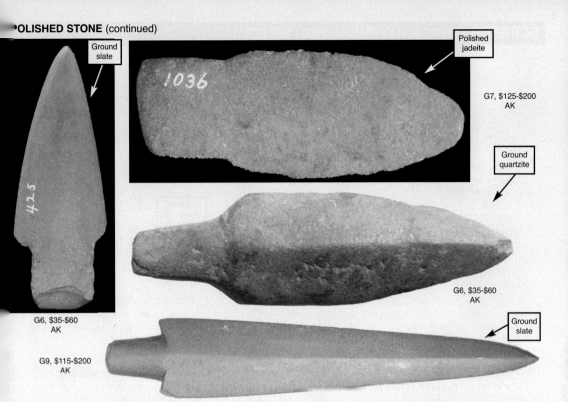

Ground slate

Polished jadeite

G7, $125-$200
AK

Ground quartzite

G6, $35-$60
AK

Ground slate

G6, $35-$60
AK

G9, $115-$200
AK

LOCATION: Alaska. **DESCRIPTION:** A medium to large size, stemmed to triangular point usually made from slate, although other lithics may be used, but are uncommon. Some examples have a median ridge running along the center of the blade. These points were probably used as knives and harpoons by the Eskimos along the coastal waters.

PORTAGE - Late Northern Archaic Tradition, 6000 - 4000 B. P.

(Also see Chignik Stemmed, Kayuk and Naknek)

LOCATION: Alaska. **DESCRIPTION:** A medium size lanceolate point with a tapered stem and a straight to slightly rounded base. Similar to *Spedis* found further south.

Gray chert

G9, $20-$35
Alaska

ST. MICHAEL LEAF - The Thule Tradition, 2000 - 400 B. P.

(Also see Chignik Leaf, Dutch Harbor Lanceolate and Naknek)

*Note: Black chert is scarce in the area

G9, *$55-$100
Alaska

Black chert

G9, $20-$35
Alaska

G9, $20-$35
Alaska

LOCATION: Alaska. **DESCRIPTION:** A medium size, broad, lanceolate point with a convex base. Blade edges are convex.

A
K

SCRAPER - Inuit/Eskimo - Historic, 2800 - 200 B.P.

(Also see Drill and Hafted Knife)

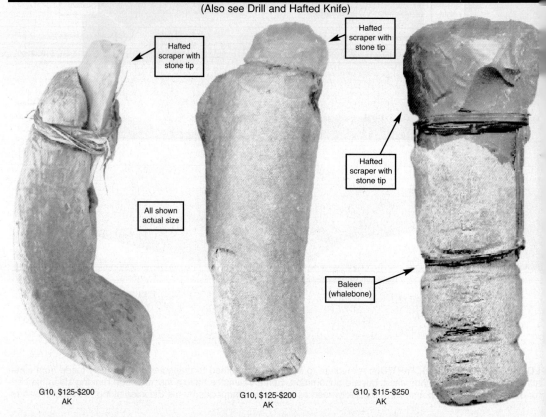

Hafted scraper with stone tip

Hafted scraper with stone tip

Hafted scraper with stone tip

All shown actual size

Baleen (whalebone)

G10, $125-$200
AK

G10, $125-$200
AK

G10, $115-$250
AK

LOCATION: Bering Sea Region, Alaska. **DESCRIPTION:** Thumb, duckbill, claw and turtleback forms are small to medium size, thick, ovoid shaped, uniface, scraping tools that are steeply beveled, especially at the the broadest end. Side scrapers are long to oval hand-held uniface flakes with beveling on the edges intended for use. Scraping was done primarily from the sides of these blades. Some of these tools were hafted.

SNOW KNIFE - Historic, 400 - 200 B. P.

(Also see Ground Stone and Ulu)

Ivory

G10, $80-$150
AK

LOCATION: Alaska. **DESCRIPTION:** A medium size knife made of ivory or bone for hafting.

SUB-TRIANGULAR - Paleo-Arctic Tradition, 11,300 - 11,000 B. P.

(Also see Chindadn and Mesa)

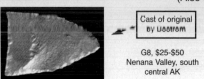

Cast of original by Uootrom

G8, $25-$50
Nenana Valley, south
central AK

LOCATION: Alaska. **DESCRIPTION:** A small size, broad, thin, triangular point made from a flake that has a straight to slightly concave base. Made during the Nenana occupation. **I.D. KEY:** Broad triangle.

1176

UGASHIK - Northern Archaic Tradition, 6000 - 4500 B. P.

(Also see Chignik Stemmed, Kotzebue Bay and Naknek)

G6, $5-$15
AK

Black chalc.

G6, $5-$15
AK

Black chalc.

G7, $12-$20
AK

LOCATION: Alaska. **DESCRIPTION:** A small to medium size point with tapered shoulders that are rounded and a broad stem with a convex base. The stem is paralled sided to slightly expanding and is usually ground.

ULU - Kodiak Tradition, 6000 - 1000 B. P.

(Also see Ground Stone, Side Knife and Snow Knife)

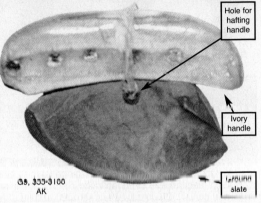

Hole for hafting handle

Ivory handle

Ground slate

G9, $35-$100
AK

LOCATION: Alaska. **DESCRIPTION:** Made from flat, thin, rocks, slate, or even jade. Handles were fashioned out of wood, ivory, or bone and often decorated with distinctive markings of the craftsmen.

G5, $35-$65
AK

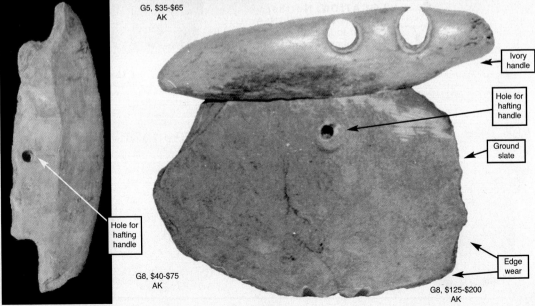

Ivory handle

Hole for hafting handle

Ground slate

Hole for hafting handle

Edge wear

G8, $40-$75
AK

G8, $125-$200
AK

A
K

UNALAKLEET (Bear type 6), Norton Tradition, 3000 B. P. - Inuit/Eskimo - Historic

(Also see Bear, Chignik Stemmed, Dutch Harbor Large Stemmed, Hafted, Kavik)

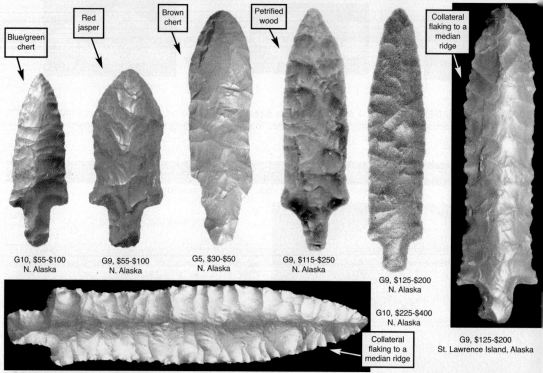

Blue/green chert

Red jasper

Brown chert

Petrified wood

Collateral flaking to a median ridge

G10, $55-$100
N. Alaska

G9, $55-$100
N. Alaska

G5, $30-$50
N. Alaska

G9, $115-$250
N. Alaska

G9, $125-$200
N. Alaska

G10, $225-$400
N. Alaska

Collateral flaking to a median ridge

G9, $125-$200
St. Lawrence Island, Alaska

LOCATION: Northern Alaska (St. Lawrence Island), North Slope, and the Northern Yukon Territory. **DESCRIPTION:** A small to medium size (2"+) lenticular point. Parallel sided horizontal transverse flaking. The stem is short to moderate and narrow. Blade edges are serrated and recurvate near the base. These may be knife forms.

WHALE - Northern Archaic Tradition, 4000 B. P. - Historic

(Also see Bear, Chignik Dart and Kavik)

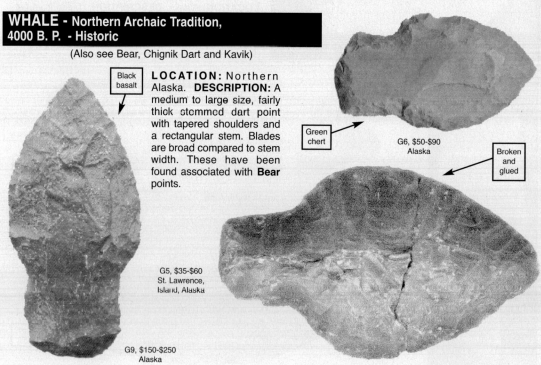

Black basalt

LOCATION: Northern Alaska. **DESCRIPTION:** A medium to large size, fairly thick stemmed dart point with tapered shoulders and a rectangular stem. Blades are broad compared to stem width. These have been found associated with **Bear** points.

Green chert

G6, $50-$90
Alaska

Broken and glued

G5, $35-$60
St. Lawrence, Island, Alaska

G9, $150-$250
Alaska

COLLECTING
OLD WORLD
PREHISTORIC ARTIFACTS

by Duncan Caldwell

© 2007 Duncan Caldwell, Pictures & Text

This section gives an overview of artifact types from Western Europe, the Sahara & the Sahel from 2.6 million to 3,000 years ago. A few tools from elsewhere appear for comparison.

This chapter includes photographic sections illustrating:
  how radically patina can differ from one face of an artifact to the other (& often should),
- various hand ax grips, showing how a few types were held,
- evidence for Neanderthal hafting of blades into compound tools,
- & proof of how large Neolithic prestige axes were hafted - in the middle, not at the end.

As in the previous edition, artifacts are presented in chronological, rather than alphabetical order, to give the reader an idea of their evolution. Furthermore, many of the artifacts are again larger than this book, so they can not be presented actual size. Instead, dimensions are given. Also, only superior specimens have been chosen in most cases, because there is not enough space to show the quality range for each type. In addition to sculptural hand-axes - which are the oldest evidence for the birth of aesthetics - there are several works of figurative & abstract prehistoric art to emphasize the expansion of assemblages with the addition of such artifacts starting roughly 45,000 years ago. Lastly, the multitude of preserved types that arose over a prehistoric period that spanned 2.6 million years as opposed to the Americas' 13,000 to 18,000 is correspondingly bigger, so this section, as opposed to the North American ones, is an overview containing gaps. All the same, by compiling this chapter with its predecessors in the 6th, 7th, 8th & 9th editions of this guide, enthusiasts may start to get a clear idea of the artifacts in the 3 regions.

RULES OF THUMB:
1)   Patinas Usually Differ from One Side to the Other:
The European and African artifacts that follow all have some kind of patina, usually a pronounced one that is different from one face to the other. This is because most prehistoric tools have just 2 main faces & tend to lie on the surface with one side exposed & the other buried both before burial and again before discovery. The part exposed to the air would be slowly adulterated by gamma radiation, lichens and wind weathering, for example, while the face lying against soil might experience silica loss and the intrusion of lime salts. An artifact's buried face could also acquire a crusty ring of minerals leached out of the surrounding soil that adhered to the artifact by tensile force and longer humidity in its shade. At the very least a stone tool would acquire soil sheen and in cold regions manganese or iron oxide concretions might "grow" from cleavage lines in frost pits. In most cases, each face would undergo several of these changes as its position shifted over hundreds of millenia.
But don't be fooled by almost unpatinated resharpening into thinking that such chipping is inevitably modern or even from a much later date than the rest of the knapping. Long experience in the field has shown that certain flake scars that are as old or nearly as old as the rest may hardly patinate. There could be several overlapping reasons for their relative failure to change color:

these facets might exhibit different geometry vis-à-vis the crystalline structure of the material - reducing porosity in their zone: even short exposure to solar radiation, gastric or other body acids, heat from fires, etc. during the tool's use may have predisposed older chipping to patination once the tool was abandoned and buried, but the surface of the latest resharpening might not have been stressed enough before burial to patinate as easily. Finally, it is true that a few tools found in highly preservative stable clay or cave deposits show only soil sheen and fine hydration mists. These account for such a negligible proportion that most collectors should simply avoid collecting Lower & Middle Paleolithic artifacts unless they exhibit intense patination, and, for surface finds, a different one on each side. There are enough fine patinated specimens that you should never have to worry about whether your pieces are authentic.

A) Dark face of an Acheulean cleaver vs. lighter face of same cleaver. Differential patination - the patina on one face is quite different from that on the other. Gravel pit find.

B) Browner side of a Mousterian Triangular biface vs. its creamier side.

C) More colorful side of a Malian Neolithic flared celt vs. its milky side.

2) Only suckers look for "perfection":

Don't expect artifacts that are often 100 times older than the oldest American ones to be unchipped. After all, many have undergone glacial periods, surviving long weathering by frost & high winds on plateaus or rolling in tumultuous thawing rivers before being deposited in gravel-beds. In fact, a collector should be comforted by a little breakage, because depending on whether the posterior chips are ancient or modern, they will show a surprising depth & variety of patinas, often on the same piece.

3) Be circumspect about famous origins:

Another point to remember is that a famous origin may increase the value of an artifact, but buyers should be circumspect. For example, in my early days, I purchased hand-axes in an auction held by France's most famous "expert" that he described as having come from the type sites of La Micoque & St. Acheul & as having been in the collection of one the greatest 19th prehistorians, de Mortillet. Later I was invited to examine large collections from those sites that had remained intact since the original excavations. The pieces I had were almost dead ringers for certain specimens from the 2 sites – but not quite. Although they had been chosen shrewdly to fool most prehistorians, the palette of patinas was slightly off, indicating subtly different lithics & geological processes. But I had no proof. Then I got a call. It was the finder of the hand-axes who had sold them directly to the "expert" with full provenance. When he had seen them being sold to me under false pretenses during the "expert's" next auction, the collector had fumed & obtained my name. The field collector pointed out tiny innocuous initials that he had put on the bifaces & provided the key for deciphering them. They were the abbreviations of his sites in the Nievre region, far from the type-sites. I was able to confirm this by checking the rest of the man's collection & even finding identical tools at the true sites. Talk about a silver lining.

But I'd learned my lesson. Even if you have just spent $50,000,000 out of an $80 million dollar budget, as one European collector is said to have done recently, read up, familiarize yourself with well provenanced collections & take claims from merchants who may be more interested in lucre than prehistory with salt. It is absolutely essential that the seller be honorable and provide a *lifetime* guarantee of authenticity.

Finally, collecting artifacts from a time span over 140 times longer than all of American prehistory combined will begin to reveal the vast iceberg of humanity's past, of which American prehistory is just the peak of the tip. As the collector of Paleolithic artifacts explores that vast new domain, he will discover unending nuances and whole zones of mystery, while developing increasing respect for the prowess of ancestors we can all truly share. To aide new-comers to this passionate field of study, I recommend not only the Handbook of Paleolithic Typology by Debénath and Dibble and Tools of the Old and New Stone Age by Bordaz, but broader books by Susan Allport, The Primal Feast, Juan Luis Arsuaga, The Neanderthal's Necklace, & Jared Diamond, Guns, Germs & Steel.

Lithics: Some of the materials from the 2 continents that this chapter concentrates on are: **For Europe:** Grand Pressigny flint - Indre et Loire & Vienne regions of France; Jablines flint - Seine et Marne; Thanatian flint - Oise & Somme valleys; jadeite, metahornblendite & dolerite - Brittany; Font-Maure jasper, France; Pelite-quartz - W Alps; Obsidian - Italy S. France, Greece; Green slate - W. Russia, Baltic states, etc. **For North Africa:** quartzite, flint, siltstone, jasper, etc. **Important sites:** Because the region and time frame are so vast, only a few almost random sites are listed. However, an effort has been made to choose fully provenanced tools from famous sites, which are referred to in the captions. "T.S." after a site indicates that it is a cultural type-site, although it should be kept in mind that other locations are often type-sites for particular traits and tools.

Prices: This section appears without price ranges. My motive for accepting Bob Overstreet's gracious invitations to contribute to these guides over the years has been pedagogical since his series represents one of the most targeted vehicles for informing a wide range of enthusiasts about the details of prehistory. But, as I've noted in previous editions, today's markets & legal systems lead to some perverse effects. One of them is counterfeiting - either of artifacts or famous provenances. Another is the wholesale elimination of vestiges from vast areas of the Sahara without prior study. Back when I contributed my first article, many African artifacts that were being sold had been collected with site data by colonial administrators while most of the available European artifacts bore collection tags dating to the 1930s or earlier. The majority of artifacts had long been in private hands or had even been de-acquisitioned by museums, so their purchase did not reward illicit digs and often saved collections from being thrown away, either by heirs or irresponsible institutions. (I will refrain from going into details, but, take my word for it, the list of museums & families is long.)

Since then, however, the supply of African artifacts has sky-rocketed. Some soil-deflated regions have been swept clean, making studies there impossible. Officials love to blame collectors for this. But almost every collector I've met has been a person of good faith who has wished both to own pieces with the fullest possible contextual information & to be able to pass them on with pride & transparency. So if only legislators & archeologists would cultivate these desires & set up synergies between collectors & researchers, instead of quixotically & self-righteously fighting market forces, they might be able to channel the market in ways which would fund research, expand scientific knowledge, and even help the poor who look for artifacts to survive.

But the ideologues of both camps are entrenched, so changes won't happen overnight. In the meantime, I look forward to providing all the expertise I can - while trying to avoid participating in a dysfunctional system.

Hand-ax & Mousterian Scraper Grips:

Hand-axes & other Paleolithic bifaces, which superficially resemble hand-axes but may have been hafted, are traditionally grouped by the geometry of their faces. But classifying a tool only on this basis can be misleading because its silhouette may change as the tool is worn, resharpened and used up. Hand-axes that are apparently quite different may just illustrate stages in the reduction sequence of a single true type. It is important to identify those types from their first stage, to determine if methods of reducing tools were also culturally specific, & to emphasize that some types are indeed particular to regions, periods & traditions. The hand-axes & bifaces below are classified not only by their silhouettes, but more importantly by:

- **their contours when seen edge-on.** Such examination reveals that certain hand-held bifaces (hand-axes) have bases that are tipped up relative to the cutting plane. This creates a <u>protective pocket</u> for the user's fingers above the material being cut & is just as intentional a design element as the contours of an artifact's face. So a protective pocket must be considered in classification. Another trait best seen from this perspective is <u>inverse beveling</u> due to the sharpening of one edge of a hand-ax, then flipping the hand-ax on its axis to sharpen the other edge. This results in opposite edges being flaked along opposite faces. Many typologists group such skewed hand-axes in a type, but inversely beveled hand-axes probably just represent advanced stages in reduction sequences.

- **the position of their grips.** True hand-axes have some sort of direct grip – whether it is an ergonomic patch of rough, rounded cortex left along a base or edge or else a "*mi-plat*" – a flat section along the rim that is perpendicular to the tool's plane. Beginners often dismiss the grip's departure from expected symmetry as breakage or an un-finished section. Instead grips testify to the care taken by the earliest toolmakers to achieve comfortable & effective designs. Since a grip's position also remains stable during reduction sequences, it is even more useful for classifying hand-axes than their changing contours.

- **an edge-on analysis of peripheral flaking, retouch, crushing, etc.** If one edge has been straightened with secondary soft-hammer retouch for cutting, whereas the opposite one has only been roughed out with hard hammer flaking or seems to have been *thinned* as opposed to sharpened, the rougher edge may have been prepared for insertion in a slotted grip that rotted away. If there is no direct grip at all – just all-around sharpness that bites into your palm when you press on one edge to cut with another - then a hafting scenario becomes almost inescapable. The use of such rim analysis led to distinctions between triangular bifaces in the 8th edition. Other tools which could be differentiated based on the distribution of straightened, thinned, crushed, resharpened, & ground edges have probably been lumped together too because their faces looked so similar that typologists thought the artifacts were the same kind. As a result, the inventiveness & cultural variety of Neanderthals probably continues to be under-estimated even by their champions.

1) Dagger grip hand-axes. These have a long "handle" composed of two facing oblique planes. Thrusting & slashing cuts. Very rare.

2) Oblique cortical grip on a concave crescent hand-ax. The grip is common, the concavity not so. A lateral cut.

3) Side grip. A rocking or sawing cut

4) Basal pocket grip. The base twists about 30 degrees away from the cutting plane, allowing fingers to be tucked into a safe pocket away from the meat or hide being prepared. Inwards lateral cuts. Aisne.

5) Crescent side-scraper grip. Such a Neanderthal tool may also have been inserted in a slotted handle like an ulu.

6) Inverse beveling seen from tip. The result of resharpening.

Proof of Hafting:

Neanderthal compound tools: The 2 photos show a much reduced Mousterian convergent side-scraper. Its most interesting feature is the thinning of the flat side of the base. This must have been done to turn the base into a peg that could be inserted and glued (with reduced birch sap or rabbit glue for example) into a handle as was the case with the 400,000 + BP flint at Schöningen. The recognition of an artifact's most telling but elusive features is one of an enthusiast's greatest pleasures, but students of prehistory should look forward to contesting their theories.

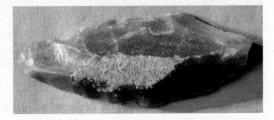

Neolithic polished axes:

1) The detail of a giant celt from Calvados shows grooves where lashing gradually ground into the ax's edge on either side of a lighter zone where the wooden handle surrounded the blade.

2) A belt of lighter patination around the middle of this ax found in a peat bog shows where the wooden handle survived long enough to impede patination until it had disintegrated.

AFRICAN, ASIAN & EUROPEAN POINT AND TOOL TYPES:

Grouping artifacts into Technological Modes:
Stone Age artifacts are currently grouped as follows:

MODE I: Oldowan. Unifacial or bifacial flaking along a cobble to make a cutting edge or remove flakes for use

MODE II: Acheulean. The first tools of a pre-determined shape not suggested by the block of stone. Working towards a mental template, the maker had to carry out dozens of gestures to achieve his goal, just like an origami master turning a sheet of paper into a swan. A sense of correctness was born – in other words, aesthetics.

MODE III: Levallois/ Mousterian/ Kombewa. The first tools of a standardized & repeated shape struck in succession from a pre-adapted core. The maker had to envision 2 successive phases at once: the core to be shaped & the products to be struck from it once the core was made. This involved planning & first occurred when modern human & Neanderthal ancestors independently reached cranial capacities of about 1,400 cc.

MODE IV: Upper Paleolithic. Blade, antler & bone tools of enormous diversity.

Archeological Periods:
The entire Stone Age fits fairly neatly into the geological **Quaternary Period**, which is currently defined as having begun 2.5 million years ago at the boundary of the Gauss/Matuyama paleomagnetic epochs. The Quaternary consists of 2 epochs: the **PLEISTOCENE** from 2.5 million until 10,000 years ago with its succession of Ice Ages, & the **HOLOCENE** from 10,000 BP till now.

Unlike in the Americas, where "Paleolithic" refers to the period from 18,000 to 8,000 B.P., in the Old World it is split into three sub-sections, each of which is linked to one or more technological Modes. The dates are approximate & shift from region to region since the modes appeared in them at different times:

1) the **Lower Paleolithic** linked to Mode I & Mode II technologies from 2.6 million to roughly 250,000 B.P.,

2) the **Middle Paleolithic** linked to Mode II & Mode III technologies from 250,000 to approximately 45,000 B.P., and

3) the **Upper Paleolithic** linked to Mode IV technologies from 45,000 B.P. to 12,000 B.P.

LOWER PALEOLITHIC (ca. 2,600,000 B.P. - 250,000 B.P.)

CHOPPER AND FLAKE TRADITION (a Mode I technology): At first *Homo habilis* &/or *Homo rudolfensis*, then *Homo ergaster* in Africa & its basic equivalent, *Homo erectus*, in Eurasia - 2.6 - 1.4 million B.P. in Africa, 1.8 million+ BP - 780,000 BP in S. Europe, with much later vestiges in Hungary, E. Asia, etc.

Oldowan I and II industries - Pebble choppers, Bifacial chopping-tools, Inverse choppers; **Clactonian flake tools:** notches, denticulates, becs. **Important sites:** Olduvai Gorge, Tanzania T.S.); Damanisi, Georgia; Longgupo, China

(1.8 million); Sangiran, Indonesia; Gran Dolina, Sierra de Atapuerca, Spain (800,000 BP); Tatoui, Romania; Orce, Greece; Clacton-on-Sea, U.K. (T.S.); Vértesszöllös, Hungary; Wimereux, France; etc.

ASIAN CHOPPER/CHOPPING TOOL TRADITION:
Important sites: Choukoutien, Patjitan, etc.

ABBEVILLEAN (Also known as the EARLY ACHEULEAN – the period of the first MODE II Technology. Mode II is defined by tapered bifaces (LCTs), which are commonly called hand-axes. Abbevillean ones were made only with direct hard hammer flaking.):
Homo ergaster & *Homo erectus* - 1,600,000 - 780,000 B.P. in Africa/ later in Eurasia)
Abbevillean hand-axes (Africa & Europe) - **Trihedral picks** (Africa) - **Amygdaloid hand-axes, Ficrons.**
Important sites: Ubeidiya, Israel; Bose Basin, S. China (app. 803,000 BP), Pingliang, China; Abbeville, France (T.S.); Konso, Ethiopia; Beni Ihklef, Algeria; etc.

MID TO LATE ACHEULEAN: *Homo erectus* to archaic *Homo sapiens* in Africa & *Homo antecessor* to *Homo heidelbergensis* in Eurasia, etc. - 780,000 - 250,000 B.P.:
NOTES: 1) The MODE II hand-axes of the later Acheulean often show *both* direct hard hammer & secondary soft hammer flaking.
2) The first MODE III technologies such as Levallois & Kombewa flake tools appeared earlier - at around 300,000 BP - in both Africa & Europe than the conventional date for the start of the Middle Paleolithic at 250,000 BP, suggesting that the Middle Paleolithic should be extended backwards.
HAND-AX TYPES: Tihodaine type cleavers (Africa), Tabel Balalt type cleaver (Africa), Kombewa flake cleavers (Africa), Chalossian pic, Lanceolate, Backed bifaces, Cordiform hand-axes, Limandes, Ovates, Discoids, Triangular (late transitional form), Elongated triangular, Fusiform hand-axes, Naviforms, Shark's tooth hand-axes, Pélécyformes, Ogivo-triangulaire, Lagéniformes, Micoquekeile, etc.
ASSOCIATED TOOLS: Kombewa flakes (Africa), Centripetal Levallois flakes, Levallois point, Levallois blades, Side-scrapers, Wooden spears (Schöningen, Germany - ca. 400,000 B.P.), Hafted knives (Schöningen).

IMPORTANT SITES (Mid-Acheulean - 780,000 - 500,000 B.P.): St. Acheul (T.S.), Soleihac & Artenac France; Petrolona, Greece; Boxgrove, U.K.; Sima de los Huesos, Burgos, Spain; Latamne, Syria; Kudaro, Georgia; Beni Ikhlef, Algeria; etc.
IMPORTANT SITES (Late Acheulean - 500,000 - 250,000 B.P.): Terra Amata & Tautavel, France; Gesher Benot Ya'aqov, Israel (tranchet cleavers); Torralba, Spain; Fontana Ranuccio, Italy; Swanscombe, U.K.; Schöningen & Karlich-Seeufer, Germany; El Ma el Abiod, Algeria; etc.

MIDDLE PALEOLITHIC (ca. 250,000 B.P. - 45,000 B.P.) – Mode III Technologies: Late *Homo heidelbergensis* to Classic *Homo neanderthalensis* (after 130,000 BP) in Eurasia, Archaic to Modern *Homo sapiens* in Africa & Middle East

TRUE MOUSTERIAN INDUSTRIES (EUROPE) First signs at 250,000 BP. Full flower 170,000 - 45,000 B.P.: 1) Mousterian in the Acheulean Tradition, 2) Denticulate Tool Tradition, 3) Quina Tool Tradition 4) Ferrassie Mousterian - **"MOUSTEROID" FLAKE TOOL INDUSTRY** (North Africa, Middle East) - **SANGOAN INDUSTRY** (Central Africa) - **ATERIAN INDUSTRY** (N. Africa), etc.
Elongated Mousterian points, Levallois points, Mousterian points (wholly retouched), Soyons points, Tayac points, Emireh points, Bifacial leaf-points - Blattspitzen (Eastern Europe), Aterian points, Raclette side-scrapers (21 types), Limaces, Burins, Cleaver hand-axes, Continuation of Micoquian hand-axes, Small to medium cordiform hand-axes (with direct soft-hammer retouching), Mousterian discs, Convex scrapers, Concave scrapers, Backed knives, First "retouchoirs" for pressure flaking, Levallois blade tools, Wooden spears (Lehringen), Borers, Non-Levallois truncated backed blades, etc.
Important sites: Le Moustier (T.S.), Fontéchevade, La Quina, Combe-Grenal, Laussel, Pech-de-l'Azé, La Chapelle-aux-Saints, Arcy-sur-Cure (France); Spy (Belgium); Monte Circeo (Italy); Neandertal (Germany); Tata, Molodova (Ukraine); High Lodge, Saccopastore, Krapina (Croatia); Mt. Carmel (Israel); Solo (Indonesia); Ain Meterchem, Kalambo Falls (Sangoan) & Charaman (T.S. Zambia), Lupemba (T.S. Congo), Pietersburg (T.S.), Howieson's Port (T.S.) & Klasies River Mouth (S. Africa); etc. **NOTE:** *According to traditional dating, based on European sites, the last 4 references are Mid Paleolithic, but typologically they anticipate the Upper Paleolithic.*

UPPER PALEOLITHIC: Mode IV Technologies (45,000 B.P. - 12,000 B.P.)

ULUZZIAN (late Neanderthals - ITALY - Circa 45,000 - 35,000 B.P.)
Crescents, Backed pionts, Burins, End-scrapers, Flake tools; Bone tools: awls, Conical points, biconical points, Etc. **Important site:** Grotta del Cavallo.

CHATELPERRONIAN (late Neanderthals - France - ca. 45,000 - 35,000 B.P.)
Châtelperronian knives, Châtelperronian points, End-scrapers, Truncated pieces, Burins, Incised tooth ornaments, Ivory pendants; Bone tools: awls, ivory pins, digging sticks, tubes, lozenge-shaped points, etc. **Important sites:** Châtelperron (T.S.), Grotte du Renne, St.-Césaire, Isturitz, Gargas, Caminade Est, Belvis, Quinçay, etc.

OTHER TRANSITIONAL MID-TO-UPPER PALEOLITHIC CULTURES: SZELETIAN (C. & E. Europe)/ LUPEMBIAN (Africa)

AURIGNACIAN (first European *Homo Sapiens sapiens*, also known as Cro-Magnons - ca. 40,000 - 28,000 B.P.)
Dufour bladelets, Retouched blades, Strangulated blades, Caminade scraper, Carinated (keeled) scraper, Nosed scraper, Plane, Dihedral burins; Bone tools: Split based atlatl points, etc. **Important sites:** Chauvet, Arcy-sur-Cure, La Ferrassie, Caminade Ouest, Dufour, Baden-Württemberg, Geissenklösterle, Vogelherd, etc.

GRAVETTIAN & PERIGORDIAN (W. Europe), PAVLOVIAN (C. Europe), KOSTIENKI (Ukraine & Russia), ETC. - *Homo sapiens* 28,000 - 23,000 B.P. - *Despite different names, the cultures of this period shared many features from the Pyrenees to Siberia, with Venus figurines made at Brassempouy in S. France sharing many stylistic aspects with those found at Kostienki, for example, although Kostienki craftsmen had a better understanding of how to align their sculptures with the grain of tusks for durability.*
Noaille gravers, Kostienki shouldered points, Font Robert points, Gravette points, Micro-Gravette points, Pointed median groove bone points, Obliquely truncated blades, Scrapers on large thin flakes, "Batons de Commandment" (wrenches), Dihedral burins, etc.
Important sites: La Gravette (T.S.), Chateau de Corbiac, Cougnac, Peche Merle, La Font-Robert, La Ferrassie, Laugerie Haute, Tursac, Predmosti, Dolni Vestonice, Avdievo, Kostienki, etc.

SOLUTREAN (France & Spain) & EPI-GRAVETTIAN (Italy, Central & E. Europe): 23,000 - 17,000 B.P.
Early Solutrean unifacial points, Mid-Sol. bifacial laurel leaf points (13 types), late Sol. shouldered points (4 types), Bifacial willow leaf points, Tanged bifacial points (Spain), Bevel based bone points, Backed bladelets, Borers, Bifacial knives, End-scrapers, Various dihedral burins, Laugerie Haute micro-scraper, Carinated scraper, Raclettes, Becs, Eyed needles, etc. **Important sites:** La Solutré (T.S.), Volgu, Lascaux, etc.

MAGDALENIAN (W. Europe), EPI-GRAVETTIAN (Italy, C. & E. Europe), KEBARIAN (Levant), IBEROMAURSIAN (N. Africa), etc. 17,000 12,000 B.P.
Teyjat points, dihedral burins, Magdalenian shouldered points, Many new microliths, Backed bladelets, Saw-toothed backed bladelets, End-scrapers, Dual burin-scraper tools, Parrot-beaked burin, Lacan burin, Carinated scraper, Thumb-nail scrapers; Bone & antler tools: Atl-atls, Harpoons (many types), Polished awls, Polished bone chisels, "lissoirs" & spatulas, Pincer tipped "navette" double ended blade grips, Engraved split bone rods, Eyed needles, wrenches, etc. **Important sites:** Gönnersdorf, Altamira, La Madeleine, Marsoulas, Pincevent, Isturitz, Niaux, Castillo, La Vache, Le Portel, Kesslerloch, etc.

MESOLITHIC: MANY DISTINCT CULTURES (end of glacial period - W. Europe: ca. 12,000 - 8,000 B.P. , Middle East: ca. 13,000 - 10,000 B.P.)

Microliths: small blade fragments retouched into geometric shapes (100s of types): Azilian points, Chaville points, Sauveterre points, Tardenois points, Capsian arrowheads, Trapezes (over 13 types), Rouffignac backed knives, Lunates, Triangles (over 11 types), Microburins, Tranchet chisels, Thumb-nail & other scrapers, Azilian Harpoons, Bone fish hooks, bone & antler mattocks, hafted adzes, etc. **Important sites:** Mas d'Azil (T.S. Early Meso.), Milheeze (Todermasaer), Ahrensbourg (T.S. early mid Meso.), Remouchamps, Conchamp (T.S.), Sauveterre la Lémance (T.S. - late mid-Meso.), Fère-en-Tardenols (T.S. - late Meso.), Shoukba & Jericho (Natufian), Gough's Cave (Creswellian), Horsham, Shippea Hill, Star Carr (Maglemosian); Otwock (Poland - Swiderian); Relilai, El Oued, Medjez (N. Africa); Mureybet (Mesopotamia: Meso. to Neo.)

NEOLITHIC: MANY CULTURES (Europe: ca. 8,000 - 5,000 B.P., Middle East: ca. 11,000 - 6,000 B.P.)

Amouq points (I & II), Byblos points, Temassinine points, Labied points, Bifacial leaf points, Tell Mureybet points; Saharan points (at least 9 families consisting of 103 groups, encompassing many more types), Chisel-ended arrowheads, French flint daggers, Sickle blades, Gouges, Chisels, Antler sleeve shock absorbers for celts, First polished celts, Antler harpoons, Eyed needles, First ceramic pottery outside Jomon (Mesolithic) Japan **Important sites:** *Europe* —> Stonehenge, Skara Brae (U.K.); Newgrange (Ireland); Barnenez, Carnac, Fort-Harrouard, Gavrinis, Filatosa (France); Michelsberg (T.S.) Belgium, Sittard (Holland); Starcevo, Sesklo, Vinca (T.S.), Butmir (T.S.), Cucuteni (T.S.), Cernavoda (Balkans); Nea Nikomedeia (Greece); *W. Asia* —> Catal Huyuk (T.S.), Hacilar, Mersin (Turkey), Jericho (West Bank), Jarmo, Hassuna, Halaf (T.S.), Jemdet Nasr (Mesopototamia), Khirokitia (Cyprus); Ali Kosh, Tépé Hissar (Iran); Dzejtun, Kelteminar; *N. Africa* —> Merimde, Badari, Fayoum (Egypt); Jaatcha, Tazina, Djerat, Redeyef, Adrar Bous III, etc. **China** —> Yangshao (T.S.).

CHALCOLITHIC & BRONZE AGE (E. Europe & Anatolia 7,500 - 3,000 B.P. / W. Europe: 5,000 - 2,800 B.P.)

NOTE: All but the most prestigious tools (& even some of those) during these periods still tended to be made of stone.

Egyptian fishtail flint knives, Gerzean flint knives, Armorican flint arrowheads, Scandanavian flint daggers based on copper & bronze models, Hardstone shaft-hole battleaxes, First Copper, then Bronze tools: Axes, Adzes, Chisels, Razors, Bronze arrowheads, Etc. **Important sites:** Cambous & Mont Bego (France); Nagada (Egypt); Hagar Qim & Mnajdra (Malta), Su Nuraxi, Sardinia; etc.

Putting The Artifacts Into Perspective

The artifacts shown below were made by a succession of human species with ever-bigger brains, who also had to adapt, in the case of the Neanderthals, to several Ice Ages. The following figures are helpful for situating each artifact in these progressions.

<u>Brian Sizes of Hominids Who Made Stone Tools:</u> Cranial capacity progressed from roughly **500 cc** at the beginning of the Stone Age, 2.6 million years ago, to approximately **1,400 cc** about 150,000 years ago. But it is also important to remember that a species did not necessarily go extinct as soon as a new species had evolved from it, so directly related species overlapped & probably made different types of tools simultaneously. Finally, brains did not expand much until more than 2.5 million years after hominids had become bipedal over 5 million years ago, so the Australopithecines & their descendant, *Homo habilis*, had brains only marginally bigger than a gorilla's **500 cc** or a chimp's **410 cc**.

Homo habilis (Africa)	2.3 - 1.5 million BP	**510 cc to 674 cc**.
Homo rudolfensis (Africa)	ca. 2 million BP	**752 cc** (skull KNM-ER 1470).
Homo ergaster (Africa)	1.9 million - 800,000 BP	**804 cc to 900 cc**.
Homo erectus (Eurasia)	1.9 million - to 54,000? BP	**813 cc to 1,225 cc** at start
		1,013 cc to 1,251 cc later on

Javan specimens of *erectus* have more robust crania than African *ergaster* but are otherwise basically the same. The name *ergaster* may be folded back into the older term *erectus*.

Homo antecessor (Europe)	ca. 800,000 BP	**App. 1,000+ cc.**

Possibly the last common ancestor of Neanderthals & our lineage, Homo sapiens

Archaic Homo sapiens (Africa)	400,000 - 250,000 BP	**1,285 cc** (Broken Hill) to
		1,400 cc (Lake Turkana).
Pre-modern Homo sapiens (Africa)	250,000 - 100,000 BP	**1,300 cc** to **1,430 cc**.
Homo heidelbergensis (Europe)	700,000 - 200,000 BP.	App. **1,000** (Steinheim) to
		1,390 cc (Sima de los Huesos).
Proto-Homo neanderthalensis (Europe)	250,000 (Ehringsdorf) & 200,000 (Biache-St.-Vaast)	
Classic Neanderthals	ca. 130,000 – 30,000 BP.	Av. **1,450 cc.** Max. **1,750 cc**
		(Amud, Israel).

Modern Homo sapiens   120,000+ - Present   Average **1,350 cc.**

The conventional average cranial capacity of modern humans is **100 cc less than the Neanderthal average.** But the average Neanderthal weighed over 168 lb. - more than the average for modern humans from any continent. So in relation to their body weight, Neanderthal brains were slightly smaller than ours. It must also be emphasized that cranial capacity by itself is NOT indicative of intelligence. Einstein's brain was twice the size of that of the great 19th century French writer, Anatole France. Because of sexual dimorphism, men have brains about 100 cc larger than a woman's of equal body weight - the same relative difference as in macaque monkeys. This difference is unconnected to cognitive functions. But it may be related to natural selection of males with better spatial orientation. Such males would have been able to mentally map landscapes & rotate images. Mental rotation may have been useful in producing the first tapered bifaces (also known as **LCTs** - large cutting tools - which are the defining trait of Mode II technology).

GLACIAL PERIODS & INTER-GLACIALS OF THE PLEISTOCENE:

Glacial periods were first defined both by moraines they left in the Alps & in outwash sediment deposited around the N. Sea. So each period has both an Alpine & Lowland name. The Alpine name appears in ***BOLD ITALICIZED CAPITALS*** & is the most common one for Old World usage. The Lowland name appears next in SIMPLE CAPITALS & the equivalent American name third. Warm to temperate inter-glacial periods, like the one we are in now, were first defined from the lowland deposits & appear between the Glacial Periods. Dates are based on oxygen isotope levels recorded from core samples extracted from ocean floors.

0 – 18,000 BP:	Inter-glacial (Although glaciers generally did not grow after 18,000 BP, fluctuating cold conditions continued until 10,000 BP when tundra animals disappeared from western Europe);		
18,000 – 67,000 BP:	***WÜRM***	= WEICHSEL	= Wisconsin
67,000 – 128,000 BP:	Inter-glacial ***UZNACH***	= EEM	= Sangamon;
128,000 – 180,000 BP:	***RISS***	= SAALE	= Illinoian;
180,000 – 230,000 BP:	Inter-glacial ***HOETTING***	= HOLSTEIN	= Yarmouth;
230,000 – 300,000 BP:	***MINDEL***	= ELSTER	= Kansan;
300,000 – 330,000 BP:	Inter-glacial ***G-M***	= CROMER	= Aftonian;
330,000 – 470,000 BP:	***GUNZ***	= MENAP	= Nebraskan;
470,000 – 540,000 BP:	Inter-glacial ***D-G***	= WAALIAN;	
540,000 – 550,000 BP:	***DONAU II***	= WEYBOURNE;	
550,000 – 585,000 BP:	Inter-glacial	= TIGLIAN;	
585,000 – 600,000 BP:	***DONAU I (DANUBE)***;		

600,000 to 2 million BP: Roughly 20 more glacial advances

CHOPPERS - Chopper & Flake Tradition: ca. 2,600,000 to 1,400,000 / 100,000 B.P. (depending on region): *Essentially Homo habilis or Homo ergaster through Homo erectus*

1) 4 1/2" *Oldowan chopper*. Foum-el-Hassan, Morocco. 1.4 to 2.2 million BP. Major wind gloss on quartzite. The flake scars aren't as clear as on the following specimen.

2) 4" *Oldowan* **chopper**. Basalt with heavy wind stippling. Taouz, Morocco. 1.4 to 2.2 million BP. A well made and dramatic specimen.

3) 3 1/2" **chopper**. Arranches, Portugal. Europe's oldest tool type – perhaps contemporaneous with Dmanisi, Georgia fossils. This one apparently closer to mid Paleolithic. Monochromatic patinated quartzite.

LOCATION: Africa and Europe as far north as Hungary.
DESCRIPTION: A cobble with 2 or more flakes struck from one side. Although choppers & chopping tools (see below) are found throughout the Stone Age, those from early sites are especially sought after as the oldest surviving vestiges of hominid tool-use:
I.D. KEY: Lower & Middle Paleolithic specimens always patinated.

CHOPPING TOOLS - Chopper & Flake Tradition: ca. 2,600,000 to 1,400,000 / 100,000 B.P. (depending on region): *Essentially Homo habilis or Homo ergaster through Homo erectus*

4) 6" x 5 1/2" **pre-Acheulean chopper**. Pointes aux Oies, France. Beneath the waves of the English Channel, the tools are in situ in peat underlying a bluff. Over 750,000 BP. Black flint turned calico in flaked area by peat acids. Massive, colorful. Unique site now covered by Nazi surf defenses & bunkers fallen from the eroded bluff & sand diverted to prevent silting of port.

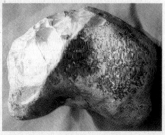

5) 6" *pre-Acheulean* **chopper**. Pointes aux Oies, France. Over 750,000 BP. Black flint turned calico. Massive, sculptural.

LOCATION: Africa, Europe as far north as Hungary. **DESCRIPTION:** A cobble with flakes struck bifacially from both sides of at least one edge, usually by alternate flaking forming a sinuous cutting edge. **I.D. KEY:** Lower & Middle Paleolithic specimens always patinated

CLACTONIAN TOOLS - European Chopper & Flake Tradition, depending on region: 1,700,000 to 500,000 B.P.: *Homo ergaster to Homo erectus to Homo antecessor*

6) 7" **Clactonian** *denticulated* knife. Sainte Adresse, France. Over 500,000 BP. Soil sheen & hydration fogging. Found 200 meters off-shore at low tide in a unique site. Cortical side grip & retouched cutting edge.
I.D. KEY: Thick flakes with percussion bulb & ripples obtained by striking a nodule against a stone anvil. Coarsely retouched with heavy hammer stone.

LOCATION: An industry without bifaces, whose official southwestern limit is Clacton-on-Sea, England. It survived in the middle latitudes of Europe as Acheulean hand-axes spread into S. Europe & east into India &, exceptionally, China. **NOTES:** The Clactonian tool set consists of choppers, chopping tools, becs (borers), dendiculates, side-scrapers & notches. Fire was known by the tradition's end. At least 3 handaxes, one clearly Micoquian, were also found in the sea at Ste. Adresse.

PRIMITIVE "ABBEVILLEAN" HAND-AXES - Early Acheulean, 1.4 million + B.P. - 780,000 B.P./Later outside Africa: *Homo ergaster to Homo erectus to Homo antecessor*

The oldest tapered idealized artifacts known are large bifaces & trihedral picks that herald the start of Mode II technology. The term LCT (Large Cutting Tool) may be applied to either of them. Both types of hand-axes were made by direct hard-stone percussion & were found with a 1.4 million year old Homo ergaster mandible in Konso, Ethiopia. The oldest datable African specimens were found in the same complex of sites below a level of volcanic tuff dated at 1.6 million BP. The oldest European specimens are more conservatively dated at roughly 650,000 BP.

AFRICAN TYPE:

7) 11" *trihedral pick* **hand-ax**. Quartzite. Beni Ikhlef, Algeria. Dated by comparison with dated series at KGA 10 in Konso, Ethiopia: at least 1.4 million years old. On the unshown ridge side, there is wind luster & desert varnish caused by Metallogenium & Pedomicrobium bacteria absorbing manganese, iron & clay particles as a sun-shield. Leaching crust. The only one this big ever seen with decorative burgundy and beige coloring.

8) 11 1/4" *Early Acheulian Lanceolate* **handax**. Bifacial as opposed to trihedral form. Western Sahara. Banded quartzite. Such huge bifaces are one of the two earliest tool types in the Konso area of Ethiopia, where they have been dated to over 1.4 million BP!

AFRICAN MID TO LATE ACHEULEAN HAND-AXES - Lower Paleolithic, ca. 750,000 - 250,000 B.P.: *late Homo erectus*

The discovery that a biface's edges could be straightened by retouching them with a soft hammer made of antler, bone or wood revolutionized bifaces around 750,000 years ago. Not only were the new hand-axes more efficient knives, but their makers could now adapt their silhouettes for specific tasks and, perhaps more importantly, as an expression of their group's particular technological culture. *The oldest artifact to have been found expressly deposited with the dead is a hand-ax dropped on top of bodies that had been dragged deep into a Spanish cave before the invention of lamps & pitched into shafts. Such hand-axes must have been charged with symbolism & represent another step in the evolution of the mind.*

9) Giant lanceolate handax. Quartzite with micro-exfoliation. One of biggest ever seen at 12". Northern Tchigheti, Mauritania. Colonial collection. Dramatic & no longer exported. Only 2 seen on market in 3 years.

10) *Giant spatulate* **handax**. Quartzite with micro-exfoliation. One of biggest ever seen at 12". Northern Tchigheti, Mauritania. Colonial collection. Dramatic & no longer exported. None seen surpassing this in size over the past several years.

11) 9" *Bifacial lagéniforme (tongue-shaped)* **handax**. Late Acheulian. Mylonite. Iringa Highlands, Tanzania. A spectacular specimen from a rare source.

12) 10" *Giant cleaver* **handax**. Mid-to-late Acheulian. Quartzite with micro-exfoliation. Northern Tchigheti, Mauritania. Colonial collection. Dramatic & no longer exported.

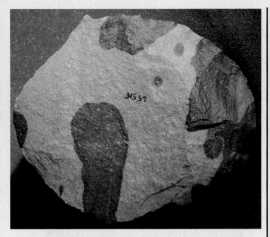

13) 8 3/4" *Flake-based* cleaver with bifacially thinned base. Late Acheulian. Tabelbalat area Algeria based on appearance. Red & tan quartzite. This side wind stippled, other side darkened. Colorful.

14) 6 1/4" *Cordiform* handax. Banded jasper and quartzite with high wind polish. Marked Mali, but probably extremely south of former Spanish Sahara. Among the prettiest materials.

EUROPEAN ACHEULEAN HAND-AXES - Lower Paleolithic, ca. 600,000 (possibly much older) - 250,000 B.P.: *Homo erectus, Homo antecessor, Homo heidelbergensis*

15) *Lanceolate* handax with *inverse double oblique grips*. Remarkable ergonomy. Chert. Among the biggest European bifaces at 9 3/4". 1920s field find in now urbanized zone; Le Tillay, Seine-et-Marne, France. Bifaces from this famous site are illustrated in Fr. Bordes' typology guides.

16) 6" *Lanceolate* handax. Pressignien flint tumbled in alluvia. Claise, Indre-et-Loire, France. An excellent example & transparent orange. Smaller specimens fall rapidly in price.

17) *Lanceolate* handax. Flint. 7 1/4". Orange patina over originally mat black Thanatian flint is typical of the brick clay of the Somme region. From the type site of the longest period in human development, St. Acheul, plus one of the finest from anywhere.

18) *Elongated ovate* handax. Gray Thanatian flint patinated by watertable. 7 1/4". One of the biggest & best proportioned from the type site of St. Acheul.

19) *Bifacial Cleaver* handax. If the angles to straight bit were not so abrupt it would be a classic *Limande*. Flint with typical orange brick clay patina of type site. 6 1/4". Cleavers are rarities in Europe as opposed to Africa and this is the best ever seen from the type site of St. Acheul itself. Lesser specimens also come from the Sahara.

20) 6 1/4" *crescent* hand-ax. Boves next door to Amiens & St. Acheul. Dark gray flint turned white by lime salt substitution for leached-out silica. Found 1883. **ID:** A concave cutting edge opposite a convex edge with an oblique grip. It is difficult to explain such hand-axes as being a step in a reduction sequence since they seem to be specific to certain sites and are exceedingly rare in those assemblages. Small cordiforms exist with frost damage or ugly material, especially in mat brown, NW African quartzite.

21) 10" *arch-backed naviform* hand-ax. Vailly-sur-Aisne, France. Sparkling quartzite with patina & crusts. The American prehistorian and frequent companion of Abbé Breuil, Harper Kelley, reported on similar giant hand-axes from the Aisne in 1963. **ID:** Arch-backed hand-axes with an oblique grip on a convex edge opposite a much straighter cutting edge that runs from the tip to the base, have been reported from the Seine northwards through the Aisne, the English Wolvercote assemblage and into central Europe.

22) 8" *arched-edge naviform* hand-ax. Montieres, France. Dark gray flint patinated white by silica loss and lime salt intrusion. For other hand-axes from the same site see François Bordes. **ID:** Whereas the *arch-backed* naviform has an oblique basal grip along the arched edge, the *arched-edge* naviform has the grip along the straighter one. On this specimen, the long bulging edge across from the grip works best with a rocking saw motion. True naviforms are double bitted & usually have a lateral grip.

23) *Naviform* handax. Quartzite. 6 3/4". Port d'Envaux. A large example of one of the rarest Acheulian types. Best seen in 3 years.

24) 5" *shark's tooth lanceolate ficron* hand-ax. **ID:** Edges not as well made as on a typical lanceolate or Micoquian. Lanceolate ficrons have slightly covex edges, Micoquian ficrons, slightly concave ones. Basal grip. Boves, next door to St. Acheul from 1883 excavation. Tri-color peat patina with fossilized worm burrow in flint. Original label, painterly colors, bold example of rare form.

25) *"Bishop's Mitre" sub-cordiform* handax, to quote the 1917 inscription on the base. Flint patinated to several colors. 4". France. Decorative & historically interesting.

26) 6" *Cordiform* handax. Acheulian. Flint. Sanvic, Seine-Maritime. Found around 1900 in a sand-pit. A large perfectly proportioned example.

27) 6 1/2" *amygdaloid* hand-ax. St. Même la Carrière, Charente. Mid-Acheulean. Extremely varied patinas from many processes. The 6 major collections in the area are black holes, sucking local artifacts in & never parting with anything.

28) 7" extremely *elongated cordiform* biface with hole through it & *tip gloss*. Bon Secour, Dreux, France. Found 1885. Dark, mat gray flint turned snowy white. All around cutting edge. The blade is so thin, it foreshadows Central European mid to upper paleo leaf points & knives. Late Acheulean to Mid Paleolithic. **HYPOTHESIS:** Although gloss on hand-axes & similar but possibly hafted bifaces may derive from soil mechanics or even the silica particles in corn roots, the author has noticed that gloss usually appears around tips, rather than elsewhere. It is hard to explain a predilection of roots for tips, so cases of tip gloss may be due to their use for digging among the silica in soil - probably for root storage organs & post pits. Hole, artisanal perfection, thinness, & 2 intriguing features. .

29) *Limande* handax. Gray flint patinated orange by watertable. 4 1/2". Bon Secour, Vernouillet, Eure-et-Loir. An especially colorful example of more typical Acheulian handaxes.

30) 9 1/4" *"Micoquian" finger-pocket hand-ax* with concave edges & lens cross-section. Heavily patinated black flint. Pommiers, Aisne. Tip thin for 2/5ths of tool's length. Seen from the side, the handle goes up at a 35 degree angle from the plane of the cutting edges – creating a sheltered space for the fingers when the knife is used for cutting flesh sideways off hide. See the Grip Demo section for a side view of a similar hand-ax. One of the biggest specimens of a type seen (rarely) from the Seine into central Europe.

31) 7 1/4" *bi-pointed, side-grip limande* hand-ax. Chevrière, Oise. Faces patinated differently: the one with cortex black, the other olive. The edge with the most cortex is actually the main cutting side. The only blunt ergonomic surface that could serve as a grip is a small patch of cortex along the opposite edge. Side-grip limande & naviform hand-axes work best with a downwards rocking & sawing motion. Rare sub-type, large size.

32) *Cordiform* handax. Late Acheulian or Mousterian. Mat black flint with some peat patina & much soil sheen. 5 1/4". An example of an only slightly patinated specimen which was probably protected where it was left by percipitated clay. The finest seen for this form for the region. Vailly-sur-Aisne, France.

33) *Miniature biconcave pebble* handax. Acheulian. Only 3". Swanscombe, Kent, UK. A rare English form due to the use of small cobbles there. This specimen belonged to Martin A.C. Hinton, the main suspect in the Piltdown Man Hoax!

OTHER EUROPEAN ACHEULEAN TOOLS -
Lower Paleolithic, ca. 650,000 (possibly older) - 250,000 B.P.: *Homo erectus, Homo antecessor, Homo heidelbergensis*

34) *Limace* Monoface with deeply invasive knapping to the base. Acheulian. Flint patinated by watertable. 4 3/4". St. Même-les-Carrières, Charente. Limace-like monofaces are far rarer than handaxes in the Acheulian tool kit.

35) 5" *Bifacial crescent* knife. Flint. St. Même-les-Carrières, Charente. The grip is around the knob in the middle of the edge opposite the ulu-like knife. An extremely rare Acheulian tool type.

THE MIDDLE PALEOLITHIC - ca. 250,000 - 45,000 B.P.: *Neanderthals & Archaic Homo sapiens*

AFRICAN MID-PALEOLITHIC TOOLS - ca. 250,000 - 45,000 B.P.: *Advanced Homo erectus variants (Broken Hill Man, Saldana Man) & "Gracile" Neanderthals (in N. Africa) to Archaic Homo sapiens*

36) A: 2" **Aterian stemmed scraper**. Petrified wood. Wind gloss. S. Algeria. **ID**: A Levallois flake which has been given a stem. One of the first indisputably hafted tools.

B: 2" **Aterian stemmed point**. Petrified wood. Wind gloss. S. Algeria. **ID**: A Levallois point that has been given a stem. The oldest stemmed point type seen. Late Middle Stone Age into Upper Paleolithic.

37) A 3" & a 3 3/4" **T-shaped tool**. W. Sahara. Tabular flint with 3 concave "spoke-shave" concavities. Wind gloss & color alteration. Some early prehistorians speculated that the longest spoke represented a bird goddess's beak while the other spokes represented her brows. Still speculating, they could be a culturally specific whittling tool or parts of a thrown snare, similar in conception to bolas. Middle Stone Age. Rare.

38) 3 1/4" T-shaped tool (or symbol). An extremely unusual specimen for 2 reasons: There are 2 concavities, not 3, & the convex section, although worked, bears significantly darker & older patina. If the narrow spoke had been a stem for hafting, one would expect the convex edge to show preparation for use as a chisel or scraper. Neither is the case. Could it be a zoomorphic or anthropomorphic representation after all? For years, the only one seen on the market. Now there are more.

39) 3 1/2" mid-Paleolithic drill made of Libyan Glass, an impactite from a meteorite explosion that vitrified dunes 29 million years ago. Earliest glass tools are from late Acheulean. W. Egypt. Transparent. Extreme wind smoothing & stippling.

40) 7" ovate biface. Wind patinated quartzite. Erg Titersine, Libya. Middle Stone Age ovates seem to be typical of the Libyan & Egyptian Sahara rather than the Western Sahara. Could they be a guide-artifact to a specific culture? The most colorful and perfect have a shield-like boldness.

41) 6 1/2" ovate biface. Libyan Desert in Egypt. Quartzite. Intense differential weathering of rock on photoed side. Other side unweathered! This piece lay like a turtle hunkered in the wind for tens of thousands of years.

42) 8 1/4" "Micoquian" lanceolate hand-ax. Libya. Beige & red quartzite. Leaching crust & aeolized on domed face. Tip unbroken, colorful, & rare type. One of 2 seen in 5 years. NOTE: Unlike true Micoquian hand-axes, from SW Europe which are localized late Acheulean to Mousterian transitional artifacts, bifaces with concave edges appeared earlier in Africa.

43) 8 1/2" fishtail cleaver hand-ax. One of two reported. Akin to both Tabelbala-Tachenghit (type 4) & tihodaine (type 5) cleavers which are common. Quartzite with micro-exfoliation & patina. Late Acheulean to early Middle Stone Age. Mauritania. ID: Like Saharan cleavers

illustrated in Overstreet editions 6 & 7, made from a huge flake with bifacial thinning along both edges. But the thinning is a tour-de-force to create a flared bit. Elegance & only 2 reported. NOTE: Type 4 has an asymmetrically tilted bit, one convex & one concave edge, an oblique base & thinning around the sides & base of the flat bottom. Type 5 has a straight bit, parallel sides, a semi-circular base & is bifacial except at the bit. Acheulean cleavers are also found in Spain, Sicily & the Middle East.

EUROPEAN MOUSTERIAN HAND-AXES, OTHER TOOLS & CORES - Middle Paleolithic, ca. 250,000 - 45,000 B.P.: *Neanderthals*

Only one of the several Mousterian cultures continued to make "hand-axes" with any regularity, the Mousterian in the Acheulean Tradition, as opposed to the Quina tradition, the Denticulate tradition, and others.

44) 6 1/2" diameter Levallois flake-tool core. From a unique site 500 meters offshore at Ault, Somme. Barnacles on back & peaty patina. This site provided so many flint nodules from a chalk cliff that have now eroded back half a kilometer that pre-Neanderthals often used cores to remove just one tool – instead of dozens as elsewhere. So the cores are among the biggest known. The workmanship is also superb.

45) 3 1/2" Quina side-scraper. One of the biggest from the type-site of this Mousterian culture: La Quina, Les Gardes, Charente. Most are half size. Found 1912. Gray chert patinated white.

46) 5" Levallois flake convergent side-scraper/crescent knife. Vailly-sur-Aisne. Black flint with soil sheen & water-table patina. Incredible preservation due to the Neanderthals' camp being covered by still waters & precipitating clay. Never tumbled or chipped. Both edges show fine scaling from the base to the tip. Rarer than most hand-ax types.

47) 4 1/2" Mousterian convergent side-scraper/leaf-blade knife. Thanatian flint typical of Picardy & the Somme. Calcite caliche on unphotoed side. Bifacial basal thinning – probably for hafting! Soissons, Aisne. Such an elegant tool bears so little resemblance to typical side-scrapers, that it seems reasonable to see it more as a finely contoured, leaf-blade knife. Dibble is correct about the reduction sequence of convergent side-scrapers to Mousterian points in some, but far from all, cases. One would expect to find the reduction sequence in all sites with double-edged side-scrapers. That is NOT the case. One would also expect many more points since they would be end products, jettisoned like cigarette butts. That is not the case either. Highly symmetrical leaf blade & crescent knives are regularly found at a few Middle Paleolithic sites, but unheard of in most others with double side-scrapers. The dismissive reduction sequence theory looks better in a drawing than in the field. Incredibly rare.

48) 4 1/2" **Mousterian monoface**. Boulogne-la-Grasse, Oise. Water table patina. A cultural indicator for an un-named aspect of the Mousterian – I'd dub it the Oise Mousterian - since it comes from an assemblage with many fine monofaces & few bifaces. Unlike on a convergent side-scraper, the flaking is invasive and not simply scaled around edges. Cortical concavity near base.

49) *Cordiform* handax. Mousterian. Gray flint turned white. 5 1/4". Villiers-Louis, Yonne. Thin cross-scetion & retouch around the edges worthy of a Gerzean knife. As fine as they get.

50) *Micoquian* handax. Cap de la Heve, Le Havre, France. True Micoquian handaxes have concave edges and are typically small. Note the barnacles on this remarkable specimen found in the English Channel. It is the best of 3 found many decades ago at a submerged site within a kilometer of the published Clactonian site off Ste. Adresse. One of the most highly sought after forms.

51) 5" *Triangular* handax. Pressignian flint patinated with lime & hydration webbing mainly on one side. Chaumussay, Indre-et-Loire, France. François Bordes wrote that the triangular handaxes reached their zenith of perfection at Chaumussay. **DESCRIPTION:** Straight or slightly convex sides, fairly straight base, often sharp, with suggestion of thinning for hafting. After the discovery of a hafted Acheulean flint in a coalmine in Schöningen, Germany, the creation of such complex tools by even the earliest Neanderthals is incontestable. Complete triangular bifaces/hand-axes are especially rare because - (1) of their thinness & consequent delicacy, (2) they were produced during the transition from the Acheulean to Mousterian, and (3) they are the first hand-axes to consistently show tip fractures suggesting impact damage (thus hafting).

52) 6" *Triangular* handax. Transitional Acheulian to Mousterian form. Flint. One side with tan patina, other creamy with concretions. Lanneray, Eure-et-Loir. All around cutting edge & geometric perfection.

53) *Giant triangular* handax. Quartzite with mineral deposits. Huge at 7 3/4". Vailly-sur-Aisne.

54) 2 3/4" **Mousterian in the Acheulean Tradition (MAT) cordiform biface**. Senonais. Max. thickness half inch. Basal thinning for probable hafting. Too small & thin to be a "hand-ax". Narrow examples may even be projectile points related to late Neanderthals' leaf points in central Europe. Colorful.

55) 2" **MAT biface**. Quartz (rare material). Manzac-sur-Vern.

56) 5" **ovate biface**. Gray flint turned yellow. Hydration webbing. Upper terrace of Loire, Nievre. The find of a decade of intensive scratching. Perfect geometry.

57) 4 3/4" **ovate biface**. Bu, Eure et Loir. Completely de-silicified in spots. A geometrical gem.

58) 7 1/2" **bifacial naviform leaf-blade**. 3 color quartzite – milky, tan & dark gray. Water-table patinas. Aisne, France. So thin & finely knapped, it resembles a gigantic Solutrean laurel leaf knife. Possibly a precursor to SZELETIAN leaf points. This is the finest & most colorful specimen seen for such a late mid-Paleolithic biface.

59) Bifacial Mousterian knife/side-scraper. Dark gray flint patinated by lime salts. 4 3/4". Malay-le-Petit, Yonne. A rare nearly rectangular biface with one sharpened long edge opposite another with crushing or other evidence of preparation for hafting. 6 are now known from a 10 kilometer square, suggesting a local variant.

60) A:Mousterian point. Creamy patination over dark gray flint. Retouched to base on one edge & halfway on other. 4". Maillot, Yonne. A splendid example.
B: Mousterian blade, heralding the first Upper Paleolithic blade-based industries. Patinated orange in boggy depression. 3 3/4". Malay-le-Petit, Yonne.

61) Mousterian point. All edges are retouched, plus basal thinning for probable hafting! Gray flint with soil sheen & creamy patination. Grignieuzeville, France. Superb specimen.

62) 2" Levallois point. Mousterian. Flint patinated orange in a peaty depression. Both edges are retouched to the base! Malay-le-Petit, Yonne, France.

63) Levallois point core. Villevallier, Yonne. 4 1/3". The ability to extract multiple points from such cores represented one of humanity's great technical innovations.

64) Levallois outre-passé flake tool. Gray flint patinated white by silica leaching & lime salt substitution. At 6 7/8", the biggest ever seen from its region. Mesnil-St.-Loup, Aube, France. Levallois flake tools, Levallois blades and Levallois points were the mainstays and basic building blocks of the Mousterian-in-the-Acheulian-Tradition tool kit. Highly decorative centripedal flake scars.

65) Mousterian "Bola". Quartzite. 3 1/2" in diameter. Malay-le-Grand, Yonne. Extremely rare to non-existant in most Mousterian sites. Often confused with concussed Neolithic hammers which are usually made of flint, whereas Mousterian "bolas" are usually quartzite.

THE UPPER PALEOLITHIC
(Sub-periods: Châtelperronian [*last Neanderthals*], Aurignacian, Gravettian, Solutrean, Magdalenian) ca. 45,000 - 12,000 B.P.: *Mainly Cro-Magnons, the name for European Upper Paleolithic modern humans were as much Homo sapiens as we are.*

SOME INVENTIONS: MEASURING SYSTEMS, ATL-ATL POINTS, NEEDLES, HARPOONS, BASKETRY & OTHER "WEAVING" TECHNOLOGIES, JEWELRY & ART:
NOTE: *Despite the fact that Upper Paleolithic tools are often much smaller than the preceding ones, they are also much rarer than most of them because:*
• *populations were extremely sparse due to often extreme glacial conditions*
• *the periods were much shorter and*
• *most sites have been off-limits to collectors for 60 or more years.*

AURIGNACIAN - ca. 40,000 (N. Europe) / 43,000 (SW Europe) - 28,000 B.P.
Hitherto associated exclusively with our species, Homo sapiens sapiens, & dated from 34,000 BP in SW Europe, but the deepest proto-Aurignacian strata in the El Castillo Cave in Spain have now been dated to 43,000 BP – about 8,000 years before firm evidence of sapiens sapiens in western Europe. Could the proto-Aurignacian have been another Neanderthal invention like the Chatelperronian? Our species may have copied Neanderthal technology as much as the other way around."

66) 5 1/2" Aurignacian calibrated antler tine. Blanchard rock shelter, Dordogne. One of the oldest examples of non-functional (in the traditional sense) notation, counting or measurement. Mathematical, musical and linguistic literacy eventually took off from the breakthrough represented by this specimen. Ca. 32,000 BP. Only one this old seen in private hands. Inestimable.

CHATELPERRONIAN - ca. 40,000 - 30,000 B.P.
Neanderthals

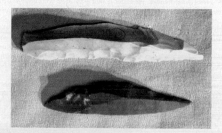

67) A: 4" Chatelperronian point. Paris, Aube – not far from Chatelperronian site at Arcy-sur-Cure. Knapping of back usually from one face. The steeply retouched back on Gravettes is usually from *both* faces. Perhaps the biggest specimen of the rarest point.
NOTE: The Chatelperronian is one of several Neanderthal cultures that represent a final flourish before they went extinct (except for a few genetic markers they seem to have left in people of European descent). Most prehistorians have a tendency to dismiss the final Neanderthal cultures as desperate attempts to cope with intruding members of our species, Homo sapiens sapiens. There has been much speculation of a deficiency of Neanderthal language, despite their well-developed hyoid bone used to anchor vocal muscles and brains that were larger than ours on average. Supposedly, our species was

also far more efficient because of its ability to manipulate symbols and a newly invented blade technology that lent itself to the manufacture of complex compound tools with insertable standardized parts. The problem is that almost all Châtelperronian layers seem to pre-date the Aurignacian ones associated with modern humans.

So the theory *may* be flawed. In fact, Neanderthals may have made jewelry and invented a blade technology *before* our lineage arrived. They may have been just as capable of invention, yet simply had less virulent microbes. Whereas our lineage had recently come out of the tropics' incredible microbial diversity - which the migrants carried within themselves (along with immunities acquired over millenia of epidemics), Neanderthals had developed in cold regions with much lower exposure to microbes. So our ancestors were walking biological bombs infecting Neanderthals directly & indirectly. Neanderthal bands would have become too small to compete in favorable areas. Mortality would have exceeded the birth rate and they would have gone extinct like the Taino before the onslaught of the Conquistadors. In the mean time, our lineage may actually have acquired some behaviors from Neanderthals - as well as vice versa. At the very least, the final Neanderthal flourishes - either independently, or in the face of disease and advancing intruders - proved Neanderthal adaptability once and for all.

B: 3 1/4" **Gravette point.** From the type-site: La Gravette, Bayac, Dordogne. Steep retouch along one edge creating a back for insertion & gluing in a slotted shaft. A true projectile point. Ca. 25,000 BP. One of the rarest Paleolithic point types.

68) A:Blade end-scraper. Upper Solutrean. East section of Laugerie Haute, Les Eyzies, Dordogne. 4 1/8".
    B: Fully Retouched Aurignacian Blade. Castelmerle, Sergeac, Dordogne. Found 1902. Still has original label. 4". Perfection & one of the rarest tools from one of the most important sites.

69) A:Double burin & parallel side-scraper all in one tool. Early Aurignacian. Lartet Rock Shelter, Les Eyzies, Dordogne. Dark gray flint patinated creams & whites. 19th C find. 5 1/4". Finest ever seen in private hands.
B: Blade end-scraper with lateral retouch to base on both sides. Upper Solutrean. Laugerie Basse, Dordogne. Flint with soil sheen & mineral patina. 6". Longest seen. **NOTE:** It should be noted that any collecting around the Dordogne's famous sites today is not only strictly forbidden but heavily policed! All the illustrated pieces come from such 19th C collections as Christy & Lartet's and often have the original labels.

70) 4 7/8" **Aurignacian to Gravettian retouched blade.** Retouch around all edges. Black flint turned white. Abri Labattut, Sergeac, Dordogne, 1912. Now a museum site.

71) 4 3/4" **Gravettian convergent side-scraper / "point".** Bergerac flint with rich patina. Reglued. From the well documented site under the lawn of the Chateau de Corbiac, Ponponne, Dordogne. Both specimens are fully retouched down to their tiny punctiform striking platforms.

72) Two Font Robert points. Both from the type site of Font Robert in the Correze. The first stemmed European point type. Gravettian. Flint with soil sheen & microscopic mineralization. Tan one 2 3/4". Black 2 7/8". Fewer than 10 seen on the market in 15 years.

73) A: Font Robert Point. From Font Robert type site in Correze. Gravettian. Flint. 2 7/8". Far rarer than contemporaneous Gravette Points or later Solutrean Laurel Leaf Points. Under ten seen in 15 years.
    B: Solutrean Laurel Leaf Projectile Point. Flint with rich but not masking patinas. 2 3/8". Carsac, Dordogne. A beautiful example of the point type which may have presaged Clovis. Prices all over the map, partly because of increasingly accomplished fakes. Two which were sold recently were almost certainly forgeries. Soil sheen is not enough – go for patina, integrity and provenance.
    C: An atypical Solutrean Shouldered Point. Dordogne with cave deposits still adhering to point. 3". Slightly cruder shouldered points continued into the Magdalenian. This is far from the best, but the best are almost all represented by fragments.

74) 2 1/2" **Solutrean bifacial lozenge point.** Only projectile of this sort seen in private hands. See Philip Smith's Le Solutréen in France for similar specimens. Laugerie Haute shelter, Dordogne. Don't confuse with almost equally rare but thicker lozenge points from Copper Age dolmens.

A MISSING LINK BETWEEN EUROPE & THE AMERICAS?

75) 3 1/4" **Solutrean laurel leaf point with *basal grinding* like on American Paleo points.** This feature has never been reported before on laurel leaves - even in Smith's encyclopedic Le Solutréen en France. Basal grinding was invented independently in several places in the world, but has never been found with so many traits shared with the earliest undisputed American tool kits. Many prehistorians suspect that a small Solutrean band may have succeeded in crossing a continuous land & ice bridge from the Pyrenees area because only American Clovis and SW European Laurel Leaf points share outre-passé flaking & lens-shaped cross sections at about the same time. Except for a single fluted point, which may represent later flux *out* of America, these features are missing at the Asian end of Berengia, where points typically have diamond-shaped cross-sections. Now that Clovis points share *3 features* with European Laurel Leaves, the case for a Solutrean migration is even harder to dismiss.

The Paleolithic population of Europe would have been demographically squeezed by advancing ice towards the peninsular dead-end of SW Europe & out onto its vast exposed continental shelves. But for a short period during the coldest phase of the last Ice Age – which occurred during the Solutrean – those shelves merged with continuous floes, ice-locked islands and other shelves rich in auks, belugas, cod and seals to make a dry passage to the Americas. Such a bridge could only have been negotiated after the invention of weather-tight clothing made possible by the eyed needle: a Solutrean invention. Similarities between the Solutrean tool set and the pre-Clovis assemblage found at Cactus Hill, Dinwiddie County, Virginia lend support to the hypothesis. A genetic marker only reported among American Indians & Basques of the Pyrenees lends further support. Although a Solutrean band may have been the first to arrive, a 9,000 year old Brazilian skeleton with features reminiscent of Micronesians suggests a possible sea voyage around the Pacific, rim. NE Asian populations living in 300 mile wide Berengia obviously got through too when the Yukon Corridor opened between the Alaskan and Canadian Ice Shields after the Solutrean. Then around 4,500 BP proto-Eskimos developed technologies to begin their remarkable expansion around the Arctic. Flint patinated with lime salt intrusion & hydration. Carsac, Dordogne. A missing link & reference specimen: True Solutrean laurel leaves are scarce as hen's teeth in private collections, but poor specimens are seen. Beware of later Clovis preforms & Saharan & Afghani Neolithic leaf points in different flints & patinas masquerading as infinitely rarer Solutrean laurel leaves!

76) 1 1/2" **Crystal Solutrean laurel leaf point**. Laugerie Haute, Dordogne. Utterly transparent. Much resharpened prehistorically but only crystal one seen outside a dozen in museums.

77) Magdalenian Harpoon. Antler. 7" of the overall 7 3/4" are original including the barbs, with only 3/4" at the tip being restored. The shaft is also broken & glued near the base and is bent by long burial. Laugerie Haute, les Eyzies. This is nearly twice as long as the only other nearly complete harpoon that came to the market (to my knowledge) over the past 5 years. It is also the only one with clear provenance.

78) 2 1/2" **Azilian Harpoon**. Transitional Upper Paleolithic to Mesolithic. Bone. La Tourasse rock shelter, Haute Garonne. The Azilian was almost named the Tourassian, since Tourasse was the first site to be described, but turned out to be both less rich than the Mas d'Azil and misdescribed, since the first excavators seem to have mixed Azilian and slightly earlier Magdalenian artifacts.

79) A broken **"Shaft Straightener"** or **"Wrench"** according to some, although I prefer the French **"Baton de Commandment"** – suggesting a scepter. Magdalenian. Antler. 5". Laugerie Basse, les Eyzies. A North American specimen exists from the Richey Clovis cache. All 3 that have come to the market in the last decade were broken, this one was the only one with partial drilling from both sides to make a second new hole! Higher if decorated. If decorated figuratively, off the charts, even if broken. Beware of fakes!

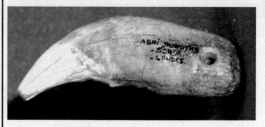

80) Cave bear fang pendant. Magdalenian. 4 1/2". From the highly documented Duruthy Rock Shelter, Sord, Landes, France (see Piette collection). Remarkable both as one of the rare examples of the earliest jewelry and as amazing evidence of the role cave bears played in Paleolithic culture. The invention of jewelry implies a new sense of self and otherness and a desire to change ones image. It also allowed individuals to differentiate themselves symbolically from each other, leading to different social roles. The repercussions of such an artifact for humans are unfathomable. After being allowed to see hundreds of collections, the author is only aware of 3 authentic cave bear fang pendants outside museums.

81) Two **Cave Bear phalange whistles**. Among the oldest known musical instruments. The smaller, 1 2/3". specimen still has its original 1863 Christy-Lartet label marked "le Moustier, Dordogne" – the first excavation at le Moustier in the first year of prehistoric studies in the Dordogne. The 2nd specimen is from the Tarté rock shelter, Haute Garonne. 2". Both pieces are heavily incised. Probably fewer than 20 authentic examples in private hands, but a Stradivarius may be easier to find.

UPPER PALEOLITHIC ART - ca. 34,000 - 12,000 B.P.

82) A delicate engraving of a **chamois on bone in its cave breccia**. Published upon discovery in main French Prehistory journal. Magdalenian. The depiction of known & drifting of symbols may have occurred in a scattered & tentative way before the upper Paleolithic but only took hold and became essential behaviors at the dawn of the new era. The oldest evidence for such behaviors comes from S. Africa and consists of geometrical incisions comparable to the calibrated Aurignacian antler tine shown above. No undisputed pieces of Upper Paleolithic art have appeared at auction in over 50 years. Inestimable.

83) Two reindeer meet as a harpoon head approaches from bottom left. Placard rock shelter, France. One of the most remarkable pieces of prehistoric art seen in private hands for 3 reasons: it appears to be a narrative – something rare in the period's art. Two, the meeting deer resemble a famous polychrome scene in the Font-de-Gaume cave. And, three, it supports the hypothesis that the first "harpoons" were used on big game. This theory is based on the concentration of harpoons at sites in dry interiors as opposed to along water. Inestimable.

84) *Paleolithic* Aboriginal **flake tool**. Basalt with red patination in flake scar on hidden base. Australia. Circa 15,000 BP. 3 3/4".

85) *Post-Contact* hifacial **disc scraper/knife & arrowhead**. Bottle glass with concretions. Rottnest Island, Australia. Only 100 years old, based on known Aboriginal activity & a dat-eable manufacturer's mark on the other side of the disc. As remarkable as Ishi's points in their testimony to the quick adaptation of Stone Age craftsmen to modern materials.

THE MESOLITHIC, ca. 14,000 – 11,000 B.P. Middle East / 12,000 - 8,000 B.P. (W. Europe) - *Homo sapiens*

SOME INVENTIONS: EARLIEST POTTERY VESSELS (JOMON, JAPAN - 12,000 B.P.); RESOURCE EFFICIENT MICROLITHIC TECHNOLOGIES; ARCHERY; SPREAD OF NARRATIVE ROCK-ART

86) Two conical Mesolithic bladelet cores. Flint. 1" & 1 1/4". From a site now flooded by a dam in Iran. Gem-stone facetting represents one of the peaks of prehistoric knapping.

NEOLITHIC - ca. 11,000 - 6,000 B.P. (Middle East) / 8,000 - 5,000 B.P. (W. Europe): *Homo sapiens*

SOME INVENTIONS: AGRICULTURE, CERAMIC VESSELS, URBANIZATION

SAHARAN POINTS, AXES & OTHER TOOLS:

87) A: Double-edged denticulate. Mauritania. Mesolithic to Neolithic. Although arrowheads from Niger to Mauritania have swamped the market in the last 6 years, few other tools have appeared – although they can be more interesting conceptually than another pointed arrowhead. Narrower serrated bladelets are also known from the European Magdalenian. Only one seen.
B: A **strangled blade**. Mauritania. Strangled blades are also one of the key artifacts of the European Aurignacian.

88) Six **lunates with steeply retouched crescent backs**. Made from blade segments. W. African Mesolithic to Neolithic. The same form occurs in the European Mesolithic – suggesting a link. Mauritanian lunates are extreme varieties of the Transverse razor arrowhead. Arrows have survived in the Sahara's aridity with lunate razors still in position. So, despite preconceptions, NOT all arrowheads are pointed! Ethnographic clues suggest that these were dipped in toxins and used to sever vessels of animals as large as giraffes. The prey would succumb over 2 or 3 days to bleeding & poisoning. Lunates could also be slotted along shafts or curved sickles to create segmented (& easily replaceable) cutting edges. The original, adaptable & light spare part. Usually unseen in collections.

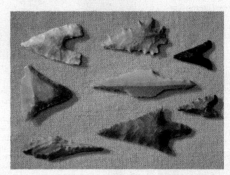

89) 7 *average* **N. African Capsian Mesolithic to Neolithic arrowheads** PLUS a **serrated point from India** for comparison. The *Transverse razor point* is similar to S. European ones & is terribly rare in NW Africa. The *barbed & stemmed point* is also found on both sides of the Mediterranean. But the notched base *Eiffel Tower points* & long tanged points are typical of NW Africa. Eiffel Tower points are never as deeply notched as *Fayoum points* (see Overstreet 6th Ed P 38 ph 97) from Egypt. The point in the center is one of the world's more unusual types – an *Escutcheon Point* described from Bir es-Sof. A bladelet has been steeply retouched to create both stem & tip. These 7 points are probably NOT contemporaries but their distribution may never be studied due to their rapid disappearance from the desert, inaccessibility to westerners and lack of funds. **NOTE:** Beware of dealers reselling these genuine & wonderful artifacts as Texas bird points and Columbia River gem points. For comparison: 1 1/16" *Spiked Xmas tree point* from India. Super rare.

90) *Fine* **green jasper points from the "Sudanese" Neolithic Tradition** of the S. Sahara & Sahel. Longest is 2 1/16". Light green point is from Niger. All others from Kiffa region, Mauritania. Amazing micro-denticulation on needle point. The workmanship of the S. Sahara, especially in the Teneré Desert, is often more impressive than that of the Capsian Tradition of the NW Sahara. But because of the poverty of the countries in question, the prices at the grassroots was lower – until recently! Suddenly the best points have jumped. Only gem-quality will tend to appreciate – despite the amazingly high premium paid by top collectors until just recently.

91) 2 1/2" **serrated V-stemmed point**. Niger. Only one of its type in huge collection.

92) A) 1 1/2" *side-toothed point* with a long bulbous stem. Best seen intact.
B) 2" white **double side-toothed point with in-curving ears**. One of the 3 masterpieces from a large collection.
C) 1 1/4" **double side-toothed quartz point**. Rarity. First described by H.J. Hugot (who found 5) in Libyca. All Mali & Niger.

93) A) 1 7/8" **Fan-eared point**. One of the few with intact barbs.
B) 1 7/8" **Fan-eared point**. One barb broken, but best overall shape & color. Probably rare as Calf Creeks. The best 2 of a huge collection. **ID:** Long wire-thin ears, often accompanied by bulbous blade. Mali & Niger.

94) 2" **double-tiered, serrated, Xmas tree point**. Best of only 2 seen from 1,000s of points. The ultimate point from the Sahel.

95) 7 3/4" **flared celt**. Mali. Rainbow flint. Paler patina on unphotoed side. Flared celts are rare suggesting a ceremonial use. Colorful common celts have flooded the market.

96) 8 7/8" *Polished & pecked* **ax**. Hard dark green stone with leaching crust. Saharan axes are often pecked into shape & polished only at the bit. One of the finest seen in recent years from the W. Sahara.

97) 5" **omphalos ax or adze**. Heavy crusting & wind erosion. S. Algeria. The central hole is too small for a strong shaft. Could this have been a totemic ax head or an elaborate pectoral ax? Although the celt form is so utilitarian that it occurs around the world, there are fabulous local variants on the polished ax. UNIQUE.

98) 7 1/8" **Early** *Gerzean Pre-Dynastic Egyptian Proto-Ripple-Flake* **Knife**. Patinated flint. Gerzean knives represent one of the highpoints of prehistoric knapping. Rarely seen on the market.

99) 8 1/4" *Thinnite shouldered* **knife** from the proto-historic phase before the first Egyptian dynasty. Patinated flint. Rarely seen.

100) 5 1/4" **grinding basin with an abstract design pecked into its domed back.** The zigzag may be a snake circling a solar egg, based on more figurative examples. The Saharan Neolithic convention for the sun was a circle or oval amid concentric pecked zones that replicate solar halos caused by suspended dust. 2 hand-held grinding basins bearing this specific design are known. Fewer than 300 portable art objects are known for the culture. **WARNING:** NON-portable rock art is being extracted from cliffs in the NW Sahara with diamond saws. Poverty, lack of local appreciation, Islamic traditions against figurative art & unscrupulous dealers have abetted pillaging of immobile petroglyphs which I hope no western dealer or collector would tolerate from his own country. There is no reason to hypocritically encourage the destruction of rock art from elsewhere, regardless of mitigating circumstances. Draw the line & stop the traffic.

EUROPEAN POINTS, AXES & OTHER TOOLS:

101) 2 **French Neolithic arrowheads: A:** 1 1/2" *transverse razor arrowhead*. Even rarer than Saharan equivalents. Only one seen with steep inverse beveling along sides. Yvelines, France. The razor arrowhead is so unusual on a world scale that its existence on both sides of the Mediterranean attests to cultural flows during the Mesolithic & Neolithic between N. Africa & Europe. Iberian & Saharan rock art from the period is also similar.
B: 2" *long-stemmed & barbed point*. Grand Pressigny, Indre et Loire. The find of a couple of lifetimes in terms of French arrowheads.

102) First Stage Ax Preform. Flint with different patination each side. Big at 10 3/4". Denmark. Rarely left at this stage with only heavy hammer knapping which makes this both a spectacularly decorative & pedagogical piece.

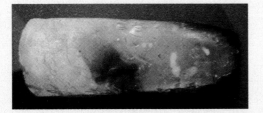

103) Polished ax. Denmark. Flint colorfully patinated by peat. 8 7/8". Spectacular 25 to 40 cm. polished Scandanavian celts exist.

104) Polished gouge. Banded flint. 5 1/2". Egtved, Jutland, Denmark. Finest seen.

105) Giant preform for a polished ax. Tabular flint. Each side has its own patina; other side is darker. At 15 1/2", one of the biggest recorded. Jablines, Seine-et-Marne. Found beside a Neolithic flint mine in the 1930s. Interestingly, no polished axes are found at the site.

106) 8 1/4" Un-polished ax. Flint with different patina on each side. Nottonville, Eure-et-Loir, France. Certain axes are so well knapped that they certainly were not preforms, representing instead fully finished prestige or currency axes.

107) Prestige ax. Banded gray flint transformed by a rich watertable patina. 7 1/8". 19th C find in Eure-et-Loir.

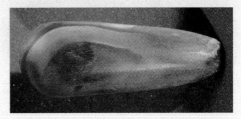

108) Polished ax. Gray flint patinated by bog. Orange one side, light yellow on other. Restored chip at bit. 7 1/4". Gaudonville, Loir-et-Cher.

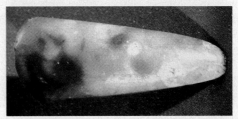

109) 7" Polished ax. Gray flint patinated orange by 5 millenia on the bottom of the Seine. Dredged from Seine at Bercy in Paris during 1890s. Where the Finance Minister's office cantilevers over the river today.

110) **Polished prestige ax**. Flint with creamy patination. At 11", it is too long and thin to have been for wood working. Maule, Yvelines, France. One of the finest French specimens. The author does not know of a single field find of this size anywhere in the country in 20 years.

111) 5 3/8" **Prestige ax**. Jadeite. Dolmen at Teillay, Ille-et-Vilaine, France. Red ochre patina on one side. As finely made as they come. This quality not seen in 7 years. Among other defects, fakes still tend to be more rectangular rather than lense-like in cross section. Beware of any deal that seems too good to be true.

112) Side-view of a 10" polished **prestige ax showing differences in color where the ax was hafted** & "rope burns" where cordage bit into the stone on either side of the ax handle! Courson, Calvados. Although a few axes have been found in their handles in peat bogs & lake sites, the author does not know of another LARGE ax blade with direct evidence not only of where the handle was placed (not at the poll, but near the middle) but also of how it was lashed.

113) 9" polished **prestige ax with a band of lighter patina around the middle of the ax where the handle survived** in peat long enough to show where it had been. Pithiviers, Loiret. Large, perfect, beautiful colors & probably unique.

114) **Polished prestige ax**. Jadeite. 6 1/8". Lighter patination around the middle provides rare evidence of how the ax was hafted! Rousset, St. Martin-de-Coux, Charente Interieur, France.

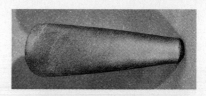

115) 6 1/2" **Polished Button Ax**. Jadeite. Vienne-en-Val, Loiret, France. One of the rarest forms of polished Neolithic axes. Only 3 seen on the market in a decade.

116) 6 1/2" **Prestige ax**. Light green jadeite patinated black on one side. 19th C find at Auneau, Eure-et-Loir with original label.

117) 10 1/2" **Ceremonial flint double pick with bi-conical pecked shaft hole**. Heavily patinated. Late Neolithic. Maintenon, Eure et Loir. The only other one known to the author is in the Chartres museum. These two totemic instruments appear to have been modeled on the first copper implements imported from Eastern Europe via the Danube corridor. One of 3 imported copper ax/adzes found in France was discovered in the same area during the 19th century.

118) 6" **Polished chisel**. Flint. Dredged from Seine at Villeneuve-St.-Georges. French Neolithic chisels must have been rare variants on prestige axes, rather than a common woodworking tool, since one will find hundreds of common celts before finding an intact "chisel".

119) **Green ax in antler sleeve**. Late Neolithic form. Found during the late 19th C in a submerged site in Chalain Lake, Jura, France. 4 3/8". Perishable material plus the finest seen in several years.

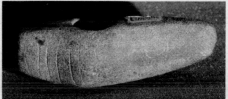

120) 4 7/8" **French engraved shaft-hole battle-ax**. Eure-et-Loir with original 19th C. label. While battle-axes are common gravegoods in northern European single male Neolithic graves, they are the find of a life-time (or more!) in southern Europe. This 19th C find is even engraved.

121) 4" **Mace-head battle-ax with a rare separated bit**. Ukraine. Hardly ever seen.

122) Macehead. Light green jadeite. 7". Dolmen in the Eure-et-Loir. Almost certainly not utilitarian, since the ends are round and highly polished. A unique piece.

123) A: 1 5/8" **Neolithic pendant** broken at the hole, but with a prehistorically engraved ax. Found in a dolmen, Eure-et-Loir. **B:** 1 3/4" **Ax-amulet pendant.** Jadeite. From a tumulus in Brittany. Formerly in the Nicaise collection described in the Lord McAlpine collection catalog. French Neolithic pendants of any kind are basically only found in funerary contexts, not fields. Pendants refering to the ax-cult are rarer still. Miniature ax pendants in other rock types are quite common in Mali & Niger.

124) 2 3/4" **Double "drill"** – in fact, probably a **pottery decorating tool**. Foissy-sur-Vanne, Yonne. Flint. Great finesse & apparently unique.

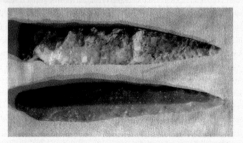

125) EUROPEAN DAGGERS: A: 6 1/2" **Scandinavian *semi-fishtail dagger***. Natural concavity in handle. Peat patina. Many thousands are known. Danish fakers place forgeries in tide pools to acquire soil sheen. Beginners should go for peat patina.
B: 7" ***Grand Pressigny dagger***. One of about 300. Pithiviers, Loiret. **ID:** Made from Neo-Levallois cores called Livres de Beurres (Pounds of Butter), which are almost unique to the Grand Pressigny region. A few similar cores have been found around Bergerac, Dordogne & Spiennes, Belgium. They were used to produce the longest & straightest blades known. The blades were delicately retouched & exported as far as Holland & the Alps for 500 years at the end of the Neolithic. Several were found at the Charavines lake site with wicker & wood handles. Micro-tracelogy shows they were used for harvesting, but most daggers in private collections – including this perfect specimen – were found before WW II in megalithic graves – underlining their ceremonial importance.

126) 6 1/2" **Danish dagger**. Gray flint patinated by peat bog. Egtved, Denmark. An above average specimen despite ding at tip. The finest examples have "stitching" up the middle of the handles. Scandanavian daggers are far more common than Southern European forms because they were regularly placed in individual male graves.

127) 7 5/8" **Grand Pressigny dagger**. Grand Pressigny, Indre-et-Loire flint patinated white on top side which is also fully polished, except for a bifacial retouch around all edges. The finest French dagger I've ever seen. An increasingly faked artifact. Reliance on provenance, previous publication & microscopic examination eliminates problems.

128) 5 3/4" **Neolithic "venus" pendant**. Silicified limestone with bituminous deposits. Northern Fertile Crescent. The shoulder holes may double as a second set of "eyes," linking it to "eye idols." Head glued back.

129) 10 1/2" **Stemmed hoe**. Basalt patinated light green & encrusted with mineral deposits. New Caledonia. An extremely ancient precontact artifact, plus the best & biggest seen.

PARADOXES OF DISCOVERY & THE LAW:

A disproportionate number of the western European artifacts above are 19th century finds because prehistoric vestiges were more easily found before quarrying was highly mechanized and gravel was conveyed blindly to crushers. A century ago, gravel pits were locally owned & their owners gave their neighbors & other collectors access. Unfortunately, European sandpits have been consolidated under huge companies including the world's largest construction materials group. These multi-nationals forbid access to non-institutional collectors – supposedly for reasons of liability and equipment theft, but also (according to their foremen) to obstruct the discovery of vestiges which might lead to calls for preservation. The institutional researchers that the monopolies must allow in (occasionally) by law are so few, have such tiny travel budgets and are so constrained by industrial lobbies that the chief archeologist of a region north of Paris told the author he rubber-stamped a huge construction project between 3 megalithic graves because he was too afraid for his job even to look. He lost his office anyway.

So it is hardly surprising that institutional researchers, who have seen their efforts attacked (even from within their governments) & salvage budgets cut, seem to have accepted a devil's bargain with quarriers: in return for the right to check top soil that doesn't interest the companies, archeologists usually don't check lower, commercially exploitable strata before a pit is opened. Such archeologists dismiss all the artifacts in lower "alluvial" strata as being displaced by currents and therefore, somehow, of no scientific interest. By this thinking, St. Acheul itself would have been a waste of time to excavate. The absurdity of such thinking is demonstrated first by such in situ Acheulean sites as ones exceptionally excavated in gravel pits at Soucy. And, secondly, by what trespassing amateurs could tell the "institutionals" they missed in some places by keeping their eyes closed. After periods of quarrying through truly tumbled alluvia, the quarrying equipment will inevitably scoop up dozens of un-eroded tools mixed with mammoth and rhino bones in clay. A true concentration that has never been tumbled, and it happens again & again. But what nobody sees, nobody has to bother with.

Too bad. When artifacts are found in such clay, which typically precipitated from becalmed backwaters on flood plains, the objects have often lain where they were put by ancient hands. Even gestures can sometimes be reconstructed. If only amateurs were working respectfully with everyone & spending their own time & gas money to watch for changes at quarries, the handful of institutional archeologists in the region, who simply can't be everywhere, would have a chance to speedily salvage some of that information with the help of volunteers - especially if the workers were motivated by finding things they could keep after proper central recording. Instead, of gaining more knowledge & saving some of what is being annihilated, everything goes to the crusher. But at least institutionals haven't compromised themselves by feeding the market or working beside enthusiasts with suspect motives.

As one prehistorian explained to the author, the discipline has also become such a question of statistics, that researchers have lost touch with pieces - and their potential aesthetics or poetry as relics of ancient human endeavor. Some institutionals make the mistake of actually disdaining finer pieces because they believe *justifiably* that too much emphasis on fine artifacts skews our perception of a site's full tool assemblage and its culture. It is true that beginning and investment-driven collecting can be uninformed & that beginners tend to be overly attracted to "prettiness." But the resulting contempt for the artifacts themselves which is a by-product of prevailing views in museums is scandalous: the author himself has found labeled bifaces in national museum dumpsters (which as a result were moved behind high spiked fences) & one of the most exalted museums is reported by some professional archeologists to have bought a crusher to destroy its "excess" handaxes. According to them, the museum's excuse is that those artifacts lack provenance and hence any "scientific" interest.

To begin with, what hubris it is for today's scientists to imagine that such pieces will never be of scientific interest!

Another excuse is said to be that the museum does not want to feed anything into the crass market where such artifacts could encourage collectors even though that market will not go away. How twisted! If the museum really wanted to subvert the market (instead of wallowing in ideological purity) it could do nothing more destructive than *dump* the museum's "useless" surpluses on collectors & make prices collapse. Such de-acquisitions would even provide such shrewd museums - which are constantly begging - with extra income while sparing the taxpayer.

But the real motive for institutional destruction of artifacts - beyond over-familiarity with them, is the doctrinaire contempt that has been growing for the group from which many great prehistorians issued and whose generosity has given birth to so many museum collections: collectors. Not surprisingly, the European laws invoked against them often date to the Fascistic period (France 1941, Italy 1939) - but are somehow perceived as "progressive". These draconian laws are easy for politicians of all stripes to continue supporting since they categorically "protect" things which are generally seen by the non-collecting public as being so rare that they should only be kept in museums.

But go figure: How can states afford to look for or curate the millions of artifacts created by humans over hundreds of thousands of years which risk destruction every year? The fact is they can't afford to and don't. The public has been kept in the dark. But is the abundance of many artifacts any reason for a museum to toss them in a crusher? I think the public would still be aghast at the destruction of such wondrously resistant reminders of our deep past and would insist on the distribution of surpluses to school collections or even to citizens who could appreciate artifacts for their tie to antiquity or sculptural beauty.

Instead, the destruction goes on - in museums & outside. At a time when agricultural, mining and construction equipment is more ubiquitous and powerful - turning over more sediment than ever before, much less is being discovered with each year. Why? Given that so many more artifacts were found in the old days when far less earth was turned over - but

turned over by hand - it's obvious that industrial nations are undergoing the archeological equivalent of genocide! Why is it happening? After all, our dutiful politicians and zealous institutionals have passed those blanket restrictions protecting vestiges. The reason is the laws themselves.

By being so categorical, sweet-sounding legislation absolves us all from having to check for perverse side effects or actual consequences. Their framers can feel honorable & move on to the next order of business. And it is undeniable that draconian laws should apply to some kinds of sites - for example, in situ deposits in caves. But when a vast pool of enthusiasts with their private funds for traveling to fields and exposures, their extra eyes and their endless legwork, are threatened and treated with contempt, then government researchers who frame the laws for politicians may have the pleasure of being purists, but deny themselves & humanity a resource that could extend researchers' range enormously. When collectors also hide their objects for fear of dispossession, rather than be encouraged by a legal system of transparency to have their pieces studied, then most potential discoveries will go un-reported and unrecognized. Finally, if a market is not allowed to operate to provide pieces with values that everyone can understand, much will even be thrown away by institutions & collectors' heirs alike - witness collections lost near Sens, Gisors & from municipal museums at Blois & the Cote d'Or.

Yet the press, which relies on museum sources for stories, seems to be unaware that there is any problem - except with collectors. In some places today any farmer with a disk-tiller or quarrier has a license to kill vestiges, but that same person is forbidden to salvage & keep a single artifact on the surface during the window between plowing and harrowing. Up in their cabs, today's workers are no longer even in touch with the soil they ravish. Embittered museum workers have even shown the author a letter from their country's Ministry of Industry to their own branch of government telling the (lesser) ministry to stop intervening to save one tiny site in a gravel pit because it was a nuisance for a multi-national. Needless-to-say, the effort was abandoned & the site destroyed. But according to government archeologists & the tame press, collectors are the enemy. Talk about scapegoats. Luckily, such laws give themselves the lie: most published sites are found during a few publicly funded construction projects for which a salvage budget is set aside out of the same good intentions that led to backfiring draconian measures. You might ask yourself: why is it that almost all prehistoric beings in European countries from dinosaurs to Neanderthals seem to have lived only on land that would end up in such projects - in other words, in the public domain? Were all those beings proto-socialists who died on land they knew would someday become public? The answer is that we are only seeing discoveries from public land because vestiges in private projects are being systematically destroyed due to the same draconian laws that mandate a salvage budget along the routes of future railroads & highways. On private construction sites, foreman after foreman has told the author that he had unwritten orders from management to obliterate anything that might ruin his schedule & even to prevent any evidence from getting out. With invasive laws, the alternative could be an imposed closure for months or even forever. Worse yet, the regulations often make the owner pay for the privilege! Whether you're in France or America, it's the same old story: apparently roughly 70 mammoths have turned up during construction just in Stark County, Ohio, but only one has been reported or saved because researchers didn't know how to get in & out in 48 hours & stick only to the patch where the first find was reported. So they weren't told of later findings. After all, what is in it for builders or any citizen under the present laws? Will their schedules be respected? Can they keep or sell vestiges? Even when they report things & their project is not postponed & their land is not requisitioned, they are often treated as culpable instead of being celebrated. So the Fascistic laws, which have been similarly framed by purists on both sides of the Atlantic, go on shooting themselves, science & the public in the foot - massively contributing to the very destruction they are (supposedly) against.

Is there an answer? Should we hire enough institutional salvage archeologists to check every public *& private* construction site? What about all the artifacts that would turn up if people looked as closely as they did in the 1880s? The museums are already so over-burdened by their reserves that they're destroying them. Does anyone really think taxpayers want to pay for still more archeologists & storage?

If only we could start over & search for synergies that would respect industry's schedules, encourage much more salvaging even if it is sometimes done speedily & by channeled amateurs who could keep their finds (& store them at their own expense) & end the atmosphere of contempt & secrecy. I bet discoveries would increase ten to a hundred-fold.

IS YOUR COLLECTION WORTHY?

Should your collection be recorded for posterity and shared with your fellow enthusiasts? If you'd like to submit photos or be an advisor, please contact Bob Overstreet by email at roverstreet1@mac.com or contact Gemstone Publishing on our toll free line at (888) 375-9800 ext. 466

When photographing your collection for submission, photos should be 300 dpi in full color with a ruler showing in the picture for reference size.

We want your help!

CHRONOLOGICAL GALLERY OF POINT TYPES

KELSEY CREEK BARBED
4,500 B.P., Warner Valley, OR, obsidian

KELSEY CREEK BARBED
4,500 B.P., Nappa Valley, CA

McGILLVRAY EXPANDING STEM
4,500 B.P., Harney Co., OR

TANGIPAHOA
4,500 B.P., S.W. MS

MOTLEY
4,500 B.P., Boone Co., MO, Burlington chert

MOTLEY
5,000 B.P., Humphreys Co., TN, Dover chert

TANGIPAHOA
4,500 B.P., S.W. MS

MOTLEY
4,500 B.P., E. Carroll Parish, LA; cache point found in 1947

MOTLEY
4,500 B.P., Dickson Co., TN, Dover chert

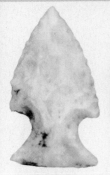

MOTLEY
4,500 B.P.,
Ashland Co., OH

BAKERS CREEK
4,000 B.P., S. IN

BULLHEAD
4,000 B.P., Harney
Co., OR

BULLHEAD
4,000 B.P., S. OR, heavy
grinding, obsidian

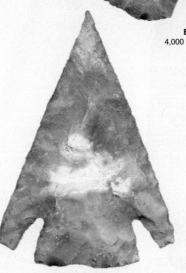

BASE TANG
4,000 B.P., Kerr Co., TX

CASTROVILLE
4,000 B.P., Kerr Co.,
TX, root beer flint

CASTROVILLE
4,000 B.P., Central TX

CASTROVILLE
4,000 B.P., Kerr Co., TX

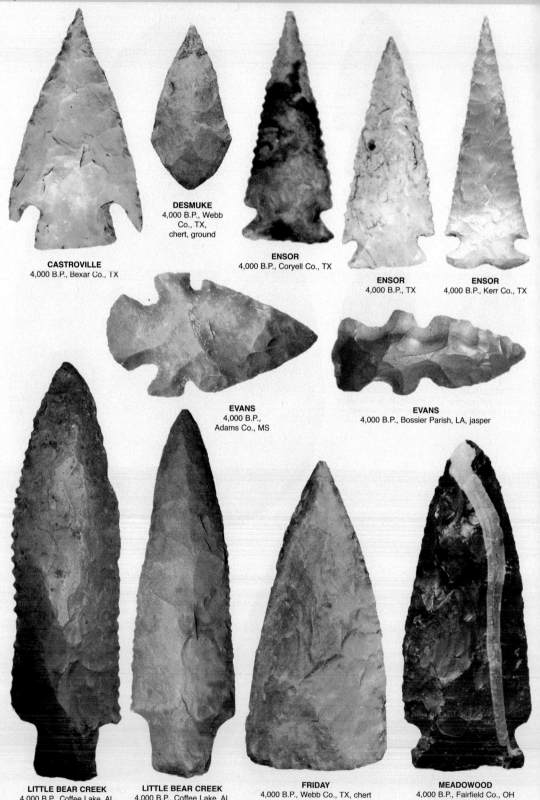

CASTROVILLE
4,000 B.P., Bexar Co., TX

DESMUKE
4,000 B.P., Webb
Co., TX,
chert, ground

ENSOR
4,000 B.P., Coryell Co., TX

ENSOR
4,000 B.P., TX

ENSOR
4,000 B.P., Kerr Co., TX

EVANS
4,000 B.P.,
Adams Co., MS

EVANS
4,000 B.P., Bossier Parish, LA, jasper

LITTLE BEAR CREEK
4,000 B.P., Coffee Lake, AL

LITTLE BEAR CREEK
4,000 B.P., Coffee Lake, AL

FRIDAY
4,000 B.P., Webb Co., TX, chert

MEADOWOOD
4,000 B.P., Fairfield Co., OH
Upper Mercer flint

CHRONOLOGICAL GALLERY OF POINT TYPES

TABLE ROCK
4,000 B.P., MO

SURPRISE VALLEY
4,000 B.P., Susanville, CA, obsidian

SURPRISE VALLEY
4,000 B.P., S. OR, obsidian

TABLE ROCK
4,000 B.P., MO

TABLE ROCK
4,000 B.P., MO

TALLAHASSEE
4,000 B.P., Jefferson Co., FL

TABLE ROCK
4,000 B.P., MO

TABLE ROCK
4,000 B.P., MO

TRINITY
4,000 B.P., Van Zandt Co., TX

TURKEYTAIL
4,000 B.P., W. KY

WILLITS SIDE NOTCHED
4,000 B.P., Warner Val. OR

WILLITS SIDE NOTCHED
4,000 B.P., CA, obsidian

WILLITS SIDE NOTCHED
4,000 B.P., Lake Co., OR

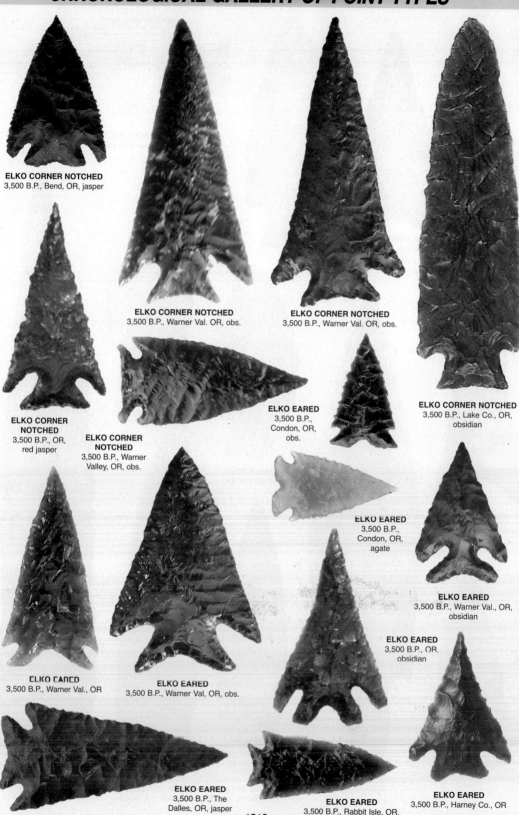

ELKO CORNER NOTCHED
3,500 B.P., Bend, OR, jasper

ELKO CORNER NOTCHED
3,500 B.P., Warner Val. OR, obs.

ELKO CORNER NOTCHED
3,500 B.P., Warner Val. OR, obs.

**ELKO CORNER
NOTCHED**
3,500 B.P., OR,
red jasper

**ELKO CORNER
NOTCHED**
3,500 B.P., Warner
Valley, OR, obs.

ELKO EARED
3,500 B.P.,
Condon, OR,
obs.

ELKO CORNER NOTCHED
3,500 B.P., Lake Co., OR,
obsidian

ELKO EARED
3,500 B.P.,
Condon, OR,
agate

ELKO EARED
3,500 B.P., Warner Val., OR,
obsidian

ELKO EARED
3,500 B.P., OR,
obsidian

ELKO EARED
3,500 B.P., Warner Val., OR

ELKO EARED
3,500 B.P., Warner Val, OR, obs.

ELKO EARED
3,500 B.P., The
Dalles, OR, jasper

ELKO EARED
3,500 B.P., Rabbit Isle, OR.

ELKO EARED
3,500 B.P., Harney Co., OR

ELKO WIDE NOTCHED
3,500 B.P., OR, obsidian

FLINT CREEK
3,500 B.P., Walker Co., AL

FLINT CREEK
3,500 B.P.,
Fayette Co., AL,
jasper

FLINT CREEK
3,500 B.P.,
Walker Co., AL

SHANIKO STEMMED
3,500 B.P., Umatilla, OR,
agate

FLINT CREEK/PONT-CHARTRAIN CROSS TYPE
3,500 B.P., Jefferson Co., MS, quartzite

FLINT CREEK
3,500 B.P., Hardin Co., TN

FLINT CREEK
3,500 B.P.
Florence, AL

FLINT CREEK
3,500 B.P., Walker Co., AL

CORNER TANG KNIFE
3,400 B.P., Kerr Co., TX, dog leg form

CORNER TANG KNIFE
3,400 B.P., Kerr Co., TX

PONTCHARTRAIN I
3,400 B.P., W. TN

GARY
3,200 B.P., Titus Co., TX

GARY
3,200 B.P., N.E. OK

PONTCHARTRAIN II
3,400 B.P., Van Zandt Co., TX

ADENA
3,000 B.P., FL, coral

GARY
3,200 B.P., Hopkins Co., TX

ADENA
3,000 B.P., S. IN

ADENA
3,000 B.P., Titus Co., TX

ADENA
3,000 B.P., S. IN

BUCHANAN EARED
3,000 B.P., Humboldt Co., NV

CHARCOS
3,000 B.P., Webb Co., TX

BUCHANAN EARED
3,000 B.P., Harney Co., OR

BEAR
3,000 B.P., AK, jasper

BUCHANAN EARED
3,000 B.P., S. OR, obsidian

EXCELSIOR
3,000 B.P., CA, jasper

EXCELSIOR
3,000 B.P., CA, jasper

KENT
3,000 B.P., LA

KRAMER
3,000 B.P.,
N.E. OK

MATAMOROS
3,000 B.P., TX

MATAMOROS
3,000 B.P., TX

MARTIS
3,000 B.P., Harney
Co., OR

OUACHITA
3,000 B.P., Van Zandt Co., TX; one of a cache

CHRONOLOGICAL GALLERY OF POINT TYPES

QUILLOMENE BAR
3,000 B.P., OR, agate

QUILLOMENE BAR
3,000 B.P., Columb. Riv.,
OR, jasper

QUILLOMENE BAR
3,000 B.P., Columb. Riv., OR, jasper

QUILLOMENE BAR
3,000 B.P., Columb. Riv., OR, agate

QUILLOMENE BAR
3,000 B.P., OR, jasper

SHUMLA
3,000 B.P., Zapata Co., TX

AÑO NUEVO
2,950 B.P., S. CA coast, basalt

PELICAN LAKE
2,600 B.P.,
Pierre, SD,
Knife River
flint

PELICAN LAKE
2,600 B.P., Prowers Co., CO,
petrified wood

PELICAN LAKE
2,600 B.P., WY, petrified wood

DARL DRILL
2,500 B.P., Kerr Co., TX

CONTRA COSTA
2,500 B.P.,
Warner Valley,
OR, obsidian

MERRYBELL III
2,500 B.P., Col. Rv., OR

MERRYBELL III
2,500 B.P., OR

DICKSON
2,500 B.P., OH

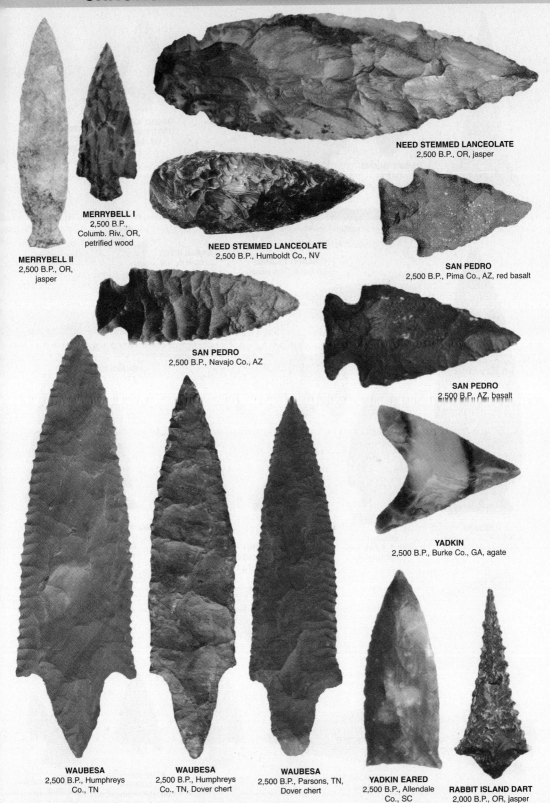

NEED STEMMED LANCEOLATE
2,500 B.P., OR, jasper

MERRYBELL I
2,500 B.P.,
Columb. Riv., OR,
petrified wood

NEED STEMMED LANCEOLATE
2,500 B.P., Humboldt Co., NV

MERRYBELL II
2,500 B.P., OR,
jasper

SAN PEDRO
2,500 B.P., Pima Co., AZ, red basalt

SAN PEDRO
2,500 B.P., Navajo Co., AZ

SAN PEDRO
2,500 B.P., AZ, basalt

YADKIN
2,500 B.P., Burke Co., GA, agate

WAUBESA
2,500 B.P., Humphreys
Co., TN

WAUBESA
2,500 B.P., Humphreys
Co., TN, Dover chert

WAUBESA
2,500 B.P., Parsons, TN,
Dover chert

YADKIN EARED
2,500 B.P., Allendale
Co., SC

RABBIT ISLAND DART
2,000 B.P., OR, jasper

CHRONOLOGICAL GALLERY OF POINT TYPES

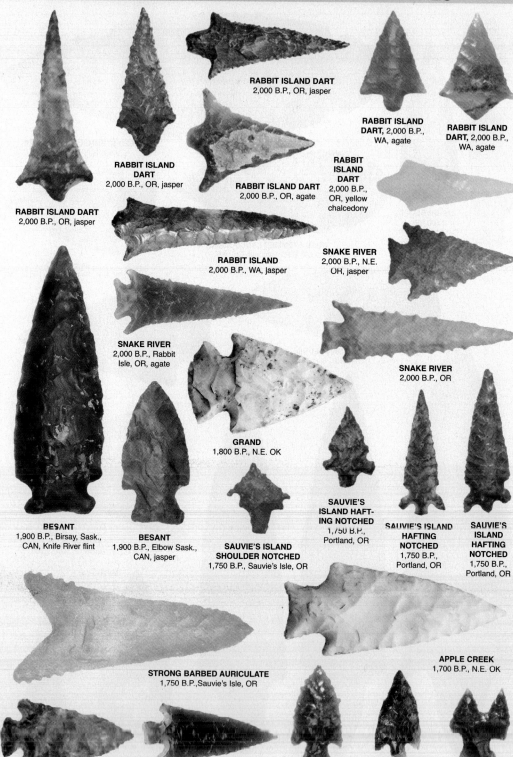

RABBIT ISLAND DART
2,000 B.P., OR, jasper

**RABBIT ISLAND
DART, 2,000 B.P.,
WA, agate**

**RABBIT ISLAND
DART, 2,000 B.P.,
WA, agate**

**RABBIT ISLAND
DART**
2,000 B.P., OR, jasper

RABBIT ISLAND DART
2,000 B.P., OR, agate

**RABBIT
ISLAND
DART**
2,000 B.P.,
OR, yellow
chalcedony

RABBIT ISLAND DART
2,000 B.P., OR, jasper

RABBIT ISLAND
2,000 B.P., WA, Jasper

SNAKE RIVER
2,000 B.P., N.E.
OR, jasper

SNAKE RIVER
2,000 B.P., Rabbit
Isle, OR, agate

SNAKE RIVER
2,000 B.P., OR

GRAND
1,800 B.P., N.E. OK

BESANT
1,900 B.P., Birsay, Sask.,
CAN, Knife River flint

BESANT
1,900 B.P., Elbow Sask.,
CAN, jasper

**SAUVIE'S ISLAND
SHOULDER NOTCHED**
1,750 B.P., Sauvie's Isle, OR

**SAUVIE'S
ISLAND HAFT-
ING NOTCHED**
1,750 B.P.,
Portland, OR

**SAUVIE'S ISLAND
HAFTING
NOTCHED**
1,750 B.P.,
Portland, OR

**SAUVIE'S
ISLAND
HAFTING
NOTCHED**
1,750 B.P.,
Portland, OR

STRONG BARBED AURICULATE
1,750 B.P., Sauvie's Isle, OR

APPLE CREEK
1,700 B.P., N.E. OK

ROSE SPRINGS CORNER
1,600 B.P., OR

ROSE SPRINGS CORNER
1,600 B.P., Warner Val., OR

**ROSE SPRINGS
CORNER**
1,600 B.P., OR

**ROSE SPRINGS
CORNER**
1,600 B.P., Harney Co.,
OR, red/black obs.

**ROSE SPRINGS
DOUBLE TIP,**
1,600 B.P., OR

ROSE SPRINGS CORNER 1,600 B.P., Humboldt Co., NV, Mah. obs.

ROSE SPRINGS KNIFE, 1,600 B.P., Humboldt Co., NV

ROSE SPRINGS KNIFE, 1,600 B.P., S. OR, obs.

ROSE SPRINGS SLOPING SHOULDER 1,600 B.P., S. OR, chalc.

ROSE SPRINGS CORNER 1,600 B.P., Warner Val, OR, Mah. obs.

ROSE SPRINGS CORNER 1,600 B.P., Warner Val., OR

ROSE SPRINGS STEMMED 1,600 B.P., Lake Co., OR

ROSE SPRINGS STEMMED 1,600 B.P., S. OR, obsidian

KNIGHT ISLAND 1,500 B.P., Stark Co., OH

GALT 1,500 B.P., W. KS

KNIGHT ISLAND 1,500 B.P., Jefferson Co., MS

MALAGA COVE LEAF, 1,500 B.P., Santa Barbara Co., CA, jasper

MALAGA COVE LEAF 1,500 B.P., Ventura Co., CA, jasper

EASTGATE 1,400 B.P., Col. Riv., OR, chalc.

EASTGATE 1,400 B.P., The Dalles, OR, jasper

EASTGATE 1,400 B.P., Humboldt Co., NV, chalc.

EASTGATE 1,400 B.P., The Dalles, OR, jasper

MALAGA COVE LEAF 1,500 B.P., Santa Barbara Co., CA, agate

MALAGA COVE LEAF 1,500 B.P., Santa Barbara Co., CA, root beer

MALAGA COVE LEAF 1,500 B.P., S. Barbara Co., CA, shale

MUMMY CAVE 1,400 B.P., Dodge City, KS

ONE-QUE 1,320 B.P., OR, jasper

ONE-QUE 1,320 B.P., OR, chalcedony

BEAR RIVER 1,300 B.P., N. UT, Bear River, jasper

PAROWAN 1,300 B.P., W. UT, chert

SCALLORN 1,300 B.P., LaSalle Co., TX

STOTT 1,300 B.P., W. KS

CHRONOLOGICAL GALLERY OF POINT TYPES

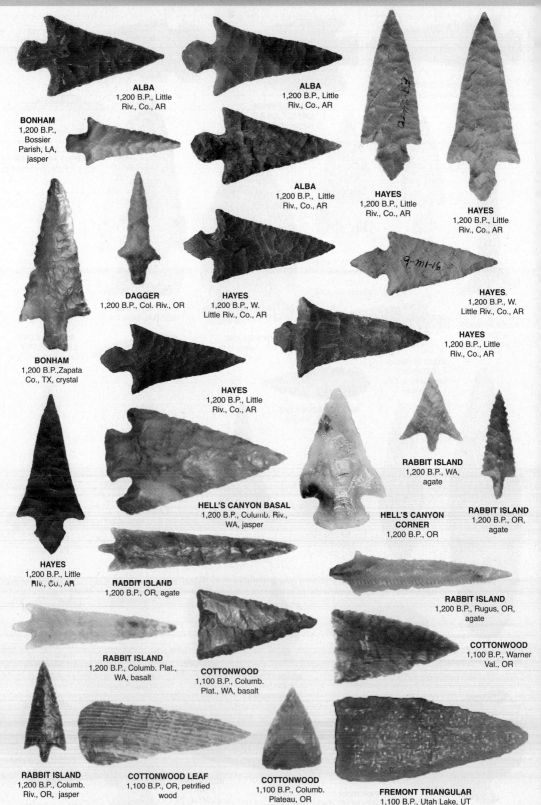

ALBA
1,200 B.P., Little
Riv., Co., AR

ALBA
1,200 B.P., Little
Riv., Co., AR

BONHAM
1,200 B.P.,
Bossier
Parish, LA,
jasper

ALBA
1,200 B.P., Little
Riv., Co., AR

HAYES
1,200 B.P., Little
Riv., Co., AR

HAYES
1,200 B.P., Little
Riv., Co., AR

DAGGER
1,200 B.P., Col. Riv., OR

HAYES
1,200 B.P., W.
Little Riv., Co., AR

HAYES
1,200 B.P., W.
Little Riv., Co., AR

HAYES
1,200 B.P., Little
Riv., Co., AR

BONHAM
1,200 B.P.,Zapata
Co., TX, crystal

HAYES
1,200 B.P., Little
Riv., Co., AR

RABBIT ISLAND
1,200 B.P., WA,
agate

HELL'S CANYON BASAL
1,200 B.P., Columb. Riv.,
WA, jasper

**HELL'S CANYON
CORNER**
1,200 B.P., OR

RABBIT ISLAND
1,200 B.P., OR,
agate

HAYES
1,200 B.P., Little
Riv., Co., AR

RABBIT ISLAND
1,200 B.P., OR, agate

RABBIT ISLAND
1,200 B.P., Rugus, OR,
agate

RABBIT ISLAND
1,200 B.P., Columb. Plat.,
WA, basalt

COTTONWOOD
1,100 B.P., Columb.
Plat., WA, basalt

COTTONWOOD
1,100 B.P., Warner
Val., OR

RABBIT ISLAND
1,200 B.P., Columb.
Riv., OR, jasper

COTTONWOOD LEAF
1,100 B.P., OR, petrified
wood

COTTONWOOD
1,100 B.P., Columb.
Plateau, OR

FREMONT TRIANGULAR
1,100 B.P., Utah Lake, UT

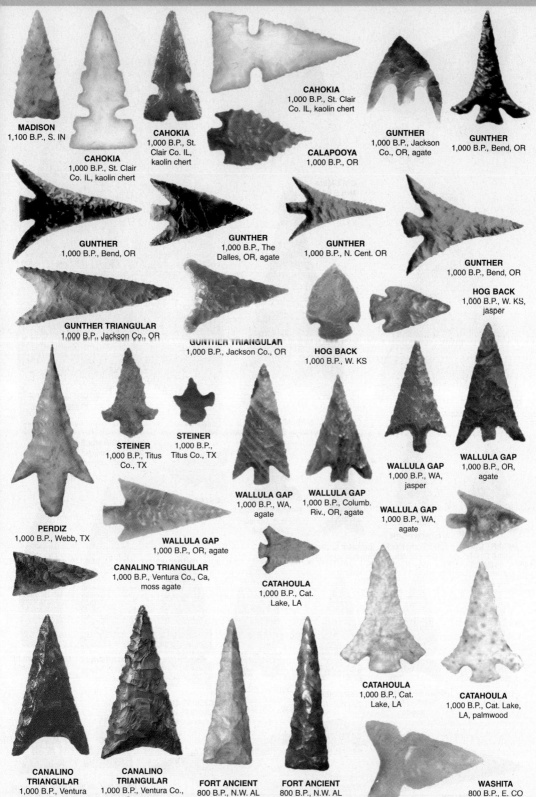

MADISON
1,100 B.P., S. IN

CAHOKIA
1,000 B.P., St. Clair
Co. IL, kaolin chert

CAHOKIA
1,000 B.P., St.
Clair Co. IL,
kaolin chert

CAHOKIA
1,000 B.P., St. Clair
Co. IL, kaolin chert

CALAPOOYA
1,000 B.P., OR

GUNTHER
1,000 B.P., Jackson
Co., OR, agate

GUNTHER
1,000 B.P., Bend, OR

GUNTHER
1,000 B.P., Bend, OR

GUNTHER
1,000 B.P., The
Dalles, OR, agate

GUNTHER
1,000 B.P., N. Cent. OR

GUNTHER
1,000 B.P., Bend, OR

GUNTHER TRIANGULAR
1,000 B.P., Jackson Co., OR

GUNTHER TRIANGULAR
1,000 B.P., Jackson Co., OR

HOG BACK
1,000 B.P., W. KS,
jasper

HOG BACK
1,000 B.P., W. KS

STEINER
1,000 B.P., Titus
Co., TX

STEINER
1,000 B.P.,
Titus Co., TX

WALLULA GAP
1,000 B.P., WA,
jasper

WALLULA GAP
1,000 B.P., OR,
agate

WALLULA GAP
1,000 B.P., WA,
agate

WALLULA GAP
1,000 B.P., Columb.
Riv., OR, agate

WALLULA GAP
1,000 B.P., WA,
agate

PERDIZ
1,000 B.P., Webb, TX

WALLULA GAP
1,000 B.P., OR, agate

CANALINO TRIANGULAR
1,000 B.P., Ventura Co., Ca,
moss agate

CATAHOULA
1,000 B.P., Cat.
Lake, LA

CATAHOULA
1,000 B.P., Cat.
Lake, LA

CATAHOULA
1,000 B.P., Cat. Lake,
LA, palmwood

**CANALINO
TRIANGULAR**
1,000 B.P., Ventura
Co., Ca, fused shale

**CANALINO
TRIANGULAR**
1,000 B.P., Ventura Co.,
Ca, agate

FORT ANCIENT
800 B.P., N.W. AL

FORT ANCIENT
800 B.P., N.W. AL

WASHITA
800 B.P., E. CO

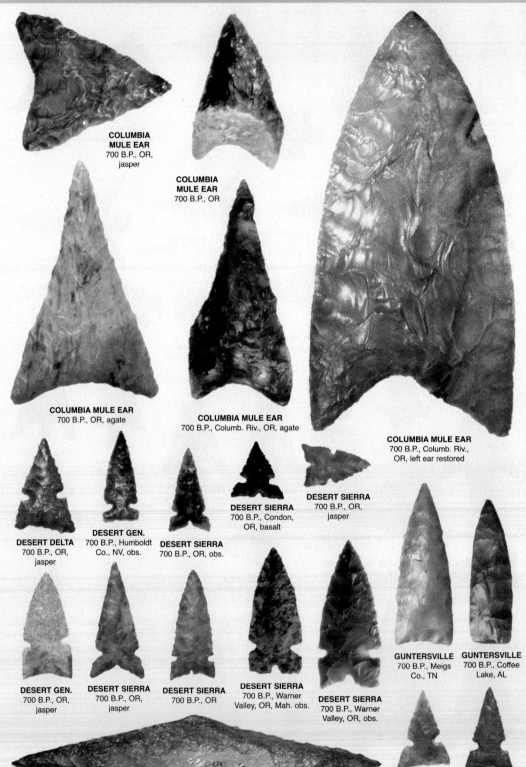

COLUMBIA MULE EAR
700 B.P., OR, jasper

COLUMBIA MULE EAR
700 B.P., OR

COLUMBIA MULE EAR
700 B.P., OR, agate

COLUMBIA MULE EAR
700 B.P., Columb. Riv., OR, agate

COLUMBIA MULE EAR
700 B.P., Columb. Riv., OR, left ear restored

DESERT SIERRA
700 B.P., OR, jasper

DESERT SIERRA
700 B.P., Condon, OR, basalt

DESERT DELTA
700 B.P., OR, jasper

DESERT GEN.
700 B.P., Humboldt Co., NV, obs.

DESERT SIERRA
700 B.P., OR, obs.

DESERT GEN.
700 B.P., OR, jasper

DESERT SIERRA
700 B.P., OR, jasper

DESERT SIERRA
700 B.P., OR

DESERT SIERRA
700 B.P., Warner Valley, OR, Mah. obs.

DESERT SIERRA
700 B.P., Warner Valley, OR, obs.

GUNTERSVILLE
700 B.P., Meigs Co., TN

GUNTERSVILLE
700 B.P., Coffee Lake, AL

HARAHEY
700 B.P., KS

LAKE RIV. SIDE
700 B.P., Col. Rv., OR, agate

LAKE RIV. SIDE
700 B.P., WA, jasper

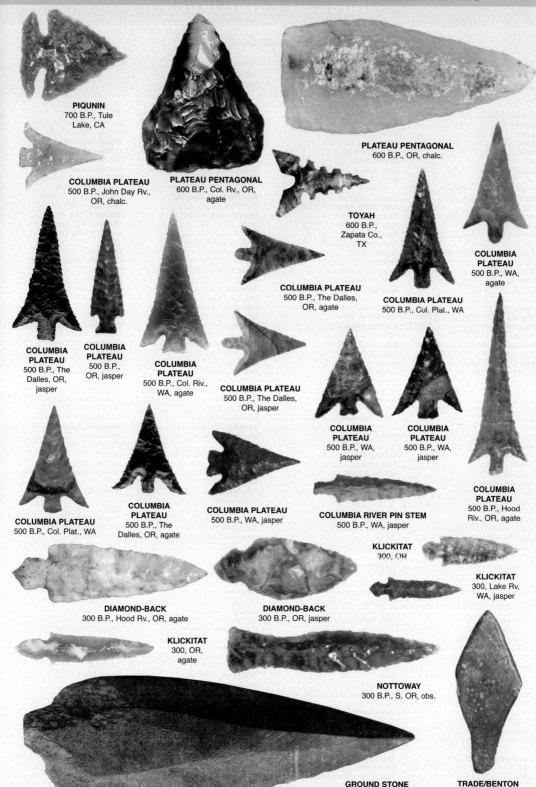

PIQUNIN
700 B.P., Tule
Lake, CA

COLUMBIA PLATEAU
500 B.P., John Day Rv.,
OR, chalc.

PLATEAU PENTAGONAL
600 B.P., Col. Rv., OR,
agate

PLATEAU PENTAGONAL
600 B.P., OR, chalc.

TOYAH
600 B.P.,
Zapata Co.,
TX

COLUMBIA PLATEAU
500 B.P., The Dalles,
OR, agate

COLUMBIA PLATEAU
500 B.P., Col. Plat., WA

**COLUMBIA
PLATEAU**
500 B.P., WA,
agate

**COLUMBIA
PLATEAU**
500 B.P., The
Dalles, OR,
jasper

**COLUMBIA
PLATEAU**
500 B.P.,
OR, jasper

**COLUMBIA
PLATEAU**
500 B.P., Col. Riv.,
WA, agate

COLUMBIA PLATEAU
500 B.P., The Dalles,
OR, jasper

**COLUMBIA
PLATEAU**
500 B.P., WA,
jasper

**COLUMBIA
PLATEAU**
500 B.P., WA,
jasper

COLUMBIA PLATEAU
500 B.P., Col. Plat., WA

**COLUMBIA
PLATEAU**
500 B.P., The
Dalles, OR, agate

COLUMBIA PLATEAU
500 B.P., WA, jasper

COLUMBIA RIVER PIN STEM
500 B.P., WA, jasper

**COLUMBIA
PLATEAU**
500 B.P., Hood
Riv., OR, agate

KLICKITAT
300, OR

KLICKITAT
300, Lake Rv,
WA, jasper

DIAMOND-BACK
300 B.P., Hood Rv., OR, agate

DIAMOND-BACK
300 B.P., OR, jasper

KLICKITAT
300, OR,
agate

NOTTOWAY
300 B.P., S. OR, obs.

GROUND STONE
300 B.P., San Juan Co., WA

TRADE/BENTON
300 B.P., W, KS,
copper

Index of Point Types

Regional Codes

Alaska - AK
Desert Southwest - SW
Eastern Central - EC

Eastern Seaboard - ES
Far West - FW
Gulf Coastal - GC

Northeastern - NE
Northern Central - NC
Northern High Plains - NP

Southern Central - SC

Abasolo (7,000) SC, SW
Abbey (6,000) GC
Acatita (3,000) SW
Addison Micro-Drill (2,000) EC
Adena (3,000) EC, ES, GC, NC, NE
Adena Blade (3,000) EC, NC, NE, SC
Adena-Mason Var. (3,000) EC
Adena-Narrow Stem (3,000) EC, NC
Adena-Notched Base (3,000) EC, NC
Adena-Robbins (3,000) EC, ES, NE, SC
Adena-Vanishing Stem (3,000) EC
Afton (5,000) NC
Agate Basin (10,200) EC, FW, NC, NE, NP, SC, SW
Agee (1,200) NC, SC
Aguaje (600) SW
Ahsahka (3,000) FW
Ahumada (4,000) SW
Alachua (5,500) GC
Alamance (10,000) EC, ES
Alba (See Hughes)
Alba (1,100) NC, SC
Albany Knife (10,000) SC
Alberta (10,000) EC, FW, NP, SC
Albion-Head Side Notched (6,500) FW
Alder Complex (9,500) FW, NP
Alkali (1,500) FW
Allen (8,500) NC, NP, SC, SW
Almagre (6,000) SW
Amargosa (4,000) FW, SW
Amos (10,000) NE
Anderson (9,000) NP
Andice (9,000) SC
Angostura (8,800) EC, NC, NE, NP, SC, SW
Año Nuevo (2950) FW
Antler (1,400) SC
Anzick (11,500) EC
Appalachian (6,000) EC, ES
Apple Creek (1,700) NC
Archaic Knife (8,000) NP
Archaic Knife (10,000) SC
Archaic Side Notched (6,000) NP
Archaic Triangle (6,000) NP
Arden (9,000) NE
Arenosa (see Langtry-...)
Arkabutla (10,500) SC
Armstrong (2450) ES
Arredondo (6,000) GC
Ashtabula (4,000) EC, NE
Atlantic Phase Blade (4,300) NE
Atlatl Valley Triangular (7,000) FW
Augustin (7,000) SW
Autauga (9,000) EC
Avonlea-Carmichael (1,800) NP
Avonlea Classic (1,800) NP
Avonlea-Gull Lake (1,800) NP
Avonlea-Timber Ridge (1,800) NP
Awatovi Side Notched (750) SW
Axtel (7,000) SC

Badin (1,000) ES
Bajada (6,000) SW
Baker (7,500) SC, SW
Bakers Creek (4,000) EC
Bandy (7,500) SC
Barber (10,000) SC
Bare Island (4,500) NE
Barnes Cumberland (see Cumberland)
Barreal (9,000) SW
Basal Double Tang (3,500) SW
Bascom (4,500) GC
Base Tang Knife (4,000) NP, SC
Base Tang Knife (10,000) FW
Basketmaker (1,500) SW
Bassett (800) SC
Bat Cave (9,000) SW
Bayogoula (800) NC, SC
Beacon Island (4,000) EC
Bear Type 1-4 (3000) AK
Bear River (1,300) FW
Beaver Lake (11,500) EC, GC, NC, NE
Beekman Triangular (4,800) NE
Belen (10,500) SW
Bell (7,000) SC
Benjamin (3,000) EC
Benton (6,000) EC
Benton Blade (6,000) EC
Benton Bottle Neck (6,000) EC
Benton Double Notch (6,000) EC
Benton Narrow Blade (6,000) EC
Benton Side Notched (6,000) EC, ES
Besant (1,900) NP
Besant Knife (1,900) NP
Big Creek (3,500) SC
Big Sandy (10,000) EC, ES, SC
Big Sandy Broad Base (10,000) EC
Big Sandy Contracted Base (10,000) EC
Big Sandy E-Notched (10,000) EC
Big Sandy Leighton (10,000) EC
Big Slough (7,000) EC
Big Valley Stemmed (4,000) FW
Billings (300) NP
Bird Arrow-Blunt (2,800) AK
Bird Spear (2,800) AK
Bitterroot (7,500) FW, NP
Black Mesa Narrow Neck (2,000) SW
Black Rock Concave (11,000) FW
Blevins (1,200) 3C
Bliss (950) FW
Blunt (11,500) EC
Boats Blade (4,300) NE
Boggy Branch Type I (9,000) GC
Boggy Branch Type II (9,000) GC
Bolen Beveled (10,500) ES, GC
Bolen Plain (9,000) ES, GC
Bone/Antler (4,500) NE
Bone Arrow (1,500) FW
Bone Arrow (2,800) AK
Bone Arrow w/Metal or Stone

points (2,800) AK
Bone Pin (11,500) FW, GC
Bonham (1,200) SC
Bonito Notched (1,050) SW
Borax Lake (8,000) FW
Bradford (2,000) GC
Bradley Spike (4,000) EC
Brewerton Corner Notched (6,000) EC, NE
Brewerton Eared Triangular (6,000) EC, ES, NE, SC
Brewerton Side Notched (6,000) EC, ES, NE, SC
Broad River (3,000) GC
Brodhead Side Notched (9,000) NE
Broward (2,000) GC
Browns Valley (10,000) EC, NC, NP, SC
Brunswick (5,000) EC
Buchanan Eared (3,000) FW
Buck Creek (6,000) EC
Buck Gulley (1,500) SW
Buck Taylor Notched (600) SW
Buffalo Gap (5,500) NP
Buffalo Stemmed (6,000) ES
Buggs Island (5,500) EC
Bull Creek (950) FW, SW
Bullhead (4,000) FW
Bulverde (5,000) SC
Burin (2,500, Merrybell Phase) FW
Burkett (2,300) SC
Burroughs (8,000) NC
Burwell (5,000) NE
Buzzard Roost Creek (6,000) EC
Cache River (10,000) EC, NC, SC
Caddoan Blade (800) SC
Cahokia (1,000) NC
Calapooya (1,000) FW
Calcasieu (5500) SC
Calf Creek (8,000) NC, SC
Camel Back (700) NP
Camp Creek (3,000) EC
Canalino Triangular (700) FW
Candy Creek (3,000) EC
Caracara (600) SC
Caraway (1,000) ES
Carlsbad (3,000) SW
Carrizo (7,000) SC
Carrolton (5,000) SC
Carter (2,500) NC
Cascade (8,000) FW
Cascade Knife (8,000) FW
Cascade-Shouldered (8,000) FW
Castroville (4,000) SC
Calahoula (3,000) SC
Catan (4,000) SC, SW
Cave Spring (9,000) EC
Cedral (see Acatita)
Cecilo Falls I (10,800) Formerly Fell's Cave, FW
Cecilo Falls II (9,500) Formerly Pay Paso, FW
Chaco Corner Notched (1,250) SW
Charcos (3,000) SC, SW
Charleston Pine Tree (8,000) NE
Chesapeake Diamond (5,500)

ES
Chesser (1,600) EC
Chignik Dart (5,000) AK
Chignik Lanceloate (5,000) AK
Chignik Leaf (5,000) AK
Chignik Stemmed (5,000) AK
Chilcotin Plateau (8,000) FW
Chillesquaque (6,000) NE
Chindadn (11,300) AK
Chipola (10,000) GC
Chiricahua (4,800) SW
Chopper (11,500) FW, SC
Cienega (2,800) SW
Circular Uniface Knife (6,000) FW
Citrus (3,500) GC
Citrus Side Notched (800) SW
Clarksville (1,000) ES
Clay (5,000) GC
Cliffton (1,200) SC
Clovis (11,500) EC, ES, FW, GC, NC, NE, NP, SC, SW
Clovis-Colby (11,500) NP
Clovis-Hazel (11,500) EC
Clovis-St. Louis (11,500) NC
Clovis Unfluted (11,500) EC, ES
Coahuila (4,000) SC
Cobbs Triangular (9,000) EC, NC
Cody Knife (10,000) FW, NP
Cohonina Stemmed (1,300) SW
Colbert (1,000) SC
Cold Springs (5,000) FW
Coldwater (10,000) EC, SC
Collins (1,500) NC
Columbia (2,000) GC
Columbia Mule Ear (700) FW
Columbia Plateau (500) FW
Columbia River Pin Stem (500) FW
Combat Wand Blade (2,500) FW
Conejo (4,000) SC, SW
Conerly (7,500) EC, GC
Conodoquinet/Canfield (4,000) NE
Contra Costa (2,500) FW
Convento (950) SW
Coosa (2,000) EC
Copena Auriculate (5,000) EC
Copena Classic (4,000) EC
Copena Round Base (4,000) EC
Copena Triangular (4,000) EC
Coquille Knife (4,500) GB
Coquille Broadneck (4,500) FW
Coquille Narrowneck (4,500) FW
Coquille Side-Notched (4,500) FW
Cordilleran (9,500) FW
Corner Tang Knife (3,400) EC, FW, NP, SC
Cortaro (4,300) SW
Coryell (7,000) SC
Cossatot River (9,500) NC
Cotaco Creek (2,500) EC
Cotaco Blade (2,500) EC
Cotaco Preform (2,500) EC
Cotaco-Wright (2,500) EC
Cottonbridge (6,000) GC
Cottonwood Leaf (1,100) FW, NP, SW

Cottonwood Triangle (1.100) FW, NP, SW
Cougar Mountain (11,000) FW
Covington (4,000) SC
Cowhouse Slough (10,000) GC
Cow's Skull (600) SW
Crawford Creek (8,000) EC
Cresap (3,000) EC
Crescent (11,000) FW
Crescent (5,000) SC
Crescent Knife (10,200) NP, SC
Crooked Creek (9,000) NE
Crowfield (11,000) NE
Cruciform I (6,000) SW
Cruciform II (3,000) SW
Crump Lake Eared (5,000) FW
Culbreath (5,000) SC
Culpepper Bifurcate (7,500) ES
Cumberland (11,250) EC, NC
Cumberland Barnes (11,250) NE
Cumberland Unfluted (11,250) NC
Cuney (400) SC
Cupp (1,500) EC, NC, SC
Cut Bank Jaw Notched (300) NP
Cypress Creek (5,000) EC
Cypress Creek (5,500) GC
Dagger (arrow) (1,200) FW
Dagger (large) (4,000) EC
Dallas (4,000) SC
Dalton-Breckenridge (10,000) NC, SC
Dalton Classic (10,000) EC, NC, NE, NP, SC
Dalton-Colbert (10,000) EC, SC
Dalton-Greenbrier (10,000) EC, SC
Dalton-Hemphill (10,000) EC, NC, SC
Dalton-Hempstead (10,000) SC
Dalton-Kisatchie (10,000) SC
Dalton-Nansemond (10,000) ES
Dalton-Nuckolls (10,000) EC, NC, NE
Dalton-Sloan (10,000) NC
Damron (8,000) EC
Dardanelle (600) SC
Darl (2,500) SC
Darl Blade (2,500) SC
Darl Fractured Base (2,500) SC
Darl Stemmed (8,000) SC
Datil (7,000) SW
Dawson (7,000) SC
Deadman's (1,600) SC, SW
Dear Arrow (see Bone Arrow)
Debert (11,000) EC, NE
Decatur (9,000) EC, ES, NC, NE
Decatur Blade (9,000) EC
Dol Carmon (550) SW
Delhi (3,500) SC
Denton (5,000) SC
Deschutes Knife (500) FW
Desert-Delta (700) FW, SW
Desert-General (700) FW, NP, SW
Desert-Redding (700) FW, SW
Desert-Sierra (700) FW, NP, SW
Desert-Stemmed (see Rose Springs)
Desmuke (4,000) SC
Dewart Stemmed (5,000) NE
Diablo Canyon Side Notched (8,000) FW
Diamond-Back (300) FW
Dickson (2,500) EC, ES, NC, SC
Disc (5,000) SW
Dismal Swamp (3,500) ES
Dolores (1,400) SW
Dorset Triangular (2,500) AK
Double Tip (see Elko, Pedernales, Samantha)
Dovetail (see St. Charles)

Drill (11,500) AK, EC, ES, FW, GC, NC, NE, NP, SC, SW
Dry Prong (1,000) SW
Drybrook Fishtail (3,500) NE
Duck River Sword (1,100) EC
Duncan (4,600) NP, SW
Duncan's Island (6,000) NE
Duran (3,000) SC, SW
Durango (4,500) SW
Durant's Bend (1,600) EC, GC
Durst (3,000) EC
Dutch Harbor Bi-Point (5,000) AK
Dutch Harbor Large Stemmed (5,000) AK
Dutch Harbor Side Notched (5,000) AK
Dutch Harbor Stemmed (5,000) AK
Duval (2,000) EC, GC
Early Eared (8,000) FW
Early Leaf (8,000) FW
Early Ovoid Knife (11,000) EC
Early Side Notched (see Archaic --)
Early Stemmed (9,000) SC
Early Stemmed (see Shaniko Stemmed)
Early Stemmed Lanceolate (9,000) FW, SC
Early Triangular (9,000) SC
Eastern Stemmed Lanceolate (9,500) EC
Eastgate (1,100) FW, NP
Eastgate Split Stem (1,400) FW, SW
Ebenezer (2,000) EC
Eccentric (see Exotic)
Ecusta (8,000) EC, ES
Eden (10,000) NC, NP, SW
Edgefield Scraper (10,500) ES, GC
Edgewood (3,000) SC
Edwards (2,000) SC
Elam (4,000) SC
Elk River (8,000) EC
Elko (3,500) FW, NP
Elko Corner Notched (3,500) FW, SW
Elko Eared (3,500) FW, SW
Elko Split Stem (2,500) FW
Elko Wide Notched (3,500) FW
Ellis (4,000) SC
Elora (6,000) EC, GC
Embudo (7,000) SW
Emigrant (900) NP
Emigrant Springs (1,200) FW
Ensor (4,000) SC
Ensor Split Base (4,000) SC
Epps (3,500) NC, SC
Erb Basal Notched (2,000) NE
Erie Triangle (1,500) NE
Eccobac (6,500) SW
Eshback (5,500) NE
Etley (4,000) EC, NC
Eva (8,000) EC
Evans (4,000) EC, NC, SC
Excelsior (2,500) SW
Exotic (5,000) EC, ES, FW, NC, SC
Fairland (3,000) EC, SC
Ferry (5,500) NC
Figueroa (3,000) SC, SW
Firstview (10,000) AK, FW, NP, SC, SW
Fish Gutter (4,000) FW
Fishspear (9,000) EC, ES
Flaking Tool (2,800) AK
Flint Creek (3,500) EC
Flint River (4,000) GC
Flint River Spike (see McWhinney)
Folsom (10,800) EC, FW, NC, NP, SC, SW
Forest Notched (3,000) NE
Fort Ancient (800) EC

Fort Ancient Blade (800) EC
Fountain Bar ((3,000) FW
Fountain Creek (9,000) EC, ES
Fox Creek (2,500) ES, NE
Fox Valley (9,000) NC
Frazier (7,000) EC
Frederick (9,000) EC
Frederick (9,000) NP, SC
Fremont Triangular (1,100) FW
Fresno (1,200) SC
Friday (4,000) SC
Friley (1,500) SC
Frio (5,000) SC, SW
Frio Transitional (3,000) SW
Frost Island (3,200) NE
Gahagan (4,000) SC
Galt (1,500) NP
Galt (Hastings) (1,500) NP
Gar Scale (1,800) SC
Garth Slough (9,000) EC, ES
Garver's Ferry (1,800) NE
Gary (3,200) NC, SC
Garza (500) SC, SW
Gatecliff (5,000) FW
Gatlin Side Notched (800) SW
Genesee (5,000) NE
Gibson (2,000) EC, NC, SC
Gila Butte (see Hodges Contr. Stem)
Gila River Corner Notched (1,350) SW
Gilchrist (10,000) GC
Glass (400) SW
Glendo Arrow (1,500) NP
Glendo Dart (1,700) NP
Gobernadora (3,000) SW
Godar (4,500) NC, SC
Goddard (1,000) NE
Gudley (2,500) SC
Gold Hill (4,500) FW
Golondrina (9,000) EC, SC
Goshen (11,250) FW, NP, SC, SW
Gower (8,000) SC
Graham Cave (9,000) EC, NC, SC
Grand (1,800) NC, SC
Graver (11,500) EC, GB, NE, NP, SC, SW
Green River (4,500) NP, SW
Greenbrier (9,500) EC, NC
Greene (1,700) NE
Greeneville (3,000) EC, ES
Ground Slate (6,000) NE
Ground Stone (300) FW
Guadalupe (1,900) SW
Guerrero (300) SC
Guilford Round Base (6,500) ES, NE
Guilford Stemmed (6,500) ES
Guilford Straight Base (6,500) ES
Guilford Yuma (7,500) ES, NE
Guntersville (700) EC
Gunther Barbed (1,000) FW
Gunther Triangular (1,000) FW
Gypsum Cave (4,500) SW
Gypsy (2,500) SW
Hafted Knife (2,000) AK
Hafted Knife (2,300) FW
Hale (Bascom) (4,000) SC
Halifax (6,000) EC, ES
Hamilton (1,600) EC
Hamilton (8,000) GC
Hamilton Stemmed (3,000) EC
Hand Axe (12,000+) FW
Hanna (4,000) NP, SW
Hanna Northern (4,600) NP
Harahey (700) EC, GC, NC, NP, SC
Harahey (see Northwestern Four-Way Knife
Hardaway (9,500) EC, ES, GC, NE
Hardaway Blade (9,500) ES
Hardway Dalton (9,500) EC, ES

Hardaway Palmer (9,500) ES
Hardee Beveled (5,500) GC
Hardin (9,000) EC, ES, GC, NC, SC
Hare Bi-Face (3,000) SC
Harpeth River (9,000) EC
Harpoon (3,000) AK, FW
Harrell (900) NC, SC
Haskell (800) NC, SC
Haskett (12,000) FW
Hatten Knife (3,000) SC
Hatwai (see Windust--) FW
Haw River (11,000) EC, NE
Hawken (6,500) NP
Hayes (see Turner)
Hayes (1,200) NC, SC
Heavy Duty (7,000) EC, ES, NC
Hell Gap (10,300) FW, NC, NP, SC, SW
Hellgramite (3,000) NE
Hell's Canyon Basal Notched (1,200) FW
Hell's Canyon Corner Notched (1,200) FW
Helton (4,000) NC
Hemphill (7,000) NC, SC
Hendricks (3,500) FW
Hernando (4,000) GC
Hi-Lo (10,000) EC, NC
Hickory Ridge (7,000) NC, SC
Hidden Valley (8,000) NC, SC
High Desert Knife (5,500) FW
High River (1,300) NP
Hillsboro (300) ES
Hillsborough (5,500) GC
Hinds (10,000) EC
Hodges Contracting Stem (1,300) SW
Hog Back (1,000) NP
Hohokam (1,200) SW
Hohokam Knife (1,200) SW
Holcomb (11,000) NE
Holland (10,000) EC, NC, NP, SC
Hollenberg Stemmed (9,500) NP
Holmes (4,000) ES
Homan (1,000) NC, SC
Hoover's Island (6,000) NE
Hopewell (2,500) EC, NC
Hopewell Blade (2,500) NE
Horse Fly (1,500) NP
Houx Contracting Stem (4,500) FW
Houx Square Stem (4,500) FW
Howard (700) SC
Howard County (7,500) NC
Hoxie (8,000) SC
Huffaker (1,000) NC, NP, SC
Hughes (1,100) SC
Humboldt (7,000) FW, SW
Humboldt Basal Notched (8,000) FW
Humboldt Constricted Base (7,000) FW, SW
Humboldt Expanded Base (see Buchanan Eared)
Humboldt Triangular (7,000) FW
Independence (6,000) AK
Intermontane Stemmed (10,500) FW
Intrusive Mound (1,500) EC
Irvine (1,400) NP
Ishi (100) FW
Itcheetucknee (700) GC
Jacks Reef Corner Notched (1,500) EC, ES, NC, NE
Jacks Reef Pentagonal (1,500) EC, NE
Jackson (2,000) GC
Jakie Stemmed (8,000) SC
Jalama (6,000) FW
Jay (8,000) SW
Jeff (10,000) EC
Jetta (8,000) SC

Jim Thorpe (6,000) NE
Johnson (9,000) EC, SC
Jude (9,000) EC, ES
Kampsville (3,000) NC
Kanawha Stemmed (8,200) EC, ES, NE
Karnak Stemmed (3,900) EC
Kaskaskia (see Trade Points)
Kavik (300) AK
Kay Blade (1,000) NC, SC
Kays (5,000) EC
Kayuk (6,500) AK
Keithville (see San Patrice)
Kelsey Creek Barbed (4,500) FW
Kennewick (11,000) FW
Kent (3,000) SC
Keota (800) EC, SC
Kerrville Knife (5,000) SC
Kessel (10,000) NE
Kin Kletso Side Notched (900) SW
Kings (4,500) NC, SC
Kinney (5,000) SC
Kirk Corner Notched (9,000) EC, ES, GC, NC, SC
Kirk Snapped Base (9,000) EC
Kirk Stemmed (9,000) EC, ES, GC, NE
Kirk Stemmed-Bifurcated (9,000) EC, ES
Kiski Notched (2,000) NE
Kittatiny (6,000) NE
Klickitat (300) FW
Kline (9,000) NE
Knight Island (1,500) EC, SC
Koens Crispin (4,000) NE
Kotzebue Bay (6,000) AK
Kotzebue Dart (6,000) AK
Kramer (3,000) NC
La Jita (7,000) SC
Lackawaxen (4,000) NE
Lady Island Pentagonal (2,500) FW
Lafayette (4,000) GC
Lake Erie (9,000) EC, NC, NE
Lake Mohave (13,200) FW, SW
Lake River Side Notched (700) FW
Lamine Knife (8,000) SC
Lamoka (5,500) NE
Lancet (11,500) EC, NP, SW
Lange (6,000) SC
Langtry (5,000) SC
Langtry-Arenosa (5,000) SC
Lecroy (9,000) EC, ES, NE
Ledbetter (6,000) EC
LeFlore Blade (500) SC
Lehigh (2,500) NC
Lehigh (4,000) NE
Leighton (8,000) EC
Leon (1,500) GC
Lerma (4,000) SW
Lerma Pointed (9,000) SC
Lerma Rounded (9,000) EC, NC, NP, SC, SW
Levanna (1,300) EC, NE
Levy (5,000) GC
Lewis (1,400) NP
Lewis River Short Stemmed (700) FW
Limestone (5,000) EC
Limeton Bifurcate (9,000) EC
Lind Coullee (11,000) FW
Little Bear Creek (4,000) EC
Little Colorado Stemmed (11,000) SW
Little River (4,500) SC
Livermore (1,200) SC
Logan Creek (7,000) NP
Lookingbill (7,200) NP, SW
Lost Lake (9,000) EC, ES, NC, NE
Lott (500) SC
Lovell (8,400) NP
Lowe (1,650) EC

Lozenge (1,000) EC
Lundy (800) NC
Lusk (8,500) NP
Lycoming Co. (6,000) NE
MacCorkle (8,000) EC, NE
Mace (1,100) EC
Madden Lake (10,700) SW
Madison (1,100) EC, ES, NC, NE
Mahaffey (10,500) NP, SC
Mahkin Shouldered Lanceolate (6,500) FW
Malaga Cove Leaf (1,500) FW
Malaga Cove Stemmed (1,500) FW
Maljamar (3,500) SW
Mallory (4,600) NP
Manasota (3,000) GC
Manker (2,500) NC
Mansion Inn Blade (3,700) NE
Manzano (5,000) SW
Maples (4,500) EC
Marcos (3,500) SW
Marianna (10,000) EC, GC
Marion (7,000) GC
Marshall (6,000) SC, SW
Martindale (8,000) SC
Martis (3,000) FW
Mason (3,000) NC
Massard (900) SC
Matamoros (3,000) SC,SW
Matanzas (4,500) EC, NC, SC
Maud (800) SC
Mayacmas Corner Notched (4,500) FW
McGillivray Expand Stem (4,500) FW
McIntire (6,000) EC
McKean (4,600) NP, SC
McKee Uniface (5,000) FW
McWhinney Heavy Stemmed (5,000) EC
Meadowood (4,000) EC, NE
Mehlville (4,000) NC
Mendocino Concave Base (5,000) FW
Merkle (4,000) EC, SC, NC
Merom (4,000) EC
Merrimack Stemmed (6,000) NE
Merrybelle, Type I (2,500) FW
Merrybelle, Type II (2,500) FW
Merrybelle, Type III (2,500) FW
Mesa (10,000) AK
Mescal Knife (700) SW
Meserve (9,500) EC, NC, NP, SC, SW
Mid-Back Tang (4,000) NP, SC
Midland (10,700) FW, NP, SC, SW
Milnesand (11,000) FW, NP, SC, SW
Mimbre (800) SW
Mineral Springs (1,300) SC
Miniature Blade (300) FW
Molalla (see Gunther)
Muntell (5,000) SC
Montgomery (2,500) EC
Moran (1,200) SC
Morhiss (4,000) SC
Morrill (3,000) SC
Morris (1,200) SC
Morrow Mountain (7,000) EC, ES, GC, NE
Morrow Mountain Round (7,000) EC
Morrow Mountain Straight (7,000) EC, ES
Morse Knife (3,000) EC, NC
Motley (4,500) EC, NC, SC
Mount Albion (5,900) NP, SW
Mount Floyd (see Cohonina Stemmed)
Mountain Fork (6,000) EC
Mouse Creek (1,500) EC
Moyote (7,000) SW
Mud Creek (4,000) EC

Mulberry Creek (5,000) EC
Mule Ear (see Columbia Mule Ear)
Mummy Cave (1,400) NP
Muncy Bifurcate (8,500) NE
Munker's Creek (5,400) NC
Naknek (6,000) AK
Nanton (1,400) NP
Nawthis (1,100) SW
Nebo Hill (7,500) NC
Need Stemmed Lanceolate (2,500) FW
Neff (3,500) SW
Neosho (400) SC
Neuberger (9,000) EC, NC
Neville (7,000) NE
New Market (3,000) EC
Newmanstown (7,000) NE
Newnan (7,000) GC
Newton Falls (7,000), EC
Nez Perce (700) FW
Nightfire (1,000) FW
Nodena (600) EC, NC, SC
Nolan (6,000) SC
Nolichucky (3,000) EC
Normanskill (4,000) NE
North (2,200) EC, NC
Northern Side Notched (7,000) FW
Northumberland Fluted Knife (11,250) NE
Northwestern Four-Way Knife (700) FW
Notchaway (5,000) GC
Nottoway (300) FW
Nova (1,600) EC
Ocala (2,500) GC
Occaneechee Large Triangle (600) ES
Ochoco Stemmed (2,500) FW
Ohio Double Notched (3,000) EC
Ohio Lanceolate (10,500) EC, NE
Okanogan Knife (4,000) FW
O'leno (2,000) GC
Oley (2,200) NE
One-Que (1,320) FW
Orient (4,000) EC, NE
Osceola (7,000) NC
Osceola Greenbrier I (9,500) GC
Osceola Greenbrier II (9,500) GC
Otter Creek (5,000) ES, NE
Ouachita (3,000) SC
Ovates (3,000) NE
Owl Cave (9,500) FW
Oxbow (5,200) NP
Padre (800) SW
Paint Rock Valley (10,000) EC
Paisano (6,000) SC
Paleo Knife (10,000) FW, NC, NP, SC
Paleo Knife (11,500) NP
Palisades (7,000) AK
Palmer (9,000) EC, ES, NE
Palmillas (6,000) SC, SW
Pandale (6,000) SC
Pandora (4,000) SC
Panoche (300) FW
Papago (see Sobaipuri)
Parman (10,500) FW
Parowan (1,300) FW, SW
Parallel Flaked Lanceolate (8,500) NE
Paskapoo (1,000) NP
Patrick (5,000) EC
Patrick Henry (9,500) ES
Patuxent (4,000) NE
Pedernales (6,000) SC
Pee Dee (1,500) ES
Peisker Diamond (2,500) NC, SC
Pekisko (800) NP
Pelican (10,000) NC, SC

Pelican Lake (2,600) NP
Pelican Lake "Keaster" Variety (see Samantha)
Pelona (6,000) SW
Penn's Creek (9,000) NE
Penn's Creek Bifurcate (9,000) NE
Pentagonal knife (6,500) EC, NE
Perdiz (1,000) SC
Perforator (9,000) EC, FW, SC, SW
Perkiomen (4,000) NE
Pickwick (6,000) EC, ES GC
Pièces Esquillées (10,000) FW
Piedmont Northern Variety (6,000) NE
Piedmont Southern Variety (see Hoover's Island) NE
Pigeon Creek (2,000) GC
Pike County (10,000) NC, SC
Pine Tree (8,000) EC
Pine Tree Charleston Variety (8,000) NE
Pine Tree Corner-Notched (8,000) EC, NC
Pinellas (800) GC
Piney Island (6,000) NE
Pinto Basin (8,000) FW, NP, SW
Pinto Basin Sloping Shoulder (8,000) FW
Pipe Creek (1,200) EC, NP
Piqunin (700) FW
Piscataway (2,500) NE
Pismo (see Rabbit Island)
Plains Knife (6,000) NP
Plains Side Notched (1,000) NP
Plains Triangular (200) NP
Plainview (11,250) EC, FW, NC, NP, SC, SW
Plateau Pentagonal (6,000) FW
Pluvial Lakes Side Notched (9,000) FW
Pogo (2,000) SC
Point Hope (3,000) AK
Point Of Pines Side Notched (850) SW
Point Sal Barbed (4,500) FW
Polished Stone (2,000) AK
Pontchartrain Type I (3,400) EC, SC
Pontchartrain Type II (3,400) EC
Poplar Island (6,000) NE
Port Maitland (2,500) NE
Portage (6,000) FW
Potts (3,000) ES
Prairie Side Notched (1,300) NP
Priest Rapids (3,000) FW
Pryor Stemmed (8,500) FW
Pueblo Alto Side Notched (1,000) SW
Pueblo Del Arroyo Side Notched (1,000) SW
Pueblo Side Notched (850) SW
Putnam (5,000) SC
Quad (10,000) EC, ES, NC
Quillomene Bar (3,000) FW
Rabbit Island Arrow (1,200) FW
Rabbit Island Dart (2,000) FW
Raccoon Notched (1,500) NE
Raddatz (5,000) NC, SC
Ramey Knife (5,000) EC, NC
Randolph (450) ES, NE
Rankin (4,000) EC
Red Horn (see Buck Taylor)
Red Ochre (3,000) EC, NC
Red River Knife (9,500) SC
Redstone (11,500) EC, ES, GC, NC, NE
Reed (1,500) SC
Refugio (4,000) SC
Rheems Creek (4,000) EC

Rice Contracted Stem
 (see Hidden Valley) NC
Rice Lobbed (9,000) EC, NC, SC
Rice Shallow Side-Notched
 (1,600) NC, SC
Rio Grande (7,500) SC, SW
Robinson (4,000) NC
Rochester (8,000) NC
Rocker (see Sudden)
Rockwall (1,400) SC
Rodgers Side Hollowed
 (10,000) SC
Rogue River (see Gunther)
Rose Springs (1,600) FW, SW
Rose Springs Contracted Stem
 (1,600) SW
Rose Springs Corner Notched
 (1,600) FW, NP, SW
Rose Springs Knife (1,600) FW
Rose Springs Side Notched
 (1,600) FW, SW
Rose Springs Sloping Shoulder
 (1,600) FW
Rose Springs Stemmed (1,600)
 FW
Rose Valley (7,000) FW
Ross (2,500) EC, NC
Ross County (see Clovis)
Rossi Expanding Stem (4,000)
 FW
Rossi Square-Stemmed
 (4,000) FW
Rossville (1,500) NE
Rough Stemmed Knife (700)
 FW
Round-Back Knife (8,000) SW
Round-End Knife (see Side
 Knife)
Rowan (9,500) ES
Russell Cave (9,000) EC
St. Albans (8,900) EC, ES, NE
St. Anne (see Varney)
St. Charles (9,500) EC, NC, NE,
 SC
St. Helena (8,000) EC
St. Michael Leaf (2,000) AK
St. Tammany (8,000) EC
Sabinal (1,000) SC
Sabine (4,000) SC
Sacaton (1,100) SW
Safety Harbor (800) GC
Salado (1,500) SW (also see
 Pueblo Side Notched)
Sallisaw (800) SC
Salmon River (8,000) FW
Salt River Indented Base
 (1,150) SW
Samantha Arrow (1,500) NP
Samantha Dart (2,200) NP
San Bruno (600) FW
San Gabriel (2,000) SC
San Jacinto (6,000) SC
San Jose (9,000) SW
San Patrice-Geneill Var
 (10,000) SC
San Patrice-Hope Var. (10,000)
 SC
San Patrice-Keithville Var.
 (10,000) SC
San Patrice-St. Johns Var.
 (10,000) SC
San Pedro (2,500) SW
San Rafael (4,400) SW
San Saba (3,000) SC
Sand Mountain (1,500) EC
Sandhill Stemmed (2,200) NE
Sandia (11,500?) SW
Santa Cruz (1,400) SW
Santa Fe (4,000) GC
Sarasota (3,000) GC
Sattler (1,400) NP
Sauvie's island Basal Notched
 (1,750) FW
Sauvie's Island Hafting
 Notched (1,750) FW
Sauvie's Island Shoulder
 Notched (1,750) FW

Savage Cave (7,000) EC, SC
Savannah River (5,000) EC, ES,
 GC, NE, SC
Saw (3,500) SW
Scallorn (1,300) NC, SC
Schustorm (1,200) SW
Schuykill (4,000) NE
Scottsbluff I (10,000) FW, NC,
 NE, NP, SC, SW
Scottsbluff II (10,000) FW, NC,
 NE, NP, SC, SW
Scottsbluff Knife (10,000) FW
Scraper (11,500) AK, EC, FW,
 NE, NP, SC, SW
Scraper-Turtleback (10,000)
 SW
Searcy (7,000) EC, SC
Sedalia (5,000) EC, NC
Seminole (5,000) SC
Sequoyah (1,000) NC, SC
Shaniko Stemmed (3,500) FW
Shark's Tooth (2,000) NE
Shoals Creek (4,000) EC
Shumla (3,000) SC, SW
Side Knife (500) FW, NP
Sierra Contracting Stem
 (6,000) FW
Silver Lake (11,000) FW SW
Simonsen (6,800) NP
Simpson (10,000) ES, GC
Simpson-Mustache (10,000)
 GC
Sinner (3,000) SC
Six Mile Creek (7,500) GC
Sixes River Knife (3,000) FW
Sizer (2,300) FW
Smith (4,000) EC, NC
Smithsonia (4,000) EC
Snake Creek (4,000) EC
Snake River Dart (2,000) FW
Snaketown (1,200) SW
Snaketown Side Notched (800)
 SW
Snaketown Triangular (1,050)
 SW
Snook Kill (4,000) NE
Snow Knife (400) AK
Snyders (2,500) EC, NC
Snyders (Mackinaw Var.)
 (2,500) EC, NC
Sobaipuri (500) SW
Socorro (3,000) SW
Sonota (1,000) NP
Soto (1,000) SW
South Prong Creek (5,000) GC
Southhampton (8,000) ES
Spedis I, II (10,000) FW
Spedis III (3,000) FW
Spedis Fishtail (10,000) FW
Spedis Triangular (10,000) FW
Spokeshave (3,000) EC, SC
Square-end Knife (3,500) EC,
 FW, NC, NP, SC
Squaw Mountain (5,000) CW
Squibnocket Stemmed (4,200)
 NE
Squibnocket Triangle (4,200)
 NE
Standlee Contracting
 Stemmed (7,500) NW
Stanfield (10,000) EC, GC
Stanly (8,000) EC, ES, NE
Stanly Narrow Stem (8,000) ES
Stark (7,000) NE
Starr (1,000) SC
Steamboat Lanceolate (5,000)
 FW
Steiner (1,000) SC
Steuben (2,000) NC, SC
Steubenville (9,000) EC
Stilwell (9,000) EC, NC
Sting Ray Barb (2,500) GC
Stockton (1,200) FW
Stone Square Stem (6,000) NC
Stott (1,300) NP
Strike-a-Lite Type I (9,000) NE
Strike-a-Lite Type II (3,000)

NE
Stringtown (9,500) EC, NE
Strong Barbed Auriculate
 (1,750) FW
Sublet Ferry (4,000) EC
Sub-Triangular (11,300) AK
Sudden Series (6,300) SW
Sumter (7,000) GC
Surprise Valley (4,000) FW
Susquehanna Bifurcated
 (9,000) NE
Susquehanna Broad (3,700) NE
Susquehannock Triangle
 (1,500) NE
Suwannee (10,000) GC
Swan Lake (3,500) EC
Swatara-Long (5,000) NE
Swift Current (1,300) NP
Sykes (6,000) EC
Table Rock (4,000) EC, NC, SC
Taconic Stemmed (5,000) NE
Talahassee (4,000) GC
Talco (800) SC
Tampa (800) GC
Tangipahoa (4,500) EC
Taunton River Bifurcate
 (9,000) NE
Taylor (9,000) ES
Taylor Side Notched (9,000)
 GC
Taylor Stemmed (2,500) GC
Tear Drop (4,000) FW
Temporal (1,000) SW
Tennessee River (9,000) EC,
 NC
Tennessee Saw (8,000) EC
Tennessee Sword, (see Duck
 River Sword)
Texcoco (6,000) SW
Thebes (10,000) EC, ES, NC, NE
Thonotosassa (8,000) GC
Three-Piece Fish Spear (2,300)
 FW
Timponogus Blade (800) FW
Tock's Island (1,700) NE
Tompkins (1,200) NP
Tortugas (6,000) EC, SC
Toyah (600) SC, SW
Trade Points (400) EC, ES, FW,
 NE, NP, SC, SW
Travis (5,500) SC
Triangular Knife (3,500) FW,
 SW
Trinity (4,000) SC
Triple T (5,500) FW, SW
Trojan (1,320) FW
Truxton (1,500) SW
Tulare Lake (11,200) FW
Tulare Lake Bi-point (8,000)
 FW
Tuolumne Notched (3,100) FW
Turin (8,500) NC
Turkeytail-Fulton (4,000) EC,
 NC
Turkeytail-Harrison (4,000)
 EC, NC
Turkeytail-Hebron (3,500) EC,
 NC
Turkeytail-Tupelo (4,750) EC
Turner (900) SC
Ugashik (6,000) AK
Uinta (1,200) FW
Ulu (6,000) AK
Unalakleet (3,000) AK
Unalaska (5,000) AK
Union Side Notched (10,000)
 GC
Uvalde (6,000) SC
Uwharrie (1,600) ES
Val Verde (5,000) SC, SW
Valina (2,500) EC
Van Lott (9,000) ES
Vandenberg Contracting Stem
 (5,000) NW
Varney (1,000) NE
Vendetta (1,750) FW
Ventana-Amorgosa (7,000) SW

Ventana Side Notched (5,500)
 SW
Vernon (2,800) NE
Vestal Notched (4,500) NE
Victoria (10,000) SC
Virginsville (5,000) NE
Vosburg (5,000) NE
Wacissa (9,000) GC
Wade (4,500) EC
Wading River (4,200) NE
Wadlow (4,000) NC
Wahmuza (9,000) FW
Waller Knife (9,000) ES, GC
Wallula Gap Rectangular
 Stemmed (1,000) FW
Wallula Gap Rectangular
 Stemmed Knife (1,000) FW
Walnut Canyon Side Notched
 (850) SW
Wapanucket (6,000) NE
Waratan (3,000) ES, NE
Warito (5,500) EC
Warrick (9,000) EC, NC
Wasco Knife (see Plateau
 Pentagonal)
Washington (3,000) EC
Washita (800) NC, NP, SC
Washita Northern (800) NP
Washita (Peno) (800)SC
Washoe (1,200) FW
Wateree (3,000) ES
Watts Cave (10,000) EC
Waubesa (2,500) EC, NC
Wayland Notched (3,700) NE
Wealth Blade (1,200) FW
Web Blade (1,500) NE
Weeden Island (2,500) GC
Wells (4,000) SC
Wendover (7,000) FW
Westo (5,000) GC
Whale (4,000) AK
Wheeler Excurvate (10,000) EC,
 GC, NC
Wheeler Expanded Base
 (10,000) EC, GC
Wheeler Recurvate (10,000) EC
Wheeler Triangular (10,000)
 EC
White Mountain Side Notched
 (000) 0W
White River (6,000) SC
White Springs (8,000) EC
Wildcat Canyon (9,000) FW
Will's Cove (3,000) ES
Williams (6,000) SC
Willits Side Notched (4,000)
 FW
Windust (10,500) FW
Windust-Alberta (10,500) FW
Windust Contracting Stem
 (10,500) FW
Windust-Hatwai (10,500) FW
Windust Knife (10,500) FW
Wintu (1,000) FW
Withlacoochee (10,500) GC
Wooden Dart/Arrow (3,500)
 FW
Wray (5,000) NP
Yadkin (2,500) EC, ES
Yadkin Eared (2,500) ES
Yana (1,500) FW
Yarbrough (2,500) SC
Yavapai (3,300) SW
Yonkee (3,200) NP
Young (1,000) SC
Youngs River Stemmed (8,000)
 FW
Zella (4,000) SC
Zephyr (9,000) SC, SW
Zorra (6,000) SC

Bibliography

Alabama Projectile Point Types, by A. B. Hooper, Ill. Albertville, AL, 1964.
Album of Prehistoric Man, by Tom McGowen, illustrated by Rod Ruth, Rand McNally and Co., Chicago-New York-San Francisco, 1975.
American Indian Almanac, by John Upton Terrell, Thomas Y. Crowell Co., New York, N.Y., 1974.
American Indian Point Types of North Florida, South Alabama and South Georgia, by Son Anderson, 1987.
American Indian Ways of Life, by Thorne Deuel, Illinois State Museum, Springfield, IL, 1968.
Americans Before Columbus, by Elizabeth Chesley Baity. The Viking Press, New York, N.Y., 1951.
America's Beginnings-the Wild Shores, by Loften Snell, National Geographic Society, Washington, D.C., 1974.
America's Fascinating Indian Heritage, The Readers Digest Association, Inc., Pleasantville, N.Y., 1978.
Americans in Search of their Prehistoric Past, by Stuart Struever and Felicia Antonelli, Holter Anchor Press, Doubleday, New York, 1979.
The Anthropology of Florida Points and Blades, by Lloyd E. Schroder, American Systems of the Southeast, Inc. West Columbia, SC 29169
The Arkansas Archeologist, Bulletin, Vol. 19, Univ. of Arkansas, Fayetteville, AR., 1978.
The Ancient Civilizations of Peru, by J. Alden Mason, Penguin Books, Ltd., Middlesex, England, 1968.
The Ancient Kingdoms of the Nile, by Walter A. Fairservis, Jr., N.A.L. Mentor Books, The North American Library, Thomas Y. Crowell Co., New York, N.Y., 1962.
Ancient Native Americans, by Jesse D. Jennings, editor, W.H. Freeman & Co., San Francisco, CA, 1978.
Antiquities of Tennessee, by Gates P. Thurston, The Robert Clarke Co., Cincinnati, OH, 1964.
An Archaeological Survey and Documentary History of the Shattuck Farm, Andover, Mass., (Catherine G. Shattuck Memorial Trust), Mass. Historical Commission, March, 1981.
Archaeology, by Dr. Francis Celoria, Bantam Books, New York, N.Y., 1974.
Archaeology-Middle America (A science program) - U.S.A., Nelson Doubleday, Inc., 1971.
The Archaeology of Essex County, by Gwenn Wells, Essex Life, summer, 1983.
Arrowheads and Projectile Points, by Lar Hothem, Collector Books, Paducah, KY, 1983.
Arrowhead Collectors Handbook, produced by John I. Sydman, Charles Dodds (author), Danville, Iowa, 1963.
Artifacts of North America (Indian and Eskimo), by Charles Miles, Bonanza Books, Crown Publ., Inc., New York, N.Y., 1968.
Beginners Guide to Archaeology, by Louis A. Brennan, Dell Publishing Co., Inc., New York, N.Y., 1973.
The Bog People (Iron-Age Man Preserved), by P.V. Glob, Faber and Faber, London, 1965.
The Book of Indians, by Holling C. Holling, Platt and Munk Co., inc., New York, N.Y., 1935.
The Chattanooga News-Free Press, Thursday, Nov. 14, 1989, page B5, U.P.I. dateline, Los Angeles, CA article by James Ryan.
Cherokee Indian Removal from the Lower Hiwassee Valley, by Robert C. White, A Resource Intern Report, 1973.
The Cherokees, Past, and Present, by J. Ed Sharpe, Cherokee Publications, Cherokee, NC., 1970.
The Columbia Encyclopedia Edition, Clarke F. Ansley, Columbia University Press, New York, N.Y., 1938.
The Corner-Tang Flint Artifacts of Texas, University of Texas, Bulletin No. 3618, Anthropological Papers, Vol.1., No. 3618, 1936.
Cro-Magnon Man, Emergence of Man Series, by Tom Prideaux, Time-Life Books, New York, N.Y., 1973.
The Crystal Skull, by Richard Garvin, Pocket Books-Simon & Schuster, Inc., New York, N.Y. 1974.
Cypress Creek Villages, by William S. Webb and G. Haag, University of Kentucky, Lexington, KY, 1940.
Death on the Prairie, by Paul I. Wellman, Pyramid Books, Pyramid Publications, Doubleday and Co., Inc. New York, 1947.
Digging into History, by Paul S. Martin, Chicago National History Museum, Chicago, IL., 1963.
Duck River Cache, by Charles K. Peacock, published by T. B. Graham, Chattanooga, TN., 1954.
Early Man, by F. Clark Howell, Time-Life Books, New York, N.Y., 1965.
Early Man East of the Mississippi, by Olaf H. Prufer, Cleveland Museum of Natural History, Cleveland, Ohio, 1960.
Etowah Papers, by Warren K. Moorehead, Phillips Academy, Yale University Press, New Haven, CT. 1932.
Eva-An Archaic Site, by T.M.N. Lewis and Madelin Kneberg Lewis, University of Tennessee Press, Knoxville, TN., 1961.
Field Guide to Point Types of the State of Florida, by Don Anderson and Doug Puckett, 1984.
Field Guide to Point Types (The Tennessee River Basin), by Doug Puckett, Custom Productions (printer), Savannah, TN.,1987.
A Field Guide to Southeastern Point Types, by James W. Cambron, Decatur, AL.
A Field Guide to Stone Artifacts of Texas Indians, by Sue Turner and Thomas R. Hester, 1985, Texas Monthly Press.
Field Identification of Stone Artifacts of the Carolinas, by Russell Peithman and Otto Haas, The Identifacs Co., 1978.
The First American (Emergence of Man), by Robert Claiborne, Time-Life Books, New York, N.Y., 1973.
Flint Blades and Projectile Points of the North American Indian, by Lawrence N. Tully, Collector Books, Paducah, KY, 1986.
Flint Type Bulletin, by Lynn Mungen, curator, Potawatomi Museum, Angola, IN., 1958.
Flint Types of the Continental United States, by D.C. Waldorf and Valerie Waldorf, 1976.
Fluted Points in Lycoming County, Penn., by Gary L. Fogelman and Richard P. Johnston, Fogelman Publ. Co., Turbotville, Pennsylvania.
The Formative Cultures of the Carolina Piedmont, by Joffre Lanning Coe, New Series-Vol. 54, part 5, The American Philosophical Society, 1964.
Fossil Man, by Michael H. Day, Bantam Books, Grosset & Dunlap, Inc., New York, N.Y, 1971.
Frontiers in the Soil, (Archaeology of Georgia) by Roy S. Dickens and James L. McKinley, Frontiers Publ. Co., Atlanta, GA, 1979.
Geological Survey of Alabama, Walter B. Jones, Geologist, University of Alabama, 1948.
The Great Histories-The Conquest of Mexico, The Conquest of Peru, Prescott, edited by Roger Howell, Washington Square Press, Inc., New York, N.Y., 1966.
Guide to the Identification of Certain American Indian Projectile Points, by Robert E. Bell, Oklahoma AnthropologicalSociety, Norman, OK., 1958, 1960, and 1968.
A Guide to the Identification of Florida Projectile Points, by Ripley P. Bullen, Kendall Books, 1975.
A Guide to the Identification of Virginia Projectile Points, by Wm. Jack Hranicky and Floyd Painter, Special Publ. No. 17, Archaeological Society of Virginia, 1989.
Handbook of Alabama Archaeology, by Cambron and Hulse, edited by David L. DeJarnette, Universtiy of Alabama, 1986.
A Handbook of Indian Artifacts from Southern New England, drawings by William S. Fowler, Mass. Archaeological Society.
A History of American Archaeology, by Gorgen R. Willey and J.A. Sabloff, Thomas and Hudson, Great Britain, 1974.
Hiwassee Island, by T.M.N. Lewis and Madeline Kneberg, University of Tenn. Press, Knoxville, TN. 1946.
How to Find and Identify Arrowheads and Other Indian Artifacts (Southeastern United States), by Frank Kenan Barnard, 1983.
A Hypothetical Classification of some of The Flaked Stone Projectiles, Tools and Ceremonials From the Southeastern United States, by Winston H. Baker, Williams Printing Inc., 1225 Furnace Brook Parkway, Quincy, MA, 1995.
In Search of the Maya, by Robert L. Brunhouse, Ballentine Books-Random House, Inc., New York, N.Y., 1974.
The Incredible Incas, by Loren McIntyre, National Geographic Society, Washington, D.C., 1980.
Indian Artifacts, by Virgil Y. Russell & Mrs. Russell, Johnson Publ. Co., Boulder, CO., 1962.

Indian Relics and Their Story, by Hugh C. Rogers, Yoes Printing and Lithographing Co., Fort Smith, AR., 1966.
Indian Relics and Their Values, by Allen Brown, Lightner Publishing Co., Chicago, IL., 1942.
Indian Relics Price Guide, by Lynn Munger, published by Potawatomi Museum, Angola, IN., 1961.
Indiana Archaeological Society Yearbook, The Indiana Archaeological Society, 1975-1986.
Indianology, by John Baldwin, Messenger Printing Co., St. Louis, MO. 1974.
Indians and Artists In the Southeast, by Bert W. Bierer, published by the author, State Printing Co., Columbia, SC, 1979.
Indians of the Plains, by Harry L. Shapino, McGraw-Hill Book Co., Inc., New York, NY, 1963.
An Introduction to American Archaeology (Middle & North America), by Gordon R. Willey, Prentice-Hall, Inc. Englewood Cliffs, NJ, 1966.
Ishi-In Two Worlds (The Last Wild Indian in North America), by Theodora Kroeber, Univ. of Calif. Press, Berkeley & Los Angeles 1965.
Journal of Alabama Archaeology, David L. DeJarnette, editor, University of Alabama, 1967.
Man's Rise to Civilization, by Peter Faro, Avon Books, The Hearst Corp., New York, N.Y., 1966.
Massachusetts Archaeological Society, Bulletin of the, by William S. Fowler, Vol. 25, No. 1, Bronson Museum, Attleboro, Mass, Oct., 1963.
The Mighty Aztecs, by Gene S. Stuart, National Geographic Society, Washington, D.C., 1981.
The Mississippian Culture, by Robert Overstreet & Ross Bentley, Preston Printinq, Cleveland, TN, 1967.
The Missouri Archaeologist (The First Ten Years, 1935-1944), The Missouri Archaeological Society, Inc., Columbia, MO, 1975.
The Missouri Archaeologist Edition, Carl H. Chapman, University of Missouri, Columbia MO.
The Mound Builders, by Henry Clyde Shetrone, D. Appleton-Century Co., New York, N.Y., 1941.
Mysteries of the Past, by Lionel Casson, Robert Claiborne, Brian Fagan and Walter Karp, American Heritage Publ., Co., Inc., New York, N.Y., 1977.
The Mysterious Maya, by George E. and Gene S. Stuart, National Geographic Society, Washington, D.C., 1983.
The Mystery of Sandia Cave, by Douglas Preston, The New Yorker, June 12, 1995.
National Geographic, National Geographic Society, Numerous issues, Washington, D.C.
The Neanderthals, The Emergence of Man Series, by George Constable, Time-Life Books, New York, N.Y., 1973.
New World Beginnings (Indian Cultures in the Americas), by Olivia Viahos, Fawcett Publ., Inc., Greenwich, CT, 1970.
North American Indian Artifacts, by Lar Hothem, Books Americana, Florence, AL, 1980.
North American Indian Arts, by Andrew Hunter Whiteford, Golden Press-Western Publ. Co. Inc., New York, N.Y., 1970.
North American Indians-Before the Coming of the Europeans, by Phillip Kopper (The Smithsonian Book), Smithsonian Books, Washington, D.C.
Notes In Anthropology, by David L. Dejarnette & Asael T. Hansen, The Florida State University, Tallahassee, FL, 1960.
Paleo Points, Illustrated Chronology of Projectile Points, by G. Bradford, published by the author, Ontario Canada,1975.
The Papago Indians of Arizona, by Ruth Underhill, Ph. D., U.S. Dept. of the Interior, Bureau of Indian Affairs, Washington, D.C.
The Plants, (Life Nature Library), by Frits W. Went, Time-Life Books, New York, N.Y, 1971.
Pocket Guide to Indian Points, Books Americana, Inc., Florence AL, 1978.
Points and Blades of the Coastal Plain, by John Powell, American Systems of the Carolinas, Inc., 1990.
Prehistoric Art, R.E. Grimm, editor, Greater St. Louis Archaeological Society, Wellington Print., St. Louis, MO, 1953.
Prehistoric Artifacts of North America, John F. Berner, editor, The Genuine Indian Relic Society, Inc., Rochester, IN, 1964.
Prehistoric Implements, by Warren K. Moorehead, Publisher, Charley G. Drake, Union City GA, 1068.
Prehistoric Implements, by Warren K. Moorehead, Publisher, Charley G. Drake, American Indian Books, Union City, GA, Amo Press, Inc., New York, NY, 1978.
Projectile Point Types In Virginia and Neighboring Areas, by Wm. Jack Hranicky and Floyd Painter, Special Publ. No. 16, Archaeological Society of Virginia, 1988.
Projectile Point Types of the American Indian, by Robert K. Moore published by Robert K. Moore, Athens AL.
A Projectile Point Typology for Pennsylvania and the Northeast, by Gary L. Fogelman, Fogelman Publ., Co., Turbotville, Pennsylvania, 1988.
Projectile Points of the Tri-Rivers Basin, (Apolachicola, Flint and Chattahoochee), by John D. Sowell & Udo Volker Nowak, Generic Press, Dothan, Alabama, 1990.
The Redskin, Genuine Indian Relic Society, Inc., published by the Society, East St. Louis, IL, 1964.
Relics of Early Man Price Guide, by Philip D. Brewer, Athens, AL, 1988.
Secrist's Simplified Identification Guide (Stone Relics of the American Indian), by Clarence W. Secrist, published by the author, Muscatine, Iowa.
Second Preliminary Report: The St. Albans Site, Kanawha County, West Virginia by Bettye J. Broyles. Number 3, West Virginia Geological and Economic Survey, 1971.
Selected Preforms, Points and Knives of the North American Indian, by Gregory Perino, Vol. No. 1, Idabel, OK, 1985.
Selected Preforms, Points and Knives of the North American Indian, by Gregory Perino, Vol. No. 2, Idabel, OK, 1991.
Selected Preforms, Points and Knives of the North American Indian, by Gregory Perino, Vol. No. 3, Idabel, OK, 2002.
Shoop Pennsylvania's Famous Paleo Site, Fogelman Publ., Co., Turbotville, Pennsylvania.
Solving The Riddles of Wetherill Mesa, by Douglas Osborne, Ph. D., National Geographic, Feb. 1964, Washington, D.C.
Southern Indian Studies, by The Archaelogoical Society of N.C., University of North Carolina, Chapel Hill, NC, 1949.
Stone Age Spear and Arrow Points of California and the Great Basin, by Noel D. Justice, Indiana University Press, 2002.
Stone Age Spear and Arrow Points of the Southwestern United States by Noel D. Justice, Indiana University Press, 2002.
Stone Artifacts of the Northwestern Plains, by Louis C. Steege, Northwestern Plains Publ., Co., Colorado Springs, CO.
Stone Implements of the Potomac Chesapeake Province, by J.W. Powell, 15th Annual Report, Bureau of Ethnology, Washington, DC, 1893-1894.
Story In Stone (Flint Types of Central & Southern U.S.), by Valene and D.C. Waldorf, Mound Builder Books, Branson, MO, 1987.
Sun Circles and Human Hands, Emma Lila Fundaburk & Mary Douglas Foreman, editors. Published by the editors, Paragon Press, Montgomery, AL, 1957.
Ten Years of the Tennessee Archaeologist, Selected Subjects, J.B. Graham, Publisher, Chattanooga, TN.
Tennessee Anthropologist, Vol. XIV, No. 2, Fall, 1989, U.T., Knoxville, 1989.
Tennessee Archaeologist, T. M.N. Lewis and Madeline Kneburg, University of Tennessee, Knoxville, TN.
Tennessee Anthropologist, Vol. 14, No. 2, 1989, The Quad Site Revisted, by Charles Faulkner
A Topology and Nomenclature of New York Projectile Points, by William A. Ritchie, Bulletin No. 384, New York State Museum, NY, 1971.
U.S. News and World Report (Weekly News Magazine) article by William F. Amman and Joannie M. Schrof-"Last Empires of the Americas," April 2, 1990 issue, Washington, DC.
The Vail Site (A Paleo Indian Encampment in Maine), by Dr. Richard Michael Gramly, Bulletin of the Buffalo Society of Natural Science, Vol. No. 30, Buffalo, NY, 1982.
Walk with History, Joan L. Franks, editor, Chattanooga Area Historical Assn., Chattanooga, TN, 1976.
Who's Who In Indian Relics, by H.C. Wachtel, publisher, Charley G. Drake, American Indian Books, Union City, GA, 1980.
The World Atlas of Archaeology (The English Edition of "Le Grand Atlas de Parcheologie"), executive editor- James Hughes, U.S. & Canada, G.K. Hall & Co., Boston, Mass, 1985.
World Book Encyclopedia, Field Enterprises, Inc., W.F. Quarrie and Company, Chicago, Ill.,1953.
The World of the American Indian (A volume in the Story of Man Library), National Geographic Society, Jules B. Billard-Editor, Washington, DC, 1989.

Time is *NOT* the enemy.
LACK OF INFORMATION IS...

Some people will tell you that once a particular generation leaves us, the collectibles they were interested in become worthless (or at least worth less).

Is that what happened with Monet? Renoir? Beethoven?

Is that what happened with Washington, Jefferson and Lincoln?

Is that what happened with Howdy Doody, Elvis or Marilyn Monroe?

How about the Lone Ranger, Tom Mix or Buck Rogers?

Collectibles are alive and well. The only enemy is ignorance.

Get your free weekly inoculation against lack of information – delivered painlessly straight to your e-mail box – from Scoop! Each week *Scoop* brings you news, auction results, interviews and insights into collecting. And did we mention it's free?

All characters ©2005 respective copyright holders. All rights r

Visit http://scoop.diamondgalleries.com/signup/ to get your free subscription!

OLD WORLD PREHISTORIC ARTIFACTS FROM HOMO HABILIS TO HOMO SAPIENS

The **Overstreet Guide**'s consultant on Old World artifacts will gladly assist collectors, auctioneers, schools and museums by providing a full range of collection services.

IDENTIFICATION & AUTHENTICATION • APPRAISALS • EXHIBITION
PLANNING DOCUMENTATION • PUBLICATION
TV BROADCASTS & EDUCATIONAL VIDEOS
TOURS OF PREHISTORIC SITES IN EUROPE AND AFRICA
and EXPERTISE FOR NATURAL HISTORY AUCTIONS

**UPPER PALEOLITHIC & NEOLITHIC
ORGANIC ARTIFACTS**

**EUROPEAN BRONZE AGE
& CELTIC ARTIFACTS**

COPPER AGE DAGGERS

I am always interested in <u>purchasing</u> and <u>exchanging</u> artifacts, as well as in turning over my collection. Needless to say, any artifacts I offer carry my <u>life-time guarantee of authenticity</u>.

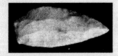

**NEANDERTHAL
POINTS**

**EUROPEAN ACHEULEAN
HAND-AXES**

DUNCAN CALDWELL
email: caldwellnd@aol.com

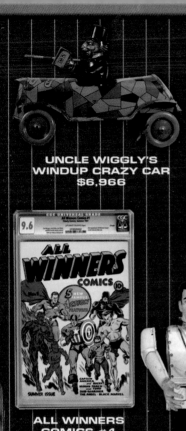

UNCLE WIGGLY'S
WINDUP CRAZY CAR
$6,966

POPEYE
POCKETWATCH
WITH BOX
$6,213

ROBIN
MEGO
FIGURE ON
RARE
KRESGE
CARD
$12,197

FANTASTIC
FOUR #1 CGC 8.0
$20,630

ALL WINNERS
COMICS #1
CGC 9.6
$95,200

DR.
FRANKENSTEIN
BATTERY
TOY
PROTOTYPE
$5,020

MARTIAN
WINDUP TOY
$5,000

MECHANICAL
BONZO BANK
$6,109

CAPTAIN AND
THE KIDS BELL
RINGER TOY $7,100

PEANUTS
SUNDAY
PAGE
ORIGINAL
ART
$41,264

REAGAN'S PERSONA
LICENSE PLATES OF
HIS 1981 INAUGURA
LIMO $14,914

THINK *BIG*, SELL *BIG*,
CONSIGN

HAKE'S AMERICANA & COLLECTIBLES · 1966 GREENSPRING DRIVE